PRESENT VALUE OF AN ANNUITY OF $1 PER PERIOD (P/A, i, n)

N	0.50%	0.67%	0.75%	1%	2%	3%	4%	5%	6%	7%	8%	9%
2	1.9851	1.9802	1.9777	1.9704	1.9416	1.9135	1.8861	1.8594	1.8334	1.8080	1.7833	1.7591
3	2.9702	2.9604	2.9556	2.9410	2.8839	2.8286	2.7751	2.7232	2.6730	2.6243	2.5771	2.5313
4	3.9505	3.9342	3.9261	3.9020	3.8077	3.7171	3.6299	3.5460	3.4651	3.3872	3.3121	3.2397
5	4.9259	4.9015	4.8894	4.8534	4.7135	4.5797	4.4518	4.3295	4.2124	4.1002	3.9927	3.8897
6	5.8964	5.8625	5.8456	5.7955	5.6014	5.4172	5.2421	5.0757	4.9173	4.7665	4.6229	4.4859
7	6.8621	6.8170	6.7946	6.7282	6.4720	6.2303	6.0021	5.7864	5.5824	5.3893	5.2064	5.0330
8	7.8230	7.7652	7.7366	7.6517	7.3255	7.0197	6.7327	6.4632	6.2098	5.9713	5.7466	5.5348
9	8.7791	8.7072	8.6716	8.5660	8.1622	7.7861	7.4353	7.1078	6.8017	6.5152	6.2469	5.9952
10	9.7304	9.6429	9.5996	9.4713	8.9826	8.5302	8.1109	7.7217	7.3601	7.0236	6.7101	6.4177
12	11.6189	11.4958	11.4349	11.2551	10.5753	9.9540	9.3851	8.8633	8.3838	7.9427	7.5361	7.1607
14	13.4887	13.3242	13.2430	13.0037	12.1062	11.2961	10.5631	9.8986	9.2950	8.7455	8.2442	7.7862
16	15.3399	15.1285	15.0243	14.7179	13.5777	12.5611	11.6523	10.8378	10.1059	9.4466	8.8514	8.3126
18	17.1728	16.9089	16.7792	16.3983	14.9920	13.7535	12.6593	11.6896	10.8276	10.0591	9.3719	8.7556
20	18.9874	18.6659	18.5080	18.0456	16.3514	14.8775	13.5903	12.4622	11.4699	10.5940	9.8181	9.1285
22	20.7841	20.3997	20.2112	19.6604	17.6580	15.9369	14.4511	13.1630	12.0416	11.0612	10.2007	9.4424
24	22.5629	22.1105	21.8891	21.2434	18.9139	16.9355	15.2470	13.7986	12.5504	11.4693	10.5288	9.7066
26	24.3240	23.7988	23.5422	22.7952	20.1210	17.8768	15.9828	14.3752	13.0032	11.8258	10.8100	9.9290
28	26.0677	25.4648	25.1707	24.3164	21.2813	18.7641	16.6631	14.8981	13.4062	12.1371	11.0511	10.1161
30	27.7941	27.1088	26.7751	25.8077	22.3965	19.6004	17.2920	15.3725	13.7648	12.4090	11.2578	10.2737
32	29.5033	28.7311	28.3557	27.2696	23.4683	20.3888	17.8736	15.8027	14.0840	12.6466	11.4350	10.4062
36	32.8710	31.9118	31.4468	30.1075	25.4888	21.8323	18.9083	16.5469	14.6210	13.0352	11.7172	10.6118
40	36.1722	35.0090	34.4469	32.8347	27.3555	23.1148	19.7928	17.1591	15.0463	13.3317	11.9246	10.7574
50	44.1428	42.4013	41.5664	39.1961	31.4236	25.7298	21.4822	18.2559	15.7619	13.8007	12.2335	10.9617
60	51.7256	49.3184	48.1734	44.9550	34.7609	27.6756	22.6235	18.9293	16.1614	14.0392	12.3766	11.0480
80	65.8023	61.8471	59.9944	54.8882	39.7445	30.2008	23.9154	19.5965	16.5091	14.2220	12.4735	11.0998
120	90.0735	82.4213	78.9417	69.7005	45.3554	32.3730	24.7741	19.9427	16.6514	14.2815	12.4988	11.1108
180	118.5035	104.6403	98.5934	83.3217	48.5844	33.1703	24.9785	19.9969	16.6662	14.2856	12.5000	11.1111
240	139.5808	119.5539	111.1450	90.8194	49.5686	33.3057	24.9980	19.9998	16.6667	14.2857	12.5000	11.1111
300	155.2069	129.5641	119.1616	94.9466	49.8685	33.3286	24.9998	20.0000	16.6667	14.2857	12.5000	11.1111
360	166.7916	136.2830	124.2819	97.2183	49.9599	33.3325	25.0000	20.0000	16.6667	14.2857	12.5000	11.1111

N	10%	11%	12%	13%	14%	15%	16%	18%	20%	25%	30%	40%
2	1.7355	1.7125	1.6901	1.6681	1.6467	1.6257	1.6052	1.5656	1.5278	1.4400	1.3609	1.2245
3	2.4869	2.4437	2.4018	2.3612	2.3216	2.2832	2.2459	2.1743	2.1065	1.9520	1.8161	1.5889
4	3.1699	3.1024	3.0373	2.9745	2.9137	2.8550	2.7982	2.6901	2.5887	2.3616	2.1662	1.8492
5	3.7908	3.6959	3.6048	3.5172	3.4331	3.3522	3.2743	3.1272	2.9906	2.6893	2.4356	2.0352
6	4.3553	4.2305	4.1114	3.9975	3.8887	3.7845	3.6847	3.4976	3.3255	2.9514	2.6427	2.1680
7	4.8684	4.7122	4.5638	4.4226	4.2883	4.1604	4.0386	3.8115	3.6046	3.1611	2.8021	2.2628
8	5.3349	5.1461	4.9676	4.7988	4.6389	4.4873	4.3436	4.0776	3.8372	3.3289	2.9247	2.3306
9	5.7590	5.5370	5.3282	5.1317	4.9464	4.7716	4.6065	4.3030	4.0310	3.4631	3.0190	2.3790
10	6.1446	5.8892	5.6502	5.4262	5.2161	5.0188	4.8332	4.4941	4.1925	3.5705	3.0915	2.4136
11	6.4951	6.2065	5.9377	5.6869	5.4527	5.2337	5.0286	4.6560	4.3271	3.6564	3.1473	2.4383
12	6.8137	6.4924	6.1944	5.9176	5.6603	5.4206	5.1971	4.7932	4.4392	3.7251	3.1903	2.4559
13	7.1034	6.7499	6.4235	6.1218	5.8424	5.5831	5.3423	4.9095	4.5327	3.7801	3.2233	2.4685
14	7.3667	6.9819	6.6282	6.3025	6.0021	5.7245	5.4675	5.0081	4.6106	3.8241	3.2487	2.4775
15	7.6061	7.1909	6.8109	6.4624	6.1422	5.8474	5.5755	5.0916	4.6755	3.8593	3.2682	2.4839
16	7.8237	7.3792	6.9740	6.6039	6.2651	5.9542	5.6685	5.1624	4.7296	3.8874	3.2832	2.4885
17	8.0216	7.5488	7.1196	6.7291	6.3729	6.0472	5.7487	5.2223	4.7746	3.9099	3.2948	2.4918
18	8.2014	7.7016	7.2497	6.8399	6.4674	6.1280	5.8178	5.2732	4.8122	3.9279	3.3037	2.4941
19	8.3649	7.8393	7.3658	6.9380	6.5504	6.1982	5.8775	5.3162	4.8435	3.9424	3.3105	2.4958
20	8.5136	7.9633	7.4694	7.0248	6.6231	6.2593	5.9288	5.3527	4.8696	3.9539	3.3158	2.4970
21	8.6487	8.0751	7.5620	7.1016	6.6870	6.3125	5.9731	5.3837	4.8913	3.9631	3.3198	2.4979
22	8.7715	8.1757	7.6446	7.1695	6.7429	6.3587	6.0113	5.4099	4.9094	3.9705	3.3230	2.4985
23	8.8832	8.2664	7.7184	7.2297	6.7921	6.3988	6.0442	5.4321	4.9245	3.9764	3.3254	2.4989
24	8.9847	8.3481	7.7843	7.2829	6.8351	6.4338	6.0726	5.4509	4.9371	3.9811	3.3272	2.4992
25	9.0770	8.4217	7.8431	7.3300	6.8729	6.4641	6.0971	5.4669	4.9476	3.9849	3.3286	2.4994
30	9.4269	8.6938	8.0552	7.4957	7.0027	6.5660	6.1772	5.5168	4.9789	3.9950	3.3321	2.4999
40	9.7791	8.9511	8.2438	7.6344	7.1050	6.6418	6.2335	5.5482	4.9966	3.9995	3.3332	2.5000

INTRODUCTION TO FINANCIAL MANAGEMENT

FOURTH EDITION

INTRODUCTION TO FINANCIAL MANAGEMENT

Lawrence D. Schall

Professor of Finance and Business Economics
University of Washington

Charles W. Haley

Rainier National Bank Professor of Banking and Finance
University of Washington

McGRAW-HILL BOOK COMPANY

New York   St. Louis   San Francisco   Auckland   Bogotá   Hamburg   Johannesburg
London   Madrid   Mexico   Montreal   New Delhi   Panama   Paris
São Paulo   Singapore   Sydney   Tokyo   Toronto

INTRODUCTION TO FINANCIAL MANAGEMENT

Copyright © 1986, 1983, 1980, 1977 by McGraw-Hill, Inc. All rights reserved. Printed in the United States of America. Except as permitted under the United States Copyright Act of 1976, no part of this publication may be reproduced or distributed in any form or by any means, or stored in a data base or retrieval system, without the prior written permission of the publisher.

1 2 3 4 5 6 7 8 9 0   VNHVNH   8 9 8 7 6

ISBN 0-07-055109-X

This book was set in Zapf Book Light by Better Graphics.
The editors were Patricia A. Mitchell, Paul V. Short, and Peggy Rehberger;
the designer was Gayle Jaeger;
the production supervisor was Charles Hess.
The drawings were done by Wellington Studios Ltd.
Von Hoffmann Press, Inc., was printer and binder.

Library of Congress Cataloging in Publication Data

Schall, Lawrence D.
    Introduction to financial management.

    (McGraw-Hill series in finance)
    Includes bibliographical references and index.
    1. Corporation—Finance.   I. Haley, Charles W.
II. Title.   III. Series.
HG4011.S33   1986   658.1'5   85-16646
ISBN 0-07-055109-X

LAWRENCE D. SCHALL is Professor of Finance and Business Economics at the University of Washington. Professor Schall received M.A. and Ph.D. degrees in economics from the University of Chicago. He has published numerous articles on various finance and economics topics, and has coauthored four books in finance, including *Theory of Financial Decisions* (with Charles Haley). Professor Schall has conducted numerous management seminars for business executives and owners, and has been a consultant to many business firms and to the U.S. government.

CHARLES W. HALEY is Rainier National Bank Professor of Banking and Finance at the University of Washington. Professor Haley received M.B.A. and Ph.D. degrees in finance from Stanford University. An active teacher and researcher in corporate finance and banking, he has designed three bank management simulations and has served as editor of the *Journal of Financial and Quantitative Analysis*. He is also coauthor of *Theory of Financial Decisions* with Lawrence Schall.

CONTENTS

In this edition our primary goal is to provide students with a thorough foundation in finance. For many students the introductory course is the only exposure to finance, and we cover all the material that we believe is essential to a comprehensive understanding of financial management. Although the text covers a wide range of topics and issues, we have treated the material at an introductory level in all cases. Our method has been to explain the main issues very carefully in order to provide the student with an intuitive understanding of finance concepts and an appreciation of the way those concepts are applied in practice.

The text does not neglect students who will be taking additional courses in finance. Basic principles, techniques, and institutional aspects needed for effective analysis of business finance cases are well covered. A foundation for more advanced theoretical courses is provided in the chapter appendixes and in Chapter 6. Throughout we have tried to ensure that our approach here is consistent with current theory. Students completing a course of study using this book should be well prepared for courses in investments because of our stress on risk and return in the financial markets and our coverage of the basic characteristics of securities and markets.

The book is designed for undergraduate one-quarter or one-semester courses, although it is unlikely that all chapters can be assigned in a single course. If supplemented by cases and readings, it will be suitable as the primary text for courses extending two quarters or more. Instructors using this text for an introductory course for MBA students will find that Chapter 6 and the appendixes to Chapters 4, 5, 8, 9, and 10 enable them to approach basic finance on a more advanced level.

We have made a special effort to provide an integrated discussion of the topics covered. Nevertheless, the book has been designed to offer great flexibility in choosing the order of presentation of most chapters. Furthermore, many chapters have one or more sections that can be deleted without any loss of continuity. Appendixes in several chapters explore major concepts in greater depth. These are intended as supplements to the basic coverage in the text and are designed for use by well-prepared undergraduate and beginning graduate students.

The first six chapters provide an introduction to the book and an introduction to finance in general. In Part 1 we examine the general nature of financial management, the financial system, taxes, the choice of business organization, compound-interest calculations, risk, and the principles of market valuation.

Parts 2 through 4 cover the basic concepts and techniques of financial management. Part 2 is concerned with long-term decisions involving investments and financing, including dividend policy. Part 3 explores techniques of financial analysis, including ratio analysis, funds flow, break-even analysis, and forecasting. Part 4 deals with the problems of managing the firm's current assets and current liabilities. The discussion in Part 4 is unusual in that the firm's working capital decisions are explicitly linked to the discussion of long-term investment and financing decisions in Part 2.

Parts 5 and 6 provide supplementary material that is often not covered in an introductory course. Part 5 offers a detailed discussion of the characteristics of the different securities issued by business firms and the procedures for issuing securities. Part 6 covers special topics including mergers and acquisitions, international financial management, and business bankruptcy.

CHANGES IN THE FOURTH EDITION

Our primary objective in revising the text was to improve its treatment of topics that are difficult for students to understand. The major changes include:

1 *A complete revision of the material in Chapters 5 and 6.* Chapter 5 is now a logical extension of the present value concept presented in Chapter 4 to the valuation of securities. This chapter now covers the efficient markets concept and, in an appendix, the term structure of interest rates. We have also placed the guide to securities quotes and sources of financial information, which had been Appendix A at the back of the book, as an appendix to Chapter 5. We have combined all the analytic discussion dealing with risk and its impact on the value of securities into Chapter 6 and simplified its presentation. Included is an intuitive explanation of why beta is a useful measure of risk.

2 *A revision of the presentation of risk in capital budgeting found in Chapter 9.* The part dealing with formal methods of adjusting for risk has been rewritten to make the discussion more accessible to students.

3 *Expanded treatments of cash management methods in Chapter 15 and letters of credit in Chapter 24.*

4 *Discussion in Chapter 3 of all tax law changes through December 31, 1984.*

5 *Revised questions and problems.* Over half of the problems are new or revised in this edition.

6 *General updating and simplification.* The text reflects more recent laws, data, and financial techniques. A general pruning of wording was undertaken to simplify the presentation and to highlight the more important points.

TEXT ORGANIZATION AND SUPPLEMENTARY MATERIALS

Although this book has been written to offer substantial latitude in selecting which chapters to cover and their order of presentation, we suggest that certain chapters be taught in a given order. Chapters 4, 5, 7, 8, 10, 12, 14, and 15 are prerequisites for certain other chapters. Specifically, Chapter 4 should precede Chapter 5, and Chapters 4 and 5 should precede all of Part 2 (Chapters 7 through 11). We recommend that the chapters in Part 2 be taught in sequence. However, these chapters can be partially rearranged to suit the needs of the individual instructor. A complete discussion of the possibilities for alternative sequences is included in the *Instructor's Manual* for the text. Many instructors may choose to assign Chapters 12, 13, and 14—which cover financial statement analysis, break-even analysis, and forecasting, respectively—early in the course. This can be done with no difficulty, although the discussion of financial leverage in Chapter 13 is most effectively taught if it is presented after Chapter 10. A sequence that we find quite workable in one quarter consists of Chapters 1 through 5, 7 through 10, 12, 14 through 17, and one or more of Chapters 18, 19, and 23; other chapters can be intermingled with these.

Students come to the basic finance course with a wide range of prior preparation in accounting, mathematics, and economics. We have assumed minimal background in these areas, but we do expect that students have had at least one quarter of accounting shortly before taking the class. Able students should be capable of mastering the material almost without regard to their previous formal course work. We have tried to make the book as self-contained as possible and, through extensive use of examples, to make it suitable for self-study.

As an aid to students, many instructors recommend a study guide when such is available. The *Study Guide* written by Thomas E. Stitzel serves as an excellent review and supplement to this book. It contains additional solved problems as well as questions in a programmed learning format. We believe that many students will find this supplement helpful.

The *Instructor's Manual* includes a substantial amount of supplementary teaching material, as well as recommended course outlines, a test bank, transparency masters, and answers to text questions and problems.

ACKNOWLEDG-MENTS

Many people have aided us in this project. Our students provided us with numerous comments that have resulted in substantial improvements over earlier versions of the text. Colleagues at the University of Washington and elsewhere have reviewed drafts of the manuscripts, and we are very grateful for their help. Our thanks go to Durwood Alkire, Henry H. Barker, William J. Bertin, Zvi Bodie, Don Boyd, Gregory Breen, Stephen G. Buell, Jess Chua, John Crockett, Fred Delva, Mark Dorfman, Eugene F. Drzycimski, Russell Ezzell, James F. Feller, John K. Ford, Michael Giliberto, John H. Hand, David Heskel, George W. Hettenhouse, Pat Hill, Gailen L. Hite, Lee Hoover, Michael H. Hopwell, Donald Houthaker, James Hugon, F. Lee Hull, Richard Johnson, Ann Kremer, Gene Laber, John B. Major, Rita M. Maldonado-Bear, Robert McDonald, Robert McGee, Judy Elmore Maese, Allen Michel, Michael Miller, Donald A. Nast, Gerald Newbould, Robert T. Patton, Gerald W. Perritt, Herb Phillips, Jerry Platt, Arthur Rasher, Bill Resler, Michael Rice, Ralph Ringgenberg, Rick Rivard, William Sartoris, William L. Scott, John Settle, Bernard A. Shinkel, Joel Shulman, Donald G. Simonson, Ronald Sprecher, Thomas E. Stitzel, Timothy Sullivan, Howard E. Van Auken, Nikhil Varaiya, Marc Vellrath, James A. Verbrugge, Jerry A. Viscione, Ernest W. Walker, Michael C. Walker, Ralph Walking, Larry White, Roger Wong, Gene Wunder, Francis Yeager, and J. Kenton Zumwalt. We are indebted to Charles D'Ambrosio, who provided us with encouragement and advice throughout the development of the book and helped us at numerous junctures. Chris Martin of Rainier National Bank gave us special assistance with the section on letters of credit in Chapter 24. Betty Schall provided us with important advice and assistance in writing Chapter 25. Paul Allen, Terence Barron, Jean-Claude

Bosch, Gregg Brauer, Susan Doolittle, Keith Hauschulz, Doug Hensler, Paul Makens, Helen Morgan, Thomas Munro, John Settle, Michael Sherry, and Kaj Svarrer developed many of the end-of-chapter questions and problems and provided us with helpful suggestions for the text material.

The editorial staff at McGraw-Hill has been a critical resource for us. Finance editors Pat Mitchell and Paul Short guided this edition through its various stages and were supportive at every turn. As editing supervisor, Peggy Rehberger was in charge of the editing and proof stages of production. Without her skill, patience, and dedication, we could not have carried it off. And we remain deeply indebted to Marjorie Singer, whose numerous recommendations and suggestions were invaluable in our writing the first and second editions; her legacy lives on in the fourth edition. Finally, the book could not have been written without the continued support of Anne Haley.

Lawrence D. Schall
Charles W. Haley

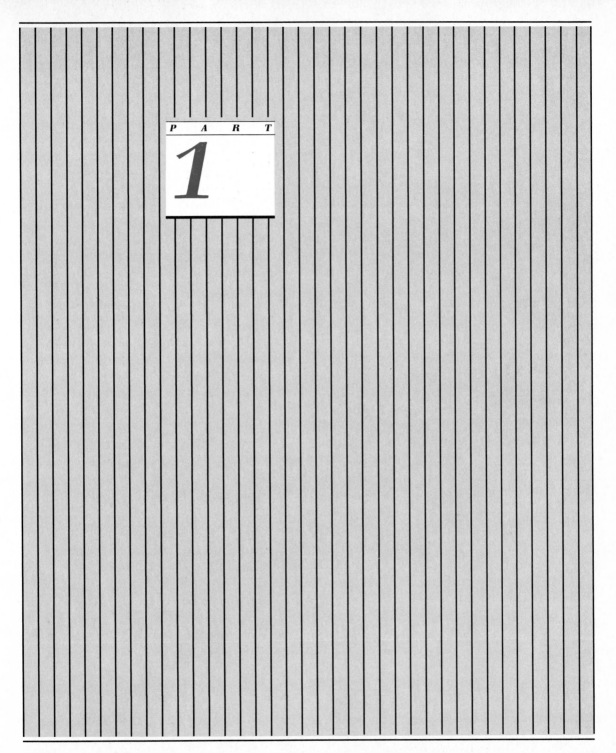

P A R T

1

THE ENVIRONMENT OF FINANCIAL DECISIONS

Part 1 consists of six chapters in which we present the general background for individual and company financial decisions. Chapter 1 is an introduction to business finance and to this text. Here we discuss the nature and objectives of financial management. In Chapter 2 we examine the American financial system: the network of financial institutions and markets that is an important part of the financial manager's environment. Chapter 3 covers other aspects of this environment, the legal form of business organizations, and the tax laws that affect financial decisions. Whereas the material in the first three chapters is largely descriptive, in Chapter 4 we develop a fundamental financial concept, the time value of money. We show here how to solve a variety of basic financial problems involving time and money. Chapter 5 explains how securities (bonds and stock) are valued in the market, and examines the theory of efficient markets. In an appendix, we discuss the term structure of interest rates. Chapter 6 explores the concept of risk and shows how risk affects the value of securities. We introduce a model of financial market equilibrium—the Capital Asset Pricing Model—and discuss its implications for financial management.

The material in Part 1 is important not just to the managers of business firms. Most of the topics covered are of equal importance to an individual concerned with such financial problems as borrowing money and choosing alternative ways of investing personal savings. The remainder of the text is almost exclusively concerned with problems faced by financial managers; but these first six chapters cover financial concepts that are useful to everyone.

This is a book about financial decisions—the financial decisions of a company. We will examine concepts which apply to giant corporations such as Exxon and General Motors and to small obscure companies which produce products you may never see. The underlying financial principles are essentially the same for all companies big or small: There are goals to be defined and facts to be considered using methods of analysis that are consistent with the goals. This book discusses those goals and presents those analytical methods within the context of important contemporary issues and the practices of modern financial management.

The financial decisions of a company can affect many groups in society. This chapter examines the two most controversial relationships: between the stockholders (owners) and management (which makes most of the decisions), and between the company and the rest of society. Each of these relationships can involve mutual benefit or serious conflict. The first part of this chapter discusses the problems that can create conflicts, and explains how these differences are, at least in part, resolved. We then inquire into the nature of finance as a discipline, and into the functions and objectives of the financial manager as a practitioner of this discipline.

THE CORPORATE OBJECTIVE

To perform effectively, the financial manager must have a clear understanding of the company's goals. We will begin by distinguishing between policies and goals. We then ask who determines the policies and goals of a company—its stockholders, management, or society—and, equally important, what goals are ordinarily pursued by firms in practice.

One of the most important goals of business firms is maximization of the owners' interest in the firm (maximization of value of the corporation's shares),[1] though nowadays social considerations can also be an important company objective—for example, helping to save energy or minimizing pollution. The policies of a company are *the strategies it employs to achieve its goals*. Company policy may involve such questions as whether to try to speed up growth by buying existing businesses, how much to invest in research and development, and what degree of risk to accept in launching new products.

A company's goals and policies are determined—theoretically —by the owners (the shareholders or stockholders) as represented by an elected board of directors. The board's responsibility is to make major policy decisions affecting the firm and to hire the day-to-day management team. In practice, however, the board of directors usually consists of a slate which is proposed by the company's management and which includes the top echelon of the management team. Thus, in reality, the shareholders delegate to management enormous powers to "run the company"—that is to say, to set its goals and shape its policies. There are two good reasons for

---

[1] As explained in Chap. 3, a corporation is a company whose owners are called "shareholders or stockholders." Each shareholder owns pieces of paper called "stock certificates" or "shares," which represent the owner's interest in the company. If a company has a total of 100,000 shares outstanding, the owner of 1000 shares owns 1 percent of the firm.

this. The first is that it would be impractical and inefficient to transmit to management the views of every stockholder on every issue. Second, the owners recognize that professional managers, because of their training and expertise, are better qualified than they are to operate the business. This delegation of authority is acceptable to most stockholders, so long as the company's performance is satisfactory in terms of dividend payments and earnings.

Owner and Management Objectives

Small businesses are usually managed by their owners. For such firms there cannot be any conflicts between owners and managers, since they are the same people. But most large firms are run by professional managers who, by law, represent the stockholders. The duty of management is to pursue the goals of the stockholders in a manner consistent with the law.

During the past decade, a whole body of financial theory—called *agency theory*—has emerged which, in part, deals with the relationship between stockholders and management and the costs imposed on stockholders when conflicts between the two exist. Conflicts between management and shareholders may arise because the managers place their own interests ahead of those of the shareholders. They may, for example, grant themselves excessive salaries and perquisites. Or management may pursue expansionary policies simply to increase the company's size even though the growth does not enhance earnings per share prospects (for some, it's more fun to manage a billion dollar company than a $500 million company; also, salaries and perquisites are generally larger the bigger the company). Or the shareholders may feel that management, in order to maintain its position, has painted an unrealistically rosy picture of the company's performance. There are many well-known cases in which management concealed major mistakes and even illegal acts. A notorious example was the Equity Funding scandal of 1973, in which audacious frauds and other hocus-pocus committed by management remained hidden from the stockholders—and from government regulatory authorities—for as long as nine years. It was ultimately revealed that the company's reported profits were nonexistent and that more than $100 million of its assets had been faked. The stockholders lost several hundred million dollars. Equity Funding's president and eighteen officers and employees of the company pleaded guilty to charges brought against them and were sentenced to varying jail terms.

But quite apart from the issue of wrongdoing, it is extremely difficult for the average shareholder to know what marks to award to management. On the one hand, it is impossible for a stockholder without exceptional expertise to know how much better the firm's performance might have been if different policies had been adopted. On the other hand, difficulties occur that are due to circumstances beyond management's control. For example, one cannot really blame cigar makers for the decline in the popularity of cigars, or blame the manufacturers of plastic toys for the sharp increase in materials costs after the oil embargo of 1973.

The question that naturally follows is "What assurances are there that management will serve, rather than exploit, the stockholders?" There are several mechanisms that protect the shareholder's position. **Stock option plans**, under which operating officers become part owners of the company, help align management's interests with the stockholders' interests. A similar function is served when part of executive compensation is a cash or stock bonus which depends on the company's earnings or on some other performance measure. Executives of many large corporations—such as International Harvester, Pillsbury, and Honeywell—have received huge bonuses under such plans. For example, in 1979 International Harvester forgave a $1.8 million loan to its chairman, Archie McCardell, because International Harvester's performance exceeded certain goals (since then the company has fallen on very hard times). There is also the threat of bad publicity by a disgruntled stockholder who can embarrass management and create discontent among other stockholders if the grievances are well founded. Stockholder complaints can result in a change of management, especially if the stockholder leading a movement is a major investor in the company. Corporate boards and managers also face legal liability for their actions. For example, since 1980 all corporate directors have had to sign the corporation's 10K report to the SEC; the effect of this has been to increase the board's accountability for the report's contents. And corporate boards now include an increasing number of outside directors who have no direct ties with management, for example, the appointments of Douglas Fraser (President of the United Auto Workers) to the Chrysler board and of ex-Congresswoman Barbara Jordan to the board of Texas Commerce Bancshares.

The possibility of an outside takeover of the company can also be a powerful deterrent to mismanagement. Although the small shareholders may not have the requisite knowledge to judge management's performance, there are well-financed outsiders who do have such knowledge. Such parties are constantly on the lookout for opportunities to purchase a company with unrealized potential. It should be pointed out that in practice, although takeovers do often occur, many takeover attempts either never go beyond the planning stage or fail. Many takeover efforts are abandoned early because of the cost. This is so whether the parties involved are outsiders or an insurgent group of stockholders. If the takeover is attempted through large purchases of stock, the price offered will have to be substantially above the current market price in order to induce existing stockholders to sell out. Furthermore, management will often successfully resist a takeover attempt by using any of a variety of tactics, including lawsuits or a merger with another firm which is friendly to management. If the takeover is targeted at electing a new slate of directors without massive purchases of stock, all the company's stockholders have to be contacted and persuaded individually to cast their votes at the annual meeting for the newly proposed slate of directors. The promotional, legal, and other expenses involved in such an undertaking run to large numbers. What's more, the chances of success—judging from the historical record—are not encouraging. To begin with, the existing board of directors has a significant advantage; it is entitled to use the company's funds to defend its position through mailings to stockholders. More important, the inertia of stockholders—

coupled with their normal distrust of insurgents or outsiders—usually ensures victory for the incumbent board, unless it is guilty of dishonesty or company performance has been conspicuously bad.

Having emphasized the large costs of stockholder revolts and takeover bids, it should be noted that takeovers are frequent occurrences. Indeed, many companies, such as Textron and International Telephone and Telegraph (IT&T), have grown into giant conglomerates by acquiring other companies and making them more profitable. A mismanaged company with depressed stock prices can be a particularly attractive acquisition if the buyer has the know-how to turn the company around.

The Corporation and Society

To Harvard economist John Kenneth Galbraith and muckraker-consumer advocate Ralph Nader, large corporations are all too often unscrupulous and antisocial, and are in dire need of house-training and socialization, preferably through strict government controls (or nationalization). They argue that, without government involvement, wealth inequalities will become unacceptably great, the environment will be ruined, and social injustice will reign unchallenged. Not so, assert economist Milton Friedman, social commentator Irving Kristol (editor of *Public Interest* and columnist in *The Wall Street Journal*), and other ardent defenders of capitalism. They hold that the primary function of a business firm is to make a profit by producing products demanded in the marketplace. Not only is an unfettered capitalism conducive to economic efficiency but, they say, perhaps more importantly, to liberty and democracy.

Unfortunately, we cannot resolve the debate here. But we *can* say that the debate is a reflection of a generally divided opinion about how much nonbusiness (government, labor, consumer groups, etc.) involvement in business decisions is best, and of the fact that substantial involvement is almost certain. Government financial intervention (for example, the 1980 $1.5 billion United States loan guarantee for Chrysler) and regulatory intervention may change form, or even diminish, but a return to the pre-1960 philosophy of "what's good for General Motors is good for the country" (quoted from Charles Wilson, former Secretary of Defense and former head of General Motors) is highly unlikely. What policies should a firm adopt and what goals should it pursue in such an environment? From a moral standpoint there is no generally acceptable answer, for people differ on what is or is not moral. From a legal standpoint, the answer is much clearer: Management should adopt policies that are lawful and which satisfy stockholder wishes. Stockholders want the value of their ownership interest to be as great as possible, which means a company policy that emphasizes earnings. Corporate stockholders generally do not like to mix their investment portfolios with their social concerns; perhaps not too surprisingly, the General Motors shareholders voted 97.27 percent against expanding the board of directors to include "public" representatives and voted 97.56 percent against the creation of a Committee for Corporate Responsibility. It should be pointed out, though, that maximization of share values usually means obeying the laws, such as antipollution statutes, that compel firms to protect society's interests. Violation of such laws can be very expensive in

The Firm's Objective

terms of government fines and hostile consumer reactions. Since share value maximization is the most important target for management, let us take a closer look at this objective.

We will assume in this book that shareholders and management (which represents shareholders) prefer policies that maximize the market value of the company's shares. Share values depend on the firm's earnings, since earnings are used to pay dividends and to reinvest in productive assets that will generate earnings in later years. But the risk as well as the level of earnings is important to shareholders. It is true that stockholders always prefer that the company achieve greater earnings per share than less. However, when a particular policy is adopted, the *future* effect on earnings is ordinarily uncertain. Shareholders may, for example, prefer policy A that provides completely safe (certain) future company earnings of $50,000 per year over "risky" policy B that will result in earnings as high as $100,000 or as low as zero, with an equal chance for all amounts between zero and $100,000. Both policies imply an average of $50,000 per year in the firm's earnings, but B is clearly less certain than A.[2] It is likely that in a market of investors who do not like risk the value of the firm's shares will be greater under policy A than under policy B. Later chapters in the book will examine in detail the impact of risk on company policy.

Using share value maximization as the objective does not mean that management is concerned with day-to-day fluctuations in the stock market. It is true that as long as existing stockholders and other investors in the market have accurate and timely information on the firm's activities, better performance will mean a higher market price for the stock. However, information may not be immediately available to investors, and there may be different views as to what the available information implies about the firm's future performance. Hence, the real concern of management is to maximize share value over the long term.

Figure 1-1 illustrates the interactions between a firm's owners, its management, and society. The details of these interactions differ from company to company. And for virtually all firms the relationships vary over time as a result of changes in our social and economic institutions.

THE KEY ROLE OF FINANCE

The Financial Manager

The financial manager plays a central role in the company. As summarized in Table 1-1, the manager's duties include budgeting, raising funds in the capital markets, evaluating investment projects, and planning the company's marketing and pricing strategies. An individual manager is often a specialist, with a knowledge of many areas of finance but particular expertise in one or two specialities. The breadth of the finance function is so great

---

[2] The average earnings under policy B are computed by simply taking the midpoint between the highest ($100,000) and lowest (zero) possible earnings outcomes, since all outcomes from zero to $100,000 are equally likely. The $50,000 is therefore a middle estimate of the earnings outcome of policy B.

FIGURE 1-1

Formulation of company objectives and policies. The firm's objectives are primarily based on owner preferences and on the economic and legal environment; however, the objectives that are sought by the firm may be affected by management attitudes. The policies to achieve the objectives are developed by management and influenced by legal and economic factors.

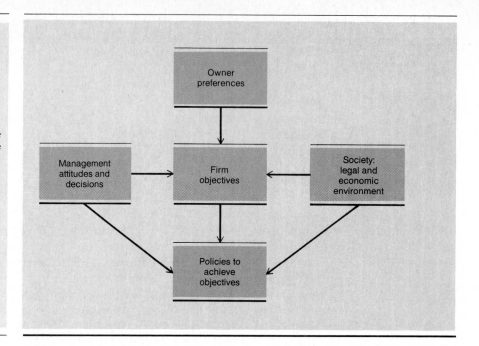

that in many companies it includes personnel from several departments and involves may echelons of management.

The crucial role played by the finance staff has not gone unrecognized in executive promotions. Finance people have headed many corporate giants, including General Motors, General Electric, CBS, Anaconda, and Twentieth Century-Fox. This ascendency of finance people to top corporate positions is not surprising. Finance is concerned with the lifeblood of a company, money: how it is obtained to finance the business and how it should be used to assure the business's success. Clearly, skill in this area is an extremely valuable asset in managing a company.

Corporate Organization

The assignment of finance functions to individuals and departments will depend upon the size of the company. The larger the company, generally the greater the degree of specialization of tasks, and the greater the proliferation of positions and departments. A smaller firm would consolidate many duties into fewer departments.

Generally, corporations are required by state law to have a president, a secretary, and a treasurer. Historically, the chief finance officer has been the treasurer. In recent years, two other positions have evolved—the controller and the financial vice president. The controller supervises most of the accounting and control functions listed in Table 1-1, and the treasurer supervises or participates in most of the remaining finance functions. The treasurer oversees the company's liquid assets, liabilities, payroll and cashier activities, credits and collections, forecasting, capital budgeting and investments, and financing. The treasurer is an active participant in long-range financial planning. In the corporate hierarchy, the financial vice president is above the usually coequal controller and treasurer. The financial vice president supervises all financial operations and planning and advises the board of directors on financial matters.

Although the finance functions shown in Table 1-1 are generally performed by staff specifically assigned to those tasks, nonfinance personnel in other areas also participate in the financial decision-making process. For example, although cost recording and control are accounting and finance functions, the determination of standard costs and the responsibility for correcting for variations from realizable standards rests with the production department. Similarly, it is the task of the sales department to estimate the level of sales for various pricing policies; this information is utilized in financial planning to estimate profit levels for each price structure. Planning funds for operations and capital budgeting is a joint decision-making process conducted by the production, sales, and finance personnel. Thus, the need for a new machine might be determined by the production department, which submits its request to the division head (who is in part a financial manager). If the expenditure is not greater than a prescribed dollar amount, say, $20,000, the decision as to whether to acquire the machine would be made at this point. If the outlay is above that amount, the requisition would be submitted for approval to the home office with the division head's recommendation (and supporting data). The home office financial staff, and perhaps the board of directors, would then approve or disapprove the proposed investment, based upon data relating to projected production and sales, and the availability of funds to finance the investment.

FINANCE AS A DISCIPLINE

The focus of this text is on the financial management of business firms; however, the field of finance is much broader. Put simply, finance is a body of facts, principles, and theories dealing with the raising (for example, by

---

TABLE 1-1
Major finance-related functions in a firm

1. Financing and investments: supervising the firm's cash and other liquid holdings, raising additional funds when needed, and investing funds in projects
2. Accounting and control: maintaining financial records; controlling financial activities; identifying deviations from planned and efficient performance; and managing payroll, tax matters, inventories, fixed assets, and computer operations
3. Forecasting and long-run planning: forecasting costs, technological changes, capital market conditions, funds needed for investment, returns on proposed investment projects, and demand for the firm's product; and using forecasts and historical data to plan future operations, e.g., planning services and uses of cash
4. Pricing: determining the impact of pricing policies on profitability
5. Other functions: credit and collections, insurance, and incentive planning (pensions, option plans, etc.)

borrowing) and using of money by individuals, businesses, and governments. Although our primary concern here will be with managerial finance, essential aspects of individual financial planning and of financial institutions will be covered.

The individual's financial problem is to maximize his or her well-being by appropriately using the resources available. Finance deals with how individuals divide their income between consumption (food, clothes, etc.) and investment (stocks, bonds, real estate, etc.), how they choose from among available investment opportunities, and how they raise money to provide for increased consumption or investment.

Firms also have the problem of allocating resources and raising money. Management must determine which investments to make and how to finance those investments. Just as the individual seeks to maximize his or her happiness, the firm seeks to maximize the wealth of its owners (stockholders).

Finance also encompasses the study of financial markets and institutions, and the activities of governments, with stress on those aspects relating to the financial decisions of individuals and companies. A familiarity with the limitations and opportunities provided by the institutional environment is crucial to the decision-making process of individuals and firms. In addition, financial institutions and governments have financial problems comparable to those of individuals and firms. The study of these problems is an important part of the field of finance.

The central topic of this text is business financial management. In addition to a knowledge of strictly company financial affairs, an appreciation of the individual's investment behavior and preferences is critical to a full understanding of managerial finance. Managers are representatives of existing shareholders; they must contract with new stockholders and creditors in raising funds. They are also concerned with financial institutions because these institutions conduct the firm's activities in financial markets. A sensitivity to the financial attitudes and concerns of these various parties is crucial to management's effectiveness.

THE ORGANIZATION OF THIS BOOK

This text provides the background and tools required for effective financial management. Of course, topics can be dealt with here only on an introductory level. Additional readings are recommended for those interested in going further. Part 1 describes the general environment for individual and company financial decisions. Financial institutions, markets, and securities, as well as basic finance concepts such as the time value of money, risk, and valuation of securities, are introduced here. Part 2 examines the long-term investment and financial structure decisions of the company. The chapters cover risk and its relationship to capital budgeting and firm financing. Capital budgeting techniques and investment risk evaluation are explained in detail. The characteristics of alternative financing methods and the problem of choosing the appropriate methods are covered. Also included is a discussion of dividend policy and its relationship to a firm's financing policy. Part 3 describes tools of analysis that are useful for evaluating company performance and planning company operations. Part 4 discusses management of short-term assets and liabilities, and the relevance of short-run planning to long-term financial and marketing strategies. Part 5 describes the process by which the company raises money to finance its operations and its relation to long-term financing sources. The various types of securities issued by a corporation and the rights of the security holder are examined. Part 6 deals with special problems confronting some firms, such as mergers, financial management in international business, and bankruptcy.

SUMMARY

The primary objective of shareholders and management is generally maximization of the value of the owners' interest in the company (maximization of the value of the firm's shares). Conflicts arise between stockholders, management, and society at large. Differences between stockholders and management can be minimized by various factors, such as stock option plans that make managers part owners, or the possibility of the company's takeover by dissatisfied parties who would replace the existing management. Socially oriented company policies are sometimes encouraged by prodding from stockholders but more often by laws (e.g., antipollution statutes). Any such laws are ordinarily viewed by management as constraints within which the company seeks to maximize profits.

The financial manager is a key person in the business organization, frequently rising to the top post in the firm. The finance function includes a wide variety of responsibilities, including budgeting and investing funds, accounting, product pricing, and forecasting.

The field of finance embraces many subareas, including personal finance, financial institutions, and managerial finance. This is a text on managerial finance, that is, on the financial management of business firms. However, we will touch upon other finance areas that are important in fully understanding business financial management.

2

THE AMERICAN FINANCIAL SYSTEM: AN OVERVIEW

The financial system provides the background for all business enterprises. This system consists of the institutions and markets that serve companies and individuals in financing the acquisition of goods and services, in investing capital, and in transferring the ownership of securities. A knowledge of our financial system is important not only for financial managers, but for informed citizens as well.

An efficient financial system is essential to a healthy economy. Its primary role is the distribution of capital in the economy. For example, the personal savings of an individual, placed in a bank, can be loaned to another individual to buy a house or to a business firm to build a plant. Thus the activity of the financial system affects every citizen.

Technically advanced nations, such as the United States, the Soviet Union, the European countries, and Japan, have complex and highly developed financial systems. In contrast, most of the nations of Asia and Africa have poorly developed financial systems. There is a clear relationship between the financial sector of a country and the development of its economy.

We begin by outlining the nature of the services provided by the financial system and the institutions providing them. We then look at the various types of securities that are issued and traded in the financial markets. Finally, we discuss the factors that determine the general level of interest rates in the economy.

SERVICES PROVIDED BY THE FINANCIAL SYSTEM

The general role of the financial system in the economy is to aid in transforming the savings (income minus expenditures on goods and services in a given time period) of some individuals and companies into **investment** (purchases of physical assets that are used to produce goods and services) by others. *The financial system provides the principal means by which a person who has saved money out of current income can transfer these savings to someone else who has productive investment opportunities and needs money to finance them.*[1] This transfer of money almost always results in the creation of a **financial asset**, which is a claim against the future income and assets of the person who issued the asset. From the viewpoint of the issuer, this claim is a **financial liability**. Therefore, for every financial asset owned by someone there is a corresponding financial liability for the issuer. Financial assets are the basic "products" of the financial system.

Types of Financial Assets

Financial assets fall into three general classes: money, debt, and stock. At the present time, money is issued by the federal government as paper currency and coins, and by some financial institutions as demand deposits and NOW accounts.[2] Debt is issued by practically everyone including gov-

---

[1] The "persons" described in this section can be individuals, business firms, farmers, governmental units, etc.

[2] Commercial banks provide demand deposit accounts (checking accounts) to everyone. Commercial banks, mutual savings banks, and savings and loan associations also issue NOW accounts to individuals and certain other types of customers such as nonprofit organizations.

ernments, whereas stock is issued only by business firms. Our emphasis in this chapter will be on the creation of debt and stock because they are issued by business firms, whereas money is issued only by the federal government and financial institutions and is the medium of exchange for transactions in goods, services, and the other financial assets. Debt and stock are very important to financial managers. The issuer of debt promises to pay the creditor a specified amount of money at a future date, whereas the issuer of stock is selling ownership of the corporation. A stockholder is entitled to a share of the profits once the claims of the debtholders are satisfied. The precise amount of money to be paid to the owner of stock is not spelled out in advance as it is in the case of debt. Thus the stockholders (owners of stock) of a firm receive income from the firm only after its creditors (owners of debt) are paid what is owed them.

There are many different types of debt assets in the financial system. We will examine the major types issued by individuals, governments, and businesses in this chapter. Chapters 16, 19, 21, and 22 will discuss in detail the kinds of debt used by business firms. An important part of financial management is the intelligent use of debt in raising money for the company.

The two basic types of stock are **common stock** and **preferred stock**. Common stock is the security that represents the ownership of corporations. The owners of the common stock of a firm are the owners of the firm. The extent of ownership by any person depends on the number of shares of common stock held by the person relative to the total number of shares outstanding. For example, if the firm has 1000 shares of common stock outstanding, someone owning 100 shares would own 10 percent of the firm. Preferred stock is much less significant than common stock in terms of the amount outstanding and as a method of financing. The owners of preferred stock are paid dividends before any dividends can be paid to the common stockowners. Many financial managers think of preferred stock as being similar to debt. When we say "stockholders" we always mean the owners of common stock, not the owners of preferred stock.

Table 2-1 shows the major types of financial assets in the economy and their owners. These data indicate both the relative magnitudes of the financial assets and their distribution among the various ownership categories. Note the importance of financial institutions as represented by the first four categories of assets. Except for currency, all these assets are liabilities of financial institutions. Financial institutions are the primary suppliers of credit to the rest of the economy as reflected by their holdings of the debts (mortgages, bonds, consumer credit, and other loans) of individuals, business firms, and governmental units.

NOW stands for "negotiable order of withdrawal" and these accounts are essentially interest-bearing demand deposits. Most credit unions offer "share draft" accounts that are similar to NOW accounts. Demand deposits could be classified as debt, since they represent money that must be paid by the issuing financial institution on the demand of the owner. However, since checks drawn on demand deposits are widely used as a means of payment, they are usually classified as money.

TABLE 2-1
Financial assets, Dec. 31, 1983 (amounts outstanding in billions of dollars)

Asset	Ownership				
	Households	Businesses	Financial institutions	Governmental units and foreigners	Total
Checkable deposits and currency	339	103	56	53	551
Time and savings deposits[a]	1,835	93	60	103	2,091
Life insurance reserves	263	—	—	—	263
Pension fund reserves	1,109	—	—	—	1,109
U.S. government securities	416	15	727	471	1,629
State and local government securities	164	4	300	8	476
Corporate bonds	62	—	482	46	590
Mortgages	184	—	1,153	214	1,551
Consumer credit	—	66	427	—	493
Other loans and securities	159	1,031	1,332	180	2,702
Corporate stock	1,520	—	535	96	2,151
Total	6,051	1,312	5,072	1,171	13,606

[a] Includes money market fund shares ($163 billion for individuals).
Source: Board of Governors of the Federal Reserve System.

The Creation and Transfer of Financial Assets

So far we have said that the general role of the financial system is to serve the saving-investment process of the economy. The basic instruments in this process are the financial assets created when money is transferred from one person to another.

A direct transfer of money occurs when a person who wants to acquire money issues a financial asset (debt or stock) and sells it to someone who has money available. For example, a person starting a small business might issue shares of stock to friends and relatives in exchange for money. He or she might also borrow money from them (issue a debt claim in exchange for money). The financial asset issued in this process is simply a piece of paper which indicates the nature of the asset and which meets legal requirements for establishing the claim (debt or stock) in case disagreements arise between the two parties involved. Financial institutions such as security **brokers** and **dealers** are often used to facilitate direct transfers. A broker is in contact with people who have money and wish to own financial assets.[3] Thus a borrower can approach a broker who will arrange for the actual transfer of money from the investor to the borrower in exchange for finan-

---

[3] These people are often called "investors" since they wish to invest in financial assets. In order to distinguish between people who *have* money to invest and people who *need* money, we shall refer to people who have money as "investors" and people who need money as "borrowers."

cial assets. A dealer actually purchases the financial assets of borrowers and then sells them to investors. Brokers simply act as "go-betweens"; they don't actually own the financial assets and they charge a commission for their services. Dealers buy and sell financial assets; their income depends on the difference between the price they pay for an asset and the price they sell it for.

Sales of financial assets by the issuer, regardless of whether brokers or dealers are involved, are called **primary market transactions**. In contrast, most of the activity of brokers and dealers involves financial assets that have been isssued *in the past* and are being sold by someone other than the person who originally issued them. There are **secondary markets** for existing financial assets just as there is a market for used cars. In these secondary markets, people who own the assets are able to sell them to others. The existence of secondary markets provides advantages to everyone. For an investor who has funds today there is a greater choice of financial assets to purchase, since the investor isn't limited to purchasing newly issued ones. Also, someone who purchased the asset in the past can raise money now by selling it rather than having to wait until the original issuer pays it off. The secondary markets are of particular importance to the owners of common stock, since these securities need never be paid off, so long as the corporation that issued the stock continues in existence.

As noted above, primary markets are those in which financial assets are originally issued. Since the amount of existing financial assets is much greater than the amount of new ones being issued, there is a great deal more activity in the secondary markets.

Indirect methods for transferring money involve the use of a group of financial institutions called **financial intermediaries**. These include banks and insurance companies. Financial intermediaries purchase the financial liabilities of firms and individuals; they also borrow by issuing their own financial liabilities. As a simple example, consider a bank that has loaned money obtained from savers to a person who is buying a house. The new financial assets that have been created here are a home mortgage owned by the bank and savings accounts owned by savers. In a direct transaction there would be only one financial asset—the mortgage owned by savers.[4] There are several advantages to money transfers performed by financial intermediaries.

1   *Flexibility and liquidity.* The intermediary is able to provide large sums of money to a borrower by pooling the savings of several investors. Moreover, the intermediary can provide investors with financial assets which may be money or readily convertible into money at the same time that it is making loans which will not be repaid for a long time.
2   *Diversification.* By purchasing the debt issues of many different borrowers, the intermediary is able to increase the chances that most of the money lent will be repaid. Therefore, it is able to provide relatively low-risk assets to investors. The federal government further decreases

---

[4] Technically, a mortgage is a pledge of property as collateral for a loan, and the debt instrument (e.g., a note) represents the financial asset. Following common usage, we use the term "mortgage" here to refer to the financial asset backed by the collateral.

the risk by insuring accounts in several types of financial institutions from losses.

3 *Convenience.* Intermediaries offer a variety of financial services to their customers besides loaning money and creating financial assets. It is convenient for a single person (individual or business) to deal with a single firm that can supply whatever services are needed.

4 *Expertise.* The intermediary, because it is continuously purchasing financial assets issued by many borrowers, becomes expert in the process. A single person, whether borrower or investor, is apt to be much less knowledgeable as to exactly what the proper form of the assets should be.

The services provided by the financial system and its component institutions also include various forms of insurance (life, health, fire, etc.), the facilitation of consumer and business transactions through the monetary system, and loans to consumers for purchase of goods and services (as compared with financing investment in productive assets). Figure 2-1 summarizes the overall structure of the financial system and the general methods of creating and transferring financial assets. Borrowers such as business firms, governmental units, and individuals raise money by issuing financial assets either directly to investors or to financial intermediaries. Investors acquire financial assets directly from the borrowers, from financial intermediaries (indirectly financing borrowers), or through purchases of previously issued securities. Brokers and dealers (including investment bankers discussed later in the chapter) facilitate the creation and transfer of new

FIGURE 2-1

The creation and transfer of financial assets.

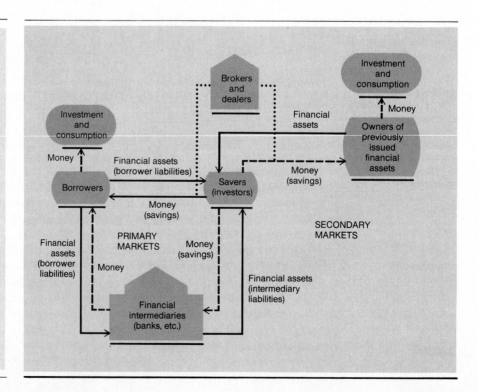

financial assets from borrowers to investors and the transfer of previously issued financial assets from their owners to investors. These financial institutions therefore compete with the financial intermediaries for the investors' favor. Now that we have a general idea of the nature of the services provided by the financial system, we will examine some of the financial institutions that play a vital role in that system.

FINANCIAL INSTITUTIONS

The financial system is composed of the financial markets and the financial institutions that, in many respects, create the markets. It is difficult to separate these two aspects of the system; however, we will look first at the financial institutions themselves and then describe the markets and the securities that are bought and sold in them.

Deposit-Type Financial Institutions

There are four types of financial institutions that accept demand or savings deposits—commercial banks, savings banks, savings and loan associations, and credit unions. They accept the money deposited by individuals, businesses, and governmental units and lend this money to other individuals, businesses, and governmental units.

Commercial banks are by far the largest type of financial institution measured in terms of the amount of financial assets they hold. There were over 15,000 commercial banks in the United States as of the end of 1984. Table 2-2 provides some insight into the diversity of their activities. They

TABLE 2-2
Financial assets held by deposit-type financial institutions (in billions of dollars)

Assets	Commercial banks		Savings and loan associations		Savings banks		Credit unions	
	1973	1983	1973	1983	1973	1983	1973	1983
Money	39	50	1	9	1	5	1	1
U.S. government securities	89	258	15	131	7	34	3	30
State and local government securities	96	162	—	1	1	2	—	—
Corporate bonds	6	13	—	—	13	22	—	—
Mortgages	119	329	227	528	73	97	1	6
Consumer credit	100	214	6	30	2	8	20	53
Other loans and securities	258	617	7	48	7	17	3	11
Miscellaneous	22	110	11	78	3	9	1	1
Total financial assets	729	1,753	267	825	107	194	29	102
Annual growth rate of financial assets, 1973–1983	9%		12%		6%		14%	

Source: Board of Governors of the Federal Reserve System.

hold substantial numbers of securities issued by governmental units, lend heavily to individuals both for purchases of homes and for other needs, and are a major source of credit to business firms (included as "other loans"). Commercial banks sometimes refer to themselves as "department stores of finance." They are very important to financial managers and their services are discussed in detail in Chapters 15 and 16.

Savings and loan associations and **mutual savings banks** acquire the majority of their funds in the form of savings deposits by individuals. They then lend those funds to finance home purchases. Both make other types of loans to individuals and business; but primarily they (1) lend to individuals who wish to buy homes and (2) accept the deposits of individuals. Savings and loan associations are found in every state. They are second only to commercial banks in assets among all financial institutions and their assets have been growing faster than the commercial banks' assets. Savings banks are not as widespread as savings and loan associations. In the Northeast, where they are very active, savings banks have aggressively expanded the financial services provided to individuals. Many savings and loan associations have become savings banks to obtain the title of "bank," which better reflects the breadth of services they now offer.

Credit unions are institutions established to provide credit to individuals who share some common bond, such as working for the same firm. While they are relatively small financial institutions, there are many of them throughout the country (approximately 20,000 at the end of 1984) and they are growing rapidly. The members of the credit union provide the funds primarily in the form of savings accounts to lend out to other members who need money. Credit unions usually provide the least expensive kind of consumer credit available.

Insurance Companies

Insurance companies can be divided into two types—life, and property and casualty. Both play distinctly different roles in the financial system and must be examined separately. To see why this is so, you must understand the nature of insurance contracts.

A basic insurance contract or **policy** involves the payment of a periodic fee or **premium** to the company in exchange for a promise to pay the insured if the peril that is being insured against occurs. For example, if you insure your house against loss through fire for $60,000 and the house burns down, you will collect $60,000 from the insurance company. The insurance company collects premiums from a large number of people to provide funds to pay the small number who actually have losses.

All basic insurance policies sold provide the insurance companies with investable funds, since the premiums are paid in advance. However, these funds are relatively temporary. To illustrate, suppose an insurance company collected $1 million in premiums at the beginning of the year on basic insurance policies covering perils for one year and sold no more insurance thereafter. By the end of the year, if the losses were as predicted, the only money left in the insurance company would be the profit on the insurance—perhaps $30,000 or so. The rest of the money would have been paid out in claims to policyholders and in operating expenses.

The distinctive features of most life insurance policies compared with basic insurance is that life insurance policies often *incorporate a savings element*. A portion of the premium paid is set aside just as if it were a savings deposit in a bank. This portion earns interest, and the total accumulates over time as more premiums are paid and interest is added. The total amount saved is called the **cash value** of the policy. Policyholders who wish to cancel their insurance get the cash value paid to them. Because of this savings element, life insurance companies accumulate large amounts of money available for investment. In this activity they perform financial intermediation just like the deposit-type financial institutions. The importance of life insurance companies to the financial system is based more on their ability to accumulate funds for investment than on their stated business of providing insurance.

As a result of the savings component in life insurance policies, life insurance companies as a group are much larger in total assets than are property and casualty insurers, which only issue basic insurance. Table 2-3 provides some information on the asset composition and growth of the two types of insurance companies. These data might also be contrasted with those for deposit-type institutions in Table 2-2. Life insurance companies hold large amounts of corporate securities and are a major source of business financing. They invest heavily in mortgages— both home mort-

TABLE 2-3

Financial assets held by insurance companies (in billions of dollars)

Assets	Life insurance		Property and casualty insurance	
	1973	1983	1973	1983
Money	2	5	1	9
U.S. government securities	4	52	5	33
State and local government securities	3	11	28	88
Corporate bonds	92	219	8	26
Corporate stock	26	65	20	48
Mortgages	81	152	—	2
Consumer credit[a]	20	54	—	—
Other loans and securities	5	28	—	—
Miscellaneous	12	52	7	22
Total financial assets	245	638	69	228
Annual growth rate in financial assets, 1973–1983	10%		13%	

[a] Policy loans.
Source: Board of Governors of the Federal Reserve System.

TABLE 2-4

Financial assets held by other financial institutions (in billions of dollars)

Assets	State and local government retirement funds		Private pension funds		Mutual funds		Finance companies	
	1973	1983	1973	1983	1973	1983	1973	1983
Money	1	7	1	2	1	1	3	5
U.S. government securities	6	87	4	69	1	42	—	—
State and local government securities	2	2	—	—	—	32	—	—
Corporate bonds	48	116	30	68	4	13	—	—
Corporate stock	20	90	91	251	38	74	—	—
Mortgages	7	15	2	5	—	—	12	18
Consumer credit	—	—	—	—	—	—	43	122
Other loans and securities	—	—	2	7	3	129	33	113
Miscellaneous	—	—	5	7	—	1	—	—
Total financial assets	84	317	135	409	47	292	91	258
Annual growth rate in financial assets, 1973–1983	14%		12%		20%		11%	

Source: Board of Governors of the Federal Reserve System.

gages, which they acquire through mortgage companies (discussed later in this chapter), and mortgages on commercial real estate.

Other Financial Institutions

There is a wide variety of other private financial institutions operating in the financial system. Some of the more important remaining financial institutions and the types of financial assets they hold are shown in Table 2-4. We will briefly discuss each of them in this section.

Pension funds are established to provide income to retired or disabled persons in the economy. Pension funds for the employees of state and local governments invest heavily in corporate bonds and stocks and some mortgages. Private pension funds established by business firms are most often managed by the trust departments of commercial banks and by life insurance companies. As can be seen in Table 2-4, the principal type of financial asset held by private pension funds is corporate stock.

Mutual funds are financial institutions established to invest the money of numerous individuals in securities of various types for the benefit of the individuals. The fund pays a fee to a management company consisting of professionals in the field of investments. These professionals manage the fund's assets, which are derived from selling "shares" to individuals. Mutual fund shares are a financial asset whose value equals the value of the securities and cash owned by the fund. The distinctive feature of mutual funds is that persons owning shares in the fund have a right to sell them back to the fund at their current asset value whenever they wish to do so. The fund is obligated to redeem the shares it issues, and mutual fund shares are not traded in secondary markets. The importance of these institutions in the financial system is that they provide an easy way for individuals to invest in a diversified portfolio of stocks and bonds. They are primarily active in the secondary markets.[5]

Mutual funds tend to specialize in their securities investments. Many funds invest almost exclusively in corporate stocks and some of these stock funds concentrate on particular areas such as energy companies or insurance companies. One fund, Japan Fund, invests in stocks issued by Japanese corporations. Some funds hold mixed portfolios of stocks and bonds and others invest only in bonds. The dominant type mutual fund is one that came into being in 1974—the money market mutual fund. Money market funds constituted more than half of all mutual fund assets at the end of 1983. They invest in short-term, low-risk securities (money market securities) issued by banks, other corporations, and the United States government. Money market securities are described later in this chapter.

Finance companies raise their money by issuing securities and borrowing from commercial banks. They use their funds to make short- and intermediate-term loans to individuals and business firms. Finance companies can be broken into three types, which are grouped together in Table 2-4. **Sales finance companies** invest in consumer installment loans, especially automobile loans; the largest sales finance company is General Motors Acceptance Corporation, a subsidiary of General Motors. They also, as a group, lend some money to business firms. **Personal finance companies** make small cash loans to individuals. Most people are aware of their activities from their substantial advertising programs. Household Finance Company and Beneficial Finance Company are personal finance companies. Finally there are companies that might be termed **business finance companies**. These firms make large cash loans to individuals and loans to business firms. Their activities are largely confined to high-risk customers who find it difficult to obtain financing from commercial banks.

Current Trends

As described above, the financial services industry in the United States is characterized by several different types of relatively specialized financial institutions. Within each type, for example, commercial banks, there are a large number of competing firms. However, the institutional structure is currently changing rapidly due to advances in technology and a variety of other social and economic factors. The trend appears to be toward an increase in competition among individual firms in the financial services industry and a decrease in the number of separate firms. Two major

---

[5] Mutual funds are a type of investment company. They are sometimes referred to as "open-end" investment companies because they are continuously selling and redeeming their shares. Mutual funds are much larger than other types of investment companies (such as "closed-end" investment companies, which do not redeem their shares) and therefore are the only type covered here.

developments are affecting the industry—deregulation and the entry of new competitors.

To understand completely the significance of what is happening requires more knowledge of how and why the financial system reached its present state than we can provide here. However, the basic picture is this. Depository financial institutions (commercial banks, savings and loans, mutual savings banks, and credit unions) once were heavily regulated by laws and government agencies as to the services they could provide, the prices they could charge or pay, and the geographic locations where they could offer their services. This extensive control by the government has been reduced significantly. The first big step was taken in 1980 with the passage of the Depository Institutions Deregulation and Monetary Control Act. This act, in part, did the following:

1 Scheduled the elimination of ceilings on the rates paid to savers by depository institutions
2 Permitted interest-bearing checking accounts (NOW accounts and share drafts) to be offered throughout the United States
3 Expanded the types of loans that can be made by savings and loan associations and credit unions
4 Provided for a partial override on state limits on interest rates charged on loans (usury ceilings)

This act was intended to permit the depository financial institutions to compete more effectively with other financial institutions such as money market funds and also to provide a more "level playing field" for the depository institutions themselves. Further developments expected are the removal of some of the geographic limitations on the depository financial institutions and removal of some more of the restrictions on the types of financial services they can offer.

The pace of deregulation is being pushed along by the entry of new competitors into the financial services industry. The premier example is Sears, Roebuck and Company. In 1981, the chief executive officer of Sears was quoted as saying that Sears seeks to become the largest financial services company in the world. Sears has made a good start toward this objective. By the end of 1984 Sears provided the following types of services: taking money and paying interest, check-writing (via a money market fund), loans, mortgages, credit cards, insurance, securities brokerage, real estate brokerage, travel services, and car rentals. In addition to these services, of course, Sears has a huge network of stores selling all sorts of products and nonfinancial services. Other firms which have expanded their financial services include American Express, Merrill Lynch, Prudential Insurance, American Can, and National Steel. The development of large firms combining a wide array of financial services to businesses and consumers along with other products and services is very recent in the United States and has created an uproar among the management of traditional financial institutions, especially commercial bankers. Thus, the bankers are pushing for further deregulation of their industry. However, Congress became concerned about the bank failures in 1983 and 1984 and did not deregulate any further at that time. What will come of all this is difficult to say, but the American financial system in 1995 could be considerably different from what it is today.

FINANCIAL MARKETS AND SECURITIES

Financial markets exist wherever financial transactions occur. By financial transaction we mean the creation or transfer of a financial asset. This contrasts with the exchange of money for real goods or services, which would not be categorized as a financial transaction. People who transfer funds from checking accounts to savings accounts are operating in the financial markets just like those who buy government bonds, common stocks, or any other financial assets. From this example we can see that the financial markets are pervasive throughout the economy. Indeed, if we include purchases of goods on credit, virtually everyone in the country is active in them.

Financial markets are usually described by the financial assets being traded. Just as we can speak of the automobile market, we can speak of the savings market or the corporate bond market. We will divide the financial markets into two general classes—money markets and capital markets. *Money markets deal in short-term debts whereas capital markets deal in long-term debts and stock.* The only markets we will examine are those that are national in scope. The stock market is a national market. It is very easy for a miner in Butte, Montana to purchase General Motors stock that was previously owned by a seventy-two-year-old retiree currently residing in Fort Myers, Florida. The basic transaction might take place within five minutes after the miner placed an order to buy and the retiree placed an order to sell the stock, although the paperwork would take several days to complete.

In contrast to the stock market, the market for consumer credit is primarily a local one. For individuals and small firms, local financial markets can be quite important; however, medium-sized and large firms are more concerned with the money and capital markets presented here.

The Money Market

Knowledge of the operations of the money market is a measure of sophistication in the financial world. The securities traded are among the most esoteric of financial assets: federal funds, commercial paper, Treasury bills, banker's acceptances, certificates of deposit, and other short-term debt instruments. To be considered a money market security, a financial asset must have little or no risk of loss to the purchaser. The money market is centered in New York but operates through a national network of commercial banks and securities dealers. It serves as the basic glue that holds the financial system together because it is the part of the financial system which acts most directly in preventing appreciable differences in local and regional interest rates. The existence of the money market, more than any other single aspect of the financial system, makes it possible to speak of a general level of interest rates that applies to the economy as a whole. In order to understand this, let us examine the financial assets that are issued and traded in the market.

Federal Funds Depository financial institutions offering checking accounts are required to have reserves as a percentage of the amount of these accounts. The bulk of these reserves are deposits in Federal Reserve banks. Federal funds are simply these deposits that can be "bought" and "sold" in the money market. A "sale" of federal funds is a *loan* by one bank to another. The loan is usually for one day only or over a weekend. The total volume of such loans can exceed $20 billion per day, and the basic trading unit is $1 million.

The interest rate on federal funds is one of the most volatile interest rates in the economy. It reflects daily, even hourly, changes in the financial markets. Most transactions in the economy for goods and services as well as for financial assets involve the use of checks drawn on deposits in commercial banks. As funds are withdrawn and deposited throughout the economy, some banks accumulate more deposits with the Federal Reserve than they need to cover their reserve requirements. Other banks have shortages. Federal funds provide a mechanism for banks with excess reserves to provide them to banks with shortages. Therefore, the demand and supply of federal funds depends on transactions throughout the economy and is sensitive to all kinds of changes in the financial system. Also, the Federal Reserve itself operates in the money markets as a means of implementing monetary policy by buying and selling United States government securities. The actions of the Federal Reserve have appreciable impact on the federal funds market, because a purchase of securities by the Federal Reserve is paid for by increasing the reserve accounts of member banks, and a sale results in a decrease in those deposits. The Federal Reserve uses the interest rate on federal funds as an index of the impact of its activities in the money markets.

Treasury Bills Every Monday at 1:30 P.M. (New York time), the U.S. Treasury closes the bidding on its weekly 91-day and 182-day debt issues. Later in the afternoon the successful bidders, primarily financial institutions, will be told how much of some several billions of dollars in bills being sold they have just bought. Payment is due and the actual bills will be delivered on Thursday. Once a month a similar process will occur for nine- and twelve-month bills. The United States government is continuously borrowing money to pay for expenditures in excess of tax receipts and to pay off maturing debt issues. Treasury bills are short-term (one year or less) debts of the federal government of the United States. The **par value** or **face value** of a bill is the amount of money that will be paid to the purchaser when the bill is due. The interest return to an investor is provided by the difference between the par value of the bills and the price the investor pays for them. This difference is called the **discount** on the bill. For example, a bill might initially be sold by the Treasury for $950 to be redeemed for its par value of $1000 a year later. The original purchaser would earn $50 on an investment of $950 if it is held for a year. There is an active secondary market in bills, and the investor can also sell the bill before it matures. The seller will receive the current market price of the bill, which will be less than the par value of $1000.

U.S. Treasury bills are the most popular of the money market securities in terms of total volume outstanding and also in terms of their use by many different types of investors, because they are backed by the United States government and have short maturities. The minimum unit of purchase is $10,000, which puts bills within the reach of many individual investors and most business firms.

Banker's Acceptances   Banker's acceptances are the oldest form of money market paper. Their equivalent was first used in the Roman Empire, and during the Renaissance the banking houses in Italy brought them to a high state of development. A banker's acceptance (or just acceptance) is a short-term debt issued by a business firm on which a large commercial bank has guaranteed payment to the investor so that it becomes a liability of the bank. In other words, a bank has backed the debt with its own credit standing. The purchaser of an acceptance does not have to worry about the risk of the borrower but only whether the bank is strong.

These securities vary in face value depending on the size of the underlying commercial transaction. They are sold at a discount from face value similar to Treasury bills. Acceptances are usually created as the result of a sale of goods from one business firm to another when the goods will be in transit for a few months as is typical in international trade, and they arise primarily from import and export activity.

Commercial Paper   Commercial paper is a short-term debt (usually three to six months maturity) of a business firm or financial institution which has been sold in the market. It is also issued at a discount from face value. This type of financing instrument is discussed in more depth in Chapter 16. As for its place in the money market, we will only point out that commercial paper is a debt issued by a private firm and that private firms (both financial and nonfinancial) have been known to fail. In 1970, Penn Central had $82 million of commercial paper outstanding when it filed for bankruptcy. Since that experience, investors have been more cautious about purchasing commercial paper, and interest rates on commercial paper have stayed well above the rates on Treasury bills.

CDs and Other Money Market Securities   Negotiable certificates of deposit (CDs) are large interest-bearing deposits in a bank. They have fixed maturities, normally under one year, and they pay interest at maturity. They cannot be withdrawn from the bank prior to their maturity date. The owners of the certificates can sell them in the money market prior to maturity, and there is an active secondary market for them.

There is another set of securities that are part of the money market—the maturing bonds of governmental units and corporations. A bond issued in 1960 that matures on December 31, 1990, was at the time of issue a long-term debt with a thirty-year maturity. However, on January 1, 1989, it will be due in one year and thus in the money market. The distinction between the bond market and the money market is somewhat arbitrary. The two markets merge for low-risk debt issues with maturities somewhere between one and three years. Also there are debt securities issued by state and local governments that have original maturities of less than one year. The United States government issues notes with maturities ranging from one to ten years, and corporations sometimes issue notes with maturities of three to ten years. Consequently, there is no way to draw a firm line that distinguishes the bond market from the money market; they blend together and strongly influence each other.

The Capital Markets

The capital markets consist of the markets in which the intermediate- and long-term securities of individuals, business firms, and governmental units are issued and traded. They are frequently subdivided into three parts—the bond market, the mortgage market, and the stock market. There are some fairly important differences among them. We will describe briefly each of the three components, focusing on obligations of individuals and governmental units.

Issuing Capital Market Securities   Before examining the capital markets in detail, it is useful to consider the procedures by which money is raised in the primary markets. There are four general methods of issuing debt and stock. One way is direct in the sense discussed earlier: The firm, individual, or governmental unit goes to someone else, usually a financial institution, and borrows the money or sells stock. More money is raised directly than by all other methods combined, and this is the only way individuals borrow. A second way is the **auction approach** used by the U.S. Treasury and described earlier in the discussion of Treasury bills. The Treasury invites bids by investors, who submit both the prices and amounts they wish to acquire. The Treasury then accepts as many bids as it needs to raise the amount of money required, taking the highest bids first. The Treasury is the only user of this method in the United States.[6] A third method used heavily by state and local governments, and to some extent by business firms (primarily gas, electric, and telephone companies) is **underwriting through competitive bids**. The borrower announces that it wishes to issue, say, $20 million in bonds to mature in twenty-five years. A single financial institution or a group of financial institutions (called a **syndicate**) can submit a bid for the entire issue. The bidder with the lowest interest cost to the issuer wins the entire issue and will then try to sell it in smaller portions to investors. The aspect that makes this procedure "underwriting" is that the winner is buying the issue to sell to someone else rather than lending the money directly. Financial institutions whose primary business is underwriting are called **investment bankers**. The fourth method, **negotiated underwriting**, is normally used only by business firms, and both bonds and stock are issued by this method. In negotiated underwritings the interest rate (or price) is set by negotiations between an investment banker and the issuing firm. This method is discussed in detail in Chapter 18.

---

[6] Bids are on the basis of price rather than interest rate since there is no interest payment on bills, and notes and bonds are issued with fixed coupon rates (refer to the next section for a definition).

The Bond Market   Bonds are debts of federal, state, and local governmental units and large corporations. They normally are issued in units of $1000 maturity or par value and have a fixed-interest payment made semiannually. The total annual interest is expressed as a percentage of the maturity value and is called the **coupon rate**. For example, a 7 percent coupon bond would pay $70 (0.07 × $1000) per year in two semiannual installments of $35 each until maturity, when the bond is to be redeemed for $1000.

While the money market is fundamentally centered in New York City, the bond market is somewhat more widespread. The issues of state and local governments in particular are traded throughout the country as are, to a lesser extent, the bonds issued by business firms. However, the focus of activity in these obligations is still New York, as it is for the issues of the federal government.

Governments and Agencies   In the language of the bond market, there are two groups of federal securities—"governments" and "agencies." "Governments" are notes and bonds issued by the U.S. Treasury and guaranteed by the federal government. They are considered to be the safest long-term debt securities available. The distinction between a note and a bond is maturity. Notes have original maturities of up to ten years, and bonds have original maturities of over ten years. Also, notes are usually issued in units of $5000, whereas bonds usually have $1000 as the minimum unit.

"Agencies" are securities issued by various federal agencies that have been established by the federal government to issue their own debt securities and use the money for a variety of purposes. The bonds issued by federal agencies have become an important part of the bond market in recent years. The major organizations and their bonds are listed in the *Federal Reserve Bulletin*. Generally the interest rates on these securities are slightly higher than comparable rates for government bonds.

Municipal Bonds   People who deal in the bond market refer to the debt issues of state and local governmental units as **municipal bonds** or "munis." The major distinguishing feature of these securities compared with all other securities in the financial markets is that the interest paid to investors is not taxed by the federal government. Since the interest is exempt from federal income taxes, these bonds are also referred to as **tax-exempt bonds**. This tax-exempt feature means that most state and local governments are able to issue bonds at lower interest costs than the federal government.

There are several types of municipal bonds. The most common are the **general obligation bonds** issued by a town, city, county, or state. These bonds are backed by the taxing power of the governmental unit involved and therefore can be considered a debt of everyone who lives in that area. Another type is **revenue bonds**. These bonds are to be paid off from the revenues derived from a specific public project. For example, roads and bridges may be financed with revenue bonds to be repaid with tolls. Dormitories and student centers at state colleges and universities are also frequently financed with revenue bonds, and student fees are used to pay them. There is a third type, **industrial development bonds**, which is of interest to business firms. These bonds are issued to build plants to attract new industry to an area. A business firm rents the plant, and the rental payments are used to repay the bonds. In effect, the local government is using the tax-exempt feature of the bonds as a way to provide cheap financing to a business firm.

Corporate Bonds   Business firms issue many types of debt; however, only large firms issue bonds. Smaller firms deal directly with lenders such as banks and insurance companies. In Table 2-1, the dollar amount of bonds outstanding is much less ($590 billion) than the amount of "other loans and securities" ($2702 billion). These "other" loans are primarily the debts of business firms, large and small, borrowed directly from financial institutions. Bonds generally have longer-term maturities than direct loans, in some cases 100 years, and are usually issued to pay for capital expenditures such as new plant equipment. The many different types of corporate bonds are described in Chapters 21 and 22.

The Mortgage Market   Although local primary mortgage markets have existed for a long time, an appreciable national secondary market for the mortgages on individual residences has developed only within the last two decades. The federal government established three major organizations to purchase mortgages from the financial institutions that originally made the loans. The three organizations are the Federal National Mortgage Association ("Fannie Mae"), which is now a semiprivate corporation; the Government National Mortgage Association ("Ginnie Mae"); and the Federal Home Loan Mortgage Corporation ("Freddy Mac"). A national market for mortgages provides several benefits; among these are the reduction of regional differences in mortgage rates and the increased availability of mortgage financing even in periods of tight money.

Most mortgages today are paid off in equal monthly (residential mortgages) or quarterly (commercial mortgages) installments over the life of the debt, which may extend to thirty or forty years. The interest rate on residential mortgages is usually somewhat higher than the rate on low-risk corporate bonds. A specialized type of financial institution, the **mortgage company**, operates in this market, as do commercial banks, savings and loan associations, and mutual savings banks. Mortgage companies are different from the other financial institutions in that they normally do not own the mortgages they originate but rather sell them in blocks to large investors such as life insurance companies and pension funds. The mortgage company collects the monthly payments and forwards them to the ultimate owner of the mortgage. Mortgage companies, therefore, act as the investment bankers of the mortgage market.

The Stock Market   When the stock market is mentioned, most people think of the New York and the American Stock Exchanges. These two stock exchanges plus ten regional stock exchanges and the over-the-counter market constitute the secondary markets for the stock issues of private corporations.

The organized stock exchanges are themselves only a way to bring buyers and sellers together via their representatives, the brokerage firms. Stock brokers are the financial institutions that buy and sell securities at the orders of their customers. Most large brokers are members of the stock exchanges and have representatives of their firm on the "floors" of the exchanges to make purchases and sales. However, the stock issues of several thousand smaller firms do not meet the criteria required for a listing on the New York Stock Exchange or the somewhat less demanding requirements of the other exchanges. A network of brokers and dealers has evolved to undertake transactions in unlisted stocks. This is the **over-the-counter market**. (It should be noted that some large companies which do qualify for listing on the stock exchanges have chosen to remain in the over-the-counter market.)

Now that we have looked at the structure of the financial system, let us examine the basic prices in the system—interest rates.

INTEREST RATES

Interest rates are the *prices* of credit. They are usually measured as an annual percentage rate of the amount borrowed; for example, 6 percent per year is $6 interest per year per $100 borrowed. Interest rates also are the earning rates on financial assets. One person's liability is another person's asset. Therefore, interest rates as prices of credit are equivalent to interest rates as earning rates—it just depends on whether you are borrowing or lending.

Different types of financial assets will have different interest rates. However, all interest rates usually vary together over time. This means that we can speak of "high" or "low" interest rates without having to be specific about the interest rate of a particular financial asset. For example, if interest rates are "high" on corporate bonds, they will usually also be "high" on home mortgages, state and local bonds, etc. The general level and variation of interest rates over the past fifty years is illustrated in Figure 2-2. Even though corporate bonds differ greatly from Treasury bills, the interest rates on these two financial assets do show similar general trends.

What causes interest rates to change over time? There are several theories that seek to explain this phenomenon. The most popular one, which is most often used by financial managers, is based on fluctuations in the supply of and demand for loanable funds. In addition, the prospects for changes in the general level of prices for goods and services, inflation or deflation, will affect the level of interest rates.

Loanable Funds

Loanable funds are the dollars available for purchases of new financial assets at a given point in time. Loanable funds, like any other commodity, are subject to the laws of supply and demand. Thus, if large amounts of dollars are available for investment, the interest rate will be low, just as the price of oranges decreases when there is a bumper crop.

The *supply* of loanable funds consists of the savings of individuals and business firms and changes in the amount of money in the economy.

FIGURE 2-2

General changes in
interest rates.
(Sources: Economic
Report of the
President; Federal
Reserve Bulletin.)

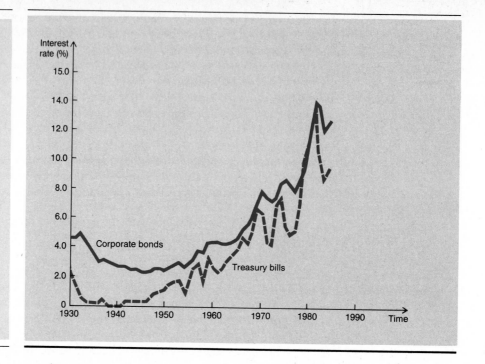

Savings is the difference between current income and current expenses including taxes and is usually the major source of loanable funds. The federal government can increase the money supply by printing more currency, but the major changes in money supply are due to the expansion of checking accounts in the banking system. Changes in the money supply are controlled by the Federal Reserve Board by adjusting the amount of reserves on deposit in the Federal Reserve banks.

The *demand* for loanable funds comes primarily from those persons who wish to borrow money to finance investment. They may include business firms that want to expand their operations or increase their productivity through modernization; federal, state, and local governments that usually spend more than they take in from taxes and must borrow funds to make up the deficit; and individuals who require funds for the purchase of houses or other durable goods. In addition, firms and individuals may wish to increase their holdings of money relative to other financial assets. This also is part of the demand for loanable funds.

As you might expect, an increase in the demand for loanable funds without a corresponding increase in the supply causes interest rates to rise until supply and demand are in balance. The general level of interest rates at any time is primarily determined by individuals' desires for current expenditures relative to their incomes (which determines savings) and the amount of investment opportunities available.

The expectation of future inflation may alter the level of interest rates by changing the supply of and demand for loanable funds. If people expect

Inflation

prices to rise in the future, there is an incentive to purchase goods and services now rather than later (at higher prices). This has the effect of reducing savings and increasing investment in productive assets.

People owning existing financial assets sell them to get money to purchase physical assets, thereby pushing down the prices of financial assets and pushing up the rates of return (interest rates) paid on financial assets. Lenders require higher interest rates because the dollars they will receive in the future in repayment of the debt will have less purchasing power due to the inflation. The result is that interest rates are higher when people expect high rates of inflation than when people expect low rates of inflation.

There is a theoretical relationship between the expected rate of inflation and observed interest rates called the **Fisher equation** after its originator, economist Irving Fisher. The observed (nominal) interest rate is considered to be the sum of two factors—the real rate of interest and the expected rate of inflation.[7]

Observed interest rate = real interest rate + expected rate of inflation

The real interest rate is determined by the productivity of investment in the economy and the preferences of individuals regarding present consumption versus future consumption. The real rate is thought to be relatively stable over time and, in the United States, to be approximately 2 percent. If the real rate of interest is 2 percent and the expected rate of inflation is 10 percent, the Fisher equation indicates that we should observe actual interest rates to be 12 percent. Figure 2-3 shows how interest rates on Treasury

[7] The equation is an approximation since factors such as taxes and uncertainty in the rate of inflation are not included. However, it has proved to be useful empirically.

FIGURE 2-3

Inflation and interest rates. Annual rates of change in the Consumer Price Index and average annual interest rates on U.S. Treasury bills of three months' maturity. (Source: Economic Report of the President, January 1982.)

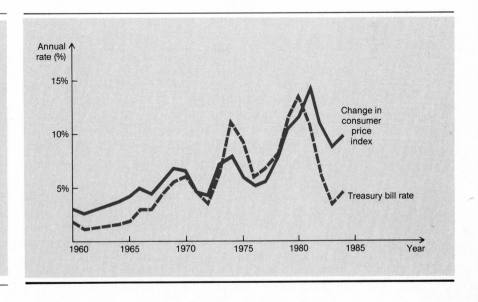

bills have moved with the rate of inflation as measured by changes in the Consumer Price Index. As you can see, the rate of inflation does appear to have a strong impact on interest rates.

SUMMARY

The primary role of the financial system is to facilitate savings and investment in the economy. Financial assets (and corresponding liabilities) are the basic products of the system. There are three general classes of financial assets—money, debt, and stock. Each of these classes may be subdivided into several types. Money consists of currency and demand deposits, and stock consists of preferred stock and common stock.

There are many different types of debt categorized by the issuer (individuals, businesses, governmental units, or financial institutions) and by the nature of the debt contract (loans, mortgages, bonds, etc.).

New financial assets are created in the primary markets. Money or goods are exchanged for a financial asset. Savers may deal directly with those persons needing money for the purchase of goods and services or indirectly through financial intermediaries.

Financial intermediaries create financial assets desired by savers, and they lend money to those who need it. The major financial intermediaries are the commercial banks, savings and loan associations, mutual savings banks, life insurance companies, and credit unions.

Many of the financial transactions in the economy do not involve the creation of financial assets. Instead, existing financial assets are purchased and sold in the secondary markets. In practice, little distinction is made between primary and secondary markets, and financial markets are most often described by the types of assets issued or traded in them. The money markets and capital markets are national in scope in contrast to the markets for savings, consumer installment loans, etc., which are local.

Short-term debt securities of business firms, governmental units, and financial institutions are issued and traded in the money markets. Money market financial assets include federal funds, Treasury bills, banker's acceptances, CDs, and commercial paper. The money market serves an important role in eliminating regional differences in interest rates.

The capital market is often divided into the bond market, the mortgage market, and the stock market. The long-term debt issues of governmental units and business firms are traded in the bond market. Mortgages on residential property owned by individuals are the principal security traded in the mortgage market. The stock market is almost completely a secondary market where previously issued shares of stock in business firms are traded.

Interest rates are the prices of credit. They differ according to the type of financial asset, and they vary over time. The general level of interest rates changes due to changes in the supply of and demand for loanable funds. Changes in expectations regarding the rate of inflation are an important factor in causing interest rates to change.

The financial system is a network of institutions and markets with pervasive effects throughout the economy. The total number of financial institutions is very large, and no single interest or even type of institution dominates. The highly developed financial system of the United States is a major contributor to the economic health of the nation.

QUESTIONS

1 What is a financial asset? How are financial assets created and transferred?
2 Explain the differences between money, debt, and stock. How does preferred stock differ from common stock?
3 If you obtain a student loan, is this a primary or a secondary market transaction? Explain.
4 The United States government issued a bond with a $6\frac{3}{4}$ percent coupon rate that matures in 1993. How much interest would you receive every six months if you bought five of these bonds which have a maturity value of $1000 each?
5 Distinguish between brokers and dealers. In which type of secondary market would you expect to find each?
6 Distinguish between money markets and capital markets. What types of assets are traded in each?
7 Why is there a difference between the interest rates on corporate Aaa bonds and U.S. Treasury bills shown in Figure 2-2?
8 "During periods of inflation it is better to be a borrower than a lender." Discuss.

PROJECT

Using Tuesday's *Wall Street Journal* as a source, collect the most recent twelve weekly values for interest rates on federal funds, ninety-day Treasury bills, a Treasury note due in 1987, and the 10 percent Treasury bonds due in 2005–2010. Plot the values on a graph (rate versus date). What conclusions can you draw? Find the articles discussing the Monday Treasury bill auctions. Why are the rates changing? (For the interest rate on the notes and bonds use the values reported as "yield.")

Benjamin Franklin once wrote, "In this world nothing is certain but death and taxes." By choosing a suitable form of organization, a business firm can outlive its original owners; however, a firm cannot escape taxes (although it can often postpone them for a long time). Taxes are an important consideration for individuals and businesses, and a general knowledge of taxation is necessary before we can discuss the problems of financial management. The form of business organization—proprietorship, partnership, or corporation—affects the taxes paid on the earnings of the business, and, therefore, the tax structure influences the choice among the alternative organizational forms. Since the topics of taxes and business organization are closely related, we cover both in this chapter.

First, we describe the various forms of business organization and discuss the factors to be considered by owners of a business in choosing among them. The remainder of the chapter examines the federal income tax and its impact on personal and business financial decisions.

BUSINESS ORGANIZATION

The three principal types of business organization are the proprietorship, the partnership, and the corporation. A **proprietorship** is a business owned by one person, a **partnership** is owned by two or more people but usually not more than ten, and a **corporation** may be owned by any number of people from one to several million. Corporations differ from partnerships and proprietorships in that the firm itself is a legal "person" apart from its owners. In a proprietorship or partnership the owners are a part of the business. As shown in Table 3-1, although proprietorships and partnerships far outnumber corporations, corporations generate 89 percent of business revenues and are a much larger economic force than the noncorporate sector.

Proprietorship

Most businesses are owned by one person and are proprietorships. A proprietorship can be established simply by beginning to sell a product or to perform some service. Except for the licensing required of many businesses, proprietorships are very easy to establish and are subject to very little government regulation. The owner is responsible personally for any debts of the business. For tax purposes, the income (or losses) of the business is part of the personal income of the owner.

TABLE 3-1
Business organizations, 1980

	Number (thousands)	Percent	Revenues (billions)	Percent
Proprietorships	12,702	76	506	7
Partnerships	1,380	8	292	4
Corporations	2,711	16	6,361	89
Total	16,793	100	7,159	100

Partnership

A partnership is owned by two or more persons. The owners must agree on how much time and money each will contribute to the business and how the profits will be divided. Partnerships are not regulated to any great extent by the government and are very easy to establish. Partnership income is taxed as the personal income of the partners. In a **general partnership** each partner is responsible for debts incurred by the business; however, profits of the business and the ownership of its assets may be divided in any way agreed on by the partners. Often there is a formally written partnership agreement specifying the arrangement.

Another type of partnership, called a **limited partnership**, is permitted in many states. In a limited partnership there must be at least one general partner. A general partner is personally liable for any of the partnership's debts. The limited partners usually invest money in the partnership and share in the profits; however, unlike the general partner, they are not personally liable for the company's debts and the most that they can lose is the amount they have invested in the business.

If a partner leaves the partnership or dies, a new partner is brought into the partnership, the old partnership dissolves. Most partnership agreements have special provisions for the purchase of the ownership interest of a partner who cannot continue in the business.

Corporation

The corporation is the most important form of business organization in the United States. Although only 16 percent of all businesses are corporations, they account for 89 percent of the total revenues of firms. Corporations are established by obtaining a charter from a state, usually the state in which the primary operations of the business are located. Large firms often choose to be chartered in Delaware because its charter provisions are more flexible than those of most other states. The corporation can own assets, borrow money, and perform business functions without directly involving its owners, who are also called **shareholders** or **stockholders**. The stockholder's ownership interest in the corporation is determined by the number of shares of common stock he or she owns. Corporations are taxed differently from other types of businesses, and the owners are not responsible for the debts incurred by the corporation. The corporation is a legal method of permitting the affairs of a business to be separated from personal affairs of its owners.

To form a corporation, the corporate founders prepare **articles of incorporation** which usually indicate the name of the proposed corporation, corporate purpose, number of directors and the names and addresses of the directors, amount of stock authorized, and the duration of the corporation (if it is to be limited). The articles are sent to the secretary of state of the state in which incorporation is sought. If the articles are approved, the corporation receives its **certificate of incorporation** and becomes a legal entity. The corporation is governed by the state's corporation laws, by the corporation's articles of incorporation, and by the corporate bylaws, which are rules drawn up by the corporation's founders and approved by the board of directors (the bylaws may be changed later by the board of directors with the shareholders' approval). The bylaws concern such matters as the rights of the shareholders (for example, whether they have the first rights to any new shares issued by the corporation), special aspects of the corporation's organization (for example, the existence of permanent committees), and how the board of directors is to be elected (for example, whether majority rule or cumulative voting is to be used).

Corporations have three important advantages over sole proprietorships and partnerships: limited liability, unlimited life, and ease in transferring ownership. The stockholders are not liable for the debts of the corporation; that is, there is limited liability for stockholders. The most that the shareholders can lose is what they have already invested in the corporation. The corporation usually has unlimited life and continues to exist even if the shareholders die or sell their shares. Relative to sole proprietorships and partnerships, transferability of ownership is especially easy for a corporation because of the convenient division of the ownership interest into shares and because of the corporation's limited liability and unlimited life features.

THE FEDERAL INCOME TAX

The federal tax on the incomes of individuals and corporations constitutes the largest single source of revenue received by any governmental unit. The income tax is determined as a percentage of *taxable income*, which is defined as total or gross income less exemptions and deductions. Tax laws influence business investment and financing decisions in several ways, which will be discussed in Chapters 7, 8, and 10. In this section we will examine some of the basic characteristics of the federal income tax. State and local income taxes vary considerably but generally follow similar patterns.

Taxation of the incomes of individuals and businesses by the federal government was authorized by the Sixteenth Amendment, which was passed in 1913.[1] Congress enacts the income tax laws (the tax code) and the U.S. Treasury Department issues detailed regulations defining or interpreting the specifics of the laws. Taxpayers are responsible for reporting their incomes to the Internal Revenue Service (IRS), which is a federal agency that collects taxes and issues rulings interpreting the tax code and the Treasury Department regulations. Federal courts resolve conflicts between taxpayers and the IRS. There is also a special court, the Tax Court, in which taxpayers may contest the rules and decisions of the IRS. This system has one primary purpose—to make sure that those taxes owed to the federal government are assessed fairly and are collected.

Below we examine the taxation of individuals and corporations. The chapter closes with a discussion of three tax factors in business decisions—depreciation, the investment tax credit, and the taxation of gains and losses realized on depreciable business assets.

---

[1] Although the Sixteenth Amendment ushered in the general income tax on a permanent basis, there was an income tax for approximately three years during the Civil War and a minor corporate excise tax (based on corporate income) beginning in 1909.

Personal taxable income equals gross income (wages, salaries, rents, dividends, interest, capital gains, etc.) *minus* business and personal deductions from gross income. Various items are excluded from gross income and are not taxable. Examples of nontaxable items are municipal bond interest, life insurance proceeds, and gifts (large gifts are subject to a separate gift tax). Business deductions from gross income include expenses and losses incurred in business. Personal deductions include interest payments (e.g., on a home mortgage), sales and property taxes, and charitable contributions. Individuals are also permitted an exemption ($1000) for each person in a family they support. Additional exemptions exist for blind or aged persons.

Gross income includes capital gain income. A capital gain results when an asset is sold for more than it cost; a capital loss results when it is sold for less than it cost.[2] If the asset was owned by the seller for six months or less at the date of sale, the capital gain or loss is **short-term**; if the asset was owned for more than six months, the gain or loss is **long-term**. All short-term gains, but only 40 percent of long-term gains, are included in taxable income. Therefore, long-term capital gains are treated very favorably. The tax treatment of a capital loss (which arises if an asset is sold for less than its original cost less accumulated depreciation) is more complicated and will not be described here. Capital gains (or losses) can be incurred on stocks, bonds, real estate, collectibles (stamps, antiques, etc.), and on most other types of assets held by individuals for investment purposes. Capital gains on assets held for personal use are taxed, but capital losses on personal assets are not tax deductible.

To illustrate the capital gain computation, assume that Clara Boyd bought 100 shares of Harbor Corporation stock on July 1, 1986 for $10 per share, a total investment of $1000. If she sold the 100 shares for $1500 on January 1, 1987 (six-month holding period), she would have a short-term capital gain of $500 and would include the entire $500 in her 1987 taxable income. If, instead, she sold the 100 shares for $1800 on January 2, 1987 (more than six-month holding period), she would have a long-term capital

---

[2] Gains on investments (e.g., stock, bonds, and real estate) and personal use assets (e.g., a home) are subject to capital gains taxation. Losses on nondepreciable investments are deducted as capital losses for tax purposes; losses on personal use assets are not tax deductible. If an asset is depreciable (only business and investment assets, and not personal use assets, may be depreciated), the gain is the sales price received minus the depreciated cost (where depreciated cost is original cost less accumulated depreciation); if this difference is negative, there is a loss equal to the depreciated cost minus the sales price received. For real property, the gain is a capital gain if straight-line depreciation was used, but may be treated as ordinary income if accelerated depreciation was used. For depreciable assets other than real estate, gains are usually, but not always, treated as ordinary income and losses are usually treated as ordinary losses. For example, assume a machine purchased for $10,000 and with a current depreciated cost of $6000 ($10,000 original cost minus $4000 accumulated depreciation). If the machine were sold for $4000, there would be an ordinary loss of $2000 ($6000 minus $4000); if the machine were sold for $10,000, there would be an ordinary gain of $4000 ($10,000 minus $6000); and if the machine were sold for $11,000, there generally would be a capital gain of $1000 ($11,000 sales price minus $10,000 original cost) and an ordinary gain of $4000 ($10,000 original cost minus $6000 depreciated cost).

gain of $800 and would include 40 percent of the $800 gain ($320) in her 1987 taxable income.[3]

The individual income tax in the United States has a *progressive rate structure*. This means that the higher a person's taxable income, the higher is the applicable average tax *rate*, where the average tax rate is simply the percentage of taxable income paid in taxes. The average tax rate varies from 0 percent to almost 50 percent, the rate depending on the amount of taxable income.[4] The tax rate also depends on the taxpayer's marital status and whether a married couple calculates taxes on the couple's joint income or on each income separately. Beginning in 1985, tax rates have been indexed to inflation so that the percentage of real taxable income paid in taxes will not be affected by inflation.[5]

Taxes on Stockholders   The tax on income from owning corporate stock takes two forms: a tax on dividends and a tax on any capital gain (or a tax savings if there is a capital loss) which is realized when the stock is sold. The first $100 of dividend income to an individual is not taxed. All dividend income over $100 is included in taxable income. A dollar of long-term capital gains is effectively taxed at a lower rate than a dollar of taxable dividends (since all of the taxable dividend except only 40 percent of the long-term gain is included in taxable income). An important implication of this tax bias in favor of long-term capital gains relative to dividends is that

---

[3] The illustration is a simplification since the effect on taxable income of a single transaction can be determined only by taking into account all of the investor's gains and losses for the year. The reason is that gains and losses are netted against each other in the computations.

[4] Personal tax rates have a "bracket" structure. To illustrate, assume (for illustrative purposes only) that the table below applies:

Taxable income	Marginal tax rate, %
$0–$10,000	0
$10,000–$20,000	25
$20,000–$30,000	30
$30,000–$40,000	40
$40,000–$50,000	45
Over $50,000	50

The *marginal tax rate* is the rate on the *last* dollar of taxable income. Thus, the tax on a taxable income of $25,000 would be $4000 (equal to 0 percent of the first $10,000 of taxable income + 25 percent of the next $10,000 of taxable income + 30 percent of the last $5000 of taxable income; the marginal tax rate is 30 percent and the average tax rate is 16 percent ($4000 tax per $25,000 taxable income). We would say that the taxpayer is in the "30 percent tax bracket." Under the existing progressive tax system, both marginal and average tax rates increase with taxable income; the maximum *marginal* tax rate is 50 percent (very roughly, on all taxable income above $50,000). As income rises, the *average tax rate* approaches but never quite equals 50 percent.

[5] For example, if your taxable income were $30,000 in 1985 and $45,000 in 1990, and if prices were to rise 50 percent from 1985 to 1990, then with indexing the percentage of taxable income paid in taxes (i.e., the average tax rate) would be exactly the same in 1990 as it was in 1985.

there is a tax advantage to a stockholder's receiving income in the form of long-term capital gains rather than dividends. This fact is relevant to corporate financial decisions, as we will discuss in later chapters.

Taxes on Owners of Small Businesses   Business income (revenues less expenses) earned by a proprietorship or partnership is treated for tax purposes as the personal income of its owners. If a small business is incorporated, the owners may have the option to be taxed either as a corporation or somewhat like a partnership.[6] If they choose to be taxed as a corporation, the corporate income tax must be paid. Any salaries and dividends paid to the owners will be taxed as their personal income; however, the salaries would be deductible in determining the corporation's taxable income but the dividends would not be deductible.

It would appear that there is little benefit in being taxed as a corporation, since the same business income is being taxed twice—once as a corporate income and again when the owners receive it in the form of dividends. However, suppose the owners wish to retain some or all of the profits in the business in order to invest in additional assets to expand the firm. The funds retained would not be taxed as dividends until dividends are paid. Therefore, dividend taxes on corporate income can be postponed. Incorporation can thereby significantly reduce the tax burden for owners of small corporations (i.e., corporations with marginal tax rates below 46 percent) if those owners have high personal tax brackets.[7]

Corporate Income Taxes

Taxable income for corporations is determined in essentially the same way as for all businesses. Business expenses including wages, salaries, materials costs, depreciation allowances, and interest expenses are subtracted from the firm's revenues for the year. Other deductions include losses from previous years and depletion allowances (such as depreciation) for oil, mining, and other extractive industries. Some types of revenues are excluded from taxable income in whole or in part; for example, interest earned on the debt securities issued by state and local governments is not subject to federal income tax.

The average corporate tax rate (percentage of corporate taxable income paid in taxes) increases with the level of taxable corporate income; that is, the corporate tax is progressive. Corporate income in 1984 was taxed using

---

[6] A small corporation with no more than thirty-five shareholders can usually elect to be taxed somewhat like a partnership, provided that it meets certain other requirements. Corporations taxed as partnerships are termed "small business corporations" by the IRS. They are also known as "S" corporations in reference to the subchapter of the tax code providing this option.
[7] For example, if Bill Reid has a personal tax bracket of 50 percent, his current tax on a proprietorship income of $50,000 would be $25,000; if the business were incorporated and paid no dividends, the current tax on $50,000 would be $8250 (using Table 3-2). That is a current tax savings of $16,750 ($25,000 − $8250). Of course, dividend taxes will be due when and if dividends are eventually paid, but that could be far in the future; until then, the corporation can be investing the $16,750 to earn additional income. If dividends are not paid, Bill Reid may only have to pay a long-term capital gains tax on the money in the corporation, if he eventually sells or liquidates the corporation.

the schedule shown in Table 3-2. Thus a corporation with $72,500 in taxable income would pay taxes of

$$(\$25,000 \times 15\%) + (\$25,000 \times 18\%) + (\$22,500 \times 30\%) = \$15,000$$

In this example, the average tax rate is 20.7 percent ($15,000/$72,500) and the *marginal* tax rate is 30 percent (since a tax rate of 30 percent applies to the *last* dollar of income, i.e., to the 72,500th dollar). In making financial decisions corporations must determine the taxes on the additional income resulting from the decision. Thus, the marginal tax rate is used.

The $15,000 tax calculated above would be the annual income tax of a corporation earning $72,500. Corporations are required (as are all taxpayers) to pay taxes essentially on a current basis. Payments of estimated taxes are made quarterly on April 15, June 15, September 15, and December 15. Thus, a corporation estimating its taxes at $15,000 for the year would pay $3750 in each quarter. If its income actually turned out to be less or more than $72,500, the corporation would either get a refund or pay more taxes at the end of the year.

Corporations, like proprietorships and partnerships, can earn capital gains. But, whereas the capital gains of proprietorships and partnerships are included in the personal taxable income of the owners, corporate capital gains are taxed at the corporate level. The corporate tax rate on the long-term capital gains is the lower of 28 percent and the corporation's regular tax rate (i.e., the corporation may apply the lower of the two in computing taxes).[8]

One difference between corporations and other businesses is that only 15 percent of dividends received from a corporation's ownership of stock in other United States corporations is included in corporate taxable income. The rationale for the exclusion from taxable income of 85 percent of dividends received is that the corporation paying the dividends has already

---

[8] That is, *all* of the long-term capital gain is subject to the 28 percent rate or the corporation's regular tax rate; this is in contrast to only 40 percent of a long-term gain which is taxable for an individual.

TABLE 3-2
Corporate income tax rates

Taxable income	Marginal tax rate, %
Up to $25,000	15
$25,001 to $50,000	18
$50,001 to $75,000	30
$75,001 to $100,000	40
Over $100,000	46

Note: An extra tax of 5 percent on income in excess of $1 million is imposed, up to a maximum extra tax of $20,250.

paid corporate income taxes on its income; the 85 percent exclusion eliminates most of the double taxation at the corporate level.

Business Losses   If a firm's taxable income is negative (i.e., expenses are greater than revenues), the firm has a loss for the year and pays no income taxes. In addition, the loss becomes a potential deduction from income in other years. The loss for the current year may be either *carried back* or *carried forward*. If the loss is carried back, the firm will receive a cash refund of taxes paid in past years. If the loss is carried forward, less taxes will be paid on income in future years than would otherwise be paid. Losses may be carried back no further than three years and be carried forward no further than fifteen years. The law requires that losses that are carried back first be deducted from the earliest year (three years ago); if taxable income in that year was insufficient to offset the loss, the remaining loss would be deducted from the second year back and so on out to fifteen years in the future.[9] To see how this works, we will consider an example. For simplicity we will assume that there is a single tax rate of 50 percent on business income.

Suppose a firm has a loss of $50,000 in 1986, and had taxable income and paid taxes in the three preceding years as follows:

	1983	1984	1985
Taxable income	$10,000	$20,000	$30,000
Taxes paid	5,000	10,000	15,000

The firm would submit a special form to the IRS covering these three years. As much of the $50,000 loss as possible would be shown as a deduction from the last three years' taxable income in order to determine the tax refund. The computations would be as follows:

	1983	1984	1985
Original taxable income	$10,000	$20,000	$30,000
Less part of 1986 loss	10,000	20,000	20,000
Amended taxable income	0	0	10,000
Taxes on amended income	0	0	5,000
Taxes previously paid	5,000	10,000	15,000
Tax refund	$ 5,000	$10,000	$10,000

[9] The taxpayer may elect not to carry back a loss at all and simply to carry the loss forward, a choice preferred by the taxpayer if, for example, the taxpayer's marginal tax rate is expected to be much higher in the future than it was during the past three years. *If* the loss is carried back, however, it must first be carried back three years, then two years, etc.

The firm would get an immediate tax refund of $25,000. The entire loss of $50,000 has been deducted from income in the three prior years.

If taxable income in the three preceding years were less than the loss in 1986, any unused portion of the loss could be carried forward. If taxable income in 1985 had been only $10,000, we would have the following:

	1983	1984	1985	Total
Original taxable income	$10,000	$20,000	$10,000	$40,000
Less part of 1986 loss	10,000	20,000	10,000	40,000
Amended taxable income	0	0	0	0
Taxes on amended income	0	0	0	0
Taxes paid	5,000	10,000	5,000	20,000
Tax refund	$ 5,000	$10,000	$ 5,000	$20,000

The firm has only been able to deduct $40,000 from prior years' income, so it would receive an immediate tax refund of $20,000. The unused portion of the loss, $10,000, would have to be carried forward and applied as a deduction from income in 1987. If income in 1987 were insufficient to use up the loss, the balance would be carried forward to 1988; if 1988 income were insufficient to use up all the remaining loss, the unused loss balance would be carried to 1989, and so on out to 2001. If the firm did not earn at least $10,000 in those next fifteen years (i.e., 1987–2001), the unused portion of the $10,000 loss carryforward would be lost as a possible deduction.

These same general rules apply to all businesses, regardless of the form of organization. However, the actual application to proprietorships and partnerships can be fairly complex when the owners have sources of income other than the business, since the losses "flow through" to their personal tax returns.

Tax Factors in Business Decisions

Three topics will be covered in this section: the concept of depreciation and its tax effects; the investment tax credit; and the treatment of gains and losses from the sale of business assets. The appendix to this chapter provides additional information on the various methods of depreciation.

Depreciation Most physical assets do not last indefinitely. Machine tools, buildings, and apple trees, for example, may have productive uses for many years, but eventually they will wear out or become obsolete and have little value to anyone. **Economic depreciation** is the decrease in the market value of an asset over a period of time, such as one year. We are concerned, however, with the depreciation provided for in the tax laws. You will recall that business expenses in general are tax deductible. If a firm pays its employees $20,000 in a year, that amount can be deducted from the firm's total income. However, if a firm spends $20,000 on a new machine, it will be able to treat only a portion of the initial cost as a deductible expense each year. The expenditure of $20,000 must be deducted in installments as depreciation over several years.

In the Economic Recovery Tax Act of 1981, the term **cost recovery** was introduced as a substitute for the term "depreciation," and the depreciation allowed under that act is defined by the **Accelerated Cost Recovery System (ACRS)**. The ACRS is described below. In most cases in this text, we will use the familiar term "depreciation" rather than "cost recovery."

The ACRS divides personal property (property other than real estate) into four classes: three-year, five-year, ten-year, and fifteen-year. Exhibit 3-1 indicates the types of assets in each class and the depreciation approach which is applicable. The accelerated depreciation method indicated in Exhibit 3-1 refers to the percentages shown in Table 3-3.[10] For example, assume a machine (five-year class life) costing $100,000 and put in service in

[10] The depreciation rates shown in Table 3-3 are roughly equivalent to 150 percent declining balance depreciation, switching at some point during the asset's life to straight-line depreciation. In Table 3-4, the depreciation for depreciable real estate approximates 175 percent declining balance switching at some point to straight-line. See Appendix 3A on declining balance depreciation.

EXHIBIT 3-1
Classes and depreciation methods for tangible personal property and certain real property

Class	Type of property	Depreciation method
3-year	Autos, light-duty trucks, tractor units for use over the road; research and development equipment; race horses more than 2 years old; horses (other than race horses) more than 12 years old; certain other short-lived assets such as special tools with a depreciable life of 4 years or less under prior law	3-year accelerated (see Table 3-3) or 3-year straight-line; optionally, straight-line over 5 years or 12 years
5-year	Machinery; equipment; public utility property with a depreciable life of 18 years or less under prior law; all other tangible personal property not in the 3-year, 10-year, or 15-year classes	5-year accelerated (see Table 3-3) or 5-year straight-line; optionally, straight-line over 12 years or 25 years
10-year	Public utility property with a depreciable life greater than 18 years but not more than 25 years under prior law; theme and amusement park property; railroad tank cars; manufactured homes; qualified coal utilization property	10-year accelerated (see Table 3-3) or 5-year straight-line; optionally, straight-line over 25 years or 35 years
15-year	Public utility property with a depreciable life of more than 25 years under prior law	15-year accelerated (see Table 3-3) or 15-year straight-line; optionally, straight-line over 35 years or 45 years

1985. Using Table 3-3, the depreciation in the five years would be $15,000 in 1985, $22,000 in 1986, and $21,000 in each of years 1987, 1988, and 1989.[11] The three years' depreciation on a $10,000 Chevrolet truck (three-year class life) put in service in 1985 would be $2500 in 1985, $3800 in 1986, and $3700 in 1987. (We are here ignoring the effect of the investment tax credit on the asset's depreciable basis; see the section below on the investment tax credit.)

Assets may be depreciated using any one of the following methods: (1) the accelerated method in Table 3-3; (2) the straight-line method over the class life; or (3) the optional approach, the straight-line method over the optional number of years stated in Exhibit 3-1.[12] Thus, the Chevrolet truck mentioned above could be depreciated as indicated earlier using Table 3-3, or on a straight-line basis over the three-year class life, or, optionally, on a straight-line basis over five years or twelve years. There is a restriction in

[11] The "half-year convention" is used for computing depreciation of assets other than real estate. Under this convention, the asset is assumed to have been acquired on July 1 of the year of acquisition regardless of when during the year it was actually acquired. Therefore, only one-half year's depreciation is allowed in the year of acquisition (assuming that the asset is held to the end of the year). The half-year convention is built into the accelerated depreciation rates in Table 3-3. If straight-line depreciation is employed, the half-year convention is used to compute the depreciation. For example, assume a $90,000 asset with a three-year ACRS class life which was purchased in 1986 and held until 1990. With a three-year ACRS class life, a full year's depreciation would be $30,000 ($90,000/3). However, since it is assumed under the half-year convention that the asset was acquired on July 1, 1986, the depreciation for 1986 would be for half a year, i.e., would be $15,000. The depreciation on the asset would therefore be $15,000 in 1986, $30,000 in 1987, $30,000 in 1988, and $15,000 in 1989.

[12] If an asset is depreciated on a straight-line basis over n years, the annual depreciation equals the asset's initial cost divided by n. Under the ACRS, salvage value is assumed to be zero.

TABLE 3-3

Cost recovery (depreciation) percentages for personal property under the ACRS for property placed in service after December 31, 1980

Recovery year	ACRS class life			
	3-yr	5-yr	10-yr	15-yr
1	25%	15%	8%	5%
2	38	22	14	10
3	37	21	12	9
4		21	10	8
5		21	10	7
6			10	7
7			9	6
8			9	6
9			9	6
10			9	6
11				6
12				6
13				6
14				6
15				6

choosing the depreciation method for an asset: All assets in the same class life category and put in service in the same year must be depreciated in the same way (e.g., all using Table 3-3, or all using straight-line over five years, etc.).

Notice that, *in computing depreciation under the ACRS we completely ignore the asset's salvage value and expected useful life*. Also, the ACRS applies only to assets put in service after December 31, 1980; assets put in service on or before December 31, 1980, follow the old depreciation guide-lines.[13]

Under the ACRS, real estate acquired after 1980 is either depreciated using the percentages shown in Table 3-4 or, if the taxpayer prefers, de-

---

[13] Depreciation was computed under the old law using the useful life and estimated salvage value of the asset or using prescribed asset lives under the Class Life Asset Depreciation Range System with no salvage value. Straight-line, declining balance, and sum-of-the-years'-digits depreciation were used in computing depreciation (see Appendix 3A on these methods).

TABLE 3-4
Depreciation percentages for real property (other than low-income housing)

Year	Month in which the asset was acquired[a]											
	1	2	3	4	5	6	7	8	9	10	11	12
1	9	9	8	7	6	5	4	4	3	2	1	.4
2	9	9	9	9	9	9	9	9	9	10	10	10
3	8	8	8	8	8	8	8	8	9	9	9	9
4	7	7	7	7	7	8	8	8	8	8	8	8
5	7	7	7	7	7	7	7	7	7	7	7	7
6	6	6	6	6	6	6	6	6	6	6	6	6
7	5	5	5	5	6	6	6	6	6	6	6	6
8	5	5	5	5	5	5	5	5	5	5	5	5
9	5	5	5	5	5	5	5	5	5	5	5	5
10	5	5	5	5	5	5	5	5	5	5	5	5
11	5	5	5	5	5	5	5	5	5	5	5	5
12	5	5	5	5	5	5	5	5	5	5	5	5
13	4	4	4	5	4	4	5	4	4	4	5	5
14	4	4	4	4	4	4	4	4	4	4	4	4
15	4	4	4	4	4	4	4	4	4	4	4	4
16	4	4	4	4	4	4	4	4	4	4	4	4
17	4	4	4	4	4	4	4	4	4	4	4	4
18	4	3	4	4	4	4	4	4	4	4	4	4
19	0	1	1	1	2	2	2	3	3	3	3	3.6
	100	100	100	100	100	100	100	100	100	100	100	100

[a] For example, if the asset were acquired in July (month 7), depreciation would be 4 percent of the asset's depreciable basis (cost) in the first year (the year of acquisition), 9 percent in the second year, etc.

preciated on a straight-line basis over eighteen, thirty-five, or forty-five years. Each property may be depreciated on the same basis or differently (e.g., one building using Table 3-4, another building on a straight-line basis over eighteen years, etc.).[14]

The Investment Tax Credit   To encourage investment by business, Congress has provided the **investment tax credit (ITC)**. It is effectively a gift by the federal government to the investing taxpayer of part of the cost of the new asset. The credit applies to most new assets used in a trade or business except real estate (with certain limited exceptions). To a limited extent the ITC also applies to used property. The amount of the ITC depends on the asset's class life under the ACRS described above (see Exhibit 3-1). A 6 percent ITC is allowed for property in the three-year class and a 10 percent ITC is allowed on assets in all other classes. The firm's tax bill for the year in which the asset is acquired is reduced by the amount of the ITC. For example, assume that a firm purchases a new drill press for $100,000 (class life of five years) and that, ignoring any ITC on the drill press, the firm owes $50,000 in taxes for the year. The ITC on the drill press would be $10,000 (10 percent of $100,000), and this would result in a reduction of $10,000 in the firm's tax bill (that is, a reduction from $50,000 to $40,000). Unused investment tax credits may be carried back three years and forward fifteen years. If an asset on which the ITC has been received is not held for a specified length of time, part or all of the ITC must be returned to the IRS (i.e., part of or all of the ITC is "recaptured"). The percentage of the ITC that is *recaptured* is shown below for property that is *not* held at least the number of years shown:

	Percentage recaptured if asset is *not* held for at least:				
	1 year	2 years	3 years	4 years	5 years
3-year property	100	$66\frac{2}{3}$	$33\frac{1}{3}$	—	—
All other property	100	80	60	40	20

Thus, if a machine with a class life of five years is disposed of $4\frac{3}{4}$ years after its purchase, 20 percent of the ITC must be returned to the IRS in the year in which the asset is disposed of; in this case, the firm would end up receiving only an 8 percent, not a 10 percent, ITC on the asset.

   The depreciable basis of an asset is reduced by one-half of the ITC taken. Thus, the total depreciation on the drill press in the above example would be $95,000 (initial cost of $100,000 *minus* one-half of the $10,000 tax credit). Appying Table 3-3, depreciation on the drill press would be $14,250 (0.15 × $95,000) in the year of acquisition, $20,900 in the next year, and $19,950 in each of the subsequent three years. To avoid this basis reduction, a smaller ITC could be elected.

[14] Beginning in 1984, automobiles, computers, and property normally used for entertainment or transportation have been significantly restricted in the amount of depreciation and investment tax credit (discussed in the next section) that can be claimed.

Gains and Losses on Depreciable Assets   This section deals with gains and losses realized on disposing of depreciable assets used in a trade or business. Although part or all of the gains are in many cases treated as long-term capital gains, the losses are generally treated as ordinary losses.[15] That is, gains may be taxed at low rates but losses can be used to offset ordinary income which is taxed at high rates (the best of both worlds!). Since there are differences between personal property (property other than real estate) and real property (real estate), we will discuss them separately.

Let's first consider personal property. Suppose a firm purchases a machine for $40,000 in 1984 and will sell the asset in 1987. Assume that the accumulated depreciation on the machine for tax purposes up to the 1987 sale date is $15,000; therefore, the book value of the asset (initial cost less accumulated depreciation) is $25,000. If the machine is sold for more than its $25,000 book value but less than its $40,000 initial cost, the entire gain (sales price − book value) is treated as ordinary income. For example, if the machine were sold for $30,000, the gain, treated as ordinary income, would be $5000; for a corporation with a taxable income greater than $100,000, the tax rate on the $5000 gain would be 46 percent. If the machine is sold for more than its original cost of $40,000, the difference between the selling price and the $40,000 original cost is treated as a long-term capital gain and the $15,000 difference between the $40,000 original cost and the $25,000 book value is ordinary income. For example, if the machine were sold for $50,000 by a corporation with a taxable income greater than $100,000, $10,000 of the gain would be treated as a long-term capital gain and be taxed at 28 percent, and the $15,000 of ordinary income would be taxed at 46 percent.[16] If the machine is sold for less than its $25,000 book value, the difference between the $25,000 book value and the selling price is an ordinary loss and is deductible from taxable income (like an ordinary business expense).

Real property is treated differently from personal property. For *nonresidential* real estate, if straight-line depreciation has been used, all of a gain (sales price minus depreciated book value) is treated as a capital gain and all of a loss is treated as an ordinary loss. If accelerated depreciation has been used, the tax treatment is the same as with personal property (see above). For *residential* real estate, if straight-line depreciation has been used, all of the gain is treated as a capital gain; if accelerated depreciation has been used, part of the gain will be treated as ordinary income (will be recaptured) and the remainder will be treated as a capital gain.[17] Assuming that the real estate (residential or nonresidential) has been used in a trade or business,

[15] Long-term gains and losses are netted against one another to compute a net long-term gain or loss for the year; similarly for short-term gains and losses.

[16] As noted earlier, the corporate tax rate on corporate long-term capital gains is the lower of 28 percent and the corporation's marginal tax rate on ordinary income (see the discussion on page 40). The machine example used here is a simplification since gains and losses on all asset sales during the year are combined in computing taxes and therefore the tax effect of a particular asset depends on other asset gains and losses.

[17] The part of the gain taxed as ordinary income equals *the lesser of* (1) the gain and (2) the accumulated depreciation that was actually taken on the building *minus* the accumulated depreciation that would have been taken *if* straight-line depreciation had been used.

any loss upon disposition of the real estate will be treated as an ordinary loss and will be deductible from ordinary taxable income.

Beginning in 1984, if a company has ordinary losses from selling assets, some of the capital gains produced by sales of other assets in later years will be treated as ordinary gains (to the extent of the earlier years' ordinary losses). For example, if Hoyt Corporation had ordinary losses of $2 million on assets sold in 1986 and, in 1987, had capital gains of $5 million on 1987 asset sales, $2 million of the $5 million of the 1987 gains would be treated as ordinary income in computing Hoyt's 1987 federal income tax.

SUMMARY

A proprietorship is owned by one individual. The owner is responsible for all of the firm's debts. For tax purposes, the income from the proprietorship is included in the owner's personal income. Partnerships are businesses owned by two or more people who share in the profits or losses. The income from the partnership is treated as personal income to the partners, and each partner is taxed according to the proportion of the business that he or she owns. The partnership dissolves if one of the partners leaves the partnershship or dies.

Corporations are legal entities established by obtaining a certificate of incorporation from the state in which the business operates. A corporation may have one or more owners who are called stockholders or shareholders; each stockholder's ownership interest in the business is determined by the number of shares of stock owned. Corporations are taxed separately from the owners. The stockholders of a corporation enjoy limited liability in that creditors of the corporation cannot require stockholders to pay any of the corporation's debts from their personal assets or incomes. Because the corporation exists apart from its owners, a stockholder can sell his or her shares to other people without involving the rest of the owners. The corporation can continue to exist even if the owners die.

An individual's taxable income is the individual's total income less a variety of exemptions, deductions, and exclusions. Personal income tax rates depend on marital status. A corporation is taxed on its net income after expenses. Both the personal and corporate income taxes are progressive in that the rates increase as income rises. A corporation can elect to be taxed as a partnership if it has no more than thirty-five shareholders and meets certain other conditions.

If a business (incorporated or unincorporated) incurs a loss for the current year, the loss may be carried back as a deduction from taxable income of the three prior years so as to produce a refund to the firm of taxes previously paid. If taxable income in the past is less than the loss, losses may be carried forward as deductions from taxable income for the next fifteen years.

Depreciation is a tax deductible expense allowed firms with certain types of business assets, including fruit orchards, machinery, buildings, and the like. The ACRS (Accelerated Cost Recovery System) assigns property, on the bais of its type, to a class life category; the class life category determines how a property may be depreciated for tax purposes. Either accelerated or straight-line depreciation may be used.

The investment tax credit is a subsidy to those who invest in depreciable assets used in a trade or business. The credit is 6 percent of the cost of the asset if the asset has an ACRS class life of three years, and the credit is 10 percent of the cost for all other eligible assets.

Part or all of a gain on disposing of a depreciable asset used in a trade or business may, in some cases, be treated for tax purposes as a capital gain. The part that is not treated as a capital gain is "recaptured depreciation" and that part is taxed as ordinary income. Generally, any losses on disposing of depreciable business assets are ordinary losses for tax purposes (i.e., are deductible from ordinary taxable income).

QUESTIONS

1 Compare and contrast the three types of business organizations. Why are large businesses almost always corporations?

2 How does being a limited partner differ from owning stock in a corporation, assuming that the percentage of ownership is the same in both cases?

3 For tax purposes how do ordinary income and capital gains income differ?

4 What are the tax advantages to a corporate stockholder of having the stock appreciate in value instead of receiving cash dividends?

5 List the advantages and disadvantages to a business of being taxed as a corporation rather than as a partnership.

6 If the total depreciation over the life of a machine is the same under all depreciation methods, what is the advantage of accelerated depreciation over the straight-line method?

PROJECT

Research and prepare a table showing percentages in terms of numbers and gross revenues (sales) accounted for by proprietorships, partnerships, and corporations for the following lines of business: grocery stores, airplane manufacturers, construction contractors, men's clothing manufacturers, and security brokers and dealers. Evaluate the variations in percentages. (Use the IRS publication *Business Income Tax Returns* for the most recent year available.)

PROBLEMS

1 In March 1986, Carl Diamond bought 2000 shares of Hedge Financial at $50 per share. The tax rate on any ordinary income from the stock is 40 percent. Ignore the dividend exclusion.

a What personal taxes on this investment would Carl have paid if he sold the stock in July 1986 for $70 per share, having received dividends of $2 per share? [Ans.: $17,600]

b What would Carl's taxes have been if he sold the stock in June of 1987 for $80 per share and received (during the fifteen-month holding period) dividends of $5 per share? [Ans.: $13,600]

2   The Flub Company forecast of taxable income for 1986 is $90,000.

a   Using the tax schedule in Table 3-2, compute Flub's estimated tax for 1986 and its expected quarterly payments.

b   Through the third quarter Flub made payments according to the estimates made in *a* above. However, at the end of the year Flub discovered that the firm had earned only $87,000 total for the year. What was the firm's fourth-quarter tax payment? [Ans.: $4237.50]

3   The Up-N Down Corporation has a seven-year history of income and expenses as shown below. What would their actual taxes paid (or received) in each year have been, making use of tax carrybacks and carryforwards? Assume a tax rate of 50 percent.

Year	1	2	3	4	5	6	7
Revenues	$15,000	$25,000	$100,000	$60,000	$ 80,000	$160,000	$40,000
Expenses	25,000	30,000	55,000	60,000	100,000	80,000	80,000

4   In 1984 the Randall Corporation purchased a $100,000 machine. The depreciable life of the machine is five years. Straight-line depreciation is used for tax purposes. Ignore the investment tax credit. Randall's tax rate is 40 percent.

a   What is the depreciation per year on the machine?

b   What is the book value of the machine on July 1, 1986?

c   How much tax must be paid on the sale if the firm sells the machine on July 1, 1986 for $40,000? Assume that this is the only asset sold by the firm during the year.

d   How much tax must be paid if the firm sells the asset for $140,000 on July 1, 1986?

5   Solve problem 4 assuming that the asset is depreciated using accelerated depreciation.

Three methods of depreciation will be described below: straight-line, declining balance, and sum-of-the-years' digits. We will illustrate the depreciation methods using an asset that cost $20,000, has a depreciable life of five years, and has a $5000 salvage value. Under the Accelerated Cost Recovery System (ACRS), salvage value is assumed to be zero in computing depreciation; however, we will assume a $5000 salvage value below in order to illustrate the general application of the depreciation methods. Under ACRS, assets may be depreciated using the straight-line method or using an accelerated method (see Tables 3-3 and 3-4) that approximates the declining balance method assuming the half-year convention (see footnotes 10 and 11). We ignore the investment tax credit in computing depreciation (see the text discussion of the investment tax credit).

Under straight-line depreciation, the annual depreciation charge is:

$$\text{Annual depreciation} = \frac{\text{initial cost} - \text{salvage value}}{\text{depreciable life}} \tag{3-1}$$

In the example, the depreciation is $3000 per year [($20,000 − $5000)/5 years].

The declining balance method (either 150 percent, 175 percent, or 200 percent declining balance) provides higher depreciation in the early years of the asset's life than it does in the later years. To calculate the depreciation allowance using the double-declining method (i.e., the 200 percent declining method), use the following formula:

$$\text{Current depreciation} = \left[\frac{2}{\text{depreciable life}} \right] \times \text{current book value} \tag{3-2}$$

where the current book value of the asset equals its original cost *minus* total depreciation to date. In our example, the depreciation allowance would be $(\frac{2}{5})\$20,000 = \$8000$ in the first year. Notice that we do not have to consider salvage value initially and that the initial book value is simply the cost of the machine. For the second year, we calculate the new book value as the cost minus the depreciation previously taken, which equals $20,000 − $8000 = $12,000. Depreciation for the second year is $(\frac{2}{5})\$12,000 = \$4800$. Later years are treated in a similar fashion. If the book value of the asset in the last year of its depreciable life is greater than the salvage value, the entire difference is taken as depreciation. In the above example, the machine would have a book value of $2592 at the beginning of the fifth year ($20,000 initial cost minus $17,408 accumulated depreciation). For the 150 percent and 175 percent declining balance methods, simply replace the 2 in Eq. (3-2) with a 1.5 and 1.75, respectively.

The sum-of-the-years'-digits method determines the depreciation in each year as a portion of the original cost less salvage value. This method also provides higher depreciation in the early years relative to the later years. To determine depreciation, we first compute a factor equal to the sum-of-the-years' digits. For example, the factor for an asset being depreciated over five years is 5 + 4 + 3 + 2 + 1 = 15. The factor may also be computed using the following formula:

$$\text{Factor} = \text{depreciable life} \times \left(\frac{\text{depreciable life} + 1}{2}\right) \qquad (3\text{-}3)$$

In the example above:

$$\text{Factor} = 5\left(\frac{5 + 1}{2}\right) = 15$$

Depreciation in year t is now determined as:

$$\text{Depreciation}_t = (\text{cost} - \text{salvage value}) \times \left(\frac{\text{depreciable life} + 1 - t}{\text{factor}}\right)$$

$$(3\text{-}4)$$

where the first year is considered year 1 ($t = 1$). The depreciation in the first year would be:

$$\text{Depreciation}_1 = (\$20{,}000 - \$5000)\left(\frac{5 + 1 - 1}{15}\right) = \$5000$$

For the second year

$$\text{Depreciation}_2 = (\$20{,}000 - \$5000)\left(\frac{5 + 1 - 2}{15}\right) = \$4000$$

The depreciation for the fifth and last year would be $1000.

A HISTORY OF FINANCE[1]

ANCIENT TIMES

When a Neolithic farmer some 7000 years ago borrowed additional seed grain to expand his land under cultivation, he had no idea what he was starting. By 3000 B.C. loans of grain and silver were commonplace in ancient Sumer. Going interest rates were $33\frac{1}{3}$ percent per year on barley loans and 20 percent per year on silver loans. Not long afterward groups of merchants established trading associations that were the predecessors of the modern corporation.

The Code of Hammurabi (about 1800 B.C.) regulated financial transactions in Babylon. Such banking operations as deposits, transfers to another party (checks), and loans were widespread by this time. Business partnerships of various types were codified, and requirements for security arrangements in loans (assets pledged to the lender) were set out. During the sixth century B.C., merchant bankers were active in Babylon. These firms engaged in activities similar to those of the great European merchant bankers of the nineteenth century, the Rothschilds: making loans to individuals, businesses, and governments; entering into partnerships with other firms to engage in some joint commercial venture; accepting, transferring, and paying interest on deposits; and purchasing existing loans secured by land (equivalent to buying a mortgage in twentieth-century secondary markets). Interest rates on loans in this period were 10 percent to 20 percent per year depending on the type of loan. Thus the Babylonians developed relatively sophisticated financial capabilities

[1] The major sources for this essay are Sidney Homer, *A History of Interest Rates* (New Brunswick: Rutgers University Press, 1963); Samuel Eliot Morrison, *The Oxford History of the American People* (New York: Oxford University Press, 1965); and Arthur Stone Dewing, *The Financial Policy of Corporations* (New York: Ronald Press, 1953).

quite early in history, and, as we shall see, there were few significant advances beyond this point for the next 2000 years.

The Greeks' contribution to finance was minimal compared with their contributions in other areas. They did develop and extend the types of loans made. By the fourth century B.C., unsecured loans became common. Interest rates were generally lower than in Babylon. A well-secured loan in second-century B.C. Athens could be obtained at an annual rate of 6 percent. On the other hand, many of the city-states of Greece had very poor credit ratings, and loans made by individuals to some cities carried interest rates as high as 48 percent per year.

A common financial arrangement throughout the Mediterranean area in ancient times was the "sea loan." Typically this was a loan secured by a ship or by its cargo made at the beginning of a voyage. If the voyage was successful, the lender was repaid; otherwise he was not. During stable periods the interest rate charged was about 30 percent. When there was active warfare or piracy, interest rates were 60 percent to 100 percent. This financial arrangement was essentially a partnership with one partner (the lender) being limited in the amount received but having first claim on any proceeds from the voyage.

The Romans, whose economy was based on agriculture and tribute from other nations, were not particularly interested in business and finance. It is known that joint stock companies with limited liability for the owners existed in Rome, but it is not clear where they originally were developed. The Romans were the original "cheap money" people. Low interest rates were considered desirable as a goal of public policy. They established a legal maximum on interest rates of $8\frac{1}{3}$ percent per year. After 443 B.C., a creditor charging more than this rate was liable for quadruple damages under Roman law. Later the

maximum rate was raised to 12 percent, where it remained for several
hundred years. During prosperous
times the actual rates charged were
usually well below the maximum,
down to 4 percent on occasion.

One shouldn't conclude from this
discussion that finance in those early
times was not very different from the
present day. Organized financial markets did not exist. Borrowing was usually undertaken to finance trade or for
personal needs, and loans were short-
term—one year or less. Large private
corporations did not exist, and governmental units were infrequent borrowers, in part due to their generally poor
credit standing. Temples in Babylon
and Greece were heavily engaged in
lending. Relatively few private banking
firms existed. The penalities for default
on a loan were severe— personal slav-
ery in Babylon and Rome.

EARLY CHRISTIANITY
AND USURY

The early Christian doctrine of usury—
the tenet that charging interest on a
loan is immoral—had a profound influence on the development of finance
for 1000 years. Loans were viewed as
an aid to a neighbor in distress. To
profit from a neighbor's distress by
charging him interest was viewed as
evil. This concept, which has philo-
sophical appeal, was applied to loans
for commercial purposes as well. The
secular authorites vacillated between
the absolute prohibition against interest demanded by the Church and the
Roman tradition of regulation and legal
maxima. Therefore, although individuals could band together in business
partnerships and share in the profits
from commercial activities, borrowing
money to engage in such activities was
inhibited.

In time some of the obvious differences in the purpose of loans became
apparent. Commercial activity began to
increase during the twelfth century,
and this forced the development of financial arrangements which avoided
the doctrine of usury while serving the
basic purpose of providing compensation to a lender. Some leaders of the
Protestant Reformation— Luther,
Zwingli, and Calvin—defended interest
on loans as proper, provided the rate
was not injurious or extortionary. Calvin fixed the maximum legal rate in
Geneva in 1547 at 5 percent per year.

THE DEVELOPMENT
OF SECONDARY
MARKETS FOR
SECURITIES

During the twelfth and thirteenth cen-
turies, two types of long-term
"securities" developed that could be
resold. The first was the "census,"
which originated early in the Middle
Ages. A census was the right to obtain
a portion of the returns from agricultural property. Originally the
returns were a share in the harvest;
later annual money payments were
substituted. A landowner could sell a
census (borrow money) on his property without the buyer (lender) being
considered a usurer. A variety of different types developed. A census might
have fixed payments and a fixed maturity and resemble a mortgage loan of
today. Some censuses were perpetuities, paying a fixed amount
forever. Others ceased with the death
of one of the parties. A secondary market of sorts existed for these contracts.
The owner of the census could sell it
to another person, but trading in these
securities was not active.

A more extensive secondary market developed in Venice. The Republic
of Venice forced its wealthier citizens
to "loan" money to the government in
order to finance its defense budget. In
return the Republic paid 5 percent per
year interest. Principal repayments
were made occasionally, depending on
the condition of the Venetian finances,
but interest payments on these loans

were made regularly for 100 years. Essentially the loans were government bonds. No paper certificates were issued, but a record of the owner of the "bonds" was kept and the ownership was freely transferable. The prices of these securities were quoted daily as an active market for them developed. Over the period in which they were outstanding, market prices varied from 20 percent of face value during wartime to over 100 percent during prosperous periods when they were being repaid.

FINANCE FROM 1100 TO 1750

The financial development of Western Europe, beginning in the twelfth century, is characterized by increasing trade and the resulting demand for short-term commerical loans and for methods of dealing in foreign exchange. Long-term debt contracts of various sorts arose in this period, including the equivalent of mortgages on real estate and of government bonds that were often perpetuities without promise of principal repayment. These government securities were issued by the independent cities of Italy and Germany and by Holland, and secondary markets developed from them. This period also saw the development of government-sponsored banks. The Bank of England was established in 1654.

What distinguishes this period from modern times are the limited nature of the financial institutions and the lack of large private corporations. Most of the banking activities were carried out through partnerships, often within a single family. Banking per se was often incidental to the basic purpose of the business—to engage in trade and commercial activities. The Medicis of Florence, who were leading bankers in the fifteenth century, are a well-known example of this. The family contained merchants, bankers, princes, and popes. They maintained offices throughout Europe, North Africa, and the Near East and engaged in a wide range of international trading and banking activities, while acquiring large land holdings and political power in Italy.

By 1750 financial affairs in Europe could be characterized as well developed in the areas of government finance and the financing of international trade. Business finance was dominated by speculators. Many companies were promoted, and their stock was actively traded. Amsterdam was the financial capital of Europe. The stock of the Dutch East India Company was traded on the Amsterdam Exchange, along with commodities and the bonds of local and foreign governments. Trading methods such as margin purchases, short sales, and futures contracts had been developed. Insurance, invented in the seventeenth century, had become a means by which private investors speculated on shipping ventures.

THE NINETEENTH CENTURY

In many respects the nineteenth century was the "golden age" of finance. The industrial revolution brought heavy demands for capital investment. New companies were formed in great numbers to exploit new technologies. Preferred stock was developed in the first half of the century, and limited liability for corporate stockholders was common by the middle of the century. The railroad boom in the United States attracted large amounts of British capital. Even the Bank of England held some American railroad bonds. Long-term interest rates were fairly low (2 to 4 percent), despite the demand for money. The invention of paper currency in the eighteenth century combined with large gold discoveries kept the money supply expanding, while rapid increases in productivity kept inflation rates down. London re-placed Amsterdam as the world's major financial center.

During this period the major consumer financial institutions were established: savings banks, "building societies" (savings and loan associations), and cooperative credit associations (credit unions). Commercial banks were almost exclusively concerned with the affairs of their business customers.

Prior to the American Revolution there were no chartered banks in the thirteen American colonies. Money was in generally short supply, and many business transactions were based on the barter of commodities. After the revolution several banks received charters from state governments. In 1791 the first Bank of the United States was chartered by Congress at the urging of Secretary of the Treasury Alexander Hamilton. The bank was founded to expand the credit available in the economy, but its charter was not renewed in 1811 because it had been badly managed and because agricultural interests in the country were opposed to renewal.

In 1816 the second Bank of the United States was chartered. As a financial institution serving the interests of the growing country, it was well conceived. Unfortunately, the bank fell prey to Andrew Jackson's mistrust of "monied interests" and its policies of keeping the paper money issued by local banks within bounds aroused intense antagonism. The second bank's charter expired in 1836. The bankers of New York City picked up the left-over pieces of the bank (which had been headquarterd in Philadelphia) and proceeded to construct a vastly greater stronghold of financial power than had been dreamed of by its original management. The ultimate result was that the farmers and frontiersmen who had opposed the bank gained nothing, but the financial center of the United States moved from Philadelphia to New York. There was not to be another central government bank in this country until the Federal Reserve Bank was established in 1913.

Historical interest rates. (Rates shown after A.D. 1200 are for long-term, low-risk securities. Earlier interest rates are for short-term debts.) (Sources: Homer, "A History of Interest Rates" and Federal Reserve Bulletin.)

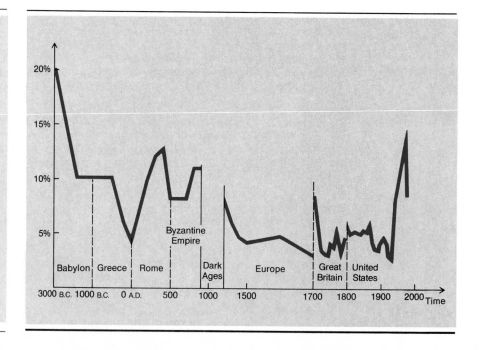

The period 1836 to 1863 was the era of "wildcat banking." Anyone could start a bank and issue currency. The currency of most of these banks was not considered to be worth its face value. The most beneficial thing that wildcat banking did was to encouarge the development of the American engraving industry. With every bank issuing its own paper currency, there was a lot of engraving work to do.

In 1863 the National Banking Act provided for the federal chartering of commerical banks (national banks) and imposed a tax on private bank currency issues that effectively eliminated them.

Nineteenth-century interest rates in the United States varied widely from one part of the country to the other. A tradition of 5 percent to 6 percent interest on long-term debt became established in the East, and rates stayed mostly in this range for secure debt instruments. In the West things were different. In specific cases mortgages on ranchland were obtained at 36 percent annual interest. Savings banks in Los Angeles at midcentury were paying 15 percent on deposits. The problem was the lack of a well-developed financial system to ease the movement of money from East to West. The discrepancies in rates spawned several political movements as well as a distrust in the West of "Eastern bankers" that persists to some extent today.

UNITED STATES FINANCE IN THE TWENTIETH CENTURY

The nineteenth century was the heyday of private financiers. In the twentieth century the federal government assumed a dominant role in the American financial system. The stock market collapse of 1929 to 1932 wiped out the fortunes of many people and dispelled the notion that Wall Street financiers had financial matters well under control. Legislation passed during the 1930s made the stock market less of a private club of speculators and stripped financial power from the major banking houses of the time by forcing a division between commerical banking and investment banking. The House of Morgan—the great banking firm established by J. P. Morgan that dominated the financial scene in the early part of the century—was split into two firms still active today as major financial institutions: Morgan, Stanley, and Company, investment bankers; and Morgan Guaranty Trust, the sixth largest commercial bank in the United Sates.

Financially the twentieth century is also characterized by the dispersion of financial power, the proliferation of financial instruments, and an emphasis on personal finance. The stock market is dominated by financial institutions that rely on individual investors for their funds. Financial institutions woo consumer accounts with all the marketing skills they can bring to bear. The average person can borrow money to finance cars, boats, and appliances. Such financing was not widely available until after World War II.

Interest rates, after staying fairly low during the early part of the century, dropped to minimal levels during the 1930s and stayed relatively low until 1965. Since then we have been living in a complex and rapidly shifting financial environment. Interest rates have moved up and down rapidly and at times have reached levels unprecedented in the history of the United States. In 1981, the United States government had to pay more than 16 percent to borrow money for two years. A reduction in the rate of inflation brought some relief in the mid-1980s as interest rates dropped in response.

The financial markets are now international in scope. The major financial centers of the world—New York, London, Hong Kong, Singapore, Zurich, and Tokyo—are closely linked together by electronic communications and financial institutions.

A well-known fact of economic life is that money is not free and can be downright expensive. In this chapter, we look at some methods of comparing cash flows that occur over time. The ability to make such comparisons is very useful for both business managers and individuals in making financial decisions. Some examples of the use of time-value techniques in dealing with business and personal financial problems are provided to illustrate the concepts.

WHY MONEY HAS TIME VALUE

In Chapter 2 we discussed the factors that determine the general level of interest rates in the economy. Essentially three elements were noted as being of major importance: (1) attitudes of individuals with respect to the importance of current consumption over future consumption, (2) the availability of opportunities for productive investment, and (3) inflation. From the viewpoint of an individual or business firm, the practical consequences are apparent. If you have some spare cash now, you can invest it in liquid and relatively riskless assets such as a savings deposit in a bank and receive more money later. If you borrow money now, you must repay a larger amount in the future (the amount borrowed *plus* interest). The result is that $100 in hand today is worth more than $100 to be received a year from now because $100 today can be invested to provide $100 plus interest next year. The existence of interest rates in the economy therefore provides money with its time value quite apart from the attitudes of any one person or the investment opportunities available to a particular firm.

In the first part of this chapter we will assume that we know the interest rate which gives money its time value. The last section is devoted to the problem of determining an unknown interest rate on a loan or investment when all the cash flows are known.

FIGURE 4-1

The cash flows associated with borrowing $200 for one year at an interest rate of 10 percent.

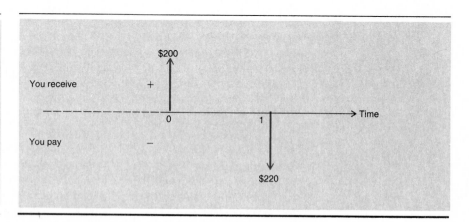

FIGURE 4-2

The cash flows
associated with
lending $200 for one
year at an interest rate
of 10 percent.

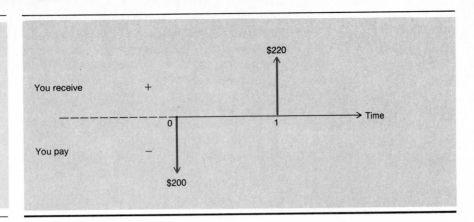

BASIC CONCEPTS

Compound Interest

If you borrow $200 for one year and agree to repay the lender $220 at the end of the year, the interest cost of borrowing is $20. The rate of interest is $20/$200 = 0.10 or 10 percent per year. All the mechanics of compound interest are illustrated in this simple example. Let's examine the basic cash flows of the example. There are really only two cash flows of importance here, your initial inflow of cash of $200 and the payment of $220 one year later. If we take the date of borrowing as time 0 and the date of repayment as time 1 (one year from time 0), these flows can be represented in the cash flow diagram shown in Figure 4-1. This diagram is drawn from the viewpoint of the borrower. If you were the lender instead of the borrower, your cash flows would be as shown in Figure 4-2.

The general relationship among the variables in the example can be expressed as

Repayment = amount borrowed plus interest payment

and, since the interest charged is usually expressed as a rate or percent of the amount borrowed

Repayment = amount borrowed + (rate × amount borrowed)

or, by rearranging the terms,

Repayment = (amount borrowed)$(1 + i)$ (4-1)

where i is the interest rate. In our example,

$$\$220 = \$200\ (1 + 0.10)$$

$$= \$200\ (1.10)$$

$$= \$220$$

Suppose that you just purchasd a used Honda from Friendly Dan, the Cycle Man, for $200. He is kind enough to give you up to one year to pay off the purchase price with only 1 percent *per month* interest charge on the outstanding balance. At the end of the first month, you would owe $200(1.01) = $202. What if you didn't pay this amount at the end of the first month? Since you owe $202 at the end of the first month, you would owe $202(1.01) = $204.02 at the end of two months. At the end of three months you would owe $204.02(1.01) = $206.06. Another way of showing the amount owed at the end of three months is

First month: (1.01)($200)
Second month: (1.01)(1.01)($200)
Third month: (1.01)(1.01)(1.01)($200)

or

$(1.01)^3$ $200 = (1.0303)$ $200 = $206.06

The interest is being compounded monthly. At the end of twelve months you would have to pay $(1.01)^{12}$ $200 = (1.1268)$ $200 = $225.36. This example illustrates the following general relationship.

If P is a present or initial amount

F is a future amount

i is the interest rate *per time period*

n is the number of time periods

then,

$$F = P(1 + i)^n \qquad\qquad (4\text{-}2)$$

In the example, P is the amount borrowed now and F is the future payment (amount borrowed plus interest). However, the formula also applies when P is the amount invested now and F is the amount received in the future (initial investment plus interest). Equation (4-2) is the basic relationship in time-value-of-money methods. All the other relationships we will discuss later are developed from this one.

The only difficult part of Eq. (4-2) is raising $(1 + i)$ to the nth power. Unless you have a calculator handy, finding $(1.01)^{12}$, for example, takes quite a while. For this reason, there are many published tables available giving values of $(1 + i)^n$ for various values of i and n. Appendix A in the back of this book contains a fairly complete set of tables of interest rate factors. Table 4-1 shows some typical values for $(1 + i)^n$. The time periods in the table can be days, months, quarters, years, or whatever time period is appropriate for your problem.

Returning to the example, if you wished to know how much you would owe on the motorcycle at the end of four months at an interest rate of 1 percent per month, you would go to the table and look across the row for four periods and under the 1 percent column, finding this value of $(1.01)^4 = 1.0406$. The amount owed at the end of four months is therefore (1.0406) $200 = $208.12.

Example Problem In 1626 Peter Minuit purchased Manhattan Island from the Indians for about $24 worth of trinkets. If the Indians had taken cash instead and invested it to earn 6 percent compounded annually, how much would the Indians have had in 1986, 360 years later?

Since Table 4-1 doesn't go out to 360, we must solve this problem in steps.

First, how much would the Indians have in 1726 at the end of the first 100 years, which is the highest value for n in the table? We see that the value of $1 at 6 percent per year for 100 years is $339.30; therefore, the value of $24 compounded at 6 percent per year for 100 years is

$$F_{100} = \$24 \ (1 + .06)^{100}$$

$$= \$24 \ (339.3)$$

$$= \$8143$$

We can now consider the $8143 as invested at $t = 0$ and see what its value would be at the end of the next 100 years compounded at 6 percent per year. At the end of the second century (1826) the $8143 invested in 1726 would again have grown by a factor of 339.3.

$$F_{200} = F_{100} \ (1.06)^{100}$$

$$= \$8143 \ (339.3)$$

$$= \$2,762,919.90$$

or approximately $2.763 million. By 1926, at the end of the third 100 years, the value would have increased another 339.3 times.

$$F_{300} = F_{200} \ (1.06)^{100}$$

$$= \$2.763 \text{ million } (339.3)$$

$$= \$937.5 \text{ million}$$

TABLE 4-1
Future compound value of $1: $(1 + i)^n$

Number of periods (n)	Interest rate per period (i)						
	1%	2%	4%	6%	8%	10%	12%
1	1.0100	1.0200	1.0400	1.0600	1.0800	1.1000	1.1200
2	1.0201	1.0404	1.0876	1.1236	1.1664	1.2100	1.2544
3	1.0303	1.0612	1.1249	1.1910	1.2597	1.3310	1.4049
4	1.0406	1.0824	1.1699	1.2625	1.3605	1.4641	1.5735
5	1.0510	1.1041	1.2167	1.3382	1.4693	1.6105	1.7623
10	1.1046	1.2190	1.4802	1.7908	2.1589	2.5937	3.1058
12	1.1268	1.2682	1.6010	2.0122	2.5182	3.1384	3.8960
15	1.1610	1.3459	1.8009	2.3966	3.1722	4.1772	5.4736
20	1.2202	1.4859	2.1911	3.2071	4.6610	6.7275	9.6463
25	1.2824	1.6406	2.6658	4.2919	6.8485	10.835	17.000
60	1.8167	3.2810	10.52	32.99	101.3	304.5	897.6
100	2.7048	7.2446	50.505	339.3	2,200.0	13,780.0	83,522.0

For the sixty years from 1926 to 1986 the $937.5 million would grow to

$$F_{360} = F_{300} \, (1.06)^{60}$$

$$= \$937.5 \text{ million } (32.99)$$

$$= \$30.93 \text{ billion}$$

This value is approximately $50 per square foot of Manhattan Island! Given current prices for Manhattan land, maybe Peter didn't make that good a buy.

Note that this problem could have been solved more simply by observing initially that $(1.06)^{360} = (1.06)^{100}(1.06)^{100}(1.06)^{100}(1.06)^{60}$. We could have simply multiplied $(339.3)(339.3)(339.3)(32.99)$ to arrive at[1]

$$(1.06)^{360} = 1288.6 \times 10^6$$

This factor multiplied by $24 provides us with $30.93 billion, the same answer as above.

Double Your Money If you look at Table 4-1 in the 6 percent column, you see that the factor for twelve periods is 2.0122. This means that $1 invested at 6 percent per year will grow to $2.01, or very nearly double, in twelve years. This is an example of a rule of thumb called the **rule of 72**. This rule works as follows: If you wish to know how long it will take to double your money at a given interest rate, divide the rate into 72 and the result is the number of years it will take. In this case $\frac{72}{6} = 12$. The rule works pretty well for most interest rates.[2] For example, the rule of 72 would say that it will take seventy-two years to double your money at 1 percent per year. In fact, it will take about seventy years. The rule says that it would take 3.6 years to double your money at 20 percent ($\frac{72}{20}$); in fact, it will take 3.8 years. The rule works the other way too. You can estimate the interest rate required to double your money in a given number of years by dividing the number of years into 72. For example, you must earn about 7.2 percent per year to double your money in ten years. The rule of 72 is a handy thing to remember.

Present Value

In the problems discussed above we were calculating the future value (or payment) of an amount invested (or borrowed) at a given rate of interest. In many problems, you would like to know the present amount that will grow

[1] This is an application of the rule for combining exponents which says that

$$N^{A+B} = (N^A)(N^B)$$

For example,

$$2^5 = (2^3)(2^2) = (8)(4) = 32$$

[2] A more accurate method is the **rule of 69**:

$$\text{Number of periods to double} = 0.35 + \frac{69}{\text{interest rate}}$$

For a development of the rule of 69 and a comparison with the rule of 72, see J. P. Gould and R. L. Weil, "The Rule of 69," *Journal of Business*, 49(3) (July 1974), pp. 397–398.

to a given future value. Suppose you are faced with the following problem. You wish to save a portion of the earnings from your summer job this year to make your first tuition payment next fall, a year from now. Tuition will be $600 and the bank will pay you 5 percent compounded annually. How much must you put in the bank now in order to have $600 next year? The future amount you need is $600 and the interest rate is 5 percent. Let P be the amount put into savings now. From Eq. (4-2) we know that

$$F = P(1 + i) \tag{4-3}$$

Solving Eq. (4-3) for P, we get

$$P = \frac{F}{1 + i} \tag{4-4}$$

and

$$P = \frac{\$600}{1.05}$$

$$= \$571.43$$

The amount $571.43 is called the **present value** of $600 to be received one year from now at the interest rate of 5 percent per year. The general relationship for the present value of a future amount to be received n periods from now at an interest rate of i per period is derived from Eq. (4-2) just as the one-period relation was. Equation (4-2) was

$$F = P(1 + i)^n$$

Solving for P,

$$P = \frac{F}{(1 + i)^n} \tag{4-5}$$

In solving problems where P is the unknown amount, if we know the value of $(1 + i)^n$, you can remember to divide the future amount by that factor in order to find the present value. Alternatively, note that Eq. (4-5) can be expressed as

$$P = F\left[\frac{1}{(1 + i)^n}\right] \tag{4-6}$$

Tables generally provide values for the term in the brackets so that when you wish to find the present value of a future amount you can *multiply* by the present value factor $1/(1 + i)^n$ rather than *divide* by the compound amount factor $(1 + i)^n$. This is done because it is easier for people doing hand calculations to multiply than divide. To take a trivial example, if $(1 + i)^n = 1.05$, then $1/1.05 = 0.9524$. Which is easier to calculate, $0.9524 \times \$100$ or $\$100/1.05$?

We can use the value of $1/1.05 = 0.9524$ to solve the previous example. From Eq. (4-6) the present value of $F = \$600$ is

$$P = \$600\ (0.9524)$$

$$= \$571.43$$

We now have two interest factors to keep track of, the **compound amount factor** $(1 + i)^n$ and the **present value factor** $[1/(1 + i)^n]$. As a way of remembering what these factors do, we use a special notation to express them. The compound amount factor is

$$(F/P, i, n) = (1 + i)^n \qquad\qquad (4\text{-}7)$$

This factor is used to find the future value of a present amount at i percent for n periods. The compound amount factor is always greater than 1.0 for i greater than zero, indicating that a present amount will always grow to a larger future value.

The present value factor is

$$(P/F, i, n) = \frac{1}{(1 + i)^n} \qquad\qquad (4\text{-}8)$$

This factor is used to find the present value of a future amount. The present value factor is always less than 1.0 for i greater than zero, indicating that a future amount has a smaller present value. A dollar in the future is worth less than a dollar today, as we said at the beginning of the chapter. Moreover, the further out in the future a dollar is, the less it is worth today. For example, at an interest rate of 6 percent the value today of a dollar received one year from now is

$$P = \$1 \ (P/F, 6\%, 1)$$

$$= \$1 \left[\frac{1}{1.06}\right]$$

$$= \$1 \ (0.9434)$$

$$= \$0.9434$$

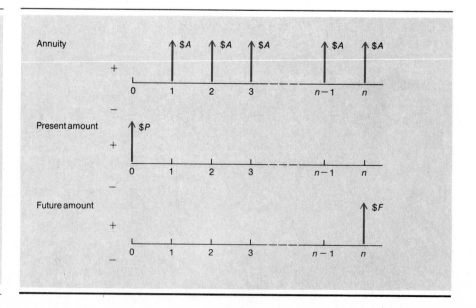

FIGURE 4-3
Cash flow diagrams.

Using Table 4-1 to obtain the value of $(1.06)^2 = 1.1236$ we see that the value today of a dollar received two years from now is

$$P = \$1 \ (P/F, 6\%, 2)$$

$$= \$1 \left[\frac{1}{(1.06)^2}\right]$$

$$= \$1 \left(\frac{1}{1.1236}\right)$$

$$= \$1(0.8900)$$

$$= \$0.89$$

Therefore, at an interest rate of 6 percent, a dollar to be received one year from now is worth 94.34 cents today, whereas a dollar to be received two years from now is worth only 89 cents today.

Note that the higher the interest rate is, the less a dollar in the future is worth today. At an interest rate of 5 percent, a dollar to be received in one year is worth 95.24 cents today, but at an interest rate of 6 percent, that dollar is only worth 94.34 cents today.

Values for all the interest rate factors for various interest rates are shown in Appendix A at the back of the book. The headings in the tables of Appendix A are based on the symbols defined above. If you look at the table for 6 percent under the column headed P/F, you will find 0.8900 in the row for $n = 2$. We will be discussing the use of these tables after we look at some more difficult problems.

Annuities

An **annuity** is a series of periodic payments or receipts of equal amounts; for example, $100 per year for ten years. A typical house mortgage repayment schedule is an annuity. Figure 4-3 shows the cash flow diagram for any annuity of $A for n periods contrasted with present (P) and future (F) amounts. As an example of one type of problem involving annuities, suppose you plan to save $1000 each summer for the next three years. You can earn 5 percent per year on this money. How much could you withdraw from the bank three years from now? A cash flow diagram of the problem we are describing is shown in Figure 4-4, where F is the unknown amount to be

---

FIGURE 4-4

The cash flows associated with a savings program.

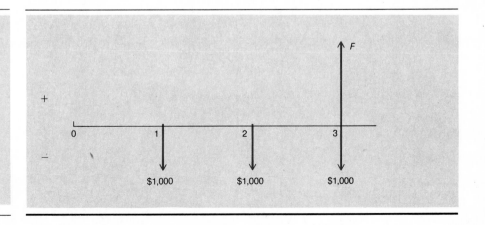

determined. From the cash flow diagram you can see that the first savings deposit planned is one year from the present. At the end of the summer two years from now you will have that $1000 plus the interest earned on it as well as a newly deposited $1000, or $1000(1.05) + $1000. Therefore, the total in the account at the end of two years will be $2050. At the end of the third summer you will have accumulated savings and interest of $2050(1.05) = $2152.50 plus an additional $1000 in new savings. You would therefore have a total future amount of $3152.50, that is

$$F = \$3152.50$$

Future Values and Annuities   There is an easier way to solve such problems. To see how, let's look at the savings program a different way. At the end of the third summer the $1000 saved in the first year would have been earning interest for two years. Therefore, the first summer's savings contributed $1000 (1.05)^2 = $1000 (1.1025) = $1102.50. The savings from the second summer earned interest for one year, $1000 (1.05) = $1050. The savings from the third year were just deposited and earned nothing. Adding them together,

$$F = \$1000 \ (1.05)^2 + \$1000 \ (1.05) + \$1000$$

$$= \$1102.50 + \$1050 + \$1000$$

$$= \$3152.50$$

We can express the computations above in terms of an annual amount A (which was $1000 in the example) and the interest rate i.

$$F = A(1 + i)^2 + A(1 + i) + A$$

Alternatively, we can write the relationship as

$$F = A[(1 + i)^2 + (1 + i) + 1] \tag{4-9}$$

The term in the brackets is another interest factor that is sometimes called the **annuity compound amount factor**.[3] It expresses the value at the end of three periods of a three-period annuity of $1 per period invested at an interest rate of i percent. We can represent this factor for n periods and i percent per period in our notation as $(F/A, i, n)$. It is used to find the future value of an annuity and always has a value greater than 1.0. Notice from Figure 4-3 that the future value F occurs at the same point in time as does the last annuity amount A; the last annuity amount therefore earns no interest. Values for the annuity compound amount factor are also found in tables such as the ones in Appendix A.

In the example above, the factor is

$$1.1025 + 1.05 + 1.0 = 3.1525$$

To solve our problem, we would need only to look in the 5 percent table in

---

[3] The general form of the annuity compound amount factor $(F/A, i, n)$ is the sum of a series of individual compound amount factors:

$$(F/A, i, n) = (1 + i)^{n-1} + (1 + i)^{n-2} + \cdots + (1 + i) + 1.0$$

Appendix A under the column headed *F/A* and along the row for $n = 3$ to find the value of 3.1525 and multiply it by $1000 to get our answer of $3152.50.

Now suppose you wanted to have $3152.50 available to you at the end of the summer three years from now. How much would you have to deposit each summer at an interest rate of 5 percent starting one year from now assuming that you save equal amounts each year? We know the answer is $1000 per year, but how can we calculate it? It's simply the reverse of the problem above. Now we are given the future amount and wish to know the annual amount.

There is a factor used to find the annuity that must be invested to provide a future value. It is called the **sinking fund factor** and is expressed as $(A/F, i, n)$. This factor is a number between zero and 1.0. In order to solve our problem, we need to know $(A/F, 5\%, 3)$. If you now look in the 5 percent table of Appendix A down the column headed *A/F* and along the row for $n = 3$, you will find

$$(A/F, 5\%, 3) = 0.3172$$

To determine the annual savings required to accumulate to a future value of $3152.50, you need to perform the following calculations:

$$A = \$3152.50 \ (A/F, 5\%, 3)$$

$$= \$3152.50 \ (0.3172)$$

$$= \$1000$$

In general, to find the annuity A given the future amount F, use the sinking fund factor

$$A = F(A/F, i, n) \tag{4-10}$$

It is worthwhile to note that the sinking fund factor is equal to the reciprocal of the annuity compound amount factor:

$$(A/F, 5\%, 3) = \frac{1}{(F/A, 5\%, 3)}$$

$$= \frac{1}{3.1525}$$

$$= 0.3172$$

The sinking fund factor is very useful in developing savings plans designed to reach a particular goal; such an example is developed later in this chapter. Many corporate bond issues require the firm to make regular payments into a sinking fund set up to retire the bonds at the end of a specified number of years. This is where the factor gets its name, since it is used to find out how large the payments (annuity) must be to make the sinking fund equal the amount of the bond issue when the bonds must be paid off.

Present Values and Annuities   In many problems you will want to know the present amount that must be invested today in order to provide an annuity for several periods. For example, suppose your grandmother wished to deposit enough money now to meet your tuition payments for the next three years of $2000 per year. The interest rate is 5 percent per year. The cash flows are shown in Figure 4-5.

One way to solve this problem is to treat it as three smaller problems of finding the present values given the future amounts.

1 How much must be invested today to provide $2000 one year from now?

$$P = \$2000 \ (P/F, 5\%, 1)$$

$$= \$2000 \left[\frac{1}{1.05} \right]$$

$$= \$2000 \ (0.9524)$$

$$= \$1904.80$$

2 How much must be invested today to provide $2000 two years from now?

$$P = \$2000 \ (P/F, 5\%, 2)$$

$$= \$2000 \left[\frac{1}{(1.05)^2} \right]$$

$$= \$2000 \ (0.9070)$$

$$= \$1814$$

3 How much must be invested today to provide $2000 three years from now?

$$P = \$2000 \ (P/F, 5\%, 3)$$

$$= \$2000 \left[\frac{1}{(1.05)^3} \right]$$

$$= \$2000 \ (0.8638)$$

$$= \$1727.60$$

The total amount that must be deposited is the sum of the three values calculated above; so

$$P = \$1904.80 + \$1814 + \$1727.60$$

$$= \$5446.40$$

This computational scheme can be written in a more general form as

$$P = \frac{A}{1+i} + \frac{A}{(1+i)^2} + \frac{A}{(1+i)^3}$$

$$= A \left[\frac{1}{1+i} + \frac{1}{(1+i)^2} + \frac{1}{(1+i)^3} \right] \tag{4-11}$$

The terms in the brackets are a simple sum of single payment present value factors. Values for such sums are tabulated as an interest factor called the annuity present value factor.[4] We can denote the factor as $(P/A, i, n)$, the present value of an annuity. The annuity begins (the first A occurs) one period *after* the present amount P occurs (this was illustrated earlier in Figure 4-3). The value for $(P/A, 5\%, 3)$ is

$$(P/A, 5\%, 3) = 0.9524 + 0.9070 + 0.8638$$

$$= 2.7232$$

This value can be found in the 5 percent table in Appendix A. For our problem above we could have determined P as

$$P = A(P/A, i, n)$$

$$= \$2000(P/A, 5\%, 3)$$

$$= \$2000(2.7232)$$

$$= \$5446.40$$

This brings up another issue: How accurate do you really need to be in calculating such values? The answer is: Not nearly so accurate as we have been in our calculations. For most practical purposes, three-place accuracy is sufficient in solving interest rate problems. An answer of $5450 is usually just as good as $5446.40. There are some business situations in which greater accuracy is desirable, but you should be able to identify them when they are encountered. The values in the tables of Appendix A are accurate to four or five figures to permit more precise results if you want them. For very precise results, a calculator or computer can be used with the formulas in

---

[4] The general relationship for the annuity present value factor is

$$(P/A, i, n) = \frac{1}{1 + i} + \frac{1}{(1 + i)^2} + \cdots + \frac{1}{(1 + i)^n}$$

FIGURE 4-5

The present value of three annual amounts.

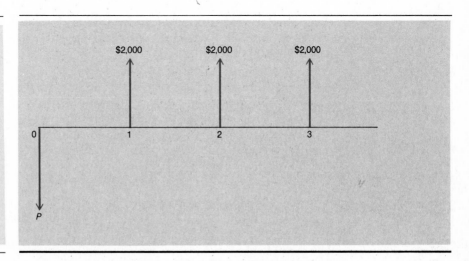

Appendix 4A at the end of this chapter. Also, many calculators have built-in financial functions for present and future values. Most of the time it is safe to round off the factors to three places.

In some problems you might want to know the annuity that can be provided from a given present amount of money. For example, suppose your grandmother (a lovely person) gave you $5446.40. You plan to deposit it in a savings account paying 5 percent and spend the entire amount plus interest over the next three years. How much could you withdraw each year with equal annual withdrawals? You know the answer already to be $2000 per year. After the third withdrawal, the deposit balance would be zero since $2000 per year is equivalent to (has the same present value as) $5446.40 today. In this case we wanted to know the annuity that results from a given present amount. The general representation of this interest factor is $(A/P, i, n)$. It is the reciprocal of the annuity present value factor

$$(A/P, i, n) = \frac{1}{(P/A, i, n)} \tag{4-12}$$

In our previous example $(P/A, 5\%, 3) = 2.7232$. The corresponding value for $(A/P, 5\%, 3)$ is $1/2.7232 = 0.3672$. You can check this by looking in the 5 percent table of Appendix A under the column headed A/P at $n = 3$.

$(A/P, i, n)$ is sometimes called the **capital recovery factor** since it can be used to determine what income is necessary to recover a capital investment given the rate of interest on the investment. It can also be called the **loan repayment factor**, since it is used to find the payments needed to pay off a loan. For example, suppose you worked for "Friendly Dan, the Cycle Man," and wished to set up monthly payment plans for motorcycle purchases. In order to find the monthly payments that would pay off a given purchase in twelve months at an interest rate of 1 percent per month, you would need to know $(A/P, 1\%, 12)$. The value of this factor is 0.0888, which you can get from the 1 percent table in Appendix A. The required payments (A) given the purchase price (P) would be

$$A = 0.0888\ P$$

For a motorcycle costing $200, the purchaser must pay $(0.0888)\$200 = \$17.76$ per month. If the cycle costs $500, the monthly payment would be $(0.0888)\$500 = \$44.40$.

Perpetual Annuities   A perpetual annuity (or "level perpetuity") is an annuity that is expected to continue forever. This type of cash flow pattern is often used for illustrative purposes both by us and by other authors because the present value of such annuities can be calculated very easily. The annuity present value factor when the number of periods becomes large (n approaches infinity) is simply $1/i$. Therefore the present value P of a perpetual annuity A beginning one period from the present is

$$P = \frac{A}{i} \tag{4-13}$$

The present value, using an 8 percent interest rate, of $100 per year beginning in one year and to be received forever is

$$P = \frac{A}{i}$$

$$= \frac{\$1000}{0.08}$$

$$= \$1250$$

**Summary of Interest
Factors**

Three pairs of interest factors are useful in solving problems involving money paid or received at different points in time. If you are using electronic calculators to solve problems, it is as easy to divide as it is to multiply and you would need to have available only one factor from each of the three pairs. But, when you are doing hand calculations, all six factors are helpful. Values for all six factors are included in tables in Appendix A under the appropriate headings. The examples given below all use the 5 percent table at $n = 5$. Appendix 4A provides an algebraic formula for each factor and instructions for using calculators to compute the factors directly.

Single Payments or Receipts   To find the future value of a present amount, use the compound amount factor:

$$F = P(F/P, i, n)$$

where

$$(F/P, i, n) = (1 + i)^n$$

This is the amount $1 will grow to in n periods invested at i percent per period. The future value of $100 invested for five years at 5 percent is $F = \$100(1.2763) = \$127.63$.

To find the present value of a future amount, use the present value factor:

$$P = F(P/F, i, n)$$

where

$$(P/F, i, n) = \frac{1}{(F/P, i, n)}$$

This is the amount that must be invested today to have $1 n periods from now at i percent per period. The present value of $127.63 to be received five years from now given a rate of 5 percent is $P = \$127.63(0.7835) = \$100$.

Annuities (Equal Payments or Receipts in Each Period)   To find the future value of an annuity, use the annuity compound amount factor:

$$F = A(F/A, i, n)$$

where

$$(F/A, i, n) = (1 + i)^{n-1} + (1 + i)^{n-2} + \cdots + (1 + i) + 1$$

This is the amount (F) accumulated by investing $1 each period for n periods at an interest rate of i per period. F is the amount accumulated at the time the last investment is made; therefore the last investment earns no interest. The future value of $100 per year for five years at 5 percent is $F = \$100(5.5256) = \$552.56$.

To find the annuity required to accumulate to a future value, use the sinking fund factor:

$$A = F(A/F, i, n)$$

where

$$(A/F, i, n) = \frac{1}{(F/A, i, n)}$$

This is the amount (A) which must be invested each period for n periods at an interest rate of i per period to obtain $1 in period n at the time the last investment is made. The last investment of amount A earns no interest. The annual savings required to accumulate to $552.56 in five years at 5 percent is $A = \$552.56(0.1810) = \$100$.

To find the present value of an annuity, use the annuity present value factor:

$$P = A(P/A, i, n)$$

where

$$(P/A, i, n) = \frac{1}{(1 + i)} + \frac{1}{(1 + i)^2} + \cdots + \frac{1}{(1 + i)^n}$$

This is the amount which must be invested to provide an annuity of $1 per period for n periods at a rate of i percent per period. The annuity begins one period after the investment is made. The present value of $100 per year for five years at 5 percent is

---

TABLE 4-2
*Interest rate of 6 percent**

n	F/P	P/F	F/A	A/F	P/A	A/P
1	1.0600	.9434	1.0000	1.0000	.9434	1.0600
2	1.1236	.8900	2.0600	.4854	1.8334	.5454
3	1.1910	.8396	3.1836	.3141	2.6730	.3741
4	1.2625	.7921	4.3746	.2286	3.4651	.2886
5	1.3382	.7473	5.6371	.1774	4.2124	.2374
6	1.4185	.7050	6.9753	.1434	4.9173	.2034
7	1.5036	.6651	8.3938	.1191	5.5824	.1791
8	1.5938	.6274	9.8975	.1010	6.2098	.1610
9	1.6895	.5919	11.4913	.0870	6.8017	.1470
10	1.7908	.5584	13.1808	.0759	7.3601	.1359

* The complete table for a 6 percent rate can be found in Appendix A

$P = \$100(4.3295)$

$= \$432.95$

To find the annuity provided by a present amount, use the capital recovery or loan repayment factor:

$A = P(A/P, i, n)$

where

$$(A/P, i, n) = \frac{1}{(P/A, i, n)}$$

This is the annuity provided for n periods by investing $1 at a rate of i percent per period. The annual income for five years provided by a present investment of \$432.95 at 5 percent is $A = \$432.95(0.2310) = \$100$.

SOLVING PROBLEMS WHEN THE INTEREST RATE IS KNOWN

Using the Tables

We have been using the tables in our examples above, but now let's examine them more carefully. Table 4-2 contains part of the table of factors in Appendix A for an interest rate of 6 percent per period. There is one such table for each interest rate included in the appendix. The range of rates provided is from $\frac{1}{3}$ to 50 percent. Each of the six factors is included in the table. In order to use the tables, you merely look up the value of the factor for the rate and number of periods desired. Note that each column in Table 4-2 is headed by the descriptive notation for the factor. The second column is headed F/P. This column contains the values of $(F/P, 6\%, n) = (1.06)^n$ for the values of n shown in the first column. For example, what is the value of $(F/P, 6\%, 5)$? Find the number in Table 4-2 that corresponds to $(F/P, 6\%, 5)$. The correct value is 1.3382.

Let's look at a problem using Table 4-2. Suppose you are trying to decide whether you should buy four tires expected to last for 20,000 miles or a set expected to last for 40,000 miles. You drive an average of 10,000 miles per year and expect to keep the car at least another four years. The 20,000-mile tires will cost \$90 now and the 40,000-mile tires will cost \$180. The cash flow diagrams for this problem are shown in Figure 4-6. Figure 4-6a shows the

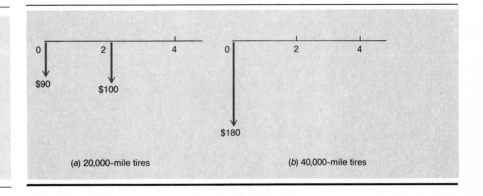

FIGURE 4-6

Cash flows from alternative tire purchases.

(a) 20,000-mile tires

(b) 40,000-mile tires

cash costs of buying 20,000-mile tires now at $90 and assumes that the same set is expected to cost you $100 two years from now. Figure 4-6b shows a single purchase of 40,000-mile tires. We will transform the two cash flows for the 20,000-mile tires to their present value. This gives us the cost of 20,000-mile tires in terms of dollars today which can be compared with the cost today of 40,000-mile tires. The present value of $90 today and $100 two years from now assuming an interest rate of 6 percent is

$$P = \$90 + \$100(P/F, 6\%, 2)$$

Look up $(P/F, 6\%, 2)$ in Table 4-2. Its value is 0.89. The present value of the cost of buying 20,000-mile tires is therefore

$$P = \$90 + \$100(0.89)$$

$$= \$90 + \$89.00$$

$$= \$179$$

Since the present value of the cost of the 40,000-mile tires is $180, you would save money with the 20,000-mile tires.

Beginning students usually encounter several difficulties involving interest rate problems. One such difficulty is recognizing the factors and tables to use in solving a particular problem. This difficulty is easily overcome with the familiarity gained from solving practice problems and reviewing the example problems on a step-by-step basis. Another difficulty arises when the cash flows in the problem are complicated and don't fit the simple examples we have been using. Here, too, practice helps, but that is not enough. There is a section later on (pages 75–78) about what to do when the cash flows vary from period to period.

A further difficulty arises when the available tables don't have the exact factor you need to solve your problem. For example, we don't have a table here for an interest rate of $7\frac{1}{2}$ percent. If your problems involve this rate, you can use any of three methods. First, you can compute the factors you need using a calculator or a computer. Formulas for the factors are provided in Appendix 4A at the end of the chapter. Second, if your problem doesn't require a high degree of accuracy, you can interpolate in the tables you do have. Interpolation is sort of like averaging two numbers to get an "in-between" value. For example, if you wish to know the compound amount factor for five years at an annual rate of $7\frac{1}{2}$ percent, you are looking for $(F/P, 7\frac{1}{2}\%, 5)$. The tables provide the following values (look them up to check):

$$(F/P, 7\%, 5) = 1.4026$$

and

$$(F/P, 8\%, 5) = 1.4693$$

The value for $(F/P, 7\frac{1}{2}\%, 5)$ will be in between these two values. Figure 4-7 illustrates the problem. Since $7\frac{1}{2}$ percent is halfway between 7 percent and 8 percent, the value for the $7\frac{1}{2}$ percent factor will be approximately halfway between the 7 percent factor and the 8 percent factor. The distance between the two factors (difference in their values) is

$$1.4693 - 1.4026 = 0.0667$$

One-half of the difference is $0.0667/2 = 0.0333$. The value for $(F/P, 7\frac{1}{2}\%, 5)$ is therefore (approximately) $1.4026 + 0.0333 = 1.4359$. Interpolation can also be used when the number of periods in your problem is not in the tables. For example, if you want $(P/A, 6\%, 41)$ and all you have is $(P/A, 6\%, 40)$ and $(P/A, 6\%, 44)$, you can interpolate between the two known values to find the unknown one. Try this problem using the 6 percent table in Appendix A. Note that 41 is one-fourth of the distance from 40 to 44. The correct answer is $15.0463 + 0.0842 = 15.1305$. Interpolation is also useful in finding unknown interest rates, as we show later in the chapter. The third method is to find someone who has a more complete set of interest tables. Banks and libraries frequently have good tables.

Variable Cash Flows

When you are faced with a problem that doesn't fit the simple situations we have been looking at, the first thing to do is to draw a cash flow diagram. Since any interest problem can be solved by applying the proper set of factors, once you identify the cash flows you can decide what factors you need. Take the example as shown in Figure 4-8a. If you wish to find the present value of the annual cash flows shown given an interest rate of 6 percent per year, either of the following two methods will work.

The first method is to consider the cash flows as being a $20 per year annuity beginning in year 2 plus a single amount of $80 in year 1, as shown in Figure 4-8b. We can first calculate the present value (P_1) of the $20 per year annuity in years 2, 3, and 4 as of the end of the first year. At 6 percent.

$$P_1 = \$20(P/A, 6\%, 3)$$

$$= \$20(2.673)$$

$$= \$53.50$$

The annuity has now been converted to a value equivalent to a cash receipt of $53.50 at the end of year 1. We can add to this figure the $80 receipt in year 1 to get the total equivalent cash receipt at this time, $80 + $53.50 = $133.50.

$$P_0 = \$133.50(P/F, 6\%, 1)$$

$$= \$133.50(0.9434)$$

$$= \$126$$

FIGURE 4-7
Interpolation.

The alternative method is to evaluate the cash flow as being an annuity of $20 beginning at the end of the first year plus a receipt of $60 in that time as illustrated in Figure 4-8c. The present value is then the sum of the present values of the two cash flows.

$$P = \$20(P/A, 6\%, 4) + \$60(P/F, 6\%, 1)$$

$$= \$20(3.465) + \$60(0.9434)$$

$$= \$126$$

As another example, suppose you wished to know what the cash flows of Figure 4-8a would accumulate to at the end of four years from today (time 0 in the figure) if deposited to earn 6 percent. Using the second method, the future value would be

$$F = \$20(F/A, 6\%, 4) + \$60(F/P, 6\%, 3)$$

$$= \$20(4.375) + \$60(1.191)$$

$$= \$159$$

Note that the $60 is compounded for only three periods since the deposit will only be in the account for that length of time from year 1 to year 4. The annuity factor, $(F/A, 6\%, 4)$, is for four periods since there are four $20 payments, one in each period.

If the cash flows vary from period to period, then you must handle each period's cash flow individually. For example, suppose you wish to find the present value of the cash flows shown in Figure 4-9. At an interest rate of 6

FIGURE 4-8

Analyzing variable cash flows.

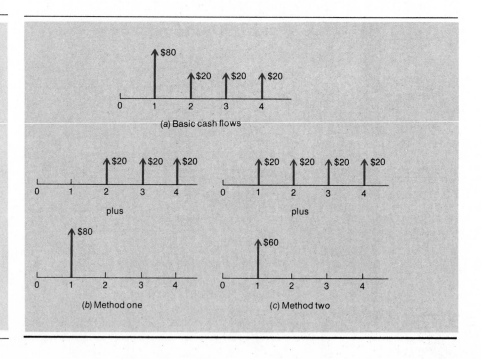

(a) Basic cash flows

(b) Method one

(c) Method two

percent per year the present value of all the cash flows is simply the sum of the present values of each one.

$$P = \$20(P/F, 6\%, 1) + \$25(P/F, 6\%, 2) + \$30(P/F, 6\%, 3) + \$28(P/F, 6\%, 4)$$

$$= \$20(0.9434) + \$25(0.8900) + \$30(0.8396) + \$28(0.7921)$$

$$= \$18.87 + \$22.25 + \$25.19 + \$22.18$$

$$= \$88.49$$

Finding future values would be done in a similar fashion but using $(F/P, i, n)$ instead of $(P/F, i, n)$. If you wish to transform a set of variable cash flows into an annuity, the easiest thing to do is to first find the present value of the cash flows, as done in the example. Then use the capital recovery factor $(A/P, i, n)$ to convert that present value into its equivalent annuity. If, for example, you wished to know the annuity equivalent to the cash flows of Figure 4-9, it can be determined by using the present value of $88.49 that we have already found.

$$A = \$88.49(A/P, 6\%, 4)$$

$$= \$88.49(.2886)$$

$$= \$25.54$$

That is, the cash flows of Figure 4-9 are equivalent to an annuity of $25.54 per year for four years at 6 percent.

Example Problem   Assume that you are twenty-five years old and wish to retire at age sixty. You expect to be able to average a 6 percent annual rate on savings over your lifetime. You would like to save enough money to provide $8000 per year beginning at age sixty-one in retirement income to supplement other sources (social security, pension plans, etc.). One problem you face is estimating how long you wish the $8000 per year to continue on retirement. Suppose you decide that the extra income need be provided for only twenty years (up to age eighty). The problem is how to organize your savings program prior to retirement so that you will have enough

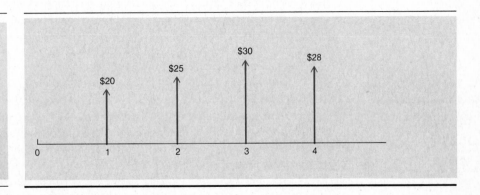

FIGURE 4-9
Variable cash flow.

money to support a supplementary retirement income of $8000 per year for twenty years. Try to draw a cash flow diagram of this problem assuming that some savings will be made each year up to age sixty.

The initial part of this problem is fairly simple. You should find the amount of money you must have at age sixty in order to provide $8000 per year for twenty years. In other words, you need to know the present value (as of age sixty) of a twenty-year annuity of $8000 per year. The factor needed is therefore $(P/A, i, n)$, the annuity present value factor

$$P_{60} = \$8000(P/A, 6\%, 20)$$

$$= \$8000(11.4699)$$

$$= \$91,760$$

At age sixty a savings account of $91,760 earning 6 percent interest per year will permit you to take out $8000 per year beginning one year after retirement and continuing for twenty years. Notice that we are making the simplifying assumption that you draw out $8000 annually. In practice, you would probably withdraw smaller amounts more frequently, for example $650 or so per month beginning at age sixty. However, the assumption of annual withdrawal is a fairly good approximation and makes the problem easier to solve. Also, for simplicity, we can round off the $91,760 to an even $92,000 as our target savings goal.

A simple savings program would be to deposit the same amount each year. To find out the annual amount invested at 6 percent needed to accumulate to $92,000 at age sixty, thirty-five years from now, what factor should be used? We wish to find the annuity that will accumulate to a future value, $(A/F, i, n)$, the sinking fund factor

$$A = \$92,000(A/F, 6\%, 35)$$

$$= \$92,000(0.0090)$$

$$= \$828$$

Therefore, you would have to save $828 per year for thirty-five years to have $92,000 at the end.

Suppose you felt that the most you could afford to save presently and until age forty-five would be $500 per year. See if you can figure out how much you would have to save each year from age forty-five to sixty in order to end up with $92,000. [Hint: The $500 saved per year for the first twenty years would be worth $500(F/A, 6\%, 20) = \$18,400$ at age forty-five. By age sixty this amount would grow to $18,400(F/P, 5\%, 15) = \$44,000.$] The answer is $2064 per year needed to be saved from age forty-five to age sixty.

Time and Timing

In this book, in problems where the cash flows cover several years, we simplify our calculations by putting all the cash received or paid during a given year at the end of the year. This is an approximation to simplify the problem. The savings-retirement problem shown earlier is an example. You would probably be making monthly deposits into your savings account during the savings period and variable withdrawals during retirement. Unless there is some reason to want a high degree of accuracy, treating the cash flows as single annual amounts is a reasonable way to keep down the complexity of a given problem. Of course, some problems demand that months or quarters or some other period be used—for example, finding the monthly payments on a mortgage. In this text, however, when we say that some amount of money is to be received in year 5, what we usually mean is that the money is assumed to be received five years from now as a single receipt.

FINDING AN UNKNOWN INTEREST RATE

In many problems you will know the amounts of all the cash flows and would like to determine what the interest rate is. Prior to the Truth in Lending Act, which went into effect in 1969, finding the true interest rate on a consumer loan was of particular importance. Now lenders usually state the rate; however, they have the option simply to tell you the total dollar finance charge, which they often do instead of giving the interest rate. Business investments are often evaluated using their **rate of return**, which is the interest rate expected to be earned by the investment.

Essentially we can identify two general situations in which you might wish to find the interest rate based on the cash flows—a loan agreement and an investment opportunity. When you are borrowing money, you generally receive an amount of money today in return for an agreement to pay more money back in the future. When you invest, you pay money out today in the expectation that you will receive more money in return sometime in the future. When you deposit money in a bank savings account, you are lending money to the bank with the expectation that the bank will pay you back with interest. Similarly, when the bank loans money to you, the bank is making an investment and expects you to pay the money back with interest.

The result is that, except for the direction of the cash flows, a loan is like an investment. The rate of return the bank earns on its investment in a loan to you is the same as the interest rate you will pay to the bank. The point is that finding interest rates on loans is the same as finding rates of return on investments. In each case the interest rate implicit in a series of cash flows is that rate which sets the present value of future cash flows equal to the initial outlay or receipt. We begin by showing how to perform the analysis of different sorts of loans and we then give examples of finding the rate of return on an investment. The stress here is on calculations by hand or using simple calculators. There are calculators and computer programs available which will calculate the interest rate for you. Some will do so only for the simple cash flow patterns described in the next sections; others will find the interest rate for variable cash flows discussed later. Even if you own one of the more powerful calculators, you should understand what the calculator is doing, and the training in this chapter will help you set up problems properly.

Simple Cash Flows

There are four payment schedules or cash flow patterns for which we can find the interest rate without using tables although tables can be used in these cases as well.

The first simple case: *You borrow money and promise to pay an equal annual amount of interest every year forever.* This is a perpetual annuity and is not a very common type of loan. (The British government has issued perpetual bonds, however.) We can use Eq. (4-13) presented on page 70 to find the interest rate

$$P = \frac{A}{i} \tag{4-13}$$

$$i = \frac{A}{P} \tag{4-14}$$

where A is the annual amount.[5] Therefore, if you borrowed $50 on the promise to pay $5 per year forever, the interest rate would be $5/$50 = 0.10 or 10 percent per year.

The second case: *You borrow money and repay the loan within one year or less with a single payment.* In this case, let P be the amount borrowed now (principal) and F be the amount repaid later. We wish to find the interest rate i given P, the principal, and future payment F.

$$F = (1 + i)P$$

$$F = P + iP$$

$$F - P = iP$$

$$i = \frac{F - P}{P} \tag{4-15}$$

$$i = \frac{F}{P} - 1 \tag{4-15a}$$

In other words, if you borrow $50 and repay $55 in one year, you are paying ($55 − $50)/$50 = 0.10 or 10 percent per year. If the loan were for less than a year, you would compute the interest rate as in Eq. (4-15), and then scale up to an annual basis. For example, if you borrow $100 for six months and repaid $105, the rate would be $5/$100 or 5 percent for six months or 10 percent per year.[6]

The third simple case: *You borrow P dollars today, pay A dollars every year for n years, and at the end pay back P dollars.* The interest rate for this type of loan is computed according to Eq. (4-14). Corporate bonds have payments like this. For example, if you borrow $50 now and pay $5 a year for six years (beginning one year from now) then pay back the $50 at the end of the sixth year, your interest cost is 10 percent per year ($5/$50). It's like a

---

[5] This can be proved mathematically using the formula in Appendix 4A for the annuity present value factor and letting the value for n approach infinity.

[6] This 10 percent figure is the annual **nominal interest rate**, assuming a 5 percent six-month rate and two six-month compounding periods. The annual **effective interest rate**, using a 5 percent six-month rate, would be 10.25 percent, which is computed as $(1.05)^2 - 1 = 10.25\%$. The 10.25 percent rate is the annual rate assuming that interest is compounded. In general, if the rate for q months, in decimals, is signified by x (for example, $x = .05$ if the rate is 5 percent), then the annual effective rate equals

Annual effective rate = $(1 + x)^{12/q} - 1$

In the example, $x = .05$, $q = 6$ (6 months), and the annual effective rate is 10.25 percent.

series of one-year loans. Think of it in this way: At the end of every year you pay the interest of $5 and pay back the original $50 borrowed, then turn around and immediately reborrow the $50. You end up on balance just paying $5 per year until the last year when you no longer borrow.

The fourth case is not as simple; it arises when the cash flows from an investment grow at a constant rate. This case is presented in Appendix 4A.

There are two more simple cash flow patterns for which the interest rate can be determined fairly quickly. However, a simple formula does not apply.[7] The first of these is where there is *a single payment but the loan is outstanding longer than one year*. Suppose you borrow $1000 and agree to pay off the borrowing three years from now with a payment of $1260. What annual rate of interest are you being charged? We know that the compound amount factor can be used to find the future payment equivalent to the principal of a loan made today.

$$F = P(F/P, i, n)$$

and in this case,

$$\$1260 = \$1000(F/P, i, 3)$$

Solving for the value of the factor, we get

$$(F/P, i, 3) = \frac{\$1260}{\$1000}$$

$$= 1.260$$

We now need to find that interest rate which provides a value for the compound amount factor of 1.260 at $n = 3$. To do this, you must go to the tables and look through them until you find the right value or one close to it. A good starting point can be found by noting that the average annual interest cost is $260/3 = $87 or roughly 8.7 percent of $1000. The exact annual interest rate will be less than the average rate since you are not really paying anything until the end of three years. If you try 8 percent first, you

---

[7] In the case of a single-payment loan (or investment) when the future payment will be made n years from now, the interest rate can be determined easily using a calculator with a power function (y^x). The procedure is as follows:

$$F = P(F/P, i, n)$$

$$F = P(1 + i)^n$$

$$(1 + i)^n = \frac{F}{P}$$

$$1 + i = \left(\frac{F}{P}\right)^{1/n}$$

$$i = \left(\frac{F}{P}\right)^{1/n} - 1$$

Find the ratio F/P and then calculate $(F/P)^{1/n}$ using the y^x function where $y = F/P$ and $x = 1/n$. In the text example, $F/P = 1.26$ and $n = 3$.

$$i = (1.26)^{1/3} - 1$$

$$= 1.080 - 1$$

$$= 8.0\%$$

will find that $(F/P, 8\%, 3) = 1.260$. Therefore, the rate you are paying is 8 percent per year.

However, what if the payment were $1275? The factor you would be looking for is 1.275, which is greater than the value for 8 percent yet less than the value for 9 percent, $(F/P, 9\%, 3) = 1.295$. The rate must be between 8 percent and 9 percent. If you wish to be more accurate than that, you can interpolate to provide a fairly good approximation. This is similar to the procedure followed earlier in the chapter, except that now we are trying to find the interest rate rather than the factor. The answer by interpolation is 8.43 percent.

The second payment pattern which can be analyzed easily using the tables is *an annuity*. For example, if a loan of $1000 requires annual payments of $250 per year for five years, what is the interest rate being charged? We know that the loan payment can be found by using the loan repayment factor $(A/P, i, n)$. Therefore,

$$\$250 = \$1000(A/P, i, 5)$$

and

$$(A/P, i, 5) = \frac{\$250}{\$1000}$$

$$= 0.250$$

Now go to the tables and try to find a value for $(A/P, i, 5)$ equal to 0.250. You know the rate will be less than 25 percent ($250/$1000) since that would apply to a perpetuity and these payments stop after five years. Try a much lower rate, say, 12 percent. $(A/P, 12\%, 5) = 0.277$. That's too large a value, so you know the interest rate must be lower than 12 percent. The lower the interest rate, the lower the payments must be. You will find that $(A/P, 8\%, 5) = 0.250$. The answer is, therefore, 8 percent. If the value of the factor for the unknown rate does not equal the value for a factor in the tables, interpolate between the factor values for the two interest rates that most closely bracket the unknown rate.

Now let's find the interest rate on an installment loan when the lender doesn't provide one. Friendly Dan advertises that you can buy a $200 motorcycle for $9 down and $9.50 per month for twenty-four months. The finance charge is the difference between the total amount of your payments and the amount you owed (borrowed) initially, or $(24 \times \$9.50) - (\$200 - \$9) = \$37$. What interest rate are you paying? The solution to this problem is similar to the one just above. You are dealing with an annuity and therefore use the formula

$$A = P(A/P, i, n)$$

Substituting in the appropriate values, we have

$$\$9.50 = \$191(A/P, i, 24)$$

$$(A/P, i, 24) = \frac{\$9.50}{\$191}$$

$$= 0.0497$$

Looking through the tables for a value of $(A/P, i, 24) = 0.0497$, we find that $(A/P, 1\frac{1}{2}\%, 24) = 0.0499$. The value for the next lowest rate in the table is $(A/P, 1\frac{1}{4}\%, 24) = 0.0485$. The interest rate therefore is between $1\frac{1}{4}$ percent and $1\frac{1}{2}$ percent per month. Interpolating to get a more exact rate,

$$0.86 = \frac{x}{0.25\%}$$

$$x = 0.22\%$$

$$(1\tfrac{1}{4} + x)\% = 1.47\%$$

Therefore, Friendly Dan is charging 1.47 percent per month, or $12(1.47\%) = 17.6$ percent per year.

Variable Cash Flows

Finding an unknown interest rate when the cash flows do not match one of the patterns shown above is more difficult. You must first set up an equation expressing the time-value equivalence of the cash flows. This equation will usually contain two or more interest factors in it involving the unknown rate.[8] Then you must try out different interest rates until you find one for which the equation will balance. This procedure is illustrated by the following example of an investment-type problem.

Suppose you would like to determine the interest rate you would earn from buying a bond and holding it to maturity. This interest rate is called the **yield to maturity** of the bond. The cash flows from buying and owning the bond are shown in Figure 4-10. The bond's current price is $850, it pays

[8] If it contains only one factor, you must have a version of one of the simple cases.

FIGURE 4-10

Cash flows from buying a bond and holding it to maturity.

an annuity of $60 per year for ten years, and it will mature in ten years paying its face value of $1000 at that time. If the price of the bond were $1000 today, we know that the yield to maturity (interest rate) on the bond would be $60/$1000 = 6 percent per year from our earlier discussion. However, since the price is only $850, we know that the yield to maturity must be greater than 6 percent. The time-value equation for the cash flows is

$$\text{Present price of the bond} = \begin{array}{c} \text{present value of} \\ \text{interest payments} \end{array} + \begin{array}{c} \text{present value of} \\ \text{principal payment} \end{array}$$

$$\$850 = \$60(P/A, i, 10) + \$1000(P/F, i, 10)$$

The problem is to find that interest rate which will make the right side of the equation equal $850. The right side of the equation is the present value (P) of the future cash receipts from owning the bond given the interest rate. We can think of the problem as finding that interest rate which will make $P = \$850$. Since we know the rate is greater than 6 percent, let's try 7 percent.

$$P_{7\%} = \$60(P/A, 7\%, 10) + \$1000(P/F, 7\%, 10)$$

$$= \$60(7.024) + \$1000(0.5083)$$

$$= \$930$$

This value of P is too large. In order to get a lower present value, we need to use a higher interest rate. Suppose we try 10 percent.

$$P_{10\%} = \$60(P/A, 10\%, 10) + \$1000(P/F, 10\%, 10)$$

$$= \$60(6.145) + \$1000(0.3855)$$

$$= \$754$$

Since the present value at 10 percent is too low, the correct rate must lie between 10 percent and 7 percent. Now that we have bracketed the true rate, we can either try some more values (8 percent or 9 percent) or we can interpolate. Let's interpolate.

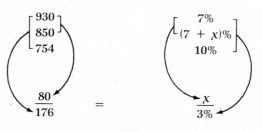

$$x = 1.35\%$$

The estimated rate is therefore 7 percent + 1.35 percent = 8.35 percent. If we wanted to get a more accurate estimate of the true rate, we could compute P at 8 percent and 9 percent and interpolate between those values instead of between 7 percent and 10 percent. The narrower the spread is, the more accurate is the interpolation. If we did this, our new estimate would be 8.26 percent. This answer is accurate to the second decimal place.

The Rate of Return on Common Stock As a final example of finding an unknown interest rate, let's look at the problem of finding the rate of return earned on an investment in common stock. Suppose you purchased ten shares of stock in a company four years ago at a price of $50 per share. Your total investment was $500 (10 × $50). The company paid you the following dividends:

	First year	Second year	Third year	Fourth year
Dividend per share	$ 2.00	$ 2.00	$ 2.50	$ 3.00
Total dividends received	20.00	20.00	25.00	30.00

The current price of the stock is $60. What rate of return have you earned on your investment if you sell the stock now? The proceeds from sale of your shares will be $600 (10 × $60). The cash flow diagram for the investment is shown in Figure 4-11. We are assuming that you have just received $30 in dividends for the current year, four years after the stock was purchased. Time is measured from the date of the original investment. To find the rate of return earned on the investment, we must find that interest rate which makes the present value of the cash receipts in years 1 to 4 equal to the amount invested. A direct expression is to treat each cash receipt as a single future amount:

$$\$500 = \frac{\$20}{1 + i} + \frac{\$20}{(1 + i)^2} + \frac{\$25}{(1 + i)^3} + \frac{\$630}{(1 + i)^4}$$

$$\$500 = \$20(P/F, i, 1) + \$20(P/F, i, 2) + \$25(P/F, i, 3) + \$630(P/F, i, 4)$$

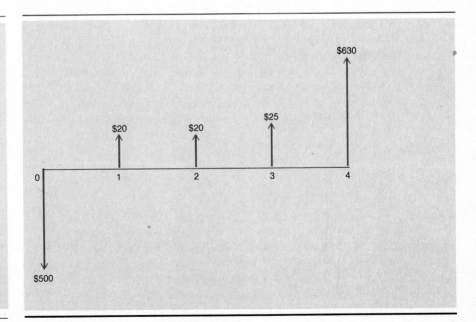

FIGURE 4-11

Cash flows from a common stock investment.

This is the most general approach and will work for any set of future cash flows. However, using this approach, you must work with as many different interest rate factors as you have future cash flows, four in this example. Often the problem can be reduced somewhat by separating out any annuities in the flows. In this case we have a two-period annuity of $20; so the following expression is also correct:

$$\$500 = \$20(P/A, i, 2) + \$25(P/F, i, 3) + \$630(P/F, i\ 4)$$

Now we need to work with only three factors instead of four.[9]

As we did in the previous example, we must try out different interest rates until we find two that bracket the true rate. Then we must interpolate between the two to estimate the value of the true rate. How can we know where to begin? There is no simple answer to the question. As you gain experience in solving these problems, your initial guesses will improve. Generally one examines the cash flow pattern and compares it with one of the simple cases discussed earlier. In this example we received $95 in dividends plus $100 capital gains for an average annual return of $49 per year. This is an average return of approximately 10 percent ($49/$500) on our investment. Since the true interest rate must be lower than 10 percent as most of the returns were not obtained until the fourth year, let's try 9 percent as a starting rate and go from there.

$$
\begin{aligned}
P_{9\%} &= \$20(P/A, 9\%, 2) + \$25(P/F, 9\%, 3) + \$630(P/F, 9\%, 4) \\
&= \$20(1.759) + \$25(0.772) + \$630(0.708) \\
&= \$500.52
\end{aligned}
$$

That is very close to $500, the initial investment. The true rate must be slightly over 9 percent, and in many practical problems, you could stop here. To get a better estimate, we must use the next higher rate in the tables, 10 percent.

$$
\begin{aligned}
P_{10\%} &= \$20(P/A, 10\%, 2) + \$25(P/F, 10\%, 3) + \$630(P/F, 10\%, 4) \\
&= \$20(1.736) + \$25(0.751) + \$630(0.683) \\
&= \$483.79
\end{aligned}
$$

This rate is obviously much too high. We can try interpolation at this point

---

[9] Although there is no advantage in this example, the following expressions are also equivalent and in many situations can be used to simplify problems:

$$\$500 = \$20(P/A, i, 3) + \$5(P/F, i, 3) + \$630(P/F, i, 4)$$

and

$$\$500 = \$20(P/A, i, 4) + \$5(P/F, i, 3) + \$610(P/F, i, 4)$$

In general, if you have a stream of future cash flows, $F_1, F_2, F_3, \ldots, F_n$, their present value can always be expressed as

$$
\begin{aligned}
P = {}& A(P/A, i, n) + (F_1 - A)(P/F, i, 1) + (F_2 - A)(P/F, i, 2) \\
& + (F_3 - A)(P/F, i, 3) + \cdots + (F_n - A)(P/F, i, n)
\end{aligned}
$$

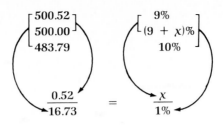

$$x = 0.03\%$$

This gives us an estimated rate of return of 9 percent + 0.03 percent or 9.03 percent per year. A still more exact figure would require use of a calculator or (preferably) a computer program. The actual rate is 9.046 percent.

SUMMARY

Interest rates give money its time value. Compound interest methods are used to solve problems when money is to be paid or received at different points in time. The basic principles of compound interest were described and illustrated through examples which serve two purposes: (1) to show how to solve problems involving compound interest and (2) to illustrate the range of problems requiring the use of compound interest techniques in real life. There are two general types of decisions that require some consideration of time value. One type of decision involves investing (or saving) money now in order to receive future cash benefits. The other type involves borrowing (or dissaving) now to make current expenditures at a cost of having less money in the future.

The present value of future income is one of the key concepts of finance. Present value provides a way to compare alternative income or cost streams that differ in time and/or amounts.

Interest rate factors are used to provide numerical solutions to financial problems. The six major interest factors are:

The **compound amount factor** $(F/P, i, n)$: This is the value n periods from now of $1 invested today at a rate of interest of i percent per period. To find the value of F of P dollars invested today, multiply P by $(F/P, i, n)$:

$$F = P(F/P, i, n)$$

The **present value factor** $(P/F, i, n)$: This is the value today of $1 to be received n periods from now given an interest rate of i percent per period. To find the present value P of F dollars to be received n periods from now, multiply F by $(P/F, i, n)$:

$$P = F(P/F, i, n)$$

The **annuity compound amount factor** $(F/A, i, n)$: This factor is the value at the end of n periods resulting from an investment of $1 per period for n periods at a rate of i percent per period. To find the future value F of an annuity of A dollars per year, multiply A by $(F/A, i, n)$:

$$F = A(F/A, i, n)$$

The **sinking fund factor** $(A/F, i, n)$: This factor is the amount that must be invested each period for n periods at i percent per period to produce $1 at the end of n periods. To find the annuity A needed to accumulate to F dollars in n periods, multiply F by $(A/F, i, n)$:

$$A = F(A/F, i, n)$$

The **annuity present value factor** $(P/A, i, n)$: This factor is the value today of an annuity of $1 provided at the end of each period beginning one period from now and ending n periods from now given an interest rate of i percent. To find the present value P of A dollars per period, multiply A by $(P/A, i, n)$:

$$P = A(P/A, i, n)$$

The **capital recovery** or **loan repayment factor** $(A/P, i, n)$: This factor is the amount of money which must be paid each period for n periods in order to pay off a loan of $1 given an interest rate of i percent. It is also the amount of money that must be received in each period for n periods to provide an interest rate of i percent on $1 invested today. To find the annuity A equivalent to P dollars, borrowed or invested today, multiply P by $(A/P, i, n)$:

$$A = P(A/P, i, n)$$

The interest factors are also used to find unknown interest rates. If the cash flow pattern does not fit one of the simple cases shown in the chapter, then a trial-and-error procedure must be used to determine the rate.

QUESTIONS

1 People often assume that an increase in interest rates will encourage more savings by individuals. Suppose that you are saving to pay for future tuition. Will an increase in interest rates cause you to save more or less money today?

2 Two banks offer savings accounts with a stated interest rate of 6 percent per year. For bank A the actual rate is $1\frac{1}{2}$ percent per quarter compounded quarterly. For bank B the actual rate is $\frac{1}{2}$ percent per month compounded monthly. Will one of the two banks provide more interest than the other assuming that no withdrawals are made from the account for one year? Why?

3 What happens to the present value of an annuity if the interest rate rises? What happens to the future value?

4 Why is $(A/F, i, n)$ called the sinking fund factor?

5 Given an investment that will provide a stream of future cash flows, what is the relationship between the present value of the future cash flows and the rate of return on the amount invested?

6 In Chapter 2 we said that an increase in the expected rate of inflation should increase interest rates. Suppose that you own a bond paying a fixed amount of money each year and read in the newspaper that inflation is expected to increase. Should you be happy, sad, or not concerned.

Obtain information about savings and savings certificate accounts offered by at least two financial institutions in your town (the number to be fixed by your instructor). Which one would appear to be the most desirable if (1) you may wish to withdraw money at any time; (2) you will not withdraw any money for at least one year; (3) you would like to withdraw interest every three months, but the principal can remain in the account for at least four years; (4) you do not intend withdrawing any money for six years.

1   What is the present value (today) of the following cash flows at an interest rate of 12 percent per year?
   a $100 received today.
   b $100 received five years from now. [Ans.: $56.74]
   c $100 received 10,000 years from now.
   d $100 received each year beginning one year from now and ending ten years from now. [Ans.: $565.02]
   e $100 received each year beginning one year from now and continuing forever.

2   Determine present values for the following cash flows and interest rates:
   a $100 is received each year beginning two years from now and ending eleven years from now. The interest rate is 12 percent per year. [Ans.: $504.48]
   b $100 is received each year for five years beginning one year from now (years 1–5), nothing is received for the next five years (years 6–10), then $100 is received each year for five more years (years 11–15). The interest rate is 10 percent per year. [Ans.: $525.22]
   c $100 is received each month for five years (sixty months). The interest rate is 15 percent per year ($1\frac{1}{4}$ percent per month). [Ans.: $4203.46]

3   What is the value of the following investments five years from now at an interest rate of 8 percent per year, 2 percent per quarter, or $\frac{2}{3}$ percent per month depending on the compounding period:
   a $100 invested today with interest compounded annually. [Ans.: $146.93]
   b $100 invested today with interest compounded quarterly. [Ans.: $148.59]
   c $100 invested today with interest compounded monthly. [Ans.: $148.98]

4   Find the future value of the following investments; the interest rate is 8 percent per year, compounded annually:
   a $100 is invested each year beginning one year from now and continuing through year 10, when the proceeds are withdrawn. [Ans.: $1448.66]
   b $100 is invested each year starting today and continuing through year 10, when the proceeds are withdrawn. [Ans.: $1664.55]
   c $100 is invested each year beginning one year from now and con-

tinuing through year 9. The proceeds are to be withdrawn in
year 10. [Ans.: $1348.66]

5   a   If you put $1000 into a savings certificate today paying interest of
10 percent per year, how much money will you have in the account after six years if no withdrawals are made from it until
then? How much of this is interest?

    b   Suppose you withdraw the interest every year. What will be your
total earnings? Why does this differ from the interest earned
in **a**?

6   If you wish to have $2000 six years from now, how much money
should you place in a savings account today that pays 8 percent interest per year?

7   How much money should you put in a savings account each month
in order to have $2000 in the account at the end of six years? As-
sume equal amounts saved each month and interest paid at a rate of
8 percent per year compounded monthly ($\frac{1}{3}$ percent per month).

8   Calculate the following:

    a   The monthly payments required on a $2000 loan bearing a 15
percent per year interest rate ($1\frac{1}{4}$ percent per month). The loan is
to be paid back in eighteen equal monthly installments.

    b   The total amount of interest paid over eighteen months for the
loan in **a**.

    c   The monthly payments on a thirty-year mortgage for $25,000. The
interest rate is 9 percent per year ($\frac{3}{4}$ percent per month).

    d   The total amount of interest paid over thirty years for the loan
in **c**.

9   The day you were born your parents bought a "baby bond" for $500.
This bond repays its purchase price plus $8\frac{1}{2}$ percent per year interest, compounded annually, on your twenty-first birthday. You have
just turned twenty-one. Happy birthday. How much money will you
be getting from your "baby bond"?

10   If you invest $500 initially plus $100 per month, beginning one
month from now, into a savings account paying 6 percent per year
compounded monthly ($\frac{1}{2}$ percent per month), how much money will
you have in the account after ten years?

11   You are considering making an offer to buy some land for $25,000.
Your offer will be to pay $5000 down and for the seller to carry a
contract for the remaining $20,000. You would like to pay off the
contract over six years at an interest rate of 12 percent per year. For
the first year you wish to pay interest only each month. For the remaining five years, you are willing to pay off the contract in equal
monthly installments. What will be your monthly payment for years
2 through 6 if the seller agrees to your terms?

12   Your great aunt left you $20,000 when she died. You can invest the
money to earn 12 percent per year.

    a   If you spend $3540 per year out of this inheritance, how long will
the money last?

    b   If you spend $2400 per year, how long will the money last?

c What is the most you can spend in equal annual amounts out of the fund for the next twenty years.

13 You are the parent of a four-year-old girl and plan to begin saving next year on her fifth birthday (on September 2, 1988) for her college education. You wish to provide $12,000 per year for four years beginning when she is eighteen. How much money in thirteen equal annual installments must be invested each year until she is seventeen (on September 2, 2000) to meet this goal if you earn 9 percent on your investment?

14 You work for a company that provides a pension plan for which the company contributes 50 percent of the amount you contribute. For example, if you specify that $100 of your monthly salary is to go into the plan, the company will add $50 to make the total contribution $150 per month. The plan guarantees an annual interest rate of 8 percent (compounded monthly). If you believe you can safely earn 12 percent per year (compounded monthly) by investing the money yourself, is it worthwhile belonging to the company plan? Assume that you plan to retire in thirty years and that you will set aside $80 per month regardless of the approach used.

15 Elizabeth Gallas has $1000 in current savings and wishes to have $10,000 five years from now to make a down payment on a house. If she can earn 9 percent per year, how much must she save each year in equal annual amounts to achieve her goal

16 Sam Rubin wants to save money to meet two objectives. First he would like to be able to retire twenty years from now and have a retirement income of $30,000 per year for at least twenty years. Second he would like to purchase a fishing boat five years from now at an estimated cost of $15,000. He can afford to save only $4000 per year for the first five years. Sam expects to earn 8 percent per year on average from investments over the next forty years. What must his minimum annual savings be from years 6 through 20 to meet his objectives?

17 One year ago you borrowed $10,000 at an annual interest rate of 15 percent ($1\frac{1}{4}$ percent per month) to be repaid in thirty-six monthly installments of $346.65 each. You have made twelve payments on the loan.

a What is the current balance remaining on the loan? (Hint: What is the relationship between the present value of the remaining payments to be made on the loan and its current balance?)

b What will be the balance owed on the loan one year from now if all payments are made as scheduled?

c What is the dollar amount of interest to be paid on the loan in the coming year? (Hint: The answers to *a* and *b* are very useful in answering *c*.)

18 Compute the annual interest rate or rate of return that you will earn on the following investments:

a A U.S. Treasury bill that has a current price of $920 and will pay $1000 at maturity one year from now. [Ans.: 8.70 percent]

b A U.S. Treasury bill that has a current price of $950 and will pay $1000 at maturity six months from now. [Ans.: 10.53 percent]

c A U.S. Treasury note selling at its maturity value ($1000), paying 12 percent coupon interest per year, and maturing in five years.

d An acre of vacation property with a current price of $5000 that you expect to be able to sell for $10,410 in six years. There are no other expenses or income from this property.

e A bond with a current price of $84 (per $100 maturity value), paying 9 percent coupon interest, and maturing in twenty years.

f A preferred stock with a current price of $90 paying $10.80 dividends per share per year forever.

19 Compute the annual interest rate for the following investments:

   a A U.S. Treasury bill which matures in ninety-one days with a quoted price of $98 per $100 maturity value.

   b A share of common stock purchased one year ago at a price of $40 per share and just sold for $48. No dividends were received.

   c A share of common stock purchased one year ago for $20 and sold yesterday for $17 after receipt of a dividend check for $1.

   d A share of common stock purchased for $20 three years ago and just sold for $20. Dividends of $1.50 were received at the end of each of the three years of ownership.

20 Determine the annual interest rate on the following debt contracts:

   a A $25,000 mortgage with monthly payments of $263.31 to be paid off in twenty-five years.

   b Solve the problem in **a** considering that the lender is charging a 2 percent fee at the time the loan is taken out so that the actual amount being lent to you is less than $25,000. [Ans.: 12.34 percent]

   c An installment loan for $2000 that has monthly payments of $69.33 for thirty-six months.

21 You need to borrow $3000 to buy a powerboat. The boat dealer offers (low, low) monthly payments of $99 for thirty-six months with an additional "balloon" payment of $300 in the last month. What annual interest rate is the dealer charging you on the $3000 loan?

22 You are considering taking out a $3000 loan from the Friendly Finance Company. They are charging a "low 12 percent annual interest rate" on a loan for twenty-four months. Your payments are determined as follows:

$$\text{Annual interest} = 12\% \text{ of } \$3000 = \$360 \text{ per year}$$

$$\text{Total due} = \text{principal plus 2 years interest}$$

$$= \$3000 + 2(\$360)$$

$$= \$3720$$

$$\text{Monthly payment} = \frac{\$3720}{24 \text{ months}}$$

$$= \$155 \text{ per month}$$

This procedure is called "add on" interest. What is the annual interest rate on this loan?

23 You are considering investing in one of the following two United States Government bonds:

Coupon rate	Maturity	Price/$100 maturity value
8%	20 years	$ 84
10	20 years	100

Your income tax rate is 40 percent and your capital gains tax rate is 16 percent. Capital gains taxes are paid at maturity on the difference between the purchase price and the maturity value. What will be your aftertax yield to maturity (rate of return after taxes) from owning these bonds to maturity?

24 Your father has asked your advice on the following problem. He has a mortgage loan on the family home that was made several years ago when interest rates were lower. The loan has a current balance of $30,000 and will be paid off in twenty years by paying $270 per month. He has discussed paying off the loan ahead of schedule with an officer of the bank holding the mortgage. The bank is willing to accept $27,000 right now to pay it off completely. What interest rate, expressed as an annual rate, would your father earn by paying off the loan now rather than making monthly payments for twenty years?

25 M. J. O'Brenen bought an apartment house two years ago with $60,000 in cash plus a mortgage loan of $90,000. The loan was made at an interest rate of 12.5 percent and requires annual payments of $13,570 for fifteen years. Rental income for the first year was $16,250 and for the second year was $18,000. M. J. just sold the property for $200,000 and paid off the mortgage.

a What was M. J.'s rate of return (pretax) on his initial investment?

b For tax purposes, depreciation on the property was $5000 per year. M. J. had a marginal tax rate of 50 percent on ordinary income and a tax rate of 20 percent on capital gains. Interest payments were tax deductible. What rate of return did M. J. earn after taxes? Assume that any gain from selling the apartment is taxed as a capital gain.

26 Two years ago Roger Hawkins invested $5000 in a savings certificate account with a six-year maturity and an annual interest rate of 9 percent compounded monthly. Interest rates are higher now and Roger is considering withdrawing the current balance in the account (no withdrawals of principal or interest have occurred) and investing the money in a higher-yielding asset. However, federal regulations require that the bank deduct a "penalty for early withdrawal" equal to the first six months' interest paid on the account.

a What is the current balance in the account?

b What will be the balance at maturity, four years from now, if no withdrawals are made?

c How much money will Roger receive if he closes out the account now?

d What interest rate must Roger earn on an alternative investment to obtain as much money in four years' time as he would have by keeping the certificate? Assume annual compounding on the alternative investment.

e If Roger keeps the certificate for one more year, will the interest rate he must earn then to make withdrawal worthwhile be higher, lower, or the same as the rate calculated in *d*? Why?

4A

**FORMULAS AND
COMPUTA-
TIONAL
METHODS**

This appendix serves as a reference and an aid to solving problems when tables that fit a particular problem are not available. Here we provide mathematical formulas for calculating the basic interest rate factors presented in Chapter 4. These formulas can be used to calculate the values for a factor for any given interest rate and time period. We also provide formulas for the present value of growing or declining streams, which were not discussed in the chapter. Finally we discuss some methods to compute the factors using the formulas.

**FORMULAS FOR THE
BASIC INTEREST
RATE FACTORS**

1 a Compound amount factor:

$$(F/P, i, n) = (1 + i)^n \qquad (4\text{-}16)$$

b Present value factor:

$$(P/F, i, n) = \frac{1}{(1 + i)^n} = (1 + i)^{-n} \qquad (4\text{-}17)$$

2 a Annuity compound amount factor:

$$(F/A, i, n) = \frac{(1 + i)^n - 1}{i} \qquad (4\text{-}18)$$

b Sinking fund factor:

$$(A/F, i, n) = \frac{i}{(1 + i)^n - 1} \qquad (4\text{-}19)$$

3 a Annuity present value factor:

$$(P/A, i, n) = \frac{(1 + i)^n - 1}{i(1 + i)^n} = \frac{1 - (1 + i)^{-n}}{i} \qquad (4\text{-}20)$$

b Capital recovery (loan repayment) factor:

$$(A/P, i, n) = \frac{i(1 + i)^n}{(1 + i)^n - 1} = \frac{i}{1 - (1 + i)^{-n}} \qquad (4\text{-}21)$$

The formulas are grouped into the three pairs of factors for which one member of the pair is the reciprocal of the other.

There are two major advantages to knowing the factors rather than relying on tables. First, you may not have tables available for the interest rate i and time period n that you require. The formulas apply to any interest rate, for example, 8.375 percent, or time period, for example, eighteen years. The second advantage is the ease with which the formulas can be programmed into programmable calculators or computers. If one of these devices is available, there is no need for tables at all when you know the formulas.

In many situations the future stream of cash payments or receipts grows or declines at constant rates. We will examine two types of growth and decline—arithmetic and compound.

**Arithmetic Growth
or Decline**

Arithmetic or *linear growth* occurs when a stream of cash increases by a constant *dollar* amount each period. For example, Figure 4-12a shows a stream of cash receipts growing at a rate of $10 per period. Similarly, Figure 4-12b shows a stream of cash receipts declining arithmetically at a rate of $10 per period. This is also called linear growth or decline because if the figures are plotted on a graph, the points lie on a straight line, dollars versus time.

The most straightforward method of evaluating such streams is to split them into two pieces—an annuity plus (or minus) the growth (decline) element. For example, the stream of Figure 4-12a can be considered an annuity of $20 per period for five periods plus a growth element of $10 per period. Similarly the stream of Figure 4-12b is an annuity of $50 per period for five periods less a decline element of $10 per period. The present value of the total stream is therefore the present value of the annuity portion plus the present value of the growth element or minus the present value of the decline element. This is illustrated in Figure 4-13 for the growing stream of Figure 4-12a. Once we calculate the present value of the stream, we can compute the equivalent annuity or future value if they are desired. Let G be the amount of growth or decline per period, $10 in the examples. We can represent the present value per dollar of growth or decline as an interest rate factor $(P/G, i, n)$ so that the present value of the growth element is

$$P = G(P/G, i, n) \qquad (4\text{-}22)$$

The formula for this factor is

$$(P/G, i, n) = \frac{1}{i} \left[\frac{1 - (1 + i)^{-n}}{i} - n(1 + i)^{-n} \right]$$

$$= \frac{1}{i} \left[(P/A, i, n) - n(P/F, i, n) \right] \qquad (4\text{-}23)$$

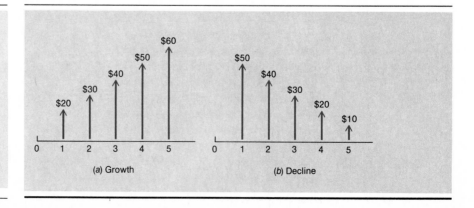

FIGURE 4-12

Arithmetic growth and decline.

(a) Growth

(b) Decline

Therefore, values for this factor can be easily calculated using tables for the two basic present value factors when they are available. Otherwise, the formulas can be used.

For example, suppose $i = 10$ percent. Then, using the tables,

$(P/A, 10\%, 5) = 3.791$

$(P/F, 10\%, 5) = 0.621$

$(P/G, 10\%, 5) = \dfrac{1}{0.10} [3.791 - 5(0.621)]$

$\qquad\qquad\qquad = \dfrac{1}{0.10} (0.686)$

$\qquad\qquad\qquad = 6.86$

The present value of the growing stream in Figure 4-12a is

$P = A(P/A, 10\%, 5) + G(P/G, 10\%, 5)$

$\quad = \$20(3.791) + \$10(6.86)$

$\quad = \$144.42$

The present value of the declining stream in Figure 4-12b is

$P = A(P/A, 10\%, 5) - G(P/G, 10\%, 5)$

$\quad = \$50(3.791) - \$10(6.86)$

$\quad = \$120.95$

Compound Growth or Decline

Compound growth occurs when a stream of cash payments or receipts grows at a constant *percentage* rate per period. For example, the rate of growth might be 10 percent period. If the initial (period 1) value is $100, and the stream grows for five periods, the values would be as shown in

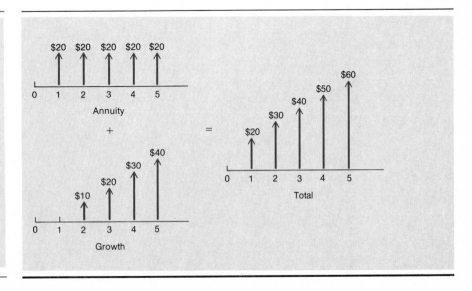

FIGURE 4-13

Annuity + growth = total.

Figure 4-14a. Note that the dollar increase in each period is not constant as in the case of arithmetic growth but increases instead. Similarly, a compound rate of decline of 10 percent per period is illustrated in Figure 4-14b.

Let F_1 be the amount of the cash flow in period 1. This is the base value which grows or declines. That is, the cash flow n periods from now is $F_1(1 + g)^{n-1}$ where g is the rate of growth or decline. The present value of such cash flow streams can be calculated from one of the two formulas presented below.[10] The choice of formula depends on the relationship between the growth rate g and the interest rate i.

1 If g equals i, then

$$P = \frac{nF_1}{1 + i}$$

(4-24)

2 If g is not equal to i, then

$$P = \frac{F_1}{i - g}\left[1 - \left(\frac{1 + g}{1 + i}\right)^n\right]$$

(4-25)

A useful special case is when n is very large (approaching infinity) and g is less than i. In this case $[(1 + g)/(1 + i)]^n$ approaches zero as n becomes large. The present value of a stream of this type is

[10] We can derive these formulas as follows: The present value of a stream of cash flows that grows or declines at a constant compound rate of g for n periods is

$$P = \frac{F_1}{1 + i} + \frac{F_1(1 + g)}{(1 + i)^2} + \frac{F_1(1 + g)^2}{(1 + i)^3} + \cdots + \frac{F_1(1 + g)^{n-1}}{(1 + i)^n}$$

(a)

Case 1: $g = i$, then (a) becomes

$$P = \frac{F_1}{1 + i} + \frac{F_1(1 + i)}{(1 + i)^2} + \frac{F_1(1 + i)^2}{(1 + i)^3} + \cdots + \frac{F_1(1 + i)^{n-1}}{(1 + i)^n}$$

$$= \frac{F_1}{1 + i} + \frac{F_1}{1 + i} + \frac{F_1}{1 + i} + \cdots + \frac{F_1}{1 + i}$$

$$= \frac{nF_1}{1 + i}$$

(b)

Case 2: $g \neq i$, multiply both sides of (a) by $(1 + g)/(1 + i)$, to obtain (c)

$$P\left(\frac{1 + g}{1 + i}\right) = \frac{F_1(1 + g)}{(1 + i)^2} + \frac{F_1(1 + g)^2}{(1 + i)^3} + \frac{F_1(1 + g)^3}{(1 + i)^4} + \cdots + \frac{F_1(1 + g)^n}{(1 + i)^{n+1}}$$

(c)

Subtract (c) from (a), to obtain

$$P - P\left(\frac{1 + g}{1 + i}\right) = \frac{F_1}{1 + i} - \frac{F_1(1 + g)^n}{(1 + i)^{n+1}}$$

$$P\left[1 - \frac{1 + g}{1 + i}\right] = \frac{F_1}{1 + i}\left[1 - \frac{(1 + g)^n}{(1 + i)^n}\right]$$

$$P\left[\frac{i - g}{1 + i}\right] = \frac{F_1}{1 + i}\left[1 - \left(\frac{1 + g}{1 + i}\right)^n\right]$$

$$P = \frac{F_1}{i - g}\left[1 - \left(\frac{1 + g}{1 + i}\right)^n\right]$$

(d)

$$P = \frac{F_1}{i - g} \qquad (4\text{-}26)$$

This is the constant perpetual growth case mentioned in Chapter 4 and used in several later chapters.

In applying Formula (4-25) we need values for $[(1 + g)/(1 + i)]^n$. For computational purposes the following approaches may be used. First, suppose that g is less than i, but n is not large so that (4-26) is inaccurate. Define a new interest rate i^*

$$i^* = \left(\frac{1 + i}{1 + g}\right) - 1 \qquad (4\text{-}27)$$

Then

$$\left(\frac{1 + g}{1 + i}\right)^n = \left(\frac{1 + i}{1 + g}\right)^{-n} = (1 + i^*)^{-n} \qquad (4\text{-}28)$$

The quantity $(1 + i^*)^{-n}$ is the present value factor $(P/F, i^*, n)$ which may be found in tables for some values of i^* and/or calculated as explained below.

If g is greater than i, we can define a new interest rate i'

$$i' = \left(\frac{1 + g}{1 + i}\right) - 1 \qquad (4\text{-}29)$$

Then

$$\left(\frac{1 + g}{1 + i}\right)^n = (1 + i')^n = (F/P, i', n) \qquad (4\text{-}30)$$

We may be able to use interest rate tables to find $(F/P, i', n)$ or calculate the value as explained below.

To illustrate the use of "interest rates" i^* and i', let's calculate the present values of the streams shown in Figure 4-14 using an interest rate i of 8 percent. Figure 4-14b is a stream with

$$F_1 = \$100$$

$$g = -0.10$$

$$n = 5$$

FIGURE 4-14

Compound growth and decline.

(a) Growth   (b) Decline

Since g is less than i, compute i^* as

$$i^* = \left(\frac{1 + i}{1 + g}\right) - 1$$

$$= \frac{1.08}{.90} - 1$$

$$= 20\%$$

We need $(P/F, 20\%, 5)$, which is available in the 20 percent table and is found to be 0.4019. Then, applying the general formula (4-25)

$$P = \frac{F_1}{i - g}\left[1 - \left(\frac{1 + g}{1 + i}\right)^n\right]$$

$$= \frac{\$100}{.08 + .10}[1 - .4019]$$

$$= \$332.28$$

The stream of Figure 4-14a has

$$F_1 = \$100$$

$$g = 0.10$$

$$h = 5$$

Since g at 10 percent is greater than i at 8 percent, compute i' as

$$i' = \left(\frac{1 + g}{1 + i}\right) - 1$$

$$= \frac{1.10}{1.08} - 1$$

$$= 1.85\%$$

Now we need to find $(F/P, 1.85\%, 5)$, which is not readily available in interest rate tables. Our choices are to use an approximation by rounding off the interest rate to fit a table we do have (in this case to 2 percent), to use interpolation in the tables, or to compute $(1.0185)^5$. Since $(F/P, 1.85\%, 5) = 1.096$, the value of the growing stream in Figure 4-14a is

$$P = \frac{F_1}{i - g}\left[1 - \left(\frac{1 + g}{1 + i}\right)^n\right]$$

$$= \frac{\$100}{0.08 - 0.10}[1 - 1.096]$$

$$= (-\$5,000)(-0.096)$$

$$= \$480$$

Calculating Interest Rate Factors

If you examine the formulas presented above, you will see that the only difficult part to calculate is $(1 + i)^n$ or $(1 + i)^{-n}$. These are the compound amount factor and the present value factor, respectively. Therefore all the other factors can be calculated easily once one of these has been found.

Although there are extensive tables for the compound amount factor available (Union Carbide Corporation publishes one, for example), a small calculator will be most useful here.

Three types of calculators available at relatively low cost will be examined.

1   "Financial" or "business" calculators usually contain $(P/F, i, n)$ as a built-in function. As we noted above, once you have a number for the present value factor $[(P/F, i, n) = (1 + i)^{-n}]$, finding any other factor is easy using the appropriate formula. These calculators often have $(P/A, i, n)$ or $(A/P, i, n)$ available so that they are very useful for solving interest rate problems. The more expensive ones calculate unknown rates as well.

2   "Scientific" calculators usually have a function described as a^x, y^x, or similar notation. Let $a = 1 + i$ and $x = n$; now $(1 + i)^n$ can be calculated with this function.

3   Calculators lacking the needed functions can also be used to compute $(1 + i)^n$ by successive multiplication. That is,

$$(1 + i)^n = (1 + i)(1 + i)(1 + i) \cdots (1 + i)$$

n times. This process is greatly facilitated if the calculator has the capacity of retaining a constant multiplier. The value of $1 + i$ is used as the constant to multiply the results of the previous multiplication until $1 + i$ has been multiplied n times. Once the first multiplication has been performed and the constant entered, $(1 + i)^n$ can usually be calculated by pressing the $=$ button $n - 2$ times. [The first multiplication gives you $(1 + i)^2$.] The most common problem with this procedure is losing count of how many multiplications have been made.

5

SECURITY PRICES

In Chapter 1 we said that the objective of financial management was to maximize the price of the firm's common stock, given legal and ethical constraints. This chapter examines how the market prices of common stock, bonds, and other securities are determined and how risk affects those prices. Appendix 5A explains how to use and interpret stock and bond price data available in financial publications. In Chapter 6 we discuss risk measurement and the impact of risk on security prices in more depth. In later chapters, we show how specific decisions by management affect stock prices.

Chapters 5 and 6 explain the four basic principles stated below. The first three principles are introduced in Chapter 5 and the fourth is explained in Chapter 6.

1 The current market price of a security is the present value of the future payments to the owner of the security.
2 The discount rate that is used to determine the present value depends on:
    a The current level of interest rates.
    b The riskiness of the income provided by the security.
    c The attitudes of investors toward risk.
3 Market prices of securities tend to reflect existing information. In investing in marketable securities you cannot profit from having information that is widely disseminated, since market prices already fully reflect that information.
4 The risk in owning a security depends on how well you can predict the future cash receipts from owning it and how well it fits with the other assets that you own.

With these points in mind, let's look first at the relationship between prices and present values.

PRICES AND PRESENT VALUES

The benefits from owning a security are the future cash flows—such as interest payments, principal payments, and dividends—that are paid to the owner. The current market price of the security is the amount of money one has to pay to obtain the future cash flows. Securities are traded in financial markets with many buyers and sellers. The price of a security at a point in time is what the highest bidders are willing to pay for the future cash flows that will be produced by the security. The question is: What is the relationship between the market price of a security and its future cash flows? A fundamental principle of finance is that *the market price of a security is the present value of its future cash flows.*

The discount rate (interest rate) used to determine the present value depends on several characteristics of the cash flows as we discuss later. For now, suppose that the cash flows are known for certain and that there is only one interest rate that applies in the market today, regardless of when the cash flows are received in the future.[1] To illustrate the equivalence of prices and present values, let's look at an example.

---

[1] Appendix 5B explains why the interest rates today may be different for different times into the future.

Suppose that the market interest rate i is 6 percent per year and you are considering the purchase of a U.S. Treasury bill maturing in one year. It will pay $1000 to the owner one year from now. The present value of $1000 one year from now at a rate of 6 percent per year is

$$\text{Present value} = \frac{\$1000}{1 + i}$$

$$= \frac{\$1000}{1 + 0.06} = \frac{\$1000}{1.06}$$

$$= \$943.40$$

If you purchase the bill at a price of $943.40, what rate of return will you earn for the year? The $1000 will pay you back the current price plus interest.

$$i = \frac{\$1000 - \text{price}}{\text{price}}$$

$$= \frac{\$1000 - \$943.40}{\$943.40} = \frac{\$56.60}{\$943.40}$$

$$= 0.06 \text{ or } 6\%$$

Purchasing the bill at a price equal to the present value of 6 percent provides a rate of return to the investor of 6 percent. If the price were not equal to the present value of $943.40, then the rate of return on the bill would not be 6 percent.

If the market interest rate is the same for all riskless securities, then dollar prices will differ among securities only to the extent that the cash payments differ in timing or amount. Exhibit 5-1 shows the market prices for several securities assuming that the market interest rate for all of them is 6 percent per year. The only things the securities shown in Exhibit 5-1 have in common are the rate of return of 6 percent provided to the purchasers of the securities and that all future payments are known for sure.

Now let's see how prices adjust to a given interest rate. For a given stream of future payments, the lower the price that is paid, the higher is the interest rate or rate of return received. This basic characteristic is illustrated using a security that pays $10 per year to the owner forever. If the price of this security is $200, investors will earn 5 percent per year.

$$\text{Rate} = \frac{\$10}{\$200} = 5\%$$

If the price is $100, investors will earn 10 percent per year.

$$\text{Rate} = \frac{\$10}{\$100} = 10\%$$

Similarly, if the price is $50, investors will earn 20 percent per year.

Suppose that the rate of interest in the market is 10 percent. If the price of a security paying $10 per year forever is $200, no one would wish to own it and the price would fall. If the price of the security were $50, everyone would find it to be an attractive investment and the price would rise. At a price of $100, this security would not be especially attractive or unattractive and there would be no tendency for the price to change. The rate of return earned on the security at a price of $100 is the market interest rate of 10 percent.

New securities issued in the market are subject to the same conditions as securities already being traded. The decisions by investors as to whether or not they wish to buy the new security, and the self-interest of the issuer, cause new securities to have the same interest rate as old securities. For example, suppose that the market interest rate is 6 percent, but a company issues bonds with a coupon rate of 5 percent. The bonds have $100 maturity value per bond and will mature in twenty years. In other words, the firm will pay $5 interest each year and $100 in year 20 to the purchaser of the bonds. From example 3 in Exhibit 5-1, we know that investors will earn 6 percent on these bonds if they pay $88.53 per bond. Since investors can earn 6

EXHIBIT 5-1

Example of security prices at an interest rate of 6 percent per year

1. *One-year bill ($100 maturity value[a])*

$$\text{Price} = \frac{\$100}{1.06}$$

$$= \$100 \ (P/F, \ 6\%, \ 1)$$

$$= \$100 \ (0.9434)$$

$$= \$94.34$$

2. *Five-year note (7 percent coupon rate,[b] $100 maturity value)*

$$\text{Price} = \frac{\$7}{1.06} + \frac{\$7}{(1.06)^2} + \cdots + \frac{\$107}{(1.06)^5}$$

$$= \$7 \ (P/A, \ 6\%, \ 5) + \$100 \ (P/F, \ 6\%, \ 5)$$

$$= \$7 \ (4.2124) + \$100 \ (0.7473)$$

$$= \$104.22$$

3. *Twenty-year bond (5 percent coupon rate, $100 maturity value)*

$$\text{Price} = \frac{\$5}{1.06} + \frac{\$5}{(1.06)^2} + \cdots + \frac{\$105}{(1.06)^{20}}$$

$$= \$5 \ (P/A, \ 6\%, \ 20) + \$100 \ (P/F, \ 6\%, \ 20)$$

$$= \$5 \ (11.4699) + \$100 \ (0.3118)$$

$$= \$88.53$$

[a] For debt securities such as bonds that pay the entire principal at maturity, the terms maturity value, principal amount, face value, and par value all refer to the same quantity.
[b] The coupon rate is the interest payment expressed as a percentage of the face value; the face value equals maturity value for these securities.

percent on other securities in the market, no one would pay the firm more than $88.53, as the rate of return would be less than 6 percent if a higher price were paid. On the other hand, if the firm offered the bonds at a price below $88.53, everyone would like to buy them since the bonds would provide a higher rate of return than available in the market. However, it would be foolish for the firm's financial managers to do this, since the firm would be paying a higher interest rate than is necessary to raise money.

Given this equality between prices and present values, let's examine how the prices and market interest rates of fixed-income securities such as bonds are determined.

FIXED-INCOME SECURITIES: BONDS

A fixed-income security provides a stream of cash payments to its owner that have been promised by the issuer (borrower) at the time the security was originally issued (when the money was borrowed). Debt contracts such as bonds and mortgages are the most common fixed-income securities, although preferred stocks are also of this type. The promised stream of cash payments are fixed at the time of issue, and the payments are the *maximum* amounts that the issuer will pay. However, if the payments are at all uncertain (risky), there is a chance that the promised payments won't be made; the issuer may default on the debt.

Let's get a better idea of what fixed-income securities are all about by looking at two bonds that are traded on the New York Exchange. One bond was issued by International Harvester (IH). It has a 9 percent coupon rate and matures in 2004. The other bond was issued by Exxon Pipeline Corporation, a subsidiary of Exxon, with a coupon rate of 9 percent and maturity in 2004. Both bonds promise to pay the owner $9 per year per $100 maturity value until maturity, and both promise to pay their maturity values (principal) on maturity. Prices for the two bonds in August 1984 were $54 for the IH bond and $73 for the Exxon bond.[2]

The yield to maturity on each bond is the interest rate on the bond given the current price and the promised payments (coupon interest and principal) for that bond. The general equation used to find the yield to maturity, i, on a bond maturing in n periods is

$$\text{Price} = \frac{\text{interest}}{1 + i} + \frac{\text{interest}}{(1 + i)^2} + \cdots + \frac{\text{interest} + \text{principal}}{(1 + i)^n} \tag{5-1}$$

or, equivalently,

$$\text{Price} = \text{interest}(P/A, i, n) + \text{principal}(P/F, i, n) \tag{5-2}$$

In 1984, both bonds had approximately twenty years until maturity ($n = 20$). To determine i for the IH bond, we used Eq. (5-2) as follows:

$$\$54 = \$9(P/A, i, 20) + \$100(P/F, i, 20)$$

---

[2] These prices were reported in *The Wall Street Journal*. Bonds usually have maturity values of $1000 per bond. Therefore, a price of $50 per $100 maturity value implies an actual price of $500 per bond.

The yield to maturity, i percent, is the interest rate that makes the equation balance. Applying the procedure of Chapter 4, we find that the yield to maturity for the IH bond was 17.3 percent. Similarly for the Exxon bond, the relationship was

$$\$73 = \$9(P/A, i, 20) + \$100(P/F, i, 20)$$

and the yield to maturity of the Exxon bond was found to be 12.8 percent. Why would anyone have paid $73 for the Exxon bond when the IH bond was only $54? If you bought the IH bond and held it to maturity and if IH made all the promised payments, you would have earned 17.3 percent per year on your investment, much more than from the Exxon bond. Why? Because investors must have believed that there was significant risk that IH would *not* make all the promised payments.

The yield to maturity on a bond is the *most* you can earn by holding it to maturity. If any of the payments are not made when due to the owners of a bond, the owners will earn less than the yield to maturity on their purchase price. For many bonds there is significant risk that you will earn less than the yield to maturity. In the case of IH, investors assessed the chance of earning less as being fairly large.

Bond Ratings and Yields

There are several ways to analyze or compare how risk affects the prices of bonds. One widely used method is based on the yield to maturity. Two bonds of the same "quality" or risk should have the same yield to maturity. Under this approach, risk is not measured precisely. Instead, bonds are classified or organized into risk groups; all the bonds within the same group should have approximately the same yield. Two financial service firms provide widely used classification systems—Standard & Poor's Corporation and Moody's Investor Services. Their classifications differ somewhat, but the two services provide comparable ratings in the lower-risk classes, as shown in Table 5-1.

Exxon bonds were rated Aaa by Moody's; IH bonds were rated B. As Moody's says about its B-rated bonds, they "generally lack characteristics of a desirable investment." By this Moody's means that a conservative investor should avoid B bonds since they are fairly risky. Generally speaking, the lower the rating for a bond, the higher will be its yield to maturity. This is so because the ratings reflect the risk of bonds as evaluated by the rating firms who are experts in this area. However, all bonds of a given rating (A, for example) don't necessarily have the same yield to maturity. Some A bonds will yield about the same as Aa bonds, and some will have yields close to those on Baa bonds. The reason is that the classification scheme is only approximate, and many investors do their own "rating." Thus, if the A-rated bonds of a particular company appear more risky than the average A-rated bond, they will have a higher yield than the average A-rated bond and vice versa. Even the highest rated corporate bonds are not riskless. There is always the possibility that a private corporation cannot pay its debts. Investors seeking the least risk can purchase U.S. government bonds. Since the U.S. government has the power to tax and to print money, it would never need to default on its obligations. The debt issues backed by the "full faith and credit" of the United States are considered to be the safest available with respect to guaranteed payment of principal and interest. Bond yields therefore scale up from the rates available on United States government securities (except for bonds with special features such as tax exempt interest or convertibility into common stock).

The yields required on bonds of a given rating are not constant over time but vary due to changes in the general level of interest rates. Also the "spread" or difference between the yields on bonds of different ratings varies over time, depending on the general outlook for the economy. Figure 5-1 shows the average yields to maturity for samples of U.S. government bonds, Aaa bonds, and Baa bonds since 1929. Note that during times of general economic uncertainty such as the 1930s the difference between the yield on the three classes of bonds widens, especially the difference between Baa and Aaa bonds, as investors require a much higher yield on the more risky Baa bonds than on the safer Aaa bonds. Compare the situation in 1932 with that of 1970. In both years the yield on Baa bonds was over 9 percent. In 1932, the higher rate on Baa bonds was due to concern over the risk of the bonds, as the Aaa rate was only 5 percent. In 1970 it was primarily due to the high general level of interest rates as reflected by the correspondingly high rates on U.S. government and Aaa bonds.

Earlier in the chapter we stated the principle that the market price of a security is the present value of the future cash flows from the security. We are now able to state a second fundamental principle:

The discount rate that determines the present value of a security's cash flows depends on the riskless rate of interest plus a premium that depends on the risk of the cash flows from the security.

The more risk there is, the higher the premium will be.

TABLE 5-1
Bond classifications

	Standard & Poor's		Moody's
AAA	Highest grade	Aaa	Best quality
AA	High grade	Aa	High quality
A	Upper medium grade	A	Higher medium grade
BBB	Medium grade	Baa	Lower medium grade
BB	Lower medium grade	Ba	Possess speculative elements
B	Speculative	B	Generally lack characteristics of a desirable investment
CCC, CC	Outright speculation	Caa	Poor; may be in default
C	Income bonds	Ca	Speculative to a high degree; often in default
DDD, DD, D	In default; rating indicates relative salvage value	C	Lowest grade

This principle is illustrated by the data shown in Table 5-2 which shows the actual average rates of return from 1926 to 1981 on four types of securities. These data show that common stocks on average have provided a much higher rate of return than corporate bonds. The corporate bonds used in the calculation all had high ratings. Even so, the corporate bonds provided higher rates of return than the government bonds and Treasury bills. In other words, investors on average have been paid premiums for risk in owning corporate bonds and common stock, and the premium was much higher for stock than it was for highly rated corporate bonds. The existence of these premiums is consistent with the idea that investors dislike risk (are risk-averse) and must be compensated for bearing it.

VARIABLE-INCOME SECURITIES: COMMON STOCK

Fixed-income securities promise to provide specified cash payments to their owners. Variable-income securities, such as common stock, do not. The yield to maturity of a bond can be calculated precisely and provides a reference point in determining its price. There is no such reference point for common stock, but there is also no ceiling on how much you can earn from owning stock.

FIGURE 5-1

Historical interest rates on United States government and corporate Aaa-rated and Baa-rated bonds.

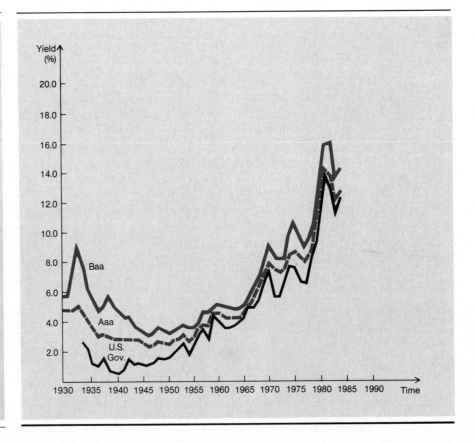

The financial returns from owning any asset come from two basic sources: periodic income (dividends on stock or interest on debt) and the amount you realize at the end of your ownership (selling price or maturity payments). In order to determine the value of the asset, you must estimate both the periodic income and the ultimate receipts from sale or maturity, and usually neither is known for sure. The returns from common stock ownership are especially uncertain since there are no promised interest or maturity payments. Future dividends are uncertain; and, since common stock has no maturity, any future sales price is uncertain as well.

Let's look at the problem of determining the value of the common stock of a corporation. Suppose you were to purchase one share of stock in Andes Company at $20 per share. One year from now you receive a dividend of $1 and sell the stock for $22. You earned $1 in dividends plus $2 in capital gains on the sale for a total of $3. Your rate of return is $3/$20 = 15 percent. Now suppose you kept the stock for two years and received dividends of $1 the first year and $1.50 the second year. At the end of the second year you sell the stock for $23.80. What rate of return did you earn? To find out you must find the rate of return i that makes the following equation balance:

$$\$20 = \frac{\$1}{1 + i} + \frac{\$1.50}{(1 + i)^2} + \frac{\$23.80}{(1 + i)^2}$$

$$= \$1\ (P/F, i, 1) + \$1.50\ (P/F, i, 2) + \$23.80\ (P/F, i, 2)$$

The rate is again 15 percent.[3] We can express the valuation relationship in a more general form. Let P_0 be the price of the stock now, D_1 be dividends in one year, D_2 be dividends in two years, and P_2 be the price at the end of the second year, two years from now. Then

[3] At $i = 15\%$

$$\$20 = \$1(P/F, 15\%, 1) + \$1.50(P/F, 15\%, 2) + \$23.80(P/F, 15\%, 2)$$

$$= \$1(.8696) + \$1.50(.7561) + \$23.80(.7561)$$

$$= \$20$$

TABLE 5-2
Average rates of return on selected securities 1926–1981

Security	Average annual rate of return	Risk premium (relative to Treasury bills)
Common stocks	9.1%	6.1%
Corporate bonds	3.6	0.6
Government bonds	3.0	0
Treasury bills	3.0	0

Source: R. G. Ibbotson and R. A. Sinquefield, *Stocks, Bonds, Bills, and Inflation: The Past and the Future* (Charlottesville, Va.: Financial Analysts Research Foundation, 1982).

$$P_0 = \frac{D_1}{1 + i} + \frac{D_2 + P_2}{(1 + i)^2}$$

$$= D_1(P/F, i, 1) + (D_2 + P_2)(P/F, i, 2) \tag{5-3}$$

Equation (5-3) applies to any stock held for two years. The use of our notation $(P/F, i, n)$ is cumbersome here so we will stop using it. Suppose a stock was held for three years. The relationship would be

$$P_0 = \frac{D_1}{1 + i} + \frac{D_2}{(1 + i)^2} + \frac{D_3 + P_3}{(1 + i)^3} \tag{5-4}$$

In general, if you owned the stock for n years,

$$P_0 = \frac{D_1}{1 + i} + \frac{D_2}{(1 + i)^2} + \cdots + \frac{D_n + P_n}{(1 + i)^n} \tag{5-5}$$

What we have developed here is a general expression to obtain a rate of return i given the purchase price of the stock, dividends paid on it, and the selling price at the end of n periods. This expression will help us determine the value of a stock.

We can consider the stream of dividends and the final price to be *forecasted* magnitudes as of today. Associated with these forecasts is uncertainty; no one can be sure what the future dividend payments and the price of common stock for a company will be. Nevertheless, investors must expect to earn a reasonable rate of return from owning the stock or else they wouldn't own it. The rate of return required by investors in the market depends on the uncertainty of the dividends and future price and on the riskless rate of interest. We will designate the rate of return *required* by investors to be k.

For example, suppose that investors in the market expect that the price one year from now of a share of stock in the Star Company will be $55 and the company is forecast to pay a dividend of $2.50 next year.[4] Also suppose that the required rate of return k is 15 percent based on investors' assessment of the uncertainty as to what the dividend and price will actually be. The price today would be

$$P_0 = \frac{\$2.50 + \$55}{1.15}$$

$$= \$50$$

P_0 is the present value of the expected $2.50 dividend and expected $55 share price using a discount rate k of 15 percent. If it actually turns out that the dividend is $2.50 and the share price is $55, the investor will have earned a 15 percent rate of return [that is, $i = 15$ percent using Eq. (5-5)]. This example reveals what we mean by the required rate of return (discount rate) k. Investors discount (value) the future dividends and share price using rate k. Valuing shares in this way means that, if future dividends and future

---

[4] We are assuming for the example that dividends are paid once per year. In practice, dividends are usually paid once per quarter.

share price turn out as expected ($2.50 and $55 in the above example), the investors will actually earn rate k (15 percent) on their investment ($50).

We can show that the value of a share can be expressed entirely in terms of the future dividends on the share. One year from now the price of the stock depends on what income (dividends) the stock is expected to provide people buying the stock then. Therefore, *the price of the stock today can be viewed as the present value of all expected future dividends, using the interest rate* k *required to compensate the owners of the stock for the time value of money and the risk of those expected dividends*. If the last payment to any owner is at time m, then [5]

$$P_0 = \frac{D_1}{1 + k} + \frac{D_2}{(1 + k)^2} + \cdots + \frac{D_m}{(1 + k)^m} \tag{5-6}$$

After time m, the price of the stock (or asset) would be zero since there would be no further income to the owners. At time m, either the assets of the firm are being liquidated or the firm is being sold in entirety to someone and all cash received from the sale is paid out. In any case, D_m is the last payment to the stockholders of the company. For many companies the last dividend may be many years into the future and therefore m is very, very large. Huge, well-established firms such as IBM and General Motors are expected to continue existence for a long time. But even for large firms, there may be considerable uncertainty as to when time m is. For example, dividends may cease due to the firm's bankruptcy, and the firm might go bankrupt any time in the future.

Equation (5-6) expresses in mathematical form the proposition that the market price (or value) of common stock is the present value of all expected future receipts (the D's) from owning the stock. This is so, regardless of whether the people now owning the stock plan to continue owning it until time m, since the value at any future time (period 3, for example) will

---

[5] As proof of Eq. (5-6), suppose you were planning to own the stock for only one year, then

$$P_0 = \frac{D_1}{1 + k} + \frac{P_1}{1 + k} \tag{1}$$

The price of the stock one year from now, P_1, must be based on what investors expect to receive in future years; for example,

$$P_1 = \frac{D_2}{1 + k} + \frac{P_2}{1 + k} \tag{2}$$

Substituting Eq. (2) into Eq. (1), we get

$$P_0 = \frac{D_1}{1 + k} + \frac{D_2}{(1 + k)^2} + \frac{P_2}{(1 + k)^2} \tag{3}$$

Now we can look at P_2 as being

$$P_2 = \frac{D_3}{1 + k} + \frac{P_3}{1 + k} \tag{4}$$

Substituting Eq. (4) into Eq. (3), we get

$$P_0 = \frac{D_1}{1 + k} + \frac{D_2}{(1 + k)^2} + \frac{D_3}{(1 + k)^3} + \frac{P_3}{(1 + k)^3} \tag{5}$$

We can continue this argument until we reach D_m, which is the last payment (including the proceeds from liquidating the company) made to owners, and we arrive at Eq. (5-6). One problem with this approach is that we have no assurance that k is the same value for each future period.

depend on the expectations regarding receipts in period 4 and thereafter. Let's look at a special case of Eq. (5-6) which is used widely in finance, constant perpetual growth.

*The Constant
Growth Model*

If investors expect dividends to be a constant amount, D dollars per year beginning one year from now and continuing forever, common stock is like a perpetuity. In this case Eq. (5-6) reduces to a much simpler relationship, which is the present value of a perpetual annuity:

$$P_0 = \frac{D}{k} \tag{5-7}$$

This formula applies when there is no growth expected in the firm's dividend payments; however, there is a more general relationship that applies when the rate of growth is constant.

Suppose that dividends per share for a firm are expected to be $1 next year. Two years from now the expected dividend is $1.06 per share. In three years the dividend is expected to be $1(1.06)^2 = 1.1236, in four years $1(1.06)^3 = 1.1910, etc. These dividends are expected to grow at a compound rate of 6 percent per year. If this growth is expected to continue for the foreseeable future (forever, to be precise), then we have an example of the constant growth case.

Let D_1 be the dividend expected in the coming year and g be the expected growth rate. The dividend in any year t is expected to be

$$D_t = D_1(1 + g)^{t-1} \tag{5-8}$$

Equation (5-8) summarizes the general situation. In our example we had:

t	1	2	3	4	$\cdots$
D_t	$1.00	$1.06	$1.1236	$1.1910	$\cdots$

The series of dividends D_t in this example can be expressed compactly using Eq. (5-8) as

$$D_t = \$1(1.06)^{t-1}$$

If the expected stream of dividend payments fits the pattern of Eq. (5-8), then we have constant growth. At time $t = 0$, the present value of this stream of dividends is

$$P_0 = \frac{D_1}{k - g} \tag{5-9}$$

Note that, when $g = 0$, Eq. (5-9) reduces to Eq. (5-7), the no-growth case.

The derivation of Eq. (5-9) was provided in Appendix 4A. The important things to know about the derivation are (1) that it is purely a mathematical result given the assumptions of constant perpetual growth (g) and constant required rate of return (k), and (2) that the growth rate g must be less than the rate of return k in order for the model to make sense.[6]

If we substitute a 6 percent growth rate and a dividend next year of $1 into the formula, we get

$$P_0 = \frac{\$1}{k - 0.06}$$

In order to do anything more, we need a value for k (or P). Suppose $k = 10$ percent. Then the price of the stock would be

$$P_0 = \frac{\$1}{0.10 - 0.06} = \$25$$

The formula can be used to illustrate the relationship between future prices and dividend streams that we discussed earlier. Suppose that expectations do not change from this year to next year and that $1 in dividends is actually paid. What will be the price of the stock next year? The price next year will be the present value of expected future dividends. Next year, the expected growth rate in dividends remains 6 percent by assumption. Also, the expected dividend one year from then will be $1.06. If k is 10 percent, the price next year will be[7]

$$P_1 = \frac{\$1.06}{0.10 - 0.06} = \$26.50$$

As of now (time 0), we are expecting a dividend of $1 and a price for the stock of $26.50, both to occur one year from now. If the required rate of

---

[6] Equation (5-9) is undefined if g equals k and is negative if g exceeds k. If g is equal to or greater than k, we can use Eq. (5-6) to show that P_0 is infinite. But, no share can have an infinite price in the world we know; and therefore no share can yield a dividend that is expected to grow, *forever*, at a rate g that equals or exceeds the discount rate k.

[7] The constant growth model implies that an equation like Eq. (5-9) applies at any point in time. For example, at time 1 (one year from now), using $D_2 = D_1(1 + g)$ from (5-8),

$$P_1 = \frac{D_2}{k - g} = \frac{D_1(1 + g)}{k - g} \qquad \text{(a)}$$

where P_1 is the price at time 1, D_2 is the dividend expected to occur at time 2, g is the expected constant dividend growth rate and k is the discount rate. In general, for the constant growth model [where $D_{t+1} = D_1(1 + g)^t$ using Eq. (5-8)]:

$$P_t = \frac{D_{t+1}}{k - g} = \frac{D_1(1 + g)^t}{k - g} \qquad \text{(b)}$$

Also, the rate of growth per period in the price of a share under the constant growth model is rate g. To see this, use (b):

Rate of growth
in stock price $\quad = \dfrac{P_{t+1} - P_t}{P_t}$
during period t

$$= \frac{\dfrac{D_1(1 + g)^t}{k - g} - \dfrac{D_1(1 + g)^{t-1}}{k - g}}{\dfrac{D_1(1 + g)^{t-1}}{k - g}}$$

$$= g$$

return is 10 percent, what should the current price be? The present value at 10 percent of $1 plus $26.50 received in one year is

$$P_0 = \frac{\$26.50 + \$1}{1 + k}$$

$$= \frac{\$27.50}{1.10} = \$25$$

We get the same price as before, which demonstrates the consistency of the "stream of dividends" approach with the "dividends plus future price" approach to stock valuation.

A final point is that Eq. (5-9) can be rewritten to express k in terms of prices, dividends, and growth rate. Solving (5-9) for k gives

$$k = \frac{D_1}{P_0} + g \qquad (5\text{-}10)$$

The first term on the right-hand side of the equation is called the *dividend yield* of the stock, dividend over price. Here the dividend yield is based on the expected future dividend, D_1. The dividend yield in our example was $\$1/\$25 = 4$ percent. Given estimates of the dividend yield and of the growth rate in dividends, g, we can use Eq. (5-10) to estimate the required rate of return on the stock. We do this in Chapter 7.

In the constant growth model, the growth rate in dividends is also the expected rate of growth of the stock price. In our example the price of the stock was expected to grow from now to next year by 6 percent, which is the same as the dividend growth rate.[8]

$$\frac{\$26.50 - \$25}{\$25} = \frac{\$1.50}{\$25} = 6\%$$

Equation (5-10) therefore reveals that the required rate of return on stock is composed of two parts: (1) expected dividend yield, D_1/P_0, and (2) the expected rate of price appreciation or capital gains rate, g.

THE EFFICIENT MARKETS HYPOTHESIS

As we discussed, a company's current stock price is based on investor expectations about future dividends and stock price. These expectations depend on the information investors have about the company and its future prospects. It would seem to follow that investors who have superior information, or who can evaluate information more effectively than others, might be able to find stocks that are likely to provide a rate of return higher than the rate required by the market; that is, they might be able to find "bargains." Some might even argue that diligently reading The Wall Street Journal (an excellent source of business information) is a path to riches.

Most investment advisors would agree though that simply reading The Wall Street Journal does not make someone—even someone who has taken four finance courses—an investment hotshot who can consistently pick

---

[8] See footnote 7.

stocks with extraordinarily high returns. The reason: Most large investors (individual and institutional) and most investment advisors (upon whom investors depend for picking stocks) either read *The Wall Street Journal* or have information sources providing the same information as does *The Wall Street Journal*. Consequently, the market prices of publicly traded stocks very quickly reflect that information. If the president of Exxon announces a major new oil discovery at 10:00 A.M. on a Monday morning, the price of Exxon stock will rise within minutes. To gain an edge, the investor must have accurate information before everyone else does. The **efficient markets hypothesis** is that information spreads quickly in the market and is reflected immediately in security prices. A type of information (for example, accounting data in a company's annual report) is "fully reflected" in prices if there is no investment strategy using that type of information that will allow an investor to do consistently better than other investors. We say that the market is *efficient* with respect to a particular set of information if market prices reflect that information. Efficient markets prevent an investor from exploiting information because prices have already adjusted to take that information into account.

Markets can be efficient with respect to some kinds of information but not others. For example, prices may fully reflect *publicly available* information but not reflect information possessed *only* by those very close to the corporation (e.g., the firm's directors and top executives). Thus, Henry Investor could not "beat the market" (earn an extraordinarily high rate of return for the risk involved) using the publicly available statistics published in *The Wall Street Journal*. But Henry might be able to make a killing by using information given to him by his Uncle Ted, a mining company geologist, on a new silver discovery in Nevada that has not been publicly announced. Of course, Henry and Ted might also have to collaborate in choosing an attorney to defend themselves against charges of illegally trading on insider information.

In the discussion below, we normally will refer to efficiency in the stock market. However, the concept of efficiency can be applied to any market; for example, the market for bonds, for potatoes, or for medical care. Most empirical research on efficiency has used stock market data. Also, recognize that when we say that a market is efficient, we *only* mean that prices fully reflect information and not that there are no brokerage fees in buying and selling stocks or that your broker can make twenty sales calls in an hour.

Types of Efficient Markets

Using types of information as the basis for categorization, Eugene Fama of the University of Chicago has conveniently categorized market efficiency as either weak form, semistrong form, or strong form. Let's look at each of these.

Weak Form Efficiency   This form of efficient markets implies that knowledge of the past price trends of stocks cannot be used to pick those stocks that will turn out, in the future, to generate extraordinarily high returns. The argument used to explain weak form efficiency is that, if everyone knows about past price trends (the information is publicly available), the current price reflects that information since it is used by investors in deciding what stocks are worth. Any investor with past price information will not have an advantage over other investors in picking stocks, since they have the same information. An enormous amount of empirical research supports the weak form efficiency notion.[9]

Semistrong Efficiency   Semistrong efficiency implies that, not only does a knowledge of past prices not provide any advantage in picking investments (weak form efficiency), but also that a knowledge of *all publicly available* information will provide no advantage. The reason is that existing prices reflect all public information, good or bad. If a firm is doing well, buyers and sellers of the stock will immediately bid the current price to a high level. If the firm is doing poorly, the stock's price will immediately fall. Unless new information is provided to the market in the future, the future price of the stock will not experience extraordinary changes. According to this hypothesis, all the information available to the market is currently impounded in market prices.

A substantial amount of empirical work has been done to test the semistrong efficiency argument. The findings offer qualified support for the theory. Supporting the efficient markets view are results that show that the market quickly adjusts to certain types of new information, such as dividend increase announcements and earnings announcements.[10] However, other studies have found that market prices may not reflect all information that could be used to earn an extraordinary rate of return.[11] Thus, asset prices probably reflect most publicly available information, but the degree of this efficiency depends on the type of information and the type of asset being traded. For example, the real estate market may not be as efficient as the stock market because information about individual properties is more costly to obtain than is information about publicly traded stocks (which are analyzed continuously by security analysts).

Strong Form Efficiency   Markets are strong form efficient if prices reflect *all* information. With strong form efficiency, an investor could not profit even from information possessed by those closest to the situation ("inside infor-

---

[9] See, for example, Arnold B. Moore, "Some Characteristics of Changes in Common Stock Prices," in Paul H. Cootner, *The Random Character of Stock Market Prices* (Cambridge, Mass.: M.I.T., 1964), pp. 139–161; Eugene F. Fama, "The Behavior of Stock Market Prices," *Journal of Business*, vol. 38, no. 1 (January 1965), pp. 34–105; Clive W. J. Granger and Oskar Morgenstern, "Spectral Analysis of New York Stock Market Prices," *Kyklos*, 16 (1963), pp. 1–27.

[10] See E. F. Fama, L. Fisher, M. Jensen, and R. Roll, "The Adjustment of Stock Prices to New Information," *International Economic Review*, vol. 10, no. 1 (February 1969), pp. 1–21; Myron S. Scholes, "The Market for Securities: Substitution versus Price Pressure and the Effects of Information on Share Prices," *Journal of Business*, vol. 45, no. 2 (April 1972), pp. 179–211; Ray Ball and Philip Brown, "An Empirical Evaluation of Accounting Income Numbers," *Journal of Accounting Research*, 6 (Autumn 1968), pp. 159–178.

[11] For example, Jaffe found that publicly available information on inside trading could have been used to select stocks which produced an above average rate of return. See Jeffrey F. Jaffe, "Special Information and Insider Trading," *Journal of Business*, vol. 47, no. 1 (July 1974), pp. 410–429.

mation"). The theory behind this is that those who have inside information (or the select group they talk to) will buy or sell the stock of the company (or whatever asset is relevant) and thereby cause its price to adjust to a realistic level in light of that information. Again the empirical results are mixed. Studies of mutual fund performance (fund managers are more likely to have inside information than are average investors) indicate that they do not consistently outperform a randomly selected portfolio of stocks of a risk similar to that of the fund.[12] This suggests that any inside information obtained by fund managers was already reflected in market prices and therefore did not, on average, produce superior results. (It could also imply that fund managers simply didn't get much inside information.)

There is also evidence that suggests that inside information can be used profitably. Niederhoffer and Osborne concluded that specialists on the major exchanges (traders on the floor of the exchanges who specialize in certain stocks) are able to use trading information to earn exceptional returns.[13] Scholes and also Lorie and Niederhoffer found that corporate officers may be able to benefit from use of privileged information.[14] It appears, therefore, that true insiders (company officers) or traders can gain by using privileged information but outsiders, such as fund managers, who get "hot tips" are less successful.

Technicians, Fundamentalists, and Middle-of-the-Roaders

In spite of the very large body of evidence in favor of weak form efficiency, many people (especially among financial practitioners) argue that an analysis of historical stock price data can be used to forecast future stock prices. They assert that research supporting weak form efficiency is based on the use of relatively simple historical price patterns such as the change in price the day before. They believe that a sophisticated "technical analyst" can, by examining very complex and subtle price patterns, often predict whether a stock's price will increase or decrease substantially in the near future. Technical analysis is the study of stock price patterns for the purpose of predicting future stock price behavior. For example, Figure 5-2 illustrates a "head-and-shoulders" formation, which technical analysts say is a sign that the stock's price will decline for some extended time period thereafter. Price patterns used by technical analysts include head and shoulders, multiple heads and shoulders, saucer, bowl, dormant bottom, and many others. The technical analysts, in effect, are arguing that the market does a poor job of interpreting historical price information, that is, that the market is *not* weak form efficient. Interestingly, the "pure" technicians claim that other types of

---

[12] For example, see M. C. Jensen, "The Performance of Mutual Funds in the Period 1954–1964," *Journal of Finance*, 33 (May 1968), pp. 389–416; N. E. Mains, "Risk, the Pricing of Capital Assets, and the Evaluation of Investment Portfolios: Comment," *Journal of Business*, 50 (July 1977), pp. 371–384.

[13] See Victor Niederhoffer and M. F. M. Osborne, "Market Making and Reversal on the Stock Exchange," *Journal of the American Statistical Association*, 61 (December 1966), pp. 897–916.

[14] See M. S. Scholes, "The Market for Securities: Substitution versus Price Pressure and the Effects of Information on Share Prices," *Journal of Business*, vol. 45, no. 2 (April 1972), pp. 179–211; James H. Lorie and Victor Niederhoffer, "Predictive and Statistical Properties of Insider Trading," *Journal of Law and Economics*, 11 (1968), pp. 35–53.

publicly available information (e.g., corporate earnings data) are more correctly used by investors in valuing securities. They argue that "money-in-the-know leaves tracks"; that is, that in using historical price information they are really obtaining information about trading by people with inside information.

A position contrasting that of the technicians is held by the fundamentalists, who believe that the important factor in forecasting a stock's future price behavior is not its past price pattern but, instead, the company's business performance (that is, expected financial condition and profitability).The fundamentalists believe that astute examination of available financial data about a company will provide a clue as to whether the share price will rise or fall. They (and their customers) believe that the market is not semistrong form efficient (prices do not reflect *all* publicly available information) but that markets are weak form efficient (current prices do reflect information about past prices).

Many analysts are "middle-of-the-roaders" or "hybrids"; that is, they blend both the technical and fundamental positions. These analysts believe that the market is neither weak form efficient nor semistrong form efficient. They feel that both historical price information and other publicly available information such as corporate earnings can be used to pick stocks that are underpriced.

Whether an analyst is a technician, fundamentalist, or a little of each, he

FIGURE 5-2

*Head-and-shoulders
price pattern for IC
Industries, Inc.*

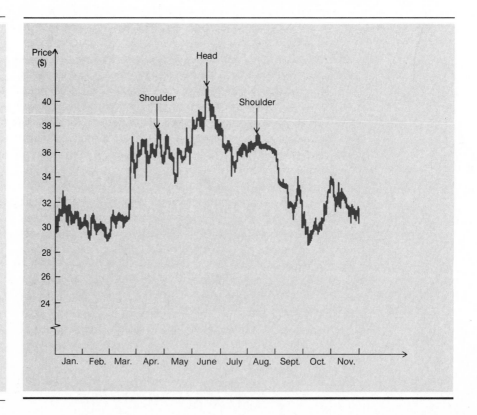

or she has the underlying conviction that studying available financial data is a way of consistently doing better than simply randomly selecting stocks. The analyst believes that current prices don't necessarily reflect the true current values of all stocks. This means that markets are not truly "efficient" in that prices do not take into account all available data about the stock and the issuing company.

Implications of Market Efficiency

We have pointed out that the evidence suggests that the market is quite efficient with respect to publicly available information and somewhat efficient in reflecting insider information. What are the implications of these findings for the investor and the financial manager?

First, we can infer that the market is not fooled by accounting manipulations which do not affect the real assets and cash flows of the firm. For example, accounting income changes which are due only to changes in how operations are reported but which do not affect cash flows (such as a switch from straight-line to accelerated depreciation for financial reporting but not for tax purposes) will not affect share prices.[15] The important point here is that the financial manager will not be able to raise share prices by sleight-of-hand tactics; all that matters is real performance (assets, liabilities, cash flows, etc.).

Second, investors and financial managers should not try to outguess the market unless they have information which is not publicly available and, even in that case, caution is warranted. With efficient markets, security prices reflect available information and therefore one cannot outsmart the market using that information. This dictum applies to an individual investor building a personal portfolio or to a firm buying marketable securities (e.g., Treasury bills, another corporation's stock or bonds, etc.) for its own account or for an employee pension fund. One can expect to earn the normal rate of return on the type of security purchased, and no more. This also applies to a financial manager who is trying to decide when to issue securities. In an efficient market, the prices of securities are unbiased estimates of security values and unless the manager has information that the market does not have, trying to time the issue of securities to take advantage of supposed "mispricing" will not, on average, provide superior results.

Third—and this is directly related to the second point above—a company should not seek a merger with another company simply because, on the basis of information that is also available to investors in the market, its management feels the stocks of the two companies form a nice stock portfolio for the stockholders. The stockholders have similar information and can create their own stock portfolios. A merger is justified only if the acquiring firm's management feels either that it has information not already reflected in stock market prices that it can use to find exceptional bargains in the market, or that a merger will produce cash flow benefits (e.g., due to

---

[15] For empirical evidence that book depreciation methods do not affect share prices, see R. S. Kaplan and R. Roll, "Investor Evaluation of Accounting Income Information: Some Empirical Evidence," *Journal of Business*, 45 (April 1972), pp. 225–257.

lower production costs resulting from economies of scale) because the merging companies mesh so well. The issue of firm diversification is discussed again in Chapters 9 and 23.

Fourth, if markets are efficient with respect to a particular type of information (e.g., publicly available information) and therefore prices fully reflect that information, then we cannot use that information to predict tomorrow's prices. That is, we cannot use the information to find temporarily undervalued or overvalued assets. For example, assume that the market is semistrong efficient (prices reflect all publicly available information). Then, the July 1 price of a share of stock fully reflects all information that is publicly available on July 1. Might you, on the basis of the July 1 information, conclude that the July 2 price will be much higher or much lower than the July 1 price? Well, if you could, then that would mean that the July 1 price did not *already* reflect the July 1 information. There would be a contradiction in assuming that prices already reflect publicly available information and also in assuming that we can use the information to predict the future price. The July 2 price is unpredictable using the July 1 information. Another word for "unpredictable" is "random." Financial theorists often say that share prices follow a "random walk," which is another way of saying that tomorrow's price is unpredictable using today's information.[16]

Fifth, with market efficiency, market prices reveal a great deal of useful information. For example, if a firm's share price has been steadily declining while stock prices in general have been stable or rising, it is clear that the market has become progressively more pessimistic about the firm's prospects. We could use this information to predict whether the firm will go bankrupt.[17] Similarly, changes in the general level of stock prices can be used to forecast ups and downs in the general economy. Stock prices depend on investors' expectations about profitability in the coming periods, and when investors anticipate a general economic downturn share prices fall. As it turns out, investors are pretty good at foretelling fluctuations in the economy. As a result, the general level of stock prices is a good leading indicator of actual business trends.

SUMMARY

The basic message of this chapter is that the market price of a financial asset is the present value of the future cash payments to the owner of the asset. When the payments are known for sure, the riskless rate of interest determines the present value. Risky streams of payments are more difficult to analyze.

Fixed-income assets, such as bonds, have a stated promised stream

---

[16] We are using the term "random walk" loosely here. Technically, prices follow a random walk if successive price changes are independent of one another and are identically distributed (i.e., have the same probability distributions). Market efficiency does not actually imply that prices conform to a random walk. Prices in an efficient market can follow a "submartingale," under which the probability distributions of price changes shift over time.

[17] On the use of share prices for this purpose, see W. H. Beaver, "Market Prices, Financial Ratios and the Prediction of Failure," *Journal of Accounting Research*, 6 (Autumn 1968), pp. 179–192.

of cash payments to the owners; variable-income assets, such as common stock, do not provide a promised stream, but instead may in the future pay more or less than the income that they are currently providing. One method of valuing fixed-income securities is based on the yield to maturity. Two fixed-income securities with the same degree of uncertainty in their payments should have the same yield for the degree of risk involved. Then the value of a fixed-income security would be the present value of the promised payments using that yield as the interest rate.

The second method of valuation is applicable to all types of income-producing assets. The value of an asset can be thought of as the present value of the expected stream of payments using (for discounting purposes) the rate of return that is appropriate for the degree of risk of the payments. For example, the value of common stock can be thought of as the present value of the expected dividends that will be paid to present and future owners of the stock.

The risk-adjusted discount rate or required rate of return that should be used in valuing the expected income from an asset depends on the general level of interest rates in the economy and the degree of risk. The greater the risk, the higher is the rate of return required by investors.

The efficient markets hypothesis states that a security's current price reflects all the information currently available to the market. The weak form of the hypothesis considers only the past price history of the security. The semistrong form considers all publicly available information including the price history. The strong form of the hypothesis considers all information that is currently known by anyone in the market. Tests of the hypothesis suggest that the market is probably fairly efficient in the semistrong sense.

QUESTIONS

1 In a world of no risk, explain why financial assets might have different prices. What is the common element to all financial assets in such a world?

2 In the world of idealized certainty (i.e., no risks, no taxes, and perfect markets for financial assets), would the following situations be possible? (In each case, support your answer.)
   a Two financial assets providing the same cash flows selling at different prices
   b Two financial assets selling at the same price but providing different cash flows to the owner
   c Two financial assets selling at the same price but providing different rates of return (interest rates)

3 Suppose that currently the yield to maturity on Aaa bonds is 9 percent. The Fritz Company is planning to issue bonds with a coupon rate of 9 percent. The bonds will be rated Aa. Will Fritz bonds sell at their face (maturity) value? Why or why not?

4 If the price of a share of common stock depends on the dividends paid to the stockholders, why do we find stocks of companies that

have never paid a dividend selling at prices greater than zero and in many cases at a high multiple of the company's earnings per share?

5 Assuming that the stock market is efficient with respect to past prices (weak form efficiency) but no more efficient than that, which of the following investment situations is likely to result in unusually high returns? Why or why not?

a The price of a stock has declined for five consecutive days. It "looks cheap and is due for a recovery."

b An analysis of General Motors' automobile sales for the past two months as reported in *The Wall Street Journal* shows that the company is experiencing increased sales of its most profitable cars. Your broker, who performed the analysis, recommends that you buy GM stock.

c In your statistics course you learned a technique for forecasting time series data. You have programmed the technique on your personal computer and are using it to forecast future stock prices based on past stock prices. You have found a stock with a current price of $40 per share that your computer forecasts will rise to $80 within one year.

6 If the stock market is strong form efficient, will anyone be able to earn unusually high returns from investing in stocks? Explain your answer. (This question draws on Appendix 5A.)

7 Explain what the figures mean in the following quotations taken from *The Wall Street Journal*.

a

Treasury bonds and notes					
Rate	Mat. Date	Bid	Asked	Bid chg.	Yld.
13s	1990 Nov n	102.4	102.12	+ .6	12.43

b

Bonds	Cur. yld.	Vol.	High	Low	Close	Net chg.
duPnt 14s91	13.	11	104	$103\frac{3}{4}$	104	$+\frac{1}{2}$

c

52 Weeks High	52 Weeks Low	Stock	Div.	Yld. %	P-E Ratio	Sales 100s	High	Low	Close	Net Chg.
46	27	DeltaAr	.60	1.8	8	699	$33\frac{1}{2}$	33	$33\frac{1}{4}$	. . .

1 Suppose that you have $10,000 to invest. Explore several alternatives open to you, using *The Wall Street Journal* and other sources of information to find the going rates of return. Try to rank these investments in increasing order of risk according to your own judgment. Estimate the risk premiums in these investments using the rate on Treasury bills for the riskless rate. Which investments would you make?

2 Using *The Wall Street Journal*, look up the prices of the 9 percent International Harvester (IH) and Exxon Pipeline bonds discussed in this chapter for each quarter during the past four years. Compute the yields to maturity for each bond and plot them on a graph over time. Relative to the Exxon bonds, what appears to have happened to the risk of the IH bonds?

1 **a** Suppose that the market interest rate is 10 percent per year. You purchase a U.S. Treasury bill that pays $1000 to its owner one year from now. How much would you pay at the most for the bill? [Ans.: $909.09]

b If you purchase the bill at a price of $909.09, what interest rate will you earn on the bill for the year?

2 A U.S. Treasury note is available in the market; it pays $100 in interest per year and $1000 at maturity two years from now.

a If the yield to maturity on the note is 10 percent, what is its current price? [Ans.: $1000]

b Given that the current price is $1000, at what price must you be able to sell the note one year from now (after the first year's interest is received) to earn 10 percent on your investment if you buy the note today? [Ans.: $1000]

c At what price would the note sell today if the interest rate is 8 percent per year? [Ans.: $1035.67]

d Given that the current price is $1035.67, at what price must you be able to sell the note one year from now to earn 8 percent on your investment if you buy the note today? [Ans.: $1018.52]

e Suppose that you purchase the note at a price of $1000 to yield 10 percent per year. One year later the market interest rate has changed to a new rate of 8 percent. What will be the price of the note at that time? [Ans.: $1018.52]

f Given your answer from **e**, what interest rate would you obtain if you sold the note after one year (after receiving interest)? What rate will you earn if you hold it to maturity instead of selling it?

g Suppose that you purchase the note at a price of $1035.67 to yield 8 percent per year. One year later the market interest rate has changed to a new rate of 10 percent. What will be the price of the note at that time? What interest rate will you earn if you sell it then? What rate will you earn if you hold it to maturity?

3 The rate of interest is 12 percent per year.

a How much should an investor pay today for a security that will pay $1000 for sure a year from now?

b How much should the investor pay for a security that pays $1000 for sure two years from now and nothing at the end of the first year?

c How much must a security pay at the end of two years to entice the investor to pay the same price as in **a**? (Nothing is paid at the end of the first year.)

4 As financial manager of Omega Industries, you have planned to issue $20 million in bonds. The coupon rate is to be 9 percent with coupon interest to be paid annually. The entire $20 million face (maturity) value will be due in ten years. Current interest rates are:

Rating:	Aaa	Aa	A	Baa	Ba	B	Caa
Rate:	8.8%	9%	9.3%	9.6%	10%	10.5%	11.2%

a What rating must the bonds have in order to sell at face value?

b If the bonds are rated Ba, what is likely to be their price per $100 face value?

c Given your answer from **b**, how much money will Omega receive from issuing $20 million face value bonds?

5 Dividends on Velocity Corporation stock are expected to grow at a rate of 12 percent per year indefinitely. Next year's dividend is projected to be $1.20 per share. The rate of return required by investors on Velocity stock is 16 percent.

a What is the price per share of Velocity stock?

b Suppose that new information came into the market which caused investors to cut their expectations of Velocity's long-run dividend growth rate in half, to 6 percent per year. Next year's dividend is still expected to be $1.20 per share. What will be the new price of Velocity stock?

c Compare the results from **a** and **b**. What do they tell you about the sensitivity of stock prices to changes in expectations?

6 The Rocky Mountain Oyster Company is expected to pay a $2.00 dividend per share of common stock next year. Rocky Mountain's current stock price is $40. Investors expect the firm's dividends to grow at a rate of 4 percent per year forever.

a What rate of return do investors require on Rocky Mountain's stock?

b Your analysis of Rocky Mountain's published financial statements suggests that the long run growth rate will be around 6 percent per year. The stock market is semistrong efficient. What rate of return should you expect to earn on Rocky Mountain's stock?

5A

SOURCES
OF FINANCIAL
INFORMATION

Information on financial markets, economic trends, and individual companies is available from a wide range of sources. Here we provide a guide to most of the major sources and show how to interpret quotations on stocks and bonds.

**DAILY SECURITIES
DATA**

Most newspapers carry some information on the daily activity in the securities market, but *The Wall Street Journal* (*WSJ*) covers more securities and provides more complete information than almost any other easily available source. The *WSJ* publishes a wide variety of articles on business and financial activities as well as data on commodity prices, foreign exchange rates, option prices, bond quotations (including both corporates and governments), and stock quotations. The data are always to be found in the last eight or nine pages of each issue.

Stock Quotations

The location of data on the trading activity of the stock issued by a particular company depends on whether the stock is listed on one of the stock exchanges or not. The *WSJ* provides information on all the listed securities that were actually traded in a given day plus information on the stock of many other companies.

Companies are shown alphabetically (names abbreviated) in three groups: NYSE Composite, Amex Composite, and Over-the-Counter. Therefore, if you are looking for information on a stock and you don't know whether it is listed or not, you must examine all three groups. The NYSE Composite provides information on stocks listed on the New York Stock Exchange and several other exchanges, excluding those stocks listed on the American Stock Exchange that are shown under Amex Composite. Other, nonlisted, stocks are shown as Over-the-Counter. An example of the information provided for listed stocks is shown in Exhibit 5-2.

EXHIBIT 5-2
Quotations for listed stocks: NYSE composite transactions, Thursday, October 4, 1984, reported in The Wall Street Journal, *October 5, 1984*

52 Weeks										
High	Low	Stock	Div.	Yld. %	P/E ratio	Sales 100s	High	Low	Close	Net chg.
$53\frac{3}{8}$	$38\frac{1}{4}$	Abt Lab	1.20	3.0	13	6,304	$40\frac{1}{8}$	39	$39\frac{3}{8}$	$-\frac{3}{4}$
71	$61\frac{1}{2}$	AlaP pf	9	14	. . .	z100	66	66	66	. . .

Both common and preferred stocks are traded on stock exchanges. The quotation for Abbott Laboratories is a common stock quotation; the Alabama Power stock is a preferred stock, as indicated by "pf" following the abbreviated name for the company. The first two columns show the highest and lowest prices at which the stock had traded during the past 52 weeks. The annual dividend is shown following the company name. Common stock dividends are calculated as four times the most recent quarter's "regular" dividend unless indicated otherwise by a footnote. Footnotes are found at the end of the list of quotations. "Yld." is the current dividend yield of the stock (dividends/price). The price-earnings ratio is the ratio of the closing price to the most recent year's earnings per share reported by the company and is provided only for common stocks, as preferred stockholders generally do not share in earnings after preferred dividends have been paid. Sales, given in hundreds, are the number of shares of the stock that were traded (bought and sold) during the day. There were 630,400 shares of Abbott Lab's common stock traded on October 4, 1984. The "z100" for Alabama Power preferred stock sales indicates that the total number of shares traded on that day was 100. The next three columns give the highest, lowest, and last price at which trading occurred on October 4. The price of Abbott Labs at the close decreased $\frac{3}{4}$ of $1 ($0.75) from the closing price on Wednesday, October 3, the previous day of trading.

Bond Quotations

The *WSJ* provides very little information on the bonds issued by state and local governments. Your best source of price and related information on these issues is a local brokerage firm. Information on new state and local issues is provided, however.

Corporate and federal government issues are covered in much greater detail. Corporate bonds may be listed on either the American Exchange or the New York Exchange, and data on listed, traded issues are provided daily. Many listed bonds do not trade every day; therefore you must often look at several days' listings before you will find data on a particular bond. Moody's manuals (see below) indicate the listing of bonds issued by corporations. Exhibit 5-3 shows example quotations for corporate bonds. Data on all bonds, notes, and bills issued by the U.S. Treasury, most bonds issued by federal agencies, and some other governmental units are provided in a

---

EXHIBIT 5-3

Listed corporate bond quotations: New York Exchange bonds, Thursday, October 4, 1984 reported in The Wall Street Journal, *October 5, 1984*

Bonds	Cur. yld.	Vol.	High	Low	Close	Net chg.
ATT $3\frac{7}{8}$ 90	5.5	67	$70\frac{1}{8}$	$69\frac{3}{4}$	$69\frac{7}{8}$	...
ATT 7s01	12	208	$60\frac{5}{8}$	60	$60\frac{5}{8}$	$-\frac{1}{8}$
Boeing $8\frac{7}{8}$ 06	cv	5	132	132	132	-1

separate section of the *WSJ*. Exhibit 5-4 shows example data for U.S. Treasury issues.

Corporate Bonds   Each bond issue that is listed on the New York Exchange that was traded on the previous trading day, is shown in *The Wall Street Journal*. As shown in Exhibit 5-3, companies such as American Telephone and Telegraph (AT&T) have more than one bond issue, and so each one must be identified separately. The identification is by company name (AT&T), coupon rate of interest (7s, pronounced "sevens," refers to a 7 percent coupon rate), and year of maturity (01, meaning 2001). The current yield is the coupon rate divided by the closing price, not the yield to maturity, which is more relevant to the investor and is explained in Chapter 5. (Compare the current yields on the two AT&T bonds, then consider that the $3\frac{7}{8}$s will mature in six years, paying $100 per $100 maturity value at that time, or a gain of $30\frac{1}{8}$ over the current price. The 7s mature in seventeen years, providing a gain of $39\frac{3}{8}$ at that time.) The "cv" for the Boeing bonds means that these securities are convertible into common stock and no current yield is provided. The "high," "low," and "close" indicate prices (per $100) maturity (or par value) during the trading day (October 4, 1984). "Net change" is the difference between the closing price on this day and the prior day's close.

Treasury Bills   U.S. Treasury bills have no coupon interest payments; they pay $1000 per bill to the owner at maturity. Bills have maturities of one year or less, and are referred to by their month and day of maturity. In Exhibit 5-4, 4-4 indicates that the bill will mature on April 4, 1985. Since bill prices

---

EXHIBIT 5-4
United States government securities quotations: Thursday, October 4, 1984, reported in The Wall Street Journal, October 5, 1984

U.S. Treasury bills

Mat.	Bid	Asked	Yield
	Discount		
4-4	10.27	10.23	10.92

U.S. Treasury notes & bonds

Rate	Mat. date		Bid	Asked	Bid chg.	Yld.
13s	1990	Nov n	102.4	102.12	+.6	12.43
12s	2008–13	August	96.27	97.3	+.9	12.37

are always less than their maturity value, the "bid" and "asked" amounts shown are the annualized discounts from maturity value. The bid on the 4–4 bill of 10.27 indicates a discount of approximately 5.135 percent since the bill matures six months from the date of the price quote. The indicated bid price was therefore $100.00 − $5.135 = $94.865 per $100 maturity value. Yield is the annual interest rate on the bill if purchased at the ask price.

Treasury Notes and Bonds   U.S. Treasury notes and bonds pay coupon interest and therefore can be identified by their coupon rate and maturity. Shown are 13 percent (13s) and 12 percent (12s) coupon rate securities. The 13 percent security matures in November 1990 and is a note as indicated by the "n" following the maturity date. The distinction between notes and bonds is based on their maturity at original issue and is not important here. The hyphenated maturity for the 12 percent bond means that the bond may be repaid (called) in 2008, but otherwise will be repaid in 2013. "Bid" and "asked" refer to dollar prices per $100 maturity value for these securities and are expressed in $\frac{1}{32}$ of $1; that is, the asked price of the 13 percent note is $102 and $\frac{12}{32}$ per $100 maturity value. "Bid change" is the change in bid price from the previous day's trading in $\frac{1}{32}$ of $1. "Yield" for these securities is the yield to maturity based on the bid price. See Chapter 5 for a discussion of yield to maturity and see Appendix 5B for reasons why the yield may vary with maturity.

SOURCE GUIDE

The table on the following page is a general guide to financial information. It is organized in two sections. The first section is a quick reference list organized by the type of information. The second section is organized by source and provides a capsule summary of the nature of the information provided in a given source.

Generally, when you are in doubt as to where to find some specific type of financial information, consult the person at the reference desk of your library.

Type of information	Sources
Current prices and yields on securities	*The Wall Street Journal, Commercial and Financial Chronicle, Bank and Quotation Record, Moody's Bond Record*, stock brokers
Average interest rates on various financial assets	*The Wall Street Journal, Federal Reserve Bulletin, Economic Report of the President*
Stock and bond market activity	*The Wall Street Journal, Statistical Bulletin of the Securities and Exchange Commission, Commercial and Financial Chronicle*
Aggregate financial data	*Federal Reserve Bulletin, Economic Report of the President*
Individual company data	Annual reports of the company, various manuals of Moody's, *Standard & Poor's Corporation Records, Fitch's Corporation Manuals, Value Line Investment Survey*
General business data	*Survey of Current Business, Statistical Abstract of the United States, Business Statistics*

Selected publications	Type of information
Business Week	General coverage of business affairs
Barron's	Security markets, individual securities, analysis of individual companies
Forbes	Analysis of individual companies, general articles on financial topics
Fortune	General coverage of business affairs, size rankings of major United States and foreign corporations, with summary data
Dun's Reviews	Bankruptcy data, average financial ratios for various industries, general financial articles
The Economist	General coverage of international business
Federal Reserve Bulletin	Wide variety of monetary, banking, and financial statistics; reviews of financial trends
Survey of Current Business	A wide variety of business statistics; see *Business Statistics* for historical data taken from this source
Monthly Bulletin of the Securities and Exchange Commission	Data on stock market activity and corporate securities issues
Monthly reviews of various Federal Reserve banks	Each Federal Reserve bank (New York, St. Louis, etc.) publishes a monthly review containing articles on financial and economic activity plus various types of data on national and regional trends

On August 24, 1981, U.S. Treasury securities maturing in one year had a yield to maturity of 17.2 percent per year whereas ten-year maturity securities had a yield of 15.3 percent. Three years later, on August 24, 1984, one-year maturity Treasury securities had a yield of 10.7 percent per year whereas ten-year maturity securities had a yield of 12.7 percent.[18] These data illustrate first that interest rates change over time for reasons explained in Chapter 2 and, second, that the rates which apply at a point in time to one maturity need not be the same as the rate for other maturities. Thus, the market interest rate on a given date depends not only on the risk of the cash flows but also on when the cash flows occur. The relationship between interest rates and the timing of a cash flow is called the term structure of interest rates or, more simply, the yield curve. The yield curves for U.S. Treasury securities on August 24, 1981 and August 24, 1984 are shown in Figure 5-3.

The yield curve is usually not "flat"; that is, interest rates usually vary with the timing of the cash flows. This poses two questions: (1) How are cash flows valued when the yield curve is not flat, and (2) what factors determine the shape of the yield curve? Let's answer the first question first.

THE TIME VALUE OF MONEY REVISITED

In Chapter 5 we established the principle that the market value of a certain (known for sure) stream of future cash flows is the present value of those cash flows. We assumed that there was only one interest rate currently applicable for all riskless streams. Now we are sayng that, in fact, the market

[18] Reported in *The Wall Street Journal*, August 25, 1981 and August 27, 1984.

FIGURE 5-3

The term structure of interest rates: August 24, 1981 and August 24, 1984.

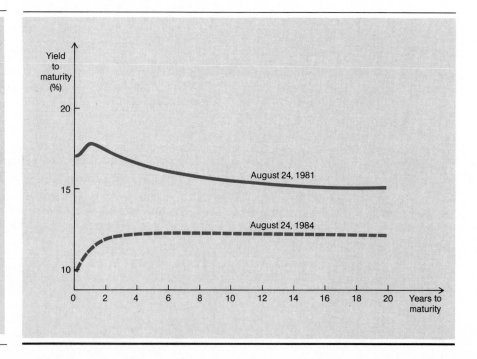

interest rate applicable to a cash flow occurring one year from now could be 11 percent whereas the interest rate applicable to a cash flow occurring two years from now could be 12 percent. What then will be the market value of an asset that pays $111 to be received for certain in one year and $125 to be received for certain in two years and nothing thereafter? The answer is quite simple: it is the sum of the present values of the two cash flows using the applicable interest rates. That is

$$V = \frac{\$111}{1.11} + \frac{\$125}{(1.12)^2}$$

$$= \$100 + \$99.65$$

$$= \$199.65$$

In general, then, we can express the value of any stream of certain future cash flows as the sum of the present values of the individual cash flows using rates i_1 for cash flows one period from now (F_1), i_2 for cash flows two periods from now (F_2), etc.

$$V = \frac{F_1}{1 + i_1} + \frac{F_2}{(1 + i_2)^2} + \frac{F_3}{(1 + i_3)^3} + \cdots + \frac{F_n}{(1 + i_n)^n} \qquad (5\text{-}11)$$

Rates i_1, i_2, i_3, etc., are the rates of interest for cash to be delivered at times 1, 2, 3, etc., respectively. These interest rates are the yield to maturity for zero-coupon securities (securities that provide only a single cash payment at maturity). These interest rates are usually referred to as zero-coupon yields. They reflect the term structure of interest rates.

There is a problem with zero-coupon yields, however—they are not directly observable in the market for known (riskless) cash flows beyond one year.[19] U.S. Treasury securities provide the closest thing we have to cash flows that are known with certainty. Unfortunately, as of 1985, the U.S. Treasury does not issue securities with a single payment (Treasury bills) beyond one year. Therefore, we use the yield to maturity on coupon-bearing Treasury securities to approximate the term structure beyond one year. Fortunately, the approximation is good enough for most purposes.[20]

THE SHAPE OF THE YIELD CURVE

Sometimes the yield curve slopes upward with long-term rates higher than short-term rates. This has been the most common shape in the twentieth century. At other times the curve is roughly flat; occasionally it is "humped"

[19] Some corporations have issued long-term zero-coupon bonds—for example, J. C. Penney. However, corporate bonds are subject to the risk of default so that the yield also includes a risk premium.

[20] For a discussion of potential problems in using yield to maturity on coupon bonds, see S. Schaefer, "The Problem of Redemption Yields," *Financial Analysts Journal*, 33 (May–June 1977), pp. 59–67. A procedure for estimating the zero-coupon yields is described by W. Carleton and I. Cooper in "Estimation and Uses of the Term Structure of Interest Rates," *Journal of Finance*, 31 (September 1976), pp. 1067–1084. Even using actual yields on Treasury securities presents some problems, because tax factors influence the yields of securities with prices different from par ($100). The yield curve in Figure 5-4 was based on securities that were selling close to $100.

with the intermediate-term rates higher than both short-term and long-term rates. In the past ten years, the curve has frequently been downward sloping with short-term rates higher than long-term rates. Figure 5-4 illustrates these four basic shapes. Several factors have been proposed to explain the shape of the curve. The three major factors are expectations of future interest rates, risk, and differences in the preferences of borrowers and lenders (investors) for different maturities.[21]

Interest Rate Expectations

Expectations of future interest rates strongly influence the yield curve. Everything else equal, when market participants (borrowers and lenders) expect interest rates to rise in the future, current long-term rates should be higher than current short-term rates. For example, suppose that the yield curve is currently flat and investors expect that interest rates will not change. The current discount rates for cash flows for all future times are equal to 10 percent. This yield curve is shown as "I" in Figure 5-5. Suppose that expectations change and market participants now expect future interest rates to rise above current levels. Current borrowers will now tend to borrow long-term (issue long-term bonds rather than short-term notes) to avoid paying higher interest rates in the future. Lenders will tend to invest in short-term assets so that they can reinvest later at higher rates. (They will buy short-term notes and avoid long-term bonds.) Prices of long-term bonds should therefore fall (since supply exeeds demand) relative to short-term notes (where demand exceeds supply). As prices fall, interest rates rise and the result will be a new equilibrium set of interest rates. The yield curve will

---

[21] For a thorough discussion of term structure theories, see James Van Horne, *Financial Market Rates and Flow* (Englewood Cliffs, N.J.: Prentice-Hall, 1978), pp. 78–135.

FIGURE 5-4

Four shapes of the yield curve.

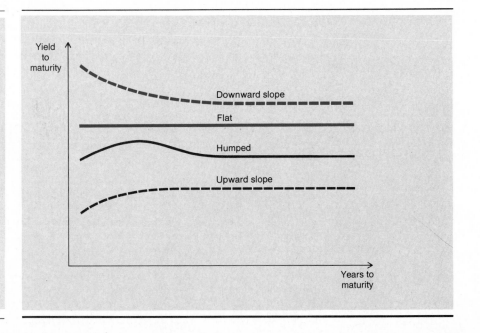

be upward sloping with long-term rates higher than short-term rates. Short-term rates may end up at 10 percent or fall to a lower level. This is illustrated by yield curve "II" in Figure 5-5. Therefore, an upward-sloping yield curve is consistent with expectations of higher interest rates in the future. Similarly, if the shape of the yield curve depends only on expectations about future rates, a downward-sloping yield curve indicates that the market believes interest rates will fall in the future and a flat yield curve indicates that no change in rates is expected.

Interest Rate Risk

Even if we are examining securities that have certain cash flows such as U.S. Treasury securities, there is risk due to changing interest rates. Investors in long-term securities are exposed to the risk that interest rates will rise, thereby making the value of the securities fall. If these investors believe that they may sell their securities prior to maturity, they will be concerned about this risk. We can say these investors are exposed to price risk. On the other hand, investors in short-term securities who plan to reinvest the cash flows in the market are exposed to the risk that interest rates will fall. Indeed all investors who plan to reinvest coupon interest payments or the proceeds from maturing securities are exposed to uncertainty in their future incomes due to changing interest rates. This is so because, if interest rates fall, the earnings on the reinvested money will also fall. We can say that these investors are subject to one sort of interest rate risk or the other. There are investment strategies that may be pursued to minimize interest rate risk for a given investor, but we will not explore them here.[22]

[22] See L. Fisher and R. L. Weil, "Coping with the Risk of Interest-Rate Fluctuations: Returns to Bondholders from Naive and Optimal Strategies," *Journal of Business*, 44 (October 1971), pp. 408–431.

FIGURE 5-5

The impact of expectations as to future interest rates on yield curves.

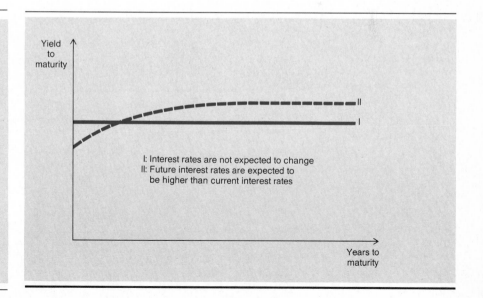

I: Interest rates are not expected to change
II: Future interest rates are expected to be higher than current interest rates

The effects of interest rate risks on the shape of the yield curve are not totally clear, but many people believe that there is liquidity preference on the part of most investors; that is, a premium must be paid in long-term rates relative to short-term rates to induce investors to give up the liquidity of short-term investment. This view is based in part on the notion that the investors are concerned about the price risk of long-term bonds because they may sell the bonds prior to maturity. To get these investors to purchase long-term bonds, a premium must be paid over the short-term rate. In addition, the major issuers of securities have long-term needs for funds (for example, corporations financing plant and equipment). They prefer to issue long-term debt because they want to be assured of the interest rate they will have to pay; if they borrow short-term, they risk that refinancing the short-term debt will involve an interest rate above current levels. A preference of investors for short-term securities and a preference of borrowers for long-term debt issues implies that the yield curve on average should be upward sloping. That is, long-term interest rates should be higher than short-term interest rates on average. For the past fifty years this, in fact, has been true. Figure 5-6 illustrates the combined effects of risk premiums on long-term bonds and expectations. Yield curve "I" is based purely on expectations and assumes that investors do not expect interest rates to change. Yield curve "II" shows how the actual yield curve looks when risk premiums are added to these expectations.

Supply-Demand Conditions

A third factor thought to influence the shape of the yield curve is the relative supply and demand for securities of different maturities apart from expectations and risk considerations. The concept here is that many of the borrowers and lenders in the market have preferences for particular maturities. Pension funds and insurance companies prefer to buy long-term

FIGURE 5-6

The impact of interest rate risk premiums on the yield curve.

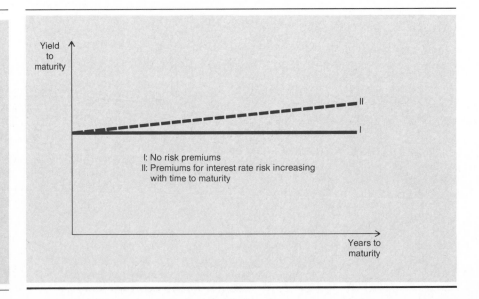

securities because they have long-term predictable obligations. These investors would rather not be bothered with the need to reinvest the proceeds from maturing short-term securities. Some corporate borrowers such as public utilities issue large amounts of long-term securities to finance new plants. Since these borrowers need the money for many years, they would rather not be bothered with the need to refinance short-term debts. If, say, the utilities want to borrow a lot of long-term money at a time when long-term investors are short of funds, long-term interest rates will tend to rise since the supply of long-term securities exceeds the demand. Conversely if long-term investors have a lot of money to invest when long-term borrowers need very little, long-term rates will tend to fall. Therefore, in order to understand the shape of the yield curve, one must examine the financial circumstances of all the major sectors of the economy. This supply-demand influence on the yield curve operates in conjunction with expectations and risk to determine the actual slope of the curve.

YIELD CURVES FOR RISKY FIXED-INCOME SECURITIES

We have been looking at government securities' yield curves for which the cash payments to the owner are assumed to be known with certainty. What about fixed-income securities paying uncertain future cash flows (that is, where there is default risk)? Although the data are less easily obtained, we can develop yield curves for fixed-income securities of different risk classes based on their yields to maturity. For example, we can estimate a yield curve for Aaa securities, a yield curve for Aa securities, etc. The result, at a point in time, should look something like the curves shown in Figure 5-7. As a frame of reference we have included the yield curve on government securities which have no default risk. Note that in Figure 5-7, as the maturity

FIGURE 5-7

The impact of default risk premiums on yield curves.

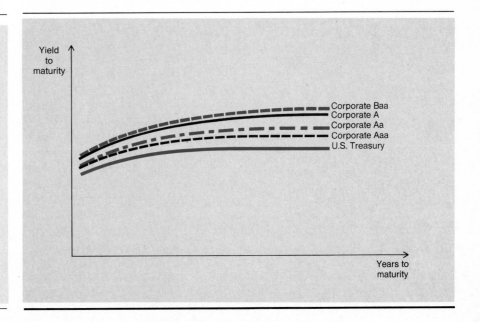

increases, the difference between the yield curves increases. For example, the difference between the yields on ten-year Baa bonds and ten-year A bonds is greater than the difference between the yields on one-year Baa bonds and one-year A bonds. This is due to the greater uncertainy in the amount that will actually be paid (greater default risk) as the distance into the future increases.[23] In principle, every borrower faces a particular yield curve at a point in time, and financial managers use this information in deciding on the maturity of debt to be issued. An understanding of yield curves is, therefore, an important part of financial management.

[23] We normally find an increasing difference in yields between yield curves of different risk classes as the maturity increases, but the differences have been exaggerated in Figure 5-7.

As any racing handicapper knows, betting at the track offers no free rides: A chance at tremendous gains by betting on a longshot is just that, a longshot. This is nothing new. Bigger potential gains usually mean bigger risks. Investors have a wide array of choices in putting their money to work earning more money for the future. The essential problem the investor faces is to choose the set of investments that has the best risk-return characteristics from the investor's standpoint. Keep in mind that an investor is concerned with the overall risk of his or her portfolio and, in assessing a particular investment, the investor should consider how much that asset will add to both the expected return and the risk of the total portfolio.

The investment choices made by investors determine the types of securities (stocks, bonds, convertibles, etc.) companies will issue and determine which firms will find it easy to obtain capital. Thus, for example, if there is optimism about the real estate market, firms with real estate-oriented activities (construction, land developers, real estate investment trusts, and so forth) will find it easier to finance investment and consequently these firms will tend to expand. Disenchantment with real estate would dampen investment in that sector of the economy. Investor attitudes therefore represent a basic determinant of where capital expenditures will take place in the economy.

What are the investment possibilities open to investors? How do they compare in terms of returns? In terms of risk? These are the subjects of this essay.

A PIECE OF AMERICAN INDUSTRY

What could be safer than owning a piece of American industry, a share of the backbone of our economy? Indeed, there is a well-known San Francisco attorney who advocates a people's capitalism with workers and management alike owning stock in their companies so that everyone can share in the rewards of being a capitalist. The seductive idea of being a part owner of the great companies of America is not without qualifications, however; even a good thing can be acquired at a price so high that the bargain is no longer attractive. In the late 1920s common stocks were touted as a guaranteed source of income and wealth. The allure was irresistible and stock prices escalated to dizzying heights. But then came disillusionment and despair as the stock market experienced the worst collapse in its history. From September 1929 to July 1932, the bears were in control. United States Steel plummeted from $262 per share to $22 per share. Montgomery Ward from $136 per share to $4 per share, and General Motors from $73 per share to $8 per share. Many lesser securities fell to less than 1 percent of their 1929 highs (or disappeared entirely).

It was not until the early 1950s that the stock market recovered from the monumental collapse of 1929–1932. Although there were several intermittent drops between 1942 and 1968, that period saw a general steep rise in equity prices. From April 1942 to December 1968, the Standard and Poor's average rose nearly fourteenfold, from 7.84 to 106.5. That is an increase of approximately 10.3 percent per year (7.1 percent per year real return, that is, when adjusted for inflation) and it doesn't include dividends paid on the stocks. The average price of stocks of smaller companies increased by considerably more. A very impressive performance and one that lulled many investors in the late 1960s into believing that it could go on forever. It didn't go on forever. From December 1968 to December 1984, the Standard & Poor's Composite rose by 54.4 percent and consumer prices rose by 197.3 percent, implying a real *decline* in the Standard

& Poor's Composite average of 48 percent over the sixteen-year period.

The above observations are supported by a number of rigorous analyses of stock performance. Fisher and Lorie studied common stock returns for the period of 1926 to 1965; the pretax return, including dividends, from 1926 to 1965 was 9.3 percent compounded annually.[1] The real pretax rate of return (the rate adjusted for inflation) was about 7.7 percent per year for the 1926 to 1965 period. For someone in a relatively high tax bracket, aftertax returns fall to 7.1 percent compounded annually before adjusting for inflation and to about 5.6 percent per year after an adjustment for inflation. A more recent study by Ibbotsen and Sinquefield found that the pretax return (dividends plus capital gains) from 1926 to 1980 was 9.4 percent for stocks (a real rate of return of about 6.3 percent per year).[2] However, Ritter and Urich found that common stocks yielded a real rate of return from 1968 to 1983 of only 1 percent per year.[3] Over very long periods of time (twenty-five years or more), stocks have usually provided what most would regard as a reasonable rate of return. But, over short or even intermediate time spans, stocks have been less predictable and have often performed poorly.

Interestingly, stocks do not in the short run appear to provide a good protection against inflation. Sharp rises in the general price level often produce declines in stock prices. Real estate, for example, seems to be a better inflation shelter in the short run. However, over the very long run, it appears that stocks do protect against inflation since revenues, expenses, and net profits all tend to increase with inflation. Of course, the long run can be a long time, and for an investor with a short planning horizon (say, under ten years), stocks may not be the ideal medium.

PLAYING IT SAFE: FIXED-INCOME ASSETS

For those whose nerves cannot tolerate the possibility of the wide daily fluctuations in wealth that can accompany stock investments, fixed-income assets may be the answer. Fixed-income securities are those that have a fixed promised dollar return (interest and principal payments), such as bonds. From 1926 to 1980 the annual pretax yield was 3.8 percent per year on long-term corporate bonds and was 3.1 percent per year on long-term United States government bonds.[4] These 50-year-average rates of return on bonds are about 6 percent less per year than those from stocks, a very substantial price to pay for the added safety of bonds. Furthermore, stocks have tax advantages that are not available on bonds.[5]

There are fixed-income investments other than corporate bonds. Perhaps the most important of these are savings accounts at financial institutions. Savings accounts yield even less than the highest-grade corporate bonds, usually at least $\frac{3}{4}$ percent less

[1] Lawrence Fisher and James H. Lorie, "Rates of Return on Investments in Common Stock: The Year by Year Record, 1926–65," *The Journal of Business*, vol. 41, no. 3 (July 1968), pp. 291–316.
[2] Roger G. Ibbotsen and Rex A. Sinquefield, "Stock, Bonds, Bills and Inflation: Historical Returns (1926–1980)," Financial Analysts Research Foundation, University of Virginia.
[3] Lawrence S. Ritter and Thomas J. Urich, "The Role of Gold in Consumer Investment Portfolios," *Monograph Series in Finance and Economics*, Salomon Brothers Center for the Study of Financial Institutions, Graduate School of Business, New York University, 1984.

[4] Ibbotsen and Sinquefield, op. cit.
[5] Long-term capital gains are taxed at a lower rate than is ordinary income. A significant portion of income from stock is in the form of long-term capital gains, whereas bond income is, on average, virtually all ordinary income.

139

INVESTING WHERE IT
COUNTS: RATES OF
RETURN ON
ALTERNATIVE
INVESTMENTS

per year and therefore savings accounts compare even less favorably on a return basis with stocks than do corporate bonds. United States government bonds, notes, and bills also yield less than do corporate bonds.

In spite of the yield disadvantage of all these fixed-income securities relative to stocks, it cannot be said that fixed-income securities are worse than stocks. It depends on the investor's taste for risk and return. For those who are very risk averse, it may be best to sacrifice the 5 percent or 6 percent in real return per year to avoid the high anxiety that they may suffer from investing in stocks.

Since interest rates move up and down with changes in inflation, short-term fixed-income securities have been a good inflation hedge. As a security matures and the investor is paid off, the funds can be reinvested at the going interest rate in the market. In periods of significant inflation, short-term fixed-income securities have outperformed stocks. Of course, long-term fixed-income assets (those that mature far into the future) suffer price declines as interest rates rise (for example, due to inflation) and these securities do not represent a good hedge against unanticipated inflation.

KEEPING YOUR FEET
ON THE GROUND

To paraphrase Will Rogers, land must be a very good investment, since the need for land is always growing but they aren't making much of the stuff anymore. How has real estate performed as an investment? It depends on the kind of real estate. The annual compound rate of increase in the price of a single-family house was 3.7 percent from 1890 to 1981 but, from 1944 to 1981 it was approximately 9 percent (stock prices rose at an average annual rate of about 6.3 percent from 1944 to 1981). From 1968 to 1983, the average

annual housing price increase was 8.6 percent. It should be mentioned that the housing price spiral did slow to around 4 percent per year by 1985. However, keep in mind that the above rates of appreciation exclude the rental income that could be provided by a house. The basic point made here is that since World War II a single-family house has been a very good investment.

Farmland is an alternative form of real estate investment, one that has experienced significant price appreciation over the years. Reilly, Marquardt, and Price found that farm real estate in the United States increased at an average rate of 3.64 percent per year from 1919 to 1974.[6] However, since World War II farmland price increases have been significantly greater. From 1968 to 1983 the average annual increase was 10 percent. By the mid-1980s, however, farmland prices were falling in many parts of the country as a severe recession struck agriculture.

Like homes and farmland, commercial, multifamily residential (apartments), and industrial real estate have been good hedges against inflation. Over long periods of time they have on average provided returns that have been competitive with stocks. A critical component of the returns on these types of properties is the tax benefit from depreciation, and, when significant changes in tax laws occur, property owners can be affected markedly. As with most investments, there are wide variations in returns depending on location and on the quality of property management.[7]

---

[6] See Frank K. Reilly, Raymond Marquardt, and Donald Price, "Real Estate as an Inflation Hedge," *Review of Business and Economic Research*, vol. 12, no. 3 (Spring 1977), pp. 1–19.
[7] For an excellent review of real estate return studies see Stephen E. Roulac, "Can Real Estate Returns Outperform Common Stocks?" *The Journal of Portfolio Management* (Winter 1976), pp. 26–43.

COLLECTING AND HOARDING FOR PROFIT

There are many kinds of assets which have historically been regarded as collectors' items or expensive consumption goods which have turned out to be extremely good investments. Examples include jewelry, precious metals, rare coins, photographs, clocks, stamps, paintings, antiques, books, and nostalgia. From the early 1970s to the end of the decade, some types of precious gems increased in value at rates between 10 percent and 20 percent per year. During the 1960s and 1970s, collectibles increased in value over 10 percent per year on average, far better than the return on stocks during the same time period. The following table shows the price increases for the 1968 to 1983 period for several of the more popular investments:

Investment	Compound annual increase in value from 1968 to 1983
Chinese ceramics	14.2%
Gold	16.6
Silver	12.6
Old master paintings	7.8
U.S. coins	17.9
Diamonds	10.1
Consumer price index	7.1

Along with the potential for large gains, there are important disadvantages to the collecting-for-profit game. First, collectibles are very risky. For example, the early 1980s saw substantial declines in the prices of gold, silver, photography collections, and many other collectibles. Even during the 1960s and 1970s, some items experienced significant price declines and other items sat for years without any appreciation. Second, most collectibles generate no income during the holding period (no interest, dividends, etc.). Third, collectibles are very illiquid and selling commissions are ordinarily high—10 percent to 25 percent or even more. This means that an item must markedly increase in price just to cover the commission on resale. Fourth, obtaining suficient knowledge—or expert advise—is more difficult with collectibles than with many other types of investments. The collectibles market is less perfect than, say, the market for investment-grade bonds or even stocks and it is very easy to overpay out of ignorance. The implication of all that is that, for most people, it is probably wise to put most of one's material wealth in other types of assets such as stocks, real estate, and bonds.

6

**RISK
AND RETURN**

Risk is present whenever future events are not completely predictable and some events are preferable to others. In Chapter 5, we showed that the price of a security is the present value of the cash flows to the owner of the security, where the discount rate used in computing the present value reflects the risk of the cash flows. This chapter explores risk in more depth. We explain how risk can be measured and how it affects the discount rates in the security market.[1] The following fundamental principle is presented:

The risk from investing in a financial asset depends on the relationship between the cash flows of that asset and the cash flows from other assets owned by an individual.

Associated with this principle is the concept of diversification, which is also developed in this chapter. We begin by looking at the problem of measuring risk.

**MEASURING RISK:
FUNDAMENTALS**

In financial decisions it is often helpful to have an objective measure of risk. Such a measure should be independent of how averse to risk a given person is (that is, how much that person dislikes risk). In other words, we would like to be able to separate the degree of risk in a situation from the feelings of different people toward bearing risk. We can then look at the question of how much risk is involved in a particular decision as a separate issue from the question of whether enough incentive is provided to warrant bearing the risk. The amount of incentive required for a given amount of risk will vary from person to person depending on how risk-averse each person is.

The main reason for having measures of risk is to enable us to make better decisions. To be useful, a risk measure should enable us to rank alternative risky ventures (such as investments). If there are two possibilities being analyzed, A and B, it is often important to know whether A is riskier than B or vice versa. A good measure of risk should also tell us *how much more risky* A is than B. Is A twice as risky or ten times as risky as B? Is B risky at all? It would be best if the risk measure had a value of zero for a riskless venture (a venture with future consequences that are now known with certainty). The risk measure should also increase numerically as the degree of risk increases.

Although we will begin our discussion by examining the case of investing in only one asset, investors are generally concerned with the risk of their total investment in many assets. The risk of investing in an asset depends on how that investment affects the overall risk of all the assets owned by the investor. For now let's assume that only one asset is owned; in a later section we will consider the implications of investing in more than one asset.

---

[1] An excellent alternative treatment of the ideas presented in this chapter can be found in Chapter 8 of Burton G. Malkiel, *A Random Walk Down Wall Street*, 2d ed. (New York: W. W. Norton, 1981).

Risk measurement procedures are usually based on a particular method of organizing financial problems—through **probability distributions**. A probability distribution is a way to describe the possible future values for a quantity. In the following example we will describe a **discrete probability distribution**, which is a distribution of a variable that can have a limited (finite) number of values (for example, the number of phone calls your stockbroker will receive before noon tomorrow). Later, we will consider a **continuous probability distribution**, which is a probability distribution of a variable that can achieve any value over some range (for example, your broker's blood pressure at noon tomorrow).

Suppose you are thinking about purchasing some of stock A, which has a current price of $50 per share and pays no dividends. If you buy it, you plan to sell the stock one year from now. The return you will get when you sell depends only on the price of the stock at the time you sell. You therefore want to consider what price the stock might sell for in one year. To illustrate the concept of a discrete probability distribution, we will assume that there is a limited number of prices your stock might achieve one year from now. You decide there is no chance that the stock will sell for less than $40 per share or more than $80 per share. You estimate that there is one chance in ten or a 10 percent chance that the price will be $40, a 20 percent chance that the price will be $50, a 40 percent chance that it will be $60, a 20 percent chance that it will be $70, and a 10 percent chance that it will be $80. The result of this analysis is shown in Exhibit 6-1 and in Figure 6-1 with the "chances" shown as decimals (20 percent is 0.2). We have labeled the vertical axis as "probability," since the "chances" are probabilities, and what you have done is to develop a probability distribution for the price of the stock.

There are two characteristics of this probability distribution that are useful in deciding whether this stock is worth owning—the expected value and the standard deviation. The **expected value** or **mean** of a probability distribution measures the average value that the variable (stock price in this case) will have. We calculate the expected value by multiplying the probability of getting each price times that price and adding up the results for all possible prices. The general equation for the expected value is

$$\text{Expected value} = p_1X_1 + p_2X_2 + \cdots + p_nX_n \tag{6-1}$$

EXHIBIT 6-1
Price of stock A in one year

Price of stock A	Probability
$40	.10
$50	.20
$60	.40
$70	.20
$80	.10

where p_1 is the probability of obtaining amount X_1, p_2 is the probability of obtaining amount X_2, etc. In this example

$$\text{Expected value} = .1(\$40) + .2(\$50) + .4(\$60) + .2(\$70) + .1(\$80)$$
$$= \$60$$

Therefore the expected price is $60. However, we know that we may not be able to sell the stock for $60. There is uncertainty as to what the price really will be.

The **standard deviation** of a probability distribution measures the dispersion or variability around the expected value. The standard deviation can be considered a measure of the reliability of the expected value and therefore a measure of the risk or uncertainty of the stock price. In other words, given an estimate of the future price as $60, the standard deviation measures how "fuzzy" that estimate is. The higher the standard deviation, the more fuzzy or spread out is the probability distribution. For example, the price of stock B in Figure 6-2b has a greater standard deviation than the price of stock A in Figure 6-2a. We are less certain about the price that will be achieved by stock B.

The standard deviation is computed by first taking the difference of each possible value from the expected value, squaring the differences, weighting the squared values by the probability of getting that price, and then summing the weighted squares. The sum is called the **variance** of the distribution and it can also be used to measure risk. The formula for the variance is

$$\text{Variance} = p_1(X_1 - \overline{X})^2 + p_2(X_2 - \overline{X})^2 + \cdots + p_n(X_n - \overline{X})^2 \qquad (6\text{-}2)$$

where p_1 = the probability of X_1

p_2 = the probability of X_2, etc.

$\overline{X}$ = the expected value of the distribution

The standard deviation is the square root of the variance

$$\text{Standard deviation} = \sqrt{\text{variance}} \qquad (6\text{-}3)$$

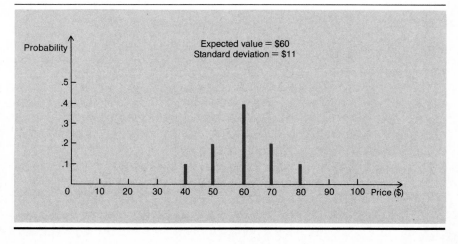

FIGURE 6-1

Probability distribution of the price of stock A.

FIGURE 6-2

Probability distributions for two stocks' prices.

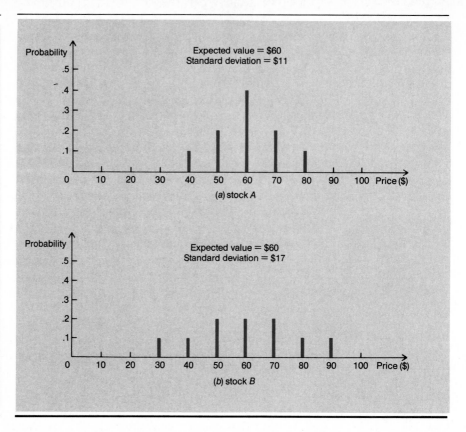

(a) stock A

(b) stock B

The standard deviation of the price of stock A (see Exhibit 6-1) is calculated as follows:

$$\text{Variance} = .1(\$40 - \$60)^2 + .2(\$50 - \$60)^2 + .4(\$60 - \$60)^2$$
$$+ .2(\$70 - \$60)^2 + .1(\$80 - \$60)^2$$

$$= .1(400)(\$^2) + .2(100)(\$^2) + .4(0)(\$^2) + .2(100)(\$^2)$$
$$+ .1(400)(\$^2)$$

$$= 120(\$^2)$$

and

$$\text{Standard deviation} = \sqrt{120(\$^2)}$$

$$= \$10.95$$

Notice that, because we are squaring dollar quantities in computing the variance, we end up with "dollars squared" in the variance. The standard deviation—the square root of the variance—is expressed in dollars, not dollars squared. So the standard deviation of the price is approximately $11.

There are four important features of the standard deviation as a measure of risk:

The Standard Deviation as a Risk Measure

1 Only differences between the expected value and the various possible values that can occur affect the size of the standard deviation. If only one value is possible, say, $60, it would have a probability of 1.0. The expected value would be 1.0($60) = $60 and the variance and standard deviation would be zero since 1.0($60 − $60)^2 = 0. Since there is no fuzziness to your estimate of $60, you are certain that the price will be $60 and there is no risk in this case. When there is no risk, the standard deviation is zero. If there is any risk at all, the standard deviation is greater than zero.

2   The differences are squared in the calculation. This means that those prices which are far away from the expected value increase the standard deviation much more than those which are close to the expected value. (The square of a large number is very much greater than the square of a relatively small number.) Therefore, using the standard deviation as a measure of risk implies that big differences from the expected value involve much more risk than small differences.

3   The squared differences are multiplied by the probability that the actual value will deviate from the expected value. Therefore, the smaller the chance a particular value will occur, the less effect it has on the standard deviation.

4   The standard deviation is the square root of the sum of the squared differences (weighted by their probabilities). This means that the standard deviation has the same measurement units as the expected value and can be compared directly with it.[2] Therefore, in the example, the standard deviation is measured in dollars.

Now that we have developed the standard deviation as a measure of risk, what can we use it for? First, it tells us something about how uncertain the price is. For most probability distributions there is very little chance that the actual value will be more than twice the standard deviation away from the expected value. In the stock *A* example, two times the standard deviation of $11 is $22. In this example, the price is certain to be between $38 ($60 − $22) and $82 ($60 + $22). We can also look at the standard deviation relative to the expected value.[3] In the example the standard deviation is 18 percent of the expected value ($11/$60 = 0.18). This tells us that the actual price is likely to be fairly close to the expected price of $60. There is only moderate uncertainty. If the standard deviation were 1 percent of the expected price instead of 18 percent, there is little uncertainty as to what the price will be. If the standard deviation were 50 percent of the expected price, then there would be a great deal of uncertainty.

The standard deviation can also be used to compare two alternatives. Suppose you evaluated stock *B* and came up with the probability distribution shown in Figure 6-2*b*. A comparison with the probability distribution for stock *A* in Figure 6-2*a* (same as stock *A* in Figure 6-1) should lead you to

---

[2] The standard deviation is a more convenient measure of risk than the variance for this reason. The variance is in terms of dollars squared.
[3] The ratio of the standard deviation to the expected value is called the **coefficient of variation** and is sometimes used as a separate measure of risk. The coefficient of variation is discussed further in Chap. 9.

the conclusion that the future price of stock B is more uncertain than the future price of stock A.

Stock B has an expected value of $60 and a standard deviation of $17, as compared with stock A, which has the same expected value and a standard deviation of $11. The standard deviation for B is larger, which reflects the greater "spreading out" of the probability distribution of B's future price. Therefore, much more uncertainty exists about the actual future price of stock B than about that of stock A.

Rates of Return

The above examples illustrate the uncertainty in future prices. However, this uncertainty is also directly translated into uncertainty about the rates of return which will be earned by an investor. For example, given that the current price of stock A is $50, let's convert the *future* prices in Exhibit 6-1 and Figure 6-1 into rates of return. An actual price of $40 at the end of the year would provide a rate of return of ($40 − $50)/$50 = −0.2 or −20 percent. That is, we had $50 invested in the stock at the beginning of the year and ended up with only $40 at the end of the year, a loss of 20 percent. We can convert all the prices into their equivalent rates of return as shown in Exhibit 6-2. We now have a "new" probability distribution as shown in Figure 6-3. Again the standard deviation is in the same units (percent) as the expected rate of return, and its value of 22 percent measures the uncertainty as to the expected rate of return of 20 percent.

Rates of return are frequently used in analyzing securities such as stocks and bonds. The basic point here is that we can translate uncertain future dollar values into their corresponding percentage rates of return given the price of the asset. We can also obtain the mean and standard deviation of the rate of return by dividing the dollar amounts by the current price. For example, the 22 percent standard deviation of the rate of return can be calculated as $11/$50.

Continuous Probability Distributions

Whenever you are dealing with a variable, such as the rate of return on a stock that can take a large number of possible values, you may wish to use a *continuous* probability distribution instead of the discrete distributions shown in Figures 6-1, 6-2, and 6-3. Since stock prices are quoted in eighths of a dollar, there are 320 (8 × 40) possible stock prices in the range of $40 to $80 for a stock and hence 320 possible rates of return in this range. If the stock might pay a dividend that is also uncertain, the number of possible rates of return would increase enormously. In Figure 6-4, a continuous distribution for the rate of return on stock A is shown along with the discrete distribution of Figure 6-3.

In a continuous distribution the probability of obtaining a single value

---

EXHIBIT 6-2
Probability distribution of rate of return on stock A

Future price	$40	$50	$60	$70	$80
Rate of return, %	−20	0	20	40	60
Probability	.1	.2	.4	.2	.1

FIGURE 6-3

Probability distribution of the rate of return on stock A.

such as a rate of return of precisely 10.0 percent is nil. Instead, we measure the probability of obtaining any value within a specified range as the area under the curve. For example, in Figure 6-4 the probability of obtaining a rate of return between 10 percent and 30 percent is 0.4 (the shaded area under the curve between the 10 percent and 30 percent rates of return in Figure 6-4). This is the same as the .4 probability of obtaining a 20 percent rate of return in the discrete distribution of Figure 6-3.

Continuous distributions are usually described by summary measures such as the expected value and standard deviation. The calculation of these measures for continuous distributions is a topic for statistics courses.

PORTFOLIO RISK AND DIVERSIFICATION

The Diversification Concept

"Don't put all your eggs in one basket" is a simple way to express the desirability of diversification. Diversification means investing in at least two assets that differ. If all your money is invested in one risky asset, the rate of return you earn depends solely on what happens to the income and market value of that one asset. If you invest in two nonidentical assets, in order for you to get a low or negative return on your money, both investments must turn out badly. Taken individually, each asset might be equally risky. How-

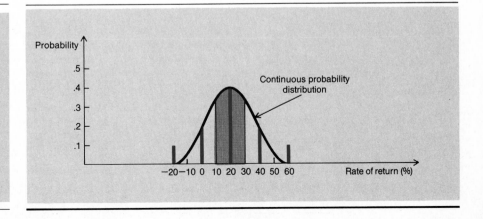

FIGURE 6-4

Continuous and discrete probability distributions of the rate of return on stock A.

ever, if you put half of your money in one and half in another, you may come out with less risk on your total investment than you would have by investing all your money in a single asset. This is so because high returns from one asset may offset low returns from the other. Investors, both individuals and firms, are concerned with the risk of their total investment, and diversification can reduce this risk.

To see how diversification can reduce or even eliminate risk, imagine that you are considering investing $200 in the stock of two different companies—a taxicab company and a bus company. During boom times, people ride in taxis and the taxi company does well, but the bus company does poorly. In recessions, people take the bus and the bus company does well, but the taxi company does poorly. Assume that the probability of boom is .5 and the probability of recession is also .5. The rates of return from the two stocks are shown in Exhibit 6-3. The expected rate of return from investing in each stock is 10% (.5 × 40% + .5 × −20%) and investing $200 in either stock by itself is risky. However, suppose that you put $100 in taxi stock and $100 in bus stock. During boom times, your investment in taxi stock will earn $40 but your investment in bus stock will lose $20, for a net return of $20 on your investment of $200 or 10% ($20/$200). In recessions, your investment in bus stock will earn $40 but your investment in taxi stock will lose $20, again for a net return of $20 or 10%. Therefore, regardless of what happens to the economy, you earn 10% on your investment and have eliminated risk.

Risk was eliminated through diversification in this example because a high return from the taxi stock was associated with a low return from the bus stock and vice versa. The statistical term for this behavior is perfect negative correlation. **Correlation** is a measure of the degree to which two variables, such as the rates of return on two stocks, move together.[4] It takes on numerical values that range between −1.0 and 1.0. In the taxicab-bus example above, the correlation was −1.0. Whenever a high return for one stock tends to occur at the same time a low return occurs for another stock, the correlation between the two stocks is negative (less than zero). If a high return for one stock tends to occur when a high return occurs for another stock, the correlation between the two is positive (greater than zero). For example, suppose a yacht company stock will return 60 percent in a boom economy and −40 percent in a recession. The yacht stock's returns are

---

[4] The correlation between two variables X and Y is calculated in two steps. First, the *covariance* is calculated. The covariance is a direct measure of the relationship between the two variables. It is expressed in the product of the units of X and Y, for example, $\$^2$.

$$\text{Covariance} = p_1(X_1 - \bar{X})(Y_1 - \bar{Y}) + p_2(X_2 - \bar{X})(Y_2 - \bar{Y}) + \cdots + p_n(X_n - \bar{X})(Y_n - \bar{Y})$$

where X_1 and Y_1 are a pair of values for X and Y occurring with probability p_1; X_2 and Y_2 are another pair of values occurring with probability p_2, etc. $\bar{X}$ and $\bar{Y}$ are the expected values of X and Y, respectively. Second, the standard deviations of X and Y are calculated according to the procedure explained earlier in the chapter. Let SD_X be the standard deviation of X and SD_Y be the standard deviation of Y. The correlation of X and Y is:

$$\text{Correlation} = \frac{\text{covariance}}{SD_X \, SD_Y}$$

EXHIBIT 6-3
Rates of return on investing in taxicab stock, bus stock, and both taxicab and bus stocks

		Rate of return earned		
	Probability	Invest all in taxicab stock	Invest all in bus stock	Invest half in each of taxicab and bus stocks
Boom	.5	40%	−20%	20%
Recession	.5	−20%	40%	20%

positively correlated (correlation of 1.0) with the returns from the taxi stock. A zero correlation would describe a situation when there is no particular relationship between the returns.

Two points were illustrated by the example. First, diversification is a way of reducing risk. By owning more than one security, you were able to eliminate all risk in the example. Unfortunately, negative correlations among security returns are quite rare since the returns of most securities available to investors tend to be dependent on the behavior of the overall economy. Therefore, security returns tend to be positively correlated, but with a correlation less than 1.0. Diversification will reduce risk but not eliminate it. The second point is that an investor should not be concerned about the risk of individual securities, but rather with the risk of the investor's total portfolio of securities, and with how investing in a particular security affects the risk of the entire portfolio.

With these points in mind, let's examine how the risk and return on a portfolio is affected by the securities in it.

Portfolio Risk and Return

The rate of return from a portfolio of securities is the weighted average of the returns from the individual securities included in it. The weights are the proportions of each security in the portfolio. For example, if you invest 40 percent of your money in a stock that returns 20 percent and 60 percent of your money in a stock that returns 5 percent, the actual return on your total investment in this portfolio will be

Actual return $= 0.4(20\%) + 0.6(5\%)$

$= 11\%$

The actual return on a portfolio tells you how well your investment has performed in the past. However, if you are trying to decide what to invest in, you are concerned with the *future* performance of your portfolio and should calculate the expected rate of return. The computation procedure for the expected returns is similar to the one used to find the actual return. Suppose that you had expected to earn 15 percent on the security that constitutes 40 percent of the portfolio and had expected to earn 10 percent on the security that constitutes 60 percent of the portfolio. Your expected return on the portfolio was

Expected rate of return $= 0.4(15\%) + 0.6(10\%)$

$$= 12\%$$

The general formula for the expected rate of return on a portfolio of n securities $(\bar{r}_p)$ is simply

$$\bar{r}_P = w_1\bar{r}_1 + w_2\bar{r}_2 + \cdots + w_n\bar{r}_n \tag{6-4}$$

where $w_1 =$ the proportion invested in security 1, etc.

$\bar{r}_1 =$ the expected rate of return on security 1, etc.

The formula for the standard deviation of the rate of return on a portfolio of n securities is rather complicated, since it contains the standard deviations of each security and the correlations between every pair of securities.[5] Instead of presenting it, we shall show numerically how diversification affects portfolio risk as measured by the standard deviation.

Suppose that you currently own stock A, which has a probability distribution of its rate of return as was shown in Figure 6-3. All your money is invested in this stock; thus the expected rate of return on your total investment is the expected rate of return on stock A, 20 percent. The standard deviation of the rate of return on stock A, and therefore on your total investment, is 22 percent. You are considering diversifying your investment by selling half of the shares you own in A and purchasing stock C. Half your investment will be in stock A and half in stock C. Stock C also has an expected rate of return of 20 percent and a standard deviation of 22 percent, the same as for stock A. Will you gain any advantage from this restructuring of your portfolio of stock?

First you should note from Equation (6-4) that the expected rate of return on the new portfolio of A and C (r_{AC}) will be 20 percent, because both securities have an expected rate of return of 20 percent. The weighted average rate of return is 20 percent since, using Equation (6-4):

$$\bar{r}_{AC} = .5(\bar{r}_A) + .5(\bar{r}_C)$$

$$= .5(20\%) + .5(20\%)$$

$$= 20\%$$

---

[5] The standard deviation for a two-security portfolio (SD_P) is calculated as the square root of the variance of the portfolio's rate of return. The variance is calculated as

$$(SD_P)^2 = w_1^2\, SD_1^2 + w_2^2\, SD_2^2 + 2w_1w_2\, Corr_{12}\, SD_1\, SD_2$$

where $\quad w_1 =$ the proportion invested in security 1

$\quad w_2 =$ the proportion invested in security 2 $(w_2 = 1 - w_1$ in this case)

SD_1 and $SD_2 =$ the standard deviations of the rates of return on securities 1 and 2, respectively

$Corr_{12} =$ the correlation between the returns on securities 1 and 2

Then

$$SD_P = \sqrt{(SD_P)^2}$$

Any benefit from diversification in this case must result from a reduction in risk as measured by standard deviation. If there is to be a benefit, the standard deviation of the rate of return on the portfolio of A and C must be lower than 22 percent, which is the standard deviation of each of A and C owned individually. Will any reduction occur? The answer depends on the correlation between the rate of return on A and the rate of return on C.

If the returns from stock A and stock C have a correlation of 1.0, then the rate of return on a portfolio of A and C together has the same standard deviation as the rate of return of stock A by itself. In this case purchasing stock C is no different from keeping all your investment in stock A because stock C achieves the same rate of return that stock A does. For example, if A has a rate of return of −20 percent, C also has a rate of return of −20 percent. In practice, the returns from two different stocks will never be perfectly correlated; most likely the correlation of returns will be greater than zero but less than 1.0. *The positive correlation of stock returns is due to the dependence of returns of most stocks on general economic conditions.* Suppose the correlation between the returns on stock A and stock C is 0.4. In this case, the standard deviation of the returns on the portfolio of A and C is 18.4 percent, less than the standard deviation of the individual stocks. Thus there is an advantage to diversifying by owning two stocks rather than one. Indeed, such an advantage will obtain for all correlations less than 1.0. The standard deviation of the portfolio of A and C for all possible values of the correlation is shown in Figure 6-5.[6] We assume in the figure that the investment is half in A and half in C, and that stocks A and C each have an expected return of 20 percent and a standard deviation of return of 22 percent. An implication of this simple example is that the correlation of the returns from a single asset with the returns from the other assets held by the investor strongly influences the risk of the total portfolio. The lower the correlation, the more effective is diversification.

Finding securities with low correlations is difficult; however, there is another way to reduce risk—increasing the number of securities in the portfolio. Increasing the diversification of a portfolio by adding additional securities whose returns are not perfectly correlated with the returns of the other securities reduces portfolio risk up to a point. This diversification effect is illustrated in Figure 6-6. We assume in this figure that each stock has (individually) an expected return of 20 percent and a standard deviation of 22 percent, the same as for stocks A and C above, and that the correlation between each pair of stock returns is 0.5. Each stock in a given portfolio is owned in equal dollar amounts. Thus, in a five stock portfolio, 20 percent is

---

[6] All results reported here and in Figure 6-5 are based on the formula in footnote 5. For example, we calculate the standard deviation of the portfolio consisting of 50 percent stock A and 50 percent stock C, when the correlation between A and C is 0.5, as follows:

$$(SD_P)^2 = w_A^2 \, SD_A^2 + w_C^2 \, SD_C^2 + 2w_A \, w_C \, Corr_{AC} \, SD_A \, SD_C$$

$$= (0.5)^2 \, (22\%)^2 + (0.5)^2 \, (22\%)^2 + 2(0.5)(0.5)(0.4)(22\%)(22\%)$$

$$= 338.8 \, (\%)^2$$

$$= \sqrt{338.8 \, (\%)^2}$$

Therefore,

$$SD_P = 18.4\%$$

invested in each of the five stocks. Figure 6-6 shows that increased diversification reduces portfolio risk. Note, however, that investing in more than ten stocks reduces risk only slightly below the level for the ten-stock portfolios. It does not take a great deal of diversification to obtain most of the benefits.

Our analysis to this point can be summarized as follows:

1　Investors who dislike risk should be concerned about the standard deviation of the rate of return on their total investment portfolios. *An implication is that, in evaluating the risk of a particular asset, what matters is how that asset affects the risk of the entire portfolio.*
2　Diversification reduces portfolio risk.
3　The contribution of an individual asset to portfolio risk depends on the standard deviation of the asset's returns, the correlation of the asset's returns with returns of the other assets in the portfolio, and the proportion of the portfolio represented by that asset.

The technique of determining how to put together a desirable investment portfolio is beyond the scope of this text. However, we have covered the basic principles here. Now we shall see what they imply for the pricing of securities in the marketplace assuming that the market is dominated by investors who understand these principles.

FIGURE 6-5

Portfolio standard deviation for different correlations between securities.

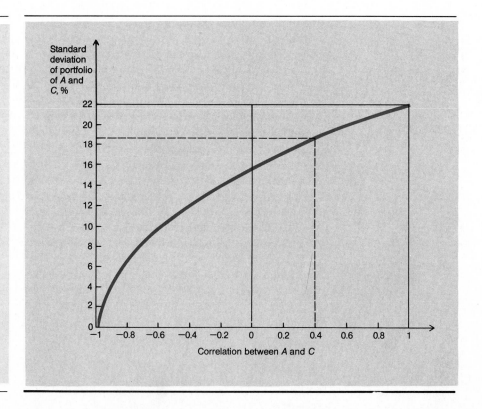

We showed in Figure 6-6 that there was a limit to the amount of risk reduction that can be achieved by diversification among positively correlated securities. This is a mathematical result and one might ask how well it applies to actual stocks. Imagine performing the following experiment. Choose *at random* portfolios of common stocks from the newspaper, each portfolio containing a *different* number of stocks. Track the performance of each portfolio by computing both its actual annual rate of return each year for several years and the standard deviation of its annual returns.[7] Now plot the standard deviation for each portfolio against the number of stocks in the portfolio. The results will look like those shown in Figure 6-7, which is very similar to Figure 6-6. Figure 6-7 shows that diversification, at least of this random variety, will eliminate some but not all risk from a portfolio. The only risk remaining in a well-diversified portfolio is the risk of the market as

[7] The standard deviation of the returns from a particular portfolio indicates how much the returns from the portfolio fluctuated from year to year over the time period studied. If the time period studied were say from 1971 to 1986, to compute the portfolio's standard deviation we would first compute the average annual rate of return on the portfolio over the sixteen-year period (equal to the sum of the annual rates of return divided by sixteen). We would then use Eq. (6-2) to compute the variance, where in Eq. (6-2): $\overline{X}$ = the average annual rate of return on the portfolio over the sixteen-year period; $p_1 = p_2 = \cdots = p_{16} = \frac{1}{16}$; and X_1 = portfolio rate of return in 1971, X_2 = portfolio rate of return in 1972, . . . , X_{16} = portfolio rate of return in 1986. The standard deviation equals the square root of the variance.

FIGURE 6-6

Impact on portfolio standard deviation of diversification among positively correlated securities.

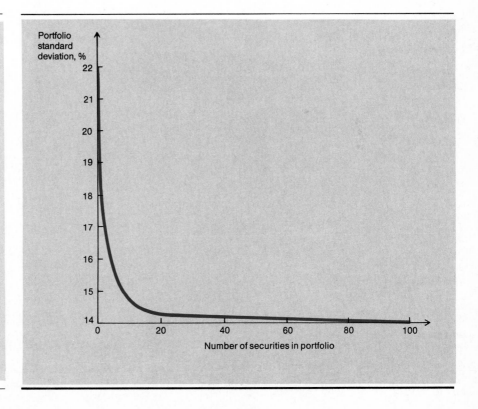

**Beta as a Measure
of Risk**

a whole (since a well-diversified portfolio is a cross section of the total market). This means that the returns from all well-diversified portfolios are highly correlated (close to 1.0) and therefore move up and down together with the entire market.

Let's assume that investors are diversified.[8] We know from the previous section that an investor is concerned with the risk of his or her entire portfolio, and that the relevant risk of a particular security is the effect the security has on the risk of the entire portfolio. This leads us to the following important proposition:

The contribution of a security to the risk of a diversified portfolio is measured by the security's beta. The higher a security's beta, the more the security raises the risk of the diversified portfolio.

A security's beta indicates how closely the security's returns move with the returns from a diversified portfolio. Since the returns from a diversified

---

[8] By "diversified" we mean that each investor's portfolio is representative of the market as a whole and that the portfolio's beta is 1.0. The same basic arguments hold as long as investors' portfolios are perfectly correlated with the market. Under certain conditions (for example, those assumed in deriving the Capital Asset Pricing Model, which is described in detail in Appendix 6A), investors who own any risky assets are best off with portfolios that are representative of the market or perfectly correlated with the market. As illustrated in Figure 6-7, ownership of even a small number of securities can provide close to complete diversification. Even if investors are not fully diversified in the sense just described (with portfolios that are identical to or perfectly correlated with the market) but are only fairly well diversified, the general concepts presented in this chapter still hold as good approximations.

FIGURE 6-7

*Impact on portfolio
standard deviation of
random
diversification.*

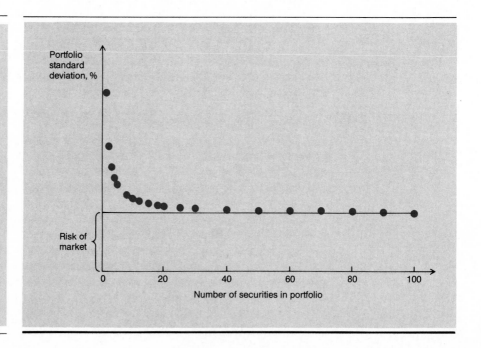

portfolio move with the market as a whole, beta also measures how closely the security's returns move with the market.[9] Securities differ in their risk and therefore in their betas. A beta of 1.0 for a given stock means that, if the total value of stocks in the market moves up by 10 percent, the stock's price will also move up, on average, by 10 percent, and if the market declines by 10 percent, the stock's price will decline, on average, by 10 percent. If a stock has a beta of 2.0, its price will, on average, rise by 20 percent when the market rises by 10 percent and fall by 20 percent when the market falls by 10 percent. And a stock with a beta of 0.5 will on average rise or fall by 5 percent as the market rises or falls by 10 percent, respectively. A stock with a -0.5 beta will, on average, rise by 10 percent when the market *falls* by 20 percent, and on average fall by 10 percent when the market rises by 20 percent (negative beta securities are extremely rare). The beta of the market as a whole is 1.0. The beta of a fully diversified portfolio of risky assets is also 1.0 since it is simply a sample of the market as a whole.

The beta of any portfolio of securities is the weighted average of the betas of the securities, where the weights are the proportions invested in each security. For example, if $400 is invested in stock A and $600 is invested in stock B (40 percent in A and 60 percent in B), and if A has a beta of 1.0 and B has a beta of 1.5, then the portfolio made up of A and B has a beta of:

Beta of the combined investment in A and B = $.4(1.0) + .6(1.5) = 1.3$

Thus, the beta of a diversified portfolio (beta = 1.0) is simply the weighted average of the betas of a large number of securities that are representative of the market (these securities comprising the diversified portfolio).

The above description of beta helps us see why beta makes sense as a measure of a security's risk. Assume that you already own a diversified portfolio of securities (portfolio's beta = 1.0) and are considering adding one more security, say stock Z. Since your portfolio is diversified, we know (from the discussion a couple of paragraphs ago) that the returns from your portfolio move with the market's overall returns (i.e., up and down together). What will adding stock Z do to the risk of your portfolio? If stock Z has a high beta (beta greater than 1.0), that is, on average its price moves closely and sharply with the market, it also on average moves closely and sharply with the value of your diversified portfolio. But that means that it will increase your portfolio's risk by making your portfolio's value bounce up and down more violently than it would if stock Z were not in the portfolio. It follows that, *for a diversified investor, a high beta security is a high risk security because adding it to the portfolio increases the risk of the portfolio.*

---

[9] Beta for stock J is usually defined as

$$\text{Beta}_J = \frac{\text{Corr}_{JM}\ \text{SD}_J}{\text{SD}_M}$$

where $Corr_{JM}$ is the correlation of stock J's return with the market return; SD_J is the standard deviation of stock J's return; and SD_M is the standard deviation of the market's return. Alternatively, beta for a security is the covariance of the security's rate of return with the rate of return on the market divided by the variance of the market's rate of return. Thus beta is simply the scaled covariance of the security's rate of return.

On the other hand, if stock Z has a low beta (beta less than 1.0) or a negative beta (beta less than 0.0), its returns on average do not move closely with the market or with your diversified portfolio. Indeed, the value of a negative beta stock on average moves contrary to the value of your portfolio, and therefore the stock reduces the risk of the total portfolio. The lesson here is that, *for a diversified investor, a low or negative beta security is a low risk security because adding it to the portfolio reduces the risk of the portfolio.*[10]

How do you determine the beta of a particular stock? A stock's beta can be estimated statistically from the history of its returns. Betas for most companies with publicly traded stock are available from investment services such as the Value Line Investment Survey and publications by the brokerage firm of Merrill Lynch. Some estimates of betas for different stocks are shown in Table 6-1. Note, however, that here betas are estimated from historical data. The beta for a firm's stock can shift over time, due to changes in the investment and financing policies of the firm and other changes in the economic condition of the firm and its industry (for example, deregulation).

Let's summarize. We have made the following points about beta as a measure of risk:

1 The value of a diversified portfolio moves with the market as a whole (up and down together).
2 Beta measures how sharply and closely a security's price moves on average with the market, and therefore (given point *1*) measures how closely a security's price moves with the returns from a diversified portfolio.
3 Adding a high beta (beta greater than 1.0) security to a diversified portfolio increases the portfolio's risk, and adding a low beta (beta less than 1.0) or negative beta (beta less than 0.0) security to a diversified portfolio reduces the portfolio's risk.

We can conclude that, in a world of well-diversified investors, a security's beta is an important indicator of risk, and therefore a determinant of what people are willing to pay for the security. In the next section, we discuss security markets and beta.

The Security Market Line

We now have a measure of risk for individual stocks (beta) that is appropriate for diversified investors who care only about the risk of their total portfolio as measured by the standard deviation of the rate of return on the portfolio. We observe that investors are generally risk-averse (that is, they prefer less risk to more risk) and not willing to bear risk without getting something for it. For securities, that something is a higher expected rate of return. However, in a market dominated by diversified investors, the relevant risk for an individual stock is how the stock's value moves with the

---

[10] As a technical note, if the investor's portfolio is representative of the market (i.e., is diversified, as assumed here), it must already contain a small amount of security Z (or a security like Z). It can be shown mathematically that the contribution of security Z to the investor's diversified portfolio's risk, given that security Z is a small fraction of that portfolio, can be measured by security Z's beta.

TABLE 6-1
Beta values for selected common stocks

Company	Beta	Company	Beta
American Airlines	1.25	Hughes Tool	1.50
American Express	1.35	IBM	1.05
Anheuser-Busch	0.75	Kellogg	0.80
Apple Computer	1.65	Lockheed	1.25
BankAmerica Corp.	1.00	Merrill Lynch & Co.	1.85
Bethlehem Steel	1.25	Nabisco	0.75
Burlington Ind.	0.95	National Semiconductor	1.50
Caesars World	1.20	Polaroid	1.00
Caterpillar Tractor	1.00	Procter & Gamble	0.70
Coca-Cola	0.80	Revlon	1.05
Con. Edison	0.65	Savannah Foods	0.45
Control Data	1.45	Sears, Roebuck	1.10
Deere	1.05	Texas Instruments	1.00
Disney Productions	0.90	Tootsie Roll Ind.	0.65
Exxon Corporation	0.85	U.S. Steel	1.05
Federal Express	1.40	U.S. Tobacco	0.80
Firestone Tire	0.95	Wang Labs-B	1.65
Ford Motor	1.15	Woolworth	0.90
General Motors	1.10	Xerox	1.00
Homestake Mining	1.20	Zenith	1.25

Source: Value Line Investment Survey, April 19, 1985

market, which we measured by beta. Given some additional conditions that are discussed in Appendix 6A, we can arrive at a theory of market risk and return called the Capital Asset Pricing Model (CAPM). The CAPM says that properly priced securities should provide an expected rate of return to investors equal to the rate of interest on riskless securities (U.S. Treasury bills) plus a premium for bearing risk. The risk is measured by the security's beta. Any security with a beta of 1.0, the same as the beta for the entire market, will have an expected rate of return equal to the rate of return expected on average for the market. In the CAPM there is a linear relationship between a stock's beta and the expected rate of return on that stock. This relationship is called the security market line and is shown in Figure 6-8.

The security market line shows the current risk-return tradeoff in the market. It should be thought of as showing what expected rates of return must be provided to investors to compensate them for bearing risk. In other words, the security market line indicates the "going" rate of return in the market for a given amount of risk. Every security having that amount of risk should provide the same expected rate of return to investors; this expected rate of return is equal to the rate of return required for that degree of risk.

We can see this more clearly by expressing the security market line as an equation.

$$k_J = i + (k_M - i)\text{beta}_J \qquad (6\text{-}5)$$

where k_J = the required rate of return for security J

   i = the riskfree rate of interest

   k_M = the expected rate of return for the market as a whole

   beta_J = security J's beta value

The symbol k will be used throughout the book to represent a rate of return required by investors in the security markets. In the CAPM, a properly priced security will provide an expected rate of return equal to the rate of return required for all securities having the same beta. If this is not true, the price will change. For example, suppose that the stock of Felix Industries has a beta of 1.5 and that the current rate of interest on U.S. Treasury securities (which is usually taken to be the riskfree rate) is 7.7 percent. The difference between the market rate of return and the riskless rate ($k_M - i$) is called the market risk premium. Assume the premium to be 6.2%, which is

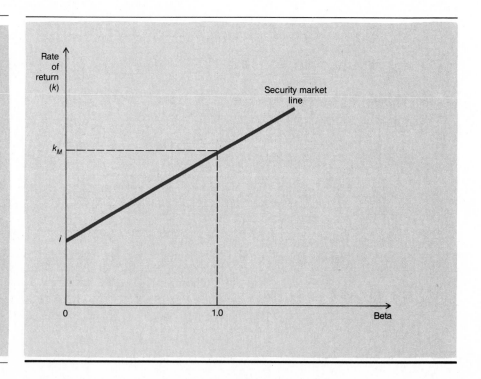

FIGURE 6-8

The security market line.

consistent with long-run historical rates of return as was shown in Table 5-2. Therefore the rate of return required in the market for stocks with a beta of 1.5 is:

$$k_J = i + (k_M - i)\,\text{beta}_J$$

$$= 7.7\% + (6.2\%)1.5$$

$$= 17\%$$

Suppose that the average investor in the market expects that Felix will pay a $2.00 dividend in one year's time and that the expected price of Felix stock in the market in one year is $28. The current price of Felix stock is $24. Thus the rate of return expected by the average investor for Felix is 25%, where this rate is calculated as follows:

$$\text{Expected rate of return} = \frac{\$28 + \$2 - \$24}{\$24}$$

$$= 25\%$$

Felix stock is underpriced as it provides too high an expected rate of return relative to the required rate of return. Investors can only expect to obtain 17 percent on other stocks in the market with a beta of 1.5 so they will be eager to buy Felix stock with its expected rate of return of 25 percent. In an efficient market, this underpricing will not persist as investors will bid the price up quickly. The price will adjust until the expected rate of return equals 17%. The price for which this is true can be calculated as the present value of the future dollar returns discounted at 17%, i.e.,

$$\text{Price} = \frac{\$28 + \$2}{1.17}$$

$$= \$25.64$$

A price of $25.64 for Felix stock provides an expected rate of return of 17%. Notice that we are using the same basic concept of the market price of a security's being the present value of its cash returns that was introduced in Chapter 5. We discount the expected return (price plus dividend) at the market discount rate of 17 percent to find the current price that provides an expected rate of return of 17 percent to the investor.

The rates of return shown by the security market line are interest rates that have been adjusted for risk. Their magnitudes are determined by the activities of all investors in the market. The market risk premium depends on the attitudes of investors toward bearing risk. The riskfree rate depends on the overall supply and demand for money in the economy. The security market line rates apply at a given point in time and are subject to change with changes in the economy. In particular we know that riskfree interest rates can change dramatically over relatively short periods of time. We know little about how the market risk premium changes and usually assume that it is constant.

The CAPM expresses the following important ideas in a relatively simple way:

1 The required rate of return on all financial assets depends in part on the riskless rate of interest.

2 Investors should be concerned primarily with risks that cannot be diversified away by holding portfolios of securities rather than single securities.

3 Investors require a premium for bearing risk, and the risk premium for a security is equal to the market risk premium times the security's beta, which measures its relative market risk.

4 If all investors are risk-averse and have similar expectations, the only way to increase the expected return from an investment in securities is to take on increased risk. Conversely, the higher the risk, the greater is the expected return.

The CAPM wraps up these ideas in a tidy package summarized by the security market line in Eq. (6-5). The CAPM is used in several ways. In Chapter 7, we show how the CAPM and beta may be used to estimate the required rate of return on a company's common stock. In Chapter 9, we discuss its application in the evaluation of risky investment projects involving real assets (as compared to financial assets). In Chapter 10, the CAPM is used to explain why the use of debt (borrowed funds) by business firms increases the risk and, therefore, increases the rate of return required by the firm's stockholders. In addition, the CAPM can be used as a basis for measuring how successful the manager of a securities portfolio has been. Financial researchers have used the model to analyze a variety of important problems in financial management and also as a way of controlling for risk in empirical research. These topics are treated in more advanced finance courses.

Although the CAPM has proved to be quite useful, there remains the questions of how well it describes the pricing of securities in actual markets. The answer is that no one is quite sure. A big problem in testing the CAPM is that the model is based on investor expectations and it is very difficult to measure and evaluate people's expectations. Despite this problem and some others, the CAPM has been supported to some extent by tests using historical data.[11] The market risk premium does appear to be positive and beta seems to be the best single measure of risk; however, we cannot very well explain the risk premiums that are observed. The empirical validity of the CAPM remains controversial. Financial experts recognize that the CAPM is too simple, and more complicated asset-pricing models have been developed. However, simplicity is itself an advantage in dealing with difficult problems. The model does contain some of the most important elements of

[11] Several tests of the CAPM are presented and discussed in M. C. Jensen (ed.), *Studies in the Theory of Capital Markets* (New York: Praeger, 1972). For a critique of the empirical work, see Richard Roll, "A Critique of the Asset Pricing Theory's Tests: Part 1: On Past and Potential Testability of the Theory," *Journal of Financial Economics*, 4 (March 1977), pp. 129–176.

financial analysis under risk, and for many practical and research problems it is still the best model available.

SUMMARY

In dealing with future monetary payments or receipts, a probability distribution is often useful in assessing the degree of risk. Two of the more important quantitative measures of risk are the standard deviation and correlation. The standard deviation measures the uncertainty as to the returns of an asset or portfolio of assets. The correlation measures the degree to which the returns of one asset vary with the returns of another asset or portfolio. The total risk of a portfolio of assets depends on the standard deviations and correlations of the individual assets.

Through diversification, investors can reduce the risk of owning risky securities. Diversification—which means investing in more than one security—reduces risk if the returns from the securities in the portfolio are not perfectly correlated with each other. The only risk remaining in a fully diversified portfolio is the risk of the market as a whole. A measure of the contribution by an individual security to the risk of a fully diversified portfolio is the security's beta.

Beta measures how closely a security's returns vary with the returns of all securities in the market. If investors are generally well-diversified, a security's beta will be an important determinant of the price of the security.

The security market line expresses the relationship between the expected rate of return required by investors and the risk of the security. In the capital asset pricing model (CAPM), the security market line is

$$k_J = i + (k_M - i) \, beta_J \tag{6-5}$$

where k_J = *the required rate of return on security J*

i = *the riskfree rate of interest*

k_M = *the expected rate of return for the entire market*

$beta_J$ = *is the value of beta for security J*

The CAPM has many uses in finance and is the dominant model of risk and return in the financial markets.

QUESTIONS

1   In 19th century England, some landowners leased their property at a fixed annual rental fee for 999 years. Today a transaction like this would be considered highly risky. Why?

2   Rank the following portfolios in order of their degree of diversification from least diversified to most diversified:

   a   Half common stock and half bonds of ITT, a company which has a wide range of business activities in many different countries.

   b   Equal amounts of stock in five firms in five different industries.

   c Equal amounts of stock in three computer companies.

   d The stocks of ten companies selected by throwing darts at a newspaper listing of stock prices.

   e Shares of a $10 billion mutual fund.

3 Suppose that you currently own 100 shares of General Motors Company stock. This is your only risky investment. Is it likely that you could achieve greater returns on your investment with less risk? Why or why not?

4 Can you think of any alternatives to the standard deviation as a measure of risk for investment returns? How would your measures compare with standard deviation? (There is no single correct answer to this question.)

5 Investors are thought to be concerned about the uncertainty in the returns on their investments as measured by the standard deviation of the returns. Why, then, should such investors be interested in the beta of a security?

6 Explain what the security market line is, using words only.

(*Note:* The following questions are based on Appendix 6A.)

7 Suppose there were a law prohibiting borrowing to invest in securities. All other assumptions of the CAPM hold. Sketch the resulting capital market line (curve). How do you think that the passage of such a law would affect the prices of securities that have large betas (for example, betas greater than 1.5)?

8 What is the difference between the capital market line and the security market line?

PROJECT

Using a source such as the Value Line Investment Survey, identify four or more stocks with betas greater than 1.2 and four or more stocks with betas less than 0.8. Examine the history of these stocks. Do the high beta stocks appear to be more risky than the low beta stocks? Do the high beta stocks appear to provide higher average returns than the low beta stocks? Can you identify any characteristics of the companies which determine whether one will have a high beta or a low beta stock?

PROBLEMS

1 You are considering purchasing stock in Massive Manufacturing Company. The current price per share is $40. You have the following expectations regarding the price of the stock one year from now (no dividends are expected):

Future price	$20	$30	$40	$50	$60	$80
Probability	0.1	0.2	0.2	0.2	0.2	0.1

a What is the price expected to be one year from now? [Ans.: $46]

b If the price turns out to be $46, what rate of return will you have earned? [Ans.: 15 percent]

c Determine the probability distribution of the rates of return on this stock. What is the expected rate of return as calculated from this probability distribution? Compare this answer to the rate of return calculated in b. Should the two be equal? Why or why not?

d Using the probability distribution of c, calculate the standard deviation of the rate of return on the stock. [Ans.: 42.13 percent]

2 Sasquatch Automotive Company is about to introduce its first product, a car that operates with sawdust as fuel. If the car sells well, the firm could make enormous profits; however, its failure could very well bankrupt the company. The current price of the stock is $20 per share. The interest rate on riskless assets is 10 percent per year. The returns from owning the stock are positively correlated with the overall economy. Your assessment of the dividends and price of the stock next year for the various possibilities and their associated probabilities is:

	Total failure	Partial failure	Partial success	Total success
Probability	.2	.3	.4	.1
Dividend	$0	$ 0	$ 1	$ 5
Stock price	$0	$10	$24	$75

a Calculate the expected total dollar return (dividend plus price) and the expected rate of return from owning one share of Sasquatch stock for one year.

b Given the above information, would you purchase the stock?

c Suppose that investors in the market on average require an expected rate of return of 25 percent on stock of this degree of risk. What price should the stock sell for if investors in general share your assessment of the prospects for Sasquatch?

d Calculate the rate of return for each possibility, given the price of $20 per share and again using the price determined in c. Compare the results of the two sets of calculations. How do changes in current prices affect rates of return given a set of future possibilities?

3 Automotive Computer Systems (ACS) sells electronic components to automobile manufacturers. Its sales, profits, and stock price are highly correlated with the economy as a whole. The current price of ACS stock is $20 per share. Your assessment of the possible dollar returns (stock price plus dividends) from owning one share of the stock for one year and their associated probabilities are as follows:

Dollar return	$14	$18	$20	$22	$24	$26
Probability	.1	.1	.3	.2	.2	.1

a What are the expected rate of return and standard deviation of the rate of return for an investment of $20 in ACS stock?

b What are the expected rate of return and standard deviation of the rate of return for an investment of $2000 in ACS stock?

c The riskless rate of interest is currently 6 percent. Does ACS stock appear to be a good investment at its current price of $20 per share?

d If other investors in the market agree with your assessment of the distributions of dollar returns from ACS stock, what will happen to the stock price?

4 The stock of Hamburger Heaven (HH) tends to perform well relative to other stocks during depressions. On the other hand, the stock of Sizzlin Steaks (SS) tends to do especially well during boom periods. The following table represents your assessment of the probabilities of boom and depression next year and of the dollar returns (dividend plus price) the two stocks will have. Both stocks are currently selling for $100 per share. Compare the expected returns obtained from investments of (1) $1000 in HH stock, (2) $1000 in SS stock, and (3) $500 in HH stock plus $500 in SS stock. Evaluate the risks of the alternative investment strategies. Which would you prefer? Why?

Economic conditions next year	Boom	Depression
Probability	.6	.4
Return of HH stock	$120	$100
Return of SS stock	$150	$ 80

5 Suppose that the riskless rate of interest is 10 percent and that we can measure risk for a security by its beta, which is 0.0 for a riskless security. The expected rate of return required by the market for a security with a beta of 1.0 is known to be 15 percent.

a Graph the security market line.

b What would be the expected rate of return on stock X, which has a beta of 0.5?

c You are considering the purchase of a stock with a current price of $50 per share. You expect to receive $3 per share in dividends next year and to be able to sell the stock for $55 in one year. What is the expected rate of return from owning the stock for one year?

d The stock in c is estimated to have a beta of 1.2. What should its expected rate of return be, according to your expectations and

the security market line of **a** above? If many other people agree
with you, what should be the price of the stock?

6 The riskless interest rate is 8 percent and the expected rate of return on
the market portfolio is 14 percent. Using the CAPM, and Eq. (6-1):

a Draw the security market line.

b What should be the expected rate of return for a security with a
beta of 2.0?

(*Note:* Problems 7, 8, and 9 are based on Appendix 6A.)

7 Miguel Martinez estimated the expected rate of return and standard
deviation for five portfolios as shown below. Miguel can borrow at a 10
percent rate of interest and can invest in riskless securities at 10
percent. Which of the five portfolios would be best for Miguel to invest
in, if Miguel is willing to assume some risk? Why?

Portfolio	A	B	C	D	E
Expected rate of return	10%	12%	14%	16%	18%
Standard deviation	9%	10%	12%	15%	20%

8 You have found that the average rate of return on a large sample of
stocks which is representative of the entire market is 12 percent. The
standard deviation of the rate of return on this sample is 6 percent.
The riskless rate of interest is 8 percent.

a What is your best estimate of the market price of risk in the capital market? Draw the capital market line.

b Draw the security market line. Why does it differ from the capital
market line?

c The stock of New Wave Computers has a beta of 1.8. What is
your best estimate of the required rate of return on this stock?

9 Gamma Computer's stock is currently selling at a price of $20 per
share. You have analyzed the company and have developed the following estimates:

Expected total dollar return in one year	$30
Standard deviation of dollar returns	$12
Correlation of Gamma's return with the market return	0.6

a Gamma stock's beta calculated from the past history of the
stock's price is 2.5. Assuming that the security market line of
problem 6 applies, is Gamma's stock correctly priced according
to your estimates?

b The standard deviation of the market's rate of return is 24 per-

cent. Given the data above, what should the price of Gamma's
stock be? [Hint: Try Eq. (6-8).]

c Based on the price calculated in b, what should be the expected
rate of return and beta for Gamma's stock? Are these values consistent with the security market line?

(*Note:* Part c is fairly difficult.)

6A

**PORTFOLIO
THEORY AND
THE CAPITAL
ASSET PRICING
MODEL**

Portfolio theory shows how investors can combine securities into portfolios that provide maximum returns for a given degree of risk. The essentials of portfolio theory were presented in Chapter 6. The Capital Asset Pricing Model (CAPM) is a theory about how the prices and interest rates on risky financial assets (securities) are determined in the capital market. The CAPM combines the principles of portfolio theory with certain assumptions regarding investor expectations and market characteristics.[12] The model provides a precise relationship between the risk of a security, as measured by its beta value, and its required rate of return. In brief, the key insights of the CAPM are:

1 A security's risk is measured by its beta value.
2 The required rate of return on a security depends on the riskless rate of interest, the market risk premium, and the security's beta.
3 Investors should own risky securities only as part of a highly diversified portfolio of such securities.
4 The only way to increase the expected rate of return from investment is to take on additional risk.

Although the assumptions made in the model present an abstract and idealized description of the capital markets, statistical analysis of actual rates of return on securities provides some support to the CAPM. Portfolio theory and the CAPM are important parts of modern finance theory and their concepts are used by security analysts, portfolio managers, and business financial managers to help them increase returns and minimize risk.

In the following pages, we develop the model in a step-by-step fashion, first examining the underlying assumptions and ideas, and then building on them. We begin with a review of portfolio theory, which is useful both in its own right and as the foundation of the CAPM.

PORTFOLIO THEORY

Portfolio theory provides investors with a method of selecting securities that will provide the highest expected rate of return for any given degree of risk or that will provide the minimum amount of risk for any given expected rate of return. Here, we present the concepts and assumptions of portfolio theory that are essential for understanding the CAPM.

Suppose that the only risk that an investor cares about is the standard deviation of the returns from the money he or she has available to invest. The investor dislikes risk and wishes to obtain as large an expected return as is possible for any given level of risk (i.e., any given standard deviation). This investor has a single period time horizon; that is, the only returns of immediate concern are those that occur one period from now. For convenience we assume that the period is one year, the funds are invested now, and that dividends or interest on the investment are received one year from

---

[12] The original development of portfolio theory is by H. M. Markowitz, "Portfolio Selection," *Journal of Finance*, 7 (March 1952), pp. 77–91. Pioneering work on the CAPM was done principally by William Sharpe and John Lintner in the mid-1960s. One of the best expositions of portfolio theory and the CAPM is W. F. Sharpe, *Portfolio Theory and Capital Markets* (New York: McGraw-Hill, 1971).

now. The returns in one year include dividends, interest payments, and the change in market value (based on selling prices) of the securities owned by the investor.

Portfolio theory assumes that the amount of money an investor has available to invest is some given amount. The investor's problem can then be analyzed entirely in terms of possible rates of return that can be earned on that given amount.

Let's now look at the options available to our investor. Suppose, for the moment, that only two securities are being considered—stock of company A and stock of company B. The investor could purchase A's stock or B's stock or any combination (portfolio) of the two; the expected rate of return and standard deviation resulting from all the possible portfolios of A and B will look something like the curve in Figure 6-9. The precise shape of the curve depends on the correlation between the returns from A and the returns from B.[13] The correlation between A and B in Figure 6-9 is 0.4. Point x on the curve shows the expected return and standard deviation for a portfolio with 50 percent of the investor's money invested in A and 50 percent invested in B.

[13] Equations that define the curve were provided in Chap. 6. For two risky securities, A and B, the expected return on a portfolio ($\bar{r}_P$) with fraction w invested in security A and $(1 - w)$ in security B is

$$\bar{r}_P = w\bar{r}_A + (1 - w)\bar{r}_B \tag{a}$$

The standard deviation of the rate of return on the portfolio (SD$_P$) can be determined by taking the square root of:

$$(SD_P)^2 = w^2 (SD_A)^2 + (1 - w)^2 (SD_B)^2 + 2w(1 - w)SD_A \, SD_B \, Corr_{A,B} \tag{b}$$

where $Corr_{A,B}$ is the coefficient of correlation between r_A and r_B.

FIGURE 6-9

*Risk and return for
alternative portfolios
of two risky stocks, A
and B.*

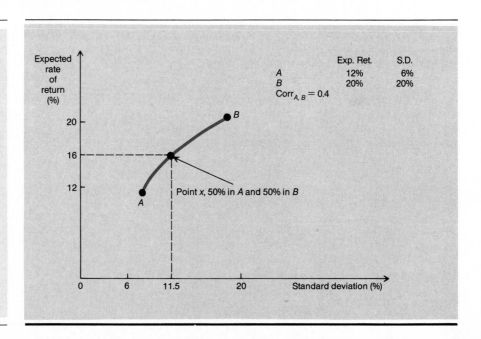

Figure 6-9 is simply a picture of the risk and expected return from the possible portfolios containing stocks *A* and *B*, including the alternatives of 100 percent in *A* and 100 percent in *B* (points *A* and *B*). Given this information the investor can choose the most desirable alternative based on his or her tastes regarding risk and return. A relatively risk-averse person might choose *A* alone, whereas most people would probably choose some combination of *A* and *B*.

The Efficient Frontier

Many more choices are open to investors. There are over 1400 different stocks traded on the New York Stock Exchange alone. Imagine that the expected rate of return and standard deviation of a large number of risky securities and of all portfolios of those assets are shown in a figure like Figure 6-10 (the shaded region in the figure). Ideally, you would like to include all the risky financial assets available for investment in the economy in this figure, so that you could consider all possible choices. If this information were available (including the ability to identify which assets are represented by every point on the figure), what could you do with it?

If you are like our investor, you will only be interested in acquiring assets or portfolios of assets that plot along the upper left edge of the shaded region. These assets and portfolios provide higher expected returns and less risk than any other risky investment shown. This curve, indicated by the heavy line from point *C* to point *D*, is called the **efficient frontier**. Given the expectations used to generate the figure, investment opportunities along the efficient frontier are better than (dominate) all other opportunities. You can achieve either a higher expected return with the same risk, or the same expected return and a lower risk, from an investment

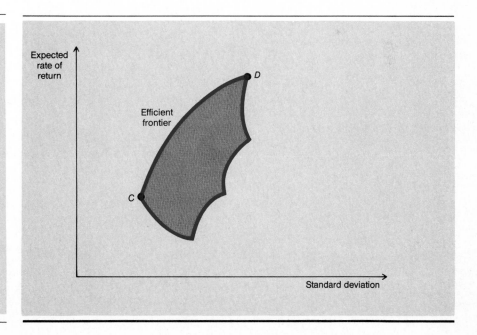

FIGURE 6-10

Risk and return for all possible portfolios of risky securities.

on the efficient frontier than from any other possible risky investment shown in the shaded region.

The concept of an efficient frontier can be applied to any number of securities under consideration for investment. The "efficient frontier" for two securities A and B is the curve connecting points A and B in Figure 6-9. Of course, the more securities that you include for consideration, the more likely you are to find superior opportunities.[14]

Borrowing and Lending Opportunities

There are, however, two other alternatives available: investing in a riskless asset (lending), and borrowing to invest additional funds in risky assets. Borrowing increases the total amount available for investment. The amount invested will be your initial capital plus the amount borrowed. Suppose for simplicity, that the rate of interest i that you can earn from investing a riskless asset is equal to the rate of interest that you pay to borrow in order to finance additional investment in risky assets. Then the risk-return combinations that you can obtain lie along a straight line passing through i, the riskless rate, and the point on the graph representing all funds invested in the risky asset (or portfolio) with no borrowing. As you increase the proportion of your initial capital that is invested in risky assets, both the expected rate of return and the risk increase. In Figure 6-11, point P represents the expected rate of return and standard deviation from investment in a portfolio of risky assets. The section of the line drawn through i and P that lies between i and P represents the possible risk-return combinations available

[14] Methods for determining the efficient frontier are provided in books and articles on portfolio theory; for example, see Sharpe, *op. cit*. The discussion here assumes that short-selling is not allowed.

FIGURE 6-11

Determining the best portfolio, when borrowing and investing in a riskless security are available.

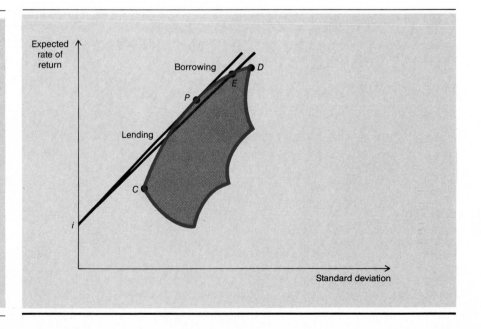

from investment in the riskless asset and in *P*. At *i*, all your capital is invested in the riskless asset; at *P*, all your capital is invested in *P*. The portion of the line extending beyond *P* to the upper right represents the risk-return combinations available from borrowing and investing the total amount (borrowed funds plus capital) in *P*. The more money that is borrowed, the greater is both the risk and expected return on your own capital.

To see how this works, suppose that you put 40 percent of your money in a riskless asset (one-year Treasury bill) offering an interest rate of 10 percent and the rest of your money (60 percent) in a portfolio of risky assets that has an expected rate of return of 15 percent and a standard deviation of 8 percent. The expected rate of return on your capital $\bar{r}_C$ will be the weighted average of the two returns.

$$\bar{r}_C = (0.4 \times 10\%) + (0.6 \times 15\%)$$

$$= 13\%$$

The standard deviation of the rate of return on your capital SD_C will be the proportion invested in the risky portfolio times its standard deviation.[15]

$$SD_C = 0.6 \times 8\%$$

$$= 4.8\%$$

On the other hand, if you were to *borrow* an amount equal to 50 percent of your capital at 10 percent interest and invest the total (150 percent of capital) in the same risky portfolio, the expected rate of return on your capital would be

$$\bar{r}_C = (-0.5 \times 10\%) + (1.5 \times 15\%)$$

$$= 17.5\%$$

We weight the 10 percent interest rate by -0.5 because you have to *pay* interest on borrowed funds equal to 50 percent of your capital. We weight the 15 percent expected rate of return on the risky asset by the proportion of your capital, 150 percent, invested in it. The standard deviation of the rate of return on your capital is still equal to the proportion of your money invested in the portfolio (150 percent) times the portfolio standard deviation.

$$SD_C = 1.5 \times 8\%$$

$$= 12\%$$

Given the mechanics of these investment alternatives, an interesting result occurs. Examine Figure 6-11 and notice that the opportunities using borrowing or lending with investment in portfolio *P* dominate all other

---

[15] To see this mathematically, assume that you invest a proportion w in risky asset A and a proportion $(1 - w)$ in riskless asset B. Since B is riskless, $SD_B = 0$. Using Equation (b) of footnote 13, the standard deviation of combination C made up of A and B is the square root of:

$$(SD_C)^2 = w^2(SD_A)^2 + (1 - w)^2 (SD_B)^2 + 2w(1 - w)SD_A \, SD_B \, Corr_{A,B}$$

$$= w^2(SD_A)^2$$

investment possibilities shown; that is, you will be able to obtain higher return with less risk.

The opportunities along the borrowing-lending line through P are also superior to borrowing or lending with any other portfolios or securities. For example, compare the line through P with the line through E, another portfolio on the efficient frontier. The opportunities provided by borrowing or lending in combination with investment in E, as represented by the line through E, are not as desirable as opportunities you have by investing in P instead. For any point on the line through E (except at i) you can find a point on the line through P that will provide a higher expected return with less risk. *Therefore, the only portfolio of risky assets of interest to the investor is P.*

The problem for the individual investor can thus be described as follows:

1   Determine the efficient frontier.
2   Find the portfolio or portfolios that, in combination with borrowing or lending, provide the best set of investment alternatives (e.g., determine the best borrowing-lending line).
3   Choose the investment package on the best borrowing-lending line that best suits the investor's tastes for risk and return.

An important point here is that, out of all the possible risky asset portfolios, there is only one (portfolio P) that the investor would consider purchasing. As we will see, unless the investor has expectations about particular securities that are greatly different from those held by most other investors in the market, the portfolio will be a highly diversified portfolio of assets similar to the portfolio of a well-diversified mutual fund.

THE CAPITAL ASSET PRICING MODEL

So far we have been discussing the situation faced by a single investor. We assumed that, in selecting a portfolio, this investor:

1   Is concerned only with the return over a single period.
2   Has a specific amount of money to invest.
3   Likes high expected portfolio return and low standard deviation of portfolio return.
4   Has estimates of the expected rates of return and the standard deviations from all portfolios of risky assets.
5   Is able to borrow and to lend at the same (riskless) rate of interest.

In addition, suppose that we assume the following:

6   Securities are bought and sold in a highly competitive market with no transaction costs (such as brokerage fees).
7   All investors have the same expectations regarding the future returns from owning securities (same expected rates of return and standard deviations for all portfolios).
8   Taxes do not bias investors in favor of one investment over another.[16]

---

[16] This assumption implies either no taxes on security returns or, if there are taxes, they do not affect the choice of which securities to own.

These assumptions describe a world in which investors may differ in their wealth and their attitudes toward risk, but in which *they all have the same opportunities and expectations*. They all dislike risk and view the standard deviation of the return on their capital as the appropriate measure of risk. They can freely invest in any combination of riskless and risky securities and can borrow, if they so desire, to finance securities' purchases. *Therefore the relationships shown in Figure 6-11 must be the same for every investor.* All investors will agree that P represents the best portfolio of risky assets to own if any risky assets are to be owned. Since all risky assets must be owned by someone, portfolio P must contain every risky security in the market. If a security is not included in P, it means that no one would want to own it, at least at its current price. The price will therefore fall. As the price falls, the security's expected rate of return will increase and eventually everyone will agree that it should be included in P. Thus, P is the *market portfolio* that contains all risky securities.[17] Given this conclusion and our assumptions, all other implications and results of the Capital Asset Pricing Model follow from the mathematics of portfolio theory.

The Capital Market Line

We designate the market portfolio as portfolio M and the rate of return on the riskless asset as i. Figure 6-12 illustrates capital market equilibrium at a point in time when all security prices have adjusted to reflect current expectations, investor attitudes toward risk, etc. All investors hold portfolios

[17] We describe a portfolio by the proportions of the various securities contained in it. The proportion of a security in the market portfolio is the total market value of that security divided by the total market value of all securities in the market.

FIGURE 6-12

Equilibrium in the capital market and the capital market line.

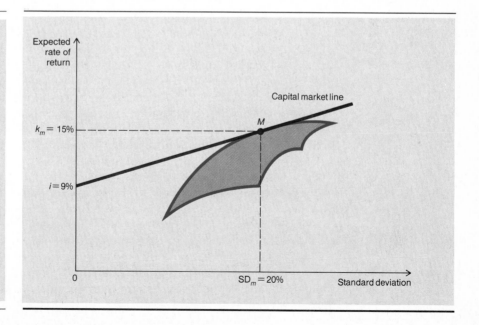

that lie along the line passing through i and M. This line is called the **capital market line**. The line can be written as an equation

$$k_C = i + s\,\text{SD}_C \tag{6-6}$$

where k_C is the equilibrium expected rate of return and SD_C is the equilibrium standard deviation of the rate of return on an investor's capital. Coefficient s is the slope of the capital market line, often called the "market price of risk," and equals

$$s = \frac{k_M - i}{\text{SD}_M} \tag{6-7}$$

where k_M is the expected rate of return and SD_M is the standard deviation of the rate of return for the market portfolio.

The capital market line shows the expected rate of return and risk for the investment alternatives available to investors from investing in M and borrowing or lending at the riskfree rate i. The investment opportunities represented by the capital market line are the best ones that are available in the market. The value of s indicates the risk-return tradeoff by investors in the market. For example, suppose that the expected rate of return on the market portfolio is 15 percent, the standard deviation for the market portfolio is 20 percent, and the riskless rate is 9 percent. From Eq. (6-6):

$$s = \frac{15\% - 9\%}{20\%}$$

$$= 0.3$$

A value of 0.3 for s means that for an increase of one percentage point in standard deviation, investors require an increase of 0.3 percentage point in expected rate of return.

The Security Market Line

Although the capital market line provides us with information about the general risk-return tradeoff in the market, it does not indicate the relationship between risk and return for individual securities. However, given the capital market line and the mathematical relationships that apply to the market portfolio and the securities that are included in the portfolio, we can develop the relationship between risk and return for individual securities.

The mathematics are complex, but the logic is as follows. Each risky security in the market is included in the market portfolio. Investors who invest in risky securities do not own a security by itself, but, as explained above, own a part of the market portfolio M which contains all risky securities. *In assessing an individual security, investors are concerned with how the total risk and return of the market portfolio is affected by including that particular security in it.* The expected rate of return on the market is simply the average rate of return on all securities in it. However, the market standard deviation depends not only on the standard deviations of the securities in the market portfolio, but also on the correlations between the securities. Consequently, the risk of an individual security for investors holding the market portfolio depends both on the standard deviation of the security's rate of return *and* the correlation of the security's rate of return with the rates of return on the other securities in the market.[18]

In equilibrium, given the capital market line, the expected rate of return on a security J is given by the security market line

$$k_J = i + s \, \mathrm{Corr}_{JM} \, \mathrm{SD}_J \tag{6-8}$$

That is, the equilibrium expected rate of return (k_J) equals the riskless interest rate (i) plus a premium for risk. This premium consists of the slope coefficient of the *capital* market line (s), which measures the risk-return tradeoff of investors, times the correlation of the rate of return on the security with the market's rate of return (Corr_{JM}) times the standard deviation of the security's rate of return (SD_J). The measure of risk here, $\mathrm{Corr}_{JM} \, \mathrm{SD}_J$, represents the contribution security J makes to the risk of the market portfolio. *All other risk associated with security J is diversified away.* For example, a security with returns that are highly correlated with the market (say, $\mathrm{Corr}_{JM} = 0.9$) and a standard deviation (SD_J) of 20 percent would have a risk of 0.9×20 percent, or 18 percent. Even when included in the market portfolio with all the other securities in the economy, most of the risk of this security cannot be diversified away. However, another security with returns that do not vary much with the market (say, $\mathrm{Corr}_{JM} = 0.2$) and a standard deviation of 25 percent would have a risk of only 10 percent $(0.2 \times 25$ percent$)$. Much of the risk of owning this security is eliminated when owned as part of the market portfolio.

One way to understand why the correlation with the market is so important in determining a security's risk is to imagine what would result if the returns from securities did not vary with any common factor. That is, if all securities' returns were uncorrelated with each other. How would the return on the market portfolio consisting of a large number of these securities behave? When some securities are experiencing high returns, others will be experiencing low returns, since all returns vary independently. If there is a sufficiently large number of securities in the market, the market portfolio's return will equal the average return for all securities with no appreciable uncertainty.[19] On the other hand, suppose that all securities' returns vary together in lock step. Then, no matter how many securities you own, the return on your portfolio will have the same uncertainty (standard deviation) as the average standard deviation of the securities in it. There are no benefits to diversification in this case.

[18] The standard deviation of any portfolio P can be determined from the following expression:

$$(\mathrm{SD}_P)^2 = \sum_{H=1}^{n} \sum_{J=1}^{n} w_H \, w_J \, \mathrm{Corr}_{HJ} \, \mathrm{SD}_H \, \mathrm{SD}_J$$

where w_H is the proportion of security H in the portfolio, and SD_H is the standard deviation of the rate of return on security H; similarly for w_J and SD_J. Corr_{HJ} is the correlation between the returns of securities H and J. In applying this formula, it is important to recognize that the correlation of a security's returns with its own returns, Corr_{HH}, is 1.0.

[19] This is based on the law of large numbers which says, in this context, that the standard deviation of the average return on the market will equal the average standard deviation of the securities in the market divided by the square root of the number of securities. Thus, with 10,000 securities, the standard deviation of the market return will be only 1 percent $(1/\sqrt{10,000} = \frac{1}{100}$ of the average of the standard deviations of the securities' returns themselves.

An alternative form of the security market line uses beta as a measure of risk. Recall from Chapter 6 that beta measures the responsiveness of a security's rate of return to the rate of return of the market. A security's beta can be expressed as

$$\text{Beta}_J = \frac{\text{Corr}_{JM}\,\text{SD}_J}{\text{SD}_M} \qquad (6\text{-}9)$$

Using this definition of beta and the equation for the slope coefficient s, Eq. (6-7), we can write the security market line of Eq. (6-8) as

$$k_J = i + (k_M - i)\,\text{beta}_J \qquad (6\text{-}10)$$

Equation (6-10) captures the basic insight of the CAPM. The expected rate of return of an individual security, in equilibrium, depends on the riskless interest rate, investor attitudes toward risk as measured by the market risk premium $(k_M - i)$, and the risk of the security measured by its beta. The security market line using beta as the risk measure for a security is shown in Figure 6-11. All portfolios and securities fall along the security market line in equilibrium. Beta for the market itself is 1.0 as implied by the definition of beta, Eq. (6-9), since correlation of the return on the market with itself is 1.0. Therefore the expected rate of return for securities with betas equal to 1.0 is the expected rate of return on the market.

Asset Prices

Equations (6-8) and (6-10) tell us what the expected rate of return will be for an asset that is priced "correctly" according to the security market line. However, it is also useful to be able to determine what the "correct" price should be directly. The ability to estimate the market price of an asset, given knowledge of the probability distribution of the asset's returns and the market parameters common to all assets (i and s), is especially convenient if the asset or security has not previously been traded in the market. For example, suppose you wish to estimate the stock price of a company that is issuing stock to the public for the first time. To do this, we restate Eq. (6-8) in terms of dollar return and prices. The resulting equation for the value of security J (V_J) is[20]

---

[20] Equation (6-11) is derived as follows:

1 The expected return (k_J) for an asset J that is "correctly priced" according to the CAPM will be [from Eq. (6-8)]

$$k_J = i + s\,\text{Corr}_{JM}\,\text{SD}_J \qquad (a)$$

2 The expected rate of return is also

$$k_J = \frac{\bar{R}_J}{V_J} - 1 \qquad (b)$$

where $\bar{R}_J$ is the expected dollar return one period from now from security J, and V_J is the current market value of security J.

3 The standard deviation of the rate of return of the security (SD_J) equals the standard deviation of the dollar return of the security (SD_{RJ}) divided by its price.

$$\text{SD}_J = \frac{\text{SD}_{RJ}}{V_J} \qquad (c)$$

4 Using relationships (b) and (c) to substitute for k_J and SD_J in (a) we can solve for V_J and the result is Eq. (6-11).

$$V_J = \frac{\overline{R}_J}{1 + k_J}$$

$$= \frac{\overline{R}_J - s \, \text{Corr}_{JM} \, \text{SD}_{RJ}}{1 + i} \tag{6-11}$$

where $\overline{R}_J$ is the expected dollar return one year from now to the owners of security J and SD_{RJ} is the standard deviation of the dollar returns. The other variables in Eq. (6-11) (s, Corr_{JM}, and i) are the same as those in Eq. (6-8). Eq. (6-11) can be used to estimate the market value of any asset for which the required data are available. Exhibit 6-4 provides an example application.

EXHIBIT 6-4
Example price calculation applying Eq. (6-11) to stock A of Figure 6-1

Stock A

Expected dollar return $(\overline{R}_A) = \$60.00$
Standard deviation of dollar return $(\text{SD}_{RA}) = \$11.00$
Correlation of stock A's returns with the market $(\text{Corr}_{AM}) = 0.6$

Market data

Slope of the capital market line $(s) = 0.3$
Riskless interest rate $(i) = 10\%$

Estimated market price (V_A)

$$V_A = \frac{\overline{R}_A - s \, \text{Corr}_{AM} \, \text{SD}_{RA}}{1 + i} \qquad \text{(Eq. 6-11)}$$

$$= \frac{\$60.00 - (0.3)(0.6)(\$11.00)}{1.10}$$

$$= \frac{\$60.00 - \$1.98}{1.10}$$

$$= \$52.75$$

P A R T

2

THE FIRM'S INVESTMENT, FINANCING,
AND DIVIDEND DECISIONS

Part 2 comprises five chapters that deal with the firm's fundamental considerations in making its investment, financing, and dividend decisions. The sequencing of these chapters roughly follows the sequence of decisions made by the financial manager. In the light of past investment, financing, and dividend decisions, the financial manager estimates the firm's cost of capital for use as a standard to evaluate proposed investments. The cost of capital is the rate of return investors require on their investment in the firm. Procedures for estimating its numerical value are presented in Chapter 7. Management then uses the cost of capital to evaluate investments of the same risk and financed in the same way as those historically undertaken by the firm. The techniques used in this process are covered in Chapter 8. Procedures for dealing with investments that differ in risk are covered in Chapter 9.

Application of the methods of business investment planning covered in Chapters 8 and 9 results in a planned capital expenditure program for the firm. The financial manager must now consider how these expenditures are to be financed. Chapter 10 examines the major sources of financing used by business firms and explains how management decides which sources to use. If this financing method differs significantly from that used in the past, the cost of capital estimate may be revised, and a change may be made in the capital budget that was initially chosen. The final financing and investment program followed by the firm depends on the cost and availability of financing.

A major source of financing is earnings retained by the firm instead of being paid out as dividends. Chapter 11 discusses the factors that influence policies for dividend payments to shareholders and how the firm formulates the policy best suited to its particular situation.

C H A P T E R

7

**THE COST
OF CAPITAL**

A company's **cost of capital** is the average rate of return required by investors in the company's securities. This average rate is often used as a minimum acceptable rate of return for new investments being considered by the firm. Under appropriate conditions, the cost of capital is the interest rate or discount rate to use in computing the market value of the cash flows generated by an investment. In this chapter we explain the conditions under which a company's cost of capital can be used to evaluate business investments. We present methods for estimating the rates that are required on the various types of securities (debt and stock) used by the firm. Then we show how to combine these rates into an estimate of the company's cost of capital.

BASIC CONCEPTS

A company's cost of capital is calculated as a weighted average of the costs of the securities used to finance the firm's investments. The cost of each type of security is multiplied by its proportion (which sums to 1.0) of the total amount of all securities issued by the firm. For example, suppose that the firm uses debt costing 5 percent and stock costing 15 percent. If the proportion of debt used is 40 percent and the proportion of stock used is 60 percent, then the cost of capital k_a is

$$\text{Cost of capital} = \text{debt proportion} \times \text{debt rate}$$
$$+ \text{ stock proportion} \times \text{stock rate} \tag{7-1}$$
$$k_a = 0.40 \times 5\% + 0.60 \times 15\%$$
$$= 2\% + 9\%$$
$$= 11\%$$

This calculation raises two questions: (1) Why is the company's cost of capital useful in evaluating investment proposals and (2) how can the components (costs and proportions) be determined? We first discuss the use of the cost of capital because this provides the basis for specifying how the components should be determined.

*Conditions for Using
the Cost of Capital*

There are two basic conditions for using the company's cost of capital to evaluate new investments.

1 The new investments being considered have the same risk as the typical or average investment undertaken historically by the firm.
2 The financing policy of the firm is not affected by the investments that are made.

The first condition means that the company's cost of capital should be used to evaluate only investments of the same risk as the average investment made in the past; that is, the new investments must not change the business risk of the firm if they are undertaken. The second condition means that the relative amounts of the different types of securities used by the firm should not change as a result of undertaking any of the new

182

PART 2
The firm's investment,
financing, and dividend
decisions

investments being evaluated; that is, the financing of the new investments must not change the financial risks of the firm.

Evaluating new investments when these conditions are not met is a much more difficult problem. We show how to deal with investments of differing risks in Chapter 9 and discuss financing issues in Chapter 10. However, the concepts developed here are useful in dealing with the more complex situations. Now let's see why the cost of capital is a proper measure of the minimum acceptable rate of return on investment when the two conditions apply.

An Illustration

Suppose a firm is considering an investment such as purchasing a new machine costing $1000 that will be financed with a debt issue of $400 and a stock issue of $600. Assume that the interest cost of the debt is 5 percent and that the stockholders require an expected rate of return of 15 percent on their investment of $600. If the cash returns from the investment are expected to continue at the same level forever and all of it is paid out in interest and dividends, how large must the annual cash flow be to justify the expenditure of $1000?

The cash flow from the investment must cover at a minimum the interest cost of the debt and provide a satisfactory dividend return to shareholders.

$$\text{Minimum acceptable cash flow} = \text{interest cost} + \text{minimum dividends}$$

$$= \text{debt rate} \times \text{debt issue}$$

$$+ \text{stock rate} \times \text{stock issue} \qquad (7\text{-}2)$$

$$= 5\% \times \$400 + 15\% \times \$600$$

$$= \$20 + \$90$$

$$= \$110$$

The minimum acceptable rate of return on this investment is the minimum acceptable cash flow divided by the amount of the investment or $110/$1000 = 11 percent. Since Eq. (7-2) expresses the minimum acceptable cash flow in terms of the financing used, let's divide both sides of that equation by the amount of the investment.

$$\frac{\text{Minimum acceptable cash flow}}{\text{Investment}} = \frac{\text{debt rate} \times \text{debt issue} + \text{stock rate} \times \text{stock issue}}{\text{investment}}$$

$$= \text{debt rate} \times \frac{\text{debt issue}}{\text{investment}}$$

$$+ \text{stock rate} \times \frac{\text{stock issue}}{\text{investment}}$$

$$= \text{debt rate} \times \text{proportion of debt}$$
$$+ \text{stock rate} \times \text{proportion of stock} \qquad (7\text{-}3)$$

$$= 5\% \frac{\$400}{\$1000} + 15\% \frac{\$600}{\$1000}$$

$$= 5\%(0.4) + 15\%(0.6)$$

$$= 11\%$$

Therefore we can compute a minimum acceptable rate of return using Eq. (7-3). Now compare Eq. (7-3) with our initial statement of the cost of capital, Eq. (7-1). The minimum acceptable rate of return and the cost of capital (k_a) are equal. If the project has an expected rate of return higher than 11 percent, it should be accepted since the cash returns from the investment will provide shareholders with dividends in excess of their minimum requirements.

We have shown by means of a simple example that the *minimum acceptable rate of return on an investment is equal to an average of the rates of return that investors require on the securities they own.*[1] This is a company's cost of capital. The concept is illustrated in Figure 7-1. This figure shows the security market line of Chapter 6 with the risks and market rates of return of the debt and stock as indicated. The cost of capital reflects the average risk (business and financial risks) of the total company and is therefore based on the risk-return relationship in the security markets as represented by the security market line.

[1] In the numerical illustration above, the debt rate used was the effective rate on debt adjusted for corporate income taxes. Figure 7-1 ignores corporate tax effects.

FIGURE 7-1

The cost of capital and the security market line.

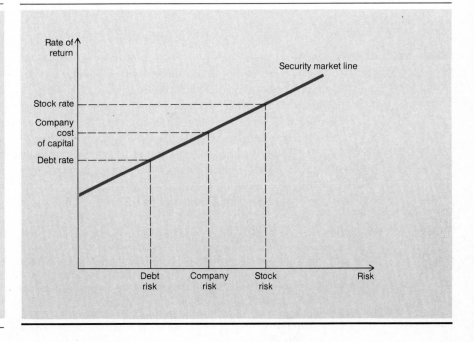

Now we have the basic concept of the cost of capital and why it is a valid measure. Let's express it as a general formula. If the firm uses n different types of financing, each type j with its own costs k_j and in proportion p_j, then the firm's cost of capital k_a is

$$k_a = p_1 k_1 + p_2 k_2 + \cdots + p_n k_n \tag{7-4}$$

If the firm uses three types of financing (for example, bonds, preferred stock, and common stock) with costs of 5, 8, and 12 percent each and in proportions 30, 20, and 50 percent, respectively, then

$$
\begin{aligned}
k_a &= p_1 k_1 + p_2 k_2 + p_3 k_3 \\
&= 0.30(5\%) + 0.20(8\%) + 0.50(12\%) \\
&= 1.5\% + 1.6\% + 6\% \\
&= 9.1\%
\end{aligned}
$$

Despite the apparent precision of the formula, the cost of capital is often difficult to estimate exactly. There are several variations of the definitions of the proportions and the costs used in the same general formula. There are also some practical problems in estimating the costs regardless of what definition is used.

Our stress here is on the underlying logic of the procedure and the basic estimates needed to determine the general magnitude of a firm's cost of capital. At this point we know that the proportions used are to be based on the financing plans of the firm and that the costs depend on the market interest rates required by investors in the firm's securities. We need now to identify the proportions and the costs more precisely so that they can be estimated from real data. Let's look at the costs first.

DETERMINING THE COST RATES

We need to know how to estimate the percentage cost rates [the k's in Eq. (7-4)] of each type of financing source used by the firm in order to calculate the average cost of capital. We will look at three types of financing used by firms: debt, preferred stock, and equity where equity includes common stock and retained earnings.[2] Although the details of each type differ somewhat, our basic procedure is similar for all of them.

The rates we wish to estimate are those which the firm must provide to investors in order to finance the firm's investments in new plant, equipment, etc. However, we don't know what those investments will be yet, since the cost of capital is used as a criterion for determining what investments to

[2] Any operational method of estimating the cost of capital for a firm involves some degree of approximation, and the procedure presented here is no exception. We are ignoring the out-of-pocket costs of raising money (underwriting fees and other flotation costs, loan set-up fees, etc.). These costs do not affect the market rates required by investors, but do affect the net dollar proceeds from borrowing and issuing stock. The presence of such costs makes the choice of investments and their financing interdependent. Simply incorporating these costs in a single cost of capital rate for the firm can lead to serious errors except in very unusual circumstances. In Chapter 10, we show how to deal with interdependent investment and financing decisions.

undertake. This would seem to pose a dilemma. We need to know the financing rates in order to get a cost of capital to evaluate investments. However, we don't know how much money will be needed and therefore can't plan the financing until we evaluate the investments. The solution to the problem is based on our two basic conditions that investment risk and financing policies remain unchanged.

We estimate the rates of return that investors in the firm's securities currently require. These security market rates reflect the current business and financial risks of the firm. The current business risk of the firm is the same as the risk of the typical or average investment made by the firm historically. Recall that the cost of capital is appropriate for evaluating only investments of this degree of risk. Similarly, the current financial risk of the firm is determined by past financing decisions. We assumed that the financing policy of the firm will not change so that we could use current market rates which reflect current financial risk.

Our procedure is, therefore, to estimate rates of return currently required by investors in the firm's securities. Under some circumstances this will be very difficult to do, and alternative approaches will be suggested to deal with these cases. However, it is important to know what the desired result is, namely, the market rates of returns which are required by the investors who supply money to the firm.

The Rate on Debt

In measuring the interest cost of debt financing, two questions arise.[3]

1 How should the use of several different types of debt be handled?
2 How should income taxes be taken into account?

The first question raises the possibility that the firm may use more than one type of debt. For example, there are several different kinds of bonds that the firm could issue. The interest and principal payments on a bond issue may be subordinated to those in other debt issues so that the investors in the subordinated bonds get paid only after the others have been paid. Since these bonds are more risky than ordinary bonds, a higher interest rate must be paid on them.

When there is more than one debt issue outstanding, we can estimate the current rate on debt by calculating the average rate.[4] For example, suppose the firm has two long-term debt issues outstanding—a "senior" bond and a "subordinated" bond, where the holders of the subordinated

---

[3] A third issue that will not be explored here is whether the promised rate (yield to maturity) or expected rate on the debt should be used. In theory, the rate of return that investors expect to earn on the debt (the **expected rate**) is more appropriate. The expected rate is less than the promised rate if there is any chance of default. However, we will use the promised rate for three reasons. First, the expected rate is difficult to estimate, whereas the promised rate can always be calculated. Second, unless the debt is very risky (rated below Ba), the promised rate produces sufficiently accurate results. Third, the promised rate is used in actual business practice.

[4] An alternative to computing the average rate on debt is to consider each type of debt a separate financing source and include it as a part of the cost of capital calculation. However, there are advantages to estimating an average rate on the debt, as will be shown when the method is applied later in the chapter.

186

PART 2
The firm's investment,
financing, and dividend
decisions

bond get paid only if the holders of the senior bond have been paid first. Let's examine a specific case. The following data are assumed:

	Senior bonds	Subordinated bonds
Maturity value	$20 million	$10 million
Market value	$18 million	$10 million
Coupon rate	9%	11%
Yield to maturity	10%	11%

The average interest rate required by the bondholders of the firm is calculated using the *market values* of both kinds of bonds and their *yields to maturity* as follows:

Total market value of bonds = $18 + $10 = $28

$$\text{Average rate on bonds} = 10\% \left(\frac{\$18}{\$28}\right) + 11\% \left(\frac{\$10}{\$28}\right)$$

$$= 10.36\%$$

We use current market value and yield to maturity in this calculation because these reflect current interest rates in the market. The firm is assumed to be able to issue new senior and subordinated bonds with an average interest rate of 10.36 percent. Maturity values and coupon rates reflect interest rates at the time the debt was originally issued, and these historical values are not relevant to current decisions.

Income Tax Effects   Our second question concerned the impact of taxes on debt rate. The answer is that the effective cost of debt is lower than the interest rate paid to creditors because the firm can deduct interest payments in the determination of taxable income, thereby reducing taxes. The amount of the reduction in taxes and the effective cost of debt depend on the tax rate. The higher the tax rate, the lower the effective interest rate on debt. For example, look at the data in Exhibit 7-1. There are two firms, A and B, that have identical earnings before interest and taxes. Firm A has no debt, whereas firm B has $2000 in outstanding debt and pays an interest rate of 10 percent. The firms' incomes are calculated using three tax rates, 0, 25, and 50 percent, and the resulting values of the net incomes are compared. If no taxes were paid, the only difference between the net incomes of the two firms would be due to the interest expense incurred by firm B of $200. In this case we would say that the effective rate on the debt was equal to the interest rate of 10 percent ($200/$2000 = 10 percent). If the tax rate is 25 percent, the impact of the debt interest on net income is only $150 due to the tax deductibility of interest. The effective rate on debt is therefore only $150/$2000 = 7.5 percent. Similarly, at a 50 percent tax rate the effective rate is only $100/$2000 = 5 percent. The general formula for the effective rate is

Effective rate = interest rate × (1.0 − tax rate)   (7-5)

where the interest rate used is the average market interest rate on the firm's debt. We use the effective rate as the cost of debt in calculating the firm's cost of capital.

The Rate on Preferred Stock

Preferred stock is similar to common stock in that it has no maturity. Once issued, it may remain outstanding as long as the firm continues in existence. Cash payments (called **preferred dividends**) to the owners of this security are a fixed amount, for example $5 per share per year, and usually no dividends can be paid to the common stockholders unless the preferred stockholders have been paid. In this respect preferred stock is much like a bond with its fixed interest payments. However, the dividends paid to preferred stockholders are not tax deductible.

The fixed cash payments to the owner plus the absence of tax deductibility means that we can estimate the rate on preferred stock by simply dividing the preferred dividend per share by the current price per share since the dividend can be considered a level perpetual payment.

$$\text{Preferred rate} = \frac{\text{dividend}}{\text{price}} \tag{7-6}$$

For example, in November 1984, Consolidated Edison's preferred stock, which pays $5 per share, was selling at a price of $40. The rate was therefore $5/$40 or 12.5 percent.

Sometimes firms have more than one issue of preferred stock outstanding. In this situation the average current rate on all preferred issues can be used as was done for debt issues.

The Rate on Common Stock

The rate on common stock (and retained earnings) is the rate most difficult to estimate. The stock rate is the rate of return required by the stockholders of the firm. However, as we discussed in Chapter 5, there are no fixed

---

EXHIBIT 7-1

Tax rates and the effective rate on debt

	0% tax rate		25% tax rate		50% tax rate	
	Firm A	Firm B	Firm A	Firm B	Firm A	Firm B
Earnings before interest and taxes	$1,000	$1,000	$1,000	$1,000	$1,000	$1,000
Interest	0	200	0	200	0	200
Taxable income	$1,000	$ 800	$1,000	$ 800	$1,000	$ 800
Taxes	0	0	250	200	500	400
Net income	$1,000	$ 800	$ 750	$ 600	$ 500	$ 400
Difference[a]		$200		$150		$100
Effective rate[b]		10%		7.5%		5%

[a] Net income of firm A − net income of firm B.
[b] (Difference in net income)/$2000 of outstanding debt for firm B.

188

PART 2
The firm's investment,
financing, and dividend
decisions

contractual payments for common stock as there are for other securities issued by the firm. Stockholders have expectations as to what future dividends are, but it's difficult for the financial manager to determine the expected values. Many firms pay no dividends for long periods of time, either because they prefer to finance through use of retained earnings to the greatest extent possible or because they have not been profitable. Several methods of estimating the rate on stock are in use. We will examine four of them here. As we will see, no method is free of problems, and often more than one is used to provide the financial manager with a reasonable estimate of the rate.

Historical Rate of Return   The first method is to determine the historical rate of return actually earned by the shareholders. Take the most recent five or ten years and calculate the rate of return earned by an investor who purchased stock at the beginning of the study period, held it to the present, and sold it at current prices. This procedure is based on the assumption that investors, on average, earn what they expect to earn. Furthermore, the method requires that (1) there were no significant changes in investor expectations as to the future performance of the firm during the study period, (2) no significant changes in the level of interest rates have occurred, and (3) investor attitudes toward risk haven't changed. Unfortunately, such conditions are very unusual, and this method must be used only with great caution. The historical rate of return often differs considerably, depending on the time period chosen.

As a simple example, suppose that five years ago the price of the firm's stock was $50. Dividends of $6 per share were paid each year, and today the stock is still selling for $50. The average rate of return for an investor who bought the stock for $50 has been $6/$50 = 12 percent per year. Using the historical method, 12 percent would be an estimate of the current required rate of return on the stock.

Estimates of Future Dividends   The second method is for the financial manager to estimate what investors expect the future dividend stream of the firm will be and to use the current price of the stock to determine stockholders' expected rate of return. The basic relationship for the price of the firm's stock was provided in Chapter 5. There we said that the price would be equal to the present value of the expected dividends given the risk-adjusted rate (k_s) required by investors. If we know the price and the expected dividends, we can determine the required rate of return from the equation.

$$P = \frac{D_1}{1 + k_s} + \frac{D_2}{(1 + k_s)^2} + \frac{D_3}{(1 + k_s)^3} + \cdots + \frac{D_m}{(1 + k_s)^m} \tag{7-7}$$

That is, given the current price P and the values for future dividends D_t, we can calculate k_s.

Determining the dividends expected by investors is not easy. However, if the firm has maintained some regular pattern of dividend payments in the past, it is not unreasonable for investors to expect this pattern to continue in the future. Suppose, for example, that for the past ten years the firm has paid an average dividend of $6 per share per year with no trend toward higher or lower payments and the earnings of the firm have also shown no trend up or down. Under these circumstances, it would be reasonable to assume that investors view the firm as paying a level perpetual dividend of $6 per share and therefore

$$P = \frac{\$6}{k_s}$$

If the current price of the stock is $50,

$$k_s = \frac{\$6}{P}$$

$$= \frac{\$6}{\$50}$$

$$= 12\%$$

A more typical firm would increase dividends over time. We know of a simple model of growing dividends that can be used to estimate k_s, the constant growth model of Chapter 5. In this model dividends are expected to grow at a compound rate of g per year. If D_1 is the dividend expected next year, then

$$P = \frac{D_1}{k_s - g} \tag{7-8}$$

or

$$k_s = \frac{D_1}{P} + g \tag{7-9}$$

To use this model, we must assume that investors expect the dividends of the firm to grow indefinitely at a rate of g. This would be reasonable if the firm had consistent growth in the past and no significant changes appear likely in the future. It may not be easy to estimate what investors expect as next year's dividend and the long-run average growth rate, but it is less difficult to do this than to try to estimate what investors expect in every future year.

As an example, suppose that, historically, dividends have grown at a rate of 6 percent per year and management expects to pay $2 per share next year. Assuming that nothing has changed about the firm that would warrant a change in expectations regarding future growth, those two figures can be used with the current price of the stock to estimate k_s. If the current price is $40, then k_s would be estimated as

$$k_s = \frac{\$2}{\$40} + 0.06$$

$$= 11\%$$

If the actual circumstances of the business do not fit the constant growth model, then the problem of estimating the required rate of return

190

PART 2
The firm's investment,
financing, and dividend
decisions

becomes much more difficult because it may be very hard to estimate the future dividends expected by investors. For example, what should be done for firms that are not paying dividends? Through 1984, Pan American Airlines had not paid any dividends since 1967. Some new businesses have never paid a dividend. For such firms some other method must be used. The historical rate of return is one possibility although, as we indicated, there are potential problems in using this method. The average rate of return earned by Pan American stockholders was negative in most of the years from 1967 through 1985 and approximately zero for the five-year period 1980–1985.

Using the Stock's Beta   A third method for estimating the stock rate k_s is based on the stock's beta value. The CAPM discussed in Chapter 6 specifies that the required rate of return on stock depends on its beta. The relationship is

$$k_s = \text{riskless rate} + \text{risk premium} \times \text{beta} \tag{7-10}$$

We can use this equation to estimate the stock rate if we have values for the riskless rate of interest, the market risk premium, and the stock's beta. We obtain the riskless rate for this purpose from the current rate on long-term government bonds as reported in publications such as *The Wall Street Journal*.[5] The market risk premium is more difficult to estimate. To obtain a rough idea of its magnitude, we can use the difference between the long-run average rate of returns on stocks and government bonds. Using the data in Table 5-2, this difference for the period 1926 to 1981 was 6.1 percentage points. Thus we estimate the market risk premium to be about 6 percentage points.

The beta for a company's stock can be obtained from published sources or estimated by the financial manager. Value Line and Merrill Lynch provide estimates of beta for the 1000 or so largest companies. For such companies, the published beta can be used. Estimating beta for a smaller company requires some statistical analysis. This is a topic for more advanced courses. In either case the value of beta is based on the historical relationship between the rate of return on the stock and the rate of return in the market. Therefore the procedure is accurate only if the business and financial risks of the firm have not changed over the period studied and are not expected to change.

As an example, beta for Pan Am's stock was estimated by Value Line to be 0.95 in 1984. Long-term government bond rates were about 12 percent in November 1984. We can therefore estimate the required rate of return on Pan Am's stock in November 1984 to be

---

[5] Some people suggest that the short-term Treasury bill rate be used as the riskless rate. This is appropriate if you wish to estimate a short-term rate on stock. We use long-term government bond rates because we wish to estimate the long-term required rate of return on stock for use in evaluating long-term investments. Our procedure is theoretically valid only under highly restrictive assumptions. However those assumptions are necessary to justify use of the CAPM to estimate long-term required rates of return.

Stock rate $= 12\% + 6\% \times 0.95$

$\qquad\qquad = 17.7\%$

Using Debt Rates   All three methods described above use historical data to estimate the stock rate. However, any use of historical data to reflect current views of investors assumes that investor views haven't changed recently. What if you are not willing to make that assumption? For example in 1981 Du Pont (a major chemical company) acquired Conoco (a major oil company) by borrowing about $4 billion. Clearly the business risk and the financial risk of the combined company might be different from that of either Du Pont or Conoco prior to the acquisition. How then in late 1981 could one estimate Du Pont's stock rate? The fourth approach takes the current rate on debt issued by the firm and assumes that the stockholders require an appreciably higher rate than that. Actual rates of return on common stocks average four to six percentage points higher than rates of return on corporate bonds. In Du Pont's case, this would imply that the company's stockholders required a rate of 18 to 20 percent since the firm's bonds were yielding around 14 percent at that time. This approach provides a very crude estimate of the stock rate, but it is based on current market rates and can be used when other approaches are suspect. It also is useful as a rough check on the magnitude of an estimate derived by another method.[6]

DETERMINING THE PROPORTIONS

In calculating the cost of capital we multiply the rate for each type of financing by the proportion of that type used by the firm. Now that we know how to determine the rates, we need to specify the proportions [the p's in Eq. (7-4)].

Several alternative ways to specify the proportions are used in practice. These include using the existing proportions on the firm's balance sheet, the proportions of financing planned for the current capital budget, the expected future financing proportions, and the current proportions of the market values of the firm's outstanding securities. Each may provide a cost of capital suitable for investment decisions in some cases; however, we recommend the use of market value proportions for two reasons.

First, it is difficult to determine the proportions of the types of financing that will be used to provide money for current and future investments before the profitability and amount of investment expenditures are known. Yet the financial manager must estimate the cost of capital before deciding which investments would be in the stockholders' interests. The current market value proportions of the firm's outstanding securities *are* known at

---

[6] There is yet another method that is sometimes used, $E/P =$ (earnings per share)/(price per share). This method can be applied to firms not paying dividends, but it requires (a) that the firm be profitable, (b) that current earnings are neither abnormally high nor low, and (c) that the firm is not expected to have investments earning more than its cost of capital on average now and in the future.

192

PART 2
The firm's investment,
financing, and dividend
decisions

the time investment decisions are made; therefore there is no need to forecast the financing methods that will be used.

Second, the best estimates of the rates associated with the various financing sources are those currently required on the firm's existing securities in the market. These rates reflect investors' assessments of the current business and financial risk of the firm and, coupled with investor expectations of future income, determine the current market value of the firm's securities. The cost of capital computed with current market rates and market value proportions is the average rate of return (adjusted for the tax deductibility of debt interest) required by investors in the firm's securities. Given the assumption that the firm's business and financial risk will not be changed, the cost of capital computed with market rates and market value proportions is a valid measure of the minimum rate of return required on new investments for them to be in the stockholders' interests. Indeed, under the assumptions used here, the present value of the expected cash flow from an investment using this cost of capital is a direct estimate of the increase in the market value of the firm's common stock from undertaking the investment. This is not true of other approaches even though they may indicate correctly, under some conditions, which investments should be undertaken.

For example, we calculate the proportions in the following way, using the market values of the securities currently outstanding:

Outstanding securities	Market value	Proportion
Debt	$ 4.0 million	0.40
Preferred stock	1.0 million	0.10
Common stock	5.0 million	0.50
Total	$10.0 million	1.00

CALCULATION OF A FIRM'S COST OF CAPITAL

Now that we know how to obtain the components, let's put them together in the calculation of the cost of capital for a firm. We will use modified data from an actual firm to illustrate the procedure.

Basic Brands, Inc. (not true name) is a consumer products company with well-established brand names. We are estimating the cost of capital for the firm at the end of 1984 for use in evaluating investment proposals in 1985. Data for Basic Brands are shown in Exhibit 7-2.

As discussed above, the required return on common stock is the most difficult value to estimate. The difficulties arise from trying to determine what shareholders are expecting with regard to the future performance of the firm. Since the firm's earnings and dividends have been growing fairly steadily since 1979 (in fact, dividends per share have risen every year for twenty-three years), the constant growth model appears appropriate. However, dividends have grown faster than earnings because an increasing percentage of earnings have been paid out. Suppose we assume that stockholders expect dividends to grow in the future at the same rate that earnings have grown at over the past six years, which is 10.8 percent per year. For 1985 let's assume $2.60 per share was expected since the firm declared a $0.65 dividend for the last quarter of 1984, which would imply an annual dividend of $2.60 if the quarterly rate were maintained. Applying Eq. (7-9), given a current stock price of $50,

$$k_s = \frac{D}{P} + g$$

$$= \frac{\$2.60}{\$50} + 0.108$$

$$= 16\%$$

What if investor expectations as to future dividends for Basic Brands were based on past dividend growth rather than past earnings growth? This would be reasonable if investors expected earnings to grow somewhat faster in the future than in the past, thereby allowing the firm to continue its high

---

EXHIBIT 7-2

Financial data for Basic Brands, Inc.: outstanding debt, preferred stock, and common stock as of December 1, 1984 (dollar figures in millions)

	Book value	Market value	Interest rate, %[a]
Bonds (7¾% due 2003)	$ 45	$ 29	13.2
Bonds (9½% due 2004)	50	42	13.2
Bonds (14% due 1992)	75	78	13.2
Other debt[b]	210	192	13.2
Total debt	$380	$341	13.2
Preferred stock[c] ($3.50)	$ 40	$ 10	14.0
Common stock	$720	$824	

	Common stock data						Average growth rate, %
	1979	1980	1981	1982	1983	1984	
Dividends per share	$ 1.45	$1.60	$1.77	$2.05	$2.28	$ 2.48	11.3
Earnings per share	2.97	3.73	4.21	4.83	4.86	4.95	10.8
Price per share	$24					$50	

Rate of return earned by stockholders 1979–1984:   18.7%

[a] Interest rates on the three bond issues and other debt were set at the rate (13.2 percent) on the recently issued debt of the firm, which is selling closest to par (14's of 1992). This was considered the best estimate of the current market rate on debt. None of the debt issues is subordinate to any other.
[b] Other debt consists of eight different types of debt, none of which is publicly traded. Market value is based on interest rates provided in the firm's annual report, using 13.2 percent as the estimated market rate that would apply.
[c] $100 par value; current market price is $25 per share.

194

PART 2
The firm's investment,
financing, and dividend
decisions

rate of dividend increase. Using the historical dividend growth rate of 11.3 percent as an estimate of future dividend growth, we get

$$k_s = \frac{D}{P} + g$$

$$= \frac{\$2.60}{\$50} + 0.113$$

$$= 16.5\%$$

Therefore, the dividend growth method gives us values for k_s of 16 to 16.5 percent. Applying the beta method, we obtain a somewhat higher number. Beta for Basic Brands was estimated to be 0.85. Interest rates on long-term government bonds on December 1, 1984, were 12 percent. Using the estimated market risk premium of 6 percent, we apply Eq. (7-10) to obtain

$$k_s = \text{Riskless rate} + \text{risk premium} \times \text{beta}$$

$$= 12\% + 6\% \times 0.85$$

$$= 17.1\%$$

The debt rate method (adding 4 to 6 percent to the debt rate to compute the equity rate) would yield values for k_s of 17 to 19 percent. Given this information and the other estimates of k_s computed above, let's use 17 percent as our estimate of equity rate k_s.

It should be apparent that estimating the stock rate is not a cookbook procedure. The best one can hope for is to be able to devise a reasonably good approximation to the "real" value, which cannot be directly observed. Note also that the actual historical rate of return to the stockholders has been 18.7 percent, which is at the high end of our estimated range. This reflects in part a stock market rally in 1984.

Given the 1984 corporate income tax rate of 46 percent, we have all the

---

Exhibit 7-3
Cost of capital calculation for Basic Brands, Inc.

	Amount[a]	Proportion[b]	Rate, %	Prop. × Rate, %
Debt	$ 341	0.29	7.1[c]	2.1
Preferred stock	10	0.01	14.0	.1
Common stock	824	0.70	17.0	11.9
Total	$1,175	1.00		14.1
		Cost of capital $k_a = 14.1\%$		

[a] These amounts are market values from Exhibit 7-2.
[b] Proportion is market value of financing type divided by total market value.
[c] Interest rate on debt is adjusted for tax rate of 46 percent. 13.2%(1 − 0.46) = 7.1%.

information needed to calculate the cost of capital for Basic Brands. The calculations are shown in Exhibit 7-3 and result in an estimated cost of capital of 14 percent. This rate would be appropriate to evaluate investment opportunities available at the end of 1984.

SUMMARY

The cost of capital for a firm is often used to evaluate investment proj-ects. It is the minimum acceptable rate of return on new investments from the viewpoint of investors in the firm's securities. The cost of cap-ital is suitable for investments with the same risks as past investments made by the firm, provided that the firm's financing policy does not change from what it has been in the past.

In order to assign a value to the cost of capital, we must estimate the rates of return required by investors in the firm's securities (including all borrowings) and average those rates according to the market values of the various securities currently outstanding. The rates are determined as follows:

1 *The debt rate is the average market interest rate on the firm's debt issues adjusted for the tax deductibility of interest. For bonds the cur-rent yield to maturity is ordinarily used as the market rate.*
2 *The rate on preferred stock is the promised dividend payment on the preferred stock divided by the price of the stock.*
3 *The stock rate is the most difficult rate to estimate. The average his-torical rate of return earned by stockholders is sometimes used as an estimate of what stockholders currently require. If the firm seems to provide a constant growth in dividends, then the expected dividend yield on the stock plus the estimated growth rate of dividends is used to estimate the rate. A third method is to use the beta of the stock, current government bond rates, and the market risk premium to esti-mate the stock rate. Another method is to base the estimated stock rate on the current interest rate of the firm's debt plus a premium for the added risk of the stock.*

QUESTIONS

1 Why is the cost of capital the minimum acceptable rate of return on an investment?
2 Under what conditions is the firm's cost of capital a valid criterion for new investment opportunities?
3 Why is it difficult to determine the rate of return required by investors in the firm's common stock?
4 Which method of calculating the rate on common stock would be most appropriate for the following firms:
   a A profitable firm that has never paid a dividend but has had steady growth in earnings.
   b An electric utility that has paid a dividend every year since 1895.
   c A firm that had grown very rapidly until two years ago, when over-

196

PART 2
The firm's investment,
financing, and dividend
decisions

capacity problems in the industry produced severe price cutting
in the firm's major product line. At the same time management
decided to invest heavily in facilities to manufacture a new product. So far the manufacturing process has not worked properly.
The firm lost $50 million last year, and the price of its common
stock has dropped 80 percent in the past two years.

5 Is the cost of debt to the firm the debtholders' required rate of return
   as measured by the yield to maturity? Why or why not?

6 If the firm has several different types of long-term debt outstanding,
   does it make any difference in principle if an average debt rate is calculated for use in computing the cost of capital rather than treating
   each debt type separately with its own proportion and rate in the
   cost of capital formula? Does it make any difference in practice?

7 Would you expect all the firms in a given industry to have approximately the same cost of capital? Why or why not?

8 Do you think that the cost of capital for a firm is fairly constant over
   time? Explain. What are the implications of your answer for business
   use of the cost of capital?

9 How could one find the cost of capital for a proprietorship or partnership? Can you think of any ways to do this? What problems are
   present for these firms that are not present for corporations?

PROJECT

Choose a business firm and estimate its cost of capital as of some particular date. The following guides may be helpful in this project:

1 A large company will be easier to obtain data for than a small com-
   .pany; however, large companies are often more complicated to
   analyze.

2 Choose a date immediately following an available annual report for
   the company. The annual report will serve as a very important source
   of data on the firm's financial affairs.

3 Appendix 5A provides additional sources of data.

4 Avoid firms with bonds or preferred stock that are convertible into
   common stock. Convertible securities are difficult to analyze.

5 Many firms use large amounts of short-term debt, have long-term
   debt with interest rates that are tied to short-term interest rates, or
   have debt denominated in foreign currencies. Treat these items as
   was done for "other debt" in the Basic Brands example in the chapter.

6 Read the footnotes to the financial statements in the annual report.
   Leases are a form of debt. Their estimated value will be found in the
   balance sheet or in footnotes.

1 Drysdale Store has the following bond issues outstanding:

	Senior bonds	Subordinated bonds
Market value	$20 million	$20 million
Maturity value	$24 million	$20 million
Yield to maturity	14%	16%
Coupon rate	10%	16%

    a What is the before-tax interest cost to the firm of each of the two types of debt issues?

    b What is the average rate on the bonds?

    c Assuming a 46 percent tax rate, what is the effective rate on the bonds?

2 Calculate the required rate of return (k_s) for common stock under the following situations:

    a Firm A has paid a $5 dividend for the past fifteen years and investors expect it to continue to do so in the future. The current price of A's stock is $40 per share.

    b Firm B's dividends per share have grown at a constant rate of 8 percent a year. Investors expect a dividend of $1.50 next year. The current price of a share of the firm's stock is $20.

    c Firm C pays no dividends and the beta for its common stock is estimated to be 1.0. The current interest rate on government bonds is 12 percent and the market risk premium is 6 percent.

3 Determine the rates to be used in a cost of capital calculation for the following securities. Assume that they are issued by different firms and that the corporate income tax rate is 40 percent.

    a A seven-year (original maturity) note with a coupon interest rate of 10 percent. The note matures in five years and has a current market price of $90 per $100 maturity value.

    b A bond issue is scheduled to mature in twenty years, bearing a coupon rate of 16 percent; however, the firm's management has announced plans to pay off the bonds one year from now after paying the interest due for the year. The bondholders would receive the maturity value at that time. The current price for the bonds as reported in the newspaper is $104.

    c A preferred stock pays $5 dividends per $100 par value. The current market price is $40.

    d The historical average rate of return earned by owners of the firm's common stock has been about 17 percent per year until very recently. The dividends of the firm have grown at an average rate of 13 percent per year over the same period. A major investment advisory service has issued a report that is somewhat critical

198

PART 2
The firm's investment,
financing, and dividend
decisions

of the firm's management and forecasts dividends and earnings to grow no faster than the overall growth rate in the general economy. The price of the firm's stock reacted sharply to the report, dropping from $100 per share to $50 per share. The long-run economic growth rate for the U.S. economy is generally thought to be 6 percent per year. The stock's dividends for next year are expected to be $5 per share.

4   Calculate the proportions to be used in calculating the cost of capital for each of the following sets of data on different firms:

a

	Balance sheet data	Market value
Bonds	$8 million maturity value	$ 8 million
Preferred stock	$4 million par value	$ 2 million
Common stock	$6 million book value	$10 million

Bond price = $100 per $100 maturity value

Preferred stock price = $50 per $100 par value

Common stock price = $10 per share

(There are 1 million shares of common stock outstanding.)

b   There are two types of securities outstanding for the firm—bonds with a maturity value of $5 million and 100,000 shares of common stock. The current market price for the bonds is $90 per $100 maturity value, and the price of the stock is $45 per share.

c

Balance sheet data	
Bonds (8% due 1992)	$10.0 million
Common stock (200,000 shares at $5 par value)	1.0 million
Surplus	1.5 million
Retained earnings	5.5 million
Total equity	$ 7.0 million

Market price for bonds = $80

Market price for stock = $60

d

Balance sheet data	
Long-term debt	$5 million
Preferred stock ($100 par)	$1 million
Book value of common stock	$6 million

Other data	
Common stock	2 million shares outstanding; current price = $4 per share
Preferred stock	These securities are not traded and no market prices are available. However, the stock is recently issued, and the dividend rate being paid by the firm is approximately equal to current market rates.
Long-term debt	Current price = $80 per $100 maturity value

5 As a financial analyst for American Resource Corporation (ARC), you have been asked to develop an estimate of the required rate of return that ARC should use in evaluating typical investment proposals. ARC's management plans to maintain its current capital structure of 40 percent debt and 60 percent equity (based on estimates of current market values). ARC's outstanding debt securities carry an average interest cost of 7.3 percent of their book value. Management estimates that the average rate in the market for new debt issues comparable to those currently outstanding would be 12 percent if the firm's financing policies are maintained. The average rate of return(dividends plus price appreciation) on ARC's common stock for the past ten years has been 22 percent. Management believes, however, that stockholders require a rate of return of 17 percent under present market conditions. ARC's tax rate is 46 percent. Is there sufficient information provided here to make the estimate called for above? If not, what is needed? If so, what is your estimate?

6 Kerry Malatesta is considering opening a bookstore in a small town which does not currently have one. She estimates that initial capital requirements would be $50,000, of which $30,000 would be borrowed at an interest rate of 15 percent and $20,000 would come from her personal funds. Given alternative investment opportunities in the capital market of comparable risk, Kerry believes that a minimum expected rate of return of 20 percent on her investment would be required to make the bookstore worthwhile. The bookstore would be incorporated and the corporate tax rate would be 25 percent (ignore personal taxes).

   a What is the minimum acceptable cash flow from the bookstore? (Assume level cash flows and ignore principal payments on the debt.)

   b What is the minimum acceptable return on the total investment in the project, given your answer from **a**?

   c Calculate the cost of capital for the bookstore and compare it to your answer for **b**.

7 The management of Kupchek Sand and Gravel (KSG) is considering expanding their business early in 1986 to meet the demands of a

200

PART 2
The firm's investment,
financing, and dividend
decisions

growing population in KSG's market area. In order to evaluate the
various alternative expansion plans, management wishes to estimate
KSG's current cost of capital. Various financial data for the firm are
given below.

Balance sheet (000s)
(December 31, 1985)

Current assets	$1,000	Current liabilities	$ 400
Fixed assets	4,000	Bonds	2,000
Total assets	$5,000	Preferred stock ($100 par value)	500
		Common stock (200,000 shares)	600
		Retained earnings	1,500
		Total liabilities and equity	$5,000

Income statement (000s)
(January 1, 1985–December 31, 1985)

Sales	$3,500
Cost of goods sold	1,200
Gross profit	$2,300
Operating expenses	1,340
Interest	160
Taxable income	$ 800
Taxes (40%)	320
Net income	$ 480
Preferred dividends	50
Earnings to common	$ 430
Dividends to common	$ 180

Historical data—common stock

	Earnings per share	Dividends per share	Avg. price per share
1985	$2.15	$0.90	$12.00
1984	2.20	0.90	12.25
1983	1.80	0.75	11.50
1982	1.60	0.70	11.75
1981	2.02	0.70	13.00
1980	1.90	0.65	10.20
1979	1.65	0.62	8.50
1978	1.42	0.58	7.25
1977	1.35	0.56	7.00

Market data (January 15, 1986)

	Bonds	Preferred stock	Common stock
Price	$780	$83.33	$12.70
Yield[a]	11.5%	12.0%	7.1%

[a] Yield for bonds is "yield to maturity"; for preferred and common stocks, yield is dividend divided by price.

The firm's tax rate is 40 percent. Beta for KSG's stock is estimated to be
0.9 and the current interest rate on government bonds is 10.4 percent.
Estimate KSG's cost of capital.

CHAPTER

8

**FUNDAMENTALS
OF CAPITAL
BUDGETING**

Each year United States nonfarm businesses spend roughly $300 billion on new plant and equipment—factories, machines, tools, pollution control equipment, and transportation facilities, among other things. Unlike current assets, which are discussed in Chapter 15, these assets, called **capital assets**, are used by the company in the physical process of producing goods and services and are ordinarily used for a number of years. Because the dollar amounts involved are so large, businesses carefully plan and evaluate expenditures for capital assets. The plan for expenditures is called a **capital budget**. The process of determining both how much to spend on capital assets and which assets to acquire is called **capital budgeting**.

This chapter presents the basic concepts of capital budgeting. The budgeting procedure is first examined and then the techniques used to evaluate proposals are described. Several important issues, including inflation and capital rationing, are discussed. The chapter ends with a look at the attitudes of business toward the various capital budgeting techniques.

**THE CAPITAL
BUDGETING
PROCESS**

Most firms prepare at least a short-run budget that indicates planned capital outlays for the current and immediately forthcoming periods. Many firms also prepare intermediate and long-term capital budgets that project capital requirements for three to five, and sometimes even ten, years into the future. Capital budgets are based on sales forecasts and on the anticipated plant and equipment needed to meet those expected sales.

Many items in the capital budget originate as proposals from plant and division management. These proposals, with supporting data, are submitted to senior management for consideration. Project recommendations may also come from top management, especially if a corporate stategic move is involved (for example, a major expansion or entry into a new market). Review of a proposed project may involve lengthy discussions between senior management and those members of lower management at the division and plant level who will be involved with the project if it is adopted. Generally, the list of proposals is studied by senior management and its staff and a subset of the list is accepted and a capital budget prepared. The budget is then submitted to the board of directors for approval.

In many cases, the process just described is modified for small dollar-value capital expenditures. For example, division managers may be permitted to spend up to some given amount, say, $50,000, for capital replacements and other outlays in a given year. All capital expenditures above that amount would require approval by central management.

A capital budgeting system under which proposals originate with top management is referred to as a **top-down system**, and one in which proposals originate at the plant and division level is referred to as a **bottom-up system**. Sometimes "top-down" signifies that approval authority rests with senior management and "bottom-up" signifies that the authority resides at lower levels. Actually, most large corporations are a mixture of both these approaches. Investment ideas emerge from below and above and authority is usually divided between senior management, which approves large projects, and division management, which has discretion up to some limit. The

202

PART 2
The firm's investment,
financing, and dividend
decisions

issue is therefore one of emphasis. Since World War II there has been a gradual shift in the direction of decentralization and a greater use of the bottom-up approach.

Economic conditions are constantly changing and even the best projections of future operations usually require revision over time. Capital budgeting is no exception. Investment plans are continually reformulated as new information regarding demand for the firm's products, changes in technology, and costs of production become available. Intermediate and long-term capital budgets are then revised accordingly. The new information not only provides a clue as to the appropriate level of future capital outlays, but it also reflects upon past investment decisions. The wisdom or error of previous decisions is revealed by the success or failure of particular projects. Information on the progress and profitability of the firm's past investments is useful in several respects. It pinpoints sectors of the firm's activities that may warrant further financial commitments; or it may call for retreat if a particular project becomes permanently unprofitable. The outcome of an investment also reflects on the performance of those members of management associated with the project. Finally, past errors and successes may provide clues regarding the weaknesses and strengths of the capital budgeting process itself.

The remainder of this chapter examines alternative procedures for evaluating investment opportunities. These techniques relate to the capital budget in two ways. First, they set forth profitability criteria that investments must satisfy in order to be accepted. The criteria are used by firms to estimate the amount of funds that they can invest profitably. These estimated amounts are incorporated into the firm's intermediate or long-term capital budget. Since these figures are only predictions of future capital outlays, they will usually have to be revised as the actual investment date approaches. At this stage the second role of capital budgeting analysis comes into play. When the time arrives to determine the exact amount to invest and where, capital budgeting techniques such as present value and internal rate of return are used. As is explained next, the analysis of an investment first requires an estimation of its cash flows.

CASH FLOW FROM AN INVESTMENT

Under each method of analysis described in this chapter, it is necessary to consider the costs and benefits of each investment opportunity. These methods for evaluating projects are based on the marginal or incremental **cash flow** from each project. The marginal cash flow from an investment is the change in total firm cash flow from adopting that investment.

Computing Cash Flow

What is cash flow, and why is cash flow the proper measure of a project's costs and benefits? Cash flow is money paid or received by the firm as a result of undertaking the project. We can express cash flow for any period in terms of the relevant costs and benefits associated with an asset (or "project") for that period:

Net cash flow fom the project = project cash inflows
$$\qquad - \text{project cash outflows}$$

$$= \text{project revenues}$$
$$\qquad - \text{project expenses other}$$
$$\qquad\quad \text{than depreciation}$$
$$\qquad - \text{project capital expenditures}$$
$$\qquad - \text{project income taxes} \qquad (8\text{-}1)$$

where project income taxes = tax rate × (project revenues
$$\qquad - \text{project expenses other}$$
$$\qquad\quad \text{than depreciation}$$
$$\qquad - \text{depreciation)} \qquad (8\text{-}1a)$$

The term in parentheses in Eq. (8-1a) is the computed taxable income from the project.[1] Project revenues in Eq. (8-1) include all cash received from customers for the firm's product (cash sales and collections of accounts receivable). Expenses other than depreciation include cash outlays for labor, materials, and other items required by the use of the asset but do *not* include interest on firm debt.

Depreciation affects the cash flow of Eq. (8-1) only through its impact on income taxes. Depreciation is not a cash expense (does not involve any expenditure of cash); it is simply a way to spread the cost of an asset (a capital expenditure) over the asset's life. From a cash flow standpoint, the capital expenditure is recorded as a cash outflow *when the asset is acquired* and not over its useful life. This will be illustrated below in an example.

It is very important to note that taxes are computed as though the project were financed entirely with equity funds. Interest on debt is not included as an expense in determining project income taxes in Eq. (8-1a). In other words, in computing aftertax cash flow, you are ignoring the method of financing the investment. Financing method is reflected in the cost of capital that takes account of the benefit derived from the tax deductibility of interest (see Chapter 7). As we will see later in the chapter, this cost of capital is used in evaluating the cash flow.

Since a project's cash flow is the change in total firm cash flow resulting from adopting the investment, a method for determining the cash flow from an investment is to compare the firm's cash flow with and without that investment. The difference between the two is the additional cash flow due to the investment. To illustrate, assume that an investment costs $1200, has a life of twelve years, has an expected aftertax liquidation value at the end of

---

[1] Cash revenues and expenses are usually not equal to taxable revenues and tax deductible expenses because revenues and expenses for tax purposes are ordinarily computed on an accrual rather than a cash basis. However, in most cases the differences can be safely ignored, as is done here. Also, capital expenditures in Eq. (8-1) include investments in current assets, such as inventory, that are required by the project. The topic is discussed in detail in Chap. 17. The fundamental principle that is applicable here is that all cash flow effects must be taken into account.

204

PART 2
The firm's investment,
financing, and dividend
decisions

the twelve years of $200, and is depreciated for tax purposes on a straight-line basis at $100 per year ($1200/12 years). (*Recall from Chapter 3 that salvage value is assumed to be zero in computing depreciation for tax purposes.*) The corporate tax rate is 50 percent. At the time the asset is acquired, the net cash flow is simply the capital expenditure, which is an outlay (a negative cash flow) of $1200. The computation in Exhibit 8-1 shows that the net cash flow for years 1 to 11 is $175. The net cash flow for year 12 is the $175 from using the asset during year 12 (computed as in Exhibit 8-1) *plus* the aftertax liquidation value of $200 that is received from selling the asset at the end of year 12; this adds up to a year 12 net cash flow of $375 ($175 + $200). The asset cash flows are shown in Exhibit 8-2.

The approach for determining and analyzing the cash flow from an investment can be summarized in the following three steps:

1   Determine the change in the firm's cash flow from acquiring the new asset. This can be done by using the Exhibit 8-1 method of comparing the firm's cash flow with and without the asset. *All* changes in cash

---

EXHIBIT 8-1
Determining the annual cash flow on an investment

	Firm's cash flow without the investment (1)		Firm's cash flow with the investment (2)		Added cash flow due to the investment (col. 2 − col. 1) (3)	
Annual revenues (*R*)		$2,000		$2,400		$400
Annual expenses other than depreciation (*E*)		1,500		1,650		150
Taxes:						
Revenues less						
expenses (*R* − *E*)	$500		$750		$250	
Less depreciation	200		300		100	
Taxable income (*TI*)	$300		$450		$150	
Tax (50% of *TI*)		150		225		75
Net cash flow (*R* − *E* − tax)		$ 350		$ 525		$175
Summary of above results:						
Revenues from the investment		$400				
Less:						
Expenses other than depreciation	$150					
Taxes	75					
Total		225				
Annual aftertax cash flow		$175				

Assumptions:

$$\text{Life of asset} = 12 \text{ years}$$
$$\text{Price of asset} = \$1,200$$
$$\text{Tax rate} = 50\%$$
$$\text{Salvage value at end of year } 12 = \$200$$

flow due to the investment must be taken into account, including any salvage value cash proceeds when the asset is sold.

2   Put the results of the step *1* computation in tabular form, showing the timing and amount of the cash flow (for example, as in Exhibit 8-2).

3   Analyze the cash flow using net present value or internal rate of return (these methods are described below) to determine whether the investment should be made.

Why is cash flow the proper measure of the costs and benefits of an investment? The answer is that cash flow represents the true inflow and outflow of purchasing power for the firm. When an asset is purchased, such purchasing power is sacrificed; when a net cash flow is earned on the asset in later periods, purchasing power is received. The future cash flow from an asset is the money generated by the asset that is available for payment to the firm's stockholders and bondholders as dividends and interest or to finance further investment. It is the stream of purchasing power provided by the asset and is therefore the measure of that asset's productivity.

A firm's cash budget (discussed in Chapter 14) and a firm's cash flow should be distinguished. The cash budget shows the forecasted cash transactions of the firm (or some subentity such as a division) for some stated time period. It is an estimate of cash receipts and cash disbursements based on an analysis of past performance and on the firm's plans for the future. A cash budget is used for planning operations and financing. Exhibit 14-4 illustrates a cash budget. The firm's forecasted cash flow [cash flow as defined in Eq. (8-1)] is readily computed using the data in the cash budget. Notice that, in contrast with the cash budget, cash flow does not include the cash effects of capital transactions (for example, interest payments, dividends, stock and bond sales, and so forth), but it represents the net cash flow generated by the firm's assets (or a single asset) that is available to those financing the company (stockholders and bondholders). Also, cash flow is often calculated for an individual investment and not just for an operating entity such as a department, division, or firm. Cash flow is used primarily to assess an investment's desirability, whereas a cash budget is ordinarily used for overall planning.

Cash Flow and Uncertainty

Generally, future cash flows are uncertain, and only estimates of these flows are available for evaluating an investment proposal. The estimate that is often used is **expected cash flow**, which will be discussed in Chapter 9. In

---

EXHIBIT 8-2
Net cash flow from the investment

Time	Net cash flow
Time 0 (when asset acquired)	− $1,200
Each year for years 1 to 11	$175
Year 12	$375

206

PART 2
The firm's investment,
financing, and dividend
decisions

the present chapter, we assume that all investments have the same level of risk. Further, we assume that a numerical estimate can be made of the cash flow in each future year from any investment. The cash flow estimate is an "educated guess" based upon available information. It is ordinarily somewhere between the highest and lowest possible figures that can be expected, in other words, a middle estimate. In Chapter 9 we will be more precise. Since in this chapter all investments are assumed to be of identical risk, all will be evaluated using the same cost of capital, k. Rate k can be viewed as the minimum acceptable rate of return on the investment. In the examples of this chapter, k will be 10 percent.

EVALUATION TECHNIQUES

After the cash flows have been estimated, they are evaluated to determine whether the investment should be undertaken. Several techniques are available to evaluate investment proposals. The chief ones are:

1   Present value
2   Internal rate of return (or simply rate of return)
3   Payback period
4   Accounting rate of return

A fifth approach that uses a profitability index will be discussed in the section on capital rationing.

Present Value

The time-value-of-money concept discussed in Chapter 4 can be used to evaluate the cash flows from an investment. The **present value** of a cash flow is what it is worth in today's dollars. Present value incorporates the time-value principle by **discounting** future dollars (computing their present value) using the appropriate discount rate (interest rate). In investment analysis, this discount rate is the cost of capital.

The present value rule states that an investment should be adopted only if the present value of the cash flow it generates in the future exceeds its cost, that is, if it has a positive **net present value** (**NPV**). The net present value of an asset equals

$$NPV = \begin{array}{c}\text{present value of}\\\text{future cash flows}\end{array} - \text{initial cost}$$

$$= \frac{CF_1}{1 + k} + \frac{CF_2}{(1 + k)^2} + \cdots + \frac{CF_n}{(1 + k)^n} - I$$

$$= CF_1(P/F, k, 1) + CF_2(P/F, k, 2)$$
$$+ \cdots + CF_n (P/F, k, n) - I \qquad (8\text{-}2)$$

where CF_1 = cash flow in period 1

CF_2 = cash flow in period 2, etc.

I = initial outlay or cost

k = cost of capital

The $(P/F, k, 1)$, $(P/F, k, 2)$, etc., terms are the present value factors discussed in Chapter 4.

If the future cash flow is a level annuity of CF per period for n periods (all cash flows are equal), then Eq. (8-2) becomes

$$\text{NPV(annuity)} = \frac{CF}{1 + k} + \frac{CF}{(1 + k)^2} + \cdots + \frac{CF}{(1 + k)^n} - I$$

$$= CF(P/A, k, n) - I \tag{8-3}$$

NPV is the net benefit that accrues to the firm from adopting the investment. A positive NPV means that the project yields a rate of return exceeding the cost of capital k. In this case, NPV is the total value in current dollars of the extraordinary return (the return above the cost of capital) earned by the investment. If a project's NPV = 0, it is just earning the cost of capital and is therefore just barely, or marginally, acceptable. If NPV is negative, less than the cost of capital is earned by the project; that is, the project is not even earning the required rate of return, and it should therefore be rejected.

In Appendix 8A, it is shown that the net present value of an investment is equal to the benefit of the investment to shareholders and that therefore net present value is a valid guide to project selection.

The Accept-Reject Decision Sometimes an investment decision involves the acceptance or rejection of a given opportunity and not the comparison of several alternatives. The present value method specifies that such an investment should be adopted if its NPV is greater than zero; if NPV = 0, it is a matter of indifference whether the project is accepted; and if NPV is less than zero, the project should be rejected.[2]

To illustrate the present value method, assume that a restaurant can buy a new sign that will increase net cash flow by attracting new customers. The choice is either to buy the particular sign or to obtain no new sign at all.

Cash flows from sign	
Initial outlay (I)	$3,500
Increase in annual cash flow for next 5 years	$1,000

The sign costs $3500, will last five years, and will increase net cash flow by an estimated $1000 in each of the next five years. Using Eq. (8-3) and assuming a cost of capital k of 10 percent, the NPV equals

---

[2] As is explained later in this section, we are assuming that the firm can obtain additional funds for investment at the cost of capital. At the end of the chapter, capital rationing (limited funds available) is considered in detail.

208

PART 2
The firm's investment,
financing, and dividend
decisions

$$NPV = \frac{\$1000}{1 + 0.10} + \frac{\$1000}{(1 + 0.10)^2} + \cdots + \frac{\$1000}{(1 + 0.10)^5} - \$3500$$

$$= \$1000(P/A, 10\%, 5) - \$3500$$

$$= \$1000(3.791) - \$3500$$

$$= \$3791 - \$3500 = \$291$$

Since the NPV of $291 is positive, the sign should be purchased. The $3791 is the value in today's dollars (the present value) of the future benefits from the asset, and the $3500 is the cost in today's dollars: The difference is the net gain, $291.

Choices between Alternatives   Many, perhaps most, investment decisions involve a choice from among several mutually exclusive alternatives rather than the simple accept-reject decision of a single alternative. Two alternatives are mutually exclusive if adopting one means that the other will not be adopted (for example, to buy machine A or machine B or neither, but not both). The present value rule dictates that the alternative having the highest NPV is best and it is accepted if, and only if, its NPV is positive (indifference if NPV = 0).

As an example, assume that a manufacturer is comparing two machines for its production line: the deluxe model, which costs $3000 and will raise net estimated cash flow by $900 per year for the next five years, and the economy model, with a smaller capacity, which costs $2000 and will raise net estimated cash flow by $610 per year for the next five years.

Cash flows of machine alternatives		
	Deluxe machine	Economy machine
Initial outlay (*I*)	$3,000	$2,000
Increase in annual cash flow for next 5 years(CF)	$ 900	$ 610

Using Eq. (8-3), we can compute the NPV of each, assuming a cost of capital of 10 percent:

$$NPV(\text{deluxe model}) = \$900(P/A, 10\%, 5) - \$3000$$

$$= \$900(3.791) - \$3000$$

$$= \$412$$

$$NPV(\text{economy model}) = \$610(P/A, 10\%, 5) - \$2000$$

$$= \$610(3.791) - \$2000$$

$$= \$313$$

The deluxe model is superior, since its NPV of $412 exceeds the economy model's NPV of $313. Further, since the deluxe model has an NPV exceeding zero, it should be purchased.

The Net Present Value Method Summarized   The net present value rule can be summarized as follows:

1   In an accept-reject decision, the investment is adopted if its NPV is positive. We are indifferent if its NPV = 0, and the investment is rejected if its NPV is negative.

2   In comparing mutually exclusive investment alternatives (at most, one alternative is to be accepted), we first determine which alternative has the highest NPV and reject all the other alternatives. We then accept the alternative with the highest NPV if its NPV exceeds zero. We are indifferent if its NPV = 0 and reject the alternative if its NPV is negative.

The above rules assume that the firm can obtain funds at the cost of capital (through borrowing, selling shares, etc.) as long as those funds can be profitably employed. Indeed, if this were not so, then "cost of capital" would have little meaning since "cost" means the price that must be paid to obtain something, in this case, capital or funds to finance investment. Later in this chapter, we will examine the case in which capital is limited or "rationed." In Chapters 9 and 10 we consider cases in which the cost of capital depends on the risk of the investment and the size of the capital budget.

The Internal Rate of Return

We can look at the above capital budgeting problems in a somewhat different way. Instead of discounting the cash flows at the cost of capital to determine net present value, we can ask the following question: What rate of return does the project earn? If the rate of return exceeds the cost of capital k, it is a profitable project since the cost of capital is the minimum required rate of return. If the project's rate of return just equals k, it is only marginal (we are indifferent as to whether it is accepted). If the project's rate of return is less than the cost of capital, it should be rejected.

Determining the IRR   In Chapter 4 (pages 79 to 87) we discussed methods for determining an unknown interest rate, for example, the rate earned on a share of stock. An internal rate of return is the rate we expect to earn on an investment project. The IRR is that rate which discounts a project's cash flow to an NPV of zero. Letting r signify the IRR, an investment's IRR is that rate r which satisfies the following relationship:

$$0 = \frac{CF_1}{1 + r} + \frac{CF_2}{(1 + r)^2} + \cdots + \frac{CF_n}{(1 + r)^n} - I$$

$$= CF_1(P/F, r, 1) + CF_2(P/F, r, 2) + \cdots$$
$$+ CF_n(P/F, r, n) - I \tag{8-4}$$

If the cash flow returns are a level annuity, that is, if $CF_1 = CF_2 = \cdots = CF_n = CF$, then Eq. (8-4) becomes

210

PART 2
The firm's investment,
financing, and dividend
decisions

$$0 = \frac{CF}{1 + r} + \frac{CF}{(1 + r)^2} + \cdots + \frac{CF}{(1 + r)^n} - I$$

$$= CF(P/A, r, n) - I \tag{8-5}$$

To illustrate the above method, assume that project H costs $3000 and generates cash flows of $2400 in the first year and $1440 in the second year. The cash flows are stated below.

Cash flows of project H
I = $3,000
CF_1 = $2,400
CF_2 = $1,440

Using Eq. (8-4), we find that the rate of return on project H is 20 percent (r = 20%) since:

$$0 = \frac{\$2400}{1.2} + \frac{\$1440}{(1.2)^2} - \$3000$$

$$= \$2000 + \$1000 - \$3000$$

Now that we have examined how an IRR is computed, let us take a closer look at what the IRR number really measures.

The Rate of Return Concept   To examine more closely what we mean by an investment's IRR assume a project requiring an initial outlay I and producing a stream of future net cash flows CF_1, CF_2, ..., CF_n, over the coming n periods. When we say that the project's IRR is some amount r, we mean that if at time 0 (now) we were to put amount I into a fund actually earning rate of return r each period, we could withdraw from the fund amount CF_1 one period from now, amount CF_2 two periods from now, and so on including CF_n n periods from now, and exactly exhaust the fund at the end of the n periods. It is similar to the idea developed in Chapter 4 of purchasing an annuity currently that pays a future income and provides a rate of return equal to the interest rate. Here, for an investment project, the price of the annuity is I, the income it provides is the CF_1, CF_2, ..., CF_n stream, and the rate of return is r. We can illustrate this concept using project H above.

The rate of return on project H is 20 percent. As illustrated in Figure 8-1, if we deposit $3000 at time 0 in a fund, we will have $3600 in the fund at time 1 assuming a 20 percent rate of return earned during the first period. Since we want to produce a cash flow CF_1 = $2400, we withdraw $2400 from the fund at time 1 and leave $1200 in the fund. One period later, at time 2, the $1200 has earned 20 percent and has therefore grown to $1440 ($1200 + 0.20 × $1200), which we can now withdraw to produce our time 2 cash flow of $1440.

A project with the cash flows I = $3000, CF_1 = $2400, and CF_2 = $1440 therefore implies that 20 percent per period is being earned on the $3000 investment.

Another insight into the IRR approach emerges by examining Eqs. (8-4) and (8-5). To compute the IRR on an investment, we plug in I and the cash flows CF_1 to CF_n into (8-4) or (8-5) and then solve for r. Since (8-4) and (8-5) are simply present value equations with the present value equal to zero, in determining r we are determining that interest rate which would imply that the investment has a net present value of zero. Keep in mind that the interest rate we used in Eqs. (8-2) and (8-3) is k, the cost of capital, and this will equal r, the IRR, only if $r = k$, that is, only if the project has an actual NPV equal to zero. (Remember in our discussion of present value that we said that if NPV $= 0$, the project is just earning the cost of capital k.) If NPV *exceeds* zero using cost of capital k, then ordinarily r exceeds k, and the project is earning a rate of return that exceeds the cost of capital.[3]

In Figure 8-2 the relationships between NPV, k, and r are shown. At the cost of capital k of 10 percent, the NPV of project H equals

$$\text{NPV(project H)} = \frac{\$2400}{1.1} + \frac{\$1440}{(1.1)^2} - \$3000$$

$$= \$2182 + \$1190 - \$3000$$

$$= \$372$$

The NPV(project H) schedule shows an NPV $= \$372$ at a discount rate of 10 percent. Each point on the schedule shows the NPV of project H along the

[3] Actually, a positive NPV necessarily implies that the investment's rate of return exceeds the cost of capital only if the investment involves an initial outlay (cost) and produces a non-negative cash flow return in future periods. This is the type of investment considered in the examples in this chapter.

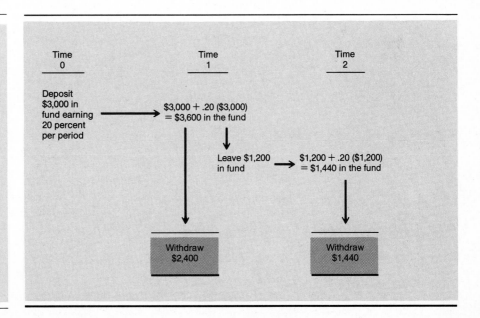

FIGURE 8-1

Internal rate of return is equivalent to interest earned on a deposit in a fund.

212

PART 2
The firm's investment,
financing, and dividend
decisions

vertical axis for each discount rate shown along the horizontal axis. Notice that if the discount rate k were 20 percent, NPV(project H) = 0; therefore, internal rate of return r for project H is 20 percent, since r is that rate which sets the NPV equal to zero [see Eq. (8-4)]. In short, we can view the internal rate of return, r, as the cost of capital which would just make the project marginally acceptable (NPV = 0). Project H would be just marginally accept-able (NPV = 0) if the cost of capital k equalled 20 percent, and therefore its IRR is 20 percent; but since k equals 10 percent, project H earns more than the cost of capital (r exceeds k) and is quite profitable (it has a positive NPV).

The Accept-Reject Decision   The IRR method requires that if a particular investment is either to be accepted or rejected (and not to be compared with some alternative investment), it should be accepted if its IRR exceeds the cost of capital. The rationale is that if an investment earns more than the cost of the funds used to finance it, it should be adopted. We can apply the rule to the restaurant sign example used earlier. The sign costs $3500 and produces a net cash flow of $1000 in each of the next five years. Using Eq. (8-5) to determine r, the IRR, we solve the following:

$1000(P/A, r, 5) = 3500

or

$$(P/A, r, 5) = 3.5$$

Using the tables, we find that r = 13.2 percent, that is, $(P/A, 13.2\%, 5) = 3.5$.[4] The project returns 13.2 percent per year, and this exceeds the cost of

_____
[4] Using interpolation (see Chap. 4), we find that $(P/A, 13.2\%, 5) = 3.5$.

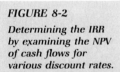

FIGURE 8-2

Determining the IRR by examining the NPV of cash flows for various discount rates.

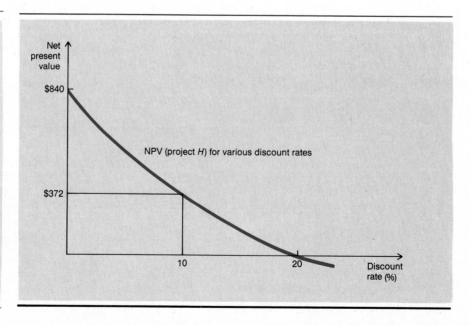

capital k of 10 percent. Therefore, the sign should be purchased, a conclusion that is consistent with that reached earlier using net present value.

Choices between Alternatives—the Incremental Approach   The IRR method can be used to compare two or more alternative investments when at most one alternative is to be accepted (mutually exclusive options). However, it is somewhat more difficult to use than is the present value method in the same situation and must be applied rather carefully. The IRR procedure consists of first determining which alternative investment is the most profitable by applying the incremental approach (described below) and then determining whether that most profitable alternative is sufficiently profitable to adopt. The alternative is adopted only if its IRR exceeds the cost of capital. (It is shown in the next section that it is incorrect to simply select the investment with the highest IRR.)

To demonstrate the method, we can refer back to the example involving a comparison between the deluxe machine (alternative D) and the economy machine (alternative E). We assume as before that the cost of capital is 10 percent. The cash flows were as shown below:

				Time			
Alternative	0	1	2	3	4	5	IRR
Deluxe machine (D)	− $3,000	$900	$900	$900	$900	$900	15.2%
Economy machine (E)	− $2,000	$610	$610	$610	$610	$610	16.0%

To compare alternatives D and E using the IRR method, we must first ask whether the additional (or incremental) investment of $1000 in D as compared with E is justified. In other words, we look at the *difference* between D and E. The difference between the cash flows of the two alternatives is:

	0	1	2	3	4	5	IRR
D − E	− $1,000	$290	$290	$290	$290	$290	13.8%

If we pick D instead of E, an additional investment of $1000 must be made and we would expect to receive an additional $290 per year for five years. The IRR on the additional investment is found to be 13.8 percent by using the IRR equation. If the firm's cost of capital k is less than 13.8 percent, then D is preferred to E; if k is greater than 13.8 percent, E is better than D. Since the cost of capital equals 10 percent (by assumption), D is preferred to E. If the cost of capital were 15 percent, then E would be chosen over D because the additional investment required by D does not provide a high enough rate of return.

The next step is to decide whether the better alternative, D, is sufficiently profitable to be acceptable. D is acceptable since its rate of return of 15.2 percent exceeds the cost of capital of 10 percent.

214

PART 2
The firm's investment,
financing, and dividend
decisions

If we have more than two alternatives available, then we must pick the best one by making a series of comparisons. Suppose there are four alternatives: A, B, C, and D. We can start off with any two and find out which one is the better of the two by the procedure just illustrated. Suppose we look at A and B first and decide that A is better. Then we could compare A with C in the same way. Suppose that A is again more profitable. Finally we must compare A with D. Suppose D is better than A. By this process we could determine that D is the best of the four alternatives. Now we need only to decide whether D is worth undertaking at all by comparing its rate of return with the cost of capital as we did above; D should be adopted if, and only if, its rate of return exceeds the cost of capital.

A common error in using the IRR method to compare two alternatives is to choose the one with the higher IRR (rather than using the incremental approach). Although this is a very natural mistake, it can mean adopting less profitable investments. This is clear from the above example since we found that, if the cost of capital were less than 13.8 percent (10 percent in the example), D was preferred to E even though D had the lower IRR (15.2 percent vs. 16.0 percent). It may appear strange that the firm should pass up a 16.0 percent investment (E) for a 15.2 percent investment (D). But, the 16 percent is *not* "passed up" since we can view D as being a package of two investments with the following characteristics:

	0	1	2	3	4	5	NPV	IRR
E	− $2,000	$610	$610	$610	$610	$610	$313	16.0%
D − E	− $1,000	$290	$290	$290	$290	$290	$ 99	13.8%
D	− $3,000	$900	$900	$900	$900	$900	$412	15.2%

Accepting D instead of E means taking on the investment package E *and* (D − E). E is an investment of $2000 with a rate of return of 16 percent and (D − E) is an investment of $1000 with a rate of return of 13.8 percent. The average rate of return on the total package [D = E + (D − E)] is 15.2 percent. Therefore, taking D over E means effectively investing in E plus another investment (D − E) that has a rate of return of 13.8 percent. If (D − E) is a good investment, which it is since 13.8 percent exceeds the cost of capital of 10 percent, you will want to take D in preference to E, since with D you in effect get investment E plus another good investment (D − E).

To further emphasize the error in simply choosing the investment with the highest IRR, assume two mutually exclusive investments, investment A involving an initial outlay of $1 and returning $10 one year hence (an IRR of 900 percent) and investment B involving an initial cost of $100,000 and returning $200,000 one year later (an IRR of 100 percent). If the cost of capital is 10 percent, the NPV(A) = $8.09 and the NPV(B) = $81,820. It should be clear that B is preferred to A even though A has the higher IRR. This is an extreme example used to highlight the need to use the incremental approach described above. Although actual situations are not so blatantly obvious, the same principle will still apply.

In the examples we just examined, the alternatives differed in the amount of initial investment; however, this is not the only situation in which simply picking the option with the highest rate of return can lead to problems. Alternatives with the same initial investment but having unequal lives or just markedly different cash flow patterns over identical lives can also present this problem (see Appendix 8B, Section 1). In general, therefore, picking the alternative with the highest rate of return can be incorrect. Instead, the incremental approach outlined here should be used.

IRR, Present Value, and Reinvestment Rate Assumptions   Although, as we just noted, simply picking the mutually exclusive investment with the highest IRR can lead to mistakes, there is a special case in which the investment with the highest IRR is best. In this case, the alternative with the highest IRR is the one that would also be chosen using the incremental IRR method or the present value method. The special case arises if the mutually exclusive investments require the same initial outlay and if the future cash flows from each investment can be reinvested by the firm in other projects which earn that investment's IRR until some particular future date, where that future date is the same for all the mutually exclusive projects. For example, mutually exclusive investments A and B might each involve an initial outlay of $1000 in 1985; A has a three-year life and an internal rate of return of 20 percent, and all future cash flows generated by A will be reinvested by the firm in other projects to earn 20 percent per year (A's IRR) until 1991; and B has a four-year life and an internal rate of return of 30 percent, and all future cash flows will be reinvested to earn 30 percent per year (B's IRR) until 1991. In this special case, B is better than A because B has the higher IRR. B would also be chosen using the incremental rate of return and the present value methods. This special case is discussed in greater detail in Section 2 of Appendix 8B. It should be pointed out that this case does *not* often occur in practice, and it is ordinarily *not* correct to choose the mutually exclusive option with the highest IRR. In general, either the incremental IRR method or the present value method should be used in choosing from among mutually exclusive investments.

There is a broader issue than the specialized case just discussed above. This issue relates to how the rate of return that can be earned on *future* investments of the firm depends on which *current* investments are adopted. As explained in Section 1 of Appendix 8B, if the profitability of future investments (regardless of how profitable) does *not* depend on which current investments are adopted, then we can ignore the future investments in evaluating current projects. This was the assumption made above in explaining the present value and IRR methods, and both these methods are completely consistent and valid in this case. There are situations, however, in which investments lead to future profitable opportunities that would not be available to the firm if the investments had not been undertaken. For example, firms that established footholds in foreign countries in the 1950s often found that they had an advantageous position in those foreign markets even in the 1980s. If the choice of current investments affects the rate of return that can be earned on future investments, then in

216

PART 2
The firm's investment,
financing, and dividend
decisions

evaluating current projects it becomes necessary to analyze the cash flows from the current investments *and* also the cash flows from the future investment opportunities that depend on the current investments. Either the present value method or the IRR method can be used to analyze these present and future project cash flows. Both present value and IRR are appropriate for such an analysis whether it is assumed that the future investments earn a rate of return equal to the cost of capital, equal to each investment's IRR, or equal to any other rate, and whether the future investments are financed by reinvesting the future cash flows from current investments or are financed by any other source. The method of analyzing this type of problem is presented in detail in Section 3 of Appendix 8B.

IRR and Present Value Compared In most situations the internal rate of return method properly applied and present value provide the same choices. The IRR approach has the advantage of providing a rate of return that is easy to interpret and for that reason is particularly popular in industry. On the other hand, computing a rate of return is usually more difficult than computing a present value, although, with electronic calculators and computers readily available, this is not a serious drawback. In addition, the incremental IRR method, as we have seen, is conceptually more complex when choosing among alternatives. Most important, in some cases the cash flows imply more than one internal rate of return or no meaningful rate of return at all.[5] In these cases, the IRR method cannot be used whereas present value can be. Finally, as is explained in the previous section and in Appendix 8B, even if special reinvestment rate assumptions are made regarding the current projects being evaluated, the present value method appropriately applied is the easiest method to use.

Overall, it is our judgment that present value is superior to internal rate of return as a capital budgeting approach. Any problem that can be treated with IRR can also be analyzed using present value, whereas the reverse is not the case. In Appendix 8A, it is shown that the gain to shareholders from an investment equals its net present value and the NPV is therefore a proper guide to selecting investments.[6]

---

[5] Some cash flows imply more than one internal rate of return or only rates of return involving $\sqrt{-1}$ (imaginary numbers). In these cases the IRR method cannot be used. Such problems will not arise if the cash flow involves an initial outflow (I_0) and positive cash flows thereafter. They can arise if some future cash flows are negative (cash outflows). For example, if an investment involves initial outlay $I_0 = \$10$, time 1 cash flow $CF_1 = \$150$ and time 2 cash flow $CF_2 = -\$140$, then the internal rates of return are 0 percent and 440 percent. For a complete discussion of the problems with the internal rate of return method, see Haley and Schall, *The Theory of Financial Decisions*, 2d ed. (New York: McGraw-Hill, 1979), Appendix 3a.

[6] If we were to take into account flotation (sales) costs of issuing securities, investor costs in buying and selling securities, and personal tax effects, net present value has to be amended (so do IRR and other capital budgeting techniques). This topic is not appropriate for discussion here but has been explored in the financial literature. One proposed approach is the use of "adjusted present value"; see S. Myers, "Interaction of Investment and Financing Decisions," *Journal of Finance* (March 1974), pp. 1–25.

The **payback period** is the length of time it takes to recover the initial investment on a project. For example, if a $1000 investment returns an aftertax cash flow per year of $400, the payback period is $2\frac{1}{2}$ years ($1000/$400). The payback period method dictates acceptance of a project only if the project has a payback period less than some level specified by management. In comparing two alternative options using this method, the one with the smaller payback period is preferred and is accepted if its payback period is less than the specified requirement.

The payback period approach has a number of problems. First, there is no consideration of returns after the required payback period. Assume that the firm has projects Q and R from which to choose and has set the required payback period at three years. Thus, only if the project recovers the entire investment within three years is the project acceptable. From Exhibit 8-3, we can see that the payback period of Q is 2 years and the payback period of R is 2.1 years. Both projects meet the three-year requirement, but Q is preferred since its payback period is less. However, notice that R returns a cash flow at time 3 of $1000, whereas Q returns only $25 after its two-year payback period. These post-payback period returns are ignored in using the method since the standard is based entirely on the time required to recover capital. Beyond the payback period, returns are disregarded. Even though payback dictates the choice of Q, at a 10 percent cost of capital the present value of Q is $-$138 and of R is $545. Present value, therefore, dictates the selection of R, the opposite result from that using payback.[7] A primary reason for the different results for the two methods is that, in contrast to payback, present value does not ignore returns beyond the payback period.

Notice secondly that payback also ignores the pattern of returns within the payback period; i.e., the time value of money is not taken into account. Compare assets S and T described in Exhibit 8-4. S and T each have a

---

[7] It is easily shown that the IRR method using incremental analysis also dictates the choice of R.

EXHIBIT 8-3
Payback period comparison

	Time	Cash flows	
		Q	R
Initial investment	0	− $1,000	− $1,000
Returns	1	200	600
	2	800	300
	3	25	1,000
Payback period		2 years	2.1 years
Net present value at cost of capital of 10 percent		− $138	$545

218

PART 2
The firm's investment,
financing, and dividend
decisions

payback period of two years and are therefore equivalent on this basis. However, since we know that a dollar received sooner is better due to the time value of money, project T is the better investment as indicated by the greater net present value of T. Payback completely fails to account for the differences in the pattern of returns.

In spite of the flaws in the payback period method, it is still widely used. Three rationales have been offered in payback's defense. First, after the required payback period the uncertainty may be so great for some projects that requiring recovery of capital within that period is a good way to avoid undue risk. However, this argument does not confront the time-value-of-money problem within the payback period illustrated above for investments S and T (Exhibit 8-4). Furthermore, risk is rarely so great that returns beyond that period should be completely ignored. As explained in Chapter 9, if risk is increasing over time, the discount rate used under the present value method can be adjusted to take this increasing risk into account. A second argument sometimes advanced in support of payback is that in practice it is generally used with other criteria which do account for the time value of money and for the post-payback period returns. But this is a roundabout way of saying that these two latter considerations must be taken into account. If this is so, why not employ the present value criterion in the first place?

The third, and probably weakest, argument used to defend payback is its simplicity. The expense of a more careful analysis is generally more than compensated for by better investment decisions. Further, with the availability of present value tables and computers, any computational advantages of payback have become negligible.

In conclusion, payback has very little to recommend it and can be highly misleading. A comparison of available approaches clearly favors the present value and IRR methods.

EXHIBIT 8-4
Payback period comparison

	Time	Cash flows	
		S	T
Initial investment	0	− $500	− $500
Returns	1	100	400
	2	400	100
	3	500	500
Payback period		2 years	2 years
Net present value at a cost of capital of 10%[a]		$297	$322

[a] $NPV(S) = 0.9091\ (\$100) + 0.8264\ (\$400) + 0.7513\ (\$500) - \$500 = \$297;$
$NPV(T) = 0.9091\ (\$400) + 0.8264\ (\$100) + 0.7513\ (\$500) - \$500 = \$322.$

The accounting rate of return (ARR) equals the average annual aftertax accounting profit generated by the investment divided by the average investment. That is,

$$ARR = \frac{\text{average annual profit from investment}}{(I + S)/2} \qquad (8\text{-}6)$$

where S is the salvage or liquidation value of the asset at the end of its useful life, and therefore $(I + S)/2$ is the average investment in the asset during its useful life. ARR is a misleading measure of the benefits from an asset for two reasons: Profit does not generally equal the asset's cash flow and may have a pattern very much different from that of cash flow and, second, the time value of money is ignored by the ARR method.

To illustrate the ARR method, assume two assets, F and G, each of which requires an initial outlay I of \$20,000. Each asset lasts for four years and is depreciated on a straight-line basis with zero salvage value (S) at the end of the four years; depreciation is therefore \$5000 per year on F or G. These data and the accounting profit for each asset are shown in Exhibit 8-5. If the cost of capital were 10 percent, asset F with a net present value of \$17,808 would be preferred to asset G with a net present value of \$15,410. But, using ARR, G is preferred to F since G's ARR of 70 percent exceeds F's ARR of 65 percent. Present value produces the correct results, and therefore ARR can lead to the wrong choices.[8]

[8] It is assumed in Exhibit 8-5 that aftertax profit equals cash flow less depreciation. This will be so if cash revenues R and cash expenses E are revenues and expenses for tax purposes. Then cash flow $= R - E -$ taxes, and profit $= R - E -$ depreciation $-$ taxes $=$ cash flow $-$ depreciation. Also, the definition of the ARR stated in Eq. (8-6) is one of many alternative definitions that have been proposed; one of these alternatives uses I in the denominator instead of $[(I + S)/2]$ as in (8-6). All the commonly proposed ARR measures are inferior to present value as capital budgeting criteria because they do not evaluate cash flow or do not *properly* take into account the time value of money.

EXHIBIT 8-5
Comparison of accounting rate of return (ARR) and present value

	Asset F		Asset G	
	Annual profit	Cash flow	Annual profit	Cash flow
1	\$11,000	\$16,000	\$ 1,000	\$ 6,000
2	11,000	16,000	1,000	6,000
3	2,000	7,000	1,000	6,000
4	2,000	7,000	25,000	30,000
Total	\$26,000	\$46,000	\$28,000	\$48,000
ARR[a]	65%		70%	
NPV		\$17,808		\$15,410

[a] ARR $=$ (Total profit/4 years) $\div$ \$10,000.

INDUSTRY USE OF CAPITAL BUDGETING TECHNIQUES

Until the 1960s, only the largest firms in capital-intensive industries employed advanced capital budgeting tools (e.g., present value and internal rate of return). Other firms used simpler and less satisfactory techniques such as payback and accounting rate of return. Although the less accurate techniques are still widely employed, a majority of the largest 250 United States firms in terms of capital outlays use either present value or internal rate of return for capital expenditure analysis. Surveys of large United States firms by Klammer and by Schall, Sundem, and Geijsbeek revealed that the use of the present value and IRR approaches has greatly increased since the 1950s.[9] By 1970, a significant majority of firms had at least one member of the company staff assigned to full-time capital budgeting. Not surprisingly, the companies using the more sophisticated capital budgeting methods were those with larger investment budgets, e.g., oil and chemical firms.

The increase in the use of present value and internal rate of return demonstrates that companies will adopt improved methods of analysis if they produce earnings benefits. The benefits accrue because better choices are made in selecting projects and in determining the amount to be invested. There is a cost to employing superior techniques, however. Since more information is required, computers may be needed to perform the analysis, and personnel with an understanding of these techniques must be found (and paid a salary commensurate with their talents). For these reasons, small firms and less-capital-intensive firms have been slower to adopt the newer approaches. However, as the costs of obtaining information and employing computers decline, and as understanding of the approaches becomes more widespread, more firms will find it profitable to modernize their capital budgeting procedures.

EXAMPLE PROBLEMS

We have introduced several techniques for assessing the desirability of capital investment projects. Of the techniques discussed, present value and internal rate of return are most likely to lead to choices that benefit shareholders. The example problems below illustrate several situations that are commonly encountered in practice. We use the present value method in the solutions; problem **13** at the end of the chapter requires that the example problems below be solved using the IRR approach. The first problem involves an asset addition that reduces costs but does not affect revenues; the second problem deals with an asset addition that increases sales *and* costs; and the third problem involves the replacement of an existing asset with a new asset. In the problems below we assume for simplicity that, for tax purposes, depreciation is spread over the asset's useful life and is computed assuming a zero salvage value for the asset. We also ignore the investment tax credit (which is discussed later in this chapter).

[9] See Thomas Klammer, "Empirical Evidence of the Adoption of Sophisticated Capital Budgeting Techniques," *Journal of Business* (July 1972); and Lawrence D. Schall, Gary L. Sundem, and William R. Geijsbeek, Jr., "Survey and Analysis of Capital Budgeting Methods," *Journal of Finance* (March 1978).

Assume that Streak Wholesalers is considering the acquisition of a delivery truck that will allow Streak to do its own shipping rather than purchase shipping services from another firm. The new asset, a truck, is not a substitute for an old one already in operation and is therefore defined here as an asset addition (rather than replacement). Suppose that the benefits from the truck would be a reduction in shipping costs. By reducing costs, the net cash flow of the firm as a whole is increased. The estimates of the costs and benefits associated with this investment decision are shown in Exhibit 8-6. Notice that although the truck reduces annual shipping costs by $15,000, additional expenses for a driver and for upkeep of the truck are also taken into account. These expenses are $13,000 per year, and therefore the return from acquiring the truck before taxes is $2000 per year. Taxes are then deducted in order to determine the aftertax benefit from making the new investment. Since the truck is a depreciable asset for tax purposes, depreciation must be deducted from the increased returns due to the truck

---

EXHIBIT 8-6
Asset addition: Asset reduces costs

Truck purchase price:
$6,400 (Truck will last 8 years with an $800 liquidation value)[a]

Returns per period for 8 years:

Reduction in shipping expenses		$15,000
Deduct: Salary for driver	$9,000	
Upkeep, gas, etc.	4,000	
Return before taxes ($15,000 − $9,000 − $4,000)		$2,000

Taxes:

Pretax return	$ 2,000
Deduct: Depreciation on truck[b]	800
Net taxable income	$ 1,200
Tax at 50% (0.50 × $1,200)	600
Increase in annual net cash flow ($2,000 − $600)	$1,400

Time	Cash flow
0 (cost)	− $6,400
1–7 (returns per year)	$1,400
8 (return)	$2,200[c]

Net present value at 10% (cost of capital):

$$\text{NPV} = \$1,400 \ (P/A, 10\%, 7) + \$2,200 \ (P/F, 10\%, 8) - \$6,400$$
$$= \$1,400 \ (4.868) + \$2,200 \ (0.4665) - \$6,400$$
$$= \$1,442$$

[a] A zero salvage value is assumed in computing tax deductible depreciation.
[b] Depreciation on a straight-line basis = $6,400 cost /8 years = $800 per year.
[c] Aftertax cash flow from use + aftertax salvage value = $1,400 + $800 = $2,200.

222

PART 2
The firm's investment,
financing, and dividend
decisions

in order to determine the part of the returns that is taxable; in the example, this taxable return is $1200. Applying a tax rate of 50 percent and subtracting the resulting taxes of $600 produces a net cash return from the asset of $1400 per year. As shown in Exhibit 8-6, the net present value of the project is $1442 and therefore the project should be accepted. The truck would be a good investment.

Asset Addition: Asset Increases Sales and Costs

In the above example, it was assumed that the firm's sales were unaffected by the acquisition of the delivery truck. The benefits from the truck were a reduction in operating expenses. It is also possible that a new investment has an impact on the firm's sales as well as upon operating costs. For example, assume that a new machine, if purchased, will enable the firm to increase annual sales by $6000, increase cost of goods sold by $2500, and increase operating expenses by $500, producing a new rise in firm's pretax cash flow of $3000 annually ($6000 − $2500 − $500). Let the new machine cost $6000 and have a five-year life with no salvage value. Using the same method as before, it is shown in Exhibit 8-7 that the change in aftertax cash flow is $2100 per year. The net present value of the machine is $1961, and it should therefore be purchased.

Replacement of an Existing Asset

Firms frequently consider the possibility of replacing assets currently in operation. Even if the old asset is economically productive, the new asset may be sufficiently more productive to warrant the replacement. In determining whether to replace, the crucial question is whether the added initial expenditure for the new asset (less the market value received from liquidating the old asset) is justified by the increase in the firm's cash flow (aftertax cash flow from new asset minus aftertax cash from the asset being replaced). That is, are the incremental cash flow benefits from the changeover sufficient to warrant the initial investment required by the replacment? An example will clarify the approach.

A new machine costing $24,000 can be acquired to replace a machine presently in use ("old" machine); the old machine was purchased four years ago for $5000 and has a current liquidation value of $3000. Assume initially that the current liquidation value of the old machine equals its book value for tax purposes and that, therefore, there is no gain or loss on sale of the old machine. (Later we explain how to deal with tax gains and losses on asset sales.) Therefore, the net outlay required to acquire the new machine is $21,000, the amount to be paid for the new machine less the amount received for the old machine. The old machine could be maintained in service for six years and the new machine has a life of six years.[10] The year 6

---

[10] The example presented below makes the simplifying assumption that the remaining life of the old asset currently being used by the firm equals the life of a new asset being considered as a replacement. This assumption, although unrealistic, allows us to present the basic approach to replacement problems. This approach is appropriate even when the lives of the old and new assets differ. However, if the remaining life of the old asset does not equal the life of the new asset, then we have to consider future replacments and we encounter the problem of comparing investments with unequal lives. This complicates the analysis but does not alter the basic method for computing or analyzing the cash flows. The problem of comparing investments with unequal lives is discussed later in this chapter.

aftertax liquidation value of the old machine will be zero and the year 6 aftertax liquidation value of the new machine will be $5000. As shown in Exhibit 8-8, the new machine will increase output and thereby raise sales by $1500, will reduce nondepreciation production expenses by $7000, and will consequently raise pretax net returns (sales − nondepreciation expenses) by $8500. The $7000 expense reduction equals the cost savings due to more efficient production with the new machine less any increased expenses involved in producing the additional units sold. The firm's aftertax cash flow increases by $6000 per year for the six years due to use of the new machine. In year 6, there is an added cash flow of $5000 due to liquidation of the new machine; the total cash flow increase in the sixth year due to the new machine is therefore $11,000 ($6000 + $5000).

As shown in Exhibit 8-8, the additional cash flows due to the replacement are an added outlay of $21,000 initially, an increase of $6000 per year for the next five years, and an increase of $11,000 in the sixth year. The cash flow has a net present value of $7956, and therefore the replacement should be made.

EXHIBIT 8-7
Asset addition: Asset increases sales

Machine purchase price:
  $6,000 (Machine will last 5 years with no salvage value)[a]

Returns per period for 5 years:

Increase in sales	$6,000
Deduct: Increases in cost of goods sold	
($2,500) and operating expenses ($500)	3,000
Return before taxes ($6,000 − $3,000)	$3,000

Taxes:

Pretax return	$3,000	
Deduct: Depreciation on machine[b]	1,200	
Net taxable income	$1,800	
Tax at 50% (0.50 × $1,800)		900
Increase in annual net cash flow ($3,000 − $900)		$2,100

Time	Cash flow
0 (cost)	− $6,000
1–5(returns per year)	$2,100

Net present value at 10% (cost of capital):
  NPV = $2,100 (P/A, 10%, 5) − $6,000
     = $2,100 (3.791) − $6,000
     = $1,961

[a] The machine has no salvage value for tax purposes and a zero estimated liquidation value in five years; therefore annual depreciation equals (machine's cost)/(machine's useful life) = $6,000/5 years = $1,200 per year.
[b] See note a.

224

PART 2
The firm's investment,
financing, and dividend
decisions

The Treatment of Gains and Losses on Asset Sales[11]   In the above problem we assumed that the current liquidation value of the old machine equalled its current book value (both $3000) and therefore there was no gain or loss on selling the old machine. If the liquidation value differs from the book value for tax purposes ("tax basis" of the asset), there will be a gain or loss on the sale of the old asset that must be included in the analysis. It is important

[11] See Chap. 3 for a discussion of gains and losses on depreciable assets.

EXHIBIT 8-8
Replacement problem

1. Initial outlay:

Price of new machine	$24,000
Current aftertax liquidation value of old machine	3,000
Net outlay for new machine	$21,000

2. Firm's annual cash flow for the next six years (years 1 to 6) with old and new machine excluding year 6 salvage value of new machine

Cash flow variable	With old machine (a)	With new machine (b)	Change due to new machine (col. b − col. a)
1. Sales	$100,000	$101,500	$1,500
2. Nondepreciation expenses	57,000	50,000	− 7,000
3. Sales − nondepreciation expenses [(1) − (2)]	43,000	51,500	8,500
4. Depreciation[a]	10,500	14,000	3,500
5. Taxable income [(3) − (4)]	32,500	37,500	5,000
6. Taxes [0.5 × (5)]	16,250	18,750	2,500
7. Net cash flow [(3) − (6)]	26,750	32,750	6,000

3. Year 6 salvage value:

Year 6 aftertax liquidation value of new machine	$5,000
Year 6 aftertax liquidation value of old machine	0
Added year 6 asset liquidation cash flow with new machine	$5,000

Time	Additional cash flow due to new machine
0 (cost)	− $21,000
1–5 (annual return)	6,000
6 (return)	11,000[b]

Net present value of replacement (at 10% cost of capital):

$$\text{NPV(replacement)} = \$6,000 \ (P/A, \ 10\%, \ 5)$$
$$+ \ \$11,000 \ (P/F, \ 10\%, \ 6) \ - \ \$21,000$$
$$= \ \$6,000 \ (3.791) \ + \ \$11,000 \ (0.5645) \ - \ \$21,000$$
$$= \ \$7,956$$

[a] Depreciation on the old machine is assumed to be $500 per year; depreciation on new machine = ($24,000/6 years) = $4,000 per year; firm's depreciation on all *other* assets = $10,000 per year.
[b] $11,000 in year 6 = $6,000 from asset's use + $5,000 aftertax salvage value.

to note that the tax effect of a gain or loss on a single asset depends on the gains and losses incurred during the period on *other* asset dispositions, since gains and losses are combined in computing taxable income. Furthermore, the tax treatment of real estate is different from the tax treatment of other business assets. The implication of all this is that no simple rule can be applied in computing the taxability of a gain or loss on an individual asset. The overall situation of the firm regarding asset gains and losses on *all* assets sold during the period must be known.[12]

To see how to treat a gain in analyzing an asset replacement, assume that the old machine in the example in Exhibit 8-8 has a liquidation value of $5000 (instead of $3000). This implies a taxable gain of $2000 (liquidation value − book value). Assume that the tax rate on the gain is 50 percnt (in light of other asset dispositions made during the period); the tax is therefore $1000 (0.50 × $2000). The current aftertax liquidation value of the old machine is $4000, the $5000 current liquidation value less the $1000 tax on the gain. This $4000 amount would replace the "current liquidation value of the old machine" of $3000 at the top of Exhibit 8-8. The net outlay for the new machine therefore becomes $20,000 ($24,000 − $4000), and the net present value of the replacement becomes $8956 instead of the $7956 shown at the bottom of Exhibit 8-8.

If an asset is sold at a loss (at less than book value), the loss is a tax deductible expense that reduces taxes payable by the firm. To illustrate, assume that the liquidation value of the old machine in the Exhibit 8-8 example is $2000 (instead of $3000), which is less than the $3000 book value. This implies a loss upon liquidation of $1000 (book value − liquidation value). The $1000 loss is tax deductible and this tax deduction reduces the firm's taxes. Assume that the tax deduction of $1000 reduces firm taxes by $500 in the example. The $500 tax benefit is added to the $2000 liquidation value to compute the net liquidation value of the old machine, which is therefore $2500. This $2500 amount replaces the $3000 at the top of Exhibit 8-8; the net outlay for the new machine therefore becomes $21,500 ($24,000 − $2500), and the net present value of the replacement becomes $7456 instead of $7956.

Problems **16** through **19** at the end of this chapter concern asset replacements that involve gains or losses on the sale of the replaced asset.

SPECIAL PROBLEMS IN INVESTMENT ANALYSIS

This section considers four issues that commonly arise in analyzing capital expenditures: comparing investments with different lives, the treatment of the investment tax credit, incorporating inflation in the analysis, and the evaluation of projects that affect one another's cash flows.

[12] Ordinarily, if an asset used in a business has been held no longer than six months when it is sold (retired), a gain on the sale is treated as ordinary income and a loss is treated as an ordinary loss in the year of sale. If the asset is not real estate and was held more than six months, a gain on the asset may in part be treated as a long-term capital gain (under Sections 1231 and 1245 of the Internal Revenue Code) if the sale price exceeds the original cost of the asset. If the sale price is equal to or less than original cost, all the gain is ordinary income because of depreciation recapture under Section 1245. The treatent of real estate (Section 1250) is more generous than the treatment of non-real estate in that a larger proportion of gains on real estate may be subject to long-term capital gains taxation.

Until now, in comparing mutually exclusive investments we have assumed that the lives of the investments were the same. Often two or more options being compared do not have equal lives. Strictly speaking, to analyze such investments using present value or IRR, it is generally necessary to evaluate them for equal periods of time. To do this, we merely ask: "What would we do after the shorter-lived asset expires, if we were to obtain it instead of acquiring the longer-lived asset?" The examples below will illustrate the problem and its solution. We will then observe that in many cases an approximation technique is adequate and that often we need not evaluate the investments for exactly equal periods of time.

Assume that a firm is comparing machines M_1 and M_2. M_1, which will last six years, costs $1000 at time 0 and will yield a net cash flow of $400 per year. M_1, if purchased, will be replaced at time 6 by M_1', which will cost $1200 and will yield $400 per year (from time 7 to time 12). M_2 will last for twelve years, will cost $1800 at time 0, and will yield $400 per year for twelve years. The point here is that the comparison should be between the NPV of M_1 and M_1' [signified NPV($M_1 + M_1'$)] and the NPV of M_2 [signified NPV(M_2)]. We can see from Exhibit 8-9 that this comparison leads us to choose M_1 now and to replace it with M_1' at time 6 rather than to obtain M_2 now, since NPV($M_1 + M_1'$) = $1048 and NPV($M_2$) = $926. It is improper to simply compare the NPV of M_1 (ignoring the replacement with M_1' at time 6) with the NPV of M_2. If we had done this, we would have chosen M_2 since NPV(M_2) = $926 and NPV($M_1$) = $742.

In the above example, the two options [option ($M_1 + M_1'$) and option M_2] had identical time durations of twelve years. Often, to establish identical durations for options being compared, it is necessary to forecast replacements many years into the future.[13] In such cases, it is ordinarily adequate to make the options only approximately, and not exactly, of the same duration.

For example, it would ordinarily be acceptable to compare the alternative of machines M_1 and M_1' (twelve-year total life) with the alternative involving M_2, even if M_2 had only an eleven- or even ten-year life; the discrepancy would be one or two years occurring a decade into the future. The importance of a time discrepancy between two investment alternatives is dependent upon three things:

1   *The shorter the discrepancy is, the less important it is.* Thus, we had to consider the replacement of M_1 and M_1' in the above example

---

[13] For example, if asset X and its future replacement each last ten years (replacement at time 10, time 20, etc.) and asset Y and each of its future replacements last thirteen years (replacement at time 13, time 26, etc.), we would have to analyze cash flows for the next 130 years (the shortest period ending when replacements of both X and Y also end). However, as noted below, adequate accuracy usually requires consideration of only a limited time period. Note also that this section assumes that investment (e.g., a replacement) in any particular time period does not depend on previous investment. Thus, in the above example, the NPV of any year 12 replacement does not depend on whether M_1 and M_1' or M_2 was used in the first twelve years. See Appendix 8B, Section 3, on analyzing investments that affect or depend on investment in other periods.

EXHIBIT 8-9
Comparison of investments with different lives

Time	Cash flows		
	M_1	M_1'	M_2
Time 0 (cost)	− $1,000		− $1,800
Time 1–6 (returns per year)	400		400
Time 6 (cost)		− $1,200	
Time 7–12 (returns per year)		400	400

$$NPV(M_1) = -\$1,000 + \$400 \ (P/A, 10\%, 6)$$
$$= -\$1,000 + \$400 \ (4.355) = \underline{\$742}$$

$$NPV(M_1 + M_1') = \$400 \ (P/A, 10\%, 12)$$
$$- \$1,000 - \$1,200 \ (P/F, 10\%, 6)$$
$$= \$400 \ (6.814) - \$1,000$$
$$- \$1,200 \ (0.5645) = \underline{\$1,048}$$

$$NPV(M_2) = \$400 \ (P/A, 10\%, 12) - \$1,800$$
$$= \$400 \ (6.814) - \$1,800$$
$$= \underline{\$926}$$

Conclusion: Buy M_1 now and replace with M_1' at time 6 since NPV(M_1 + M_1') exceeds NPV(M_2).

cause a six-year discrepancy between M_1 and M_2 was too large to ignore.

2   *The further into the future the life discrepancy is, the less important it is.* For example, if we were considering alternative buildings for a vacant piece of land, we could ordinarily compare the NPV of a building with a forty-year life with the NPV of a building with a fifty-year life and ignore what each would be replaced with at the end of its life. The ten-year discrepancy occurs forty to fifty years into the future and can be ignored in most cases. The reason is that the NPV of cash flows occurring far in the future is usually very small.[14]

3   *The closer is the rate of return on future investments to the cost of capital, the less important are any time discrepancies.* This is because the NPV = 0 for any future investment that just earns the cost of capital. *If the NPV on future investment is zero, then the time discrepancy can be ignored.* For example, assume that M_1' in the above exam-

---

[14] Even a very large net present value far into the future has a small value when discounted to the present using an economically realistic discount rate. For example, $1,000,000 at time 50 discounted to time 0 (now) has a value of $8500 if the discount rate is 10 percent $[(P/F, 10\%, 50) = 0.0085]$. Of course, the larger is the future amount, the further into the future it must be for it to become insignificant when discounted to the present.

228

PART 2
The firm's investment,
financing, and dividend
decisions

ple has the cash flows shown below instead of those shown in
Exhibit 8-9.[15]

Time	Cash flow of M_1'
t_6 (cost)	$-\$1,200.00$
t_7-t_{12} (returns per year)	$\$275.55$

$$\text{NPV}(M_1') \text{ at time } 6 = \$275.55(P/A, 10\%, 6) - \$1200$$
$$= \$275.55(4.355) - \$1200$$
$$= \$1200 - \$1200 = 0$$

$\text{NPV}(M_1') = 0$; that is, *it adds nothing* to the NPV of M_1 and M_1' combined. We can just ignore M_1' and directly compare the six-year asset M_1 with the twelve-year asset M_2. Assuming that M_1 and M_2 have the cash flows and NPVs as shown in Exhibit 8-9 and M_1' has the cash flows and NPV shown above, the $\text{NPV}(M_1 + M_1') = \text{NPV}(M_1) = \$742$, since $\text{NPV}(M_1') = 0$. We choose M_2 since $\text{NPV}(M_2) = \$926$, which exceeds $\text{NPV}(M_1)$ of $\$742$.

To summarize, in order to provide an exactly correct comparison between mutually exclusive options, the two alternatives must have equal lives. An alternative here refers to a particular course of action that ordinarily involves an investment now and may involve further investments (replacements) in the future. Often it is not practical or possible to establish equal lives for two alternatives. In this case, it is generally correct to ignore time discrepancies if they are small, or if they occur far into the future, or if the rates of return on investments subsequent to the ones being considered are close to the cost of capital (that is, if such future investments have small NPVs).

The above conclusions also apply if we are using the IRR approach in comparing alternatives. We must ordinarily use equal lives for the alternatives for an exactly correct answer. However, as with the present value method, this rule is subject to the above qualifications.

The Investment Tax Credit

To encourage investment by business, Congress enacted the **investment tax credit**. The credit applies to most new physical business assets other than real estate (and in certain cases to real estate). To a limited extent, it also applies to the purchase of used assets. In the year the asset is acquired, the firm's tax bill is reduced by the amount of the tax credit. The credit is 10 percent of the cost of the asset for most assets, and is 6 percent for other eligible assets. Further details on the investment credit are provided in Chapter 3.

To illustrate how the investment credit is taken into account in capital budgeting, assume that the firm has a taxable income of $200,000 from its

---

[15] If M_1' cost $1200 at time 6 and yields $275.55 per year for years 7 through 12, it has an IRR of exactly 10 percent [$(A/P, 10\%, 6) = 0.2296$]. At a cost of capital of 10 percent, the NPV of M_1' is zero at time 6, as is shown in the text computation below.

other operations and pays $100,000 in income taxes on this income. The tax credit on a $1000 investment is $100 (10 percent $\times$ $1000). This credit is deducted from the taxes owed for the period; i.e., the firm's taxes become $99,900 ($100,000 − $100). In effect, this means that the aftertax cost of the asset is only $900. That is, in purchasing the asset, the firm must invest $1000 but gets $100 in a tax reduction from the government, the net outlay being $900. In computing the net present value of the asset, the initial investment I is $900.[16] As noted in Chapter 3, the depreciable basis of the asset is the initial cost ($1000) less one-half of the investment credit ($50), i.e., is $950. (In the problems to this chapter, we assume for simplicity that the depreciable basis of an asset is its initial cost.)

In capital-intensive industries, e.g., oil, chemicals, automobile manufacturing, and especially public utilities, the investment tax credit can be a very significant factor. For example, the credit reduced Du Pont's United States income taxes in 1977 by $70.6 million—and that's a sum of some consequence even to an industrial giant like Du Pont.

Inflation and Capital Budgeting

There was a time, not so long ago, when inflation was viewed by most Americans as a problem solely of less-developed countries. This illusion was dispelled during the Vietnam and post-Vietnam era, as inflation assumed the archvillain's role in the United States economy. Economists are still divided as to what causes inflation. Fortunately, the financial manager's task is enormously simpler than that of the macroeconomist.

In an inflationary environment, the financial manager should know how to incorporate inflation into capital budgeting analysis. The job is surprisingly simple. The capital budgeting analyst should merely predict the actual dollar cash flows that will occur, taking into account the inflationary trend. For example, if the firm sells product X and the aftertax cash flow generated by sale of a single unit is expected to rise (due to inflation and any other factors) at the rate of 5 percent per year from the current level of $1, then the aftertax cash flow to be discounted is $1 per unit of product X sold this year, $1.05 per unit next year, $1.1025 (= 1.05 $\times$ $1.05) the year after next, and so forth to year 5, when the cash flow will be $1.276 per unit. Thus, the firm should use its expectations regarding inflation to estimate the actual dollar

---

[16] If the time period is defined as a year (the usual approach in practice), treating the ITC as a benefit at time 0 (when the investment is made) or at time 1 (one year after the investment is made) will normally provide an adequately accurate analysis in actual situations. Corporations pay estimated taxes on a quarterly basis, with one-half of the year's taxes due on the fifteenth day of each of the third month and the sixth month after the close of the fiscal year (e.g., one-half due on March 15 and one-half due on June 15 if the fiscal and calendar years are the same). The estimated tax is ordinarily based either on the taxes expected to be due for the current year or on the previous year's actual taxes paid (the choice depending on the current year's taxable income relative to the previous year's taxable income). Whether it is more accurate to treat the ITC as a benefit at time 0 or at time 1 (one year later) depends on when during the fiscal year the investment is made and on whether estimated taxes are based on the current or previous year's taxable income. A refined analysis would define the time period as less than a year (e.g., a month or a quarter) and would treat the ITC as a benefit in the periods in which the ITC tax savings are received in the particular situation; this degree of refinement is unusual in practice.

230

PART 2
The firm's investment,
financing, and dividend
decisions

cash flows to be earned, and then use those expected actual flows in the analysis. The inflationary trend must be estimated, and usually this is done by selecting an estimate made by economists or by forecasting firms such as Chase Econometrics and Data Resources. These forecasts are sometimes published in financial periodicals or are available for a fee from the forecasters.

The appropriate discount rate to employ is still the market rate currently used by investors to discount cash flows of a similar risk. *Market rates take into account inflationary expectations*, and a greater expected rate of inflation will mean that investors will require a higher rate of return. This is the reason that interest rates on bonds and the borrowing rate at banks (including the prime rate charged the banks' biggest and least risky customers) increase as inflation accelerates. Figure 8-3 illustrates the similar historical patterns of the general price level and market discount rates (an average of long-term Baa bond rates in the figure).

The essence of this approach is that the proper rate to apply in discounting a cash flow is the rate investors apply to cash flows of similar risk. This rate will necessarily take into account inflationary trends. To illustrate the method, assume that a store is considering the purchase of a display case for $1500 that has an anticipated useful life of three years. If there were no inflation, the added sales due to the display case would be $2500 per year, increased cost of goods sold would be $1300, added nondepreciation expenses (i.e., expenses other than depreciation) would be $200, and the rise in the firm's taxes would equal $300. Thus, aftertax cash flow from the

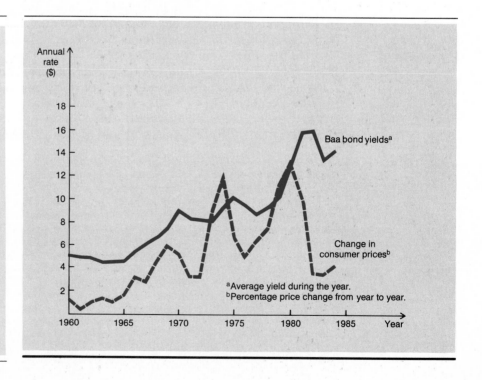

FIGURE 8-3

The behavior of market interest rates and changes in the general price level for goods and services. (Source: Economic Report of the President)

case would equal $700 per year ($700 = $2500 − $1300 − $200 − $300) for three years. However, with the expectation of continued inflation, the selling price of the product and the magnitude of the costs will rise. Assume that the expected cash flows (taking into account inflationary expectations) are as shown in Exhibit 8-10.

Notice from the table that the impact of inflation on sales may differ from the impact on costs. Let the discount rate appropriate to the cash flow be 12 percent; that is, the rate of return required by investors for cash flows of similar risk is 12 percent. The net present value of the display case is the discounted value of the cash flows in Exhibit 8-10 less the $1500 initial cost of the case; that is,

$$\text{NPV} = \frac{\$750}{1.12} + \frac{\$800}{(1.12)^2} + \frac{\$900}{(1.12)^3} - \$1500$$

$$= 0.8929(\$750) + 0.7972(\$800) + 0.7118(\$900) - \$1500$$

$$= \$448$$

The expected future dollar cash flows are discounted, and the current market discount rate used by investors is used for discounting. The cash flows are estimated so that they reflect anticipated inflation, and the current discount rate reflects the inflationary expectations of investors.

Interrelated Investment Opportunities

Up to this point we have considered investment choices that either involved accepting or rejecting a particular project or involved a choice between two mutually exclusive options, e.g., whether the truck purchased would be a Ford or a Chevrolet. Frequently, however, two or more investments are being evaluated, any or all of which can be accepted. Furthermore, the investments may affect one another's profitability. In this case, the decision involves selecting the set of investments having the highest net present value and accepting the set if its net present value is positive. To illustrate, assume that Blue Grass Realty owns two adjacent plots of land, plot 1 and

---

EXHIBIT 8-10
Cash flows from the display case with inflation

	Year 1		Year 2		Year 3	
Increase in sales		$2,700		$2,900		$3,200
Deduct:						
Increase in cost of goods sold	$1,400		$1,500		$1,600	
Increase in other nondepreciation expenses	250		275		300	
Increase in taxes	300		325		400	
Total deductions		1,950		2,100		2,300
Change in firm's aftertax cash flow		$ 750		$ 800		$ 900

232

PART 2
The firm's investment,
financing, and dividend
decisions

plot 2. Intuitively we know that what is constructed on plot 1 may influence the profitability of what is constructed on plot 2. The two land uses are economically interdependent. Blue Grass has decided that its only options for plot 1 are to construct a rest home on it or leave it vacant; its only options for plot 2 are to construct an amusement park on it or leave it vacant. Its options are therefore to construct the rest home and not the amusement park, to construct the amusement park and not the rest home, to construct both, or to construct neither. Assume that to leave both plots vacant produces a zero cash flow and requires a zero investment. Also assume for simplicity that all options involve the same risk and the same cost of capital of 10 percent.[17] The costs and payoffs of each decision involving the construction of one or both of the amusement park and rest home are shown in Exhibit 8-11. It is not surprising that the total cash flow from both the amusement park and rest home together ($24,000) falls far short of even the rest home alone ($50,000 per year). The home would not be too restful (and patrons therefore few) with merry-go-round music and children's screams wafting through the air. The net present value of the rest home on plot 1, with plot 2 left vacant (no amusement park), is the highest of the three choices, and would be the option selected, since its present value of $200,000 is positive.

The above example suggests a general guideline for analyzing a set of interdependent options.[18] If we have any set of investments which have *interdependent* cash flows, e.g., investments A, B, and C, the following procedure is appropriate in determining the best course of action:

[17] If different options involve different risk, then they will warrant different discount rates (costs of capital). For example, if the rest home were riskier than the amusement park, the former might warrant a 14 percent discount rate and the latter a 10 percent discount rate; and the two together might justify an 11 percent discount rate. The issue of differing risk is discussed in Chap. 9.

[18] For a detailed analysis of cash flow interdependencies, see Haley and Schall, *The Theory of Financial Decisions*, chap. 3.

EXHIBIT 8-11
Interrelated investment opportunities

	Only amusement park	Only rest home	Amusement park and rest home
I_0	$100,000	$300,000	$400,000
Annual expected perpetual aftertax cash flow	$ 12,000	$ 50,000	$ 24,000
Net present value at 10%[a]	$ 20,000	$200,000	−$160,000

[a] NPV(only amusement park) = $12,000(10) − $100,000 = $20,000 where 10 is the 10% annuity present value factor for a perpetual annuity (see Appendix A); NPV(only rest home) = $50,000(10) − $300,000 = $200,000; NPV(amusement park and rest home) = $24,000(10) − $400,000 = −$160,000.

1 Determine the combinations of the interdependent options that are possible. For three interdependent options, A, B, and C, if none is mutually exclusive of any of the others (that is, all can be simultaneously adopted), then the possible combinations (which involve adopting at least one option) are:

A but not B or C   B and C but not A

B but not A or C   A and C but not B

C but not A or B   A, B, and C together

A and B but not C

2 Determine the initial outlay, the future aftertax cash flows, and the net present value of each of the combinations of options identified in step *1* above (seven combinations in the above example of A, B, and C).

3 Choose the combination of options analyzed in step *2* above with the highest net present value. If that highest net present value is positive, adopt that combination; if negative, reject that combination along with all the other combinations; if zero, you are indifferent concerning investment in that combination, and reject all the other combinations.

This procedure was followed in the amusement park–rest home example. In step *1*, we defined the combinations of options as the amusement park and not the rest home, rest home and not amusement park, or both. In step *2*, we determined the initial outlay, future cash flows, and net present value of each option (shown in Exhibit 8-11). In step *3*, we chose the rest home alternative since it had the highest net present value and that net present value was positive.

Are all options of the firm interdependent in some way, and must every combination of investment opportunities be analyzed in choosing a capital budget? Fortunately, the problem is not as bad as that. Although strictly speaking all a firm's activities are somewhat dependent (i.e., affect one another's profitability), many options are approximately independent and can therefore be evaluated as separate projects. For example, if plots 1 and 2 of Blue Grass Realty were in different parts of the city, the land uses on each could be individually evaluated. In that case, the rest home on plot 1 could be accepted or rejected, and the amusement park on lot 2 could be independently accepted or rejected. We would then not have to consider as a separate possibility the construction of both the amusement park and the rest home. Notice that if we had done this in the case of the adjacent (and therefore interdependent) plots described in Exhibit 8-11, we would have erroneously accepted the amusement park and the rest home, since each if done without the other has a positive net present value ($20,000 and $200,000, respectively). *With interdependencies that are significant we cannot consider each investment option individually.* This is so since the cash flow figures relating to the options as individual investments do not apply if more than one of the investments are undertaken. This is clearly illustrated in Exhibit 8-11, since the cash flow of the amusement park and rest home together ($24,000) is not equal to the cash flow of the amusement park alone ($12,000) plus the cash flow of the rest home alone ($50,000).

234

PART 2
The firm's investment,
financing, and dividend
decisions

As a closing point, note that investments can be geographically near one another and still be economically independent. For example, if a new roof on a firm's manufacturing plant does not affect the profitability of a new truck, then the roof and truck are independent. If the roof and truck were independent of all other investment options being considered, then the project evaluation procedure would involve evaluating the roof and truck separately. The roof would be built if, and only if, its net present value were positive, and the truck would be purchased if, and only if, its net present value were positive.

CAPITAL RATIONING

Sometimes, only limited funds are available for investment and, at least in the short run, no additional capital is obtainable from external sources. This might occur if the decision unit is not an entire firm but a division with a given capital allocation for investment determined by the parent company. The problem is how the division manager should use the funds that are available. Capital constraints are also common for government agencies with fixed appropriations.[19]

The present value approach to treating the capital constraint problem is to invest the funds that are available in that set of projects with the highest total net present value. That is, the goal is to maximize the net present value of the entire current investment.[20] For example, assume a fixed sum of $100,000 is available for an investment. Also, assume that the firm can invest in some combination of projects A through D. The data associated with each project are shown in Exhibit 8-12. Assume that A and B are mutually exclusive (cannot both be done), as would be so, for example, if A were a restaurant and B were a gas station on a given plot of land that has room for only one or the other. Also note that since we have only $100,000 to invest, we cannot do both C and D, nor can we do both A and D, because each combination involves an initial outlay of $110,000. Therefore, given the mutual exclusivity of A and B and the budget constraint of $100,000, the possible project combinations are A and C, B and C, and B and D. If B and C are done, there is $10,000 left over, since together they require only $90,000 of the $100,000 available. In Exhibit 8-13 the net present value of each

[19] If the reason that the firm cannot obtain capital at an acceptable rate (acceptable cost of capital) is that outsiders realistically view the firm's investment opportunities as unattractive, no capital rationing exists. This would simply be a case of a firm with investment opportunities that do not offer sufficient risk-return qualities to attract investors. Similarly, capital rationing does not exist just because credit is tight and funds in the economy are extremely expensive; the firm's resulting high cost of capital should nevertheless be used to evaluate current investments. If the company's investments do not provide a rate of return at least equal to this cost of capital (i.e., imply a positive NPV), they should be rejected since the firm can earn the cost of capital by simply investing (lending) its funds in the market. No investment that is inferior to such market opportunities should be accepted.

[20] We are assuming in this discussion of capital rationing that the constraint on funds exists only in the current period and not in future periods. The same general concepts apply with multiperiod constraints, but the analysis is far more complex; an additional consideration that becomes important with multiperiod constraints is the rate at which funds can be reinvested by the firm in each period. For a proof of the validity of the method presented here, see Edwin Elton, "Capital Rationing and External Discount Rates," *Journal of Finance* (June 1970).

feasible combination of projects is shown. The $60,000 net present value of the combination of A and C equals the net present value of A ($40,000) plus the net present value of C ($20,000), which were stated in Exhibit 8-12. The net present value of a combination of B and C equals the sum of the net present values of B and C, and the net present value of the combination of projects B and D equals the sum of the net present values of B and D. Note that the $10,000 that is unspent if B and C are adopted has a *net* present value of zero since, if it is invested at the market rate, the benefits received will be worth $10,000, producing a net present value of zero.[21] Since the net present value of the combination of projects A and C is the greatest, as can be seen from Exhibit 8-13, this is the combination that should be selected.[22]

The above method for dealing with a capital constraint problem is valid because investors want the cash flow generated by the investment to have

[21] In order for an investment to have a positive NPV, the present value of the investment's future returns must exceed the investment's initial cost. The $10,000 invested at the going market rate of return will produce future benefits with a present value of $10,000, and therefore the investment has a zero *net* present value (i.e., a zero extraordinary return).

[22] Dynamic programming can greatly facilitate the analysis of the combinations of investment opportunities. This problem is often referred to as the "knapsack problem": see Harvey M. Wagner, *Principles of Operations Research*, 2d ed. (Englewood Cliffs, N.J.: Prentice-Hall, Inc., 1975).

EXHIBIT 8-12
Net present values of the firm's investment opportunities with capital rationing

Opportunity	Present value of future returns (1)	Initial outlay (2)	Net present value (col. 1 – col. 2) (3)
A	$90,000	$50,000	$40,000
B	50,000	40,000	10,000
C	70,000	50,000	20,000
D	65,000	60,000	5,000

EXHIBIT 8-13
Net present values of alternative firm capital outlays with capital rationing

Possible combinations of opportunities	Net present value of entire capital budget[a]
A and C	$60,000[b]
B and C	30,000[c]
B and D	15,000

[a] Computed by adding the net present values from Exhibit 8-12; for example, the net present value of A and C is $40,000 + $20,000, the sum of the net present values of A and C.
[b] A and C is the best combination.
[c] See text discussion and footnote 21 on why the unspent $10,000 is not added to the $30,000 in computing the net present value.

236

PART 2
The firm's investment,
financing, and dividend
decisions

the highest value possible. This value is determined by discounting the cash flow at the market interest rate appropriate to the riskiness of the cash flow.[23] The method is quite general and can be applied to investments even if they are interdependent (if they affect one another's cash flows or are mutually exclusive). However, if all the firm's investments are independent of one another (they do *not* affect one another's cash flows and are *not* mutually exclusive), then a simplification of the above procedure is possible. (It is extremely important to note that this profitability index procedure should *not* be used in comparing mutually exclusive options or in analyzing investments that, if adopted together, will affect one another's cash flows.) *The procedure is to rank the firm's investments by the ratio of the net present value per dollar of initial investment that they provide (NPV/I), and then select those investments with the highest NPV/I until the budget is exhausted.* NPV/I is referred to as the **profitability index.**[24] This procedure selects for adoption the combination of investments within the budget constraint that has the highest total net present value.

To illustrate, assume that the firm has up to $100,000 to invest and no more. Exhibit 8-14 indicates the firm's investment opportunities, their costs (I), NPVs, and profitability indices. The firm should invest its funds in projects A through F, a total outlay of $98,000. This leaves $2000 ($100,000 budget limit minus $98,000 invested). The $2000 is insufficient to accept either of the remaining opportunities with positive NPVs (G and H), and so the $2000 can be held for future investment, be paid out in dividends, or be used to reduce company debt.

A problem may arise in using the above procedure that involves those investments that are just marginally acceptable (on the border between being accepted and rejected, for example, E, F, and G in Exhibit 8-14). The problem can arise if the projects that are accepted on the basis of highest profitability index do not fully exhaust the capital available. Thus, let the NPV of project G in Exhibit 8-14 equal $1200 instead of $1000; G's profitability index would become 0.24, still below the profitability index of project F. Using the above profitability index procedure, A through F would still be selected and G would be rejected. However, notice that it would be more profitable (a higher total NPV for all projects combined) to select G and

---

[23] For a complete discussion, see Elton, op. cit. Notice that the investments that make up the capital budget can differ in risk (for example, A, B, and C may be of different risk). As will be explained in Chap. 9, the cash flow from any combination of investments should be discounted at that rate appropriate to the riskiness of the total cash flow generated by that combination of investments. Thus, in the example, the cash flow from A and C might be discounted at 10 percent whereas the discount rate for the cash flow from B and C might be 12 percent. In this chapter we are assuming that all investments have the same risk and are therefore evaluated using the same cost of capital (discount rate).

[24] The profitability index is also often defined as (NPV + I)/I = (present value of future net cash flows)/(initial outlay); this ratio is sometimes referred to as the benefit-cost ratio and using this ratio to rank investments leads to the same decisions as using the profitability index as defined here. Also, I is in some contexts defined as the present value of present and future capital outlays associated with the investment; for capital rationing in the *current* period, it is proper to define I as *current* capital outlays, as is done here. Multiperiod capital rationing is not examined here (see footnote 20).

reject E and F since the NPV of G is now $1200, whereas the total NPV of E and F is only $1100.[25] Therefore, the profitability index procedure is misleading in this case in selecting from among the marginal investments. The way to avoid an error of this type is simply to examine the investments close to the budget limit (the marginal investments) and make sure that an error is not being made.

It should be pointed out that completely inflexible budget constraints are not common for large businesses. This is particularly true in the long run, that is, if sufficient time is available to inform sources of capital of the firm's profitable investment opportunities. A budget constraint means that a limited quantity of capital is available *regardless of the profitability of the company's investments*. Such a limited capital situation can arise for small businesses because of the inability of management to convince outside sources of capital of the attractiveness of the company's opportunities.[26] A large firm with profitable investments can usually either borrow additional funds or sell additional shares of stock to finance the investments. Of course, it will have to pay the going rates on the acquired funds, but this will be reflected in the cost of capital used to evaluate the investments. Similarly, if a division of a company has attractive projects, the division head can generally present his or her proposals to central management, which will ordinarily allocate funds to the division if the investment proposals merit support.

---

[25] With E and F we have $2000 left over. However, the *net* present value of any investment of that $2000 will be zero; that is, the value of what is received on the investment of $2000 will equal $2000. Any investment outside the firm that earns just the normal rate of return has a zero *net* present value. All the investments with positive net present values should be included in the analysis of Exhibit 8-14 in determining the allocation of the $100,000.

[26] See footnote 19.

EXHIBIT 8-14
Simplified present value procedure for capital rationing

Project	Initial outlay (*I*)	NPV	Profitability index (NPV/*I*)
A	$50,000	$80,000	1.6
B	10,000	15,000	1.5
C	20,000	10,000	0.5
D	$98,000 { 15,000	6,000	0.4
E	2,000	800	0.4
F	1,000	300	0.3
G	5,000	1,000	0.2
H	3,000	300	0.1
I	4,000	0	0

SUMMARY

The enormous cost of new capital equipment purchased each year by United States industry has motivated firms to carefully budget capital expenditures. Most firms prepare short-run budgets, and many companies plan capital outlays for the next three to five years. These budgets are estimates and are often revised as new information becomes available.

The additional aftertax cash flow generated by an invesment is the relevant measure of the investment's productivity to the firm. The cash flow can be evaluated using present value, internal rate of return, payback, or benefit-cost. Using present value, a project should be accepted only if its net present value is positive. In comparing mutually exclusive investment alternatives (alternatives only one of which can be accepted), that with the highest net present value is the most profitable and should be adopted provided that its net present value is positive.

The internal rate of return (IRR) method specifies that only investments with an IRR greater than the cost of capital should be accepted. In comparing mutually exclusive options, the incremental method should be used. This method determines whether the additional cash flows of one alternative relative to another justify the former's acceptance. The IRR approach is often more cumbersome to use than is present value and in some cases is not applicable because of analytical problems. Present value is therefore recommended as the preferred evaluation technique.

The payback period method dictates acceptance of projects only if they return the cost of the investment within a specified period of time (the payback period). This method ignores the time value of money and does not take into account cash flows after the payback period. The accounting rate of return method requires that the investment with the highest accounting rate of return be adopted if the rate exceeds a specified level. As with payback, this method ignores the time value of money. Payback period and accounting rate of return are distinctly inferior to net present value and internal rate of return as capital budgeting criteria.

The use of sophisticated capital budgeting techniques has been primarily limited to large, capital-intensive firms. However, present value and IRR are rapidly gaining in acceptance and may eventually replace payback, accounting rate of return, and other less accurate methods.

If investments being compared are not of the same life, then a completely correct analysis usually requires that future investments be taken into account. In many situations this is not necessary, however, and the net present values of the investments can be directly compared in the usual manner, or the incremental IRR method can be applied.

The investment tax credit allows a tax rebate when a new asset is acquired. For capital budgeting purposes, the tax rebate should be viewed as a reduction in the initial cost of the asset.

In the presence of inflation, the firm should still use the actual cash flows that are anticipated in computing NPV. Furthermore, the discount rate that is appropriate is, as in the case of no inflation, that rate used by investors to discount cash flows with a similiar risk to the one being analyzed. This approach is valid, since the cash flow and the discount rate

*will both take the inflation into account and the investment's NPV will be
its net benefit to the stockholders in terms of current dollars.*

*Investment opportunities may affect one another's cash flows if both
are adopted, for example, a gas station and a restaurant next door to one
another. In this case, the cash flows and net present values from undertaking each project alone and from undertaking them together must be
computed. That combination of opportunities (an opportunity taken alone
or with one or more of the interrelated opportunities) that produces the
highest NPV is best and should be adopted if its NPV is positive.*

*A capital rationing problem exists if the firm does not have and can-
not obtain (through borrowing or selling new shares) sufficient funds to
adopt all projects with a positive NPV. In this case, the firm should adopt
that set of investments not exceeding its budget constraint which has
the highest total NPV. Under certain conditions, a shortcut analytic approach is applicable which specifies that the firm should adopt those
investments with the highest profitability indices. A budget constraint
generally does not exist for large firms. Such a constraint is ordinarily a
short-run problem that may occur for small firms or for corporate divisions.*

QUESTIONS

1   What information is required to determine the cash flow from an in-
    vestment opportunity?
2   Why do we use cash flow in evaluating an investment?
3   Depreciation is a noncash expense. Why, then, is it necesary to com-
    pute depreciation in order to perform a proper cash flow analysis?
4   Intuitively, what does an internal rate of return show?
5   What are the advantages and disadvantages of the net present value
    method relative to the internal rate of return method?
6   The TOPCOA Industrial Corporation has been using the payback
    evaluation technique for a number of years. Recently, you have been
    hired by the firm as a financial analyst. Prepare a convincing memo
    to the vice president for finance explaining your rationale for using
    another technique of investment evaluation. In your memo you want
    to be objective. Are there any situations in which the payback period
    method can be useful in capital budgeting analysis?
7   A recent graduate of the Wellduke Business School commented:
    "Capital budgeting is simple; just divide the investment's net income
    after taxes by the amount of the investment and compare this to the
    cost of financing the investment. If the return on investment is
    greater than the cost of financing, accept the investment." Comment
    critically.
8   Define the terms "cost of capital," "discount rate," and "minimum
    acceptable rate of return," and explain why they are equal to one an-
    other in project evaluation.
9   Strictly speaking, all activities of a firm are interdependent; that is,
    they affect one another's cash flows. Therefore any new investment

240

PART 2
The firm's investment,
financing, and dividend
decisions

in some way—directly or indirectly—affects the cash flows of every other investment the firm adopts. Since this is so, how can we justify ever evaluating a new investment by itself, i.e., without considering how it affects the cash flows of every other investment we are considering? What are the advantages and disadvantages of ignoring interdependencies?

10 Early in the chapter it was noted that intermediate- and long-term capital budgets are revised periodically. As a part of such a revision process, suppose a firm is reviewing the progress of a specific venture that has been in operation for five years. Outline the considerations that are relevant in performing the review process.

11 Assume that the federal government is considering the following four new policies to stimulate investment by private firms:

a Raise the investment tax credit on new assets from 10 percent to 15 percent.

b Allow firms to deduct 5 percent of the cost of new assets from their taxable income in the year the asset is acquired.

c Pay firms a cash subsidy of 5 percent of the cost of new assets in the year the asset is acquired.

d Allow firms to increase depreciation above what is currently allowed in the year an asset is acquired by 5 percent of the cost of the asset and to reduce future years' depreciation on the asset by 5 percent of the asset's cost; that is, to allow firms to accelerate depreciation by raising the current depreciation deduction by 5 percent of the asset's cost with an equal reduction in future depreciation.

Carefully compare these four policies in terms of the probable relative impact of each on a firm's level of investment.

PROJECT

Refer to library sources (e.g., the *Federal Reserve Bulletin*, the *Economic Report of the President*, the *Survey of Current Business*) and examine the past annual levels of investment, national income, federal income taxes, profits, and dividends in the United States. Try to find breakdowns of investment by industry or by sector of the economy. Also investigate forecasts of investment by industry, by sector, and for the entire United States economy.

PROBLEMS

[Note: In the following problems, ignore the investment tax credit unless otherwise indicated. Also, in computing depreciation for tax purposes: (1) assume a zero salvage value for the asset; (2) assume that the asset was acquired on January 1 of the year of acquisition, i.e., assign a full year's depreciation to the year in which the asset is acquired; and (3) unless otherwise indicated, assume that depreciation is spread over the asset's useful life.]

1 Arbor Instruments has annual cash revenues of $750,000, annual cash expenses of $250,000, and annual depreciation of $200,000. These figures are expected to remain the same permanently, if Arbor continues to subcontract out to other companies certain phases of its production process. If Arbor invests $300,000 in new machinery and discontinues the subcontracting, it will be able to increase its sales and reduce its per unit costs. With the new machinery, the firm's annual cash revenues will increase to $890,000 and annual cash expenses will increase to $270,000. The new machinery has a ten-year life, with no salvage value for tax purposes and no expected end-of-life liquidation value. The machinery will be depreciated for tax purposes on a five-year accelerated basis using the ACRS. At the end of the ten-year life of the machinery, the company's cash flow will return to what it would have been without the new machinery unless a replacement for the machinery is purchased at that time. The firm's tax rate is 50 percent, both with and without the new equipment.

a Set up a cash flow analysis table for this problem like Exhibit 8-1 in the text to determine the cash flow from the machinery. Refer to Chapter 3 for the necessary information to compute the ACRS depreciation.

b Assuming that the appropriate discount rate on the investment is 15 percent, use the net present value method to determine whether the investment should be made.

2 Platonic Sportswear just bought a new loom for $90,000. The salvage value for computing depreciation and the estimated liquidation value of the asset at the end of three years are both zero. The future cash flow and profit generated by the loom are:

Year	Cash flow	Profit
1	$50,000	$20,000
2	50,000	20,000
3	35,000	5,000

Compute the following for the loom:

a Internal rate of return [Ans.: IRR = 24.9 percent]

b Net present value using a cost of capital of 15 percent [Ans.: NPV = $14,298]

c Payback period [Ans.: 1.8 years]

d Accounting rate of return [Ans.: 33.3 percent]

3 If the cash inflows from the loom in problem 2 could be kept fully invested until the end of year 3, earning a rate of return of 30 percent per year, how much would the cash flow accumulate to at the end of year 3? [Ans.: $184,500]

4 P. Carter ("Bubbles") Dodd IV speculates in political memorabilia. He

242

PART 2
The firm's investment,
financing, and dividend
decisions

purchased a truckload of Hubert Humphrey 1968 Presidential campaign posters and buttons for $8000. Bubbles expects to be able to
sell the truckload in one year for $10,000 (net of taxes). The memo-
rabilia generate no other cash flows. Bubbles' cost of capital is 20
percent. Using both the net present value method and the IRR
method, determine whether Bubbles should purchase the truckload
of memorabilia. [Ans.: NPV = $333 and IRR = 25%; therefore Bub-
bles should purchase the memorabilia]

5 Assume that the investment described in problem 4 will give Bubbles
   Dodd a return of $10,000 in two years. Using the information in
   problem 4, apply the net present value method and the IRR method
   to determine whether Bubbles should make the investment.

6 Little Pumpkin Cookie Shoppe is considering the purchase of a new
   cookie cutting machine. The cookie cutter will cost $30,000 and, be-
   cause of increased cookie output, will increase net cash flow by
   $6000 per year for the next ten years. The cookie cutter has a zero
   liquidation value at the end of its useful life of ten years. Little
   Pumpkin's cost of capital is 20 percent. Compute the cookie cutter's:
   a NPV
   b IRR
   c Payback period

7 Dimples Baby Products is deciding whether it should buy a new vegetable masher for manufacturing its product "Vegey Goo," a smooth,
   creamy, vegetable pablum for infants. The masher will cost $40,000
   and will increase the firm's cash flow by $8000 per year for the next
   fifteen years (assume that the first $8000 occurs one year hence). At
   the end of the fifteen years it is expected that the masher can be
   sold for $4000 (this is net of taxes). What is the masher's:
   a NPV using a cost of capital of 15 percent?
   b IRR?
   c Payback period?

8 Flag Carwash is considering the purchase of new car wash equipment in order to expand its operations. Two types of options are
   available: a low-speed system with an $18,000 initial cost and a high-
   speed system with a $26,000 initial cost. Each system has a twenty-
   five-year life and a zero end-of-life liquidation value. The net cash
   flows associated with each investment are:

	Low-speed system	High-speed system
Initial cost	$18,000	$26,000
Annual cash flow for years 1 through 20	$2,800	$3,900

a Analyze the above problem using the NPV method. Perform the
   analysis for each of the following costs of capital:

1 12 percent [Ans.: NPV(low-speed system) = $7416
NPV(high-speed system) = $9400]

2 14 percent

3 16 percent

Compare your results for the three cases.

b Analyze the problem using the IRR method, using each of the above costs of capital (12 percent, 14 percent, and 16 percent).

9 Hank Sykes and his wife, Hyacinth, have long dreamed of owning their own business. A recent inheritance has made realizing this dream possible. Cranberry farming has a particular attraction for the Sykes because Hank's family has for generations been in farming and both Hank and Hyacinth have very strong hands and arms (which will help in working the cranberry bog). The Sykes can acquire 40 acres of cranberry bog land for $8000 per acre. In addition to the bog land cost, a capital investment of $48,000 will be necessary to set up operations. The $48,000 in capital assets will be depreciated on a straight-line basis over twelve years. Assume also a zero market value of the capital assets at the end of the fifteen years. Each acre of land is expected to yield 150 barrels of cranberries per year, and berry prices are antipicated to remain at $20 per barrel indefinitely. Cash expenses will be 30 percent of the gross receipts from selling the cranberries. In addition, the Sykes will pay themselves total annual salaries of $30,000 ($15,000 each), which is what they would have to pay two other people to perform the work of operating the cranberry farm and exactly what the Sykes can earn in alternative employment. This $30,000 in salaries to the Sykes is to be deducted in computing company cash flow. The Sykes plan to sell the bog land in fifteen years, and they expect the land to increase in value at the rate of 5 percent per year over that time period. The tax rate applicable to all company income except the gain from selling the bog land is 30 percent; the tax rate on the gain from selling the bog is 15 percent. The appropriate discount rate on the firm's cash flows is 12 percent. Answer the following:

a Why must the salaries of Hank and Hyacinth be included among company expenses in computing the firm's cash flow? Would the $30,000 in salaries have to be deducted as an expense if the Sykes decided not to pay themselves a salary?

b Compute each year's net cash flow from the investment in the cranberry business.

c Should Hank and Hyacinth invest in the cranberry bog?

10 Elixir Press is considering a $300,000 capital outlay for a new printing press which will reduce printing costs. The press will last twenty years and will have a zero liquidation value at the end of the twenty years. Nondepreciation cost reductions resulting from the new press are forecast at 3 percent of the current $2 million per year. Elixir's annual revenues of $4 million will remain unaffected. The press will

244

PART 2
The firm's investment,
financing, and dividend
decisions

be depreciated over twelve years on a straight-line basis; this depreciation will be added to a current depreciation allowance for the firm of $500,000 per year on existing plant and equipment. The firm's tax rate is 50 percent. The new press will be eligible for a 10 percent investment tax credit. Elixir's cost of capital is 15 percent.

a Set up a cash flow analysis like Exhibit 8-1 in the text for this problem.

b Compute the net present value, internal rate of return, payback period, and accounting rate of return for this project. Should the project be adopted?

11 Assume that Elixir Press buys the printing press described in problem 10. In addition, assume that Elixir, as a result of purchasing the new printing press, could reduce the sales price of its unabridged dictionary from $50 to $48. Because of the price reduction, the number of books sold will rise from 80,000 to 85,000, and production costs will rise from $2 million to $2.04 million. Except for these additional effects of the new press, all the facts stated in problem 10 still apply. Which one of the three following options should Elixir adopt?

a Purchase the new press but keep its old price ($50) and old output (80,000 units).

b Acquire the new press and cut its price (to $48) and increase its output to 85,000 units.

c Not purchase the press and simply keep its old price ($50) and output (80,000 units).

Use the present value method to solve this problem. Assume that Elixir's cost of capital is 15 percent.

12 Consider the following three projects, each of which has an investment cost of $130 and a life of three years.

Year	Net cash flow		
	A	B	C
1	$90	$ 20	$ 40
2	60	70	30
3	30	110	100

a Which project is called for by the payback method?

b Compute NPV for each project at discount rates of 0 percent, 5 percent, 10 percent, 15 percent, 20 percent, and 30 percent. Plot the results (with NPV on the vertical axis). Which investment is superior for each of these discount rates?

c Find the IRR of each project.

d Note that IRR corresponds to the rate where the curve crosses the horizontal axis. From your plot, make some inference as to why two projects cannot be compared by comparing IRR.

13 Solve the problems of Exhibit 8-6 (page 221), Exhibit 8-7 (page 223), and Exhibit 8-8 (page 224) using the internal rate of return method.

14 Sandra Hayden owns a large microcomputer retail outlet. She is considering a new location for her store, and has the opportunity to purchase a store in the main business district for $500,000 (land $200,000, building $300,000). The store will require an additional $60,000 outlay for remodeling. Its depreciation base for tax purposes will be $360,000 ($300,000 for the building plus $60,000 for the remodeling improvements), and the depreciation will be on a straight-line basis over eighteen years (i.e., depreciation will be $20,000 per year). Sandra plans to use only half of the available space in the new store for her own business and will lease out, under a twenty-five-year lease, the other half of the store for $30,000 per year. At the end of the twenty-five years, the entire structure will be demolished (assume that the removal costs will be negligible and can be ignored). The value of the land at the end of the twenty-five years is expected to be $400,000.

Sandra is now at the end of the tenth year of a twelve-year lease at her present location, but she can get out of the lease by paying a $5000 tax deductible penalty. Her tax deductible lease payments at the current location are $10,000 per year. At the end of the twelve-year lease, Sandra can get a renewal for an additional twenty-five years at $14,000 per year.

Sandra's annual cash revenues are $840,000, and her cash expenses other than lease rentals and taxes are $500,000. These items will remain unchanged if Sandra stays at her present location, but will increase by 40 percent if she moves to a new location. Sandra's tax rate is 50 percent and she uses a 15 percent cost of capital for discounting cash flows. Should Sandra move to the new location?

15 Solve problem 14 but assume that the value of the land at the new location will increase at 5 percent per year over the twenty-five-year period and assume that the new property will be sold by Sandra at the end of the twenty-five years. Also, assume that a 20 percent tax rate will apply to the gain from selling the property at the end of the twenty-five years (the gain will equal the value of the land at the end of the twenty-five years minus the $200,000 original cost of the land). Assume no real estate brokerage costs or sales taxes in selling the property.

16 Pepé's Ski Shop is contemplating replacing its equipment for injecting foam into the linings of downhill ski boots to provide a custom fit. The foaming machine currently in use was purchased eight years ago for $24,000, has been completely depreciated, and has a current market value of $4200. Pepé is considering the following two *mutually exclusive* alternative replacements:

Alternative 1: A similar but larger-capacity machine costing $45,000. Pepé estimates that this machine will increase annual revenues by $18,000 and increase annual nondepreciation expenses by $6500, implying a net pretax cash flow increase of $11,500 per year over its estimated fifteen-year life. It is expected that the new machine will have an actual aftertax liquidation value of $2000 at the end of

246

PART 2
The firm's investment,
financing, and dividend
decisions

fifteen years. The machine will be depreciated for tax purposes on a straight-line basis over fifteen years (assume a zero salvage value for computing depreciation).

Alternative 2: The latest in boot-foaming technology—a high-pressure machine capable of injecting a new ultralight foam with exceptional insulating characteristics and high resistance to breakdown. Since ultralight foam represents the frontier in ski boot technology, Pepé anticipates that cachet-conscious skiers will pay a premium to have boots foamed by this process. As a result he estimates that this process will provide an increase in annual revenues of $36,000 and an increase in annual nondepreciation expenses of $15,500, implying an increase in annual pretax cash flow of $20,500 over the fifteen-year life of the process. This alternative requires an initial outlay of $75,000 for equipment. The equipment is expected to have a zero actual liquidation value at the end of fifteen years. The machine will be depreciated for tax purposes on a straight-line basis over fifteen years (assume a zero salvage value for computing depreciation).

Pepé estimates his cost of capital at 12 percent, uses straight-line depreciation on all his equipment, and faces a marginal tax rate of 40 percent for the foreseeable future. The 40 percent tax rate applies to all taxable income, including any gain from selling the old foaming machine.

a Pepé has offered you a new pair of ski boots if you can help him make the correct choice. Should Pepé select alternative 1 or alternative 2? Assume no investment tax credit.

b If the equipment of alternatives 1 and 2 qualified for the 10 percent investment tax credit, would your recommendation change?

17 Quintet Packing, Inc. (QP) bought a wrapping machine three years ago at a price of $26,000. The machine's remaining lifetime is estimated to be ten years; then the machine must be scrapped (salvage value for depreciation purposes = expected end-of-life liquidation value = 0). Depreciation of this machine is $2000 per year. Since QP bought the machine, however, there has been continuous technical development so that the wrapping machine models now available are more efficient (lower variable production cost per unit). Furthermore, the manufacturer of the wrapping machine is at present developing a new model with added features that will enable the packaging company to increase output. This new model will be available in one year. QP's tax rate is 50 percent.

QP wants to know what the best action would be right now. There are three possibilities to consider: (1) continue with the old machine, (2) replace the old machine now with the more efficient model already available, or (3) replace the old machine after one year with the new, improved model.

If the old machine is not replaced, QP's annual cash flows for the next ten years have been estimated to be:

1. Sales revenues	$250,000
2. Cash expenses	130,000
3. Pretax cash flow [(1) − (2)]	120,000
4. Depreciation	32,000
5. Taxable income [(3) − (4)]	88,000
6. Taxes [(0.50) × (5)]	44,000
7. Net cash flow [(3) − (6)]	76,000

Depreciation (in the table above) on the old machine is $2000 per year, and depreciation on all other assets is $30,000 per year. The data on the old and new machines are:

Old machine
Original purchase price: $26,000
Current book value: $20,000
Salvage value after 10 years: 0
Current liquidation value: $24,000
Expected liquidation value in one year: $9,000

New machine bought today
Purchase price: $35,000
Expected lifetime: 10 years
Liquidation value after 10 years: $5,000
Expected to reduce cash expenses by 10% to $117,000 per year

New machine bought next year
Purchase price: $35,100
Expected lifetime: 9 years
Liquidation value after 9 years: $10,000
Expected to increase sales revenues by 10% to $275,000 per year and to reduce cash expenses to $121,000 per year

QP uses straight-line depreciation. The tax rates are 50 percent for ordinary income and 30 percent for long-term capital gains. Assume that any gain realized from selling a machine (gain = sale price − depreciated book value) is taxed as ordinary income (at a tax rate of 50 percent) if the sale price is less than or equal to the original purchase price paid for the machine. What action should QP take if its cost of capital for evaluating alternatives is 15 percent? Assume that depreciation on an asset for tax purposes is computed using a zero salvage value for the asset.

18 The management consulting firm of Toady, Chill & Minion (TCM) is evaluating two computer systems to meet its needs over the next ten

248

PART 2
The firm's investment,
financing, and dividend
decisions

years (all depreciation is on a straight-line basis with no salvage value assumed). TCM is considering the two following choices:

Choice A: Buy ten used Apple II's and four Apricots for $20,000. These computers are depreciable for tax purposes over three years, with no salvage value assumed. It is expected that the computers will be sold after two years for total proceeds of $4000 (net of taxes). The Apples and Apricots will be replaced by an advanced IBM system which is expected to last eight years and which is expected to cost $60,000. The IBM system will be depreciated over three years, with no salvage value for tax depreciation purposes. It is expected that the IBM system will be sold at the end of the eight-year holding period (ten years from now) for $5000 (net of taxes).

Choice B: Buy a new IBM system for $70,000. The system will last for ten years and will have a zero salvage value for computing depreciation for tax purposes. The system will be depreciated over three years. It is expected that the IBM system will be sold in ten years for $1000 (net of taxes).

The services provided over the next ten years under choice A and choice B are the same. Also, we know that both choice A and choice B have a positive NPV; the problem is to choose the better of the two alternatives. TCM is in the 40 percent tax bracket and has a 15 percent cost of capital. Is choice A or choice B preferable?

19 Alvarez Corporation manufactures chemical products and is evaluating two new processes for producing a particular compound. Demand for the compound will be small during the next five years and will then increase. Process A requires equipment that is appropriate for small output levels; A will be replaced in five years with process B, which will utilize equipment with an eighteen-year life. B is capable of meeting large output requirements. The alternative to using processes A and B is to install currently (time 0) process C, which employs equipment with an estimated life of twenty years. The costs of A, B, and C are:

Time of outlay	Expected capital outlay for process		
	A	B	C
Now (time 0)	$1.5 million		$3 million
Five years hence		$5 million	

The future annual net cash flows from each process are:

Time of cash flow (years)	Annual cash flow		
	A	B	C
1–5	$500,000		$400,000
6–20		$800,000	$700,000
21–23		$800,000	

The discount rate is 12 percent. Answer the following:

a Should the firm adopt A and B or adopt C? Justify your approach. (What about the three-year time discrepancy between the A-B combination and C?)

b If the life of process C were only fifteen years instead of twenty years, would your approach to the problem be different? Explain.

20 A packaging machine has an expected life of eight years and costs $114,000. The machine is eligible for the 10 percent investment tax credit. The expected aftertax net cash flow from the machine is $20,000 per year in the first five years and $30,000 per year in the last three years. The asset will be depreciated on a straight-line basis over five years. Assume that one-half of the investment tax credit is deducted from the cost of the machine in computing the cost basis for depreciation purposes; that is, assume that only $108,300 of the asset's costs can be depreciated.

a What will the firm charge off as depreciation expense on the machine each year?

b If the cost of capital is 16 percent on the machine, what is the machine's NPV?

21 A parcel of land was worth $200,000 on January 1, 1986. The increase in the general level of prices (inflation) was 6 percent during the year from January 1, 1986 to December 31, 1986.

a If the real value of the land (value in terms of purchasing power) was the same on December 31, 1986 as on January 1, 1986, what was the dollar value of the land on December 31, 1986? [Ans.: $212,000]

b If the real value of the land was 10 percent greater on December 31, 1986 than it was on January 1, 1986, what was the dollar value of the land on December 31, 1986? [Ans.: $233,200]

22 Arthur Deco purchased a small Rembrandt for $300,000. The net cash flow from holding the painting during the coming three years will be zero; the only future cash flow will be the cash proceeds from selling the painting, which Art plans to do in three years.

a If the painting increases in value by 10 percent per year during the next three years, what will its dollar value be in three years? In this case, if Art sells the painting in three years, what pretax annual rate of return has he earned on the property during the three years?

b If after three years the painting has increased in value to $450,000, is Art concerned about the inflation rate that occurred during the three-year period? Why?

c If Art expects to earn a pretax annual real rate of return of 5 percent on the painting and he expects an annual inflation rate of 7 percent, what does he expect the dollar value of the painting to be in three years?

d Assume that at the end of the three-year period the Rembrandt is worth $500,000. Also assume that the inflation rate during the three-year period was 4 percent per year. Suppose that Art Deco

250

PART 2
The firm's investment,
financing, and dividend
decisions

sells the painting at the end of the third year and pays $40,000 in capital gains taxes. What is the aftertax real rate of return per year that Art earned on the painting?

23 The Rainbow Paint and Dye Company wants to know whether to go ahead and market a promising new product, Formula Z paper dye. The firm is calculating depreciation on a five-year basis. Formula Z will be phased out and replaced by a still more advanced dye process after five years. The table below indicates relevant projected cost and revenue data for each of the ensuing five years stated in *beginning of 1986 prices.*

	1986	1987	1988	1989	1990
Revenues	$200,000	$260,000	$360,000	$330,000	$298,000
Depreciation expenses	24,000	24,000	24,000	24,000	24,000
Selling expenses	40,000	30,000	15,000	10,000	5,000
Production costs	107,000	138,000	202,000	174,000	161,000

Assume that the above flows occur at the *end* of the year (end of 1986, end of 1987, etc.). All of the above projections are at *beginning* of 1986 prices; i.e., they assume there will be no inflation after 1985. But in fact substantial inflation is expected. The projected inflation rate is 9 percent per year over the five-year period, and this rate is expected to apply uniformly to all prices (except depreciation). The 9 percent rate is the best estimate of top economists and is the forecast generally acccepted by the public. Depreciation is expected to equal the amounts shown in the table above. However, all the cash flow items in the table (all the items other than depreciation) will be greater in nominal terms by an amount just sufficient to adjust for inflation; thus, the dollar amounts *in purchasing power terms* will be those stated in the table. Therefore, to compute the expected *dollar* cash flows, the data in the table (except depreciation) must be inflated by an inflation factor; for example, by (1.09) for the end of 1986 cash flows, by $(1.09)^2$ for the end of 1987 cash flows, etc.

The investment needed to initiate the Formula Z project is $120,000 at the *beginning* of 1986. At the end of 1987 all assets associated with the Formula Z project will be sold for $100,000 (in *beginning* 1986 prices). The firm's tax rate is 50 percent, and this tax rate is applicable to all net income and to any dollar gain on selling the assets at the end of 1990 (there is a gain if the asset is sold for a price that exceeds its end-of-1990 book value). If the firm's current cost of capital is 16 percent, is this project worthwhile? In solving the problem keep in mind that actual dollar amounts should be used, *not* amounts stated in beginning of 1986 dollars.

24 Aerobic Health Foods is a chain of health food restaurants based in

California and the Northwest. Aerobic is considering three methods of stimulating business: (A) a blitz advertising campaign, (B) replacement of existing restaurant signs with new signs, and (C) the use of computerized robot waiters at all the restaurants. The initial outlays for each alternative are:

Investment	Initial outlay
A. Advertising campaign	$500,000
B. Signs	300,000
C. Computerized waiters	900,000

If A is done but B and C are not, A has an NPV (present value of future cash flows less the $500,000 initial outlay) of $275,000. If B is done but A and C are not, B has an NPV of $100,000. The advertising attracts customer attention to the signs. The NPV of doing both A and B is $450,000. The NPV of the robot waiters, C, is $90,000. C's NPV does not depend on whether A or B is adopted, and the NPV of A or B does not depend on whether C is adopted. Assuming that the firm has no budget constraint (can obtain funds at the cost of capital to finance any investment with a positive NPV), which of investments A, B, and C should Aerobic adopt? [Ans.: Adopt A, B, and C]

25 Solve problem 24 assuming that the firm can invest only $900,000; that is, the firm has a $900,000 capital constraint. [Ans.: Adopt A and B]

26 The Piker Paper Products Company currently manufactures paper napkins, towels, tissues, and bags. The company has been considering expanding its successful business. It is evaluating three options:
A. Expand its paper bag line.
B. Produce custom ordered and printed bags.
C. Expand into a line of paper party accessories.
The returns from A, B, and C are as follows:
A. The expansion of the paper bag line will require an initial investment in machinery of $150,000 and an additional initial outlay of $40,000 for plant improvements. The present value of the future cash flows generated by A is $250,000.
B. Custom ordered and printed bags would call for a relatively small current investment of $50,000 for the purchase and installation of a printing press. The present value of the future cash flows from B is $95,000.
C. To expand into a party accessories line will require a printing press somewhat more sophisticated than that needed for B. Also, new cutting and fabricating machinery will be needed. The required initial outlay is $275,000. The present value of the future cash flows from C is $380,000 assuming A and B are not done.
If A and B (but not C) are both done, a more efficient higher-capacity

252

PART 2
The firm's investment,
financing, and dividend
decisions

bag line will be justified. The total outlay for A and B together will be $260,000, but because of increased efficiency and lower operating costs the present value of the future cash flows generated by A and B together is $410,000.

If B and C (but not A) are done, the printing press used in the party accessories line will also be available for the custom printing of bags. This option would therefore eliminate all but $10,000 of the initial investment required for B. The initial outlay for B and C together is therefore $285,000. There are no other interdependencies between B and C.

If A and C (but not B) are done, there will be no interdependencies. The party accessory line will not compete with the bags for sales, and the production operations will be separate. The initial outlay for A and C together is therefore $465,000, and the present value of the future cash flows from A and C is $630,000.

If A, B, and C are all done, the advantages noted above from doing both A and B and from doing both B and C will still be available. However, the adoption of all three projects will require added plant space requiring an additional plant expansion cost of $200,000. If A, B, and C are done, the initial outlay will be $615,000, and the present value of future cash flows from A, B, and C will be $790,000.

Which options should Piker Paper Products adopt?

27 Magnum Calculators is considering a number of plant improvement investments and has allocated $315,000 to do the job. Under consideration are the following projects. Assume that the net annual cash inflows are all perpetuities.

Project	Outlay	Net annual inflows
A. Computerize stamping and assembly	$300,000	$57,000
B. Revamp assembly line	100,000	20,000
C. Increase warehouse space	100,000	12,000
D. Install new climate control system	20,000	22,000
E. Expand shipping dock	30,000	7,500

Not all these projects can be considered independently of one another. The following information may help clarify some of the relationships:

A and B are alternative (mutually exclusive) proposals for the same assembly line.

If A is done, then the option of expanding the shipping dock (E) would cost only $10,000 because it could be done conveniently by the contractors on A.

If B is done, then $5000 can be saved on the installation of the shipping dock (E). Also, under these circumstances, there would be an increase in shipping efficiency, so that the shipping dock expansion would generate $9000 per year instead of $7500.

All other combinations are independent (do not affect one another's cash flows). The cost of capital is 15 percent. Which projects should be adopted?

28 Rubicon Longevity Powders, Inc., manufactures flavored health potions. Rubicon is in an expansion mode and plans to add new flavors to its line. It has $2 million to invest. The four new flavors that it is considering are lime (L), potato (P), raspberry (R), and zucchini (Z). Market research has revealed that distinctly different groups of consumers prefer each of the four flavors and that L, P, R, and Z are consequently entirely independent of one another (adding any of these flavors to Rubicon's line will not affect the cash flows from any of the other flavors). The data for L, P, R, and Z are shown below:

Investment	Initial outlay	Present value of future cash flow from the investment
Lime (L)	$300,000	$800,000
Potato (P)	250,000	120,000
Raspberry (R)	400,000	700,000
Zucchini (Z)	500,000	425,000

Which flavors (L, P, R, and/or Z) should Rubicon add to its line?

29 Solve problem 28 but assume that L has a present value of future cash flows equal to $550,000 instead of $800,000.

30 The Plush Mountain Shopping Center Association is an incorporated entity comprising the merchants in the center. As a corporation, the center has accumulated $450,000 in cash. The $450,000 is the maximum amount Plush Mountain has available for investment. The center would like to begin a development on an adjacent vacant plot of land which it can buy for $220,000. On this land it can do one or more of the following:

A. Build a three-tier parking structure.
B. Build an ice-skating rink to be operated by the corporation.
C. Build and operate a movie theater.
D. Erect a fabulous sign advertising the shopping center.

The parking structure will cost $120,000 to build (in addition to the acquisition of the land for $220,000), and by providing added customer convenience, is expected to yield an NPV of $75,000. The skating rink will cost $150,000 over and above the land acquisition, and will yield an NPV of $90,000. The theater will cost $180,000 in addition to the land cost and will yield an NPV of $100,000. All NPVs

254

PART 2
The firm's investment,
financing, and dividend
decisions

are computed with the $220,000 cost of the land included in the initial outlay.

The land can accommodate both the skating rink and the same amount of parking space if the three-tier parking building and the rink are built as a single structure. The parking structure would cost only $90,000 to build over and above the cost of the rink, and the combination skating rink–parking building would yield an NPV of $290,000. The parking structure would provide needed parking for the rink. Similarly, the theater and parking structure could be done for a *total* of $225,000, excluding the land, yielding an NPV of $275,000. The rink plus the theater would be infeasible because of insufficient parking. D may be done for $40,000, and no matter which of A, B, or C are done, D yields an NPV of $90,000 *if* the land has been acquired (i.e., not net of the $220,000 land cost); D would therefore not be done alone. Rank all the possible investment combinations and select the best combination that can be done for no more than $450,000.

31 Gourmet Fast Foods has the following projects available during the coming year:

Project	Initial outlay	Net present value
A	$ 40,000	$11,000
B	100,000	28,000
C	120,000	25,000
D	200,000	45,000
E	240,000	65,000
F	300,000	95,000
G	300,000	80,000

Assuming: (1) the initial outlay is the only cash outflow for each project, (2) the projects are *not* mutually exclusive, and (3) the cash flows of the projects are *not* interdependent:

a Rank the projects in order of desirability on the basis of profitability index.

b If the firm has a limited capital budget of $680,000, which projects should it choose?

c The cash flows for project F are revised as follows:

Project	Initial outlay	Net present value
F	$280,000	$90,000

Now answer **a** and **b** again.

32 Gear Corporation has the following projects available during the coming year:

	Initial outlay	Net present value	Internal rate of return
A	$ 200,000	$ 300,000	25%
B	500,000	500,000	15
C	300,000	540,000	30
D	1,000,000	1,200,000	22
E	700,000	600,000	18
F	500,000	200,000	20
G	3,000,000	1,500,000	10
	$6,200,000		

The projects are not mutually exclusive; that is, acceptance of one project will not exclude acceptance of any of the others. Furthermore, adoption of any one of the projects does not affect the cash flows from adoption of any of the other projects. A cost of capital of 15 percent was used to calculate net present values.

a Rank the projects according to their internal rates of return and according to their profitability indices.

b The firm is able to raise only $2,000,000 to finance the entire capital budget. Which projects should the firm choose?

c What is the total net present value of the projects chosen in b?

8A

WHY AN INVESTMENT'S NET PRESENT VALUE EQUALS ITS BENEFIT TO CURRENT STOCKHOLDERS

In calculating the net present value for project selection in the text of this chapter, we assumed that a project's NPV is the net gain to stockholders from the project. Criteria for investments under the NPV technique are:

1 If the firm can obtain funds (borrow funds or sell new shares) to finance profitable investments, for mutually exclusive investments, the one with the highest positive NPV should be adopted; and, in making accept-reject decisions, an investment should be adopted if and only if its NPV is positive.

2 If the firm faces a budget constraint, the set of projects with the highest positive total NPV should be adopted.

In this appendix, we explain why the NPV of a project equals the gain to current ("old") shareholders from that project. Current or old shareholders are those who own the firm when the investment decision is being made and do *not* include any new shareholders who buy additional shares of the company's stock that are sold to finance the investment. We will consider two kinds of financing of the investment: first, the use of idle cash (described below) and, second, the use of borrowing or selling new shares.

FINANCING WITH THE FIRM'S CASH

Idle cash is cash that has a value equal to its face value because it does not produce an above-average rate of return by serving the firm in a productive capacity. The cash has a value equal to its face amount *and is the property of stockholders*. If the cash is spent, it is therefore a sacrifice of that cash by the company's shareholders.

An investment paid for with idle cash is an exchange of cash in the amount I (amount of investment) for the newly acquired assets. The value of the cash given up is I; for example, an investment I of $100,000 of idle cash is a sacrifice by stockholders of the $100,000. The new asset obtained by investing I provides the firm with an added future cash flow. The net gain equals the present value of the returns from the investment less the cost of investment. That is, the net gain to stockholders equals

$$\begin{pmatrix} \text{Gain to} \\ \text{stockholders} \end{pmatrix} = \begin{pmatrix} \text{the present value of the} \\ \text{future cash flow from the} \\ \text{new assets acquired} \end{pmatrix} - \begin{pmatrix} \text{cash surrendered} \\ \text{in making the} \\ \text{investment} \end{pmatrix}$$

$$= \frac{CF_1}{1 + k} + \frac{CF_2}{(1 + k)^2} + \cdots + \frac{CF_n}{(1 + k)^n} - I$$

$$= NPV$$

Terms CF_1, CF_2, ..., CF_n are the cash flows from the project in periods 1, 2, ..., n; k is the discount rate; and I is the initial investment in the project (the cash expended on the project). The above relationship indicates that the net gain to shareholders is simply the NPV of the project. The net present value method is therefore appropriate if the investment is financed with idle cash.

We wish to show that if the funds to finance new investment are acquired by selling *new* shares (in amount S^N) or through borrowing (selling new bonds in amount B^N), the the effect on the wealth of current shareholders (those owning the "old" stock) from the investment and its financing will equal the investment's NPV. This net wealth gain will be reflected in a rise in the market value of the firm's old shares by an amount equal to the project's NPV. Old shares refer to the stock outstanding *not* including the new shares issued (S^N).

To show that the effect on the value of the firm's *old shares* from a project is the project's NPV whether it is financed with new stock S^N, new bonds B^N, or a combination of the two, assume the following:

S = the market value of the old shares assuming the investment in a new project is made and is financed with some combination of new stock and new bonds

S' = the market value of the old shares assuming the investment is *not* made

B = the market value of the firm's old bonds (not including new bonds to finance the investment) if the investment is made

B' = the market value of the old bonds if the investment is *not* made

S^N = the market value of new shares sold to finance the investment

B^N = the market value of new bonds sold to finance the investment

V = the market value of the firm (value of all outstanding stocks and bonds) if the new investment is made

V' = the market value of the firm if the new investment is *not* made

New shares S^N and new bonds B^N are issued to finance investment and are not issued if there is no investment. Therefore, with investment of amount I financed with S^N and B^N we know that

$$S^N + B^N = I \tag{8-7}$$

For example, new investment of amount \$100,000 might be financed with \$40,000 of new stock and \$60,000 of new borrowing (bonds); thus, $I = \$100,000$, $S^N = \$40,000$, and $B^N = \$60,000$.

Since, by definition, the value of the firm equals the value of all outstanding stocks and bonds, with the investment the firm's value is

$$V = \begin{pmatrix} \text{value of the} \\ \text{firm with the} \\ \text{investment} \end{pmatrix} = \begin{pmatrix} \text{value of all shares} \\ \text{outstanding with} \\ \text{the investment} \end{pmatrix} + \begin{pmatrix} \text{value of all bonds} \\ \text{outstanding with} \\ \text{the investment} \end{pmatrix}$$

$$= S + S^N + B + B^N \tag{8-8}$$

Furthermore, the value of the firm if the investment is *not* undertaken (signified by V') equals

258

PART 2
The firm's investment,
financing, and dividend
decisions

$$V' = \begin{pmatrix} \text{value of the firm} \\ \text{without the} \\ \text{investment} \end{pmatrix} = \begin{pmatrix} \text{value of all shares} \\ \text{outstanding without} \\ \text{the investment} \end{pmatrix} + \begin{pmatrix} \text{value of all bonds} \\ \text{outstanding without} \\ \text{the investment} \end{pmatrix}$$

$$= S' + B' \tag{8-9}$$

We know that the change in the value of the old shares due to the investment equals $S - S'$, the value of the shares with the investment less the value without the investment. By rearranging (8-8) it is clear that $S = V - B - B^N - S^N$ and by rearranging (8-9) we know that $S' = V' - B'$. Subtracting S' from S, the change in old share values is

$$S - S' = (V - B - B^N - S^N) - (V' - B')$$

$$= V - B - B^N - S^N - V' + B'$$

$$= V - V' - (S^N + B^N) - (B - B') \tag{8-10}$$

From Eq. (8-7) recall that $(S^N + B^N) = I$ and let $(B - B') = 0.$[27] Equation (8-10) becomes

$$\begin{pmatrix} \text{Change in old share value} \\ \text{due to the investment} \end{pmatrix} = S - S' = (V - V') - I \tag{8-11}$$

The change in the firm's total value in Eq. (8-11), $V - V'$, is the additional value of the firm due to the investment. $V - V'$ is the present value of the future cash flow from the new assets. Since I is the current cost of the new assets, it follows that the right-hand side of Eq. (8-11) is the NPV of the new investment. Therefore, if investment is financed with funds from the sale of some combination of new stocks and bonds, the increase in the value of the old shares equals the net present value of the investment.

An example will help clarify the above concept. Assume that the firm is considering an investment outlay of $10,000 that would be financed with $6000 from borrowing ($B^N = \$6000$) and $4000 from the sale of new stock ($S^N = \$4000$). If the new investment *is not* adopted, the value of the currently outstanding stock would be $500,000 ($S' = \$500,000$) and the value of the currently outstanding bonds would be $400,000 ($B' = \$400,000$). The value of the firm (V') therefore would be $900,000. Assume that if the new investment *is* adopted, the value of the firm would be $915,000 ($V = \$915,000$), the present value of the additional aftertax cash flow to stockholders and bondholders from the new assets therefore being $15,000 (the

---

[27] The assumption that $B - B' = 0$ means that the new investment and its financing by selling additional shares or bonds does not affect the value of the *old* bonds. If the value of the old bonds were affected by a new investment—for example, by reducing the likelihood of bankruptcy (thereby making the old bonds less risky and consequently more valuable)—then the value of the new investment to stockholders would equal the investment's net present value less the change in the value of the old bonds. This assumption that the old bonds do not change in value is made throughout this book and is generally made in actual business practice. This is because it not only simplifies the analysis but is ordinarily a realistic assumption. For a discussion of this point, see Haley and Schall, *The Theory of Financial Decisions*, chap. 12.

EXHIBIT 8-15
Equality of NPV and the change in old share values

	Without the investment	With the investment
1. Value of old shares	$500,000	$505,000
2. Value of old bonds	400,000	400,000
3. New stock sold for the investment	0	4,000
4. New bonds sold for the investment	0	6,000
5. Value of all stock outstanding [= (1) + (3)]	500,000	509,000
6. Value of all bonds outstanding [= (2) + (4)]	400,000	406,000
7. Value of firm (V) [= (5) + (6)]	900,000	915,000

Gain to old shareholders = rise in value of old shares = $505,000 − $500,00 = $5,000. Net present value of the investment = (present value of future cash flows from the investment) − (cost of investment) = (V − V') − I = ($915,000 − $900,000) − $10,000 = $5,000.

rise in the value of the firm's total aftertax cash flow being $915,000 − $900,000). The *net present value of the investment* is therefore $5000, $15,000 less the cost of the assets of $10,000. *The increase in the value of the old shares* is consequently $5000. The data associated with the problem are shown in Exhibit 8-15.

8B

*CHOICES
BETWEEN
MUTUALLY
EXCLUSIVE
INVESTMENTS:
INTERNAL RATE
OF RETURN
VERSUS
PRESENT VALUE*

The three sections of this appendix cover the following:

1 The use of the present value and internal rate of return methods in comparing mutually exclusive investments assuming either that future investment opportunities are not dependent on current investments or that all future investments will yield exactly the cost of capital. We show that the present value or the *incremental* IRR method must be used and that simply selecting the investment with the highest IRR is usually not the proper approach, that is, it can lead to adoption of the less profitable investment.

2 The special case mentioned on page 215 in which the best investment from among a set of mutually exclusive investments is the one with the highest IRR. In the discussion below, it is shown that the investment with the highest IRR is the best one as long as certain conditions hold. It is also the investment that would be chosen using the incremental IRR method or the present value method.

3 The general approach for analyzing investments when the firm's future investment opportunities *depend on which investments are currently adopted.* This approach is valid whether the future reinvestment rates (the rates of return on future investments) are equal to the firm's cost of capital, the current investments' IRRs, or some other rate.

We assume throughout this appendix that the firm can obtain funds at the cost of capital. Capital rationing was considered in a separate section in the body of Chapter 8.

*1. FUTURE
INVESTMENTS
INDEPENDENT
OF CURRENT
INVESTMENTS*

It should be noted at the outset that if the profitability of future investment opportunities is not dependent on current investments, then it is correct to evaluate current investments using the present value and IRR techniques described in the text, with the incremental IRR approach applied if one is selecting from among mutually exclusive alternatives. This is true regardless of the rate of return that the firm expects to earn on future investments as long as those future investments do not depend on currently adopted projects. In this case, the *current* projects are accepted or rejected on the basis of the cash flows that they generate, and the *future* projects are accepted or rejected on the basis of the cash flows that they generate. Both present and future projects are evaluated using the firm's cost of capital, either as a discount rate or as a minimum acceptable rate of return.

A second important point is that, in evaluating current investments, we can ignore any future project that depends on current investments as long as that future project is expected to earn a rate of return not exceeding the firm's cost of capital. The reason that such future investments can be ignored is that all future projects earning less than the cost of capital will not be adopted, since they have a negative NPV (and so are irrelevant), and all future projects earning exactly the cost of capital have a zero net present value and therefore do not affect shareholder wealth (they are just marginally acceptable). In this situation, we can apply the present value and internal rate of return methods to the cash flows of current investments as explained in the text. In this section of Appendix 8B the use of the present value and incremental rate of return methods will be illustrated for the present case that allows us to ignore *future* investments. In this case it is ordinarily incorrect simply to select the mutually exclusive investment with the highest IRR. This was shown to be so in the text (pages 213–215) if the investments being compared require different initial outlays. We show below that choosing the investment with the higher IRR can lead to errors even if the mutually exclusive investments have the same lives and require the same initial outlay. Either the incremental rate of return method or the present value method should be used.

To illustrate the principles involved, assume that the firm has two mutually exclusive investment opportunities, A and B, which each require an initial outlay now of $1000. The cash flows from A and B are shown in Exhibit 8-16. Assume that the cost of capital is 10 percent. Observe that although the 30 percent internal rate of return of B, $r(B)$, exceeds $r(A) = 20$ percent, the net present value of A, NPV(A), of $283 exceeds NPV(B) = $204. A is the superior investment. Also, notice that the incremental rate of return is 14 percent, which exceeds the cost of capital of 10 percent; therefore the incremental IRR method also correctly leads to a choice of A over B. Figure 8-4 shows the net present values of A and B for various discount rates. If the discount rate (cost of capital) is less than 14 percent, the NPV(A) exceeds NPV(B) (the case in the example where the cost of capital was assumed to be 10 percent); if the cost of capital were exactly 14 percent, NPV(A) = NPV(B) and we would be indifferent between A and B; and if the cost of capital were greater than 14 percent, NPV(B) would exceed NPV(A) and B would be preferred to A.

EXHIBIT 8-16
Cash flows from mutually exclusive investments A and B

	A	B	A − B
Time:			
Now	− $1,000	− $1,000	$ 0
Year 1	50	1,200	− 1,150
Year 2	100	100	0
Year 3	1,536	40	1,496
IRR (r)	20%	30%	14%[a]
NPV (at 10% rate)	$283	$204	$79

Conclusion: Choose A since $283 exceeds $204.

[a] The 14% rate is the IRR of the (A − B) cash flows; the added outlay of $1,150 in year 2 produces an added return of $1,496 in year 4, the rate of return being 14% per year. Since 14% exceeds the cost of capital rate of 10%, A is superior to B using the incremental IRR method [the (A − B) increment has an IRR that exceeds the cost of capital].

Assume that the firm is comparing two or more mutually exclusive investments and that conditions **a**, **b**, and **c** below apply to those investments:

a. All the investments involve the same initial (current) dollar outlay.

b. Each investment provides the firm with the special opportunity to reinvest the investment's future cash flows at a rate of return equal to the investment's IRR.

c. The reinvestment opportunity described under **b** above lasts until T periods from the current investment (i.e., the funds can remain reinvested earning the internal rate of return until T periods hence), where T is the same for all the mutually exclusive opportunities being compared *and* T is no less than the life of the longest lived of the mutually exclusive investments (e.g., if the longest-lived investment has a five-year life, T is no less than five years).

Conditions **a**, **b**, and **c** were noted in the text on page 215. It was observed that **a**, **b**, and **c** hold infrequently in practice. In those cases in which **a**, **b**, and **c** do hold, the mutually exclusive investment with the highest IRR is also that which provides the highest NPV and is the investment that would be chosen using the incremental rate of return method. We will use an example to show this.

Assume that investments C and D are being evaluated by the firm at time 0. The firm's cost of capital is 10 percent. C and D each require an initial outlay of $1000 (condition **a**). The cash flows of C and D are shown in Exhibit 8-17. The IRR of C [signified $r(C)$] is 20 percent, and the future cash flows from C can be reinvested until time 5 at a rate of return of 20 percent per period; that is, by investing in C now, the firm obtains the opportunity to

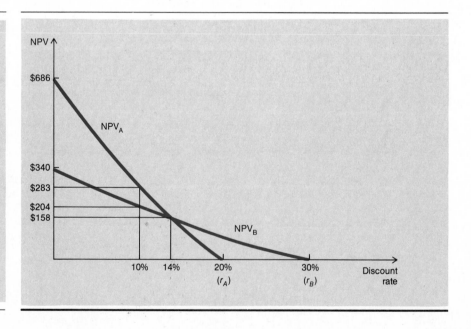

FIGURE 8-4

The NPV of investments A and B at different discount rates.

reinvest C's future cash flows in new projects that also earn 20 percent per period (until time 5). C is identical to A in Exhibit 8-16 except that we are now assuming that the future cash flows from A are reinvested at A's IRR. The IRR of D, $r(D)$, is 35 percent, and the future cash flows from D can be reinvested to earn 35 percent until time 5. Thus, condition b is satisfied. Note that T in condition c is equal to 5 in this example; therefore, condition c is satisfied since 5 is greater than the three-year life of project C, the longer-lived project. Since the firm's cost of capital is only 10 percent, we know that the firm will, if C is adopted, reinvest C's cash flow at the reinvestment opportunity rate of 20 percent and will, if D is adopted, reinvest D's cash flow at the reinvestment opportunity rate of 35 percent. Assuming such reinvestment, the firm will accumulate at time 5 the terminal amount $V_5(C) = \$2488$ if C is adopted and amount $V_5(D) = \$4484$ if D is adopted. $V_5(C) = \$2488$ results by investing, at a rate of 20 percent per period, C's time 1 cash flow of $50 for four periods (to time 5), reinvesting C's time 2 cash flow of $50 for three periods, etc. $V_5(D) = \$4484$ results by reinvesting at 35 percent per period D's time 1 cash flow of $1350 for four periods to time 5. Notice that for any T in condition c (where $T = 5$ in the present example)

$$V_T = (1 + r)^T I = (F/P. r, T)I \tag{8-12}$$

Equation (8-12) follows, since reinvesting all cash flows at the internal rate of return r is equivalent to simply investing I for T periods with all funds kept invested for the T periods earning rate r per period. This is like putting I in a bank account earning r each period and leaving all interest in the account along with the principal until the end of the T periods.

The objective is to maximize the present value of the returns from the investment (using the cost of capital) and, using (8-12),

---

EXHIBIT 8-17

Comparing mutually exclusive investments with cash flows that are reinvested at the internal rate of return

	C	D
Time:		
Now	− $1,000	− $1,000
Year 1	50	1,350
Year 2	50	0
Year 3	1,596	0
IRR (r)	20%	35%
NPV of above cash flows		
at 10% (ignoring reinvestment)	$286	$227
Year 5 terminal amount (V_5)	$2,488	$4,484
NPV of V_5 at 10%	$545	$1,784

Conclusion: Choose D since $1,784 exceeds $545.

264

PART 2
The firm's investment,
financing, and dividend
decisions

$$\text{NPV(C)} = \frac{V_5(C)}{(1 + k)^5} - I \tag{8-13}$$

$$= \frac{[1 + r(C)]^5 I}{(1 + k)^5} - I = \frac{(1.2)^5 \, \$1000}{(1.1)^5} - \$1000$$

$$= \frac{\$2488}{(1.1)^5} - \$1000 = \$545$$

$$\text{NPV(D)} = \frac{V_5(D)}{(1 + k)^5} - I \tag{8-14}$$

$$= \frac{[1 + r(D)]^5 I}{(1 + k)^5} - I = \frac{(1.35)^5 \, \$1000}{(1.1)^5} - \$1000$$

$$= \frac{\$4484}{(1.1)^5} - \$1000 = \$1784$$

Notice from Eqs. (8-13) and (8-14) that as long as C and D involve the same I, T, and cost of capital k—which is the case here since $I = \$1000$, $T = $ five years, and $k = 10$ percent for both investments—the investment with the higher V_T is preferred. We can see from Eq. (8-12) that this is equivalent to choosing the investment with the higher internal rate of return.

Although simply selecting the alternative with the highest IRR is the easiest selection method under the present assumptions (a, b, and c above), it should be clear that the net present value method also leads to the correct choice. The procedure is simply to compute the terminal value, V_T, of each mutually exclusive investment and choose the investment with the highest terminal value since, with the same initial outlay and T for all the investments, highest terminal value also means highest NPV.

3. REINVESTMENT RATES IN GENERAL

In general, if future investment opportunities are affected by current investments, then those future opportunities must be taken into account in evaluating projects. All effects of current investments on the future cash flows must be taken into account, including future capital projects and returns from those projects. The net present value or incremental IRR methods can be applied in this case. It is not in general correct to choose the investment with the highest internal rate of return.

To illustrate the correct approach, assume that the firm is comparing mutually exclusive investments E and F that require current outlays of $2000 and $5000 in the current period. E has a life of two years (returns annual cash flows of $1500 at the end of years 1 and 2), and the funds from E can be reinvested at a 20 percent rate of return until the end of year 4. E also provides the opportunity to invest an additional $1000 at the end of the third year (three years hence) at 20 percent per year for one year. After year 4, investment E provides no special reinvestment opportunities, and all funds are withdrawn from E and its reinvestment projects at the end of year 4. Exhibit 8-18 describes these cash flows.

Investment F is a three-year project (returns annual cash flows of $2500 from years 1 through 3) but provides no special reinvestment opportunities.

Do we choose E or F? *The preferred investment is that with the greater net present value of future cash flows, taking into account any reinvestment opportunities earning more than the cost of capital. The objective is to choose that investment plan which maximizes the net present value of cash flows.*

The net present value of E is computed by assuming that the $1500 cash flows of years 1 and 2 are reinvested to earn 20 percent per year until the end of year 4; $1000 is also invested at the end of year 3 until the end of year 4 at a rate of return of 20 percent. The total amount accumulated at the end of year 4 [$V_4(E)$] is $5952. The net present value of E is computed as follows:

$$\text{Amount accumulated at end of year 4 with E} = V_4(E)$$

$$= \$1500(1.2)^3 + \$1500(1.2)^2 + \$1000(1.2)$$

$$= \$5952$$

$$\text{Present value of new funds invested in E} = I(E) = \$2000 + \frac{\$1000}{(1.10)^3} = \$2751$$

$$\text{Net present value of E [NPV(E)]} = \frac{V_4(E)}{(1.10)^4} - I(E)$$

$$= \frac{\$5952}{(1.10)^4} - \$2751 = \$1314$$

For investment F, the net present value equals

$$\text{NPV(F)} = \frac{\$2500}{1 + 0.10} + \frac{\$2500}{(1.10)^2} + \frac{\$2500}{(1.10)^3} - \$5000$$

$$= \$2500(P/A, 10\%, 3) - \$5000$$

$$= \$2500(2.487) - \$5000 = \$1218$$

Since NPV(E) = $1314 exceeds NPV(F) = $1218, E is preferred; and since NPV(E) is positive, E should be adopted.

EXHIBIT 8-18
Cash flows from investment E and reinvestment

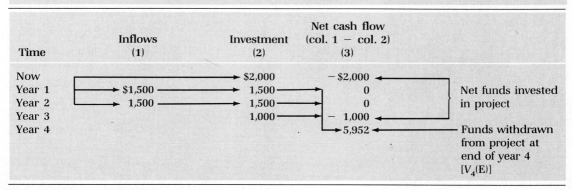

Time	Inflows (1)	Investment (2)	Net cash flow (col. 1 − col. 2) (3)	
Now		$2,000	− $2,000	Net funds invested in project
Year 1	$1,500	1,500	0	
Year 2	1,500	1,500	0	
Year 3		1,000	− 1,000	
Year 4			5,952	Funds withdrawn from project at end of year 4 [$V_4(E)$]

9

RISK ANALYSIS AND CAPITAL BUDGETING

In Chapter 8 we assumed that all investments being considered for inclusion in a company's capital budget had the same risk as those undertaken in the past, on average, by the firm. Thus the firm's cost of capital could be used as a discount rate or minimum acceptable rate of return in evaluating the desirability of each investment project. Projects normally vary in their risks and the firms cost of capital will not be the proper discount rate to use in evaluating all of them. The analysis of risky investment projects is one of the most difficult and debated issues in finance. Many different approaches are used and no single approach is generally recognized as best in all situations.

In this chapter we present several procedures for evaluating investments that differ in degree of risk. We begin with an explanation of the problem and follow this with a description of some relatively simple procedures that do not require the explicit measurement of risk. Then we show how to analyze the estimated cash flows of an investment to determine which of the economic factors affecting the cash flows may be the major contributors to the project's risk. Next we explain how risk can be measured using probability distributions of a project's cash flows. We then describe how risky projects are evaluated and how the risk assessment procedures discussed earlier in the chapter are used in the evaluation. In the final section we apply the Capital Asset Pricing Model to evaluate risky investments.[1]

PROBLEMS IN EVALUATING RISKY INVESTMENTS

Suppose that you are the financial manager of a company and that three different investment projects have been proposed. The first project involves the burning of industrial waste to produce steam to generate electricity for the firm's use. The second project is to increase the production capacity of the firm. The third is to begin manufacturing a new product. Each of these investments is risky in the sense that no one currently knows for certain what the future cash flows resulting from these investments will be. The degree of uncertainty is different for each project and may also vary over time for a particular project. For example, the cash flows from generating electricity are probably more certain than those from manufacturing the new product. The cash flows from generating electricity next year are probably more certain than those from generating electricity ten years from now.

The initial step in any project analysis is to choose a method of project evaluation. The choice will depend on the costs and benefits of each possible method. Some methods in this chapter require significant time and expense. These methods are usually reserved for large-scale risky projects for which accurate risk estimates may prevent management from making costly errors. The authors know of a firm that built a $50 million semiconductor plant based on very limited analysis. The plant turned out to be a $50 million disaster and has been shut down. Management admits (privately)

---

[1] Problems in the financing of investments and of interactions between investment and financing decisions are covered in Chap. 10.

that if they had more carefully analyzed the risks at the beginning, they would not have made this mistake. When the project cash flows are relatively certain or when the potential cost of an error is small, extensive risk analysis is not economically advisable.

All methods of analyzing a risky project have three things in common:

1 A framework for analysis
2 An assessment of the project's risk
3 An adjustment for the degree of risk

Procedures for assessing risk and adjusting for it vary among different methods of analysis. The financial manager may assess risk by judgment or by an elaborate computer analysis of the project's cash flows. The manager may adjust the cash flow estimates to reflect their risk or may adjust the discount rate used to compute the present value of the cash flows. Most of the methods found in theory and in practice use the discounted cash flow approach described in Chapter 8 as their basic framework. The methods discussed here are based on this framework with some variations.[2]

INFORMAL METHODS OF RISK ANALYSIS

There are three methods of risk analysis found in practice that use discounted cash flow techniques and that do not require numerical measures of risk. All are based on managerial judgment as to the risk of a project. They are:

1 Use of conservative estimates of project cash flows
2 Use of judgment as to whether the project is sufficiently profitable to compensate for its risk
3 Use of a classification system for projects with prespecified minimum acceptable rates of return (discount rates) for each classification

All three methods share a common problem; they do not directly consider how investors will value the cash flows from a project that is undertaken. Therefore, they are not very accurate in determining whether undertaking a project will benefit the owners of the firm. To compensate for this inherent lack of accuracy, the methods are relatively easy to apply. Under the proper conditions, all of them can provide reasonable results.

Conservative Estimates

Perhaps the oldest and still most widely used method of dealing with risk is to make conservative estimates of the cash flows. The firm's cost of capital is used to evaluate the cash flows from all projects regardless of their risk. For example, as a financial manager evaluating the proposal to manufacture a new product, you might take the sales projections and reduce them by 20 percent. Then you might increase the cost per unit manufactured by 10 percent. If the project's revised cash flows have a positive net present value based on the firm's cost of capital, you might then decide the project

---

[2] A theoretical procedure for adjusting the cash flow estimates to their "certainty equivalents" is presented in Appendix 9A. In this procedure, riskless interest rates are used to determine the present values of future, adjusted cash flows.

268

PART 2
**The firm's investment,
financing, and dividend
decisions**

is worthwhile undertaking. There are three major problems with this procedure. First, it does not handle low-risk projects very well. If the project offers significantly less risk than the typical firm project, it may be erroneously rejected unless it is extremely profitable.[3] Second, the procedure requires a great deal of judgment by the financial manager. To properly account for risk, high-risk cash flows should be adjusted differently from low-risk cash flows. Without additional analysis, it isn't clear how large the adjustment should be (10 percent, 20 percent, or what?). Third, if the people who originate the projects find out that you are adjusting their estimates, they are likely to compensate by providing overly optimistic estimates. This can result in a game played between the financial manager and operating personnel that does not contribute to sound decisions or to good personal relationships.

Judgmental Risk Evaluation

Under the most common procedure using judgmental risk evaluation, the financial manager computes, or asks the project originator to compute, the project's internal rate of return. The financial manager decides whether the internal rate of return is "high enough" given the perceived risk of the project. This judgment of the financial manager is based on past experience and current conditions in the capital markets. The firm's cost of capital may be used as a comparison rate. For example, suppose the internal rate of return on a project is calculated to be 16 percent based on the best available estimates of the future cash flows. The firm's cost of capital is estimated to be 12 percent. If the project is thought to be only slightly more risky than the typical project or less risky, it will be undertaken. If the project is thought to be extremely risky, it will be turned down. A capable financial manager can use this approach with some success, avoiding large errors. It is often used in small- and medium-sized firms.

Project Classification

In many large firms with decentralized decisions, a more formal procedure, project classification, is used. The project classification method is based on the assumption that broad groups of projects will have similar risks. Classification schemes in use are typically based on the purpose of the project and on the product line of the division. The corporate finance staff will estimate a separate cost of capital for each division as if the division were an independent firm. Frequently estimates of the cost of capital for other firms in industries similar to the division's industry are made using the techniques described in Chapter 7. For example, a diversified petroleum firm might estimate separate costs of capital for its divisions: exploration and development, tanker operations, pipelines, petrochemicals, refining, and

---

[3] If a project's cash flows have less risk than is typical for the firm's past investments, a discount rate that is less than the firm's cost of capital is needed to correctly compute the net present value of the expected cash flows. Therefore, using the firm's cost of capital as the discount rate will cause some desirable investments to be rejected even when the expected cash flows are properly discounted. Applying conservative estimates to the cash flows compounds the problem. This type of error can be minimized in the application of the conservative cash flow estimate method by using a low discount rate for all projects, perhaps even the interest rate on United States government bonds.

marketing. Within each division several different discount rates for projects might be established. A relatively low discount rate might be used for cost reduction investments involving known technology. An average discount rate might be used for investments involving expansion of existing facilities or cost reduction investments using new technology. A high discount rate might be used for investments involving new products. These discount rates are provided to division financial managers for use in their evaluations of projects.

Project classification has two major advantages. First, when interest rates are relatively stable, the discount rates do not have to be changed often. Therefore, they can be estimated with some care initially.[4] Second, once in place, they are objective criteria that can be communicated throughout the organization. This inhibits the game playing that may occur when more judgmental methods are used.

The major disadvantage of project classification in its application is that the classification schemes used by most companies are very limited and do not recognize risk differences among projects within the same classification. For example, not all new products in the petrochemical division are likely to be of equal risk. Likewise, there may be several alternative methods of producing a product all involving similar levels of technology. However, some methods may be more readily adaptable to different products than others, making investment in these production methods less risky. Ford Motor Company closed down one of the most efficient (low-cost) V8 engine plants in the world because the plant could not be used economically to produce the small engines then in demand. However, other Ford plants that were less efficient at engine production in general were also more flexible and Ford transferred production to them. The investment in these, more flexible plants was less risky than investment in the V8 engine plant.

SENSITIVITY ANALYSIS

The approaches described in the preceding section used estimates (expected values) of the cash flows for a project and various forms of judgmental risk evaluation. Most of the procedures used to measure the risk of a project require the development of probability distributions. However, the first technique we examine, sensitivity analysis, may be used alone or in conjunction with analysis of probability distributions.

The net cash flow from a project depends on many variables, each of which must be estimated. For example, suppose we wish to calculate the net cash flow from a project to generate electricity from industrial waste to replace power currently being purchased from the electric utility. We must estimate the investment outlay, the amount of waste available for burning, the costs of operating and maintaining the generating equipment, the amount of electricity generated, and the probable price of the electricity if

---

[4] The frequent, large changes in interest rates during the past decade have reduced this advantage. For example, the average rate on Aaa corporate bonds increased by over three percentage points during 1981. Corporations should now review their discount rates at least once a year. Some firms revise their discount rates quarterly.

270

PART 2
The firm's investment,
financing, and dividend
decisions

we continue to purchase it from the electric utility rather than generate it. Sensitivity analysis is a systematic way to determine which of the factors affecting project cash flow are most important. The method is used to assess the degree of risk in the project and indicates areas where additional effort to produce better (less uncertain) estimates might be justified. The basic procedure is to recalculate the net present value using assumptions that differ from those used to produce the original net cash flow estimates. The purpose of the analysis is to assess how "sensitive" the net present value is to changes in assumptions about the underlining economic factors.[5] There are many variations in this basic procedure; we illustrate one approach below.

Suppose that the electricity generating project has estimated cash flows as shown in Exhibit 9-1. The firm uses the project classification method and 9 percent is the discount rate normally applied to cost reduction projects by the firm. Given these estimates, the NPV of the project is positive, indicating that the project is acceptable. As financial manager, you decide to perform a sensitivity analysis by first examining how sensitive the esimated NPV is to an error of 10 percent in the estimates of the economic factors affecting the cash flows. To do this, you recalculate the NPV using revised values for each factor taken one at a time, as shown in Exhibit 9-2. Here the initial cost and annual depreciation are assumed to be known so that these components need not be investigated further.

From the data in Exhibit 9-2 you find that the NPV is most sensitive to errors in the forecasts of the price of electricity and the volume of power generated. If the forecasts are off 10 percent in the wrong direction, the NPV of the project falls from a positive $27,000 to a negative $69,000. The NPV is also fairly sensitive to errors in the life of the project. On questioning the plant manager, who originated the project, you find that the volume of power is unlikely to vary much more than 2 percent from forecast as the supply of industrial waste (fuel) is ample and the technology is well known. The major sources of risk in this project are uncertainties in the future price of electricity and the life of the project. At this point, sensitivity analysis has made its contribution. You have zeroed in on the crucial risk factors in the decision: the electricity price and the project's life. The next step could be an attempt to estimate the probability distribution of net cash flow. In applying probability analysis, which is described below, the major effort would be placed on estimating the probability distribution of the electricity price and the project life since these are now known to be critical variables.

---

[5] Sensitivity analysis can be summarized as follows:

a Develop numerical estimates of the partial derivatives of the dependent variables (NPV or IRR) with respect to the economic variables (e.g., electricity price) that determine net cash flow.

b Evaluate the degree of uncertainty of those variables having large impacts (large partial derivatives).

c Use the information to assess the project's risk or as a guide to where additional efforts in refining estimates (reducing uncertainty) might be made.

Other possibilities include examining alternative "scenarios" for combinations of electricity price, project life, operating costs, etc. Sensitivity analysis is a flexible method that provides useful information; but it does not tell you what decision should be made.

EXHIBIT 9-1
Electricity generating project with equal annual cash flows assumed

Initial cost $1,000,000

Estimated life .... 10 years

Depreciation $100,000/year

Operating costs $50,000/year

Power generated .... 1 million kwh/year

Price of purchased electricity .... $0.25/kwh (expected average price over 10 years)

Tax rate .... 40 percent

Discount rate .... 9 percent

Electricity savings = (price) × (power generated)

= $0.25 × 1 million kwh

= $250,000

Taxes = (tax rate) × (electricity savings − operating costs − depreciation)

= 0.4 ($250,000 − $50,000 − $100,00)

= $40,000

Net cash flow = electricity savings − operating costs − taxes

= $250,000 − $50,000 − $40,000

= $160,000

Present value of net cash flow = (6.4177)$160,000 = $1,027,000 (rounded)

NPV = $27,000

EXHIBIT 9-2
Sensitivity analysis of electricity generating project

Factor	Estimate	Revision	Revised net cash flow	Revised NPV
Life	10 years	9 years	No change	− $41,000
Operating costs	$50,000	$55,000	$157,000	$8,000
Power generated	1 mil. kwh	900,000 kwh	$145,000	− $69,000
Electricity price	$0.25	$0.225	$145,000	− $69,000
Tax rate	40%	44%	$156,000	$1,000

The most advanced techniques of project risk analysis use the probability distributions of the cash flows from the project.[6] There are two problems here—first, how to obtain the distributions and, second, what to do with them once you have them. Our emphasis is on the second problem since the project originator is usually the one who provides the probability distributions for the financial manager to evaluate.

Recall from Chapter 6 that a probability distribution may be either discrete or continuous. Figure 9-1 illustrates the two types. The choice of which type to use in project analysis depends on convenience and the degree of accuracy needed in describing the possible values that may occur. In this chapter we use discrete distributions throughout for convenience. Summary measures are commonly used to describe a probability distribution. The **expected value** (mean) of the distribution is a measure of where the center is. The **standard deviation** (or variance) measures the spread of values around the expected value. The **correlation coefficient** is a measure of the relationship between two variables. There are several other statistical measures, but these three are the ones most frequently used.

Financial managers often use estimated probability distributions to assess the degree of risk in a project. Once the risk is assessed, an adjustment to the discount rate or the project's expected cash flows will be made. The adjustment for the degree of risk can be done by judgment or by objective calculations. Objective methods for risk adjustment are still in the process of development; however, we illustrate one such method based on the Capital Asset Pricing Model later.

Measuring Risk

In Chapter 6 we discussed the use of the standard deviation as a measure of uncertainty. In dealing with the cash flows from a project, however, an alternative measure is useful. To illustrate the issues, let's look at a project

[6] Readers who do not feel comfortable with the concept of probability distribution, standard deviation, etc., should review Chap. 6, pp. 142–147 before proceeding with this section.

FIGURE 9-1

Discrete and continuous probability distributions.

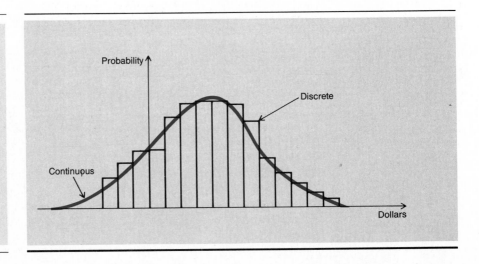

that uses industrial waste to generate electricity. The initial equipment investment is known to be $1 milliion, and the investment has an economic life of five years.[7] Probability distributions of the net cash flow from the project for years 1 and 5 are shown in Figure 9-2. The degree of uncertainty in the cash flows increases with time. This is shown both by the standard deviation of cash flows ($80,000 in year 1 versus $240,000 in year 5) and by another measure, the coefficient of variation (.4 in year 1 versus .8 in year 5).

Coefficient of Variation   The coefficient of variation (CV) of a probability distribution is defined as

$$CV = \frac{\text{standard deviation}}{\text{expected value}} \tag{9-1}$$

In computing the CV, the standard deviation is divided by the expected value in order to adjust for the scale or magnitude of the cash flow. The standard deviation measures the uncertainty of the cash flow and is measured in the same units (dollars here) as the expected value. The coefficient of variation provides a relative measure of uncertainty that can be expressed in percentage form. For example, the year 1 coefficient of variation can be expressed as 40 percent. When dealing with cash flows, the coefficient of variation provides a better measure of the uncertainty than does the standard deviation. To take an extreme example, suppose that the standard deviation of cash flow A and of cash flow B is $20,000. Also assume that the expected value of cash flow A is $20,000 whereas the expected value of cash flow B is $2 million. CV for A is 1.0, or 100 percent, whereas CV for B is .01, or 1 percent. For practical purposes, cash flow B is virtually certain whereas

---

[7] In many cases the initial cost and life of an investment are also uncertain. Uncertainty in the amount of initial investment poses some special problems for analysis that are dealt with in more advanced texts.

FIGURE 9-2

Electricity generation project net cash flows.

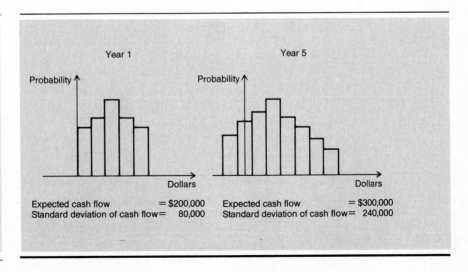

	Year 1			Year 5	
Expected cash flow	= $200,000		Expected cash flow	= $300,000	
Standard deviation of cash flow	= 80,000		Standard deviation of cash flow	= 240,000	

274

PART 2
The firm's investment,
financing, and dividend
decisions

cash flow A is highly uncertain. This difference in uncertainty is reflected by the coefficient of variation but not by the standard deviation.

Correlation in Project Risk Analysis   We have identified two related measures of the uncertainty of a project's cash flow—the standard deviation and the coefficient of variation. However, only part of the uncertainty affects the risk of the project, the part that cannot be diversified away by investors in the firm. This part depends on the correlation of the project's cash flow with the returns from the other assets owned by the investors. We discuss diversification and its implications regarding corporate decisions in more detail later in the chapter; for the moment, we need to show how it affects project risk.

Two points are relevant here. First, any project of the company is owned by the company's shareholders and is therefore a part of the portfolios of assets owned by the shareholders. Second, the risk of a project (from the shareholders' perspective) depends on how it affects the risk of the shareholders' portfolios, and this depends on how the project blends with the rest of those portfolios. For any given standard deviation of cash flow from the project, the higher is the correlation of the project's cash flows with the cash flows of the other assets in the shareholders' portfolios, the more the project increases the risk of the portfolios and therefore the greater is the project's risk.[8]

If you are a manager of a company trying to maximize the market value of the company's shares, what should you suppose about the asset compositions of the portfolios owned by your existing shareholders and by potential shareholders (who establish the market price for your company's stock)? For most United States companies, the best assumption is that existing and potential investors in your company's shares have diversified portfolios with returns that move closely with the United States economy. On average, the economy is simply the sum total of all investors' portfolios and is therefore a reasonable measure of what investors own.

If we assume that the cash flows from investors' portfolios move closely with the economy, then, for any given standard deviation of cash flow from a project, the higher the correlation of the project's cash flows with the economy, the more the project increases the risk of investors' portfolios and the higher is the risk of the project. Estimating the correlation of a project's cash flows with the economy may be done by an analysis of historical relationships such as the relationship between the price of electricity and GNP. Often the cash flows of the project will be very highly correlated with the cash flows of an existing operating unit or division within the firm. In such cases the historical correlations between the cash flows of the division and the economy may be used as an estimate of the correlations of the project's cash flows with the economy. Alternatively, there may be another firm which has observable cash flows similar to those of the project. The historical correlation for this firm could be used. Determining an appropri-

---

[8] For details on the relationship between a single asset's standard deviation and correlation with the portfolio's returns and the effect of the asset on the portfolio's risks, see Chap. 6 (the sections on Portfolio Risk and Diversification, Risk and Return in the Securities Markets, and Appendix 6A).

FIGURE 9-3

*An example of the
input and output for
the simulation analysis
of an investment.*

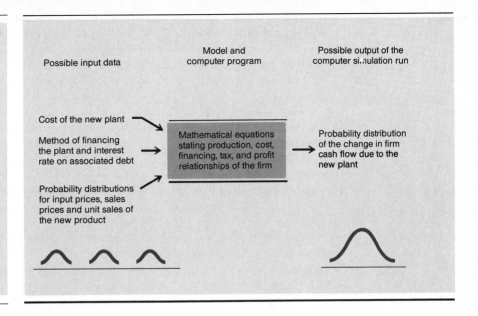

Possible input data

Model and
computer program

Possible output of the
computer simulation run

Cost of the new plant

Method of financing
the plant and interest
rate on associated debt

Probability distributions
for input prices, sales
prices and unit sales of
the new product

Mathematical equations
stating production, cost,
financing, tax, and profit
relationships of the firm

Probability distribution
of the change in firm
cash flow due to the
new plant

ate correlation can be a difficult task, but some estimate must be made to properly assess the risk of the project.

ESTIMATING PROBABILITY DISTRIBUTIONS

Two techniques used in estimating probability distributions should be known by the financial manager. They are simulation and decision tree analysis. We look at each one separately.

Simulation

If complete probability distributions for the cash flows are desired, computer simulation is normally used. This approach is typically applied to large-scale projects where the benefits of the complete analysis are sufficient to justify the time and effort involved. The basic procedure is to estimate, for each time period, separate probability distributions for each uncertain factor affecting net cash flow (sales price, labor cost, etc.). The probability distributions may be discrete or continuous. A computer program that contains the equation for net cash flow [Eq. (8-1), for example] generates values for each factor from its probability distribution for the first time period of the project's life and computes the net cash flow. This process is repeated for each period of the analysis to produce a set of net cash flows for the project. Then a new set of net cash flows is generated by the same procedure. After many such cash flows have been developed, the result is a series of probability distributions for the net cash flow, one for each time period. The mean (expected) value for each period, the standard deviation, and any other desired measures are calculated by the computer program. The reason computers are used is that a large number of computations is involved. The simulation process for analyzing investment in a manufacturing facility to produce a new product is illustrated in Figure 9-3.

In some situations, the development of probability distributions of net cash flows requires an evaluation of future decisions. Decision tree analysis is used in these cases. Decision tree analysis is usually done with a diagram that has "branches," thus the name. The branches reflect alternative future decisions and possible states of the world. For example, suppose that you are trying to decide whether to invest $1 million in a pilot plant for a new process to produce synthetic rubber. Based on the results of the pilot plant operations, you will then decide whether or not to proceed with synthetic rubber manufacturing. The probability of favorable results from the pilot plant is .5 and the probability of unfavorable results is also .5. The net cash flow from the project will depend on whether demand for the product is high or low as well as on the cost of the manufacturing process as obtained from the pilot plant operations. Figure 9-4a illustrates the original problem.

The idea behind decision tree analysis is that, of all the possible future decisions, you should include only the ones you might actually make in deciding whether to invest in the pilot plant today. If the outcome of the pilot study is unfavorable, the best future decision is not to invest in a synthetic rubber plant since the present value of the future cash flows, even when there is high demand for the product, is less than the cost of building a full-scale plant. There is no need to consider the possibility of investing in the plant when it will not be profitable to do so. On the other hand, if the outcome of the pilot study is favorable, building the full-scale plant appears to be the best decision. At worst, under conditions of low demand, the plant is a break-even investment. Therefore, the alternative of not building the plant when the pilot study is favorable can be eliminated from consideration. Decision tree analysis shows how to prune out future possibilities and, therefore, to develop more accurate probability distributions. Figure 9-4b illustrates the results of the pruning.

COMPANY DIVERSIFICATION AND PROJECT ANALYSIS

We noted earlier that, for large United States companies, the correlation of a project's cash flows with the United States economy was an important measure of risk from the perspective of the firm's stockholders. We did not consider the impact of the project on the risk of the firm itself. Should the firm be considered a portfolio of projects and should management try to minimize the risk of the firm's portfolio? The answer is *no*. The reason is that investors are able to diversify on their own, and they are not willing to pay extra for a firm's shares just because the firm is diversified; that is, they are not willing to pay a premium for someone else (firm management) to do what they can do themselves.

To illustrate the above point, assume that firm A could buy firm B (which is in a line of business different from A's) and thereby diversify. The new firm would be called firm AB. Also assume that the total income of firm AB is exactly equal to the sum of the incomes of firms A and B separately (i.e., there are no economies of scale or other savings from combining). Will investors pay more for the shares of firm AB than for the shares of firms A and B separately? That is, will the value of firm AB be greater than the sum of the values of firms A and B if unmerged? The answer is *no*. Even if firms A and B were separate, the investors could do their own diversifying by simply buying shares in firm A and shares in firm B; they don't need a merger to produce the diversification benefits. The values of firms A and B if they are not merged (V_A and V_B) will reflect the diversification benefits investors can gain from combining shares of A and B into portfolios and will equal the value of the merged firm (V_{AB}), that is, $V_{AB} = V_A + V_B$. The same principle

FIGURE 9-4

An example of a decision tree analysis.

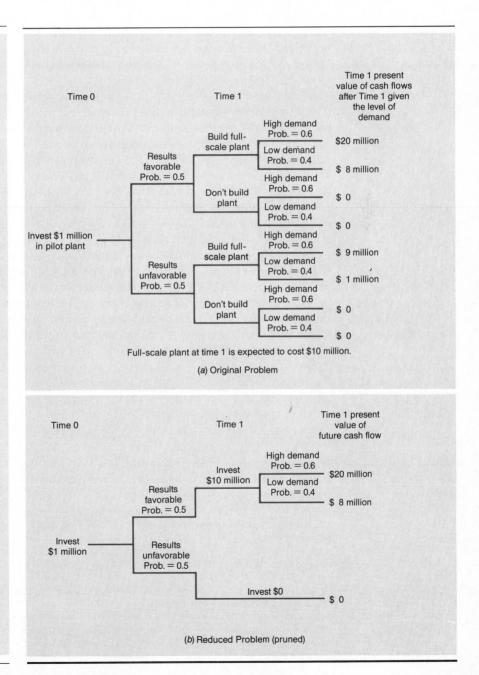

(a) Original Problem

(b) Reduced Problem (pruned)

278

PART 2
The firm's investment,
financing, and dividend
decisions

applies if B is not a separate firm but is simply a new project of firm A. The value of project B to the firm is simply V_B, the value of the income stream from B to investors. That is, we simply use the appropriate risk-adjusted market discount rate to discount the cash flow from B. We do not have to worry about how the income stream from project B correlates (diversifies with) the income stream from firm A.[9]

The important message is that, since investors can do their own diversifying, firms do not have to be concerned with diversification and can ignore correlation between project returns.[10] Management's job is to find projects with positive net present values; in other words, projects generating cash flows with values to investors that are greater than the projects' costs.

RISK AND PROJECT EVALUATION

So far we have been examining methods of analyzing and measuring the risk of a project. Sensitivity analysis is used to determine the economic factors and cash flow components that are the major sources of uncertainty for the project. Simulation and decision trees are used to generate probability distributions. We looked at three summary measures of a cash flow distribution (standard deviation, coefficient of variation, and correlation) and discussed their importance in measuring risk. Now let's see how we can use the information from cash flow probability distributions to evaluate an investment project.

Suppose that you are provided the following data for a project: the expected net cash flows (including the initial outlay), the standard deviations of the cash flows, and the correlation of each period's cash flows with the economy. An example of such data is shown in Exhibit 9-3. What do you do next? One possibility is to compute the internal rate of return for the project, which is 16.6 percent, and use judgment to determine whether the internal rate of return is high enough to justify undertaking the project. The difference between this approach and the "judgmental risk evaluation" method described earlier is that now you have numerical risk measures of the project's cash flows to aid in making a judgment. Of course, to apply judgment in this case you will need experience in dealing with the risk measures as well as knowledge of current capital market conditions. An alternative procedure is to compute the net present value of the project.

Project Net Present Value

To apply the net present value technique, the present value of the cash flow in each period must be computed. Since the risk of the cash flows in Exhibit 9-3 varies from period to period, the discount rates applicable to the cash

---

[9] If CF_A is the cash flow stream of firm A without project B, CF_B is the added flow provided by project B, and CF_{AB} is firm A's cash flow if it adopts project B (where $CF_{AB} = CF_A + CF_B$), then it follows that: $V_{AB} = V_A + V_B$, where V_{AB} is the value of firm A if project B is adopted, V_A is the value of firm A if project B is not adopted, and V_B is the value that CF_B would have as an individual stream in the market. The principle that the total value of a set of combined income streams (V_{AB}) equals the sum of the values of the streams separately ($V_A + V_B$) is commonly referred to as the "value additivity principle."

[10] The firm may be able to benefit from a reduction in costs associated with financial planning and financial distress if the uncertainty in the firm's cash flows is reduced. This benefit of diversification is very difficult to quantify and informal, judgmental procedures are used to account for it.

cash flow, we can determine the rate of return or discount rate that would apply to the cash flow if it were available in the capital market. A set of such discount rates could then be used in Eq. (9-2) to estimate the market value of the cash flows from an investment. Once we have discount rates for all the cash flows from an investment, the rates can be used to discount the expected cash flows to obtain the net present value from undertaking the investment. If the net present value is positive, the investment is desirable; if the net present value is negative, the investment should not be undertaken.

For example, suppose that $k_M = 14$ percent, $i = 8$ percent, and therefore the market risk premium $(k_M - i)$ is 6 percent. Also assume that we have a project with an expected cash flow one year from now of $100, an expected cash flow two years from now of $150, and no further cash flows after that. Let the initial outlay on the project be $175. If the cash flow one year from now has a beta value of 1.0, using Eq. (9-5) we compute the discount rate for that cash flow as

$$k_1 = 8\% + (6\%)1.0$$

$$= 14\%$$

Similarly if the cash flow two years from now has a beta of 1.2, the value of k_2 is:

$$k_2 = 8\% + (6\%)1.2$$

$$= 15.2\%$$

The net present value of the project is therefore:

$$NPV = -\$175 + \frac{\$100}{1.14} + \frac{\$150}{(1.152)^2}$$

$$= \$25.75$$

Since the NPV is positive, the project should be accepted.

The major difficulty with the above approach is estimating the betas. The nature of the problem is a topic for advanced courses, but we will indicate some approaches to the solution. A cash flow's beta depends on the correlation of the cash flow with the economy and the cash flow's coefficient of variation. The larger are these two measures of risks, the larger is the beta of the cash flow.[13] However, little more can be said about estimating individual cash flow betas without much more discussion.

[13] Beta for an asset A which has a single cash flow occurring one period from now can be expressed as:

$$Beta_A = \left(\frac{1 + i}{k_M - i}\right)\left(\frac{1}{1 - s \, Corr \, CV} - 1\right)$$

where i = the riskless interest rate
k_M = the expected rate of return on the market portfolio
s = the slope of the capital market line [see Eq. (6-7)]
Corr = the correlation of asset A's cash flow with the market
CV = the coefficient of variation of asset A's cash flow

The relationship for multiperiod cash flows is more complex. For an analysis of some of the difficulties in using asset betas, see S. C. Myers and S. M. Turnbull, "Capital Budgeting and the Capital Asset Pricing Model: Good News and Bad News," *Journal of Finance*, #32 (May 1977), pp. 321–332.

282

PART 2
The firm's investment,
financing, and dividend
decisions

An alternative to estimating the beta for each period's cash flow is to estimate a single average beta for the entire stream of cash flows from the project. This beta can then be used to determine a single discount rate for all the cash flows. Of course, if the cash flows differ in their risk, this approach is only an approximation. A way to determine a single beta is to identify an asset already existing in the market which has cash flows that are similar in risk to the cash flows from our project. We can estimate the beta for the existing asset and use it for our project. For example, if our investment project is a steel mill, we could look at the betas of steel companies to estimate the project's beta.

In conclusion, there is no easy solution to the problem of evaluating risky investment projects. All known methods involve some degree of judgment by the financial manager and many require extensive analysis without providing a definite answer. We have presented an overview of the tools available at this time.

SUMMARY

Not all investment opportunities available to business firms have the same risk. Good decisions about which investments to make require that differences in risk be reflected in the analysis of those investments. Most of the methods used in practice are based on managerial judgment about project risk. Firms using discounted cash flow analysis typically adjust the discount rate or minimum acceptable rate of return to reflect the degree of risk. High-risk projects are evaluated using a higher discount rate than low-risk projects. In some cases, the estimates of project cash flows are lowered to reflect their risk.

Numerical risk analysis techniques include sensitivity analysis and the estimation of the probability distributions of the cash flows. Sensitivity analysis is done by revising the estimates of the components of the expected cash flows from the project to see how much the net present value changes as a result of the revision. Computer simulation is used to estimate the probability distribution of the cash flows for large-scale projects. The probability distributions of the cash flows are developed by repetitive sampling from probability distributions of the components of the cash flows. Decision tree analysis is used to eliminate from consideration those future outcomes that would result only if management made poor future decisions.

The primary measures of risk that are obtained from probability distributions are the standard deviations of the cash flows and their correlations with the economy. The coefficient of variation equals the standard deviation of a cash flow divided by the expected value. It is superior to the standard deviation as a risk measure because it compensates for the size of the cash flow. If the owners of the firm are well diversified, the firm's managers need not be concerned about diversification of the firm's investments. Each investment opportunity can be evaluated on its own merits.

Numerical risk measures can be combined with judgment to produce discount rates that reflect the risks of the cash flows. The Capital Asset

Pricing Model provides an objective method of determining discount rates based on the betas of the project's cash flows.

QUESTIONS

1 Why might the use of conservative cash flow estimates for projects cause rejection of more low-risk projects than high-risk projects?

2 Is judgmental risk evaluation better suited to small firms or to large firms? Why?

3 What is the major advantage of the project classification approach relative to judgmental risk evaluation?

4 Why is the standard deviation of an investment's cash flow an inadequate measure of the investment's risk?

5 What are we assuming about investors in the firm when the correlation of a project's cash flow with the economy is used as one of the measures of the project's risk?

6 Assume that a firm has raised $10 million by selling new shares and bonds to finance its entire current capital budget, which involves investing in many individual projects. What is the reasoning for using different risk-adjusted discount rates for investments of different risk if they are financed from the same $10 million source of funds?

7 If you are considering an investment in an apartment building and have estimated the expected future cash flows from the building, how might you go about estimating a proper discount rate for the investment to determine the apartment's net present value?

8 Midwest Resources engages in several distinct lines of business organized into separate divisions including natural gas pipelines, natural gas exploration and development, coal mining, and electric power generation. The financial manager has carefully estimated discount rates for each line of business for use in capital budgeting decisions at the divisional level. Each division is provided with the discount rate to be used for projects in that division. New discount rates are calculated quarterly. Evaluate the approach used by Midwest.

9 Discuss the practical limitations of:
   a Performing computer simulations over more than a two- or three-year horizon period.
   b Doing a decision tree analysis for more than a two- or three-year period.

PROJECT

Visit one or more large firms in your area and inquire how the firms perform their capital budgeting analyses. Among the questions you might want to ask are:

1 How much does the firm spend each year on capital outlays?

2 What capital budgeting techniques are employed (present value, IRR, payback, accounting rate of return, etc.)?

3 If a cost of capital is used, how is the cost of capital determined and what is its numerical magnitude?

284

PART 2
The firm's investment,
financing, and dividend
decisions

4 If cash flow is used in evaluating projects, how is it computed?
5 How is risk assessed for a particular investment, e.g., using probability distributions, subjective assessment without quantification, no assessment at all, etc.?
6 How is risk accounted for in analyzing investments, e.g., by using risk-adjusted discount rates?

PROBLEMS

1 National Music Company uses the project classification method of evaluating investment proposals. The minimum acceptable rates of return for different types of projects are:

Cost reduction = 9%
Expansion of existing products = 12%
New products = 16%

As chief financial officer you have received the following proposals:
a Installation of new equipment to reduce costs of manufacturing guitar strings. Initial outlay is $300,000. Annual savings after tax is $45,000 per year for ten years.
b A plant to produce electronic violins. Only one firm—a competitor of National Music Company—currently manufactures this product. Initial outlay is $2 million. Annual net cash flow after taxes is $500,000 for six years.

Which investment (a, b, both, or neither) do you recommend that National undertake?
2 Clearcut Lumber Company is considering investment in a new plywood manufacturing facility. The initial cost of the plant will be $400,000. Annual cost and revenue items are shown below. The discount rate is 15 percent. Perform a sensitivity analysis on this project. Clearcut's effective tax rate is zero.

Economic life of plant = 20 years
Volume of plywood produced = 2 million square feet per year
Price per square foot of plywood sold = $0.25
Labor cost per square foot of plywood produced = $0.05
Lumber cost per square foot of plywood produced = $0.10
Operating costs of plant = $100,000 per year

3 a Rank the following projects according to their coefficients of variation:

Project	Expected cash flow	Standard deviation of cash flow
A	$ 40,000	$ 10,000
B	400,000	16,000
C	500,000	150,000
D	800,000	160,000

b If each project has a correlation with the economy of 0.4, which project is the most risky from the perspective of a highly diversified stockholder?

4 Norton Sports owns bowling alleys and tennis courts throughout the United States. Norton is evaluating a new project that will house a variety of sports facilities, including tennis, bowling, and swimming, in one location. The initial (time 0) cost of the project will be $4.5 millon. The project is regarded by Norton as quite risky. The estimated expected annual cash flows and their associated discount rates for computing present values are shown below:

Time	Expected annual cash flow	Risk-adjusted discount rate
1	$400,000	12%
2	600,000	16%
3 and thereafter	800,000	18%

Norton management feels the higher discount rate is appropriate for more distant future cash flows because of markedly increasing uncertainty about them.

What is the net present value of the project?

5 Rework the synthetic rubber plant example shown on pages 276–277, showing both the original problem and the reduced problem under the following revised conditions:

a If the full-scale plant is not built, the pilot plant has a salvage value of $0.5 million. Otherwise the salvage value is zero.

b If results from the pilot plant are unfavorable and a full-scale plant is built, the present value of the cash flows at time 1 under low demand conditions is $4 million.

6 Agglomerated Industries is evaluating a facility to produce a new breakfast product. The product which is referred to internally as "Ham-Z," consists of soy meal and fish protein flavored to taste like ham. The initial cost of the facility is $3 milliion. In analyzing this project, you discovered that the success or failure of the product would probably be known after the first year. If the product is successful, the first-year cash flow is expected to be $300,000. If Ham-Z continues in production, the cash flow in the second year and beyond is expected to be $500,000 into the indefinite future. The discount rate applicable to these cash flows is 12 percent. If the product is a failure, cash flow in the first year is expected to be −$100,000 (a net outflow). If Ham-Z production continues, the cash flow in the second and subsequent years is expected to be $150,000 per year. The discount rate applicable to these cash flows is 15 percent. It is also possible to sell the Ham-Z facility at the end of the first year, thereby obtaining a cash flow of $2 million in addition to the cash flows resulting from the first year's operations. No additional cash flows will result if this alternative is chosen.

286

PART 2
The firm's investment,
financing, and dividend
decisions

a Set up a decison tree for the Ham-Z project.

b Try to reduce (prune) the tree.

c Suppose that the probability of success is 0.5 and, therefore, the probability of failure is 0.5. The year 1 present value of cash flows expected in the second year and beyond can be treated as a cash flow at the end of the first year. Compute the expected cash flow for year 1 using the reduced decison tree. If the discount rate applicable to this cash flow is 20 percent, should the Ham-Z project be undertaken?

7 The National Music Company has decided to estimate a separate discount rate for the electronic violin project of problem **1b**. The beta for the project is thought to be the same as the beta of the firm currently manufacturing the product. The estimated beta is 2.0. The riskfree rate is 8 percent and the market risk premium is 6 percent. Should National undertake the project?

8 As a financial analyst in the gas pipeline division of Midwest Resources, you have been given the task of estimating a discount rate to be used in evaluating typical (normal risk) projects in the division. The chief financial officer of Midwest has specified that divisional discount rates must reflect current capital market rates and the degree of risk in the division.

a Will the CAPM help you in this task? What are the advantages and disadvantages of using it?

b How will you estimate the beta for a typical project?

c Suppose that you estimate the division's beta to be 0.8. The current rate on U.S. Treasury bonds is 10 percent and the market risk premium is thought to be 6 percent. What discount rate would you recommend?

(**Note:** Problems **9** and **10** are based on Appendix 9A.)

9 A project has an expected cash flow two years hence of $100. The certainty equivalent factor $a_2 = 0.90$ for this cash flow and the riskless interest rate is 12 percent. What risk-adjusted discount rate applies to this cash flow? [Ans.: Discount rate = 18.1 percent]

10 Four Seas' Bounty Fish Packing, Inc., is evaluating a capital project that will require a current outlay of $500,000. The cash flows from the project will begin one year later and are stated below. The riskless rate is 12 percent, and the risk-adjusted discount rate Four Seas has decided to use on the investment is 18 percent. Four Seas has also estimated the certainty equivalent factors for each year, which are indicated below.

Year	Expected cash flow	Certainty equivalent factors (a_t)
1	$100,000	0.912
2	100,000	0.880
3	200,000	0.695
4	400,000	0.921

a Verify that the net present value is the same for this investment whether the firm uses the risk-adjusted discount rate of 18 percent or uses the certainty equivalent approach.

b Is the above set of certainty equivalent factors equivalent to the 18 percent risk-adjusted discount rate? Why or not not? To answer this question, for each year (years 1 to 4) separately compute the risk-adjusted discount rate that would be appropriate for discounting that year's expected cash flow. To compute the risk-adjusted discount rate, use the certainty equivalent factors (a_t) shown above and the riskless rate.

c Consider the alternative set of certainty equivalent factors a_t' shown below and determine the risk-adjusted discount rate that would be appropriate for discounting each year's expected cash flow. (This is done as in b above.)

Year	Expected cash flow	Alternative set of certainty equivalent factors (a_t')
1	$100,000	0.949
2	100,000	0.901
3	200,000	0.855
4	400,000	0.811

d What can you conclude from the results of a, b, and c above?

CERTAINTY EQUIVALENTS AND RISK-ADJUSTED DISCOUNT RATES

Throughout this text the discount rates used to evaluate cash flows are "risk-adjusted." The discount rate that applied to a zero-risk cash flow is identified as the "riskless" rate of interest. The firm's cost of capital reflects the average risk of the firm's securities as shown in Figure 7-1. The security market line of Chapter 6 shows the relationship in the market between risk and the required (risk-adjusted) rate of return on a security. The dominant theme of Chapter 9 is how to determine what (risk-adjusted) discount rate to use to evaluate the cash flows from a project. However, there is an alternative to the use of risk-adjusted discount rates, the **certainty equivalent approach**. Here we present this approach and show how it is applied to business investment decisions.

RISK ANALYSIS USING CERTAINTY EQUIVALENTS

The certainty equivalent approach to analyzing risky investments is to determine the riskless cash flow stream that is just as good as the risky cash flow anticipated from a project and then to discount that riskless stream at the riskless rate of interest to obtain its present value.

To illustrate, assume that investment S is being evaluated and that it will require an initial $300 outlay (for simplicity, assume that this initial cost is known with certainty) and will generate an expected cash flow of $100 per year during the next two years and an expected cash flow of $200 in the third year. Assume that the correct risk-adjusted discount rate for the cash flows is 10 percent and that the riskless rate of interest is 6 percent (rate of return earned in the economy on riskless assets). We could use the procedure described in Chapter 8 and simply compute the NPV of the asset using the 10 percent discount rate. An alternative is to use the certainty equivalent approach, which involves determining the riskless future stream of returns that has the same value to investors as does the risky cash flow stream from the asset. Exhibit 9-4 is an example of such riskless amounts.[14] Thus, in this illustration, investors currently (when initial outlay of $300 is made) would be indifferent between receiving $96 one year hence for certain and owning the risky asset year 1 cash flow with expected dollar return of $100. That is, investors are currently indifferent between a sure thing of $96 received in year 1 and the cash flow probability distribution with an expected level of $100. Similarly, investors currently would be just as happy to know that they will receive $93 for certain in year 2 as they would be to own the risky asset year 2 stream that has an expected payoff of $100 in year 2. And investors are currently indifferent between receiving $178 in year 3 and receiving the risky asset's year 3 cash flow with an expected value of $200. The reason investors are indifferent between the

---

[14] The numbers in col. 2 of Exhibit 9-4 are those, as shown below, that are consistent with a riskless interest rate of 6 percent and a risk-adjusted discount rate of 10 percent. In general, for investors who do not like uncertainty, we know that the numbers in col. 2 must be less than those in col. 1 for any cash inflows that are uncertain.

riskless stream and the risky stream with a *higher* expected level is that investors do not like risk. The asset provides an *expected* return of $100 in year 1, but the amount that actually will occur might be much less, for example, perhaps only $80 or even less; so, investors would be just as happy with $96 for sure.

Column 3 in Exhibit 9-4 shows the certainty equivalent factors, a_t, where the t subscript stands for the time period. Factor a_t states the amount of money received for certain in future period t that is just equivalent (just as good in the eyes of investors) to a period t cash flow probability distribution with $1 of expected return. Thus, investors are currently indifferent between $0.96 received for certain in year 1 and a year 1 cash flow probability distribution from project S with an expected level of $1. The lower is a_t, the less the year t risky cash flow is worth, i.e., the riskier it is perceived as being.[15] A lower a_t means that fewer dollars received for certain in year t are equivalent for the year t risky stream. In the example of Exhibit 9-4, we are assuming that investors view the stream as more risky as they look further into the future; for this reason, a_t is decreasing as t increases, falling from $a_0 = 1$ down to $a_3 = 0.89$.

The above discussion implies that

$$\left(\begin{array}{c}\text{Risky period } t \text{ cash flow} \\ \text{with expected level CF}_t\end{array}\right) \text{ has the same value as}$$

$$\left(\begin{array}{c}a_t\text{CF}_t \text{ received for} \\ \text{certain in period } t\end{array}\right) \tag{9-5}$$

Equation (9-5) states that the present value to investors of the risky cash flow equals the present value of the equivalent riskless amount a_tCF$_t$. That is,

[15] Actually, a_t depends on both the perceived riskiness of the period t cash flow and how investors feel about incurring risk in period t. Therefore, a decline in a_t as t rises could occur because of increased risk or because of an increased dislike of risk, or both, as t increases. For simplicity we are assuming in the text discussion that the dislike of risk, or risk aversion, is the same for all t; given this assumption, a fall in a_t with greater t necessarily implies more risk as t rises, i.e., as we look further into the future.

EXHIBIT 9-4
Certainty equivalents for asset S

Time (t)	Expected cash flow (1)	Riskless amount equivalent to risky flow (2)	Certainty equivalent factor a_t (col. 2 ÷ col. 1) (3)
Now	− $300	− $300	1.00
Year 1	100	96	.96
Year 2	100	93	.93
Year 3	200	178	.89

290

PART 2
The firm's investment,
financing, and dividend
decisions

Present value of
the risky cash flow
discounted at
risk-adjusted rate k_t
$$= \frac{CF_t}{(1 + k_t)^t}$$

$$= \frac{a_t CF_t}{(1 + i)^t} = \begin{array}{l} \text{present value of} \\ \text{the riskless amount} \\ \text{discounted at the} \\ \text{riskless rate } i \end{array} \qquad (9\text{-}6)$$

In Eq. (9-6), k_t is the risk-adjusted discount rate used to discount the period t expected cash flow, CF_t; i is the rate of return in the economy earned on riskless assets (the riskless rate of interest) and is therefore the rate used by investors to discount riskless amounts.[16] We use the riskless rate i in Eq. (9-6) to discount $a_t CF_t$ since $a_t CF_t$ is a riskless amount, i.e., is a riskless dollar amount that would be equally desirable as the risky cash flow from the asset.

In the Exhibit 9-4 example, $k_t = k = 10$ percent for all t. That is, the certainty equivalent factors a_t imply that investors view the cash flow risk as justifying a 10 percent risk-adjusted rate of return to discount the cash flow. To see this, let's use (9-6) and compute the net present value of the cash flows using the risk-adjusted discount rate method and the certainty equivalent method. Using a risk-adjusted discount rate of 10 percent, the NPV equals (where I is the initial outlay)

$$NPV = \frac{CF_1}{1 + k} + \frac{CF_2}{(1 + k)^2} + \cdots + \frac{CF_n}{(1 + k)^n} - I \qquad (9\text{-}7)$$

$$= \frac{\$100}{1.10} + \frac{\$100}{(1.10)^2} + \frac{\$200}{(1.10)^3} - \$300$$

$$= \$91 + \$83 + \$150 - \$300 = \$24$$

Using the certainty equivalent approach, with $i = 6$ percent, the net present value equals

$$NPV = \frac{a_1 CF_1}{1 + i} + \frac{a_2 CF_2}{(1 + i)^2} + \cdots + \frac{a_n CF_n}{(1 + i)^n} - I \qquad (9\text{-}8)$$

$$= \frac{(.96)\$100}{1.06} + \frac{(.93)\$100}{(1.06)^2} + \frac{(.89)\$200}{(1.06)^3} - \$300$$

$$= \$91 + \$83 + \$150 - \$300 = \$24$$

NPV in Eqs. (9-7) and (9-8) must be equal since they are simply two different ways of computing the same value. We can use a risk-adjusted rate k which is greater than i, as in (9-7), or, instead, we can adjust the cash flows in the numerator to take care of risk and then discount the risk-adjusted cash flows at the riskless rate, as in (9-8). Both the risk-adjusted discount rate k

---

[16] The riskless rate is assumed here to be constant over time to simplify the discussion. All relationships can be generalized to nonconstant rates by setting $i = i_t$.

and the certainty equivalent factors a_t are selected so as to correctly reflect the riskiness of the investment.

An important characteristic of using a constant discount rate to value risky cash flows is illustrated by the certainty equivalent factors in Exhibit 9-4. The certainty equivalent factors decline from 1.0 to 0.89 which means that the cash flow is riskier the further we look out into the future. Using a constant discount rate $k = 10$ percent is apparently consistent with this increasing risk since it produces the correct present value in Eq. (9-7) of \$24. Let's examine this in a more general format.

RISK ADJUSTMENT IN DISCOUNT RATES

Using Eqs. (9-2) and (9-3), we can express net present value as

$$\text{NPV} = \frac{CF_1}{1 + k_1} + \frac{CF_2}{(1 + k_2)^2} + \cdots + \frac{CF_n}{(1 + k_n)^n} - I \tag{9-9}$$

where k_t is the risk-adjusted discount rate for discounting the period t expected cash flow CF_t. We also know that, using certainty equivalents, NPV also equals (where i is the riskless rate)

$$\text{NPV} = \frac{a_1 CF_1}{1 + i} + \frac{a_2 CF_2}{(1 + i)^2} + \cdots + \frac{a_n CF_n}{(1 + i)^n} - I \tag{9-10}$$

The NPVs in (9-9) and (9-10) are equal, and so is each term in (9-9) equal to the corresponding certainty equivalent term in (9-10); that is,

$$\frac{CF_t}{(1 + k_t)^t} = \frac{a_t CF_t}{(1 + i)^t} \tag{9-11}$$

Equation (9-11) implies

$$a_t = \frac{(1 + i)^t}{(1 + k_t)^t} = \left[\frac{1 + i}{1 + k_t}\right]^t \tag{9-12}$$

and, that

$$k_t = \frac{1 + i}{(a_t)^{1/t}} - 1 \tag{9-13}$$

Notice from Eq. (9-12) that if k_t is the same for all t, that is, if we use the same discount rates for all future period cash flows regardless of how far into the future the flows will occur, then a_t falls as t rises. For example, if $k = 10$ percent and $i = 6$ percent, then $a_1 = .96, a_2 = .93, a_3 = .89$ (these were the figures in Exhibit 9-4). But with a_t falling as t gets bigger, we are saying that risk is becoming greater the further into the future cash flow occurs, since, as explained in the text, a smaller a_t means that the cash flow is riskier (investors are willing to take a smaller certain amount for each dollar of expected cash flow). For any constant k ($k_t = k$ for all t) in (9-12), a_t must decline as t rises, implying that a constant k means rising risk. (See Figure 9-5.)

If the risk is constant, then the a_t in (9-12) are the same for all t and k_t must decrease as t increases. For example, with $i = 6$ percent and $a_t = .96$ for all t, substituting these values into Eq. (9-13) we find that $k_1 = 10$

FIGURE 9-5

Behavior of k_t for
different risk
assumptions. If k_t falls
less sharply (or is
constant or rising)
than the constant risk
schedule indicates,
then risk is assumed
to be rising; if k_t falls
more sharply than the
constant risk schedule
indicates, then risk is
assumed to be falling.

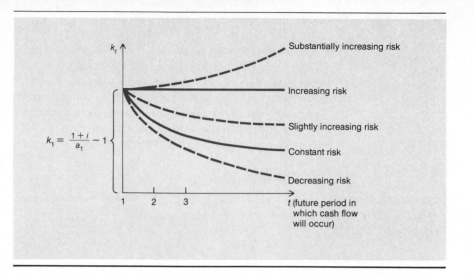

percent, k_2 = 8.2 percent, k_3 = 7.4 percent, etc. Having risk constant as we
look into the future means that we use a smaller and smaller k for cash
flows further into the future in computing a present value in Eq. (9-9). This is
illustrated in Figure 9-5.

CONTROLLING RISK

Risk is not simply a take it or leave it matter—risk can be changed and controlled by any of a variety of techniques at management's disposal. Below we discuss ways of making costs (operating and financing) and revenues more predictable. We note more than once that these risk reduction strategies are often not free, and whether they are profitable in a particular situation will depend on circumstances.

INSURANCE

Perhaps the purest antidote for risk is **insurance**. There are many kinds of insurance, including insurance to cover physical damage, theft and loss of life or health (for example, of a key business executive), loss of revenues (e.g., to provide a lessor with insurance against a lessee's not paying the lease rentals), and even default on a mortgage. Leasing rather than buying an asset is a way of purchasing insurance against a large decline in the salvage value of the asset; part of the lease rental is really a fee to the lessor (the asset's owner) for bearing the salvage value risk.

LONG-TERM ARRANGEMENTS

Peabody International, a major energy and environment control firm, found that costs often ran far ahead of expectations, largely because of inflation. The solution: Peabody often obtains fixed commitments from subcontractors before placing its own bids on new projects. The risk reduction strategy used by Peabody involves a long-term contract which guarantees the supply of a critical input at a prearranged price. The same strategy is being used when a company negotiates a long-term credit line with a bank: The company is guaranteeing a supply of funds even if there's a general credit crunch. A firm can also reduce uncertainty about its ability to

sell its product by negotiating a long-term sales contract with a customer.

INDEXING

Risks due to uncertainty about the future purchasing power of the dollar (inflation uncertainty) and about future interest rates can be shifted from one party to another by agreeing beforehand to make adjustments as prices or interest rates change in the future. For example, labor contracts and supply contracts often have **escalator clauses** under which the price of the good or service being supplied is adjusted for inflation. The **real price** (i.e., the price in terms of dollars of a fixed purchasing power) is thereby held constant. Variable rate mortgages carry interest rates which move up and down with the general level of interest rates (for example with the United States Treasury bill rate). This means that the mortgage lender is always assured of receiving an interest rate which is at least roughly in line with current interest rates. Long-term supply contracts for goods or services that involve price indexing actually protect both the buyer and the seller against inflation risks since the indexing is a way of keeping the real price (that is, the price in terms of purchasing power) constant. With a fixed price and no indexing there is uncertainty about what the real price will be. If inflation is greater than expected, the supplier will be worse off and the buyer will be better off than expected; but, if inflation turns out to be lower than expected, the supplier will be better off and the buyer worse off than expected.

The same then applies to interest rate indexing. The lack of interest rate indexing was a boon to borrowers and a disaster to savings and loan institutions in the early 1980s. During the 1970s, savings and loan companies used depositors' money (on which they were paying 5 percent or 6 per-

294

PART 2
The firm's investment,
financing, and dividend
decisions

cent) to make long-term mortgage loans at 7 percent to 9 percent. When interest rates went up at the end of the 1970s and the early 1980s, depositors withdrew their funds from savings and loan institutions and put the money into money market funds and other instruments which earned high interest rates. The savings and loan institutions then had to borrow money at far above the 7 percent to 9 percent they were earning on the mortgages in order to stay solvent. The only alternative was to sell the old mortgages at large discounts. If the mortgage interest rates had been indexed to the general level of interest rates, the savings and loan institutions would not have faced this disaster. But, mortgage borrowers would have been worse off since, with indexing, the interest rates on their mortgages would have risen with the general level of interest rates. On the other hand, if interest rates on mortgages had fallen (to, say, 6 percent) rather than risen, the mortgage borrowers would have been worse off than if the mortgage interest rates had been indexed to the general level of interest rates. Without indexing and with a general fall in interest rates, mortgage borrowers have the choice of either continuing to pay high interest rates on their mortgages or of paying off their old high interest rate mortgages (usually with a hefty prepayment penalty) and reborrowing at a lower interest rate.

IMPROVING INFORMATION

If you reach inside a box without peeking inside first, you have no way of knowing whether you are going to find a $100 bill or be bitten by a cobra. A simple look inside would resolve the risk. The same concept applies to investments: Risk can be reduced (although not usually completely eliminated) by obtaining more information before accepting a project and by maintaining a current flow of information about those projects which have been adopted. Obtaining information, and properly evaluating that information, is perhaps the key technique for reducing risk. An extreme example of this is the use by Turner Construction Company of a computerized system which uses up-to-date information on work progress, costs, weather, and other relevant factors in scheduling and controlling projects. Information and information analysis is not free and should be expanded only as long as the incremental benefits exceed the incremental costs. Usually, though, at least a small investment in information collection and analysis is justified.

CHANGES IN MODUS OPERANDI

Different methods of producing or marketing a product can have different risks. Rotary well drilling is faster than cable drilling, but it involves the risk of drilling right past a water table, the result being an unusable well. Acting as an intermediary (broker) between a computer lessor and a user involves less inventory risk than buying computers from a manufacturer and either selling or leasing them to users, since computers can become obsolescent almost overnight. This realization at one time motivated Itel Corporation to change its method of operation (Itel has since had its problems for other reasons). Whether adopting the lower-risk approach is desirable will depend on the relative costs and returns, as well as risks, of the available choices.

OPTIONS

An **option** is an arrangement which gives the optionholder the right to compel someone else to do something. Options take many forms. The right to buy (or sell) a building for $1 million at any time over the next year, the right to obtain up to $500,000 from a bank at any time over the next year under a revolving credit line, or the right to purchase up to 5000 tons of coal at any time over the next three years are all options. Options reduce risk for the optionholder by providing flexibility, by providing additional choices. This involves less risk than having to adopt a fixed course of action with fewer choices (for example, of buying, or of not buying, the building or the coal now, or of borrowing or not borrowing the money now). An option is not a "heads I win, tails you lose" transaction; the optionholder must pay a price for the option. This price may take the form of a fixed dollar amount; for example, I pay you $25,000 now for the option to buy your building for $1 million at any time over the next year (if I don't buy, you keep the $25,000). The option price may also take the form of a fee per unit time; for example, $\frac{1}{2}$ percent per year on any part of the $500,000 credit line *not* drawn down (borrowed). Since the option has a price, a decision must be made as to whether the added flexibility afforded by the option is worth the price. That depends on the situation.

HEDGING IN THE FUTURES MARKETS

You manufacture a chocolate-coated candy called Chocolate Surprise. You are about to sign a one-year fixed-price contract to supply Chocolate Surprise to a national chain of food stores. There is a great deal of uncertainty concerning the price of cocoa over the coming year and you would like to eliminate this risk without having to store huge quantities of cocoa. There is a very simple way to solve this problem: Purchase cocoa for future delivery by buying cocoa futures contracts in the commodities futures market. The buyer of a futures contract is entitled to delivery of the commodity at a specified future date and at a price that is agreed upon today. Commodity futures markets exist for most agricultural products, minerals, and metals. Futures markets also exist for certain types of financial instruments (for example, United States Treasury bills) and this provides a way to hedge against future changes in interest rates (see Inflation and Innovation in the Financial Markets, pages 343–350).

10

FINANCING DECISIONS AND CAPITAL STRUCTURE

The preceding discussion of capital budgeting showed how investment opportunities are evaluated and combined into a planned capital budget. In this chapter we examine the problems faced by a financial manager in deciding how to obtain the money needed to finance a given capital budget. We look at the four major financing sources used by firms—debt, preferred stock, common stock, and retained earnings—and examine the methods used to plan a complete financing program.

After describing each source of financing, we show the impact of alternative financing plans on the returns and risks to the firm's owners. Then the problem of long-run policy as to financing sources is examined, and we discuss how the policy chosen affects the cost of capital used to evaluate investment opportunities. This chapter covers the basic financing decisions that must be made by the financial manager and the implications of those decisions for capital budgeting.

CHARACTERISTICS OF FINANCING METHODS

Debt, preferred stock, and common stock are alike in one essential feature. They are sources of money that are *external* to the firm and its operations, as opposed to retained earnings, which represent an *internal* source of funds. Provided that management can convince other people of the desirability of investing in or loaning money to the firm, there is virtually no limit to the amount of money that can be raised from external sources.[1] Retained earnings are internal to the firm, and the amount of money that the firm can raise by retaining earnings is strictly limited by the profits of the firm and the amount paid in dividends to its owners.

Common stock and retained earnings share an important feature. They both represent money contributed by the firm's owners rather than by its creditors or preferred stockholders. The owners of the firm receive income only after all obligations due its creditors and preferred stockholders have been paid.

Table 10-1 provides a partial breakdown of the financing used by nonfinancial corporations from 1956 to 1983. Notice first that the major source of financing throughout the entire period is internal funds (retained earnings and depreciation). Second, debt financing is second to internal funds, and is sometimes used almost as heavily as internal funds. Third, although common stock and preferred stock are relatively minor sources of financing in aggregate, they can be quite significant for an individual firm in a given year. One of the purposes of this chapter is to explain why internal funds and debt tend to be used rather than common stock and preferred stock in financing investment.

Debt Financing

When a business firm raises money by borrowing, it must promise to repay the money borrowed (the principal) plus interest. These principal and interest payments are spelled out in the debt contract, which stipulates

---

[1] There is no practical limit to the amount of money the firm can raise as long as those with funds to invest in the firm (new stockholders or lenders) feel that the money will be invested in assets that provide an acceptable rate of return. However, the cost of financing may be quite high, particularly for small firms and firms with very risky investments.

when and how much money must be paid by the firm. If the payments are not made on time and in the proper amount, the debtholders can take a variety of actions to force payment, depending on the terms of the debt agreement. They may take some of the firm's assets, cause management to be fired, or even force the firm to sell all its assets and thereby force it out of business. They can prevent any payments being made to shareholders (owners) or preferred stockholders before the debtholders have been paid. The debtholders have priority over the other security holders in receiving money from the firm. An important feature of debt financing is that the amount of money to be paid to the debtholders is limited to what has been specified in the debt agreement. For example, if the firm owes a bank $2 million, which is to be paid in one year with interest of $200,000, the bank must be paid $2.2 million, but only this amount.[2] Debt financing also differs from the other sources in that interest payments are tax deductible. As we noted in Chapter 7, the effective cost of debt financing is less than the interest rate paid to the debtholders due to the tax deductibility of the interest. (See Exhibit 7-1.)

Many different types of debt agreements are used by business firms, but for the purpose of this chapter these three characteristics—priority over other security holders, tax deductibility of interest, and limits on amount— are the most important. From the viewpoint of debtholders, the limitation on interest and principal payments to them also means that they are very concerned with the degree of certainty of these payments, as in the case of bonds discussed in Chapter 5.

*Preferred Stock
Financing*

Preferred stock has characteristics that are intermediate between debt and common stock. Preferred stock is similar to debt in that the payments to preferred stockholders—preferred dividends—are usually limited in

[2] There may be additional charges if the firm fails to make the required payments, but these too would be specified in the debt agreement.

TABLE 10-1
*Financing sources used by nonfinancial corporations, as a percentage
of total financing*

	Internal funds	Debt	Common and preferred stock
1956–1960	68.8%	26.8%	4.4%
1961–1965	66.4	32.6	1.0
1966–1970	58.4	39.3	2.3
1971–1975	52.1	42.8	5.1
1976–1980	56.9	41.0	2.1
1981–1983	72.6	25.1	2.2

Sources: U.S. Department of Commerce and the Board of Governors of the Federal Reserve System.

298

PART 2
The firm's investment,
financing, and dividend
decisions

amount to a fixed dividend rate per share. Preferred dividends have priority over common stock dividends. The preferred stockholders must be paid before common stock dividends can be paid; but if no common stock dividends are to be paid, preferred dividends need not necessarily be paid. Unlike debt interest, failure to pay preferred dividends does not expose the firm to the adverse consequences of failing to pay interest. Also, preferred stock rarely has a maturity; the face (par) value need never be repaid by the firm.

The preferred stockholders are protected by several features commonly found in preferred stock agreements. The dividends are usually **cumulative**, which means that any dividends not paid when due remains as an obligation of the firm. No dividends to the common stockholders can be paid until *all* the preferred dividends that are owed to date have been paid. For example, if a firm fails to pay a $6 per share preferred dividend for four years in a row, a total of $24 (4 × $6) in back dividends plus the current dividend of $6 must be paid in year 5 before the firm can pay any dividends to common stockholders in year 5. Failure to pay preferred dividends for a specific number of years often permits the preferred stockholders to elect some of the firm's directors and to gain some control over the firm's policies. Finally, if the firm is liquidated, preferred stockholders have priority over the firm's owners. The face value of the preferred stock must be paid to its holders before the common stockholders can receive any proceeds from the sale of the firm's assets.

Common Stock Financing

A firm can raise money by issuing common stock and selling the shares to investors, who become new owners if they were not already stockholders of the firm. Let us assume here that a firm raising money by issuing common stock is selling the stock to new investors as opposed to its existing owners ("old" owners).[3]

The sale of common stock divides the ownership of the firm into two parts—that part owned by the old owners and that part owned by the purchasers of the new stock. Suppose that 20,000 shares are held by the old owners and an additional 5000 shares are sold. There would now be 25,000 shares outstanding. The original owners who had 100 percent of the firm now have only 80 percent (20,000/25,000), and the new shareholders who bought 5000 shares have 20 percent (5000/25,000). If the firm now pays $100,000 in dividends, the money must be distributed equally among the shares. In this example, the old shareholders would be entitled to 80 percent of $100,000 while the new shareholders would be entitled to 20 percent of $100,000.

The amount of money raised by issuing a given number of new shares depends on what the new shareholders believe their proportionate interest in the firm is worth. Suppose that the total value of the firm's stock after financing (therefore, including the new shares) and investment has taken place is expected to be $1 million. The new shareholders would then be

---

[3] As we will discuss in Chap. 11, this is not always true, but the assumption greatly simplifies the discussion without making any significant difference to the results.

willing to pay 20 percent of $1 million, or $200,000, to the firm for 5000 shares. This amounts to $40 per share ($200,000/5000). In practice, management decides how much money is needed ($200,000), estimates the price that new investors will be willing to pay for the shares ($40), and from this information determines the number of shares that must be issued (5000).

The shareholders as owners have voting rights through which they elect the firm's directors, who determine corporate policy and affect the shareholders' earnings. The new shareholders therefore acquire 20 percent of the voting power. In many cases firms are reluctant to sell common stock because the new shareholders may not agree with the policies followed by the management elected by the old shareholders. This is especially true of small businesses where the old shareholders usually are the firm's management. For example, the president of a small company who is also its largest shareholder might lose control of the business if the company sold a large enough number of shares to other people. The new shareholders could then determine policy or even fire the president.

A major advantage of common stock financing over debt financing is the absence of any requirement to make payments to the shareholders. If the firm borrows money and then runs short of cash when a debt payment comes due, it may have to sell some of its assets to make the payment or even be forced out of business by the creditors. On the other hand, the firm does not have to pay dividends to its shareholders, and it never has to repay the money the new shareholders invested. The owners of common stock who wish to get back their original investment must either find someone to buy their stock or try to have the company liquidated. Common stock financing has only slight advantages over preferred stock financing in these respects since failure to pay a preferred dividend is not nearly so serious as failure to pay interest, and the money obtained from sale of preferred stock never need be repaid.

Retained Earnings

Retained earnings are the profits remaining in the firm after dividends are paid. As we indicated earlier, the major differences between retained earnings and the other three financing sources are that retained earnings are limited in the amount available but do not require raising money from "outsiders" (lenders or new stockholders). However, financing with retained earnings reduces the dividends that can be paid to the firm's current owners. This means that the availability of retained earnings depends not only on the earnings of the firm, but also on the policies of the firm regarding dividend payments. We will discuss dividend policies in some detail in Chapter 11; for now, we will only note that firms generally try to avoid reducing their level of dividend payments even in the face of temporary reductions in earnings. This policy makes the amount of retained earnings (profits less dividends) available in any given year highly variable with profits. Therefore, the financial manager cannot rely on the availability of this source to finance investment.

Although it reduces the current money available for dividends, using retained earnings increases the future amount of money available for dividends to the current owners. The reason for this is that, if the firm uses

300

PART 2
The firm's investment,
financing, and dividend
decisions

debt, it must pay the lenders interest in the future, thereby reducing the money available for future dividends; and if preferred stock is issued, preferred dividends must be paid in the future. If common stock financing is used, future dividends must be paid to the new shareholders as well as to the old ones.

It is important to recognize that the firm does not have to rely exclusively on the earnings retained from the current year's profits. Most managements forecast their investment needs several years into the future. Given this forecast, it is possible to begin to retain earnings and temporarily invest in financial assets prior to planned investment in profitable opportunities.

Retained earnings substitute most directly as an alternative to common stock, since both represent investment by owners (old or new) of the firm. However, the use of common stock may present problems in maintaining control of the firm by the original shareholders. For this reason many small firms avoid common stock issues. Also the firm must pay various fees and costs to issue stock that are avoided when retained earnings are used (see Chapter 18).

At this point we have already begun to list some of the advantages and disadvantages of each source of financing. The basic characteristics of each one are summarized in Table 10-2. Let us examine more directly the considerations in choosing the means of financing investment.

ANALYZING EXTERNAL FINANCING METHODS

Financial managers base their financing decisions on the firm's forecasted capital budget. The period of time covered and the amount of care taken in developing this forecast will depend greatly on the size of the firm and its particular situation. A small firm whose present plans are only to acquire a new delivery truck may not do more than estimate when and at what price the truck is to be acquired. A large firm embarking on a major expansion program may forecast its financing needs for several years. For the purposes of this chapter, we assume that the financial manager has undertaken this forecasting-planning process and has developed a clear picture of how much money is needed, during the next year, plus some idea of the likely financing requirements of the firm in the more distant future.[4] The manager knows what sources of financing are currently available and the prices, interest rates, and other characteristics of each source. A critical part of the financial manager's job is deciding on and arranging for external financing. We will discuss the problem of choosing among debt, preferred stock, and common stock first, assuming that external financing is needed. Later we will examine the use of retained earnings.

Impact on Shareholder Earnings

To see how the choice of financing affects the returns to current owners, let's look at an example. Auric Mining Company is planning the development of a mine and processing plant on land owned by the firm. At the present time this land is the firm's only asset. The development costs are

---

[4] Forecasting financial requirements is obviously an important problem for the manager, and methods for doing this are provided in Chap. 14.

$1 million to be paid in the first year. The expected cash flow before taxes from the operation is $480,000 per year. We will assume that all cash flow from the mine will be paid out in taxes, dividends, and interest and that the cash flow is expected to continue forever. The corporate tax rate is 50 percent and the aftertax cash flow is therefore $240,000, assuming, for simplicity, that no depreciation or depletion allowances are available. Suppose that the owners of Auric don't have any money of their own to finance this venture and that the firm does not have any cash. The $1 million in development costs must be raised by borrowing the money, by issuing preferred or common stock, or by some combination of these methods. Let's look at common stock financing first so that we have a basis for the contrast with debt and preferred stock financing.

Common Stock   If common stock is issued, the new stockholders will share in the future cash flows. Their share will depend on the percentage

TABLE 10-2
Characteristics of financing sources

Debt	Preferred stock	Common stock	Retained earnings
1. Firm must pay back money with interest.	1. Similar to debt in that preferred dividends are limited in amount to rate specified in agreement (like interest rate).	1. Money is raised by selling ownership rights.	1. Lowers amount of money available for current dividends but can increase future dividends.
2. Interst rate is based on risk of principal and interest payments as perceived by lenders.	2. Dividends are not legally required, but no common dividends can be paid unless preferred dividends are paid; also usually cumulative, and passing dividend for a stated number of years may give preferred stockholders voting rights.	2. Value of stock is determined by investors.	2. Stockholders forego dividend income, but they do not lose ownership rights as occurs if new common stock is issued.
3. Amount of money to be repaid is specified by debt contract.	3. No maturity but usually callable.	3. Dividends are not legally required.	3. Funds are internal— no need for external involvement.
4. Lenders can take action to get their money back.	4. Usually no voting rights except as per (2) above.	4. Creates change in ownership.	4. Cost of issuing securities is avoided.
5. Lenders get preferred treatment in liquidation.	5. Preferred dividends are not tax deductible.	5. Shareholders have voting rights.	
6. Interest payments are tax deductible.		6. Common dividends are not tax deductible.	

302

PART 2
The firm's investment,
financing, and dividend
decisions

ownership they obtain in the firm in return for the $1 million they will be investing in it. The percentage ownership will be a bargain struck between the present owners, as represented by the firm's management, and the investors. In general, the investors will demand at least that the expected rate of return to them will equal the rate of return available in the financial markets on investments of comparable risk. As we know from Chapter 6, the relationship between risk and return in the financial markets is shown by the security market line. If the financial manager acts in the best interests of the *present* owners of Auric, no greater rate of return should be provided to the *new* stockholders than that minimum required. Suppose the required rate of return is 12 percent per year. Then to raise $1 million, stock investors must expect to receive 12 percent per year on $1 million, which is $120,000 per year on the average. The $120,000 represents 50 percent of the aftertax cash flow expected from the mine. Under these conditions, new shareholders must obtain 50 percent of the stock of the company in return for their investment of $1 million. The present owners will be left with the remaining 50 percent of the stock and an expected cash return of $120,000 per year. These values are shown in Exhibit 10-1.

Preferred Stock   Preferred stock may be issued to finance the mine. The dividend rate that must be provided to preferred stockholders will reflect the risks borne by them. Since the preferred stock of a company is usually a less risky security than the common stock, let's assume that the required dividend rate is 10 percent. Preferred dividends on a $1 million preferred

---

EXHIBIT 10-1
The impact of debt and stock financing on expected income

	Common stock	Preferred stock	Debt
Before-tax cash flow *E.B.I.T*	$ 480,000	$ 480,000	$ 480,000
Interest	0	0	(80,000)
Taxable income	$ 480,000	$ 480,000	$ 400,000
Taxes (at 50%)	(240,000)	(240,000)	(200,000)
Earnings after taxes	$ 240,000	$ 240,000	$ 200,000
Preferred dividends	0	100,000	0
Earnings to common	$ 240,000	$ 140,000	$ 200,000
Income to new stockholders	$ 120,000	0	0
Income to original owners	$ 120,000	$ 140,000	$ 200,000

Common stock financing:	$1 million raised from new stockholders, in return for 50% of the company's shares
Preferred stock financing:	$1 million raised from investors with a dividend rate of 10% per year
Debt financing:	$1 million raised from lenders with an interest rate of 8% per year

stock issue would therefore be $100,000, and the original owners would receive $140,000, as shown in Exhibit 10-1. Under this financing plan, the original owners expect to receive $20,000 more in dividends than if common stock is issued because the rate of return required by the preferred stockholders is less than that required by new investors in common stock.

Debt Suppose that the $1 million could be raised by borrowing the money at an interest rate of 8 percent per year. Lenders generally do not require as high an interest rate as stockholders because the risk is less. Interest would amount to 8 percent of the $1 million borrowed, or $80,000 per year. The expected aftertax cash flow available to the original owners would therefore be $200,000, as shown in Exhibit 10-1. The original owners would therefore expect to receive $80,000 per year more in income if debt financing were used instead of common stock ($200,000 − $120,000) and $60,000 more if preferred were used ($200,000 − $140,000). These income differences are due to two factors. First, the interest rate on the debt (8 percent) is lower than the rate of return required by new shareholders (12 percent) or by preferred stockholders (10 percent). Of the $80,000 difference between debt and common stock, $40,000 is due to the difference in rates (4 percent of $1 million). Of the $60,000 difference between debt and preferred, $20,000 is due to the difference in rates (2 percent of $1 million). Second, the interest on the debt is tax deductible, and this accounts for the remaining $40,000 difference for both common and preferred stock. When debt financing is used, we see from Exhibit 10-1 that the firm pays only $200,000 in taxes instead of the $240,000 in taxes paid with preferred and common stock financing. Therefore, the original owners benefit both from the lower interest rate on the debt and the tax deductibility of interest.

EBIT-EPS Analysis

An obvious question at this point in the analysis is what happens if the mine doesn't earn $480,000 before interest and taxes each year? We need to examine other levels of earnings. A common method used to evaluate the impact of financing decisions on shareholder income is to analyze the relationship between earnings before interest and taxes (EBIT) and earnings per share (EPS). Since the original stockholders will own the same number of shares regardless of the method of financing, EPS (earnings to common divided by the number of outstanding shares) is directly related to the income belonging to the original owners (EPS × number of original shares = original owners' income). The level of EBIT varies from year to year depending on how successful the firm's operations are. The analysis involves taking each financing method proposed and plotting on a graph the EPS that would result from a given value of EBIT. The relationship between EPS and EBIT for each financing method is a straight line. When the lines representing each method are plotted on the same graph, we can compare them. To see how this works. let's use the Auric Mining data in a general procedure. (In the Auric example, EBIT = before-tax cash flow.)

1 We need information on the existing financing (all common stock in this example) used by the firm and related data:

304

PART 2
The firm's investment,
financing, and dividend
decisions

a The tax rate (50 percent)
b Interest per year on outstanding debt (none)
c Preferred dividends (none)
d Number of shares outstanding (50,000)

2 We need the terms of the alternative financing methods:
a Debt: interest on debt (8 percent on $1 million = $80,000)
b Preferred stock: preferred dividends (10 percent of $1 million = $100,000)
c Common stock: number of shares to be issued (50,000)[5]

3 Since the graphical relationship between EPS and EBIT for any given financing method is a straight line, only two points on the graph are needed to completely determine the line.[6] Therefore, given the above information in 2, we need to compute earnings per share at two different levels of earnings before interest and taxes for each financing method. Choice of the two EBIT values is not critical; however, they

---

[5] Since new shareholders must own 50 percent of the firm according to the earlier analysis, they must acquire the same number of shares as held by the original owners. The 50,000 figure for the number of shares held by the original owners is simply assumed; from that assumption the number that must be issued follows.

[6] The relationship between EPS and EBIT can be expressed as

$$\text{EPS} = \frac{(\text{EBIT} - \text{interest})(1 - \text{tax rate}) - \text{preferred dividends}}{\text{total number of shares outstanding}}$$

The financing method chosen fixes the values for interest, the number of shares, and preferred dividends. So long as the tax rate is a constant, this relationship is a straight line.

EXHIBIT 10-2
Calculation of the impact of financing methods on earnings per share

	Common stock		Preferred stock		Debt	
EBIT	$ 200,000	$ 600,000	$ 200,000	$ 600,000	$200,000	$ 600,000
Interest (old debt)	0	0	0	0	0	0
Interest (new debt)	0	0	0	0	(80,000)	(80,000)
Taxable income	$ 200,000	$ 600,000	$ 200,000	$ 600,000	$120,000	$ 520,000
Taxes	(100,000)	(300,000)	(100,000)	(300,000)	(60,000)	(260,000)
Earnings after taxes	$ 100,000	$ 300,000	$ 100,000	$ 300,000	$ 60,000	$ 260,000
Preferred dividends (old)	0	0	0	0	0	0
Preferred dividends (new)	0	0	100,000	100,000	0	0
Earnings to common (1)	$ 100,000	$ 300,000	$ 0	$ 200,000	$ 60,000	$ 260,000
Number of old shares	50,000	50,000	50,000	50,000	50,000	50,000
Number of new shares	50,000	50,000	0	0	0	0
Total common shares (2)	100,000	100,000	50,000	50,000	50,000	50,000
EPS [(1)/(2)]	$1.00	$3.00	$ 0	$4.00	$1.20	$5.20

are usually chosen to be representative of levels of EBIT that the firm might have. Calculations of EPS at EBIT = $200,000 and EBIT = $600,000 are shown in Exhibit 10-2. The results of the calculations are plotted on a graph (Figure 10-1).

Figure 10-1 shows that at EBIT levels of over $160,000, the debt issue provides higher values for EPS than does common stock, whereas when EBIT is below $160,000, the common stock issue is better. This number can be verified by calculation (recommended as an exercise). Debt provides higher EPS than preferred stock at all levels of EBIT. Preferred stock provides higher EPS than common at levels of EBIT greater than $400,000.

Financial Leverage   Figure 10-1 illustrates the concept of **financial leverage**.[7] Financial leverage refers to the response of shareholders income to changes in EBIT and is created by debt or preferred stock financing with fixed interest and dividend payments. If the firm is financed entirely with common stock, a given percentage change in EBIT results in the same

---

[7] It is also referred to as "trading on equity." The British use the term "gearing."

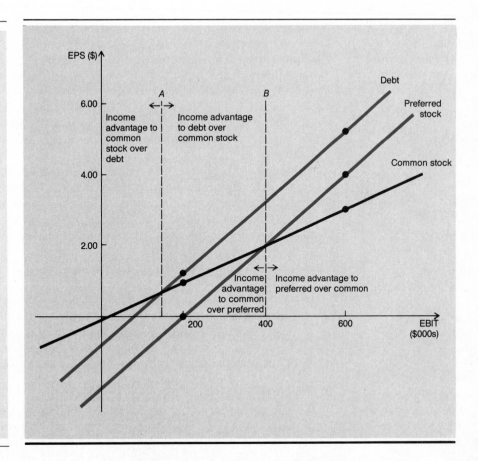

FIGURE 10-1

Impact of alternative financing methods on EPS.

306

PART 2
The firm's investment,
financing, and dividend
decisions

percentage change in EPS. A 10 percent increase in EBIT results in a 10 percent increase in EPS. However, the use of debt or preferred stock financing increases the responsiveness of EPS to changes in EBIT. For example, when EBIT is $400,000, both common stock and preferred stock financing provide earnings of $2 per share (EPS = $2). A 50 percent increase in EBIT to $600,000 increases EPS with common stock financing to $3, also a 50 percent increase. If preferred stock is used, a 50 percent increase in EBIT leads to an EPS of $4, a 100 percent increase. Financial leverage works both ways, down as well as up. The percentage reduction in EPS is greater than a given percentage of reduction in EBIT when debt or preferred stock financing is used. We will look more explicitly at the negative effects of leverage when we consider risk.

Businesses that have a lot of debt outstanding relative to their assets are often said to be "highly levered," since shareholder income tends to be more variable for such firms than for firms using less debt. A more precise measure of the degree of financial leverage than the proportion of debt used is the ratio of interest payments to EBIT (assuming no preferred stock is used).[8] Lenders and financial managers use this ratio (or its reciprocal) in evaluating the use of debt by the firm. Additional measures are discussed in Chapter 12.

Impact on Shareholder Risk

Although debt and preferred stock financing provide income advantages over common stock if the firm does well, they increase the risk if it does not. The most risky financing from the viewpoint of the stockholders is debt because interest and principal payments are contractual obligations of the firm. Preferred dividends need not be paid when earnings are poor, and the money raised from preferred stock financing need never be repaid. Since debt offers the greatest income advantage and the greatest risk, we will focus our discussion here on the choice of debt relative to common stock. We consider preferred stock again later.

There are two types of risk to the owners of a firm, business risk and financial risk. Financial risk depends on the method of financing whereas business risk depends on the nature of the firm's operations. Business risk is directly related to the uncertainty as to the firm's ability to earn a satisfactory rate of return on its investments over the long run. It involves

---

[8] The degree of financial leverage can be expressed more generally as a multiplier of the percentage change in EBIT; that is,

Percentage change in EPS = leverage multiplier × percentage change in EBIT

The leverage multiplier can be calculated from the leverage ratio as follows:

$$\text{Leverage ratio} = \frac{\text{interest} + [\text{preferred dividends}/(1 - \text{tax rate})]}{\text{EBIT}}$$

Notice that this ratio equals interest/EBIT when there are no preferred dividends.

$$\text{Leverage multiplier} = \frac{1}{1 - \text{leverage ratio}}$$

For example, with debt financing, interest is $80,000; at an EBIT of $480,000, the leverage ratio equals .167, and the multiplier is 1.2. A 10 percent increase in EBIT from $480,000 will therefore increase EPS by 12 percent.

uncertainty as to the demand for the firm's products and the prices of the products. It is related to the degree of control the firm has over its costs, and how readily its assets can be converted into cash if the need arises. Business risk depends on the quality of the firm's management and the ability of management to react to unforeseen events. Fundamentally then, business risk involves uncertainty as to the long-run profitability of the firm (EBIT) and its investments and to the potential value of the firm in liquidation, if it cannot be operated at a profit.

If there were no business risks, the firm could finance as it pleased without affecting the risk to its owners and without paying a high interest rate. If the Auric Mining Company, its owners, and its creditors knew for sure that the mine would produce $480,000 per year forever, there would be absolutely no risk to the owners from borrowing $1 million at an interest rate of 8 percent per year since the $80,000 interest payments could always be paid from the earnings of the mine. If desired, the firm could be completely out of debt in a few years by paying the aftertax cash flow to the lenders until the $1 million debt was paid off. However, the returns from business investments are never certain. Let's look at Auric's financing problem when there is business risk in the mining investment.

To keep the problem simple and to isolate the source of risk, suppose that the costs of mining and the amount of product (gold) to be mined are known for sure. However, the price is uncertain. There are three possible prices.[9] At the low price the mine will provide only $60,000 per year in before-tax cash flow net of the costs of mining the gold. At the middle price, the mine will provide $480,000 per year, and at the high price the mine will provide $600,000 per year. The probability of the high price is .35, the probability of the middle price is .55, and the probability of the low price is .10. The expected cash flow *before taxes* is therefore

Expected cash flow = .35($600,000) + .55($480,000) + .10($60,000)

= $480,000

which equals the before-tax cash flow used in Exhibit 10-1.

If high or middle prices are obtained, there is no problem with debt financing. We can see from Figure 10-1 that the income benefits of debt financing are substantial for EBIT of $480,000 and $600,000. However, there is a 10 percent chance that only $60,000 per year will be generated from the mine due to the low price of gold. If the firm must pay $80,000 in interest on the debt, sufficient money is not available from the mine's operations to meet this obligation. So what will happen? The answer in practice will depend on several things. Auric's owners might continue to operate the mine for a while, paying the $20,000 per year deficit ($80,000 − $60,000) out of their own pockets if they have hopes that prices will increase in the future. Failure to pay the interest would force the firm into bankruptcy and

---

[9] A more realistic assumption that provides the same results is that the "prices" are average price levels for the product. It is not necessary to assume that the price of gold will be constant at, for example, $400 per ounce. The actual price could vary over time, say, between $350 to $450 while averaging $400.

308

PART 2
The firm's investment,
financing, and dividend
decisions

the mine would be sold for whatever it would bring. The lenders would have first claim on the proceeds from such a sale up to $1 million principal amount of the debt. Under the circumstances of the example it is unlikely that the entire property could be sold for as much as $1 million, and so the lenders would take a loss and the owners would receive nothing.[10] In any case, the firm, its owners, and its creditors would be in trouble.

Also, the interest rate charged by lenders will be affected by the possibility that the mine will incur losses. If the entire $1 million is raised from debt and lenders require 8 percent on a safe loan, they will charge a higher rate on this loan; they may even not be willing to lend this amount of money.

In this simple example, the risk to the lender can be eliminated by the firm not borrowing so much money. Suppose only $750,000 is borrowed at 8 percent. The firm is then obligated to pay only 0.08($750,000) = $60,000 per year, which would be covered even in the worst case. Prudent financial managers would limit the amount borrowed to a level where they are confident that the interest can be paid from the firm's income. Exceeding this point subjects the firm and its owners to excessive risk and may also be costly due to higher interest rates being charged.

Using even limited amounts of debt is likely to increase the risk of losses for a firm. A more general situation is depicted in Figure 10-2. The curves in this figure were drawn assuming the firm's earnings before interest and taxes are represented by the probability distribution shown by curve *A*. Curve *A* is also the income to all shareholders before taxes if no debt is issued. Curve *B* illustrates the effects of financing with some given amount

---

[10] This assumes that Auric is a corporation and that the owners are not personally liable for the debt. Otherwise, the lenders would try to make up any losses by instituting legal action to claim personal assets of the owners.

FIGURE 10-2

Effects of debt financing on stockholder income. Curve A shows EBIT for the firm, which equals stockholder income before taxes when debt is used. The fixed interest payment increases the probability of loss from that shown as the crosshatched area under A to that shown as the hatched area under B.

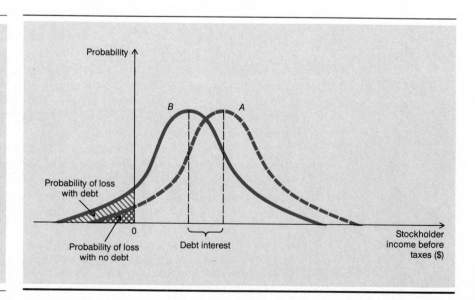

of debt on shareholders' income before taxes. The fixed interest charges change curve *A* to curve *B*. Notice that the likelihood of the firm's incurring a loss has increased appreciably due to the use of debt. Generally the more debt that is used, the greater the risk of loss.

A third aspect of the risk of debt is its impact on the variability of shareholder income. From our discussion of financial leverage, we know that debt financing increases the responsiveness of earnings per share to changes in earnings before interest and taxes. Therefore, the use of debt (or preferred stock) amplifies the inherent variability of EBIT and increases the variability of shareholder income.

For example, suppose that earnings before interest and taxes for the first year of Auric's operations are $200,000 and in the second year are $180,000, a decline of 10 percent. The effects of this decrease in EBIT on Auric's owners are shown in Exhibit 10-3 assuming that the entire investment of $1 million is being financed completely either with common stock or with debt at an 8 percent interest rate. The decrease in income to the original owners is 17 percent with debt financing as compared with the 10 percent decrease with stock financing. With common stock financing all changes, positive or negative, in income are shared among all the shareholders, whereas with debt financing, the lenders receive a fixed interest payment and all changes are borne by the original owners.

Leverage and Beta   EBIT-EPS analysis is widely used by financial managers because it provides a simple picture of the consequences of alternative financing methods; however, more sophisticated techniques are available. One approach is to consider the impact of alternative methods on the stockholder's risk as measured by beta. In Chapter 6 we used beta as a summary measure of the risk of a financial asset based on the Capital Asset Pricing Model (CAPM). A precise analysis of the impact of financing on beta is a topic for more advanced courses. Here we provide the basic idea. The beta of a firm's common stock depends on the amount of leverage used by

---

EXHIBIT 10-3
The impact of debt and common stock financing on the variability of income

	Common stock		Debt	
	First year	Second year	First year	Second year
EBIT	$ 200,000	$180,000	$200,000	$180,000
Interest	0	0	(80,000)	(80,000)
Taxable income	$ 200,000	$180,000	$120,000	$100,000
Taxes (at 50%)	(100,000)	(90,000)	(60,000)	(50,000)
Net income	$ 100,000	$ 90,000	$ 60,000	$ 50,000
Income to original owners	$ 50,000	$ 45,000	$ 60,000	$ 50,000
Dollar change	−$5,000		−$10,000	
Percentage change	−10%		−17%	

310

PART 2
The firm's investment,
financing, and dividend
decisions

the firm. Measuring leverage as the ratio of debt (and preferred stock) to the total value of all securities issued, beta of the common stock increases with leverage. This is illustrated in Figure 10-3a.[11] Since the risk to the stockholders increases with increased leverage, the stockholders' required rate of return also increases as shown in Figure 10-3b. The problem for the financial manager is to determine how the *value* of the firm's stock will be affected. The higher expected income from leverage will be discounted at a higher rate. Thus the trade-off between risk and return is analyzed in terms of the impact of financing decisions on the value of the firm's stock.

Financial Leverage and Value

We assume that management will want to choose the financing method that provides the greatest financial benefit to current stockholders of the firm. The financial benefits to stockholders are obtained from current dividends and the value of their stock. However, the choice among external financing methods does not affect current dividends, so we first examine the problem of how the choice of external financing effects stock value. To highlight the issues, we focus on the choice between debt and common stock. The impact of financing leverage on value is one of the most difficult and heavily debated topics in finance. Divergences of opinion exist among financial managers and among financial theorists. Ultimately the financing decision is a matter of judgment for the financial manager. Here we present what is currently known about the problem.

The No-Tax Case   Let's examine the simplest possible situation to provide a base for understanding the problem as found in practice. Suppose that a firm's securities (debt, preferred stock, and common stock) are issued and

[11] The relationship shown in Figure 10-3a was developed from numerical examples by applying the CAPM to several different probability distributions. It applies when the firm issues risky as well as riskless debt.

FIGURE 10-3

The effects of leverage on securities' betas and rates of return in the CAPM.

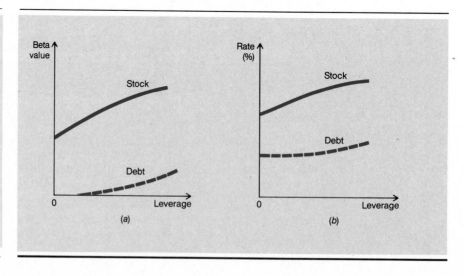

traded in a perfect capital market.[12] All investors in the market have the same probability distributions for the future returns from any securities or from any investments undertaken by the firm. Assume also that there are no costs or penalties (such as legal fees and disruption of operations resulting from default) incurred by the firm if it defaults on debt payments, although the debtholders may take over the firm.[13] All debt issues are perpetual bonds; only interest payments are required. For now we assume that there are no corporate or personal income taxes. Under these conditions, how do financing decisions affect the value of a firm's common stock? Let's use the Auric Mining example to explore the problem.

Recall from page 307 that the expected income from the mine is $480,000 per year. As before, $1 million must be raised to undertake the investment. Our choice is between debt financing at an interest rate of 8 percent or common stock financing. Investors in common stock are assumed to require an expected rate of return of 12 percent if no debt is used. All income will be paid out as dividends and interest.

If only common stock financing is used, the total market value of the outstanding stock will be the present value of the expected dividends to the stockholders. The expected dividends are a perpetual stream of $480,000 per year since there are no corporate income taxes. The value of the dividends is

$$\text{Market value} = \frac{\text{expected dividends}}{\text{required rate of return}}$$

$$= \frac{\$480,00}{0.12}$$

$$= \$4 \text{ million}$$

If the total market value of common stock is $4 million and if $1 million in stock has been sold to new investors, the value of the original owners' stock must be $3 million. What, then, will the original owners' stock be worth if debt rather than common stock is used to raise $1 million? Financial theory tells us that in this situation the original owners' stock will also be worth $3 million with debt financing.[14] Therefore the value of the original owners' stock is not affected by the financing decision. This is because of two conditions implied by our assumptions. First, the total income being received by investors (stockholders and bondholders) does not depend on

---

[12] In perfect capital markets, transactions (buying, selling, and issuing securities) involve no transaction costs (such as brokerage fees); investors have equal, costless access to information; and there is a large number of buyers and sellers of securities, none of whom is individually able to affect market prices.

[13] This assumption means that the act of default and the subsequent actions by lenders do not reduce the level of EBIT below what it would have been in the absence of the contractual obligations that have been unfulfilled due to the default (that is, what the EBIT would have been if the firm had been all equity financed).

[14] The original analysis of the problem was done by F. Modigliani and M. H. Miller, "The Cost of Capital, Corporation Finance, and the Theory of Investment," *American Economic Review*, 48 (June 1958), pp. 261–297. The same conclusion can be reached by application of the CAPM to the problem.

312

PART 2
The firm's investment, financing, and dividend decisions

how the firm is financed. Second, the total value of the income is the same regardless of how it is split up among different types of securities.[15] (The value of a pie stays the same regardless of how you slice it.) To see how this works, let's look at Auric Mining when debt is used.

In Exhibit 10-4 we show what interest and expected dividend payments will be for various combinations of debt and common stock financing. We have assumed here that the interest rate on debt increases as the amount of debt issued increases. Notice that total payments to security holders is the same under present assumptions regardless of the financing package chosen. Since Auric needs $1 million, raising only $250,000 in debt implies that $750,000 in new common stock must be issued. The values of the various securities issued by the firm are also shown. These values are based on the proposition that the total value of the firm's securities is $4 million and therefore the value of the original owners' shares remains at $3 million regardless of the choice of financing. In addition this analysis implies that the required rate of return on stock increases with the leverage of the firm. We show a measure of leverage (interest/EBIT) and the expected rate of return on total stock given the expected dividend payments and stock values. Figure 10-4 shows the general behavior of security values and rates of return for the no-tax case. In Figure 10-4c the firm's cost of capital is also plotted. Notice that it is unaffected by the degree of leverage used even though the rates on stock and debt increase with leverage. This implies that the firm's investment decisions are unaffected by the choice of financing in this simplified situation.

[15] We sketch out the formal argument in Appendix 10A.

EXHIBIT 10-4
Impact of financial leverage on required rates of return with no taxes

Debt issued	$ 0	$ 250,000	$ 500,000	$ 750,000	$1,000,000
Interest rate	—	6%	6.5%	7.0%	8.0%
Expected EBIT	$ 480,000	$ 480,000	$ 480,000	$ 480,000	$ 480,000
Interest	0	15,000	32,500	52,500	80,000
Dividends = net income	$ 480,000	$ 465,000	$ 447,500	$ 427,500	$ 400,000
Total returns (dividends + interest)	$ 480,000	$ 480,000	$ 480,000	$ 480,000	$ 480,000
Interest/EBIT	0.0	0.03	0.07	0.11	0.17
New stock issued	$1,000,000	$ 750,000	$ 500,000	$ 250,000	$ 0
Value of old stock	3,000,000	3,000,000	3,000,000	3,000,000	3,000,000
Total stock value	$4,000,000	$3,750,000	$3,500,000	$3,250,000	$3,000,000
Debt and stock value	$4,000,000	$4,000,000	$4,000,000	$4,000,000	$4,000,000
Required rate on stock[a]	12%	12.4%	12.8%	13.2%	13.3%

[a] Calculated as dividends/total stock value.

The Effects of Corporate Income Taxes   Suppose that Auric pays corporate income taxes, but all other assumptions remain the same.[16] If the corporate tax rate is 50 percent, only $240,000 in shareholder income is provided from the mine with common stock used to raise $1 million, as was shown in Exhibit 10-1. The market value of an expected dividend stream of $240,000 is $2 million given a required rate of return of 12 percent. Since $1 million in stock is sold to new investors, the original owner's stock is worth $1 million with stock financing.

The effect of debt financing is significantly different with corporate income taxes than it is in the no-tax case. Since interest payments are tax deductible, issuing $1 million in debt with required interest payments of $80,000 causes shareholder income to drop from $240,000 to $200,000 with the debt issue as shown in Exhibit 10-1. In the no-tax case we found that the required rate of return on stock was 13.3 percent for $1 million in debt financing (see Exhibit 10-4). We note that the financing leverage is the same

[16] In general, interest rates in the capital market would probably be different with corporate taxes than with no corporate taxes. We have kept the same rate structure to highlight the important differences between the tax and no-tax cases for an individual firm.

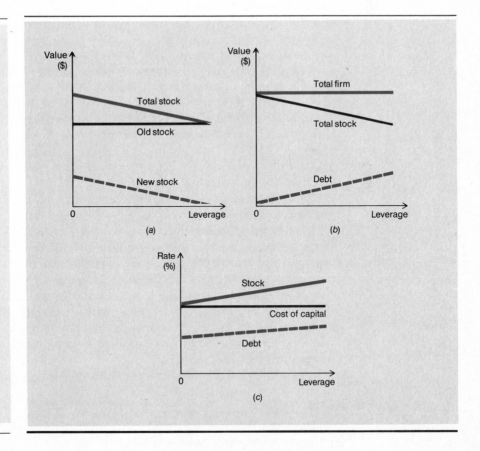

FIGURE 10-4

The effects of leverage on securities' values and rates of return with perfect markets and no taxes.

314

PART 2
The firm's investment,
financing, and dividend
decisions

in both cases. Our measure of financial leverage, interest/EBIT, is not affected by taxes.

$$\frac{\text{Interest}}{\text{EBIT}} = \frac{\$80,000}{\$480,000}$$

$$= 0.167$$

If the degree of leverage is the same, the risk-return relationship in the capital market is the same, and the business risk is the same, then the required rate of return on stock should be the same.

Indeed financial theory tells us that this is so.[17] With a required rate of return of 13.3 percent and expected dividends of $200,000 per year, the stock value with $1 million in debt financing will be

$$\text{Stock value} = \frac{\$200,000}{0.133}$$

$$= \$1,500,000$$

Since the value of the original owners' shares with stock financing was only $1 million, the stockholders will prefer debt financing.

To understand why debt increases value, consider the total cash payments made to security holders (i.e., to stockholders and bondholders). In the no-tax case the amount of money paid in dividends and interest is expected to be $480,000 per year regardless of the financing method used. With taxes, debt financing increases the total expected payments from the firm because the firm pays lower taxes. When common stock is used, the total expected payments to security holders are $240,000 (all dividends) and the firm pays taxes of $240,000. When $1 million in debt is issued, expected total payments to security holders rise to $280,000 ($200,000 dividends plus $80,000 interest) and taxes drop from $240,000 to $200,000. By financing with debt instead of common stock, $40,000 more is expected to be paid to security holders and $40,000 less is expected to be paid to the government. The value of the additional $40,000 is reflected in a higher value for the old stock with debt financing.

The implications of this analysis when the amount of debt issued varies are shown in Exhibit 10-5.

Compared to the no-tax case of Exhibit 10-4, we see that taxes reduce the net income (dividends) to stockholders. However, the degree of financial leverage (interest/EBIT) is the same at each level of debt and, therefore, the required rate of return on the stock is the same as in the no-tax case. We calculate the total value of the stock as the present value of the income to the stockholders. Notice that the total value of stock declines as the amount of debt issued increases. However, by issuing more debt, we are issuing less new stock. The value of the original shareholders' stock increases with the increased use of debt.

Figure 10-5 displays the data of Exhibit 10-5 in graphical form. Leverage

[17] See Haley and Schall, op. cit., p. 301. This result is an implication of both the Modigliani-Miller analysis of the problem [F. Modigliani and M. H. Miller, "Taxes and the Cost of Capital: A Correction," *American Economic Review*, 53 (June 1963), pp. 433–443]. and of the CAPM when the Security Market Line is the same under the tax and no-tax cases.

EXHIBIT 10-5
Impact of financial leverage on stock value with corporate income taxes

Debt issued .... $	0	$ 250,000	$ 500,000	$ 750,000	$1,000,000
Interest rate	—	6%	6.5%	7.0%	8.0%
Expected EBIT .... $	480,000	$ 480,000	$ 480,000	$ 480,000	$ 480,000
Interest	0	15,000	32,500	52,500	80,000
Taxable income .... $	480,000	$ 465,000	$ 447,500	$ 427,500	$ 400,000
Taxes (@ 50%)	240,000	232,500	223,750	213,750	200,000
Net income .... $	240,000	$ 232,500	$ 223,750	$ 213,750	$ 200,000
Interest/EBIT	0	0.03	0.07	0.11	0.17
Required rate on stock[a]	12%	12.4%	12.8%	13.2%	13.3%
Value of total stock[b]	$2,000,000	$1,875,000	$1,750,000	$1,625,000	$1,500,000
New stock issued	$1,000,000	$ 750,000	$ 500,000	$ 250,000	0
Value of old stock[c]	$1,000,000	$1,125,000	$1,250,000	$1,375,000	$1,500,000

[a] From Exhibit 10-4.
[b] Value of total stock = net income (dividends)/required rate on stock.
[c] Value of old stock = value of total stock − new stock issued.

FIGURE 10-5
The effects of leverage on securities' values and rates of return with perfect markets and corporate taxes.

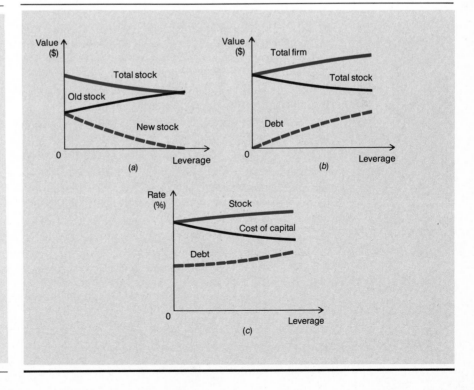

316

PART 2
The firm's investment,
financing, and dividend
decisions

is measured as interest/EBIT. In Figure 10-5*a*, the values of the old stock and new stock issued sum to the total stock value. Notice as the degree of leverage increases, total stock value declines but the value of the old stock increases. In Figure 10-5*b*, the value of the stock plus the value of the debt equals the total value of the firm. Note that total firm value increases with leverage. In Figure 10-5*c*, the behavior of the required rates on debt and stock and of the firm's cost of capital are shown. Notice that, despite the increased rates on debt and stock, the cost of capital decreases as leverage increases under the assumptions here.

We have found that the existence of corporate taxes coupled with the tax deductibility of interest implies that debt financing is superior to common stock. What about financing with preferred stock? Preferred dividends are not tax deductible; therefore, preferred stock financing results in the same value for the original owners' stock as common stock financing. The implications for small business finance are interesting. Although we won't analyze the problem in detail, we can indicate the general results. The advantage of debt financing results from a reduction in *corporate* income taxes. If a business is not paying corporate taxes,[18] then the no-tax case applies and there is no advantage to debt relative to any other method of obtaining money from external sources, such as bringing in a new partner.

The Effect of Personal Taxes   Taxes on the income received by investors in the firm's securities (personal taxes) greatly complicates the analysis. Personal taxes affect the choices among all types of financing including retained earnings. We discuss the impact of these taxes on dividend–retained earnings policies in Chapter 11. Here we present the implications for the use of external financing methods, especially debt. The basic idea is quite simple. United States tax law treats income from the ownership of corporate debt securities (interest) less favorably than it treats income from common and preferred stock (dividends and capital gains).[19] This difference in tax treatment should affect the relative values of the different types of securities. It is difficult to say in general what the relative values will be, but we can indicate the direction of the effect.

Income to common stockholders comes in the form of increases in the value of their stock (capital gains) and dividends. Capital gains in particular are taxed at lower rates than are dividends and interest for most taxpaying investors. To illustrate the point, suppose that the effective personal tax rate on interest paid by Auric is equal to 50 percent, the same rate as Auric's corporate income tax rate, and that the effective personal tax rate on the

[18] The business may be a proprietorship, a partnership, or a small corporation that has elected to be taxed as a partnership. See Chap. 3.

[19] The first $100 of dividend income (on common or preferred stock) received by an individual stockholder is not taxed. Furthermore, 85 percent of dividends (common or preferred) received by a corporation on stock owned in United States corporations is not taxable to the recipient corporation. All interest income received by an individual or a corporation is fully taxable. Also, the tax rate on long-term capital gains (most of which are generated by common stock and real estate) is only 40 percent of the tax rate on ordinary income; interest income and taxable dividend income are taxed at the ordinary income tax rate.

income to stockholders is zero.[20] This is obviously an extreme case but emphasizes the effects of personal taxes. Exhibit 10-6 shows the aftertax income received by Auric security holders with all common stock financing and all debt financing. In this example, the higher personal tax on interest income offsets the lower corporate tax (zero) on interest paid. The total income for security holders produced by Auric net of all taxes is the same regardless of the choice of financing.

The above example was meant only to illustrate how personal taxes (which favor equities) can compensate for corporate taxes (which favor debt). Of course, the extent to which personal tax effects offset corporate tax effects depends on the corporate tax rate and on the personal tax rates on debt and equity income. Personal tax rates vary widely among investors. Because of this, the overall tax system (i.e., personal and corporate taxes) does not completely favor either debt or equity financing, but rather encourages a mixture of both debt and equity in the economy.[21]

[20] This might be approximately true if all earnings are retained and invested to increase the value of the stock and the stockholders defer capital gains taxes by holding their stock indefinitely.

[21] The basic idea is that investors with very high personal tax rates will end up with more aftertax income (net of corporate and personal taxes) if the firm issues them stock (since for them the personal tax on debt interest more than wipes out the corporate tax savings from using debt); and investors with low personal tax rates will end up with more aftertax income if the firm issues them debt securities (since for them the personal tax on debt is not enough to wipe out the corporate tax savings from using debt). The result will be that firms in the economy will issue both debt and equity securities, with high-tax-bracket investors owning equities and low-tax-bracket investors owning debt securities. These points are developed in detail in M. H. Miller, "Debts and Taxes," *Journal of Finance*, 32 (May 1977), pp. 261–275; and H. De Angelo and R. W. Masulis, "Optimal Capital Structure Under Corporate and Personal Taxation," *Journal of Financial Economics* (March 1980), pp. 3–29.

EXHIBIT 10-6
The combined effects of corporate and personal taxes on investors' income

	Common stock issued	Debt issued
EBIT	$480,000	$480,000
Interest	0	80,000
Taxable income	$480,000	$400,000
Corporate income tax (@ 50%)	240,000	200,000
Income to stockholders	$240,000	$200,000
Personal taxes on stock income (@ 0%)	0	0
Personal taxes on interest income (@ 50%)	0	$ 40,000
Total income to investors' pretax	$240,000	$280,000
Taxes on investor income	0	40,000
Aftertax income obtained by investors	$240,000	$240,000

318

PART 2
The firm's investment,
financing, and dividend
decisions

Complications in Practice   If the world were as simple as was assumed above, life would be much easier for financial managers and they would be paid lower salaries. Some of the complications found in practice provide advantages to debt financing whereas other factors favor common stock.

First, the capital markets are not perfect. Information is not costlessly available to everyone; there are costs to investors in buying and selling securities, etc. The lack of perfection in the market implies, primarily, that there may be situations where debt financing (or preferred stock financing) may be unusually costly relative to common stock or vice versa. The financial manager must be alert to market conditions and consider them in making financing decisions. Investment bankers can often provide helpful advice as to the current market situation.

Second, there are legal fees, investment banking commissions, and other expenses involved in issuing securities. This topic is examined in Chapter 18. Here, it is sufficient to know that, generally, it will be more expensive for a firm to issue preferred stock than to issue debt and more expensive to issue common stock than to issue either debt or preferred stock.

Third, the use of debt financing increases the possibility that the firm may be forced to default on its debt obligations. We examine the consequences of bankruptcy in Chapter 25; here we need only to point out that there are severe costs associated with default. There is often serious disruption of the firm's business activity as top management spends time in negotiations with lenders while lower management starts thinking about alternative jobs. Customers for the firm's products and services begin to look for other sources of supply. The firm may have profitable investment opportunities at the same time its existing business is doing poorly. The firm may be forced to delay or forego making these investments because it cannot finance them. There are also legal and other expenses associated with the legal proceedings in bankruptcy situations. As the firm uses increased amounts of debt financing, the probability that it may default at some future time also increases. At some point the expected costs of default will become large enough to offset any other advantages to debt. At this point other sources of financing will be preferred.

Firms with large amounts of outstanding debt may have other problems. Lenders are reluctant to lend additional money to firms that are highly levered, and they may either not lend the money or charge a very high interest rate to compensate for their exposure to risk. Potential lenders and investors in the firm's securities may not agree with management. They may be unwilling to commit large amounts of new money to a corporation that is already highly levered. This problem may be especially significant for firms with relatively high business risks. The general opinion of financial experts is that, beyond some point, additional leverage is undesirable. This opinion is reflected in the concept of an optimal capital structure.

Optimal Capital Structure   The term *capital structure* means the proportions of different types of securities issued by the firm. The optimal (best) capital structure is the set of proportions that maximize the total value of the firm. Although the concept of capital structure applies to all types of securities, for simplicity we will continue to examine only debt and common stock. Figure 10-6 illustrates the general concept as applied to the Auric Mining example. In Figure 10-6a, the two components of total stock value (value of original owners' stock and value of new stock issued) are shown. In Figure 10-6b, the total value of all the firm's securities, debt plus stock, is shown. Notice that maximum value for the original owners is reached in the same range as maximum value for the entire firm. Management should use the proportion of debt to total value (or, equivalently, that degree of financial leverage) that maximizes the value of the firm since this provides the highest financial return to the original owners.[22]

Contrast the situation depicted in Figure 10-6 with that shown in Figure 10-5. In Figure 10-5 the value of the old shares and the total value of all securities increases with the amount of debt issued. In Figure 10-6, increasing debt is only desirable up to a point; beyond the optimal range, value declines and no more debt should be issued.

How is the financial manager to determine where the range of maximum value is? This is a tough problem. Financial managers must formulate their own policies. One source of information is the behavior of the prices of

[22] This is true provided that there are no differences in current dividends. When particular financing choices affect current dividends (as when retained earnings are used), current dividends plus the value of the original owners' shares is a better measure of owner benefits.

FIGURE 10-6

An illustation of optimal capital structure.

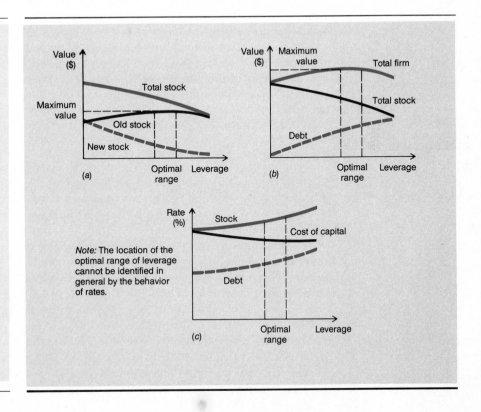

Note: The location of the optimal range of leverage cannot be identified in general by the behavior of rates.

320

PART 2
**The firm's investment,
financing, and dividend
decisions**

the firm's securities. If the price of the firm's stock drops on announcement of a new financing program, this is an obvious sign that the planned financing will move the firm outside of the optimal range. Institutional lenders such as banks and insurance companies provide the financial manager with their views on the desirability of financing programs. If the firm must pay unusually high interest rates for its debt issues, this may be a sign that too much debt is being issued. A lowering of ratings on the firm's bonds by the bond-rating agencies is another sign. The firm's investment bankers, who are experts in the issuance of securities, are a major source of information and advice.

Capital Structure and the Cost of Capital   Given that management is able to determine the optimal capital structure for the firm, how does this affect the cost of capital? The required rates of return on the firm's securities, debt and stock, will depend on the capital structure chosen. Figure 10-6c shows the behavior of debt rates and stock rates as leverage is increased. Since these rates depend on the capital structure decision, it is important that management measures the cost of capital when the firm has a capital structure in the optimal range; that is, when the firm's value is maximum. Otherwise the computed cost of capital may be seriously in error.

   Once management has established the optimal financing policy and allowed time for the securities markets to adjust to the policy, the cost of capital can be measured as described in Chapter 7. The general procedure was and is to determine the current proportions of the outstanding securities and to estimate current capital market rates as inputs to the cost of capital computation.

   There are some adjustments to the cost of capital approach that may be necessary under some conditions. These adjustments will be discussed in a later section of the chapter, after we consider financing through internal funds.

**RETAINED
EARNINGS AND
INTERNAL FUNDS**

Debt, preferred stock financing, and common stock financing force the financial manager to bargain with "outsiders." Lenders and investors must be convinced of the stability and profitability of the firm's present operations and of the desirability of new investment if they are to provide money at a reasonable cost to the firm and its present owners. The precise terms of these external financing sources will be determined by negotiations between management and the people providing the money. In any case the use of external financing reduces the future income available to the present owners. Financing investment by reducing cash and securities accumulated from the earnings of prior periods and by retaining cash generated from current operations does not present these difficulties. Instead the problem is to convince current shareholders (and perhaps current lenders) that the funds are best used for investment rather than for paying dividends or repaying debt before it is due. Usually this is an easier task because current shareholders and debtholders have already made a commitment to the future of the firm. Indeed, the firm has no legal obligation to pay debtholders prior to the scheduled principal and interest payments. The shareholders present a different problem, however.

The following type of problem has arisen for many companies. Suppose the shareholders have become accustomed to receiving on average about 50 percent of the profits as dividends. Profits and dividends have been growing at an average rate of 5 percent per year for several years. Management is about to embark on a major capital expenditure program that will probably continue for several years. New products will be manufactured and production facilities will be expanded. Management anticipates that these will be profitable investments to make, although only the current opportunities have been evaluated in detail. In any case, some current decisions will commit the firm to investing large amounts of money for two or three years. Based on forecasts of current and future cash flows, a continuation of the 50 percent payout of dividends would imply substantial external financing, at least part of which would have to be in the form of common stock. The use of debt to cover all additional requirements would, in management's judgment, be unwise, as the required amounts would subject the firm to excessive risk. The resulting capital structure would be outside the optimal range. Informal discussions with potential lenders have confirmed this judgment.

Given these circumstances, should management change the dividend policy of the firm to provide additional internal funds, plan to issue common stock as needed in the face of the uncertainties of future market conditions, try to borrow more money, or reduce investments? Notice that each of the above alternatives implies a cost to the current shareholders.

Foregoing profitable investments is not in the best interest of the stockholders unless there is no way to finance them at a reasonable cost. We have shown how the use of too much debt places the firm in a vulnerable position and will produce a lower value of the firm's stock. Therefore the source of the money must be either retained earnings (which implies lower dividend payments) or the sale of common stock. We feel, as do many financial theorists and managers, that usually the shareholders would be better off receiving lower dividends than having the firm issue common stock. This is so for several reasons:

1 If the firm retains earnings instead of paying higher dividends and issuing stock, the price per share of stock should be higher since earnings per share and future dividends per share will be higher if new stock is not issued. The shareholders could therefore get cash benefits from the investment by selling some of their stock. They would receive capital gains on the stock rather than dividends, and a dollar of capital gains is worth more after personal taxes than is a dollar of dividends since capital gains are taxed at a lower rate than dividends. (We consider personal taxes in more depth in Chapter 11.)

2 There is a variety of costs (legal fees, commissions, etc.) associated with issuing common stock. These costs can amount to over 25 percent of the total dollars of stock issued.

3 Temporarily investing retained earnings in marketable securities for purposes of future investment increases both the safety of the firm and its financial flexibility. Selling securities generally provides cash

322

PART 2
The firm's investment,
financing, and dividend
decisions

more quickly than would turning to external sources (borrowing or issuing stock) for funds. When the investment is to be made, the securities are liquidated and the proceeds used to finance the capital expenditure. On the other hand, if conditions change for the worse, sales of these securities bring cash quickly to meet debt payments, pay dividends, or pay expenses. Moreover, the existence of these funds does not preclude other financing if desirable. Their absence forces management to seek external sources to finance investment.

4 Sale of common stock may create control problems for the current owners of the firm.

Accordingly, we can see that there are sound reasons for preferring to finance investment through funds generated from operations and accumulated as marketable securities.

Despite the usual advantages to financing with retained earnings, this method of financing is not always possible or desirable. Shareholders may react very negatively to receiving lower dividend payments. It is one thing not to increase dividends as earnings rise and another to reduce them from prior levels. Shareholders may depend upon a given level of dividends, and reducing the dividends may force them to sell shares (and incur brokerage fees) to finance personal expenditures. The higher prices for the firm's stock due to the investment program may not be achieved immediately, and shareholders could be hurt under these conditions. Also, a reduction in dividends may actually cause temporary declines in the firm's stock. Investors may interpret the reduction of the dividend as evidence of weakness in the firm.

It may also be true that the amount of money available from not paying dividends would not be sufficient to avoid issuing some stock if the investment program is to be maintained. Under these conditions management is likely to be reluctant to risk even temporary declines in the stock price and may continue to pay dividends to support the price. Management will attempt to achieve a balance between the dividends paid and the increased number of shares needed to be sold. It should be clear that, whenever a firm issues stock and also pays a dividend, in effect it is using some of the stock sale proceeds to pay the dividends. This is not an uncommon occurrence.

THE IMPACT OF FINANCING ON INVESTMENT

The firm's cost of capital is the standard by which investment projects having the same business risk as the firm are evaluated. We have seen that the magnitude of the cost of capital depends on the firm's capital structure. Therefore the impact of financing decisions on investment decisions is conveyed through the use of the cost of capital. However, there are situations where the procedures of Chapter 7 used to estimate the cost of capital will not provide an appropriate measure for use in evaluating investment projects, even though the projects have the same business risk as the firm. We will consider three common problems here: (1) changes in financing policies, (2) financing large capital budgets, and (3) costs of issuing new securities.

Suppose that the financial manager has determined that the present capital structure of the firm is inappropriate. Economic conditions may have changed, or new management may have decided that past policies are not optimal. In any case, calculation of a cost of capital using current proportions of outstanding securities will not reflect the proportions to be maintained in the future. In addition, the required rates of return on the securities are likely to change as capital structure changes. In theory, the solution is simple. A new capital structure for the firm is obtained by issuing new securities and retiring outstanding ones. For example, debt can be rapidly reduced by selling stock and using the proceeds to retire the debt. Once the new capital structure has been achieved, the market rates on the securities can be measured and a new cost of capital can be calculated using the new proportions.

In practice, major changes in capital structure are not often made rapidly. There are several types of costs and fees that would be incurred, such as costs of issuing new securities and penalities imposed on early retirement of debt. Instead, firms usually move gradually toward a new capital structure by disproportionate use of one financing source over another for several years. This procedure has the advantage of not only keeping costs down, but also permitting financial managers to assess the effects of the new policy, to "feel their way" toward the optimal range.

An operational solution to the problem of estimating the new cost of capital when changes are being made gradually is to use, not the current proportions of financing sources, but *the planned future proportions*. The rates used are those currently in effect. We assume here that the new policy has been announced to the market so that current rates on the firm's securities reflect the market's assessment of this new policy. The rates must be continually reevaluated as the actual capital structure changes, but this must be done in any case as capital market conditions change.[23]

For example, if the financial manager believes that an appropriate capital structure for the firm is 30 percent debt, 10 percent preferred stock, and 60 percent common stock, then these are the proportions to be used in calculating the average cost of capital. The new financing policy is announced to the market, and new rates for the firm's securities are estimated based on the prices of outstanding securities after the announcement has been made. These rates are then used with the planned future proportions to calculate a new cost of capital.

The problem associated with the size of the capital budget can be most simply posed in terms of an example. Suppose that a firm with $10 million in assets is planning its capital expenditure program for the coming year. The financial manager has calculated the firm's cost of capital (using the procedure of Chapter 7) and has found it to be 12 percent. Would it make any difference if the capital expenditures for the year were $10 million or $1 million, given that all investments have positive net present values (all

---

[23] The theoretical solution to this problem is complex, but the solution recommended here serves as a reasonable approximation.

324

PART 2
The firm's investment,
financing, and dividend
decisions

internal rates of return greater than 12 percent)? In most cases the answer would be yes.

If the firm were investing only $1 million, the money probably could come from internal funds and readily available debt (e.g., a bank loan). If the firm is operating profitably and has not exceeded its debt capacity, neither lenders nor shareholders would be disturbed by a $1 million capital budget. However, suppose that the firm must raise $10 million, thereby doubling its assets in one year. In this case, new shares of common stock must be issued or substantial new debt acquired, or, more likely, both sources will be used. In any case, to raise this much new money compared with the past financing requirements of the firm is likely to cause lenders and stockholders to require a higher rate of return than in the past, thereby causing the true cost of capital to be more than 12 percent.

There are several explanations why the cost of capital increases as the capital budget gets larger:

1 If the size of the capital budget is large relative to the size of the firm, external financing from new sources is probably needed. New investors, both stockholders and lenders, will be asked to provide the firm with the money needed to undertake the investment. New investors generally have a more pessimistic view of the firm's future than do "old" investors and often require a higher rate of return because of a greater perceived risk.
2 Investors may also doubt the ability of management to control so much growth. That is, they may believe that the investments taken individually could be profitable, but will not be profitable if undertaken simultaneously. Many new people would have to be hired, trained, and organized; existing production processes may be disrupted; and so on. Therefore the investments may be viewed as being more risky.
3 The firm will incur issue costs if the volume of investment forces it to issue new securities (rather than use internal funds and direct loans from financial institutions). Issue costs pose special problems and are discussed later in this chapter.

Figure 10-7 shows how the size of the capital budget affects the firm's cost of capital. For small budgets the cost of capital for new financing (marginal cost of capital) is the same as the current cost of capital for the firm. As the amount invested and financed increases, the cost of capital for the new financing increases, causing the current cost of capital for the firm to rise. This means that the current cost of capital is not a reliable standard for evaluating new investments when the volume of investment proposals is large relative to the present size of the firm. Basing investment decisions on the current cost of capital may cause so many investments to be included in the capital budget that the firm's current cost of capital rises, thereby making some of those investments unprofitable to undertake.

For example, suppose that the capital budget would be $10 million if 12 percent were used as the discount rate. That is, there are $10 million in new investments with a positive net present value using a discount rate of 12 percent. However, the $10 million could only be raised at a marginal cost of

16 percent. The correct cost of capital for $10 million in new investment is 16 percent, not the current cost of capital for the firm, which is less than 16 percent. However, if the cost of capital is 16 percent, many of the investments included in the capital budget when 12 percent was used will now be rejected. The internal rate of return on these rejected opportunities is greater than 12 percent but less than 16 percent. The total amount of planned expenditures might be significantly decreased, say, to $3 million, if the minimum acceptable rate of return is set at 16 percent. But if the firm invests only $3 million, the cost of capital for new financing is likely to be less than 16 percent. In Figure 10-7, the cost of capital for $3 million is approximately 12 percent (point *a*). Now the firm may be undertaking too little investment, rejecting investments that offer rates of return less than 16 percent but greater than 12 percent.

The proper capital budget must be determined by finding that amount of expenditures having a cost of capital less than any projects included in the budget but with no profitable projects excluded. The problem is illustrated in Figure 10-8. The expected rate of return on the least profitable or marginal investment included in a given capital budget is plotted for different sizes of capital budget. This is the curve that falls as the amount invested increases. In other words, the firm has relatively few projects that have high expected rates of return but quite a few that have low expected rates of return. All investments here are of the same risk, the average business risk of the firm. The cost of capital for new financing is the same curve depicted in Figure 10-7. Using a cost of capital of 16 percent will result in a capital budget of $3 million (point *b*), but a $3 million capital budget can be financed at a cost of capital of 12 percent (point *a*). In this hypothetical case the optimal capital budget has expenditures and requires new financing of $7 million (point *c*). The minimum rate of return on any investment accepted and the cost of capital for new financing are both 13 percent.

In practice, financial managers do not have precise numbers that en-

FIGURE 10-7

The impact of the size of the capital budget on the cost of capital for new financing.

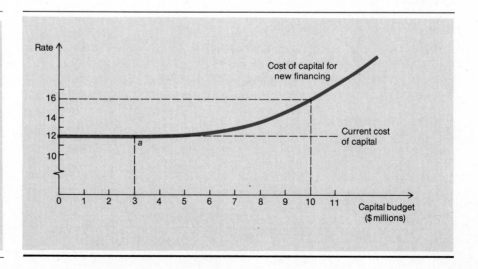

326

PART 2
**The firm's investment,
financing, and dividend
decisions**

able them to draw curves like those in Figure 10-8 and compute an exact answer. The cost of capital curve is especially hard to estimate, and more than two curves are required for investments that differ in risk. Instead, the financial manager evaluates the costs and difficulties involved in raising enough money to support the planned capital budget. If financing is a problem, those investments that were only marginally profitable when evaluated using the original estimate of the cost of capital are eliminated from the capital budget. A revised capital budget is developed and financing requirements are examined. This process is continued until management decides that the returns expected from the remaining projects in the capital budget are sufficient to justify the cost of financing them, and the budget is approved. In other words, the actual process produces results that come close to the ideal case shown in Figure 10-8.

Issue Costs

Whenever the firm raises money from external sources, it incurs some initial costs. These costs include expenses such as legal fees, costs of printing stock and bond certificates, and fees paid to underwriters. All costs associated with the process of raising money are called issue costs or flotation costs to distinguish them from the ongoing costs of the payments made to the suppliers of the money—for example, the interest paid to bondholders. Issue costs vary with the type and amount of external financing used. Stock issues cost more than bond issues. Bond issues cost more than bank loans. Large securities issues have higher dollar costs, but lower costs per dollar raised than do small issues. We examine issue costs in more detail in Chapter 18. See Table 18-1 for data. Here we are concerned with how these costs of financing affect the firm's investment decisions.

One way to incorporate issue costs in the investment decision is to include them as part of the cost of capital. Issue costs are one reason that

FIGURE 10-8

*Determination of the
optimal capital budget
and new financing.*

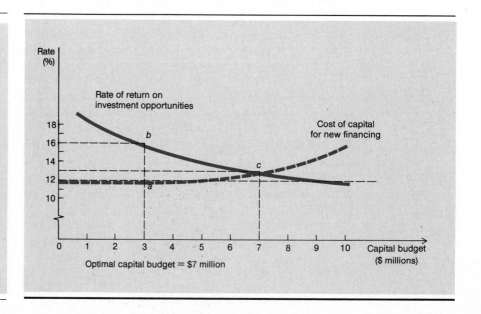

the cost of capital increases as the amount of financing increases. The approach presented here is quite simple and provides good results in a variety of situations. The method assumes that the firm maintains the same capital structure over time and that issue costs are a constant proportion of the dollar amount raised for each type of security issued.[24]

We need to deal with two concerns. First, we must adjust the cost of each external financing source to include issue costs. Second, we must recognize that the cost of retained earnings differs from the cost of issuing common stock. As we will see, the cost of retained earnings is less than the cost of common stock. Therefore, the financial manager will use retained earnings first. However, the amount of financing from retained earnings is limited by the profits of the firm. If more equity is required to finance investments than is available from retained earnings, common stock must be issued. The use of this more expensive source of equity causes the cost of capital to increase.

A general procedure for estimating the cost of each financing source is as follows:

1   Determine the net amount of money that the firm will receive from the financing source after deducting issue costs.
2   Solve for the effective cost (k) of the financing source.

In the case of debt financing, the effective cost is the discount rate that makes the present value of the aftertax payments equal to the net amount received. That is,

Net amount = present value of future principal and interest payments

$$= \frac{X_1}{1 + k} + \frac{X_2}{(1 + k)^2} + \cdots + \frac{X_n}{(1 + k)^n} \tag{10-1}$$

where $X_1, X_2, \ldots, X_n$ are the payments made to the lender net of any taxes associated with the financing. For example, suppose that the cost of issuing $1 million of ten-year bonds is $50,000. The bondholders are paying $1 million in cash, but the firm is receiving $950,000 after all expenses and discounts. The net amount of money the firm will have to use for investment is therefore the gross proceeds of $1 million less the issue costs of $50,000—$950,000. The issue costs on a debt issue are deductible for tax purposes, but they must be amortized over the life of the debt on a straight-line basis. In this example there would be a tax deduction of $5000 per year for ten years resulting from the issue costs of $50,000. Assume that the tax rate for the firm is 40 percent. The tax saving from the issue costs is therefore $2000 per year (0.40 × $5000). Suppose that the interest rate on the $1 million loan is 10 percent; therefore, the interest payments on the bonds are $100,000 per year, all of which is tax deductible. At a 40 percent

[24] The method presented here provides only approximate results, as do all existing methods that include flotation costs through a cost of capital adjustment. More exact methods are significantly more complicated. For a discussion of this issue, see John Ezzell and R. Barr Porter, "Flotation Costs and the Weighted Average Cost of Capital," *Journal of Financial and Quantitative Analysis*, XI, 3 (1976) pp. 403–414.

328

PART 2
The firm's investment,
financing, and dividend
decisions

tax rate, the aftertax interest cost is \$60,000 per year $[(1 - \text{tax rate}) \times \$100,000]$. The annual net aftertax cash payment resulting from the bond issue is the annual aftertax interest expense less the annual tax savings from the issue cost deduction:

$$\text{Annual aftertax interest} = \$60,000$$

$$\begin{aligned} \text{Less: Annual tax savings from} \\ \text{issue cost deduction} &= \underline{\quad 2,000} \\ \text{Annual aftertax payment} &= \underline{\underline{\$58,000}} \end{aligned}$$

To find the aftertax cost of the debt, we must now solve for the interest rate on the net amount received, \$950,000. The annual aftertax payments are \$58,000. At the end of ten years the firm must pay back \$1 million. Therefore, we can solve for the effective aftertax cost of the debt as the rate that makes the present value of the future aftertax principal and interest payments equal to the net amount received:

$$\$950,000 = \$58,000(P/A, k, 10) + \$1,000,000(P/F, k, 10)$$

$$k = 6.5\%$$

In the absence of issue costs, the effective cost of the debt financing would be 6 percent $[(1 - \text{tax rate}) \times 10\%]$. In this example, issue costs of only 5 percent of the amount issued (\$50,000/\$1 million) significantly raises the effective cost of the debt, from 6 percent to 6.5 percent.

Common stock and preferred stock have indefinite maturities. For these sources we can calculate the effective financing cost by multiplying the estimated market rate by the gross amount of the issue divided by the net amount received:

$$\text{Effective rate} = \text{market rate} \times \frac{\text{gross amount}}{\text{net amount}}$$

For example, suppose that you have estimated the market rate on your company's stock as 15 percent. A stock issue of \$2 million will have issue costs of \$180,000 (issue costs on stock are not tax deductible). The net amount received from this stock issue will be \$1,820,000 (\$2,000,000 − \$180,000). We compute the effective cost of the stock issue as

$$\text{Effective rate} = 15\% \times \frac{\$2,000,000}{\$1,820,000}$$

$$= 16.5\%$$

For retained earnings we use the market rate on the firm's stock. In the above example, 15 percent was the market rate. Since use of retained earnings avoids the issue costs associated with common stock, no stock will be issued until all available retained earnings have been exhausted. Under the conditions of this analysis, there will be an increase in the cost of capital once we start issuing stock to finance the capital budget. The marginal cost of capital with stock financing is greater than the marginal cost of capital with retained earnings financing because of stock issue costs.

The marginal average cost of capital is the minimum rate of return required on investments of the same risk as the firm. To combine the costs of the individual financing sources and obtain the marginal average cost of capital, we need to know the capital structure proportions for the firm (using the market values of the firm's outstanding stock and debt to compute the proportions). Suppose that these proportions are 60 percent equity and 40 percent from debt. We have two marginal costs of capital—one with retained earnings as the source of equity, and one with new common stock as the source of equity. Using the 6.5 percent cost of debt, the 15 percent cost of retained earnings, and the 16.5 percent cost of new common stock:

With retained earnings:

$$MCC = 0.6 \times 15\% + 0.4 \times 6.5\%$$

$$= 11.6\%$$

With common stock:

$$MCC = 0.6 \times 16.5\% + 0.4 \times 6.5\%$$

$$= 12.5\%$$

Suppose that any capital budget in excess of $6 million would require the use of common stock. Then the minimum acceptable rate of return on investment for capital budgets over $6 million would be 12.5 percent. If the capital budget is $6 million or less, the minimum acceptable rate of return is 11.6 percent. We show this graphically in Figure 10-9.

Issue costs are only one factor causing the marginal cost of capital to rise as the size of the capital budget increases. Under more realistic condi-

FIGURE 10-9

The impact of issue costs for common stock on the marginal cost of capital

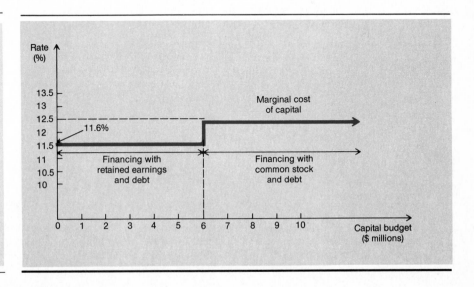

tions, the marginal cost of capital increases without the distinct jump shown in Figure 10-9.[25]

SUMMARY

Business firms finance their investments from four major sources: debt, preferred stock, common stock, and retained earnings. The characteristics of each source are summarized in Table 10-2.

In developing a plan for financing the firm's capital budget, the financial manager must consider the risks and returns provided by alternative plans. Debt financing increases the financial leverage of the firm and, therefore, both the risk and the return. Debt financing amplifies the basic business risk of the firm. Financial risk is the increase in total risk caused by the use of debt. This is the risk borne by stockholders and the firm because of the requirements to pay the debt interest and principal when due.

An analysis of the financing problem of business firms leads to the following conclusions:

1 Under idealized conditions with no income taxes, there are no advantages or disadvantages to any given financing plan from the viewpoint of the firm's stockholders.
2 Under idealized conditions with corporate income taxes (but no personal taxes), debt financing provides an advantage over other financing sources because of the tax deductibility of interest.
3 In practice there exists an optimal range for the capital structure of the firm. If the firm finances outside of this range, the value of the firm will decline.

Flexibility in future financing is provided by retaining earnings. Internal financing with retained earnings means that less current dividends will be paid than would be the case with external financing (new stock or debt). Stockholders may be better off receiving lower current dividends for several reasons. First, the price of the firm's stock should increase, reflecting the additional money invested in the firm, and there are personal tax advantages to capital gains instead of dividends. Second, issue costs of common stock are avoided. Third, with internal financing present owners are better able to retain their control of the firm.

When a firm changes its financing policy, its cost of capital is likely to change. The cost of capital should be calculated using the planned future proportions of the various financing sources and the current rates on its securities.

The cost of capital may be affected by the amount of financing re-

---

[25] Figure 10-9 assumes that the only factor affecting the cost of capital is issue costs on new equity that are a fixed proportion of the dollar amount raised. In practice, issues costs per dollar raised vary with the amount raised. Also, as we discussed earlier, the perceived risk of the capital budget (and therefore the cost of capital) can depend on the size of the capital budget. These complications, and others, generally cause the cost of capital to increase gradually as the amount of funds obtained increases.

*quired to support the planned capital budget. The capital budget may
require revision to ensure that the returns expected from the least profitable investments being undertaken are sufficient to justify the costs of
financing them.*

QUESTIONS

1 Compare and contrast debt with preferred stock as alternative methods of financing.

2 What are the major differences between retained earnings and other
sources of financing?

3 Financial institutions, such as banks, finance their assets with a very
high percentage of debt (considering demand and savings deposits
as forms of debt). How are they able to do this without exposing
their stockholders to a great deal of risk?

4 Describe what happens if a firm finances investment by issuing common stock at an "unreasonably" low price because of unusual
conditions in the security markets. How is this "bad" for the current
owners of the firm?

5 From 1945 to 1965 the economy achieved high rates of growth, financial markets were relatively stable, and interest rates on long-term
debt for major corporations did not vary much and were fairly low
(3 to 4 percent). Profits also grew substantially during this period.
How did these factors influence the types of financing used? (See
Table 10-1.)

6 Regulated monopolies such as electric utilities and telephone companies use much more debt and preferred stock than do industrial
corporations. Why do you think this is so?

7 If the corporate income tax were substantially reduced (say, to a flat
rate of 10 percent), how would the types of financing used by corporations be affected?

8 If dividends on common stock and preferred stock were tax deductible expenses for the corporation, what would be the impact on the
choice of financing?

9 Company A is in a high-risk business whereas company B is in a
low-risk business. Sketch on one graph the behavior of the total
value of the firm's securities for each of the two firms as a function
of the degree of leverage used under realistic assumptions concerning the impact of leverage. Assume that the stock values of the two
firms would be equal if neither firm used any leverage.

PROJECT

Estimate the relative proportions of debt, preferred stock, common stock,
and retained earnings used as financing sources for each of the past ten
years by nonfinancial corporations. Examine the level of long-term interest rates, corporate profits, and the behavior of the stock market over the
same period. Try to explain the variations in financing methods used
over this period. See Appendix 5A for sources of this information.

1 The Sands Corporation currently has 1.8 million shares of common stock outstanding. Management has developed a capital budget calling for total expenditures of $2.4 million in the next six months.

   a If new stock can be issued at a price of $12 per share, how many shares must be issued to finance the entire capital budget from common stock?

   b What will be the percentage of the firm's stock held by the new shareholders if shares are issued in a? [Ans.: 10 percent]

   c Last year Sands paid a dividend of $0.50 per share. Management plans to maintain this dividend rate. What were the total dividends paid by the firm last year? What will be the total dividends paid in the coming year if new shares are issued and the dividend rate is maintained? What percentage of the dividends paid in the coming year will be received by the new shareholders?

2 The financial manager of Cheetah Freightlines is considering issuing either debt or preferred stock to finance trucks costing $3 million. The interest rate on debt will be 10 percent whereas the required dividend rate on preferred stock will be 12 percent. The firm's tax rate is 40 percent.

   a What annual interest payments will be required on the debt issue?

   b How much in additional earnings before interest and taxes must be generated from the new trucks to cover interest on the debt?

   c What annual dividends will be required on the preferred stock issue?

   d How much in additional earnings before interest and taxes must be generated from the new trucks to cover preferred dividends?

3 The Peachy Computer Company started in business five years ago manufacturing home computers. The firm has grown rapidly and there are now 100,000 shares of common stock outstanding, largely owned by management. Last year's income statement is shown below. Peachy's chief designer, P. I. Tracy, has developed a new

Peachy Computer Company

	Last year actual	Next year projections			
		Stock issue		Debt issue	
Sales	$1,000,000	$1,000,000	$3,000,000	$1,000,000	$3,000,000
Expenses	680,000	800,000	1,600,000		
Operating profit	$ 320,000				
Interest	0				
Taxable income	$ 320,000				
Taxes (50%)	160,000				
Earnings	$ 160,000	$ 100,000			$ 550,000
Earnings per share	$1.60	$0.63			$5.50

combination computer, TV, and telephone in a single package. In order to manufacture this product, new facilities will be required involving a total investment of $2 million. Two financing alternatives are being considered: issuing 60,000 shares of stock or borrowing the $2 million at an interest rate of 15 percent per year. Management has considered two possible future sales projections: a pessimistic projection of $1 million and an optimistic projection of $3 million, as shown in the table on page 332.

  a   Calculate the values needed to complete the table.

  b   Develop an EBIT-EPS graph for the two alternatives.

  c   Draft a statement to the chief executive officer, A. P. Ricot, explaining the advantages and disadvantages of the alternative financing methods as illustrated by the data in the table and your graph.

4   Pants Inc., is a retail clothing store financed entirely with common stock (100,000 shares outstanding). The firm is planning to open a new outlet in a suburban location. The capital investment in the new store will be $200,000. The financial manager of Pants is looking into two possible methods of financing—common stock at the current price of $5 per share or debt at an interest rate of 10 percent.

  Pants' management is concerned about the risk associated with the new store and its financing. They have quantified their beliefs regarding the firm's earnings before interest and taxes as shown below (dollar amounts in thousands). Assume no taxes. (Note: This problem assumes an understanding of the concepts covered in Chapter 9.)

Probability	.1	.4	.4	.1	EV[a]	SD[b]	CV[c]
EBIT (no new store)	$(10)	$50	$ 80	$130	$64	$34	0.53
EBIT (with new store)	$(15)	$75	$120	$185	$95	$49	0.52

[a] Expected value.
[b] Standard deviation.
[c] Coefficient of variation (SD/EV).

  a   Find the probability distribution of EPS without the new store and its financing and the probability distributions of EPS with the new store under the two financing plans (all debt and all stock).

  b   Explain the differences in the three probability distributions. What kind of risk has increased or decreased?

  c   What will be the likely impact of the choice of financing on (1) the required rate of return for the new store and (2) the stock price?

5   Central Pipelines is being formed to build and operate a gas pipeline in the Midwest. The pipeline is estimated to cost $1.4 billion and is expected to earn (EBIT) $196 million per year forever. (Assume no

334

PART 2
The firm's investment,
financing, and dividend
decisions

taxes will be paid and all earnings will be distributed as dividends and interest.)

a Assume that, if the plant is financed entirely with common stock, stockholders will require a 14 percent rate of return. What will be the total market value of Central if only common stock is issued in financing the pipeline?

b Assuming perfect capital markets and no costs to bankruptcy, what will be the total value of Central if $600 million in bonds are issued at an interest rate of 10 percent as part of the financing package?

c Given that bonds are issued as in b, calculate the rate of return required by stockholders on Central's common stock.

d Assuming that the pipeline will be built, how should it be financed?

6 The Quasar Corporation has no outstanding debt or preferred stock. Management estimates that the required rate of return on Quasar common stock is currently 14 percent. The total market value of the stock is $40 million. An expansion program is planned that will involve $20 million in capital expenditures over the next two years. The estimated net present value of these investments is $5 million based on the current cost of capital of the firm. Therefore, assuming that only equity (common stock and retained earnings) is used to finance the expansion and that capital market rates do not change, the value of the firm's stock would be $65 million in two years.

Quasar's financial manager has suggested that debt be used to finance at least part of the $20 million. The following estimates have been developed:

Debt issued	Debt interest rate, %	Total common stock value	Rate on stock, %	Total value of Quasar securities
$ 0	—	$65 million	14.0	$65 million
5 million	10	62 million	14.2	
10 million	10.2	58 million	14.7	
15 million	10.6	53 million	15.2	
20 million	11	47 million	16.5	

a Determine the total value of Quasar's securities and its cost of capital for each financing alternative given that Quasar's tax rate is 40 percent.

b What financing plan would you recommend and why? (Hint: See Figure 10-6 and discussion.)

7 The QX Corporation has the following investment proposals which passed preliminary screening:

Proposal	Initial outlay	Expected rate of return
A	$ 100,000	30%
B	400,000	25
C	1,200,000	20
D	1,000,000	18
E	800,000	15
F	1,000,000	14
G	2,000,000	13
H	1,500,000	12
Total	$8,000,000	

The firm's current cost of capital is estimated at 11.5 percent. However the financial manager has determined that financing the entire budget of $8 million would result in a higher cost of capital for the firm. Only $3 million could be raised without increasing the cost of capital. The costs of new financing in incremental amounts are estimated to be as follows:

Incremental new financing	Cost of incremental new financing, %
$3.0 million	11.5
2.0 million	12
1.5 million	13
1.0 million	14
0.5 million	15

What should the firm do?

8 Shula Industries is planning to issue $5 million in twenty-year maturity bonds. The bonds will bear a 12 percent coupon rate of interest and be issued at par. The cost of issuing the bonds will be $400,000. Shula's tax rate is 40 percent. What is the effective, aftertax cost of the bonds?

9 In order to finance its capital budget, Shula Industries may have to issue $3 million in common stock. The cost of issuing these securities will be $500,000. Shula's financial manager has estimated that the market rate on stock is 16 percent. What is the cost of the common stock for use in calculating a marginal cost of capital for Shula?

[*Note:* Problems **8** and **9** must be solved before problem **10** can be solved.]

10 Shula Industries maintains a capital structure of 40 percent debt and 60 percent equity. Suppose that Shula issues the securities described in problems **8** and **9** in order to finance its capital budget. What is the marginal cost of capital for Shula?

10A

**THE
MODIGLIANI-
MILLER
ANALYSIS
OF CAPITAL
STRUCTURE
AND VALUE**

As discussed in Chapter 10, under idealized conditions in the capital markets and in the absence of taxes and bankruptcy costs, the value of a firm is unaffected by its financing. Both the total value of a firm's securities and its cost of capital are independent of its capital structure. In this appendix we will provide an illustration of the original analysis of Modigliani and Miller (MM) that provides these results and present the major arguments against the applicability of their results.

THE MM ANALYSIS

Consider two firms that have identical business risks and (for ease of illustration) the same expected level of earnings before interest and taxes. We assume that all business risk is based on the probability distribution of EBIT and that these two firms have identical distributions. Leverage Inc., has $1 million of 8 percent bonds outstanding, and Equity Inc., has no debt. Data on the two firms are shown in Exhibit 10-7. The question at issue here is what the market value of Leverage's common stock and therefore its total value will be. If there is an advantage to debt financing, the total value of Leverage will be greater than that of Equity. If debt financing is undesirable, Leverage's value will be less than Equity's. We can solve the problem by examining the consequences of first assuming that debt reduces value and then assuming that it increases value. If we find that neither assumption is reasonable, then, logically, total value must be the same for the two firms. In addition, arguing the point in this way will be helpful in illustrating the underlying characteristics of the analysis.

Suppose that the total value for Leverage's securities is only $3.5 million compared with Equity's $4 million. Debt financing has reduced the value of

---

EXHIBIT 10-7
Basic data

	Leverage, Inc.	Equity, Inc.
EBIT	$480,000	$480,000
Interest	80,000	0
Dividends	$400,000	$480,000
Market value—bonds	$1 million	0
Market value—stock	?	$4 million
Total market value	?	$4 million

Leverage. Its bonds are worth $1 million, and its stock is worth $2.5 million. Consider an investor who wishes to purchase the rights to an income stream with the risk of Equity. For an investment of $400,000, the investor could purchase 10 percent of Equity's stock and for this amount would have an expected income of 10 percent of Equity's income, or $48,000. The investor now considers investing in Leverage. The investor could purchase 10 percent of Leverage's bonds at a cost of $100,000, which would provide $8000 interest and 10 percent of Leverage's stock at a cost of $250,000 with expected dividends of $40,000. The investor's total expected income from Leverage's securities would be $48,000, and *this income would have a probability distribution identical to that of the income from 10 percent of Equity's common stock*. This is so because the investor would own a 10 percent share in Leverage's earnings before interest and taxes just as he or she would have from purchasing Equity's common stock. The data describing these alternative transactions are shown in Exhibit 10-8. But note that purchasing a 10 percent claim against Leverage's income would cost the investor a total of only $350,000. Obtaining the same expected income ($48,000) from Equity stock would cost the investor $400,000. If you were the investor, which choice would you make? Obviously you would prefer to buy Leverage's securities. In a perfect market, identical substitutes cannot sell at different prices. If all investors agree on the probability distributions of the two firms, their securities must sell at prices that provide the same returns. Either Equity's stock must sell for less than $4 million or Leverage's stock and bonds must sell for more than $3.5 million. *In any case the total value of*

EXHIBIT 10-8
Assume debt lowers value

Market value of Leverage's bonds .... $1.0 million
Market value of Leverage's stock .... 2.5 million
Total market value of Leverage .... $3.5 million

Equity's stock value = total value = $4 million

1. Purchase 10% of Equity's stock

Purchase cost = $400,000
Dividend income = $48,000/year

2. Purchase 10% of Leverage's stock and bonds

	Purchase cost	Income
Bonds	$100,000	$ 8,000/year
Stock	250,000	40,000/year
Total	$350,000	$48,000/year

Investors would prefer 2, investing in Leverage's stock and bonds.

338

PART 2
The firm's investment,
financing, and dividend
decisions

Leverage's securities cannot be lower than the value of Equity's; otherwise investors would all prefer to purchase a combination of stocks and bonds issued by Leverage rather than to purchase Equity's stock.

The result established by this example is that a firm using debt financing cannot lower its value below what it would be with all stock financing because investors can always undo the leverage by purchasing a combination of stocks and bonds issued by the firm. However, remember that we are assuming that the probability distribution of EBIT is not affected by financing.

What about the possibility that Leverage's value will be greater than Equity's? Suppose that Leverage's stock has a market value of $3.2 million and a total value of stock plus bonds of $4.2 million. A similar analysis can be performed in this case and the results are shown in Exhibit 10-9. Now investors desiring securities with the same risk as Equity's would purchase Equity's stock because they can get a better return than by purchasing 10 percent of Leverage's stock and bonds. However, what about an investor who is willing to trade off some risk in order to achieve a higher rate of return on the investment? An investment of $400,000 in Leverage's stock will provide the investor with an expected return of $50,000 per year, or 12.5 percent ($50,000/$400,000), as compared with only $48,000 per year, or 12 percent, if $400,000 is invested in Equity's stock. Such an investor has another alternative, however. Under the assumptions of this analysis, the investor can borrow at the same interest rate that the company can by using stock as security for the loan. Suppose the investor takes $375,000, borrows an additional $125,000 at 8 percent, and purchases Equity stock with the total amount ($500,000). The results are shown in Exhibit 10-10. The inves-

---

EXHIBIT 10-9
Assumes debt increases value

Market value of Leverage's bonds .... $1.0 million
Total market value of Leverage's stock .... 3.2 million
Total market value of Leverage .... $4.2 million

1. Purchase 10% of Equity's stock

   Purchase cost = $400,000

   Dividend income = $48,000/year

2. Purchase 10% of Leverage's stock and bonds

	Purchase cost	Income
Bonds	$100,000	$ 8,000/year
Stock	320,000	40,000/year
Total	$420,000	$48,000/year

Investors would prefer 1, investing in Equity's stock.

tor's net income is $50,000, the same as if the investor purchased Leverage's stock, and the out-of-pocket outlay is only $375,000 instead of $400,000. Since investors would rather hold Equity's stock alone than a combination of Leverage's stock and bonds, or they would prefer to borrow to invest in Equity's stock rather than hold Leverage's stock by itself, Leverage's stock value must be less than $3.2 million (or Equity's stock must be worth more than $4 million).

One final point is worth making. Suppose the market value of Leverage's stock and bonds is $4 million, made up of $3 million of stock value and $1 million of bond value. Equity's stock value and total value are both $4 million. An investor seeking higher risk and return could invest in Leverage's stock or borrow to invest in Equity's stock. Is risk and return from these two alternative strategies the same given the same dollar outlay by the investor? Exhibit 10-11 evaluates the returns achieved by the two strategies for three different levels of EBIT. Remember, Leverage and Equity are assumed to have identical probability distributions of EBIT (EBIT for the two firms have a correlation of 1.0). We see from Exhibit 10-11 that identical returns are achieved by the two investment alternatives: They have identical risks.

We have just shown that Leverage's total value cannot be greater than Equity's total value. We have also shown that Leverage's total value cannot be less than Equity's value. Thus, in the absence of taxes, the values of Leverage and Equity are equal and, therefore, a firm's total value (equity plus debt) does not depend on its financial structure.

Leverage with Corporate Taxes

MM used arguments similar to those above to examine the impact of corporate taxes. They found, as we discuss on page 314, that debt provides a benefit to the firm because of the tax deductibility of interest payments. The implication of their analysis in this case is that the value of the firm is maximized when its capital structure contains only debt. Although this

---

EXHIBIT 10-10
Using personal borrowing when debt is assumed to increase value

1. Purchase 12.5% of Leverage's stock

    Purchase price = $400,000

    Dividend income = $50,000/year

2. Borrowing to invest in 12.5% of Equity's stock

	Purchase cost	Income
Stock	$ 500,000	$ 60,000
Borrowing	(125,000)	(10,000)
Net	$ 375,000	$ 50,000

Investors would prefer 2, borrowing to invest in Equity's stock.

340

PART 2
The firm's investment,
financing, and dividend
decisions

EXHIBIT 10-11
Assessing the risk from two investment strategies

	EBIT for leverage and equity		
	$80,000	$480,000	$600,000
Leverage interest	$80,000	$ 80,000	$ 80,000
Leverage dividends	0	400,000	520,000
Strategy A:			
Investor income	$ 0	$ 40,000	$ 52,000
Equity dividends	$80,000	$480,000	$600,000
Strategy B:			
Investor dividends	$ 8,000	$ 48,000	$ 60,000
Investor interest	(8,000)	(8,000)	(8,000)
Investor income	$ 0	$ 40,000	$ 52,000

Strategy A
   Investor purchases $300,000 of Leverage's stock, which has an aggregate market value of $3 million. Investor owns 10% of Leverage's stock.

   Out-of-pocket investment = $300,000

Strategy B
   Investor borrows $100,000 at 8% interest rate and buys $400,000 of Equity's stock, which has an aggregate market value of $4 million. Investor owns 10% of Equity's stock.

   Out-of-pocket investment = $300,000

Conclusion: Both strategies provide the same income regardless of the level of EBIT for the firms; therefore the risk is the same for the two strategies.

extreme result is impractical because the Internal Revenue Service would never permit interest payments of this magnitude to be tax deductible, the inference is that firms should use as much debt as they possibly can, subject only to the restrictions of the IRS and the willingness of creditors to lend to the firm.

   The results of the MM analysis can be summarized as follows:

A   The only benefit of debt financing (relative to equity financing) is the reduction in corporate income taxes due to the tax deductibility of debt interest.

B   There is no disadvantage of debt financing relative to equity financing.

Implications for Financing   If a firm is not paying corporate income taxes, the financing decision is irrelevant. It doesn't matter one way or the other whether or not debt is used. A firm paying corporate taxes should maximize its use of debt. Debt is superior to any other financing source.

There are four conditions that must be met in order to validate the MM analysis and produce the above results:

1 No costs are imposed on the firm when it defaults on debt payments or goes bankrupt.
2 Investors must be able to do their own borrowing, using "homemade leverage," if they desire higher returns (with higher risk) than the returns provided by debtfree or low-debt firms.
3 Investors must able to undo the leverage achieved by a corporation by purchasing a proportionate share of all the outstanding claims against corporate income.
4 Personal taxes must be neutral with respect to the choice between debt and equity.

Critics of the MM position have focused their attack on the realism of assuming these four conditions. We can separate these criticisms into two groups. The first group of criticisms is direct toward result A, that the only benefit from debt financing is due to the tax deductibility of interest. The second group of criticisms is directed toward point B, that there is no disadvantage to debt even if used very heavily. We summarize the various arguments below.

Arguments Supporting Additional Benefits from Debt

1 The risk of leverage as perceived by an individual investor borrowing money is different from the investor's perception of the risk of leverage when the corporation borrows the money. Corporate leverage and homemade leverage are not perfect substitutes from the standpoint of the person doing the borrowing. Therefore, individuals will prefer that the corporation rather than they do the borrowing. One reason for this difference is risk in the limited liability of a corporate stockholder. If the corporation borrows and goes bankrupt, individuals lose at most their investment. If the individual borrows to finance stock purchases and the stock becomes worthless, the creditors can take over assets owned by the individual to pay off the debt.
2 The interest rate charged by lenders may be greater for an individual than for a corporation. Therefore, it will be cheaper from the viewpoint of the stockholders to have the corporation do the borrowing.
3 There are legal limitations inhibiting homemade leverage. Mutual funds and trust funds that invest heavily in common stock cannot borrow, and so these investors may prefer corporations with debt.

Arguments Implying a Disadvantage to Debt

1 The firm is likely to incur costs and suffer penalties if it does not meet its promised principal and interest payments. Legal expenses, disruption of operations, and loss of potentially profitable investment opportunities may result. As the amount of debt in the capital structure increases, so does the probability of incurring these costs. Consequently there are disadvantages to debt, and excessive use of debt may reduce the value of the firm. This is one of the most telling arguments against result B on page 340.
2 Investors seeking to undo excessive leverage will incur transaction

342

PART 2
The firm's investment,
financing, and dividend
decisions

costs (brokerage fees from buying and selling securities) that would otherwise not need to be paid. Therefore the securities of highly levered firms will sell at somewhat lower prices than MM would predict.

3 Much corporate debt is not marketable. It consists of loans made by banks and other financial institutions. Thereore, investors cannot undo excessive leverage because they cannot purchase a proportionate share of the outstanding claims (stock and debt) against the firm's income.

4 Many institutional investors such as banks and life insurance companies cannot legally purchase low-rated bonds such as those issued by a highly levered corporation. Therefore the interest rates on highly rated, "investment grade" bonds are significantly lower than those on more risky bonds.

5 As firms in general increase their use of debt financing, they provide increasing amounts of interest which is taxed as ordinary income at the expense of capital gains on the stock which is taxed at lower rates. At some point the corporate tax advantage of debt may be offset by the personal tax disadvantages.

6 The existence of risky borrowing by the firm (risky in the sense that the firm might not be able to repay the debt) can cause the firm to adobt a less profitable investment strategy than it would if it had no risky debt outstanding.

SUMMARY

The Modigliani-Miller (MM) analysis implies that firms are indifferent concerning the method of financing (all combinations of debt and equity are equally good) if there are no taxes, but, with corporate taxes, firms should be financed with virtually all debt. However, the MM model assumes away many factors that can imply that a particular blend of debt and equity financing is best for a given firm.

We should add that existing theoretical models provide only a partial explanation of empirically observed corporate financing behavior, and there are serious difficulties in empirically measuring the impact of leverage on firm value. We do observe that capital structures differ across industries and that, for industries comprising firms with roughly comparable business risks (such as utilities and banks), it is often the case that the firms within an industry have similar capital structures. It is not clear whether this similarity in financing policies is due to "herd instinct" or to a correct determination of optimal capital structure by the companies' managers. The question of optimal capital structure remains a contentious issue in finance.

"May you live in interesting times," is an ancient Chinese curse. One of the aspects of our times that contributes to its "interest" is inflation. **Inflation** is an increase in the general level of prices for goods and services. The reverse of inflation is **deflation**, a reduction in the general level of prices. For the past forty years we have been experiencing some inflation almost continuously, and since 1965 it has become a serious problem for us. The degree of inflation we have faced recently is illustrated by the behavior of an index of consumer prices developed by government statisticians. The figure on this page indicates the severity of the inflation since 1965. This essay is an overview of the consequences of inflation, the problems it creates, and the reactions of individuals and firms to it.

THE FINANCIAL
IMPACT OF INFLATION

Inflation has two major financial effects. It reduces the value of money and it may increase risk. Here let's look at the impact of inflation on the value of money, and what individuals and businesses are doing to protect themselves against the reduction in the value of the dollar.

The basic impact of inflation is straightforward: A given amount of money will purchase less in the future than it does today. This means, for example, that people living on a fixed income of $500 per month will find it impossible to maintain their standard of living as time passes. Their money income stays the same, but they become poorer as the amounts of goods and services they can buy with their $500 monthly income declines. If prices are increasing at a rate of 10 percent per year, then peoples' incomes must increase at least 10 percent per year for them to stay even. A similar logic applies to investments. If the rate of inflation is 10 percent per year and the rate of return on the investment is 6 percent per year, you are actually earning a negative 4 percent per year on the investment in terms of your ability to purchase goods and services. To gain from the investment, you must earn more than the 10 percent per year inflation rate.

Individuals and businesses have

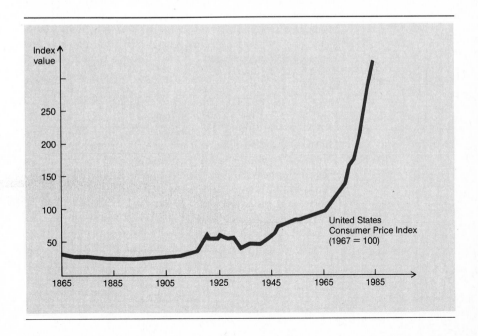

United States
Consumer Price Index
(1967 = 100)

344

PART 2
The firm's investment,
financing, and dividend
decisions

been doing several things to protect themselves against inflation. Employees demand cost of living pay increases. Labor unions seek contracts with employers that provide inflation escalators. These escalators increase wages automatically if the Consumer Price Index or some other measure of the price level increases. For example, a contract might provide that an increase of 10 percent in the Consumer Price Index would result in a 10 percent increase in wage rates. The number of workers covered by major labor contracts with cost of living escalators increased at an unprecedented rate during the 1970s. Congress has responded to pressures from retired people by including cost of living adjustments in social security payments and federal pensions.

Business firms are reluctant to enter into long-term, fixed-price contracts to supply goods and services. Instead they will include some provision for increasing prices in the future depending on the degree of inflation. Similarly, long-term leases for commercial real estate include escalators of various sorts so that lease payments will rise with inflation. However, the most significant changes have occurred in the financial markets.

INNOVATIONS IN THE FINANCIAL MARKETS

When inflation increases unexpectedly and interest rates increase as well, borrowers are benefited but lenders hurt. In the early 1980s, the hurt to savings and loan associations from interest rate increases was so severe that large numbers of them ceased to operate as separate firms. In order to protect themselves against unanticipated increases in inflation, lenders have developed many new financial arrangements. Moreover some borrowers, in order to appeal to lenders (investors), have developed some ideas of their own.

Most of the innovations in financing can be characterized as belonging to one of two types:

1 Variable (instead of fixed) interest rates
2 Equity participations where the lender shares in any increases in the value of the assets being financed

In addition there have been innovations such as "zero-coupon" bonds, which protect investors from decreases in interest rates and several home mortgage plans with payments that increase (contractually) over time to match anticipated increases in a borrower's ability to pay.

Mortgage lenders have been particularly innovative in designing variable or adjustment rate mortgage loans. Traditionally home mortgages have been long-term, fixed-interest-rate contracts between the borrower and the lender. The critical question for someone buying a house was "can we afford the monthly payment?" However, once the monthly payment on a loan was determined (based on the interest rate on the loan, the amount loaned, and the loan's maturity) that payment was fixed over the entire term to maturity. Now the question is more difficult to answer. Some mortgages (rollovers) have an interest rate and monthly payment that is fixed only for the first five years. At the end of five years, the interest rate may change to the current interest rate and a new monthly payment is determined to run for another five years. Rollover mortgages have been the dominant type of mortgage loan in Canada for many years. There are also many variable rate mortgages with interest rates that change semiannually. The new rate is based on an index such as the cost of funds of savings and loan associations, the national average rate on new mortgages, the six-month Treasury bill rate, or whatever index agreed to by the borrower and lender. Loans also differ in whether the change in interest rate on the mortgage is reflected in a change in the monthly payment or the loan's maturity date. Often the maturity changes, keeping the same monthly payment. When interest rates increase substantially, however, the monthly payment may not even be enough to pay the monthly interest on the loan. When this happens, the monthly payment is usually increased to make sure the loan will eventually be repaid by the monthly payments. In some cases, the monthly payments are not changed but the loan balance is increased and a balloon payment is required at maturity. We show most types of home mortgages in the table below.

Varieties of home mortgages

Mortgage type	Interest rate	Maturity	Payments
Conventional	Fixed.	Fixed, often 30 years.	Fixed over term of the loan.
	May be scarce when interest rates are climbing, because lenders do not want to risk being locked into lower income.		
Adjustable rate or variable rate (ARM or VRM)	Indexed to a market rate (for example, 6-month Treasury bill rate). Starting rate may be lower than on conventional because borrower shares risk of rising rates with lender.	Fixed, but sometimes can be extended in lieu of increase in monthly rate rises.	May change when interest rate changes or only at specified intervals, such as annually or every 3 to 5 years. If payments do not increase with interest rates, result may be negative amortization (see GPM below).
Graduated payment (GPM)	Fixed.	Fixed.	Low at start. Increase gradually as predetermined during first 5 or 10 years, then level out.
	Because of lower starting payments, may appeal to young borrowers who anticipate increased income in future years. *Caution:* Early payments may not cover interest due. Unpaid interest is added to outstanding principal, increasing the debt. This is called *negative amortization*, and borrowers may get a shock if they decide to sell in a few years and discover reduced equity in the property. However, some GPMs may include arrangements to prevent negative amortization.		
Graduated payments adjustable	Adjustable as in ARM or VRM.	Fixed, up to 40 years.	Similar to GPM. During first 10 years may be less than required to fully amortize loan. Adjusted within that period and every 5 years thereafter to insure full payment.
	Federal savings and loans and mutual savings banks were authorized in July 1981 to offer this mortgage, which combines graduated payments with adjustable interest rates. Payment adjustments may be quite large because of these two areas of change.		

(Continued)

Mortgage type	Interest rate	Maturity	Payments
Renegotiable rate (RRM)	Fixed for 3 to 5 years, then renegotiated.	Short-term loan (3 to 5 years) but amortized over longer term, usually up to 30 years.	Payments will change as interest rate changes.
	Short-term loan is automatically renewable; but if new interest rate is not acceptable, the borrower must either refinance or sell the property. The interest rate increases permitted each year and over the life of the loan may be limited.		
Shared appreciation (SAM)	Fixed.	Fixed.	Fixed.
	In return for lower interest rate the borrower agrees to share with the lender a percentage of any increase in the value of the home—at specified future dates or when it is sold, whichever occurs first. This plan may appeal to first-home buyer as a way to make the purchase affordable. But remember, increase in value must be shared with the lender; sharing a *decrease* in value may or may not be part of the agreement.		
Wraparound (WRAP)	Fixed.	Fixed.	Fixed.
	The lender combines an existing mortgage on the property (bearing a lower rate) with a new mortgage for the balance needed (at a higher rate) to provide a lower overall cost to the borrower. This is possible only if the existing mortgage is assumable by the buyer. (All FHA and VA mortgages are assumable.)		
Balloon payment	Fixed or adjustable.	Fixed. Traditionally 5 years but may be shorter or longer.	Fixed, usually based on 20- to 30-year amortization, but at end of term debt will not be fully paid. Borrower must pay off remaining "balloon" balance or refinance at prevailing rates.
	Because of short term and balloon payment, the down payment may be as little as 5 percent.		
Reverse annuity (RAM)	May be adjustable.	May be fixed with refinancing option.	Loan due when home is sold or upon death of borrower.
	This plan calls for periodic payments to homeowners based on a loan against their equity in a home. It is designed to appeal to older persons who may be having difficulty living on reduced incomes.		
"Take-back"	Usually fixed.	Usually short term.	Usually a high down payment. May call for balloon payment at maturity.
	This is a loan by the seller of the property, who agrees to take the mortgage in order to facilitate the sale.		

Varieties of home mortgages (continued)

Mortgage type	Interest rate	Maturity	Payments
Federal Housing Administration (FHA) insured	Set by FHA. Usually more favorable because of protection afforded lender. Seller may have to pay "points," an amount to raise lender's return to market levels.	Fixed.	Fixed or graduated, depending on FHA options.
	Available from lenders approved by FHA. Properties to be mortgaged must meet FHA requirements.		
Veterans Administration (VA) guaranteed	Fixed. Lower than others but seller may have to pay points.	Fixed. Usually 25–30 years.	Fixed or graduated, depending on VA options.
	Terms are eased because of VA guarantee. No or low down payment. Veterans should check with VA for eligibility requirements and for other assistance related to housing.		
Buy-down	Below market rate, for a specified period or for the life of the loan.	Fixed.	Fixed for term of the buy-down, usually increases thereafter.
	A seller or home builder pays an amount to a lender "up front," who then gives to buyers below-market rate loans. The borrower should realize this arrangement may increase the purchase price of the home.		

Source: Charting Home Mortgages, Federal Reserve Bank of Philadelphia, January 1982.

Adjustable interest rates are found in many types of debt contracts other than home mortgages. Some banks are offering variable rate consumer installment loans. The majority of bank loans to corporations have interest rates that change daily. Corporations have been issuing five- to ten-year bonds with variable interest rates usually linked to Treasury securities' rates. In 1982 banks and thrift institutions began offering variable rate time deposits for Individual Retirement Accounts (IRAs).

Equity participations have also become widely used. **Equity participation** means that the supplier of money, the lender, shares in any increases (or decreases) in value of the asset being financed. Most of this activity has been in real estate financing. A **shared-appreciation mortgage (SAM)** has a low, fixed rate of interest, but gives the lender a share of any appreciation of the property. In a typical SAM the interest rate is 33 percent lower than the prevailing standard mortgage rate (for example, 8 percent rather than 12 percent). However, when the property is sold the lender gets 33 percent of any increase in the value of the real estate being financed. Under some agreements, the lender can collect its share of the appreciation after a given number of years (normally ten years) even if the borrower hasn't sold the property (the value being determined by a professional appraiser). Another type of equity participation involves the lender's sharing in the revenues from an income-producing property, such as an office building or shopping center. Some life insurance companies have gone so far as to be co-owners of the property, becoming limited partners of the real estate developer.

ARE FINANCIAL FUTURES IN YOUR FUTURE?

Not all the innovation has been confined to the financing area. The variability of interest rates and the desires of businesses and financial institutions to protect themselves against unexpected changes in interest rates has encouraged the development of a new type of financial security—**financial futures**. A **futures contract** is simply an agreement between two parties (individuals or firms) to exchange at some future date an asset for cash at a price that is fixed today. If you agree on January 31 to buy 100 ounces of gold on July 31 at a price of $400 per ounce from your local gold dealer, you have just created a six-months futures contract with the dealer. On July 31 you will have to put up $40,000 and the gold dealer will have to put up the 100 ounces of gold. In this contract $400 is the futures price of gold for delivery on July 31. The current (January 31) price of gold for immediate delivery is called the cash price.

One problem with this arrangement is that both you and the dealer have to have a great deal of trust in each other. The dealer trusts you to have $40,000 on July 31 and you trust the dealer to have the 100 ounces of gold to sell to you on July 31. To avoid this problem (and others), organized markets have been established for buying and selling futures contracts.

There are established futures markets for gold, orange juice, wheat, coffee, and many other commodities. Standardized futures contracts are bought and sold in these markets. All contracts in a given commodity are for a fixed quantity; for example, 100 ounces of gold, 50,000 pounds of cotton, and 10 metric tons of cocoa.

Delivery dates are limited to one day in each month so that only the month of delivery need be specified; for example, July 1987, gold futures. The delivery months available for trading at any point in time are limited and vary with the commodity. For example on June 20, 1985, prices were quoted for twelve gold futures contracts listed in *The Wall Street Journal* ranging from July 1985 to February 1987. There were only four gasoline futures listed, ranging from July 1985 to October 1985.

Futures prices at a given point in time reflect expectations of market traders as to the future cash prices of the commodity. For example, if the cash price of gold six months from now is expected to be higher than the current cash price, the futures price of gold for delivery in six months will be greater than the current cash price. As expectations change, so do futures prices. **Futures prices** are not the cost of buying or selling a contract; they are the price per unit of the commodity in the contract for future delivery (i.e., the price the buyer of the contract agrees to pay for the commodity on the delivery date). In order to buy or sell a contract, you must "post margin" and pay a commission. For example, if you buy a July futures contract for 100 ounces of gold at $400 per ounce in the futures market, the broker with whom you place the order (e.g., Merrill Lynch) will require you to place money in a margin account, about 5 percent of the value of the contract for most commodities. Thus, for a $40,000 gold contract, the required margin would be about $2000. The broker will also charge you a commission, say, $50, for purchasing the contract for you. Once you have purchased this contract, you may either hold it and take delivery of the gold (which is handled through your broker) or, anytime before the July delivery date, sell a July futures contract for 100 ounces of gold, thus "closing out your position." This latter alternative is the most likely. Less than

3 percent of traded contracts are settled by delivery of the actual item. Your gain or loss on the two transactions (purchase and sale of the contract) will depend on what has happened to the July futures price of gold. If the price of July futures has risen since you bought the contract, upon closing out your position you will receive the difference between the prevailing futures price and the $400 futures price when you purchased the contract (less commissions). Thus, for example, if the futures price has risen to $440 per ounce when you close out your position, you will net $4000 less commissions on the deal [($440 − $400) × 100 ounces]. $4000 is a rather nice return on your investment of $2000 in the margin account!

What happens if the price of July gold futures falls instead? Each day your margin account will be reduced by the loss on the contract for that day. When your account drops below a minimum level (maintenance margin), which depends on the contract, you will be asked by your broker to either post more margin (put more money in your account) or to close out your position.

Suppose that you think the price of gold will fall. You can speculate on falling gold prices by selling a gold futures contract. Notice that, when selling contracts in the futures markets, you do not need to own the commodity. If you sell a July gold futures contract in January, you are obligating yourself to hand over 100 ounces of gold in July. You can either be prepared to have 100 ounces of gold to settle the contract, or buy a July futures contract prior to the July delivery date. Buying a July contract gives you the right to obtain 100 ounces of gold on the same delivery date as the contract you sold. Therefore, buying a July futures contract at anytime before the delivery date will enable you to close out your position without actually having to deliver the gold. So that you

don't forget to cover your position, your broker will remind you to close out any open positions prior to the expiration dates of the contracts you own.

Although commodity futures have been used for years, financial futures are a recent development. A financial futures contract is simply a futures contract involving financial assets rather than commodities. The financial assets for which there are active futures markets include foreign currencies (e.g., British pounds), thirteen-week Treasury bills, four- to six-year Treasury notes, fifteen-year Treasury bonds, ninety-day commercial paper, and others. Financial futures can be used to speculate on changes in interest rates (security prices) just as commodity futures can be used to speculate on changes in commodity prices. If you think short-term interest rates are going to rise, sell a one-year Treasury bill futures contract, say, at a price of $90.50. (Prices are stated per $100 of face value.) If interest rates do rise, the price will fall, say, to a price of $89.50. You can close out your position by buying a contract at $89.50. Since each contract in one-year Treasury bills is for $250,000 face value, you will earn $2500 from the transaction. Financial futures have much lower margin requirements than commodity futures, ranging between 0.15 percent to 2 percent of the face value of the contract. You would need only $900 in margin for a single one-year Treasury bill contract.

Financial futures are used by businesses and financial institutions to protect (hedge) against changing interest rates. For example, an airline might be planning to issue $10 million in long-term fixed-rate bonds in six months' time, when a new airplane is to be purchased. The financial manager could protect the airline from an increase in interest rates by selling 100 long-term Treasury bond futures contracts now. The contracts have a face value of $100,000 each so 100 contracts have a face value of $10 million. The financial manager would be planning to buy 100 contracts six months later when the bonds are issued. If interest rates do rise, the gains on the futures transaction will help to offset the higher interest rate on the bond issue. Of course, if interest rates fall, there will be losses on the futures transaction. But in this case the airline will benefit from the lower interest rates on the bonds. In 1981 Pillsbury wished to protect itself from higher interest rates on its short-term borrowing. It sold $60 million in Treasury bill contracts. Interest rates did rise and Pillsbury purchased $60 million in contracts, closing out its position with a profit of $225,000 to help offset its higher borrowing costs. Futures have a bright future as financial managers become adept in using them.

11

DIVIDEND POLICY AND RETAINED EARNINGS

A corporation can use its earnings to pay dividends to its stockholders, or it can use the funds for other purposes, such as retirement of debt or financing new investments. An increase in dividends involves the payout of firm cash to its shareholders. If management does not want the dividend increase to affect the firm's asset base or level of debt (i.e., if investment policy and financial structure policy are not to change), then the firm will have to issue additional shares to finance the added dividends. A "pure" dividend policy change (i.e., one requiring no alteration of the firm's investment and financial structure policies) involves a change in dividends and an equal dollar change in new share sales (an increase in both or a decrease in both). In general, however, there may be simultaneous changes in more than one policy. For example, a company may decrease its dividend and use the funds to expand its investment (a mixture of dividend policy and investment policy changes), to pay off some of its debt (a mixture of dividend policy and financial structure policy changes), or to increase investment and retire debt (a simultaneous change in all policies). The implications of all this is that dividends, investment, and financing are very closely related.

In the first section of this chapter, we describe the dividend payment procedure. We then discuss the various factors that influence the firm's dividend policy and examine the alternative dividend policies that are followed in practice. Later sections of the chapter cover dividend reinvestment plans, stock dividends and splits, and share repurchases.

THE DIVIDEND PAYMENT PROCEDURE

Generally, firms pay dividends once per quarter, that is, four times per year. Normally, dividends are set at a level that the firm feels is sustainable even during the years of poor earnings. The firm projects its anticipated earnings and desired long-term payout ratio given the investment opportunities it anticipates, and sets a dividend payout ratio that it feels it can maintain. This dividend, which is planned with the firm's long-run situation in mind, is referred to as the **regular dividend**. In addition, some firms pay an **extra dividend** at the end of the year once the firm's earnings are known and investment needs have been determined.

The first step in the dividend payment procedure is the announcement by the board of directors that a specified dividend will be paid to shareholders of record at some particular future date. For example, the board of directors of Serrento Corporation announces on February 15, 1986, that dividends of $0.50 per share will be payable to all shareholders of record on March 18, 1986, payment being made on April 8, 1986. A shareholder of record on a given date is someone who is recorded on the company's books at the close of business on that date as the owner of specific shares of stock. In the example, if Serrento Corporation were informed on March 18, or before, of a transfer of shares, the new owner (buyer) receives the dividend; if the corporation were notified of the sale on March 19 or thereafter, the old owner (seller) receives the dividend.

Since there is a lag of several days from the time a sale transaction takes place to the time the firm is informed of the transaction, a sale on, say, March 16 would not generally be recorded on the company's books until

352

PART 2
The firm's investment,
financing, and dividend
decisions

after the record date of March 18, that is, the seller would still be entitled to the dividend. Because of this lag, the practice is that the right to the dividend goes with the stock up to, but not including, four business days before the record date; a buyer of the stock four business days before the record date or thereafter does not acquire the right to the dividend. The stock is referred to as **ex-dividend** four days before the record date or thereafter, since the stock no longer provides the right to the dividend. For example, assume that Bill Seller owns 100 shares of Serrento Corporation stock. There are five business days between Tuesday, March 11, 1986, and March 18, 1986. Therefore, if Bill Seller sells the stock on or before March 11, 1986, the purchaser, Alex Buyer, also acquires the right to the dividend; but if Alex Buyer purchases the stock on March 12 or thereafter, the claim to the dividend remains with Mr. Seller, that is, the stock is ex-dividend. The ex-dividend date is March 12.

The price of the firm's stock will reflect that it has gone ex-dividend. Going ex-dividend will cause the price of the stock to fall by approximately the amount of the dividend. In our example, assuming no other cause for the stock price to change, a share of Serrento stock would sell for $0.50 per share (the amount of the dividend per share) less on March 12 than it did on March 11. If Serrento stock sold for $30 per share on March 11, it would sell for approximately $29.50 per share on March 12. This is so since the buyer of the stock on March 11 is also entitled to the $0.50 dividend; a buyer on or after March 12 is not entitled to the dividend. The dividend checks would be mailed by Serrento Corporation on April 8, 1986, to shareholders of record on March 18, 1986.

FACTORS AFFECTING THE DIVIDEND DECISION

The factors that are important in setting a dividend policy are the profitability of the firm's investment opportunities, taxes, legal considerations, liquidity and debt needs, and various costs that result from the firm's pursuing a particular dividend policy. Let's look at each of these factors.

Profitability of the Firm's Investment Opportunities

If the company cannot invest profitably, earnings can be paid out in dividends. On the other hand, if profitable opportunities exist, earnings can be used for their financing. A zero dividend payout is not uncommon for young, rapidly growing firms with good investment opportunities. Financing investments from profits (internal financing) may be preferable to paying larger dividends and financing investments by selling new stock and bonds, because the firm's shareholders prefer capital gains income to dividend income (see the discussion of taxes below). Furthermore, raising external capital involves transaction costs (for example, flotation costs), which are completely avoided by using internally generated funds from operations. Even if current projects are unattractive, when a profitable future investment is foreseen, it may be advisable to invest present earnings in liquid assets (for example, marketable securities) so that the funds will be available later to finance the investment.

Taxes

Shareholder Taxes   As was explained in Chapter 3, shareholders pay ordinary income taxes on dividends and pay capital gains taxes on long-term capital gains (gains on assets held more than six months).[1] These taxes encourage firms to finance investment internally from retained earnings and so keep dividends lower than would be the case if capital gains were not allowed a tax advantage. Why is this so? Each dollar that is *earned and retained* by the firm as cash or invested by the firm in a productive asset raises the value of the firm and, therefore, the value of the currently outstanding shares. The retained earnings thus raise the price of a share and generate capital gains. *When the share is sold* by a stockholder this price rise (gain) is taxed as a capital gain. If, on the other hand, the firm were not to retain the earnings but to pay them out in dividends, a tax on the dividend at the ordinary tax rate would be payable *immediately* by the stockholder. Thus, the return as a capital gain involves a lower tax rate and, in addition, permits investors to postpone their tax payments until they sell the stock. Also note that stockholders who earn capital gains on their stock instead of receiving dividends and who want to receive cash in the current period can simply sell *some* of their shares to obtain the cash; stockholder income will then be in the form of a realized capital gain, which is taxed at a lower rate than would be the same amount of income received as dividends. The point here is that the lower effective tax rate on capital gains encourages firms to pay lower dividends (that is, to retain more funds and thereby generate more capital gains) than they would if dividends and capital gains were subject to the same effective tax rate.

If the tax bias in favor of capital gains were eliminated and dividends and capital gains were taxed at the same rate and at the same time, retained earnings financing would lose its tax advantage for stockholders. A probable result would be higher dividends and greater use of external financing of investment by corporations.[2] It must be kept in mind that at this point we are considering only personal tax effects; as we will see, some of the other factors (tax and nontax) influencing dividends may bias in favor of dividend income rather than capital gains.[3]

Tax on Excessive Firm Retentions Is a corporation able to pay out no dividends and permit its shareholders to earn all income in the form of capital gains? It can, *if* the funds that would have been paid in dividends are

[1] There are certain exceptions to this. The tax law specifies that the first $100 of total dividends (dividends from all United States company stock owned) received by an individual shareholder is tax-free. Therefore, those receiving very small dividend income ($100 or less) will prefer that income to an equal dollar amount of capital gain (which is taxable). Under another special tax provision, if a corporation pays out, as a dividend, all the proceeds from liquidating a division, those dividends are subject to capital gains tax treatment. If U.S. corporation X owns shares in another U.S. corporation, Y, X pays corporate taxes on only 15 percent of any dividends received on the corporation Y shares.

[2] It is easily shown that if investors incur negligible brokerage fees in buying and selling securities and if information about a firm can be obtained by investors at a nominal cost, then a tax bias in favor of capital gains relative to dividends implies that firms will never finance an investment by selling new shares if the investment can be financed from retained earnings. That is, management will reduce dividends to provide funds for an investment before it will sell new shares to obtain the funds. On this see R. C. Stapleton, "Taxes, the Cost of Capital and the Theory of Investment," *The Economic Journal* (December 1972), pp. 1273–1292.

[3] The dividend policy implications of taxes and various other relevant factors are discussed later in this chapter in the section "The Dividend Policy Debate."

354

PART 2
The firm's investment,
financing, and dividend
decisions

used to purchase productive assets by the firm and not merely retained in the form of cash and cash substitutes (stocks and bonds, Treasury bills, etc.). If the firm accumulates cash and cash substitutes beyond a limit deemed reasonable by the Internal Revenue Service in meeting the firm's liquidity needs, a special surtax will be imposed on the firm's improper accumulations. Although this penalty is unlikely to be imposed, it does discourage flagrant attempts by corporations to avoid paying dividends.

Corporate Taxes   From Chapter 10, you will recall that the tax deductibility of interest encourages firms to use more debt financing (and therefore less equity financing) than they would if interest were not tax deductible. This means that more of the corporation's cash flow will be paid out as interest on debt and less will be paid out as dividends.

Legal Commitments and Requirements

Contractual Restrictions   The contract between the firm and its creditors or between the firm and its preferred stockholders may include constraints on the firm's activities for protection of the lenders' or preferred stockholders' investments (see Chapter 21). A common constraint is that dividends may be paid only out of profits earned in periods after the debt contract becomes effective. Preferred stock contracts, which provide for cumulative dividends to preferred stockholders, stipulate that there will be no dividend payment to common stockholders until current and all unpaid past preferred dividends have been paid (for details, see Chapter 21).

Statutory Constraints on Capital Impairment   Most state laws provide that dividends in the form of cash or property may not exceed retained earnings (accumulated profits) plus paid-in surplus. That is, the firm may not pay dividends if the owners' equity (assets minus liabilities) is no greater than the outstanding stock's total par value or, if the stock has no par value, the outstanding stock's "legal" or "stated" capital (a value designated by the firm's board of directors). This requirement is imposed to ensure that the assets of the firm exceed liabilities by a minimum cushion in order to protect the creditors. This cushion (the par value of the firm's stock) may be small in relation to the assets and liabilities of the firm, but it nevertheless provides at least some safety margin to creditors. A second statutory limitation on dividends often applies if the firm is insolvent. Most states prohibit an insolvent firm from paying dividends.[4]

The Firm's Liquidity and Debt Needs

A firm will generally hold some liquid assets, such as cash and marketable securities, to meet planned or unexpected cash requirements. The rate of return on such liquid assets, net of the costs of supervising them (for example, the costs of managing the portfolio of marketable securities), is generally low, and excessive accumulation of such assets is therefore unprofitable. To eliminate excess liquid assets, unneeded cash and proceeds from selling excess marketable securities can be paid out as a dividend or be

[4] The definition of insolvency varies from state to state. In some cases it means that the firm is simply unable to pay its debts, whereas, in other states, it means that assets are less than liabilities.

used to retire debt. A deficiency of liquid assets may encourage the company to curtail dividends.

Costs of External Financing and of Dividend Payments   A firm may maintain a low dividend payout so that it can avoid external financing of its investments. The greater is the cost of obtaining external financing, the greater will be the incentive to finance internally from the firm's profits. The costs of external capital include underwriting costs, brokerage commissions and fees, bank loan set-up costs, legal and accounting fees, and the expense of management's time in arranging outside financing. These costs are avoided by financing internally. Furthermore, the transaction costs involved in paying dividends (e.g., bookkeeping and postage costs) are avoided if no dividends are paid. The firm's out-of-pocket expenses are always less with internal financing than with external financing.

Stockholder Transaction Costs   Investors incur costs when they buy or sell an asset such as stock. In the case of stock, this cost appears as a brokerage commission and as time spent by the shareholder in conducting the transaction. If shareholders want cash for living expenses or for investments in different assets (for example, in the shares of other firms), the transaction costs to them will be less if they have dividend income than if they have to sell their shares in order to obtain the cash. From a purely transaction cost standpoint (for example, ignoring tax considerations), investors who want cash will prefer dividends to capital gains of the same dollar amount.

On the other hand, some shareholders may prefer to keep their capital invested. If the firm pays them a dividend, they have to reinvest it themselves and pay a brokerage commission. But, if the firm retains the dividend and invests it, shareholders will receive a capital gain that involves no transaction costs to them. In contrast to those who want cash and prefer dividends, investors who wish to keep their funds in the firm prefer income in the form of capital gains rather than in the form of dividends.

Because of differing preferences among investors for capital gains and dividends, firms with high dividend payouts will tend to attract investors who want cash income (dividends), and firms with low dividend payouts will tend to attract investors who want to keep their funds invested. This attraction of investors to companies with dividend policies that meet the investors' preferences is referred to as the **clientele effect**. The clientele effect encourages corporations to maintain stable, predictable dividends because most investors do not like uncertainty about the timing and magnitude of their dividends and capital gains. Unexpectedly low dividends may force a shareholder to sell shares to raise cash (which means brokerage fees and perhaps the payment of capital gains taxes). Unexpectedly large dividends for investors who had planned to keep their funds invested will mean the cost of reinvesting the cash (brokerage fees) and the immediate payment of taxes on the dividends received. It follows that firms with unstable, unpredictable dividend policies will be relatively unattractive to investors. The shares of such companies will sell for a lower price than they would if the company had a stable, predictable dividend.

THE FIRM'S DIVIDEND POLICY

Two important dimensions of a firm's dividend policy are:

1 *Dividend stability:* whether dividends remain fixed or fluctuate from period to period
2 *Long-run dividend payout ratio:* the long-run average percentage of earnings paid out in dividends

Policy variables **1** and **2** are distinct from one another. Dividends can be stable or unstable whether the percentage of earnings paid out as dividends is high or low.

In examining the two policy variables, we will consider the factors the firm must evaluate in determining its optimal policy and the empirical evidence concerning United States corporate behavior. The actual experience of corporations indicates which factors are most important.

Dividend Stability

Alternative Policies and the Evidence   Regardless of the policy determining the long-run dividend payout ratio, year-to-year fluctuations in dividends may follow any one of several guidelines:

1 *Stable dividend payout ratio.* This policy requires that the percentage of earnings paid out (dividend payout ratio = dividends ÷ earnings) each year is held stable. The result is dividends that fluctuate proportionately with earnings.
2 *Stable dollar dividend.* The dollar level of dividends is relatively stable from period to period or follows a steady upward or downward trend over time.
3 *Stable dollar dividend plus an "extra" dividend.* The company pays out a stable (in dollar level) regular dividend plus an added dividend at the end of particularly prosperous years.

Historical evidence suggests that whereas the first policy is rare, a stabilized dollar dividend is maintained by most major United States corporations. The third policy is practiced by a small minority, perhaps 10 percent, of large firms, with General Motors the most prominent example.

Figure 11-1 shows that earnings (net aftertax income) have historically been far more volatile than dividends, although both have trended upward since the 1930s depression. A classic study by John Lintner indicated that firms adjust their dollar dividends only gradually as earnings vary from year to year.[5] He also found resistance by corporations to reducing dividends below the amount paid in the previous period. Later studies by Brittain and by Fama and Babiak provided results generally consistent with those of Lintner.[6]

[5] See John Lintner, "Distribution of Income of Corporations among Dividends. Retained Earnings, and Taxes," *American Economic Review*, 46 (May 1956), pp. 97–113.
[6] See John A. Brittain, "The Tax Structure and Corporate Dividend Policy," *American Economic Review* (May 1964), pp. 272–287; Eugene F. Fama and Harvey Babiak, "Dividend Policy: An Empirical Analysis," *Journal of the American Statistical Association* (December 1968), pp. 1132–1161.

An Explanation of Dividend Stability   The primary goal of company policy is to benefit shareholders. To justify a stable dollar dividend policy, we must show that stockholders are made better off by this policy. Several explanations for investors' preferring stable dollar dividends have been suggested.

First, investors may use dividends to cover living expenses, which are usually rather stable from period to period. A radical decline in dividend income may force investors to sell shares to obtain funds for living expenses, and a radical rise in dividends may produce excess cash that investors will want to reinvest. Selling shares or investing dividends involves brokerage fees and other expenses, including the investor's time. These costs are avoided if dividends are stable and predictable and the investor consequently does not have to sell shares or reinvest dividend income.

Second, the level of current dividends conveys information to investors on the *future* dividend-paying capacity (earning capacity) of the firm. If

FIGURE 11-1

Aftertax profits, dividends, and retained earnings of U.S. corporations. (Source: Federal Reserve).

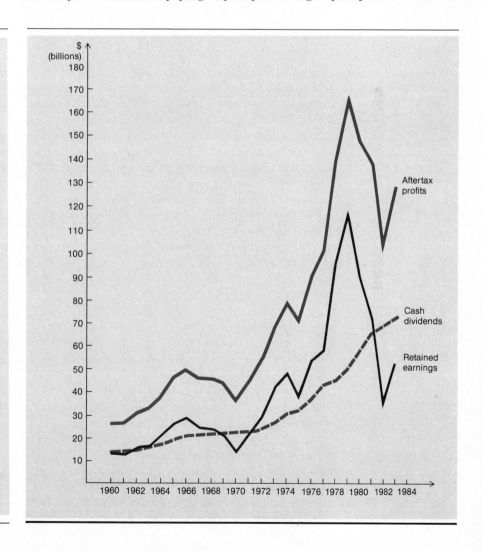

358

PART 2
The firm's investment,
financing, and dividend
decisions

investors know that the firm will raise or lower dividends only if management foresees a permanent earnings increase or decrease, respectively, then the level of dividends informs investors about management's expectations about earnings. A cut in dividends implies poor earnings expectations, no change implies earnings stability, and a dividend increase implies management's optimism about earnings. On the other hand, a company with an erratic dividend poicy is, in effect, not providing such information, thereby increasing the risk of the shares. Stable dividends that are based on long-run earning power of the company therefore reduce share riskiness and consequently increase the value of the shares to investors.

A third factor encouraging stable dividends is the requirement by many states that financial institutions, for example, mutual savings banks, insurance companies, and mutual funds, may invest in only those stocks with good dividend records. These institutions are a significant force in the market, and their demand for the company's stock can enhance its price (which benefits the shareholders). Also, federal laws covering pension plans encourage the purchase of stocks with high, stable dividends.

Long-Run Dividend Payout Ratio

The above discussion concerned the first aspect of dividend policy, stability from year to year. We noted that firms tend to keep dividend payments stable from period to period. The second aspect of dividend policy is the long-run average percentage of earnings that the firm pays out in dividends. The firm may plan a high or low long-run dividend payout ratio regardless of its policy concerning period-to-period stability. In actuality, we find that, although most firms have relativley stable dollar dividends, firms differ markedly in terms of their long-run payout ratios. Large, mature companies such as General Motors, Du Pont, and Exxon tend to have high dividend payout ratios, whereas smaller, rapidly growing firms, such as Bally Manufacturing, Hewlett-Packard, and Tandy, often have low dividend payout ratios or pay no dividends at all. The question arises as to whether there is a "correct" dividend policy for a given firm or indeed for all firms. Below, we address this issue and provide guidelines for setting a company's dividend policy.

The Dividend Policy Debate

There is controversy as to whether dividend policy matters at all! There are two schools of thought: the **imperfect markets school**, which argues that dividend policy matters, and the **perfect markets school**, which argues that dividend policy is irrelevant.

The imperfect markets school holds that various types of imperfections (transaction costs, costs of obtaining information, and tax biases) make dividend policy important. One branch of this school asserts that a firm is better off paying *small dividends* and financing investments internally than it would be paying larger dividends and financing investments externally by selling new shares. Internal financing is viewed as superior (cheaper) to external equity financing because, with the former, the firm's current owners earn income as capital gains rather than as dividends (an advantage due to personal tax effects; see the discussion of shareholder taxes earlier in this chapter).[7] Also, flotation costs are avoided with internal financing, and dividend payment accounting and postage costs are avoided if these dollars are reinvested rather than paid out as a dividend. Using internal rather than external equity financing therefore means a lower cost of equity capital and a lower average cost of capital for evaluating investments. An implication is that the cost of capital and the level of investment will depend on the type of equity financing that is available. Thus, it is argued, a firm will invest more if it has internal funds available than if it has to resort to the more costly external equity financing.

A second branch of the imperfect markets school contends that firms should pay *large dividends* even if it means selling new shares to do so. The argument goes something like this: "Firms should pay large dividends even if new shares have to be sold to finance the dividends because investors need the dividends for living expenses. Large dividends provide the needed income without the shareholders' having to sell their shares (which would involve brokerage fees). Although firms incur costs in selling new shares to pay dividends, firm managements are more astute in choosing the proper time to sell (that is, they can sell shares when the stock is overpriced and then store up the cash proceeds to pay big dividends for several periods); investors, on the other hand, are less astute and may, if dividends are small, be forced to sell their shares when they are underpriced. Second, by paying large dividends the firm is showing that it can *really* generate cash returns for the shareholders. That is, dividends are viewed by investors as less risky than capital gains and therefore the firm's shares will be worth more if income is in the form of dividends rather than capital gains." The argument that management is more astute in timing the sale of shares assumes that management has better information about share price trends and values than do shareholders. This is a debatable point which has not been resolved. However, the second argument concerning the advantage of paying dividends to reduce share risk is clearly specious. When a firm sells shares to pay dividends, it is doing nothing more than what shareholders could do for themselves (since shareholders could sell their own shares and receive the proceeds directly). A firm policy of selling shares each period to pay dividends therefore provides shareholders with no reduction in share risk and no benefits.[8]

Imperfect markets theory advocates of both the small and the large dividend payment persuasions hold that, because of brokerage fees and

---

[7] For theoretical arguments and empirical evidence consistent with this view see, for example, M. J. Brennan, "Taxes, Market Valuation and Financial Policy," *National Tax Journal*, 22 (December 1970), pp. 417–427; R. H. Litzenberger and K. Ramaswamy, "The Effect of Personal Taxes and Dividends on Capital Asset Prices: Theory and Empirical Evidence," *Journal of Financial Economics*, 7 (June 1979), pp. 163–195; and R. C. Stapleton, op. cit. (footnote 2).

[8] Some arguments in favor of higher dividends to reduce share risk actually involve changes in firm investment policy; that is, these arguments involve a confusion between dividend policy and investment policy effects. For the debate on this point and on other related points, see M. J. Gordon, "Dividends, Earnings and Stock Prices," *Review of Economics and Statistics*, 41 (May 1959), pp. 99–105; M. J. Brennan, "A Note on Dividend Irrelevance and the Gordon Valuation Model," *Journal of Finance*, 26 (December 1971), pp. 1115–1122.

360

PART 2
The firm's investment,
financing, and dividend
decisions

other imperfections, firms should maintain a *stable* dividend (see the previous section on dividend stability). As is discussed in the next section, the *smoothed residual dividend policy* conforms to the imperfect markets view. It dictates that the firm should maintain a stable dollar dividend and set the dividend level so that equity investment (investment not financed by borrowing) is financed internally (with retained earnings) to the greatest possible degree rather than by selling new shares since internal financing is cheaper.

Confronting the imperfect markets school are those who believe that dividend policy does not matter. We will call this the perfect markets school. The members of the perfect markets school hold that the costs of internal and external equity financing are the same and therefore that the type and level of investment made by the firm do not depend on whether funds are raised internally or externally. The firm can, in any period, choose whatever dividend it deems appropriate, and any excess of equity investment over internally available funds will be financed by selling new shares.

The perfect markets theory begins with a famous proof by Miller and Modigliani that dividend policy is irrelevant in a world of no imperfections (that is, no transaction costs, no tax biases, etc.).[9] Modigliani and Miller do assume risk and uncertainty, however. Perfect markets theory proponents then go on to argue that transaction costs are not all that great and other imperfections do not really matter. For example, the tax bias favoring capital gains relative to dividends is not important because, through various types of tax shelters, dividend tax rates can be reduced to capital gains tax rates.[10] Furthermore, there is no need to stabilize dividends just to convey a positive image to investors; informed investors (informed by financial analysts who specialize in gathering, analyzing, and disseminating information about companies) will value the firm on the basis of its underlying financial health, not on the basis of its dividend policy. Finally, since some investors prefer high dividends and low capital gains (for example, financial institutions which may invest in only those firms with good, stable dividend records), and other investors prefer low dividends and high capital gains, there is a clientele for the shares of a firm regardless of its dividend payment policy.[11] In short, the market price of a firm's shares does not depend in any significant way on dividend policy.

[9] M. H. Miller and F. Modigliani, "Dividend Policy, Growth and the Valuation of Shares," *Journal of Business*, 34 (October 1961), pp. 411–433.

[10] See M. H. Miller and M. S. Scholes, "Dividends and Taxes," *Journal of Financial Economics*, 6 (December 1978), pp. 333–364.

[11] See F. Black and M. S. Scholes, "The Effects of Dividend Yield and Dividend Policy on Common Stock Prices and Returns," *Journal of Financial Economics*, 1 (May 1974), pp. 1–22. Black and Scholes argue that all dividend policies we observe at equilibrium for a particular type of firm (one with similar investment and financial structure policies) must be equally desirable (must produce the same share values) or some firms would switch to a different dividend policy which produces higher share values. That is, all dividend policies we have observed must be equally good (must produce like share values) because inferior policies will be abandoned by firms.

Who is right? Well, let's look at the evidence.[12] A study by Fama, which supports the perfect markets view, concludes that the evidence is consistent with the notion that a firm's investment and dividend policies are independent.[13] A study by Black and Scholes largely supports Fama's findings.[14] These results confront a significant body of contrary findings supporting the imperfect markets theory. Pye examined 330 United States firms and found that an abnormally low proportion of firms that issued new stock also paid dividends.[15] This suggests that firms tend to utilize retained earnings to finance investment before employing external stock financing. Similar conclusions were reached by Higgins, who found that, consistent with the residual payout policy, dividends vary positively with earnings and negatively with investment.[16] Dhrymes and Kurz found that a desire to maintain stable dividends may hamper investment by reducing internal funds available for capital expenditures. Furthermore, their results suggest that investment reduces the dividend payout, as predicted by a residual payout policy.[17] Baumol, Heim, Malkiel, and Quandt observed that the rate of return earned on internally financed investment was significantly lower than that earned on investments financed externally.[18] This is consistent with the view that more must be earned on externally funded capital outlays because external financing is most costly. Litzenberger and Ramaswamy found that investors may prefer a dollar of capital gains to a dollar of dividends, suggesting that stockholders do not want increased dividends which are financed by new share sales (which reduce the owners' capital gains by diluting their ownership in the firm).[19]

What are the implications if you are setting your company's dividend policy? First, shareholders will likely want the company to maintain a stable dividend from period to period. As explained earlier, radical declines in dividends may force some shareholders to sell shares, and sharp rises in dividends may force some shareholders to reinvest the excess dividend. These transactions and the associated brokerage fees and other costs are avoided if dividends are stable.

Second, the firm's shareholders are probably best off if the company has

---

[12] For a pointed discussion of the state of uncertainty concerning dividend policy, see Fischer Black, "The Dividend Puzzle," *Journal of Portfolio Management*, 2 (Winter 1976).

[13] See E. F. Fama, "The Empirical Relationships between the Dividend and Investment Decisions of Firms," *American Economic Review*, 64 (June 1974), pp. 304–318.

[14] See Black and Scholes, op. cit. (footnote 12).

[15] See Gordon Pye, "Preferential Tax Treatment of Capital Gains, Optimal Dividend Policy, and Capital Bugeting," *Quarterly Journal of Economics* (July 1972), pp. 226–242.

[16] See Robert C. Higgins, "The Corporate Dividend-Saving Decision," *Journal of Financial and Quantitative Analysis* (March 1972), pp. 1527–1541.

[17] See P. Dhrymes and M. Kurz, "Investment, Dividends, and External Finance Behavior of Firms," in R. Ferber (ed.), *Determinants of Investment Behavior* (New York: National Bureau of Economic Research, 1967).

[18] See W. J. Baumol, P. Heim, B. G. Malkiel, and R. E. Quandt, "Earnings Retention, New Capital and the Growth of the Firm," *The Review of Economics and Statistics*, 52 (November 1970), pp. 345–355.

[19] See R. H. Litzenberger and K. Ramaswamy, op. cit. (footnote 7).

362

PART 2
The firm's investment,
financing, and dividend
decisions

a long-term policy of minimizing reliance on new shares to finance operations. If necessary, sell shares if internally generated cash and borrowed funds are insufficient to finance investment. But, because taxes on shareholders are so important, do not regularly sell additional shares to pay bigger dividends. An added dollar of dividends financed by new share sales raises the existing shareholders' dividends by one dollar and reduces their capital gains by roughly one dollar. This increases shareholder taxes because dividends are taxed more heavily than are capital gains. The tax advantage of capital gains over dividend income means that shareholders are generally made worse off if the company sells stock to pay bigger dividends. The name for a policy of stable dividends with minimum reliance on new share financing is the **smoothed residual dividend policy**, which is discussed below.

Third, if the company has excess cash that it wants to pay out to shareholders, it is better from a tax standpoint to buy back shares from the shareholders than to pay them dividends. As explained at the end of this chapter, dividends are taxed at the ordinary income tax rate, which is much higher than the long-term capital gains tax rate that usually applies to any gains on shares that a stockholder sells back to the company.[20]

Residual Dividend Policy

The most prominent dividend policy based on the theory that internal financing is cheaper than external financing is referred to as the **residual dividend policy**. Many companies follow this strategy.

Let's begin by examining the residual concept. Funds for corporate investment come from borrowing, retained earnings, and the sale of stock. We refer to investment funded by equity capital sources (retained earnings and stock sales) as **equity investment**. In each period, management determines the proportions of new investments to be financed by borrowing and by equity capital. The desired proportions depend on financial market conditions and on target debt levels set by management. The dividend *under a residual dividend policy* equals the amount left over from earnings after *equity* investment. If equity investment equals earnings, no dividends are paid. If equity investment is greater than earnings, no dividends are paid and new shares are sold to cover any equity investment not covered by earnings. And, if equity investment is less than earnings, *all* such investment is covered from earnings (no new shares sold) and what is left over from earnings is paid out as a dividend. *Dividends are therefore merely a residual remaining after all equity investment needs are fulfilled.* Notice that a residual policy minimizes the use of external equity financing (sale of new shares) since, by this policy, equity investment has a higher-priority claim to earnings than do dividends.

Corporations have employed three general approaches in putting the

---

[20] For example, Arrow Corporation could pay $100 to a shareholder either by paying the shareholder a $100 dividend or by buying $100 worth of the shareholder's Arrow Corporation stock. The shareholder pays a much larger tax on the $100 dividend than on the $100 received for the Arrow stock. For details, see the section on repurchasing stock at the end of this chapter.

residual dividend poilcy into practice. Before describing these approaches, we will define the following variables:

D_t = dividend paid in year t

I_t^e = investment in year t that is financed from equity sources (retained earnings and stock sales)

E_t = earnings in year t

q_t = dividend payout ratio in year t where $q_t = \dfrac{D_t}{E_t}$

1 *Pure residual dividend policy.* Following this approach, the corporation will set the dividends paid each year so that, if equity investment I_t^e equals or exceeds earnings E_t, then dividends will be zero; and if I_t^e is less than E_t, then dividends will be

$$D_t = E_t - I_t^e$$

2 *Fixed dividend payout ratio.* Dividends under this approach equal a constant proportion (q_t) of yearly earnings. This can be expressed as

$$D_t = q_t \cdot E_t$$

If the percentage paid in dividends is 40 percent, for example, this would equal

$$D_t = q_t \cdot E_t = 0.4E_t$$

The percentage q_t is set so that, over the long run, dividends are equal to earnings minus equity investment.

3 *Smoothed residual dividend policy.* Under this approach, dollar dividends have a stable pattern. Dividends over the long-run equal earnings minus equity investment (dividends are zero if, on average, equity investment exceeds earnings).

Exhibit 11-1 shows dividends for 5 years under each of the above three approaches. Under the fixed dividend payout ratio policy the ratio (percent) used is 40 percent. The pure residual dividend policy can produce highly

---

EXHIBIT 11-1
Earnings, equity investment, and dividends of a company using a residual payout policy

	Year					Total
	1	2	3	4	5	
Earnings E_t	$140	$180	$130	$200	$150	$800
Equity investment I_t^e	80	60	130	110	100	480
Pure residual dividend D_t	60	120	0	90	50	320
Fixed dividend payout ratio dividend D_t (ratio = 0.4)	56	72	52	80	60	320
Smoothed residual dividend D_t	50	60	60	70	80	320

364

PART 2
The firm's investment,
financing, and dividend
decisions

volatile dividends, particularly if investment and earnings move in opposite directions from period to period (from years 2 to 3 and from years 3 to 4 in the Exhibit 11-1 example). The fixed dividend payout ratio residual dividend policy lets dividends fluctuate directly with earnings and will be as volatile as those earnings.

The smoothed residual dividend strategy generally produces the most stable dollar dividend. In a period in which earnings exceed dividends plus equity investment (years 1, 2, and 4 in Exhibit 11-1), the firm increases its holdings of liquid assets (cash and marketable securities). These holdings are used later for dividends and investment in periods in which dividends plus investment exceed earnings (years 3 and 5). The smoothed residual policy minimizes dependence on external financing of equity investment and provides a stable dollar dividend.

The residual dividend policy refers to the second policy variable on page 356, the long-run dividend payout ratio. All three residual dividend policies—pure residual policy, fixed payout ratio residual policy, and smoothed residual policy—follow the same basic long-run dividend payout ratio strategy: They set the ratio so that, on average over the long run, dividends will equal what is left over from earnings after the earnings are used to finance equity investment. But these three residual dividend policies differ with regard to the first policy variable on page 356, dividend stability. A pure residual policy does not seek stability, whereas the fixed dividend payout ratio residual policy achieves stability in terms of the payout ratio, and the smoothed residual dividend policy achieves stability in terms of the dollar level of dividends.

DIVIDEND REINVESTMENT AND OTHER BENEFIT PLANS

Many firms allow stockholders to request that the firm not pay them a dividend but, instead, that it automatically reinvest the dividend in the company's shares. AT&T, Exxon, General Motors, and Uniroyal are among the numerous firms providing this option. Automatic reinvestment is easier and less costly in terms of brokerage fees than would be reinvestment of a dividend by the stockholders themselves (by using the dividend to buy the firm's stock on the open market). Stockholders who do not want to reinvest in the company can simply choose to receive the dividend. It should be pointed out that the automatic reinvestment of a shareholder's dividends still necessitates the shareholder to pay ordinary income taxes on the dividend, so there is no tax advantage from automatic reinvestment. The advantage of the plan lies in the opportunity to avoid brokerage fees in purchasing additional shares of the company's stock.[21]

Automatic dividend reinvestment plans have been available since the late 1960s. Lately companies have heightened the attraction of reinvestment by offering shareholders the chance to purchase new shares at a discount below the stock's market price. These discount-reinvestment plans—

---

[21] In some cases, a shareholder of a utility may elect to exclude from taxable income part of the dividends received from the utility.

known as DRPs—have been offered by some of the best-known corporations, incuding AT&T, Allied Chemical, Kemper, and Crocker National. A discount of approximately 5 percent from the existing market price is common. The DRP plans have become so popular that some companies have provided dividend reinvestment to preferred stockholders and interest reinvestment to bondholders (allowing the preferred stockholders and bondholders to purchase shares of the firm's common stock at a discount).

Another bonus offered by many companies to stockholders is the opportunity of discount purchases of the company's merchandise. A stockholder of Borden Company should not be surprised to find accompanying the quarterly dividend check an offer to buy a five-pound pippin (wheel) of cheddar cheese for 20 percent below retail value. A stockholder of Cope Allman International Ltd. could add an adventurous wardrobe touch by purchasing a sheepskin jacket at a 10 percent discount. Other companies making available similar merchandise benefits to shareholders include J. J. Heinz, Quaker Oats, Castle and Cooke, and GAF Corporation.

All of the above benefits are meant to raise the firm's share price by making the shares more attractive. Many stockholders of a company may personally avail themselves of a dividend reinvestment plan or a bargain sale of merchandise. Those shareholders who do not care to take advantage of these programs also benefit if the programs appeal to investors in the market and consequently raise the company's share price.

STOCK DIVIDENDS AND STOCK SPLITS

A stock dividend is a dividend payment in the form of additional shares of stock instead of cash. A stock split is essentially the same. When a stock splits, shareholders are given a larger number of shares for the old shares they already own. In either case, each shareholder retains the same percentage of all outstanding stock that he or she had before the stock dividend or split.[22] Thus, for example, a 10 percent stock dividend would mean that each shareholder was given one share of stock for every ten shares already owned. Under a two-for-one stock split, each shareholder would be given one additional share of stock for every share already owned, thus doubling the number of shares owned by each stockholder.[23]

The effects of a stock dividend or a stock split can be summarized as follows:

---

[22] There is a difference in the accounting procedure for treating stock dividends and stock splits. To record a stock dividend, the fair market value of the stock is transferred from the retained earnings account to the paid-in capital account. In contrast, a stock split merely requires restating the par value of the stock; e.g., a two-for-one split of stock with an initial par value of $10 per share would only necessitate a change in the par of the common stock to $5 per share.

[23] If a stockholder is entitled to a fraction of a share under a stock dividend or split, then the company will pay cash in place of the fractional share. For example, with a 2 percent stock dividend, a stockholder with ten shares is entitled to two-tenths of a share (2 percent × 10 shares). The firm would pay the stockholder two-tenths of the fair market value of a share in cash. If the market price per share were $20, the stockholder would receive $4 (0.2 × $20).

366

PART 2
The firm's investment,
financing, and dividend
decisions

1 There is no change in the firm's assets or liabilities or in shareholders' equity (assets less liabilities), and there is no change in the *total* market value of the firm's shares.
2 There is a fall in *per share* earnings, book value, and market price, and an offsetting rise in the number of shares held by each stockholder. Each stockholder, therefore, has no change in the total book value, total earnings, or total market value of all shares held since he or she owns the same percentage of the firm after the stock dividend or stock split as before.

A stock dividend or split does not change the assets of the firm, since nothing is received by the firm for new shares issued. The firm's debt is also unchanged by the stock dividend or split, since the debt is in no way involved. It follows that the total shareholders' equity (the firm's total assets less debt) is also unchanged. Since shareholders each retain their old percentage of the total shareholders' interest, each has the same claim to real assets after the stock dividend or split as before. The total value of a stockholder's shares will consequently be the same before and after the new shares are issued. The stockholders therefore do not gain or lose as a result of the new shares. An example will clarify this point.

Assume that the X. Y. Zoro Company (XYZ Co.) is planning a 25 percent stock dividend (one new share paid for each four already owned). The stock dividend will increase the number of shares outstanding from 800,000 to 1 million. The firm's assets, the firm's debt, the stockholders' equity (assets minus debt), and the firm's income are left unchanged. Since the number of shares outstanding has increased, however, the *per share* book value, earnings, and market price decline. This is shown in Exhibit 11-2. Why has market price fallen in the same proportion as earnings and book value? Because a share of stock is nothing more than a claim on the assets and earnings of the firm; if the assets and earnings per share fall exactly by 20 percent, as is the case here, then it is reasonable for the share price to also fall by 20 percent. Notice that the shareholder is completely unaffected by the stock dividend. This is so because the fall in the figures per share in Exhibit 11-2 are exactly compensated for by the increase in the shareholder's number of shares owned. Consequently, the total book value, total earnings, and total market value of the shares the stockholder owns are the same after the stock dividend as before. To see this, assume a shareholder owned 100 shares of XYZ stock before the stock dividend and owns 125 shares after the stock dividend. The total book value of the shares owned *before* the stock dividend was $1000 (100 shares owned × $10 per share); the total book value *after* the stock dividend of 25 shares is also $1000 (125 shares owned × $8 per share). Total earnings on the shareholder's shares are also unchanged since earnings on the shares before the dividend were $200 (100 shares × $2 earnings per share) and earnings after the dividend are also $200 (125 shares × $1.60 earnings per share). Nor does the total market value of the shareholder's portfolio change; it was $4000 (100 shares × $40 per share), and after the stock dividend is still $4000 (125 shares × $32 per share).

In short, all that has happened is that the firm has printed extra pieces of paper called additional shares and distributed them proportionally to all stockholders. The shareholder is unaffected and still owns the same fraction of the firm's equity. The firm's equity does not change since the firm's total assets, debt, and earnings are unchanged. No one benefits or loses from the stock dividend (or split), except for a possible minor increase in share price because the stock enters a more attractive price range (see discussion below).

The New York Stock Exchange defines a stock split as a stock dividend that exceeds 25 percent (more than one share per four shares owned), and a stock dividend as a distribution of additional shares up to 25 percent of those outstanding. The distinction is arbitrary, and the principles described above apply fully to stock dividends and to stock splits.

Sometimes a firm *reduces* the number of shares outstanding through a **reverse split**. Each shareholder is required to exchange with the corporation the shares owned for a smaller number of shares, e.g., to exchange each four shares owned for one share in return. This action frequently follows a decline in the price of the company's stock over several years. Colt Industries, Studebaker, and United Whelan are among corporations that have engaged in a reverse split after suffering financial difficulties. Except for a possible minor benefit from having per share stock price in a popular price range, as with a stock split, a reverse split has no impact on the corporation's operations or on shareholder wealth. It is merely an exchange of claims (shares) with the same total value; for the stockholder, it is akin to receiving a $5 bill in exchange for five $1 bills.

Why do firms issue stock dividends or effect stock splits if there is no gain or loss involved? It has been argued that additional shares may benefit shareholders by reducing the stock's price range and thereby allowing investors to purchase round lots (multiples of 100 shares) rather than odd

---

EXHIBIT 11-2
The effects of a stock dividend

	Total for firm before and after stock dividend	Per share figures before stock dividend (800,000 shares outstanding)[a]	Per share figures after stock dividend (1 million shares outstanding)[b]
Equity book value[c]	$ 8,000,000	$10	$ 8
Earnings[d]	1,600,000	2	1.60
Market value of shares	32,000,000	40	32

[a] This column is the total for the firm (col. 1) divided by 800,000.
[b] This column is the total for the firm (col. 1) divided by 1 million.
[c] Equity book value equals firm assets less liabilities as represented on the company balance sheet.
[d] Earnings equals net income to shareholders after taxes and after interest on debt.

368

PART 2
The firm's investment,
financing, and dividend
decisions

lots (less than 100 shares). The advantage here would be to reduce the brokerage fees since they are greater on odd-lot purchases than on round-lot purchases. This effect, however, is probably insignificant, since the brokerage fee differentials are not great. Empirical research suggests that any benefits that occur from stock dividends or stock splits are insignificant. The evidence indicates that share price increases are due to earnings and associated cash dividend increases and not to stock dividends or splits.[24]

REPURCHASING STOCK

Corporations sometimes repurchase some of their own shares from stockholders; e.g., General Electric may buy back some General Electric stock from its own shareholders. Stock purchased by the issuing firm is referred to as **treasury stock**. The corporation can purchase its shares in the open market (like any investor buying shares through a broker), through a direct private transaction with the stockholder or through a tender offer (an announcement to shareholders that the firm will buy back a specified number of shares at a particular price during a stated time period). Open market purchases are more common and generally smaller in magnitude than tender offers. Private purchases are least important. Shares purchased as treasury stock are not retired but are held by the firm for possible resale or for use as payment, for example, in buying another company.

Treasury stock carries no stockholder privileges; thus it receives no dividends and does not have the voting right. If treasury stock is resold, it is again outstanding (is no longer treasury stock) and carries with it the same rights and privileges associated with the other outstanding common stock of the firm. A sale of treasury stock is essentially the same as the sale of any other stock issued by the company.

Treasury stock is *not* an asset of the firm. If the firm owns a share of its own stock, it owns a claim against itself (like owing yourself money). To see this, merely imagine that the firm holds some treasury stock and then destroys that stock (say, burns the certificates). Has the firm lost anything in the process? No, except the paper certificates that have been destroyed. In effect, by burning the certificates, the corporation has eliminated equity ownership claims against itself. Contrast this with securities of *other* companies owned by the firm. If the firm owns securities issued by another company, these securities are assets since they are claims against the real assets of the other company.

Why would a firm purchase its own shares? One good reason is to provide the company's shareholders with tax savings. A company can pay out cash to its stockholders either by paying dividends or by buying back some of the stockholders' shares. Treasury stock purchases can have a tax advantage for the shareholders as compared with dividend payments. Divi-

---

[24] Empirical studies suggest that stock dividends produce no benefits for stockholders, for example, see C. A. Barker, "Evaluation of Stock Dividends," *Harvard Business Review*, 36 (July–August 1958), pp. 99–114; E. Fama, L. Fisher, M. Jensen, and R. Roll, "The Adjustment of Stock Prices to New Information," *International Economic Review* (February 1969), pp. 1–21; J. A. Millar and B. D. Fielitz, "Stock Split and Stock-Dividend Decisions," *Financial Management* (Winter 1973) pp. 35–45.

dends are taxed on an ordinary tax basis, whereas any gain realized from *selling shares back to the corporation* is taxed as a capital gain. For example, assume that Alice Brown originally bought 200 shares of the company's stock for $6 per share, but the stock is currently selling for $10 per share (an unrealized gain of $4 per share). Assume that Alice Brown's ordinary tax bracket is 45 percent but the capital gains rate would be 18 percent. If the firm were to pay her a dividend of $100, all of that dividend would be taxable as ordinary income, resulting in a tax of $45. But if the company were to pay her $100 for ten of her shares, she would realize a gain of $40 (10 shares × $4 realized gain per share); the capital gains tax on the $40 gain would be $7.20 (18 percent capital gains rate × $40 gain) rather than the $45 of tax on the dividend. It should be noted, however, that if the treasury stock purchase does not meet certain requirements, the entire distribution ($100 in the above example) will be treated as a dividend (subject to ordinary income taxation) and not as a sale of stock subject to capital gains treatment.[25]

Another motive for treasury stock purchases is the existence of government controls limiting dividends. Such controls existed during a wage-price freeze in the early 1970s. Firms repurchased shares in record amounts during that period.

Companies sometimes purchase treasury shares to block a takeover bid by an outside group. Management may believe that the outside purchaser will mismanage the company; or the members of management may be worried about their jobs (new owners sometimes fire old managers). Thus, if an outsider were offering $40 per share to existing shareholders for their stock, the firm might make a counter-bid of $45 per share. Companies sometimes buy the shares of existing shareholders who threaten to attempt a takeover of the company unless their shares are purchased for an amount above the going market price (see the essay The Merger Game after Chapter 23 for details).

Firms may buy back shares to obtain shares for a particular use, for example, for a stock option plan (under which the shares are sold to employees) or for acquiring another company (the stock being used as payment for the purchased company). Purchases of treasury stock for specific uses is a questionable practice. It is generally easier and cheaper

---

[25] A treasury stock purchase (stock repurchase) is *not* treated as a dividend to the shareholder (and is treated as a sale of stock subject to capital gains tax treatment) if any *one* of the following four conditions holds:

1 The percentage ownership of the shareholder falls by more than one-fifth (e.g., if 10 percent of the firm's shares is owned by the shareholder before the repurchase and less than 8 percent is owned after the repurchase) *and* the shareholder owns less than 50 percent of the firm's shares after the repurchase.
2 All the shareholder's stock in the company is acquired under the stock repurchase.
3 The repurchase is not "equivalent to" a dividend. Indications that the repurchase is equivalent to a dividend would be a history of the corporation's not paying significant dividends or a repurchase that is pro rata among the shareholders (same percentage of each shareholder's stock acquired under the repurchase).
4 The repurchase of railroad stock under some conditions of bankruptcy.

If none of the above four conditions holds, then a purchase of a shareholder's stock will normally be treated as a dividend subject to ordinary income taxes.

370

PART 2
The firm's investment,
financing, and dividend
decisions

simply to issue additional shares. Issuing shares involves none of the brokerage fees or other transaction costs usually associated with treasury stock purchases.

What happens to a company's stock price when the company buys back its shares? Several empirical studies have found that, on average, the stock's price permanently increases after a share repurchase is announced, and that the share repurchase tends to be followed by extraordinary earnings increases for the company.[26] One interpretation of this is that before a repurchase is decided on by management, management foresees an earnings rise that is not yet foreseen by the market. Management concludes that the shares are undervalued and has the company repurchase its shares. But investors know that when shares are repurchased, it often signals that the company's management believes the shares are undervalued because of likely future earnings increases. This motivates investors to bid up the share's price when the stock repurchase is announced. The price rise is sustained after the share repurchase because the company's earnings actually turn out to be high.

SUMMARY

Earnings can be paid out as dividends or be retained for internal use. The level of dividends a firm chooses to pay is influenced by a variety of factors.

1 *Taxes.* Personal taxes on shareholders favor capital gains relative to dividends and encourage the company to reinvest earnings rather than to pay them out in dividends. Taxes on the firm's excess retentions of cash and cash substitutes encourage companies to pay dividends. Corporate income taxes, because of interest tax deductibility, favor debt financing; in the long run this reduces equity financing and reduces the firm's *total* dividends relative to what they would be if interest were not tax deductible.

2 *Investment opportunities.* Exceptional corporate investment opportunities encourage reinvestment of earnings and low dividends.

3 *Contractual restrictions.* Dividends may be restricted by debt or preferred stock contracts and by state regulations prohibiting payment of dividends if stockholders' equity does not exceed the par or stated value of outstanding stock.

   Some earnings may be used to increase the firm's liquidity or to pay off debts rather than be paid out as dividends. The transaction costs in raising external funds and in paying dividends encourage the firm to finance investment with retained earnings and to therefore curtail dividends. Because of the transaction costs paid by stockholders in buying and selling shares, for example, brokerage fees, stockholders prefer that dividends are stable rather than erratic. Investors differ

---

[26] See, for example, L. Y. Dann, "Common Stock Repurchases: An Analysis of Returns to Bondholders and Stockholders," *Journal of Financial Economics*, 9 (June 1981), pp. 113–138; and T. Vermaelen, "Common Stock Repurchases and Market Signalling: An Empirical Study," *Journal of Financial Economics*, 9 (June 1981), pp. 139–183.

*regarding the proportions of their income that they prefer in dividends
and in capital gains. A firm will therefore attract a "clientele" or type of
investor preferring the company's particular dividend payout policy. This
clientele ordinarily wants the company to follow its established dividend
policy and to maintain relatively stable (unerratic) dollar dividends.*

*Two important aspects of dividend policy are stability from period to
period and the long-run proportion of earnings paid out in dividends.
Dividend payments are relatively stable because investors prefer predictable and level rather than volatile dividend income.*

*Two theories have been formulated to explain corporate dividend
policy. The imperfect markets theory holds that dividend policy is quite
important, whereas the perfect markets school argues that dividend policy is irrelevant. One branch of the imperfect markets school argues that
firms should use earnings to finance profitable investments rather than
pay out the earnings as dividends; another branch argues that firms
should pay out a portion of their earnings as dividends even if it means
financing investments by selling new shares. One dividend strategy con-
forming to the imperfect markets theory is the smoothed residual
dividend policy. Under this policy, there is an attempt to keep the dollar
level of dividends equal to earnings less equity investment (investment
that is not financed by borrowing). Additional shares are sold only if
there is an unexpected shortage of cash to maintain a stable dividend
and meet investment needs, as would be so, for example, if a very large
project is undertaken that completely absorbs earnings and excess liquid
reserves.*

*Stock dividends and stock splits merely involve the distribution of
additional shares of stock to the firm's stockholders. Since stockholders
retain their original fractions of the firm, they neither gain nor lose from
the stock dividend or split.*

*Stock that is repurchased by the issuing firm is called treasury stock.
Companies repurchase their own shares to produce tax benefits for
shareholders, to avoid government constraints on dividends, to fight a
takeover bid by another company, or to obtain stock for a particular purpose (e.g., for use in a stock option plan).*

QUESTIONS

1 In what way are dividend policy and retention of earnings related to
the financing of the firm's investments?

2 Investors presumably buy a firm's shares in order to receive a return
on their investment. Further, it would seem that the more profitable
are the firm's investments, the higher that return would be. Since the
return to shareholders can take the form of dividends, why do we
say that more profitable investment opportunities for the firm *lower*
the firm's dividend payments?

3 It has been repeatedly stated that as long as a firm has a *productive
use* for them, earnings should be retained. What do you think the
term "productive use" means?

4 How can stockholder income tax considerations affect the dividend
policy of firms?

372

PART 2
The firm's investment,
financing, and dividend
decisions

5 It has been said that the tax deductibility of interest *lowers* a firm's total dividend payments. What is a rationale for this proposition?

6 Why might a firm borrow $100,000 and simultaneously pay a dividend of $100,000; that is, wouldn't it be wiser not to borrow and pay no dividend since there are transaction costs in borrowing (e.g., bond flotation costs) and in paying a dividend (accounting costs, postage, etc.)?

7 It is stated in the text that the personal income tax bias in favor of capital gains relative to dividend income leads firms to pay less dividends than they would pay if no such bias existed. In a particular year, in determining whether to change its level of dividends from the previous year, would you expect personal income taxes to be more of a consideration for a large corporation with one million shareholders, or to a small company earning $1 million per year and having only six shareholders?

8 What role do stockholder transaction costs play in determining corporate dividend policies?

9 What are the major factors that ordinarily would discourage a firm from issing new shares to raise funds to pay higher dividends on existing shares? What might offset these factors and encourage a firm to sell shares and use some or all of the proceeds to pay dividends? Explain.

10 How can a stable dividend policy be said to reduce the riskiness associated with the shares on which the cash dividends are paid?

11 Describe the "perfect markets" theory of dividend policy and contrast it with the imperfect markets view.

12 If Poe Sleep Tablets declared a cash dividend on March 14, 1986, payable to all shareholders of record on April 25, 1986, and you bought the stock on April 23, 1986, were you a shareholder of record? In other words, would you be entitled to receive the cash dividend? If nothing else affected the price of Poe's stock and the company declared a $1 cash dividend, what would you expect the price of the stock to be when it went ex-dividend? Assume the stock was selling at $30 just prior to the ex-dividend date.

13 When a firm buys back some of its shares from stockholders it pays money for those shares (treasury stock). Yet, we say that the treasury stock is not a real asset of the firm (the treasury stock could be destroyed with no loss) since it is simply a claim of the firm against itself. Why would the firm pay money for treasury stock if it is not an asset? Aren't remaining stockholders (those who have not sold their shares back to the company) worse off as a result of the treasury stock purchase since the company has paid out dollars for something that isn't really an asset? Explain.

PROJECTS

1 Find three stocks that have recently split and examine their price behavior before and after the splits.

2 Ascertain the dividend policy of a company in your area by talking

with the firm's management. Inquire as to why the particular policy is followed and analyze the policy in light of the discussion of this chapter. Consider whether the policy is in the best interest of stockholders.

1 Nielson Services, Inc., had 1986 earnings of $2,000,000, retained $800,000 of these earnings, and had 200,000 shares outstanding. What were the dividends per share? [Ans.: Dividends = $6/share]

2 Dan Verdi owns 2000 shares of Gamma Chemicals, which he bought in 1974 for $10 per share. The tax rate on Dan's dividend income is 50 percent, and the tax rate on long-term capital gains (gains on the sale of stock held more than six months) is 20 percent. In 1986, Dan received $0.60 per share in dividends from the Gamma Chemicals stock. Dan sold 500 shares of his Gamma stock at the end of 1986 for $25 per share. Answer the following:

  a What were Dan's dividends and realized capital gains in 1986 on the Gamma Chemical shares (realized capital gains equal gains on shares that are sold)? [Ans.: Dividends = $1200 and realized capital gains = $7500]

  b What taxes did Dan pay in 1986 on the Gamma Chemical stock? [Ans.: Tax on dividends = $600; tax on realized capital gains = $1500]

3 On January 1, 1986, Arlene Hoffman purchased 400 shares of Zorn Metals, Inc., (ZM) for $15 per share and 200 shares of Amour Utilities (AU) for $10 per share. The dividends and end-of-year share prices for ZM and AU are shown in the table below for the years 1986 and 1987. Arlene Hoffman is in the 40 percent tax bracket, and this rate is applicable to all dividend income from ZM and AU. Assume that the tax rate on any long-term capital gain (gain on stock held more than six months) is 16 percent.

Dividends and price per share of Zorn Metals (ZM) and Amour Utilities (AU)		
	1986	**1987**
Zorn Metals (ZM):		
Dividends/share during year	$ 1	$ 2
Price per share on December 31 (ex-dividend)	20	25
Amour Utilities (AU):		
Dividends/share during year	1	1
Price per share on December 31 (ex-dividend)	10	30

  a Compute the dividends Arlene received during 1986 and compute the increase in the value of her ZM and AU shares during

374

PART 2
The firm's investment,
financing, and dividend
decisions

1986. What is the total return (dividend plus share value increase) for each stock?

b Compute the taxes paid by Arlene in 1986 on her ZM and AU stock if she sold no shares in 1986.

c Assume that Arlene sells half her ZM shares and half her AU shares on December 31, 1987. Compute the total taxes paid by Arlene in 1987 on all her ZM and AU shares.

4 Magic Clinics, Inc., a national chain of health maintenance organizations, had earnings of $20 million in 1985. Since 1975, earnings grew at a steady rate of 11 percent per year. Dividends in 1985 were $9 million. Earnings in 1986 were exceptionally high, $30 million, and investment was $14 million. It is expected that earnings will not stay at the high level but will settle back down to the long-run 11 percent per year growth rate (expected 1987 earnings of around $24,642,000, etc.). Assuming each of the following, what were dividends in 1986?

a Magic follows a stable long-run dividend payout ratio of 45 percent.

b Magic follows a stable dollar dividend payout policy.

c Magic follows a pure residual dividend policy; assume that 30 percent of the 1986 investment is financed with debt.

d 1986 investment is financed 60 percent with debt and 40 percent with retained earnings. All earnings not invested are paid out as dividends.

e 1986 investment is financed 30 percent with debt, 30 percent with retained earnings, and 40 percent from the sale of new shares. All earnings not invested are paid out as dividends.

5 Signet, Inc., has shares with a market value of $1,500,000 and debt of $700,000. Signet's management is considering two dividend policy alternatives: (I) to pay no dividends on existing shares; and (II) to sell new shares that provide net (net of any flotation costs) proceeds to Signet of $370,000 and then immediately pay the $370,000 to existing (not including new) stockholders.

a Assume that the flotation costs in selling the new shares are zero.

(1) Compare the total value of the firm's shares under policies I and II (value of existing shares under I compared with the value of the existing and new shares under II). [Ans.: The value of the shares under policies I and II is $1,500,000]

(2) Compare the wealth position (dividends and value of shares owned) of existing shareholders under policies I and II.

(3) What factors favor policy I? When might policy II be justified?

b Assume that under policy II the new shares are sold for a price of $400,000 (assume this to be a fair price) and that flotation costs are $30,000; the $370,000 difference is received by Signet and paid as a dividend. Answer questions 1, 2, and 3 under *a* above.

c Compare the results under *a* and *b* above and observe how stock issuance flotation costs discourage the use of stock flotations simply to pay dividends.

6 The board of directors of Doric Electronics is meeting to determine the dividend to be paid to common shareholders during the next year (1988). Doric has profitable investment opportunities amounting to $15 million for 1988 and expects 1988 income after taxes to be $25 million, which can be retained or paid out as dividends. Doric has a target book debt to book equity ratio of 40 percent and pursues a pure residual dividend policy. The firm's current (before the new investment) book debt to book equity ratio exactly equals its target of 40 percent. How much should Doric pay out in dividends in 1988?

7 Assume that Doric Electronic's has, as in problem **6**, $25 million in expected 1988 aftertax earnings, $15 million in investments, and a firm target debt-equity ratio (using book values) of 40 percent. However, assume that because of past policies the company has the following balance sheet:

Balance sheet, December 31, 1987		
Assets $100,000,000	Debt	$ 45,000,000
	Equity	55,000,000
		$100,000,000

If Doric wishes to attain its target debt to equity ratio of 40 percent, how much should the firm pay out in dividends in 1988?

8 HMS Incorporated is planning an investment in dress manufacturing equipment in order to increase production by 125 percent. The new equipment will cost $3,500,000 and HMS's current-period aftertax earnings are $11,250,000. HMS plans to maintain its present debt-equity ratio (in book terms) of 1/4.

a If HMS follows a pure residual dividend policy and has 1,000,000 shares outstanding, what should the current-period dividend per share be?

b If HMS maintains a fixed dividend payout ratio of 85 percent, how much new (external) equity financing will be required in the current period?

9 King Lear Engineering, Inc. (KLE) forecasts that total net income for the next five years will equal $25 million and total capital investment will equal $20 million. KLE wishes to formulate a short-run dividend policy that meets all three following objectives:

1 Maintain an average dividend payout ratio over the five-year planning period of 50 percent (but not necessarily 50 percent in each year).

2 Provide shareholders with a "stable" dividend stream over the planning period—where "stable" connotes either level, increasing at an approximately constant rate, or increasing from period to period by approximately equal dollar increments.

376

PART 2
The firm's investment,
financing, and dividend
decisions

3 Maintain KLE's current debt-equity ratio (in book value terms) of 3/7 in every year.

KLE will continue its current policy of financing strictly with debt or equity (no preferred stock). Answer questions **a** and **b** below for each of the three different anticipated scenarios (in the table which follows) for the behavior of annual net income (E_t) and annual capital investment requirements (I_t) over the five-year planning horizon.

Year (t)	Scenario I		Scenario II		Scenario III	
	E_t	I_t	E_t	I_t	E_t	I_t
1	$ 4.13	$ 3.30	$ 7.00	$ 3.00	$ 4.00	$ 2.90
2	4.56	3.65	1.00	3.90	4.10	3.70
3	4.99	3.99	5.80	4.50	3.70	4.10
4	5.44	4.35	6.00	4.50	6.00	5.40
5	5.88	4.71	5.20	4.10	7.20	3.90
	$25.00	$20.00	$25.00	$20.00	$25.00	$20.00

(all dollar amounts in millions)

a What are the annual equity financing requirments (I_t^e) under each scenario?

b What would the annual dividends be under each scenario if KLE followed a "pure residual" dividend policy? Would such a policy be consistent with KLE's three stated short-run policy objectives? Why or why not?

10 Consider the following projections for Hoff Instruments, Inc.:

Year	EBIT
1988	$1,000,000
1989	1,500,000
1990	1,900,000
1991	2,200,000
1992	2,500,000

Hoff has (December 1987) total assets of $2,300,000, liabilities (all in the form of bonds paying a 14 percent coupon rate with ten years to maturity) of $1,000,000, and equity of $1,300,000. As Hoff's financial manager, you are considering alternative future dividend policies in light of the fact that Hoff is undergoing a $1,250,000 capital expansion program over the next five years. The expansion will take place at equal dollar costs in each of the next five years ($250,000 each year) and will be half-financed with equity funds. The debt financing will be in the form of six-year $125,000 notes, with one note issued in each of the five years 1988 to 1992. Each note requires interest payments of 15 percent annually ($18,750 per year) with all the principal ($125,000) paid at the end of six years. Assume that Hoff's tax rate is 40 percent.

a What would be the dividend in each of the next five years under a pure residual dividend policy?

b Determine the dividend payout ratio and each year's total dividend payout assuming that Hoff follows a long-run residual payout policy with a stable dividend payout ratio. Determine the dividend payout assuming that total equity investment plus dividends over the five years exactly equals total earnings over the five years. Cite any years in which new external financing might be required.

c Suggest a schedule of dividends for the next five years assuming a smoothed residual dividend schedule. The total dividends plus equity investment over the five years need only approximate total earnings over the five years.

d Having made the recommendations called for in *a*, *b*, and *c* of this problem you have noticed that the dividend growth under the expansion plan as it is now (given any one of the three policies in *a*, *b*, and *c*) would be much faster than the 10 percent rate Hoff has had to date. You feel that Hoff might not be able to maintain such a trend through the 1990s. The board of directors has decided that it does not want to convey to investors the impression that the rapid rate of dividend increase can be permanently sustained. Comment on the following courses of action that Hoff might adopt to reduce dividend payments:

(1) Retire some of the outstanding 14 percent bonds.

(2) Finance the expansion plan completely with retained earnings.

(3) Enlarge the expansion program and finance the added expansion with retained earnings.

(4) Acquire liquid assets with funds in excess of those required to maintain a 10 percent to 14 percent dividend growth rate.

(5) Adopt an alternative dividend policy (perhaps a stable dollar dividend plus an "extra" dividend).

11 Auckland Woolens has declared a 50 percent stock dividend. Its shares are selling for $60 each. You own 1000 shares.

a How many shares will you have after the stock dividend is paid?

b What would you expect the price of the shares to be after the stock dividend is paid?

12 On March 24, 1986, the directors of Lyle's Worm Farms, Inc., declared a 2 percent stock dividend payable on May 10 to stockholders of record on April 14.

a On what day would you have had to buy stock in order to be a shareholder of record?

b At the time the company announced the stock dividend, it also announced that it will omit its $0.10 cash dividend, which it had paid in each of the four previous quarters. Furthermore, at the

378

PART 2
The firm's investment,
financing, and dividend
decisions

time the stock dividend and the cash dividend omission were announced, it was also pointed out that for the six years prior to March 1985, the company had paid $0.50 quarterly. What does this information suggest about Lyle's Worm Farms, Inc.?

c   On April 8, the day on which the common stock went ex-dividend, the price per share of stock was $11.25. If all else remained the same between April 7 and April 8, what would you have expected the price of stock to have been on April 7? (Hint: Consider just the impact of the stock dividend. The market price already reflects the fact that the cash dividend has been eliminated.)

13   Ranger Forest Products has 3 million shares of common stock outstanding, and earnings per share are $4. Ranger has a dividend payout ratio of 40 percent. The firm is considering a 3 for 1 stock split to lower the price of the common stock from $120 per share to a more attractive level. What will be the effect of the stock split on

a   EPS?

b   Dividends per share?

c   Price per share?

d   Total market value of the firm's shares?

e   The value of the holdings of Tab McKinley, who currently owns 1000 shares of Ranger stock?

14   Martha Burney owns 4000 shares of Generic Brands Corporation. Martha paid $20 per share for the stock in 1982. In July 1986, Generic paid a dividend of $0.50 per share and in August 1986 made a treasury stock purchase, buying up 15 percent of all outstanding Generic Brands stock. Martha sold 1000 of her 4000 shares back to Generic for $30 per share. In 1987 Martha sold her remaining 3000 shares in the market for $35 per share. Assume that Martha's tax rate on dividend income is 40 percent and that her tax rate on long-term capital gains is 16 percent.

a   What tax did Martha pay on her 1986 Generic dividends and on the capital gain she realized on the shares she sells back to Generic in 1986?

b   What capital gains tax did Martha pay on the Generic shares she sold in 1987?

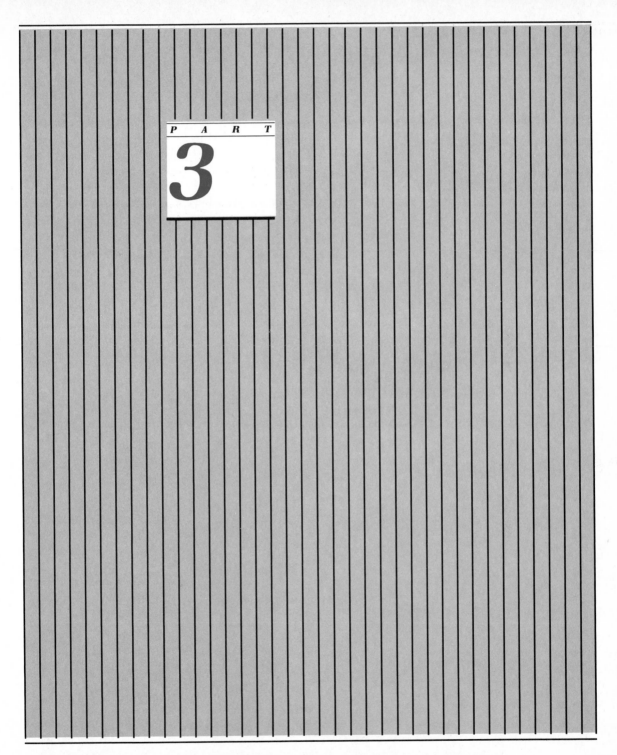

FINANCIAL ANALYSIS AND FORECASTING

Part 3 covers several important techniques for evaluating and forecasting financial data. Chapter 12 presents the two major approaches for analyzing financial statements: ratio analysis and funds flow analysis. Chapter 13 deals with profit planning. Profits are shown to depend on fixed and variable production costs, on sales volume, and on financial leverage. Chapter 14 examines techniques for forecasting important financial variables, such as sales, costs, and cash flows. Good forecasts are critical to effective financial planning by management.

All the analytical methods covered in Part 3 use accounting data to evaluate a company's current activities and to plan for the future. They are useful both to financial managers and to those outside the firm, such as financial institutions that lend money to the company and investors who purchase the company's securities.

12

FINANCIAL STATEMENT ANALYSIS

The body of information describing even the smallest firm is enormous. To be useful, this information must be organized into an understandable, coherent, and sufficiently limited set of data. Financial statement analysis can be very helpful in this respect. Data from a firm's financial statements can be used to determine the firm's financial ratios and flow of funds. The company's financial ratios can be compared with target values that are deemed appropriate for the company. The **funds flow statement** shows how a firm obtained and used the resources at its disposal during a time period. It can also pinpoint areas of mismanagement and potential danger. As with all shortcut methods of analysis, ratios and funds flow data must be used only in the light of other relevant facts.

FINANCIAL STATEMENTS

We will be concerned primarily with two types of firm financial statements: the **balance sheet** and the **income statement**. The balance sheet states the company's assets, liabilities, and stockholders' equity (net worth) at a *particular date*, for example, at December 31, 1987. The balance sheet of Macro Toy Company is shown in Exhibit 12-1. Asset values are usually shown at cost (what the company paid for the assets), and the stated liabilities indicate the amount owed. Stockholders' equity is simply the difference between assets and liabilities.

The income statement reveals the performance of the company during a *particular period of time*, for example, for the year ended December 31, 1987. It shows the revenues from sales and various costs, including interest

---

EXHIBIT 12-1
Macro Toy Company balance sheet as of December 31, 1987

Assets		Liabilities	
Cash	$ 70,000	Accounts payable	$ 150,000
Marketable securities	30,000	Notes payable to bank (8%)	200,000
Accounts receivable, net	450,000	Accruals	20,000
Inventories	350,000	Federal income taxes payable	80,000
Total current assets	$ 900,000	Total current liabilities	$ 450,000
		Mortgage bonds (6%)	150,000
Gross plant and equipment	$2,100,000	Debentures (7%)[a]	400,000
Allowance for depreciation	(500,000)	Total liabilities	$1,000,000
Net plant and equipment	$1,600,000		
		Stockholders' equity	
		Common stock	$ 500,000
		Retained earnings	1,000,000
		Stockholders' equity	$1,500,000
Total assets	$2,500,000	Liabilities plus equity	$2,500,000

[a] The annual sinking fund contribution is $25,000.

expense and taxes, which the company has incurred during the period. Macro Toy Company's income statement is presented in Exhibit 12-2.

There are two other frequently used financial reports, the statement of retained earnings and the sources and uses of funds statement. The statement of retained earnings indicates the magnitude and causes of changes in the firm's retained earnings due to the year's activities. Retained earnings are the accumulated corporate profits that have been kept by the company over the years, that is, earnings not paid out in dividends, not used to purchase back the firm's shares (treasury stock), etc. The sources and uses of funds statement—which is discussed later in this chapter—shows where the company obtained funds during the year and how the funds were used.

RATIO ANALYSIS

Types of Ratios

The people whose job it is to analyze a firm's financial position will differ in the ratios they find useful. For example, short-term creditors are primarily interested in the firm's short-run performance and level of liquid assets (cash, marketable securities, accounts receivable, etc.). Long-term creditors

---

EXHIBIT 12-2
Macro Toy Company income statement for year ended December 31, 1987

Net sales		$5,400,000
Cost of goods sold		4,400,000
Gross margin on sales		$1,000,000
Operating expenses:		
Selling	$200,000	
General and administrative[a]	330,000	
Lease payments	20,000	
Total operating expenses		550,000
Operating income		$ 450,000
Add: Other revenues (interest on		
marketable securities plus royalties)		3,000
Operating income plus other revenues		$ 453,000
Less other expenses:		
Interest on bank note	$ 16,000	
Interest on mortgage	9,000	
Interest on debentures	28,000	
Total interest expense		53,000
Income before taxes		$ 400,000
Federal income taxes (at 50%)		200,000
Net income (net profit)[b]		$ 200,000
Dividends		$ 30,000
Increase in retained earnings		170,000

[a] This includes depreciation expense of $100,000.
[b] This equals net income available to common shareholders since there are no preferred dividends.

and stockholders are concerned with the long-term as well as the short-term outlook. Management uses all the financial ratios to gauge performance.

How to determine what ratio levels are satisfactory is discussed later in this chapter. But first, using an example, we will describe the ratios that are especially useful in financial analysis. We will then explore how ratio analysis should be used in actual business applications and where the necessary information for computing ratios can be found.

Any given ratio reflects a particular aspect of a company. But usually that's not sufficient. That particular ratio and what it indicates must be viewed in the context of other ratios and other facts concerning the company. A historical illustration of this point is the case of Penn Central Corporation, which shortly before its collapse in 1970 had a seemingly safe ratio of debt to total assets. Amazingly, the perilous condition of Penn Central was generally undetected even by sophisticated analysts and financial institutions. Their error was a failure to perceive the company's operations were generating insufficient cash flow and that its assets were highly illiquid (primarily real estate and railroad properties that could not readily be sold at a reasonable price). The credit "crunch" of early 1970 made it impossible for Penn Central to borrow enough to stave off a liquidity crisis, and bankruptcy ensued. In this case, the relationship between debt and assets, isolated from other considerations, was misleading.

Four types of ratios are used in analyzing the financial position of a company.

1 **Liquidity ratios** indicate the company's capacity to meet short-run obligations.
2 **Leverage ratios** indicate the company's capacity to meet its long-term and short-term debt obligations.
3 **Activity ratios** indicate how effectively the company is using its assets.
4 **Profitability ratios** indicate the net returns on sales and assets.

Each of these four types of ratios will be defined and examined within the context of an example involving the Macro Toy Company.

Macro Toy Company manufactures games for children and adults. Relative to other firms in its industry, Macro is highly innovative and is willing to take above-average risks in developing and marketing new products. In addition to its regular line, the company produces a number of expensive, special-order toys. Because of its innovativeness and special-order service, the firm is somewhat more risky than the toy industry as a whole. Furthermore, the company recently discontinued production of an unprofitable product, resulting in significant unutilized capacity at its plant.

Exhibits 12-1 and 12-2 show the balance sheet and income statement of Macro for the year ended December 31, 1987. The ratios describing Macro's financial condition were calculated from data in these two statements and are listed in column 5 of Table 12-1. Table 12-1 also shows ratios in column 3 that are considered average for the toy industry; and in column 4 it shows ratios that Macro must meet under current circumstances if it is to maintain its aggressive and innovative policies, and yet remain financially healthy and attractive to investors and creditors.

TABLE 12-1
Ratio definitions and values for Macro Toy Company

Ratio (1)	Ratio formula (2)	Industry average (3)	Appropriate ratio level for Macro Toy Company (4)	Actual Macro Toy Company ratios (5)
Liquidity ratios				
Current	$\dfrac{\text{Current assets}}{\text{Current liabilities}}$	2.4	2.6	2.0
Quick	$\dfrac{\text{Current assets} - \text{inventory}}{\text{Current liabilities}}$	1.2	1.7	1.22
Leverage ratios				
Debt	$\dfrac{\text{Total debt}}{\text{Total assets}}$	0.45	0.4	0.4
Debt-equity[a]	$\dfrac{\text{Long-term debt}}{\text{Stockholders' equity}}$	.48	.43	.37
Times interest earned	$\dfrac{\text{Earnings before taxes} + \text{interest}}{\text{Interest charges}}$	6	6.5	8.55
Fixed-charges coverage	$\dfrac{\text{Income available for meeting fixed charges}}{\text{Fixed charges}}$	3.2	3.5	3.85
Activity ratios				
Inventory turnover	$\dfrac{\text{Cost of goods sold}}{\text{Average inventory}}$	5	9	11
Average collection period, days	$\dfrac{\text{Average accounts receivable}}{\text{Average credit sales per day}}$	56	46	30
Fixed-assets turnover	$\dfrac{\text{Sales}}{\text{Fixed assets}}$	11	10	3.375
Total assets turnover	$\dfrac{\text{Sales}}{\text{Total assets}}$	7	6.5	2.16
Profitability ratios				
Gross profit margin, %	$\dfrac{\text{Sales} - \text{cost of goods sold}}{\text{Sales}}$	12	14	18.5
Net operating margin, %	$\dfrac{\text{Operating income}}{\text{Sales}}$	5	6	8.33
Profit margin on sales, %	$\dfrac{\text{Net income}}{\text{Sales}}$	2.6	3	3.7
Return on total assets, %[b]	$\dfrac{\text{Net income} + \text{interest}}{\text{Total assets}}$	8	9	10.12
Return on equity, %[c]	$\dfrac{\text{Net income}}{\text{Stockholders' equity}}$	9.5	11	13.33

[a] Sometimes current debt or total debt, rather than long-term debt, is used in computing this ratio.
[b] Return on total assets as defined here [(net income + interest)/total assets] is sometimes referred to as the "operating return on total assets." Also, the term "return on total assets" is often used to refer to net income/total assets; however, as explained on pages 401 to 403, the ratio (net income/total assets) is not very meaningful.
[c] See footnote 8, page 395, for a company with preferred stock as well as common stock outstanding.

Later in this chapter, we will demonstrate the methods used to determine the values of the ratios in column 4, which are considered financially appropriate for Macro's particular situation.

Liquidity Ratios Liquidity ratios measure the firm's ability to fullfill *short-term* commitments out of its liquid assets. Assets are "liquid" if they are either cash or relatively easy to convert into cash (for example, through sale). Short-term creditors are generally very interested in the liquidity ratios. The current ratio and the quick ratio are the most commonly used liquidity ratios.

Current Ratio The current ratio equals current assets divided by current liabilities. Current assets are viewed as relatively liquid, which means they can generate cash in a relatively short time period. Current liabilities are debts that will come due within a year. If the current ratio is too low, the firm may have difficulty in meeting short-run commitments as they mature. If the ratio is too high, the firm may have an excessive investment in current assets or be underutilizing short-term credit.

For Macro the current ratio equals

$$\text{Current ratio} = \frac{\text{current assets}}{\text{current liabilities}}$$
$$= \frac{\$900,000}{\$450,000}$$
$$= 2$$

A poor current ratio may imply that only one or that several of the specific current assets and liabilities are at an undesirable level. Thus, a low current ratio could mean that cash, marketable securities, accounts receivable, or inventory should be increased. Similarly, a low current ratio may mean that one or more of the debts—accounts payable or notes payable, or accruals, or provisions for taxes—should be reduced.

Macro's current ratio is 2. However, as indicated in Table 12-1, the acceptable current ratio for Macro is 2.6. It might seem that current assets equal to twice current liabilities should be sufficient. However, recall that Macro is a high risk business. Macro's special-order toy inventories are not very liquid, and are potentially salable only at a large discount. Furthermore, there may be a delay in collecting accounts receivable. The firm could sell the accounts receivable to a factor (a firm specializing in the purchase of accounts receivable from other companies). But, even if the receivables are sold, less than the $450,000 owed to Macro by its customers (see balance sheet, Exhibit 12-1) would be realized since the factor will demand a profit on the transaction. In short, Macro's current position should be improved and is a justifiable concern to management and to the firm's short-term creditors.

Quick Ratio or Acid Test Ratio The quick, or acid test, ratio measures the firm's ability to meet short-term obligations from its most liquid assets. In this case, inventory is not included with other current assets because it is generally far less liquid than the other current assets. The quick ratio equals current assets, excluding inventory, divided by current liabilities. That is,

$$\text{Quick ratio} = \frac{\text{current assets} - \text{inventory}}{\text{current liabilities}}$$

$$= \frac{\$900,000 - \$350,000}{\$450,000}$$

$$= 1.22$$

The quick ratio for Macro reflects the same weak position reflected by the current ratio. Macro's quick ratio of 1.22 is significantly less than the acceptable level of 1.7 shown in col. 4 of Table 12-1. The same reasons for concern that applied to the current ratio are relevant here.

Leverage Ratios   Leverage ratios measure the extent of the firm's total debt burden. They reflect the company's ability to meet its short- *and* long-term debt obligations. The ratios are computed either by comparing fixed charges and earnings from the income statement or by relating the debt and equity (stockholders' investment) items from the balance sheet. Leverage ratios are important to creditors, since they indicate whether or not the firm's revenues can support interest and other fixed charges, as well as whether or not there are sufficient assets to pay off the debt if the firm liquidates. Shareholders, too, are concerned with leverage, since interest is a company expense that increases with greater debt. If borrowing and interest are excessive, the company may become bankrupt.

The more predictable are the returns of the firm, the more debt will be acceptable, since the firm will be less likely to be surprised by circumstances that prevent fulfilling debt obligations. Utilities have historically had relatively stable incomes; they have also been among the industries with the heaviest debt. In contrast, furniture manufacturers and auto producers are cyclical businesses and normally include a far lower proportion of debt in their capital structures.

Recall that Macro is more risky than most firms in its industry. Consequently, a more conservative level for the leverage ratios is warranted. For this reason, the three leverage ratio levels indicated in Table 12-1 that are appropriate for Macro (col. 4) differ from those for the industry as a whole (col. 3).

Debt to Total Assets Ratio   This ratio equals total debt (total liabilities) divided by total assets. That is, using the Exhibit 12-1 balance sheet data,

$$\text{Debt to total assets ratio} = \frac{\text{total debt}}{\text{total assets}}$$

$$= \frac{\$1.0 \text{ million}}{\$2.5 \text{ million}}$$

$$= 0.4$$

The debt to total assets ratio is also called the debt ratio. Generally, creditors prefer a low debt ratio since it implies a greater protection of their position. A higher debt ratio generally means that the firm must pay a higher interest rate on its borrowing; beyond some point, the firm will not be able to borrow at all.

Macro's debt ratio of 0.4 is satisfactory in that it is less than the maximum acceptable level of 0.45 for the firm indicated in Table 12-1. Recall that Macro's current ratio and quick ratio were too low. Since the firm's overall leverage is not excessive, it could reduce its current liabilities and keep total debt (long-term debt plus current liabilities) at a satisfactory level by borrowing long-term and using these funds to retire some of its short-term (current) obligations. Thus, Macro might borrow an additional $100,000 on a long-term basis (long-term debt rises from $550,000 to $650,000 in Exhibit 12-1) and use the money to pay off $100,000 in current liabilities (reducing current liabilities from $450,000 to $350,000). This would not affect the firm's debt ratio (total debt remains at $1,000,000), but by reducing current liabilities, it would produce a more satisfactory relationship between current assets and current liabilities.

Debt to Equity Ratio This ratio equals the firm's debt divided by its equity, where debt can be defined as total debt or as long-term debt. We will use long-term debt since it is so frequently employed, and because it provides added information not provided by the debt ratio discussed above. Using Exhibit 12-1 data, the debt-equity ratio equals

$$\text{Debt-equity ratio} = \frac{\text{long-term debt}}{\text{stockholders' equity}}$$

$$= \frac{\$550,000}{\$1,500,000}$$

$$= 0.37$$

where Macro's long-term debt equals its mortgage bonds plus its debentures. A high debt-equity ratio (using long-term debt in the numerator) implies that a high proportion of long-term financing is from debt sources, that is, the firm is using a great deal of financial leverage. Long-term creditors generally prefer to see a modest debt-equity ratio since it means greater protection (a larger equity cushion) and a greater stake in the company's future for equity holders (implying a greater stockholder motivation to see the company prosper).

Macro's debt-equity ratio is satisfactory since it is less than the maximum desirable level of 0.43 specified in Table 12.1. Therefore, Macro can increase its long-term borrowing (e.g., to pay off some current liabilities, as discussed above) and still maintain an acceptable debt-equity level.

Times Interest Earned Ratio The times interest earned ratio equals earnings before interest and taxes (EBIT) divided by interest. EBIT can be computed by simply adding interest expense ($53,000) to income before taxes ($400,000). In Exhibit 12-2, the times interest earned ratio equals net income before taxes plus interest expense all divided by interest expense:

$$\text{Times interest earned ratio} = \frac{\text{EBIT}}{\text{interest expense}}$$

$$= \frac{\$400,000 + \$53,000}{\$53,000}$$

$$= 8.55$$

Times interest earned reflects the firm's ability to pay interest out of earnings. Macro's times interest earned ratio of 8.55 means that Macro's earnings available to pay interest is 8.55 times the interest that is due. From Table 12-1, this is more than the appropriate level for Macro of 6.5. Creditors can feel confident that the interest will be paid, since interest is amply covered by EBIT. Notice that the numerator in the ratio, EBIT, is earnings *before* interest expense and taxes since all of EBIT is available for payment of interest. If interest equalled Macro's EBIT of $453,000, times interest earned would be 1; the company could just pay its interest and would pay no corporate income taxes since taxable income would be zero (earnings before interest and taxes − interest expense = taxable income, that is $453,000 − $453,000 = 0). Keep in mind that EBIT fluctuates from year to year, and it may in the future fall far short of current EBIT. Therefore, a current times interest earned ratio greatly exceeding unity is desirable because it means that interest on currently outstanding debt will very likely be paid in coming years.

Fixed-Charges Coverage Ratio   The fixed-charges coverage ratio equals income available to meet fixed charges divided by fixed charges. Fixed charges include all fixed dollar outlays, including debt interest, sinking fund contributions, and lease payments. A fixed charge is a cash outflow that the firm cannot avoid without violating its contractual agreements. The firm periodically deposits money in a sinking fund that is eventually used to pay off the principal of the long-term debt for which the fund was set up (see Chapter 21 for details). Lease payments are made by Macro to lessors (owners) of equipment that is used by Macro in its operations. The fixed-charges coverage ratio therefore equals[1]

Fixed-charges coverage ratio

$$= \frac{\text{income available for meeting fixed charges}}{\text{fixed charges}}$$

---

[1] The bond agreement may require the firm to make periodic payments into a sinking fund that will eventually be used to retire the debt. If the sinking fund contribution is not made, the firm defaults. Sinking fund payments are not tax deductible and therefore must be made from the firm's aftertax income. Notice that the fixed-charges coverage ratio is the number of dollars available from current operations to pay fixed charges divided by the amount that *must be* earned before taxes to assure the payment of fixed charges and also pay the firm's taxes. Fixed charges other than sinking fund payments are tax deductible, and therefore to cover them the firm need only earn pretax amounts equal to those fixed charges. However, to cover the non-tax-deductible sinking fund contribution of $25,000, the firm must earn more than $25,000 in pretax returns. Thus, assuming a corporate tax rate of 50 percent,

$$\frac{\text{Pretax dollars needed}}{\text{to cover sinking fund}} \times (1.0 - \text{tax rate}) = \text{sinking fund payment}$$

and therefore,

$$\frac{\text{Pretax dollars needed}}{\text{to cover sinking fund}} = \frac{\text{sinking fund payment}}{1.0 - \text{tax rate}}$$

$$= \frac{\$25,000}{1.0 - 0.5} = \frac{\$25,000}{0.5} = \$50,000$$

The firm needs $50,000 in pretax earnings to cover the $25,000 in sinking fund payments.

$$= \frac{\text{operating income} + \text{lease payments} + \text{other income}}{\text{interest} + \text{lease payments} + \text{before-tax sinking fund contribution}}$$

$$= \frac{\$450,000 + \$20,000 + \$3000}{\$53,000 + \$20,000 + \$50,000} = \frac{\$473,000}{\$123,000}$$

$$= 3.85$$

The fixed-charges coverage ratio is significant since it indicates how much income there is to pay for all fixed charges. Macro's position is satisfactory since its actual ratio of 3.85 exceeds the minimum acceptable level of 3.5 for the firm, as shown in Table 12-1.

Activity Ratios   Activity ratios show the intensity with which the firm uses its assets in generating sales. These ratios indicate whether the firm's investments in current and long-term assets are too small or too large. If investment is too large, it could be that the funds tied up in that asset should be used for more productive purposes. For example, the firm may have unused plant capacity that it could sell and then use the proceeds in some profitable way. If investment is too small, the firm may be providing poor service to customers or inefficiently producing its product. For example, the firm might benefit from an increase in inventories because current stocks are inadequate to efficiently service customers.

There are two basic approaches to the computation of activity ratios. Under the approach shown here, we assume that the purpose of the analysis is to evaluate average performance over the year. Therefore, average levels of the assets for the year are used. The alternative approach would be to examine whether current (for example, December 31, 1987) levels of the assets are at proper levels. Under this latter approach the end-of-period levels of the assets would be used.

We will assume for simplicity that the asset balances for Macro did not fluctuate much during the year and that end-of-year asset balances approximate the average asset levels during the year. However, to illustrate the technique for computing an average asset level when there are variations during the year, we assume in computing the inventory turnover ratio that Macro's inventories did change significantly during the year. End-of-year asset balances are used for all the other ratios. It will also be assumed throughout that sales did not fluctuate significantly during the year.[2]

Inventory Turnover   Inventory turnover equals cost of goods sold divided by average inventory. Therefore, both balance sheet and income statement data must be used. Inventory may have changed significantly

---

[2] If sales fluctuate during the year, it is not correct to compare annual sales with asset balances (either end-of-year or a simple average for the year) in computing activity ratios. For example, the accounts receivable at December 31 reflect sales during the latter part of the year, and therefore average daily sales in the latter part of the year should be compared with the accounts receivable at year-end to compute the implied collection period. If performance over the entire year is to be assessed, then a separate collection period should be computed for several points during the year, for example, using quarterly accounts receivable balances and each quarter's sales. Also see footnote 4, this chapter.

during a given year, and it is particularly important here to use a yearly average rather than the year-end inventory amount. For Macro, the beginning-of-the-year inventory is not shown on the balance sheet in Exhibit 12-1. But let's assume that beginning (December 31, 1986) inventory was $450,000; the balance sheet shows that the December 31, 1987, inventory is $350,000; therefore

$$\text{Average inventory for year} = \frac{\$450,000 + \$350,000}{2}$$

$$= \$400,000$$

and

$$\text{Inventory turnover} = \frac{\text{cost of goods sold}}{\text{average inventory}}$$

$$= \frac{\$4,400,000}{\$400,000}$$

$$= 11$$

Since inventories are valued in terms of their cost, cost of goods sold rather than sales was used in computing inventory turnover in our example. Although sales is less accurate than cost of goods sold for calculating this ratio, sales is often used in practice. Also, if inventory fluctuates seasonally, for example, is high at the middle of the year but low at the beginning and end of the year, then it's somewhat complicated to calculate the average. Nevertheless, the average should be used.[3]

Inventory absorbs fluctuations in deliveries so as to avoid stockouts. A low inventory turnover implies a large investment in inventories relative to the amount needed to service sales. Excess inventory ties up resources unproductively. On the other hand, if the inventory turnover is too high, inventories are too small and it may be that the firm is constantly running short of inventory (out of stock), thereby losing customers. The objective is to maintain a level of inventory relative to sales that is not excessive but at the same time is sufficient to meet customer needs (see Chapter 15).

A substantial portion of Macro's business is special-order merchandise that is not inventoried, and consequently Macro's appropriate inventory turnover ratio is higher (since inventories are lower) than for the industry. However, Macro's inventory turnover of 11 is higher even than the level of 9 deemed appropriate for the firm (see Table 12-1) and may suggest that Macro is understocked with inventory. It may also be that inventories are being used with exceptional efficiency. Further investigation would be needed to provide the answer.

Average Collection Period   The average collection period is a measure of how long it takes from the time the sale is made to the time the cash is

---

[3] For example, with quarterly data available, the average could be computed by taking inventories at the beginning of the year plus each end-of-quarter inventory balance and dividing the total by 5. An even more accurate average would be the inventory balance at the beginning of the year plus each end-of-month inventory balance all divided by 13.

collected from the customer. To compute this figure, the average credit sales per day is determined by dividing the year's credit sales by 360. The average credit sales per day is then divided into year-end accounts receivable or into average accounts receivable for the year. Assume for simplicity that the level of accounts receivable has not varied significantly during the year and that year-end and average accounts receivable are therefore about the same.[4] Also assume that all Macro Toy Company's sales are made on credit. Thus,

$$\text{Average credit sales per day} = \frac{\text{annual credit sales}}{360 \text{ days}}$$

$$= \frac{\$5,400,000}{360 \text{ days}}$$

$$= \$15,000/\text{day}$$

$$\text{Average collection period} = \frac{\text{accounts receivable}}{\text{average credit sales per day}}$$

$$= \frac{\$450,000}{\$15,000/\text{day}}$$

$$= 30 \text{ days}$$

The average collection period indicates the firm's efficiency in collecting on its sales. It may also reflect the firm's credit policy. If customers are given more time to pay, then the collection period will generally be greater. A long collection period is not necessarily bad, since a stringent credit policy requiring customers to pay faster may lead to a reduction in sales. However, the longer time in collecting on sales from a lax credit policy is a cost to the firm, and it can only be justified if it produces greater sales. The sooner the firm receives the cash due on sales, the sooner it can put that money to work earning interest. That is, the cost of a long collection period is a return (interest) lost on these funds.

Given that the firm has a particular credit policy (it requires payment by customers within a given time period), some acceptable average collection period is implied. If the collection period is too long, remedial measures must be implemented. The weakness may be slow billing procedures, ineffective incentives to get customers to pay on time, or poor selection of customers in extending credit. Macro's collection period of thirty days is

[4] If sales are stable during the year but accounts receivable fluctuate significantly during the year, an average rather than a year-end accounts receivable estimate would be preferable, It should be noted that with seasonal or other fluctuations in credit sales during the year the average collection period computed as shown in the text above will also fluctuate during the year *even though* collections are stable over the year (that is, even though the fraction of credit sales still uncollected one month after the sale, two months after the sale, etc., is the same from month to month). Also, with fluctuating sales, a stable collection period figure may be implied even though collections are slowing (deteriorating). The implication is that the average collection period figure must be used with caution if the business has significant credit sales fluctuations during the year. On this point, see Wilbur G. Lewellen and Robert W. Johnson, "Monitoring Accounts Receivable," *Harvard Business Review* (May–June 1972).

well within the acceptable level for the firm of forty-six days (shown in Table 12-1).

Fixed-Assets Turnover   This ratio is computed by dividing net sales by fixed assets (net plant and equipment) and equals

$$\text{Fixed-assets turnover} = \frac{\text{sales}}{\text{fixed assets}}$$

$$= \frac{\$5,400,000}{\$1,600,000}$$

$$= 3.375$$

This ratio indicates how intensively the fixed assets of the firm are being used.[5] An inadequately low ratio implies excessive investment in plant and equipment relative to the value of the output being produced. In such a case, the firm might be better off to liquidate some of those fixed assets and invest the proceeds productively (or to pay off its debt, or to distribute the proceeds as dividends).[6]

Macro has an exceptionally low fixed-assets turnover of 3.375 relative to the proper level of 10 shown in Table 12-1. Recall that Macro's plant has significant unused capacity. The implication is that the firm would do better to move to smaller facilities unless it anticipates a significant increase in production and sales.

Total-Assets Turnover   Total-assets turnover equals sales divided by total assets; therefore,

$$\text{Total-assets turnover} = \frac{\text{sales}}{\text{total assets}}$$

$$= \frac{\$5,400,000}{\$2,500,000}$$

$$= 2.16$$

Total-assets turnover reflects how well the company's assets are being used to generate sales. Total-assets turnover for Macro is well below the appropriate level of 6.5 shown in Table 12-1. This is due to the excessive investment in fixed assets noted earlier. Recall also that the firm has an inadequate current ratio (current assets/current liabilities). Therefore, if it were to liquidate some of its fixed assets, such as plant and equipment, some of the funds generated could be used to increase current assets (such as inventories) or to decrease current liabilities (for example, pay off the bank notes) so as to raise the current ratio to an acceptable level.

---

[5] If fixed assets have changed significantly during the year an average fixed-asset level for the year should be used (see the average inventory calculation for the inventory turnover ratio). Average assets would also be used in computing the total-assets turnover ratio and the return on total assets.

[6] The use of a balance sheet (book) asset value (cost less accumulated depreciation) as a measure of the market liquidation value of the asset may be misleading, particularly if market values have changed since the asset was purchased by the firm. However, book magnitudes usually provide a useful, albeit rough, estimate of the company's situation.

Profitability Ratios   Profitability ratios measure the success of the firm in earning a net return on sales or on investment. Since profit is the ultimate objective of the firm, poor performance here indicates a basic failure that, if not corrected, would probably result in the firm's going out of business.

Gross Margin   The gross profit margin is gross profit (sales minus cost of goods sold) divided by sales. Thus, for Macro,

$$\text{Gross profit margin} = \frac{\text{sales} - \text{cost of goods sold}}{\text{sales}}$$

$$= \frac{\$5,400,000 - \$4,400,000}{\$5,400,000}$$

$$= 18.5\%$$

Macro's gross profit margin is very impressive since it far exceeds the target of 14 percent shown in Table 12-1.

The gross margin reflects the effectiveness of pricing policy and of production efficiency (that is, how well the purchase or production cost of goods is controlled). Of course, if the gross margin is increased by raising the price of the firm's product, the product may become uncompetitive, producing a falloff in sales. Therefore, a company may find it advantageous to lower the price, and therefore lower the gross profit margin, if it increases sales so much as to increase total profits.

Net Operating Margin   The net operating margin equals net sales minus the sum of cost of goods sold and operating expenses, all divided by net sales. That is,

$$\text{Net operating margin} = \frac{\text{operating income}}{\text{sales}}$$

$$= \frac{\text{sales} - \text{cost of goods sold} - \text{total operating expenses}}{\text{sales}}$$

$$= \frac{\$5,400,000 - \$4,400,000 - \$550,000}{\$5,400,000}$$

$$= \frac{\$450,000}{\$5,400,000}$$

$$= 8.33\%$$

The net operating margin indicates the profitability of sales before taxes and interest expense. Nonoperating revenues (for example, interest on marketable securities and royalties) are not included in the returns, and nonoperating expenses (such as interest) are not deducted. Nonoperating income and expense items are those not directly associated with the production or sale of the firm's product (note that interest expense is a financing cost and not a production cost). The purpose of this ratio is to measure the effectiveness of production and *sales* of the company's product in generating pretax income for the firm. For any given level of sales, the higher the net operating margin the better. Macro's net operating margin of 8.33

percent is superior to both the industry average of 5 percent and the level of 6 percent deemed appropriate for Macro.[7]

Profit Margin on Sales   This ratio equals net income divided by sales.

$$\text{Profit margin on sales} = \frac{\text{net income}}{\text{sales}}$$

$$= \frac{\$200,000}{\$5,400,000}$$

$$= 3.7\%$$

By itself, profit margin on sales provides little useful information since it mixes the effectiveness of sales in producing profits (reflected by the net operating margin) with the effects of the method of financing on profits (since net income is after deduction of interest on debt and of taxes, which are affected by interest). Macro's appropriate profit margin on sales shown in Table 12-1 is the level management seeks given its current debt level; it would be misleading to compare Macro's profit margin on sales with the profit margin of companies with different degrees of debt financing. In contrast, the net operating margin (operating income/sales) is useful since it reflects pricing policy relative to costs, a useful index for decision making. Later in this chapter, we will see that profit margin on sales is used, in combination with another ratio, to compute return on investment.

Return on Total Assets   This ratio equals net income plus interest on debt, divided by total assets.

$$\text{Return on total assets} = \frac{\text{net income} + \text{interest expense}}{\text{total assets}}$$

$$= \frac{\$200,000 + \$53,000}{\$2,500,000}$$

$$= 10.12\%$$

Return on total assets is the total after-corporate-tax return to stockholders and lenders on the total investment that they have in the firm. It is the rate of return earned by the firm as a whole for all its investors, including lenders. Macro's rate of return on total assets of 10.12 percent is

---

[7] The net operating margin can be expressed as

Net operating margin $= 1 -$ operating ratio

where the operating ratio is equal to (cost of goods sold + operating expenses)/sales.

   The ratio of operating income to total assets could be used to measure the effectiveness of sales and pricing policies and of operations in generating income. This ratio is useful in gauging efficiency since it abstracts from financing effects (operating earnings are earnings before deductions for interest on debt and taxes). Notice that this ratio can be computed from ratios described in the text since

$$\frac{\text{Operating income}}{\text{Total assets}} = \frac{\text{operating income}}{\text{sales}} \times \frac{\text{sales}}{\text{total assets}}$$

$$= \text{net operating margin} \times \text{total-assets turnover ratio}$$

significantly above the appropriate rate for the firm of 9 percent shown in Table 12-1. In an overall sense, Macro can therefore be viewed as a successful company.

Return on Equity   This ratio equals the net income available to common stockholders (i.e., net income minus dividends on any preferred stock) divided by the common stockholders' equity.[8]

$$\text{Return on equity} = \frac{\text{net income to common}}{\text{common stockholders' equity}}$$

$$= \frac{\$200,000}{\$1,500,000}$$

$$= 13.33\%$$

Management's objective is to generate the maximum return on shareholders' investment in the firm. Return on equity is therefore the best single measure of the company's success in fulfilling its goal. Macro's return of 13.33 percent is well above the minimum desired level of 11 percent. In the next section we will discuss interrelationships between various ratios and will show how return on equity can be expressed in terms of many other ratios.

Use of Ratios: Macro Company Revisited

So far, we have defined fifteen ratios and noted their significance. Below, we explain how the firm's target ratio levels—deemed appropriate for the firm—relate to industry ratio levels. We then discuss ratio interrelationships and ratio trends. Finally, we discuss certain problems with using financial statement information.

Firm Standards versus Industry Averages   Companies that produce the same products generally confront similar problems. This would seem to imply that to evaluate a firm, it would be reasonable to compare that firm's ratios with the average ratio levels for companies in the same industry. This is valid in some cases, but it's only a rough approximation—sometimes very rough! There are at least two reasons that industry averages must be used cautiously.

First, as with individual firms, entire industries may be prosperous or sick. Using an industry standard to evaluate a firm implies that the industry performance is satisfactory on the average. However, this is not so for ailing industries (for example, railroads). To make the judgment that an individual firm within the industry is healthy because it conforms to industry averages would be wrong in such cases. However, it would be fair to say that if a firm's ratios are as good as the industry's, it is likely that the firm's manage-

---

[8] For a firm with preferred stock as well as common stock outstanding, a separate return on total equity (common stock and preferred stock) and on common equity alone can be computed. The return on total equity equals (net income)/(common and preferred equity); and the return on common stock equals (net income − dividends due preferred stock for the period)/(common stock equity); common stock equity equals total equity minus preferred equity (where preferred equity = preferred par *plus* preferred paid-in surplus).

ment is doing at least an average job in view of industrywide conditions, for example, conditions relating to demand for the industry's products or to supply of its inputs.

Second, companies within an industry vary in size and the individual firm's products and services are not all exactly the same. This implies possible differences in risk and operating conditions. Therefore, the same ratio levels may not be appropriate for all companies in the industry. For example, some firms in the publishing industry may produce lower-risk technical and reference materials, whereas other firms publish higher-risk fiction and popular magazines. Riskiest of all is the underground press, which has had great successes, such as *The Village Voice* and *L. A. Free Press*, but many diasters, such as the *San Francisco Balloon* and *The Washington Rebel*.

Another thing to consider is that many firms straddle more than a single industry. To evaluate these firms properly, it is necessary to take into account the proportion of their activities in each industry. It may even be advisable to calculate separate sets of ratios for operations in each industry. The larger is the firm being analyzed, the more likely it is that it will have multi-industry activities and that separate ratios for several lines of activity will have to be computed.

What standards should be used to establish the proper ratios for a particular firm? From the shareholders' standpoint, ratios should be at those levels which mean that the company will generate the best stream of net income over time—simply put, income per share with most desirable risk-return properties. Creditors seek assurance that their principal and interest on the debt will be paid, implying a preference on their part for the firm to be prosperous and for the liquidity and leverage ratios to be equal to or greater than some minimal safe level.

The inventory turnover ratio and operating ratio values should imply that the firm is expanding sales and minimizing costs for any given level and quality of output. Excessive debt means an unacceptable likelihood of default on the debt, something that should be avoided since bankruptcy is disastrous to shareholders and to creditors. This risk is reflected in the liquidity and leverage ratios. The profitability ratio should reflect an adequate return on investment given the risk of the company's activities. In any case, a firm's particular objectives and circumstances must be reflected in the ratio levels that are deemed appropriate for the company. Industry averages can, in most cases, offer no more than a general guide. The firm's ratios should coincide with the industry average ratios only if the firm's objectives and circumstances are typical of the industry and the industry is made up of successful and well-managed companies.

In establishing the appropriate ratio levels for Macro Toy Company (column 4, Table 12-1), it was assumed that the industry ratio levels (column 3) were satisfactory for an average firm in the toy industry. That is, the industry is efficient and moderately prosperous and therefore provides a good average standard of performance. Macro Toy Company, however, is not representative since it has an exceptionally high volume of special-order sales and is relatively risky (greater uncertainty regarding future sales or costs, earnings, etc.). Because there is more than average risk, this firm should have a lower debt ratio and a higher interest coverage, as well as a higher than normal profitability (to compensate for greater risk). This is reflected in the appropriate ratio values for Macro, which differ from the values of the ratios for the entire industry. Also, since Macro does many special-order projects, it will not require as large an inventory of finished products as competing companies with primarily mass production products. Therefore, Macro needs a higher inventory turnover ratio (a lower level of inventory relative to sales) than do its competitors in the industry.

Interrelationship of Ratios   Ratios must be evaluated together, not individually. For example, Macro Toy Company has a low current ratio (inadequate liquidity) but a better than adequate debt ratio, interest coverage, and profitability. The firm, therefore, is in a good position to seek additional long-term debt or equity financing if needed. As noted earlier, the current ratio could be improved (increased) by increasing long-term debt and using the proceeds to pay off short-term debt. Recall also that the firm has a high fixed-assets ratio, implying that some of the production facilities could be sold and the funds used to reduce current liabilities. Even if the firm does not reduce its current (short-term) liabilities, creditors can take note that the firm will be able to resort to long-term financing or sell its fixed assets to pay off short-term debts when they come due. Short-term creditors must be concerned not only with the current liquidity position of the firm, but also with its overall position. The current or quick ratios alone do not reveal the entire story. Indeed, another firm with an excellent current ratio but rapidly deteriorating overall position might be far riskier for creditors. This is not to suggest, however, that the liquidity ratios are irrelevant. Higher liquidity ratios mean that the firm is better prepared to pay off debts that are coming due, without having to resort to long-term borrowing (which may be expensive or even impossible if the company is in financial distress).

Expressing the return on equity in terms of other ratios is especially revealing:

$$\text{Return on equity} = \underbrace{\underbrace{\frac{\text{net income}}{\text{operating income}}}_{} \times \underbrace{\frac{\text{operating income}}{\text{sales}}}_{\text{net operating margin}}}_{\text{profit margin on sales}} \times \underbrace{\frac{\text{sales}}{\text{total assets}}}_{\substack{\text{total-assets} \\ \text{turnover}}} \times \underbrace{\frac{\text{total assets}}{\text{equity}}}_{\substack{1 + \\ \text{debt-equity ratio}^9}}$$

Notice from the above equation that, even if one of the above four ratios comprising return on equity is low, return on equity may still be high. For example, if the net operating margin is very low compared with those of

---

[9] [Total assets/equity] = [(equity + debt)/equity] = 1 + [debt/equity] = 1 + debt-equity ratio.

other firms in the industry, the return on equity may be high if the firm has a high total-assets turnover ratio or high debt ratio (assets are large relative to equity). An example of this might be a firm which cuts the sales price of its product (and therefore lowers its operating income and its profit margin on sales) but consequently greatly expands its sales (producing a high total-asset turnover) and therefore has a high return on equity. Another example is a firm which has a great deal of debt relative to equity (i.e., a large debt ratio and therefore a large total-assets/equity) but has a pretax return on investment which exceeds the interest rate (and therefore has a satisfactory profit margin on sales).[10] The high [total-assets/equity] ratio can mean very large return on equity. This situation is common in the real estate industry. These examples illustrate that a particular ratio level may appear only satisfactory or even poor (for example, a low net operating margin or a high debt ratio), but this may be part of a calculated strategy of management to achieve a high overall performance (a high return on equity). One benefit of expressing return on equity in terms of other ratios, as in the above equation, is that it reveals how policy changes in various areas can affect return on equity. It provides some insight into what factors determine firm profitability.

Trends Over Time   Historical information can be useful in diagnosing a firm just as it is in medically diagnosing a patient. Whether the fever is rising or falling can be as important as its level. When a firm's weaknesses are revealed, the immediate reaction is to consider remedies. However, if trends indicate that the situation is improving, it may be that no remedy is needed. Indeed, attempted remedies may make things worse.

Time trends are important in another sense. Pricing and credit policies, production methods, and other areas of managerial control can be varied, all affecting the firm's performance. A survey of past policies and their effects on the firm, as reflected in such performance measures as the above ratios, can be a very helpful guide in formulating future policies.

An additional word of caution regarding the forecasting of future trends: Historical data are suggestive but not conclusive. A financial variable changing in one direction in the past may not continue to move in that direction in the future. Therefore, to determine if a variable is settling at some level or maintaining its trend, additional information regarding the company and the industry must be obtained.

Examining Macro's trends over time in Figure 12-1, notice that the liquidity ratios at the end of 1986 and 1987 are markedly below the levels of previous periods, implying that the current and quick ratios may be only

---

[10] Note that interest is a tax deductible expense. Also, *if* an investment earns (before corporate taxes) more than the interest rate paid on borrowed funds used to finance the investment, the investment will generate additional profit for the firm's owners. Of course, the sword cuts both ways: If the investment return is less than the interest rate, losses will be produced by the investment. An implication is that, simply raising [total assets/equity] (that is, raising the debt-equity ratio for any given level of total assets and any given operating income) will not necessarily raise return on equity. This is so because greater debt means more debt interest expense, which in turn means lower net income and lower [net income/operating income] since more of the operating income must be paid out to creditors.

temporarily depressed. Inadequate liquidity may, therefore, not reflect chronic mismanagement, but merely an extraordinary situation that will soon be corrected. However, the fact that the liquidity deficiency in 1987 is even greater than at the end of the previous year suggests that the problem should be investigated.

The debt ratio has not changed much. From Figure 12-1, we see that sales have declined due to the discontinuation of an unprofitable line. This has increased profits per dollar of sales (increase in the operating margin) but has also created unused plant capacity and a resulting fall in assets turnover (sales/fixed assets and sales/total assets). The firm's profitability has increased, suggesting that the rise in the operating margin has more than compensated for the fall in sales. Of particular interest to the analyst would be projections of future sales. Additional information would be needed to formulate such a sales forecast.

We should point out that in order to properly forecast a company's future performance (and the implied financial ratios), it is essential that the forecaster have some understanding of the company's production, marketing, and financial plans. The economic feasibility of those plans (in light of data concerning the firm, the industry, and the economy as a whole), and the ability of the company's management to fulfill its plans, should be carefully studied in any evaluation. Financial statement data alone are

FIGURE 12-1

Time trends of the Macro Toy Company financial ratios.

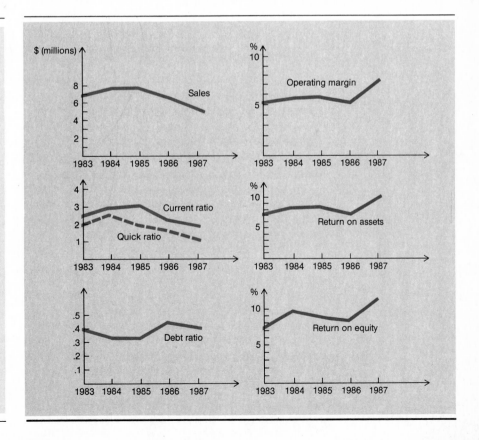

ordinarily insufficient for the task. A close familiarity with the circumstances behind the financial statements is essential.

The analysis of ratio interrelationships and trends over time is the essence of many modern techniques of financial statement analysis. Several ratios can be simultaneously considered with each ratio weighted by its relative importance (the weights being determined by a statistical study of historical data); the weighted average of the ratio magnitudes gives a number which can be used for predictive purposes, for example, to forecast financial distress. This approach is used in what is referred to as "discriminant analysis." Another ratio technique for forecasting performance involves analysis of rates of change in ratios over time. The traditional method of examining only a few ratios at one point in time is gradually being replaced by these more effective approaches.[11]

Using Financial Statement Information Financial ratios are generally based on balance sheet and income statement figures. However, there are potential problems with these numbers.

Balance sheet asset figures do not ordinarily equal the actual market values of the assets, and balance sheet liability figures often do not equal what it would actually cost to retire the outstanding liabilities. Assets are listed on the balance sheet at cost (what the company paid for the asset) less depreciation, or, for certain assets (e.g., marketable securities and inventories) at the *lower* of cost or market. Therefore, for Macro Toy Company in Exhibit 12-1, the actual market value of plant and equipment might be $5 million and the actual market value of inventories might be $450,000, even though the figures shown on the balance sheet are $1.6 million and $350,000, respectively. Furthermore, the debentures shown on the balance sheet at $400,000 may have a market value of, say, only $350,000 (that is the company could retire the bonds by buying them in the market for only $350,000).[12]

Similar observations apply to the income statement. The quantities shown on the income statement are not actually cash flows in the period covered by the income statement (for example, the year 1987 in Exhibit 12-2), but, instead, are amounts computed according to generally accepted accounting principles. For example, in Exhibit 12-2, although depreciation is included as a general and administrative expense, depreciation is not an actual outlay during 1987. Rather, it is some percentage of what was spent on plant and equipment in past periods. Similarly, net income shown on the income statement is an amount computed according to generally ac-

[11] On the use of multiple ratios and ratio changes over time see E. I. Altman, "Financial Ratios, Discriminant Analysis and the Prediction of Corporate Bankruptcy" *Journal of Finance* (September 1968), pp. 589–609; W. H. Beaver, "Market Prices, Financial Ratios, and the Prediction of Failure," *Journal of Accounting Research* (Autumn 1968), pp. 179–192; B. Lev, *Financial Statement Analysis: A New Approach* (Englewood Cliffs, N.J.: Prentice-Hall, 1974); and G. Foster, *Financial Statement Analysis* (Englewood Cliffs, N.J.: Prentice-Hall, 1978).

[12] The $400,000 shown on Macro's balance sheet in Exhibit 12-1 is the amount Macro borrowed when it issued the debentures. If, on balance sheet date December 31, 1987, interest rates are much higher than the 7 percent rate on the bonds, the bonds would sell in the market for much less than $400,000. On bond values and market interest rates, see Chapter 21.

cepted accounting principles. This net income is usually not, for example, equal to the dividends paid during the year or to the change in the shareholders' wealth during the year. The change in shareholders' wealth during the year equals the dividends *plus* capital gains (change in the market value of the company stock) for that year.

What does all this mean for ratio analysis? First, we should note that, except for long-term assets like plant and equipment, balance sheet values for assets and liabilities are usually "in the ball park" and are therefore good rough measures of actual asset and liability magnitudes. Ratios based only on these values are therefore generally quite useful. Whenever long-term assets are included in a ratio, though, market values for those assets should also be obtained unless there is good reason to believe that the balance sheet figures approximate true market value. Market values for assets are often shown as supplementary information on the balance sheet.

Second, although income statement net income is only one version of income (it is conventional historical cost income computed under generally accepted accounting principles), it is useful as a very rough guide for assessing and comparing companies. It is not the only guide, however. Another basis of evaluation is funds flow, which we discuss later in this chapter.[13]

DU PONT SYSTEM

Around World War I the DuPont Company introduced a method of financial analysis that has won general recognition for its usefulness and has, in one form or another, been adopted by most major United States firms. Its purpose is to provide management with a measure of performance in the form of a return on investment, or ROI. Two common versions of ROI are net income to total assets, Eq. (12-1) below, and return on equity, Eq. (12-2) below (this is the same return on equity discussed earlier).

$$\text{ROI (total assets)} = \frac{\text{sales}}{\text{total assets}} \times \frac{\text{net income}}{\text{sales}} = \frac{\text{net income}}{\text{total assets}} \tag{12-1}$$

$$\text{ROI (equity)} = \frac{\text{sales}}{\text{total assets}} \times \frac{\text{total assets}}{\text{stockholders' equity}} \times \frac{\text{net income}}{\text{sales}}$$

$$= \frac{\text{net income}}{\text{stockholders' equity}} \tag{12-2}$$

The issues of interest here are: Which of the two above equations is more useful? How can the firm control its ROI if it is too low? And, perhaps most important, how good a measure of performance is ROI?

If a choice is to be made between the two ROI equations, the second

---

[13] In addition to conventional historical cost income, the accounting profession has developed two other income measures, current cost income and general price level adjusted income (also referred to as historical cost–constant dollar income). Still other bases for evaluation that are used are current and forecasted firm dividends and current and forecasted firm operating cash flow. As a practical matter, ratio analysis based on the balance sheet and income statement (as described in the chapter) is still the most widely used method of evaluation. It is likely, though, that techniques using actual cash flows rather than income statement net income will become increasingly important in the future.

should be selected. Net income is the return to those providing *equity* capital, that is, the dollar return on equity. The proper measure of return *on total assets* is *not* net income divided by total assets [Eq. (12-1)] but is net income *plus* interest on debt divided by total assets (this is the return on total assets ratio that was discussed earlier in this chapter). Although Eq. (12-1) is often used in practice, it is very misleading and can produce results at variance with Eq. (12-2) and with the return on total assets ratio described earlier (see page 394). Indeed, it is easily shown that one company can have a greater return on equity and a greater total return (net income + interest) on total assets than another firm but still have a lower ROI using Eq. (12-1) because the latter firm—the one with the higher ROI using (12-1)—has less debt.[14] Our conclusion is that if we want to measure return on total assets, we should use the (net income + interest)/total assets ratio previously described in this chapter. On the other hand, if we wish to use net income as the numerator in an ROI index of performance, then we are interested in return on net worth and we should use Eq. (12-2), which is also a valid measure of performance.

Can the firm raise its ROI by increasing its assets turnover (sales/total assets) or by increasing its margin on sales (net income/sales)?[15] Assets turnover is dependent on the company's line of business. Retailers such as grocery stores and automobile dealers generally have high assets turnovers, whereas utilities, real estate-based service companies (such as hotels), and the capital-intensive manufacturers ordinarily have relatively low assets turnovers. Assets turnover tends to decline as the period of time required for the company to produce the product increases and as the proportion of costs going into physical plant increases. Table 12-2 presents ratios for several industries. Assets turnover can be increased by the more efficient use of available assets and the elimination of any excess capacity (unused plant). However, there is ordinarily an upper limit on assets turnover that is determined by the nature of the business.

Profit margin on sales is highly sensitive to pricing policy (which is influenced by competitive conditions), cost control, and the level of sales. Profit margin tends to increase with the level of sales because of the existence of fixed operating costs, such as depreciation on plant (this is referred to as "operating leverage," which is discussed in Chapter 13). Firms that keep per unit costs down and keep sales up are those with high sales profitability and usually high ROIs. Profit on sales generally varies more within a given industry than does assets turnover.

[14] For example, assume that firm A has profits of $1.1 million, assets of $10 million, and no debt; so, ROI (total assets), ROI (equity), and return on total assets are 11 percent. Compare this to firm B that has profits of $1 million, assets of $10 million, and debt of $4 million and pays $400,000 per year in interest. Firm B has an ROI (total assets) of 10 percent (less than firm A's) but has a higher ROI (equity) ($1 million/$6 million = $16\frac{2}{3}$ percent), and a higher return on total assets [($1 million + $400,000)/$10 million = 14 percent] than does firm A. Therefore, using ROI (total assets), firm A is outperforming firm B; but using ROI (equity) and return on total assets, firm B is outperforming firm A.

[15] As is clear from Eq. (12-2), ROI (equity) is also dependent upon the ratio of total assets to stockholders' equity. As shown in footnote 9, this ratio can be expressed in terms of the firm's debt ratio since we know from a balance sheet that total assets equal firm total liabilities plus stockholders' equity.

Regardless of the ROI measure that is used [Eq. (12-1), Eq. (12-2), or return on total assets described earlier in the chapter], ROI is only a very rough measure of performance. Only under very unusual circumstances will the actual rate of return being earned on the firm's assets equal the computed ROI. This is due to the definition of ROI, which uses accounting net income rather than cash flow and uses accounting depreciation in computing net income and net assets. Accounting depreciation is generally not equal to actual depreciation, and therefore net income and asset values are distorted. In spite of these deficiencies, it is true that ROI and the real rate of return tend to move together; a high ROI over several accounting periods ordinarily means a high real rate of return, and therefore, ROI is a rough index of performance. It can be used in comparing the relative performance of different firms or of divisions within a firm.

Since the mid-1960s, ROI has been the target of criticism as a basis of performance measurement. The central issue is that ROI is not a very accurate index of true rate of return earned on the company's assets. Although ROI is likely to survive for some time, it is also likely that the ROI concept will eventually be significantly altered or abandoned in favor of more useful measures of performance.

SOURCES OF INFORMATION ON FIRM AND INDUSTRY RATIOS

Data for computing the ratios of particular firms can be obtained from the annual and interim financial reports of the firm and from investment advisory services such as Moody's, Standard & Poor's, and Value Line. Brokerage houses, particularly those with large research departments, distribute financial information on all companies listed on the national exchanges and on some of the larger firms traded in the over-the-counter

TABLE 12-2
Ratios for various industries

Industry	$\dfrac{\text{Sales}}{\text{Total assets}}$	$\dfrac{\text{Sales}}{\text{Equity}^b}$	$\dfrac{\text{Income}^a}{\text{Sales}}$	$\dfrac{\text{Income}^a}{\text{Equity}^b}$	$\dfrac{\text{Debt}}{\text{Equity}^b}$
Grocery and meat retailers	5.84	15.0	1.4%	20.3%	1.5
Auto retailers— new and used	4.59	14.4	1.5%	21.6%	2.1
Motels, hotels, and tourist courts	.71	1.7	6.7%	11.4%	3.7
Water utilities	.22	.5	18.2%	9.1%	1.5
Detective agencies	3.43	7.3	2.8%	20.4%	3.8
Aircraft manufacturers	1.36	4.3	4.7%	20.2%	1.6

[a] Before-tax income.
[b] Total stockholders' equity.
Source: Robert Morris Associates.

market. Data can also be obtained from the firm directly. However, company officials may be reluctant to provide a great deal of help for fear of violating Securities and Exchange Commission "inside information" regulations or of disclosing information valuable to competitors.

There are several sources of information on the various sectors of the economy (for example, manufacturing, retailing, wholesaling) and on particular industries. Some of these sources are noted below.

Dun & Bradstreet   Dun & Bradstreet annually publishes key business ratios, including fourteen key ratios for firms in 125 types of retailing, wholesaling, manufacturing, and construction. A large sample of data is used in computing each of the ratios, and values are provided for the upper quartile (top fourth), median, and lowest quartile (bottom fourth).

Robert Morris Associates   In its annual statement studies, this association of bank loan officers provides ratio data on 156 lines of business activity. Eleven ratios are provided for each line with the information derived from the financial statements of firms that the banks deal with. A breakdown is provided showing the relationship of the ratio levels to firm size, although the companies in the samples tend to be large.

Trade Associations   Many trade associations compile data on financial ratios for various industries. Examples are the National Retail Furniture Association and the National Hardware Association.

Government Agencies   The Federal Trade Commission and the Securities and Exchange Commission jointly publish the *Quarterly Financial Report for Manufacturing Corporations*, which provides income statement and balance sheet data based upon a wide sample of manufacturing corporations. The data analysis is presented by industry groups and by firm asset size. The United States Department of Commerce and the Small Business Administration frequently publish studies covering large and small businesses, often including information on the standard financial ratios.

Other Sources   In its semiannual publication, *The Barometer of Small Business*, the Accounting Corporation of America provides income statement and balance sheet data for companies grouped by sales volume and by geographic region. The National Cash Register Company publishes information on expense percentages for firms in fifty-seven lines of business.

THE PURPOSES OF RATIO ANALYSIS

Ratios are a shortcut method of conveying certain crucial facts about a firm's operations and financial situation. When creditors provide funds to a firm, their primary interest is the future capacity of that company to repay the debt. This is true of short-term and long-term lenders. Before extending a loan, banks and other financial institutions generally apply ratio analysis to a prospective borrower's financial statements. The results of the analysis can be a determining factor in whether or not the loan is made. Ratio analysis is also among the tools used by Moody's and Standard & Poor's in rating the bonds of corporations.

Short-term creditors are particularly concerned with the firm's liquidity ratios, since the existing or near-term current assets are generally used to liquidate short-term debts. The overall condition of the firm, however, is also important, because the general financial health of a firm reflects its ability to repay even short-term debt. A strong current asset position can deteriorate rapidly if the company is losing money or is reducing its current assets through capital investment or payments to creditors or stockholders. On the other hand, even if the firm's current liquidity position is weak, if its long-run financial strength seems assured, short-term creditors will be protected as long as the company can borrow funds from long-term sources to pay off short-term liabilities. Therefore, the long-run outlook for the firm is relevant to short-term lenders to the extent that it affects the borrower's capacity to obtain additional outside financing as a means of repaying short-term debts.

Long-term lenders are concerned with any financial ratio that reflects the ability of the firm to meet long-run debt requirements. They are concerned with the liquidity ratios as a measure of both the firm's policy and ability with respect to liquidating short-term debt. The leverage ratios interest lenders because they reflect how much the company is presently in debt. Only in exceptional situations would the lender examine activity ratios, since for most lending purposes the profitability ratios offer a sufficiently good measure of the firm's operating effectiveness.

In evaluating the firm as an investment prospect, security analysts frequently examine the financial ratios. The analyst is interested in the desirability of the firm's stocks and bonds as an investment and in any information reflecting upon the firm's operating efficiency and financial strength. For regulated industries—for example, utilities, airlines, and railroads—financial ratios will be of interest to government agencies, both for the purpose of appraising the financial health of the regulated firm and for rate setting (setting the prices the firms may charge customers).

The management of a firm is concerned with all aspects of its operations and its relations with creditors, investors, and the government. The firm's ability to fulfill commitments to creditors (liquidity and leverage ratios) and to minimize costs (activity and profitability ratios) determines whether it will meet its ultimate objective of providing shareholders with a maximum return (reflected in the profitability ratios). Financial ratio analysis is therefore not just a device for outsiders. It is also useful as a managerial tool.

FUNDS FLOW ANALYSIS

The determination of the sources of cash flowing into the firm and the uses of that cash by the firm is referred to as sources and uses of funds analysis, or simply, as funds flow analysis. We are using "funds" here to refer to cash; later in this section we will examine funds flow using working capital as funds. Funds flow analysis provides a comprehensive view of a firm's receipts and outlays. It is particularly useful for monitoring how well a firm realizes its established plans for obtaining funds (from its sales as well as its lenders and investors) and for using those funds. Lenders are interested in a sources and uses statement because it provides an excellent overview of what transpired during the year.

Funds (cash) sources and uses are associated with specific types of changes:

Sources of funds involve:

1 A decrease in assets, or
2 An increase in liabilities, or
3 An increase in stockholders' equity (from a rise in paid-in capital or in retained earnings)

Uses of funds involve:

1 An increase in assets, or
2 A decrease in liabilities, or
3 A decrease in stockholders' equity (from a decrease in paid-in capital or in retained earnings)

Sources of generating cash are selling assets (decrease in assets), borrowing money (increase in liabilities), issuing and selling new shares (an increase in paid-in capital), or retaining net income earned rather than paying it out in dividends (an increase in retained earnings).

These funds would then be used in the following ways: to purchase assets (an increase in assets), to retire debt (a decrease in liabilities), to retire common or preferred stock by purchasing it or calling it in (decrease in paid-in capital and perhaps retained earnings), or a loss (negative income) incurred by the firm (a decrease in retained earnings).[16] Since every dollar must have a source and a use, the total sources of funds must equal the total uses of funds.

An example will help to clarify the concept of sources and uses of funds. In the illustration we will first use the **comparative balance sheet approach** for determining the sources and uses of funds during the period. This approach is based on changes in each balance sheet account from one statement date to the next. Exhibit 12-3 shows the balance sheet figures for the Macro Toy Company for the periods ending December 31, 1986, and December 31, 1987, and the differences between them are either sources or uses of funds. Notice that a decrease in assets is a source of funds, and an increase in assets is a use of funds. For example, Macro's net accounts receivable decreased by $150,000 during the year, reflecting collections on those accounts (a source of funds). Inventories rose by $70,000, and this rise involved a use of funds.

Increases in liabilities and owners' equity accounts are sources of funds and decreases are uses of funds. Exhibit 12-4 summarizes the transactions generating funds and requiring (using) funds.

For example, the $15,000 rise in Macro's accruals (amounts owed to

---

[16] A company is said to "call" its preferred stock or bonds when it exercises its right to buy back the security from the preferred stockholder or bondholder at a price specified in the initial preferred stock or bond contract (for details, see Chap. 21).

those providing goods or services to Macro) is a source of funds (funds in effect lent to Macro by the suppliers). The $25,000 decrease in Macro's mortgage bonds is a use of funds to pay off some of that debt.

The data from the sources and uses statement of Exhibit 12-3 suggest healthy performance and growth. Retained earnings increased by $170,000; debt declined by $40,000 (a decrease in accounts payable, mortgage bonds and debentures of $60,000, and an increase in accruals and federal income taxes payable of $20,000); and assets expanded by $150,000. These data used in conjunction with the other measures of financial position (for example, income statement, various ratios, and an assessment of the firm's business plans) would provide a complete picture of Macro's condition.

Two areas of confusion concerning the sources and uses statement should be mentioned. First, notice that net income and dividends do not appear as a source and a use of funds, respectively. This is because the two have been netted to produce the "increase in retained earnings" entry. The $170,000 of increase in retained earnings (source of funds) is really the difference between the net income of $200,000 (a source) and dividends of $30,000 (a use). The net income and dividends figures for Macro are shown in Exhibit 12-2 on page 382. Note that since we are illustrating the comparative balance sheet approach to funds flow analysis, we use balance

---

EXHIBIT 12-3
Macro Toy Company comparative balance sheets and sources and uses of funds (cash) statement (in thousands of dollars) for the year ended December 31, 1987

	Dec. 31, 1986	Dec. 31, 1987	Sources	Uses
Assets				
Cash	$ 100	$ 70	$ 30[a]	
Marketable securities	20	30		$ 10
Net accounts receivable	600	450	150	
Inventories	280	350		70
Gross plant and equipment	1,790	2,100		310
Allowance for depreciation	(440)	(500)	60	
Total assets	$2,350	$2,500		
Liabilities and stockholders' equity				
Accounts payable	$ 160	$ 150		10
Notes payable	200	200		
Accruals	15	20	5	
Federal income taxes payable	65	80	15	
Mortgage bonds	175	150		25
Debentures	425	400		25
Common stock paid-in capital	480	500	20	
Retained earnings	830	1,000	170	
Total liability and stockholders' equity	$2,350	$2,500	$450	$450

[a] The decrease in cash of $30,000 is indicated as a "source" in order to balance sources and uses since, ignoring the cash account, uses of cash minus sources of cash equal $30,000. We can view the $30,000 decline in cash as a source since it involves drawing $30,000 out of the firm's cash balances, and that is a "source" of cash.

sheet data (that is, we use retained earnings figures and not net income and dividends figures, which are income statement data). Of course, we could deviate somewhat from the comparative balance sheet approach in Exhibit 12-4 and include the $200,000 of net income as a source of funds, and the $30,000 in dividends as a use of funds, with no entry for the increase in retained earnings.

The second area of confusion relates to depreciation. Notice in Exhibit 12-2 on page 382 that depreciation expense was $100,000 during 1987, but the change in the allowance for depreciation indicated in Exhibit 12-3 on page 407 was only $60,000. The reason for this is that there were asset retirements during 1987 and, when the assets were retired, the allowance for depreciation associated with those retired assets (in the amount of $40,000) was written off the books (that is, cancelled).[17] The change in the allowance for depreciation during the period was therefore:

Allowance for depreciation, 12/31/86	$400,000
Depreciation expense during 1987	100,000
Allowance for depreciation associated with assets retired during 1987	(40,000)
Allowance for depreciation, 12/31/87	$460,000
Change in allowance for depreciation during 1987	$ 60,000

In the above comparative balance sheet analysis of Macro Toy Company we used cash as funds. We could also have done the analysis defining funds

---

[17] When an asset is disposed of or retired, the entry to the books is:

	Debit	Credit
Proceeds from asset dispositions	xxx	
Allowance for depreciation on retired asset	xxx	
Loss on disposition sale	xxx	
Gross book value of retired asset		xxx
Gain on disposition sale		xxx

For Macro Toy Company, assume that the total book value of the retired assets in the example was $70,000, the allowance for depreciation $40,000 (therefore a net book value of $30,000), the disposition sale proceeds $45,000, and therefore the gain on the sale $15,000 (proceeds − net book value). The entry would be:

	Debit	Credit
Proceeds from asset dispositions	$45,000	
Allowance for depreciation on retired assets	40,000	
Gross book value of retired assets		$70,000
Gain on disposition sale		15,000

EXHIBIT 12-4
Macro Toy Company statement of sources and uses of funds (cash), 1987 (in thousands of dollars)

Sources of funds (cash)		
Assets	Decrease in cash[a]	$ 30
	Decrease in accounts receivable	150
	Increase in allowance for depreciation	60
Liabilities	Increase in accruals	5
	Increase in income taxes payable	15
Owners' equity	Sales of additional common stock	20
	Increase in retained earnings	170
		$450

Uses of funds (cash)		
Assets	Purchase of marketable securities	$ 10
	Increase in inventories	70
	Increase in gross fixed assets	310
Liabilities	Decrease in accounts payable	10
	Decrease in mortgage bonds	25
	Decrease in debentures	25
		$450

[a] See footnote a, Exhibit 12-3.

as working capital (current assets minus current liabilities). Using working capital, we would have examined changes in all nonworking capital accounts (all accounts other than those that include current assets or current liabilities) and identified those changes as sources and uses of working capital.[18] Rather than explore the comparative balance sheet method of computing sources and uses of working capital, let's look at an approach for determining the sources and uses of funds which does not use comparative

[18] The reader is invited to perform this exercise. The sources of working capital in the example total $250,000 and this is computed by adding the $60,000, $20,000, and $170,000 amounts in the Sources column of Exhibit 12-3. The uses of working capital total $360,000 and this is computed by adding the $310,000, $25,000 and $25,000 in the Uses column of Exhibit 12-3. The net change in working capital for 1987 is therefore a decrease of $110,000 ($360,000 − $250,000). For a further explanation of the sources and uses of working capital, see the discussion below in the text on the statement of changes in financial position. Note that, although the computed change in working capital for 1987 will of course be the same whether the comparative balance sheet method (Exhibit 12-3) or the statement of changes in financial position method (Exhibit 12-5) is used, the total funds (working capital) uses will differ between the two methods. The total funds sources will differ also. With the former method, sources and uses total $250,000 and $360,000, respectively, whereas with the latter method (see Exhibit 12-5), sources and uses total $350,000 and $460,000. The differences arise because different accounts are used to obtain the $110,000 working capital change for the period.

balance sheets and which ordinarily uses working capital to define funds (although the method can also use cash to define funds). This alternative approach simply identifies the fund sources and uses and categorizes them as associated with operations (i.e., generated by net income and depreciation), with investment (i.e., with acquiring new assets or retiring old assets), and with capital transactions (with financing activities, for example, borrowing or retiring debt, selling new shares, paying dividends). The **statement of changes in financial position** itemizes the sources and uses of funds and is included in a company's annual report. Funds here are normally defined as working capital. Such a statement for Macro Toy Company is shown in Exhibit 12-5.

The sources and uses shown in Exhibit 12-5 indicate the changes in

EXHIBIT 12-5
Macro Toy Company statement of changes in financial position for the year ended December 31, 1987 (in thousands of dollars)

Sources of funds

Net income	$ 200
Depreciation	100
Disposal of plant (at net book value)[a]	30
Proceeds from sale of newly issued common stock	20
Total	$ 350

Use of funds

Dividends paid to stockholders	$ 30
Expenditures for plant and equipment	380
Retirement of mortgage bonds	25
Sinking fund payment on debentures	25
Total	$460

Decrease in working capital	$ 110
Working capital at beginning of year	560
Working capital at end of year	450

Increase (decrease) in working capital by element

Cash	$ (30)
Marketable securities	10
Net accounts receivable	(150)
Inventories	70
Accounts payable	10
Accruals	(5)
Federal income taxes payable	(15)
Decrease in working capital	$(110)

[a] See footnote 17, this chapter, for the details on the asset disposition. The proceeds from the disposition are $45,000, made up of $30,000 to cover the disposed assets' net book value, and a $15,000 gain (which is included in net income).

working capital caused by the change in the item indicated. For example, the $200,000 in net income was a source of working capital during the year.

Notice that since funds are working capital and not cash in Exhibit 12-5, it is necessary to provide a separate statement that breaks down working capital into its components in order to identify the component changes. This statement is shown at the bottom of Exhibit 12-5.

It should be pointed out that depreciation is not really a source of funds in the strict sense of the word but is instead, a *noncash charge* that was deducted in computing net income. Depreciation is only a bookkeeping entry and does not involve an expenditure of funds. Depreciation must therefore be added back to net income to get the funds generated by operations. The table below shows the relevant figures for Macro.

Funds from operations (aftertax)	$ 300,000
Depreciation (noncash charge)	(100,000)
Net income (net profit)	$ 200,000
Dividends (actual cash payment)	(30,000)
Increase in retained earnings	$ 170,000

In Exhibit 12-5, net income and depreciation are shown as funds sources, and dividends are separately indicated as a use. This contrasts with the comparative balance sheet approach of Exhibits 12-3 and 12-4 where income and dividends were netted against one another to produce a net source of $170,000 because of an increase in retained earnings.

As we will see in Chapter 14, which examines budgeting and forecasting, planning requires a forecast of future sales, capital transactions, and applications of funds in purchasing assets and retiring liabilities. Data based on forecasts can be used to prepare a projected or pro forma sources and uses statement. This statement is, in effect, a plan of action based on expected future cash inflows and outflows associated with production, sales, and existing contractual obligations. This statement summarizes a firm's expected financial activities for a specified time period. It is useful both as a planning tool for management and as an indication to creditors of the firm's future capacity to meet its debt obligations.

SUMMARY

Ratios provide the analyst with a set of summary measures of the firm's debt burden, operating efficiency, and profitability. There are four types of financial ratios:

Liquidity ratios indicate the firm's ability to fulfill short-run commitments.

Leverage ratios indicate the firm's debt burden.

Activity ratios indicate how effectively a firm uses assets.

Profitability ratios indicate the net returns on sales and assets.

The ratios are computed from data in a firm's balance sheet and income statement and then compared with levels considered desirable for the firm. In determining what ratio levels would be desirable for a particular company, the average ratios for that company's industry are a helpful guide, recognizing that adjustments should be made to fit the firm's special circumstances. For example, if the company is riskier than the industry average, it may warrant a higher liquidity and a lower debt ratio. Interrelationships between ratios should be examined since each ratio reflects only one aspect of the company. Weakness in one area may be compensated for by strength in another. Changes in ratios over time should be examined, since this information may reveal whether a problem is being solved or new remedies are needed. Deteriorating ratios may also signal difficulties not yet present but looming over the horizon. In computing financial ratios, balance sheet and income statement figures should be used with caution because they may not be the quantities appropriate for the ratio computations.

Data on individual firms, industries, and sectors of the economy are available from a variety of sources. These sources include the company being analyzed, private data collection services and financial institutions, trade associations, and government agencies.

Ratios can be helpful to the firm's short- and long-term creditors, to investors and investment analysts, to government agencies, and to the firm's management. Regardless of the user's purpose, however, ratios provide only a partial description of a firm and should be used in combination with other available information.

Funds flow analysis identifies all sources and uses of funds (cash or working capital) by the firm during the year. The sources and uses statement can be useful to management and to creditors, since it offers a comprehensive view of company activities.

QUESTIONS

1   It is said that a balance sheet measures stocks and an income statement measures flows. Explain.

2   What is a shortcoming of the current ratio as an indicator of the firm's ability to meet short-term obligations?

3   Why would a stockholder ordinarily prefer to see the firm with a current ratio of 3 than a current ratio of 10?

4   Sartre Meditation, Inc., is a nationwide chain of transcendental meditation training studios. Except for its small home office in Faroot, New York, Sartre rents all its studios under long-term leases; on the average, the leases currently have eight years to expiration. In computing all its financial ratios, neither the leased assets' values nor the lease obligations are included on the balance sheet; however, lease rentals are included as expenses on the income statement. Sartre owns its small home office building, and there is an outstanding mortgage on the building, which is the firm's only interest-bearing debt. The entire building is occupied by Sartre employees and no

place is rented to outside tenants. Seventy-five percent of Sartre's noninterest expenses are in wages to transcendental meditation experts, with most of the remaining 25 percent going for rent on the studios and advertising; depreciation on the home office building is negligible relative to total expenses. Sartre is generally viewed as being in a very risky type of business.

Harding Poker Chips and Playing Cards, Incorporated, has been in business since 1920 and has well-established, stable markets for its products and highly predictable costs. The firm's new manufacturing facility in Cleveland, Ohio, is its main fixed asset. Harding leases no assets but does have some long-term bonds outstanding.

Assume that Sartre and Harding are both expertly managed and each firm has financial ratios that are appropriate to this line of business. With no further information, what would you expect regarding the relative magnitudes of the ratios stated below for Sartre and Harding (for example, which firm has the larger debt ratio, etc.)? Explain your choice.

a Debt ratio
b Times interest earned
c Fixed-charges coverage
d Inventory turnover
e Fixed-assets turnover
f Total-assets turnover
g Return on total assets
h Return on net worth

5 Is it possible for a firm to have a consistently high profit margin on sales and yet be unable to meets its debt obligations?

6 Why is it important to analyze the trends in financial ratios as well as their levels at a particular point in time?

7 Sonny Smiles owns a surfboard manufacturing company, Surf, Inc., and is seeking additional capital from the bank for expansion. Sonny tells William Folde, the bank loan officer and Sonny's golf chum, "My firm is a winner and expansion is clearly justified. Why, over the past three years the profit on sales has averaged 1.3 times the industry average and the profit on total assets has averaged 1.1 times the industry level." Evaluate Sonny Smiles' argument.

8 What types of ratios would the following investors be particularly interested in? Explain.

a Banks specializing in short-term loans to commercial enterprises
b Pension funds wishing to purchase shares of common stock for their portfolios
c Individuals purchasing twenty-year bonds
d A firm's management

9 Why is depreciation considered a source of funds?

10 In analyzing a firm's balance sheets for December 31, 1987, and December 31, 1988, state whether each of the following is a source or a use of cash:

a Purchase of a new machine for $300,000
b $500,000 received from sale of land
c Sale of 2000 shares of common stock for $25 per share
d Issuance of $2,500,000 in twenty-year bonds

e Repurchase of 3000 shares of common stock
f Decrease of $5000 in the allowance for depreciation
g Income after taxes of $20,000
h Dividend payments of $0.50 per share on 100,000 shares out-
standing
i Decrease in accounts receivable resulting from a get tough policy
toward customers
j Change in inventory from $250,000 in 1987 to $340,000 in 1988

PROJECT

First refer to *Dun's Review* or to the Robert Morris Associates' *Statement*
and examine the financial ratios of different industries. Try to account for
the differences. Then obtain the financial statements of two firms in different industries and compare their ratios with the industry averages. Try
to account for the differences between your firms and the averages for
their industries.

PROBLEMS

1 The 1987 balance sheet and income statement for Roland, Inc., are
shown below. Also shown are the standards (target ratios) set by
management for the company. Compute the financial ratios for
Roland and compare them with the standards. Evaluate Roland's
performance using the standards.

Roland, Inc., balance sheet, December 31, 1987

Assets	
Cash	$ 120,000
Marketable securities	80,000
Accounts receivable, net	800,000
Inventories	1,000,000
Gross plant and equipment	2,000,000
Allowance for depreciation	(800,000)
Total assets	$3,200,000

Liabilities and equity	
Accounts payable	$ 300,000
Notes payable	500,000
Accruals	40,000
Long-term debt	860,000
Common stock	500,000
Retained earnings	1,000,000
Total liabilities and equity	$3,200,000

Roland, Inc., income statement for year ended December 31, 1987

Net sales		$6,000,000
Cost of goods sold		4,500,000
Gross margin on sales		$1,500,000
Operating expenses:		
Selling	$525,000	
General and administrative	375,000	
Total operating expenses		900,000
Operating income		$ 600,000
Other revenues		26,000
Gross income		$ 626,000
Less:		
Interest on long-term debt	$110,000	
Interest on notes payable	86,000	
Total interest		196,000
Income before taxes		$ 430,000
Federal income taxes		145,000
Income after taxes		$ 285,000

	Roland	Standard for comparison
Current ratio	—	2.1
Quick ratio	—	1.1
Debt ratio	—	.5
Times interest earned	—	4.0
Fixed-charges coverage	—	3.2
Inventory turnover[a]	—	7.0
Average collection period[a]	—	34 days
Fixed-assets turnover	—	4.0
Total-assets turnover	—	2.0
Net operating margin	—	12%
Profit margin on sales	—	5%
Return on total assets	—	16%
Return on equity	—	20%

[a] Based on balance sheet and income statement figures.

2 Handy Tools, Inc., is a chain of hardware stores in the Midwest. In
the 1970s and early 1980s Handy Tools expanded from one small
store in Princeville, Illinois, to one hundred twenty-five stores in
eight states. A large percentage of Handy Tools' sales is on credit.

During the mid-1980s Handy faced increased competition and declining profitability. Handy Tools ratios for the years 1984, 1985, and 1986 are shown in the table below.

	1984	1985	1986
Current ratio	2.4	2.7	2.6
Debt ratio	0.4	0.52	0.6
Inventory turnover	7	11	15
Average collection period (days)	43	41	40
Fixed-assets turnover	5	7	8
Total-assets turnover	3.5	4	5
Net operating margin, %	10	8	3
Profit margin on sales, %	6	5	3
Return on total assets, %	15	9	7
Return on equity, %	19	14	4

a Using the 1984 ratio levels as the standard of comparison, what ratios appear to have deteriorated by 1986?

b What might explain the ratio deterioration and what action might Handy Tools undertake to bring the ratios back in line?

3 Meteor Cabs pays 40 percent of its taxable income in taxes (taxable income = EBIT − interest expense). The table below shows the balance sheet figures and certain ratios for Meteor as of the end of each of the indicated three years.

Balance sheet	1984	1985	1986
Assets			
Current	$500	?	$1,500
Plant & equipment	$900	?	?
Liabilities			
Current	$200	$250	?
Long-term	?	?	?
Stockholders' equity	$600	$680	$ 700
Other data			
Current ratio	?	2.8	5.0
Debt ratio	?	0.60	0.72
EBIT	$280	?	$510
Interest expense	$130	$182	?
Taxes	?	$ 76	?
Times interest earned	?	?	1.7
Return on equity	?	17%	?

a Fill in the unknown amounts (signified by ?) in the table. Total
   sales over the 1984 to 1986 period remained constant.

b Assume that during the years 1984, 1985, and 1986 the firm sold
   new shares (no old shares were retired) in the following
   amounts:

Year	Funds received (paid-in capital) from selling new shares
1984	$100
1985	80
1986	15

Using your answer to **a**, determine the amount of dividends paid
during 1985 and 1986.

c Assume that you are analyzing Meteor's situation as of December
   31, 1986. Using your answers to **a** and **b**, what is your diagnosis
   of Meteor?

4 Penetro Inc., manufactures industrial detergents and cleansers. Penetro currently (December 31, 1986) has assets of $1,000,000, total
   liabilities (short-term and long-term combined) of $400,000, and
   equity of $600,000. Penetro's 1986 income statement is shown below.

Penetro, Inc., income statement for year ended December 31, 1986

Net sales		$900,000
Cost of goods sold		500,000
Gross margin on sales		$400,000
Operating expenses:		
Selling	$ 60,000	
General and administrative	100,000	
Lease payments	40,000	
Total operating expenses		200,000
Operating income		$200,000
Less interest on debt		50,000
Income before taxes		$150,000
Federal income taxes (40%)		60,000
Net income		$ 90,000
Dividends		50,000
Increase in retained earnings		$ 40,000

Penetro's management has decided to undertake immediately (on January 1, 1987) a major expansion. The firm will issue $500,000 of new
equity and $500,000 of new debt (interest rate of 12% per annum) to

raise the funds to purchase another chemical company for cash (the purchased company has no debt). After the expansion the firm will have to make annual sinking fund payments of $50,000. Penetro's 1987 pro forma income statement (including income from the purchased company) is shown below.

Penetro, Inc., pro forma income statement for year ended December 31, 1987

Net sales		$2,000,000
Cost of goods sold		1,000,000
Gross margin on sales		$1,000,000
Operating expenses:		
Selling	$140,000	
General and administrative	100,000	
Lease payments	40,000	
Total operating expenses		280,000
Operating income		$ 720,000
Less interest on debt		120,000
Income before taxes		$ 600,000
Federal income taxes (40%)		240,000
Net income		$ 360,000
Dividends		160,000
Increase in retained earnings		$ 200,000

a What times interest earned ratio and fixed-charges coverage ratio are implied for 1987 by Penetro's pro forma 1987 income statement and the other information provided above?

b What are the 1986 and 1987 profitability ratios for Penetro that are implied by the 1986 income statement, the 1987 pro forma income statement, and other information provided above? Use the December 31, 1986, equity to compute the 1986 profitability ratios, and use the December 31, 1987, equity to compute the 1987 profitability ratios.

5 Scan Technologies, Inc., manufactures geological equipment. Although Scan's sales have increased each year from 1983 to 1986, profits have remained very low. Furthermore, future sales for 1987 and beyond are highly uncertain because of the entry of new competition into the field. In comparison with other companies in the same industry, Scan Technologies, Inc., is smaller, less well established, and consequently a riskier enterprise. However, except for Scan's greater sales uncertainty, Scan is very similar to other companies in the industry (in terms of personnel, types of products, and methods of production). The industry is growing steadily and is composed mostly of competitive, well-managed firms.

   a Compute the key ratios for Scan for the years 1983 through 1986. (See tables on pages 419–420).

b Graph the trends in each of the ratios.

c Comment on any strengths or weaknesses you found in *a* and *b*.

d What changes do you recommend to improve Scan's condition?

Scan Technologies, Inc., comparative end-of-year balance sheets (all figures in $000's)

	1983	1984	1985	1986
Assets				
Current assets				
Cash	$ 20	$ 37	$ 30	$ 32
Securities	10	3	5	0
Accounts receivable, net[a]	32	41	45	54
Inventories[a]	88	112	119	134
Total current assets	$ 150	$ 183	$ 199	$ 220
Fixed assets				
Gross plant and equipment	$ 530	$ 620	$ 710	$ 830
Reserve for depreciation	(78)	(96)	(116)	(152)
Net plant and equipment	$ 452	$ 524	$ 594	$ 678
Total assets	$ 602	$ 707	$ 793	$ 898
Liabilities				
Current liabilities				
Accounts payable	$ 18	$ 29	$ 45	$ 51
Accrued wages & salaries	12	15	18	19
Taxes payable	14	16	20	18
Bank loan (10.0%)	15	44	57	59
Total current liabilities	$ 59	$ 104	$ 140	$ 147
Long-term liabilities				
Mortgage (7.5%, 20 yr)	$ 96	$ 88	$ 78	$ 67
Debentures (12%)	60	60	60	60
Subordinated bonds (12%)	75	125	175	275
Total long-term liabilities	$ 231	$ 273	$ 313	$ 402
Total liabilities	$ 290	$ 377	$ 453	$ 549
Stockholders' equity				
Stockholders' equity				
Common stock ($10 par)	$ 150	$ 150	$ 150	$ 150
Additional paid-in capital	50	50	50	50
Retained earnings	112	130	140	149
Total stockholders' equity	$ 312	$ 330	$ 340	$ 349
Total liabilities and stockholders' equity	$ 602	$ 707	$ 793	$ 898

[a] Accounts receivable at end of 1982 were $28,000. Total inventory at end of 1982 was $72,000.

Scan Technologies, Inc., comparative income statements (all figures in $000's)

	1983	1984	1985	1986
Net sales	$840	$980	$1,020	$1,210
Cost of goods sold	691	803	828	1,002
Gross margin on sales	$149	$177	$ 192	$ 208
Operating expenses:				
Selling	$ 30	$ 33	$ 36	$ 48
General and administrative	42	45	58	50
Lease payments	20	20	20	20
Total operating expenses	$ 92	$ 98	$ 114	$ 118
Operating income	$ 57	$ 79	$ 78	$ 90
Other revenues:				
Income from securities	$ 5	$ 6	$ 4	$ 1
Royalties	2	2	3	3
Total other revenues	$ 7	$ 8	$ 7	$ 4
Gross income	$ 64	$ 87	$ 85	$ 94
Other expenses:				
Interest on bank loan	$ 0	$ 4	$ 5	$ 7
Interest on mortgage	8	8	7	7
Interest on debentures	7	7	7	7
Interest on subordinated bonds	7	13	25	31
Research	10	15	21	24
Total other expenses	$ 32	$ 47	$ 65	$ 76
Net income before taxes	$ 32	$ 40	$ 20	$ 18
Federal income taxes (at 50%)	16	20	10	9
Net income available to shareholders	$ 16	$ 20	$ 10	$ 9
Dividends	$ 1	$ 2	$ 0	$ 0
Increase in retained earnings	15	18	10	9

1986 industry ratios

Ratio	Industry 1986 level
Current ratio	1.50
Quick ratio	0.50
Debt ratio	0.40
Times interest earned	5.12
Fixed-charges coverage	2.00
Inventory turnover	7.00
Average collection period (days)	15.00
Fixed-assets turnover	2.50
Total-assets turnover	1.75
Net operating margin	10%
Profit margin on sales	5%
Return on total assets	9%
Return on equity	10%

6 Elaine Percy has the following target ratios that she wants her firm, Camden Products, to achieve:

Debt-equity ratio = 0.25
Inventory turnover ratio = 5
Return on equity = 22.5 percent
Profit margin on sales = 10 percent
Current ratio = 3
Fixed-asset turnover ratio = 3
Average collection period = 36 days

In computing the average collection period, a 360-day year was assumed. Also, all ratios using balance sheet figures are computed here using December 31, 1987, balance sheet figures. Camden's sales are entirely on a credit basis and they total $900,000 per year. Assuming that Camden has achieved the above targets in 1987, fill in the blanks in the balance sheet below.

Camden Products balance sheet for the year ended December 31, 1987			
Cash	$30,000	Accounts payable	_____
Accounts receivable	_____	Short-term notes	
Inventory	_____	payable	$20,000
Total current assets	_____	Current liabilities	_____
Fixed assets	_____	Long-term debt	_____
		Equity	_____
Total assets	_____	Total liabilities and equity	_____

7 The balance sheet, income statement, and certain other relevant information for Reggie Corporation, a manufacturer of quality sports apparel, are shown below and on page 422. Study the information given and then solve the problems that follow.

Additional Information:

Dividends paid = $12,000
Market price per share for common stock (year-end) = $10.50
Quick ratio = 1.2
Working capital
  (current assets − current liabilities) = $100,000
Inventory turnover ratio = 5.5
Average collection period
  (assuming 360 day year) = 36 days

$$\frac{\text{Total liabilities}}{\text{Stockholders' equity}} = 1.75$$

a Complete the balance sheet and income statement (fill in appropriate data where question marks are shown).
b Calculate the following:

(1) Current ratio
(2) Earnings per share
(3) Return on common stockholders' equity (%)

(4) Fixed-assets turnover
(5) Times interest earned
(6) Net operating margin (%)

Reggie Corporation balance sheet, December 31, 1986

Assets

Cash	?
Marketable securities	$ 35,000
Accounts receivable (net of bad debt allowance)[a]	?
Inventory[a]	?
Total current assets	?
Plant and equipment (net of depreciation)	?
Total assets	?

Liabilities

Accounts payable[a]	?
Notes payable—bank (12%)	$ 50,000
Other current liabilities	10,000
Total current liabilities	?
Long-term debt (10%)	$180,000
Common stock (40,000 shares, $1 par)	40,000
Retained earnings	120,000
Total liabilities and stockholders' equity	?

[a] Monthly levels of accounts receivable, inventory, and accounts payable have not varied significantly during the year; average levels and end-of-year levels are therefore approximately equal.

Reggie Corporation income statement for year ended December 31, 1986

Sales (all credit sales)	$600,000
Cost of goods sold	?
Gross profit	?
Selling and administrative expense	100,000
Operating income	?
Interest expense	24,000
Income before taxes	?
Income tax (50% tax rate)	?
Net income	?

---

8 The 1986 and 1987 balance sheets for Inland Adhesives, Inc., are

shown below. Indicate whether each balance sheet change is a
source or a use.

a Prepare a sources and uses of funds statement for Inland Adhesives, Inc., using the comparative balance sheet approach.

b Assume that Inland Adhesives, Inc., had income after taxes of
$300,000 in 1987. Explain the change in retained earnings shown
above from $350,000 to $450,000.

c What transaction or transactions could account for the change in
gross fixed assets and in the allowance for depreciation?

Inland Adhesives, Inc., comparative balance sheets (in thousands of dollars)				
	Dec. 31, 1986	Dec. 31, 1987	Source	Use
Assets				
Cash	$ 60	$ 180	_____	_____
Marketable securities	90	140	_____	_____
Net accounts receivable	240	180	_____	_____
Inventories	250	360	_____	_____
Gross fixed assets	780	720	_____	_____
Allowance for depreciation	(220)	(180)	_____	_____
Total assets	$1,200	$1,400	_____	_____
Liabilities and owners' equity				
Accounts payable	$ 150	$ 270	_____	_____
Notes payable	200	100	_____	_____
Accruals	100	180	_____	_____
Long-term debt	300	250	_____	_____
Common stock	100	150	_____	_____
Retained earnings	350	450	_____	_____
Total liabilities and owners' equity	$1,200	$1,400	_____	_____

9 Using the data from problem **8**, also assume that the following figures apply to Inland Adhesives, Inc., for the year ended December
31, 1987 (in thousands of dollars):

Net income	$300
Depreciation expense	$200
Disposal (retirement of old assets at net book value)	$ 60
Proceeds from new shares issued	$ 50
New long-term borrowing	$100
Retirement of old debt	$150
Expenditures for new plant and equipment	$240
Dividends paid to stockholders	?

a What were the dividends paid during 1987?

b Prepare a Statement of Changes in Financial Position for the year ended December 31, 1987, for Inland (see Exhibit 12-5 in the text).

c If the expenditure for new plant and equipment of $240,000 were not indicated above, could you determine that figure from the other information that is provided in the question? Explain.

A company's financial statements are an extremely important source of information about the business. The statements should indicate where the company is now, where it has been, and provide useful clues about where it is going. Without the kind of information provided by financial statements, it is almost impossible to evaluate a company. This reliance on financial statements makes it critically important that the data provided are accurate, that is, truthful, and, equally important, that the variables being measured are relevant to the financial statement user's purposes.

GARBAGE IN,
GARBAGE OUT

There is a familiar warning to computer users that computer analysis of bad data will produce poor results: garbage in, garbage out. Highly sophisticated financial analysts using inaccurate financial statement data will generally get misleading results. This can be very costly.

Bad information can be unintentionally or intentionally included in the financial statements. Unintentional errors are most likely in areas where judgment is required, for example, in valuing assets. An example is National Cash Register, the Dayton, Ohio, computer company that wrote off $135 million in obsolete inventory (inventory that some say should have long before been revalued). The result was a "big bath" represented by a $60 million loss in a single year.

The most notable cases of misleading financial statements provided by a company have involved fraud, usually without the knowledge of the company's auditors. A classic case involved the fraudulent overstatement of the inventories and accounts receivable of McKesson & Robbins, Incorporated for the year ended December 31, 1937. The fraud was engineered by the president of the corporation and several of

his subordinates. Phony invoices, advices, and other documents with fictitious vendors were prepared to conceal a cash outflow of nearly $25 million, only $3 million of which came back to McKesson in collection of receivables or other cash receipts. Although the auditors, Price Waterhouse & Co., were not involved in the fraud, their audit did fail to spot what had been going on. The accounting firm paid heavily for what happened: it returned over $500,000 in audit fees earned from 1933 to 1937.

History's most spectacular case of financial reporting fraud occurred in the early 1970s and involved the complicity of some of the guilty company's auditors. From 1965 to 1972, the chairman and many members of the top management of Equity Funding Corporation of America and its main subsidiary, Equity Funding Life Insurance Company, created $2 billion of phony life insurance policies on nonexisting persons. The policies were then sold to other life insurance companies for cash and the returns from these sales were included in Equity Funding's growing reported earnings. The bogus assets Equity Funding created in this manner greatly exceeded the $75 million in total profits reported over its entire thirteen-year history. The implication is that the company, which had been the darling of Wall Street for many years, may very well have always been a losing operation— a shocking revelation, particularly to those who invested in the company on the basis of its 25 percent annual compound "earnings" growth record. Some of the auditors of Equity Funding were aware of the scheme and were eventually convicted for fraud, along with the involved Equity Funding executives.

What degree of assurance does the reader of an audited financial statement have that the auditors have made an honest effort to uncover any management attempts to distort the reported figures? It appears that fraud is clearly the exception, but it is impossible to know how many unexposed plots have succeeded. It is possible, however, to describe what auditors say they do and what responsibility they are willing to assume. Until recently, CPA firms held that their function was not to uncover management fraud but rather to ensure that the information provided in the financial statements was presented in accordance with generally accepted accounting principles. Since the late 1960s attitudes have changed and, although the CPA companies are not willing to assume responsibility for management dishonesty, the auditors do now employ auditing procedures specifically designed to detect fraud. They are especially cautious about a company showing certain danger signals, such as inadequate working capital or credit, numerous lawsuits (especially by the firm's shareholders), difficulties in collecting from important customers, and inadequate internal controls and auditing.

Although the alert auditor investigates any observed signs of management fraud, the accounting profession is probably right in stating that even a moderately clever management can fool the auditors if it makes a determined effort to do so. To adopt foolproof fraud detection auditing techniques to be applied to all companies, or even to just those companies showing danger signals, would be prohibitively costly. The conclusion for the financial statement user is that there are no guarantees. The only consolation is that it appears that fraud is the infrequent exception and not a common occurrence.

ACCOUNTING WIZARDRY

A good magician does not need a blindfolded audience to create illusions; a quick hand or a confusing sequence of events will do the trick. And the accounting does not need false data to blindfold the reader, proper arrangements and good combinations of numbers are often sufficient to produce the desired result. We can call this accounting wizardry: the appropriate selection of accounting principles to produce a particular conclusion. Accounting principles often permit more than one approach for treating a given financial event. It is this flexibility that allows the accountant wide discretion in computing a company's earnings or balance sheet figures. The accountant has discretion in allocating revenues or costs in such areas as officers' bonuses, revenue recognition on long-term projects, and the treatment of pension costs. Some other important examples follow.

Depreciation

A company can use one depreciation method on its financial statements and a different depreciation method for tax purposes. On the financial statements, for example, the company could maximize current earnings by minimizing depreciation with the straight-line method; at the same time it could use accelerated depreciation to reduce taxable income in order to minimize current taxes.

Inventory Valuation

Valuation of inventories used up during a period affects reported earnings. LIFO (last in, first out) assumes that the inventories sold during the period were the last inventories purchased, whereas FIFO (first in, first out) assumes that the inventories sold during the period were the oldest inventories in stock. In periods of rising inventory prices (such as during times of inflation), LIFO implies a higher value to inventories sold, a higher cost of goods sold, and therefore lower earnings than FIFO. It should be pointed out that with increasing inventory prices, the use of LIFO for tax purposes produces lower taxable income and therefore lower taxes. A firm should generally use LIFO during periods of increasing inventory prices. By law, if a company uses LIFO for tax purposes it must also use LIFO on its financial statements. Thus, if a company uses FIFO on its financial statements simply to report higher earnings, it must also use it in computing taxable income and must therefore pay higher taxes. Use of FIFO is a costly way to pump up reported earnings.

Research and Development Costs

In some instances accounting principles allow research and development costs to be expensed during the period incurred (that is, completely deducted as an expense) or capitalized (recorded as an asset to be depreciated over several years). Current earnings are greater if the research and development costs are capitalized rather than expensed.

Investment Tax Credit

When a firm receives an investment tax credit for acquiring assets during a period, it can either show the credit as a reduction in taxes paid during the period (the "flow-through" method) or it can amortize the credit over the life of the asset (the deferral method). For example, if a company buys an asset with a ten-year life for $1 million and receives a $100,000 tax credit, its financial statements can show a $100,000 reduction of current taxes. Alternatively, it can spread the $100,000 over a ten-year period, showing a $10,000 reduction in taxes each year. To maximize current aftertax income reported on the financial statements, the firm would use the flow-through method.

Implications for Financial Statement User

What does all this mean for the user of financial statements? First, it means that in interpreting a given year's earnings, the analyst should know which accounting principles were used. Were the computations done on a conservative or liberal basis and what are the implications for both current and future earnings? The notes to the financial statements generally indicate which accounting principles were used. However, it is often impossible to figure out what the figures would have been had different accounting principles been employed. This is an area in which the accounting profession has done a rather poor job.

Second, most accounting choices that increase one year's earnings will decrease the earnings in one or more future periods by the same amount. That is, accounting wizardry generally involves allocation of revenues and expenses to time periods so that more in one year means less in another year. This means that an overstatement of earnings for one period will usually result in an earnings understatement in one or more other periods. An implication is that examination of reported results for several consecutive time periods will ordinarily give a good picture of what the results on average would have been had different accounting choices been made. Therefore, evaluation of a company using financial statement figures should involve analysis of several years' results and not just the results for a single year.

We should point out that, although there is a great deal of room for mischief in managing earnings by making the appropriate accounting choices, the accounting profession in recent years has made an effort to encourage accurate and meaningful financial reporting. There has been an attempt to require that the accounting method used be the one that best fits the economic situation. Although there remains substantial opportunity for accounting wizardry, the possibilities are significantly less than they once were.

CURRENT VALUES VERSUS HISTORICAL VALUES

Financial statement figures are primarily historical-cost-based rather than current-cost-based. In most cases, balance sheet asset values equal that was paid for the asset (less accumulated depreciation) and not what the assets are currently worth. Liabilities are generally shown at the amount that was borrowed, not what would be required to retire the debt.[1] The result is that balance sheet book values may not indicate the actual financial position of the company.

The income statement has failings similar to those of the balance sheet. Revenues and costs are computed on an accrual basis using historical quantities. Thus, depreciation—which is included among expenses—may not equal what is actually being spent to replace plant and equipment. Cost of goods sold is based on the historical cost of inventories used up during the period and not on the inventories' current replacement cost. In short, accounting income (that is, conventional historical cost accounting income) does not equal cash flow and does not equal economic income (the increase in the shareholders' wealth during the period from holding the firm's shares). Interestingly, though,

there is abundant evidence that a company's share price rises when its accounting income turns out to be greater than expected, and falls when its accounting income turns out to be less than expected.[2] This implies that accounting income contains information which investors find highly useful in valuing shares. There is also evidence that share price does not permanently react to unexpected changes in income or income forecasts that do not have cash flow implications (e.g., a change in depreciation method for firm financial statement reporting but not for computing income taxes); that is, investors apparently "see through" accounting manipulations which do not have real implications for the firm's financial position.[3]

Many of the problems with accounting figures (both balance sheet

---

[1] For example, assume that in 1960 ABC Company issued $5 million of forty-year bonds at face value (i.e., for $5 million) and that the bonds had a coupon yield of 5 percent per year. Because of much higher interest rates in 1986, the bonds might have a 1986 market value of only $3 million. This means that ABC Company could go into the market and buy back its bonds and retire the debt for approximately $3 million, not the $5 million shown on the balance sheet.

[2] See, for example, R. Ball, "Anomalies in Relationships Between Securities' Yields and Yield Surrogates," *Journal of Financial Economics*, 6 (June 1978), pp. 103–126; H. A. Latane and C. P. Jones, "Standardized Unexpected Earnings—1971–1977," *Journal of Finance*, 34 (June 1979), pp. 717–724; W. H. Beaver, R. Clarke, and W. F. Wright, "The Association Between Unsystematic Security Returns and the Magnitude of Earnings Forecast Errors," *Journal of Accounting Research*, 17 (Autumn 1979), pp. 316–340; D. Givoly and J. Lakonishok, "The Information Contents of Financial Analysts' Forecasts of Earnings," *Journal of Accounting and Economics*, 1 (December 1979), pp. 165–185.

[3] See, for example, T. R. Archibald, "Stock Market Reaction to Depreciation Switchback," *The Accounting Review*, 47 (January 1972), pp. 22–30; R. S. Kaplan and R. Roll, "Investor Evaluation of Accounting Information: Some Empirical Evidence," *Journal of Business*, 45 (April 1972), pp. 225–257; W. H. Beaver and R. E. Dukes, "Interperiod Tax Allocation and δ-Depreciation Methods: Some Empirical Evidence," *The Accounting Review*, 48 (July 1973), pp. 549–559; and S. Sunder, "Stock Price and Risk Related to Accounting Changes in Inventory Valuation," *The Accounting Review*, 50 (April 1975), pp. 305–316.

and income statement) are due to inflation and this has not gone unnoticed by the accounting profession. Statement of Financial Accounting Standards No. 33 requires large corporations to present certain inflation-adjusted data (including two additional measures of income—historical cost constant dollar income and current cost income) in their financial statements. This new disclosure requirement is not a complete solution to the problem, one of which is to provide cash flow rather than just accrual amounts. But it is a significant step in the right direction.

What is the implication for the financial manager who uses accounting data to do financial analysis (including ratio analysis)? It is that accounting figures ordinarily provide useful but very rough measures of financial position and performance. Comparisons based on these figures are far from meaningless. However, the figures are only approximations of what we are really interested in, namely the actual current dollar amounts (market values, cash flows, etc.) which are relevant in making financial decisions.

C H A P T E R

13

**BREAK-EVEN
ANALYSIS
AND THE
MEASUREMENT
OF LEVERAGE**

The level and risk of a company's profits are very important to its stock-holders and determine the value of the company's shares. This chapter is concerned with the firm's underlying cost factors that affect profits. Break-even analysis, the first topic to be discussed, examines the relationship between output, profits, and costs. It also considers pricing and cost structure changes that can contribute to greater profitability. The latter half of the chapter discusses leverage, which is the existence of fixed costs (costs that do not vary with output) among the company's costs. Operating leverage is due to the existence of fixed production costs, whereas financial leverage is due to the presence of fixed financing costs (interest). Both operating leverage and financial leverage are major determinants of the level and variability of company profits.

**BREAK-EVEN
ANALYSIS**

Like ratio and funds flow analysis, break-even analysis is used to analyze financial data. Break-even analysis deals with the relationship of profits to costs, to pricing policy, and to volume of output.[1] A knowledge of this relationship enables a financial manager to maximize income (profits) by specifying production methods, pricing, and output volume.

Break-even analysis is primarily concerned with:

1 How income varies with changes in sales volume (if cost structure and output prices are unchanged)
2 How income varies with changes in costs and prices

Net income (that is, aftertax income) equals revenues from sales less all costs, including depreciation, interest on debt, and taxes, as well as labor, materials, advertising, and other current expenses. By comparing the income from different levels of output, under different cost and price structures, the financial manager can choose the best strategies for investment (which products to produce and how) and for marketing (lower sales price versus increased advertising, for example).

We will first discuss the nature of production costs and then proceed to break-even analysis.

**Fixed and Variable
Costs**

Fixed costs are expenditures that *do not vary as output changes*. The cost of office and factory space and equipment, the cost of an executive staff to oversee operations and a production staff to supervise production, real estate property taxes, etc., are usually fixed costs.

Variable costs are expenditures that *vary with the level of output*. Production materials, direct labor, power for production equipment, shipping services, and office materials used directly for purchasing and billing are ordinarily variable costs.

[1] Break-even analysis can be used to examine the relationship of revenues and operating costs (ignoring financial costs such as interest); such an analysis deals with the impact of sales fluctuations on earnings before interest and taxes. The discussion presented here will deal, instead, with the impact of sales fluctuations on the firm's pretax and aftertax income (after deducting interest).

431

CHAPTER 13
**Break-even analysis
and the measurement
of leverage**

Most costs may be classified as variable or fixed depending upon any of the following:

1   The magnitude of the change in output
2   The amount of time required to change the cost
3   The length of time the change in output is expected to last

If the expenditure varies with output, the cost is variable; if it does not, the cost is fixed. Let's consider each of these cases.

1   Some costs will be fixed in the long and short run, but only for certain ranges of output. For example, a machine may have a production capacity of 50,000 units annually and be the most economical machine to use for any output between 30,000 and 50,000 units. Over the range of 30,000 to 50,000 units, machine cost is fixed; that is, the same machine is used and neither more nor fewer machines are employed. Outside the 30,000-to-50,000 range, machine cost may be variable. Thus, a rise above 50,000 units annually will necessitate additional machinery; machine cost will therefore vary if output rises above 50,000 units.

2   Some costs may be varied if enough time is available but are fixed (cannot be varied) in the short run. For example, a new manufacturing plant may take three years to construct. Existing plant capacity may be 100,000 units of output annually, with production above 70,000 units requiring much higher labor costs due to round-the-clock operation and overtime pay for workers. The company experiences an increase in annual demand from 55,000 to 95,000 units. In the short run (less than three years), the size of the plant cannot change; production plant cost (depreciation, property taxes, etc.) is fixed over the three-year period, even though output has risen from 55,000 to 95,000 units. In the long run (more than three years), the company will expand its plant capacity so as to produce the 95,000 units more economically; in the long run, plant costs are variable.

3   Some changes in output can result in fixed or variable costs. For example, if a decrease in output is considered temporary (perhaps less than one year), a company may be reluctant to reduce its executive staff or certain segments of its production staff. The cost of their salaries is considered fixed. However, if the downturn is permanent, the firm may decide to reduce its staff or liquidate its plant and equipment. These costs are then variable because they change with output. Similarly, the machine discussed in **1** above may be the most economical means of producing 30,000 to 50,000 units annually; but, if yearly output were to fall permanently below 30,000 units, a smaller machine might be warranted. In the long run, machine cost would be variable for output declines to below 30,000 units annually.

Break-even analysis can be applied for short-run changes in output, in which case some costs are fixed due to the time considerations in **2** and **3**, or for long-run changes, in which case such costs are variable. In the discussion below, we will assume that output variations are short run and

some costs are fixed, either because they can't be changed in the short run
(as in **2**) or because it isn't profitable to change them simply to respond to
temporary changes in output (as in **3**).

The costs considered in our discussion of break-even analysis which
will be fixed and variable are:

    Fixed costs:
        Depreciation on plant and equipment
        Minimum maintenance costs on plant and equipment
        Salaries and wages of executive and research staff
        Rentals on long-term lease agreements
        Office expenses
        Advertising expenses (if not dependent on output)
        Interest on debt
    Variable costs:
        Direct labor wages
        Materials costs
        Sales commissions and salaries

To illustrate the cost relationships, assume that Arcan Corporation has
the fixed costs and variable costs listed in Exhibit 13-1.

Arcan's fixed costs are $200,000; whatever output during the year may
be, these costs are unaffected. For each unit of output, the firm must incur
an additional $10 of cost; that is, variable cost is $10 per unit. Arcan's total
variable cost depends on the level of output. Exhibit 13-2 shows the costs
and sales revenues for Arcan at various output levels. Figure 13-1 illustrates
these data. The diagonal total cost line in Figure 13-1 shows the total costs

---

EXHIBIT 13-1
Costs of Arcan Corporation

Fixed costs:

Depreciation	$100,000
Plant maintenance	15,000
Executive salaries	40,000
Lease rentals	8,000
Office expense	12,000
Advertising	5,000
Interest on debt	20,000
Total	$200,000

Variable costs per unit of output:

Labor	$ 3.00
Materials	5.00
Sales commissions	2.00
Total	$10.00

EXHIBIT 13-2
Arcan Corporation cost and profit schedule

Units sold x	Total fixed cost F	Total variable cost vx	Total cost $F + vx$	Sales px	Pretax income (loss) Profit[a] (loss) (sales − total cost)	Net income (loss)[a]
0	$200,000	$ 0	$200,000	$ 0	$(200,000)	$(100,000)
10,000	200,000	100,000	300,000	150,000	(150,000)	(75,000)
20,000	200,000	200,000	400,000	300,000	(100,000)	(50,000)
30,000	200,000	300,000	500,000	450,000	(50,000)	(25,000)
40,000	200,000	400,000	600,000	600,000	0	0
50,000	200,000	500,000	700,000	750,000	50,000	25,000
60,000	200,000	600,000	800,000	900,000	100,000	50,000
70,000	200,000	700,000	900,000	1,050,000	150,000	75,000

Unit selling price p = $15.00
Fixed costs F = $200,000
Unit variable cost v = $10.00
Total cost $(F + vx)$ = $200,000 + $10x
Break-even point = 40,000 units

a Net income refers to aftertax income. We assume a tax rate of 50%. With a loss, we assume a tax credit equal to the tax rate times the loss (a tax loss carryback)

FIGURE 13-1

Cost and sales relationships and the break-even point.

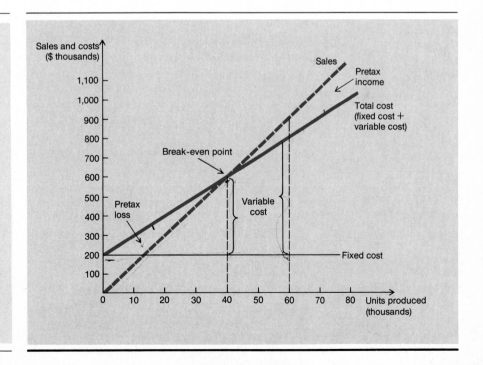

(fixed plus variable) for each level of output. This line corresponds to the total cost column in Exhibit 13-2.

Income and Interest Cost

Break-even analysis can be used to examine the effect of changes in sales on income (either before-tax or aftertax) or on earnings *before* interest and taxes (EBIT). The impact on pretax income and aftertax income (earnings after deducting interest and taxes) will be examined here. Pretax income equals revenues minus all fixed and variable costs; fixed costs (signified as F) include depreciation *and interest*, since both of these are deducted in computing a company's income. Aftertax income (i.e., net income) equals pretax income minus income taxes paid by the firm.

Interest is a fixed cost that arises from **financial leverage** (borrowing); interest is a financial fixed cost. Lease payments are treated here as operating fixed costs.[2] The other fixed costs listed in the previous section are also operating fixed costs. Operating fixed costs create **operating leverage**. Operating leverage is the presence of operating fixed costs in the firm's cost structure. Thus, financial leverage arises from financial fixed costs and operating leverage arises from operating fixed costs. Fluctuations in income due to sales variations are affected by *both* financial leverage and operating leverage, since *all* fixed costs (both financial and operating) are deducted in determining income. Therefore, in break-even analysis using income, we deduct interest as a fixed cost.

In the later sections of this chapter, we will *not* deduct debt interest as a fixed cost in examining operating leverage, since interest is not an operating cost. However, we will deduct interest as a fixed cost when we consider financial leverage and combined leverage (combination of operating and financial leverage).

Measuring Profitability

To calculate profitability using break-even analysis, revenue from sales must be compared with costs. Assume that Arcan sells its output at a price of $15 per unit. Total sales, costs, and income for each level of output are shown in Figure 13-1 and stated in Exhibit 13-2.

At what level of output should the firm operate for maximum profitability, and at which level must it operate in order to just "break even," that is, earn zero income? In answer to the first part, the firm will generally be somewhat uncertain as to the ultimate demand for its product. From Figure 13-1 and Exhibit 13-2, we can see that income increases as the number of units sold increases, assuming the unit variable cost of $10 and sales price of $15. Therefore, Arcan Corporation will seek to maximize its sales. But sales depend as much upon customer demand for the product as upon the willingness of a firm to sell the product. The firm may not be able to sell as much as it is capable of producing. Future demand is generally uncertain and subject only to an estimate.

What sales are necessary for Arcan to break even? We can see from

---

[2] Technically, lease payments are both financial *and* operating fixed costs; the "interest" portion (net return to the lessor) of the lease payment is a financial fixed cost to the lessee, and the rest of the lease payment, which is a return to the lessor to cover the cost (depreciation) of the asset, is an operating fixed cost to the lessee (is like depreciation).

435

CHAPTER 13
Break-even analysis
and the measurement
of leverage

Exhibit 13-2 that income is zero at sales of 40,000 units. This break-even point of 40,000 units is also illustrated in Figure 13-1 by the intersection of the total-cost and sales curves. Sales below 40,000 units mean losses, and sales above 40,000 units generate income.

Before analyzing the above problem algebraically, we should clearly understand what is being assumed about the relationship of costs and revenues to sales. We are assuming that certain costs are fixed (at $200,000) over the range of output being considered, that variable costs per unit ($10) are constant over the range of output, and that sales price per unit ($15) is fixed. Later in the chapter we will consider variations in sales price and the effect on the analysis if variable costs per unit change as output changes.

Determining the Break-Even Point

We can solve for the break-even point by trial and error (just by scanning the numbers in Exhibit 13-2 or by examining Figure 13-1) or algebraically. The following variables are needed for an algebraic solution:

x = number of units sold
F = fixed costs = $200,000
v = variable cost per unit = $10
p = sales price per unit = $15
x_b = level of x at the break-even point (break-even x)

We know that

Pretax income = total sales − total costs

$$= px - (vx + F)$$

$$= px - vx - F$$

$$= x(p - v) - F \tag{13-1}$$

At the break-even point, both pretax and net (aftertax) income are zero. Therefore, to solve for the break-even output x_b, set pretax income in Eq. (13-1) equal to zero and solve. Thus, using (13-1), at the break-even point

$$x_b(p - v) - F = 0$$

$$x_b = \frac{F}{p - v} \tag{13-2}$$

and, therefore

$$\text{Break-even } x = x_b = \frac{F}{p - v} = \frac{\$200,000}{\$15 - \$10} = 40,000 \text{ units}$$

Notice that 40,000 units is the same as the value determined by examining Exhibit 13-2 and Figure 13-1.

What if we want the break-even level of dollar sales? This is just the sales price p times the break-even point in units (x_b). That is,

$$\text{Break-even dollar sales} = px_b = p\left(\frac{F}{p - v}\right)$$

$$= \$15\left(\frac{\$200,000}{\$15 - \$10}\right) = \$600,000$$

From Exhibit 13-2 we see that the dollars of sales at the break-even point of 40,000 units are in fact $600,000. This is also shown in Figure 13-1.

The quantity $(p - v)$ in Eqs. (13-1) and (13-2) is called the **contribution margin**. The contribution margin equals the increase in pretax income from an added unit sold. From Eq. (13-2) we can see that the break-even output x_b is fixed costs divided by the contribution margin.

Sales Price and Cost Changes

Break-even analysis can be useful in analyzing policies which affect sales (for example, changing sales price) or which affect the level of fixed or variable costs. For example, by lowering its sales price, the company may be able to increase total sales. A decline in sales price reduces the contribution margin $(p - v)$ and thereby raises the break-even point x_b, as can be seen from Eq. (13-2). In Figure 13-2, a lower sales price implies a fall in the slope (decrease in steepness) of the total sales schedule. Although income per unit of sales decreases, total sales and income may actually rise. This is illustrated in Figure 13-2. If the decrease in sales price from p_1 to p_2 produces an increase in units sold from q_1 to q_2, then income will increase.

Alternative marketing strategies can be compared using the break-even analysis. The firm might be comparing a new long-term advertising campaign with the alternative of a price reduction in order to increase sales. If the advertising campaign adds amount A to fixed costs, then we could compare the relative benefits of the lower prices with the benefits of the advertising. In Figure 13-3 we see that adoption of the advertising campaign raises sales to q_2 (assuming that unit sales price remains at p_1). Comparing

FIGURE 13-2

Effects of a change in sales price.

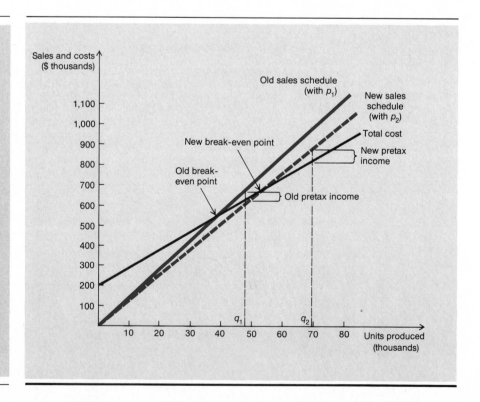

437

CHAPTER 13
Break-even analysis
and the measurement
of leverage

*Nonlinear Break-
Even Analysis*

Figures 13-2 and 13-3, we see that advertising increases income by more than the increase due to the lower sales price strategy in Figure 13-2. This firm will therefore seek to increase sales and income by advertising rather than by lowering its sales price.

In the previous discussion it was assumed that costs increased linearly with output; each added unit has the same variable cost. Although this may be valid for some ranges of output, it is not likely to hold over the entire range for an actual firm. Thus, the variable cost of the twenty thousandth unit may be higher or lower than the variable cost of the ten thousandth unit. In Figure 13-4 the cost of an additional unit of output (unit variable cost) is assumed to decrease and then to increase as production increases. Since income equals sales minus total cost, at point q^* the firm's income is maximized (maximum vertical distance between sales and total cost).[3] Notice that there are two break-even points q_b and q_b'. All sales between q_b and q_b' produce positive income. Notice that even if customers demand more than q^* units, the firm will not produce them, since beyond q^* profits are decreasing, that is, profits are greater by selling only q^* units.[4]

[3] At q^*, the *slope* of the total-cost schedule equals the slope of the sales schedule, implying that the price of output equals the variable cost (marginal cost) of the q^*th unit of output.

[4] The firm may in the short run produce more than q^* as a service to customers so that their patronage will not be lost. However, as long as costs and product price do not change (i.e., as long as the sales and cost schedules in Figure 13-4 remain valid), the firm will not produce beyond q^* in the long run since q^* maximizes profit.

FIGURE 13-3

*Effects of a change in
fixed costs.*

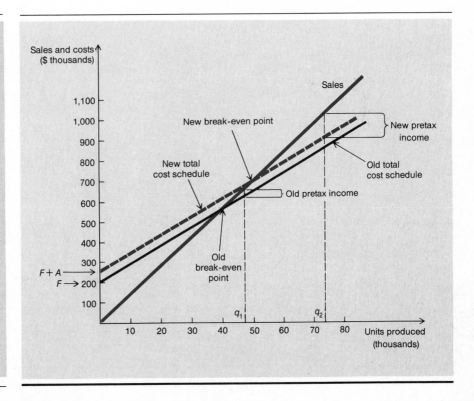

Where will the firm operate? As with linear costs, demand for the firm's product is uncertain, and therefore so is the level of sales and production. The firm will not be willing to maintain production and sales above q^* since income is decreasing above that level of output. As long as sales are between q_b and q^*, the firm will earn income. If sales happen to fall below q_b, we can see from Figure 13-4 that the firm will suffer a loss. If this continues, the firm will eventually go out of business. An essential point here is that the exact level of sales is generally unpredictable. The figures tell us only what the firm's income will be for each level of sales. This also was true with linear costs. The analysis using nonlinear costs is essentially very similar to that using linear costs.

Limitations of Break-Even Analysis

Even with nonlinear costs, break-even analysis has serious limitations. As we noted earlier, the distinction between fixed and variable costs depends on several assumptions, including the output range that is relevant and the time period involved. A change in assumptions may necessitate an entirely new analysis (new numbers and diagrams). Furthermore, the fixed and variable costs and the price at which the product is to be sold are assumed to be known at each level of output. In real situations, there is often uncertainty as to what costs and price will be for any particular output level. If this uncertainty is incorporated into the break-even framework, the analy-

FIGURE 13-4
Nonlinear costs.

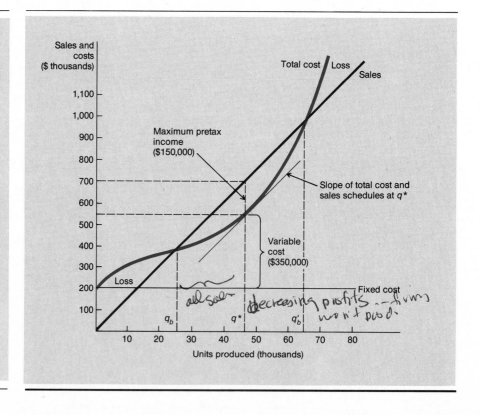

439

CHAPTER 13
Break-even analysis
and the measurement
of leverage

sis may become unwieldy and another approach may be required. Simplicity is both the virtue and weakness of break-even analysis. Although it can be helpful as a rough guide to decision making, it generally falls far short of being a complete planning tool.

THE CONCEPT OF LEVERAGE

Leverage is the existence of fixed costs among a firm's costs. It is useful to categorize leverage as operating and financial. Operating leverage depends on the company's operating fixed costs (fixed costs other than interest on debt), such as administrative costs, depreciation, advertising expenditures, and property taxes. Financial leverage, which was examined in Chapter 10, depends on financial fixed costs (interest expense, loan fees, etc.). We will see that operating and financial leverage can be joined together to provide a measure of total or "combined" leverage. Before proceeding, assume the following definitions:

F_0 = operating fixed costs (administrative costs, depreciation, etc.)
F_f = financial fixed costs (interest expense, loan fees, etc.)
F = total fixed costs = $F_0 + F_f$
EBIT = earnings before interest and taxes (i.e., pretax income plus interest expense) = $px - vx - F_0 = x(p - v) - F_0$

Operating Leverage

Operating leverage arises when there are fixed *operating* costs in the firm's cost structure. Fixed operating costs do *not* include debt interest (a fixed *financial* cost). With positive (i.e., nonzero) fixed operating costs, a change of 1 percent in sales produces more than a 1 percent change in EBIT. A measure of this effect is referred to as the degree of operating leverage (DOL) and it equals

$$\text{Degree of operating leverage (DOL)} = \frac{\text{percentage change in EBIT}}{\text{percentage change in units sold}}$$

and this can be shown to equal[5]

$$\text{DOL} = \frac{x(p - v)}{x(p - v) - F_0} \tag{13-3}$$

where x is the output level at which DOL is computed, and p, v, and F_0 are unit sales price, unit variable cost, and operating fixed costs, respectively. Recall that operating fixed costs F_0 for computing DOL *exclude* interest on firm debt since interest is a financial fixed cost.

[5] Equation (13-3) for DOL is derived as follows:

$$\text{EBIT} = x(p - v) - F_0$$

$$\Delta\text{EBIT} = \Delta x(p - v) \qquad \text{since } p, v, \text{ and } F_0 \text{ do not change } (\Delta \text{ means "change in")}$$

$$\frac{\Delta\text{EBIT}}{\text{EBIT}} = \frac{\Delta x(p - v)}{x(p - v) - F_0}$$

$$\frac{\Delta\text{EBIT}/\text{EBIT}}{\Delta x/x} = \frac{\Delta x(p - v)/[x(p - v) - F_0]}{\Delta x/x} = \frac{\Delta x(p - v)}{x(p - v) - F_0} \cdot \frac{x}{\Delta x}$$

$$= \frac{x(p - v)}{x(p - v) - F_0} = \text{DOL}$$

The greater is a firm's DOL, the more its EBIT will vary with sales fluctuations. We can see from Eq. (13-3) that the firm's cost structure (fixed and variable costs) determines its DOL for any given sales price p. In Exhibit 13-3, two firms with different cost structures are compared. Clear Glassworks has lower fixed costs and higher per unit variable costs than Strand Paper. Both firms charge $10 ($p$) for each unit sold. Notice that at an output of 50,000 units, both firms have the same profits ($60,000). However, as sales fluctuate, the EBIT of Clear Glassworks fluctuates far less than the EBIT of Strand Paper. Strand Paper has a higher DOL. We can see this by computing the DOL for each firm at an x of 50,000 units.

DOL of Clear Glassworks at an output of 50,000 units

$$= \frac{x(p - v)}{x(p - v) - F_0} = \frac{50,000(\$10 - \$7)}{50,000(\$10 - \$7) - \$90,000} = 2\frac{1}{2}$$

DOL of Strand Paper Co. at an output of 50,000 units

$$= \frac{50,000(\$10 - \$5)}{50,000(\$10 - \$5) - \$190,000} = 4\frac{1}{6}$$

The above computations indicate that a 1 percent change in sales will produce a $2\frac{1}{2}$ percent change in EBIT for Clear Glassworks and a $4\frac{1}{6}$ percent change in EBIT for Strand Paper. The EBIT of the firm with the higher DOL (Strand) shows a greater variation with a change in sales. From Exhibit 13-3, you can see that an increase in Strand's sales from 50,000 units to 60,000 units (a 20 percent rise) will raise EBIT from $60,000 to $110,000, an $83\frac{1}{3}$ percent rise ($4\frac{1}{6}$ times the 20 percent sales rise). The same 20 percent

---

EXHIBIT 13-3
Cost and profit schedules for Clear Glassworks and Strand Paper Company

Clear Glassworks				Strand Paper Company			
Units sold x	Sales px	Total operating cost	EBIT (sales − total cost)	Units sold x	Sales px	Total operating cost	EBIT (sales − total cost)
10,000	$100,000	$160,000	$(60,000)	10,000	$100,000	$240,000	$(140,000)
20,000	200,000	230,000	(30,000)	20,000	200,000	290,000	(90,000)
30,000	300,000	300,000	0	30,000	300,000	340,000	(40,000)
40,000	400,000	370,000	30,000	40,000	400,000	390,000	10,000
50,000	500,000	440,000	60,000	50,000	500,000	440,000	60,000
60,000	600,000	510,000	90,000	60,000	600,000	490,000	110,000
70,000	700,000	580,000	120,000	70,000	700,000	540,000	160,000
80,000	800,000	650,000	150,000	80,000	800,000	590,000	210,000

Unit selling price p = $10   Unit selling price p = $10

Operating fixed costs F_0 = $90,000   Operating fixed costs F_0 = $190,000

Unit variable operating cost v = $7   Unit variable operating cost v = $5

Total operating variable cost vx = $7x   Total variable operating cost vx = $5x

Total operating cost $(F_0 + vx)$ = $90,000 + $7x   Total operating cost $(F_0 + vx)$ = $190,000 + $5x

EBIT break-even point = 30,000 units   EBIT break-even point = 38,000 units

441

CHAPTER 13
Break-even analysis
and the measurement
of leverage

increase in unit sales for Clear Glassworks will increase EBIT from $60,000 to $90,000, only a 50 percent rise ($2\frac{1}{2}$ times the 20 percent increase in sales). Notice from the table that a fall in sales below 50,000 units causes a greater percentage decline in Strand's EBIT than in Clear Glassworks' EBIT. A high DOL means large EBIT if sales are great and large losses if sales are depressed. DOL is therefore a measure of firm risk. A high DOL indicates a high risk (a high variability of EBIT if sales vary), as in the case of Strand Paper.

The DOL is also important in production planning. For example, the company may have the opportunity to change its cost structure by introducing labor-saving machinery and thereby increasing fixed capital costs and reducing variable labor costs. This rise in fixed costs and decline in variable costs will increase DOL. In this case, a financial manager would want to evaluate the probability that sales will be high so that the firm can enjoy the increased earnings of increased DOL—and the probability that sales will be low, in which case the higher fixed costs and higher leverage would be disadvantageous. The greater the likelihood of high sales, the more attractive will be the shift to a higher DOL (higher fixed operating cost and lower variable operating cost) method of production.

Operating leverage is often incorrectly used as a synonym for "business risk." Business risk refers to the uncertainty or variability of the firm's EBIT. A company with a highly unpredictable EBIT has high business risk. It is true that the greater is the DOL, the more sensitive is EBIT to a given change in unit sales and that, everything else being equal, a higher DOL means higher business risk. But risk also depends on two other factors: the variability of the firm's sales and the variability of the company's cost and price structures. Let's examine these two other factors.

Assume first that output price and the company's cost structure are known (p, F_0, and v are known, as was the case in our computation of DOL). The DOL indicates how EBIT will change with sales; but, to evaluate the variability of EBIT (the company's risk), we must also know something about the variability of sales. A company with large fixed and low variable costs—for example, a utility or an office building—will have a large DOL, but it may have extremely stable revenues and consequently a stable EBIT and low risk. Conversely, a firm with low fixed operating costs and high variable costs, and therefore a low DOL, may have very unpredictable sales and a highly unpredictable or variable EBIT—for example, a construction firm with most of its costs being wages, material purchases, and equipment rentals.

EBIT can vary not only because sales fluctuate but also because of changes in the company's output price and costs, that is, changes in p, F_0, and v. Indeed, unit sales might remain fixed while EBIT gyrates wildly because of cost or price variations. Also, if price and costs are uncertain, DOL is uncertain, since DOL is defined in terms of p, F_0, and v. In this case, the use of DOL in evaluating business risk is somewhat limited.

The main point here is that DOL is only one measure that can be useful in some situations for determining the behavior of EBIT. The analysis must also examine sales variability and, in many instances, must take into account uncertainty regarding output price and cost structure.

Recall from Chapter 10 that financial leverage arises when a company borrows funds. A firm with no debt obligations has no financial leverage. To illustrate the impact of debt on earnings (net income) per share, assume that $500,000 is required to set up the operations of Clear Glassworks. Three financing options are described in Exhibit 13-4 and the impact on firm earnings (net income) is shown in Exhibit 13-5: case A, all equity financing (stockholders' investment $500,000); case B, $400,000 of equity and $100,000 of debt financing; and case C, $300,000 of equity and $200,000 of debt financing. The interest rate on all debt is 10 percent.

The degree of financial leverage (DFL) is a measure of the extent of the company's borrowing and is represented by the following formula:

$$\text{Degree of financial leverage (DFL)} = \frac{\text{percentage change in EPS}}{\text{percentage change in EBIT}}$$

which equals

$$\text{DFL} = \frac{\text{EBIT}}{\text{EBIT} - F_f} \tag{13-4}$$

where, as before, F_f is interest on debt (fixed financial costs) and EPS refers to aftertax earnings (net income) per share.[6] Using the data in Exhibit 13-5, DFL at 50,000 units for cases A, B, and C equals:

Case A: $\text{DFL} = \dfrac{\$60,000}{\$60,000 - 0} = 1.0$

Case B: $\text{DFL} = \dfrac{\$60,000}{\$60,000 - \$10,000} = 1.2$

Case C: $\text{DFL} = \dfrac{\$60,000}{\$60,000 - \$20,000} = 1.5$

[6] Equation (13-4) for DFL can be derived as follows:

$$\text{EPS} = \frac{(1 - T)(\text{EBIT} - F_f)}{n} \tag{a}$$

where T = corporate tax rate

F_f = financial fixed costs

n = number of shares

The change in EPS due to a change in EBIT equals

$$\Delta\text{EPS} = \frac{(1 - T)\Delta\text{EBIT}}{n} \tag{b}$$

since T, F_f, and n are constants (do not change as EBIT changes). Therefore, the percentage changes in EPS equals

$$\frac{\Delta\text{EPS}}{\text{EPS}} = \frac{[(1 - T)\Delta\text{EBIT}]/n}{[(1 - T)(\text{EBIT} - F_f)]/n} = \frac{\Delta\text{EBIT}}{\text{EBIT} - F_f} \tag{c}$$

The degree of financial leverage equals the percentage change in EPS divided by the percentage change in EBIT which, using (c), equals

$$\text{DFL} = \frac{\Delta\text{EPS}/\text{EPS}}{\Delta\text{EBIT}/\text{EBIT}} = \frac{\Delta\text{EBIT}/(\text{EBIT} - F_f)}{\Delta\text{EBIT}/\text{EBIT}}$$

$$= \frac{\text{EBIT}}{\text{EBIT} - F_f}$$

443

CHAPTER 13
Break-even analysis
and the measurement
of leverage

EXHIBIT 13-4
Three alternative financing plans for Clear Glassworks

Case	Total financing	Debt proportion, %	Dollars of debt (10% interest rate)	Dollars of equity	Number of shares outstanding
A	$500,000	0	$ 0	$500,000	5,000
B	$500,000	20	$100,000	$400,000	4,000
C	$500,000	40	$200,000	$300,000	3,000

Therefore, a 1 percent change in EBIT produces a 1 percent change in EPS if Clear Glassworks has no debt, a 1.2 percent change in EPS with $100,000 in debt, and a 1.5 percent change in EPS with $200,000 in debt. Notice from Exhibit 13-5 that *the greater is the leverage, the wider are fluctuations in the return on equity*. This is illustrated in Figure 13-5, where rate of return on equity for each level of EBIT is graphed for funding plans A, B, and C; the steeper the schedule, the greater the change in earnings for a unit change in EBIT.

Combined Leverage

Combined leverage is the measure of the total leverage due to both operating and financial fixed costs. It is easily computed using the DOL and DFL formulas. The degree of combined leverage (DCL) equals

$$\text{Degree of combined leverage (DCL)} = \frac{\text{percentage change in EPS}}{\text{percentage change sales}}$$

which equals

$$\text{DCL} = \frac{x(p - v)}{x(p - v) - F} \tag{13-5}$$

where, as before, $F = F_0 + F_f = $ total (operating plus financial) fixed costs.[7] For Clear Glassworks, at an output of 50,000 units ($x = 50,000$) and debt of $100,000,

---

[7] Equation (13-5) for DCL can be derived by observing that DCL = DFL × DOL; that is,

$$\text{DOL} \times \text{DFL} = \frac{\text{percentage change in EPS}}{\text{percentage change in EBIT}} \times \frac{\text{percentage change in EBIT}}{\text{percentage change in sales}}$$

$$= \frac{\text{percentage change in EPS}}{\text{percentage change in sales}} = \text{DCL}$$

Therefore, using Eqs. (13-3) and (13-4),

$$\text{DCL} = \text{DOL} \times \text{DFL} = \frac{x(p - v)}{x(p - v) - F_0} \times \frac{\text{EBIT}}{\text{EBIT} - F_f} \tag{a}$$

But, EBIT $= x(p - v) - F_0$, and substituting this into (a) (and noting that $F_0 + F_f = F$),

$$\text{DCL} = \frac{x(p - v)}{x(p - v) - F_0} \times \frac{x(p - v) - F_0}{x(p - v) - F_0 - F_f} = \frac{x(p - v)}{x(p - v) - F}$$

which is DCL in Eq. (13-5) in the text.

EXHIBIT 13-5
Illustration of financial leverage—Clear Glassworks

Units sold	EBIT[a]	Interest on debt[b]	Taxes[c]	Net income (loss) (EBIT − interest − taxes)	Earnings per share (net income/ no. of shares)[d]	Rate of return on equity, %[e]
A. No debt; equity investment = $500,000 (5,000 shares at $100 per share)						
10,000	$(60,000)	0	$(30,000)[f]	$(30,000)	$(6.00)	− 6
20,000	(30,000)	0	(15,000)[f]	(15,000)	(3.00)	− 3
30,000	0	0	0	0	0	0
40,000	30,000	0	15,000	15,000	3.00	3
50,000	60,000	0	30,000	30,000	6.00	6
60,000	90,000	0	45,000	45,000	9.00	9
70,000	120,000	0	60,000	60,000	12.00	12
80,000	150,000	0	75,000	75,000	15.00	15
90,000	180,000	0	90,000	90,000	18.00	18
B. Debt = $100,000; equity investment = $400,000 (4,000 shares at $100 per share)						
10,000	$(60,000)	$10,000	$(35,000)[f]	$(35,000)	$(8.75)	− 8¾
20,000	(30,000)	10,000	(20,000)[f]	(20,000)	(5.00)	− 5
30,000	0	10,000	(5,000)[f]	(5,000)	(1.25)	− 1¼
40,000	30,000	10,000	10,000	10,000	2.50	2½
50,000	60,000	10,000	25,000	25,000	6.25	6¼
60,000	90,000	10,000	40,000	40,000	10.00	10
70,000	120,000	10,000	55,000	55,000	13.75	13¾
80,000	150,000	10,000	70,000	70,000	17.50	17½
90,000	180,000	10,000	85,000	85,000	21.25	21¼
C. Debt = $200,000; equity investment = $300,000 (3,000 shares at $100 per share)						
10,000	$(60,000)	$20,000	$(40,000)[f]	$(40,000)	$(13.33)	−13⅓
20,000	(30,000)	20,000	(25,000)[f]	(25,000)	(8.33)	− 8⅓
30,000	0	20,000	(10,000)[f]	(10,000)	(3.33)	− 3⅓
40,000	30,000	20,000	5,000	5,000	1.67	1⅔
50,000	60,000	20,000	20,000	20,000	6.67	6⅔
60,000	90,000	20,000	35,000	35,000	11.67	11⅔
70,000	120,000	20,000	50,000	50,000	16.67	16⅔
80,000	150,000	20,000	65,000	65,000	21.67	21⅔
90,000	180,000	20,000	80,000	80,000	26.67	26⅔

[a] See Exhibit 13-3 for the computation of EBIT for Clear Glassworks.
[b] Interest rate on debt is 10%, interest on debt = 0.10 × debt.
[c] The tax rate is assumed to equal 50%; taxes = 0.50 × (EBIT − interest on debt).
[d] It is assumed that there are 5,000, 4,000, and 3,000 shares of stock outstanding in cases A, B, and C, respectively. Earnings per share equal net income of the firm divided by the number of shares outstanding.
[e] Rate of return on equity = (net income)/(equity investment) = (net income per share)/$100, where $100 = equity investment per share.
[f] A negative tax means a tax credit due to a negative taxable income [negative (EBIT − interest on debt)].

445

CHAPTER 13
Break-even analysis
and the measurement
of leverage

$$DCL = \frac{50,000(\$10 - \$7)}{50,000(\$10 - \$7) - (\$90,000 + \$10,000)} = \frac{\$150,000}{\$50,000} = 3.0$$

where, $F = F_0 + F_f = \$90,000 + \$10,000$. At an output of 50,000 units, each 1 percent variation in sales will cause a 3 percent change in EPS. In Exhibit 13-5, a 10 percent rise in sales to 55,000 units will increase earnings per share from $6.25 to $8.125 (a 30 percent increase in EPS) since

$$
\begin{aligned}
EPS_{55,000 \text{ units}} &= EPS_{50,000} + EPS_{50,000} \times (\% \text{ change in EPS}) \\
&= EPS_{50,000} + EPS_{50,000} \times (DCL \times \% \text{ change in sales}) \\
&= EPS_{50,000} + EPS_{50,000} (3.0 \times 10\%) \\
&= \$6.25 + 6.25(30\%) = \$8.125
\end{aligned}
$$

A greater DOL or DFL will raise DCL. DCL is a measure of the overall riskiness or uncertainty associated with stockholders' earnings that arises because of operating and financial leverage.

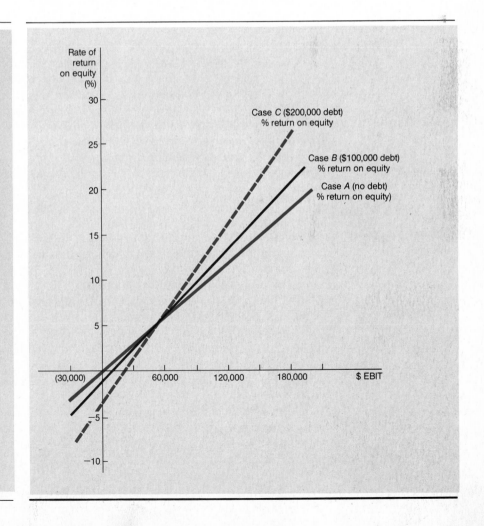

FIGURE 13-5

Variability of the rate of return on equity increases with greater leverage.

SUMMARY

Break-even analysis is used to assess the effects of changes in the firm's sales volume, or in cost and price structure, on company profits. An important factor is the relationship between fixed and variable costs. Fixed costs do not vary with output changes, whereas variable costs do vary with output. Most costs can be classified as fixed or variable, depending upon the situation. Break-even analysis can be used to examine the effect of changes in sales price and cost structure on firm profitability. Although linear costs are often assumed in break-even analysis, nonlinear costs as well as variable price can also be assumed. The technique can therefore be adapted to realistic assumptions and often serves as a useful tool in financial planning. However, break-even analysis can become unwieldy if many policy alternatives are being compared. It is therefore generally used in combination with other analytical approaches.

Operating leverage is due to fixed operating costs, such as depreciation on property taxes. The greater are fixed costs relative to variable operating costs, the more variable will be earnings before interest and taxes (EBIT) and the higher will be the firm's degree of operating leverage (DOL). Operating leverage is not the only cause of fluctuations in EBIT, since EBIT can also change with variations in the company's cost structure (level of fixed or per unit variable cost) or sales price.

Financial leverage occurs when the company borrows money. The greater is the firm's debt, the greater will net aftertax earnings per share change due to a given change in EBIT. The degree of financial leverage (DFL) increases directly with increased borrowing. The degree of combined leverage (DCL) indicates the percentage change in net aftertax earnings due to a 1 percent change in sales. DCL rises as operating leverage and financial leverage rise and is therefore a measure of the impact of operating and financial fixed costs on the variability of net income.

QUESTIONS

1 Define and give examples of fixed costs and variable costs.
2 Explain how the following may change the classification of a cost into the fixed or variable class:
   a The magnitude of a change in output
   b The amount of time required to change the cost
   c The length of time the change in output is expected to last
3 Explain what is meant by "contribution margin."
4 In each of the following situations explain what happens to the break-even point in units:
   a The selling price increases and all other variables remain unchanged.
   b The fixed cost increases and all other variables remain unchanged.
   c The variable cost increases and all other variables remain unchanged.
5 In the text it is said that DOL and business risk are often incorrectly

447

CHAPTER 13
Break-even analysis
and the measurement
of leverage

used as synonyms. Explain why such usage is incorrect and point
out the differences between DOL and business risk.

6 Define the degree of financial leverage (DFL) and explain why it is a
measure of risk.

7 Define the degree of combined leverage (DCL) and explain how DCL
depends on operating and financial leverage.

PROJECT

Obtain the financial statements of two companies in different industries
and compare the firms in terms of the relationship between fixed costs,
variable costs, and sales. Assume that the sales price and variable cost
per unit of output of one of the companies is the same for all levels of
production and compute the company's break-even level of sales, its degree of financial leverage, its degree of operating leverage, and its degree
of combined leverage. Hint: To compute break-even dollar sales, note
that:

$$\frac{\text{Break-even}}{\text{dollar sales}} = px_b = p\left(\frac{F}{p-v}\right) = \frac{F}{1-\dfrac{vx}{px}} = \frac{F}{1-\dfrac{\text{variable costs}}{\text{sales}}}$$

PROBLEMS

1 Pardo Crystal sells Swiss jars for $80 each. Pardo's annual fixed costs
are $100,000 and its variable cost per jar is $30.

    a Calculate the firm's break-even point in number of units.

    b Calculate the firm's break-even point in dollar sales.

    c What is the company's pretax income if 5000 jars are sold?

2 Sparkle Pens manufactures a single product, its famous "Smoothie
Pen." Each Smoothie pen requires a variable cost of $2 (for labor, ma-
terials, etc.). The annual fixed costs at the Smoothie plant are
$120,000 for rent, $40,000 for depreciation of equipment, and mis-
cellaneous other costs of $90,000. Each Smoothie pen is sold by
Sparkle Pens for $5.

    a What are Sparkle Pen's annual total fixed costs and per unit (per
pen) variable cost?

    b What is Sparkle Pen's break-even point in units and in dollar
sales?

    c What is pretax income at 100,000 units?

    d What is the contribution margin?

    e Assume that Sparkle Pens is selling 100,000 units per year and has
the costs and unit sales price indicated in **a** through **d** above. The
company has the opportunity to add a new machine that greatly
lowers labor costs; the machine will increase annual fixed costs to
$275,000 but will lower per unit variable costs to $1.50. If Sparkle
Pens maintains its sales price at $5 and output at 100,000 units,
will adding the new machine increase pretax income?

    f Assume that Sparkle Pens is selling 100,000 units and has the
costs and sales price indicated in **a** through **d** above. The com-

pany can lower the sales price to $4 per unit and thereby raise sales to 150,000 units. What is the effect of the sales price change on pretax income?

3 Rand Collections Limited sells miniature gold-plated replicas of famous sports, political, and entertainment personalities. Each miniature is sold by Rand for $200. Rand's fixed costs are $200,000. In 1986, Rand sold 6000 miniatures. Total variable costs for 1986 were $600,000.

   a What was the company's pretax income in 1986?
   b How many miniatures must the company sell just to break even?
   c For 1987, the company expects a 25 percent increase in fixed costs.

      1 What is the new break-even point in units (miniatures) if the price remains at $200?
      2 By how much should the price per miniature be increased in order for the company to make the same profit as in 1986, assuming that variable costs and the number of miniatures sold remain at the 1986 level?
      3 The production manager believes that efficiency-increasing measures could be introduced in 1987 which would reduce per unit variable cost. Assuming that the selling price remains at $200 per miniature, what reduction in the variable cost would result in the same break-even point (in units) as in 1986?

4 Mickey Mars, president of Pestgo Chemicals, a producer of pesticides, has provided the following data and forecast for the company:

Current sales	$15 million
Forecasted sales in 5 years	$20 million
Current variable cost	80% of sales
Current total (operating and financial) fixed cost (including depreciation of $300,000)	$1.5 million

It has recently come to Mars' attention that the firm's high labor and maintenance costs are the result of the obsolete equipment and deteriorating condition of one of the company's plants. Consequently, Mars is considering the replacement of the plant with a new, automated facility. Mars estimates that the new facility will have variable costs equal to 60 percent of sales revenues but annual fixed costs (including depreciation) will increase over their former level (under the obsolete plant) by $3 million.

   a Calculate the current earnings before taxes (EBT) of Pestgo.
   b What is the sales break-even point for the new plant?
   c What is the EBT for the old plant at the forecast level of sales of

449

CHAPTER 13
Break-even analysis
and the measurement
of leverage

$20 million? What is the EBT for the new facility at the forecast level of sales of $20 million?

d Compute the degree of operating leverage (DOL) for both the new and the old facilities at the current level of sales and the forecast level of sales. Assume that operating fixed costs are $1 million.

5 Brighton Bantamwagon Dealers sells new Bantamwagons, a modern lightweight English camper automobile. In 1986, Brighton's earnings before interest and taxes were $400,000. On January 1, 1986, Brighton increased its debt from $200,000 (on which annual interest cost was $20,000) to $700,000; the annual interest on the additional debt is $60,000. The company's tax rate is 40 percent.

a What would Brighton's degree of financial leverage be if it did not increase its debt from $200,000 to $450,000?

b What is the 1986 degree of financial leverage using the actual 1986 figures?

c In 1986, what percentage change in aftertax earnings per share (EPS) would result from a 40 percent increase in EBIT?

d In 1986, what percentage increase in EBIT would bring about a 10 percent increase in EPS?

e In 1986, Brighton sold 200 campers for $10,000 per camper. Brighton's fixed operating cost was $300,000 and total variable operating cost was $1.3 million. What was the degree of combined leverage using the actual 1986 figures?

f Suppose the 1986 EPS is $3. What would EPS be if unit sales increased by 20 percent?

g Compute DOL and check the relation DCL = DOL × DFL using the data and results of **b** and **e**.

6 Broderick Corporation currently has a degree of combined leverage (DCL) of 3 and a degree of operating leverage (DOL) of 1.5. Broderick plans to purchase new machinery to replace old machinery. The new machinery will increase fixed operating costs but decrease variable costs per unit. Broderick's management believes the DOL will be 1.8 after the investment. Management considers a DCL of 4.5 to be the highest acceptable degree of combined leverage for the firm.

a Calculate the degree of financial leverage before the investment and the maximum acceptable degree of financial leverage after the investment.

b If the new EBIT is expected to be $6,000,000, what is the maximum amount of fixed financial cost the corporation will be able to cover?

c Suppose the fixed financial costs (interest, lease payments, etc.) are $2.4 million before the investment. What is the maximum amount of new borrowing that management will consider to be acceptable if the firm can borrow at an interest rate of 15 percent?

7 Hydro, Incorporated, has just recovered from a severe slump in business and has projected sales of $3,600,000 for next year. Based on

the existing production equipment, total fixed operating costs and total variable operating costs are expected to be $1,200,000 and $1,800,000, respectively, so that the EBIT will be $600,000. The selling price per item produced is $50. The firm has a $1,500,000 five-year note outstanding on which it pays interest of 15 percent. Hydro plans to pay off the five-year note with funds borrowed at a lower interest rate. The production manager has suggested the modernization of the old equipment. This would result in a 30 percent increase in fixed operating costs and a 20 percent decrease in per unit variable operating costs.

The general manager agrees with the modernization plan as long as the firm's risk, as measured by the DCL, does not change. This could be made possible by the refunding of the outstanding five-year note. Hydro will borrow $1,500,000 from the bank in order to pay off the note. How much lower must the interest rate on the new $1,500,000 loan be for the modernization plan to become acceptable in the eyes of the manager? Assume that sales price and sales will be unaffected by the cost changes. (Hint: DCL = DFL × DOL)

FINANCIAL FORECASTING AND PLANNING

In Chapters 12 and 13 we discussed financial analyses that are based on past and current financial performance. Although these techniques are helpful in judging what the future performance of the firm may be, they are not forecasts of future performance. To maintain and increase the profitability of the firm, the financial manager must be able to anticipate its future needs for cash. Financial forecasting allows the financial manager to make educated guesses about the future financial condition of the firm. The financial manager also develops budgets that indicate, as time passes, whether the forecasts are proving to be accurate. In this chapter we look at the problem of forecasting future cash requirements and the general financial condition of the firm. We then show how these forecasts are used to develop plans and budgets.

Forecasts are important for several reasons:

1 Cash forecasts show when and how much new financing will be needed, given current operating and investment decisions. This information is used by the financial manager to plan the financing of the firm and to arrange for external sources of funds, such as debt and stock.

2 The data obtained from forecasts provide a basis for the decisions regarding cash management and investment in marketable securities. This is discussed in Chapter 15.

3 Budgets prepared from forecasts provide a way to maintain control over the firm's financial affairs and signal changing conditions that are reflected in the cash flows of the firm. (For example, if cash were expected to increase by $100,000 in June and the increase turned out to be only $50,000, the financial manager would want to know what happened.)

4 Lenders such as commercial banks are favorably impressed by careful financial planning, especially on the part of small businesses where such planning is frequently not done. Evidence of financial planning is very helpful in obtaining loans.

In general, forecasting permits the financial manager to be more effective in monitoring the firm's financial affairs, in controlling and investing cash, and in developing financing. These activities increase profits and reduce risk and are therefore vital to the continuing success of the firm.

FORECASTING SINGLE FINANCIAL VARIABLES

Forecasts of the total financial condition of the firm are normally developed from forecasts of individual financial variables. For example, to develop a balance sheet for some future period, it is necessary to forecast accounts receivable and inventory. The forecasts of individual accounts are combined into a forecast of the complete balance sheet. In this section we will look at several approaches to forecasting single financial variables. In the next section we will show how the forecasts of single variables can be combined into an integrated forecast of the financial condition of the firm—balance sheets, income statements, and cash flows.

Most forecasts combine objective analysis of historical data with the subjective insights of the forecaster. In the descriptions of trend, ratio, and statistical forecasting methods that follow, we focus on the objective analytical techniques. When we show how the forecasts of single variables are combined into a forecast of the firm's cash flows, income statement, and balance sheet, examples of objective forecasts modified by management to reflect its judgment will be presented.

Trend Forecasts

Trend forecasts rely solely on historical information about the variable being forecast. The most elementary trend forecast is to predict "no change" from the current value of the variable when information available suggests that there will be no change. For example, if management does not plan to issue or retire any common stock, it would forecast "no change" in common stock outstanding. "No change" forecasts are also used when there is a complete lack of information as to the extent and direction of any change that may occur, in other words, when the current value is the only information available.

More commonly, trend forecasts are based on past trends and seasonability. For example, if sales have grown at an average rate of 8 percent per year, then a forecast for next year's sales might be 8 percent above current levels. Past seasonal patterns are also considered. If sales in December are typically 15 percent of annual sales, then it would seem reasonable that sales for next December might be 15 percent of forecast sales for the year.

All trend forecasts are essentially a projection of recent historical values for the variable into the future. A basic technique used in analyzing the past history of a variable is to plot the values over time. For example, suppose we wish to forecast the level of inventory next month (month 13). The history of inventory levels over the past twelve months is illustrated in Figure 14-1. Based on this history we would forecast inventory in month 13 to be I^*. There are statistical techniques available for performing such projections mechanically; their use is covered in statistics courses.

Forecasting Based on Relationships between Variables

Trend forecasts are useful, but they do not take into account what else is expected to happen in the firm or the economy. For example, suppose government and private economists are forecasting that a recession will occur next year. If you were forecasting sales of General Motors cars, you might want to forecast lower sales regardless of recent car sales trends, because car sales are affected by general economic conditions. Similarly, if you were forecasting income statement accounts such as cost of goods sold and earnings before interest and taxes, you would want the forecasts for each account to be consistent with forecasted sales. In developing forecasts of single financial variables, the financial manager will want to be sure the forecasts are consistent with each other. Forecasts of one variable are frequently based on a forecast for another variable, which we refer to as the **base variable**.

The levels of assets, liabilities, revenues, and expenses are known to be related to sales volume. The most obvious examples are the revenue and expense accounts; however, assets such as accounts receivable are also related to sales. An increase in sales will usually result in an increase in the level of accounts receivable.[1] Therefore, given a forecast for sales, it is often useful to forecast accounts receivable (or collections) based on past relationships with sales. For example, suppose that the average collection period of the firm is thirty days. This means that there are about one month's sales in accounts receivable. A forecast of accounts receivable for the end of December would equal the sales forecast for December.

Using Ratios in Forecasting   The simplest relationship between two variables is the ratio of the two. Gross margin is a ratio of gross profit to sales. Ratios, such as those discussed in Chapter 12, can be used in forecasting as follows:

1   The ratio itself is forecast or estimated using historical data. Frequently the average value of the ratio over the past year or two is used, although sometimes a trend forecast with adjustments for seasonality is made. For example, if the firm's gross margin has averaged 30 percent in the past, it might be forecast to remain at 30 percent.
2   The base variable is forecast (sales). The base variable here is the denominator of the ratio. In many cases someone else's forecast of the base variable is used. For example, the marketing manager may provide the financial manager with a sales forecast.
3   The individual financial variable is forecast as

Variable = ratio × base variable

For example, if sales for next year are forecast to be $10 million and the gross margin is forecast to be 30 percent,

Gross profit = gross margin × sales

= 0.30 × $10 million

= $3 million

Sales are the most common base variable in forecasts using ratios since

[1] Of course if the increase in sales were confined to customers who pay cash, then an increase in accounts receivable would not occur.

FIGURE 14-1

A trend forecast of inventory.

most of the financial variables of the firm are related to sales, at least in the long run. A forecast of sales is often used to provide long-term forecasts for variables that are not directly related to sales in the short run. Plant and equipment would not be likely to vary with sales on a month-to-month basis. However, a forecast of plant and equipment needed by the firm five years from now might be based on the past average ratio of these assets to sales. Accounts payable (and payments to suppliers) are primarily related to purchases. In the short run, purchases may differ appreciably from sales levels. In the short run, therefore, a forecast of accounts payable should be based on expected purchases. In the long run, however, purchases and sales are apt to move together in a fairly stable relationship since goods must be purchased before they can be sold. Therefore, a forecast of sales serves indirectly as a forecast of purchases, and consequently the average ratio of accounts payable to sales can be used as a reasonable basis for a long-range forecast of accounts payable given the sales forecast.

Although sales are the most common base for forecasts using ratios, the general method may be applied using other bases. For example, inventory, wages, or electricity costs might be more related to production levels than to sales. Given a forecast of production, the historical ratio of wages to production might then be used to forecast future wage payments. Similarly, if the ratio of accounts payable to inventory tends to be a constant ratio, a forecast of inventory could serve as a base to forecast accounts payable.

Graphical and Statistical Methods   Suppose that it is now 1987 and we wish to forecast inventory levels over the next five years, 1988 to 1992. Either trend or ratio methods may be used; however, there are more accurate alternatives. One of the less complicated of these alternatives is to examine the past relationship between inventory and sales as illustrated in Figure 14-2. Each point on the graph represents the particular values of inventory and sales for a given year.

FIGURE 14-2

Forecasting inventory using historical relationships with sales.

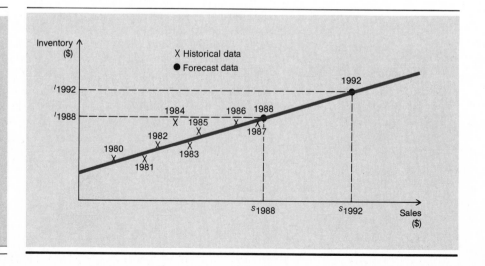

There is a general tendency for higher sales to require higher inventories. Suppose we fit a straight line to these as indicated in Figure 14-2. The line may be drawn by hand or it may be estimated using statistical methods. The line shows the average past relationship between inventory and sales. If the points lie on a line through the origin (sales and inventory equal to zero), a fixed ratio between sales and inventory would be indicated. Since they do not, the ratio method would not provide accurate forecasts in this case.[2] Given the sales forecast for 1988, inventory for 1988 is forecast as shown. Similarly the 1992 sales forecast is used to provide an inventory forecast for 1992.

This approach is quite general because it can be based on the relationship between any two items of interest. For example, accounts payable could be related to inventory just as inventory was related to sales in the above case. A forecast of inventory could then be used in conjunction with the line relating accounts payable to inventory to forecast accounts payable.

More elaborate techniques are also available. Statistical techniques can be used to fit a straight line to the data rather than drawing it by hand. It is possible to fit curved lines rather than straight lines if a curved line describes the relationship better. It is also possible to use more than one variable to forecast another. For example, inventory could be related to both the level of sales and the change in sales from the prior period, or it could be related to sales and production. A major advantage of statistical methods is that they provide measures of how well the fitted relationship matches the actual data. Such methods are generally covered in statistics courses.

Problems in Forecasting

The forecasting methods we discussed are "scientific" in the sense that two people applying the same method to generate a forecast should arrive at the same result. Repeatable results, however, do not guarantee accurate forecasts. As we noted earlier, good forecasting relies on good judgment combined with an objective analysis of the data. Therefore a financial manager should approach a forecast by considering the choice of methods available, using the ones that are judged to provide the most reliable results, and deciding whether objective methods alone will be accurate. A financial manager, for example, may want to forecast earnings by multiplying the sales forecast by the expected profit margin. The profit margin can be based on historical patterns, but it might be better to consider the firm's future outlook for prices and costs. If the firm has just undertaken a major cost reduction program, it would not seem reasonable to use historical profit margins as a basis for forecasting future profits. Management can also utilize the judgment of economists as to the future prospects of the industry and the economy. If the economy is headed for increased inflation, then

---

[2] The equation for the line is

$$I = a + bS$$

where I is inventory, S is sales, and a and b are constants. The ratio of inventory to sales is

$$\frac{I}{S} = \frac{a + bS}{S} = \frac{a}{S} + b$$

Therefore the ratio is not constant with respect to sales levels unless a is zero.

the forecast of sales and prices should take that information into account. Here, the judgment of the financial manager may be much more accurate than scientific methods.

FINANCIAL FORECASTING

So far we have discussed forecasting as if we were solely concerned with the future value of a particular financial variable. However, financial managers usually are more interested in forecasting the total picture. They will use one of the more comprehensive financial forecasting methods—the **cash flow method** or the **balance sheet method**. Both of these approaches forecast the cash position of the firm and make use of single-variable forecasts.

The cash flow method forecasts the cash available to, or needed by, the firm by focusing on the payments and receipts of cash over time. The balance sheet method forecasts the balance sheet accounts of the firm and also the firm's cash position. Since there are differences in the information provided by each method, a comprehensive financial forecast requires the use of both. Both start with a sales forecast, and both require a forecast of the firm's income statements. Generally, someone other than the financial manager (such as the marketing manager) is responsible for forecasting sales. Similarly, for manufacturing firms, production schedules are also normally provided by someone else (such as the production manager).

The sales forecast is the backbone of a comprehensive financial forecast because many of the other variables are related to sales. A production schedule, for example, cannot be developed in the absence of a forecast for sales. Any of the methods of forecasting single variables may be used in developing the sales forecast; however, it is important that the financial manager be aware of how the forecast has been developed. In particular, the sales forecast used for financial forecasting should be the best estimate available and not a sales target or goal developed to motivate sales personnel. Careful attention must be paid to competitive conditions within the firm's industry, the outlook for the general economy, and any other factors (such as technological changes in other competing industries) that may have a significant impact on the firm's future sales.

Income Statement Forecasts

We used simple income statement forecasts in Chapter 10 in order to examine the impact of alternative financing methods on the firm's profits. Income statement forecasts are widely used in financial planning since an important consideration in any financial decision is the impact of the decision on the firm's profits. The critical variable in any income statement forecast is the sales forecast. The financial manager usually takes the sales forecast provided by the marketing manager and uses it as the base variable in forecasting the variable costs of the goods and services sold. The financial manager will also forecast other income (for example, interest income on securities investment), operating expenses, interest on debt, depreciation, and any other expenses that may be incurred during the forecast period. Given all income and expense items, the financial manager can calculate income taxes owed to the government and arrive at a forecast of net income (profits) for the firm.

Interest costs on outstanding debt and interest income on present securities investment can be forecast accurately since the financial manager knows the interest rates on debt and securities. However, interest costs of new debt and interest income on new securities cannot be forecast accurately until a cash flow or balance sheet forecast has been made. The amount of new borrowing and the cash available for investment are important results from the forecast. Yet neither a cash flow forecast nor a balance sheet forecast can be completed without having an income statement forecast. Fortunately, these interest items are rarely large relative to other financial variables. Therefore standard procedure is either to ignore the interest on new debt and new securities investment or to use a "no change" forecast from the previous year. Once a preliminary estimate of borrowings and securities investment has been made, the forecast can be revised to reflect these items more accurately. This is part of the planning and budgeting process discussed later in the chapter. Exhibit 14-1 illustrates a simple income statement forecast. A more realistic example is included in the next section.

Cash Flow Forecasts

To develop a cash flow forecast for the firm, the financial manager must estimate the cash receipts and payments of the firm over the forecast period. The primary sources of cash receipts are cash sales and collections of accounts receivable. Other cash receipts may result from the sale of assets, the maturing of securities investments, and the proceeds from issuing debt or common stock. Cash payments are made for a wide variety of purposes. They include salaries and wages paid by the firm to its employees, payments to suppliers of goods and services, government taxes, dividends, scheduled payments of principal and interest to lenders, and plant and equipment expenditures. Cash flow forecasts are most often used for

---

EXHIBIT 14-1
Income statement forecast example (dollar figures in thousands)

	Year 1	Year 2	Year 3	Forecast for year 4	Forecasting method used
Sales revenues	$800	$1,000	$1,000	$1,200	Marketing judgment
Cost of goods sold	480	600	600	720	Historical ratio to sales
Gross profit	$320	$ 400	$ 400	$ 480	
Operating expenses ...	100	120	145	174	Trend growth rate
Operating profit	$220	$ 280	$ 255	$ 306	
Other income	10	4	20	20	Same as most recent year
Interest expense	(40)	(64)	(50)	(50)	Same as most recent year
Profit before taxes	$190	$ 220	$ 225	$ 276	
Federal income taxes ..	82	91	90	110	Same tax rate as most recent year (40%)
Net profit	$108	$ 129	$ 135	$ 166	

monthly plans although they may be made for longer or shorter periods of time.

Large firms often make daily forecasts for the coming month, monthly forecasts for the coming year, quarterly forecasts for the next year or two, and annual forecasts for several more years. This type of forecasting permits the financial manager to plan the firm's financing requirements several years into the future while focusing on short-run needs which can be forecast relatively more accurately and which require current decisions.

An Example   Suppose that the financial manager of the Snip Tool Company wishes to forecast monthly cash flows for the 1988 fiscal year beginning October 1, 1987. Snip manufactures a complete line of lawn and garden tools. Its sales are highly seasonal since half of the sales of Snip's products

---

EXHIBIT 14-2

Snip Tool Company financial statements for the fiscal year ending Sept. 30, 1987 (dollar figures in thousands)

Balance sheet at Sept. 30, 1987

Assets		Liabilities and stockholders' equity	
Cash	$ 100	Accounts payable	$ 160
Securities	150	Accrued expenses	90
Accounts receivable	180	Mortgage (current)	50
Inventory	620	Current liabilities	$ 300
Current assets	$1,050	Mortgage (8%)	600
Plant and		Common stock	2,000
equipment (net)	3,000	Retained earnings	1,200
Other assets	50	Total liabilities and	
Total assets	$4,100	stockholders' equity	$4,100

Income statement Oct. 1, 1986 to Sept. 30, 1987

Net sales	$5,500
Cost of goods sold[a]	4,550
Gross profit	$ 950
Operating expenses	330
Operating profit	$ 620
Other income	10
Less interest on debt	(70)
Profit before taxes	$ 560
Federal income taxes	270
Net profit	$ 290
Dividends	120
Additions to retained earnings	$ 170

[a] Includes depreciation of $150, labor expenses of $1,650, and materials expenses of $2,750.

are made in only four months (February through May). As is common for firms with seasonal sales, Snip's fiscal year does not coincide with the calender year.[3] Snip's financial statements for the year ending September 30, 1987 are shown in Exhibit 14-2.

The marketing manager estimates sales for next year to be $6 million, with monthly sales as shown in Exhibit 14-3. In forecasting monthly collections, the financial manager must consider the past payment habits of the firm's customers as well as the terms of sale. Snip asks its customers to pay within thirty days, but in the spring months many customers delay payment due to their cash flow problems. Accordingly, the financial manager uses the historical monthly relationship between collections and sales to forecast collections, as shown in Exhibit 14-3. For the first three months, sales made in one month are forecast to be collected in the next month. Then, as indicated in the exhibit, collections begin to slow down in relation to sales. In August, the firm's customers again begin paying within thirty days.

Despite the high degree of seasonality of sales, Snip's production is

[3] Fiscal years are established for convenience in preparing annual accounting statements. Seasonal firms often pick a time when they are not busy to begin their fiscal year. For example, department stores commonly start their fiscal year on February 1 because their inventories and sales are low then. Financial planning for a seasonal firm should be done at a slack time because maximum financial stress usually occurs when the firm is extremely busy and the degree of stress should be planned for in advance.

EXHIBIT 14-3
Snip Tool Company forecasts of sales, collections and accounts receivable

Month	Sales	Collections	Accounts receivable (end of month)
October 1987	$ 200,000	$ 180,000 [a]	$ 200,000
November	200,000	200,000	200,000
December	400,000	200,000	400,000
January 1988	400,000	300,000 [b]	500,000
February	600,000	300,000 [c]	800,000
March	800,000	500,000	1,100,000
April	900,000	700,000	1,300,000
May	900,000	850,000	1,350,000
June	500,000	900,000	950,000
July	500,000	700,000	750,000
August	400,000	750,000	400,000
September	200,000	400,000	200,000
Total	$6,000,000	$5,980,000	

[a] September 1987 accounts receivable assumed collected in October.
[b] December sales not fully collected in January.
[c] Half of the sales made in January will not be collected until March. This collection pattern is assumed to continue through July.

maintained at an even rate throughout the year. This enables the firm to stabilize its manpower requirements and achieve significant economies in production costs. In the past Snip's material costs have been about 50 percent of sales and labor costs have been about 30 percent of sales. The financial manager expects these historical relationships to hold for 1988 as well. The production manager has indicated that normal (level) production schedules will be followed for 1988 and no changes in year-end (September 30) inventories are planned. Since 1988 sales are forecast to be $6,000,000, Snip's labor expenses for 1988 will be forecast as 0.30($6,000,000) = $1,800,000 and materials expenses will be forecast as 0.50($6,000,000) = $3,000,000. Since no change in materials inventory is planned, purchases of materials for the year will equal materials expenses, $3,000,000. With level production schedules, these forecasts imply that purchases of material will be about $250,000 per month ($3,000,000/12) and labor expenses will be about $150,000 per month ($1,800,000/12). By a similar analysis, operating expenses are forecast to be $360,000 for 1988, or $30,000 per month. Labor and operating expenses are paid in cash monthly; however, purchases are not cash payments. The cash outflow occurs when payment is made to suppliers. Snip normally has thirty days to pay for its purchases and pays on time. Any materials bought by Snip will be paid for in the month following their purchase. Note that at the end of September 1987 (Exhibit 14-2), Snip owed $160,000 to its suppliers (accounts payable). Therefore, in October 1987 Snip will be paying $160,000 to them.

Other cash flows that must be forecast include income tax payments, investment expenditures on plant and equipment, interest and principal payments on debt, other income from investments in securities, and new financing. Expenditures on plant and equipment are usually planned well in advance. Snip currently plans to build a new warehouse whose total cost will be $100,000, with $50,000 being spent in October and $50,000 in November. In addition, replacement and upgrading of the firm's production facilities will require $30,000 per month for the next ten months beginning in October. Therefore, monthly plant and equipment expenditures will be $80,000 for October and November, and $30,000 for December through July. Income taxes will be paid as equal installments in December, April, June, and September based on the income forecast for the year. An income statement forecast is needed to estimate income taxes. This must be done before the cash flow forecast can be completed.

A forecast of Snip's monthly income statements is shown in Exhibit 14-4. Using the sales forecast of Exhibit 14-3, Snip's financial manager estimates cost of goods sold as 80 percent of sales (30 percent labor plus 50 percent materials) plus depreciation expense. Depreciation expense is forecast based on the depreciation schedules for existing assets plus the depreciation that will be taken on depreciable assets acquired during the year. This is estimated to be $160,000. The expense is prorated against the sales in each month. The easiest method to do this is to take the percentage of depreciation for the year ($160,000) to sales for the year ($6,000,000):

$$\text{Annual percentage} = \frac{\$160,000}{\$6,000,000} = 2.7\%$$

EXHIBIT 14-4

Snip Tool Company forecast income statements, October 1987 to September 1988 (dollar figures in thousands)

	Oct.	Nov.	Dec.	Jan.	Feb.	Mar.	April	May	June	July	Aug.	Sept.	Total[a]
Sales	$200	$200	$400	$400	$600	$800	$900	$900	$500	$500	$400	$200	$6,000
Cost of goods sold[b]	165	165	331	331	496	661	744	744	413	413	331	165	4,960
Gross profit	$ 35	$ 35	$ 69	$ 69	$104	$139	$156	$156	$ 87	$ 87	$ 69	$ 35	$1,040
Operating expenses	30	30	30	30	30	30	30	30	30	30	30	30	360
Operating profit	$ 5	$ 5	$ 39	$ 39	$ 74	$109	$126	$126	$ 57	$ 57	$ 39	$ 5	$ 680
Less interest on debt[c]	5	5	5	5	5	5	5	5	5	5	5	5	60
Profit before taxes	$ 0	$ 0	$ 34	$ 34	$ 69	$104	$121	$121	$ 52	$ 52	$ 34	$ 0	$ 620
Federal income taxes[d]	0	0	17	17	35	52	60	60	26	26	17	0	310
Net profit	$ 0	$ 0	$ 17	$ 17	$ 34	$ 52	$ 61	$ 61	$ 26	$ 26	$ 17	$ 0	$ 310
Dividends[e]			30			30			30			30	120
Additions to retained earnings	0	0	(13)	17	34	22	61	61	(4)	26	17	(30)	190

[a] Totals may not agree with sums of rows due to rounding.
[b] Including depreciation of $160 for the year, $150 as per 1984, plus $10 additional for new assets.
[c] Net of other income; same as 1984, preliminary assumptions.
[d] 50% tax rate is used.
[e] Planned for 1988; same as 1987.

Then add this to the estimated labor and materials percentage (80 percent) to get cost of goods sold as a percentage of sales (82.7 percent). So monthly cost of goods sold is forecast as 82.7 percent of monthly sales. Other expenses, such as electricity, which are included in cost of goods sold but which are forecast separately (not in relation to sales) can be treated similarly to depreciation and added into the cost of goods sold percentage.

The other items on the income statement that are forecasts (rather than calculations) are operating expenses and interest on debt discussed above. A line for dividends is included. Dividends are forecast based on the dividend policy set by management. Dividend payments will depend in part on the forecast of net income for the year and also on financing requirements. Therefore, dividends, like interest, are a preliminary estimate. Interest payments are forecast as "no change" from the prior year as per the discussion in the section on income statement forecasts. Note that in order to get a cash flow forecast, we need a forecast of income taxes. These income tax projections are derived from the income statement forecast, and, therefore, the income statement forecast must precede the cash flow forecast. Having calculated income taxes, let us examine the cash flow forecast for Snip.

Monthly cash flow forecasts are shown in Exhibit 14-5. The forecasts are based on the assumptions in the text and on the income statement forecasts. The bottom row of Exhibit 14-5, "Cumulative funds required," provides the information of most interest to the financial manager. This figure shows the total amount of money that must be available each month from financing sources outside of the firm. We have assumed that the financial manager will maintain average minimum cash balances of $100,000 (no change from September 30, 1987) and that securities will be sold before any borrowing is done. The forecasts of cumulative funds required indicate that the financial manager must begin to arrange for financing immediately because $90,000 will be required by the end of October. At the peak, in February, the firm must have $1,078,000 from some source in order to support its operations. However, by August the firm will be able to repay all outside financing and will have $223,000 available for investment in securities or for other purposes. These extra funds will not be available for long since only $120,000 will remain by the end of September, 1988.

Although the issues involved in determining minimum cash balances, investing in securities, and financing seasonal operations will be examined in Chapters 15 and 16, this example shows the value of the cash flow forecast for Snip's financial manager. Having projected the cash needed and available for fiscal 1988, the manager is in a good position to arrange for financing and to develop an accurate plan or budget for the period. Snip's financial manager relied on knowledge of past performance in making many of the original assumptions. The payment habits of customers and estimates of labor and material costs as a percentage of sales were all based on historical information. Current plans for investment in plant and equipment also were used. A forecast of the cash flows for an entire fiscal year provides the Snip Tool Company with a consistent projection of its needs and financial expectations for the coming year.

EXHIBIT 14-5
Snip Tool Company preliminary cash flow forecast, October 1987 to September 1988 (dollar figures in thousands)

	Oct.	Nov.	Dec.	Jan.	Feb.	Mar.	April	May	June	July	Aug.	Sept.
Operating cash receipts												
Collections of accounts receivable	$ 180	$ 200	$ 200	$ 300	$ 300	$ 500	$ 700	$ 850	$ 900	$ 700	$ 750	$ 400
Operating cash payments												
Payments to suppliers	$ 160	$ 250	$ 250	$ 250	$ 250	$ 250	$ 250	$ 250	$ 250	$ 250	$ 250	$ 250
Wages–production	150	150	150	150	150	150	150	150	150	150	150	150
Operating expenses	30	30	30	30	30	30	30	30	30	30	30	30
Total payments	$ 340	$ 430	$ 430	$ 430	$ 430	$ 430	$ 430	$ 430	$ 430	$ 430	$ 430	$ 430
Net operating cash flow	$(160)	$(230)	$(230)	$(130)	$(130)	$ 70	$ 270	$ 420	$ 470	$ 270	$ 320	$ (30)
Other cash inflow (outflows)												
Plant and equipment outlays	(80)	(80)	(30)	(30)	(30)	(30)	(30)	(30)	(30)	(30)		
Mortgage payments and other interest[a]				(51)								
Federal income tax[b]			(17)				(104)		(146)	(49)	(10)	(43)
Dividends[c]			(30)			(30)			(30)			(30)
Net cash inflow (outflow)	$(240)	$(310)	$(307)	$(211)	$(160)	$ 10	$ 136	$ 390	$ 264	$ 191	$ 310	$(103)
Cash available–securities	150											
Funds required (available)	$ 90	$ 310	$ 307	$ 211	$ 160	$ (10)	$(136)	$(390)	$(264)	$(191)	$(310)	$ 103
Cumulative funds required (available)	90	400	707	918	1,078	1,068	932	542	278	87	(223)	(120)

[a] Principal $25 every six months: interest 8% per annum paid every six months on outstanding balance plus additional $10 interest payment in August (see footnote c, Exhibit 14-4).
[b] Due December, April, July, and September. See Exhibit 14-4 for estimates.
[c] Planned, same as 1987

Forecasted or **pro forma**[4] **balance sheets** can be used to provide estimates of funds required and available just as the cash flow forecast does. Therefore, a balance sheet forecast can serve as an alternative to a cash flow forecast. Long-term forecasts (over one year) are often made using only pro forma balance sheets ánd income statements; however, for short-term forecasts, such as the Snip example, a balance sheet forecast serves only as supplementary data and utilizes figures from the cash flow forecast so that the two forecasts are consistent. Accordingly, the procedure used to forecast the balance sheet depends on whether a cash flow forecast has been made. We will first show how a pro forma balance sheet is developed based on a cash flow forecast using the Snip Tool Company example. Then we will discuss the forecasting problem when only pro forma balance sheets and income statements are desired.

Supplemental Balance Sheet Forecasts　Given income statement and cash flow forecasts covering a period of time, developing a pro forma balance sheet for the end of the period is primarily a problem of computation rather than forecasting. A supplemental balance sheet must be based on the assumptions and estimates used to forecast the income statement and cash flows of the firm; otherwise the balance sheet would not be consistent with the other forecasts. The general procedure used to forecast balance sheet accounts is as follows:

$$\begin{array}{c} \text{Ending balance} \\ \text{(forecast)} \end{array} = \begin{array}{c} \text{beginning balance} \\ \text{(known)} \end{array} + \begin{array}{c} \text{flows in} \\ \text{(forecast)} \end{array} - \begin{array}{c} \text{flows out} \\ \text{(forecast)} \end{array}$$

The financial manager takes the current value of the account (beginning balance) and adds the net change in the account derived from the income statement and cash flow forecasts (flows in − flows out) to arrive at the forecast value for the end of the period (ending balance). For example, accounts receivable is forecast as:

$$\begin{array}{c} \text{Ending} \\ \text{accounts} \\ \text{receivable} \end{array} = \begin{array}{c} \text{beginning} \\ \text{accounts} \\ \text{receivable} \end{array} + \begin{array}{c} \text{sales on} \\ \text{credit} \\ \text{during period} \end{array} - \begin{array}{c} \text{collections} \\ \text{during} \\ \text{period} \end{array}$$

Notice that the figure for sales comes from the income statement forecast and the figure for collections comes from the cash flow forecast so that the ending balance of accounts receivable is derived from these forecasts.

Suppose that Snip's financial manager wishes to forecast two supplemental balance sheets—the balance sheet for February 28, 1988, because that is when the need for financing is the greatest, and the balance sheet for September 30, 1988, because that is the end of the forecast period. In practice, a complete set of monthly balance sheets is usually developed.[5]

Snip's two pro forma balance sheets and the assumptions used to

---

[4] Forecasted income statements are called pro forma income statements.

[5] Most businesses use computer programs to calculate pro forma financial statements. Electronic spreadsheet programs such as Lotus 1-2-3 and Multiplan are available on personal (micro) computer systems costing less than $4000. However, to use such programs effectively, you need to understand the principles explained in this chapter.

generate them are shown in Exhibit 14-6. If all calculations are performed correctly and are consistent with the forecasts of the income statement and cash flows, the balance sheet will balance as it does here.

The balance sheets show the amounts of assets and liabilities of the firm and permit the financial manager to see the relationships between them. These data can be analyzed using the procedures of Chapters 12 and 13. In

---

EXHIBIT 14-6
Snip Tool Company balance sheet forecasts (dollar figures in thousands)

	Feb. 28, 1988	Sept. 30, 1988	Assumptions
Cash	$ 100	$ 100	$100 minimum
Funds available	0	120	From Exhibit 14-5.
Accounts receivable	800	200	From Exhibit 14-3.
Inventory	1,200	620	See Example A below.
Current assets	$2,100	$1,040	
Plant and equipment (net)	3,183	3,240	See Example B below.
Other assets	50	50	Same as Sept. 30, 1987.
Total	$5,333	$4,330	
Funds required	$1,078	0	From Exhibit 14-5.
Accounts payable	$ 250	$ 250	From text.
Taxes payable	52	0	From Exhibits 14-4 and 14-5.
Accrued expenses	90	90	Same as Sept. 30, 1987.
Mortgage (current)	50	50	Repayment schedule (Exhibit 14-5).
Current liabilities	$ 442	$ 390	
Mortgage (8%)	575	550	Repayment schedule (Exhibit 14-5).
Common stock	2,000	2,000	Same as Sept. 30, 1987.
Retained earnings	1,238	1,390	Sept. 30, 1987-value plus additions
Total	$5,333	$4,330	from Exhibit 14-4.

Example A

Beginning inventory	(Sept. 30, 1987)	$ 620	(Sept. 30, 1987)	$ 620
Plus production	(Oct.–Feb.)	2,067	(Oct.–Sept.)	4,960
Less cost of goods sold	(Oct.–Feb.)	1,487	(Oct.–Sept.)	4,960
Ending balance	(Feb. 28, 1988)	$1,200	(Sept. 30, 1988)	$ 620

Example B

Beginning net plant and equipment	(Sept. 30, 1987)	$3,000	(Sept. 30, 1987)	$3,000
Plus additions to plant and equipment	(Oct.–Feb.)	250	(Oct.–Sept.)	400
Less depreciation ($13.33/month)	(Oct.–Feb.)	67	(Oct.–Sept.)	160
Net plant and equipment	(Feb. 28, 1988)	$3,183	(Sept. 30, 1988)	$3,240

addition, lenders usually require supplemental balance sheets for the times when the need for funds is greatest.

Primary Balance Sheet Forecasts   Pro forma balance sheets may also be the primary method of forecasting funds required and available: A cash flow forecast will not be made. This is most often used in long-range forecasting and planning. A general procedure for three- to five-year forecasts is presented below:

1   Annual income statements are forecast. Included is a preliminary estimate of dividend payments.
2   Individual balance sheet accounts are forecast using one of the single-variable methods.
3   The retained earnings account is forecast using the income statement forecast of additions to retained earnings (net income less dividends) and the beginning balance in the account.
4   The balance sheet is balanced by "plugging in" additional cash or funds required as needed. That is, all assets and liabilities (including equity accounts) are forecast by whatever method the financial manager considers to be the most accurate. But total assets must equal total liabilities plus equity. If the sum of all assets forecast is less than the sum of liabilities plus equity, then the firm must have additional assets (funds available) so that balance is achieved. Similarly, if the sum of liabilities plus equity is less than the asset total, additional liabilities (funds required) must be obtained.

As an example of the balancing procedure, look at the Snip forecast in Exhibit 14-6. On the balance sheet for February 28, 1988, suppose that all assets and liabilities have been forecast except "Funds required." There must be an additional liability of $1,078,000 so that the balance sheet balances. This number could be calculated as:

Funds required = total assets − (liabilities + equity)

$$= \$5333 - (\$442 + \$575 + \$3238)$$

$$= \$5333 - \$4255$$

$$= \$1078$$

Similarly, the balance sheet for September 30, 1988, must have an "extra" $120,000 on the asset side (funds available) to be in balance.

**FINANCIAL PLANS
AND BUDGETS**

Financial managers forecast in order to plan and use forecasts to indicate whether or not their plans for the future are consistent with the goals of the firm. Forecasts therefore are a major part of the planning process. Management uses forecasts to anticipate problems so that action may be taken to alleviate them. Promotional campaigns may be developed to increase sales. Equipment may be purchased to reduce the costs of production or to increase the productive capacity of the firm. Such decisions affect the financial aspects of the firm's operations and must be planned well in advance of their implementation. Once management has determined a plan of action for the future, these plans are incorporated into a written **financial budget**. A financial budget is a formal statement of expected values of the financial variables of the firm over a future period. There may be a number of separate budgets for the various activities of the firm showing in detail management's plans for the future. For example, the capital budget would indicate expenditures on the capital projects planned over the budget period. The budget for operating expenses would be broken down by expense categories. The separate, detailed budgets are summarized in a cash budget that shows the various cash flows of the firm similar in form to the cash flow forecast shown in Exhibit 14-5. However, a cash budget would include the sources for financing planned in the future and the use of funds available.

There are two general approaches to developing a financial budget for the total firm—**top-down and bottom-up**. Top-down planning begins with a set of overall goals for the firm for the planning period. Then the activities that must take place in order to reach those goals are developed. This approach is most commonly used in long-range planning. Suppose, for example, that management establishes a goal of increasing earnings per share at an average rate of 10 percent per year over the next five years. Management then must determine the revenues that must be obtained in order to reach that goal. These revenue goals are then considered for their implications with respect to the assets required to achieve them, the production requirements, financing requirements, and so forth. The result of this approach is an overall plan or budget for the firm that is consistent with the goal established.

The bottom-up approach begins with estimates of the component activities of the firm. Each product line sold by the firm or each division might be forecast individually. Budgets are established for each area and then added together to provide a total financial plan for the firm. This approach is more like the forecasting procedure discussed earlier in which forecasts of single financial variables are combined into an integrated forecast of cash flows, income statements, and balance sheets.

In large firms both approaches are often used. Management may develop a general plan based on goals it has established. Forecasts of the firm's activities are then made, added together, and compared with the general plan. This dual procedure provides information on aspects of the firm's operations that must be given more attention. Also, it tells management whether the original goals are realistic.

Once the budgets have been established, they may then be used as a means of controlling the firm's operations. Lower-level management personnel can be provided with budgets for their own areas of responsibility and can be asked to operate within the confines of their budget. Budgets used in this way make it more likely that the firm's actual operations will approximate the overall plan.

If actual results deviate appreciably from the budgeted values, management investigates the reasons for the deviations. Depending on the reasons, either the budget will be revised to reflect changing conditions in the firm's environment or action will be taken to bring the firm's operations back into line with the plan.

The planning and budget process in large corporations usually involves a department whose sole activity is planning, and the process is more complicated than we have indicated here. In small firms, planning is usually limited to a forecast of cash flows and financial statements for the coming year and a preliminary plan for financing.

SUMMARY

Forecasting and planning the future financial condition of the firm are important parts of financial management. There are several basic techniques for forecasting single financial variables. These methods are:

1 The use of historical trends for the variable to forecast future values.
2 The use of the ratio of two variables to forecast one given a forecast of the other.
3 The application of statistical methods to historical data to determine the relationship between one or more variables; then one variable can be forecast using forecasts of the others.
4 The application of judgment and subjective evaluation of the future.

The forecasts of individual financial variables can then be combined to develop complete forecasts of the firm's financial position over time. There are two general approaches that may be used. The cash flow method focuses directly on movements of cash into and out of the firm. The balance sheet method relies on forecasts of individual balance sheet accounts. Income statement forecasts are used with both approaches. Each forecast provides somewhat different information about the financial condition of the firm over time, and both may be calculated if the financial manager wishes to have a complete forecast of the financial aspects of the firm's operations.

Forecasts are used as part of the planning and budgeting process of the firm. Budgets are formal plans used as an aid in controlling the firm's operations. Two approaches to planning are in common use. The top-down approach begins with some general goals for the firm for the planning period, and then the activities necessary to achieve these goals are estimated. The bottom-up approach starts with estimates for the separate parts of the firm. These separate plans or budgets are then combined to provide a total plan. Often both approaches are used to ensure consistency of separate budgets with the general goals established by management. The budgets for individual departments or operating units of the firm enable a firm's management to control its operations.

QUESTIONS

1 Why is forecasting an important part of the financial manager's job?
2 How do "trend" forecasts differ from "ratio" forecasts?
3 Under what circumstances would a "no change" forecast be best?
4 What is a "base variable"? What's the most common base variable in financial forecasting, and why is it used so often?

5 A scientific forecasting method provides the same results when used by different people. Does this mean that scientific methods provide the best forecasts?

6 What are pro forma financial statements?

7 What are the principal operating sources of cash receipts for a business firm?

8 There are two general approaches to forecasting a firm's balance sheet at a given future date. What are the two approaches, and under what circumstances is each one used?

9 Describe the two planning procedures discussed in the chapter.

PROJECTS

1 Obtain the annual reports for at least the past two years of a company (may be assigned by your instructor). Using data from the earlier financial statements, forecast the balance sheet and income statement for the year of the most recent annual report that you obtained. Assume that you have accurately forecasted the sales volume for the most recent year; that is, use the year's actual sales as a base variable. Compare your forecasts of all the data other than sales with the actual results. Try to determine why any major errors (greater than 5 percent) occurred.

2 Develop a financial forecasting model for the Snip Tool Company, using an electronic spreadsheet and the data in the text. Check your results against Exhibits 14-3, 14-4, 14-5, and 14-6. Then prepare new forecasts for fiscal 1988, based on revised sales forecasts of $5.5 million and $6.5 million for the year. Assume that the same seasonal patterns as shown in Exhibit 14-3 will be maintained; i.e., monthly sales will equal the same percentages of annual sales that are implied by the data in Exhibit 14-3.

PROBLEMS

1 Make the following forecasts using the method indicated:

a Operating expenses have increased at an average rate of 8 percent per year for the past five years. Last year, operating expenses amounted to $50,000. Forecast operating expenses for next year using a trend forecast. [Ans.: $54,000]

b The cost of goods sold has averaged 75 percent for the past three years. Next year's sales are forecast to be $900,000. Forecast cost of goods sold for next year using the ratio method. [Ans.: $675,000.]

c General and administrative (G & A) expenses have been as follows:

Year	1983	1984	1985	1986
G & A	$90,000	$99,000	$110,000	$120,000

Forecast G & A expenses for 1987 using the trend method.

d A construction equipment dealer's bad debt losses as a percentage of average annual accounts receivable have been a fairly steady 2.0 percent per year. As a percentage of sales, bad debt losses have varied between 0.2 percent and 0.4 percent. In good years many of the firm's customers pay cash; however, the dealer also offers extended credit terms to six months. Sales are forecast to be $3.5 million next year and accounts receivable are expected to average $600,000. Forecast bad debt losses using the ratio method.

2 AAA Rentals has the following history of sales as of 1986:

Year	1986	1985	1984	1983	1982	1981	1980
Sales (millions)	$7.1	$7.0	$6.9	$6.6	$6.4	$6.1	$5.5

a Comparing 1986 sales with 1980 sales, calculate the average annual percentage increases over the six-year period. Forecast 1987 sales using this figure.

b Apply a graphical approach to forecasting 1987 sales by fitting a straight line to the data from 1980 to 1986.

c From an inspection of the data, is there any other forecast that you feel might be better than the forecasts in **a** and **b**?

3 Given the historical data shown, prepare a forecast for purchases in 1988. The value of goods produced (production) in 1988 is forecast to be $2.1 million.

Year	1987	1986	1985	1984
Production (millions)	$2.00	$1.80	$1.75	$1.60
Purchases (millions)	$0.70	$0.55	$0.60	$0.53

4 Given the sales forecast and other information shown below, prepare forecasts of collections and accounts receivable for January, February, and March. Assume that accounts receivable are collected, on average, two months after the sales are made.

	November	December	January	February	March
Sales	$150,000	$175,000	$175,000	$200,000	$225,000
Accounts Receivable	350,000	325,000			
Collections	250,000	200,000			

5 The financial manager of Pinewood Furniture has found from experience that the collections of accounts receivable in a given month can be estimated as being 10 percent of the current month's sales plus

60 percent of the previous month's sales plus 30 percent of the sales made two months ago. For example, a forecast of August collections would equal 10 percent of August sales + 60 percent of July sales + 30 percent of June sales.

At the beginning of January, a sales forecast for the year is as follows:

Month	Sales (thousands)	Month	Sales (thousands)
January	$100	July	$180
February	$100	August	$150
March	$120	September	$100
April	$140	October	$ 80
May	$200	November	$ 70
June	$200	December	$ 70

Last November sales were $60,000, and last December sales were $60,000. Accounts receivable as of December 31 are $69,000.

Using the above data, forecast monthly collections and end-of-month accounts receivable balances of January through December.

6 As of January 1986, Kachina Distributors had recorded the following sales and average inventory:

Year	Sales ($000)	Average inventory ($000)
1978	$ 800	$400
1979	1,000	450
1980	1,200	560
1981	1,300	500
1982	1,400	600
1983	1,800	680
1984	1,750	800
1985	2,000	760

The financial manager would like to know what the average level of inventory is likely to be in 1987. Sales of $3.0 million have been forecast for 1987.

a Obtain forecasts of 1987 inventory in the following ways:
  1 Use the ratio of inventory to sales estimated over the last two years of data.
  2 Use a "trend" approach.
  3 Use a simple graphical method to estimate the relationship between inventory and sales.

b Compare the three forecasts obtained in **a** and discuss their validity.

7 Last year's income statement for Texas Minerals is shown below. Sales for next year are expected to be $600,000. Interest expense is expected to stay the same. The corporate income tax rate will be 20 percent on the first $25,000 of income and 40 percent on income over $25,000. The other income statement items are expected to maintain their past relationship to sales. Forecast next year's income statement using these assumptions.

	Last year	Next year (forecast)
Sales	$500,000	$600,000
Cost of goods sold	300,000	_____
Gross income	$200,000	
Operating expenses	50,000	
Interest expense	4,000	_____
Income before taxes	$146,000	
Income taxes	55,900	
Net income	$ 90,100	_____

8 Income statements for the past two years for Fiber Products are shown below. Sales for 1988 are forecast to be up 20 percent over 1987. Operating expenses are expected to follow their most recent trend. Interest expense is projected to increase to $40,000 because of a planned issue of long-term debt. Management expects that the average income tax rate will be 30 percent in 1988. Other income is not expected to change. All other income statement items are expected to maintain their past relationships to sales. Forecast the 1988 income statement for Fiber Products based on these assumptions.

	1986	1987	1988 (Forecast)
Sales	$1,400,000	$1,500,000	
Cost of goods sold	746,000	800,000	_____
Gross income	$ 654,000	$ 700,000	
Operating expenses	225,000	250,000	_____
Operating income	$ 429,000	$ 450,000	
Less interest expense	(19,000)	(25,000)	
Plus other income	10,000	10,000	_____
Income before taxes	$ 420,000	$ 435,000	
Income taxes	160,000	174,000	_____
Net income	$ 260,000	$ 261,000	_____

9 An analyst working under you has prepared the partially completed

balance sheet forecast shown below. He doesn't know what to do next. Can you complete the forecast for him? The minimum acceptable cash balance is $30,000. [Ans.: Cash = $50,000]

Assets		Liabilities and equity	
		Financing required	————
Cash	————	Accounts payable	$100,000
Accounts receivable .	$150,000	Other liabilities	50,000
Inventory	300,000	Current liabilities	
Current assets ..	————	Long-term debt	$200,000
Fixed assets	600,000	Stockholders' equity	750,000
Total assets	════	Total liabilities and equity	════

10 The analyst of problem 9 has just entered your office looking very upset. He informs you that he forgot that additional capital investments had been planned that would result in a forecast value of $700,000 for fixed assets instead of $600,000 shown above. Revise the forecast balance sheet to reflect the new information. How much new financing will be needed?

11 Develop a pro forma balance sheet in the following form for the end of next year given the data provided. Sales for next year are forecast to be $2.0 million.

Assets		Liabilities and equity	
Cash	————	Financing required ..	————
Accounts receivable .	————	Accounts payable ...	————
Inventory	————	Long-term debt	————
Fixed assets	————	Common stock	————
		Retained earnings ...	————
Total	════	Total	════

Minimum cash balance = $50,000
Accounts receivable = 15% of annual sales
Inventory = 12% of annual sales
Fixed assets = No change from current level of $850,000
Accounts payable = 4% of annual sales
Long-term debt = $240,000 based on present plans
Common stock = $200,000 (no change)
Retained earnings = $480,000 (current level) plus any additional earnings retained during year
Net income = 5% of annual sales (no dividends planned)

12 The financial manager of Omega Industries wishes to have a forecast for the firm's balance sheet three years from now at the end of year 3. You have been assigned to the task and provided the format and data shown below. Complete the assignment.

Assets		Liabilties and equity	
Cash	_____	Financing required ..	_____
Accounts receivable .	_____	Accounts payable ...	_____
Inventory	_____	Long-term debt	_____
Fixed assets	_____	Common stock	_____
		Retained earnings ...	_____
Total	=========	Total	=========

Year	1	2	3
Sales forecast	$1,000,000	$1,100,000	$1,200,000

Minimum cash balance = 3% of annual sales
Accounts receivable = 10% of annual sales
Inventory = $50,000 + 12% of annual sales
Fixed assets = $400,000 plus $20,000 per year
Accounts payable = 50% of inventory
Long-term debt = $300,000 less $30,000 per year principal repayment
Common stock = $200,000 (current value; no new issues planned)
Retained earnings = $150,000 (current value) + total additions
Net income per year = 4% of annual sales
Dividends per year = 40% of net income

13 Asian Imports must pay for the goods it purchases one month after receiving them. The firm orders goods based on expected sales so that the goods are received in the month of the anticipated sales. To ensure sufficient inventory will be available, Asian keeps a minimum base stock worth $60,000 (at cost). Approximately 40 percent of dollar sales are cash sales to retail customers. The remaining 60 percent consists of sales to dealers who pay two months after the sale is made. Cost of goods sold (purchase cost of goods) averages 75 percent of dollar sales. The sales manager has prepared a sales forecast for the next four months (January–April) as shown on page 475. As financial manager, you wish to develop monthly forecasts of cash receipts from sales and payments to suppliers.

Month	Total sales	Cash sales	Collections	Total receipts	Purchases	Payments to suppliers
November	$160,000	$64,000	$60,000	$124,000	$120,000	$ 80,000
December	200,000	80,000	72,000	152,000	150,000	120,000
January	80,000					
February	100,000					
March	120,000					
April	120,000					

Notes: Figures shown for November and December are actual. Collections shown are sales made in September and October; payments shown are due to October and November purchases.

a Prepare the cash flow forecasts using the format shown above.
b What are your forecasts for accounts receivable and accounts payable at the end of April?

14 The Deep Six Company manufactures depth sounders for fishing boats. In early January, Deep Six's financial manager, Valerie Steinberg, is in the process of developing a monthly cash flow forecast for the first six months of 1988. Total sales for 1988 are forecast to be $3 million. The following information is available:

Month	Sales forecast ($000's)
January 1988	$ 50
February	70
March	200
April	500
May	900
June	600
Six-month total	$2,320

Sales in November and December 1987 were $40,000 and $20,000, respectively. The depth sounders are sold to retailers who generally buy on credit. It is estimated that 10 percent of sales are for cash, 70 percent are collected in the month following sales, and 20 percent are collected in the second month following sales. Even though sales are quite seasonal, production is maintained at an even rate throughout the year. No changes in year-end (December) inventories are planned.

Valerie has observed the following historical relationships over the past several years:

Cost of raw material = 50% of sales
Cost of labor = 30% of sales

These relationships are expected to hold during the coming year as well. The raw materials will be purchased evenly over the year in relation to production needs. Payments for raw materials are made during the month following purchase. Labor costs and operating expenses are paid in the month incurred. Total operating expenses are forecast to be $120,000 for the next six months and, like raw materials and labor, will not vary appreciably from month to month. Total depreciation for the next six months is expected to be $60,000 and is included in the cost of goods sold.

Expenditures on plant and equipment are forecast to be $30,000 per month from April through June. Deep Six has an outstanding

---

Deep Six Company financial statements for the fiscal year ending December 31, 1987.

Balance sheet at December 31, 1987 (dollar figures in thousands)

Cash	$ 75	Accounts payable	$ 140
Securities	100	Accrued expenses	30
Accounts receivable	150	Mortgage (current portion) .	100
Inventory	800	Current liabilities	$ 270
Current assets	$1,125	Mortgage	1,400
Plant and equipment (net) .	5,000	Common stock	3,000
Other assets	45	Retained earnings	1,500
Total	$6,170	Total	$6,170

Income statement for the year ended December 31, 1987
(dollar figures in thousands)

Net sales	$2,700
Cost of goods sold[a]	2,268
Gross profit	$ 432
Operating expenses	220
Operating profit	$ 212
Other income	2
Less interest on debt	(74)
Profit before taxes	$ 140
Federal income taxes[b]	70
Net profit	$ 70

[a] Includes materials expenses of $1,350, labor expenses of $810, and depreciation of $108.
[b] 50 percent tax rate.

mortgage, which requires principal payments of $50,000 in June. Interest expenses are estimated to average $9000 per month. The Deep Six Company will continue to pay $10,000 per quarter in dividends in March and June as they did for the last two years. A minimum cash balance of $75,000 is required. Quarterly income taxes of $20,000 are due in each of April and June. Deep Six pays taxes each quarter based on its estimated total taxes for the year. The tax rate is 50 percent.

Given this information, do the following:

a Develop monthly income statement and cash flow forecasts for the coming six months, January–June.

b Develop a balance sheet for the month in which the maximum amount of financing is needed as determined in **a**.

c Develop monthly balance sheets for the coming six months, January–June. (Note that the balance sheet asked for in **b** will be included here.)

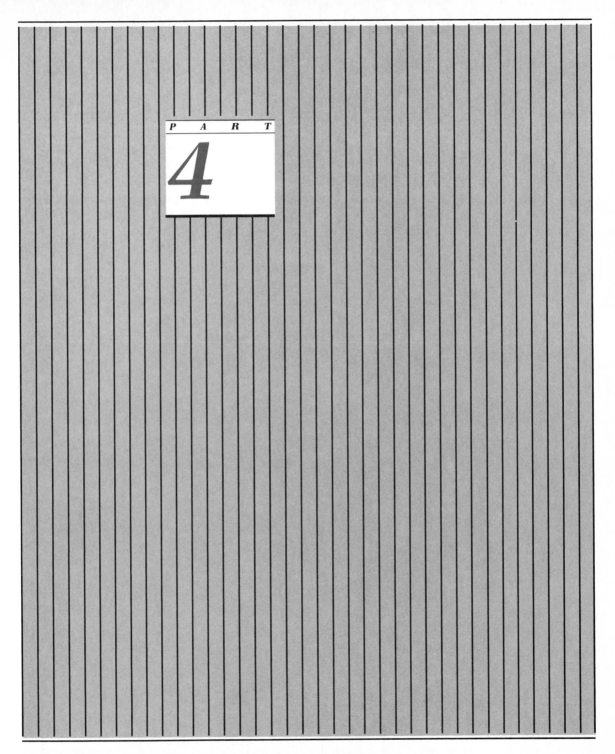

P A R T

4

WORKING CAPITAL MANAGEMENT

Working capital management is the management of a company's current assets and current liabilities. Chapter 15 shows how the basic investment concepts of Chapter 8 are modified to deal with the special characteristics of inventory, accounts receivable, cash, and securities—all of which constitute current assets of the firm. Chapter 16 describes the major sources of short-term financing—trade credit (accounts payable), bank loans, and commercial paper—which constitute the most important current liabilities of the firm. Chapter 17 shows how current asset decisions affect the method of financing and link together concepts developed in Part 3 and in the previous chapters of Part 4.

15

*CURRENT
ASSET
MANAGEMENT*

The four major types of current assets are cash, securities, accounts receivable, and inventory. The basic principles of asset investment discussed in Chapters 8 and 9 apply to these assets, as well as to long-term assets such as plant and equipment. However, each type of current asset has unique characteristics that the financial manager must consider in deciding how much money should be invested in that particular asset. In this chapter we describe the four types of current assets and examine the decisions that determine the level of investment in each.

Managing current assets requires more attention than managing plant and equipment expenditures. The financial manager cannot simply decide that the inventory investment, for example, should be $1 million and stop there. The level of investment in each current asset varies from day to day, and the financial manager must continuously monitor these assets to ensure that desired levels are being maintained. In most cases the desired level is, itself, a changing quantity. For example, the desired level of inventory for the Snip Tool Company of Chapter 14 at the end of February 1988, when its sales are very high, would not be the same as the desired level at the end of September 1988, when its sales are very low (see Exhibit 14-6).

Since the amount of money invested in current assets can change rapidly, so does the financing required. Mismanagement of current assets can be costly. Too large an investment in current assets means tying up capital that can be more productively used elsewhere (or it means added interest costs if the firm has borrowed to finance the investment in current assets). Excess investment may also expose the firm to undue risk if inventory cannot be sold or accounts receivable cannot be collected. On the other hand, too little investment also can be expensive. For example, insufficient inventory may mean that sales are lost since the goods that a customer wants to buy are not available. The result is that financial managers spend a large percentage of their time managing current assets because these assets vary quickly and a lack of attention paid to them may result in appreciably lower profits for the firm.

We begin with a discussion of the general rules that apply to investment in any current asset. Then we discuss each asset separately, first inventory, next accounts receivable, and then cash and securities. Three aspects of each asset will be examined:

1 The basic characteristics of the asset and how it is used by firms
2 The benefits and costs associated with the level of investment in the assets
3 The risks involved in investing in the asset

*PRINCIPLES OF
CURRENT ASSET
INVESTMENT*

The same general rules developed for the firm's investment decisions in Chapters 8 and 9 apply to current assets with some modifications that reflect their unique characteristics. First, although the amount of investment in any current asset ordinarily varies from day to day, the average amount or level over a period of time is used in current asset analysis. Using an average greatly simplifies planning. Second, both the dollar level of investment and the type of current assets held are important decision variables. Think of the inventory of a dealer in construction equipment. The dealer must decide how many bulldozers to keep in stock, as well as whether to stock bulldozers or dump trucks. From the viewpoint of the financial manager, all the decisions as to particular items add up to an average level of inventory for a given item, and these averages for all items add up to the total average inventory investment of the firm. The result is that there is a very large number of alternative levels of investment in each type of current asset. Therefore, in principle, current asset investment is a problem of evaluating a large number of mutually exclusive investment opportunities.

Solution of this problem by the methods presented in Chapter 8 requires that:

1 The financial manager estimates the costs and benefits from each alternative.

2 The net present value must be calculated for each alternative given the discount rate (cost of capital) appropriate to the degree of risk involved.

3 That alternative with the highest net present value be chosen.

However, the net present value approach is rarely used in practice. There are too many alternatives that must be evaluated, and they must be regularly reevaluated since the most profitable level of investment depends on the sales volume of the firm, which is continually changing. Procedures to handle the computational requirements exist, but differ for each asset. Net present values also are somewhat difficult to calculate and interpret for current assets.

So, instead of net present values, an alternative method is used: maximize average net profit with the amount invested treated as its equivalent annual cost. Let us explore this further.

Net Profit and Net Present Value

Suppose we are investing $1000 and will continue to receive $100 per year so long as we keep the $1000 invested. At any time, we can choose to withdraw our $1000 and the annual cash flow of $100 stops. This type of investment is described as being **reversible** since the transaction can be "reversed"; we can get the amount of the investment back if we want to. A savings account is a reversible investment. Current assets are usually evaluated as reversible investments.

One characteristic of reversible investments is that net present values are difficult to interpret. How would you calculate the present value of the above investment given a discount rate of 8 percent?

$$NPV = -\$1000 + \frac{\$100}{1.08} + \frac{\$100}{(1.08)^2} + \cdots + \frac{\$100}{(1.08)^n} + \frac{\$1000}{(1.08)^n}$$

$$= -\$1000 + \$100(P/A, 8\%, n) + \$1000(P/F, 8\%, n)$$

The above NPV is the present value of the net gain, or profit, from the investment. But there is a problem as to what time period n to use. The net present value depends on the time period you choose. However, the nice thing about reversible investments is that *when* the investment period ends is generally not important. To see this, let's calculate the annuity that has a present value equal to the net present value computed above. This annuity is the average net profit per period from the investment.

$$\text{Net profit} = \text{annuity} = \text{NPV}(A/P,\, 8\%,\, n)$$

$$= [-\$1000 + \$100(P/A,\, 8\%,\, n) + \$1000(P/F,\, 8\%,\, n)](A/P,\, 8\%,\, n)$$

$$= \$100(P/A,\, 8\%,\, n)(A/P,\, 8\%,\, n)$$
$$- [\$1000 - \$1000(P/F,\, 8\%,\, n)](A/P,\, 8\%,\, n)$$

But, $(P/A,\, 8\%,\, n) = 1/(A/P,\, 8\%,\, n)$, so

$$\text{Net profit} = \$100 - \$1000[1 - (P/F,\, 8\%,\, n)](A/P,\, 8\%,\, n)$$

The first term on the right-hand side of the above equation is the annual cash flow of $100. The second term is the annual capital cost of the investment of $1000, and this equals 8 percent of $1000 regardless of the number of periods n of the investment.[1]

Therefore,

$$\text{Net profit} = \$100 - 0.08(\$1000)$$

$$= \$100 - \$80$$

$$= \$20$$

The $80 is the annual capital cost of the $1000 investment at an 8 percent discount rate, and the annual net profit of $20 does not depend on when the investment is reversed. The result is that we can use net profit per period as a criterion for choosing among alternative reversible investments. The investment with the highest value of net profit per period is also the investment with the highest net present value, regardless of when the investment is reversed. Investments with positive NPVs have positive net profits; investments with zero NPVs have zero net profits; and investments with negative NPVs have negative net profits.

Many inventory decisions are made on the basis of minimizing cost. The same procedure as above is valid here. Instead of minimizing the net present value of costs, it is easier to minimize total annual cost where the annual capital cost of the investments is the discount rate times the amount invested. We will discuss this further in the next section, which deals specifically with inventory.

---

[1] The annual capital cost of an investment of a given amount is the annuity that has the same present value as the amount invested. In other words, we convert an initial amount invested into its equivalent annuity. The annual capital cost for any reversible investment is the discount rate k times the amount of the investment. We can show this mathematically by expressing the interest rate factors in their algebraic form from Appendix 4A.

$$[1 - (P/F,\, k,\, n)](A/P,\, k,\, n) = [1 - (1 + k)^{-n}]\left[\frac{k}{1 - (1 + k)^{-n}}\right] = k$$

Stating our results more generally, if the discount rate is k percent:

$$\text{Net profit} = (1 - \text{tax rate}) \times (\text{annual cash revenues} \\ - \text{annual cash costs}) - k(\text{investment}) \tag{15-1}$$

$$\text{Total cost} = (1 - \text{tax rate}) \times (\text{annual cash costs}) \\ + k(\text{investment}) \tag{15-2}$$

where net profit [Eq. (15-1)] and total cost [Eq. (15-2)] are expressed (following standard practice) as dollar amounts per year.

In the analysis below we will treat current asset investments as reversible and therefore select policies that maximize net profit or minimize total cost. The choice between a profit or cost approach depends on the particular problem being analyzed.

INVENTORY

Managing the level of investment in inventory is like maintaining the level of water in a bathtub with an open drain. The water is flowing out continuously. If water is let in too slowly, the tub is soon empty. If water is let in too fast, the tub overflows. Like the water in the tub, the particular items in inventory keep changing, but the level may stay the same. The basic financial problems are to determine the proper level of investment in inventory and to decide how much inventory must be acquired during each period to maintain that level. Let's examine the various types of inventory to see how each type is used.

Types of Inventory

Business firms keep inventories for many different purposes. Firms that operate equipment often maintain inventories of spare parts so that breakdowns can be quickly repaired. All firms must have some inventories of office supplies such as paper, pencils, and pens. The three most important types of inventory for most business firms are raw materials, work-in-process, and finished goods. Raw materials consist of goods purchased from another firm that are used to manufacture a product. Work-in-process inventory contains partially completed goods in process of production. Finished goods are goods ready for sale. The classification of a particular item depends on the kind of business being discussed. For a coal mining firm, coal is finished goods. For a steel mill, coal is raw materials, as it will be used in the production of steel. Similarly, steel is finished goods for a steel mill, but raw materials for an automobile manufacturer. Once goods have been produced in a form suitable for the consumer (automobiles, refrigerators, furniture, canned food, etc.), they are classified as finished goods. For example, an automobile dealer purchases automobiles from the factory; therefore in a sense they might be considered raw materials for the dealer. However, since the dealer sells a car essentially as it is to the consumer, the stock of automobiles is considered finished goods.

The inventory of a manufacturing firm contains all three major types of inventory. Wholesalers, retailers, and other firms involved in the distribution of goods from the manufacturer to the ultimate consumer hold finished goods that have been purchased from another firm. The level of investment in inventory differs greatly for firms in different industries. Table

15-1 shows inventory as a percentage of assets for different types of firms. The figures shown are industry averages. You might speculate on why firms

<table>
<tr><td>The Basic Inventory
Decision</td><td>Although the benefits, costs, and risks vary for every kind of inventory, all inventories have two characteristics in common: (1) Costs must be incurred to acquire inventory and (2) there are costs to holding inventory. Let's analyze this basic case before considering other aspects of inventory investment.</td></tr>
</table>

Although the benefits, costs, and risks vary for every kind of inventory, all inventories have two characteristics in common: (1) Costs must be incurred to acquire inventory and (2) there are costs to holding inventory. Let's analyze this basic case before considering other aspects of inventory investment.

Inventory is constantly being used up. This is true regardless of the type of inventory. Raw materials and work-in-process inventories are used in production. Finished goods are being sold. The rate at which the inventory is being used up is called the **usage** or **sales rate**, depending on the type of inventory. We can express this rate as S units of goods per year. For example, a steel mill may be using 10 million tons of coal per year. A grocery store may be selling 50,000 cans of chicken soup per year. To replace the inventory that is being used up, **orders** must be made. An order may be placed with a supplier (coal mine) or within the production facility of the firm. The person managing the finished goods inventory of a steel mill places an order for more steel bars with the production manager of the mill. An order is for some quantity Q.

TABLE 15-1
Average inventory investment for selected businesses

	Inventory/Assets, %
Manufacturers:	
Aircraft	48.0
Apparel	35.0
Drugs	21.0
Lumber	19.0
Petroleum refining	7.0
Wholesalers:	
Footwear	51.0
Drugs	45.0
Lumber	30.0
Petroleum products	15.0
Retailers:	
Shoes	64.0
Drugs	58.0
Department stores	45.0
Lumber	37.0
Gasoline stations	7.0
Miscellaneous:	
Soft drink bottlers	13.0
Laundry and dry cleaners	10.0
TV stations	0.1

Sources: Robert Morris Associates and Federal Trade Commission.

If the usage rate is constant, orders are made at even intervals for the same amount each time, and inventory goes to zero just before an order is received. In this case, the number of units in inventory will be as shown in Figure 15-1. For example, suppose that the usage rate is 1200 units per year (100 per month) and orders of 100 units are placed every month. When an order is received, there will be $Q = 100$ units in stock. the amount in stock will be reduced, on average, 100 units/30 days $= 3\frac{1}{3}$ units each day, and at the end of the month inventory will be zero.

The average number of units in stock will be $Q/2$. The average level of investment in this item will be the cash outlay required to acquire each unit (C) times the average number of units.

$$\text{Average investment} = \frac{CQ}{2} \tag{15-3}$$

If the cost per unit is $20, average investment in this item will be 20(\frac{100}{2}) =$ $1000.

From the viewpoint of the person managing the inventory, the basic decisions are how much to order, Q, and when to place the order. From the viewpoint of the financial manager, the decision is what level of investment should be made, $CQ/2$. Regardless of who makes the decision, there are four important types of costs that will be incurred: acquisition costs, order costs, holding costs, and the capital costs.

Acquisition Costs and Quantity Discounts Acquisition costs are the cash costs per period of acquiring inventory (either making goods or buying them). These costs can be calculated as the cash outlay per unit C times the usage rate S,

$$\text{Acquisition cost} = CS \tag{15-4}$$

FIGURE 15-1

Inventory levels over time when usage rate is constant.

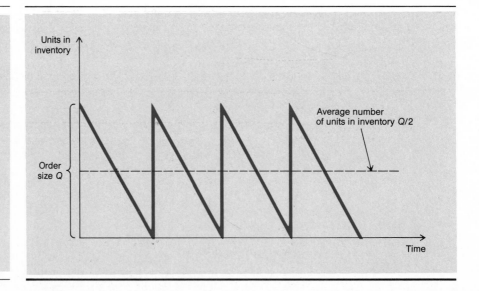

For purchased goods, C is the purchase price; for goods produced by the firm, C is the cash cost per unit produced. Determining C for goods produced by the firm is a difficult problem in cost accounting, so we shall use purchased goods in our examples to keep the variables in the problem clearly defined.

If neither the usage rate S nor the cash outlay per unit C is affected by the order quantity or investment decision, the level of acquisition costs will not affect the decision regarding the level of Q. That is, if acquisition cost is a constant value regardless of the inventory decision, this cost can be ignored in making the decision. However, acquisition costs may vary because of quantity discounts on purchased goods, so let's consider this more realistic situation. Note that, although the present example involves purchased goods, the acquisition costs of goods produced by the firm may also vary with the amount ordered; the analysis here also applies to this case.

A **quantity discount** is a reduction in price for ordering more than a minimum quantity of goods at a time. Quantity discounts are usually expressed as a percentage reduction in list price. For example, a discount of 10 percent on orders of 500 units or more for an item with a $20 list price means that the unit price will be $18 ($20 $-$ 0.10 $\times$ $20) if the firm orders at least 500 units at a time. Often discounts are available at several levels of order quantity. For example:

Discount, %	Amount ordered (Q)	Price (C)
0	1–99	$20.00
5	100–499	19.00
10	500–999	18.00
15	1,000 and over	17.50

Quantity discounts are normally given to reflect the savings in costs to the supplier from filling large orders. Special, temporary discounts are also occasionally offered when a supplier is overstocked on an item and wishes to reduce inventory quickly.

The effect of a quantity discount is that acquisition cost depends on the quantity ordered Q since the cash outlay per unit C varies with Q. Remember that in analyzing the basic decision we are assuming that the usage rate S is constant. To calculate acquisition cost, we must specify a value for Q. If Q is fifty units, we see from the table above that C = $20 and with a usage rate S = 1200 units per year it follows from Eq. (15-4) that

Acquisition cost = $20 $\times$ 1200

$\qquad$ = $24,000 per year

If Q = 500, then C = $18, and

Acquisition cost = $18 $\times$ 1200

$\qquad$ = $21,600 per year

Order Costs   Order costs are the costs that vary with the *number* of orders. In the basic model we assume that every time an order is made, a fixed dollar cost is incurred. For inventories such as work-in-process and finished goods produced by the firm, order costs include any costs of setting up equipment to produce the item. For these inventories the term "set-up costs" is used. Typical types of order and set-up costs are shown in Table 15-2.

The dollar cost of orders in a period depends on how many orders are made in the period and the cost per order. The number of orders per period is

$$\text{Number of orders per period} = \frac{\text{usage rate}}{\text{quantity per order}}$$

$$= \frac{S}{Q} \tag{15-5}$$

With a usage rate of 1200 units per year, if each order is for 10 units, 120 orders must be made per year. However, if 100 units are ordered at a time, only twelve orders per year must be made.

Define the cost per order for a given inventory item as *f*. The order cost per period for the item is

$$\text{Order cost} = \text{cost per order} \times \text{number of orders}$$

$$= f\frac{S}{Q}$$

$$= \frac{fS}{Q} \tag{15-6}$$

For example, if the cost per order *f* is $25 and twelve orders are made per year ($Q = 100$, $S = 1200$), the annual order cost for the item will be

$$\text{Annual order cost} = \$25 \times 12$$

$$= \$300$$

Holding Costs   Holding costs are costs due to holding (owning) inventory. Typical kinds of holding costs are shown in Table 15-2. Generally holding cost is calculated as a percentage of the average dollar investment in inventory. The financial manager determines the holding cost rate *h* by

---

TABLE 15-2
Typical costs of ordering and holding inventory

Order and set-up costs	Holding costs
Transportation costs	Storage costs
Clerical costs of making orders	Fire insurance
Costs of placing goods in storage	Property taxes
Downtime on equipment	Spoilage and deterioration

adding up the cost rates for the various kinds of holding costs. For example, suppose the following costs are estimated as percentages of the dollar value of inventory:

$$
\begin{aligned}
\text{Storage costs} &= 2.5\% \text{ per year} \\
\text{Property taxes} &= 1.0\% \text{ per year} \\
\text{Other holding costs} &= 0.5\% \text{ per year} \\
\hline
\text{Holding cost rate } h &= 4.0\% \text{ per year}
\end{aligned}
$$

The holding cost per period is the rate h times average investment in inventory [defined by Eq. (15-3)].

Holding cost = holding cost rate × average inventory investment

$$
= h\frac{CQ}{2}
$$

$$
= \frac{hCQ}{2} \tag{15-7}
$$

If 100 units are ordered each time ($Q = 100$) with a price of $19 per unit ($C = \$19$), average investment will be $950 ($19 × $\frac{100}{2}$). With a 4 percent annual holding cost rate,

Annual holding cost = 0.04 × $950

$$
= \$38
$$

Capital Cost Capital cost is the minimum annual dollar return required on the money tied up in inventory. As we discussed earlier in the chapter, a reversible investment can be evaluated on the basis of total costs [Eq. (15-2)] including the capital cost defined here. The discount rate k that applies to investments in inventory may differ for items according to the risk of investing in them. The risks in inventory investment are discussed in the next section. For now we will take the discount rate as given for the item in question.

Capital cost = discount rate × average inventory investment

$$
= k\frac{CQ}{2}
$$

$$
= \frac{kCQ}{2} \tag{15-8}
$$

Given a discount rate k of 10 percent per year and an average investment of $950 ($C = \$19$, $Q = 100$).

Capital cost = 0.10 × $950

$$
= \$95
$$

Total Cost The total cost of inventory for the basic model can now be expressed by plugging the cost elements we have developed thus far into the general total-cost equation [Eq. (15-2)]:

Total cost = (1 − tax rate) × (acquisition cost + order cost
+ holding cost) + capital cost

$$= (1 - \tau) \times \left(CS + \frac{fS}{Q} + \frac{hCQ}{2}\right) + \frac{kCQ}{2} \tag{15-9}$$

where τ is the tax rate. The capital cost is not multiplied by $(1 - \tau)$ since k is an aftertax discount rate. (In this book, all discount rates used for investment decisions are rates that apply to after-corporate-tax cash flows; this includes the average cost of capital defined in Chapter 7 and used in Chapter 8.) The decision variable in this equation is Q, the quantity ordered. Alternatively, we would express the total-cost equation as

$$\text{Total cost} = (1 - \tau) \times \left(CS + \frac{fCS}{2I} + hI\right) + kI \tag{15-10}$$

where I is the average level of investment $(I = CQ/2)$. Regardless of which way the equation is written or whether Q or I is considered to be the decision variable, we wish to minimize total cost.

We will examine two approaches to finding the minimum cost solution. First we will present a special case of the basic model that applies when acquisition costs do not vary with order quantity; then we will show the more general solution.

The EOQ Model   When acquisition costs do not vary with the quantity ordered, the quantity to be ordered that minimizes total cost in Eq. (15-9) can be calculated from a formula. This optimal amount to order is often called the **economic order quantity** or "EOQ" and the formula for its value is

FIGURE 15-2

*Total cost of inventory
when acquisition costs
do not vary with
quantity ordered.*

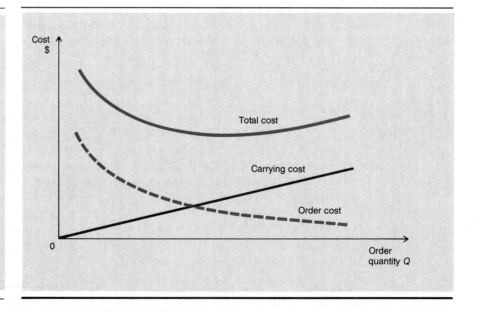

$$EOQ = \sqrt{\frac{2(1 - \tau)fS}{(1 - \tau)\,hC + kC}} \qquad (15\text{-}11)$$

The EOQ formula is derived by manipulating the total-cost equation [Eq. (15-9)] to find the value of Q that minimizes total cost. This is done in Appendix 15A. A graph of total costs and its two major components, order costs and carrying costs, are shown in Figure 15-2. Carrying costs are holding costs plus capital cost. Both holding costs and capital cost increase with the amount ordered whereas order costs decrease as the quantity ordered increases.

Suppose that the following values are given:

Usage rate	S = 1200 units per year
Cost per order	f = $25 per order
Holding cost rate	h = 4% per year
Discount rate	k = 10% per year
Tax rate	τ = 48%
Price per unit	C = $20 per unit for all order quantities

Then, plugging these values into the formula,

$$EOQ = \sqrt{\frac{2(1 - \tau)\,fS}{(1 - \tau)\,hC + kC}}$$

$$= \sqrt{\frac{2(0.52)(25)(1200)}{(.52)(0.04)(20) + (.10)(20)}}$$

$$= \sqrt{\frac{31{,}200}{2.42}} = \sqrt{12{,}893}$$

$$= 113.55 \text{ units}$$

Since fractional units are probably not possible to order, the optimal amount to order would be 114 units.[2]

Solving the Basic Model   The EOQ formula applies only when acquisition costs are not affected by the quantity ordered. To solve the more general case including the possibility of quantity discounts (or any other variations in acquisition costs), the easiest method is to calculate total cost for different amounts to be ordered (Q) given values for the other variables in Eq. (15-9). The value of Q that minimizes total cost can be read from a table of the results of the calculation or determined from a graph of the results.

Exhibit 15-1 shows several such calculations using the example data, and Figure 15-3 is a graph of total cost as the quantity ordered increases. The "jumps" in the curve reflect the quantity discounts provided at quantities of 100, 500, and 1000 units ordered. As can be seen both from Exhibit

---

[2] Total cost does not change very much for orders between 100 and 125 units, so a more convenient order quantity than 114 units, such as 100 units or 120 units (10 dozen), might well be used in practice.

15-1 and Figure 15-3, total cost is minimized at $Q = 500$ units, which means that average inventory investment in this item is

$$I = \frac{CQ}{2}$$

$$= \frac{\$18 \times 500}{2}$$

$$= \$4500$$

The basic inventory decision is to find the order size or average level of investment that produces a minimum total cost. Small, frequent orders allow a low level of investment that has low holding cost and low capital cost, but frequent orders are expensive because of order costs and because quantity discounts may not be available. Large, infrequent orders keep order costs down and may provide quantity discounts that cause high holding cost and high capital cost. The best inventory decision is the one that balances all types of costs so that total cost is minimized.

EXHIBIT 15-1
Total cost calculated for various order quantities

Total cost = (1 − tax rate) × (acquisition cost + order cost + holding cost)
              + capital cost

Quantity Q	Acquisition cost CS	Order cost $\dfrac{fS}{Q}$	Holding cost $\dfrac{hCQ}{2}$	Capital cost $\dfrac{kCQ}{2}$	Total cost
50	$24,000	$600	$ 20	$ 50	$12,850
100	22,800	300	38	95	12,130
120	22,800	250	46	114	12,120
200	22,800	150	76	190	12,160
300	22,800	100	114	285	12,250
400	22,800	75	152	350	12,350
500	21,600	60	180	450	11,810
800	21,600	38	288	720	12,120
1,000	21,000	30	350	875	11,990
1,200	21,000	25	420	1,050	12,200

Assumptions		Quantity discount schedule	
Usage rate S = 1,200 units per year		Quantity (Q)	Price (C)
Cost per order f = $25 per order		1–99	$20.00
Holding cost rate h = 4% per year		100–499	$19.00
Discount rate k = 10% per year		500–999	$18.00
Tax rate τ = 48%		1,000 and over	$17.50

An alternative way to think of the basic inventory decision is that increasing investment in inventory provides benefits from a reduction in order costs and from the possibility of quantity discounts. This benefit is offset by the increase in holding costs and the requirement that inventory investment provide a satisfactory rate of return, the discount rate k. Now let's look at some other benefits from inventory investment that are not directly related to order quantity.

Avoiding Stockouts　In our development of the basic model we implicitly assumed that the usage rate was known precisely and that we knew exactly when an order would be received once it was placed. These assumptions are not usually valid in practice. Suppose the firm tried to use the solution developed above. The average usage rate is 1200 units per year or 100 units per month. Every five months an order will be placed for 500 units. If it takes a month between the time an order is placed and the time it is received, an order must be placed when the inventory reaches 100 units, which is one month's supply. What happens if the demand for the item is greater than 100 units in the month before the order is received or if the order takes forty-five days to arrive? The firm will not have enough units in stock to satisfy the demand. This is called a stockout.

Stockouts are expensive. If the inventory item is finished goods, the customer may buy the goods from someone else; therefore, the profits on the sale will be lost. Even if the customer is willing to wait until the goods arrive, some goodwill is lost. If a firm is often not able to supply goods when

FIGURE 15-3

Total cost of inventory as a function of order quantity.

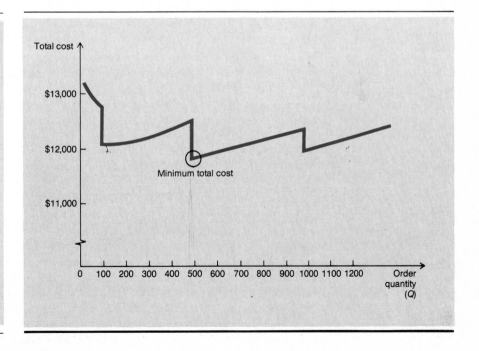

customers want them, its reputation suffers and it will lose business—more business than just the orders that were not filled for lack of inventory.

Stockouts of raw materials or work-in-process can cause the production process to stop. This will be expensive because employees will be paid for time not spent in producing goods or, if they are temporarily laid off, the firm will be assessed higher unemployment taxes. Some production processes are so expensive to shut down that management will go to great lengths to avoid running out of raw materials. There exists a company whose business is flying parts to automobile assembly plants so that they won't have to shut down when they run out of a critical item. The cost to the automobile manufacturer of having parts flown in by private jet planes can be several times the cost of the parts themselves. However, paying the high cost of transportation is preferable to shutting down an entire plant.

To avoid stockouts, firms maintain **safety stocks** of inventory. Safety stock is the minimum level of inventory desired for an item given the expected usage rate and the expected time to receive an order. In our example, if an order is placed when the inventory reaches 150 units instead of 100 units, the additional 50 units constitute the safety stock. The manager expects to have 50 units in stock when the new order arrives. The safety stock protects the firm from stockouts due to unanticipated demand for the item or to slow deliveries. Increasing the amount of inventory held as safety stock reduces the chances of a stockout and therefore reduces stockout costs over the long run. The level of inventory investment is, however, increased by the amount of the safety stock.

The best level of safety stock for a given item depends on how much a stockout costs and on the variability of usage rates and delivery times. If the usage rate and the delivery time can be forecast with a high degree of accuracy and if the cost of a stockout is small, then little or no safety stock will be needed. If the circumstances are not so favorable, then a significant investment in safety stock will be desirable.

A simple solution to the problem is to examine the costs associated with a given level of investment in safety stock.

$$\text{Safety stock costs} = (1 - \text{tax rate}) \times (\text{expected stockout cost} \\ + \text{holding costs}) + \text{capital cost} \qquad (15\text{-}12)$$

Holding cost can be calculated as the holding cost rate times the dollar investment in safety stock. Capital cost is the discount rate times safety stock investment. Expected stockout cost must be estimated at various levels of inventory investment. Given the cost estimates, we wish to find that level of investment which minimizes total cost. Exhibit 15-2 illustrates a solution to the problem given the assumptions shown. Minimum cost is achieved at 100 units of safety stock and an investment of $1800.

A complete solution to the problem of determining the proper level of safety stock for an item is complex and beyond the scope of this text. For example, the frequency of orders affects the number of stockouts for any given level of safety stock. Therefore the order quantity decision affects the safety stock decision and, in general, the two decisions must be analyzed together. Since some costs, such as loss of customer goodwill, are very difficult to estimate accurately, safety stocks are typically established by rules of thumb and managerial judgment. Depending on the type of inventory, avoiding stockouts is important to production or marketing management. The financial manager's role in the decision is often that of reminding other members of management that money invested in inventory should earn at least the cost of capital. Therefore, total avoidance of stockouts by maintaining large safety stocks is usually not the best solution.

Marketing Benefits   So far we have discussed the benefits and costs of investing in individual inventory items. We have not considered the decision as to what items to stock. Generally the wider is the variety of items stocked, the higher the inventory investment will be. What benefits are derived from stocking many types of inventory?

Most items in raw materials and work-in-process inventories of man-

---

EXHIBIT 15-2

Total cost of safety stock investment

Total cost = (1 − tax rate) × (expected stockout cost + holding cost) + capital cost

Investment Cu	Expected stockout cost sN	Holding cost hCu	Capital cost kCu	Total cost
$\ \ \ 0	$2,000	$\ \ 0	$\ \ 0	$1,040
450	1,200	18	45	680
900	800	36	90	525
1,800	400	72	180	425
3,600	0	144	360	435

Assumptions and definitions

Investment Cu = cash outlay per unit C × number of units of safety stock u
Cash outlay per unit C = $18
Holding cost hCu = holding cost rate h × investment Cu
Holding cost rate h = 4% per year
Capital cost kCu = discount rate k × investment Cu
Discount rate k = 10% per year
Tax rate τ = 48%
Expected stockout cost sN = stockout cost per stockout s × number of stockouts per year N
Stockout cost per stockout s = $40

Stockout estimates

Safety stock u, units	Number of stockouts per year N
0	50
25	30
50	20
100	10
200	0

ufacturing firms are necessary in that production cannot proceed without them. The decision as to what items produced by the manufacturer will be kept in finished goods inventories depends on the frequency of customer orders for the item, the time required to produce it, how important rapid delivery times are to customers, and the costs of carrying the item in stock. However, the demand for an item may depend on whether it is normally available. This problem is similar to the problem of determining the proper level of safety stocks. In both cases the sales and profits foregone as a result of not having an item in stock must be evaluated.

A further consideration is the extent to which having a more complete inventory in terms of the number of items stocked increases sales of all items. Most customers purchase more than one item at a time. A manufacturer who stocks a complete line of products is likely to obtain more business on each item than one who stocks only the items in greatest demand.

The decision as to which items to stock is of particular importance to distribution firms such as retailers and wholesalers, since their businesses are based on the availability of goods to meet their customers' demands. Inventory decisions are therefore very much related to the marketing approach used by the firm.

For example, Levitz Furniture Corporation virtually revolutionized furniture retailing early in the 1970s by its marketing strategies that included maintaining an unusually large variety of furniture in stock. As a result, inventory investment for Levitz was over 50 percent of total assets as compared with the industry average of 36 percent in 1974.

Inventory Speculation   During periods when the prices of purchased items are rising rapidly, firms have an incentive to invest more heavily in inventory than is indicated by the minimum cost calculation. If management believes the price of an item will increase by 10 percent in the next month, substantially more of that item may be ordered than normal. **Inventory speculation** is the term used to describe this extra investment.

The financial manager must keep speculative investment in inventory within prudent limits, since it can be both expensive and risky if carried to extremes. During inflationary periods, interest rates are usually high and so the discount rate is high. An unusually large inventory may require the firm to rent additional storage space as well as to incur all the normal holding costs. There is always the possibility that demand for the item will fall and the firm will be stuck with a large inventory for a long time. This possibility raises the problem of risk in inventory investment. The risks are not inconsequential, so let's look at them.

*Risks in Inventory
Investment*

The main risk in inventory investment is that the market value of inventory may fall below what the firm paid for it, thereby causing inventory losses. The sources of market value risk depend on the type of inventory. Purchased inventory of manufactured goods is subject to losses due to changes in technology. Such changes may sharply reduce final prices of the goods when they are sold or may even make the goods unsalable. This risk is, of course, most acute in products embodying a high degree of technological sophistication, for example, electronic parts. Distributors of electronic calculators and digital watches experienced this problem in the early 1970s as prices dropped over 50 percent in less than a year. In some cases the current retail price was less than the price charged by the manufacturer a few months earlier. Essentially, firms shouldn't have a lot of buggy whips in stock when buggies are becoming obsolete.

There are also substantial risks in inventories of goods dependent on current styles. The clothing industry is particularly susceptible to the risk of changing consumer tastes. A merchant with a large stock of blue denim pants is in trouble if corduroy becomes the fashion.

Agricultural commodities are a type of inventory subject to risks due to unpredictable changes in production and demand. A bumper crop of a commodity like corn or cocoa can send prices plummeting. Of course, there is also the potential for shortages in these commodities, which cause rapid price rises.

All inventories are exposed to losses due to spoilage, shrinkage, theft, or other risks of this sort. Insurance is available to cover many of these risks and, if purchased, it is one of the costs of holding inventory.

The financial manager must be aware of the degree of risk involved in the firm's investment in inventories. The manager must take those risks into account in evaluating the appropriate level of inventory investment. This can be done by including predictable losses as part of the holding costs and by applying a higher discount rate to those items that are subject to greater risks.

MANAGING ACCOUNTS RECEIVABLE

Accounts receivable is the total of all credit extended by a firm to its customers; therefore this balance sheet account represents unpaid bills owed to the firm. From the viewpoint of the financial manager the dollar amount of accounts receivable can be divided into two parts. One part represents the cash outlays made by the firm in providing the goods that have been sold. The other part is the difference between the cash outlay and the selling prices of the goods. The cash outlay portion is the actual investment by the firm in accounts receivable; the remainder represents accounting profits. The nature of accounts receivable is illustrated by the following example.

Suppose a wholesaler of automobile parts buys mufflers from the manufacturer at a price of $20 each. The wholesaler has invested $20 in each muffler in inventory plus cash expenses associated with inventory investment (holding costs and order costs) of $1 per muffler on average. The cash outlay per muffler is $21. The firm sells ten mufflers to a garage for $26 each on credit. It costs the wholesaler $5 cash expenses to sell and deliver the ten mufflers. The cash outlay by the firm is now $215 for the ten mufflers, $200 initial cost plus $10 inventory expense plus $5 selling and delivery expense. The garage owes the wholesaler $260 for the ten mufflers. This is an account receivable. The cash investment (out-of-pocket costs) in this account is $215 and the remaining $45 represents accounting profits. What has happened is a transformation of real assets, mufflers owned by the wholesaler, into a financial asset, money owed by the garage to the wholesaler.

What if the garage never pays for the mufflers? The wholesaler will lose the $215 it has spent in acquiring, holding, and selling the goods—nothing more.[3] The $215 therefore measures the investment made by the wholesaler in this account.

The basic decision to be made regarding accounts receivable is how much credit to extend to a given customer and on what terms. However, the financial manager sets policies that have a great deal to do with this decision, and it is these policies that we will examine. Let us begin with an analysis of credit extension to a single customer and then see how general credit policies affect this decision and therefore the total investment in accounts receivable.

The Credit Decision

Business firms extend credit to three groups of customers—other business firms, individual consumers, and governmental units. We will confine our analysis to firms selling either to other businesses or to individuals. Governmental units are similar enough to business firms to require no special treatment in an introductory discussion.

Consumer Credit   Businesses selling goods to individual consumers normally provide some sort of credit terms for purchases. The major exceptions are the supermarkets. However, most small merchants do not provide this credit directly themselves; they accept **credit cards**. Sales made with credit cards do not create accounts receivable for the merchant; the issuer of the card (a bank, American Express, etc.) pays the merchant when it is notified of the charge. The issuer of the credit card has the accounts receivable. Large merchants (such as department stores) usually extend credit directly to the consumer. Sales made on credit by these merchants do create accounts receivable for them.

All credit decisions are based primarily on the creditor's assessment of the customer's likelihood of payment. Setting a maximum on the amount of credit offered to a customer limits the exposure of the firm to the risk that the customer won't pay. In deciding to provide credit to a customer, the credit manager must evaluate the chances of nonpayment and estimate the benefits of extending credit. The benefits result from the additional sales obtained and any interest or fees charged for the credit. Consumer credit extending beyond thirty days usually carries with it an interest charge.

Risk assessment is a quantitative analysis of the likelihood that a customer won't pay for goods purchased on credit, and it assists the credit manager in deciding whether credit should be extended to a particular customer. Consumers applying for credit supply information about themselves that the firm evaluates. The firm may also seek information about customers from a credit bureau. Credit bureaus gather information on the credit history of people and sell it to businesses extending credit. People

---

[3] The $45 that was added to the firm's pretax profits when the sale was recorded is a "loss" from the perspective of the firm's accounting, but the net effect of $45 profit less $45 loss is zero.

who have failed to pay their bills in the past are viewed as greater credit risks than those who have an unblemished credit record. The information supplied by the individual and the credit bureau is evaluated in terms of the firm's experience with customers having similar characteristics. For example, firms have found that people who own their own home are more likely to pay their bills than those who rent. On the basis of this evidence renters would be looked upon less favorably than home owners when they apply for credit. The types of information asked for may include employment history, income, home ownership, checking and savings accounts, other assets, outstanding debts, etc. The extent of the information asked for depends on the size of the typical credit purchases at the firm. If a large amount of credit is being extended, more information will be requested.

The end result of this risk assessment is the classification of a credit customer into one of a set of **risk classes**. Large firms may use computerized statistical methods. An example classification scheme is shown in Exhibit 15-3.

The general credit policy of the firm will specify which classes of customers will be extended credit. Since the considerations of general credit policy are similar for both business customers and consumers, we will discuss them together after we look at the credit decision for business customers.

Business Credit   The majority of the sales by one business firm to another are made on open account. That is, the buyer is not required to pay for the goods immediately on receiving them and does not sign a formal debt contract. The buyer is asked to pay for the goods within a specified period, typically thirty days. The seller may also offer a discount or reduction in the cost of the goods if payment is made sooner. For example, the buyer might get 1 percent off the amount of the invoice if payment is made within ten days. The **credit terms** of the seller involve the specification of the type of account (open account or some other arrangement), the credit period (when payment is due), the size of the discount, and a discount period. A description of various credit terms is provided in Chapter 16 (see Table

---

EXHIBIT 15-3
Risk classification

Class	Average loss ratio, %
1	Negligible
2	0.5
3	1.0
4	4.0
5	10.0
6	25.0
7	50.0

16-1). In addition, the seller usually sets a limit on how much credit will be extended to a particular customer. Once the customer has reached the limit, no further sales on credit are made until some of the amount owed is paid off.

Generally, the credit terms of a company selling in a particular market are competitively determined in the market. The firms in a given line of business usually have very similar credit terms, and the credit terms of a firm will apply to all its customers. Credit terms are not normally varied from customer to customer. This is true of consumer credit as well. The decisions regarding a particular customer are whether or not to extend credit at all and what the maximum amount extended should be.

In making the decision to extend credit to a particular firm, the credit manager will seek information about its financial condition and past history. The primary source of information is credit agencies, such as Dun and Bradstreet, that provide credit ratings and credit reports on firms throughout the country. From this information the credit manager will attempt to determine the degree of risk involved in extending credit to the customer. In other words, the credit manager tries to estimate how likely it is that the firm will pay its bills. If the amount of credit involved is large, and if a cursory investigation suggests that the financial condition of the firm is weak, the credit manager may seek additional information by requesting financial statements from the firm. Techniques such as ratio analysis are often used to evaluate the financial condition of the firm. However, even if there is a significant chance of loss present, the credit manager must also consider the potential profits to be gained from selling to the customer. If the credit manager turns down the request for credit, the customer is likely to buy from someone else. A firm that has no bad debt losses is likely to be turning away many customers to whom it would be profitable to extend credit. Once a customer has been identified as being risky, the limits on credit become important. By restricting the amount of credit extended to a customer with financial problems, the potential loss is limited.

The techniques developed to classify consumers as to credit risk are not easily applied to business firms. Assessing the risk of extending credit to a business firm is much more of an art than a science, and experienced credit managers tend to rely heavily on their assessment of the "moral character" of the firm's owners and managers as it relates to their tendency to pay their creditors. However, if the credit manager has not had past dealings with the people requesting credit, the manager must rely on financial data and on the firm's past record with respect to other creditors.

Customer Attributes   Credit managers base their evaluations of the risk in extending credit on their assessments of the attributes of the particular customer. Customer attributes can be summarized by the "five C's" of credit—character, capacity, conditions, capital, and collateral.

> **Character** is a customer's own desire to pay off debts. As indicated above, experienced credit managers consider this to be the most important attribute.

Capacity is the ability of a customer to pay debts as reflected in the cash flows of the individual or firm.

Conditions are the general economic circumstances of the firm's industry or the individual's employment.

Capital refers to the financial strength of the customer, which depends primarily on the customer's net worth relative to outstanding debt obligations.

Collateral is any asset that the customer has available to pledge against the debt.

These attributes are assessed by examining financial data for the customer and by obtaining credit reports from firms that provide this service such as Dun and Bradstreet (for businesses) or credit bureaus (for individuals).

Credit Policy

Decisions regarding extension of credit to particular customers of the firm are based in part on general credit policy. If the firm has a policy of being fairly restrictive as to its credit terms and the customers to whom it will extend credit, it will have a lower investment in accounts receivable, lower bad debt losses, and very likely lower sales volume. Conversely, as the firm provides easier credit terms and sells on credit to poorer credit risks, its sales will rise but so too will its bad debt losses and level of accounts receivable.

Alternative credit policies can be evaluated by the net profit approach [Eq. (15-1)] outlined earlier in the chapter. The financial manager must estimate the cash revenues (collections of accounts receivable plus cash sales) the firm will obtain from each credit policy. Cash expenses and the amount of investment are also estimated for each credit poilcy. Given these estimates plus the discount rate k and the firm's tax rate τ

$$\text{Net profit} = (1 - \tau)(\text{cash revenues} - \text{cash expenses}) - k(\text{investment}) \tag{15-13}$$

The credit policy that provides the highest net profit should be established. To see how an evaluation of net profit is done, let's look at an example.

Suppose the financial manager is considering the adoption of five different credit policies, A through E. To determine which of these policies should be pursued, we first need to know the impact on accounts receivable, revenues, and expenses. Exhibit 15-4 displays values for these variables. No accounts receivable are shown for policy A. Credit policy A is selling for cash only. Naturally there are no bad debt losses with this policy. Policy B provides credit for low-risk customers who will pay on time. There are no bad debt losses for policy B, but there are some accounts receivable equal to fifteen days of sales. Policy C involves selling on credit to more risky customers, and occasionally the firm will have bad debt losses. Also, these customers will take longer on average to pay for the goods sold to them on credit. Policies D and E involve selling to even more risky customers on longer credit terms. Of course, the advantage of providing credit is the increase in the sales (revenues) for the firm. In order to evaluate these alternative policies, we need to know the net revenues after taxes from the sales volume achieved. The aftertax revenues provided by each credit policy are shown in column 7 of Exhibit 15-4.

As we discussed in connection with inventory policy, a decision on the level of investment in an asset requires us to consider the amount of investment. Exhibit 15-5 shows the investment required for each credit policy. The key figures are in column 3, "Total investment"; however, these figures are simply the sums of the data in columns 1 and 2. Note first that the values for "Cash investment in accounts receivable," column 1, are not the same values as shown for accounts receivable in Exhibit 15-4. The figures in column 1 of Exhibit 15-5 are 80 percent of the corresponding figures for accounts receivable in Exhibit 15-4. The remaining 20 percent is accounting profit. As we discussed at the beginning of the section on accounts receivable, cash investment is less than the value of accounts receivable on the firm's financial statement. The 80 percent figure reflects acquisition costs plus costs in stocking and selling the goods.

Another important aspect of Exhibit 15-5 is the inclusion of inventory investment. Note that increasing sales are assumed to require additional inventory. Two questions might occur to you. First, why are we including inventory in a credit policy analysis? Second, if it is proper to do it here, why didn't we include accounts receivable in the inventory example earlier in this chapter? Taking the second question first, we assumed that usage (sales) rates were constant in our examples. Therefore, accounts receivable were unaffected by the inventory decisions examined. So our answer to the first question is that we include inventory here because, whenever there is a choice among alternative policies causing differences in the sales volume of the firm, the impact on the investment in all current assets of the firm must

---

EXHIBIT 15-4
The impact of alternative credit policies on revenues and expenses

Credit policy	Annual revenues (1)	Accounts receivable (2)	Acquisition cost of goods sold (3)	Bad debt losses (4)	Operating cost (5)	Net revenues before taxes (6)	Net revenues after taxes (7)
A	$ 60,000	$ 0	$ 42,000	$ 0	$12,000	$ 6,000	$ 3,120
B	120,000	5,000	84,000	0	21,000	15,000	7,800
C	150,000	12,500	105,000	300	25,000	19,700	10,244
D	170,000	21,000	119,000	1,300	28,500	21,200	11,024
E	180,000	30,000	126,000	2,500	30,000	21,500	11,180

Assumptions and definitions

Acquisition cost per unit sold = 70% of selling price
Net revenues = annual revenues − acquisition cost − operating cost − bad debt losses
Aftertax revenues = $(1 − \tau)$ net revenues
Tax rate τ = 48%
Operating costs = holding and order costs of inventory plus sales commissions, collection expenses, and other costs of accounts receivable

be considered. This is so regardless of the nature of the decisions being made—whether they involve new production methods, marketing strategies, personnel policies, or whatever. Unless the firm sells services for cash, an increase in sales will almost always require an increase in accounts receivable and inventory.[4] This added investment in the firm must be evaluated by the financial manager.

A general procedure for dealing with such problems is to determine the optimal inventory investment for each credit policy given the sales (usage rate) estimated for each policy and then, given the amount of inventory to be held, to proceed with the analysis as shown in this section. In other words, each inventory level shown in column 2 of Exhibit 15-5 can be viewed as having been determined by an analysis similar to that performed earlier. Since the amount of inventory investment differs for each credit policy, that investment must be included in the analysis.

The remaining factor in the equation for net profit [Eq. (15-13)] is the discount rate k. Suppose that $k = 10$ percent; then net profit can be calculated as shown in Exhibit 15-6. We see that a maximum net profit of $7494 is achieved with credit policy C. This leaves us with the question of how risky is investment in accounts receivable, since the degree of risk affects the discount rate k.

Risk in Accounts Receivable

Accounts receivable is generally considered a relatively low-risk asset. The basic risk is due to the possibility that the firm will not be able to collect all that is owed to it by its customers. Under normal circumstances the total bad debt losses a firm will experience can be forecast with reasonable accuracy, especially if the firm sells to a large number of customers and does not change its credit policies. These "normal" losses can be considered purely a cost of extending credit. The real risk arises from the possibility that a significant number of the firm's customers may suddenly get

---

[4] Even a service firm selling for cash might wish to increase its holdings of cash and securities if volume increases substantially. We will discuss this in more detail in the next section of this chapter.

EXHIBIT 15-5
Investment for alternative credit policies

Credit policy	Cash investment in accounts receivable (1)	Investment in inventory (2)	Total investment [(1) + (2)] (3)
A	$ 0	$ 7,000	$ 7,000
B	4,000	14,000	18,000
C	10,000	17,500	27,500
D	16,800	19,800	36,600
E	24,000	21,000	45,000

EXHIBIT 15-6
Net profit for alternative credit policies

Credit policy	Net revenues after taxes[a] (1)	Total investment[b] (2)	Capital cost (3)	Net profit (4)
A	$ 3,120	$ 7,000	$ 700	$2,420
B	7,800	18,000	1,800	6,000
C	10,244	27,500	2,750	7,494
D	11,024	36,600	3,660	7,364
E	11,180	45,000	4,500	6,680

Net profit = net revenues after taxes − capital cost
Capital cost = discount rate k × total investment
Discount rate k = 10%

[a] From col. 7, Exhibit 15-4.
[b] From col. 3, Exhibit 15-5.

into financial difficulties. For example, suppose an appliance dealer is located near a large industrial plant and 90 percent of its accounts receivable represent credit sales to the plant's employees. If, for some reason, the plant shuts down for an extended period of time, the dealer is likely to be unable to collect a large portion of the accounts receivable. There are companies that provide insurance against unusual losses (credit insurance), and this is one way to reduce the risk. In most cases, accounts receivable is not a particularly risky asset and the discount rate that should be used in evaluating a credit policy is less that the firm's weighted average cost of capital.

CASH MANAGEMENT

In current practice, the term cash management refers to the general problem of managing the firm's cash balances (currency and demand deposits), cash flows (receipts and collections), and short-term investments in securities. There are several reasons for firms to invest in cash and securities and we will discuss them in this section. We will also examine the problem of managing the cash flows of the firm. Let's begin by examining the securities held by business firms.

Investment in Securities

Firms often invest in securities because they have excess funds that they wish to invest temporarily or even over the long term. There are several reasons for this.

Firms with seasonal sales patterns usually have periods of one or more months during which they have excess funds. This usually occurs in the months immediately after the peak sales period. At this time inventory and accounts receivable reach their low point of the year and collections of accounts receivable exceed cash outflows. An example of a firm with this pattern is Snip Tool Company in Chapter 14. Firms in industries where sales vary substantially over the business cycle often retain excess cash during recessions in anticipation of an upturn in the economy. As business improves, the funds will be used to finance the additional inventories and accounts receivable needed to suppport increased sales.

Some firms try to maintain a semipermanent "ready reserve" of securities to ensure that funds will be available to meet unexpected needs for cash. This reason for holding excess funds is sometimes called the **precautionary motive**. The practice of maintaining precautionary balances is characteristic of conservative financial managers.[5] Interestingly, most firms that do this have ready access to bank credit that serves as an alternative source of funds in emergencies and therefore make precautionary balances somewhat unnecessary. An exception might be small firms operating in risky lines of business. For these firms a ready reserve could prove highly desirable.

Another reason for holding excess funds is to meet a large planned payment of cash in the near future. Firms often accumulate funds in order to meet taxes, dividends, or payments on long-term debt. A similar situation arises when the firm has raised long-term capital to invest in a new plant. Such financing is often arranged in advance of the actual need for the funds, and the proceeds from the sale of the firm's securities are temporarily invested in other securities prior to paying for the plant.

In cases such as these, most financial managers will invest in money market securities, often planned so that the securities will mature just before the cash is needed. In the case of precautionary balances, the funds at maturity will be reinvested. The main advantage of money market securities is that they may be sold very quickly with little chance of loss due to changes in interest rates. Table 15-3 lists some methods of short-term investment used by large corporations. Small firms usually confine their investments to Treasury bills, bank (time or savings) deposits, and commercial paper.

There are situations in which firms will accumulate excess funds and invest them over long periods of time. These usually involve the planned long-run expansion of the firm and a desire on the part of the financial manager to finance anticipated needs with internally generated funds rather than with new debt or stock. Bendix Corp. accumulated $500 million of short-term securities in early 1982 to be used to finance future acquisitions. Also, funds may be accumulated to retire an issue of long-term debt either prior to or at maturity. In such cases the funds may be invested in long-term debt securities or even common stock.

The decisions as to specific investments in securities depend greatly on conditions in the securities markets and on the circumstances of the firm. The financial managers of large corporations have become very astute in

---

[5] There is a reason for holding liquid assets called the speculative motive, which is not so important for business firms. Cash and short-term securities may be held in order to speculate on a possible increase in interest rates. This would *not* be typical of a conservative financial manager.

TABLE 15-3
Methods of short-term investment used by large corporations

Type	Description	Maturities	Marketability	Minimum denomination[a]
U.S. Treasury bills *other federal agency issues* *Fanny May*	Obligation of U.S. government. Treasury issues 3- and 6-month bills weekly, 9-month and 1-year bills monthly. Sold on a discount basis.	Up to 1 year	Excellent	$10,000
Commercial paper: finance company	Unsecured notes of finance companies sold directly to investors who may specify maturity desired. May be coupon bearing but normally sold on a discount basis.	3 to 270 days	None, although issuer may be willing to redeem early.	$1,000[b]
Commercial paper: dealer	Unsecured notes of major industrial firms and financial institutions sold through commercial paper dealers. Sold on a discount basis.	15 to 270 days	Generally limited to the issuing dealer.	$100,000
Negotiable certificates of deposit	Certificates of time deposits at a commercial bank. Interest paid at maturity. Insured up to $100,000 by Federal Deposit Insurance Corp.	Usually less than 1 year, but may be longer	Good, for major banks	$100,000
Prime banker's acceptance	Time drafts (orders to pay) issued by a business firm (usually an importer) and "accepted" by a bank. Bank effectively guarantees payment to investor. Sold on a discount basis.	Rarely over 6 months	Good, for major banks	$25,000

Short-term tax exempts	Notes of states, municipalities, and other political subdivisions and local agencies. Project notes of public housing agencies may be backed by U.S. government. Interest is exempt from federal income tax.	Up to 1 year	Good	$1,000
Repurchase agreements	Purchase of securities with a guarantee to repurchase by the issuer of the agreement. Essentially a collateralized note. U.S. government obligations are most commonly used. Issuers are usually banks and securities dealers. Known as "repos" or "RPs."	1 day to several weeks	None	$100,000
Eurodollars	Dollar-denominated time deposits in banks or branches outside the United States. Used by multinational corporations.	Usually 30 to 180 days	Variable	$100,000
Foreign securities and deposits	Wide variety available, subject to exchange risks and tax considerations.	Up to 1 year	Variable	Variable

[a] The amounts shown are the minimum values in normal practice. Exceptions do exist.
[b] Minimum order is $25,000.

floating rate
preffered
Stock mutual
funds
 - div part float of it
 - tax exempt @ (≈80% of it)
 - pretty liquid

Money market
mutual
funds

their management of cash and securities. Let's look at the process of managing the cash balances and cash flow through the firm.

Why Do Firms Hold Cash?

Most payments and receipts of business firms involve checks drawn on demand deposits at commercial banks.[6] Businesses typically pay their employees and suppliers with checks and their customers pay them in the same way. Relatively few transactions involve the use of currency, and these are primarily retail sales. We will use the term cash to refer to both currency and demand deposits.

Business firms hold cash for basically the same reasons individuals do—to have funds available to meet checks drawn on their accounts. The amount of cash that should be held depends not only on the withdrawals from the account but also on the deposits of checks received. If you know that every day you will be depositing $100 and that $100 of your checks will be withdrawn, you might think that the average bank balance at the end of the day would be zero. However, this isn't so. When you deposit a check, the bank may not let you withdraw funds until the check has been cleared—in other words, until the funds have been withdrawn from the account on which the check was drawn. Normally the funds will be available within three days. Therefore you would need to have made three days' of deposits to your account in order to have funds available to pay your checks. In this example, your bank balance (total value of checks deposited less total withdrawals) would have to be $300. At any given time, there will be no more than $100 in your account available for immediate withdrawal.

Moreover, deposits and withdrawals are usually made at irregular intervals. One day you might deposit nothing and the next day $300. The checks you have written are likely to arrive at your bank at unpredictable times. Therefore you must keep higher average balances in order to ensure that funds will be available at all times.[7] As a consequence, cash balances must be maintained to permit the normal transactions of the business. This is sometimes referred to as the **transactions motive** for holding cash.

There are other reasons for holding cash. Commercial banks encourage firms to maintain demand deposits as a means of paying the bank for some of the services it provides, instead of charging fees for the services. Such services include not only the processing of the firm's checks, but also purchasing securities for the firm and providing credit information on new customers of the firm. Companies borrowing money from a bank are often required to maintain a specified amount of cash on deposit with the bank. Demand deposits held to compensate banks for services and loans are called **compensating balances**.

[6] Many of these transactions are made electronically. Firms and government agencies may pay their employees by delivering a magnetic tape to a central processing facility that automatically transfers funds from the firm's demand account to the accounts of each employee. In most large cities, individuals can pay bills by telephoning into a bank's computer and instructing the computer to transfer funds from their accounts to the account of the business to which they owe money.

[7] An alternative is to have an overdraft privilege where the bank automatically lends you money to cover checks exceeding your available balance. Interest is charged on the loan.

For large firms, the compensating balance requirements of their banks are a major factor determining the average amount of cash held. Funds available in excess of normal cash requirements are usually invested in securities to provide a return. These excess funds may be automatically invested by the firm's banks in overnight repurchase agreements, which are described in Table 15-3. This arrangement is called a "sweep" account because excess cash is "swept" into investments. Aggressive financial managers try to keep cash balances to the barest minimum sufficient to meet transaction requirements and to compensate the bank.

Cash Control and Concentration

Keeping cash balances at the minimum level requires careful management, especially for companies that have offices and banks in multiple locations. Efficient cash management requires that financial managers know the balances in all corporate bank accounts on a timely basis. For large corporations which deal in millions of dollars, timely means daily. The information may be obtained via telephone, telecopier, or other means. Major banks now offer balance reporting through computer terminals at the financial manager's office. The manager can access required information on the terminal regarding any account covered by the system. Given this knowledge, the manager can decide where funds should be transferred or invested.

Concentration of cash is the simplest way to gain control of it. Once excess balances in the firm's banks have been identified, the next step is to concentrate the money in an account at one of the firm's major banks. This bank is called a **concentration bank**. The fastest way to move money from one bank to another is wire transfer. Funds transferred by wire become available for use the same day. There are two wire transfer systems in use in the United States. The Fed Wire is operated by the Federal Reserve System and money transfers are done by bookkeeping entries on the accounts of the banks in the Federal Reserve System. The Bank Wire is a private wire service subscribed to by banks. Transfers over the Bank Wire are made by entries to accounts of the banks which are members. Because wire transfers are relatively more expensive ($3–$6 per transfer) than other methods of moving money such as checks, they are most often used for transferring amounts in excess of $5000. Systems are now available that allow the financial manager to initiate a wire transfer directly from a computer terminal. These systems can reduce the cost of the transfer.

An alternative to wire transfer is a **depositary transfer check**, which costs only a few cents. These are checks without signatures which are payable only to the account in the firm's concentration bank and drawn on one of the branch office local bank accounts. The firm's local managers notify the head office after depositing money in the local accounts. The concentration bank issues the checks on the instructions of the head office for deposit in the concentration account. Automated depositary transfer services are also available from many banks. Under an automated system, the local managers telephone amounts to be transferred to the concentration bank, which then creates electronic fund transfers from the local accounts to the concentration account. Once the cash has been concentrated at a single account, it can be invested.

Cash flow management is the management of collection and disbursement procedures with the following objectives:

1 Collection from customers as quickly as possible so that the funds will be available to the firm as soon as possible (e.g., to earn interest);
2 Payment to vendors and other parties as slowly as possible so that the funds will remain available to the firm as long as possible (e.g., earning interest).

Both individuals and firms have a cash flow management problem.

The individual's strategy for efficient cash flow management is relatively simple. Checks are deposited as soon as possible and bill payments are delayed as long as possible without incurring a finance charge. Credit cards and charge accounts are particularly useful in this respect since the time between purchase and payment can run as long as several months in some instances (with no interest charge). Both business firms and consumers essentially attempt to do the same thing—to minimize the time they are providing someone else with free credit (an interest-free loan) and to maximize their own free credit. This free credit is called "float."

Float is money in the process of being collected. It is measured in dollar-days. Therefore $4 million in float can be $1 million for four days, $2 million for two days, $0.5 million for eight days, or any other combination of amount and time with a product of $4 million dollar-days. Float is measured in this way because it translates directly into cash balances. For example, if you can collect money owed to you more quickly, you will have more cash on average over time. A permanent reduction of $1 million in the float arising from collections will provide an increase of $1 million in available cash. There are several different types of float, but the two basic types are collection float and disbursement float.

Collection float is money being received by the firm from its customers. Once a customer has initiated the payment, by mailing a check for example, the firm has collection float. The float ends when the firm has the payment credited to its account *as collected funds available for investment or other uses.* The collection float therefore arises both from the time it takes a check to go through the mail system and get deposited into the bank, and from the time it takes a deposited check to clear through the bank system and become available for withdrawal. Collection "float time" is the amount of time from the moment a customer's check is mailed to the firm to the moment the money becomes available to the firm. For example, if a firm receives $1 million per day in payments and it takes six days on average from the time a check is mailed to the time the money actually becomes available to the firm, this firm's average collection float is $6 million. The collection float time is six days.

Businesses attempt to reduce collection float time by several methods. One method of reducing float time involves establishing a **lock box** (a special post office box) in an area where there are many customers. Customers are instructed to send their payments to this address. A local bank picks up the checks and deposits them in the firm's account with that bank. After the checks have cleared, the funds are available to the firm. A lock box system can reduce float time by one to four days. If checks are being received at a rate of $100,000 per day, reduction of three days frees $300,000 of cash for use by the firm.

Another method of reducing float time is to persuade customers to permit the use of pre-authorized checks which are issued by the company or the company's bank, payable to the company, and drawn on the customer's account. The customer signs an agreement with the company to allow these checks to be issued at specific times and for specific amounts. Pre-authorized checks are used primarily in situations where the customer is making a regular monthly payment of a fixed amount, for example, insurance payments and mortgage payments.

Perhaps the most important thing any firm can do is simply to make sure all checks received are deposited immediately. Large firms that may have accounts with many banks also need to be careful to maintain a close watch over balances in each account so that excess cash does not build up. Any cash not needed in an account can be invested to earn interest.

Disbursement float is money being paid by the firm to its employees, suppliers, creditors, etc. Disbursement float time is the time period from the moment the firm initiates payment (puts a check in the mail) to the moment the cash leaves the firm's account. This float can be measured as the difference between the balance shown on the firm's checkbook and the cash balance recorded in the firm's account at the bank. For example, suppose that your bank account averages $20,000 more than the balances recorded on your checkbook. On average you have $20,000 in checks that have been written but have not yet cleared your account at the bank. This is disbursement float. It can also be measured directly as was done for collection float. Suppose that a firm writes $4000 in checks each day and it takes five days on average before those checks reach the firm's bank. The firm would have $20,000 ($4,000 times five days) in disbursement float and its bank balance would be $20,000 higher on average than its checkbook balance. Firms like to have a large disbursement float in that they want their outstanding checks to take a long time to clear. The longer the delay in clearing, the longer the company has use of the money.

Just as it is important to accelerate collections, it is important to maintain close control over the timing of payments to avoid early payments whenever possible. There are several procedures for achieving this control which are called "controlled disbursement." One procedure is the use of zero balance accounts. Such accounts allow a firm to write checks without having any money on deposit. Each day, the financial manager is notified of the value of the checks arriving at the bank drawn on the account. The amount needed to cover the checks is wired from a central account. Large firms may have several such accounts around the country. In their attempts to increase disbursement float, some firms have adopted the practice of maintaining accounts in banks that have remote locations relative to the parties they are paying so that the checks take longer to reach the banks.

For example, a firm located in Atlanta, Georgia might maintain an account with a bank in Spokane, Washington on which checks would be written to pay suppliers in the Southeast. Since many of the methods of increasing disbursement float impose losses on other people in devious ways, they seem somewhat disreputable and are not widely advertised by the firms that practice them. The Federal Reserve has actively discouraged banks from selling firms remote disbursement.

Efficient cash management is more difficult for large national firms which have many local facilities paying bills, a number of bank accounts, and customers all over the country. Firms with international operations have even greater problems. However, the sums of money involved are generally large enough to justify the use of specialists to keep close watch over cash flows. A one-day speedup in receipts or a one-day slowdown in disbursements may not be terribly important to a firm with cash flows of $1000 per day. For a firm with cash flows of $1 million per day, a one-day speedup means that $1 million in additional funds is available. At 9 percent interest, which has often been available in recent years, $1 million provides interest income of $90,000 per year, which will easily cover the salary of a full-time specialist whose job is to synchronize the firm's cash flows.

Evaluating Cash Management Methods

Regardless of the size of the firm and the complexity of its operations, the same basic approach to analyzing alternative methods of cash management may be used. This is to compare the costs involved in more efficient management of cash with the benefits derived from the cash released. All cash management methods involve some costs—fees paid to banks, time spent by financial managers, and salaries of personnel. There may also be investment in specialized equipment such as computer terminals or communication devices. The primary benefit arises from the earnings on cash available for investment in securities or other purposes (reducing debt, for example). If no investment in equipment is involved, we can use net profit [Eq. (15-1)] as the basis for our evaluation; the problem is to estimate the cash revenues and cash costs. Since investment is zero, we can ignore taxes and can use net revenue as defined in Eq. (15-14):

$$\text{Net revenue} = \text{annual cash revenues} - \text{annual cash costs} \qquad (15\text{-}14)$$

Annual cash revenues are normally estimated by first determining the cash provided by the system. To be accurate, the daily average of the cash released should be determined for each month of the year. Then the financial manager must consider how the cash will be used. Normally the cash would be used either for temporary investment in securities or to reduce short-term loans. In each case the cash can be thought of as providing interest revenues to the firm. Thus, depending on the situation in a given month, either the monthly interest rate on short-term investments or the monthly interest rate on short-term loans would be used to multiply the daily average balance for the month to obtain cash revenues for that month. The cash revenues over a twelve-month period are then added to estimate annual revenues. The reason for this procedure is that the cash provided tends to fluctuate considerably from day to day and from month to month. Therefore, to obtain an accurate evaluation, the annual values must be estimated with some attention to monthly variations. For firms with stable cash flow patterns without pronounced seasonality, the annual average could be used without proceeding through the detailed analysis.

Typically, historical data are used to estimate the monthly average cash provided. These values are then projected into the future based on expected increases in firm activity (sales). Often the firm's bank is willing to provide help in this analysis, if the firm is considering use of the bank's cash management system. A bank competing for the firm's account is also quite likely to provide estimates of the cash released.

To illustrate the procedure, an example calculation of daily average cash provided for a week is shown below.

Day:	Mon	Tues	Wed	Thurs	Fri	Sat	Sun
Cash provided (000's):	$1,200	$1,000	$800	$1,200	$2,000	$2,000	$2,000
Total for week: $10,200			Daily average: $1,457				

Thus the daily average cash provided in this example is $1.457 million. If this cash can be invested to earn 8 percent per year, cash revenues received by the firm for the week were $(.08/52) \times \$1.457$ million, which equals $2242. Suppose that additional fees charged by the bank and other operating expenses incurred by the firm amount to $1500. Assuming no investment is involved, the firm had a positive net revenue from the cash management system of $742 ($2242 − $1500). A complete analysis of establishing a new cash management system requires an evaluation period longer than one week; we recommend one year.

If a cash management system involves equipment investment, neither a net revenue nor a net profit approach is appropriate because equipment expenditures are not reversible (see the discussion of reversibility in the section on net profit and net present value at the beginning of this chapter). The normal capital budgeting procedures described in Chapters 8 and 9 must be used to evaluate such systems, but the cash revenues can be estimated using the procedures described here.

SUMMARY

This chapter described the problems of determining the level of investment in current assets. Investment in current assets differs from fixed-assets investment because the amount may vary substantially over short periods of time and the investment is reversible. For these reasons, net profit or total cost is used to evaluate alternative average levels of investment.

Decisions regarding manufacturing inventory are complicated by the nature of the manufacturing process, which varies from industry to industry. The general considerations regarding raw materials and finished goods inventories are, however, similar in many respects to those regard-

ing the finished goods inventories of retailers and wholesalers. The factors influencing the decision to invest in inventory include costs of holding inventory, costs of ordering new stock, availability of quantity discounts, and the costs of stockouts. A safety stock of inventory is often carried to reduce the chances of stockouts. There are risks to carrying inventory due to the possibilities of variation in the market value of the goods held and possible deterioration, theft, or spoilage. In addition, the benefits from increased investment are uncertain. The minimum acceptable rate of return or discount rate for inventory investment should reflect the inventory's risk as well as the basic time value of money.

The level of accounts receivable depends primarily on the sales volume of the firm and its credit policy. The basic decisions are whether or not to extend credit to a given customer and what the maximum amount of credit should be. The general credit policy of the firm provides a basis for these decisions and affects the sales volume of the firm. Restrictive credit policies reduce bad debt losses and the amount of investment in accounts receivable relative to sales. However, restrictive policies also limit sales. An evaluation of alternative credit policies must consider the impact of additional sales volume on the investment in inventory as well as on accounts receivable.

The management of cash and marketable securities involves four considerations: (1) the minimum cash balance, (2) the amount of excess funds to be invested in marketable securities, (3) the particular securities to be purchased, and (4) efficient management of the firm's cash flow. Financial managers attempt to reduce collection float and to control disbursements in order to increase the funds available for other uses.

In evaluating cash management systems, an analysis of net revenue (annual cash revenues less annual cash costs) is used when no investment is needed. Otherwise standard capital budgeting procedures apply.

QUESTIONS

1 What is a "reversible" investment and why is reversibility an important characteristic for analyzing current asset investments?

2 How do the concepts of "net profit" and "total cost" as used in this chapter differ from the normal accounting concepts of profit (net income) and cost?

3 How would the following developments affect the level of investment in inventory by a firm? Specify which types of inventory costs have changed (if any) and whether the costs have increased or decreased.
   a Faster and cheaper transportation of goods.
   b Using an existing computer to generate purchase orders.
   c Expectations of greater future inflation.
   d Changing from English measures (pounds, inches) to metric measures (kilograms, centimeters). Discuss both the short-run and the long-run impact.
   e Increasing the number of models in a product line.
   f An increase in the price per unit of purchased goods.

4 Would you expect the discount rate for investment in an inventory

of cocoa to be higher, lower, or the same as the discount rate for investment in an inventory of chocolate bars? Why?

5 In what sense does "safety stock" provide "safety" to a firm? Is there such a thing as being "too safe"?

6 There is potential conflict in inventory decisions between the views of the financial manager and the marketing manager. Why? Why would there be a possible conflict between the financial manager and the production manager regarding inventory?

7 What are the major costs and benefits in establishing a severe credit policy as compared with a more lenient credit policy?

8 In the past four years, the Z Company has not experienced a bad debt loss in its accounts receivable. Sales and profits have increased 10 percent over this period. Evaluate the performance of the Z Company's credit manager.

9 How would you adjust the credit policy of your firm in the following situations? Be as specific as you can.
   a You are trying to attract customers in a wider geographic market.
   b Your customers are paying, on average, thirty days after payment is due.
   c You are asked to manufacture a custom product for a small firm and you are unsure of its financial condition.

10 If accounts receivable are $200,000 as of the end of the year for the Abacus Company, is the firm's investment in accounts receivable $200,000? Why or why not?

11 Does the credit policy of a firm affect its discount rate for investment in accounts receivable? In what ways?

12 The marketing manager of your firm has suggested installing an electronic communications network connecting all the firm's plants and offices around the country. As financial manager, would you find such a network useful in managing the firm's cash position? What kinds of information would you want and how would you use the information?

13 Suppose you are considering various alternative means of investing $2 million that will be needed in ninety days to pay federal income taxes. What alternatives would you consider?

14 A representative of Big City National Bank is trying to obtain your firm's demand deposit account. As part of the bank's sales pitch, a "lock box" system is being heavily promoted. How interested would you be in this system if you were the financial manager of the following businesses:
   a A nationwide chain of self-service laundromats
   b An auto parts wholesaler selling primarily to service stations in the Kansas City metropolitan area
   c A manufacturer of speaker cabinets made on custom order selling to hi-fi dealers on the West Coast
   d A mail-order retail clothing business that allows its customers fifteen days to inspect the merchandise before they have to pay

15 Within the past fifteen years or so retail merchants who provide

charge accounts, gasoline companies with credit cards, and similar businesses have shifted from billing all customers at the end of each month to "cycle billing." With cycle billing, customers are billed throughout the month. For example, customers whose last names begin with "A" may be billed on the first day of the month, those with last names beginning with "L" in the middle of the month, those with last names beginning with "Z" at the end of the month. Any given customer is billed at the same time each month.

a As a customer of a firm who has just switched over, would the change matter to you? In considering the change, would it make any difference whether your personal income is received weekly rather than monthly?

b Discuss the advantages and disadvantages of cycle billing to the business firms. Consider the impact on accounts receivable, cash flows, and any costs involved.

PROJECTS

1 Interview the manager of a small local business and find out how current assets are managed. What kinds of decisions are made regarding inventory, accounts receivable, and liquid assets? Does the manager try to minimize cash balances by investing in securities or interest-bearing deposits? What constraints are placed on demand deposit balances by the firm's bank? (*Note*: This project could be done by teams rather than individuals.)

2 Suppose you are an assistant to the manager of a small business. The firm has $100,000 cash that will not be needed in its operations for six months. Using *The Wall Street Journal* or other sources, develop a recommendation to the manager concerning how the money should be invested. Include in your recommendation an estimate of the earnings to be achieved and discuss any risks your investment strategy entails.

PROBLEMS

1 Perform the indicated calculations using a discount rate of 10 percent per year and an income tax rate of 40 percent:

a Net profit for a reversible investment of $2000 which provides $1200 in additional annual cash revenues and $400 in additional annual cash costs. [Ans.: $280]

b Total cost for a reversible investment of $1500 with annual cash costs of $600. This is one of several alternative investments that all provide the same level of annual revenues. [Ans.: $510]

c Calculate the net present value for the investment in **a** assuming that funds are withdrawn (investment is reversed) in five years' time. Check your calculation by using two equivalent procedures.

d Calculate the present value of costs for the investment in **b** assuming that funds are withdrawn in ten years' time. Check your calculation by using two equivalent procedures.

2 The manager of a farm supply store is evaluating two alternative levels of investment in seed inventory, A or B. Relevant data for the two alternatives are shown below:

	A	B
Average dollar investment	$1,000	$2,000
Monthly cash revenues	$ 600	$ 800
Monthly cash costs	$ 200	$ 390

The discount rate for this investment is 1 percent per month. The income tax rate is 40 percent. In six months' time (at the end of the season) inventories of this item will be reduced to zero. The manager expects to realize the amount invested at that time.

a Calculate the monthly net profit (as defined in this chapter) for the two alternatives. [Ans.: A = $230, B = $226]

b Calculate the net present value for the two alternatives. [Ans.: A = $1333, B = $1310]

c Which alternative is best? Does it matter whether net profit or net present value is used to decide on the alternative?

3 An electronics store sells on average twenty volt-ohm meters (VOMs) per month. VOMs are currently ordered in lots of forty at a time, and the purchase price per VOM is $25.

a What is the store's average investment in VOMs assuming no safety stock is maintained? [Ans.: $500]

b If it costs $5 to place an order for VOMs, what are the annual order costs? [Ans.: $30]

c Suppose holding costs average $0.06 per dollar invested per year. What are the annual holding cost of VOMs? [Ans.: $30]

d Given a discount rate of 12 percent per year for inventory investment, what is the annual capital cost of inventory investment? [Ans.: $60]

e Given a tax rate of 25 percent, what is the total cost of this inventory policy excluding acquisition costs? [Ans.: $105]   *leave out acquisition cost*

4 Using the data of problem 3, calculate the total costs (excluding acquisition costs) for the following additional order quantities: 20 VOMs per order and 60 VOMs per order. The purchase price per VOM is $25 regardless of the amount ordered.

a What order quantity (20, 40, or 60) provides minimum total costs?

b Would inclusion of acquisition costs affect your decision in this case? Why or why not?

5 Suppose the supplier of the VOMs in problem 3 offers the following quantity discounts from the base price of $25 per VOM.

VOMs per order	0–49	50–99	100–199	200 or more
Discount from base price	0%	5%	10%	12%

What inventory policy minimizes total cost? (Assume that VOM orders are in multiples of twenty.)

6 Midwest Electronics manufactures instruments for medical tests. The sales manager of Midwest has been concerned about losing sales because of the low levels of inventory the firm carries. An analysis of losses due to stockouts carried out by a task force set up to investigate the problem suggests the following relationship between average minimum inventory levels and stockout losses:

Average safety stock investment	$100,000	$150,000	$200,000	$250,000
Annual stockout losses (pretax)	$ 50,000	$ 20,000	$ 6,000	0

Holding costs for this type of inventory average 8 percent per year per dollar of inventory. The firm's tax rate is 40 percent, and management estimates the discount rate applicable to this type of investment to be 10 percent.

As financial manager of Midwest Electronics, what level of safety stock would you recommend?

7 The K Company has accounts receivable of $400,000 at the present time. The average manufacturing cost of goods sold is 60 percent of the selling price. The pretax profit margin for the company is currently 12 percent. The cost of holding finished goods inventory is 5 percent of manufacturing cost. Sales people are paid 8 percent of their dollar sales in commissions. What is the actual cash investment in accounts receivable for this firm? [Ans.: $284,000]

8 A furniture manufacturer has a line of computer stands. The direct manufacturing cost of this product averages 60 percent of the selling price. Shipping, handling, and sales-related expenses are 15 percent of the selling price. Sales are made to dealers on open account and, on average, accounts are paid sixty days after a sale is made. The firm's sales of this product are currently $20,000 per month. What is the firm's current cash investment in accounts receivable for the product line?

9 Krypton Associates is a consulting firm specializing in industrial security. Clark Kent handles the firm's financial affairs. The firm bills its clients at the end of an assignment on terms net 30; that is, the customer is supposed to pay within thirty days after the billing date. Lately Clark has been alarmed about a buildup in accounts receivable and the pressure placed on the firm's cash position caused by the resulting slowdown in collections. He is also concerned about the bad debt losses the firm has experienced. After analyzing the situation with some care, Clark was able to classify the firm's clients into two groups, normal risk and high risk. Data for the two classes of clients are shown below:

	Annual revenues	Annual operating costs	Annual bad debt losses	Current accounts receivable
Normal risk	$120,000	$ 90,000	$1,000	$10,000
High risk	60,000	50,000	5,000	20,000
Total	$180,000	$140,000	$6,000	$30,000

The marginal tax rate of the firm's partners is 50 percent, and they feel that a 20 percent discount rate would be appropriate in assessing the desirability of extending credit to high-risk clients. The dollar investment in accounts receivable is difficult to evaluate because the major investment is in time spent by the partners on the client's problems; however, for purposes of analysis Clark decided to consider the foregone revenues from the investment of time as being part of the cash outlay in the accounts receivable. The level of $20,000 in accounts receivable of high-risk clients is, therefore, estimated to reflect $15,000 in cash investment.

Should Krypton Associates stop extending credit to high-risk clients, assuming that this business would be lost entirely if such a policy were implemented? Base your decision on the "net profit" from accepting high-risk clients.

10 The Save-More Company operates a chain of drugstores in California. The firm's financial manager, C. K. Wu, is investigating the impact of establishing a new credit policy for the firm. For many years Save-More extended credit only to a select number of customers who were known personally by the company managers of their stores. In an effort to increase sales and to compete more effectively, management changed its policy two years ago to one of extending thirty days of credit to anyone who asked for it. This policy proved successful in increasing sales but also caused a tremendous increase in accounts receivable and bad debt losses. C. K. thought that, by being somewhat more selective in extending credit and by adding an interest charge to accounts more than thirty days overdue, most of the benefits of the wide-open policy might be retained while reducing costs. The following estimates were requested by C. K. from the marketing staff and are based on an analysis of customer accounts (dollar figures are in thousands):

Credit policy	Annual sales	Cost of goods sold	Operating costs	Average inventory	Accounts receivable
Restrictive	$40,000	$24,000	$10,000	$6,000	$1,000
Selective	$50,000	$30,000	$12,500	$7,000	$6,000
Wide open	$55,000	$33,000	$13,500	$7,500	$8,000

(*Note*: Operating costs include bad debt losses.)

C. K. estimated that the interest charge on accounts extending past thirty days under the selective policy would provide an income of $250,000 per year in addition to the sales revenues shown above for this policy. He was also aware that the actual cash investment in accounts receivable would be somewhat less than the book figures shown, but he wasn't sure how this should be handled. He did know that the firm's accountants estimated that $0.20 out of every dollar of sales went to costs associated with handling, storing, and selling goods. This figure included, however, salaries of some store personnel that do not vary appreciably with sales volume. About $0.05 out of the $0.20 fell into this category.

Another thorny issue was the question of what discount rate should apply. Senior management of Save-More had differences of opinion on this topic. The chief executive officer leaned toward application of the company's average cost of capital (currently estimated to be 14 percent) to investments in inventory and accounts receivable on the grounds that such investments constituted the majority of the assets of the firm. The marketing manager thought this was too high for such relatively secure assets as accounts receivable and pointed out that the major increase in investment was in this asset. He recommended that a rate of 10 percent apply. C. K. thought both positions had merit and in the case of the restrictive and selective policies a rate of 10 percent would indeed be appropriate. However, he thought that the firm's average cost of capital, 14 percent, should be used to evaluate the wide-open policy, because the risks of this policy more closely approximated the overall risk of the firm.

Evaluate the three credit policies and develop a recommendation as to which one should be implemented. Show how your findings depend on the discount rate(s) you use. Use a tax rate of 40 percent.

11 The financial manager of the CM Company has analyzed both the collection and the disbursement operations of the firm. It takes six days on average for CM to obtain cash from its collections once its customers initiate payment. On the other hand, it only takes four days from the time CM sends checks to its suppliers and employees until the checks clear CM's bank account. CM's sales are entirely on open account. Sales are currently averaging $20,000 per day and disbursements average $18,000 per day.

a How large is CM's collection float? [Ans.: $120,000]

b How large is CM's disbursement float?

c If CM maintains a minimum cash balance of $40,000 on its own books, how large will its average balance be at the bank? [Ans.: $112,000]

12 The Steak 'n Tater Company (STC) is franchiser of a national chain of fast-food restaurants. The company sells a variety of supplies to its franchisees, and its cash receipts average $400,000 per day. Based on an analysis of the payments received, STC's management estimates that it takes seven days on average between the time a check is mailed to the firm and the time the money is actually available for use.

a How much money is being tied up by the seven-day delay? [Ans.: $2,800,000]

b Suppose that the delay could be reduced to five days. How much additional money would be available for other uses?

c The company's bank has indicated that by introducing special handling of the checks and going to a lock box system the delay could be reduced from seven days to three days. In order to do this, however, the bank says that STC must increase its demand deposits by $600,000; that is, the firm's average balance must increase by that amount. In addition, the firm would incur a variety of additional costs amounting to $70,000 per year. The financial manager of STC plans to invest the money freed by the new cash management system in marketable securities yielding 10 percent per year. Is the new system worth implementing?

13 American Packing Company (APC) maintains banking relationships with twelve banks around the country. Currently a bank in Chicago handles all transactions in the central states region. Cash receipts processed through the bank average $1 million (600 checks) per day. The bank requires that demand deposit balances of $500,000 be maintained for this service; no fees are involved. APC's financial manager expects to earn 9 percent per year on short-term securities investments. (Daily check volume is based on 365 days per year.)

a The bank has offered to renegotiate the terms of its agreement with APC. The bank wants to institute a per check charge for processing of $0.05 plus a new (lower) compensating deposit balance. As financial manager for APC, what is the maximum balance you would be willing to accept, given that you have the alternative of staying with the existing arrangement?

b A bank in Kansas City has approached APC with the suggestion that it handle all Kansas and Missouri transactions, currently $200,000 per day. You believe that this arrangement would reduce cash receipt time by $1\frac{1}{2}$ days for transactions in the two states. The Kansas City bank wants a flat fee of $10,000 per year for the service; no balances would be involved. The Chicago bank has indicated that it would require only $450,000 in balances (as compared to the existing requirements of $500,000) if APC uses the Kansas City bank for Kansas and Missouri transactions. What do you recommend?

In Chapter 15 we showed how to find the order quantity that minimizes the total cost of inventory investment. The solution method was to calculate total cost [Eq. (15-9)] for different order quantities and to find the minimum either numerically or by examining a graph. The total-cost equation is

Total cost = (1 − tax rate) × (acquisition cost + order cost + holding cost) + capital cost

$$= (1 - \tau) \left(CS + \frac{fS}{Q} + \frac{hCQ}{2} \right) + \frac{kCQ}{2} \tag{15-9}$$

Suppose that acquisition cost does not vary with order quantity in this equation. Acquisition cost is therefore constant, insofar as the decision regarding Q is concerned, and it will not affect the decision. All variables except Q in Eq. (15-9) are assumed to be constants unaffected by the value of Q. Under these conditions, we can derive a formula for the value of Q that minimizes total cost, Q^*. This value is the economic order quantity in Eq. (15-11). This appendix provides the derivation of Eq. (15-11).

We wish to minimize the total-cost function

$$\text{Total cost} = TC = (1 - \tau) \left(CS + \frac{fS}{Q} + \frac{hCQ}{2} \right) + \frac{kCQ}{2}$$

To do this, calculate the derivative of the total-cost function with respect to Q, the decision variable in this case, and solve for the value of Q that will make the derivative equal to zero (this value of Q is Q^*).

$$\frac{d(TC)}{dQ} = (1 - \tau) \left(\frac{hC}{2} - \frac{fS}{Q^2} \right) + \frac{kC}{2}$$

$$(1 - \tau) \left(\frac{hC}{2} - \frac{fS}{(Q^*)^2} \right) + \frac{kC}{2} = 0$$

$$(Q^*)^2 \left(\frac{hC}{2} + \frac{kC}{2(1 - \tau)} \right) - fS = 0$$

$$(Q^*)^2 = \frac{2(1 - \tau)fS}{(1 - \tau)hC + kC}$$

$$Q^* = \sqrt{\frac{2(1 - \tau)fS}{(1 - \tau)hC + kC}} \tag{15-11}$$

The economic order quantity Q^* is the value of Q that minimizes total cost when per unit acquisition costs do not vary with order quantity Q. Besides the convenience of having a simple way to calculate Q^*, Eq. (15-11) is also useful because it indicates how Q^* and therefore the average invest-ment in inventory $CQ^*/2$ is affected by the variables in it. In particular we can see that, as usage rates (sales rates) S increase, the economic order quantity Q^* and the average investment in inventory also increase. However, the increase in investment is not directly proportional to S, but rather proportional to $\sqrt{S}$. Suppose we rewrite Eq. (15-11) in terms of the average level of inventory investment I and rearrange terms

$$I = \frac{CQ^*}{2}$$

$$= \frac{C}{2}\sqrt{\frac{2(1 - \tau)fS}{(1 - \tau)hC + kC}}$$

$$= \left[\sqrt{\frac{(1 - \tau)fC}{2[(1 - \tau)h + k]}}\right]\sqrt{S} \tag{15-15}$$

The variables inside the brackets are all cost factors and usually don't change very much. The usage rate S is subject to change. From the formula it is clear that an increase in usage rate with no change in costs will increase average inventory investment in proportion to the square root of S, which is less than S.

ELECTRONIC BANKING

The future is now. After two decades of discussion, the application of computers and electronic communication devices is starting to change the basic means by which individuals, governmental units, and business firms transfer money. There are advantages to everyone in the changes that are taking place, but there is also much controversy. What is happening, and why is so much fuss being made?

ELECTRONIC BANKING SERVICES

Electronic banking services mean increased convenience for the customer. The primary element for individuals is a plastic card with a magnetic strip on the back. A shove of the card into a machine permits the person who owns the card to withdraw cash from his or her bank account (checking or savings), transfer money between checking and savings accounts, borrow money, and pay off a loan. In many places this can be done at any time during the day or night, seven days a week. The machine may be imbedded in the outside wall of a conventional bank office or found in a shopping center mall, an airline terminal, a supermarket, or an employee cafeteria. As the services expand nationally, a Californian visiting Washington, D.C., will be able to undertake many of the same sorts of transactions 3000 miles away from home. Approximately 33 percent of bank customers now use these machines.

Other electronic banking services include automatic deposit of payroll, dividend, and social security payments. The money is directly deposited into the person's bank account with no action on the recipient's part. Retail purchases may be paid for by electronic transfers from the purchaser's account to the retailer's account or through a loan extended electronically. Some transactions may be made over the telephone or through a cable television hookup from the person's own home.

The result for the consumer is a reduction in the cost (including time) of making a variety of financial transactions. Electronic banking makes it easier for people to obtain cash, make payments, and deposit money at any time of day and at many physical locations.

A variety of electronic banking services are being offered to businesses. Funds transfer across the United States by wire has been available for many years. A firm in Boston that wishes to pay another firm in Phoenix can do so in a few minutes if desired. Many large banks offer cash management services such as the ability for a corporate treasurer to determine on a computer terminal in the treasurer's office the current balances in the company's deposit accounts at any one of its fifty banks. Orders to transfer funds from one account to another can be transmitted and effected immediately. Banks also provide the ability to "sweep" any excess cash out of the company's demand accounts into interest-bearing repurchase agreements. For the corporate treasurer, electronic banking has become a normal part of business.

IMPACT ON FINANCIAL INSTITUTIONS

The most controversial aspect of electronic banking is the elimination of traditional barriers to competition among financial institutions.

One impact, therefore, is increased competition that may imply lower prices for financial services. In addition, electronic banking facilities are expensive to establish. These expenses plus lower prices would appear to imply lower profits for financial institutions. However, the cost per financial transaction is expected to drop dramatically as the volume of electronically processed transactions increases. Automatic teller transactions are already much cheaper (21 cents per transaction) than those processed by a teller in a bank (52 cents per transaction). It is also much cheaper to install an automatic teller ($40,000) than a new branch ($400,000). The result is that smaller accounts become more desirable (profitable). The net impact on profits is not clear at the present time. The potential for increased competition in the provision of financial services is quite clear, however.

Electronic banking should significantly affect a major barrier to competition for consumer accounts due to laws restricting depository financial institutions from establishing branches outside a limited geographic area. Banks headquartered in one state cannot build branches in other states and therefore have not been able to compete effectively in those other states for consumer accounts. In many states, especially in the South and Midwest, banks are limited to operating from a single office. These geographic limits on branching have not prevented banks around the country from competing for large corporate accounts, partly because corporations conduct much of their business by telephone, and partly because the loans and deposits of these customers are large enough to pay for the banks to send people to the corporation offices when personal contact is needed. Consumers and small businesses call on the banker. Therefore, those banks with nearby offices attract consumer and small business customers more readily than do banks with offices that are far away. Electronic banking reduces the need for small customers to come to the bank. Therefore, the geographic location of bank branches becomes less important in the customer's decision on where to bank.

The existence of so much present and prospective competition means that many cost savings provided by electronic banking will be passed on, at least in part, to customers. Those firms that invest heavily in electronic banking may not reap extraordinary profits. However, those that wait too long before investing are apt to find themselves losing a substantial portion of the consumer market.

IMPLICATIONS FOR BUSINESS FIRMS

Consumer electronic banking has some implications for business firms. Retailers are substantially reducing their losses from bad checks by utilizing check guarantee systems offered by many banks. When a customer writes a check to the retailer in payment for goods or for cash, the retailer can electronically verify that the check is good provided the customer has a card issued by the bank. The bank will guarantee all checks that have been verified; thus the retailer is not exposed to the possibility of losing money from accepting a bad check. The use of electronic means to pay bills will reduce the time needed for collections, thereby reducing accounts receivable and freeing cash for use elsewhere in the business.

Firms that pay their employees by direct deposit will gain reductions in the cost of processing payrolls. However, they will also have to have the money on deposit when payment is made and can no longer rely on some employees taking a few days to cash their payroll checks.

Overall, the major benefits of electronic banking will go to consumers and to the firms that offer the most effective electronic banking services. One thing is clear. Barring the imposition of stringent controls by the government, the market for consumer financial services will be in a state of flux for years to come.

16

SHORT-TERM FINANCING

After planning investment in current assets and forecasting funds required by the firm over the coming year, the financial manager must arrange for financing. The general principles of financing decisions were examined in Chapter 10. After deciding on the combination of debt and equity sources to be used, the financial manager must decide on the particular types of debt financing. Short-term borrowing is typically used to finance temporary investments in current assets. In this chapter we will discuss the principles used by the financial manager in deciding what types of short-term financing to obtain. In Chapter 17 we will examine the problem of how much short-term financing should be used relative to long-term financing.

This chapter will be divided into two main sections covering:

1 The characteristics of major sources of short-term financing, such as bank loans. We will evaluate the advantages and disadvantages of each source of credit and analyze the cost of each credit source to the borrower.
2 The pledging of inventory and accounts receivable to lenders as security for short-term credit. We will describe the types of secured debt agreements used by businesses for short-term financing.

MAJOR SOURCES OF SHORT-TERM FINANCING

In choosing a source of short-term financing, the financial manager will be concerned with the following five aspects of each financing arrangement:

1 *Cost.* Generally the financial manager will seek to minimize the cost of financing, which usually can be expressed as an annual interest rate. Therefore, the financing source with the lowest interest rate will be chosen. However, there are other factors that may be important in particular situations.
2 *Impact on credit rating.* Use of some sources may affect the firm's credit rating more than the use of others. A poor credit rating limits the availability, and increases the cost, of additional financing.
3 *Reliability.* Some sources are more reliable than others in that funds are more likely to be available when they are needed.
4 *Restrictions.* Some creditors are more apt to impose restrictions on the firm than are others. Restrictions might include dollar limits on dividends, management salaries, and capital expenditures.
5 *Flexibility.* Some sources are more flexible than others in that the firm can very easily increase or decrease the amount of funds provided.

All these factors must usually be considered before making the decision as to the sources of financing.

The three primary sources of short-term financing for business firms are, in descending order of importance, trade credit, loans from commercial banks, and commercial paper. Both trade credit and commercial paper are unsecured forms of credit, whereas banks make both secured and unsecured loans. A secured loan is one for which the borrower pledges specific assets as security for the loan. Automobile loans are secured consumer loans. Business firms usually pledge accounts receivable or inventory as security for short-term loans. In this section we will consider only unsecured types of credit from the three major sources; secured financing arrangements are covered later in the chapter.

Trade Credit

Trade credit for a business firm is equivalent to a charge account for a consumer. When a firm (the purchaser) buys goods from another firm (the supplier), it normally does not have to pay for those goods immediately. During the period of time before payment becomes due, the purchaser has a debt outstanding to the supplier. This debt is recorded on the purchaser's balance sheet as a liability, **accounts payable**. The corresponding account for the supplier is, of course, accounts receivable, which was discussed in Chapter 15. Normal business transactions therefore provide the firm with a source of short-term financing, trade credit, because of the time between delivery and payment. The amount of financing depends on the volume of purchases and when the purchases are paid for. For example, suppose the firm purchases $1000 of goods every day from its suppliers and always pays thirty days after the invoice date. The firm would have 30 × $1000 = $30,000 of accounts payable or trade credit outstanding at all times.

An attractive feature of trade credit as a financing source is that it responds readily to an increase in the firm's purchases such as might occur during a seasonal buildup of inventory. If purchases double to $2000 per day, accounts payable will double to 30 × $2000 = $60,000, if the firm continues to pay on a thirty-day schedule.

The cost to the firm for utilizing this financing source depends on several factors, one of which is the credit terms granted by the firm's suppliers. Table 16-1 shows the different terms under which goods are sold. These terms vary considerably according to the industry involved. As we indicated in our discussion of accounts receivable, credit terms tend to be fairly similar within a given industry. However, some suppliers may provide more lenient terms than others. If the quality, price, and service provided by the more lenient firms are not inferior to those provided by others, purchasing from those suppliers *may* be to our advantage. Why isn't it *surely* to our advantage?

The answer depends on the nature of the credit terms offered and our alternatives. Suppose two suppliers of comparable products offer the following ordinary credit terms. Supplier A sells on terms 2/10, net 30, and supplier B sells on terms 2/10, net 60 (see Table 16-1). Since B offers better terms than A, you might think that it is clearly better to buy from B. However, the cash discounts offered by both are the same, 2 percent if the account is paid within ten days.

Suppose you are considering purchasing from B and waiting for sixty days before making payment. The cost of foregoing a cash discount (that is, of paying after the ten-day discount period) can be expressed as an annual interest rate as follows:

Annual interest rate = rate per period × number of periods per year

$$= \frac{\text{discount}}{100\% - \text{discount}} \times \frac{365 \text{ days}}{\text{payment period} - \text{discount period}} \quad \textbf{(16-1)}$$

TABLE 16-1
Terms of sale

Terms	Definition	Use
CBD	Cash before delivery: goods must be paid for before shipment is made.	High-risk customers.
COD	Cash on delivery: goods are shipped to customer, who must pay the shipper before taking possession.	High-risk customers or those for whom credit information is lacking.
SDBL	Sight draft—bill of lading attached: when goods are shipped, a draft for the purchase price plus a bill of lading (shipping document) is sent to firm's bank for payment. Firm must pay for goods in order to obtain bill of lading needed to get goods from shipper.	Automobile manufacturers, meat packers, and fruit and vegetable canners are typical sellers. Sometimes used by others when large shipments are made.
Net cash (net 7 days; net 10 days; bill to bill)	Goods must be paid for in 7 or 10 days depending on industry. Bill to bill terms require payment on previous delivery when a new one is made.	Retail store purchases of tobacco, produce, fresh meat, and dairy products.
Ordinary terms (2/10, net 30; 2/10, net 60; 1/15, net 30; net 30, etc.)	Terms of 2/10, net 30 provide a discount of 2% if payment is made within 10 days of the invoice date; otherwise payment is due in 30 days.	Many lines of business. Most common trade credit terms.
Monthly billing (2/10, EOM, net 30; 2/10, prox., net 30; 8/10, EOM)	A single payment for all purchases made before the 25th of one month is made in the next month. A cash discount for payment within the first 10 days (2/10) may be quoted. EOM stands for "end of month"; "prox." is an abbreviation of *proximo*, Latin word for "next."	Apparel trades, lumber, books, and other lines of business where several orders may be placed during a given month by the purchasing firm.
Seasonal dating (net 30, January 1; net 30, October 1; 2/10, net 30, January 1)	Payment for all goods shipped prior to the indicated date (Jan. 1) is due per the rest of the terms (net 30; 2/10, net 30).	Businesses with distinct seasons, such as toys, Christmas cards, and school textbooks.
Consignment	Payment for goods is made after they are sold by purchasing firm. Title to the goods remains with original supplier until sale by purchasing firm.	May be used in any business but commonly for rack jobbers in supermarkets, magazines, and photographic supplies.

In the example above the discount is 2 percent, the payment period is sixty days, and the discount period is ten days. Therefore the annual interest rate is

$$\text{Annual interest rate} = \frac{2\%}{100\% - 2\%} \times \frac{365 \text{ days}}{60 \text{ days} - 10 \text{ days}}$$

$$= 0.0204 \times 7.3$$

$$= 0.1489 \text{ or approximately } 15\%$$

The reasoning behind this formula is that, if you do not pay within ten days, you must pay 100 percent of the invoice price of the goods. If you do pay within ten days, you will pay only 98 percent (100% − 2%) of the invoice price. The first ten days (discount period) do not cost you anything. The amount of financing you are really getting after ten days is therefore 98 percent of the invoice price, but you are incurring a dollar cost of 2 percent of the price for the privilege of delaying payment. The ratio 2%/(100% − 2%) expresses the basic interest cost of foregoing the discount for the period involved, .0204 or 2.04 percent. If you pay sixty days (payment period) after the invoice date, you have really gotten only an additional fifty days (payment period − discount period) of credit. You are therefore paying 2.04 percent for fifty days of credit. At an annual rate this amounts to 365 days/50 days × 0.0204 = 15 percent per year.

If you were to buy from supplier A and pay thirty days later, it would cost you 37 percent [2%/(100% − 2%) × 365 days/(30 days − 10 days) = 0.37]. By this measure B is still a better deal.[1] However, do you really want to pay 15 percent for short-term financing from supplier B? If you have money invested in securities at 10 percent or can borrow from the bank at 12 percent, you would probably rather take the cash discount no matter which supplier you buy from. Therefore it might not make any difference to you, since both suppliers offer the same discount. If A provided better service, you would prefer A in this case.

Using Eq. (16-1) to compute the annual interest rate enables the financial manager to determine the cost of foregoing cash discounts. This cost is the basic interest cost of trade credit financing. There are other factors that are also important in assessing the desirability and possibilities of using this source of short-term financing.

The dollar volume of a firm's purchases determines the amount of trade credit financing available to it. This type of financing arises only from the firm's not paying immediately for its purchases. As such, it is flexible and very convenient, but rather limited in amount. Trade credit does not provide a direct source of cash to pay other bills. Purchases provide goods, not cash. Moreover, a firm that persistently does not pay its bills when due is apt to develop a poor credit rating. Suppliers may become reluctant to provide credit, requiring the firm to purchase on COD or even CBD terms (see Table 16-1). This can present problems for the firm in several ways.

[1] If payment to A were delayed for sixty days, the interest cost would be the same as for B. However, in this case the account is overdue and this may cause problems in the future as discussed below.

First, the firm may not be able to find alternative sources of credit (for example, a bank loan). In this case the amount of inventory that the firm can carry may be severely limited, and therefore its sales and profits will fall. Second, the loss of trade credit imposes a cost on the firm and that is not inconsequential. Suppose that the Tight Company is purchasing on terms of net 30 (no cash discount) and is paying after sixty days. If purchases are $1000 per day, the firm would have $60,000 of accounts payable. If Tight paid within thirty days, it would have accounts payable of $30,000. However, delaying payment to sixty days gives Tight a poor credit rating, and suppliers could require the firm to pay cash for goods ordered. Its accounts payable would then shrink to zero. Suppose Tight can borrow from the bank at a rate of 12 percent. If the firm pays its suppliers on time (within thirty days), it will have $30,000 of free credit from suppliers and $30,000 of bank credit at 12 percent. If instead, Tight delays payment to sixty days, it may be required to borrow the entire $60,000 at 12 percent. By paying on time, the firm would be paying 12 percent on $30,000 and 0 percent on $30,000 for an average rate of 6 percent on its short-term financing of $60,000. On the other hand, by delaying payment, Tight would end up paying 12 percent on $60,000. The interest cost of delaying payment is twice the cost of paying on time; in addition, the firm acquires a bad credit reputation.

Moreover, COD terms impose costs of their own on the firm. Fees are charged by the shipper to collect payment, and cash discounts are not offered to COD customers. Of course, if alternative sources of credit are very expensive and if suppliers are relatively forgiving, it may be desirable to "stretch the payables" (as paying late is called). Occasionally delaying payment or paying only a few days later can be done without disturbing suppliers. However, this practice can be expensive for the firm if carried to extremes.

Bank Loans

The second major source of short-term financing for business firms is loans from commercial banks. Short-term commercial bank loans are generally made in the form of a note—a written and signed statement in which the borrower agrees to repay the loan when it is due and to pay interest. Notes may be payable on demand by the bank (demand notes), or payable in thirty days, ninety days, or one year (thirty-day notes, ninety-day notes, etc.). This is in contrast with trade credit, where the only evidence the supplier has of money owed is the purchase request and the invoice. In this section we will discuss some general characteristics of unsecured bank loans. Secured loans are described in more detail in the next section.

Seasonal Loans   Seasonal loans have traditionally been the basic type of credit provided by banks to business firms. Such loans are called self-liquidating as they are used to finance temporary increases in inventory and accounts receivable, which are soon converted into cash to repay the loan. For example, textbook publishers have a well-defined pattern of seasonal borrowings. Their borrowings begin in Februrary, as inventory accumulates and books are shipped out to the schools and bookstores, and reach their peak in September/October, at which time payments start pouring in. The majority of seasonal loans are unsecured, although in recent years an increasing number of them have involved collateral. A typical seasonal loan is based on a line of credit previously requested by the firm and approved by the bank.

A **line of credit** is an informal agreement by the bank to lend up to a stated maximum amount to the firm. The bank does not have a legal commitment to supply the funds when the firm requests them, but banks tend to feel a moral obligation to do so. The procedure works as follows for a firm that has been a regular customer of the bank. At the low point of the season, the financial manager estimates funds required for the coming year and then asks the bank for a line of credit equal to the maximum expected need for funds. Let's assume it is $100,000. Usually the firm will provide the bank with its most current financial statement and may include forecasted financial statements to support its request. A financial forecast is especially desirable if the firm is requesting a significant increase in the line of credit. If everything looks reasonable to the bank, one of its officers will write a letter to the firm indicating the amount of the line, the interest rate, and usually a statement that the firm should be "out of the bank" (not borrowing) for at least one or two months during the year. This latter provision is intended to ensure that the loan is really a short-term seasonal loan and does not involve permanent financing. The firm will then borrow money as it needs it in the form of thirty- or ninety-day notes, where the total outstanding cannot exceed the credit line.[2]

There is another type of credit arrangement, similar to a line of credit, called **revolving credit**. In this case, the bank makes a legal commitment to extend credit up to the maximum. Revolving credit agreements usually involve both seasonal and longer-term financing and extend over several years. The bank may require a fee based on the unused portion of the credit. For example, if the maximum is $500,000 and the firm is currently borrowing $300,000, a fee such as 0.5 percent per year might be charged on the $200,000 not being used in addition to the interest on the $300,000 borrowed. Since revolving credit agreements are most often longer term in nature, they will be discussed again in Chapter 18.

Bankers consider seasonal lines of credit to be one of the most desirable types of loans to make. The interest rates are often lower on this type of loan than on any other that might be requested by a given firm. However, banks usually require that a firm borrowing under a line of credit maintain a minimum average demand deposit with the bank. This amount is called a **compensating balance** and is expressed as a percentage of the loan. For example, a compensating-balance requirement of 15 percent means that, if the firm is borrowing $100,000, its minimum average checking account at

---

[2] In Europe such lines are often executed by the firm's simply writing checks on its account. If there are insufficient funds in the account to cover the checks, the bank will honor the overdraft and create a loan. This arrangement is more flexible since the firm isn't confined to borrowing money over an entire thirty-day period if it needs the funds for only fifteen days. We may see this type of loan commonly available to business firms in the United States in the next few years. Many banks already offer overdraft loans to individuals.

the bank must be $15,000. In addition, there may be a compensating-balance requirement on the unused portion of the credit line. This is invariably a lower percentage than that for the borrowed portion. For example, if the credit line of this borrower were $150,000, then the compensating balance on the unused portion might be 8 percent. When the firm is borrowing $100,000, $50,000 of the credit is unused and an additional $4000 (0.08 × $50,000) balance in the firm's bank account would have to be maintained. Compensating balances would therefore be $15,000 (15 percent of $100,000) on the borrowed portion and $4000 (8 percent of $50,000) on the unused portion for a total of $19,000.

What is the impact of compensating-balance requirements on the cost of the loans? The answer depends on what the average balances of the firm would normally be. If the firm would normally maintain $10,000 average balances, in order to have $19,000 in its account an additional $9000 must be borrowed merely to meet the requirement. Suppose the interest rate on the $100,000 borrowed is 12 percent. The firm really has use of only $91,000 since $9000 of the total borrowed must be kept in the bank to meet the compensating-balance requirements. The firm would be paying $12,000 (0.12 × $100,000) per year to get $91,000, and therefore the effective rate of interest would be $12,000/$91,000 = 13.2 percent. On the other hand, if the firm were planning to keep $20,000 in its account in any case for transaction purposes, the required compensating balance of $19,000 would not affect the cost of the loan. In this case, the effective interest rate on the $100,000 loan would be 12 percent.

Interim Financing   Short-term bank loans are often used for the initial financing of construction by contractors or of plant and equipment investment by business firms where the ultimate financing will be long term in nature. This use of short-term loans is called **interim financing** (bridge financing), as the loans are intended to cover the funds needed in the interim before the long-term money is made available (bridge the gap between need for funds and availability of long-term financing). Such loans are found most frequently when money is being spent over several months in the construction of apartment houses, shopping centers, or industrial plants. Real estate developers may obtain a commitment from a long-term lender such as an insurance company to provide funds when a project is completed and the bank supplies funds during the period of construction. Manufacturers may use this type of loan prior to issuing long-term securities to finance a new plant. The alternative procedure for these firms would be to issue the securities in advance of their need for funds and invest the proceeds in marketable securities.

Interest Rates on Bank Loans   The interest rates on business loans are determined through personal negotiations between the banker and the borrower. The riskier the borrower, the higher is the interest rate on the loan. However, bankers have traditionally refused to make loans to high-risk borrowers, forcing such borrowers to find other sources of credit. Loan rates are usually scaled upward from the bank's prime rate, the rate charged on credit lines to businesses with excellent credit ratings. Major corporations can borrow money in large amounts for 30 days or less at interest rates below the prime rate, although for most business loans the prime rate is the lowest rate available. The prime rate moves in jumps whenever there are significant changes in money market rates. Figure 16-1 shows the prime rate compared with the interest rate on commercial paper for the past few years.

The interest on a loan may be paid in three different ways: the one used is a matter of agreement between the bank and the borrower. The true cost to the borrower depends on which of the three methods is adopted. **Ordinary interest** is paid at the maturity of the note. If you borrow $10,000 at 8 percent per year and repay the loan with interest at the end of one year, you will pay $800 in interest at that time. The true interest rate is 8 percent. The second method of paying interest is used when the bank **discounts** the note. The interest is deducted from the face value of the note when the loan is made. For example, suppose a firm borrows $10,000 on a discount basis for one year at a stated rate of 8 percent per year. The firm would receive only $10,000 − $800 = $9200, the loan amount less the $800 interest. At the end of the year, the firm would pay $10,000. The true interest rate here is determined by dividing the interest by the amount actually received; that is, the rate would be $800/$9200 = 8.7 percent. If the loan is discounted, the true interest rate is therefore higher than the stated rate.

The third method of paying interest is based on a **floating rate**. The interest rate on these loans varies or "floats" with the bank's prime rate using a relationship that is specified in the loan agreement. For example, the rate might be specified as "prime plus 1 percent." Interest would be

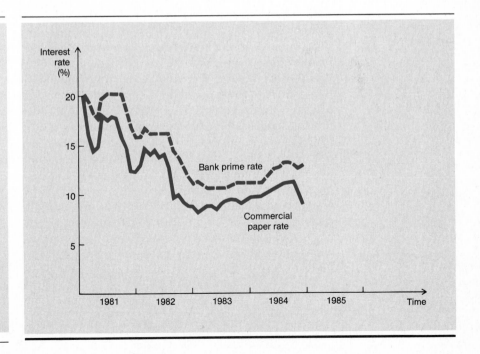

FIGURE 16-1

Bank prime rates and commercial paper rates. (Source: Federal Reserve Bulletin.)

calculated on the loan each day by adding 1 percent to the prime rate, then expressing the result as a daily equivalent rate [(prime rate + 1.0 percent)/365 days] and multiplying by the loan balance to compute the daily interest. Each month the bank would ask the firm to pay the interest owed from the previous month. In this case, the actual cost of the loan can be determined only after it has been paid off. For the past few years, the majority of business loans have been of this type.[3]

Commercial Paper

Commercial paper is a short-term marketable security sold by business firms to investors—usually other firms, small banks, and financial institutions. It is an unsecured debt of the firm issuing the paper and usually has a maturity of 270 days or less to avoid the registration requirements of the Securities and Exchange Commission (see Chapter 18). Most commercial paper is issued by financial institutions (finance companies and bank holding companies); however, large nonfinancial corporations are also important users of this method of short-term financing. Just prior to the Penn Central bankruptcy in 1970, medium-sized corporations had also begun to issue commercial paper in significant quantities. Penn Central had $80 million in commercial paper coming due that it could not repay or refinance. Only three weeks prior to the company's filing for bankruptcy, its commercial paper was considered to be of very low risk. After Penn Central defaulted on its commercial paper, investors became very cautious and reluctant to purchase any commercial paper not issued by companies of the highest financial reputation. The market recovered, but only those firms with excellent credit ratings and which need $10 million or more can easily find dealers to sell the paper for them.

Many large companies sell their paper directly to investors using their own salespeople who call on potential buyers. Approximately half of the commercial paper outstanding at any given time is sold direct. This large proportion is due to the huge borrowing through direct sales of a few finance companies such as General Motors Acceptance Corp., Ford Motor Credit, and General Electric Credit. However, most issues of commercial paper market their paper through dealers who do the actual selling to investors. Dealers charge about $1000 per $1 million (one-tenth of 1 percent) for this service. The main advantage of commercial paper over short-term bank loans is the cost. The interest rate for prime-rated (low-risk) issues of commercial paper is normally lower than the prime rate charged by commercial banks. Moreover, there are no compensating-balance requirements. Most issuers find it desirable (or even necessary) to have lines of credit with commercial banks to backstop their issues of commercial paper. This is to provide protection to the firm in the event that it has financial problems when it has to repay commercial paper that is coming due. Banks charge about one-half of 1 percent for such backup lines. The commercial paper market is highly impersonal, and investors are understandably reluctant to purchase the issues of shaky firms. Commercial banks, however, are gener-

---

[3] See Table 1.34 in each issue of the *Federal Reserve Bulletin* for information on terms of lending.

ally more willing to stand by a customer who gets into difficulty and not to require payment when the loan is due. This is one of the major advantages of bank loans as compared with commercial paper. Figure 16-1 provides an historical comparison between commercial paper rates and bank loan rates.

SECURED BORROWING

Firms whose credit ratings are not sufficiently high to qualify them for unsecured loans or commercial paper are often required to pledge a portion of their assets to the lender as security for a loan. The pledged assets are called **collateral** for the loan. The advantage to the lender is that if the firm is liquidated, the lender has first claim against the assets pledged as security. This means that the lender is provided additional protection against loss (in addition to a general claim against the firm's assets) if the firm gets into trouble. We will discuss the problems associated with financial distress and bankruptcy in Chapter 25; however, it should be clear that the lender is usually the party that requires security. Since there are costs involved in establishing and maintaining the security, it is rare that a firm which could borrow on an unsecured basis would elect to pledge assets to secure the loan.

There are several sources for secured short-term loans, with commercial banks, finance companies, and factors being the most important. The most common business assets pledged as security are accounts receivable and inventory. We will look at the use of these two assets separately as financing arrangements differ more by the asset pledged than by the particular lender providing the money.

Accounts Receivable as Collateral

Accounts receivable represent money owed to a business by the individuals or firms to which it has extended credit. Ordinarily, as we discussed in Chapter 15, accounts receivable represent a fairly safe asset for a firm to hold. They usually serve as excellent collateral for loans for the same reasons. In order for a lender whose loan is fully secured by accounts receivable to take a loss, not only must the firm fail but also the money owed to the firm must be uncollectible. From the lender's point of view, however, this does not mean that there is little or no risk in loans secured by accounts receivable. The goods sold by the firm may be returned by the purchaser for various reasons, perhaps because they are defective. This would reduce the amount that could be collected. The firm may be extending credit to high-risk customers in order to increase sales. Thus the accounts receivable could be subject to large bad debt losses. Also, there is the possibility that the borrower may falsify records to show nonexistent accounts. Therefore, lenders rarely loan the full amount of accounts receivable pledged when collateral is deemed necessary.

There are two common approaches to using accounts receivable as collateral. The simpler approach, which is less costly but involves more risk for the lender, is to lend money using all the firm's accounts receivable as collateral. This is called a **general lien** on accounts receivable. The lender may be willing, for example, to loan up to 75 percent of outstanding accounts receivable as part of a secured credit line. The firm is obligated to tell the lender on a regular basis the amount of accounts receivable outstanding. The firm can borrow, as with any credit line, up to the agreed maximum amount.

Another approach is for the borrower to present invoices to the lender as collateral in sufficient amount to cover the amount of the loan; however, the lender may reject some of the accounts as being too risky. In other words, lenders can select the accounts on which they are willing to base loans. In such cases, since lenders have some control over the quality of the collateral, they will be willing to loan a higher percentage of the face value, sometimes 90 percent or more.

As we said, the cost of such arrangements is usually high. The borrower has the costs and problems associated with presenting accounts to the lender, and the lender has the costs involved in keeping track of the accounts pledged. For this reason lenders charge an additional fee to cover costs for secured loans. Finance companies make such loans and will usually charge higher rates than a bank since they are frequently lending to firms that are too risky to qualify for bank credit even on a secured basis.

Factoring   Instead of pledging accounts receivable for a loan, some firms sell their accounts receivable to a **factor**. The sale of accounts receivable is called **factoring**. The factor is a financial firm that specializes in this business. Historically, factoring has been most common in the textile industry and most factors were located in the Northeast, although other types of firms also utilize factors and they are found throughout the United States. The typical factoring arrangement is more than just a way to raise money; it usually includes services. The factor may provide credit analysis of the customers and collection of payments due, thereby relieving the firm of most if not all of the expense of maintaining a credit department. The factor may also provide temporary unsecured financing to the firm in addition to the funds furnished by sale of the accounts receivable. While factoring is generally considered an expensive method of financing, these additional advantages may make it the preferred method of short-term financing for some firms.

Credit Cards   The widespread use of bank credit cards has virtually revolutionized the financing of accounts receivable at the retail level. Major retailers have for many years provided charge accounts for their customers. With the introduction of bank credit cards, smaller retailers can provide equivalent services to customers holding such cards. From the customer's point of view, acceptance of his or her card by a retailer is as convenient as the extension of credit by the retailer. The retailer is paid immediately by the bank upon submission of the credit invoice; thus the retailer has no investment in accounts receivable and does not actually extend the credit.

For this service the retailer pays the bank a percentage (for example, 3 percent) of the invoiced amount. The arrangement has many of the same characteristics as a complete factoring agreement. The bank does all the credit analysis on the customer and provides immediate funds just as a factor does. The two major differences between a credit card agreement and factoring are, first, credit card customers are consumers whereas the customers of a firm factoring its accounts receivable are other businesses and, second, a credit card customer does not usually perceive the retailer as extending credit whereas the customer of the factoring firm does. This loss of customer identification with the retailer (the customer does not have a charge account at the particular store) is one of the reasons that many large retailers have been reluctant to abandon use of their own charge account systems.[4]

*Inventory as
Collateral*

Many types of inventory are easily sold and serve as fairly good security for short-term loans, whereas other types of inventory are valueless as collateral from a lender's point of view. The major consideration in the suitability of inventory as a means of securing a loan is the marketability of the inventory. Work-in-process inventories (goods still in the manufacturing process) are almost never considered suitable, since such partially completed products are almost impossible to sell. Many raw materials such as grain, primary metals, and industrial chemicals are good collateral since a ready market exists for them. Manufacturers' finished goods inventories and retail inventories may or may not be good collateral depending on the nature of the goods. New cars, appliances, paper, and lumber are usable as collateral. Clothing, perishable goods, and specialized equipment are not very usable. If an inventory is suitable collateral, the lender will advance some percentage of the total value. The more stable the market value of the inventory, the higher the percentage will be. For example, a commodity such as cocoa, which is subject to wide price variations, would have a lower percentage than a commodity like wheat, which generally does not vary as much in price.

There are several ways in which a lender can gain a secured interest in inventory. Since each of the methods has a somewhat different implication for the cost and flexibility of the financing arrangement, we will consider each separately.

General Lien   Just as was true of accounts receivable, the lender can obtain a lien against all or part of the firm's inventory, whatever the specific items may be. This type of arrangement is very easy to set up, but it doesn't provide much security since there is no telling what the inventory will be like in the event of the firm's liquidation. Since the lender cannot maintain good control over the quality of the collateral, the amount loaned as a percentage of the inventory's value is likely to be small, unless collateral is not a significant element in the credit decision of the lender. The interest rate may also be somewhat higher for this type of inventory loan.

Floor Planning   Floor planning is a type of security arrangement often used in financing automobile dealers, farm and industrial equipment dealers, and sellers of consumer durable goods. Under this type of agreement the goods are specifically identified by the serial numbers of the items in stock.

---

[4] A retailer with charge accounts is able to direct specific advertising to its customers and can include promotional material with the bill, etc. However the existence of so many people with credit cards puts continuous pressure on stores to accept the cards. Many stores now accept credit cards and also offer their own charge accounts.

When an item is sold, the proceeds are supposed to be given to the lender in repayment of the loan against that item. As new inventory is purchased, the borrower signs a form describing the items purchased and specifying the terms of the agreement. The lender then pays the supplier for the goods. Periodically a representative of the lender checks out the current inventory of the dealer to make sure that all items covered by the floor plan are still in stock.

Floor plan agreements are fairly inexpensive to administer and provide all the flexibility most borrowers require. The security from the lender's point of view is good provided that the merchandise has not been sold without the lender's being notified. Unfortunately this happens often enough to mean that lenders cannot consider such plans totally secure.

The lender may be a bank, a finance company, or even the manufacturer of the product. Manufacturers engaging in this type of arrangement usually do so in order to encourage their dealers to carry a complete line of goods to boost sales. When such financing is available from the manufacturer, it often carries lower interest rates than the dealer would be able to get from a financial institution.

Warehousing Arrangements   Under warehousing arrangements a third party controls the borrower's access to the goods held as security. Since this party must be paid for its services, this is a relatively expensive procedure. There are two basic types—**field warehouses** and **public warehouses**. In field warehousing arrangements, the warehousing company establishes an area on the borrower's premises as a field warehouse. The company is supposed to maintain strict control over the inventory so that the lender should be able to find out at all times exactly what inventory is there. The borrower has ready access to the goods since they are stored on the borrower's property; however, they must be accounted for continuously. Even with the degree of control afforded by this type of arrangement there have been cases of fraud. The most spectacular case was the Allied Salad Oil scandal of 1963, which caused over $100 million of losses to the lenders involved. Money was lent on salad oil supposedly stored in a field warehouse (large tanks). The tanks turned out to contain water with a little oil floating on top.

Even tighter control over the inventory used as security is provided by public warehouses. In this case the inventory is held in a physical location apart from the borrower's place of business and under control of the warehousing company. The major disadvantage of this type of security arrangement is the cost to the borrower of obtaining the goods for use or for sale. Goods may be moved out of the warehouse only with the consent of the lender. Of course the warehousing company must also be paid for its services. This is the most expensive form of security arrangement.

SUMMARY

The factors that affect the types of short-term financing chosen are interest cost, impact on credit rating, reliability, restrictions, and flexibility. The credit rating of the firm affects the availability of financing and the terms of financing.

Trade credit (accounts payable) is a very important source of credit to small firms and is used to some extent by all firms. Credit terms vary considerably from industry to industry. The amount of trade credit available to the firm depends on its volume of purchases and its credit rating. A major advantage of trade credit as a source of financing is that it increases as the firm's activity increases. The cost of using trade credit is the amount of any discounts foregone so long as the firm pays its bills when they are due. Delaying payment past the due date, while often done, tends to have an adverse impact on the firm's credit rating and may result in suppliers' refusing to provide credit.

Loans from commercial banks are a major source of short-term credit to businesses. Compensating balances are often required by banks. A compensating balance is an amount that the firm must maintain in its checking account with the bank and is stated as a percentage of the credit line. The interest rate charged on a bank loan depends on the credit standing of the firm and the level of short-term interest rates in the economy. The lowest rate charged by banks on credit lines is called the prime rate. Banks sometimes deduct the interest from the principal of the loan in advance. This increases the effective rate of interest.

Commercial paper is a short-term debt security issued by large firms and financial institutions. It can be issued directly to investors or sold through dealers. While the interest cost of commercial paper is usually lower than the rates charged by banks, if the firm becomes unprofitable, it may have trouble refinancing its commercial paper issues.

Lenders such as commercial banks may require a firm whose credit rating is weak to pledge assets as security for a loan. Accounts receivable and inventory are often used as collateral. Accounts receivable are usually the best collateral since the risk to the lender is less with these assets. There are several methods used by lenders to obtain a security interest in accounts receivable. Generally the more control the lender has over the pledged accounts, the less risk there is to the lender but the cost of administering the loan is greater. Lenders frequently require a fee in addition to the interest charge to compensate them for the costs of administration. Factoring is the sale of accounts receivable, but it may also involve other services. Credit cards reduce or eliminate the need of retailers to provide credit to their customers. The credit card company provides the credit, and the merchant is paid immediately on presentation of an invoice.

Inventory may also be pledged as security for a loan. The suitability of inventory as collateral depends on its marketability and on the predictability of its price if it is sold. Floor planning, field warehousing, and public warehousing are methods used by lenders to keep track of inventory used as collateral.

QUESTIONS

1 "The objective of a financial manager is to minimize the cost of financing when seeking short-term funds." Comment on this statement considering other factors that may affect the choice of short-term financing arrangements.

Rank the three major sources of short-term financing in terms of availability to the following types of business:

    a A large manufacturer with a high credit rating

    b A medium-sized manufacturer with a good credit rating

    c A small retailer with a fair credit rating

3 What is the basic cost of trade credit and why is it a cost?

4 What determines the amount of trade credit to a firm?

5 "The cost of incurring a bad trade credit reputation is simply the cost of obtaining financing from other sources." Do you agree? Why or why not?

6 Distinguish between a credit line and a revolving credit from the viewpoints of the lender and borrower.

7 Which types of short-term financing would you expect to be used by the following firms:

    a A small open-air market selling fresh seafood and eggs

    b An apparel shop specializing in clothing for taller women

    c A large metropolitan department store

    d A dealer selling new and used cars

    e A contractor constructing the coolers for nuclear reactors

    f A finance company with branch offices nationwide

    g A partnership selling and servicing Whirlpool appliances

8 In 1978 the outstanding short-term borrowings of Pillsbury Co. varied between $30 million and $40 million, mostly in commercial paper. The assistant treasurer, Frances Gamble, reportedly said (*Business Week*, July 8, 1978) that banks were not used "unless we owe them a favor." She also indicated that Pillsbury did borrow from its banks once in the past three years "to let them know we want a line there if we need it." Why do you think Pillsbury uses commercial paper rather than bank loans as a normal practice? Why did the company use bank loans at all in the preceding three years?

9 Are accounts receivable generally considered a better source of collateral than inventories? Why or why not?

10 Given that the following firms use secured financing arrangements, would they be more likely to be pledging inventory, accounts receivable, or both as collateral? Why?

    a A company manufacturing custom electronic equipment for major aerospace firms

    b A wholesale lumber dealer

    c A retail appliance (refrigerators, etc.) store

    d A children's clothing manufacturer

11 Distinguish between the following types of secured financial arrangements in terms of advantages and disadvantages to the borrower:

    a Factoring

    b General lien

    c Floor planning

    d Warehousing arrangements

Obtain a recent annual report of a nonfinancial business. Analyze the sources of short-term financing currently used by the firm. Have the amount or composition of short-term financing sources changed from the previous year? Estimate their costs to the extent possible. Be sure to read the footnotes to the balance sheet, where much of the detail on financing will be found.

1 Fun Furs purchases $300 per day from suppliers whose terms are net/30.

    a If Fun Furs pays its bills on time, what will its accounts payable balance be? [Ans.: $9000]

    b Suppose sales (and purchases) increase 20 percent over previous levels, what will the new accounts payable balance be? [Ans.: $10,800]

    c At the new level of purchases in **b**, how much additional financing could Fun Furs obtain by paying, on average, fifteen days late? [Ans.: $5400]

2 Fred's Hobby Shop is a small proprietorship located in an urban shopping center. The terms on purchases of models from a wholesaler are 4/10, net 60. How much would it cost Fred to forego the discount and pay in sixty days rather than ten days? [Ans.: 30.4 percent per year]

3 Suppose that Fred of problem **2** can purchase from either of two wholesalers. The first wholesaler offers terms given in problem **2** while the second offers a trade discount of 2/15, net 30. Fred can borrow from a bank at 12 percent per year interest cost. What are your recommendations?

4 An approximate formula for the cost of trade credit is often used in place of Eq. (16-1). The approximation is

$$\frac{\text{Annual}}{\text{interest rate}} = \text{discount} \times \frac{360 \text{ days}}{\text{payment period} - \text{discount period}}$$

    a For each of the following trade credit terms calculate the annual interest rate using the exact formula Eq. (16-1) and the approximate formula above assuming that bills are paid when due:

        1 2/10, net 30   **3** 3/10, net 30

        2 2/10, net 60   **4** 5/10, net 90

    b Compare your results in **a** for the two formulas. How accurate is the approximation? Would the size of normal monthly purchases under the given terms (for example, $10,000 per month vs. $100,000 per month) affect your findings as to the accuracy of the approximation?

5 Compute the interest cost of foregoing discounts [using Eq. (16-1)] for the following terms assuming bills are paid when due:

a EOM, net 30
b 2/10, EOM, net 30
c 2/15, prox., net 30
d 3/10, net 30, October 1

6 Dryland State Bank has granted Camino Yacht Company Incorporated a line of credit of $400,000, under the stipulation that Camino maintain a 15 percent compensating balance in its deposit account with the bank on any loans outstanding and a 10 percent compensating balance for the unborrowed portion of the credit line. Dryland also charges Camino an interest rate of 12 percent for funds borrowed.

a If Camino borrows $300,000 on the line of credit, what is the dollar amount that must be maintained in Dryland as a compensating balance? [Ans.: $55,000]

b What is the effective interest rate on Camino's borrowings of $300,000 assuming the firm would normally (i.e., even if Camino did not obtain the line of credit) keep $20,000 in the account? [Ans.: 13.58 percent per year]

7 Bank A offers a one-year loan at an interest rate of 15 percent per year, where the interest is paid at the end of the year when the loan matures. Bank B offers to loan at a stated rate of 14 percent per year but deducts the interest at the beginning of the year. Which bank offers the lower cost financing?

8 The Last National Bank has offered the Scale Fish Company a choice of alternative terms for Scale's annual line of credit of $6.0 million. The bank will charge a flat 12 percent annual rate on all borrowings, or is willing to charge 11.5 percent if Scale will maintain a 20 percent compensating balance on outstanding loans and a 10 percent compensating balance on the unused portion of the line. In the absence of compensating-balance requirements, Scale's average deposit balances would be $600,000. As financial manager of Scale you have estimated the following loan needs for the coming year. Which loan terms would you choose? (Treat any additional deposit balances needed as a reduction in funds available from the line.)

Month	Jan.	Feb.	Mar.	Apr.	May	June	July	Aug.	Sept.	Oct.	Nov.	Dec.
Loan needed: (millions)	$0	$0	$1.0	$1.0	$2.0	$3.0	$5.0	$5.0	$3.0	$2.0	$2.0	$0

9 Northern Lights requires additional short-term financing of $12.0 million. It has excellent relationships with its bank and its suppliers, and a high credit rating in general. The company maintains normal deposit balances of $400,000. The following sources are available:

a Trade credit. Purchases average $300,000 per day on terms of

2/10, net 30; the $12 million financing need was based on payment within 10 days.

b A 12 percent loan from the bank that will require 15 percent in compensating balances to be held on deposit with the bank.

c Commercial paper bearing a 11.5 percent interest rate. In order to issue the paper, the firm must maintain backup lines of credit with a bank. The bank will charge an annual fee of 0.5 percent of the credit line and require the firm to maintain 10 percent of the line as deposits at the bank.

Evaluate the cost of each of these three sources. How should Northern Lights obtain the $12 million needed?

C H A P T E R

17

WORKING
CAPITAL
MANAGEMENT

In Chapters 15 and 16 we examined the principles of investment in the major types of current assets and the choice among the major sources of short-term financing. We will now look at issues in the overall management of current assets and current liabilities, which is called **working capital management.**[1] This chapter therefore serves as a summary of current asset management and financing and it draws on Chapters 12 and 14 as well.

This chapter is divided into three sections. In the first section we discuss the concept of working capital. The second section contains the central concern of the chapter, the interrelationships between current assets and current liabilities and the choice between short-term and long-term financing. The last section covers the relationship between current assets, current liabilities, and long-term investment decisions.

WORKING CAPITAL:
DEFINITIONS

Working capital has traditionally meant current assets. The term originated in simpler times when the economy was based on agriculture. Fruit and vegetable processors, meat packers, and commodity dealers purchase agricultural products, process them, and sell them. Agricultural production is a seasonal business and normally the products are sold prior to the next season. Thus, at the beginning of the season these firms have very low levels of current assets. As crops are harvested, processed, and sold, current asset levels increase dramatically. The current assets of these firms are financed almost entirely with short-term sources. As inventory is sold, accounts receivable collected, and short-term debt repaid, both current asset and current liability levels are lowered until the bottom of the seasonal cycle is reached, typically in the late spring. This is "capital at work." The term "working capital" is still frequently used as a synonym for current assets, and the term "net working capital" is used to mean the quantity that results from subtracting the dollar value of current liabilities from the dollar value of current assets. In this book we use the term "working capital" to mean current assets minus current liabilities (that is, as a synonym for net working capital), since this is more common in practice. Working capital management includes the management of all the types of current assets and short-term financing sources discussed in Chapters 15 and 16. It also includes the decisions as to the appropriate amount of long-term financing used in financing the current assets of the enterprise.

Working capital represents the portion of current assets financed with long-term debt and equity. Any firm with a current ratio greater than 1.0 has positive working capital. For a given level of current liabilities, the greater the working capital of the firm, the larger is its current ratio. Long-term debt agreements often contain provisions requiring the firm to maintain a minimum level of working capital. Such provisions are intended to provide a degree of safety to the lender under the assumption that current assets are more likely to maintain reasonable liquidating value than other assets of the firm.

What determines the amount of working capital for a firm? Obviously,

---

[1] To understand this chapter, you should have studied Chapters 12, 14, 15, and 16.

working capital is determined by the level of current assets and the level of current liabilities, since working capital is simply the difference between the two. But what considerations by management lead them to operate with a particular level of working capital? First, as noted above, the firm's long-term lenders may have something to say about it. However, there are other reasons for the financial manager to be concerned with the problem. Let's examine them.

THE WORKING CAPITAL DECISION

A major theme of this chapter is the interrelated nature of current asset and current liability decisions. We noted in Chapter 15 that decisions regarding accounts receivable could not be made without considering the implications for inventory investment. Further, any business decision that results in increased sales and collections for the firm is likely to mean that larger average cash balances will be needed or that a new cash management system will be desirable. Therefore all the current asset decisions are related. Now consider some of the links between current assets and current liabilities.

A decision to increase purchased inventories will mean higher purchases in the short run as inventory investment is increased. If sales increase, purchases must increase to maintain a constant level of inventory, and growing sales will usually require greater inventory investment and purchases. Unless the firm purchases on cash terms, an increase in purchases will lead to an increase in accounts payable. Thus a portion of the increase in inventory will be financed "automatically" with trade credit. The amount of trade credit financing will depend on decisions regarding payments. Inventory decisions therefore are linked to trade credit decisions.[2]

We discussed the use of inventory and accounts receivable as collateral for loans in Chapter 16. Thus, for firms unable to obtain unsecured financing, the nature and quality of these current assets affect the availability and terms of short-term financing. We also noted in Chapter 16 that banks often require compensating balances as part of their loan terms. This means that the short-term financing decision influences the level of cash held.

The procedures discussed in Chapters 15 and 16 for analyzing and evaluating current asset and current liability decisions took into account the major interactions that might influence the decision. However, we can see now that these procedures are approximations to broader problems of working capital management.

How do financial managers deal with these complex interactions? The primary tools are the pro forma financial statements presented in Chapter 14. Alternative working capital policies are evaluated by forecasting their impact on the cash flows, balance sheets, and income statements of the firm. For example, decisions that require heavy use of short-term secured credit also require the availability of appropriate collateral. In making their

[2] This problem has been analyzed in Charles W. Haley and Robert C. Higgins, "Inventory Control Theory and Trade Credit Financing," *Management Science*, 20 (December 1973), pp. 464–471.

FIGURE 17-1

The firm's assets over time.

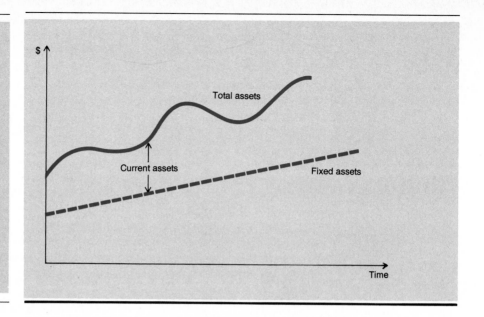

decisions regarding the appropriate amount of short-term financing to support forecasted current asset investment, financial managers use the matching principle as an important guide.

The Matching Principle

The **matching principle**, one of the oldest principles in finance, can be stated as follows:

Finance short-term needs with short-term sources, and finance long-term needs with long-term sources.

The idea expressed in this principle is to "match" the maturity of the source of funds to the length of time the funds are needed.

The underlying logic is that, in the long run, the firm will be exposed to less risk and lower financing costs if the matching principle is followed. If the firm finances long-term needs with short-term borrowing, it will have to refinance (reborrow) its short-term debts as they become due, thereby exposing itself to added transaction costs (accounting and legal costs, fixed borrowing fees by lenders, etc.) and to the risk that new borrowing will be available only at higher interest rates with onerous terms. If the firm finances short-term needs with long-term sources, there will be times when there are excess funds that may have to be invested in low-yielding securities.

To see how the matching principle is applied, let's examine a graph of the total assets of the firm over time. For simplicity we will break the assets into only two types, current assets and fixed assets. Current assets include cash, marketable securities, accounts receivable, and inventory; fixed assets are long-term assets such as plant and equipment. In Figure 17-1 the fixed assets are shown increasing at a steady rate, as we are assuming a growing firm. Current assets are added to fixed assets to arrive at total assets. The matching principle states that the fixed assets of the firm should be financed with long-term sources (long-term debt plus equity), but what about current assets? Notice that in Figure 17-1 current assets have their ups and downs over time but they, too, are increasing on average. To see this more clearly, we can look at just the current assets over time in Figure 17-2. We have divided the current assets held by the firm into two types: temporary current assets and permanent current assets. Permanent current assets are the minimum investment in current assets that management has determined as being appropriate to support the current sales of the firm.

From Figure 17-2 the matching principle indicates that permanent current assets in addition to fixed assets should be financed with long-term sources. Only temporary current asset investment would be financed with short-term sources. The matching principle is not always followed by financial managers, in part because it does not consider the "permanent" short-term financing that arises from trade credit and some other current liabilities. As the firm's sales grow over time, its current liabilities increase apart from any explicit decisions made by financial management. Increases in sales result in increased employment and therefore higher average levels of wages and salaries payable. Increases in the volume of purchases lead to increased accounts payable (trade credit) even if all discounts are taken. Higher profits lead to higher taxes and therefore higher taxes payable. Thus a portion of increases in permanent current assets is financed by spontaneously generated increases in current liabilities. Only the increase in permanent working capital (permanent current assets minus permanent current liabilities) is to be financed by long-term sources under the matching principle. Furthermore, financial managers may be willing to trade off some risk in order to reduce financing costs. In order to understand this

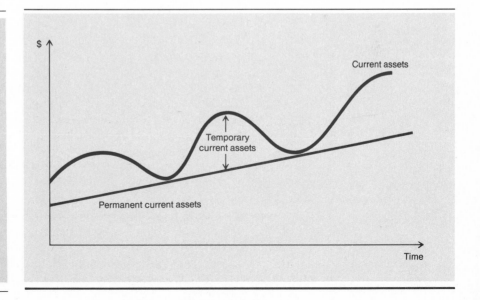

FIGURE 17-2

The firm's current assets over time.

tradeoff between risk and financing cost we need to know about yield curves.

The Yield Curve

For most of the twentieth century interest rates on short-term debt securities have been less than interest rates on long-term debt securities. The typical situation is illustrated in Figure 17-3. A graph of interest rates on debt securities of a given type relative to the maturity of the debt is called a **yield curve**. At any point in time the financial manager of a firm can construct a yield curve showing the interest rate that the firm would have to pay on debt of a given maturity. In the typical case, the interest rate on short-term debt is less than the interest rate on long-term debt. However these relationships change over time. Often, short-term rates exceed long-term rates. For example, throughout 1981 the prime rate on bank loans was several percentage points higher than the interest rate on long-term Aaa bonds.

Yield curves can be developed for the securities of any borrower. The primary yield curve in the economy is the interest rate–maturity relationship for United States government securities. The financial manager must understand the information provided by these relationships. The government securities yield curve is thought to be determined by three factors:[3]

1 The current level of short-term interest rates[4]
2 The expectations of investors and borrowers as to future interest rates
3 Premiums for risk of ownership of long-term securities (also called liquidity premiums)

[3] A more comprehensive discussion of this topic is in Appendix 5A. We provide only the basic ideas here.
[4] See Chapter 2 for a discussion of the factors determining the current level of short-term interest rates.

FIGURE 17-3
A typical yield curve.

When investors believe that interest rates will rise in the future, they will want to purchase short-term securities planning to reinvest at maturity at the higher rates. Thus the prices of short-term securities will rise, forcing down the interest rates on those securities. Simultaneously the prices of long-term securities will fall as investors sell them to buy short-term securities, and interest rates on long-term securities will rise. Conversely, when investors believe interest rates will fall, short-term interest rates will rise and long-term interest rates will fall as investors shift from short-term securities to long-term securities. The process stops when investors estimate that it is no longer profitable to make such shifts and the market comes into equilibrium. Thus, the yield curve reflects current expectations regarding future interest rates. However, expectations are not the only factor influencing yield curves. Even for securities issued by the United States government, investors must bear some risk due to possible changes in interest rates. An increase in interest rates causes the prices of fixed income securities to fall. The longer the maturity of the security, the larger is the decline in price for a given change in interest rates. Thus long-term bonds are riskier than short-term bonds or bills. The result is that long-term bonds provide higher yields than short-term bonds to compensate investors for the additional risk.[5]

For business firms, long-term debt carries an additional premium because the interest and principal payments become less certain the further into the future they are; that is, there is more risk that the firm will default. Even AT&T bonds are risky in this sense. You may be fairly confident that AT&T will be able to pay its debts in 1990, but what about AT&T bonds maturing in 2005? Are you sure that satellite technology or some other factors will not put AT&T in a difficult financial position then? If you are not sure about AT&T, how about Burlington Northern Railroad, or IBM? These firms appear very safe today, but who knows what problems they might have in the future. The result is that the long-term debt of a business carries a higher risk premium than its short-term debt because of the difficulty in predicting long-run future outcomes.

The existence of risk premiums on long-term debt presents a dilemma to the financial manager. Financing exclusively through short-term debt has a lower expected interest cost to the firm, but it also is riskier. When the firm finances through twenty-year bonds, management knows the interest and principal payments that must be paid over the next twenty years if the firm is to avoid bankruptcy. If one-year notes are used, they must be repaid when due. If new securities must be issued to repay the one-year notes, the interest payments required after the first year are uncertain. Future interest payments will depend on the general level of interest rates at the time of the

---

[5] Actually, the reason for higher interest rates on long-term debt instruments (positively sloped yield curve) is more complicated than described here. The shape of the yield curve depends on expected inflation, the preferred holding periods of investors, and the supply of debt instruments. However, since the yield curve for United States government securities is ordinarily positively sloped, it is likely that investors feel that the risk of long-term securities is greater than that of short-term securities, that is, the "risk premium" is larger the greater the term to maturity.

refinancing and the risk of the business at that time. Exclusive use of short-term debt would probably result in negative working capital for most firms and lenders often do not like to see current ratios of less than 1.0 for the firms to which they are providing credit. Moreover, use of short-term debt to finance permanent current assets and fixed assets means that the firm must continually refinance the debt as it comes due. Poor operating results in any year can make this difficult and expensive.

The pressure on financial managers remains. Should they strive for lower costs of financing by heavy use of short-term debt or should they reduce risk by following the matching principle? There is no clear-cut answer.

Liquidity

Liquidity for a firm is best defined as the ability to raise cash when needed. Assets are liquid if they can be rapidly converted into cash. Money market securities are an excellent source of asset liquidity. Potential liabilities (unused available credit) also provide liquidity. For example, if a firm has a line of credit of $200,000 and is currently borrowing only $50,000, it has $150,000 of liquidity from this borrowing source. Note that for assets, the larger is the amount held by the firm, the greater the firm's liquidity. Similarly, for potential liabilities the larger are the firm's potential liabilities, the greater its liquidity. Thus, a firm with a credit line of $200,000 that is borrowing only $50,000 has more liquidity than another firm with the same credit line but borrowing the full $200,000. To the extent that the firm has large investments in assets that are readily convertible into cash and has a large potential for increased borrowing, it is liquid.

There are two aspects to liquidity—planned liquidity and protective liquidity. Planned liquidity involves nothing more than the planning we stressed in Chapter 14. The financial manager must forecast cash needs and plan how those needs are to be met—either through reductions in assets (usually cash and marketable securities) or through increases in liabilities (drawing down established credit lines). Protective liquidity is the ability to meet unexpected cash demands. Unexpected cash demands are net cash outflows greater than those originally forecast. Unexpected cash demands can arise for many reasons. In some cases cash is needed to undertake unexpected investment opportunities. The inability to raise sufficient cash to undertake these investments results in foregone profits. In other cases cash is needed because of unexpected outflows—for example, a recall of defective products or a sudden increase in the prices of purchased goods. Cash may be needed because cash inflows are less than anticipated—for example, a strike that stops production, a slowdown in collections due to recession in the economy, a breakdown in a critical manufacturing step that cannot be fixed quickly, or a technological breakthrough that causes prices to drop dramatically.

Given the general uncertainty regarding cash flows, conservative financial managers maintain substantial liquidity. These managers make sure that they have committed credit lines well above the amount they expect to need. If the firm uses commercial paper, backup lines with banks will be maintained. They will keep marketable securities as a precautionary invest-ment.

In all cases the appropriate level of working capital is greatly influenced by the inherent characteristics of the business. For example, policies that would be considered fairly safe and conservative for an electric utility (such as having a current ratio of 1.2) would be considered highly risky for firms in most other industries. Therefore, in evaluating alternative policies the finan-cial manager should take into account the particular operating charac-teristics of the business. A helpful guide is to compare the firm's working capital position with those of other firms in the same industry, using procedures such as those discussed in Chapter 12. It is also essential to take into account the special features of the firm since all companies in a given industry are not exactly alike.

WORKING CAPITAL AND BUSINESS EXPANSION

From our analysis of cash, accounts receivable, and inventory, we know that the amount of investment in current assets is closely related to the firm's sales volume. We also know that increased sales and inventory require higher purchases of raw materials or goods for resale and thus lead to increases in accounts payable. Further, in our discussion of financial fore-casting in Chapter 14, we observed that part of the firm's other short-term liabilities depends on the general level of firm activity, wages payable, for example. This means that a firm planning investments in plant and equip-ment in order to expand output and sales must also plan for an increase in current asset investment. This increase in current assets, however, will be financed at least in part by "natural" costless increases in current lia-bilities.[6] But as long as some of the increased current assets are financed from sources other than current liabilities (that is, from cash flow from operations or from new stock or long-term debt), the result will be an increase in working capital investment by the firm. This additional invest-ment must be considered in the analysis of the desirability of expansion and be included as part of the total investment of the project.

As an example, consider a firm planning to invest $1 million in a plant to manufacture snowshoes. The expected annual sales from the facility are $1.8 million with anticipated aftertax cash flows of $200,000 per year. As-suming these cash flows will continue in perpetuity, the rate of return on the plant investment might be thought to be 20 percent ($200,000/ $1,000,000). But wait. The financial manager must estimate the additional investment in raw materials, work-in-process, and finished goods inventory. Total additional inventory investment might be 20 percent of annual sales, or $360,000. If the firm purchases additional raw materials at a rate of $50,000 per month on terms of net 30, increased accounts payable will be (at no cost to the firm) $50,000. If the snowshoes will be sold on terms of net 60, accounts receivable will average two months' sales or 2 × ($1.8 million/12) = $300,000.

---

[6] Here we would include only accounts payable that will be obtained when all discounts are taken. If discounts are foregone, trade credit is not costless and must be considered as part of the overall financing plan.

The cash investment in these accounts is $200,000 (the cost of producing the goods sold to create the accounts receivable). The firm will probably also need additional cash balances to support the production and collection activity, say, 1 percent of annual sales, or $18,000. Additional current liabilities excluding any discretionary short-term financing might be 2 percent of annual sales, or $36,000. A summary of the additional working capital required is shown below.

Cash balance needed	$ 18,000
Cash investment in accounts receivable	200,000
Inventory investment	360,000
Total investment in current assets	$578,000
Less: Accounts payable	50,000
Other current liabilities	36,000
Required investment in working capital	$492,000

This additional investment in working capital must be included as part of the total investment. Thus total investment in the project will be $1 million in plant plus $492,000 in working capital for a total of $1,492,000. The actual rate of return on this project is therefore only 13.4 percent ($200,000/ $1,492,000).

Clearly, the financial manager would be making a big mistake to ignore working capital in evaluating the desirability of expansion. How is the manager to determine the amount of working capital needed? In theory each asset and liability must be analyzed in detail according to the principles of Chapters 15 and 16. However, this is usually too time-consuming for the degree of accuracy possible given the normal uncertainties inherent in any major expansion. Instead, the manager will use approximations based on the forecasting techniques of Chapter 14.

In addition to including working capital investment as part of initial investment, any anticipated changes in the level of investment over the life of the project must be included. Additions to working capital due to forecasting increases in sales volume reduce net cash flow in the period when the increase occurs. Reductions in working capital increase net cash flow. At the end of the investment period, working capital due to the project will fall to zero. The reduction in working capital investment is part of the salvage value of the total project (is a cash inflow).

SUMMARY

Working capital management is the management of current assets and current liabilities of the firm, which must be considered as a total package because of the many links between current assets and current liabilities. Working capital equals current assets minus current liabilities. Working capital is therefore the portion of the firm's current assets that is financed with long-term debt, preferred stock, and equity.

The matching principle states that short-term needs for money should be financed with short-term financing sources and that long-term needs for money should be financed with long-term sources. If the matching principle is followed, temporary investments in current assets should be financed with current liabilities such as trade credit, commercial paper, and short-term bank loans.

The relationship between interest rates and maturities of debt securities at a point in time is called a yield curve. The yield curve is determined by current short-term interest rates, by expectations of investors and borrowers as to future interest rates, and by the risk premiums required by investors. From the perspective of investors, the greater is the maturity of the debt, the more risky it is to own. However, from the perspective of the financial manager of a business firm, financing with short-term debt is more risky than financing with long-term debt.

Liquidity for a firm is the capability to raise cash quickly when it is needed. Assets provide liquidity if they can be rapidly converted into cash. The ability to borrow cash also provides liquidity. The financial manager should plan to provide liquidity for anticipated future cash needs. In addition, it is desirable for the firm to have liquidity available for unexpected cash needs.

Working capital requirements are an important part of capital budgeting decisions and should be included in the evaluation of each project.

QUESTIONS

1 Some data for two companies are shown below. Which one do you think has the more liquidity? Why?

Working capital	Company A	Company B
Current assets	$2,000	$2,200
Working capital	$1,500	$ 800
Total assets	$5,000	$5,000

2 The two partners of Kale and Collard Enterprises recently had the following argument:

Kale: "At the end of this year we expect our growth in sales to require an increase in current assets of $400,000. In view of this need I suggest we seek long-term financing."

Collard: "On the contrary, the $400,000 increase is due entirely to increased accounts receivable and inventory, for which $60,000 will be needed only for a few months. We should finance this $400,000 in additional current assets with a current liability such as a short-term bank loan."

Can you help Kale and Collard?

3 Indicate for the following situations whether you would expect the

working capital of the firm in each case to increase, to decrease, or to remain at current levels. Explain why.

a An electronics manufacturer has just completed new facilities that are expected to enable the firm to increase sales by 30 percent.

b A clothing manufacturer discovers that a large part of the firm's inventory is unsalable and is therefore worthless.

c A pencil manufacturer receives a large special order for an odd-sized pencil not normally produced.

d The financial manager of a large corporation has received a staff study that indicates the corporation's liquidity is much too low because of increased uncertainty in the future cash flows and profits of the firm.

4 What is the matching principle?

5 Which one of the following three cases best describes a firm that is applying the matching principle? What financing policies do the other two firms appear to be using?

a Firm A maintains a low current ratio compared to other firms in its industry although its proportion of debt to total assets equals the industry average. Sales for the firm have increased each year for the past four years at a stable rate.

b Firm B has substantial credit lines available at commercial banks and is a frequent issuer of commercial paper; however, it often has no outstanding bank loans or commercial paper. The sales of this firm are somewhat seasonal and sales increased at annual rates varying between 4 percent and 20 percent over the past five years.

c Firm C is a highly seasonal industry and its sales growth has been irregular. It often has substantial holdings of marketable securities in contrast to other firms in the industry and its working capital as a percentage of total assets is well above the industry average.

6 As financial manager of the Curve Company you have observed that for the past twelve months interest rates on long-term debt securities of Curve have averaged two percentage points higher than the rates on short-term debt. In recent weeks interest rates in the economy have risen. The differential between long-term and short-term interest rates for Curve has decreased to one percentage point. What do you think is happening?

7 What are the two general sources of liquidity for a firm?

8 How does planned liquidity differ from protective liquidity?

9 Since liquidity is desirable, why don't all firms have lots of liquidity?

10 Bismark Shipyards is planning a new shipyard. Will the amount of working capital investment that must be considered in the decision depend on whether the new yard is a replacement for an existing facility or is in addition to existing facilities? Why or why not?

Plot the current yield curve for United States government securities and the yield on these securities one year ago. Try to explain why they appear as they do and what has changed from last year to the present. (A source for yields on United States government securities is *The Wall Street Journal*.) In your analysis do not include yields on any bonds that have coupon rates of $4\frac{1}{4}$ percent or less as yields on these securities are strongly influenced by special tax considerations. (They may be redeemed at par in settlement of estate taxes.)

(*Note*: For ease of calculation in all the problems below, assume that a year contains 360 days.)

1 Determine the working capital for a company with the following balance sheet.

Assets		Liabilties and net worth	
Cash	$ 500	Notes payable	$ 3,000
Accounts receivable	8,500	Accounts payable	2,500
Inventory	6,500	Long-term debt	6,000
Equipment	9,500	Net worth	13,500
Total	$25,000	Total	$25,000

2 As financial manager for Trident Electronics, you have completed the two-year cash flow forecast shown below. All cash inflows and outflows have been forecast, given the minimum cash balance of the firm, except that any new financing required and temporary investments in securities are not included in the cash inflows and outflows. Cash discounts are assumed to be taken when available. (Dollar figures are in millions.)

Quarter	1	2	3	4	5	6	7	8
Cash inflow (outflow)	$2.2	$(6.5)	$(4.0)	$1.3	$4.0	$(2.0)	$2.0	$(0.5)
Cumulative inflow (outflow)	$2.2	$(4.3)	$(8.3)	$(7.0)	$(3.0)	$(5.0)	$(3.0)	$(3.5)

a How much "permanent" financing appears to be needed by this firm?

b Given your answer from *a*, what is the maximum "temporary" financing required and when does it occur? [Ans.: $5.3 million in quarter 3]

3 As Trident Electronics' financial manager (problem 2), you must develop a financial plan for the firm.

a Evaluate the following alternative financing proposals submitted by your staff. Which ones are consistent with the matching principle? Might any fail to meet the financing needs of the firm? Are any particularly unsuited for the firm in other ways?

1 Obtain a line of credit for $3.0 million and issue $5.5 million of long-term debt in quarter 2.

2 Plan to issue ninety-day commercial paper as needed.

3 Obtain a two-year revolving credit agreement with a limit of $8.5 million.

4 Obtain a line of credit for $5.5 million and issue $3.0 million in long-term debt in quarter 2.

5 Issue $3.0 million of common stock in quarter 2 and use trade credit as needed.

6 Plan to finance with ninety-day bank loans as needed.

b Examine the implications of financing alternatives 1, 4, and 6, assuming the following:

1 Interest rate on long-term debt will be 15 percent.

2 Interest rate on line of credit will be 14 percent.

3 Interest rate on temporary investments will be 12 percent.

You should determine the actual loans and investments that will be outstanding in each quarter and the total cost of the three financing plans over the two-year period, treating the interest received on securities as an offset to interest expense on debt. Rank the three alternatives with respect to interest cost and with respect to financing risks. What do you observe?

4 Flake Enterprises is expecting sales next year to be $4.4 million, up $400,000 from last year. Inventory is expected to increase from $800,000 to $880,000 in order to support the higher level of sales. Purchases of goods average 60 percent of sales, and Flake pays its suppliers within 20 days, on average, taking all discounts available. How much of the $80,000 increase in inventory investment will be financed by spontaneous trade credit?

5 Estimate the liquidity readily available for the following companies:

a Firm A has $40,000 in U.S. Treasury bills and bank credit lines of $200,000. The firm has no bank loans currently outstanding.

b Firm B has no marketable securities and a bank credit line of $400,000. The firm is currently borrowing $150,000 from its bank.

6 Brigham Corporation is planning to build a new printing plant. The plant is expected to provide additional sales as follows:

First year	Second year	Third year and on
$2.0 million	$2.5 million	$3.0 million per year

That is, the plant is not expected to be producing at its maximum capacity of $3.0 million per year until the third year after opening.

The financial manager of Brigham estimates that, for every dollar of sales, $0.30 must be invested in current assets. If all discounts are taken and all bills are paid on time, accounts payable average $0.05 per dollar of sales for products similar to those being produced in the new plant. Other current liabilities, such as wages payable, typically average $0.03 per dollar of sales. Estimate the working capital investments required for the new mill. How do these requirements affect the cash flows associated with the project?

7 In January 1985, Robert Anderson, financial vice-president of Summit Company, ran into Elena Serrano at O'Hare International Airport. The two friends had not seen each other since their graduation in 1975 from business school. Over a drink Mr. Anderson told about the growth of Summit and the financial policies that had been used to support the firm's rapid growth. Ms. Serrano, who was a commercial loan officer in a large Los Angeles bank, was highly interested in the firm's limited use of bank credit. Mr. Anderson explained how Summit was able to grow while maintaining self-sufficiency in its capital requirements.

"The keys to our ability to operate with minimal outside financing are our ability to obtain good credit terms from our suppliers and our efforts to keep our investment in current assets at a relatively low level. We insist that our suppliers provide us with substantial credit and, in fact, they have little choice in the matter since extending credit is standard practice in the industry. On the other hand, we minimize our investment in current assets by maintaining tight control of cash, encouraging fast payment from our customers, and keeping close watch on inventory. In particular, we offer more liberal discounts for fast payment than is standard practice for our industry; but look at our collection period compared with the industry average. On average we are getting paid off twenty days earlier than our competitors. By speeding inflows and taking advantage of the supplier credit available, we are pretty much self-financing and need relatively little bank borrowing. With the prime rate now at 11 percent, that's important. Some months, of course, we do get a little tight and need to borrow, but as soon as we get any spare cash we pay off the debt and put any left over into securities. We can get 8 percent now on Treasury bills and better than 8.25 percent on CDs if we have $100,000 or more to invest."

Since both people had some time to kill between flights, they decided to spend some time reviewing Summit's financial policies. Ms. Serrano was particularly intrigued by Summit's limited use of bank credit and wondered whether she had an opportunity here to generate some business. Her bank had a "loan production office" in Seattle where Summit had its facilities.

Company Background   Summit Company is a manufacurer of quilted outerware, primarily designed for skiing, hiking, and similar outdoor activities. The company had been an operating division of a diversified corporation whose primary line of business was basic chemicals. In 1981 the division was sold to four investors including Mr. Anderson and another person, who were employees of the parent corporation. The two managers found two other people interested in the investment prospects of Summit to purchase the firm. From the beginning the firm was forced to be as self-sufficient as possible since none of the four original stockholders could contribute additional capital. In addition, Summit was burdened with significant debt as part of the buyout agreement. The firm's long-term debt was owed to the original parent corporation. Exhibit 17-1 shows Summit's balance sheet as of December 31, 1984.

The high debt-equity ratio when Summit was established and the lack of separate operating history had severely limited the amount of credit initially available from the firm's bank. The bank had been willing to loan up to $50,000 secured by accounts receivable and limited to 80 percent of receivables outstanding. This was sufficient to take care of Summit's seasonal credit needs. As the financial condition of the firm became more secure, the bank no longer required the accounts receivable as collateral. Mr. Anderson viewed the credit line as the major contribution to the firm's financial flexibility and tried to keep borrowings below the limit whenever possible. More recently the bank had indicated a willingness to explore setting up an unsecured line of credit of as much as $200,000. The interest rate on such a line would probably be 1 percent over the prime rate.

Sales for the company had grown at a compound rate of 20 percent per year since its inception, reaching a peak of $3.4 million in 1986. (See Exhibit 17-2 for the 1984 income statement.) After a somewhat shaky first year, profits had also grown substantially and had been entirely retained in the business.

Financial Policies Mr. Anderson decided that the firm would have to obtain substantial credit from suppliers to finance its growth

---

EXHIBIT 17-1
Summit Company, December 31, 1984 ($000s)

Assets		Liabilities and equity	
Cash and securities	$ 100	Accounts payable	$ 320
Accounts receivable	240	Accrued expenses	30
Inventory	520	Current long-term debt	90
Current assets	$ 860	Current liabilities	$ 440
Net plant & equipment	740	Long-term debt @ 12%	540
		Common stock & retained earnings	620
Total assets	$1,600	Total liabilities and equity	$1,600

without additional outside financing. He actively sought out suppliers who would offer the longest payment terms even though in some cases this involved purchasing somewhat higher-priced materials. He told Ms. Serrano "In many cases I have been able to obtain terms of sixty days from my suppliers in contrast to the 2/10, net 30 that is customary. Those people who continue to offer us 2/10, net 30 have been generally willing to let us go forty-five days or even sixty days without any hassling.

"On the other hand, we have really been able to speed up our collections. Our sales are split evenly between types of customers. We make private label goods for several department stores and mail order firms. We offer them terms of 2/10, net 30, and almost all of them pay within ten days. Our own Summit line is sold through sporting goods stores throughout the West. We are forced to give these people a larger discount of 4/10, net 60 in contrast to our competition, who mostly offer 2/10, net 60, but it's well worth the difference. Forty percent of these customers pay us within ten days and we have also been able to expand our outlets because of the better discount.

"Our inventory policies also contribute to our success. At year-end 1984, with sales at an annual rate of about $3.6 million, our in-

---

EXHIBIT 17-2
Summit Company income statement, year ending December 31, 1984 ($000s)

Sales		$3,400
Materials	$1,500	
Labor	800	
Overhead	200	
Cost of goods sold		2,500
Gross margin		$ 900
Selling and advertising		320
General and administration		290
Net interest expense		80
Profit before taxes		$ 210
Income taxes		90
Profit after taxes		$ 120

Industry averages	
Net income/sales	5%
Net income/assets	6%
Accounts receivable/sales	12%
Inventory/sales	30%
Accounts payable/sales	7%

ventory was only 14 percent of sales, well below the industry average. One reason is our reliance on private label sales that are manufactured to order. We do not need to stock finished goods for these customers. We are able to keep finished goods of the Summit line to a minimum by limiting the sizes, colors, and styles that we offer. Admittedly, this has cost us some sales as we are occasionally out of stock on an urgent order. We are also able to maintain smaller purchased inventories by this approach. In the long run, our marketing strategy dictates relative expansion of our own, more profitable line and this will mean additional inventory. For now, we are really able to make our cash go a long way."

a Evaluate the working capital policies of Summit.

b What changes would you recommend and why?

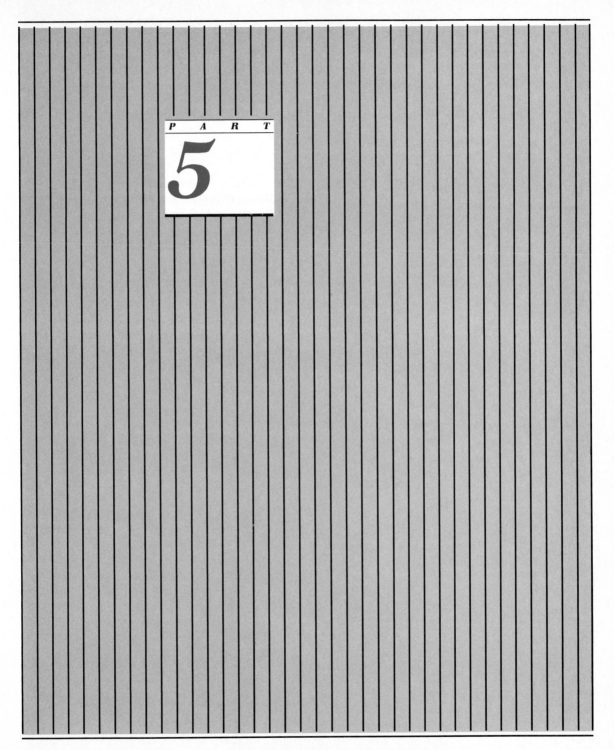

SOURCES OF LONG-TERM CAPITAL

Part 5 discusses the alternative sources of long-term capital available to the firm. Chapter 10 provided general guidelines for selecting the best combination of capital sources. Chapters 18 through 22, which comprise Part 5, explain the procedures used in raising money and provide a detailed description of each type of security that may be issued by corporations.

Chapter 18 explains how capital is raised through direct arrangements with financial institutions such as banks or insurance companies, or by selling securities to the public. Chapter 19 describes various forms of leasing arrangements, indicates why leasing may have advantages over purchasing, and explains how the financial manager decides whether to lease or purchase a particular asset. Chapters 20, 21, and 22 describe the major types of securities a company can issue: common stock, debt, preferred stock, convertibles, and warrants. The rights and privileges of security holders and the associated obligations of the firm are important considerations in choosing which kinds of securities should be issued.

18

RAISING INTERMED- IATE- AND LONG-TERM FUNDS

When a business firm needs money to pay for new assets or to pay off debt obligations that are coming due, the financial manager must choose a source for the money. In Chapter 10 we examined the problem of choosing among debt, preferred stock, common stock, and retained earnings. In Chapter 16 the nature and use of short-term debt sources were presented. We now look at some more technical aspects of the decision and the process by which firms raise money. Our discussion focuses on debt issues with maturities of more than one year and on stock issues.

For example, suppose that as the financial manager of a business you have decided that the firm should borrow $10 million—what happens next? What decisions should be made and whom should you talk to about providing this money? The answers to these questions are the subjects of this chapter.

GENERAL DECISIONS IN RAISING FUNDS

There are two related decisions to be made once the firm has determined the amount of financing needed and the type of financing to be used (debt, common stock, or some other type). The financial manager must choose between public or private financing, and then the maturity of any debt to be issued must be fixed. A **public security issue** is sold to individual and institutional investors. The actual selling is usually handled by an investment banker, who buys the securities from the firm and sells them to investors. If a **private security issue** is chosen, the firm approaches one investor or a small number of investors directly and sells the securities to them. This process is also called private placement. Usually the investors in a private issue are financial institutions such as insurance companies.[1] While a number of factors influence the choice between public and private financing, the major considerations are the size and type of financing needed. Common and preferred stocks are usually sold as public issues, whereas debt is issued publicly and privately. Large issues of long-term debt (over $10 million and over ten years) are more often public issues, whereas smaller and shorter-term debt issues are more often private ones. There will be more on these points later.

Once the financial manager has decided that debt with a maturity greater than one year is appropriate, the particular maturity must still be chosen. Is it to be two years or forty years? The traditional answer to this question is the same "matching principle" discussed in Chapter 17, namely, that the maturity of the debt should match the period of time for which the money will be needed. While this principle makes much sense when applied to the question of short-term versus long-term financing, it is not

---

[1] The terms "issuing securities" or "securities issues" as used in practice generally connote public issues of debt and stock. In the interest of simplicity in our discussion we employ these terms in their broader sense of the agreements between a firm and the people of firms which have supplied money to it. Similarly the term "investor" tends to be associated with a person or firm who either purchases public issues of debt and stock or owns common stock. It normally does not apply to financial institutions making direct loans to a business firm. We use "investor" in its broader sense as one who has invested money in the firm or owns its securities, regardless of the nature of the investor.

nearly so helpful in the decision as to whether the debt should have a maturity of five years or of ten years. Traditionally, maturity of debt is determined by the economic life of assets acquired with the money raised. There is an implicit assumption that the use of any debt is temporary in that once the "need" has passed the debt will be retired. However, as we have seen in Chapter 10, many firms will plan to maintain debt as a normal part of their outstanding securities. This means that as old debt issues mature, they will be repaid with new debt issues, not by selling assets or drawing down cash balances. Determining debt maturity for these firms is largely a decision as to how often the firm wishes to refinance its debt. We will return to this problem at the end of the chapter after some of the factors that influence the decision have been discussed.

A comment on nomenclature is appropriate here. In the financial world, "short-term" generally refers to debt with a maturity of less than one year. This usage is quite common. The words used to describe longer-term financing arrangements are not so well-defined. Many people use "intermediate-term" to refer to maturities of over one year and up to ten years, and reserve "long-term" for maturities over ten years. However, "long-term" may also be used to describe maturities in excess of five years. The five- to ten-year area is therefore somewhat fuzzy. To one person a $7\frac{1}{2}$-year loan may be intermediate-term and to someone else it may be long-term. In this text we will not attempt any special definition, but we will use "long-term" rather loosely to refer to any debt issue with a maturity in excess of one to two years. We will not distinguish "intermediate-term" from "long-term" because for our purposes the distinction is not very meaningful.[2]

Let us turn now to the procedure involved in making a public issue of securities.

PUBLIC SECURITIES ISSUES AND INVESTMENT BANKING

Most companies making a public issue of debt or stock use the services of an investment banker, who does the actual selling of the securities. In some situations, firms do try to sell the securities to the investors themselves. This is called a direct securities issue and, for nonfinancial corporations, is largely confined to common stock. In this section we will examine the functions of investment bankers. Direct issues of common stock are covered in Chapter 20.

Firms use investment bankers to sell securities to investors when it is cheaper and easier than doing it themselves. Investment bankers specialize in selling new securities issues. They are familiar with the desires of investors as to the type and features of securities and are organized to contact potential buyers. They normally earn their money on the difference be-

---

[2] There is a variety of historical reasons for making such distinctions. For example, people would consider intermediate-term debt as temporary, whereas long-term debt would be considered permanent. Moreover, certain types of debt issues tend to have intermediate-term maturities (term loans), whereas others tend to have long-term maturities (bonds). Modern financial managers do not appear to be concerned with whether a given debt issue is intermediate- or long-term, but rather with the particular characteristics of alternative issues. Maturity is only one such characteristic.

tween the price at which they acquire the securities from the firm and the price at which the securities are sold to investors. Let us look at a typical issue and the procedure that is followed.

Most public issues are sold through **negotiated underwriting**. In this process a firm chooses an investment banker, negotiates the price and conditions of the issue, and sells it to the banker. Underwriting is the process whereby the investment banker purchases the issue from the firm at a given price and then sells it as best he can. In an underwritten issue, the investment banker bears the risk that it will not sell well. In contrast, the firm is guaranteed a fixed price. Alternative procedures are also possible.

Some firms, primarily railroads and public utilities, use **competitive bidding**, rather than negotiation, both to pick the investment banker and to determine the price of the issue. In a competitive bidding situation, the firm announces that it wishes to issue securities and invites bids from investment bankers. On large issues several investment bankers join together in a syndicate and submit a single bid for the group. The firm specifies the type of security and any conditions or features that it has. The investment bankers then submit bids on the price (or interest rate) for the issue, and the banker making the best bid is awarded the issue.

Regardless of whether the investment banker is chosen by negotiation or bidding, the banker acts as an underwriter. Another approach is for the firm to ask an investment banker to sell its securities on a **best efforts or agency** basis. In this case the investment banker is not acting as an underwriter but merely sells the securities for a commission. This procedure is used either by very large firms, which are confident that their securities will sell fairly easily, or (much more frequently) by very small firms, when the investment banker feels the risks of an unsuccessful issue are too high. Table 18-1 provides information on the relative amounts of securities issued through investment bankers. Notice that 71 percent of the dollar volume of all issues is underwritten. Also note that, whereas almost all bonds, notes and preferred stock are underwritten, a large portion of common stock is sold on an agency basis (27 percent) or direct (7 percent).

TABLE 18-1

Corporate securities issues by method of issue during 1983 (dollar figures in millions)

	Underwritten		Agency basis		Direct		Total	
	Amount	Percent[a]	Amount	Percent[a]	Amount	Percent[a]	Amount	Percent[a]
Bonds and notes	$16,059	97	$ 152	1	$ 339	2	$16,550	100
Preferred stock	$ 4,768	99	$ 16	*	$ 28	*	$ 4,812	100
Common stock	$19,903	66	$8,286	27	$2,180	7	$30,369	100
Total issues	$40,730	71	$8,454	15	$8,287	14	$57,470	100

[a] Percentages are based on row totals.
* Less than 0.5%.
Source: Monthly Statistical Review, Securities and Exchange Commission.

A typical security issue begins with discussions by the firm's financial manager with one or more investment bankers. At this stage the investment banker can provide helpful advice to the firm, especially regarding investors' reactions to debt policy, the possible features or conditions of a debt issue, and an estimate of the price or interest rate that investors will require. The financial manager will usually ask for a written proposal as to what the security issue might be and, when discussions are carried out with more than one banker, the proposals provide a basis for choosing among them. The investment banker chosen in this process is called the **originating house**. Large firms often establish continuing relationships with an investment banker that may last for many years. For large issues, other investment bankers may be brought in to form the underwriting syndicate. The originating house will normally serve as the manager of the syndicate and underwrite the largest portion of the issue.

The fees paid to the investment banker for undertaking the issue can be divided into two parts—underwriting commissions and sales commissions. As their names imply, the underwriting commission is the portion that represents the payment for risk bearing and the sales commission represents the payment for doing the actual selling of the securities. The manager of a syndicate is compensated for this job out of the underwriting commission, and the remaining part (after expenses are deducted) is paid to the members of the syndicate in proportion to their original share of the underwriting. Sales commissions are based on the actual sales of the syndicate members.

The division of the fees is not too important to the firm issuing the securities; it is the total amount that is most relevant. Table 18-2 provides some data on the costs of issuing securities through a negotiated underwriting. Notice that issue costs as a percentage of the proceeds decline rapidly until the issue size reaches about $10 million. Also note that the underwriting commission for common stock is higher than the commission for debt. The difference is due to the greater price fluctuation of common stock and hence the greater risk borne by the underwriter.

Once agreement has been reached between the investment banker and the issuing firm, an investigation and evaluation of the firm will be made. If new plant and equipment are going to be acquired through the proceeds of the issue, engineering firms may be hired to analyze the technical aspects of the assets. An accounting firm may be called in to audit the firm's accounts.

A major portion of the preissue activity of the investment banker consists of meeting the requirements imposed by the state and federal agencies regulating new issues. Most of these requirements involve the disclosure of information regarding the company's operations and financial condition, the ownership of outstanding securities by officers and directors of the firm, and any legal problems the firm may be having. The regulatory authorities are especially concerned that the relevant facts about the company are fully disclosed and that incorrect information is not given to potential investors. The purpose of this regulation is, therefore, to protect the purchasers of the securities from basing their decisions to buy on erroneous information and to provide sufficient, accurate information so that a thoughtful decision can be made.

The final price or interest rate to the firm is not usually set until after the registration procedure has been completed. If the firm is issuing bonds and already has outstanding bonds that are being traded in the bond market, the interest rate will be set slightly higher than the current rate in the market. Similarly, if the firm is issuing stock and its stock is currently traded in the stock market, the offering price of the stock will be somewhat lower than the market price at the end of registration. In both cases, how much different the terms of the issue will be from the market rate or price will depend on how stable the market has been recently and is a matter of negotiation between management and the investment banker. The problem facing a firm that has never had a public issue of the security in question is more difficult.

If the firm is issuing bonds and there are no publicly traded bonds outstanding, management and the investment banker must decide what the proper interest rate should be. They will rely primarily on comparisons with other firms that do have outstanding bonds. In addition they may ask for the bonds to be rated by one of the firms that provide such services (as was discussed in Chapter 5, page 106). If management and the investment banker know that bonds will be rated A, for example, then they will use the current interest rate on A-rated bonds as a basis for determining the rate on the issue. The rating firms charge a fee for this service that is part of the cost of issuing the bonds. Rating increases the marketability of a bond issue,

TABLE 18-2
Costs of issuing corporate securities[a] (cost expressed as a percentage of issue amount)

Size of issue ($ millions)	Debt, %	Preferred stock, %	Common stock, %
$0–$0.49	12.3	14.5	23.7
$0.5–$0.99	11.0	12.2	20.9
$1–$1.9	10.5	9.8	16.9
$2–$4.9	6.2	5.2	12.4
$5–$9.9	3.1	2.5	8.1
$10–$19.9	1.9	1.8	5.9
$20–$49.9	1.4	1.7	4.6
$50–$99.9	1.2	1.6	3.7
$100 and over	1.0	2.4	3.0

[a] Data are averages for issues during 1971–1972 except for debt issues of less than $2 million and preferred stock issues of less than $5 million, for which averages from 1961–1972 are used. Small public issues of debt and preferred stock are relatively rare.
Sources: *Cost of Flotation of Registered Issues* 1971–1972, Securities and Exchange Commission, Washington, D.C., December 1974, and Investment Bankers Association.

since the existence of a rating reduces the amount of work needed by investors to decide whether they wish to buy the issue. For this reason most public debt issues are rated, regardless of whether the firm has currently outstanding bonds or not.

Pricing a New Issue
of Common Stock

A firm making its first public issue of common stock is said to be **going public**. Prior to going public the firm would have only a few shareholders, who purchased their stock directly from the firm or who were the founders of the firm and their families. Now, either the firm needs more equity capital than can be provided by retained earnings or the original owners wish to sell a part of their interest in the firm to others. Going public almost always substantially increases the number of shareholders in the firm. There is no established market price for such firms, and an estimate must be made by the firm's management and the investment banker as to the market value of all the firm's shares once the stock is issued. Once the total market value has been estimated, the estimated price per share is simply the market value divided by the total number of outstanding shares. For example, suppose that the market value of the firm is estimated to be $1 million and there will be 200,000 shares outstanding after issue. Then the estimated price per share is

$$\text{Price} = \frac{\$1,000,000}{200,000 \text{ shares}} = \$5 \text{ per share}$$

Here we are not concerned about the number of *new* shares to be issued, only the total number that will be outstanding after issue. The problem then is to estimate the market value of the common stock.

The basic principles required to estimate the value of common stock were presented in Chapter 5. There we developed the idea that the value of an asset was the present value of the income produced from it. From the viewpoint of the owners of a firm's common stock, the relevant income is the dividend stream paid by the firm. There are two practical problems that complicate the direct application of this principle to estimate the market value of a firm. First, it is difficult to estimate what investors might forecast the long-run dividend stream to be. Second, as we know from Chapter 7, it is difficult to estimate the required rate of return on common stock if the stock does not already have a market price. Depending on the history and future prospects of the firm, an assessment of its market value may or may not be possible through a straightforward application of the basic principles. Let us first examine a situation where it is a reasonable approach.

The Constant Growth Model   Suppose that the net income and dividends of the firm have risen at a fairly regular rate over the past several years, say 7 percent per year. Neither management nor the investment banker has any reason to believe that the future performance of the firm will differ much from the past. If the two parties believe that investors will evaluate the firm in a similar manner, the constant-dividend growth model used in Chapters 5 and 7 would be appropriate. The value of the stock, S can be estimated using the relationship

$$S = \frac{D}{k - g}$$

where D = expected dividend payment next year to all shareholders

k = rate of return required by investors

g = long-run dividend growth rate

Let us suppose that the firm expects to earn $100,000 and pay $40,000 in dividends next year. Given a growth rate of 7 percent, the only other factor is k. In Chapter 7 we discussed the problem of estimating k. Indeed, we used the above model in a situation where we knew the current price of the firm's shares. Since the value of the shares is what we are trying to estimate here, we need an alternative approach to estimating the required rate of return. This is the same problem we faced in Chapter 9 where we were concerned with estimating a discount rate for a single project. Similar procedures may be used here. Management and the investment banker may have some idea of the required rate of return based on their knowledge of the securities market and the firm. The rates of return on shares of other companies that are similar to this firm and whose stocks are traded in the market may be used to get some idea of the "going rate." The beta of the firm may be estimated and the Capital Asset Pricing Model used to determine the discount rate. Let us suppose that, based on one of these procedures, the required rate of return is estimated to be 11 percent. We now have sufficient informaton to use the formula above to estimate the total market value of the firm's stock.

$$S = \frac{\$40,000}{0.11 - 0.07}$$

$$= \frac{\$40,000}{0.04}$$

$$= \$1,000,000$$

Unfortunately, the constant growth model using historical growth rates is not often applicable. Most firms going public do not have a record of stable growth in income and dividends. Many of them have never paid any dividends and do not plan to do so for some time because of their need for money to finance investments. Also, investors are unlikely to use historical growth rates for the firm blindly in their assessment of its future potential. If the firm has grown much more rapidly than the economy or its industry in the past, investors will probably not expect such high rates of growth to continue indefinitely. In these cases an alternative approach may be used.

Comparative Price-Earnings Ratios   Perhaps the most popular method of pricing stock is the use of comparative price-earnings ratios. The ratio of market price to earnings per share (*P/E*) can be used to compare stock prices of firms. To use *P/ E* as a valuation method, the ratios are computed for several firms similar to our firm that have publicly traded stock. In addition, the *P/E* ratios for other firms that have recently gone public are examined. The financial conditions, growth prospects, managements, and any other relevant information about these other firms are compared with the same attributes of our firm. From this examination a subjective judgment is made as to what might be an appropriate *P/E* for the firm. The most important factor that affects the value used is expected future growth in earnings. The resulting ratio multiplied by current net income provides an estimate of the market value of the stock.

$$S = P/E \times \text{net income} \tag{18-2}$$

Once we have the total market value *S*, it is a simple matter to estimate the price as outlined earlier.

The *P/E* method is simply a systematic way to estimate the value of the firm's stock using as much information as possible. However, a great deal of judgment necessarily enters into the process. This is not bad, but it does mean that management and the investment banker may well reach different estimates even though they have the same basic data. The two parties will then have to discuss the question until they either agree on a proper price or terminate the deal. If too high a price is set, the underwriter will lose money. If too low a price is set, the current owners of the stock will not receive full value on the sale. Ultimately, the market will determine the actual value when the stock is sold and will reveal whose price estimate was the more accurate. However, prior to sale, the issue price is purely the result of a bargaining process.

Advantages of Underwriting

The investment banker provides a variety of services including counseling on the type and terms of the securities to be issued and maintaining a market for common stock after issue. For small companies going public, this latter service can be quite valuable, as it provides the old shareholders with an opportunity to sell some of their stock more easily than before. A public issue of common stock handled by an investment banker also reduces the chances of the original owners losing control of the company to outsiders. The stock will be sold to many investors rather than to only a few, making it less likely that the new shareholders will be able to agree that current management should be replaced. This is an important consideration for firms that are controlled by a few people and yet need substantial new equity to finance investments. Finally, there is the advantage of knowing exactly how much money will be raised and at what cost. The firm receives the money when the underwriter pays for the entire issue. The alternative is to have the sale of the securities occur over a period of time with varying prices (or interest rates) depending on the reaction of investors and changing economic conditions. In an underwritten issue the investment banker bears these risks.

Regulation of Public Issues

Public securities issues must comply with a variety of state and federal regulations. In 1911, the Kansas state legislature passed one of the first laws regulating securities issues. A member of the legislature remarked at that time that the new law would prevent sellers of securities from promising the "blue sky" to unsophisticated investors. As a result, such state regulations are called **blue sky laws**. Generally state requirements impose some minimum standards for disclosure of the business and financial affairs of the issuing firm and regulate the activities of investment bankers and securities broker-dealers. The laws in some states set limits on the percentage of the issue that can be paid in compensation to the investment banker.

The principal federal laws in this area are the Securities and Exchange Acts of 1933 and 1934. The 1934 act established the Securities and Exchange Commission (SEC) as the primary federal regulatory agency responsible for securities issues and trading. The 1933 act was specifically directed toward regulation of new securities issues. The major result of this law was to force firms issuing securities to the public to disclose fully any information relevant to an investor in the new security being offered. Before a security can be issued, the firm must file a registration statement containing this information that must be approved by the SEC before the securities can be issued. The registration process may take two to four months to complete. In addition, copies of a condensed version of the registration statement must be available to prospective investors before they purchase the securities. This package of information is called a **prospectus**.

For purposes of SEC regulation a public issue is one that will be sold to more than approximately twenty-five investors; however, not all public issues need be registered with the SEC. The major exceptions are:

1   Small issues, less than $1.5 million in amount during a single year
2   Issues limited to purchase by citizens of a single state
3   Debt issues with maturities of less than 270 days (commercial paper is in this category)
4   Firms in industries already regulated by another federal agency (for example, railroads, which are regulated by the Interstate Commerce Commission)

From an investor's viewpoint it is important to remember that the SEC *does not* prevent firms from issuing trashy securities. Stock may be greatly overpriced, or debt may have too low an interest rate for the risk involved. The firm may even be doing illegal things such as paying bribes to foreign governmental officials. The firm may be unprofitable and close to bankruptcy. All the SEC requires is that complete and accurate information be disclosed. It is up to the individual investor to sort out the trash.

Shelf Registration: Rule 415

In November 1983, following an 18-month trial period, the SEC gave permanent approval to Rule 415, which authorizes a process for issuing securities called **shelf registration**. Under shelf registration, a company need only register a security offering once in a period of two years. After the registration has been approved by the SEC, the firm can issue securities at any time and in any amounts during the two-year period, so long as the total amount issued does not exceed an amount specified in the registration. For example, a company might register $100 million in bonds. Six months later, the company could issue $50 million, and a year later issue another $40 million without going through another registration. A final issue of $10 million could be made, or not, at the company's discretion. Indeed, none of the $100 million need be issued. Shelf registration provides the company with a great deal of flexibility and convenience. It avoids the need for multiple registrations, and therefore saves on issue costs. In addition, the time required to issue is greatly reduced. With a shelf registration in place, it is possible for a company to raise capital in a few days. A phone call from the financial manager to the firm's investment bankers is sufficient to initiate the process, and the issue might be sold to investors before the day is over. The company will not receive the cash for several days, but it is assured of the financing within a few hours. Shelf registration is only available for the debt securities of large corporations, but it has become the normal procedure for issuers that meet the minimum size limits set by the SEC.

PRIVATE PLACEMENT

The distinguishing differences between public and private issues include the number of buyers of the securities and the extent of contact between the firm issuing the securities and the buyers. In a public issue many investors will purchase the securities, whereas a private issue will involve only a few investors. A firm making a public issue will not normally have any contact with the investors prior to their becoming stockholders or bondholders of the firm. In a private issue, the firm will be discussing the terms of the issue directly with prospective purchasers. Common stock is much less likely to be privately placed than are debt and preferred stock. In recent years, less than 5 percent of common stock financing has been through private placements, whereas about 20 percent of bond and preferred stock financing has been privately placed.

Public versus Private Issues

Private issues have some definite advantages over public issues. For one thing the firm is spared the time, trouble, and expense of having to register the issue with the SEC and to comply with its requirements. Moreover, since the main requirements of public issues involve disclosure of information about the company, many firms dislike the idea of having to "tell it all" to their employees, their competitors, and the general public. Privately placed debt issues provide advantages if the firm gets into difficulties later on. The firm can discuss the problem directly with the lender and make modifications in the debt agreement. For example, a scheduled loan payment might be delayed or refinancing arranged with the same lender (usually at a higher interest rate). This is much more difficult to do when there are many holders of a public debt issue.

However, private issues have some disadvantages. First, the investor-lender may monitor the operations of the firm much more carefully than the purchaser of a public issue. In the case of common stock financing, the investor or investor group is more likely to try to gain control of the firm. Second, the interest rate paid on debt issues is likely to be higher and the price of common stock issues lower if they are private placements. Therefore, the advantage of lower issue costs for private issues may be partially or completely offset by the higher rate of return required by a private investor.

This is especially true for large issues because issue costs tend to be relatively smaller for them (see Table 18-2). Shelf registration has also reduced the cost of public issues for large corporations. Third, it is more difficult to finance large amounts privately than it is to make a public issue. The result is that larger securities issues tend to be public issues, whereas smaller issues tend to be private.

The feature that distinguishes different private placements is not *what* securities are issued, but *who* provides the money. Therefore we will look at some of the major private sources of intermediate- and long-term financing.

Commercial Banks

Business firms acquire money from commercial banks through two long-term debt arrangements—mortgages and term loans. A mortgage is a loan secured by real estate—land and buildings—that is repaid in periodic installments.[3] Mortgage loans to business firms are similar to mortgage loans to individuals except that the maturity of the loan is usually less for business mortgages. Mortgage loans to people buying a house to live in (**residential mortgages**) usually are repaid over a period of twenty to thirty years. Business mortgages (usually called **commercial mortgages**) infrequently extend past twenty years and may be repaid over only five years. Residential mortgages almost always require equal monthly payments, whereas commercial mortgages are often repaid quarterly.

Term loans may or may not be secured by assets of the firm. Payment schedules are highly variable but do not extend beyond ten years. A typical term loan would be paid off in quarterly installments over a period of three to five years. Term loans differ from mortgage loans in that the principal payments are usually the same amount each quarter (or month), whereas the interest payments are based on the outstanding balance of the loan. A mortgage normally involves the same amount of cash payment each period. For example, suppose that a firm could borrow $100,000 for ten years using either a mortgage or a term loan with quarterly payments required. The interest rate on both loans is 8 percent per year, or 2 percent per quarter. The mortgage loan would require a payment each quarter, for forty quarters, of $3656 calculated as

$$A = \$100,000 \ (A/P, 2\%, 40)$$
$$= \$3656$$

The term loan would require a principal payment of $100,000/40 = $2500 per quarter plus interest on the outstanding balance. In the first quarter the interest would be $100,000 × 0.02 = $2000, and so the total payment would be $2000 + $2500 = $4500 in the first quarter. However, in the last quarter the loan is outstanding, the interest payment would be $2500 × 0.02 = $50 for a total payment of $2550. Therefore, a term loan of the same maturity as a mortgage would involve higher initial cash payments than the mortgage and lower payments later on.

There are some other features of term loans that are important. They

---

[3] The term "mortgage" has a particular legal definition. Our use includes other types of loans secured by real estate (e.g., deeds of trust) as well.

will often carry **restrictive provisions** or constraints on the firm. For example, the loan agreement may require that the firm not pay any dividends in excess of earnings for the year or that the firm maintain working capital equal to a fixed percentage of long-term debt. Most term loans made by banks are **variable rate** loans. That is, the interest rate may vary over the life of the loan. The rate is usually expressed as a fixed percentage over the bank's current prime rate.[4] For example, the agreement might read that the rate will be "1 percent over prime." If the current prime rate were 9 percent, the current interest rate on the loan would be 10 percent. It is standard practice to vary the interest rate on the loan whenever the prime rate changes. Thus, if the prime rate on February 15 changes from 9 percent to 8 percent, the interest rate on all loans made under this type of arrangement would be adjusted downward. If the prime rate changed again on February 22, the new rate would immediately apply. Under this system, the bank charges the firm periodically (monthly or quarterly) the amount of interest owed for the prior period.

The uncertainty in the interest payments on variable rate loans has concerned financial managers of business firms. They now often attempt to negotiate a ceiling on the average interest rate over the period of the loan. Such a ceiling is called a **cap**. A loan agreement might specify a cap of, say, 15 percent. This means that if interest rates rise and stay over 15 percent for a long time, future interest payments made by the firm will be reduced so that the 15 percent cap is not exceeded on average. This does not mean that the rate in any given period cannot exceed 15 percent, only that the average interest rate paid on the loan must not be greater than 15 percent per year.

Revolving credits, as we mentioned in Chapter 16, are a type of term loan. With a revolving credit, the bank has made a formal commitment to the borrower to continue lending up to the maximum amount stated in the revolving credit agreement until the end of the agreement. Three years is a typical period for such an agreement to run. Revolving credits have a variable interest rate (changing when the prime rate changes) that is computed on the daily balance of the amount loaned. As noted in our discussion of bank credit lines in Chapter 16, compensating deposit balance requirements or fees are common. So long as the borrower abides by the terms of the loan (restrictive provisions, etc.), the bank is legally obligated to continue lending. Often, at the end of the revolving credit agreement, there is a provision that the loan may be converted into an ordinary term loan with a regular repayment schedule. Revolving credits are heavily used by large corporations because of the flexibility they provide to the borrower.

Insurance Companies

Life insurance companies are another important source of long-term debt financing for business firms. Term loans, mortgages, and bonds with maturities of over ten years are the types of financing available. Besides the longer maturity, insurance company term loans differ from bank term loans in that

---

[4] Base rates other than the prime rate are becoming common in loans to large corporations. The rates used include the rate on short-term certificates of deposit and LIBOR (London interbank offering rate), which is an interest rate in the London market for money loaned between banks.

a penalty is often assessed for payments made ahead of schedule. In addition, these loans usually carry a provision prohibiting the firm from prepaying by refinancing the loan in order to gain a lower interest rate. The loans may be made at a fixed rate of interest and the insurance company does not want the firm to be able to repay the loan early by issuing new debt at a lower rate, because the insurance company would then only be able to invest the money at the lower rates. Since banks generally prefer shorter maturities than insurance companies, it is quite common for a bank and an insurance company to participate in the same loan. In a fifteen-year term loan, the principal payments made in the first seven years might go to the bank whereas the payments made in the last eight years would go to the insurance company. Of course, the interest would be paid on the balance owed to each party and the interest rate may differ on the two portions, with the rate paid to the bank often being lower than the rate paid to the insurance company.

High interest rates and inflation in the period 1979 to 1982 encouraged the insurance companies to shorten the maturities, to require variable interest rates, and to add **equity kickers**. Equity kickers are such features as convertibility to common stock, warrants, or the right to share in the income in real estate being financed. We discuss convertible bonds and warrants in Chapter 21.

One of the most interesting term loans ever made was a $250 million term loan by Prudential Insurance Company to Chrysler Corporation in 1954. The maturity of the loan was 100 years, with the entire balance due in 2054. Chrysler "took down" the loan in four annual installments of $62.5 million each so that the full amount was not borrowed until 1958. There was a provision in the loan agreement that after 1964 either party could convert the loan into a twenty-year term loan to be repaid annually. The interest rate on the original loan was $3\frac{3}{4}$ percent; however, the rate would drop to $3\frac{1}{2}$ percent if the twenty-year option were taken. Needless to say, with much higher interest rates prevailing in 1964, the insurance company took the option as soon as it could and Chrysler had to begin paying off the loan. The loan was completely paid in 1984, thirty years after the initial borrowing.

Government Financing

The federal government provides financing to business firms in several ways, although much of it is short-term. Some government financing does extend longer than one year. Advance payments on defense contracts are frequently made. For items with long lead times in development and production, these payments amount to intermediate-term financing.

The Small Business Administration (SBA) has the authority to make loans to small business in general and has special provisions for low-income and other economically disadvantaged persons. The SBA also may guarantee up to 90 percent of a loan made by a private lender (for example, a bank) to a qualified borrower. Loans made or guaranteed by the SBA are ordinarily repaid in monthly installments. Generally, the SBA prefers to guarantee a loan rather than to lend the money directly. Also, neither direct loans nor guarantees will be made unless the firm is unable to get loans on reasonable terms from private sources. Interest rates on SBA or SBA-guaranteed loans are usually below the rates on normal loans made by financial institutions.

Another source of financing, which has been a topic of considerable debate, is provided by local governments—**industrial revenue bonds.** Industrial revenue bonds are issued by a city or county to build a plant that is then leased to a business firm. The interest on bond issues of $5 million or less is exempt from federal income tax, and the bonds therefore have a relatively low interest rate. The lease payments made by the firm are used to pay off the bonds. The bonds themselves are issued through investment bankers who acquire the issue through competitive bidding. The business firm negotiates with the local officials on the lease payments and conditions for the use of the plant. The purpose of this type of financing is to attract business firms to an area by providing them with low-cost facilities. From the viewpoint of the financial manager this is a cheap way to finance a plant. The U.S. Treasury, however, feels that this method of financing encourages the issuance of too many securities with tax exempt interest. That is why large issues are not tax exempt, but Congress has been unwilling to eliminate the tax exemptions entirely.

Small Business Investment Companies   Small business investment companies (SBICs) are private firms licensed under the Small Business Investment Act of 1958 and organized to provide long-term debt and equity financing to small business. The SBA will provide long-term debt at low interest rates to an SBIC in amounts that depend on the equity capital of the SBIC.

The SBIC may use its capital only to finance small businesses. The SBA has criteria (which it changes from time to time) for defining "small business." An SBIC may either lend the funds or purchase common stock of the small business. Stock accounts for slightly over half of the financing provided by SBICs. Frequently, the SBIC will purchase convertible debentures (unsecured bonds that can be converted into common stock). The SBIC may not extend financing to a single business in a total amount that exceeds 20 percent of the SBIC's equity capital.

SBICs receive very generous federal tax treatment. Any dividends received from its investments are exempt from the corporate income tax. A loss on its investments is treated by the firm as an ordinary loss (deductible from operating income) rather than as a capital loss. Furthermore, in determining their personal income taxes, the owners of the SBIC may deduct a loss on their investment in the SBIC as a deduction from ordinary income rather than as a capital loss.

In spite of the considerable government incentives to SBICs, they have had only varying success. The history of the SBICs suggest that finding good small business opportunities has generally been quite difficult and costly. Many of the investments made have been to firms which are close to the upper limit of the size requirements for a "small business." The result is that SBICs provide only a minor portion of the financing needs of small businesses.

In addition to those above, there are many corporations, partnerships, and individuals who provide financing for business firms. One type of financial institution, leasing companies, is discussed in the next chapter. Business finance companies provide one- to ten-year loans on purchases of equipment. The manufacturers of large, expensive equipment often offer long-term financing to purchasers. There are many venture capital firms and individuals who are willing to provide equity money to promising companies. The more organized groups (including many SBICs) often provide management consulting to a business in which they have invested money.

Many people argue that small businesses have more difficulty in obtaining long-term financing than large businesses. It is certainly true that smaller firms must often pay a high price for the money they raise, for a variety of reasons. However, there is usually no shortage of money for those willing and able to pay the price.

SUMMARY

A firm can raise money by public offerings of its securities and by private placement. A public securities issue is sold to many investors at terms announced in advance, and large issues must be registered with the Securities and Exchange Commission. Private placement involves direct negotiations between the issuing firm and a few investors and need not be registered with the SEC.

Investment bankers sell the new securities issues of companies to the public. Investment bankers provide several services including advice on the terms of an issue, underwriting, and selling the securities to investors. The underwriting service transfers the risk that the securities will not be purchased at their offering price from the firm to the investment banker. The banker buys the securities from the firm at one price and sells them to the public at a higher price. The difference between the two prices is the compensation to the investment bankers.

In the negotiations between the firm and the investment banker, setting an appropriate price for the securities is a critical problem. For debt issues, a rating is usually obtained from the rating agencies and the interest rate is based on the rates available in the market for debt with the same rating. Pricing a new issue of common stock is especially difficult. Several approaches are used, but the most popular involves estimating an appropriate price-earnings ratio for the stock.

An alternative to a public issue of securities is private placement. In this procedure, the firm may directly negotiate with a few investors or lenders or it may employ the services of an investment banker to act as the firm's representative in the negotiations. The major advantages of private issues of securities are the lower issue costs and the elimination of delays due to registration requirements on public issues. The terms of private debt issues are also more easily modified later on. In recent years there has been an increase in the private placement of common stock although debt issues still are the more likely candidates for this approach.

*Commercial banks and life insurance companies are the major finan-
cial institutions offering long-term funds directly to businesses.
Commercial banks offer term loans and mortgages, and life insurance
companies offer term loans and bonds. Other sources include federal
agencies, local governments, finance companies, SBICs, and wealthy
individuals.*

QUESTIONS

1 How does a public securities issue differ from a private securities
   issue?
2 What factors will be considered by the financial manager in choosing
   between a public issue of common stock and a private issue of common stock?
3 Would the following firms be more likely to use private placement or
   a public issue? Why? All the firms wish to issue long-term debt.
   a A local appliance dealer.
   b A medium-sized ($20 million annual sales) electronics manufac-
      turer.
   c An electric utility company serving customers in three states.
   d A large electronics manufacturer whose research staff has made
      a major technological breakthrough. Financing is needed to ex-
      ploit this new technology as rapidly as possible.
4 What are the distinctive characteristics of an underwritten securities
   issue as compared with other methods of raising money?
5 Why would a corporation use negotiated underwriting rather than
   obtain competitive bids?
6 How is an investment banker compensated for services provided to
   the corporation?
7 What services are performed by an investment banker in a negotiated underwriting?
8 "Large, well-known corporations have no real need for the services of
   an investment banker. There is little done by the investment banker
   that cannot be done by the financial staff of the corporation." Evaluate this statement.
9 How does a revolving credit arrangement differ from a line of credit?
10 In recent years many large corporations have made public issues of
   five-year maturity notes. These notes pay fixed interest to the purchaser, and the principal value is paid in full at maturity. Speculate
   on why corporations might choose to issue such notes rather than
   to obtain term loans of the same maturity.
11 In what ways do governments aid businesses in obtaining financing?
12 Suppose you are managing an SBIC. What kinds of businesses would
   you be interested in financing through common stock purchases?

PROJECT

Obtain the prospectus for a recent security issue (may be provided by instructor). Review the prospectus in general. What types of information
does it contain? Determine the following:

1 The issuing firm and the investment banking firm.
2 The type of security and the terms (price or interest rate of the issue).
3 What type of issue it is (negotiated, etc.).
4 How much the issue is costing the firm.
5 How much the investment banking firm is getting paid.

PROBLEMS

1 Using the data in Table 18-2, estimate the dollar costs that would be incurred by a firm for issuing the following securities:
   $2 million in debt.
   $12 million in debt.
   $2 million in preferred stock.
   $2 million in common stock.
   $12 million in common stock.

2 If the total market value of common stock is estimated to be $5 million, at what price should the stock sell if 200,000 shares will be outstanding after going public? What would the price be if 500,000 shares were to be outstanding? [Ans.: $25; $10]

3 The Enterprise Company plans to raise $2 million through its first public stock issue. The total market value of stock after issue is estimated to be $8 million. There are presently 100,000 shares outstanding held by the Kirk family.
   a How many new shares must be issued to raise $2 million? [Ans.: 33,333 shares]
   b What is the estimated price per share of the stock after the issue is sold?
   c The firm's investment bankers believe that a desirable initial price per share for a firm such as Enterprise is $20. They recommend that, prior to issuing the new stock, the old stock should be "split" with the current shareholders to receive additional shares of stock in proportion to their current holdings. If Jim Kirk owns 50 shares, how many new shares would Jim receive if the investment banker's recommendation were followed?

4 Krypton, Inc., is planning a public issue of stock. Price-earnings ratios for similar firms in the same industry average twelve times earnings. The firm's earnings are $3 million and 2 million shares will be outstanding after issuing the stock. What is a likely issue price per share?

5 The financial manager of a firm planning to go public estimates that investors will require an expected rate of return on the stock between 12 percent and 14 percent. Earnings and dividends are each expected to grow at an average rate somewhere between 6 percent and 8 percent per year over the long run. Management plans to pay $240,000 in dividends next year. What is the range of possible current market values for the common stock of this firm?

6 As financial manager of Robot Manufacturing, you have estimated that you will need to raise $20 million in long-term debt over the

next two years. You have decided to evaluate the three alternatives shown below on the bases of net cost to the firm (ignoring timing of the costs over the two years) and risk. What are the costs and risks of the alternatives? Assume that $10 million is needed this year (now), and $10 million is needed next year (twelve months from now). Which of the following three options would you recommend?

1 Issue $20 million in long-term debt this year at an interest rate of 10 percent. Issue costs will be $400,000. The excess funds will be invested in a one-year Treasury bill yielding 8 percent.

2 Issue $10 million in long-term debt this year and $10 million next year. Issue costs are expected to be $300,000 for each issue. The interest rate on the debt issued this year will be 10 percent. You expect interest rates to be stable over the next eighteen months, and therefore you expect to be able to issue debt next year at 10 percent.

3 Borrow $10 million in short-term debt this year at an interest rate of 9 percent, issue $20 million in long-term debt next year, and use $10 million of the proceeds to repay the short-term debt. There are no issue costs on the short-term debt; the cost of issuing the long-term debt is expected to be $400,000. The interest rate on the debt issue next year is expected to be 10 percent.

7 Laidback Log Cabins Co. is planning its first public issue of common stock. The demand for the precut log cabins produced by Laidback has been increasing at a rate of 18 percent per year for the past five years and the firm's earnings and dividends have had comparable growth. The firm will pay a $1.20 per share dividend next year from earnings of $3.00 per share, based on the total number of shares to be outstanding after the issue. B. C. Riddle and Company, an investment banking firm, has proposed to Laidback management that stock be issued at a price of $24 per share.

a What is the price-earnings ratio that Riddle is applying to the firm?

b What required rate of return is implied by the price of $24 if investors' expectations of the future are consistent with the history of the firm? [Ans.: 23 percent]

c As financial manager, you believe that investors may be somewhat more pessimistic than past history would indicate. You consider a 10 percent growth rate per year to be a conservative estimate of the long-term growth potential of the firm. Furthermore you have carefully estimated the rates of return required by investors in stocks issued by other housing companies. These seem to range between 14 percent and 16 percent. What range of issue prices for the common stock would you feel is appropriate for Laidback given this set of estimates?

d Price-earnings ratios of other housing companies range from 7 to 12. What range of stock prices for Laidback is implied by these P/E ratios?

e Given your analysis in a through d, how would you respond to Riddle's proposal?

VENTURE CAPITAL

Invest $50,000 and get back $5 million three years later? Sounds great—where do you sign up? Invest $50,000 and get back not one thin dime? Find some other pigeon. Both these results, however, are possibilities in the great financial game of venture capital investment. Venture capital is money invested in a new business by people who usually have no interest in managing the firm, although some will provide advice. The venture capitalist normally receives common stock in return for the money invested. The hope and expectation of the venture capitalist is that the business will turn out to be very profitable. If this occurs, the stock will be worth much more than its initial cost. Unfortunately, many new businesses never become profitable. Indeed, a large percentage fail after a few years and the stockholders receive little or nothing.

WHO ARE THE VENTURE CAPITALISTS?

Venture capital comes from a surprisingly wide variety of sources. The traditional suppliers of this type of financing for new businesses are wealthy individuals. These people typically form partnerships or corporations with $5 million to $30 million in capital that will be invested in several new businesses. One always hopes that the winners will more than compensate for the losers and that the investors will end up obtaining significantly higher average rates of return than would be obtained from more conventional investments. Also, the returns from venture capital investments are capital gains and therefore are subject to a lower tax rate than dividends and interest. If you are in a high tax bracket, you are not very interested in dividends or interest. Lately, however, other people have been getting into the act.

Investment bankers establish venture capital sections to nurture small, growing firms. When these firms grow large enough to go to the market with public issues of stocks and bonds, the investment bankers who helped them grow expect to handle the issues. Of course, earning high returns on their investment is not irrelevant to these investment banking firms.

Many commercial banks, such as Bank of America, First National of Boston, and First National of Chicago, have established small business investment companies (SBICs) to provide venture capital. Again there are two reasons for the bank's interest. One is profit, and the other is to be better able to attract and serve business customers of the bank. Some small acorns grow into mighty oaks, and the bank that aided the process can expect to retain the banking business of the firm as it grows.

Another group of venture capitalists consists of large corporations such as General Electric, Exxon, Texaco, and Xerox. The corporations are attracted in part because of the prospects of higher returns on their venture capital investments than on conventional investments in their business. However, the corporations also hope to gain access at an early stage to new ideas and technology that will benefit other aspects of their operations. *Venture Capital Journal* estimated that 90 percent of the $11.5 billion in venture capital available in 1984 came from partnerships and corporate subsidiaries.

Venture capitalists, therefore, come in all shapes and sizes. They may be SBICs owned by a bank, by an insurance company, by a few individuals, or by publicly held companies with their own traded common stock. They may be investors in a limited partnership organized around a talented person who acts as the general partner. There are a few foreign venture capital funds investing in the United States as well as some domestic "business development companies," which are a type of mutual fund authorized by Congress in

1980. Even some cities and states, such as Buffalo, Alaska, California, and Massachusetts, have established taxpayer-financed venture capital firms to aid small businesses. About the only thing they have in common is their interest in finding new firms that need money and that have good prospects.

WHAT KIND OF VENTURES ATTRACT CAPITAL?

The classic recipient of venture capital is a person with limited financial resources, with an idea for a new product involving high technology, and with business sense (or teamed with someone who has business sense). For example, Steven Jobs and Stephen Wozniak, both in their twenties, built their first computer in Jobs' parents' garage in 1976. The demand for their machine was too great for them to produce it by themselves, so they enlisted two older men with marketing and manufacturing experience. One of them took a 50 percent pay cut to join the fledgling company and the other invested $91,000 of his own money. The four entrepreneurs raised $600,000 from venture capitalists to start the Apple Computer Company. When Apple went public in 1980, Steven Jobs (age 25) owned stock valued at $165 million. The other people didn't do so badly either. Venture capitalist Arthur Beck, who invested $57,600 in Apple, ended up with stock worth $14 million three years later. However, almost any type of business can attract venture capital provided there are reasonable prospects of future profits. *Patient Care*, a magazine for doctors, was launched with the support of American Research and Development Corporation, one of the largest and most successful venture capital firms. The company that introduced Minute Maid frozen orange juice was helped by J. H. Whitney and Company, a highly successful partnership. Home Health Care of America was able to launch a home intravenous feeding service with backing from Kleiner, Perkins, Caufield, and Byers, a very successful San Francisco partnership. Federal Express, an airline that delivers small packages overnight, was aided by New Court Securities Corporation.

There are definite advantages to being located in an area where there is a large number of venture capital firms. The Boston and San Francisco metropolitan areas are hot spots of venture capital activity. There are both a large number of venture capital firms and a large number of businesses started with the aid of venture capitalists in these two areas. New York, Massachusetts, California, Illinois (Chicago area), and Texas are the top states in number of venture capital firms. Location is important to the business seeking venture capital because the venture capital firms like to keep fairly close watch over the businesses they invest in, and they also provide management advice and guidance to the businesses.

Surprisingly, it is possible to be *too small* to interest most venture capitalists. Most venture capital is invested in amounts over $1 million. One of the largest venture capital deals involved Amdahl Corporation. This computer company was established in 1970 with $46 million in venture capital riding on the strength of Gene Amdahl's reputation as the architect of the IBM 360 computers.

Perhaps the most critical feature of a business seeking venture capital is the people involved. Whenever the heads of successful venture capital firms are asked what they look for in a potential investment, they respond "creative," or "talented," or "high-quality" management. People rank first and products second.

Virtually any asset that can be purchased can also be leased. A **lease** is a contract between the owner of an asset, called the **lessor**, and another party, called the **lessee**, who makes periodic payments to the owner for the *right* to use the asset. From the introduction of leasing by Phoenician shipowners 3000 years ago until the mid-1960s, only a few types of assets could be leased and the volume of lease transactions was not very large compared with the volume of purchases. However, in recent years the volume of leasing and the range of assets available for lease has grown dramatically. In addition to the well-established leasing operations in computers, office equipment, transportation equipment (railroad cars, autos, aircraft, ships), and machinery, leasing arrangements now extend to such areas as shipping containers, nuclear fuel cores, medical equipment, and pollution control devices. Approximately one-fifth of all new equipment in the United States is leased. A striking example of the importance of leasing is Anaconda Aluminum's $138,000,000 reduction mill near Sebree, Kentucky, which is entirely leased. That single plant represents approximately 3 percent of the entire United States aluminum production capacity. Even the United States Navy began leasing ships in 1971 when Congress failed to appropriate funds for the purchase of needed fuel tankers. Leasing, indeed, has come of age.

WHO PROVIDES LEASES?

As we noted, at least two parties are involved in a lease—the lessor (owner) and the lessee (user). In a **leveraged lease**, there is also a lender (for example, an insurance company), from whom the lessor borrows the funds to purchase the assets. Sometimes, a **lease packager** or an investment bank will arrange the lease agreement for a fee without participating directly as a lessor, lessee, or lender. In terms of dollar volume, the most important lessors of equipment are the manufacturers themselves; they represent roughly half the equipment leasing done in the United States. Banks account for approximately one-third of the equipment leasing, with most of the rest done by independent leasing companies.

TYPES OF LEASES

Operating Lease

An **operating lease** is a short-term lease (lease term is only a small fraction of the useful life of the asset). A long-term lease which allows the lessee (and sometimes the lessor) to cancel the lease at any time is also referred to as an operating lease. The lessor may provide services under the lease agreement such as maintenance, insurance, and the payment of property taxes. Vehicles, computers, copiers, amusement equipment, display fixtures, and furniture are among the assets commonly acquired on an operating lease basis. The term "operating lease" also refers to a lease which is not classified under accounting rules as a capital lease (see the discussion later in this chapter on accounting for leases).

Financial Lease

A **financial lease** (or **finance lease**) involves an intermediate or long-term commitment by the lessor and lessee. If the asset is equipment, the lease duration will generally equal at least half of the expected useful life of the assets. Maintenance or other services are not generally provided by the lessor under a financial lease although this is subject to negotiation.

Assets often covered by financial leases include real estate, office equipment, medical equipment, railroad cars, airplanes, and construction equipment. If the asset is real estate, the lessor may be an individual or a business firm, frequently an insurance company. An equipment lessor is commonly a manufacturer, a finance or leasing company, or a commercial bank. A common procedure for leasing equipment is for the lessee to determine the equipment it wants to lease and to settle on a purchase price with the manufacturer. The firm then finds a leasing company or bank, which will purchase the asset and lease it to the firm for a rental which provides an adequate return on the lessor's investment.

A financial lease will often provide a means for the lessee to continue possession of the property after the expiration of the initial lease. This may be allowed for under a renewal option that permits the lessee to obtain a new lease at a specified rental after the initial lease expires. The lease may also contain a purchase option that gives the lessee the right to buy the asset for a particular price at the lease's expiration.

The lease payment is a fixed obligation of the lessee and, as with debt interest, failure to make the rental payment can result in insolvency and bankruptcy court action. Although the lessor's claim against the lessee in the event of bankruptcy is usually somewhat less stringent than that of most creditors, it does provide for repossession of the leased asset and at least partial payment to the lessor of lease rentals applicable to the remaining term of the lease. Perhaps more relevant is that, for the going concern, leases involve a fixed charge like debt payments, and therefore fluctuations in firm income are absorbed by the lessee. In other words, a financial lease, like debt, involves the benefits and dangers of leverage.

Sale and Leaseback

A firm may sell an asset it already owns to another party and then lease it back from the buyer. In this way the firm can obtain cash (proceeds from the sale) and still have use of the asset. This arrangement is called a **sale and leaseback**. Financial leases (rather than operating leases) are virtually always used in sale and leasebacks. The lease will ordinarily provide for an option either to renew the lease or to purchase the asset at the end of the lease term.

As with an ordinary financial lease, the buyer and lessor under a sale and leaseback agreement will frequently be an insurance company if the asset is real estate, or a leasing firm, finance company, or commercial bank if the asset is equipment. The lease provisions are the same as those described for financial leases in general.

Full-Service Lease

Under a full-service lease the lessor maintains and insures the assets and pays property taxes on the asset. This is similar to a **maintenance lease**, which obligates the lessor to provide maintenance services. A full-service lease is the opposite of a **net lease**, under which the rent payment is "net," i.e., the lessee pays maintenance costs, insurance, and property taxes.

Leveraged Lease

A **leveraged lease,** *or* **third-party lease,** involves a third party—a lender—in addition to the lessor and lessee. The lessor borrows part of the asset's purchase price from the lender, and the lease rentals are used to service the loan, any excess going to the lessor. Both the depreciation (for tax purposes) and the investment tax credit on the asset are allocated to the lessor. The loan is on a nonrecourse basis, i.e., the lender has a claim against the asset and the lease rentals if there is default on the loan but the lender may not demand additional payments from the lessor. Therefore, even in the unlikely event that the asset becomes worthless and the lessee becomes bankrupt, the most that the lessor could lose would be the down payment that it made in purchasing the asset. Of course, the loan will carry an interest rate which adequately compensates the lender for the risks involved.

Large lease transactions (e.g., the lease of a plane or ship) may involve the creation of a **trust** that acquires the asset to be leased. The trust obtains the funds to purchase the asset by selling an equity (ownership) interest in the trust to the lessor and selling **mortgage bonds** to other investors. These bonds are usually guaranteed by the lessee (that is, the lessee pays them off if the trust defaults on the bonds).[1] The periodic lease payments go to the trust, which uses them to pay off the bonds. Whatever is left over after making the bond payments is income to the ownership (lessor) interest in the trust.[2] This arrangement allows the lessor company to borrow some of the funds through the trust (by issuing the mortgage bonds) to cover the asset's cost, while at the same time limiting the lessor's liability on the bonds (since the lessee guarantees the bonds).

Table 19-1 summarizes the characteristics of the major types of leases.

[1] This means that if the trust defaults on the bonds, the bondholders can take possession of the trust's assets (including the leased assets); and if the assets are not worth enough to repay what is owed on the bonds, the lessee must pay what is still owed. The lessor is not liable for the bonds.

[2] Income from the trust and the investment tax credit on the asset are allocated to the lessor in computing corporate income taxes. The taxable trust income (or loss) is the rental payments less interest deduction on the mortgage bonds less depreciation on the asset.

TABLE 19-1
Types of leases

Type of lease	Parties involved	Duration	Does lessor maintain asset?
Operating lease	Lessor and lessee	Short-term	Often yes
Financial lease	Lessor and lessee	Long-term	Generally no
Sale and leaseback	Lessor (buyer) and lessee (seller)	Long-term	Generally no
Full-service	Lessor and lessee	Generally short-term	Yes
Leveraged lease	Lessor, lender, and lessee	Long-term	Generally no

**DEFINING A LEASE
FOR TAX AND
ACCOUNTING
PURPOSES**

*True Leases
and the IRS*

With a **true lease** the lessor retains the tax benefits of ownership and the lessee deducts the lease rentals for tax purposes. The lessor claims the depreciation, owns the leased equipment at the end of the lease, and receives the investment tax credit (unless, by agreement between the lessor and lessee, the tax credit is passed on to the lessee). Even if two parties regard an agreement as a lease, the agreement is a true lease (that is, a lease for tax purposes) only if it conforms to certain guidelines set forth in the law. If the agreement does not conform to the guidelines, the transaction will be treated for tax purposes as a *sale* of the asset to the user; this is so regardless of the intent or desires of the "lessor" and "lessee."

Three major guidelines appear in the tax law for determining whether an arrangement between a user and provider of an asset is a lease. The first and oldest guideline is Revenue Ruling 55-540, which essentially states that a transaction is a lease only if the lease rental payments do not effectively provide the "lessee" with an ownership interest in the asset.[3]

In 1975, the Internal Revenue Service issued Revenue Procedure 75-21, which covers leveraged leases and, in practice, also covers direct leases; this guideline expanded upon Revenue Ruling 55-540. Revenue Procedure 75-21 stipulates that for a transaction to be deemed a lease for tax purposes:[4]

1 The lessor must maintain at least a 20 percent "at risk" investment in the asset throughout the lease term.[5]
2 The residual value of the asset must equal 20 percent of the original cost of the asset without taking into account general inflation or deflation (i.e., netting out any value changes due to inflation or deflation); and the remaining useful life of the asset at the end of the lease term must be the larger of one year or 20 percent of the original estimated useful life of the asset.
3 The lessee may not have the right to buy the asset from the lessor for a price less than fair market value, and the lessor may not have the right to require any party (including the lessee) to buy the asset.
4 The lessee may not finance the asset's cost (e.g., by lending money to the lessor) and may not guarantee any indebtedness incurred by the lessor in connection with the asset.
5 The lessor must show that it expects to profit from the transaction apart from the tax benefits provided by the asset under the lease arrangement.

---

[3] Evidence that ownership is being acquired would be, for example, if the lease rental were far above fair rental value or if the lessee had the option to purchase the asset for a price which is materially less than fair market value at the time the purchase option could be exercised.

[4] Only the major provisions of Revenue Procedure 75-21 are stated below.

[5] **At risk investment** is the sum of cash invested in the asset by the lessor plus any recourse debt incurred by the lessor in acquiring the asset. With **recourse debt** the creditor may legally demand payment of the debt, as well as take claim to the asset, if the lessor defaults on the debt. With **nonrecourse debt**, the loan is at most collateralized by the asset and the creditor may not turn to the borrower for payment if the borrower defaults on the loan. The 20 percent investment in the asset is computed by dividing the cash investment plus recourse debt by the depreciated tax basis of the asset; the depreciated tax basis of the asset at any point in time equals the original cost of the asset minus accumulated depreciation for tax purposes.

The major thrust of the above criteria is that the lessor must retain some of the nontax benefits of owning the asset (e.g., a material salvage value) and must assume some of the risks and responsibilities of ownership (e.g., of obtaining financing).[6]

The Economic Recovery Tax Act of 1981 (ERTA) temporarily changed the rules of the leasing game (the law was later changed again) for *corporate* lessors; the lease guidelines under ERTA have generally been referred to as the "safe-harbor" leasing provisions.[7] Under ERTA, a corporate lessor and a lessee could elect to treat a transaction as a lease for tax purposes as long as the lessor maintained at least a 10 percent " at risk" investment in the leased asset throughout the lease term and the lease had a duration satisfying a certain specified constraint.[8] ERTA made it much easier to deem a transaction a true lease since it imposed no constraints on the financing of the asset (except for the 10 percent at risk lessor investment), on the level of the lease rentals, on the existence of a bargain purchase option (e.g., an option allowing the lessee to buy the asset for $1 at the end of the lease term would be acceptable), or on the profitability of the asset for the lessor. Companies with tax losses (who therefore could not take the investment tax credit or depreciation deductions) could easily arrange leases with profitable companies which could use the tax shelters to reduce their corporate income taxes. Under such leases the tax benefits enjoyed by the lessor would in part be passed on to the lessee in the form of low lease rentals.

After passage of ERTA, many firms chose to lease rather than to own operating assets. For example, in 1981 Ford sold to IBM $1 billion of machinery, equipment and tooling (representing almost all of Ford's 1981 domestic capital spending). Ford had purchased the assets in 1981 but, because of its continuing losses, would not have been able to benefit from investment tax credits or depreciation. By selling the assets to IBM and then leasing them back, Ford ended up ahead by well over $100 million in cash. IBM received large tax savings by using the investment tax credits and depreciation to reduce its tax bill.

In the years after 1981, Congress changed the tax law several times. The revisions included a phaseout of the safe-harbor provisions and an introduction of certain new incentives to leasing. The new law that has emerged provides benefits to leasing that are far less than those under ERTA but somewhat more than those under the pre-ERTA tax law.

Accounting for Leases

The Financial Accounting Standards Board (an arm of the American Institute of Certified Public Accountants) requires, under FASB Statement 13, that leases be classified *by the lessee* as either capital leases or operating

---

[6] If a lease arrangement does not meet the five criteria, the IRS or the courts may still allow the arrangement to be treated as a lease for tax purposes. The likelihood of treatment as a lease is greater the more closely the lease satisfies the five criteria.

[7] ERTA specified that, to be eligible for safe-harbor treatment, the lessor must be a corporation (or a group of corporations); the lessee need not be a corporation.

[8] A failure to elect to have the lease fall under the safe-harbor provisions would mean that the old law (in effect, Revenue Ruling 55-540 and Revenue Procedure 75-21) would apply to the lease.

leases. A **capital lease** transfers most or all of the benefits and risks of ownership to the lessee. If a lease is not a capital lease, it is an operating lease.[9] If one or more of the following conditions are met, the lease is deemed a capital lease by the lessee:[10]

1 The lease transfers ownership of the asset to the lessee at the end of the lease term.
2 The lease provides for a bargain purchase option.
3 The lease term equals or exceeds 75 percent of the asset's useful life.
4 At the beginning of the lease term, the present value of the lease payments equals or exceeds 90 percent of the current fair market value of the asset.[11]

If the lease is a capital lease, the balance sheet of the lessee shows the present value of the lease rental payments as an asset ("leased property under capital leases") and as a liability ("capital lease obligations"). This is illustrated in Exhibit 19-1.

---

[9] For excellent reviews of the FASB's Statement 13 (Statement of Financial Accounting Standards No. 13: Accounting for Leases) see J. J. Kalata, D. G. Campbell, and I. K. Shumaker, "Lease Finance Reporting," *Financial Executive* (March 1977), pp. 34–40; L. Schachner, "The New Accounting for Leases," *Financial Executive* (February 1978), pp. 40–47; J. R. Deming, "An Analysis of FASB No. 13," *Financial Executive* (March 1978), pp. 46–51.

[10] For a *lessor*, a lease is a capital lease if it meets one or more of the four conditions stated in the text below *and* if there is reasonable certainty concerning both the receipt of the lease rentals and the magnitude of the costs to be incurred by the lessor in connection with the lease. It is possible that a lease be categorized as a capital lease by the lessee but, because of uncertainties concerning rentals or lessor costs, be classified as an operating lease by the lessor.

[11] The interest rate used to compute the present value of the lease rentals is the lessee's incremental borrowing rate; however, if the lessee knows the lessor's implicit internal rate of return on the lease transaction, the lower of that rate and the lessee's marginal borrowing rate is used.

EXHIBIT 19-1
Balance sheet of a firm with capital lease obligations

Assets:	
Current assets	$1,000,000
Property and equipment	6,000,000
Leased property under capital leases	2,000,000
Liabilities and shareholders' equity:	
Current liabilities	$3,000,000
Long-term debt	1,000,000
Capital lease obligations	2,000,000
Shareholders' equity	3,000,000

Back in Chapter 8, it was explained that the net benefit to the firm from purchasing an asset is its net present value. The asset should be purchased only if the net present value is positive. Leasing is an alternative way to obtain use of an asset. To determine whether leasing or buying an asset is better, the net present value of the asset's cash flows to the lessee under the lease must be compared with the net present value of the asset if purchased. The option (lease or purchase) with the greater net present value is superior and the asset is acquired if, and only if, that superior option has a zero or positive net present value (a zero net present value means that the superior option earns just the minimum acceptable rate of return). The analysis proceeds in the following steps:[12]

1 Compute the net present value of the asset's cash flows if the asset is purchased [signified NPV(purchase)]; this step is *identical to* that described in Chapters 8 and 9 (since Chapters 8 and 9 were concerned with the evaluation of an asset purchase).
2 Compute the net present value of the cash flows generated for the firm by the asset if it is leased [signified NPV(lease)].
3 Compare NPV(purchase) with NPV(lease). The option—purchase or lease—with the higher NPV is superior, and the other option should be rejected. The superior option should be adopted if, and only if, its NPV is zero or positive.

The remainder of this section explains how the above analysis is performed. Before illustrating the approach, though, we should explain why it is generally *not* correct to use NPV(purchase) to accept or reject projects and *then* to do the lease versus purchase analysis of the accepted projects. Such a method would mean that any asset with a negative NPV(purchase) would be rejected and would not be considered further. Thus, it is possible that an asset have a negative NPV(purchase) but a positive NPV(lease), in which case rejecting the asset because NPV(purchase) is negative would mean passing up a good opportunity (the opportunity to lease the asset). For example, if a machine has an NPV(purchase) of $-\$500$, under this method we would drop the machine from further consideration. But, if NPV(lease) = $800 for the machine, by rejecting the machine we would be losing the $800 present value obtainable with a lease. The approach recommended here prevents this type of mistake. Admittedly, there are cases in

---

[12] The lease or buy analysis presented here in the text assumes that firm debt and leasing are independent and is based on an equivalent method described in L. D. Schall, "The Lease or Buy and Asset Acquisition Decisions," *Journal of Finance* (September 1974). If debt and leasing are interdependent, Eq. (19-3) must have an additional term, $\tau \, \Delta R$, $p\Delta R$ is the change in firm interest expense due to a change in firm debt resulting from leasing (on this see Schall, ibid., footnote 10). For a detailed analysis of the debt-leasing interdependency using a model consistent with the one presented here, see S. C. Myers, D. A. Dill, and A. J. Bautista, "Valuation of Financial Lease Contracts," *Journal of Finance* (June 1976). For a discussion of other leasing issues see M. H. Miller and C. W. Upton, "Leasing, Buying, and the Cost of Capital Services," *Journal of Finance* (June 1976); W. G. Lewellen, M. S. Long, and J. J. McConnell, "Asset Leasing in Competitive Capital Markets," *Journal of Finance* (June 1976).

which it is clear (even without any formal present value analysis) that an asset should be acquired and that the only decision is whether to lease the asset or purchase it. In this case, we could either use the method recommended in this chapter or we could simply compute the net advantage to leasing the asset, and then lease it only if the net advantage is positive; the net advantage to leasing approach is described in Appendix 19B.

We should also point out that the method illustrated below assumes that leasing the asset does not affect the firm's borrowing against other assets; Appendix 19A discusses the complications which arise in the analyses when leasing does affect the level of firm debt.

With purchase of the asset, the firm assumes all the risks and benefits of ownership, including risks associated with the sale value (salvage value) of the asset when the firm no longer needs it. The company pays all the costs of maintaining the asset, e.g., upkeep expenses and property taxes. If the firm borrows to finance the asset, it pays interest and principal on that debt. All maintenance expenses, debt interest, and depreciation on the asset are tax deductible. The firm can also ordinarily take the investment tax credit on the asset (see Chapter 8). On the other hand, with a lease the firm receives the benefits from using the asset but has no claim on its salvage value (which is reserved for the asset's owner). The lessee must make lease payments and may also be required to cover some or all of the maintenance expenses on the asset. Lease payments and lessee expenses associated with the asset are tax deductible for the lessee. The lessee cannot deduct depreciation on the asset, since this is a tax deduction for the lessor (owner). The investment tax credit may be taken by the lessor or, with certain restrictions, be passed on to the lessee (this is subject to negotiation between the lessor and the lessee). The lessor will likely charge a higher lease rental if the tax credit is passed on to the lessee than if the lessor retains the credit.

The cash flow from purchasing the asset is computed in the manner described in Chapter 8. This cash flow in year t, CF(purchase)$_t$, equals[13]

$$\left\{ \begin{array}{c} \text{Cash flow in year } t \\ \text{with purchase of asset} \end{array} \right\} = \text{CF(purchase)}_t$$

$$= \text{revenues}_t - \text{expenses}_t$$
$$- \text{capital expenditures}_t - \text{taxes}_t$$

$$= \text{revenues}_t - \text{expenses}_t$$
$$- \text{capital expenditures}_t$$
$$- \tau \, (\text{revenues}_t$$
$$- \text{expenses}_t - \text{depreciation}_t) \qquad (19\text{-}1)$$

---

[13] To include the investment tax credit (see Chaps. 3 and 8 for details on the credit), the credit is treated as an aftertax cash inflow when it is received, normally in the year in which the asset is purchased. The example in Exhibit 19-2 shows how the credit is incorporated into the analysis. We assume here that the lessee does not get the investment tax credit on the asset; as noted earlier, upon meeting certain requirements, the lessor may allow the lessee to receive the credit instead.

where τ is the corporate tax rate. Equation (19-1) is identical to Eq. (8-1). "Capital expenditures" in Eq. (19-1) represents any additional capital outlays during the life of the asset (e.g., a new roof or lighting fixtures if the purchased asset were a manufacturing plant). If the asset is sold (e.g., near the end of its useful life), there is a cash inflow equal to the net aftertax proceeds from selling the asset, and this is reflected in Eq. (19-1) as a negative capital expenditure (i.e., as a positive cash flow). The example in Exhibit 19-2 on page 593 illustrates how salvage value is treated. As explained in Chapter 8, in Eq. (19-1) interest on debt is not included in expenses. CF(purchase)$_t$ is discounted using the firm's cost of capital if the purchased asset is financed in the same way (same proportions of debt and equity financing) and is of the same risk as the company's other assets. The discount rate will differ from that used on the firm's other assets if the asset's financing or risk differs from that of the firm's other assets. The method for determining the discount rate in this latter case is described in Chapter 9. The analysis of an asset purchase is identical to that described in Chapters 8 and 9. Once we have estimated the discount rate, k, we compute the net present value with purchase, which equals

$$\text{NPV(purchase)} = \frac{\text{CF(purchase)}_1}{1 + k} + \frac{\text{CF(purchase)}_2}{(1 + k)^2}$$

$$+ \cdots + \frac{\text{CF(purchase)}_n}{(1 + k)^n} - I \qquad (19\text{-}2)$$

CF(purchase)$_n$ includes the net aftertax salvage value of the asset assuming it is sold in year n. I is the initial cost of the asset.

With leasing, the cash flow in year t from the asset, CF(lease)$_t$ equals

$$\left\{ \begin{array}{c} \text{Cash flow in year } t \\ \text{with leasing of} \\ \text{the asset} \end{array} \right\} = \text{CF(lease)}_t$$

$$= \text{revenues}_t - \text{expenses}_t - \text{lease rental}_t - \text{taxes}_t$$

$$= \text{revenues}_t - \text{expenses}_t - \text{lease rental}_t$$
$$- \tau(\text{revenues}_t - \text{expenses}_t - \text{lease rental}_t)$$
$$(19\text{-}3)$$

The expression in parentheses is the taxable income from the asset if it is leased. All of CF(lease)$_t$ goes to the company's stockholders [since there is no debt used to finance the asset and CF(lease)$_t$ is net of the lease rental payments]. The appropriate discount rate for CF(lease)$_t$ is a rate that reflects the riskiness of CF(lease)$_t$. This lease cash flow is likely to be riskier than CF(purchase)$_t$ since CF(purchase)$_t$ is the *total* aftertax stream to equity *and* to any debt used to purchase the asset, whereas CF(lease)$_t$ is the net cash flow over and above the amount payable to the lessor; that is, CF(lease)$_t$ is an equity cash flow after meeting the fixed charge in the form of the lease payment. The rate k_L for discounting CF(lease)$_t$ will therefore normally exceed the rate k in Eq. (19-1) for discounting the less risky CF(purchase)$_t$.[14] The important point here is that *the discount rate used to discount any cash flow is the rate that is appropriate given the risk of that cash flow; therefore, if CF(purchase)$_t$ is less risky than CF(lease)$_t$, k in Eq. (19-2) will be less than k_L in Eq. (19-4).* (The reader may find it helpful to review the discussion of risk-adjusted discount rates on pages 279 to 282.) The net present value of the lease cash flow equals

$$\text{NPV(lease)} = \frac{\text{CF(lease)}_1}{1 + k_L} + \frac{\text{CF(lease)}_2}{(1 + k_L)^2} + \cdots + \frac{\text{CF(lease)}_n}{(1 + k_L)^n} \qquad (19\text{-}4)$$

Leasing is superior if NPV(lease) exceeds NPV(purchase), and purchase is superior if NPV(purchase) exceeds NPV(lease). The superior choice, lease or purchase, is accepted only if its NPV is zero or positive. For example, if NPV(lease) = \$2000 and NPV(purchase) = \$1000, lease is superior since NPV(lease) exceeds NPV(purchase); and the asset should be leased since NPV(lease) is positive. However, if NPV(lease) = $-\$1000$ and NPV(purchase) = $-\$1500$, lease is superior to purchase (it's less bad), but leasing is rejected along with purchase since NPV(lease) is negative. In this situation, acquiring the asset by lease or by purchase is unprofitable.

A numerical illustration will help to clarify the approach outlined above. Assume that the firm can purchase, for \$3000, an asset with a useful life (to the firm) of five years. It is expected that the asset will be sold after five years for \$200 (net of any taxes on the sale) and depreciation for tax purposes is to be on a straight-line basis, that is, \$600 per year for five years (\$3000/5 years). (Recall from Chapters 3 and 8 that, in computing depreciation for tax purposes, salvage value is assumed to be zero.)[15] Purchase of the asset will increase the firm's expected revenues by \$2400 per year and will raise its expected operating expenses (not including depreciation or debt interest) by \$1000 per year. The corporate income tax rate is 50 percent. The invest-

---

[14] To clarify the point that the discount rate used to discount CF(purchase) in Eq. (19-1) is likely to be less than the discount rate applicable to CF(lease) in (19-3), notice that (19-1) is *not* net of payments to creditors (interest and principal) who may provide part of the funds to finance the firm's acquisition of assets. CF(purchase) is funds flow from the asset that goes to *both* shareholders and creditors and is therefore discounted using a rate (cost of capital) that is a *weighted average* of the firm's equity discount rate (signified k_s) and the firm's debt rate (signified k_B). For example, assume an asset with a CF(purchase) of \$100 per year, where \$60 per year is to go to shareholders and \$40 per year is to go to bondholders, and let k_s = 12 percent and k_B = 9 percent. The rate k_s to discount the \$60 equity cash flow (signified CF$_e$) would be 12 percent, the rate k_B to discount the \$40 debt cash flow would be 9 percent, and the rate to discount the total \$100 flow (signified k) would be between 9 percent and 12 percent, say, 10 percent (k = 10 percent). Observe that CF$_e$ = CF(purchase) $-$ debt payments = \$100 $-$ \$40 = \$60. The equity rate k_s is greater than the weighted average k because equity flow CF$_e$ is riskier, due to financial leverage (see Chaps. 10 and 13), than total cash flow CF(purchase). Notice now that CF(lease) in Eq. (19-3) is net of the firm's lease payments. Deducting the lease payments is similar to deducting debt payments from CF(purchase) to compute CF$_e$. CF(lease) is like CF$_e$ in that both are riskier than the total cash flow from the asset before deduction of the fixed charges (debt or lease). It follows that CF(lease) of (19-3) is likely to be riskier than CF(purchase) of (19-1).

[15] We will ignore here the effect of taking the investment tax credit on the allowable depreciation deduction.

ment tax credit on the asset is $300. Assume that the discount rate for the asset is 10 percent. As shown in Exhibit 19-2, NPV(purchase) = $1214.

The firm can also lease the asset for a yearly rental of $700. With the lease, the increase in expected revenues from using the asset is $2400 (as with purchase) and the increase in the firm's expected nondepreciation expenses is $900 (this differs from the $1000 increase in expenses with purchase since it is assumed that $100 of the asset's maintenance expenses will be covered by the lessor). The discount rate to be used in discounting the expected net cash flow from leasing the asset is 15 percent. This rate exceeds the 10 percent discount rate with purchase because we are assuming that the lease cash flow [Eq. (19-3)] is riskier than the purchase cash flow [Eq. (19-1)] (see footnote 14 and the associated text discussion). Exhibit 19-3 shows the lease computations. Since NPV(lease) = $1341, and, as shown in Exhibit 19-2, NPV(purchase) = $1214, the asset should be leased.

CONSIDERATIONS IN THE LEASING DECISION

The decision to lease or not to lease is often based in practice on certain commonly held notions about leasing. Below we examine these notions.

Availability of cash

It is sometimes argued that leasing imposes less of a current cash drain on the firm than purchase, thus freeing capital for other purposes. This argument is correct in the unusual situation in which the firm can lease the asset but cannot borrow to buy the asset (and cannot buy the asset on an installment payment basis, which is in effect a borrowing arrangement). If

---

EXHIBIT 19-2

Computation of the net present value of purchasing the asset

Year (1)	Revenues (2)	Nondepre-ciation expenses other than debt payments (3)	Depre-ciation (4)	Taxes {0.50[(2)− (3) − (4)]} (5)	Aftertax salvage value (6)	Net cash flow [(2) − (3) − (5) + (6)] (7)	10% Present value factor (8)	Present value of net cash flow[a] [(7) × (8)] (9)
1	$2,400	$1,000	$600	$400		$1,000	0.9091	$ 909
2	2,400	1,000	600	400		1,000	0.8264	826
3	2,400	1,000	600	400		1,000	0.7513	751
4	2,400	1,000	600	400		1,000	0.6830	683
5	2,400	1,000	600	400	$200	1,200	0.6209	745
								$3,914

NPV(purchase) = present value of future cash flows − cost of asset + investment tax credit
= $3,914 − $3,000 + $300 = $1,214

[a] Figures are rounded.

EXHIBIT 19-3
Computation of the net present value of leasing the asset

Year (1)	Revenues (2)	Nondepreciation expenses other than lease and debt payments (3)	Lease rental (4)	Taxes {0.50[(2) − (3) − (4)]} (5)	Net cash flow [(2) − (3) − (4) − (5)] (6)	15% Present value factor (7)	Present value of net cash flow[a] [(6) × (7)] (8)
1	$2,400	$900	$700	$400	$400	0.8696	$ 348
2	2,400	900	700	400	400	0.7561	302
3	2,400	900	700	400	400	0.6575	263
4	2,400	900	700	400	400	0.5718	229
5	2,400	900	700	400	400	0.4972	199
							$1,341

NPV(lease) = present value of net cash flows with leasing = $1,341

[a] Figures are rounded.

the firm can purchase the asset using borrowed funds, the immediate cash outlay may be no greater than with leasing. Lease arrangements often require deposits or advance rental payments when the lease is set up, and these immediate cash payments may equal or exceed any equity investment (down payment) required in purchasing the asset.

Effect on the firm's borrowing capacity

Lenders (as well as shareholders) pay serious attention to the company's ability to service its debt. Too much debt restricts the firm's capacity to borrow further. What of leasing? Is leasing a method of obtaining assets on credit without the penalty of a reduced capacity to incur additional debt? Clearly, a lease imposes a fixed charge on the firm and poses a similar threat to the firm's solvency as does debt (leaseholders can demand payment just as creditors can).[16] At issue here is whether lenders view the lease in this way or merely ignore outstanding leases in computing fixed charges of the firm. Until recently, leases often were not properly acknowledged by cred-

[16] Leases and debt do differ in certain important respects. First, a lessor may obtain the asset being financed at the end of the lease term, whereas a creditor does not receive a physical asset. Second, creditors have a stronger claim than do lessors against a firm in the event that the borrower (lessee) firm suffers financial distress. Although both the lessor and a secured lender have a claim against the asset if payments are not properly made, there may be an amount due in excess of the value of the asset. The creditor can sue for that deficiency whereas a lessor is limited to one year's lease payment from a bankrupt firm and to three years' lease payments from a firm under reorganization. Third, a borrowing firm can always dispose of an asset and pay off the debt when it chooses but, if it leases the asset, it cannot necessarily terminate possession of a leased asset unless there is a lease cancellation option or the right to sublease the asset. That is, a lessee may be locked into an asset, whereas this can be avoided if the asset is owned. Fourth, constraints on the firm are more likely to be imposed by creditors than by lessors (for example, that the firm maintain a particular level of working capital, of net worth, etc.).

itors. Therefore, the firm's ability to incur added debt was greater if the firm leased assets rather than purchased them with borrowed funds. Now, however, leases are usually recognized as fixed obligations similar to debt. This change in attitude is in part due to pressure from the Securities and Exchange Commission and The American Institute of Certified Public Accountants for improved financial disclosure by firms. As described earlier in the section on Accounting for Leases, financial statements now disclose major assets held under a lease and disclose the associated rental payment obligation. Because leases as well as debt are now taken into account by lenders, leasing and borrowing have similar effects on the firm's borrowing ability.

Convenience

Leasing is a very convenient way to obtain the services of an asset for a short period of time. Except for tax considerations, leasing is economically equivalent to buying an asset from a dealer and, at the time of purchase, negotiating an agreement to sell the asset back to the dealer for a predetermined price. Leasing has emerged in part to meet the needs of those who want short-term use with no uncertainty about cost (e.g., no uncertainty about what can be obtained for the asset when it is no longer needed). Furthermore, for those with a very short-term need for an asset, leasing is especially practical because it involves fewer legal costs and lower taxes than purchase and resale; purchase and resale would require two transfers of title and perhaps state sales taxes on each transfer.

Avoidance of Restrictions on the Firm

Lenders frequently impose restrictions on the firm with the idea of improving the firm's capacity to pay off the loan. Examples are limits on dividends, subordination clauses, and restrictions on new investment or sales of firm property. Lease agreements may also include such constraints, but they are less frequent and are often less restrictive. However, in contrast with debt, a lease may involve constraints on the use of the leased property, for example, how many hours per week a machine may be used. These restrictions are meant to protect the asset (since it is still owned by the lessor) rather than to enhance the lessee's rental-paying ability.

Avoiding the restrictions of a debt arrangement by leasing instead is not costless. The debt restrictions protect the lender and reduce the lender's risk, thereby reducing the interest the lender demands on the debt. If a lessor does not require similar restrictions, the risk for the lessor will be greater than for a lender and, to compensate for this, the lease rentals will provide a higher rate of return to the lessor than to a lender. The benefit to the lessee firm of no restrictions on its operations is reflected in higher lease payments. Whether the lack of restriction is worth the added cost will depend on the situation.

Shifting of Risk of Obsolescence

Is leasing a way for an asset user to escape the risk that the asset will become obsolete and worthless? The answer is yes, but normally at a cost. Even with a financial lease, the lease term can be sufficiently short (e.g., 50 percent of the asset's expected economic life) that the lessee can avoid holding an obsolete asset. Alternatively, the lease may be long-term but have a cancellation clause (which allows the lessee to cancel the contract during its term). Therefore, the risk of obsolescence can be shifted to the lessor. But, here again the rental price on the asset will mirror the costs borne by the lessor. To be willing to assume the obsolescence risk, the lessor will require a higher rental than if such risk were assumed by the lessee. In effect then, the lessee ends up paying for the obsolescence risk.[17] But what if the lessor is better able than the user (lessee) to find a use for a somewhat outdated asset? This might occur because of the lessor's superior access to many potential users of the asset. Under these conditions, the cost of obsolescence may be less under leasing than under purchase by the user. This advantage will be at least partially passed on to the lessee (in the form of lower lease payments) as lessors compete for customers in a competitive market. In this case, the asset user (lessee) may gain by leasing rather than buying the asset since the impact of obsolescence is lower with lease than with purchase.[18]

Salvage Value

The owner of the asset receives salvage value (residual value); but the higher the expected salvage value, the lower the lease rentals need be in order that the lessor earn a satisfactory return on its investment. The anticipated salvage value is therefore reflected in the lease payments required on an asset, and there is no implied gain to a firm from owning relative to leasing. Indeed, if the lessor firm is especially capable of finding productive economic employment of the asset after it is used by the lessee, the salvage value may be greater for a lessor than for a user-lessee. This advantage would make leasing more economical than purchase by the user firm.[19] On the other hand, if the user anticipates that the asset will have a higher future value than others (lessors) expect—as might occur, for example, if the asset were real estate—then the firm might wish to purchase. This is a gamble on the part of the firm's management that its expectations are more likely to be fulfilled than those of the lessor.

An example that illustrates, in the extreme, how important residual value can be in some cases involves Gulf Oil's lease of a property in West Texas. In 1925, Gulf negotiated a fifty-year lease of the Waddell Ranch oil properties owned by wildcatter W. H. McFadden. Because oil output during the fifty-year lease was unexpectedly restricted by the Texas Railway Commission (which sets oil extraction rates in Texas), much of the oil remained in the ground when the lease expired in 1975. Gulf Oil foresaw this during

---

[17] Even if the lessee pays the lessor for assuming the obsolescence risk, there may be an advantage for the lessee in this arrangement in that the lease rental payments are predictable (since they are specified in the lease contract), whereas the future impact of obsolescence on the value of the asset is uncertain. Therefore, the lessee is in a more predictable position by leasing rather than by buying. But, again, it should be emphasized that the lessee pays a higher rental to the lessor for having the latter assume the less predictable position. Whether the asset user is willing to pay the extra amount to a lessor in order to shift the uncertainty to the lessor (rather than for the user to buy the asset) will depend upon the particular circumstances.

[18] If there are dealers who buy and sell used assets and who, like lessors, have good access to potential asset users, leasing may offer no advantage relative to purchase and eventual resale to a used-asset dealer.

[19] See footnote 18.

the late 1960s and sued to have the lease extended. The Texas Supreme Court ruled against Gulf, declaring that the lease specified fifty years and the unexpected intervention of the Texas Railway Commission did not alter that fact. The stock of Southland Realty Company, the owner of Waddell Ranch, rose sharply after the court decision.

Tax Considerations

The firm can depreciate the asset for tax purposes if it purchases the asset but not if it leases the asset. The purchaser can also take the investment tax credit (ITC) on the asset. However, since a *lessor* gets depreciation deductions and the ITC and *will in a competitive market pass at least some of the tax benefits on to the lessee in the form of lower rental charges*, we cannot assume that depreciation and the ITC encourage purchase rather than lease by the user. Also, under the tax code the lessor can let the lessee have the ITC if this is agreed upon by the lessee and lessor; thus, the firm need not purchase the asset in order to get the ITC.

In short, tax factors encourage that choice between leasing and purchase which minimizes the total taxes associated with the asset's use and ownership (ownership by the user with purchase or by the lessor with lease). Whether lease or purchase is preferred on the basis of tax considerations depends on such factors as the lessor's and lessee's tax brackets, the method of depreciating the asset (straight-line or accelerated), and the degree to which the asset is debt financed by its owner (the user under purchase or the lessor under a lease). These factors vary from case to case and the impact of taxes will therefore depend on the particular situation.

SUMMARY

Under a lease, the user of an asset (the lessee) pays the owner (the lessor) a rental per period for the usage right. An operating lease is a short-term lease whereas a financial lease covers a major portion of the asset's useful life. A sale and leaseback contract provides for the sale of the asset by the user, who then leases it back from the purchaser. A full-service lease requires that the lessor provide services to the lessee, including maintenance of the asset, payment of property taxes and insurance, etc. A leveraged lease (or third-party lease) involves not simply the lessor and lessee but also a lender who ordinarily provides a major portion of the asset's purchase price. The loan is on a nonrecourse basis, i.e., the lender has a claim to the asset and to the rental payments due under the lease but may not turn to the lessor for any amounts owed on the loan.

The tax law specifies requirements which must be met in order that a transaction be treated as a lease for tax purposes. Financial statements prepared in accordance with the guidelines set by the Financial Accounting Standards Board must disclose major leases. If the lease is a capital lease under these guidelines, the lessee lists, on its balance sheet, the present value of the future lease rentals as an asset and as an obligation (much like debt).

The purchase and lease alternatives for acquiring an asset can be evaluated by comparing their cash flows. The alternative with the higher net present value of cash flows is preferred and is adopted if its net present value is positive or zero.

A firm may prefer to lease rather than purchase because a lease imposes less of an immediate cash drain on the firm; but this is only true if the firm cannot borrow to buy the asset. Lease obligations are generally viewed by creditors as a form of debt, and they will reduce the firm's ability to borrow in the same way that borrowing to purchase an asset will. Leasing is an especially convenient and economical way to obtain the short-term use of an asset since it involves fewer legal costs, and sometimes lower total sales taxes, than a purchase. Leasing is a way to avoid the restrictions imposed by lenders and is a way to shift the risks of obsolescence; but the lease rental will reflect the risks borne by the lessor. The presence of a high salvage value on an asset does not imply that purchase is better than lease since the lease rental will take into account the salvage value the lessor will realize on the asset. Tax considerations may favor lease or purchase by the asset user, depending on the particular circumstances.

QUESTIONS

1 Describe the major difference between an operating lease and a financial lease.
2 What is a leveraged lease?
3 How is the discount rate used to evaluate a lease determined? Is the discount rate for evaluating the purchase of an asset the same as that used for evaluating the lease? Explain fully.
4 "The neat part about leasing is that there is less cash drain on a company than if it buys the asset outright." Evaluate this statement.
5 What rationale, if any, can be given for listing the leased assets and the present value of lease payments on the balance sheet?
6 Restrictive provisions are more often found in debt contracts than in lease contracts. Furthermore, the return required by lessors is usually greater than that required by creditors. Reconcile these facts.
7 How does a lease affect the cost of asset obsolescence to the asset user?
8 "The trouble with leasing from the lessee's standpoint is that the lessor, not the lessee, gets the advantage of taking depreciation for tax purposes." Evaluate this statement.
9 How do the expectations of the lessee and the lessor concerning an asset's salvage value affect the attitudes of each with regard to what is an acceptable lease rental?
10 Describe in words the proper way to evaluate a lease.

PROJECTS

1 Select a major asset used by one or more firms in your area and find out how you would negotiate the lease and the purchase of the asset.
2 Select several assets that can both be purchased and leased. For each asset, obtain data on the purchase price and the lease rental

charged for the asset (assume some lease duration), and obtain an estimate of the likely salvage value of the asset at the end of the lease term you assume. Find out how the asset is depreciated under current tax law and the amount of any investment tax credit allowed on the asset. Compute the aftertax rate of return earned by the lessor on the asset. Assume that the lessor is in the 46 percent tax bracket, and assume that the lessor pays the purchase price you determined for the asset.

PROBLEMS

1 Rocket Technologies is evaluating the purchase or lease of new equipment. The estimated increase in annual revenues is $200,000, and the estimated increase in operating expenses is $90,000, regardless of whether the asset is purchased outright or leased from the manufacturer. The equipment costs $300,000 to purchase and has an estimated life of eight years, at the end of which time it can be sold for an aftertax salvage value of $20,000. If the asset is leased, the annual payments come to $50,000, payable at the end of each year for eight years. The company plans to depreciate its new equipment on a straight-line basis over five years (assume zero salvage value for tax depreciation computations). The proper discount rate with which to evaluate the leased equipment is 20 percent; for the purchased equipment, it is 18 percent. The firm's tax rate is 40 percent. If Rocket Technologies purchases or leases the equipment, it will not get the investment tax credit. What should Rocket Technologies do—purchase, lease, or not acquire the equipment? Show all calculations.

2 Your firm, Data Consultants, is considering the lease or purchase of a new computer. The new computer will replace an existing computer which, although usable, has insufficient capacity for many of the software programs you want to run. Assume that you can ignore any salvage value of the existing computer because it has been fully depreciated for tax purposes and has virtually no market value. The new computer will allow you to serve additional clients, and, if you purchase it, will raise your *before-tax* net cash flow by $40,000 per year. If you buy the computer, you will have an immediate cash outlay of $100,000 for the purchase price. The computer will last five years, at the end of which time you expect to be able to sell it for an aftertax value of $5000. You will depreciate the computer over five years on a straight-line basis with no salvage value (depreciation of $20,000 per year). You can also lease the computer for five years for $30,000 per year for the first two years and $35,000 per year for the remaining three years. The lease payments are payable at the end of each year. The lessor will maintain the computer, a savings to you of $3000 per year in maintenance costs. Leasing the computer will raise your before-tax net cash flow by $43,000, before deducting the lease rental. You will take the 10 percent investment tax credit if you buy the computer, and will also get the credit if you lease it. Your tax

bracket is 40 percent. You will use an 18 percent discount rate to compute all present values (with purchase or lease). Should you purchase the computer, lease it, or not acquire it at all?

3 You just sold your business and are considering a number of proposals on how you should invest your cash. Knox Corporation, a major builder in your city, has offered to construct and lease out an office building which Knox wants to sell you for $2,000,000. If you buy the property, you will receive a rental of $200,000 per year for the first five years, and $300,000 per year for the following thirteen years. You expect to sell the property at the end of the eighteen year period for an aftertax price of $1.5 million. You will depreciate the building over eighteen years on a straight-line basis; the building has a depreciable basis of $1,800,000 and depreciation will be $100,000 per year. The building is not eligible for the investment tax credit. Knox will manage and maintain the building, but you will pay the local property taxes (which are tax deductible for federal income tax purposes) of $30,000 per year. Your tax rate is 40%. You want at least a 15% aftertax return on your investments. Should you buy the building from Knox? Assume that you will pay cash for the property.

4 At the recent board of directors meeting of Durham Corporation, one of the directors argued that the company would be better off if it leased assets rather than bought them with borrowed money. He commented, "After all, you won't have a balance sheet showing debt on it. And that's good, 'cause we can borrow later on if we want to." Another director pointed out that lease payments are viewed as the equivalent to fixed charges on debt and that no one would be fooled by the lease versus debt issue. A third director thought the company would have to capitalize the leases in order to depict the true nature of the balance sheet.

If the firm has $20 million in assets before acquiring new assets, show what the balance sheet would look like under each of the proposed systems if the firm were to lease the assets or buy them with borrowed money. The cost of the assets to be acquired is $3 million. The firm can borrow the money to finance them at the market rate of 8 percent a year for twenty years. The annual lease payments, if the assets are leased, will be $160,000 for the twenty-year period. The company currently has a book debt-equity ratio of $\frac{3}{7}$.

5 Lark, Inc., can purchase or lease a machine. Lark is in the 40 percent tax bracket. The data in the table on page 601 apply with purchase and lease. The asset will be used by Lark for seven years (purchased and sold in seven years or leased for seven years). The aftertax salvage value of the asset at the end of the seven years is expected to be $3,500. Assume that the annual revenues ($4,200), annual expenses ($1,300 with purchase and $1,100 with lease), and annual depreciation ($2,500) occur at time 1, 2, . . . , 7; the seven annual lease rental payments begin now and continue to time 6 (six years from now).

Lark, Inc.

Purchase

Purchase	
Purchase price	$21,000
Investment tax credit (10%)	$2,500
Life of machine	7 years
Expected aftertax salvage value of machine	$3,500
Added annual firm revenues from using the machine	$4,200
Added annual firm expenses from using the machine	$1,300
Annual depreciation (using straight line)	$2,500
Discount rate on aftertax cash flow	16%

Lease	
Lease rental (payable at the beginning of the year, i.e., now, at time 1, at time 2, . . . , at time 6)	$2,500 per year
Length of lease	7 years
Investment tax credit	Retained by lessor
Added annual firm revenues from using the machine	$4,200
Added annual firm expenses from using the machine (not including lease rental)	$1,100
Discount rate on aftertax cash flow	20%

Using the above information, determine whether Lark should purchase the machine, lease the machine, or not acquire the machine.

Note: Problem **6** requires knowledge of Appendix 19A; and problem **7** requires a knowledge of Appendix 19B (Appendix 19A is helpful background).

6 Sun Technologies will either purchase or lease new equipment on January 1, 1987. The company will replace the equipment in five years whether it purchases or leases it. Sun's tax rate is 50 percent. With purchase: (a) the purchase price of the equipment is $2 million; (b) the equipment will have an expected January 1, 1992, aftertax salvage value of $200,000; (c) the equipment will be depreciated over five years (at $400,000 per year); (d) the investment tax credit on the equipment is $200,000; (e) the equipment will produce a $1.6 million increase in annual firm revenues and an $800,000 increase in annual firm nondepreciation operating costs; and (f) the discount rate in computing NPV(purchase) is 11 percent.

With lease of the equipment: (a) the annual lease rental is $600,000 payable on January 1 of each year from 1988 to 1992 (five payments); (b) the discount rate for discounting the net equity cash flow from leasing the asset (col. 8 of Exhibit 19-5 on page 606) is 12 percent; (c) the equipment will produce a $1.6 million increase in annual firm revenues and an $800,000 increase in annual firm non-depreciation operating costs (same as with purchase); and (d) Sun Technologies will reduce its other debt by $1 million which we assume would have been payable at 10 percent per annum in the following installments:

Payment date (1)	Principal (2)	Interest (3)	Total [(2) + (3)] (4)
Jan. 1, 1988	$163,797	$100,000	$263,797
Jan. 1, 1989	180,177	83,620	263,797
Jan. 1, 1990	198,194	65,603	263,797
Jan.1, 1991	218,014	45,783	263,797
Jan. 1, 1992	239,818	23,982	263,800

Determine whether Sun Technologies should purchase or lease the equipment. You may round all figures to the nearest thousand dollars.

7 Melody Corporation will either purchase or lease a fleet of automobiles on June 15, 1986. The fleet is essential to Melody and therefore the decision to obtain it has been made; the remaining decision is whether to purchase or lease the fleet. Melody's tax rate is 40 percent.

   With purchase of the fleet: (a) the purchase price of the fleet is $600,000; (b) the fleet will be kept by Melody for four years and then be sold for an expected aftertax salvage value of $50,000; (c) the fleet will be depreciated over three years by Melody ($200,000 in depreciation per year); (d) the investment tax credit on the fleet is $36,000; (e) the firm operating expenses will be $5000 per year more with purchase than with lease (because the lessor would pay $5000 per year in maintenance costs on the fleet); (f) the firm will increase its current debt (to finance the purchase) by $200,000, payable at 12 percent per annum over four years, with equal amortization payments on the debt on June 15, 1987, June 15, 1988, June 15, 1989, and June 15, 1990. Assume that the tax deductible interest on the $200,000 of debt would be $24,000 for June 15, 1987, $19,000 for June 15, 1988, $13,400 for June 15, 1989, and $7100 for June 15, 1990.

   With lease of the fleet: (a) the annual lease rental will be $160,000 payable on June 15, 1987, June 15, 1988, June 15, 1989, and June 15, 1990; (b) the investment tax credit will be retained by the lessor; (c) Melody will reduce its other debt by $400,000, which we assume would have been payable at 12 percent per annum in equal annual installments on June 15, 1987, June 15, 1988, June 15, 1989, and June 15, 1990.

Assume that the discount rate applicable to the additional firm cash flow with lease (relative to purchase) is 13 percent per year. What is the net advantage to leasing (NAL), and should Melody Corporation purchase or lease the fleet?

19A

LEASE OR PURCHASE ANALYSIS WHEN LEASING AND FIRM DEBT ARE INTER-DEPENDENT

DEBT AND LEASE INTERDEPENDENCE

We pointed out in the text that Eq. (19-3) assumes that leasing an asset does not affect the firm's borrowing against other assets. This assumption is a simplification since borrowing and leasing both represent fixed obligations which must be periodically serviced by the firm, and the firm may wish to limit the *total* amount of such obligations (assuming any given set of productive assets being used by the firm). Leasing an asset might therefore motivate the firm to have a debt level which is lower than it would have if the asset were purchased. To illustrate how the lease or purchase problem is solved if debt and leasing are interdependent, assume that, with purchase, the following data apply to the asset:

Firm tax rate (τ) = 50 percent
Purchase price of asset = $2000
Useful life of asset = five years
Expected year 5 salvage value of asset = $100
Additional annual firm revenues from the asset = $1500
Additional annual firm nondepreciation operating expenses due to the asset = $750
Annual depreciation (for tax purposes) on the asset = $400
Investment tax credit = $200

Assume that the $2000 asset purchase price would be financed 50 percent with debt and 50 percent with equity, i.e., $1000 from each financing source. The firm's balance sheet without the asset and with the asset assuming purchase is shown below.

A.

Firm balance sheet without the new asset		
Assets	$10,000	Debt $5,000
		Equity $5,000

EXHIBIT 19-4
Amortization schedule of $1000 debt retired with lease

Year (1)	Principal payment (2)	Interest payment (3)	Total payment (2) + (3) (4)
1	$167	$90	$257
2	182	75	257
3	198	59	257
4	216	41	257
5	237	21	258[a]

[a] To amortize the debt with *equal* installments would require $257.10 per year.

B.

Firm balance sheet with purchase of the new asset

Assets	$12,000	Debt	$6,000
		Equity	$6,000

The asset can be leased for a rental of $550 per year. Assume that the firm has a target of financing assets 50 percent with equity and 50 percent with *debt and/or lease obligations*. The firm's balance sheet with the lease of the new asset is shown below.

C.

Firm balance sheet with lease of the new asset

Assets	$12,000	Debt	$4,000
		Lease obligation (present value of lease payments)	$2,000
		Equity	$6,000

The $12,000 in balance sheet C assets includes the $2000 asset acquired under the lease. Notice that because of leasing the asset the firm has reduced its debt from $5000 in balance sheet A to $4000 in balance sheet C. The purpose of this $1000 debt reduction is to make the firm's debt *plus* lease obligations equal the $6000 of debt which would exist with purchase of the asset (see balance sheet B).

What is the cash flow impact of reducing firm debt by $1000 because the asset is leased? First, there is an immediate cash outlay of $1000 to retire the debt.[20] Second, there is a cash saving in future periods since interest and principal on the $1000 debt need no longer be paid. Third, there is a tax effect since the firm's tax deductible debt interest is lower than before. Assume that the retired debt of $1000 would have been amortized over a five-year period and carried an interest rate of 9 percent per annum. The amortization payments on the debt are shown in Exhibit 19-4. Given the above information, let's now examine how we could make the lease or purchase decision.

---

[20] The amount needed to retire the $1000 debt could actually be more or less than the $1000. For example, a 10 percent bond might be issued for $1000 and be callable at $1050; if interest rates fell to, say, 8 percent after the bond was issued, the bond would have a current market price greater than $1000; in this case to retire the bond the firm would either have to buy the bond in the market or call it for $1050 (either way it would cost more than $1000 to retire the bond). On the other hand if interest rates rise after the bond's issuance, say, to 12 percent, the bond could be purchased in the market for less than $1000 and retired.

To decide whether to purchase the asset, lease it, or not acquire it at all, we apply the following three steps:[21]

1 Compute the net present value of the asset's cash flows if the asset is purchased [signified NPV(purchase)]; this step is the same as step 1 on page 589.

2 Compute the net present value of the cash flow generated by the asset if the asset is leased [signified NPV(lease)]; this step is similar to step 2 on page 589 except that we will now take into account firm debt changes which result from leasing the asset.

3 Compare NPV(purchase) with NPV(lease). The option—purchase or lease—with a higher NPV is superior, and the other option should be rejected. The superior option should be adopted if and only if its NPV is zero or positive. This step is identical to step 3 on page 589.

Step 1 is shown in Exhibit 19-5. Under step 2 we have to take into account the change in the firm's debt from $5000 (balance sheet A) to $4000 (balance sheet C) which results from leasing the asset. As noted earlier, to retire the $1000, 9 percent debt a $1000 current payment to the creditor is necessary if the asset is leased. But, by repaying the debt, interest and principal payments are reduced by the amounts shown in Exhibit 19-4.

[21] Like other methods presently available in the literature, the lease versus purchase methods described in the text and in Appendixes 19A and 19B ignore personal tax effects, financial distress cost effects, and certain other costs of debt and leasing (e.g., the costs associated with monitoring agreements between the firm and its creditors or lessors). The methods presented here provide useful approximations in most practical situations.

EXHIBIT 19-5

Computation of the net present value of purchasing the asset

Year (1)	Revenues (2)	Nondepreciation expenses other than debt payments (3)	Depreciation (4)	Taxes $\{0.50[(2) - (3) - (4)]\}$ (5)	Aftertax salvage value (6)	Net cash flow $[(2) - (3) - (5) + (6)]$ (7)	10% Present value factor (8)	Present value of net cash flow[a] $[(7) \times (8)]$ (9)
1	$1,500	$750	$400	$175		$575	0.9091	$ 523
2	1,500	750	400	175		575	0.8264	475
3	1,500	750	400	175		575	0.7513	432
4	1,500	750	400	175		575	0.6830	393
5	1,500	750	400	175	$100	675	0.6209	419
								$2,242

NPV(purchase) = present value of future cash flows − cost of asset + investment tax credit
= $2,242 − $2,000 + $200 = $442

[a] Figures are rounded.

Instead of CF(lease)$_t$ of Eq. (19-3) on page 591, we have the following equation for years 1 through 5:

$$\begin{aligned}
\text{CF(lease)}_t = {} & \text{revenues}_t - \text{expenses}_t - \text{lease rental}_t \\
& + \text{principal and interest saved}_t - \tau(\text{revenues}_t \\
& - \text{expenses}_t - \text{lease rental}_t + \text{interest saved}_t) \qquad (19\text{-}4a)
\end{aligned}$$

$$\begin{aligned}
= {} & \text{Eq. (19-3)} + \text{principal saved}_t \\
& + (1 - \tau)(\text{interest saved}_t) \qquad\qquad\qquad\qquad (19\text{-}4b)
\end{aligned}$$

The computations are shown in Exhibit 19-6 (on the following page). We are assuming that the lessor pays $100 of the asset's annual maintenance expense and therefore with lease the nondepreciation expenses other than lease and debt payments (col. 3 of Exhibit 19-6) are $650 per year, $100 less than the $750 nondepreciation expenses with purchase (col. 3 of Exhibit 19-5). NPV(lease) is $291, which is less than NPV(purchase) of $442; the present value of future aftertax cash flows is $151 greater with purchase. Therefore, purchase is preferred. The 14 percent discount rate in Exhibit 19-6 for discounting the net cash flow from leasing the asset is that rate which reflects the risk of the cash flow being discounted. The cash flow being discounted is like that of Eq. (19-3) *plus* a debt stream of principal and aftertax interest [see Eq. (19-4b) above]; since it is a mixture of the risky steam of Eq. (19-3) and a lower risk debt stream, it has a lower risk than the CF(lease)$_t$ of Eq. (19-3).

EXHIBIT 19-6
Computation of the net present value of leasing the asset

Year (1)	Revenues (2)	Nondepreciation expenses other than lease and debt payments (3)	Lease rental (4)	Decrease in debt principal payments (5)	Decrease in debt interest payments (6)	Taxes[a] $\{0.50[(2) - (3) - (4) + (6)]\}$ (7)	Net cash flow $[(2) - (3) - (4) + (5) + (6) - (7)]$ (8)	14% Present value factor (9)	Present value of net cash flow[a] $[(8) \times (9)]$ (10)
1	$1,500	$650	$550	$167	$90	$195	$362	0.8772	$ 318
2	1,500	650	550	182	75	188	369	0.7695	284
3	1,500	650	550	198	59	180	377	0.6750	254
4	1,500	650	550	216	41	171	386	0.5921	229
5	1,500	650	550	237	21	161	397	0.5194	206
									$1,291

NPV(lease) = present value of cash flows with leasing − current amount needed to retire $1000 debt
= $1,291 − $1,000 = $291

[a] Figures are rounded.

It was explained in the text that, in general, it is not correct to decide whether or not to accept an investment using capital budgeting procedures and then, if the investment is acceptable, decide whether to lease the asset or to purchase it. The problem with this method is that the asset may have a negative NPV(purchase) and therefore be rejected even though its NPV with lease [NPV(lease)] is positive. That is, we would have rejected the profitable opportunity to lease the asset. In some situations, however, it is obvious (without any formal present value analysis) that a particular asset is so profitable that it should be acquired. In this case a shortcut approach to the lease or buy analysis is possible: We can simply compute the new present value of the difference between the cash flows with lease and the cash flows with purchase. The present value of the cash flow differences is the **net advantage to leasing**, or NAL. If NAL > 0, leasing is better; if NAL < 0, purchase is better; and, if NAL = 0, purchase and lease are equally desirable.

To illustrate the NAL method, we will use the example of Appendix 19A. The reader may find it helpful to review Appendix 19A. As before we will assume the following with purchase of the asset:

Firm tax rate (τ) = 50 percent
Purchase cost of asset = $2000
Useful life of asset = five years
Expected year 5 salvage value of asset = $100
Additional annual firm revenues from the asset = $1500
Additional annual firm nondepreciation operating expenses due to the asset = $750
Annual depreciation for tax purposes on the asset = $400
Investment tax credit = $200
Increase in firm debt due to purchase of the asset = $1000

Exhibit 19-7 indicates the increase in firm debt payments resulting from the added $1000 of firm debt if the asset is purchased, where we are assuming an interest rate of 9 percent on marginal firm borrowing.

EXHIBIT 19-7
Payments on additional $1000 with purchase of the asset

Year (1)	Principal payment (2)	Interest payment (3)	Total payment [(2) + (3)] (4)
1	$167	$90	$257
2	182	75	257
3	198	59	257
4	216	41	257
5	237	21	258[a]

[a] To amortize the debt with *equal* installments would require $257.10 per year.

The asset can also be leased for $550 per year, in which case the data in Exhibit 19-6 apply (see page 608). With lease, the firm will *reduce* its debt by $1000 and firm debt payments will *fall* by the amounts shown in Exhibit 19-4 (see page 604). We are assuming for simplicity that the firm's marginal borrowing rate is 9 percent and therefore Exhibits 19-4 and 19-7 are the same; they both show debt payments associated with a $1000 debt repayable at 9 percent interest over a five-year period.

The firm will have $2000 more debt with purchase than with lease, but with lease the firm will have a $2000 lease obligation (see balance sheets A, B, and C on pages 604–605). The added debt payments on the $2000 debt equal the sum of the amounts in Exhibits 19-4 and 19-6; Exhibit 19-8 shows the added debt payments on the $2000 of debt. Column 5 of Exhibit 19-8 indicates the corporate tax savings due to the payment of debt interest. Each dollar of interest paid reduces corporate taxes by $1 times the corporate tax rate (here assumed to be 50 percent).

To compute the net advantage to leasing (NAL), we must look at the difference in firm cash flows with leasing and with purchase. If the asset is leased, there is no cash outlay at time 0 (when the asset is acquired); however, if the asset is purchased, there is a net current cash outlay of $1800, the purchase price of the asset ($2000) *minus* the $200 investment tax credit on the asset. Therefore, the time 0 benefit from leasing the asset equals

Time 0 advantage of leasing = $1800

The *future* cash flow differences between leasing and purchase for years 1 through 5 can be determined by comparing Exhibits 19-5 and 19-6 (pages 606 and 608). Exhibit 19-9 shows the differences between the aftertax cash flows with lease and purchase. Column 7 is the difference between the firm's cash flow with lease and with purchase; since the figures are all

---

EXHIBIT 19-8
Payments on added $2000 debt with asset purchase

Year (1)	Principal payment (2)	Interest payment (3)	Total payment [(2) + (3)] (4)	Firm tax savings due to interest tax deductibility [tax rate × (3)] (5)
1	$334	$180	$514	$90
2	364	150	514	75
3	396	118	514	59
4	432	82	514	41
5	474	42	516[a]	21

[a] To amortize the debt with *equal* installments would require $514.20 per year.

EXHIBIT 19-9
Computation of the net advantage to leasing

Year (1)	Added aftertax operating expenses with purchase[a] (2)	Depreciation tax savings with purchase[b] (3)	Aftertax salvage value (4)	Aftertax lease rental[c] (5)	Interest tax savings with purchase[d] (6)	Added cash flow with lease [(2) − (3) − (4) − (5) − (6)] (7)	9.02% Present value factor (8)	Present value [(7) × (8)] (9)
1	$50	$200		$275	$90	$(515)	0.9173	$ (472)
2	50	200		275	75	(500)	0.8414	(421)
3	50	200		275	59	(484)	0.7718	(374)
4	50	200		275	41	(466)	0.7079	(330)
5	50	200	$100	275	21	(546)	0.6493	(354)
								$(1,951)

Net advantage to leasing = $1,800 − $1,951 = −$151 = −$151 < 0; therefore, purchase is preferable to lease.

[a] Equal to (1 − tax rate) × (col. 3 of Exhibit 19-6 *minus* col. 3 of Exhibit 19-5).
[b] Equal to (tax rate) × (col. 4 of Exhibit 19-2).
[c] Equal to (1 − tax rate) × (col. 4 of Exhibit 19-6).
[d] Equal to col. 5 of Exhibit 19-8.

negative, firm cash flow is smaller with lease than with purchase in years 1 through 5. The $1800 time 0 benefit with lease therefore requires a future sacrifice in years 1 through 5. To compute the NAL, we first determine the present value of col. 7 (which equals − $1951); the − $1951 means that the present value of the *future* firm aftertax cash flows with leasing is $1951 *less* than the present value of the *future* aftertax cash flows with purchase. We therefore deduct the $1951 from the $1800 to compute the NAL, implying an NAL of − $151. Leasing is therefore inferior to purchase since it produces a present value of aftertax cash flows which is $151 less than with purchase. This is the same as the result arrived at in Appendix 19A (see page 607).

How did we arrive at the 9.02 percent discount rate in col. 8 of Exhibit 19-9 which we used to compute the present value? The 9.02 percent rate is that rate which is appropriate given the risk of the cash flow in col. 7. This discount rate must produce the same $151 advantage with purchase as was calculated in Appendix 19A since the Appendix 19A approach and the NAL approach must be consistent with one another. An alternative approach for computing the present value of the cash flows in Exhibit 19-9 is to discount each of cols. 2, 3, 4, 5, and 6 separately, using the rate appropriate to the risk of the cash flow being discounted. If the discount rates selected are correct, the NAL must equal the − $151 implied by the Exhibit 19-5 and 19-6 computations (assuming, of course, that the discount rates used in Exhibits 19-5 and 19-6 are correct). In practice, selecting the proper discount rate for computing a present value is very difficult and usually a good ballpark estimate is the best that can be hoped for.

COMMON STOCK

This chapter discusses in detail the rights of shareholders. Management is concerned with this issue because it is the shareholder whom management is supposed to serve. Furthermore, in raising additional capital through new share sales, the rights accorded the new shareholders determine both the price received for the new shares and the "piece of the pie" that is being given away to the new shareholders. This issue is therefore relevant to corporate financing decisions, e.g., in choosing between selling new shares and borrowing the funds instead.

It should be pointed out that we have already discussed many features of common stock. In Chapters 1 and 2 we defined the stockholders as the firm's owners and described the financial institutions through which shares are traded. Chapter 3 described some of the characteristics of a corporation and the taxation of stockholder income. Chapter 10 examined common stock financing and Chapter 11 concerned dividend policy. What we have not yet looked at are the various rights and privileges associated with share ownership. The first part of this chapter discusses this topic from the standpoint of the shareholder. Later we consider some additional problems and considerations important to management decisions.

RIGHTS AND PRIVILEGES OF STOCKHOLDERS

Income

The right of shareholders to the firm's income is referred to as **residual**; that is, shareholders receive what is left after all other investors in the firm have been paid. For example, if income before taxes and interest on debt is $100,000, and if interest on debt is $60,000, stockholders receive before-tax earnings in the current period of $40,000 ($100,000 − $60,000 = $40,000). However, if interest on debt is $120,000, stockholders incur a loss of $20,000 ($100,000 − $120,000 = −$20,000). Of course, if losses are great enough, the firm may become bankrupt and even the bondholders may not receive all that is due to them; in this case, stockholders lose their entire investment. But being in a residual position also has advantages. If the firm earns $500,000 during the current period, bondholders receive only their fixed interest, say, $60,000, and stockholders receive $440,000. Along with the greater risk of a residual interest goes the chance of a greater reward. This is the concept of financial leverage, which was discussed in Chapters 10 and 13.

The income to stockholders may be retained by the firm or be paid out as dividends. Dividends are paid after they are declared by the board of directors. In most cases, the firm's income exceeds the dividends and some of the period's aftertax income is retained by the firm. The retention causes an increase in the value of the firm's shares. For example, if the firm earns $200,000 during the year and pays dividends of $120,000, the value of the firm's shares will rise by $80,000 ($200,000 − $120,000 = $80,000).[1] The

---

[1] In reality, share prices will probably not rise by exactly $80,000. This is so because of differential taxes on capital gains and dividends. Furthermore, note that when it is stated here that share values will rise by $80,000, this means that the retained earnings will have an upward effect on share prices of $80,000. Factors other than current retained earnings (e.g., general stock price trends, expectations about the firm's future earnings) may also be affecting share values, causing them to rise by more or less than $80,000.

shareholders have therefore received benefits in two forms: first, dividends of $120,000, and second, an increase in the value of their shares (a capital gain).[2] Companies that reinvest a large fraction of their earnings will have low dividend payments relative to earnings but will have higher than average share value increases each year; that is, more income to shareholders will be in the form of capital gains.

Control

In theory, stockholders control the firm through their right to elect the board of directors of the corporation. The board of directors, in turn, appoints the members of the management who supervise the daily operations of the company. In practice, stockholder control is somewhat limited. Most often, management selects the board of directors. At the time of the election, management sends stockholders proxy statements requesting that the shareholders assign to management the right to vote their stock. Of course, shareholders may give their proxies to some outside dissident group; however, this is the exception rather than the rule. Stockholders who neither appear at the stockholders meeting nor give their proxies to someone else to vote do not exercise their right to vote, and those who do vote consequently elect the new board of directors. Shareholders usually sign and return the proxies they have received from existing management or simply fail to exercise their vote. Only a small fraction of stockholders attend most annual meetings. As a result, management usually retains control of the corporation and chooses the board of directors.[3] Effective control of a corporation generally does not require even 50 percent ownership of the outstanding common stock. The inertia or apathy of shareholders often ensures that a minority position retains control. Successful takeover by an outsider group is usually possible only after existing management has clearly mismanaged the company for an extended period of time. A more detailed description of the voting process is presented later in this chapter.

Some firms have both voting and nonvoting common stock. For example, the class A common stock may have the right to vote, whereas the class B common stock may not. The nonvoting stock may or may not have an identical claim to dividends, income, and assets as the voting shares. Even if the different classes of stock differ only in voting rights, the nonvoting shares usually have a slightly lower market value since the voting privilege is a valuable right.

---

[2] An increase in the price of a stockholder's shares is referred to as capital gain whether or not the shares are sold by the stockholder. The capital gain is referred to as **realized** if the shares are sold for cash (the gain is realized in the form of cash).

[3] Rebelling against the annual stockholders meeting as a waste of time and money, some years ago J. B. Fuqua, chairman of Fuqua Industries, polled his stockholders on their reaction to the idea of discontinuing such meetings. He received 99 percent support. Although Delaware law would have allowed discontinuing the annual meetings, they are required by the New York Stock Exchange for all listed firms. So the meetings continue even though no more than a dozen of the Fuqua shareholders (out of 18,000) generally attend.

The **preemptive right** is the right of existing stockholders to maintain their share of the ownership of the corporation by purchasing any new shares issued by the corporation. For example, if the corporation has outstanding 100,000 shares of common stock and plans to issue 50,000 new shares, a stockholder owning 100 of the 100,000 outstanding shares (0.1 percent) will have the right to purchase 50 of the 50,000 new shares (0.1 percent) before those new shares are offered to anyone else.

Common law provides for the preemptive right. However, some states deny the preemptive right by statute unless it is specifically included in the corporate charter; in other states, the preemptive right exists unless denied under the corporate charter. If the firm issues securities that are convertible into common stock, existing shareholders are generally permitted under the preemptive right to purchase these convertible securities before they are offered to outsiders. Even when the preemptive right exists, it does not apply to new common stock which is used as payment for property or as payment in a merger acquisition, and does not apply to the resale of treasury stock (that is, the sale of stock which was previously bought back by the firm from shareholders) or to the issuance of stock to employees (for example, under a stock option plan). Stockholders may waive the preemptive right upon management's request, for example, if the preemptive right is a hindrance to issuing new shares.

The preemptive right is an important protection to shareholders. Without this right, management could issue stock to individuals favorably inclined to management and thereby retain control of the company. The preemptive right also protects shareholders against dilution of their financial interest in the firm. *If additional shares are sold to new stockholders at a price below the stock's current market price, owners of the old shares will suffer a fall in the market value of their holdings.* For example, assume a firm with 100,000 shares of common stock but no bonds outstanding and a market value of $10 per share; the market value of the firm is therefore $1 million (100,000 × $10). The firm is to issue 50,000 new shares at $4 per share, thereby raising $200,000 of new capital. After issuance of the new stock, the value of the firm is approximately $1,200,000 ($1,000,000 + $200,000 raised by issuing new stock) and there are 150,000 shares outstanding. The market value per share of the stock is $8 ($1,200,000 divided by 150,000 shares = $8) instead of the preissuance price of $10. The original stockholders lose $2 per share of stock owned. The preemptive right ensures that current stockholders get the first chance to buy any new shares at $4 per share. The procedure by which stockholders exercise the preemptive right is discussed below in the section on stock rights.

A stockholder has the right to obtain information from management regarding the firm's operations. However, this right is not unlimited, and applies only if the release of such information will not injure the competitive position of the firm. This limitation is imposed in order to protect other stockholders. A stockholder who feels that management is withholding information about its malfeasance or gross negligence in managing the company may take the case to the courts. This is an example of the general rule that management's control is protected unless a determined (and often very expensive) effort is undertaken to reduce or eliminate that control.

Claim on Assets under Bankruptcy

The stockholders' right to the firm's assets is residual. Other claimants (e.g., creditors and preferred stockholders) have a prior claim to the company's assets. If the firm fails to make required interest and principal payments to creditors, control of the firm may shift from shareholders to creditors. The firm's assets may be sold and the creditors paid off, or the firm may continue to be operated under court supervision until creditor claims have been met.

Right to Transfer Shares

In the discussion of business organizations in Chapter 3, we noted that one advantage of the corporation is the ease with which a shareholder can transfer his or her ownership claim to another investor. No permission is required from management or from other stockholders if a particular shareholder wishes to sell his or her shares. Furthermore, in contrast to sole proprietorships or partnerships, the corporation continues to exist regardless of any changes in ownership because of transfers of stock by shareholders. A shareholder may directly sell his or her stock to another party merely by signing that stock (on the back of the certificate) over to the buyer. If the stock is publicly traded, the shareholder may also transfer the stock through a broker. The purchaser of the stock (or the broker) sends the stock certificate, which has been transferred to the purchaser, to a transfer agent representing the corporation. The transfer agent then issues a new certificate under the name of the purchaser so that the new owner may be listed on the firm's books as the owner of record. The new shareholder is now entitled to receive dividends on the shares and has all the rights and privileges associated with stock ownership.

Limited Liability

Because the corporation is a distinct entity under the law, a stockholder is not liable for the debts of the corporation. In contrast, the owner of a sole proprietorship or a general partner of a partnership would be personally liable for the debts of the business.

This corporate shield between the stockholder and the firm's creditors, however, is not impenetrable in all cases. If the corporation is used by its stockholders for illegal or morally reprehensible purposes, the stockholders may become liable for the *corporation's acts*. However, for large corporations, this qualification is of less significance, and shareholders are generally protected from liability for the firm's debt.

STOCKHOLDER VOTING

We noted earlier that one of the rights of stockholders is to elect the board of directors of the corporation. Two types of voting systems are in general use—majority rule and cumulative voting.

Unless otherwise provided by statute or by the corporate charter, the will of the majority of those voting is effective in electing the board of directors. Each share entitles its owner to one vote; an owner of 100 shares has 100 votes. Each position on the board of directors is voted on individually. Therefore, if six positions were to be filled, an owner of 100 shares would cast 100 votes for a candidate for position 1, 100 votes for a candidate for position 2, etc. Thus, if the firm has 100,000 shares outstanding, a group with 50,001 shares acting together could elect the candidate it prefers for each position and prevent election of any directors by the minority. For this reason an alternative voting system has evolved, one which gives the minority a greater opportunity for representation on the board. This system is cumulative voting.

Under cumulative voting each shareholder receives a number of votes equal to the number of his or her shares times the number of directors to be elected. For example, if six directors were to be elected, a shareholder with 100 shares would have 600 votes. A shareholder's votes may be applied in support of one candidate or they may be spread over a number of candidates. With six directors to be elected, a shareholder with 600 votes could cast all 600 votes for a given candidate, or say, 400 votes for one candidate and 200 for a second candidate, etc. Under both the majority rule and cumulative voting systems, those candidates receiving the most votes are the ones elected to the board of directors. If six positions on the board were to be filled, and there were twelve candidates, the six candidates with the most votes would win. However, whereas under the majority rule system a majority is able to elect all members of the board, under cumulative voting a significant minority is assured of at least some representation on the board, if it properly distributes its votes among the candidates.

To illustrate the differences between the majority rule and cumulative voting systems, assume that a firm has five directors to be elected and twelve candidates seeking election. Suppose that the firm has a total of 10,000 shares outstanding. Since there are five directorship openings, each share of stock is entitled to five votes under the cumulative voting method; an owner of 100 shares has 500 votes. An owner of 100 shares could distribute all 500 votes in any manner between the twelve candidates, e.g., 50 votes for each of candidates 1 through 10, or all 500 votes for candidate 1.

The number of shares that must be controlled in order to guarantee the election of a particular number of directors can be calculated by the following formula:

$$\text{Number of shares needed to elect desired number of directors} = \frac{n \times d}{D + 1} + 1 \tag{20-1}$$

where n = total number of firm shares outstanding

$\quad\quad d$ = number of directors stockholders desire to elect

$\quad\quad D$ = total number of directors to be elected

Using this equation in the above example, in order for a group of share-holders to be sure of being able to elect one director it would have to have 1667 shares,[4] since

$$\frac{10{,}000 \times 1}{5 + 1} + 1 = 1667\tfrac{2}{3} \text{ or } 1667$$

If the group were to vote its 1667 shares for one candidate (e.g., for candidate 6), then the group would be assured of electing that candidate regardless of how the majority group (which owns the remaining 8333 shares) were to cast its votes. In order to elect two directors, the minority group would have to have 3334 shares.[5] With 3334 shares, the minority group would have 16,670 (5 × 3334) votes. If it were to cast exactly half its votes for candidate 6 and half of its votes for candidate 7, it would be assured of electing these two candidates regardless of how the majority voted (the majority would own the remaining 6666 shares and therefore have 5 × 6666, or 33,330, votes).[6] Exhibit 20-1 illustrates this situation for the majority rule and cumulative voting systems. We assume that the majority group prefers candidates 1 through 5 and that the minority group prefers candidates 6 through 10. Under the majority rule system, the majority with 6666 shares would be able to elect all five directors.

ISSUING NEW SHARES

We noted in Chapters 10 and 18 that, to finance company operations, the firm may issue new shares of stock. In this section we will examine how the firm records the stock issuance on its books and how **par value** differs from a stock's market value. We will then look at the use of stock rights and its implications for the company's stockholders.

Recording a Stock Issue

When a company issues new shares it ordinarily receives, in payment, cash from the investors buying those shares. To show how this is recorded by the firm, assume that Infotex, Inc., has issued 1 million new shares at $11 per share (the price paid by those buying the stock) and that the flotation costs (fees to investment bankers) are $1 million. The net proceeds of Infotex from the sale are $10 million. On its books, Infotex records the sale by increasing

---

[4] Fractions are dropped in the equation.

[5] Using the formula $[(10{,}000 \times 2)/(5 + 1)] + 1 = 3334\tfrac{1}{3}$, that is, 3334 shares by rounding off the fraction.

[6] If we wished to know how many directors we could elect with a given number of shares owned, rearranging the terms in the equation we find that

$$\text{Number of directors that can be elected with shares owned} = \frac{(q - 1) \times (D + 1)}{n}$$

where q is the number of shares owned. A stockholder owning 4000 of the 10,000 shares outstanding could therefore elect two directors since

$$\frac{(4000 - 1) \times (5 + 1)}{10{,}000} = 2.4 \text{ or } 2 \text{ directors}$$

EXHIBIT 20-1

Comparison of majority rule and cumulative voting systems

Candidate	Majority rule		Cumulative voting	
	Votes	Election results	Votes	Election results
1	6,666	Elected	6,667	Elected
2	6,666	Elected	6,667	Elected
3	6,666	Elected	6,667	Elected
4	6,666	Elected	6,665	Not elected
5	6,666	Elected	6,664	Not elected
6	3,334	Not elected	8,335	Elected
7	3,334	Not elected	8,335	Elected
8	3,334	Not elected	0	Not elected
9	3,334	Not elected	0	Not elected
10	3,334	Not elected	0	Not elected
11	0	Not elected	0	Not elected
12	0	Not elected	0	Not elected

Note: The majority group casts all its votes for candidates 1 through 5; the votes for the other candidates are cast by the minority group.

both cash and stockholders' equity by $10 million. If the stock has a par value (explained below) of, say, $5 per share, the $10 million increase in stockholders' equity is made up of a $5 million rise in each of the par value and paid-in surplus on the balance sheet. Paid-in surplus is the amount above par value received by a corporation for shares it sells. Exhibit 20-2 shows the balance sheet changes for Infotex from the stock sales assuming that the stock has a par value of $5 per share.

Par value is a per share amount assigned to the corporation's stock by the board of directors. The use of a par value is meant to protect creditors, since in many states the law requires that corporations not make payments to stockholders which reduce shareholders' equity below the total par value of outstanding shares.[7] For example, Infotex cannot reduce stockholders' equity below $20 million after the new shares are issued since this is the total par value of Infotex stock (see Exhibit 20-2).

In some states, corporations are required to set a "stated value" per share rather than a par value per share. As with par value, the firm is not permitted to pay dividends which reduce owners' equity below its stated value (stated value per share times the number of shares outstanding).

A distinction should be made between par or stated value and the

---

[7] Shareholders' equity (or the firm's net worth) consists of paid-in capital (what stockholders paid the firm in purchasing the shares) plus retained earnings. This is equal to the firm's assets minus liabilities.

market value of the shares when issued. Generally, the firm will issue new shares at a market price significantly above par or stated value. Except for the restriction placed upon payments to shareholders described above, it is the market price of the shares upon issue (the amount received by the firm for issuing the stock, ignoring flotation costs) that is of significance to shareholders and management. This market price is what new investors are willing to pay for the firm's shares, and is what management feels is at least a fair payment for the ownership interest being sold to those investors. Generally, it will be market price and not par or stated value that will be of interest in analyzing the financial decisions of the firm.

Rights Offerings

Earlier in the chapter we explained that preemptive rights protect the shareholder's position in the firm. If preemptive rights exist, the corporation must issue **rights** (technically called stock subscription warrants) to existing stockholders when the firm is raising capital through the sale of new shares of common stock. A right is an option to purchase stock at the issue price (also called the subscription price or exercise price) of the new shares. One right is issued for each share of currently outstanding common stock; however, the number of rights needed to purchase a new share depends on the terms of the rights offering. Let's examine how the financial manager plans the rights offering.

Planning the Rights Offering Suppose that Crown, Inc., is considering a rights offering and that the relevant data are as follows:

EXHIBIT 20-2
Recording the issuance of new shares by Infotex, Inc.

	Balance sheet		Change in balance sheet figures
	Before new shares are issued	After new shares are issued	
Assets			
Cash	$ 5,000,000	$15,000,000	$10,000,000
Other assets..............	60,000,000	60,000,000	0
Total assets	$65,000,000	$75,000,000	$10,000,000
Liabilities and owners' equity			
Liabilities	$30,000,000	$30,000,000	
Owners' equity			
Par value...............	15,000,000	20,000,000	$ 5,000,000
Paid-in surplus	10,000,000	15,000,000	5,000,000
Retained earnings........	10,000,000	10,000,000	0
Total liabilities and owners' equity..............	$65,000,000	$75,000,000	$10,000,000

Shares outstanding	1,000,000
Market price per share	$25
Total value of shares outstanding (1,000,000 shares $\times$ $25)	$25,000,000
Funds to be raised	$5,000,000

In order to ensure that all rights are exercised, the firm will set the subscription price for the new shares at a level somewhat below the market price of $25. If the exercise price were set near $25, say, $24, a small decline in the stock's market price (e.g., to $23) would prevent any rights from being exercised (since no one would pay $24 for a share selling in the market at $23). Therefore, Crown's manager sets the subscription price for new shares at $20. Since the firm plans to raise $5 million in new funds and will receive $20 per new share, it follows that

$$\text{Number of new shares} = \frac{\text{funds to be raised}}{\text{subscription price per new share}}$$

$$= \frac{\$5,000,000}{\$20 \text{ per new share}} = 250,000 \text{ new shares}$$

We know that one right is issued on each of the 1 million original shares. Since the firm wishes to sell only 250,000 new shares, if all rights are to be surrendered in obtaining new shares, the firm must require that four rights be surrendered for each new share purchased. That is,

$$\frac{\text{Number of rights}}{\text{(to buy a new share)}} = \frac{\text{number of rights issued}}{\text{number of new shares}}$$

$$= \frac{1,000,000 \text{ rights}}{250,000 \text{ new shares}} = 4 \text{ rights per new share}$$

Therefore, a stockholder must surrender four rights plus pay the subscription price of $20 to obtain one new share.

Effects of a Rights Offering

The effect of a rights offering on the price of the firm's stock is stated in Exhibit 20-3 and illustrated in Figure 20-1. On March 15, Crown, Inc., announces that rights will be issued on June 15 to all shareholders of record

---

EXHIBIT 20-3
Price per share before and after the rights offering

A.	Value of firm's shares before rights offering	$25,000,000
B.	Number of shares outstanding before offering	1,000,000
C.	Value per share before rights offering [A/B]	$25
D.	Cash proceeds from rights offering added to firm's assets	$5,000,000
E.	Value of firm's shares after rights offering [A + D]	$30,000,000
F.	Number of shares outstanding after offering	1,250,000
G.	Value per share after rights offering [E/F]	$24

on May 15 (those recorded on the company's books on May 15 as share-holders). However, there is a delay between the date of a stock sale transaction and the date the transaction is recorded on the corporation's books. Anyone owning the stock on May 8 (five business days before May 15) will still be the stockholder of record on May 15 and will be entitled to the rights. Therefore, a buyer of the firm's stock on or before May 8 will buy the stock **rights-on** and will receive the rights; a buyer on May 9 or thereafter will buy the stock **rights-off** or **ex-rights** and will not receive the rights. Since each share of stock entitles the owner to one right, *the rights-on price of a share is equal to the rights-off price plus the value of a right.* In the example, the value of a right is $1 (the computation is explained below). This is illustrated in Figure 20-1.

What is the market value of a right and the impact on the shareholder of the rights offering? The right has a value because of the opportunity it provides to purchase the firm's shares at less than the stock's market value. The value of a new share received upon exercising the right will take into account that

1 There are 25 percent more shares outstanding after the new stock issue than before the issue.
2 The firm receives $5 million from selling the new shares.

FIGURE 20-1

Price per share with a rights offering announced on March 15. The last day that the stock sells rights-on (sells at $25) is May 8; on May 9, the stock sells rights-off (sells at $24).

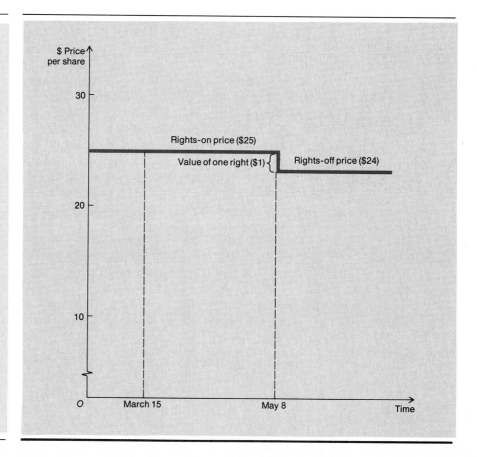

Before the rights offering, the value of each share of stock was $25 (see Exhibit 20-3). If we assume that the added $5 million received for the stock raises the total value of the shareholders' interest by $5 million, then the value of all the firm's stock will increase from $25 million to $30 million. Since the rights offering raises the number of shares to 1,250,000, the new price per share will be $24 ($30 million divided by 1,250,000 shares = $24). The new share price we are referring to here is the market value of a share *after* the new shares are issued (this is the rights-off or ex-rights value referred to earlier).

Now let us determine the value of a right. It takes four rights plus $20 to buy a new share with a value of $24. What are the four rights worth? The answer is $4, since with four rights a buyer of a new share saves $4 (i.e., only pays $20 for a share worth $24); one right is therefore worth $1. We consequently have a formula for determining the value of a right:[8]

$$\text{Value of one right} = \frac{\left(\begin{array}{c}\text{market price of one}\\ \text{share rights-off}\end{array}\right) - (\text{subscription price})}{\begin{array}{c}\text{number of rights required to}\\ \text{obtain one new share}\end{array}}$$

$$= \frac{\$24 - \$20}{4} = \$1$$

Notice that, in Figure 20-1, as a share of stock goes from rights-on to rights-off status on May 9, the value of the share falls by the $1 value of the right.

Value of a Rights Offering to Shareholders Clearly, stockholders should not simply let their rights expire without selling or exercising them. By exercising rights, stockholders can acquire shares at a price ($20 in the example) less than a share's market value ($24). By exercising rights, stockholders can make a $4 profit per share by buying the stock at $20 and selling each share for $24. Or stockholders can simply sell their rights for $4 (see above discussion). Does this imply that a rights offering makes the shareholder richer? The answer is no. It is easy to show that the rights offering makes the shareholder neither better off nor worse off *as long as the rights do not expire without being exercised or sold.* In fact, the shareholder can always sell the appropriate number of his or her rights and use the proceeds to exercise the remaining rights and be exactly in the same position as before the rights offering. By way of illustration, assume in the example above that investor George Goodwin owns 600 shares of Crown, Inc., stock before the rights offering. The value of his portfolio before the rights offering is $15,000 (600 shares × $25 per share = $15,000). Since Goodwin owns 600 shares, he receives 600 rights. Assume that Goodwin sells 500 of his rights

---

[8] The value of a right can also be expressed in terms of the rights-on value of the stock:

$$\text{Value of one right} = \frac{(\text{market price of one share rights-on}) - (\text{subscription price})}{(\text{number of rights required to purchase one share}) + 1}$$

$$= \frac{\$25 - \$20}{4 + 1} = \$1$$

See the text discussion of rights-on value.

for $500. He has 100 rights remaining and can purchase 25 new shares (four rights per new share are required) for $20 each (subscription price); the total cash outlay for the twenty-five new shares is $500 (25 × $20). The $500 used to purchase the new shares is exactly the proceeds he received from selling 500 rights. Goodwin now has a total of 625 shares, each worth $24 (rights-off value); just as before the rights offering, his portfolio is worth $15,000 (625 shares × $24).[9]

Of course, Goodwin can reduce the value of his holdings in the firm by selling his rights. On the other hand, if he feels that the firm is a good investment, he might increase his investment in the firm by exercising all his rights.[10] Given the above relationships, he will not be provided with any improved selling or buying opportunities in the firm's stock merely as a result of the rights offering.

The point of the above example is that the rights offering itself does not produce any costs or benefits for the shareholders (except for any lower underwriting fees with a rights offering relative to a public offering; this is discussed in the next section). If the firm were to invest the new funds in an exceptionally profitable venture (earning more than the firm's cost of capital), shareholders would benefit. However, the benefit in this case is due to the profitability of the investment and not to the rights offering. The same benefit could be obtained by selling shares to outsiders (at a price which reflects the share's true value) and then making the investment. The resulting price behavior of the stock after the offering will depend upon the impact of the investment on the future earnings of the firm.

It was noted earlier that the preemptive right protects current shareholders from a dilution of their investment and control. It does this by preventing management from selling new shares to outsiders for less than their true worth.[11] However, even without the preemptive right the firm could avoid a dilution of shareholders' investment by placing a price on new shares *sufficiently high to reflect their true worth.* Outsiders buying the new stock would pay for what they get and the old shareholders need suffer in no way. Therefore, if management is acting in the interests of shareholders and sells new shares for their true value, the preemptive right is not

---

[9] The sale of 500 rights and exercise of 100 rights (purchase of 25 new shares with a cash payment plus 4 rights per new share) reduces the stockholder's percentage ownership of the firm from 0.6 percent (600 shares owned/100,000 shares originally outstanding) to 0.5 percent (625 shares/125,000 shares outstanding after the rights offering). However, the value of the firm's shares has increased from $25 million to $30 million because of the $5 million raised by the firm under the rights offering. The shareholder's portfolio therefore does not change in value (0.006 × $25,000,000 = 0.005 × $30,000,000).

[10] If Goodwin exercises all his rights (sells none of them), he must invest an additional $3000 ($3000 = 150 shares × $20 per share) but will continue to own 0.6 percent of the firm's shares (600 shares out of 100,000 before the rights offering and 750 shares out of 125,000 after the offering). The value of Goodwin's portfolio of shares rises from $15,000 (600 shares × $25 per share) to $18,000 (750 shares × $24 per share), an increase of $3000, which is exactly the additional amount invested in the firm. There is therefore no net gain for the investor.

[11] In the example, if the firm had simply sold new shares to outside investors for $20 per share without issuing rights to old shareholders, old shareholders would have suffered a loss of $1 per share owned (since the stock price fell from $25 to $24 per share).

necessary. The right exists *as a protection to shareholders in those instances in which management is not acting in good faith.*

The empirical evidence bears out what we have said. Studies by Smith (of the United States stock market) and Marsh (of the British stock market) show that the rights offering itself does not cause a significant change in the rights-on value of the share (the rights-off value plus the value of the right), that is, shareholders are neither benefited nor hurt by the rights offering.[12] This was found to be true regardless of the subscription price of the new shares (i.e., regardless of the discount offered to new shareholders). Another interesting finding was that the success of a rights offering is not dependent on whether the stock market is rising or falling.

Advantages of Rights Offerings   In addition to ensuring that the position of current shareholders is not jeopardized, external equity financing via a rights offering has certain advantages. Rights offerings are generally much less expensive in terms of brokerage and underwriting fees than is a public sale of stock. This is a real saving to the firm and its shareholders. Since the shares in a rights offering are sold directly to investors who have a favorable view of the firm's prospects (since they are willingly the firm's current shareholders), the rights method is a low-cost means of offering the new shares to a receptive market. A public offering is a more costly and indirect means of reaching potential buyers. With a rights offering, even if some of the existing shareholders sell their rights, a large percentage of them generally exercise the rights and buy additional shares of the firm. The costs of issuance to the firm under a rights offering may be less than half the flotation costs involved in a public issue.

Rights also provide shareholders with the opportunity to borrow a high proportion of their investment in the new shares. The margin requirement for purchasing shares under a rights offering is generally less stringent than the requirement for purchasing other listed shares.[13] For example, whereas an investor might be allowed to borrow only up to 50 percent of the funds used to buy other listed shares, 70 percent might be allowed for purchasing shares under a rights offering. This provides the investor with a wider range of alternatives in building a portfolio.

THE LISTING OF STOCK

A corporation is referred to as **closely held** if it has relatively few shareholders. An existing group of shareholders may wish to keep the company closely held in order to maintain privacy or to retain full control over operations (and not be answerable to a dissident group of stockholders). However, if a firm has 500 or more shareholders and total assets in excess of

---

[12] See C. W. Smith, "Alternative Methods for Raising Capital: Rights versus Underwritten Offerings," *Journal of Financial Economics*, 5 (December 1977), pp. 273–307; P. R. Marsh, "Equity Rights Issues and the Efficiency of the UK Stock Market," *Journal of Finance*, 34 (September 1979), pp. 839–862.

[13] The Federal Reserve Board sets a limit on the percentage of the purchase price of a listed stock that one can finance with borrowing. Buying with funds that are in part or wholly borrowed is known as buying **on margin**.

$1 million (both conditions must apply), it must publicly disclose its financial position by filing an annual statement with the SEC.[14]

The shares of a **publicly held** corporation are owned by the general public. These shares are traded publicly in the over-the-counter market or on one of the thirteen organized exchanges in the United States. From the standpoint of the firm, it is debatable whether a listing provides significant gains. As was explained in Chapter 2, both over-the-counter and listed stock transactions usually involve brokers who act as intermediaries between buyers and sellers of the stock. SEC regulations are essentially the same for listed and unlisted companies. One might expect a benefit from listing since some financial institutions are permitted (under state laws) to own only listed stocks, and since listed securities enjoy somewhat greater publicity (e.g., trading volume in the stock and price quotations are published in more newspapers if the stock is listed). However, it is not clear from the empirical evidence that the market price of a company's stock is enhanced merely because it is listed on an exchange.[15]

If a firm lists its stock, it must file papers with the exchange and with the SEC. The various exchanges have minimum listing requirements pertaining to assets, earnings, number of shares outstanding, and number of shareholders. The SEC requires that the firm publish both quarterly earnings reports and annual overall financial statements.

SUMMARY

Ownership of common stock entitles the stockholders to the following:

To receive the residual portion (after other investors, e.g., creditors, are paid) of the firm's income

To elect the board of directors

In many cases, to purchase any new firm shares before they are sold to outsiders (preemptive right)

To inspect the company's books

To transfer their shares

To be immune from liability to the corporation's creditors

To own a residual claim to the firm's assets in the event of liquidation

The election of the board of directors may be conducted under the majority rule or cumulative voting procedures. Under the majority rule, ownership of a majority of the shares ensures the power to elect the entire board, whereas under the cumulative voting method votes are distributed so that a significant minority is assured of representation on the board.

The firm's decision with regard to the timing and size of a new stock

---

[14] If the company has securities that are convertible to stock, owners of the convertible securities are added to the number of shareholders to determine whether the minimum of 500 shareholders is met (e.g., 400 stockholders and 100 owners of bonds convertible into stock would satisfy the requirement).

[15] See J. C. Van Horne, "New Listings and Their Price Behavior," *Journal of Finance* (September 1970), pp. 783–794.

issue will depend upon the productivity of the funds to the firm and the cost of the funds. When any new shares are issued for sale, the existence of the stockholders' preemptive right gives stockholders the opportunity to buy the new shares before they are issued to outsiders. For each share of stock already owned, the shareholder receives one right.

The stockholder can exercise the rights and buy additional shares of stock by surrendering the rights and paying a stipulated price for each new share purchased. The rights can also be sold to someone else who may then exercise them. The preemptive right and the use of rights in issuing new shares have two principal advantages. First, the right protects the shareholder against management's issuing new stock to outsiders at a price below its reasonable value. Second, in terms of flotation costs, the use of rights is a more economical method than a public offering.

A publicly held corporation—that is, one that is owned by many stockholders—may have its stock traded on the over-the-counter market or on an organized exchange. Securities traded on an exchange are referred to as listed. Listing of a stock requires fulfillment of both exchange and SEC requirements.

QUESTIONS

1. Itemize the rights of common stockholders. For each right you itemize, indicate whether it invariably attaches to common stock or its inclusion depends upon the terms of the stock offering, which vary from one stock to another.

2. "As an investor in a firm's common stock, I am really interested in only one thing, namely, that I get a rate of return consistent with the level of risk I assume. The management of a company cannot do anything more for me than that, so all this business about the rights and privileges of stockholders mentioned at the very beginning of the chapter is just so much baloney." Evaluate this statement.

3. "If an unprofitable company wishes to issue additional shares, no matter what provisions the shares contain in the contract, the shares are not likely to have much value." Comment on the validity of this statement.

4. Explain the advantages and disadvantages of having a residual claim on the income of the firm.

5. If a firm earns $200,000 and retains half of it, how much would you expect the value of its shares to increase assuming there are no other influences except earnings retention on the value of the shares?

6. What is a proxy statement?

7. American Telephone & Telegraph Company has over 3 million shareholders, no one of whom owns more than one-tenth of one percent of the outstanding shares. Of what value do you think the voting "privilege" is to each of these shareholders? Explain fully.

8. Elwood Corporation, a closely held computer manufacturing firm located in Issaquah, Washington, has fifteen shareholders. The company is incorporated in the state of Washington, and the one

shareholder who owns more than 51 percent of the voting shares controls the firm. Of what value is the voting right in this case? Explain fully.

9 A shareholder of Quantum Corporation can purchase under a rights offering ten shares of Quantum stock for $10 per share, $2 per share below the current $12 per share market price. Does this mean that the shareholder's wealth is greater with than without the rights offering? Explain.

10 Of what value is the preemptive right provision in common shareholder agreements?

11 Differentiate between majority rule voting and cumulative voting.

12 What relationship, if any, exists between par value and market value? Explain fully.

13 What is a "shareholder of record"? If you sell your Miles Brewing Company stock on June 7, 1986, when do you cease to be a shareholder of record?

PROJECTS

1 Obtain from your state's secretary of state (or other appropriate official) information on the requirements for forming a corporation in your state and the rights and privileges of stockholders. Compare the provisions of your state law with those outlined in this chapter.

2 Obtain from a local stock brokerage firm or from financial publications (e.g., *Barron's*) data on a recent rights offering. Observe the behavior of the stock's price as the stock goes from a rights-on to a rights-off basis.

PROBLEMS

1 Oslo Logistics, Inc., has outstanding $15,000,000 in 10 percent long-term bonds (thirty years maturity) and 400,000 shares of common stock (with a current market value of $30 per share). Oslo pays taxes at the rate of 40 percent. Show the aftertax earnings per share for this corporation if earnings before interest and taxes are $6,000,000, are $2,000,000, and are $200,000. In the last case, explain how the bond obligation is paid.

2 Twain Corporation is having an election of directors. There are five directors to be elected. If there are 400,000 shares outstanding, how many shares are needed to ensure the ability to elect one director if Twain Corporation uses (a) majority rule voting and (b) cumulative voting? How many shares are needed to elect two directors under each method?

3 Vivaldi Silver, Inc., uses majority rule voting to elect its eight-member board of directors. Vivaldi has 2000 shareholders and 1 million shares outstanding. Two slates of directors are running for election this year. Slate A is preferred by 600 stockholders, who hold 600,000 of the 1 million outstanding shares. Slate B is preferred by 1400 shareholders, who hold 400,000 shares.

a How many votes are cast in all, assuming all votes are cast?

    b Which is the minority slate?

    c Can any of the minority slate be elected?

    d Show how votes will be cast for each position?

4 Suppose that Vivaldi Silver in problem **3** has instead a cumulative voting rule, and that the above-described contest for the board of directors takes place.

    a How many minority members can now be elected?

    b Show how the votes are cast for each position to achieve the result in *a*.

5 Below is the balance sheet of Rose Foods, Inc., before it issued 200,000 shares of new common stock at a price of $30 each. The underwriting fees aggregated 5 percent of the total sale. Show the net effect on the company's balance sheet of the sale of the new stock. Assume that the new stock has a par value of $5 per share.

Assets	
Cash	$ 7,000,000
Other assets	56,000,000
Total assets	$63,000,000
Liabilities and owners' equity	
Liabilities	$25,000,000
Owners' equity	
Comon stock ($5)	1,000,000
Paid-in surplus	5,000,000
Retained earnings	32,000,000
Total liabilities and owners' equity	$63,000,000

6 If Garbo Testing, Inc., issues 400,000 new shares of common stock to existing shareholders at a price of $50 per share, what would you expect the price of the common shares to be if it was $80 a share before the issue? There were 800,000 shares outstanding before the new shares were issued.

7 Carono Corporation plans to sell 100,000 shares of new stock to existing shareholders. It has 400,000 shares outstanding. The selling price of the new shares will be $30. The current market price of the outstanding shares is $40.

    a How many rights are needed to buy one new share?

    b What is the value of each right?

8 You own 150 shares of Java, Inc. The company decides to offer new shares to existing shareholders at the rate of one new share for each ten shares held. The current market price per share is $60. The subscription price is $55. What is the value of the right before the ex-rights date?

9 Abecedarian Corporation announced on August 2 a rights offering of 20,000 new shares at a subscription price of $41. The rights offering is for shareholders of record as of October 20, and the rights are to be issued on November 20. A buyer of the stock on or before October 13 is entitled to the rights, whereas a buyer on October 14 or thereafter is not (stock goes "ex-rights" on October 14, five *business days* before October 20). Three rights are required to purchase one new share and one right will be issued for each share outstanding on October 20. The market price of Abecedarian as of August 2 is $45. Assume there are no changes in the market value of the stock except those due to the rights offering.

a What is the value of one right?

b Can you infer how many shares are outstanding on October 20?

c Trace the market price of a share of Abecedarian from August 2 to November 20.

Long-term debt and preferred stock are often referred to as **fixed-i[ncome]
securities** because the firm promises the security owner a fixed a[nd]
income (fixed interest on the debt or fixed dividends on the preferred st[ock].
We see from Table 21-1 that long-term debt and preferred stock are imp[or]-
tant sources of capital. This chapter first discusses the general characteristics of long-term debt and then examines some novel forms of debt. The
last section describes preferred stock.

LONG-TERM DEBT

Debt is usually referred to as long-term if the term of the loan is at least ten
years. Although there are many forms of long-term debt, all debtholders are
guaranteed a prior claim over stockholders to the firm's income. That is,
*creditors receive what is contractually promised to them before stock-
holders receive anything.*

A **bond** is a long-term promissory note issued by a corporation. The
contract between the corporation and lender is referred to as the **bond
indenture.** The indenture ordinarily specifies that the creditor will receive

TABLE 21-1
New issues of securities by United States corporations (in millions)[a]

	Common stock	Preferred stock	Bonds	Total
1968	$ 3,946	$ 637	$17,383	$21,966
1969	7,714	682	18,347	26,744
1970	7,240	1,390	30,315	38,945
1971	9,291	3,670	32,123	45,090
1972	9,694	3,367	28,896	41,957
1973	7,642	3,337	21,049	32,025
1974	3,994	2,253	32,066	38,311
1975	7,405	3,458	42,756	53,619
1976	8,305	2,803	42,380	53,488
1977	7,861	3,916	42,015	53,792
1978	7,526	2,832	36,872	47,230
1979	7,751	3,574	40,208	51,533
1980	16,858	3,632	53,199	73,688
1981	23,552	1,797	45,092	70,441
1982	25,449	5,113	54,076	84,638
1983	44,366	7,213	46,971	98,550

[a] Gross proceeds (offering prices times number of units sold).
[b] *Source:* Federal Reserve Bulletin.

regular interest payments, usually semiannually, during the term of the debt and then receive the **face value** or **maturity value** of the bond at the date of maturity. For example, a twenty-year, $1000 bond promising a **coupon rate** of 10 percent per year sold on January 1, 1986, will pay $100 per year (.10 × $1000) until January 1, 2006; the $100 annual interest will commonly be paid in two $50 semiannual installments. On the maturity date, January 1, 2006, the corporation will also pay the lender the bond's maturity value of $1000.

The Value of a Bond

What is the *market value* of the twenty-year, $1000 bond described above? That is, what value do investors place on this bond in the bond market? The market value equals the discounted value (present value) of the dollar payments promised to the bondholder using the market interest rate to discount those payments. The market interest rate is the rate of return required by investors on the bond and was referred to in Chapter 5 as the bond's *yield to maturity*. If the annual market interest rate on comparable securities were 10 percent, then you will recall from Chapter 5 that the market value of the bond would be[1]

$$V = \frac{\$100}{1.10} + \frac{\$100}{(1.10)^2} + \cdots + \frac{\$100}{(1.10)^{20}} + \frac{\$1000}{(1.10)^{20}} = \$1000$$

This bond has a market value equal to its face value of $1000.

A bond generally does not sell for its face value. The bond could sell for more or for less than $1000, depending upon the market interest rate used to discount the payments received by the bondholder. Recall that the coupon rate is only used to compute the annual coupon payments paid by the firm, $100 in the example. To determine the value the bond would have to someone seeking a 12 percent return on investment, we find the present value of the coupon and maturity payments at 12 percent.[2]

$$V = \frac{\$100}{1.12} = \frac{\$100}{(1.12)^2} + \cdots + \frac{\$100}{(1.12)^{20}} + \frac{\$1000}{(1.12)^{20}} = \$851$$

If an investor were to purchase the bond for $851 and hold it for twenty years, the return on this investment would be 12 percent per year (assuming that the firm actually pays the interest and principal, i.e., does not default). If investors demand a 12 percent rate of return on the firm's bonds, the firm's bonds will sell for $851 (since $851 is the price investors will pay for the bonds). Notice that the coupon of $100 per year is only part of the net return to the bond investor. The rest of the return is in the form of a capital gain, the capital gain equaling $149—the $1000 received by the bondholder in year 2006 less the $851 paid in 1986. This difference between maturity value and 1986 market value, which equals $149 in the example, is called the **discount** on the bond. Thus, if the firm were to sell its bond initially for $851, it would be selling them at a discount of $149.

[1] Using the factors of Chapter 4, V = $100(P/A, 10%, 20) + $1000(P/F, 10%, 20) = $100(8.5136) + $1000(.1486) = $1000.
[2] Using the factors of Chapter 4, V = $100(P/A, 12%, 20) + $1000(P/F, 12%, 20) = $100(7.4694) + $1000(.1037) = $851.

The bond may also sell at a **premium**. If investors demand an 8 percent return on their investment, the value of the bond to them is[3]

$$V = \frac{\$100}{1.08} + \frac{\$100}{(1.08)^2} + \cdots + \frac{\$100}{(1.08)^{20}} + \frac{\$1000}{(1.08)^{20}} = \$1196$$

An investor paying $1196 for the bond and holding it to maturity will earn an annual 8 percent return on the investment of $1196. If the firm were to issue the bond for $1196, it would be issuing the bond at a premium of $196 ($1196 − $1000).

The real interest rate (market rate) that investors demand and earn on a bond was referred to above as the yield to maturity. The yield to maturity was 12 percent in the case of the bond selling at a discount, and was 8 percent in the case of the bond selling at a premium.[4] The coupon rate was 10 percent in both cases, and is important only in that it is used to compute the coupon (interest) payable in dollars each year to the bond-holder. The coupon rate should not be confused with the real interest rate or yield. If the bond sells at neither a discount nor a premium, then it has a present value equal to its face value, and its coupon rate and yield to maturity are equal. In the example, if the bond has a present value of $1000, its yield to maturity and coupon rate are both 10 percent. The relationship between the coupon rate, market rate, and bond discount or premium is shown in Figure 21-1. If the market rate is less than the coupon rate, the bond sells at a premium, and if the market rate exceeds the coupon rate, the bond sells at a discount.[5]

Income Priority

Creditors are in a preferred position relative to stockholders with regard to corporate income—that is, they receive what is promised to them before the stockholders receive anything. A bondholder is promised a payment each year (coupon rate × face value of bond), plus a payment at the end of

---

[3] Using the factors of Chapter 4, $V = \$100(P/A, 8\%, 20) + \$1000(P/F, 8\%, 20) = \$100(9.8181) + \$1000(.2145) = \$1196$.

[4] Notice that the yield to maturity is similar to the internal rate of return discussed in Chap. 8. The yield to maturity is the rate of return earned on the bond *assuming that the firm does not default* (default means that promised payments are not met) since the interest and face value payments that are discounted are those promised by the firm.

[5] For simplicity, we are assuming in the computation that interest is paid once per year and is discounted at the annual rate. Since the interest is actually paid semiannually, another approach often used in practice involves discounting each semiannual interest payment using a six-month rate of $k/2$, where k is the *annual* nominal interest rate and $k/2$ is the rate that applies to each six-month time interval. To illustrate, if the bond in the text example has a yield to maturity k equal to 8 percent, then the value of the bond equals

$$V = \frac{\$50}{1 + k/2} + \frac{\$50}{(1 + k/2)^2} + \cdots + \frac{\$50}{(1 + k/2)^{40}} + \frac{\$1000}{(1 + k/2)^{40}}$$

$$= \frac{\$50}{1 + 0.04} + \frac{\$50}{(1 + 0.04)^2} + \cdots + \frac{\$50}{(1 + 0.04)^{40}} + \frac{\$1000}{(1.04)^{40}}$$

$$= \$50(P/A, 4\%, 40) + \$1000(P/F, 4\%, 40)$$

$$= \$50(19.793) + \$1000(0.2083) = \$1198$$

In the remainder of this chapter we will simply compute values by discounting the annual interest payments at the annual interest rate.

the life of the bond (maturity or face value). Whatever is left after these payments is available to shareholders. For example, assume that the firm has bonds outstanding which promise $80,000 per year in coupon interest payments. The income to shareholders is shown for three cases in Exhibit 21-1. Notice that the bondholders always get $80,000 if the firm has the resources to make the payment. In case 3, the firm has a current loss but still pays the coupon of $80,000. Shareholders receive what is left over after taxes and interest ($60,000, $10,000, and a loss of $10,000, in cases 1, 2, and 3, respectively).

*Provisions of the
Bond Contract*

General Provisions   Bonds may be secured or unsecured. Unsecured bonds, called **debentures**, are usued against the general credit of the corporation, whereas secured bonds are backed by a pledge of specific assets. This section discusses general provisions that apply to both kinds of bonds. The special characteristics of unsecured and secured bonds are examined later.

Keep in mind that a provision in the bond agreement that protects the bondholders generally means greater constraints on the firm. The provision makes the bonds more attractive to lenders and means the firm can borrow at a lower interest rate than without such a provision. Whether a particular provision is included in a bond contract will depend on the company's situation (which determines how burdensome the provision is) and on the attitudes of lenders (how much they value the provision).

Terms and Enforcement of the Bond Agreement   The bond contract or indenture specifies the terms agreed upon by the corporation and

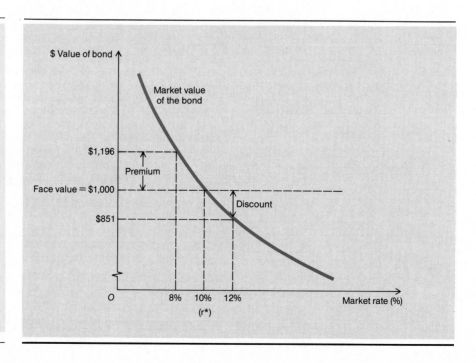

FIGURE 21-1

The relationship between the bond's market price, the coupon rate, and the market interest rate. Coupon rate = r* (r* = 10 percent in the example). If the market interest rate is less than r*, then the bond sells above face value and at a premium. If the market interest rate is greater than r*, the bond sells for less than face value and at a discount.

bondholders. The indenture stipulates the payments to be made by the corporation to the bondholders, the identity of any property that is pledged, the call provisions, and any restrictions on the firm to protect the interests of the bondholders. These restrictions are called **protective covenants**. They relate to the right of the firm to pay dividends, to the need to maintain a given level of working capital, and to any other requirements needed to ensure the capacity of the firm to meet its debt obligations. Such restrictions are an important protection to bondholders.

A **trustee**, frequently a commerical bank, is assigned to represent the bondholders by ensuring that the bond contract meets legal requirements and that the corporation fulfills the terms of the debt contract once the bonds are issued. If the corporation violates a provision of the bond indenture (for example, to pay interest and principal, or to maintain a particular net worth position), it is in **default**. It is the duty of the trustee to protect the bondholders if the firm is in default. Bond issues in excess of $1 million and registered with the Securities and Exchange Commission are subject to the Trust Indenture Act of 1939. This federal act provides that the indenture terms must be clear and not deceptive and that the trustee act strictly in behalf of the bondholders.

Call Provision The call provision in the bond agreement provides that the firm can repurchase ("call") the bonds after they are issued at some stipulated **call price**, which is generally above the face value of the bonds. The difference between the call price and the bond's face value is referred to as the **call premium**. For example, if a $1000 (face value), thirty-year, $7\frac{1}{2}$ percent bond can be called by the firm for $1075, the call premium is $75 ($1075 − $1000). The premium is frequently equal to one year's coupon payment ($75 on a $7\frac{1}{2}$ percent, $1000 bond). Sometimes the call premium declines over time; it might be $75 the first year the bonds are outstanding,

---

EXHIBIT 21-1
Bondholder income priority

	Case 1	Case 2	Case 3
Earnings (sales minus operating costs) before interest and taxes (EBIT)	$200,000	$100,000	$ 60,000
Interest payable on bonds	(80,000)	(80,000)	(80,000)
Earnings before taxes (EBT)	$120,000	$ 20,000	$(20,000)
Taxes (0.50 × EBT)	(60,000)	(10,000)	10,000[a]
Net aftertax earnings	$ 60,000	$ 10,000	$(10,000)

[a] If a firm incurs a loss (negative EBT), then it may receive a rebate on past taxes paid equal to the tax rate times the loss, in this case equal to 0.50 times the $20,000 loss; this reduces the loss by the amount of the rebate. Such a rebate is available as long as the firm has profits in the previous three years against which losses have not already been taken (carried back). Losses in a period can also be carried forward for five years.

$72.50 the second year, and so on, the premium declining by $2.50 per year for thirty years to zero at the maturity date.

Investors would prefer that there be no call provision, since it means that the firm can force them to sell back their bonds at a particular price. For example, assume that a $1000, 8 percent, twenty-year bond is issued on January 1, 1986, at par (that is, for $1000) and has a call provision that allows the firm to repurchase the bond at any time for $1050. The investor pays $1000 for the bond and, if the firm does not call the bond, will receive an interest payment of $80 per year for twenty years, plus $1000 at the end of that period. Assume that interest rates in the market fall to 6 percent because of a change in economic conditions after the bond is issued and the firm decides to call the bond on January 19, 1988. The corporation will probably wish to call the bond in this case, since it can now borrow at 6 percent instead of 8 percent. Is the investor worse off than if the firm could not call the bond? The answer is clearly yes. If there were no call option, the value of the bond (using a 6 percent discount rate) would be $1217—the present value of $80 per year for eighteen years (January 1988 to January 2006) plus the present value of the $1000 face value received in eighteen years.[6] However, the firm pays the bondholder only $1050 (the call price) for the bond. To compensate the bondholder for the call provision disadvantage, bonds with such a provision generally pay a somewhat higher coupon rate. Thus, if the $1000 bond were issued at par, without a call provision it might have a coupon rate (and yield to maturity) of 7 percent, providing a promised coupon of $70 per year; with the call provision, the bond issued at par might have a coupon rate (and yield to maturity) of 8 percent, providing a promised coupon of $80 per year.

Sinking Fund Provision   The bond agreement may include a sinking fund provision that requires the corporation to retire a given number of bonds in certain specified years. The funds for retirement are transferred to a trustee who retires the bonds. The stipulated means of retirement may be calling the bonds or purchasing them in the open market. For example, if the firm issued $10 million of twenty-year bonds on January 1, 1986, it might agree to retire 5 percent of the bonds ($500,000 of par value) in each year beginning in 1987. Sinking fund provisions vary significantly and may require that only some or all of the bonds be retired before maturity. The sinking fund retirements may begin immediately or several years after issuance of the bonds. For example, for the twenty-year bonds issued on January 1, 1986, the indenture might require the retirement of 5 percent of the bonds in the years 1996 to 2005, with the remaining bonds retired at maturity on January 1, 2006.

Retiring bonds under a sinking fund agreement reduces the company's outstanding debt. This reduces the risk of the remaining debt by diminishing the company's debt burden.

---

[6] Using the factors of Chap. 4, the value of the bond = V = $80(P/A, 6%, 18) + $1000(P/F, 6%, 18) = $80(10.828) + $1000(0.3503) = $1217.

Other Provisions A bond indenture restriction might limit the dividends the firm may pay, or might require the firm to maintain a minimum current ratio or level of working capital. A limitation on the amount of further company borrowing is common. Particularly for small firms, there may be restrictions on corporate officers' salaries or on company investments. Some bonds are convertible into common stock; convertible bonds are discussed in Chapter 22.

Unsecured Debt

Nature of Bondholder's Claim Unsecured bonds, or debentures, are backed by the general credit of the corporation—that is, by all the firm's assets that are not pledged as security on secured debt. These bonds are not secured by any specific property. Large corporations with excellent credit standing—for example, AT&T, General Motors, and Sears, Roebuck—are those most likely to issue debentures instead of secured bonds. The type of assets owned by the firm also affects the choice between issuing secured or unsecured debt. Whereas a railroad with large fixed assets may find it advantageous to issue secured bonds, a firm with liquid or intangible assets, as for example, a publishing company (whose assets may largely be in the form of copyrights and goodwill), will generally have to resort to unsecured debt.

Bond indentures frequently include a **negative pledge clause**, stipulating that no new debt will be issued by the firm that takes priority over the debentures in their claim to the firm's assets. This may apply to assets acquired in the future as well as to those already owned by the firm.

Subordinated Debentures One issue of debt is subordinated to another if it has a lower-priority claim to the firm's assets in the event of bankruptcy. If debt issue A is subordinated to debt issue B then, in the event of firm liquidation, the issue B creditors must be fully paid (all principal and interest due) before the issue A creditors are paid anything. The indenture specifies which debt has the preferred position relative to the subordinated debentures. Debentures are often subordinated to bank loans and other short-term debt. Subordinated debt allows the firm to increase its borrowing without jeopardizing the security position of senior debt. Thus the firm can obtain senior loans at a relatively low interest cost by specifying that any further debt will assume a subordinate position. The effect of subordination in the case of liquidation is described in Chapter 25.

Secured Debt

Nature of Claim The distinguishing feature of a secured bond is that particular corporation assets are specified in the bond indenture as security on the debt. In the event of bankruptcy, the secured bondholder has first claim to the assets securing those bonds. A **mortgage** is used to pledge real property (land or buildings), and a **chattel mortgage** is used to pledge personal property (property that is not real property).

Priority of Debt   A given secured bond issue may have a senior claim to specific assets, in which case the bonds would be referred to as **first mortgage bonds**. The claim to the assets may be subordinate to that of other creditors, in which case the bonds carry a junior mortgage on the property and would be referred to as second mortgage bonds or third mortgage bonds, etc. This situation is analogous to the familiar first, second, and third mortgages on residential real estate.

The mortgage contract may have a **closed-end provision**, which prohibits the firm from issuing further debt *of the same priority* against the same property. For example, if the firm has $5 million of first mortgage bonds covered by a mortgage on $10 million worth of property, a closed-end provision would prevent the firm from issuing further first mortgage bonds on the property, but it may allow the issuance of second mortgage bonds on that property. If the mortgage were an **open-end mortgage**, the firm would be allowed to issue further first mortgage bonds against the property. Clearly, first mortgage bonds under a closed-end mortgage contract are less risky for investors than under an open-end mortgage contract. Thus, in the above example, if the $5 million in bonds were secured by a closed-end first mortgage, and the firm were to issue additional bonds worth $1 million, the new bonds would be subordinated to the $5 million of first mortgage bonds. In this case, if the firm in liquidation were to realize $5 million on the assets, the first mortgage bonds would be fully paid and the second mortgage bonds would receive nothing. Under an open-end first mortgage contract, however, the additional $1 million of new bonds have equal priority with the initial $5 million of bonds; with $5 million realized on the liquidation of the assets, all bondholders would receive $83\frac{1}{3}$ cents on each dollar of debt ($5 million realized on assets/$6 million of debt). The bond contract may also provide for a **limited open-end mortgage**, which allows the issuance of further first mortgage bonds up to a given limit. In the above example, the limited open-end mortgage might allow the issuance of an additional $2 million of first mortgage bonds beyond the initial bond issue of $5 million.

Property Securing the Debt   A mortgage may relate to specific land and buildings or may be a **blanket mortgage** covering all the real property owned by the corporation. Instead of a mortgage (which is a security interest in real property), the firm may use personal property as collateral on the bonds. If equipment is used, bonds are referred to as **equipment trust certificates**. This type of security has been used frequently by railroads. Sometimes securities (stock or bonds owned by the corporation) or inventory or other intangible assets (e.g., patents) are used as collateral, in which case the debt securities issued by the corporation would be referred to as **collateral trust bonds**. Collateral trust bonds are most frequently issued by railroads and by holding companies (companies whose primary assets are the stock issued by its subsidiaries).

To strengthen the security position of the bondholders, the bond indenture may include an **after-acquired property clause**. This provides that any property acquired by the firm in the future will also serve as collateral for the bonds. in addition to the after-acquired property clause, the bond contract may permit the firm to issue a specified amount of additional debt secured by the same property as the bonds.

An illustration of a mortgage bond is provided by Inland Steel's first mortgage $8\frac{7}{8}$ bonds, maturing on April 15, 1999. The properties securing the bonds are the following:

1 The Indiana Harbor Works and certain parcels of land in East Chicago, Indiana
2 Certain iron ore properties in Michigan and Minnesota
3 The coal properties of the company in Jefferson County, Illinois
4 Approximately 400 acres of vacant land in Porter County, Indiana

The mortgage is open-ended, with the indenture permitting the issuance of additional debt under the mortgage so long as interest is adequately covered by the firm's income.

The Advantages of Long-Term Debt

Bonds offer the attraction to investors of providing a fixed stream of returns with a relatively high degree of safety. On the other hand, bondholders do not share in any exceptional profitability that the firm may achieve and generally do not have the right to vote. Bonds appeal to investors willing to sacrifice the chance of extraordinary gain for safety of return.

The company must weigh several advantages and disadvantages of raising additional capital by issuing debt rather than new shares of common or preferred stock. As explained in Chapters 3 and 10, since interest is tax deductible whereas payments to other security holders are not, the aftertax cost of debt capital may be lower, at least up to some level of borrowing. Of course, as discussed in Chapter 10, the corporate tax advantage of debt may be at least partially offset by the personal tax advantage of common stock. Also, the firm will want to limit its borrowing so as to avoid increasing the possibility of bankruptcy. Shareholders also benefit from the fact that the bondholders do not participate in any extraordinary profits and do not enjoy the voting privilege. Offsetting these advantages is the added risk to the firm of incurring the fixed-debt commitment. Except for income bonds (see discussion below), periodic interest coupon payments must be met or the firm will be in default. Furthermore, in the case of bonds (including income bonds) the firm must retire the bonds at maturity by paying their face value. These debt commitments must be met regardless of the corporation's profitability. In addition, many bond indentures include restrictions on the firm's operations, e.g., on working capital and dividend payments. In short, the greater safety provided to bondholders implies greater risk to shareholders.

Conditions in the securities markets may influence the choice between new debt and new equity financing. Bond prices and stock prices sometimes move in opposite directions, or in the same direction but to a different degree. The market price reflects what the firm will receive on any new securities it issues. In obtaining outside capital the firm will tend to find it advantageous to issue bonds if bond prices are relatively high (interest rates low) and share prices low, and to issue stock when stock prices are relatively inflated and bond prices are low (interest rates high).

The firm's choice of capital structure depends on the predictability of cash flows. Greater predictability means that the company can borrow more without running the risk of default. A greater chance of default causes lenders to charge a higher rate of interest. Shareholders are also generally averse to excessive company borrrowing because company bankruptcy is undesirable to them just as it is to creditors.

SOME NOVEL FORMS OF DEBT

In addition to the standard forms of debt described above, a variety of less conventional debt instruments have evolved. Below, we briefly examine several of those debt forms: income bonds, industrial development bonds, variable (floating rate) bonds, low coupon bonds, put bonds, and project financing debt.

Income Bonds

Income bonds are unsecured debt requiring payment of interest only to the extent earned by the firm. For example, if the annual interest on the bonds is $100,000 and the firm earns only $50,000 (before interest and taxes), the company has to pay only $50,000 interest on the income bonds. If the firm has earned $150,000, $100,000 in interest would be paid on the income bonds.

Income bonds have been used by companies whose capacity to meet interest and principal payments is questionable, for example, after corporate reorganizations (especially railroad reorganizations). Income bonds have also been used by some small companies as a replacement for outstanding preferred stock. An advantage of income bonds is that interest on those bonds, as on other bonds, is tax deductible. Preferred stock dividends are not tax deductible. The advantages of preferred stock are that the stock never need be retired (whereas all corporate bonds must have a maturity date for the interest to be tax deductible) and that preferred dividends need not be paid even if earned during the year.

Income bond indenture provisions vary. Interest payments are sometimes cumulative; that is, if not paid in a given period, they must be paid in future periods if earned by the firm. Sinking fund provisions are common, and some income bonds are convertible into common stock.

Industrial Development Bonds

Industrial Develpment Bonds (IRBs), also called industrial revenue bonds, are issued through state or municipal agencies to raise funds which are used by private corporations to finance ventures (for example, $1 million for a McDonald's restaurant in Wetumpka, Alabama). The unique feature of these bonds is that the interest paid on the bonds is not taxable income to the bondholder and, therefore, the interest rate on the bonds is relatively low. Although the IRBs are issued under the auspices of a state or municipal agency, the bonds are the debt of the corporation for whom the IRBs have been issued. The governmental agency is not liable if the corporation defaults on the bonds. Often, the bond proceeds are used by the corporation to buy plant and equipment (frequently pollution control equipment). In other cases, the government agency will take the proceeds and buy an asset (for example, a factory) and then lease the factory to the corporation;

the lease rentals are set so that they are just sufficient to pay of the IRBs. IRB financing has blossomed (exploded!) in recent years. The number of firms using IRBs is enormous and includes such companies as Boise Cascade, K-Mart, McDonald's Corporation, Georgia Pacific, ITT, Monsanto, and Weyerhaeuser. This type of financing is of coure controversial bcause it involves a tax subsidy to business (due to the tax exempt interest on the bond).

Variable Rate (Floating Rate) Bonds

A **floating rate bond** pays interest which fluctuates with prevailing interest rates, rather than being fixed over the life of the bond. For example, the interest rate on Citicorp's 1992 floating rate bond is 1 percent above the rate on ninety-day Treasury bills. In 1980, General Motors Acceptance Corporation issued ten-year notes which yielded 13.45 percent during the first two years and a floating yield thereafter (adjusted annually and tied to the ten-year Treasury bond rate). Petro-Lewis sold bonds in 1980 with an interest rate which varies with the price of "sweet" crude oil from West Texas.

The rationale behind variable interest rate debt is that, in a period of highly uncertain and volatile interest rates, many borrowers and lenders do not want to engage in a long-term fixed interest rate contract. One option, of course, is to borrow or lend on a short-term basis at the going market interest rate and to continue to do so from period to period. An alternative is a long-term floating rate security. A floating rate security provides the borrower and lender with what is equivalent to a series of short-term loans. An advantage of the variable rate security relative to the series of short-term loans is that the borrower and lender do not have to incur the trouble and transaction costs of reborrowing or relending every few months on a short-term basis. Also, the borrower is assured of long-term financing with a long-term loan, whereas this is not necessarily so with short-term debt (the firm may simply be unable to renew or renegotiate a short-term loan).

Low Coupon Bonds

The shockingly low 7 percent coupon on Northwest Industry's, Inc., thirty-year bonds issued in 1981 did not reflect a general decline in interest rates (bonds with similar ratings were yielding roughly 14 percent at the time). The Northwest Industry's bonds were sold at a 47 percent discount from par ($527.50 price for a bond with a $1000 face value payable at maturity); the yield to maturity on the bonds was 13.5 percent. Even more extreme is General Motors Acceptance Corporation's ten-year debentures which have a zero coupon!

What are the advantages of low coupon debt? **Low or zero coupon bonds** are issued at a discount (that is, at below face value) and are referred to as original discount bonds. These bonds provide most or all of the cash payment (interest and principal) when the bond matures. This may be attractive to a lender (bondholder) who does not want the inconvenience of reinvesting periodic interest payments or who wants to lock in his or her investment at current interest rates. An ordinary bond which pays high coupon payments involves uncertainty about the rate of return the bond-holder will be able to earn in the future by reinvesting those coupons. Also, low coupon bonds are generally callable at a price far above the issuance price (for example, at face value), which means that even if market interest rates fall and the bond's price rises substantially, the bonds will not be called (this inability to call a bond at a reasonable price is, of course, a disadvantage to the issuing firm). Low coupon bonds do have the disadvantage that, even though the coupon is small or zero, the bondholder must pay income taxes on a pro rata share of discount as well as taxes on the coupon.[7] Apparently, investors have found these bonds to be especially attractive because they have sold with yields to maturity roughly $\frac{1}{4}$ percent to $\frac{3}{4}$ percent below comparably rated regular bonds.

Low coupon bonds allow the borrower to postpone to maturity most or all of the interest and principal payments on the loan. This means that, in effect, the firm is able to borrow more money for a longer period of time. Furthermore, each year the firm may deduct for tax purposes a part of the bond discount even though the discount isn't paid until maturity.[8]

Put Bonds

Put bonds allow the bondholder to return the bonds to the issuer in return for a cash payment equal to the bond's face (par) value. For example, in 1976 Beneficial Corporation issued bonds which mature in 2001 and which allow the bondholder, after June 15, 1983, to turn in the bond to Beneficial in return for the par value of $1000. In return for the put option, put bonds yield a little less than ordinary bonds.

Project Financing

Project financing involves debt which is a claim against a particular project, and not against the parent company. These are privately placed loans, usually with major banks. The projects for which such financing has been made available have generally been very large (commonly mineral extraction and mineral processing projects). Project financing allows the parent corporation to limit or even eliminate its liability exposure (the degree to which the parent is liable is subject to negotiation). Of course, liability limitation is not free since the banks will charge an interest rate which reflects the loan's risk.

PREFERRED STOCK

Preferred stock is a hybrid of debt and common stock financing. Preferred stockholders have a prior claim relative to common stockholders to the firm's income after interest and taxes and to the firm's assets in the event of bankruptcy. Preferred stock is subordinate to all debt with regard to earnings and assets. Preferred shareholders generally have voting privileges on certain matters. The firm need not pay dividends on preferred stock if it so chooses, so long as it also fails to pay common stock dividends. Therefore, the existence of preferred stock does not increase the probability of firm bankruptcy. Indeed, any added capital provided by the issuance of pre-

---

[7] For example, assume a twenty-year, 4 percent, $1000 bond which is issued for $400 (implying a yield to maturity of approximately 12 percent). In computing taxable income, a bondholder would have to include each year in his other ordinary income (not capital gains) both the $40 coupon *and* $30 of amortized discount ($600 discount divided by twenty years).

[8] Thus, in the illustration of footnote 7, the corporation could deduct each year for tax purposes the $40 coupon *and* the $30 of amortized discount.

ferred stock reduces the likelihood of bankruptcy by increasing the firm's capital.

Dividend Payments

Characteristics of Preferred Stock

Par Value   Preferred share dividends are generally stated as a percentage of the preferred's par value, e.g., a dividend of 8 percent of par with a par of $100 would be $8 per year.[9] Similarly, 8 percent preferred stock with a par of $50 would pay $4 (0.08 × $50) in annual dividends. If the preferred stock does not have a par value, the dividend payment is merely stated by itself, e.g., as an annual dividend of $8 per preferred share.

Priority of Payment   Preferred dividends must be paid before any dividends can be paid to common stockholders. All debt interest takes priority over payments to preferred shares.

Cumulative Dividend   Usually, a **cumulative dividend provision** is included in the preferred stock agreement that requires that all past unpaid dividends on the preferred stock must be met before any dividends can be declared on the common stock. For example, if the firm has a $10 million (par) 8 percent preferred stock issue outstanding, the annual preferred dividend would be $800,000. Assume that the firm did not pay dividends in 1985 and 1986 but is considering paying a dividend on the common stock in 1987. Under a cumulative preferred dividend provision, before the common dividend can be paid, the preferred dividends owed for 1985 and 1986, plus the preferred dividend for 1987, must first be paid—a total preferred dividend of $2,400,000 ($800,000 for each of the years 1985, 1986, 1987).

The cumulative dividend provision is important protection for the preferred stockholders. Since preferred dividends need be paid only when common stock dividends are also paid, without the cumulative provision the firm could greatly reduce preferred dividends by paying large infrequent dividends on the common stock instead of paying smaller annual dividends. Thus, in the example above but with noncumulative preferred stock, payment of large dividends to common stockholders once every three years would require a payment of $800,000 to preferred stockholders only once every three years; however, paying even a small dividend to common stockholders each year would require an $800,000 dividend on the preferred every year.

Adjustable Dividends   Infrequently, preferred stockholders may participate equally (or up to a stipulated level) with common stockholders in

[9] The par value of preferred is similar to the par value of a bond and is used to express the dividend payment (as a percentage of par). The *market value* of a share of preferred is rarely equal to its par value. Market value equals the present value of future dividends on the preferred using the market discount rate (*not* the dividend rate as a percentage of par). For example, assume a $100 par preferred paying an annual 8 percent dividend ($8 dividend = 0.08 × $100), and assume that the preferred is not expected to be called in the future (perpetual dividend). If investors want to earn 10 percent on their investment in the stock, its market value is the $8 dividend discounted at 10 percent, which equals $8(*P/A*, 10%, ∞) = $8(10.0) = $80. An investor paying $80 for the preferred stock will earn 10 percent annually on the $80 investment as long as the stock is held, assuming that the dividend is actually paid each year.

receiving dividends. Such preferred stock is referred to as **participating preferred**. With fully participating preferred, the dividend distribution involves payment first to preferred stock up to the stipulated amount (e.g., $8 per share on 8 percent $100 preferred), then a dividend payment on each common share equal to that paid on a preferred share, and finally, equal payment of the remaining dividends to the common and preferred stock.

Adjustable rate preferred (ARP), which became popular in the mid-1980s, pays dividends that are pegged at a fixed relationship to government security interest rates (e.g., to the highest of the rates on three month Treasury bills, 10-year Treasury bonds, and 20-year Treasury bonds). There is generally a stipulated maximum and minimum dividend rate, for example, the ARP agreement might specify that the annual rate never fall below 10 percent or rise above 14 percent. A variant of the ARP is the **convertible adjustable preferred (CAP)**, which has an adjustable dividend but is also convertible to common stock at the option of the preferred shareholder. Many companies have issued ARPs or CAPs, including Sears Roebuck & Company, Northern Trust Corporation, GATX, and Tidewater, Inc.

Priority of Claim on Assets   If the firm is in liquidation, creditors must be fully paid before preferred and common stockholders receive anything. After payment to creditors, the preferred stockholders are paid the par value of their shares, plus any preferred dividends in arrears or for the current period. Anything remaining goes to the common shareholders.

Voting Rights   Preferred stockholders usually have only limited voting privileges. Consent of the preferred stockholders may be required for the issuance of additional securities with an equal or higher-priority claim on the firm's assets or earnings, e.g., the issuance of additional debt. Sometimes, the preferred stockholders may elect a minority number of directors, e.g., two out of seven. This privilege of electing directors may be contingent upon the failure of the firm to pay preferred dividends for some specified number of periods.

Other Provisions

Callability   The corporation may retain the right to call the preferred shares, generally at a price above par. For example, the firm may be able to call its $100 par preferred shares by paying the shareholders $108 per share, the call premium in this case being $8.

Sinking Fund Provision   Periodic retirement of the preferred stock under a sinking fund arrangement may be required, although this provision is far less common than it is with bonds.

Convertibility   The preferred stock may be convertible into common stock at the option of the holder. The preferred stock may also be issued as a **unit** with warrants to purchase common stock (the unit is the combination of the share of preferred stock and a specified number of warrants).

Restrictions on the Firm   The preferred stock agreement may require the corporation to maintain a specified current ratio or level of working capital before dividends may be paid on the common stock. A limit may be placed on the issuance of additional debt or preferred stock. The objective of these conditions is to insure the ability of the firm to pay preferred dividends and to protect the preferred shareholder's investment in the company.

An Actual Preferred Stock Issue   On February 26, 1974, the Appalachian Power Company offered for sale 200,000 shares of 8.52 percent cumulative preferred. The par value of the stock was $100, implying an annual dividend of $8.52 per share (8.52 percent × $100). However, the offering, or selling, price per share to investors was $101 per share, thereby providing them with an actual annual dividend yield of 8.44 percent ($8.52/$101). These terms are shown below.

Shares (000's)	Par value	Annual dividend yield (dividend/par)	Offering price	Actual yield (dividend/offering price)
200	$100	8.52%	$101	8.44%

The stock is callable as a whole or in part at varying prices over time: at $110.28 from the date of issuance through February 28, 1979; at $108.94 through February 28, 1984; at $105.82 through February 28, 1989; and at $103.59 thereafter. Some of the conditions designed to protect the preferred stockholders' interest were as follows:

1   Consent of the holders of a majority of the total number of preferred shares then outstanding is needed to issue additional preferred stock unless the firm's net income and gross (pretax) income relative to preferred dividends (on old and any new preferred stock) and interest on the firm's debt are at certain specified levels.
2   Consent of the holders of a majority of the total number of preferred shares is required for the firm to issue or assume additional unsecured debt, if the result is to cause the firm's debt burden to exceed a certain specified level.
3   Dividends on the firm's *common stock* will be restricted if the firm's debt-equity ratio exceeds a specified level.

This issue contains most of the provisions that we described earlier.

The Use of Preferred Stock

From the investor's standpoint, preferred stock has the advantage of yielding a relatively safe and steady return. Since dividends received from domestic corporations are 85 percent tax-free to a corporate investor (whereas all bond interest income is taxable to a corporate investor), some firms find the preferred stock of other corporations a desirable investment. Because of the tax advantage to corporate investors of dividend income relative to interest income, preferred shares often have lower yields than bonds (since corporate investors bid up the prices of the preferred). This can mean a lower aftertax yield for an individual (noncorporate) investor, since dividend income received by an individual does not receive the same favored tax treatment as does dividend income received by a corporation.

Preferred stock is, of course, not risk-free. Because of its lower-priority position relative to bonds, preferred stock is subject to a greater risk of nonpayment. A company is less likely to be able to pay preferred dividends than debt interest, and, in the event of the company's bankruptcy, creditors are paid before any payment is made to preferred shareholders. Also, because preferred stock has no fixed maturity date, it has greater price variability (as interest rates in the market change) than do fixed maturity bonds. The greater risk and often lower yield of preferred stock relative to bonds makes preferred stock a poor investment medium for most individual investors.

Preferred stock has three advantages for the issuing firm:

1 The preferred shareholders' returns are generally limited so any extraordinary company profits go to the common shareholders.
2 Nonpayment of the preferred dividend does not place the firm in default, as is the case if interest on debt is not paid.
3 Control of the firm remains with the common shareholders.

In merger situations, preferred stock (as well as common stock) has an additional advantage over debt. Suppose firm *A* is buying firm *B* and uses the securities of firm *A* as payment. The use of firm *A* bonds as compensation to firm *B* owners would produce a taxable gain to the sellers at the time of sale. On the other hand, if firm *A* stock (voting preferred or common) were used, the gain would generally not be taxable until the firm *B* owners were to sell the firm *A* stock that they received in the merger.

Balancing the advantages of preferred stock are several disadvantages. The dividend payments on preferred, and the preferred's claim to the firm's assets under bankruptcy, take priority over the common shareholders' claims, a disadvantage to stockholders that would not apply if additional common stock were issued. Furthermore, dividends to preferred stock are not tax deductible as is interest on debt—a disadvantage to the firm. The consequence is that the residual income to common stockholders is less with preferred stock than with debt, even if the coupon rate on the debt equals the dividend rate on the preferred.

The lower cost of debt was explained in Chapter 10. To illustrate this point, in Exhibit 21-2 the net income to common shareholders, assuming $5 million of 6 percent bonds outstanding (annual interest of $300,000), is compared with the net income to common shareholders with $5 million of 6 percent preferred stock outstanding (annual preferred dividends of $300,000). The common shareholders' net income is $850,000 with debt, but only $700,000 with the preferred stock, simply because interest is tax deductible whereas preferred dividends are not.

THE REFUNDING DECISION

Refunding is the issuance of new securities to retire old debt or preferred stock. The old securities may be retired by calling them or by purchasing them in the open market. A firm will consider refunding if the cost of borrowing has declined since the old securities were issued. The method of computing the gain from refunding is described below.

The refunding problem can be viewed as a firm's investment decision, since it involves obtaining funds (e.g., through borrowing) and then using those funds for a profitable purpose (retiring old debt or preferred). The refunding is desirable only if the net present value of the resulting aftertax cash flow is positive, as in any investment decision. The initial outlay of the refunding (a cash outflow like the investment outlay under capital budgeting) is the difference between what is paid out to purchase the old securities less what is received from new bond or preferred investors on issuing the new securities. In the case examined below, this initial outlay is equal to (1) the flotation costs of the new security plus (2) the call premium on the old security. The benefits of the refunding operation equals the reduction in aftertax payments to debt (or preferred stock). These benefits must then be discounted to determine their present value. The refunding is desirable only if the present value of the benefits exceeds the initial outlay. In discounting the cash flow benefits, the current aftertax market interest rate in the firm's debt is used as a discount rate. This is the rate that properly reflects the risk involved with the debt-associated cash flows being discounted.

Assume that Vista Corporation has a $100 million, 9 percent (coupon rate) bond issue outstanding, with twenty years remaining to maturity. The bonds were issued five years ago at par ($100 million) with a flotation cost of $2.5 million (Vista netted $97.5 million on the issue). These flotation costs are being charged off for tax purposes as an expense at the rate of $100,000 per year ($2.5 million/25 years).[10] If the bonds are called, the unamortized portion of the flotation costs ($2 million) will be deductible for tax purposes when the bonds are called. Vista's tax rate is 50 percent. Vista can call the bonds for $107 million. The call premium is therefore $7 million, and this premium is tax deductible as an expense (like interest) *in the year the bonds are called*.[11] Vista has been informed by its investment bankers that the firm

---

[10] The bonds had twenty-five years to maturity when they were originally issued.

[11] The $7 million call premium is deductible in the year the bonds are called. Since the firm's tax rate is 50 percent, deducting the $7 million from taxable income reduces taxes by $3.5 million, and this $3.5 million tax saving is subtracted from the $7 million to produce an aftertax call premium cost of $3.5 million.

EXHIBIT 21-2
Income effects of debt and preferred stock

	Debt	Preferred Stock
Income before interest and taxes	$2,000,000	$2,000,000
Less interest on debt	300,000	0
Income before taxes	$1,700,000	$2,000,000
Taxes (at 50%)	850,000	1,000,000
Income after taxes	$ 850,000	$1,000,000
Dividends on preferred stock	0	300,000
Net income to common stockholders	$ 850,000	$ 700,000

can issue between $95 million and $105 million in new debt at an interest cost of 6 percent. The firm is considering the issue of $100 million of 6 percent bonds that will involve flotation costs of $3 million. Assume for simplicity that the interest on the old bonds was paid right before the refunding and that interest is paid yearly (therefore, the next interest payment on the old debt is due in one year). Now we can compute the net present value of the refunding.

Initial Outlay   The initial outlay equals the aftertax cash outflow to retire

Face value of old bonds		$100 million
Call premium	$ 7 million	
Less tax benefit from deducting call premium	(3.5 million)	
Aftertax call premium cost		3.5 million
Less tax benefit from write-off of $2,000,000 in unamortized flotation costs (tax rate × $2,000,000)		(1.0 million)
Cash outflow		$102.5 million
Price of new bonds	$100 million	
Less flotation costs	(3 million)	
Cash inflow		97.0 million
Initial outlay (cash outflow − cash inflow)		$ 5.5 million

Annual Savings   Refunding affects interest and flotation costs. Both costs are tax-deductible and therefore reduce the company's taxes.

Interest Cost   Recall from Chapter 10 that interest cost equals 1 minus the corporate tax rate times the interest paid since interest is tax deductible. Therefore, assuming a corporate tax rate of 50 percent:

Aftertax interest expense on old debt ($100 million × 0.09 × 0.5)	$4.5 million
Aftertax interest expense on new debt ($100 million × 0.06 × 0.5)	3 million
Annual savings on interest	$1.5 million

where the 0.5 in the above computation is (1 − tax rate) = (1 − 0.5) = 0.5.

Tax Benefits from Amortization of the Flotation Costs   Flotation costs of the new issue are $3 million. This amount may be deducted for tax purposes over the life of the twenty-year bonds in the amount per year of

$$\frac{\$3 \text{ million}}{20 \text{ years}} = \$150,000 \text{ per year}$$

The $150,000 is deducted as an expense. The flotation costs on the old bonds would have been $100,000 per year and would also have been tax-deductible. The deduction for flotation costs has therefore increased by $50,000 a year. Since flotation costs can be used as a tax deduction, each added dollar of flotation costs deduction reduces taxes by that dollar times the tax rate. The flotation cost tax benefit of refunding equals[12]

$$\text{Tax benefit from increased flotation costs amortization} = \text{tax rate} \times \text{added flotation costs}$$

$$= 0.50 \times \$50,000 \text{ per year}$$

$$= \$25,000 \text{ per year}$$

The total benefit per year equals the sum of the aftertax interest saving plus the increased tax saving on amortization of flotation costs, that is,

$$\text{Annual savings} = \$1,500,000 + \$25,000$$

$$= \$1,525,000$$

The savings are realized in each of the forthcoming twenty years.

Now we determine whether the stream of benefits computed above is sufficient to warrant the initial cost of the refunding. We must compute the net present value of the cash flows. This is done as follows:[13]

$$\text{Aftertax cost of new debt} = (1 - \text{tax rate}) \times \text{interest rate}$$

$$= 0.5 \times 6\% = 3\%$$

Present value factor for a 20-year annuity at 3% = $(P/A, 3\%, 20)$ = 14.877

Present value of $1,525,000 per year for 20 years = $14.877 \times \$1,525,000$

$$= \$22,687,425$$

Initial outlay = $5.5 million

Net present value of refunding operation

$$= \text{present value of annual savings} - \text{initial outlay}$$

$$= \$22,687,425 - \$5.5 \text{ million}$$

$$= \$17,187,425$$

[12] Each dollar of any tax deductible expense, flotation costs included, reduces taxable income by $1 and thereby reduces taxes by the tax rate × $1. For example, assume that Vista's taxable income before any flotation cost deduction is $1 million and the corporate tax rate is 50 percent. With the old flotation cost deduction of $100,000, taxable income = $1,000,000 − $100,000 = $900,000 and corporate taxes equal the tax rate × $900,000 = 0.5 × $900,000 = $450,000. With the new bonds, the flotation cost tax deduction is $150,000 annually, taxable income = $1,000,000 − $150,000 = $850,000, and corporate taxes = 0.5 × $850,000 = $425,000. The new bonds increase the flotation cost deduction by $50,000 (from $100,000 to $150,000) and therefore reduce taxes by the tax rate × increase in flotation cost deduction = 0.5 × $50,000 = $25,000.

[13] For a discussion of the use of the aftertax cost of debt versus the pretax cost of debt for discounting the benefits from refunding, see A. R. Ofer and R. A. Taggart, Jr., "Bond Refunding: A Clarifying Analysis," *Journal of Finance* (March 1977).

The net gain from refunding is $17,187,425. It is therefore better to refund the existing bond issue than to keep it outstanding for 20 years. However, these are not the only two alternatives, and a complete analysis would consider not only refunding now, but refunding one year from now, two years from now, etc. Refunding one year from now may be better than refunding currently. For example, if, in the above illustration, we expected interest rates to fall significantly below 6 percent, we might want to postpone the refunding. However, if we expected interest rates not to decline below 6 percent, refunding now would likely be the best strategy.

It must be emphasized that the refunding was so attractive in the above example because the firm could call the old bonds for only $106 million. If there were no call provision, the bonds would sell for a value that would make refunding less attractive, even unattractive. If the old bonds were viewed by investors (bondholders) as having the same risk as the new debt, the yield to maturity on the old bonds would be approximately 6 percent (the same as the interest rate on the new debt) and their market value would be about $135 million.[14] Without a call provision, the firm would have to pay at least $135 million for those old bonds to retire them by purchasing them in the open market. Refunding under these conditions would clearly not have been a good choice.

The above example involved the refunding of a debt issue. Refunding preferred stock involves a similar computation. Problem 7 at the end of the chapter involves a preferred stock refunding decision.

SUMMARY

Long-term debt and preferred stock are fixed-income securities since they provide the investor with a promised series of future payments. The interest and face value are specified for bonds, and the dividend rate is stated for preferred stock. Creditors have a prior claim to the company's income and to the company's assets if the company liquidates. The firm must pay the interest and the maturity value on its debt as agreed upon in the bond contract, or the firm defaults and is subject to legal action. In contrast, the firm is not obligated to pay dividends on the preferred stock unless dividends are also paid to common stockholders. Thus, rather than increasing the probability of bankruptcy, the issuance of preferred stock lessens bankruptcy risk by raising the total assets of the firm, thereby strengthening the capacity of the company to meet its debt obligations.

The value of a bond is the discounted worth of the coupon (interest) payments and maturity value. This discounted value may differ from the bond's face or maturity value, depending upon the interest rate investors use to discount the bond payments. The debt agreement, or indenture, may include provisions to protect bondholders, such as the requirement that the firm maintain a given working capital position, restrict dividends, refrain from issuing further debt of the same class, or

---

[14] $135 million = $9 million $(P/A, 6\%, 20)$ + $100 million $(P/F, 6\%, 20)$ = $9 million(11.47) + $100 million(0.3118).

periodically retire part of the debt issue. The tax deductibility of interest is a strong inducement to the use of debt. This inducement does not exist for preferred stock, since preferred dividends are not tax deductible to the paying corporation.

In addition to the conventional types of debt that are most commonly used, there is a variety of rather novel debt forms. The forms include income bonds, industrial development bonds, variable rate (floating rate) bonds, low coupon bonds, put bonds, and project financing.

Preferred stock dividends must be paid before any dividends can be paid on the common stock. Dividends are usually cumulative; that is, before any dividends can be issued on the common stock, there must be payment of all past preferred dividends as yet unpaid. Preferred stock may be participating, in which case preferred shareholders receive dividends on an equal basis with common stockholders.

Financing with debt and preferred stock, rather than with additional common stock, allows existing common stockholders to retain company control and to retain claim to any extraordinary company profits. Debt has the added advantage of interest tax deductibility, whereas preferred stock does not involve the default risk associated with debt. The choice between debt and preferred stock as a method of financing will depend upon the volatility of the firm's income and upon its existing capital structure. Even a relatively stable company may issue preferred stock rather than additional debt if its existing debt burden is great.

QUESTIONS

1   Describe the nature of the promise made to debtholders as opposed to the promise made to stockholders.
2   Explain the financial manager's motivation to use debt.
3   Define: bond, indenture, face value, and coupon rate.
4   Describe how one goes about placing a value on a bond.
5   Why is it that bonds usually do not sell at face value? Explain fully.
6   Distinguish between debentures and mortgage bonds.
7   What role does the trustee assume when bonds are issued?
8   Under what conditions do you think a firm would call its bonds?
9   Of what value is the cumulative feature found in preferred stock issues?
10 How can a bond or preferred stock refunding decision be viewed as an investment decision?
11 "In the text of this chapter, the discount rate used to evaluate a refunding decision is the aftertax cost of debt to the firm. I thought the firm's average cost of capital was supposed to be used to evaluate capital budgeting decisions. How come the authors used the rate they did?" Answer this question.

PROJECT

Obtain from a stockbroker a prospectus for a new bond issue. Examine the provisions concerning priority of payment, collateral (if applicable), restrictions on the firm (on dividends, working capital position, etc.), and any other matters discussed in this chapter.

1 Find the value of a bond that matures in sixteen years, has a face value of $1000 and a coupon rate of 14 percent, and pays interest annually. Bonds of similar quality and maturity have a yield to maturity of 13 percent. [Ans.: $1066]

2 Find the value of a bond that matures in twelve years, has a face value of $1000 and a coupon rate of 10 percent, and pays interest annually. Bonds of similar quality and maturity have a yield to maturity of 16 percent.

3 Purdee Corporation is planning to issue twenty-five year bonds with a face value of $1000 per bond to finance expansion of its plant. The bonds pay interest once per year. The market rate of interest (yield to maturity) on bonds of the same risk and maturity as the proposed Purdee issue is 12 percent.

   a If Purdee issues the bonds with a 15 percent coupon, what price will one bond sell for? With a 12 percent coupon? With a 9 percent coupon?

4 Below is the balance sheet, *before* liquidation, of Madison Ring Company, Inc. The debt is in the form of A bonds and B bonds. Assume that the firm is liquidated after having defaulted on its debt, and that it receives $0.50 on a dollar (book value) for all of its assets. What would the debtholders be entitled to if there were no subordinated debt (i.e., neither A bonds or B bonds subordinated to the other)? What would debtholders obtain if the B bonds were subordinated to the A bonds? What do the shareholders get in each case?

Madison Ring Company balance sheet		
Total assets		$700,000
Liabilities:		
A bonds	$250,000	
B bonds	150,000	
Total liabilities	$400,000	
Net worth	300,000	
Total liabilities and net worth		$700,000

5 Primabella Fabrics is planning a capital expansion next year to meet the increasing demand for its products. It estimates that it will need $10 million and plans to issue preferred stock to finance the expansion. The preferred will have a par value of $100 and an 11 percent dividend. Primabella does not plan to retire the preferred in the foreseeable future. It has found that similar issues of preferred (same risk and maturity characteristics) are yielding 12 percent. Assume that flotation costs are zero.

   a What price can Primabella expect to receive for a share of the preferred?

b How many shares must it issue to finance the planned expansion? [Ans.: 109,091 shares]

c What are the advantages of a preferred issue over a bond issue?

6 In 1985 Hickok Pharmaceuticals floated a $30 million bond issue scheduled to mature in 2005. Since interest rates were relatively high at the time of issuance, Hickok attached a 12.5 percent coupon to the bonds in order to sell them at a par value of $1000 per bond. Flotation costs for the issue were $750,000 which Hickok is amortizing over the life of the bond issue for tax purposes. Hickok's tax rate is 40 percent. The bond indenture stipulates that Hickok may call the bonds after 1986 at a price of $1050 per bond. Recently the prime rate has fallen and Hickok's investment bankers have notifed the firm that it can now issue $30 million in bonds at par with a coupon rate of 9.5 percent to mature in fifteen years. Flotation costs on the new issue would amount to $877,500. The bankers also mentioned that they do not expect the interest rate to fall lower in the near future. The finance officers of Hickok are meeting to determine whether or not they should refinance the old bonds in light of the information given by the investment bankers. What do you advise? (Note: You may round off percents to the nearest $\frac{1}{2}$ percent, e.g., 6.4 percent rounded to 6.5 percent or 7.8 percent rounded to 8 percent, before performing present value computations.) Analyze the problem assuming that the present date is January 1988, just after interest has been paid on the old bonds.

7 Beam Utility Services is considering refunding an old preferred stock issue. There are 40,000 shares of the preferred outstanding. Beam is paying a $12 dividend per year on each share. The par value is $100 per share, and Beam can call the stock at $102 per share. Beam's financial analysts feel that they can issue 40,000 new shares of preferred at their par value of $100. Since the market rate of interest on similar issues is 11 percent, the analysts feel that if the preferred promises an $11 dividend it can be sold at par, thus saving the firm $40,000 annually in dividends. Flotation costs on the new issue would be $80,000; this $80,000 cost is completely deductible in the current year. Beam is in the 40 percent tax bracket. Assume that the call premium on the outstanding preferred stock is *not* tax deductible. Should Beam refund the preferred stock issue?

22

CONVERTIBLES
AND WARRANTS

The securities used most often by corporations to raise long-term capital are common stock, bonds, and preferred stock. Convertibles and warrants are alternatives to these three basic securities. Convertibles and warrants have the special feature that either can be converted at the will of the owner into the issuing company's common stock. In this chapter we describe these securities and explain why they appeal to investors and to companies seeking capital.

CONVERTIBLES

Convertible bonds and preferred stock can be converted at the discretion of the security's owner into the common stock of the issuing firm. The owner may convert at any time or choose never to convert. The investor's decision regarding conversion is discussed below.

Conversion Price and Conversion Ratio

The **conversion price** is the dollars of par value of the convertible security paid per share of common stock acquired through conversion.[1] For example, if the conversion price of the stock is $50, a $1000 (par value) bond can be converted into twenty shares of common stock. That is,

$$\text{Conversion price} = \frac{\text{par value of convertible security}}{\text{number of common shares received}} \qquad (22\text{-}1)$$

$$= \frac{\$1000}{20} = \$50$$

Similarly, if a share of convertible preferred with a par value of $100 is convertible into two shares of common stock, the conversion price is $50.

The **conversion ratio** is the number of common shares received for converting the convertible security. In the examples above, the conversion ratio is 20 for the convertible bond and 2 for the convertible preferred.

The convertible security agreement may contain a provision for a varying conversion price over time; for example, a bond may be convertible into 10 shares of common stock from 1980 to 1982, into $9\frac{1}{2}$ shares of common stock from 1983 to 1985, and so on. Less frequently, the conversion option completely expires after a number of years.

The conversion ratio is adjusted if stock dividends or a stock split is declared. The adjustment ensures that holders of the convertible security will maintain their proportional shares of the firm's common stock. For example, a 10 percent stock dividend would result in a 10 percent increase in the conversion ratio.

---

[1] See Chaps. 20 and 21 on par value.

Investment Value of the Convertible Security   The **investment value** (pure security value) of a convertible security is the value that the security would have if it were not convertible but had all its other features. Investment value equals the present value of the interest plus maturity value of a convertible bond, or the present value of the dividend payments anticipated on a convertible preferred. For example, the investment value of a $1000 par 5 percent convertible bond with twenty years to maturity is the present value of the interest payments of $50 per year, plus the present value of the $1000 maturity value received twenty years hence. Applying the bond valuation procedure at the beginning of Chapter 21, if the market interest rate on bonds of comparable risk but lacking the conversion option is 7 percent, the investment value of the bond is

$$\text{Investment value} = \frac{\$50}{1 + 0.07} + \frac{\$50}{(1 + 0.07)^2}$$

$$+ \cdots + \frac{\$50}{(1 + 0.07)^{20}} + \frac{\$1000}{(1 + 0.07)^{20}}$$

$$= \$50(P/A, 7\%, 20) + \$1000(P/F, 7\%, 20)$$

$$= \$50(10.594) + \$1000(0.2584) = \$788 \qquad (22\text{-}2)$$

A convertible security's market value will generally exceed its investment value. Why is this so? Because the investor not only receives the coupon (interest) payments and the maturity payment (or, with preferred stock, the preferred dividend payments) but also has the *additional advantage* of being able to convert the security into common stock at his or her option. The market value of a convertible equals its investment value plus the value of the option to convert.

Conversion Value of the Convertible Security   The **conversion value** of a security is the market value of the stock into which it is convertible. For example, assume that a $1000 bond is convertible into twenty shares of common stock with a market value of $46 per share. The conversion value of the bond is $920 (20 × $46). That is,

Conversion value = (number of shares of common stock received upon
conversion) × (market price per share of common
stock)

= (conversion ratio) × (market price per share of
common stock)   (22-3)

If the market price of the common stock is high, conversion value can exceed investment value. Conversion value is shown in Figure 22-1; it rises as the market price of the common stock rises. Notice that conversion value can also be less than investment value, if the price of the common stock is low. Recall that our 5 percent bond has an investment value of $788, which in no way depends on the price of the common stock. But conversion value does depend on the market price of the common. If that market price were

$30 per share, the conversion value would be $600 (20 shares × $30 per share), which is less than the investment value of $788. If the price per common share were $50, the conversion value of the convertible bond would be $1000, greater than investment value. Thus, conversion value can be above or below investment value depending upon whether the price of the common stock is high or low.

Market Value (Market Price) of the Convertible Security   We have decided that the market value of the convertible security cannot be less than its investment value because the convertible security's market value equals the investment value of the bond or preferred stock plus the value of the right to convert. It is also true that market value can never be less than conversion value—this is so since the security is always worth at least as much as the common stock into which it can be converted. For example, if we know that we can convert a bond into $920 worth of stock ($920 conversion value), then we know that the convertible bond must be worth at least $920. Therefore, *market value is never less than investment value and never less than conversion value.*

The market value of the convertible security may exceed the investment and conversion values. Since the security also offers the option to convert, a premium above investment value may be paid for the convertible. The market value may also exceed the conversion value, since a convertible

---

FIGURE 22-1

Investment and conversion values of a convertible bond.

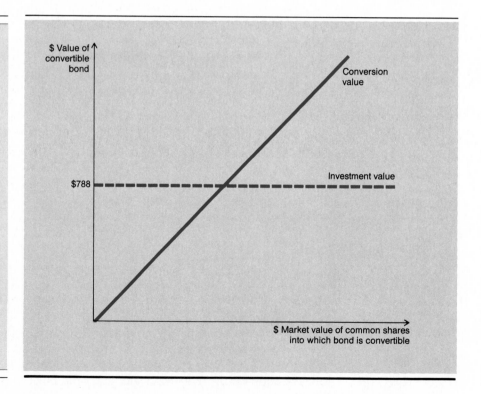

security not only offers the stock if one wishes to convert *but also has the investment value floor that common stock does not have.*

To illustrate, assume that the convertible bond in the above example has an investment value of $788 and is convertible into twenty shares of common stock with a market price of $60 per share; the conversion value of the bond is $1200, the market value of the twenty shares of common stock. But which is better, owning the convertible bond or owning the twenty shares of common stock? Clearly, the bond. The bond can always be converted into the twenty shares of common stock, so it must be worth at least as much as the twenty shares of common stock. The bond also has a "floor value," as explained above, equal to its investment value; no such floor exists for the twenty shares of common stock. Thus, if the common stock were to fall to $30 per share, the twenty shares of common stock would be worth $600. However, the convertible bond's value would not fall to $600; it would fall no further than the investment value floor of $788.[2] This added advantage of the convertible security gives it a value above the twenty shares of stock into which it can be converted (its conversion value). Of course, if the prices of the common stock and the convertible become extremely high, the investment value may become almost irrelevant and the value of the convertible security may approach its conversion value. For example, if the price of the common stock were $100 per share, conversion value of the convertible bond would be $2000 (20 shares × $100 per share). If it is extemely unlikely that the common stock will fall significantly, the floor provided by the investment value does not provide much of an advantage, and the convertible bond's market value will approximate its conversion value.

In summary, the market value of a convertible security will never be less than, and will generally exceed, both its investment value and its conversion value. See Figure 22-2. The **conversion premium** is the amount by which the market value of the convertible exceeds the higher of its investment and conversion values (shaded area in Figure 22-2).

Dilution Effects of Conversion

Conversion generally lowers the earnings per share on the common stock. Let's see why. Assume that the firm has $10 million of twenty-year, 6 percent convertible bonds outstanding (not yet converted), which are convertible into common stock at a conversion price of $50 (therefore convertible into 200,000 shares of common). The firm also has 1 million shares of common stock outstanding before conversion. From Exhibit 22-1, which summarizes

---

[2] For the investment value to remain at $788, the market interest rate in Eq. (22-2) must be 7 percent. If the general level of interest rates rises and the stock's price falls, e.g., if the interest rate in Eq. (22-2) rises to 8 percent, the investment value would become $50(P/A, 8%, 20) + $1000(P/F, 8%, 20) = $705, which still exceeds the $600 value of the shares; the convertible bond would therefore have a market price of at least $705. If the interest rate on the bond were 10 percent in Eq. (22-2), then the investment value would be $50(P/A, 10%, 20) + $1000(P/F, 10%, 20) = $574; in this case, the convertible bond would be worth at least $600, since the bond's value must be no less than its investment value ($574) or the value of the stock into which it can be converted ($600).

the position of the firm before and after conversion, we see that the earnings per share on the common stock drop from $3.30 to $3 due to conversion.[3] To see how this same concept works for convertible preferred stock, see problems **3** and **5**.

Appraisal of Convertible Securities

Many investors find convertible securities attractive because they provide a relatively safe investment income (and therefore an investment value floor) with the possibility of a large gain if the common stock appreciates significantly. However, the investor pays for the conversion right since the yield on a convertible security is less than that on a comparable security without the conversion privilege. For example, a twenty-year, $1000 nonconvertible bond of the firm with a coupon rate of 8 percent ($80 per year in interest payments) might sell at its face value of $1000, whereas a convertible bond

[3] It is possible that conversion will lead to a rise in earnings per share. This will occur if earnings per share before conversion are less than added aftertax earnings from eliminating the fixed charges, i.e., interest or preferred dividends on the convertible security divided by the number of new shares due to conversion. For example, assume that in Exhibit 22-1 the firm's convertible bonds were convertible into 50,000 shares of common stock instead of into 200,000 shares. After conversion there are 1,050,000 shares of common stock with earnings of $3.43 per share, which exceeds the preconversion earnings per share of $3.30. This occurred since earnings before conversion of $3 were less than added earnings from eliminating the interest on the convertibles divided by the number of new shares ($300,000/50,000 shares) = $6.

FIGURE 22-2

Value of a convertible bond. The market value of the convertible bond is never less than the investment value or conversion value. The market value of the convertible approaches conversion value if the common stock has a very high market value. The shaded area is the conversion premium, which is the excess of the convertible's market value over the higher of investment value and conversion value.

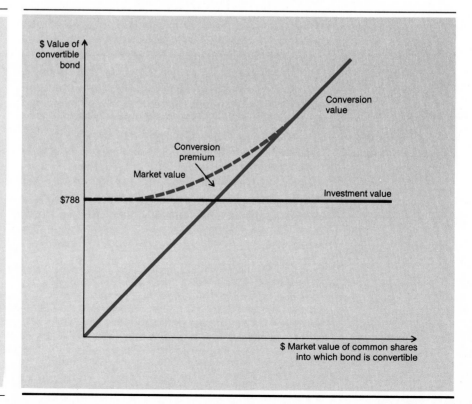

with a coupon rate of only 6 percent ($60 per year in interest payments) might also sell at its face value of $1000. The nonconvertible bond yields 8 percent and the convertible bond yields 6 percent. The difference in yield is due to the conversion feature of the 6 percent bond. That is, investors are willing to accept the lower yield on the convertible bond because of the convertibility privilege.

It should be pointed out that convertible bonds often have a lower-priority position (subordinated position) than some or all of the issuing company's other debt obligations. The investor will want to take this factor into account.

The firm's decision to sell a convertible security must be based, like all financing decisions, on the firm's particular situation and on security market conditions. There is no reason to suppose that convertibles are, on the average, superior to other financing vehicles. It may appear that there is an advantage to the firm because convertible bonds or preferred stock can be sold at a yield less than that required if the securities were nonconvertible. However, whether such an advantage exists depends on the future trend in the company's common stock price. If the firm's stock does not appreciate much in value, then the common stockholders are better off since conversion will never occur. But if the firm prospers and the value of its stock rises, conversion will occur and the convertible security holders will effectively have bought the company's common stock at a bargain price. In this case, the firm's common shareholders are worse off than they would have been if the firm had initially issued nonconvertible securities. Therefore, the company's decision to issue convertibles essentially involves a gamble on the future course of the firm's stock.

Benefits may be provided by convertibles if the firm wishes to increase its debt (or preferred stock) outstanding in the short-run, but to replace the debt later with common stock financing. If the firm were to issue nonconvertible bonds now and stock later to pay off those bonds, it would incur flotation costs twice—now, and later when the stock is sold. With convertibles it could issue convertible debt now, which would be converted into

---

EXHIBIT 22-1
Effect of conversion on earnings per share

	Before conversion	After conversion
Earnings before interest and taxes	$7,200,000	$7,200,000
Bond interest.............................	600,000	0
Earnings before taxes.....................	$6,600,000	$7,200,000
Taxes (at 50%)	3,300,000	3,600,000
Earnings after taxes	$3,300,000	$3,600,000
No. of shares of common stock.............	1 million	1.2 million
Earnings per share.......................	$3.30	$3.00

common stock at the later date, with flotation costs incurred only in the current period. If a rise in the firm's common stock in a later period is anticipated, so that conversion can be expected to occur, this approach will avoid the refunding costs associated with replacing the nonconvertible debt with common stock.

Generally, convertible issues have a call provision that provides the firm with a means of compelling convertible security holders to convert to common stock if the stock price rises sufficiently. If the conversion value of the convertible security rises above the call price, the firm can merely call the securities and conversion will be forced. For example, assume a $1000 convertible bond convertible into twenty shares of City Corporation common stock. Let the call provision allow the firm to call the convertible for $1100. Assume that the price per share of City common stock is $65. The conversion value of the bond is $1300 (20 shares × $65 per share). City Corporation can call the bond, and security holders have the choice of converting or surrendering their bonds for the call price. An investor who does not convert receives the call price of $1100; an investor who does convert receives twenty shares of common stock with a total value of $1300. Obviously, investors will convert.

WARRANTS

A warrant is an option to buy a specified number of the firm's common stock at a stated price per share. Recall that a convertible security required surrender of the security in exchange for the common stock. A warrant requires a surrender of the warrant, *plus* the payment of additional cash—called the **exercise price**—in order to obtain the common stock. Warrants are issued by corporations for cash to investors who may exercise them (i.e., buy the stock) or may resell them to other investors. A warrant is like a stock right except that rights are issued free to existing stockholders who may sell them or exercise them by buying new shares (see Chapter 20). Warrants do not have to be exercised when they are bought but generally expire at a given date, although some are perpetual. Alleghany Corporation, Atlas Corporation, and Tri-Continental Corporation are among the few firms that have issued perpetual warrants.

In some cases, the exercise price of the common stock varies—generally moving upward—over time. For example, Indian Head warrants that expire in 1990 allow the owner to purchase one share of common stock at $25 per share until May 15, 1975, at $30 per share until May 15, 1980, at $35 per share until May 15, 1985, and $40 per share until May 15, 1990.

Warrants are often issued with other securities (usually bonds or preferred stock) in a unit or package. The warrants in this case may be "detached" and sold separately by the investor.

Valuation of a Warrant

Theoretical Value of a Warrant The **theoretical value** of a warrant equals the market value of the common stock purchased with the warrant minus the total exercise price paid for the shares. This is analogous to the conversion value of a convertible security. The theoretical value equals

Theoretical value of a warrant

$$\begin{aligned} = &\ (\text{market price of common stock} - \text{exercise price}) \\ &\times (\text{number of shares purchased with one warrant}) \quad (22\text{-}4) \end{aligned}$$

For example, assume that Makitbig Company has warrants outstanding, each of which entitles the holder to purchase two shares of Makitbig Company stock for $40 per share. These warrants expire on December 31, 1988. If Makitbig common stock were selling for $45 per share, using Eq. (22-4) the theoretical value of the warrant would be

Theoretical value of Makitbig warrant $= (\$45 - \$40) \times 2 = \$10$

By owning a warrant we can buy two shares of stock from the company for $10 less than buying the shares on the open market. The theoretical value can therefore be defined as the discount on the company's common stock that is allowed the warrantholder. If investors buy warrants *for their theoretical value* and exercise them, they end up paying the same price for the company's common stock as they would if they were to buy the common stock directly in the market.

What if the market price of the common stock were equal to or below the exercise price? Then the theoretical value of the warrant would be zero (a warrant will never have a negative value).

Market Value of a Warrant An investor willing to purchase the common stock at its market price would willingly pay the theoretical value for a warrant, since it can be immediately exercised and the common stock obtained. The theoretical value represents the minimum market value of the warrant. Warrants, however, also offer investors the added option of holding the warrant instead of purchasing shares.

Since warrants do not provide their owners any dividends or interest payments, they do not have any investment value comparable to that for a convertible security. The market value of a warrant is due entirely to its potential conversion into common stock. However, the market price of a warrant is generally greater than its theoretical value. The difference between the market price of a warrant and its theoretical value is called the **premium** on the warrant. Let's see why premiums arise and how they depend on the price of the stock.

Suppose the price of Makitbig stock in the example above is $40. The $40 exercise price of the Makitbig warrants is therefore equal to the stock price and the theoretical value of the warrants is $0. Will the market price and premium for the warrants be $0? Of course not. The owner of a Makitbig warrant will be able to realize a positive dollar return from owning the warrant if the stock price rises above $40 (the exercise price of the warrant) at any time prior to the expiration date of the warrant. The warrant will sell at a positive price (and premium) so long as there is a chance that the price of Makitbig common will exceed $40 prior to expiration of the warrant. Since the stock price is currently at $40, the chances are very good that the stock will rise in price (unless the warrant will expire momentarily) and therefore the premium will be relatively large. However, suppose that the stock price is $30, well below the exercise price. The theoretical value of the warrant is $0 in this case, just as before. But now, in order for the warrant to provide a positive dollar return from exercising it, the stock price must rise significantly above its current level. Therefore, the price (and premium) of the warrant will be much lower if Makitbig stock is selling for $30 than it would be if Makitbig stock were selling for $40. We can conclude that the further below the exercise price ($40) is the current price of the stock, the lower will be the warrant's premium and market price (market price = premium since the market price is less than the exercise price of $40).

What happens to the market price and the premium on the warrant if Makitbig's stock price goes over $40? The warrant's market price will rise reflecting the higher theoretical value of the warrant, but the premium will decrease. Therefore, at stock prices well above the exercise price, the market price of the warrant becomes approximately equal to its theoretical value; that is, the premium vanishes. This decline in the premium is due to the reduced advantage of owning the warrant relative to exercising it. To see why this is so, let's assume for a moment that the premium is a constant $5 regardless of Makitbig's stock price. As we will see, this assumption of a constant premium is not reasonable. Furthermore, for illustrative purposes, suppose that investors expect that Makitbig stock will provide the same probability distribution of annual rates of return at any given price for the stock. The assumed distribution is

---

EXHIBIT 22-2
Returns from Makitbig warrants

	Current stock price					
	$40		$45		$50	
Current market price of warrant[a]	$ 5		$15		$25	
Future stock price[b]	$32	$56	$36	$63	$40	$70
Dollar return from warrant[c]	$ 0	$32	$ 0	$46	$ 0	$60
Rate of return on warrant[d]	−100%	540%	−100%	207%	−100%	140%
Expected dollar return[e]	$16		$23		$30	
Expected rate of return on warrant[f]	220%		53.3%		20%	

[a] Theoretical value plus $5 premium.
[b] Based on constant probability distribution of rate of return applied to given stock price.

Probability:	0.5	0.5
Rate of return:	−20%	40%

For example, if the current stock price is $40, the future stock price will be either [$40 − .20($40)] = $32 or [$40 + .40($40)] = $56.
[c] Assumes warrant for two shares of stock is exercised if stock price exceeds exercise price of $40. Thus, for example, if the current stock price is $40 and the future stock price is $56, the dollar return from the warrant = 2 × ($56 − $40) = $32.
[d] Equals [(Dollar return from warrant/current market price of warrant) − 1] × 100%.
[e] Based on equal probabilities of occurrence of 0.5. For example, $16 = .5($0) + .5($32).
[f] Based on equal probabilities of occurrence of 0.5. For example, 220% = .5(−100%) + .5(540%) = 220%.

| Probability: | 0.5 | 0.5 |
| Rate of return: | −20% | 40% |

The expected rate of return on the stock is therefore 10 percent [$0.5 \times (-20\%) + 0.5 \times (40\%)$].

Exhibit 22-2 shows the rates of return expected on Makitbig warrants assuming that they will expire in one year and hence will be exercised within one year if it is profitable to do so. Observe that the expected rate of return declines as the stock price rises due to the increased theoretical value of the warrant plus our assumed constant premium of $5. Thus, for example, if $5 is a reasonable premium from the perspective of investors when the stock price is $40, the $5 premium is too high when the stock price is $45. The actual premium will decrease as the stock price increases. Therefore, in Exhibit 22-2, the premium will be less at a stock price of $45 than at a stock price of $40, and the premium will be less at a stock price of $50 than at a stock price of $45. As the stock price becomes very high, the premium almost completely disappears and the market price of the warrant will approximate its theoretical value.[4]

The general behavior of the price of Makitbig's warrants is illustrated in Figure 22-3. The market price of the warrant equals the premium for stock

[4] As the stock price goes up, both the expected rate of return on the warrant for any given fixed premium and the risk decline. Therefore, the net impact is difficult to analyze, but under reasonable assumptions it is possible to show that the premium should decline as the stock price rises (this is what we observe in practice). On this, see Paul A. Samuelson, "Rational Theory of Warrant Pricing," *Industrial Managment Review* (Spring 1965).

FIGURE 22-3

Value of Makitbig warrants.

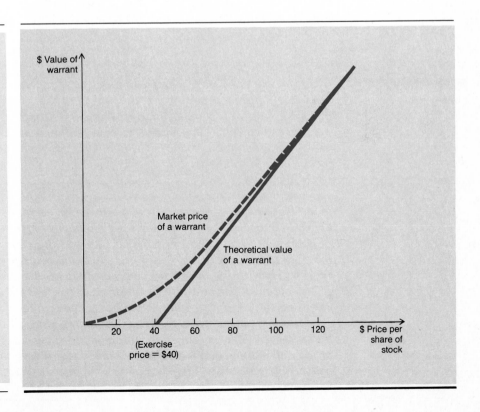

prices below the exercise price of $40. For stock prices below $40, changes in the market price of the warrant are the result of a changing premium. The market price of the warrant increases for stock prices above $40 due to the increased theoretical value; however, the premium declines as the stock price increases due to the reduced advantage of holding the warrant relative to exercising it.

Appraisal and Use of Warrants

Warrants have value beyond their theoretical value because they provide the opportunity of owning the common stock if the warrants are immediately exercised and the alternative of holding the unexercised warrant. As explained in the previous section, one may wish to hold the unexercised warrant rather than the common stock since it offers the potential for a very high rate of return. Of course, there is also a high risk of loss. Also, until the warrants are exercised, the warrantholder receives no voting privileges or dividends.

The attraction of warrants for investors has led to their frequent use, especially by small dynamic firms as part of units of bonds, preferred stock, or common stock. A unit might be composed of a bond plus a warrant or of several shares of common stock plus a warrant. Various such combinations have appeared. Although warrants have characteristically been the tool of the smaller firm, in April 1970 AT&T, in a monumental offering, obtained $1.57 billion on an issue of bonds and warrants. This was the first time in over fifty years that the New York Stock Exchange accepted warrants for listing. As it turned out, the price of AT&T stock declined and the warrants become practically valueless, with few of them being exercised. Since 1970, other large firms have issued warrants, many of which are also listed on the New York Stock Exchange.

SUMMARY

A convertible bond or preferred stock can be transformed into the common stock of the corporation at the option of the holder. The value of a convertible as an income-producing security—providing bond interest or preferred dividends—is referred to as its investment value. The market value of the common stock into which the security can be converted is its conversion value. The convertible's market value is the price it sells for in the market, and this value will generally exceed both investment value and conversion value. Conversion increases the number of common shares outstanding and usually decreases earnings per share. A convertible provides the investor with a relatively safe return in the form of interest or preferred dividends and, in addition, the potential opportunity to participate in the firm's growth and stock price increase. However, because of the conversion advantage to the investor, the firm can pay a lower interest rate or lower preferred dividend rate than would be the case if the conversion option were not included. Whether a convertible is attractive to a given investor will depend upon the investor's risk-return preferences and expectations regarding the future price of the company's common stock. Similarly, the firm's decision to issue a convertible security will depend upon management's expectations regard-

ing the company's stock price. An advantage of convertible securities is that they allow the firm, in effect, to issue debt in the short run and stock in the long run (when the convertible is converted into common stock) without incurring flotation costs on two separate issues.

The purchase of a warrant entitles the holder to purchase the company's common stock at a specified price on any date preceding the warrant's expiration. A warrant has a theoretical value equal to the market value of the stock obtained with the warrant less the price paid for the stock upon exercise. The theoretical value is the discount provided the warrantholder on the price of the common stock. The market value of the warrant will at least equal, and will generally exceed, its theoretical value. Although historically the device of small firms, warrants have recently enjoyed increased popularity as a financing method of larger companies.

QUESTIONS

1 What is the investment value of a convertible security? Explain.
2 Explain what is likely to happen to the investment value of a convertible if the general level of interest rates rises.
3 Why is it that a convertible security's market price will generally exceed its investment value?
4 "Convertible securities can be sold with a lower coupon rate than nonconvertible securities. This means that their cost to the firm is less than that of nonconvertible securities." Comment on this statement.
5 What should the holder of a convertible bond do if the bonds are called for redemption and the bond is selling:
   at call price
   below call price
   above call price
6 Will dilution in earnings per share of common caused by conversion of convertible securities cause a decline in the value of the shares?
7 What are the major differences between a warrant and a convertible security?
8 In terms of their earning dilution effects, compare the conversion of a convertible bond into the company's common stock with the exercise of a warrant to acquire the firm's stock.
9 "If the theoretical value of a warrant is equal to the market price of that warrant, an investor should be indifferent between the purchase of the warrant *and exercising it* and the purchase of the stock." Evaluate this statement, assuming there are no trading costs to consider.
10 Why might it be advantageous to hold a company's warrants rather than its common shares?

PROJECT

Select a convertible bond and obtain quarterly price data for a two-year period (for data, see, for example, *The Wall Street Journal*). For each quarter determine the convertible's investment value, conversion value, market value, and conversion premium. Satisfy yourself that the ideas presented in this chapter are valid for the convertible you selected.

Also obtain two years of quarterly price data for a warrant. Identify the warrant's market price and theoretical value for each quarter. Consider the market price and theoretical value behavior in light of the chapter material.

PROBLEMS

1 If the market price of a common share is $90, and you hold a warrant entitling you to purchase ten shares at a price of $50 per share, what is the theoretical value of the warrant? [Ans.: Theoretical value = $400]

2 Rumley, Inc., has outstanding an issue of $1000, 14 percent subordinated convertible debentures that are callable, will mature in ten years, and are convertible into common stock at a conversion price of $50. The market price of the common stock is $70. What is the conversion value of the convertible bonds? [Ans.: Conversion value = $1,400]

3 A $100 par value preferred stock is convertible into common stock at a conversion price of $50, and the preferred stock is selling in the market at $250 per share. The preferred's investment value is $130. What is the approximate market price of the common stock? Show any calculations you make. [Ans.: Price of common stock = $125]

4 Assume that you own a $1000 convertible bond of the Barber Company maturing in six years. These bonds have a 13 percent coupon rate. The bonds are convertible into twenty shares of common stock. In addition, the bonds are callable at a call price of $1150. The Barber Company straight bonds (i.e., nonconvertible, noncallable) currently sell to yield 15 percent and Barber's stock is selling at $55 a share. The straight bonds have the same risk as the convertibles would have if they didn't have the conversion feature.
   a What is the conversion ratio for the convertible bond?
   b What are the conversion price, conversion value, and investment value?
   c What is the bond's current market value floor?
   d What is the minimum price of the common stock at which shareholders will convert if the convertible bonds are called? (Ignore personal taxes in your computation.)
   e Suppose the stock's price falls to $45 a share. In this case, what would be the bond's market value floor?

5 Lionel Pidgeon Industries has a $120 million, ten-year, 13 percent convertible bond issue outstanding. The company also has 120,000 shares of $11\frac{1}{2}$ percent, $500 par convertible preferred stock outstanding. Both the bonds and the preferred stock are callable. The bond's conversion price is $30 and the preferred conversion ratio is 20. The company is now in a position to call either or both issues. The current year's earnings before interest and taxes are expected to be $95 million. The firm currently has 1.5 million shares of common stock

outstanding. Its tax rate is 50 percent. Show the effect on earnings
per share of

  a Conversion of the bonds only.

  b Conversion of the preferred stock only.

  c Conversion of both bonds and preferred stock.

  d Assume that the bonds' conversion price is $50 (instead of $30).
Show what happens to EPS upon conversion of the bonds only
and comment on the result.

6 Consider a $1000, 12 percent convertible, twenty-year bond maturing
ten years from now. The bond is convertible into common stock at a
conversion price of $50. The bond is also callable at $1120. Currently
this bond is trading at $1100, and the common stock of the same
firm sells at $42 a share. Straight bonds of this quality and maturity
are currently traded on the market to yield 11 percent.

  a What is the conversion premium paid on the convertible bond?

  b At what common stock price would the holders of the convertible bond be indifferent between surrendering the bond if called
or converting? (Ignore personal taxes in your computation.)

  c Suppose that the price per share for the common stock remains
at $42, but the going rate of interest falls to 9 percent. What is
the minimum possible market value of the bond?

7 A share of Karma Corporation's common stock sells for $60. One
warrant will purchase three shares of the common stock at an exercise price per share of $38. What is the theoretical value of the
warrant?

8 A warrant sells for $115 and entitles the owner to purchase ten
shares of stock at an exercise price of $9 per share. The common
stock sells for $20 per share.

    What is the theoretical value of the warrant?

    What is the premium at which the warrant is selling?

9 Fruhan, Inc., needs to raise $5 million to introduce a new engine oil
additive. The company would like to sell common stock, but the
market is somewhat depressed and management believes that the
current $25 a share for its stock does not reflect its true value. Two
alternatives are being considered: (**a**) sell 5000 12 percent convertible
bonds (each with a par value of $1000) with a conversion ratio of 20
or (**b**) sell 5000 12 percent bonds, each with a par value of $1000 and
each with twenty warrants attached, with each warrant good to buy
one share of common stock at $32. With **a** or **b**, Fruhan will receive
$5 million in cash (the bonds are sold at par with zero underwriting
costs). Before adopting **a** or **b**, the firm has the following liabilities
and equity position:

Short-term loans	$ 500,000
Common stock, $10 par	2,000,000
Retained earnings	500,000
Total claims	$3,000,000

The firm's rate of return on assets before interest and taxes is 30 percent; its tax rate is 50 percent. Thus the EBIT before a or b is adopted is $900,000 (30% × $3,000,000). The rate of return (in terms of EBIT) on investment of any new capital raised under a or b will also be 30 percent.

a Show the liabilities and equity position of the firm for both alternatives a and b *after* conversion.

b Assuming that the firm invests all of its available funds, compute the earnings per share (EPS) for alternatives a and b. Explain the differences, if any.

c What considerations other than EPS could be important in reaching a decision as to which alternative to use?

In the spring of 1973, two events occurred in Chicago that sparked minor revolutions in the theory and practice of finance, created excitement among investors, caused concern in the chambers of the United States Congress, and generated long hours for the staff at the Securities and Exchange Commission. In April the Chicago Board of Trade launched a new venture, the Chicago Board Options Exchange (CBOE), an organized exchange for the trading of options in common stocks. A few weeks later the May–June issue of the *Journal of Political Economy* (published by the University of Chicago) was mailed out to subscribers. In the *Journal* was an article by two academicians, Fischer Black and Myron Scholes, entitled "The Pricing of Options and Corporate Liabilities." The "Option Pricing Model" developed by Black and Scholes has since taken a position in financial theory second only to the "Capital Asset Pricing Model" of Chapter 6.

Since 1973 the trading volume in options has exploded. For popular companies such as IBM and Kodak, more shares are now involved in options trading than in the stock themselves. In the academic literature there has been a parallel increase in journal articles analyzing options and other financial contracts using the perspective of option pricing theory. What are these options that people are so excited about and what new insights has the analysis of options provided? The answers to these questions are the topic of this essay.

THE OPTIONS MARKETS

Have you ever received a rain check when you tried to purchase an item on sale at a store but found the item was out of stock? If the store gives you a slip of paper saying that you can buy the item at the sale price when the item comes in, the store has given you a **call option** on the item. A call option in common stock is the right to purchase the stock at a fixed price ("exercise price" or "striking price") during a set period of time. A typical call contract provides the purchaser with the right to buy 100 shares of a particular stock at any time up to and including the expiration date of the call, which may be thirty days to one year from the time the call was first written. Note that the holder of a call does not have to buy the stock (or the item at the store); the call provides the option of buying or not buying at the holder's discretion. Warrants (discussed in Chapter 22) are a special type of call option issued by a company on the company's stock. A **put option** is the right to sell a given number of shares of a particular stock at a specified exercise price during a set period of time. The holder of a put has the option of selling or not selling the stock.

Options have been used in real estate transactions for many years. Land developers often purchase options on individual parcels of land in the process of attempting to put together a large enough area to make a development project economically feasible. Stockbrokers and dealers have traditionally bought and sold options for their customers. The opening of the CBOE meant that an organized market existed for purchase and sale of options on common stock. In particular, a good secondary market for options now exists. Thus, for example, the investor in a call option that will expire in six months has the choice of:

1. Selling the option to another investor at any time in the next six months
2. Exercising the option (buying the underlying stock for the price fixed in the contract) at any time in the next six months
3. Holding the option until it expires

Similarly, the holder of a put option can sell it to someone else, exercise it, or simply hold it until expiration. With an organized exchange it is now easy for the investor to find out what the current value of the option is, and the investor knows that it will be easy to sell the option at any time. These are the same sorts of advantages that exist for investors in stock listed on the stock exchanges as compared with those that trade "over-the-counter."

For whatever reasons, individuals and financial institutions have flocked to the options market. In 1973, 1.1 million option contracts traded on the CBOE; in 1974 volume went to 5.6 million. At this point other exchanges began options trading. The Amex, Philadelphia, Pacific, and Midwest stock exchanges began listing options. By 1980, the annual total volume of stock underlying the options traded exceeded the volume of actual shares traded on the New York Stock Exchange. The growth of the options market has dramatically exceeded expectations.

BUYING AND SELLING OPTIONS

An individual may write or buy a call option and may write or buy a put option. As explained above, the *buyer* of an option is entitled to purchase the underlying stock (a call option) or to sell the underlying stock (a put option) at the exercise price if the option is exercised within the specified time period. The *writer* of an option assumes the other side of the transaction. The writer of a call option is obligated, under the option agreement, to sell the underlying stock at the exercise price if the option is exercised before the option expires. The writer of a put option is obligated to buy the underlying stock at the exercise price if the option is exercised before the expiration date. For every call option and every put option there

is a writer and a buyer; the individual investor may assume either of these roles.

To buy or write an option, an individual need only contact a securities broker. The broker will conduct the transaction, in return for which a commission is charged. A commission is charged both when an option is purchased or written and when it is exercised (it is generally the case that a commission is paid when a security—e.g., a share of stock—is purchased and again when it is sold).

Only the shares of certain companies have been approved for options trading on the exchanges. For the shares to be approved, there must be at least a certain number outstanding, the per share price must exceed a specified minimum, and the trading volume in the shares must exceed a certain level.

In addition to the strategy of buying or writing a put or call option, an investor can also engage in a **spread** or a **straddle** transaction. A spread position involves writing and buying calls (or writing and buying puts) on the same underlying stock, but the options have a difference in maturity date, striking price, or both. An example of a spread would be holding a call option to buy 100 shares of Ideal Corporation common stock at $50 per share and also writing a call option for 100 shares of Ideal stock with an exercise price of $55 per share. A straddle involves writing and buying an equal number of puts (or calls) for the same underlying stock, where the puts (or calls) bought and written have the same exercise price and the same expiration date. Writing a put and buying a put covering 100 shares of Ideal stock, both with an exercise price of $50 and both expiring on April 20, 1986, would be a straddle. An investor in a straddle generally anticipates wide price fluctuations in the underlying stock but is unsure as to whether the movement will be up or down.

APPLICATIONS OF OPTIONS ANALYSIS

The discussion of warrant valuation in Chapter 22 applies equally well to other forms of call options. Moreover, the concept of an option has far broader applications than simply to real estate deals and to options on common stock. Common stock itself can be viewed as an option on the company. For example, suppose a firm has only one type of liability against it, a bank loan that must be paid in full in sixty days. The stockholders of the firm have an option on the firm. The exercise price of their option is the payment due on the debt. If the stockholders believe the firm is worth more than the amount due on the debt, they can pay the bank and own the firm's assets. Otherwise they can let their option expire and the bank will own the firm.

Consider a much different application, a fixed-rate long-term loan with prepayment possible (that is, the borrower is permitted, if he or she chooses, to pay off the loan before maturity). The borrower in this case has been provided with an option to prepay the loan. If interest rates go up, the borrower need only make the required payments. If interest rates decline, the borrower can get a new loan at the lower rate and pay off the old loan. This option is valuable to the borrower; however, it is obtained at the expense of the lender. The lender has an incentive not to give something for nothing; therefore the lender may charge a somewhat higher interest rate on such loans (that is, a higher interest rate than if prepayment were forbidden), or more commonly, include penalties for early repayment.

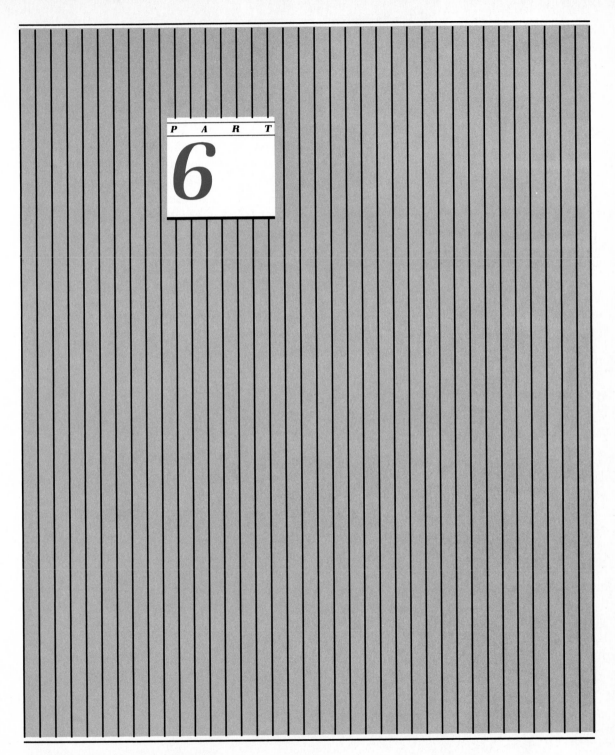

P A R T

6

SPECIAL TOPICS

Part 6 discusses several issues relating to some—but not all—business firms. Chapter 23 covers mergers and acquisitions—when they are justified and how management should analyze a potential merger in determining its advisability. Chapter 24 examines the problems faced by companies that conduct foreign trade or that have subsidiaries in foreign countries (multinational companies). Foreign exchange transactions are discussed and the methods used by firms in financing exports and imports are described. The last part of the chapter deals with multinational companies and the special problems faced by the financial managers of such firms. Chapter 25 discusses business bankruptcy and how management and creditors cope with business failure.

C H A P T E R

23

*HOLDING
COMPANIES,
MERGERS, AND
CONSOLIDA-
TIONS*

This chapter discusses how and why two or more separate companies combine into one company. The common term for this combination process is "merger." The sections that follow describe the various kinds of business combinations, how firms arrange a merger, why they merge, and how a company decides whether or not a merger is a good idea. The Merger Game, which follows this chapter, examines the strategies companies use in taking over other companies and defending themselves against takeovers, and discusses the use of investment bankers who help companies in formulating and carrying out those strategies.

*HOLDING
COMPANIES,
MERGERS,
CONSOLIDATIONS,
AND DIVESTITURES*

A **holding company** is a corporation that has working control of one or more other corporations, called **subsidiaries**, through ownership of the subsidiaries' common stock. The sole purpose of the holding company is to own shares in other corporations. The holding company may achieve sufficient influence for control with as little as 20 percent, or an even smaller fraction, of a subsidiary's stock.

Holding companies are subject to an added tax on profit. Fifteen percent of dividends received by the holding company from the domestic (United States) corporations in which it has an investment are taxed as corporate income.[1] If the holding company and the corporations it controls were merged into a single firm, this added tax could be avoided.[2]

A **merger** or **consolidation** is the unification of previously separate companies into a single corporation. Technically, a merger occurs if one of the two or more combining firms survives (e.g., if firm *A* and firm *B* merge and the new firm is called firm *A*). A consolidation is the union of firms into a new firm (e.g., firm *A* and firm *B* combined to form firm *C*). The merger or consolidation of firms that are in similar lines of business, e.g., two food wholesalers or two appliance manufacturers, is referred to as a **horizontal combination**. A **vertical combination** joins firms that are engaged in different stages of production of the same type of product, e.g., an oil producer and a refiner. A **conglomerate** is any group of firms in different lines of business that are controlled by a single corporation. The controlled firms in a conglomerate may be separate corporate entities (subsidiaries) or unincorporated divisions of the parent.

Since mergers, consolidations, and other business combinations involve essentially the same financial issues, we will use the term "merger" to refer to either a merger or a consolidation. Also, since one of the firms in a merger

---

[1] For example, if corporation J pays holding company H $100 in dividends, $15 of these dividends would be taxable at the corporate tax rate. If the corporate tax rate were 40 percent, then company H would pay $6 in taxes on the dividends (0.40 × $15).

[2] Actually, the tax on 15 percent of dividends can be avoided if the holding company and its subsidiary form all or part of a consolidated group of corporate entities and file a consolidated federal income tax return. One of the requirements for a consolidated group is that the holding company own at least 80 percent of the subsidiary's stock.

survives, the surviving firm can be viewed as acquiring the other (nonsurviving) firm; if firm A survives and firm B does not, we will often refer to the merger as the acquisition of firm B by firm A.

A **divestiture** (often referred to as a **spinoff**) is the sale of a division or subsidiary; it is the opposite of a merger. The failure to realize any benefits from a merger acquisition often motivates companies to divest themselves of previously acquired firms. Such giants as RCA, American Can, and ITT have recently engaged in massive sell-offs of unwanted subsidiaries.

A **leveraged buyout** is a transaction in which a company, or a subsidiary or a division of a company, is bought by private investors who borrow to finance the purchase. Typically, the assets of the purchased company are used to collateralize the borrowing of the purchaser, and the acquired business is a publicly traded firm (or subsidiary or division of a publicly traded firm) which is taken private (not publicly traded) after the buyout. Very frequently, the private investors purchasing the company are existing managers of the business. For example, in 1984 Dupont sold, for $500 million, the commodity chemical operations it got in its 1981 purchase of Conoco. The buyers were Conoco managers, and their financing was from a group of bankers and insurers lead by Manufacturers Hanover Trust and Prudential Insurance.

MERGER PROCEDURE

Negotiating the Merger

A merger is usually arranged through negotiations between the managements of the firms concerned. The negotiations are ordinarily initiated by the acquiring firm, which offers cash or securities to the other firm's stockholders. After a merger agreement has been worked out by the firms' managements, the agreement must then be approved by the companies' boards of directors. For the combination to proceed, approval must be secured from the stockholders of both firms; a majority—and frequently two-thirds—of the outstanding shares of each firm must be voted in favor of the merger. Following this and the filing of any papers with the state governments in which the corporations are domiciled, the exchange of assets for securities is made and the merger is consummated.

Mergers are not always friendly matches. Frequently, when firm A indicates an interest in purchasing firm B, the latter company's management spurns the advance. Firm A may attempt to circumvent the firm B management. One approach is to obtain the proxies (voting power) of the firm B shareholders and undertake a proxy fight. If firm A wins the proxy fight (that is, gets more proxies than firm B management does), it can vote to oust the firm B management and then proceed to promote the merger. Proxy fights are expensive and usually unsuccessful for the outsiders. An alternative strategy for circumventing the firm B managment is for firm A to buy the firm B shares. This may begin with firm A's purchasing some of the shares in the open market and then announcing that it will purchase some or all of the remaining firm B shares directly from the firm B shareholders. The offer announcement is called a **tender offer**. Tender offers sometimes succeed and sometimes don't, but they are more often successful than proxy fights. In response to the tender offer, the hostile firm *B* management may use various legal and financial tactics to fend off firm *A* (for details, see "The Merger Game," which follows this chapter). Sometimes there are competing tender offers, with several companies offering to buy the shares of a particular "target" (the term for a company which another company wants to buy).

Antitrust Laws

The Federal Trade Commission and the Justice Department both have the power to prevent a merger if it will, or potentially will, reduce competition. This power results primarily from three statutes: the Sherman Act of 1890, the Federal Trade Commission Act of 1914, and the Clayton Act of 1914 (as amended by the Celler-Kefauver Act of 1950). In special cases, a merger can also be disallowed by other government agencies such as the Department of Transportation or the Federal Communications Commission. For example, Civil Aeronautics Board approval is necessary for one airline to take over another airline.

A merger may be blocked if it substantially lessens or tends to lessen competition in a line of business. The courts have wide discretion in defining the relevant product line and geographic area of competition. For example, in its decision that Du Pont's control over the cellophane market did not constitute a monopoly, the courts defined the relevant market to include all types of wrapping (of which cellophane represents only a small fraction) rather than cellophane alone (over which Du Pont had a monopoly). In contrast, Reynolds Metals was forced to divest itself of Arrow Brands because of the combined firm's share of the sales of aluminum foil to florists alone. The absence of clear guidelines on what will and what will not be acceptable to government antitrust officials or the courts injects an added element of uncertainty to merger activities.

Companies may not be allowed to merge even if the threat to competition is only potential. Procter & Gamble, which had entered the bleach market in a big way by purchasing giant Clorox, was forced to divest itself of Clorox because the courts felt that the merger removed Procter & Gamble as a potential competitor of Clorox. The rationale for ordering the divestiture was that keeping P & G "on the fringes" of the market as a watchful potential entrant into the market would prevent Clorox from abusing its strong market position.

January 1982 saw two dramatic events in United States antitrust history—a settlement between the U.S. Justice Deparment and American Telephone and Telegraph Company, which resulted in AT&T's breakup; and the end of the government's thirteen-year antitrust suit against IBM, with the U.S. Justice Department simply dropping the case. Under the AT&T settlement, AT&T divested itself of its local telephone operating companies (by distributing stock in the companies to AT&T stockholders); the total physical assets of those companies is roughly $80 billion. In return, AT&T was allowed to retain its three remaining major components: its Western Electric manufacturing subsidiary, its Bell Laboratories research arm, and its long-distance operations—a combined entity with approximately $40 billion in physical assets. Additionally, AT&T was freed of restrictions from entering new markets, including cable television, newspapers, telecommunications, and computers.

The IBM victory reflected in large part changing market conditions. During the thirteen-year battle between IBM and U.S. Justice Department, IBM's dominance in the computer field deteriorated as new technologies developed and as domestic and foreign competitors entered the market. This relative decline of IBM was in some measure due to the antitrust suit itself. To avoid strengthening the government's case in the suit, IBM was reluctant in the early and mid-1970s to use its full muscle in competing with other companies. It was only in the late 1970s that IBM again fought aggressively for market share. But, by that time, the industry had changed and many new and vigorous competitors had emerged. In 1982, IBM's competitive environment became still more ominous as another giant, AT&T, was unleashed from government constraints.

The Form of Property Exchanged

One firm's acquisition of another firm may involve a merger, the purchase of a controlling interest in the other firm (that is, a purchase of a majority of its stock), or the purchase of the other firm's assets. In each case, the buying company can pay cash, its securities (the buyer's common stock, preferred stock, bonds, etc.), or some combination of the two.

With a merger, acquiring firm A obtains all the assets and liabilities of selling firm B and the two companies are consolidated under single control. The shareholders of both firms must vote in favor of the merger. Usually at least two-thirds approval of the shareholders of each company is required. If, instead, A buys the stock of B but no formal merger occurs, approval by neither firm's shareholders is required. A problem does arise, though, in that complete consolidation of the two firms may be blocked by a recalcitrant shareholder of B; of course, if firm A owns a sufficient fraction of firm B's stock, it can deal with this situation by voting the shares of B in favor of a merger and then merging the two companies. The third option—the purchase of B's assets—does not require the approval of firm A's shareholders and requires the approval of the seller B's shareholders only if a major portion of B's assets are sold. Furthermore, A can pick and choose the assets it prefers and does not assume B's liabilities (some of which may be hidden). Firm B can either retain the proceeds from the asset sale or distribute them to shareholders.

Should firm A pay cash or securities in the acquisition? Firm A may prefer to pay cash if it has excess cash available; if not, it will have to issue debt or equity securities to make the purchase. Expectations concerning the price of A's stock are also relevant. For example, even if A has excess cash available, if its management feels that the firm's stock price is unreasonably inflated, management may prefer to use stock rather than cash (or stock rather than debt securities) in the purchase. Since what is paid in the acquisition is a matter of negotiation between A and B, the desires of the shareholders of firm B also affect the form of payment. The firm B shareholders will more likely prefer cash to firm A stock the better are the alternative investment opportunities available to the firm B shareholders and the less optimistic are the firm B shareholders about the future trend in the price of firm A stock. Taxes also affect the choice of form of payment in an acquisition. This is discussed next.

Tax Considerations

The taxes of the buyer and the seller in an acquisition depend on whether the acquisition is taxable or tax-free. Although the tax laws are quite complex, the primary condition that must be met for an acquisition to be tax-free is that a major part (how much depends on whether stock or assets are acquired and on other details) of the payment by buyer A to seller B be in the form of voting stock (common or preferred) of firm A. This is so whether the acquisition is an asset purchase, a purchase of stock, or a formal merger. If the acquisition is not tax-free, it is taxable.

Under a taxable exchange, the shareholders of selling firm B pay capital gains taxes (or take capital losses) on the sale just as though they had sold their shares in the stock market. Under a tax-free exchange, the firm B shareholders pay no taxes currently but may owe taxes in later years. The acquiring firm's taxes are also affected in that, with a taxable exchange, the tax basis (depreciated value for tax purposes) of the acquired firm's assets reflects the purchase price paid in the acquisition; with a tax-free exchange, the acquired assets have the same tax basis as before the merger.

To illustrate a taxable and tax-free exchange assume that Bear Transportation Industries buys Honey Bus Company, Inc. Honey's physical assets are ten buses which were purchased by the firm in 1983 for $500,000; the buses are being depreciated on a straight-line basis over five years ($100,000 per year in depreciation) and, in 1986, have a depreciated book value of $200,000. Assume that, because of inflation and good maintenance, the buses' market value is $400,000. In 1986 Bear buys Honey for $600,000. Assume that Honey's shareholders paid $500,000 for their shares in 1984. Exhibit 23-1 shows the tax consequences of the acquisition; it is clear that, from a tax standpoint, the Honey shareholders are better off with a tax-free exchange but Bear is better off with a taxable exchange. In general, sellers prefer (from a tax standpoint) a tax-free exchange if they have a gain (as do the Honey shareholders) and prefer a taxable exchange if they have a loss (for example, if the Honey shareholders had originally paid $700,000 rather than $500,000 for their shares). Similarly, buyers prefer a taxable exchange if the current values of the assets exceed their depreciated values to the seller (as in the above example), and they prefer a tax-free exchange if the current asset values are lower than their depreciated values.

Another relevant tax factor is the taxability of dividends received by one corporation from another corporation in which it owns stock. If firm A were to buy less than 80 percent of firm B's stock, 15 percent of any dividends paid by firm B to firm A would be included in firm A's taxable corporate income. This dividend tax at the corporate level is avoided if firm A owns 80 percent or more of firm B. This tax consideration might influence firm A in its choice between purchasing stock in firm B, purchasing firm B's assets, or effecting a formal merger with firm B.

EXHIBIT 23-1
Tax consequences of taxable and nontaxable acquisition

	Taxable acquisition	Nontaxable acquisition
1. Tax consequences for Honey shareholders	A long-term capital gain of $100,000 is recognized in 1986.	No capital gain is recognized in 1986; the capital gain is deferred until the Honey shareholders sell their Bear stock.[a]
2. Tax consequences for Bear	The tax basis of the buses for computing Bear's depreciation is the buses' actual $400,000 value; depreciation over the remaining 2-year life of the buses will be $200,000 per year ($400,000/2 years).	The tax basis of the buses for computing Bear's depreciation is the buses' old basis of $200,000; depreciation over the remaining 2-year life of the buses will be $100,000 per year ($200,000/2 years).

[a] If the Honey shareholders were to sell the Bear stock in 1991 for, say, $900,000, they would have a long-term capital gain of $400,000 (= $900,000 sales price *minus* $500,000 original cost of the Honey shares).

MERGER TRENDS

During the 1960s mergers and acquisitions in this country reached an historic peak, exceeding the previous high achieved during the boom of the late 1920s. As indicated in Figure 23-1, the uptrend in business combinations from the early 1930s to the end of the 1960s (1968 was the peak year) was followed by a sharp decline and, in recent years, a recovery. The post-1968 decline resulted in large part from more vigorous anti-trust law enforcement, more stringent tax laws, and poor performance by many conglomerates that had grown through merger. In addition, during the 1960s, the availability of desirable acquisition candidates declined (and their prices rose) as many of these companies were purchased. By the mid-1970s, a cautious realism emerged out of the hyperemotional enthusiasm of the 1960s and the negativity of the early 1970s. In the 1960s, firms often made acquisitions without carefully considering the ultimate consequences. The result, in many cases, was severe disappointment for the acquiring company. The largely intuitive and hasty approach is now shunned, and acquisition decisions usually follow exhaustive study. Outside experts (particularly commerical and investment banks, CPA firms, and merger specialists) are often used in the merger process. Merger evaluation and analysis will be the subject of much of this chapter.

REASONS FOR MERGER

Our analysis of investment opportunities in Chapters 8 and 9 focused on investments in new assets which involved the *internal* expansion of the firm. Mergers involve the acquisition of other business entities and are referred to as *external* expansion. The primary benefits of mergers are the resulting synergies and tax savings.

Mutual benefits produced by the merger are called **synergies**. Examples are lower costs of production, management, financing, research, and marketing. The most common economies are reductions of duplicate fixed costs of production and management, since fewer plants and smaller total managerial staff may be needed as a result of the merger. Even if the merged firms produce different products, it is often possible to reduce accounting and personnel departments and top-level managerial staffs simply by eliminating duplication and inefficiencies. Research economies may also be achieved by eliminating similar research efforts and the repetition of mistakes already made by the other firm's researchers. Marketing economies may be produced through savings in advertising (by reducing the need to attract each other's customers), and also from the advantages of offering a more complete product line since a wider product line may provide larger sales per unit of sales effort and per sales person. A saving often arises from consolidating departments involved with financial activities, e.g., accounting, credit, billing, and purchasing. And, there may be significant economies of scale in acquiring capital through public offerings. Flotation costs per dollar of capital raised drop rapidly as issue amounts increase up to $10 million (see Chapter 18, Table 18-2).

Strategic pricing advantages may also accrue through the acquisition of monopolistic power or something approaching it. However, this advantage involves serious legal risks and may be short-lived because of enforcement of antitrust regulations.

The concept of synergy was the rationale used by many conglomeratiers during the 1960s to justify their ambitious expansion into many

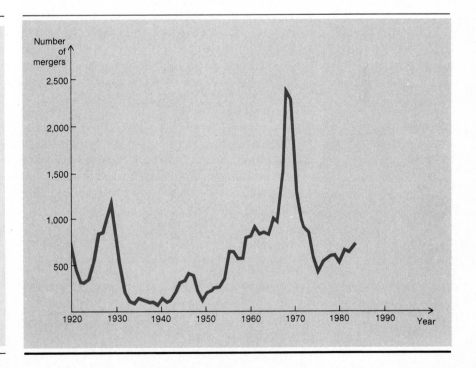

FIGURE 23-1

Historical trends in mergers and acquisitions by manufacturing and mining concerns.

unrelated industries. The idea was that by placing many companies under a single management, a cross-fertilization of ideas and managerial expertise would result. In some cases it worked, or at least the conglomerates in question were successful. Notable examples are Textron, ITT, and MCA. But there are also casualties, including such former high fliers as Ling-Temco-Vought, Whittaker Corporation, and Memorex Corporation, all of which expanded into various unrelated fields and suffered large losses. Even Litton Industries, once the archetype of the successful conglomerate, experienced severely deflated earnings and financial difficulties in the early 1970s that necessitated a major overhaul of operations. By the 1980s, Litton had reorganized and returned to profitability. However, the days of glory were long past.

The mixed results of acquisition are also reflected in the experience of otherwise successful corporate giants that strayed into unfamiliar areas. Boise Cascade's failure in mobile home and engineering ventures, RCA's enormous losses in computers, Union Carbide's unprofitable diversification into petroleum, pharmaceuticals, and semiconductors, and Amcord's unsuccessful diversification into non-cement-related areas are prominent examples. Of course, there are also examples of unsuccessful mergers of companies within the same industry. The important point here is that in most cases the likelihood of achieving synergistic benefits from merger is enhanced if the acquiring company expands into fields with which it is familiar. Although this would appear to be good common sense, it is a principle that has often been ignored.

Tax Benefits

There are two major tax considerations favoring merger. First, the tax treatment of liquidations of stock to raise money to pay estate taxes is very generous. As a result, the heirs of a company's deceased owner often find it advantageous to sell their inherited stock in the company to another firm. The second tax consideration relates to the offsetting of profits and losses for tax purposes. With merger, the losses (or tax credits) of one company can be used to offset the profits of the other. The result is that lower total taxes are paid by the combined company. For example, if firm A were earning $3 million per year and firm B were losing $1 million per year, a merged company composed of firm A and firm B would have a net income of $2 million per year (assuming no synergies or diseconomies from the merger). Without merger, firm A would pay taxes on $3 million of income and firm B would pay no taxes; whereas with merger taxes would have to be paid only on income of $2 million.[3] Similarly, firm B may have unused

---

[3] If the firm incurring the loss can carry back its losses against past profits and thereby receive a rebate of past taxes, no gain from merging with a profitable company would accrue. Losses can also be carried forward, so that in future profitable years previous losses can be deducted from the profits, thus reducing taxable income by that earlier loss. However, the firm must wait for this carryforward benefit until it makes a profit. Furthermore, losses can be carried back only three years and forward fifteen years, implying that continuous losses over many years (e.g., due to large research outlays) may never be canceled against profits. In this case of extended losses, a merger with a currently profitable firm would be advantageous. On loss carrybacks and carryforwards, see Chapter 3.

investment tax credits which could be used to reduce firm A's tax bill if the two firms were merged.

Internal Versus External Growth

Instead of acquiring another company, a firm could, of course, atttempt to build the operation from scratch through internal investment.[4] But, sometimes external expansion (merger) has special advantages. Expansion is more rapid if an existing firm is purchased. In some cases, it may be impossible to duplicate an operation, particularly if a patent or mineral right is monopolized by that company or if the product manufactured has a commanding position in its market. Even if duplication is possible, an attempt to create a similar business operation internally is usually more risky than acquiring a going concern. A newly created operation may not be able to match an existing company's performance record, or acquire similar product markets and staff. This risk element is magnified if the industry of the acquired company already has adequate capacity. Increasing that capacity through internal investment would therefore be profitable only if an existing producer were displaced, whereas a business combination would merely involve consolidating existing capacity. The latter would probably be the less risky alternative.

Keep in mind that, although acquiring an existing firm can have the advantages over internal investment noted above, the stockholders of the takeover candidate will ordinarily demand a price for their stock that reflects the company's value. For the would-be purchaser, this price may be high enough to negate the advantages of merger over internally generated expansion.

Portfolio Diversification: A Poor Rationale for Mergers

You remember from Chapter 6 that portfolio diversification is a way for an *investor* to reduce risk. Does it follow that a *firm* should diversify (e.g., by buying other companies) in order to provide its shareholders with less risky returns (that is, with returns from a diversified portfolio of corporate assets)? Is firm diversification *for diversification's sake alone* a good rationale for corporate merger? In general, the answer is no. The reason is that investors can do their own diversifying and there is no advantage to shareholders from companies doing their diversifying for them. An investor could buy 1 percent of firm A's shares and 1 percent of firm B's shares, and this would be just as good as buying 1 percent of a merged company made up of firms A and B. Merger will produce no benefits for shareholders simply as a result of firm diversification. For merger to produce benefits, there must be greater total cash flows from the merged firms, for example, as a result of operating synergies or tax savings.[5]

---

[4] Internal investment should be contrasted with internal financing of investment, where the latter refers to the use of retained earnings (earnings not paid out as dividends) rather than externally raised funds (through the sale of new stock or through borrowing) to finance investment. On internal and external financing, see Chap. 11.

[5] The reader should review the Chap. 9 discussion of Company Diversification and Project Analysis on pages 276–278; the same underlying principle applies to firm asset diversification whether it is accomplished through ordinary capital investments or through merger acquisitions.

Two usually minor exceptions to the rule that firm diversification does not pay should be mentioned. First, a firm may be able to reduce the possibility of financial distress (that is, of not having sufficient cash to service debt) or even bankruptcy by merging with a company which has cash flows which follow a different pattern.[6] A second exception applies to stockholders who have most of their wealth invested in a single stock. For example, assume that Curly Mills has most of his savings tied up in the stock of Mills Mills Incorporated (MM Inc.). Also assume that Curly paid $2 per share for the stock and the stock is now selling for $10 per share. If Curly wants to diversify, he will have to sell his MM Inc. stock and pay capital gains taxes. However, if MM Inc. diversifies, Curley can achieve diversification without selling his stock and can thereby avoid the capital gains taxes. This kind of situation is particularly relevant to closely held family corporations.

DO MERGERS PRODUCE GAINS?

Do mergers produce gains for investors? The evidence is that the selling firm's shareholders enjoy significant gains from a merger but that the buying firm's shareholders experience no significant gains or losses (some studies show small average gains or losses for buyers).[7] Using different data samples, the average percentage premium above premerger share price paid by the buyer for the seller's stock was found by Shad to be 20 percent, by Mandelker to be 14 percent, and by Bradley and Korn to be 53 percent.[8] Premiums vary enormously and are sometimes more than 100 percent. For example, in 1981 Standard Oil Company of Ohio paid a 130 percent premium for Kennecott Corporation. Amax, Inc., *rejected* a bid from Standard Oil Company of California which involved a premium of over 100 percent, presumably because it was too low. The premium paid by Du Pont for Conoco was a "mere" 80 percent.

The moral we can draw from the above evidence is clear: it pays to be bought. This fact has not been overlooked by the investment community. The investor newsletters of the large brokerage firms regularly list companies which are potential "targets" (companies targeted for acquisition by other companies). Merger "arbitragers" speculate in stocks of firms which are likely merger candidates. And investment bankers and law firms provide

[6] For example, if High Corporation's cash flow tends to be high during booms and low during recessions and Low Corporation's cash flow tends to be low during booms and high during recessions, merging High and Low will result in a merged company with a cash flow which is more insulated from the business cycle than the cash flow of either High or Low alone.

[7] See, for example, S. R. Shad, "The Financial Realities of Mergers," *Harvard Business Review* (November–December 1969) pp. 133–146; G. Mandelker, "Risk and Return: The Case of Merging Firms," *Journal of Financial Economics* (December 1974), pp. 303–335; T. C. Langetieg, "An Application of a Three-Factor Performance Index to Measure Stockholder Gains from Merger," *Journal of Financial Economics* (December 1978), pp. 365–383; P. Dodd and R. Ruback, "Tender Offers and Stockholder Returns: An Empirical Analysis," *Journal of Financial Economics* (December 1977), pp. 351–373. For an excellent collection of papers on the consequences of corporate mergers, see *Journal of Financial Economics* (April 1983).

[8] See Shad, op. cit. and Mandelker, op. cit.; and see J. W. Bradley and D. M. Korn, "Bargains in Valuation Disparities: Corporate Acquiror versus Passive Investor" *Sloan Management Review* (Winter 1979), pp. 51–64.

advice—often on a continuing basis—to company managements who are worried that another firm might come along and offer a large premium to the company's shareholders and effect a takeover (on this, see "The Merger Game" following this chapter).

We should be careful in interpreting the finding that buyers on average neither gain nor lose significantly from a merger. First, since buyers are normally much larger than sellers, it may be that the changes in the buyer's stock price from the merger is simply not ordinarily large enough to be picked up by empirical tests. A company with shares worth $1 billion might buy another firm for $100 million and gain, or lose, $20 million as a result; but a gain or loss of $20 million is only 2 percent of the buyer's equity value, simply a small blip that is not easy to detect from available data (especially since many other factors affect the company's share price). Second, none of the merger studies takes into account the costs incurred by the acquiring company in pursuing a long-term merger program (these costs may have been incurred over many years). It might be that, if the costs were netted out, we would find that acquiring firms actually end up with net losses from their merger activities.

ANALYZING AN ACQUISITION

The shareholders of both the acquiring and the acquired firms want the merger to improve their wealth positions. Only if the long-run returns per share of common stock of the acquiring firm are improved is the merger acceptable to the buyer. Similarly, the seller is better off only if the cash or securities received in the merger are worth more than the securities surrendered. We will now examine how the price paid for an acquired firm is determined. For clarity, purchase with cash and purchase with securities will be examined separately.

Purchase with Cash

If the payment for the selling company is in cash, then the decision from the standpoint of the buyer can be handled in the same way as any new investment using the capital budgeting methods described in Chapters 8 and 9. Only if the net present value of the aftertax net cash flow from the new assets is positive is the acquisition a good investment. The simplest case is that in which only the assets and not the liabilities of the selling firm are obtained. In this case, the investment in the assets [I of Eq. (8-2) of Chapter 8] for computing the acquisition's net present value is simply the cash price paid for the assets.

If the acquisition for cash also involves the assumption of the selling firm's liabilities, the present value of the seller's debt that is assumed must be added to the cost of the assets (cash paid to the seller's stockholders) to determine the initial outlay in computing NPV. The acquisition then would be acceptable to the buyer only if the present value of the future aftertax flow from the acquired firm exceeds the cash paid to the seller's stockholders plus the present value of the seller's debts that are assumed. For example, if firm A merges with firm B by paying firm B's stockholders $1 million in cash and also assumes firm B's liabilities of $500,000, the computation of the net present value of the acquisition is as shown in Exhibit 23-2. It is assumed in the example that the assets of firm *B* will generate an aftertax cash flow of $180,000 per year for twenty-five years and that the discount rate on the new investment is 10 percent.[9] Notice that the situation here is therefore identical to a capital budgeting decision in which firm *A* buys $1.5 million in assets and finances the acquisition with $500,000 of debt and $1 million in retained earnings (the firm's cash). In both cases, firm *A* ends up with firm *B*'s assets and an added debt of $500,000. The Exhibit 23-2 computation produces an NPV of $133,860, implying that the merger is profitable to firm *A*.

In determining their willingness to sell their shares for $1 million, firm *B*'s stockholders will have analyzed the anticipated future performance of firm *B* without the merger, tax effects, and other considerations discussed earlier. Only those shareholders who want the funds to spend on current consumption, or to reinvest in what they view as better opportunities than firm *B*, will be satisfied with the merger agreement. To assure that the selling firm's stockholders will approve the acquisition, the price per share offered by the acquiring firm for the selling firm's stock is often significantly above the stock's premerger market price.

[9] This discount rate will depend upon the risk ot the investment. It is assumed here for simplicity that the firm's debt-equity ratio will not be significantly changed as a consequence of the merger. On these points, see Chaps. 7 and 9.

EXHIBIT 23-2
Evaluating the purchase for cash of company B by company A

Pretax cash flow from new assets		$ 300,000
Less taxes:		
Pretax cash flow	$300,000	
Depreciation	60,000	
Taxable income	$240,000	
Tax (0.50 × taxable income)[a]		120,000
Aftertax cash flow		$ 180,000
Initial outlay:		
Payment to *B*'s (seller's) stockholders		$1,000,000
Assumption of *B*'s debt		500,000
Total initial outlay		$1,500,000

Applicable cost of capital adjusted for risk of the investment = 10%

$$\text{NPV} = \$180,000 \ (P/A,\ 10\%,\ 25) - \text{initial outlay}$$
$$= (9.0770 \times \$180,000) - \$1,500,000$$
$$= \$133,860$$

Conclusion: Merger is profitable since NPV = $133,860.

[a] A corporate tax rate of 50 percent is assumed.

In a merger in which stock is issued in payment to the selling firm's stockholders, stockholders will find the merger desirable only if the value of their shares is higher with the merger than without the merger. The number of shares that the buying firm (A) will issue in acquiring the selling firm (B) is determined as follows:

1   The acquiring firm will compare the value per share of firm A with and without the merger.
2   The selling firm will compare the value of firm B with the value of the shares that they would receive from firm A under the merger.
3   The managements of firms A and B will negotiate the final terms of the merger in light of 1 and 2; the ultimate terms of the merger will reflect the relative bargaining positions of the two firms.

The fewer of A's shares that A must pay B, the better off are the stockholders of A and the worse off are the stockholders of B. However, for the merger to be effected, the shareholders of both the buying firm and the selling firm will have to anticipate some benefit from the merger.

To illustrate points 1, 2, and 3 for a simple case (Exhibit 23-3), we will assume that the value of a share can be computed by applying an appropriate price-earnings ratio to its current earnings.[10] Assume that the expected

---

[10] The analysis applies regardless of how investors value shares. For example, if the value of a share is equal to the present value of expected future dividends (see Chapter 5), then in Exhibit 23-3 substitute "Dividends per share" for "Earnings per share" in row 3, and substitute "Price-dividend ratio" for "Price-earnings ratio" in row 5; the price-dividend ratio for the perpetuity case considered here is simply $(1/k)$, where k is the discount rate for computing the present value of the dividends and $(1/k)$ is the perpetuity factor $(P/A, k, \infty)$. Rather than expected future dividends, one could also discount expected future equity cash flow (firm cash flow minus payments to creditors) to value the firm's shares. Until recently, earnings analysis was a more popular method than discounted cash flow (or discounted dividends) for evaluating merger prospects. By the mid-1980s, however, large companies had come to rely as heavily on the discounted cash flow approach as on earnings analysis in assessing merger candidates.

EXHIBIT 23-3
Premerger and postmerger financial data

	Premerger firm A	Premerger firm B	Postmerger firm A
1. Current earnings per year	$200,000	$100,000	$350,000
2. Shares outstanding	50,000	10,000	?
3. Earnings per share [(1)/(2)]	$4	$10	?
4. Price per share	$40	$100	?
5. Price-earnings ratio [(4)/(3)][a]	10X	10X	10X
6. Value of firm [(2) × (4)]	$2,000,000	$1,000,000	$3,500,000
7. Expected annual growth rate in earnings in foreseeable future	0	0	0

[a] The price-earnings ratio equals either [(4)/(3)] or [(6)/(1)].

annual earnings of firms A and B without merger are $200,000 and $100,000, respectively, a total of $300,000 per year. Earnings are expected to remain level in the future. With merger, the expected total annual earnings are $350,000, an increase of $50,000 per year due to the economies generated by the merger. The information missing from Exhibit 23-3 cannot be supplied until the number of firm A's shares to be issued in purchasing firm B is determined. In Exhibit 23-4 the effects of issuing 20,000, 30,000, and 37,500 new shares of firm A in purchasing firm B are shown. With 20,000 new shares there are 70,000 postmerger firm A shares and B's stockholders obtain two-sevenths (20,000/70,000) of the merged firm, that is, obtain shares worth $1 million ($\frac{2}{7} \times$ $3.5 million postmerger firm value). The merger has no effect on firm B's shareholder wealth, since the value of the firm B stock surrendered is also $1 million. The exchange ratio in col. b is the number of new firm A shares issued (20,000) per firm B share obtained (10,000), which equals 2. Firm A's stockholders have shares worth $2.5 million after the merger and are therefore $500,000 better off as a consequence of the acquisition.[11]

If 37,500 new firm A shares were issued, firm B's shareholders would own a fraction ($\frac{375}{875}$) of the postmerger firm with a total share value of

[11] We can compute the number of shares which makes the shareholders of A no better and no worse off (signify this number as n_A^*, where $n_A^* = 37,500$ in the example), and the number of shares which makes the shareholders of B no better and no worse off (signified n_B^*, where $n_B^* = 20,000$ in the example). Let n_A' be the number of firm A shares before the merger ($n_A' = 50,000$ in the example). n_A^* and n_B^* satisfy the following equations:

$$\text{Value of firm } A \text{ shares without merger} = \left[\frac{n_A'}{n_A' + n_A^*}\right] \times \left[\text{value of firm } A \text{ shares after the merger}\right] \tag{a}$$

$$\text{Value of firm } B \text{ shares without merger} = \left[\frac{n_B^*}{n_A' + n_B^*}\right] \times \left[\text{value of firm } A \text{ shares after the merger}\right] \tag{b}$$

where $[n_A'/(n_A' + n_A^*)]$ in (a) is the fraction of postmerger firm A owned by the A shareholders after the merger if n_A^* shares are paid; and $[n_B^*/(n_A' + n_B^*)]$ in (b) is the fraction of postmerger firm A owned by the B shareholders after the merger if n_B^* shares are paid.

EXHIBIT 23-4
Impact of alternative numbers of firm A's shares issued to buy firm B on the total value of shares owned by stockholders of firms A and B

Number of firm A's shares issued to firm B stockholders (a)	Exchange ratio [(a)/10,000 firm B's shares] (b)	Number of firm A's shares outstanding after merger [50,000 + (a)] (c)	Postmerger fraction of firm owned by firm B shareholders [(a)/(c)] (d)	Value of shares owned by firm B shareholders [(d) × $3.5 million] (e)	Postmerger fraction of firm owned by original firm A shareholders [50,000/(c)] (f)	Value of shares owned by firm A shareholders [(f) × $3.5 million] (g)
20,000	2	70,000	$\frac{2}{7}$	$1,000,000	$\frac{5}{7}$	$2,500,000
30,000	3	80,000	$\frac{3}{8}$	1,312,500	$\frac{5}{8}$	2,187,500
37,500	3.75	87,500	$\frac{375}{875}$	1,500,000	$\frac{500}{875}$	2,000,000

$1,500,000. Firm A's stockholders would own a fraction $(\frac{500}{875})$ of the merged company's shares and have shares worth $2 million. In this case, firm B's stockholders gain and firm A's stockholders neither gain nor lose from the combination. For any number of shares issued between 20,000 and 37,500 (e.g., 30,000), both firm A's stockholders and firm B's stockholders benefit from the merger. If less than 20,000 shares were offered to B, B's stockholders would lose in the exchange, and exactly 20,000 shares would leave B's stockholder with no gain or loss. Similarly, an offer of more than 37,500 shares of firm A's stock for firm B would result in a reduction in the wealth of firm A's stockholders, and exactly 37,500 shares would leave A's stockholders no better and no worse off. Since A's and B's shareholders want a gain from the merger, the final bargain must be between 20,000 and 37,500 of firm A's shares paid for firm B.

What will the ultimate bargain produce? That depends on the relative bargaining positions of firm A and firm B. If firm A has many other merger candidates of equal desirability to firm B, little more than 20,000 shares might be necessary to induce firm B to negotiate. If firms similar to B are rare and B's owners are aware of that fact, and if, in addition, many other merger-hungry firms such as A are seeking merger partners, close to 37,500 shares might be required to buy firm B. This is largely what has happened in recent years. Successful small companies are actively sought by larger firms for marriage, the result being high prices for the small companies.

The above example simplifies the problem in several respects. First, as noted earlier, the stockholders of the two firms may have differing expectations regarding the futures of the firms if left unmerged and if merged. Furthermore, earnings may be growing and not level, as in the above illustration. Thus, for example, firm A might be growing rapidly, firm B growing slowly, and the new merged firm might have an expected growth rate close to that of firm A. In this case, firm B's shareholders would be trading shares with a claim to low growth earnings for shares with rapidly increasing earnings. The greater the growth potential of the new shares of the merged company relative to the old firm B's shares, the fewer the new shares firm A needs to issue to acquire firm B. Indeed, firm B's stockholders might be willing to trade in their shares for new shares with lower *current* earnings because of the greater growth rate in earnings per share. For example, if current earnings of firm B were $100,000 and growing at 2 percent per year, the owners of firm B might be willing to trade these shares for firm A's shares providing current earnings of only $80,000 but a growth rate of, say, 10 percent per year. In short, future earnings are as important (usually more important) than current earnings in determining the desirability of the merger to the parties concerned.

Are the book values and liquidation values of firm B's assets, and the quantity of firm B's liquid assets, relevant in appraising firm B as an acquisition possibility? None of these factors was mentioned above. We can begin by dismissing book values entirely since they are based on historical costs and generally do not reflect real economic worth.

To obtain cash (for example, for exploiting investment opportunities), firm A can issue its own securities (debt or equity) or sell some of its assets;

it can also buy a company that has excess liquid assets (that are readily converted to cash), or buy an illiquid company and either sell some of its fixed assets or issue securities against those assets. That is, there are many ways to obtain liquidity and they should be compared on the basis of overall cost and benefit. It is true that purchasing a company with surplus liquidity is a convenient way to obtain cash, but it is clearly not the only way or necessarily the cheapest way.

ACCOUNTING TREATMENT OF MERGERS

In accounting practice, a merger is recorded as a purchase or as a pooling of interests. The primary differences between the two methods are in the value placed on the assets of the purchased firm for representation on the combined entity's balance sheet and for computing depreciation for the combined firm and in the representation of the combined firms income after merger. Note that the treatment of a merger for tax purposes (taxable or nontaxable) is an issue that is separate from whether a merger is a pooling or a purchase; it is the latter topic that we discuss in this section.

Under the purchase method, the acquired assets are carried on the books at the price paid (in cash or stock) for the selling company's stock plus any liabilities of the selling company assumed by the acquiring firm. To illustrate, assume that firm A purchases firm B by paying firm B's shareholders in firm A stock worth $1,500,000 (fair market value of the stock) and assume that the purchase method of accounting is used. From the premerger balance sheet in Exhibit 23-5 note that the firm B's owners' equity is only $800,000 and therefore the acquisition involves a $700,000 premium over book value paid to firm B's owners ($1,500,000 in firm A's stock for $800,000 of equity interest). This means that firm B's assets are being valued at $700,000 more than they appear on firm B's books, that is, are valued at $1,700,000. The acquired assets are valued on the postmerger books at $1,700,000; total assets are therefore $4,700,000 for the combined company ($3 million of firm A's assets + $1,700,000). The depreciation deduction (for

---

EXHIBIT 23-5
Premerger and postmerger balance sheets of firms A and B under the purchase method and the pooling of interests method of accounting for the merger

	Premerger balance sheets		Postmerger balance sheet of merged firm	
	Firm A	Firm B	Purchase method	Pooling of interests method
Assets (net of depreciation)	$3,000,000	$1,000,000	$4,700,000	$4,000,000
Liabilities	1,000,000	200,000	1,200,000	1,200,000
Owners' equity	2,000,000	800,000	3,500,000	2,800,000

accounting purposes) for the merged company in forthcoming years will be computed using the $4,700,000 as the depreciation base.

Under the pooling of interests approach, the assets are valued just as they were on the acquired firm's books. The depreciation base for the combined company will consequently be $4 million. Thus, if a merger involves payment for a firm's shares in excess of their book value, a pooling of interest involves lower asset values and lower depreciation charges in future periods (and therefore higher accounting income) than does a merger accounted for as a purchase.

The second difference between purchase and pooling is that with purchase the income on the financial statements of the acquiring firm includes the income of the acquired firm only from the date of the merger, whereas with pooling the income of the acquiring firm is restated retroactively to include the income of the acquired firm in all previous periods. For example, assume that firm A buys firm B on July 1, 1986, and that A has earned $3 million per year since its beginning in 1960. B has earned $1 million per year since its beginning in 1970. With purchase, A's financial statements after the merger will show 1986 earnings of $3,500,000 ($3 million of A's earnings plus the earnings of B after the July 1, 1986 merger) and will show pre-1986 earnings of $3 million (that is, will not include any of B's earnings in the premerger years). In contrast, with pooling, the earnings of A will be stated as $4 million for all years from 1970 (when B was started) to 1986, that is, the earnings of the two firms are simply combined for all time periods. Thus, when the historical earnings of firm A are presented in firm A's financial statements after the merger, those historical earnings will appear to be larger if the merger of A and B was a pooling of interests than if the merger was a purchase.

We have assumed thus far that the price paid for the acquired firm does not include a premium above the fair market value of the acquired firm's assets if those assets were sold individually. Such a premium is commonly referred to as goodwill and arises if the acquired firm has added value from such things as a strong market position, unusually talented personnel, and so forth. Goodwill is amortized in the financial statements and therefore deducted in computing the earnings reported to stockholders; however, the amortized goodwill is not deductible for tax purposes. Accounting earnings will be negatively affected by the amortized goodwill with purchase accounting but not with pooling of interests accounting, since the latter records assets at book values rather than at the purchase price.

Opinion 16 of the Accounting Principles Board of the American Institute of Certified Public Accountants specifies the conditions under which a pooling of interests accounting for a merger may be used. If these conditions are not met, the merger is to be treated as a purchase. One condition that must be satisfied for the pooling of interests method to be applicable is that the owners of the acquired firm must maintain their proportionate ownership claim (with voting rights) in the surviving firm. This would occur if they received voting common stock in payment for their stock in the acquired firm, whereas it would not occur if preferred stock, bonds, or cash were exchanged for the selling firm's shares. Use of the pooling of interests approach also requires that the combined entity intends to retain most or all of the purchased assets for at least two years after the merger and that the purchase be effected in a single transaction (no payments contingent upon the firm's future performance).

SUMMARY

A holding company is a firm that controls one or more other companies (called subsidiaries) through ownership of the subsidiary firms' common stock. In this chapter we use the term "merger" to signify the combination of two or more firms into one. Mergers take many forms, including horizontal, vertical, and conglomerate combinations. A merger may result from a friendly agreement between the managements of the combining companies (with the approval of the shareholders of both companies) or may involve the unfriendly takeover of one company by another. An unfriendly takeover ordinarily entails the buyer's purchase of the seller's shares by means of a tender offer. The Federal Trade Commission, the U.S. Justice Department, and certain other government agencies can block a merger if it will reduce competition.

A company can purchase a controlling interest in another company, can buy the other company's assets, or can combine with the other company through merger. A purchase can involve payment in the form of cash or of the securities of the purchasing company. A purchase is taxable to the selling firm (or its stockholders) if payment is in cash or bonds, whereas the taxes are postponed (a nontaxable exchange) if the voting stock of the purchasing firm is used in payment. From a tax standpoint, the sellers will usually prefer a nontaxable exchange whereas the acquiring firm will usually prefer that it be taxable. The buying company prefers a taxable purchase because this generally implies a higher depreciation base (higher depreciation deductions for tax purposes) in future years. The choice between payment in voting stock or in cash or nonvoting securities may also depend upon nontax considerations, such as the availability of excess cash in the buying company's coffers, the desire for cash by the selling firm's stockholders, and the expectations regarding the future performance of the acquiring firm's stock that would be used as payment in the purchase. A merger can produce benefits in the form of production economies, tax reductions, and reduction of risk through diversification. External growth through merger can provide certain advantages over internal expansion, including greater speed, lower risk, and the ability to purchase assets only obtainable by buying another firm. Merging simply to produce a better portfolio of assets for shareholders is generally a poor policy since shareholders can do their own diversifying.

In a purchase for cash, the decision to sell will be based upon a comparison by the sellers of the cash offered for their firm with the value of the firm being sold. The purchasing firm can treat the purchase as a capital budgeting problem, purchasing the new company only if the net cash flow from the acquired enterprise has a present value exceeding the purchase price. If payment is in the form of stock of the purchasing company, although a capital budgeting approach is still valid, an easier approach is to examine earnings per share with and without the merger. For both parties to agree to the merger, the shareholders of both firms must perceive an increase in their wealth positions. Particularly if there are real benefits from the merger (for example, production economies or tax benefits), both parties can gain—that is, both can end up with stock worth more than the value without the merger.

From an accounting standpoint, a merger is treated as a purchase or as a pooling of interests. The primary differences between the two methods are in recording the value of the acquired firm's assets on the acquiring firm's balance sheet and in the representation of the combined firm's historical earnings.

QUESTIONS

1   Contrast a holding company, a merger, and a consolidation.
2   Differentiate between horizontal and vertical combinations.
3   State the steps involved in a tender offer.
4   Certain production economies can result from mergers. What are some of these economies?
5   How can a reduction in the variability (uncertainty) of firm income occur through merger?
6   Explain when one can regard a reduction in the income uncertainty or variability resulting from a merger as a good thing, that is, as a benefit of the merger. When is it not a benefit?
7   What advantages are there to external growth through merger? Disadvantages?
8   What advantages does the straight purchase of assets have over a merger?
9   From a taxation point of view the form of payment for acquired firms can be important. Explain why. If only tax conditions were important, what form of payment would the seller and the buyer prefer?
10 It has been argued that a prosperous firm can acquire firms with operating losses and thereby incur a tax savings. Explain how this can come about.

PROJECT

Find an example of a tender offer being advertised in *The Wall Street Journal*. If you owned 100 shares of stock of the firm for which the tender offer is being made, would you be willing to tender your shares? You should analyze the offer carefully before making your decision (see Appendix 5A on sources of information about the firm involved).

PROBLEMS

1   What are the tax advantages of merging Camper Farms and Sandman Sleepwear, where Camper has an annual taxable income of $8 million and Sandman has an annual loss of $5 million? Assume that Camper has a 40 percent tax rate and that Sandman pays no taxes.

2 Melody Dance Studios is contemplating the acquisition of Grange Theaters. Melody can acquire Grange Theaters for $7 million but must pay off Grange's $4 million in liabilities. The pretax cash flow from Grange Theaters is estimated at $2 million a year for twenty years. The $7 million in Grange Theaters' assets are to be depreciated over twenty years on a straight-line basis (with no salvage value). At the end of the 20 years Melody expects to sell Grange Theaters for an after tax price of $10 million. Melody is in a 40 percent tax bracket, and Grange Theaters will be operated with no debt. Investments with risk comparable to that of Grange Theaters should yield 20 percent after taxes. Determine whether the acquisition is advisable for Melody.

3 Vertigo Pharmacologies is considering the acquisition of Olsen Pills. Vertigo can buy Olsen for $2.5 million. Olsen's annual pretax cash flow is forecast at $1.3 million forever. Depreciation for tax purposes is forecast at $200,000 per year forever. In the purchase, Vertigo will assume $800,000 of Olsen's liabilities. Vertigo is in the 40 percent tax bracket. Vertigo estimates that a fifteen percent aftertax rate of return is appropriate for its investment in Olsen Pills. Should Vertigo buy Olsen? Show all calculations.

4 Type-It Inc. is considering a merger with Write-It Inc. The data below are in the hands of both boards of directors. The merger is expected to generate significant production economies and increased earnings. The issue at hand is how many Type-It shares Write-It should get. Both boards are focusing their attention on earnings per share, for this potentially affects the value of the shares to be received and given. Both boards have agreed that the number of shares to be considered should be 200,000, 400,000, and 600,000. Construct a table demonstrating the potential impact of each scheme on each set of shareholders.

	Without merger		With merger
	Type-It	Write-It	
Earnings per year	$5,000,000	$1,500,000	$7,350,000
Shares outstanding	300,000	100,000	?
Earnings per share	$16.67	$15	?
Price per share	$50	$45	?
Price-earnings ratio	3X	3X	3X
Value of firm	$15,000,000	$4,500,000	$22,050,000

5 Scratch Fur is considering a merger with Trap Inc. The data below are in the hands of both boards of directors. The issue at hand is how many shares of Scratch should be exchanged for Trap. Both boards are considering three possibilities: 20,000, 25,000, and 30,000

shares. Construct a table demonstrating the potential impact of each
scheme on each set of shareholders.

	Scratch	Trap	Combined
Current earnings per year	$150,000	$90,000	$312,500
Shares outstanding	60,000	200,000	?
Earnings per share	$2.50	$.45	?
Price per share	$20	$3.60	?
Price-earnings ratio	8X	8X	8X
Value of firm	$1,200,000	$720,000	$2,500,000

6 Firm *A* acquires all of firm *B*'s stock by paying the firm *B* shareholders $90 million of firm *A* shares (which were issued to make this
acquisition). The premerger balance sheets of the two firms are set
forth below. Show how the balance sheet of the combined firm will
look under both the purchase method and the pooling of interests
method of accounting.

	Firm *A*	Firm *B*
Assets	$200,000,000	$95,000,000
Liabilities	80,000,000	30,000,000
Owners' equity	120,000,000	65,000,000

It's a rare week that the financial press does not report the details of at least one corporate courtship turned sour, with one company desperately fleeing the unwanted attentions of the other. This essay describes some of the tactics, and some of the tacticians, involved in this popular drama. We begin by describing two megamergers: the Socal purchase of Gulf Corporation (the largest takeover in U.S. history) and the DuPont acquisition of Conoco.

THE SOCAL-GULF MERGER

When T. Boone Pickens offered $65.00 per share—$5.00 above book value—for giant Gulf Corporation stock, it was not quite clear whether Pickens thought he could pull it off or really expected to end up a winner by being a "loser." In the end, Pickens was outbid by Standard Oil Company of California (Socal) which purchased Gulf for $80.00 per share. Pickens and his partners lost the contest for Gulf but pocketed a $760 million profit for their efforts.

The drama began on August 11 1983 when T. Boone Pickens' Mesa Petroleum and several deep-pocketed partners began buying Gulf stock at $39.00 per share. By October 14 the group had spent $630 million dollars for 14.5 million Gulf shares, 8¾% of Gulf stock. Gulf executives were disdainfully shocked by the specter of tiny Mesa (1983 sales of $433 million), attempting a takeover of huge Gulf (1983 sales of $28.9 billion). Gulf immediately attempted a legal ruse to derail Mesa by making Gulf, a Pennsylvania corporation, into a Delaware corporation. Because of differences in the corporation laws in the two states, the change would make it harder for Pickens to get on the Gulf board of directors. Picken's Mesa group countered with a proxy fight, which it subsequently lost. After the proxy victory, Gulf mistakenly assumed it was secure from further Mesa group overtures and went about its business. Gulf was so confident that it even turned down a $70.00 per share offer from Arco.

Pickens, observing the $70.00 price that Arco was willing to pay, made a tender offer for Gulf stock on February 23, 1984 at $65.00 per share, borrowing to the hilt to finance the purchase. Pickens set a March 14th deadline on the offer, giving Gulf virtually no time to marshall a defense. With institutional investors readily tendering their shares to Pickens, Gulf management desperately announced that Gulf was for sale to the highest bidder. In the end, Socal made the winning bid of $80.00 per share. The contestants at the end were Arco with a bid of $72.00 per share, a complex leveraged buyout bid from Kohlberg, Kravis, Roberts and Company, and the successful $80.00 per share offer from Socal. The Kohlberg, Kravis, Roberts and Company offer would have meant that existing Gulf managers would take the company private. The clear winners in this contest were the Gulf shareholders, most notably the latecomers T. Boone Pickens and his partners, who alone made a $760 million profit on their $1 billion investment in Gulf stock.

THE DU PONT-CONOCO MERGER

It didn't appear at the time to be an especially noteworthy occasion. Dome Petroleum's chairman, John Gallagher and its president, William Richards, had come to see Conoco's chairman, Ralph E. Bailey, to discuss the possible acquisition by Dome of certain Conoco properties in Canada. Dome's proposal was for it to purchase 20 percent of Conoco's stock in a public tender offer and then surrender the stock to Conoco in exchange for the Canadian properties. Bailey listened but was noncommittal. Somehow, Gallagher misunderstood and thought that he had the go-ahead. About a week after the meeting, on May 5, 1981, Dome made its tender offer for 20 percent of the Conoco shares at $65 per share, about $15 more than the price Conoco shares had been trading at in recent weeks. The response of the stockholders was more than Dome had anticipated. Banks, pension funds, and other institutions held a majority of Conoco stock and were eager to sell not just 20 percent, but 51 percent—control of Conoco—to Dome at the $65 tender price. Although Conoco had huge oil, gas, and coal holdings, estimated by some to be worth $160 per share, Conoco had been having trouble with the United Mine Workers and had worrisome exposure because it held large reserves in Libya. Nevertheless, $65 per share was a bargain price for a controlling interest in Conoco. At least that was the view of Edgar Bronfman, Chairman of Seagram, which had recently been outbid by Fluor Corporation in an attempt to buy St. Joe Minerals. On May 31, Bronfman met with the Conoco board and proposed that Seagram buy for cash, at $70 to $75 per share, 35 percent of Conoco. Bronfman even agreed to a "standstill agreement" under which Seagram would vote with management for the next fifteen years. But the Conoco board was not satisfied with this proposal, since after the fifteen-year pact expired Seagram could effectively control the company. The discussions reached an impasse and Bronfman left. Meanwhile, on another floor at Conoco headquarters, Dome was negotiating with Conoco an exchange of $245 million in cash plus the 2 million shares of Conoco it had bought through its tender offer in return for Conoco's Canadian oil and gas properties.

At this point, Conoco was not sure what Seagram would do next. As a precaution Conoco asked investment bank Morgan Stanley to prepare a list of potential "white knights" which might be interested in merging with Conoco should Seagram decide to attempt a takeover. Over the coming weeks, Du Pont's chairman, Edward Jefferson,

heard about the goings-on at Conoco and on June 24 called Bailey to inquire about the matter. The next day, on June 25, Seagram made a tender offer for 41 percent of Conoco's stock at $73 per share. Shearson Loeb Rhoades and Lazard Frères were now serving as Seagram's investment bankers. After the Seagram tender offer, Mobil and Texaco called Bailey. Bailey spurned the Mobil advances. The Conoco board also decided against the Texaco offer of $85 per share in cash because of potential antitrust problems. Bailey then called Du Pont's Jefferson to propose a merger. Du Pont accepted, but only on the condition that it could buy 16 million shares from Conoco's treasury for $87.50 a share before making a public tender offer. On July 6, Du Pont made its offer for all of Conoco's outstanding shares: $87.50 for the first 40 percent of the stock and 1.6 Du Pont shares per Conoco share for the remaining Conoco shares.

On July 12, Seagram counterattacked by raising its bid to $85 per share for 51 percent of Conoco's stock. Du Pont responded by increasing its offer to $95 per share for the first 40 percent of the stock and 1.7 shares of Du Pont shares per share of Conoco for the rest of the stock. On July 16 a new player entered the game: Mobil announced it would pay $90 a share for the first 50 percent of Conoco and Mobil securities worth $90 per share for the remainder.

Over the next three weeks, Du Pont, Seagram, and Mobil increased their offers in a bidding war which ended on August 5 with Du Pont's victory. In the end, Seagram acquired 28 million Conoco shares which it exchanged for 47.5 million new Du Pont shares. Seagram thus became the largest single Du Pont stockholder, with 20.1 percent of the stock (the Du Pont family and trusts own approximately 19.8 percent).

After the merger, the total market value of Du Pont stock was about $11 billion. The merger had created a new energy-chemical giant. Du Pont now had a guaranteed source of petroleum and ownership of the nation's largest single coal reserve; in 1981 Conoco's proven United States reserves were 403 million barrels of oil, 2.7 trillion cubic feet of natural gas, and 14 billion tons of coal. In exchange for Conoco, the Conoco shareholders (including Seagram) received cash and Du Pont stock worth nearly $7.5 billion.

KNOWING HOW TO SAY NO IMPOLITELY

If an acquiror has sufficient resources and determination, it can at some price induce the shareholders of a target firm to sell out. But without the cooperation of the target firm's management—cooperation that is often absent—the target may carry too high a price tag to be acceptable to the potential acquiror. The acquiror has several methods for attempting to purchase another company: peaceful negotiation with the other company's management, a proxy fight, or a purchase of the target firm's shares (in the open market or through a tender offer). If the peaceful approach doesn't work, the most common takeover tactic is to simply sidestep the target's management and try to buy its shares.

The target's management may resist a merger because it feels the offer is inadequate, that the combination does not make good business sense, that the target's management will be replaced if the takeover succeeds, or for some other reason. In these situations, the acquisition attempt is regarded as hostile—the result often being a furious attempt by the target's management to protect its "sleeping beauty" from the grasp of the attacking "black knight." Many companies keep "black books" listing defense tactics known in the trade as "shark repellent." In addition to simply appealing to the company's shareholders not to sell their shares to the shark, there are numerous defensive weapons available to the target's management.

One technique to repel an attacker is to find a "white knight," another merger partner that will pay a higher price, provide a better operating fit, or offer a more attractive future to management than is expected if the black knight succeeds. Socal was the white knight that rescued Gulf from T. Boone Pickens. Du Pont was a white knight for Conoco, which was battling it out against black knights Seagram and Mobil. A variation of the white knight stratagem is the "lockup." The lockup involves the target's selling stock or a part of the company to a friendly buyer, thereby making a takeover either less attractive or more difficult. For example, Pullman, Inc. granted options to Wheelabrator-Frye Inc., to purchase parts of Pullman's operations. This reinforced Pullman in its attempts to ward off McDermott, Inc. A special breed of lockup was attempted by Continental Airlines when, to thwart a hostile takeover attempt by Texas International Airlines, it proposed to give its employees a 51 percent ownership of Continental by issuing new shares and in effect selling the shares to its employees under an employee stock ownership plan (ESOP). Although the plan never materialized, it was interesting testimony to the ingenuity of human beings under siege.

Still another tactic was used by St. Joe Minerals Corporation to block a $45 per share bid by Seagram. St. Joe's management threatened to liquidate the company (sell off its assets and distribute the proceeds to its shareholders). The issue was ultimately resolved when Fluor Corporation bought St. Joe for $60 per share, more than Seagram was willing to pay.

Legal ploys are common defenses. The target firm can take the attacker to court so as either to delay or block the merger, an approach used, for example, by Conoco against Seagram, McGraw-Hill against American Express, and Continental Airlines against Texas

International Airlines. A farsighted management may adopt another tack: to change the rules of the game by encouraging shareholders to amend the corporate charter so that a very large majority of shares (e.g., 80 percent) is needed to approve a merger.

Another legal stratagem is the "poison pill," a deterrent to potential acquirors which becomes effective if a takeover is attempted or succeeds. For example, the corporate charter might be amended to include a provision that the company buy back (redeem) at a high specified price the shares of the minority shareholders who do not sell their shares to an acquiring firm. The idea here is that paying off the minority shareholders could wipe out a major portion of the company's assets, making it an unattractive acquisition. Another poison pill would involve according to the company's shareholders the right to buy shares in an acquiring company at a significant discount from market price, if a hostile takeover were to succeed.

One way to avoid being acquired is to beome an acquiror. There are several variants of this approach. One is to simply buy other firms, financing the purchases with new stock. Expanding the size of the company and the number of shares makes it more costly and more difficult for another firm to obtain control. An extra edge is gained if, in purchasing other companies, the target makes an acquisition that might result in antitrust action if the hostile acquiror were to succeed in effecting the merger. The target company can also buy back its own shares from the firm attempting the takeover. The payment for the stock (often referred to as "greenmail") virtually always produces a large profit for the firm selling back the target's shares. Under the buy-back agreement, the aggressor agrees to cease from any further takeover attempts for some period (say 10 years). The largest "greenmail" payment to date was the 1984 repurchase by Texaco of 9.9% of its stock from the Bass

Brothers (Texas Oil folks) for $1.28 billion. Other major buy-backs were Walt Disney's 1984 purchase of 11.1% of its stock from Saul Steinberg for $325.5 million, Gulf and Western's 1983 acquisition of 9.4% of its stock from Carl Lindner for $210.1 million, and Warner Communications 1984 buy-back of 8.6% of its stock from Rupert Murdoch for $181.6 million. Many critics have argued, with good justification, that "greenmail" is the target management's way to prevent a takeover that may jeopardize the management's jobs. The target's shareholders, of course, foot the bill.

The heated struggle between Curtiss-Wright, the aerospace conglomerate, and Kennecott Corporation, the nation's largest copper company, illustrates two other aggressive defense tactics: the target making a target out of the aggressor, and the countertender offer for one's own shares. A couple of years after losing a 1978 proxy fight to take over Kennecott, Curtiss-Wright announced that it was going to increase its stock holdings in Kennecott from 14.3 percent to 25 percent. Kennecott management began to fear a takeover attempt by Curtiss-Wright. They decided on a preemptive strike: a Kennecott takeover of Curtiss-Wright. The copper company offered $40 per share for Curtiss-Wright, nearly twice the then going price. In response, Curtiss-Wright made a $44 (and then a $46) counteroffer for its own stock, thereby blocking Kennecott. Kennecott then started buying Curtiss-Wright stock in the open market and eventually accumulated 32 percent of the company's shares. In the end, in early 1981, Kennecott and Curtiss-Wright negotiated a truce which included Kennecott's exchanging the Curtiss-Wright shares it held for the Kennecott shares held by Curtiss-Wright. Shortly thereafter, in 1981, Standard Oil of Ohio bought Kennecott for $2 billion.

Many managements have arrived at the same conclusion: If you can't save the ship, at least save the captain. This idea has spawned a rash of bailout agreements between companies and their managements to protect top officers from the unpleasantness of a takeover by another company. For example, Conoco chairman Ralph Bailey was guaranteed his salary through April 1, 1989—a perc worth $3.5 million. Wetterau Inc., a St. Louis food company, agreed to grant huge cash payments to sixteen executives—including $1.25 million to its chairman—if the company were unwillingly acquired. Needless to say, this type of "golden parachute" arrangement has become highly controversial. Indeed, under a new tax provision enacted in 1984, if the parachute payment is more than three times the executive's annual compensation during his or her last five years of employment, a large tax penalty is imposed on the executive receiving the payment and on the company making the payment.

THE MERGER BROKERS

Companies looking for a merger partner or trying to defend themselves against hostile takeovers often turn to specialists—investment bankers, lawyers, accountants, proxy solicitors, and public relations firms. Expert advice does not come cheap. Four months of legal and strategic battling was involved in the successful 1980 effort by Pullman Inc. to fight off McDermott Inc., and instead be acquired by Wheelabrator-Frye Inc., for $646 million. The total fees to investment bankers, lawyers, accountants, and others paid by the three companies was $17 million. First Boston alone collected $6 million. The $13.4 billion purchase of Gulf by Socal produced $63 million in fees to investment bankers ($46.5 million to Salomon Brothers and Merrill Lynch for advising Gulf Oil, and $16.5 million to Morgan Stanley for helping Socal). In the $7.5 billion Du Pont-Conoco merger, First Boston (which advised Du Pont) and Morgan Stanley (which advised Conoco) each received approximately $15 million.

Failure to consummate the transaction does not derail the gravy train. Forest products company Mead Corporation successfully fought a nine-month battle to prevent its takeover by Occidental Petroleum. The fight cost the two firms $15 million.

Ordinarily the investment bankers' fee is the largest professional expense in a major takeover. In a transaction involving several hundred million dollars, investment bankers advising the buyer will customarily receive $1.5 million to $3 million. Sometimes the fee is tied to the success of the offer. When Phillip Morris paid $515.5 million for 7-Up ($47 per share), Lehman Bros. received $1.9 million in fees instead of the $3,150,000 that it would have received if the purchase had been at the earlier tender offer price of $41 per share.

The seller's investment banker usually earns a percentage of the purchase price, roughly in the neighborhood of one-half percent, although this can vary from 0.1 percent for billion-dollar deals to well over 1 percent for transactions under $100 million. The fee is likely to be higher for hostile takeovers than for peaceful ones. First Boston's $6 million fee in the Pullman-Wheelabrator merger was about 1 percent of the purchase price. A common guideline on small deals is the 5–4–3–2–1 formula, under which the merger specialist gets a 5 percent commission on the first $1 million of the merger's cost, 4 percent on the second million, and so on.

Are the professionals who provide the advice and counsel worth the cost? Although in some cases companies have partially supplanted the services of investment bankers with those of the somewhat less expensive financial consulting firms, it is almost certain that as long as there are mergers—especially of the hostile variety—the services of bankers and lawyers will be in demand.

24

**INTER-
NATIONAL
FINANCIAL
MANAGEMENT**

Companies that buy and sell goods outside their own countries face special problems not confronted by purely domestic businesses. The companies must deal in currencies of different countries, not simply the domestic currency. Furthermore, countries differ in their laws, taxes, business practices, and degrees of economic stability. Management must understand and adjust to the conditions in each country in which it does business. This chapter examines the special problems that arise with international transactions. The first section describes the factors influencing the rates of exchange among the world's currencies. Then the methods that have been developed to finance purchases of goods in international trade are described. The last section of the chapter deals with the multinational company, a business firm with operations in more than one country.

CURRENCIES AND EXCHANGE RATES

Suppose you are planning a trip to Germany. You will need to have German currency, or Deutsche marks (DM), so that you can make purchases while you are there. How many marks can you obtain with, say, $500? The relationship between the values of two currencies is called the **exchange rate**. The exchange rate between dollars and marks can be stated as dollars per mark or marks per dollar; for example, $0.50 per mark or DM2.0 per dollar. At this exchange rate $500 would exchange into (purchase) 2.0 × $500 = DM1000. Note that one exchange rate is the reciprocal of the other: 0.5 = (1/2.0). Exchange rates of major world currencies, expressed both as dollars per foreign currency unit and as currency units per dollar, are listed in *The Wall Street Journal* each day. The names of several countries' currencies and exchange rates relative to United States dollars are shown in Table 24-1. Notice the wide range of relative currency values that exist at a point in time. In addition, Table 24-1 indicates that precise wording is needed when dealing with foreign currencies. It is not sufficient to say a bushel of wheat sells for $2.50. You must say whether it is $2.50 United States, $2.50 Australian, or $2.50 Canadian. Similarly, more than one country denominates its currency in pounds, in pesos, in francs, and so forth.

Factors Determining Exchange Rates

Exchange rates are determined in the foreign exchange market and reflect the supply and demand for each currency. The demand for a given country's currency is based on people's needs to make payments in that currency, plus speculative demand, plus government demand. Payments requiring foreign exchange are made for several reasons: purchases of goods being exported from the country, purchases of goods and services by foreign tourists in the country, financial assets being acquired by foreign investors, and direct investments in plant and equipment by foreign corporations establishing productive facilities in the country. Speculative demand for a currency is based on expectations that the currency will appreciate (increase in value) relative to other currencies. Government demand reflects attempts by the government of a country to maintain its currency's value relative to the values of other currencies.

The supply of a currency in the foreign exchange market comes from people who presently own the currency and wish to exchange it for foreign currencies. Importers who wish to pay for goods purchased abroad buy foreign currencies, thus supplying their own currency to the foreign exchange market. Tourists exchange their home country's currency for the currencies of the countries they are visiting. Anyone holding currency X who would prefer to hold some other country's currency is a source of supply of currency X. For example, if you are a citizen of country X and are worried about high rates of inflation, political instability, or possible confiscation of your assets in country X, you might prefer to transfer funds out of country X into more secure assets in country Y.

Inflation Although changes in exchange rates result from changes in the supply and demand for currencies, this explanation does not provide a very helpful answer to the question of why exchange rates change. We must look for the more fundamental factors that affect the supply and demand for currencies. One factor is the relative rate of inflation in different countries. If the rate of inflation is 10 percent per year in country X and 1 percent per year in country Y, the purchasing power of country X's currency is declining faster than the purchasing power of country Y's currency. As a result, the exchange rate of country X's currency will tend to decline relative to country Y's currency. If people could freely transfer money from one country to another and could freely purchase goods and services throughout the world, the goods and services that can be purchased for $100 in the United States, for example, would be the same as those available in France if $100 is

TABLE 24-1
Selected currencies and exchange rates

Country	Currency	Exchange rate (U.S. $)	
		January 1985	January 1984
Australia	Dollar	.815	.906
Austria	Schilling	.045	.050
Canada	Dollar	.755	.801
France	Franc	.103	.116
Germany	Deutsche mark (mark)	.315	.356
India	Rupee	.079	.093
Italy	Lira	.00051	.00059
Japan	Yen	.0039	.0043
Mexico	Peso	.0044	.0060
Netherlands	Guilder	.279	.316
Spain	Peseta	.0057	.0063
Sweden	Krona	.110	.122
Switzerland	Franc	.376	.447
United Kingdom	Pound	1.113	1.408

Source: Federal Reserve Bulletin.

exchanged into French francs. Exchange rates therefore tend to vary so as to provide similar purchasing power in each country. Differences in inflation rates among countries result in changes in exchange rates.

Interest Rates   A second factor influencing exchange rates is relative interest rates. If investors can earn 4 percent interest per year in country Y and 8 percent per year in country X, they will prefer to invest in securities of country X provided that the rate of inflation is the same in both countries. As people buy currency X with currency Y, the exchange rate of country X's currency will appreciate relative to country Y's. The increased demand for securities in country X relative to country Y also tends to reduce the interest rate differential between the two countries. This occurs because the prices of country X's securities rise (reducing their yield to new investors) and the prices of country Y's securities fall (increasing their yield to new investors).[1]

Government Policies and Other Factors   Governments have an enormous influence on exchange rates through tariffs, quotas, foreign exchange restrictions, and fiscal and monetary policies (which affect inflation and interest rates). In addition, the political stability of a country affects the risks of investing in that country. Governments often actively intervene in the foreign exchange markets, buying and selling currencies to support the value of their currency relative to others. In some cases governments do not allow their currencies' values to be established in the foreign exchange market. For example, the communist countries are not tied into the international financial system, and their exchange rates are set by government decree.

*Spot and
Forward Rates*

The **spot** rate of exchange between two currencies is today's rate of exchange for currencies being bought and sold for immediate delivery. The **forward** rate of exchange is a rate agreed on today with the actual delivery of the currency to take place at a *future* time, usually 30, 90, or 180 days from now. Forward exchange rates are therefore prices set today for currency exchanges that will occur in the future.

Forward rates may be greater than the current spot rate (premium) or less than the current spot rate (discount). For example, on February 1, 1985 the following exchange rates were quoted in *The Wall Street Journal* (for transactions on January 31, 1985):

	British pounds (£)	German marks (DM)
	1.1310	0.3163
30–day futures	1.1274	0.3169
90–day futures	1.1213	0.3184
180–day futures	1.1160	0.3206

---

[1] The interest rate (yield) provided by a financial asset is inversely related to its price (see Chap. 5).

The first figure shown in each case was the spot rate for that day, $1.131 per pound for example. The other rates are the forward rates for contracts of the time specified. Forward rates on the pound are at a discount from the spot rate, whereas forward rates for the mark are at a premium. Purchase of a forward contract for exchange of £100 into dollars 180 days later (July 31, 1985) would assure the purchaser that £100 could be exchanged into $111.60 (£100 × $1.1160) regardless of the spot rate in effect on July 31, 1985.

Covering Investment Positions in the Forward Market   Contracts for future exchanges are used to "cover" a position (investment) in a particular currency. For example, suppose interest rates in Great Britain are 10 percent per year and interest rates in the United States are 6 percent per year. You have $10,000 (United States) that you could invest in a British security which will mature in 180 days. The spot rate for British pounds is $2; that is, $10,000 will purchase £5000. If you exchange your dollars into pounds and invest in the British security, you will have about £5250 180 days from now (principal plus 5 percent since the investment is for half of a year). At that time you wish to exchange the pounds back into dollars. You could make the exchange at the spot rate prevailing then, whatever it turns out to be. In this case you would run the risk of having the pound depreciate relative to the dollar. That is, instead of being able to acquire $2 for each pound ($10,500), you might only be able to obtain $1.90 per pound or $9975 (1.90 × £5250). Receiving $9975 in six months' time from an investment of $10,000 is not desirable. You would have been much better off investing at 6 percent

---

EXHIBIT 24-1
Using a futures contract to cover a foreign investment position

---

Basic investment:

$10,000 exchanged at current spot rate of $2 per pound to provide £5,000
£5,000 invested at 10% per year to yield £5,250 in 180 days

Returns from uncovered position:

Spot rate[a]	$2.04	$2.00	$1.96	$1.90
Dollar return[b]	$10,710	$10,500	$10,290	$9,975
Rate of return[c]	14.2%	10%	5.8%	−0.5%

Returns from covered position:

Forward rate (180 days) = $1.98 per pound
Dollar return = £5,250 × $1.98 per pound = $10,395
Rate of return = 3.95% for 180 days or 7.9% per year

---

[a] Possible values for exchange rate between British pounds and United States dollars (dollars per pound) in effect 180 days from initial investment.
[b] Dollar value of £5,250 at indicated spot rate.
[c] Annual percentage rate earned on initial dollar investment when returns from British investment are exchanged into dollars.

per year in the United States if this were to happen. This is called an "uncovered" position because what you actually earn on the investment depends on future exchange rates. Exhibit 24-1 shows some possible outcomes for different exchange rates.

Alternatively, you could cover the investment by executing a contract in the forward exchange market to exchange £5250 into United States dollars 180 days from now. The rate of exchange in this contract is the forward rate. Suppose the forward rate is $1.98 per pound on a 180-day futures contract. You will exchange £5250 for $10,395 (1.98 × £5250) in 180 days, and you will earn 7.9 percent per year on your investment in British securities as contrasted with 6 percent in United States securities.[2]

Forward exchange markets thus provide a way to protect against future changes in exchange rates. They are used by investors in foreign securities, banks, and companies engaged in international transactions. Forward exchange markets also provide a means to speculate on changes in exchange rates. The failure of Franklin National Bank in 1974 was in part due to massive losses from forward exchange market speculation.

FINANCING INTERNATIONAL TRADE

In a typical domestic purchase of goods by one business firm from another, the goods are shipped and the purchaser is billed for their value. The seller provides trade credit to the purchaser as discussed in Chapter 16 and bears the risk that the purchaser will not be able to pay for the goods. The credit risks are generally greater in international transactions than in domestic ones. Sellers have less reliable information about purchasers in another country, and it is more difficult to collect debts in a foreign country. Shipping times are much greater in international trade; the goods may be in transit for months. Therefore, the financing burden is much greater because, while the goods are being shipped, neither seller nor purchaser has access to them and yet someone must be financing them. There also may be exchange rate risk associated with the transaction. In this section we describe some of the methods used to deal with foreign exchange risk, credit risk, and financing in international trade.

Foreign Exchange Risk

There is no foreign exchange risk if the buyer (importer) is willing to pay the seller (exporter) when the goods are ordered. The two parties need only agree on the price of the goods—taking into account the current exchange rate between the currencies of the two countries—and complete the transaction. For example, suppose that a United States department store wishes to import 10,000 meters of silk from Thailand. The price of the silk, exported by a Thai silk mill, is to be 200,000 baht (Thai currency). The exchange rate is 20 baht per United States dollar, so the price in United States dollars is $10,000. If the department store immediately buys 200,000 baht and pays the silk mill when it orders the silk, there is no exchange risk and there is no credit risk. However, most international trade involves delayed payments.

Whenever payment is delayed, there is a risk that the exporter's cur-

---

[2] This type of transaction is called **covered interest arbitrage.**

rency will appreciate relative to the importer's currency, but not the reverse. This is so because importation of goods involves money moving from importer to exporter, and because the exporter ultimately wants payment in its own currency. Assuming that no strategy is used to eliminate exchange risk (see next section), the importer's currency will be exchanged for the exporter's currency when the importer pays for the goods. The risk is that the importer's currency will buy fewer units of the exporter's currency than it did when the goods were sold. If the goods are invoiced in the importers currency, the exporter is exposed to the exchange risk. If the goods are invoiced in the exporter's currency, the importer is exposed to the exchange risk.

Suppose that the silk in the example above will be in transit three months and that the Thai exporter is willing to extend credit for this time. If the silk is invoiced at a price of $10,000 (the importer's currency), the silk mill is exposed to the risk that $10,000 will be worth less than 200,000 baht in three month's time; that is, that the baht has appreciated relative to the dollar. If the silk is invoiced at a price of 200,000 baht (the exporter's currency), the department store is exposed to the risk. If the baht appreciates relative to the dollar, it will take more than $10,000 to purchase 200,000 baht when payment is made.

Eliminating Exchange Risk

How can the exchange risk of a delayed payment be eliminated? One way is to cover the transaction in the forward exchange markets. If the goods are invoiced in the importer's currency (dollars, for example), the exporter bears the risk. The exporter can eliminate this risk by selling a forward contract to deliver the importer's currency in exchange for the exporter's currency at the time the sale is made. For example, if the Thai silk mill provides ninety days of credit and invoices the goods at a price of $10,000, it will be receiving $10,000 in ninety days (which it will then convert to baht). Suppose the mill sells a contract for delivery of $10,000 in ninety days' time in exchange for baht. If the forward rate on a ninety-day futures contract is the same as the current spot rate ($0.05), under the forward contract the exporter will be able to deliver the $10,000 and receive 200,000 baht in ninety days' time, regardless of what happens to the exchange rate in the meantime. If the forward rate is at a discount or premium, the amount of baht to be received will be different from 200,000, but in any case the amount will be known at the time the forward contract is made. Indeed, the price of the goods is likely to depend in part on the length of time for which credit will be extended and the cost of covering the transaction in the forward exchange markets.

If the goods are invoiced in the exporter's currency (baht, for example), then the importer bears the exchange risk. In our example, the United States department store could eliminate the risk by selling a forward contract to deliver dollars in exchange for baht at a fixed exchange rate. The contract would be for the amount of dollars needed to obtain 200,000 baht at the ninety-day forward rate.

An alternative method of eliminating exchange risk is through money market transactions. The delayed payment is an asset for the exporter (account receivable) and a liability for the importer (account payable). The party exposed to the exchange risk can eliminate it by creating an offsetting liability or asset in the foreign currency. Suppose that the silk in our example is invoiced at a price of $10,000 to be paid in three months. The Thai exporter has a dollar receivable and is exposed to the exchange risk. The mill could eliminate the risk by obtaining a dollar loan which has a total principal and interest payment of $10,000 at the end of three months. The proceeds from the loan (the present value of $10,000 discounted at the interest rate on the loan) can be exchanged into baht immediately. At the end of the three months, the exporter uses the $10,000 payment on the receivable to pay off the loan.

On the other hand, if the silk is invoiced at a price of 200,000 baht, the United States department store has a baht payable and is exposed to the exchange risk. The store can eliminate the risk by immediately exchanging dollars into baht and investing in a Thai security (asset) which will pay 200,000 baht in three months time. The proceeds from the security can be used to pay the silk mill when the 200,000 baht payment is due in three months.

An analysis of the costs of protection against exchange rate risks is complex and beyond the scope of this book. In many instances firms do not choose to protect against the risk because the costs are too great.

Letters of Credit

As we noted above, immediate payment by the importer (buyer) to the exporter (seller) eliminates the exchange risks of deferred payment and allows the exporter to avoid bearing any credit risk. However, immediate payment means that the importer has money tied up in the goods while they are in transit. Moreover, the importing firm owns goods that will not be in its control and available for inspection for some time. The sellers of any product have an incentive (profits) to ease the problems faced by their customers in acquiring those goods. Only when credit or political risks are very great will the seller demand cash in advance. In some cases, sales will be made on open account, as is customary in domestic transactions. Between these two extremes, a variety of specialized financial arrangements have been developed to facilitate international trade. The most widely used arrangement is based on a **letter of credit**. A letter of credit is a written statement made by a bank that it will pay out money if specified conditions are met. There are several different types of letters of credit; here we will describe the one most often used in United State imports—an irrevocable letter of credit issued by a United States bank.

Import Letters of Credit Suppose a United States importer wishes to buy goods from a foreign company. The importer orders the goods, asking the seller firm to ship under a letter of credit. The two parties reach agreement on prices, method of shipment, etc. The importer then applies for a letter of credit from a commercial bank. This letter of credit, sent to the exporter, authorizes the exporter to obtain money from the bank by presenting the required documents supporting the sale and shipment of the goods. The exporter is likely to use a bank in its country to handle the paperwork (the

EXHIBIT 24-2
Sample letter of credit

RAINIER NATIONAL BANK
WORLD BANKING DIVISION
P.O. Box 3966 Seattle, Washington 98124 U.S.A.

DATE: January 10, 1985

IRREVOCABLE COMMERCIAL
LETTER OF CREDIT

OUR NO. SEA-92000   ADVISING BANK NO.

ADVISING BANK

Thai Military Bank, Ltd.
34 Phayathai Road
Bangkok 4, Thailand

APPLICANT

Osgood & North
906 Fourth Avenue
Seattle, Washington 98104

BENEFICIARY

Thai Silk Mills Ltd.
P.O. Box 128
Bangkok, Thailand

AMOUNT

US $10,000.00 (TEN THOUSAND AND
NO/100 US DOLLARS)

EXPIRY

March 11, 1985 in Thailand

YOU ARE AUTHORIZED TO DRAW ON US YOUR DRAFTS AT Sight
FOR 100% INVOICE VALUE WHEN ACCOMPANIED BY THE FOLLOWING DOCUMENTS:

Signed Commercial Invoice in quintuplicate;
Packing List in duplicate;
Certificate of Origin;
Beneficiary's Certificate that one set of non-negotiable documents has been airmailed
   to Applicant and Seattle Custom Broker, P.O. Box 1092, Seattle, Washington 98123;
Full Set of Clean On Board Marine Bills of Lading issued to the order of shipper
   and blank endorsed, evidencing shipment not later than March 5, 1985, Marked
   Freight Collect and Notify Applicant and Seattle Custom Broker, P.O. Box 1092,
   Seattle, Washington 98123;

SHIPPING TERMS: FOB Vessel, Thailand Port
COVERING: 10,000 Meters Thai Silk

THE AMOUNT OF ANY DRAFT DRAWN UNDER THIS CREDIT MUST BE ENDORSED ON THE REVERSE OF THE ORIGINAL CREDIT. ALL DRAFTS
MUST BE MARKED "DRAWN UNDER RAINIER NATIONAL BANK LETTER OF CREDIT NUMBER SEA-92000 DATED 1-10-85 "

SHIPMENT FROM: Thailand | PARTIAL SHIPMENTS | TRANS-SHIPMENT
TO: Seattle, Washington | Prohibited | Permitted

SPECIAL INSTRUCTIONS:
All bank charges other than those of the issuing bank are for the account of the beneficiary.
Buyer Insures. This letter of credit is available with us by payment and with any bank
for negotiation. The negotiating bank is to forward all documents to us in one airmail.

Drafts and documents to be presented for negotiation not later than 10 days after the Bill of Lading date.

Except so far as otherwise expressly stated, this documentary credit is subject to the "Uniform Customs and Practice for Documentary Credits" XXXX 1983
Revision), International Chamber of Commerce Publication No. XXX 400

WE HEREBY AGREE WITH THE DRAWERS ENDORSERS AND BONA-
FIDE HOLDERS OF DRAFTS DRAWN UNDER AND IN COMPLIANCE
WITH THE TERMS OF THIS CREDIT THAT SUCH DRAFTS WILL BE
DULY HONORED ON DUE PRESENTATION TO THE DRAWEE IF
NEGOTIATED ON OR BEFORE EXPIRY DATE.
jmt

ADVISING BANK NOTIFICATION

Authorized Signature   Authorized Signature   Place, date, name and signature of the advising bank.

04284 R7-79

negotiating bank). A sample letter of credit is shown in Exhibit 24-2. A glossary of the terms used in the letter and in international trade is shown in Table 24-2.

Notice that there are four parties involved in this transaction—the importer (Osgood and North), the importer's bank (Rainier National Bank), the exporter (Thai Silk Mills), and a bank that will notify the exporter that the letter of credit has been issued (Thai Military Bank). The letter of credit is *irrevocable* by the issuing bank if the *bank* promises to pay the money provided the conditions specified in the letter of credit are met. In such transactions when the importer's bank issues the letter of credit, neither the

TABLE 24-2
Definitions of some terms used in international trade[a]

Term	Definition[b]
Accept; acceptance	To agree to pay on a designated date a draft drawn on the party accepting; an acceptance is an accepted draft. (Rainier National Bank would be the party accepting the draft.)
Beneficiary	Party in whose name a letter of credit has been issued or a draft drawn (Thai Silk Mills).
Bill of lading	Document showing that the goods were received by the carrier ("vessel" in which the goods are to be shipped). A "clean" bill of lading shows no indications of defects in the goods or their packing.
Certificate of origin	Document showing the country where the goods originated (Thailand).
Commercial invoice	The bill for the goods issued by the exporter (Thai Silk Mills).
Draft	Instrument by which one party directs another party to make a payment. (Thai Silk Mills would draw a draft against the letter of credit from the Rainier National Bank. The mill might direct the Rainier National Bank to pay $10,000 to Thai Military Bank for the mill's account.)
Free on board (FOB)	A term of sale indicating the point at which the exporter stops paying for transportation costs and the importer begins paying. (Thai Silk Mill would pay all costs involved in getting the silk on the boat. Osgood and North would have to pay for marine insurance and the ocean voyage.)
Open	To establish or issue, as in "to open a letter of credit."

[a] Excluded are those terms defined in the text and included in the glossary at the end of the book.
[b] Remarks in parentheses refer to the text example and Exhibit 24-2.

exporter nor the exporter's bank need have any knowledge of the credit worthiness of the importer. All the credit risk to the exporter is absorbed by the importer's bank, which is in a good position to evaluate the credit of the importing firm. The credit standing of the importer's bank becomes the only concern of the exporting firm and its bank.

Financing under Letters of Credit

Letters of credit are used to reduce the credit risk borne by the exporter. They may or may not involve financing. The letter of credit (L/C) in Exhibit 24-2 specifies that the exporter can draw a draft at sight. This means that the exporter will receive an immediate payment of $10,000, the amount specified in the L/C, when the required documents are presented to the issuing bank (Rainier). Therefore the importer (Osgood & North) is financing the goods in transit. Financing under an L/C is done through the use of time drafts. A time draft is payable at a future date rather than at sight and its tenor (time to payment) will be specified in the L/C, for example, 90 days. The payment may be made either 90 days from the date of the draft or 90 days from sight, as specified in the L/C. A time draft is used when the exporter is providing financing of the goods in transit but does not want to assume the credit risk of a sale on account to the importer.

Time drafts also provide the basis for banker's acceptances, a money market security described in Chapter 2. A banker's acceptance is created if the bank issuing the L/C stamps "accepted," with the signature of an authorized bank officer and date on the face of the time draft. The draft then becomes a legal obligation of the bank and a negotiable security. The exporter can sell this security immediately to raise cash at a discount from its face value or can borrow money at a relatively low rate of interest, using the banker's acceptance as collateral for the loan. The cost of this financing may be paid by the importer or by the exporter depending on their agreement, and is usually lower than other financing methods available to the firms. Of course, for this service the bank charges a fee, which can be as high as 2 or 3 percent if the importer is financially weak. Banker's acceptances are widely used in financing international trade.

THE MULTINATIONAL COMPANY

A multinational company, or MNC, is a company that has direct investments (produces a product or products) in more than one country. The importance of the MNC is highlighted by the fact that every one of the fifty largest (in sales) United States manufacturing concerns is a multinational! As of 1985, the total foreign assets of these firms was approximately $250 billion. Although the United States is the dominant home of MNCs, Britain, Switzerland, West Germany, Canada, and Japan have, in the aggregate, invested outside their borders approximately as much as has the United States. By 1985, direct foreign investment in the United States totalled approximately $150 billion.

The Profit Motive

Four major factors encouraged United States companies to establish subsidiaries abroad. The first was the desire to avoid foreign tariffs against United States goods. For example, to sell its American-made product in

France, a cosmetics manufacturer would have to pay a French tariff, but there would be no tariff to pay if the products were manufactured by its subsidiary in France. The decline in trade barriers during the last twenty years has made this advantage less important.

A second factor encouraging the growth of MNCs has been the lower production costs overseas. In recent years, however, wages in other countries have risen more sharply than have American wages; consequently much of the cost advantage has eroded.

A third influence was American technical and managerial superiority. This advantage, too, has dwindled in the face of mounting competition from the MNCs of other countries and the increased sophistication of the foreign nations in which the United States MNCs operate.

The fourth factor that has encouraged United States investment abroad is tax benefits accorded companies which have foreign operations. Taxes are discussed later in this chapter.

The Counterforce: Foreign Investment in the United States

The insignia of United States industrial giants have long been familiar to Europeans and Canadians, as well as to the peoples of many less industrialized countries. But, until recently, foreign direct investment in the United States has been less than meager. Now, however, the inflow of foreign investment is accelerating. Britain has been a leader through such English firms as the British American Tobacco Company, the British Land Company, Slater-Walker Securities, Barclays Bank Ltd., and Lloyds Bank Ltd. of London. Switzerland's huge Nestle Alimentana, France's Michelin, and West Germany's Volkswagen are other standard-bearers of the foreign invasion. Total foreign direct investment in the United States was approximately $70 billion in 1985, and it has been rising at over $4 billion annually in recent years.

The Extraordinary Risk of Foreign Investment

Political Risk   Although few foreign ventures are as ill-fated as Anaconda's copper investments in Chile or some of the international oil firms' holdings in the Middle East, the risk of foreign expropriation—or, at least, controls—is an ever-present threat to multinational enterprises. The danger is particularly great for investments in natural resources in underdeveloped countries, since such resources often represent a large portion of the national wealth and are regarded by the nationals as "part of the country."

To deal with the risk of foreign government intervention confronting United States companies abroad, the United States government established the Overseas Private Investment Corporation (OPIC). This agency insures against losses due to inconvertibility into dollars of amounts invested in the foreign country or of any income from those investments. Other OPIC programs insure against expropriation and nationalization and against losses due to war or revolution. Only certain properties can be insured, and each project must be individually approved for eligibility. The fees charged by OPIC—a specified percentage of the value of the insured property—are the same for all firms and all investments, regardless of risk, but they do vary depending upon whether the coverage is for inconvertibility , expropriation, war, and so forth.

Exchange Rate Risk   There are two major risks associated with exchange rate changes. The first is the purely **monetary risk** that an exchange rate change will alter the dollar value (that is, the value expressed in the parent company's currency) of the assets and liabilities of the foreign subsidiary. The second type of exchange rate risk arises from the possible impact of an exchange rate change on the competitive position of the parent and of foreign subsidiaries; we will call this **exchange rate business risk**.

To illustrate the above risks, assume that Blass Products Inc., a United States company, has a subsidiary in England, Blass Ltd. Blass Ltd. has assets worth £100,000 and liabilities of £60,000. Suppose that the exchange rate is $2 per pound, implying that, in United States dollars, the subsidiary's assets are worth $200,000 and the liabilities total $120,000. If the pound increases in value to $3 per pound, there would be an increase in the dollar level of the Blass Ltd.'s assets to $300,000 and liabilities to $180,000. *A rise in the value of the foreign currency (the pound) causes a dollar gain on the foreign assets (the assets can be converted into more dollars) and a dollar loss on the foreign liabilities (more dollars would be required to pay off the liabilities).* On the other hand, if the pound fell in value to $1 per pound, there would be a decrease in the dollar level of Blass Ltd.'s assets to $100,000 and a decrease in its liabilities to $60,000. *A decline in the value of the foreign currency causes a dollar loss on the foreign assets (the assets can be converted into fewer dollars) and a dollar gain on the foreign liabilities (fewer dollars would be required to pay off the liabilities).* The figures in this example are shown in Exhibit 24-3.

From Exhibit 24-3 it is clear that, if Blass Ltd.'s assets exceed liabilities (positive equity), there is a net gain if the pound rises in value in terms of dollars and a net loss if the pound falls in value in terms of dollars. This highlights an interesting point: The risk exposure depends on foreign assets minus foreign liabilities, that is, on the foreign subsidiary's equity. Thus, when one £1 = $2 the equity is $80,000. If the pound appreciates to $3, the equity increases to $120,000; this gain of $40,000 equals a gain of $100,000 on the assets (which increase in dollar value from $200,000 to $300,000) minus a loss of $60,000 on the liabilities (which increase in terms of dollars from $120,000 to $180,000).[3]

From the above example it follows that, if a company expects the value of the foreign currency (for example, the pound) to rise in terms of dollars, it will want to have large assets and minimal liabilities denominated in the foreign currency. The opposite holds if the company expects foreign currency to fall in terms of dollars.

Why does the parent company care if the *dollar* value of its equity in a foreign subsidiary changes? If the parent never expects to convert the foreign holdings into dollars, and never expects to make further dollar investments in the foreign subsidiary, the parent shouldn't care. But this is unusual. Foreign subsidiaries of United States corporations often repatriate

---

[3] In this chapter we are concerned with financial and economic issues and not with accounting rules of financial disclosure. For details on accounting guidelines as they relate to international operations, see Statement of Financial Accounting Standards No. 52.

profits to the United States, and the more dollars that are received the better. Put simply, since repatriation is virtually always at least a possibility, the greater the dollar amount that can be brought home as dividends, or as the liquidation proceeds from selling the subsidiary, the better.

The second exchange rate risk relates to the impact of the exchange rate change on the competitive position and long-run profitability of the parent corporation and its subsidiaries. We call this risk exchange rate business risk. To illustrate, assume that Blass Ltd. manufactures technical instruments which are made using English labor and materials (that is, not imported inputs) but which are sold primarily outside England. Imagine that the British pound falls in value, causing the foreign price (i.e., in currencies other than the pound) of Blass's product to fall. This makes Blass's product more competitive, thereby increasing sales. Since the cost (in terms of pounds) of production will not be directly affected because the inputs of production are British, the increased foreign demand for Blass Ltd.'s products will mean greater profits (as measured in pounds).[4] On the other hand, if the pound were to appreciate in terms of dollars, Blass Ltd.'s competitive position would deteriorate and sales would decrease, thereby reducing the firm's profits in terms of pounds.[5]

Companies can eliminate both the purely monetary risk and the business risk of exchange rate changes. The methods of eliminating exchange rate monetary risk described on pages 705–707 had one common feature: They all involved reducing to zero the net exposure of the company in terms of a foreign currency. That is, any claims to the foreign currency (for example, holdings of the foreign currency, assets in the foreign country, etc.) must be exactly offset by liabilities denominated in that foreign currency. Thus, a parent corporation can eliminate exchange rate monetary risk by, for example, making sure that its net equity position in a foreign

[4] The effect on profits in terms of dollars will depend on the effect of the pound devaluation on sales and also on the change in the dollar value of the pound. Thus, there could be an increase, decrease, or no change in Blass Ltd.'s profits in terms of dollars.
[5] But the change in profits as measured in dollars might increase, decrease, or not change at all (see footnote 4, this chapter).

EXHIBIT 24-3

Impact of an exchange rate change on the dollar balance sheet of a British subsidiary

	If exchange rate is £1 = $2		If exchange rate is £1 = $3		If exchange rate is £1 = $1	
	In pounds	In dollars	In pounds	In dollars	In pounds	In dollars
Assets	£100,000	$200,000	£100,000	$300,000	£100,000	$100,000
Liabilities	60,000	120,000	60,000	180,000	60,000	60,000
Equity	40,000	80,000	40,000	120,000	40,000	40,000

subsidiary is zero. For example, Blass Products Inc., could have Blass Ltd. borrow £40,000 (see Exhibit 24-3), convert those pounds to dollars, and repatriate the dollars to the United States; after this transaction, Blass Ltd. would have assets worth £100,000 and liabilities of £100,000 and Blass Products Inc., would have a zero equity position in Blass Ltd. An alternative strategy would be for Blass Products Inc. to sell £40,000 for dollars in the forward markets; gains or losses in a forward contract would be exactly offset by losses or gains on its equity position in Blass Ltd.[6]

Protecting against the second kind of exchange rate risk—exchange rate business risk—is more difficult, but is possible in some cases. The basic strategy is internationally diversifying output or sources of input supply so that exchange rate changes for one currency can be offset by shifting production or input purchases to places where the exchange rate has not shifted disadvantageously. For example, a rise in the value of the pound might depress Blass Ltd.'s export sales (by making its product more expensive to foreigners). If Blass Products also has a subsidiary making the same product in another country which has a currency which has not appreciated, or has depreciated, the decline in Blass Ltd.'s sales might be made up by sales of the other subsidiary. Similarly, with the rise in the value of the pound, it might behoove Blass Ltd. to switch its purchases of input X from a domestic (English) supplier to a foreign supplier (since the rise in the value of the pound has made imports into England less costly in terms of pounds). Clearly, international diversification for production and input purchases is not always easy or practical, especially if there are important advantages in locating production in particular places (e.g., where technical skills are available) or in one place (because of economies of scale). Also, a particular input may be obtainable only from a single source so that diversification of sources may not be possible.

Asset Management and Investment   Management of the cash balances of an MNC is similar to cash management by domestic firms, but there are some complications. An MNC may hold cash balances in a number of countries. If it has central control over cash balances, it may attempt to pool its cash, for the most part, in areas in which safety, liquidity, and yield are highest. Central money pools are usually held in countries that have major money market centers and strong currencies; funds may also be held in countries with low tax rates (tax havens). Obviously, there is an incentive to channel income into the subsidiaries located in tax havens. Exchange restrictions may make pooling impossible in some cases, and they provide one reason that MNCs may wish to deal with large multinational banks that

---

[6] For example, assume that the one month forward rate is $2 per pound and that Blass Products Inc. sells £40,000 forward for $80,000, where delivery is to be made in one month (for simplicity, we will ignore taxes, interest, and transaction costs). If after one month the pound has depreciated in value to one pound equals one dollar, Blass Products will have suffered a $40,000 decline in the value of its equity position in Blass Ltd.; however, it will have made a $40,000 profit on its forward contract since, to cover the contract, it can buy £40,000 in the market for $40,000 and exchange (under the forward contract) the £40,000 for $80,000, thus producing a $40,000 profit.

can maintain complete and up-to-date information on worldwide exchange restrictions.

Multinational companies often have inventories dispersed throughout the world, with a significant portion in transit over long distances. Furthermore, the company may need to maintain safety stocks in countries with potential import restrictions. These problems make inventory management more difficult for an MNC than for a purely domestic business. Accounts receivable management can involve the added complication of receivables denominated in a foreign currency. Accounts receivable are generated whenever trade credit is extended to a foreign buyer.

What discount rate should a parent use in evaluating its investments in foreign subsidiaries? As with domestic investments, it should be a rate which reflects the risks associated with the flow of aftertax dollars that will be generated for the parent over the life of the investment. The risks of foreign investment include the underlying business risks of the investment, political risks (e.g., that the entire investment will be expropriated), and foreign exchange risks (since the dollars received from a foreign investment will depend on the exchange rate for converting the foreign subsidiary's income into dollars). After taking into account all these factors, the dollar cash flow probability distribution can be estimated. Foreign investments can be evaluated along with domestic investments in developing a capital budget. Assuming that all the relevant factors affecting cash flows from foreign investments have been incorporated in estimating the cash flow's probability distribution, the discount rate (for computing a present value) applicable to a particular foreign investment is the same as the discount rate applicable to a domestic investment with an identical aftertax cash flow probability distribution.

Management of Debt and Equity   Roughly half of the funds used by foreign subsidiaries are provided by cash flow from operations. The subsidiaries also obtain funds from parent companies in the form of equity, loans, and supplies of inventory and other physical assets without payment within normal time periods. Loans from parent companies to subsidiaries are often more desirable than equity investment—partly because foreign exchange controls imposed by governments are likely to make it easier to secure repayment of loans than return of equity. Supplying physical assets is convenient when a subsidiary is assembling products produced by the parent company. Funds are in effect supplied as long as payment by the subsidiary is delayed.

Short-term borrowing by a subsidiary is likely to be conducted in the country in which the subsidiary is operating—from multinational banks in some cases, and from local banks when knowledge of the business situation by the local banks is of advantage. Many United States firms have established finance subsidiaries to raise funds for their industrial subsidiaries in foreign countries. The finance subsidiaries may be based in tax-haven countries or incorporated in a state such as Delaware with minimum corporate regulatory requirements.

Finance subsidiaries are likely to borrow in the Eurodollar and Eurobond markets. A **Eurodollar** is simply a commerical bank deposit of dollars in a bank outside the United States.[7] Eurodollar loans are usually made to prime borrowers in relatively large amounts ($500,000 or more). Eurodollar loans vary in maturity from one day to as much as fifteen years, and may have fixed interest rates or floating rates. Large Eurocurrency loans may be syndicated with many banks participating. The bank that syndicates the loan seeks participants, structures the loan, and services the loan as needed. The model for such loans is the United State domestic multibank floating rate term loan. The interest rate is stated as a spread above the London interbank offering rate (LIBOR), with adjustment at predetermined intervals.

When long-term funds are needed, borrowing in the Eurobond market may be involved. Bonds are issued, usually in strong currencies such as dollars or Deutsche marks, but sometimes in special currency units. Interest costs are usually lower than for other borrowing in European capital markets, but higher than in the United States. However, disclosure requirements of the Securities and Exchange Commission and costs of such disclosure, which would have to be met for borrowing in the United States, are avoided. It appears from some recent research that voluntary disclosure in the Eurobond market is attractive to investors and favored by companies since it avoids some onerous requirements of the SEC.

Borrowing in the United States is a final alternative available to foreign subsidiaries, and this may be desirable if dollar funds are needed at a time when Eurodollar rates are very high.

Repatriating Funds   The ultimate objective of foreign investment is a flow of dollar returns to the parent. This "repatriation of funds" can be accomplished in various ways including dividends on stock owned in the subsidiary; interest and principal payments on parent loans to the subsidiary; payments for goods or services provided by the parent to the subsidiary (this includes payments for assets and inventories, fees for management services, etc.); and royalties for the use of patents, copyrights, and trade names. The form of the payments of the parent affects the company's ability to repatriate the funds and also affects the taxability of the payments (see next section). Many governments restrict the flow of capital to other countries. Dividends are more likely to be restricted than are interest and principal payments on debt, royalties, and payments for goods and services supplied by the parent. Therefore, in financing a subsidiary, it may be better to provide financing which is not repayable as dividends, for example, by making a loan to a subsidiary or by selling the subsidiary goods or services (with repayment scheduled to meet the subsidiary's needs). Of course, governments are aware of the games that can be played by foreign-owned subsidiaries, and knowing how far one can go in avoiding a particular

[7] For example, assume that Peugot sells 200 Peugots to an American auto dealer for $1 million and that the American sends Peugot a check for $1 million drawn on Chase Manhattan Bank. Peugot deposits the $1 million check at the Banque de Paris which, as a result, has a $1 million credit to its account with Chase Manhattan Bank. Peugot has a $1 million demand deposit claim against the Bank of Paris. The $1 million deposit is a Eurodollar deposit.

government restriction on capital flows is essential in planning funds repatriation.

Taxes   United States companies must pay United States income taxes on dividends received from foreign subsidiaries. Furthermore, a subsidiary must pay taxes in the country in which it is based. Many countries have a tax agreement with the United States under which a United States company, in computing its United States tax on foreign dividends, is allowed to deduct the foreign taxes it has paid. To illustrate, assume that Raleigh Textiles has a subsidiary in two foreign countries, Lowtax and Hightax. The corporate tax rate in Lowtax is 30 percent and the corporate tax rate in Hightax is 60 percent. Hightax also imposes a 10 percent withholding tax on dividends paid to the United States parent. Raleigh's United States tax bracket is 46 percent. The subsidiaries in Lowtax and Hightax both have $100 in pretax profits they wish to repatriate to the United States. Exhibit 24-4 illustrates the tax computation for both subsidiaries.[8]

In computing foreign taxes, expenses (interest on debt, payments to the parent for goods and services, royalties to the parent, etc.) are generally deductible. Therefore, one way for a parent to finance a foreign subsidiary and simultaneously minimize foreign taxes is for the parent to make a loan to the foreign subsidiary or to provide the subsidiary with goods and services. In computing the foreign business taxes, interest on the loan and

---

[8] If certain conditions are met, the U.S. parent corporation can postpone paying U.S. income taxes on profits of its Lowtax foreign subsidiary by not repatriating those profits to the United States. One of these conditions is that the U.S. parent own no more than 50 percent of the controlling stock of the foreign subsidiary. If this 50 percent condition and certain other requirements are not satisfied, the foreign subsidiary's income will be classified as Subpart F income, in which case all of the subsidiary's income will be taxed whether or not repatriated (e.g., as dividends) to the U.S. parent.

EXHIBIT 24-4
Foreign and United States taxes on foreign subsidiary income

		Lowtax		Hightax
1. Profit before tax		$100		$100
2. Foreign corporate tax		30		60
3. Aftertax profit		$ 70		$ 40
4. Dividend withholding tax		0		4
5. Dividend to U.S.		$ 70		$ 36
6. U.S. tax on $100 profit	$46		$46	
7. Credit for foreign tax rates paid (up to the 46% due under U.S. law)	30		46	
8. U.S. taxes due [(6) − (7)]		16		0
9. Aftertax dividend [(5) − (8)]		$ 54		$ 36

payments for the goods and services are generally tax deductible expenses for the subsidiary. The parent can also extract funds from the subsidiary by levying royalties or management fees, both of which are tax deductible expenses in the foreign country. These strategies to minimize foreign taxes are well known and should be considered only in light of expert tax counsel.

A special tax benefit is provided to corporations engaged in export activities and meeting certain other requirements. These companies are referred to as "foreign sales corporations" (which generally replaced, beginning in 1985, "domestic international sales corporations" or DISCs). The tax benefit takes the form of postponement of U.S. federal income taxes on part of the income earned by the foreign sales corporations. Ordinarily, the foreign sales corporation is a subsidiary of a United States parent corporation that has established the foreign sales corporation to tax-shelter income earned from the parent's export operations.

Financial Control   The international finance function is more complex than the finance function in domestic firms because of the factors discussed in the preceding sections. There are clearly advantages to centralizing financial control—taxes may be minimized by maximizing profits in certain countries, borrowing may be more advantageous in certain countries, and there are possibilities for eliminating duplication of financial activities. Forms of organization, however, depend heavily on historical factors and may not be as logical as might be desired. The most that can be said at present is that at least some decisions are typically made at the corporate headquarters level—decisions concerning repatriation of funds, approval of intersubsidiary financing, hedging and currency swaps, and acquisition of funds, especially medium-term or long-term funds.

The Future of MNCs

Unless there is a radical change in economic trends, MNCs will increase their relative importance as a part of the world economy. But increased size will probably be achieved at the price of greater government scrutiny and regulation. Critics have demanded—with some success—that the power of the MNC be curtailed. A more vigorous enforcement of antitrust regulations and the appearance of new forms of regulation are likely. Particularly in less developed countries, governments have demanded control and eventual ownership of foreign firms operating within their borders. It seems probable that in most cases the new rules of the game for MNCs will strike a balance between government laissez faire and total state control. Failure to achieve such a balance would almost certainly have regressive repercussions on world economic development.

SUMMARY

When a company conducts part of its business outside its own national boundaries, it faces a much more complicated environment. The financial manager must consider the consequences of a broader range of political and economic risks. One of the most important differences be-

tween domestic and international financial transactions is that the monetary units or currencies vary from country to country.

Exchange rates express the relationships between currencies of different countries. The spot rate is the rate on current exchanges of currencies, and the forward rate is the current rate on future exchanges. Differences between spot and forward rates reflect expectations of future changes in foreign exchange rates and differences in interest rates among countries.

Changes in foreign exchange rates are caused by differences in inflation rates among countries, by differences in interest rates, and by governmental action. Businesses and individuals use the forward exchange market to protect themselves from possible losses due to changes in exchange rates.

Special financing procedures have been developed to facilitate international trade. The most commonly used financing methods are based on letters of credit issued by commercial banks.

Most major United States firms are multinational. United States companies have invested abroad to avoid trade restrictions and to use cheaper foreign labor and because United States firms have often enjoyed a competitive advantage due to their superior technical and managerial skills. These factors are becoming less important, and consequently the gap between new United States investment abroad and new foreign investment in the United States has diminished.

United States subsidiaries abroad enjoy a tax advantage under United States law since foreign earnings are not taxed until repatriated (paid to the United States parent). Furthermore, foreign income taxes paid are deducted from the United States taxes due (a tax credit).

Foreign investment often involves political risk and risk due to the possibility of exchange rate fluctuations. The manager of a multinational firm has problems not faced by a domestic firm manager. These problems include cash and inventory transfers between countries, use of special credit devices in trade (for example, letters of credit), raising short- and long-term funds in different countries, and maintaining efficient control over foreign subsidiaries that may be subject to different governmental controls and that follow different commercial practices.

Although there has been criticism of MNCs in recent years, they will almost certainly continue to grow as the world economy expands and becomes more integrated. However, the growth will likely be accompanied by more stringent governmental regulations over MNC activities.

QUESTIONS

1 What risks are greater in international business than in domestic business?
2 What factors cause the exchange rate between two countries' currencies to change?
3 What is the difference between the spot rate and the ninety-day forward rate of exchange between two countries' currencies? Be specific and illustate by means of an example (can be hypothetical).

4 Suppose you are planing to spend a semester at a German university. Six months from now, room, board, and tuition will cost 3000 marks. What could you do to be sure in advance of the dollar cost of your expenses?

5 Why would an exporter wish to sell goods under a letter of credit rather than on open account?

6 In an import letter of credit with payment to be made using a 180-day time draft, what is being financed, who is being financed, and who is providing financing?

7 Is there any exchange risk when imports are purchased using a letter of cedit? Why or why not?

8 What factors have motivated United States firms to invest abroad?

9 How do changes in exchange rates affect the income of multinational corporations?

PROJECTS

1 Identify a local firm that has some type of international transactions (imports or exports) and interview one of its executives. Find out how the firm handles its financing problems and deals with exchange risks.

2 Pick a large United States corporation and, using its annual report and articles in business periodicals, outline the extent of its international activities. What countries does it do business in, and how much business of what sort does it do there? What percentages of the corporation's sales and profits stem from its international operations? Are its international operations expanding at a greater or slower pace than are its domestic operations?

3 Interview a local banker regarding the bank's engagement in international activities. What kinds of services does the bank provide for its business and individual customers in the international area? How active is the bank itself overseas?

PROBLEMS

1 Use the foreign exchange rates for January 1985 in Table 24-1 to calculate the amount of United States dollars the following currencies will exchange for.

1. 100 Deutsche marks	[Ans.: $31.50]
2. 100 Rupees	
3. 100 Pesos	
4. 10,000 Lira	[Ans.: $ 5.10]
5. 10,000 Yen	

2 Obtain a recent copy of *The Wall Street Journal* and calculate the currency exchanges of problem *1*. How do these figures compare to those obtained in problem *1*?

3   Use the exchange rates in Table 24-1 for January 1985 to calculate
    the following:
    a   How many Italian lira can be acquired for $5.10 U.S.? [Ans.: see 4
        in table in problem 1]
    b   How many Mexican pesos can be acquired for $.44 U.S.?
    c   How many Swedish krona can be acquired for $22 U.S.? [Ans.: 200
        krona]
    d   How many British pounds can be acquired for $500 U.S.?

4   Use the exchange rates in Table 24-1 for January 1985 to calculate
    the following:
    a   How many Dutch guilders can be acquired with $100 U.S.?
    b   How many French francs can be acquired with $100 U.S.?
    c   How many French francs can be acquired with 358.42 Dutch
        guilders?
    d   How many British pounds can be acquired with $100 Canadian?

5   Suppose *The Wall Street Journal* reports the following exchange
    rates for country Flint whose currency is the stone:

Flint (stone)	0.2400
30-day futures	0.2380
90-day futures	0.2365
180-day futures	0.2305

    a   Is the forward rate on the stone at a discount or premium rela-
        tive to the dollar?
    b   Suppose you executed a thirty-day futures contract to exchange
        100,000 stones into United States dollars. How many dollars
        would you get thirty days from now? [Ans.: $23,800]
    c   Suppose you executed a 180-day futures contract to exchange
        $100,000 U.S. into stones. How many stones would you get 180
        days from now?

6   Suppose that interest rates in Sandland are 24 percent per year
    whereas United States interest rates are 8 percent per year. You are
    considering investing $10,000 for 180 days (one-half year) in Sandland
    securities but are concerned about exchange rate risk. Sandland's
    currency is the camel. You find the following quotations in the
    newspaper ($U.S.):

Sandland (camel)	0.1000
30-day futures	0.0980
90-day futures	0.0970
180-day futures	0.0950

    a   What is your net gain in United States dollars from investing in
        Sandland securities relative to United States securities assuming
        the exchange rate in 180 days equals today's spot rate?

b What is your net gain from an uncovered position if the spot rate does not change?

c Suppose the camel depreciates 10 percent relative to the dollar in the next 180 days. What is your net gain (or loss) from an uncovered position relative to a United States investment?

d What is your net gain or loss from a covered position?

e What do you conclude from this analysis? Are there any other factors you should consider before your final decision?

7 Merrimar Corporation is a United States corporation with major subsidiaries in ten countries. Its French subsidiary, Pied Bleu, manufactures shoes and is headquartered in Paris, France. Pied Bleu has assets of 20 million francs and liabilities of 8 million francs.

a What is Pied Bleu's equity position (assets − liabilities) in francs and in dollars, if the exchange rate is $1 = 10 francs (one dollar is worth ten French francs). [Ans.: 12 million francs and $1.2 million]

b What is Pied Bleu's equity position in francs and in dollars, if the exchange rate is $1 = 5 francs? What is the gain or loss in dollars due to an exchange rate change from $1 = 10 francs to $1 = 5 francs?

c What is Pied Bleu's equity position in francs and in dollars, if the exchange rate is $1 = 16 francs? What is the gain or loss in dollars due to an exchange rate change from $1 = 10 francs to $1 = 16 francs?

8 Perform the calculations in problem 7, assuming that Pied Bleu has assets of 8 million francs and liabilities of 20 million francs.

In the preceding chapters, we analyzed ongoing firms with sufficient revenues to service their debt and to avoid default. This chapter examines those cases in which default is likely or has already occurred. We begin the chapter by explaining what failure means. Then we discuss historical trends and the most frequent causes of failure. The remainder of the chapter explores how the firm and its creditors deal with financial distress.

DEFINITION OF FAILURE

The failure of a firm can be economic or contractual. A firm is an **economic failure** if it cannot be operated profitably even if it were properly managed and debtfree. The best solution to economic failure is liquidation of the firm. **Financial failure** (or **contractual failure**) occurs when the firm is unable to meet its contractual obligations to its creditors. Financial failure can occur whether or not a firm is an economic failure.

A firm that is an economic failure may terminate and liquidate its assets even if it is not a financial failure. **Liquidation** means the termination of the firm as a going enterprise and the sale of the assets for the price that they will bring in the market. Whenever the firm's value as an ongoing enterprise is less than its value in liquidation, liquidation is justified. Firms in this condition are often referred to as "being worth more dead than alive." For example, a firm may have no debt and be earning $10,000 a year. However, if the liquidation value of its assets were $500,000, the firm would be earning only 2 percent on its assets ($10,000/$500,000 = 2 percent). The firm should liquidate. In short, if a firm is an economic failure though not a financial failure, it should be liquidated.

In the remainder of this chapter we will look at firms suffering from financial failure and perhaps from economic failure. If the financial failure is accompanied by economic failure, the firm should and probably will be dissolved and liquidated. If the financial failure is not accompanied by economic failure, the firm may continue in existence under either a voluntary adjustment or a reorganization.

Bankruptcy is a condition in which the firm is unable to pay its debts (is a financial failure) and its assets are surrendered to the court for administration. Bankruptcy proceedings may not result in liquidation but may provide for an arrangement or a reorganization under which the firm continues to operate. The voluntary remedies used to prevent bankruptcy are discussed below. Then, the bankruptcy process under the Bankruptcy Reform Act of 1978 and its amendments is examined.

FREQUENCY AND CAUSES OF FAILURE

Figure 25-1 shows the failure rate of business firms since 1929. Research by Dun and Bradstreet and by others indicates that failure is particularly common among new firms—those that have been in existence less than five years.[1] Furthermore, as might be expected, the failure rate is lower for large firms and is lower in times of prosperity than during periods of recession and depression. Large firms are not, of course, immune to failure, as evidenced by the recent and highly publicized failures of Wilson Foods, Braniff Airlines, and Manville Corporation. The most important single cause of business failure has historically been the inability of the company to effectively promote the product and generate sufficient sales. Difficulties in collecting on receivables and in controlling operating expenses have also been frequent causes of failure.

The sharp increase in the business failure rate since 1978 (see Figure 25-1) has been largely due to three factors: recessions, high interest rates, and a liberalized bankruptcy law which has made bankruptcy filing and failure easier for U.S. businesses. Even with a strong economy and moderate

[1] Under the Dun and Bradstreet's definition of failure, business failures include firms that ceased operations following assignment or bankruptcy; ceased with a loss to creditors after such actions as execution, foreclosure, or attachment; voluntarily withdrew leaving unpaid obligations; were involved in court actions such as receivership, reorganization, or arrangement; or voluntarily compromised with creditors.

FIGURE 25-1

Historical business failure rate per 10,000 concerns.

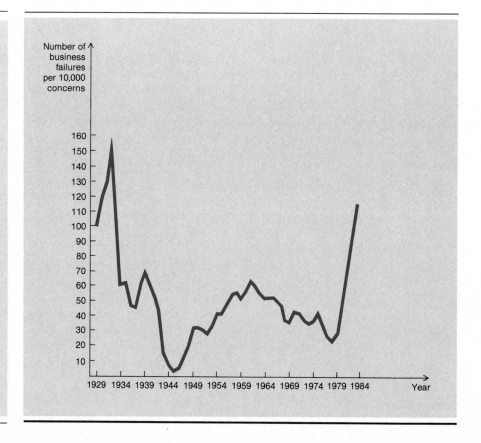

interest rates, the new legal environment is likely to mean a continuation of a higher rate of bankruptcy than in past decades.

VOLUNTARY REMEDIES FOR FINANCIAL DISTRESS

If a firm is unable to meet its commitments to creditors, an agreement to avert bankruptcy may be reached between the firm's creditors and owners. The agreement may take one of several forms, depending on circumstances, but it usually results in a continuation of the firm under existing ownership. In some cases, however, the firm may be terminated. Below we will consider adjustments that allow the firm to survive.

It is important to stress that voluntary agreements are *voluntary*—no court or trustee supervises the settlement. Any creditor who refuses to take part in the agreement may press a claim, blocking the agreement for all creditors. However, this may result in more financial loss to the creditor than would cooperating with the other creditors to arrange a settlement with the debtor. Often small claims—those under $50 or $100—are fully paid, with the creditors having the larger claims remaining as parties to the voluntary agreement. Those creditors participating in the accord with the firm will usually appoint a committee among themselves to deal with the debtor firm. Voluntary solutions to the financial distress of the firm include extension, composition, and temporary assumption of firm control by creditors.

Extension

In an **extension** the creditors agree to *postpone* payments on the debt for a given period in order to mitigate the debtor firm's current difficulties. To get the creditors to agree to the extension, the firm's owners may have to provide security, such as mortgages on the firm's assets or the personal property of the company's owners.

Composition

Under a **composition**, creditors agree *to receive less* than the amount originally owed to them, for example, $0.80 for every dollar of debt. Creditors may agree to a composition because they feel that the only other alternative is to force the firm into bankrupty and liquidation, with the possible result that they would receive even less than under the composition.

Creditor Management of the Firm

An agreement may be reached under which a creditor's committee representing the creditor group assumes temporary control of the firm. The hope is that the committee will be able to ameliorate the situation sufficiently for the debts to be retired, after which old management can resume control.

GENERAL BANKRUPTCY PROVISIONS

The United States Congress has the power to establish laws regulating those corporations, partnerships, individuals, and others in financial distress. Congress enacted the National Bankruptcy Act of 1938 to provide such laws. This act was amended several times over the years to adjust to changing conditions. It was completely repealed in 1978 and a new statutory structure, The Bankruptcy Reform Act of 1978 (known as the Bankruptcy Code) was enacted. This act streamlines and consolidates many former procedures as well as introduces numerous innovations.[2] The Code was extensively amended in 1984, primarily to correct certain jurisdictional problems, but some substantive amendments were also made. The Code provides for court-supervised adjustments in a firm's capital structure that make survival of the firm possible. When adjustments are not feasible, liquidation under the Code is possible.

Chapter 11 of the Code deals with debtor reorganizations. Chapters 7 and 11 contain all the remedies available to corporations. Most liquidations are covered by Chapter 7. Chapter 13 provides for a remedy for individuals and businesses which are neither corporations nor partnerships and which have unsecured debts less than $100,000 and secured debts of $350,000 or less. Under a Chapter 13 plan, the debtor generally must be able to reduce its debt within thirty-six months. An unsuccessful Chapter 13 plan may be converted to a Chapter 11 plan or to a Chapter 7 liquidation.

Either the debtor or the creditors or stockholders may initiate a petition if the firm is insolvent, as defined by the Bankruptcy Reform Act. Under the act, *insolvency* means that the firm is not paying its debts as they come due, or that, within 120 days before the involuntary petition is filed, a custodian (other than a trustee) was authorized to take charge of all or substantially all of the debtor's property. A hearing is held after the filing of an involuntary petition if the debtor challenges the petition. At the hearing, the bankruptcy court determines whether the firm is insolvent under the above definition.

CHAPTER 11 REORGANIZATIONS

Under Chapter 11 reorganizations, a debtor may petition the bankruptcy court for a reorganization under which the debtor will eliminate its debts by making only partial or delayed payments to creditors. A creditor, a creditors' committee, or the stockholders may file a plan if the debtor fails to do so within 120 days after filing the petition.

The firm's creditor and ownership claims are divided into classes containing claims similar in type. Each secured claim is normally in a class by itself. Common stock and preferred stock would not be in the same class even if held by the same person. Within each class of creditors, two-thirds of the amount of debt and a numerical majority of the claims must approve of the plan for the class itself to be deemed to have approved the plan. The stockholders are represented in one or more classes of "equity security holders." Holders of two-thirds of the amount of stock in each class must approve the plan for the class to approve it.

In order for the classes of claims against the firm to make an informed decision on the proposed plan, the proponent of the plan must make a

---

[2] The Bankruptcy Code contains four titles. Only Title I concerns us here because Titles II–IV are very technical in nature. The seven chapters of Title I (all odd-numbered) contain all substantive statutory laws concerning bankruptcy: Chapter 1 contains general provisions; Chapter 3 covers the court administration of a case; Chapter 5 deals with creditors' claims; Chapter 7 explains the liquidation process; Chapter 9 has special rules and procedures for municipalities; Chapter 11 (of particular relevance here) consolidates the debtor relief provisions of the repealed Chapters X, XI, and some of Chapter XIII of the old Bankruptcy Act.

disclosure statement to each class before its vote on the proposal. Disclosure statements are specifically exempted from compliance with either federal or state securities law, but the Securities and Exchange Commission (SEC) may be heard by the court on whether or not sufficient information is being disclosed. The court will probably attach great weight to the SEC's opinion, but it is not bound by it. The SEC will normally only be interested in a case in which the debtor is a large, publicly owned firm.

After the necessary disclosures are made, their adequacy has been determined by the court, and the classes of claims have voted, the bankruptcy court will confirm or reject the proposed plan. The court must accept a plan when it complies with the applicable laws and regulations; it is proposed in good faith; necessary disclosures are made to the court; and the various classes of claims or interests have either accepted the plan, or it is fair and equitable to each dissenting class. "Fair and equitable" is defined by the statute to mean that each creditor of that class will receive no less than it would under a Chapter 7 liquidation or no less than the amount of its security interest, if any. The Code divides the secured debt into two parts: a "secured claim" is the value of the collateral and an "unsecured claim" is the difference between the amount of the debt and the collateral's value. After claims with priority over the secured creditor are fully paid, the secured creditor is paid the value of the collateral in full; the remaining amount due (the unsecured claim) is paid to the same extent as are other claims of that class.

After the plan is confirmed, the payments in cash, property, or securities are made to the creditors and stockholders, and the debtor discharged from all affected debts (however, if the debtor is a corporation or a partnership and if the plan involves the complete liquidation of the debtor, special rules apply).

The reorganization plan may provide for the issuance of new securities to the firm's creditors in order to reduce the debt payment burden. Often, the firm's assets are only sufficient to cover some of the debt claims, in which case the equity claims of stockholders and the claims of some or all unsecured creditors may be completely eliminated, that is, entirely unpaid and dissolved.

Reorganization and Priority

Under reorganization, new securities are issued to some or all of the firm's creditors and perhaps to its preferred and common stockholders, depending upon the value of the firm upon reorganization. Generally, senior claims are honored in full before junior claims receive anything. However, as noted below, in some circumstances the rule may be modified. To illustrate priority in settling the firm's claims, assume that the firm's balance sheet as of the end of the period preceding the petition for reorganization was as shown in Exhibit 25-1. Remember that balance sheet asset figures are at book value ($18 million) and not at liquidation value. Assume that the estimated liquidation value of the firm's assets is $4 million, but its going concern value is estimated to be $6 million. The estimated value of the securities to be issued under the new capital structure created under reorganization is $6 million. The total liabilities of $8 million exceed the new value of the firm, and consequently the old stockholders receive nothing under the reorganization. The stockholders' equity interest in the firm has been eliminated because the firm is insolvent (assets of $6 million are less than liabilities of $8 million). Assume that the $6 million in new securities to be issued will be in the form of $2 million in 6 percent bonds, $1 million in $6\frac{1}{2}$ percent subordinated debentures, $1 million in 7 percent preferred stock, and $2 million in common stock. Values of the claims of each creditor and the distribution of the new securities to those creditors are shown in Exhibit 25-2. The holders of the notes receive $3 million in new bonds and new subordinated debentures in satisfaction of their original $3 million claim. The subordinated debenture holders receive new preferred stock and new common stock worth a total of $2,250,000, and the general un-secured creditors receive $750,000 in common stock. Thus, only the note holders receive new securities with a value equal to the original claim against the firm. This is because the notes are repaid before the subordi-nated debenture holders receive anything.[3]

The Code may allow priorities which differ from those shown above. For example, senior creditors with large claims may wish to allow the old stockholders to retain some interest in the firm. This may be done over the protests of the junior creditors if the dissenting classes of junior creditors are to receive a "fair and equitable" portion of the proceeds from implemen-tation of the plan.

A business in a Chapter 11 reorganization may reject certain ongoing contracts it has made if the rejection will aid in the reorganization. Several court cases have dealt with a debtor corporation's rejection of collective bargaining agreements. Congress specifically addressed the issue of collec-tive bargaining agreements in the 1984 amendments to the Code. The debtor now cannot reject a collective bargaining agreement unless it follows certain rather stringent procedures. It is now more difficult for a debtor

---

[3] The distribution of securities parallels the distribution of cash under liquidation, as de-scribed in the section below on liquidation.

EXHIBIT 25-1
Balance sheet

Assets	$18,000,000
Liabilities	
Notes payable	3,000,000
Subordinated debentures[a]	4,000,000
General unsecured creditors	1,000,000
Stockholders' equity	10,000,000

[a] Subordinated to the notes payable. The general unsecured creditors are not affected by the subordination.

corporation to modify its collective bargaining agreements without the consent of the employees' union.

Decision to Reorganize or Liquidate

In evaluating the reorganization plan, the court, the security holders, and the SEC, if involved, must decide whether the firm's going concern value after reorganization will exceed its liquidation value. Reorganization is justified only if the firm is not an irreversible economic failure. If, even after a reorganization, it is likely to be an economic failure, the firm should be liquidated and not reorganized.

To estimate the going concern value, future revenues, costs, and earnings must be forecast, using available information regarding expected sales, labor and material input costs, and any other factors relating to the firm's operations. Of course, as with any forecast, only rough estimates are possible. The choice between reorganization and liquidation will vary from situation to situation. For example, if the firm were a chain of retail clothing stores that had overexpanded into unprofitable geographic regions, liq-

---

EXHIBIT 25-2
Old claims and new claims under reorganization

Old security	Old claim	New claim with reorganization[a]
Notes	$3,000,000	$3,000,000
Subordinated debentures	4,000,000	2,250,000
General unsecured debt claims	1,000,000	750,000

Distribution of new securities under new claim with reorganization

Old security	Received under reorganization
Notes	$2,000,000 in 6% bonds $1,000,000 in 6½% subordinated debentures
Subordinated debentures	$1,000,000 in 7% preferred stock $1,250,000 in common stock
General unsecured debt claims	$750,000 in common stock

[a] Because in this illustration the debentures are subordinated only to the notes, the general unsecured creditors are unaffected by the subordination and therefore receive what they would if no subordination agreement existed (per dollar owed this equals the amount contractually owed divided by the dollars available for the debt repayment). Since the securities distributed have a value of $6 million but creditor claims equal $8 million, general unsecured creditors receive 75 percent ($6,000,000/$8,000,000) of their claim, i.e., $750,000 in securities (0.75 × $1,000,000). The remaining $5,250,000 in securities is divided between the notes and subordinated debenture holders; however, since the notes are senior to the debentures under the subordination, they are paid in full (securities worth $3 million) and the remaining $2,250,000 in securities goes to the debenture holders.

uidation value of the land and buildings might be very high but the business itself would be an economic failure. Even better management could not generate the sales needed to make the firm profitable. Therefore, liquidation would be preferable to an attempt to reorganize in this case. On the other hand, the firm might be a poorly managed manufacturing firm with good markets for its products and owning specialized equipment with little liquidation value. Reorganization under these circumstances might be more reasonable than liquidation.

LIQUIDATION

If the creditors estimate that the going concern value of the firm is less than its liquidation value, they may seek to liquidate the firm's assets and distribute the proceeds among the creditors. There are two ways to effect liquidation: assignment and bankruptcy. Under either, the proceeds from the liquidation are distributed among the firm's creditors. The remainder of the chapter explores these topics in detail.

Liquidation under Assignment

Under an assignment, the firm and its creditors privately settle the firm's debt. The courts are not involved. A trustee is generally appointed by the creditors to supervise the orderly liquidation of the firm's assets and the distribution of the proceeds. Not infrequently the trustee is the adjustment bureau of a local or national creditors association.

All creditors must consent to the settlement, since any one of them is free to block it and place the firm in bankruptcy through court action. As noted below, the priority rule applies under a bankruptcy liquidation; that is, senior claims are ordinarily fully paid before junior claims are met at all. Therefore, for senior claimants to agree to an assignment, they will demand priority treatment. If they are denied priority, they may move to throw the firm into bankruptcy. Consequently, the settlement under assignment will generally conform to the priority rule. The priority ranking of claimants is covered below examining liquidation under bankruptcy.

Generally, liquidation under an assignment is less costly than under bankruptcy in terms of both legal and accounting expenses and time involved. Furthermore, the creditors have the opportunity to select a trustee who may be more effective than a court-appointed trustee in selling the firm's assets because of greater familiarity with the firm's line of business or greater legal flexibility in handling the sale. However, bankruptcy may be preferred by one or more creditors. Some creditors may not agree to the proposed distribution of proceeds under the assignment or may feel for other reasons that their rights would be better protected by court supervision of the liquidation. Furthermore, a creditor may prefer to pursue bankruptcy proceedings than to privately seek unanimity of agreement by a large number of creditors under an assignment.

Liquidation under Bankruptcy

If a reorganization fails or a voluntary liquidation cannot be worked out, a firm may enter into a liquidation under Chapter 7 of the Code. (The procedure is the same whether the firm itself voluntarily files for bankruptcy or an involuntary bankruptcy petition is filed by the creditors.) The federal bankruptcy court appoints a referee who then arranges a meeting of the creditors. At the meeting, claims are proved and a trustee is elected by the creditors. The trustee's responsibility is to liquidate the firm's assets in an orderly manner and to distribute the proceeds to the claimants. Upon completion of the payment to the creditors, the trustee prepares an accounting that is presented to the creditors and to the referee.

Under the priority guidelines provided by Chapter 7 the distribution of the proceeds from liquidation must conform to the following priority of claims (highest priority first):

1 Expenses associated with preserving, supervising, and liquidating the bankrupt's estate. These are called administration expenses.
2 Unsecured claims arising after the filing of an involuntary petition but before the appointment of a trustee.
3 Wages, salaries, and commissions, not to exceed $2000 per claimant, earned within ninety days prior to the filing of the bankruptcy petition.
4 Claims for contributions to employee benefit plans arising within 180 days before commencement of the proceeding or the debtor's cessation of business, whichever occurs first. This item is limited by a statutory formula.
5 Certain consumer claims, not exceeding $900, arising from purchase, lease, or rental of goods or services.
6 Some government tax claims.
7 Secured and unsecured creditors, claims in order of priority.
8 Payment of dividends to preferred stockholders.
9 Payment of dividends to common stockholders.

Item 7 needs some clarification. Secured creditors have first right to that property which was used to secure their claims. To the extent that such property is insufficient to cover the amount owed to them, the secured creditors join the unsecured creditors in dividing the remaining liquidation proceeds. If the proceeds from the sale of the security property more than meet the secured claims, the remaining funds are used to pay unsecured creditors. If proceeds from sale satisfy creditor claims, then the remaining amount is payable to stockholders.

To illustrate the distribution under the above rule, assume that Falling Timber Paper Products, Inc., is to be liquidated. The claims against the firm are shown in Exhibit 25-3. Assume that the liquidation value of the assets is equal to $5.4 million, but that the firm's going concern value under reorganization would be only $1 million. Therefore, liquidation is justified. Also assume that the $3 million in notes are secured by a mortgage on the Falling Timber production plant that is sold by the trustee for $2 million. Finally, a total of $400,000 is spent to cover the costs in items 1 through 6 in the list, including those associated with the trustee's expenses in liquidating the estate, wages and commissions to employees, consumer claims, any creditor expenses, and taxes. Therefore, the proceeds available for distribution to creditors and stockholders are $5 million ($5.4 million in proceeds less $400,000 in expenses). The distribution is shown in Exhibit 25-3.

The funds available for settlement of all claims are $5 million. This amount is less than the debt of $8 million. Therefore, none of the proceeds is paid to the residual common shares, since all creditors must be reimbursed before stockholders receive anything. The mortgage notes have first claim to the $2 million received from sale of the plant representing security on those notes. This leaves $3 million (of the $5 million) for distribution to cover the $6 million of remaining debt ($1 million still owed on the notes, $4 million owed on the subordinated debentures, and $1 million owed to general unsecured creditors). If the debentures were not subordinated to the notes, the $3 million would be distributed by percentage of amount owed to total debt remaining in meeting the remaining $6 million of claims. In this case, each creditor would receive $0.50 for each dollar owed. This is shown in the second column at the bottom of Exhibit 25-3. With subordination, a different distribution occurs. The general unsecured creditors are unaffected by the subordination of the debentures to the notes, and they

EXHIBIT 25-3
Distribution of proceeds under liquidation of Falling Timber Paper Products, Inc.

Type of claim	Old claim	Received under the liquidation
Notes (secured by mortgage)	$ 3,000,000	$3,000,000
Subordinated debentures	4,000,000	1,500,000
General unsecured debt claims	1,000,000	500,000
Common stockholders	10,000,000	0
Total	$18,000,000	$5,000,000

Computation of the distribution:

Liquidation proceeds available for distribution	$5,000,000
Amount paid to secured note holders on sale of mortgaged property	2,000,000
Available to note and debenture holders and general unsecured creditors	$3,000,000
Total claims remaining ($8,000,000 less payment of $2,000,000 on secured notes)	$6,000,000

Distribution of remaining $3,000,000 to cover total remaining claims of $6,000,000

Type of claim	Claim remaining	Claim on liquidation proceeds without subordination	Claim on liquidation proceeds with subordination
Notes	$1,000,000	$ 500,000	$1,000,000
Subordinated debentures	4,000,000	2,000,000	1,500,000
General unsecured creditor claim	1,000,000	500,000	500,000

consequently receive the same amount as they would if there were no subordination, that amount being $500,000. This leaves $2,500,000 for distribution to the notes and subordinated debentures. The notes are fully repaid before the subordinated debentures receive anything. Therefore, $1 million is paid to the note holders and the remaining $1.5 million goes in payment to holders of the subordinated debentures.

Although this example is relatively simple, it illustrates the way proceeds from liquidation are distributed under Chapter 7. In all cases, however complicated, the underlying guideline is that superior claims are paid in full before junior claims receive anything. This principle is followed regardless of the complexity of the firm's capital structure.

SUMMARY

Failure of a corporation is economic if the company cannot earn a reasonable return on its investments. Failure is contractual or financial if the firm cannot meet its commitments to creditors. A company that is an incurable economic failure (whether or not it is a financial failure) should go out of business and liquidate its assets, since it cannot earn a reasonable return on investment. With financial failure but no economic failure, the firm will have to make some adjustment in order to satisfy unpaid creditors. This adjustment may involve only postponement of payment on the debt or may require the extreme remedy of a corporate reorganization.

Some private agreements between the firm and its creditors to avert bankruptcy are extensions, compositions, or temporary assumption of managerial control of the firm by creditors. Under an extension, creditors accept a postponement of their payments, whereas under a composition the creditors accept only partial payment in satisfaction of the debt.

Adjustments that permit the company to continue in existence may also be effected through court action under Chapter 11 of the Bankruptcy Code. Under Chapter 11, a firm may petition the court to approve a plan that provides for settlement of the company's debts and specifies the steps required for a reorganization. The reorganization can also be initiated by the firm's creditors. After the court approves the petition, a trustee may be appointed to draw up the reorganization plan and to supervise the company's assets until the plan goes into effect. However, the old management will often be left in control. Under reorganization, the old securities of the corporation are retired and new securities are issued to those people with claims against the company. Creditors with senior claims usually receive securities with a value covering the amount owed to them before junior claimants receive anything.

If a company is an economic failure, it will be liquidated. Liquidation may proceed under a private settlement between the company and its creditors or with court supervision under Chapter 7 of the Bankruptcy Code. In either case, senior claimants are ordinarily fully paid before junior claimants receive anything.

1 Distinguish between economic failure and financial failure.
2 Under what conditions should a firm be liquidated?
3 Distinguish among the three basic types of voluntary remedies of financial distress: extension, composition, and temporary assumption of control of the firm by creditors.
4 What rationale can you give for creditors' accepting less than the face value of their claim when a firm is financially distressed?
5 What is a reorganization plan?
6 On what basis is a decision to reorganize or liquidate a bankrupt firm made?
7 What is the priority of claims rule as it is used in reorganizations and liquidations? When may it be modified?

Talk with a lawyer who specializes in bankruptcy cases and inquire about the significance of legal costs, accounting fees, and so on, that are involved in bankruptcy. Ask about the importance of business disruptions caused by creditor (or trustee) takeover if the bankrupt firm is not liquidated but is continued by the creditors as a going enterprise.

1 The book value of the assets of Melancholy Paints, Inc. is shown below. The notes are subordinated to the bank loans. The going concern value of Melancholy Paints is $2 million. ($2 million is the value of the company's debt and equity if the firm continues to operate.)

Melancholy Paints, Inc. balance sheet		
Assets		$15,000,000
Liabilities:		
Bank loans	$3,000,000	
Subordinated notes	2,000,000	
General creditors	7,000,000	
Total liabilities		12,000,000
Stockholders' equity		$ 3,000,000

What will each type of creditor and stockholder receive under each of the following assumptions:
a The firm's assets are liquidated for $15 million.
b The firm's assets are liquidated for $12 million.
c The firm's assets are liquidated for $8 million.
d The firm's assets are liquidated for $4 million.
2 The book value of Marginal Foods, Inc. assets is shown on page 735. The liquidation value of the assets is $25 million. Assume a going concern value of $35 million. Also assume the bonds are subordi-

nated to all other liabilities. Marginal has defaulted on its debt and is in bankruptcy. Determine how much the stockholders and each class of creditor will receive.

Marginal Foods, Inc. balance sheet		
Assets		$40,000,000
Liabilities:		
General creditors	$15,000,000	
Notes payable	5,000,000	
Subordinated bonds	16,000,000	
Total liabilities		36,000,000
Stockholders' equity		$ 4,000,000

3 Tutu Corporation is facing reorganization under Chapter 11 of the Reform Bankruptcy Act with the following existing capital structure:

	Book value
Bonds	$ 30,000,000
General unsecured creditors	40,000,000
Preferred stockholders	50,000,000
Common stockholders	100,000,000
	$220,000,000

The trustee for the reorganization has estimated the liquidation value of Tutu's assets at $100 million and the value of Tutu as a going concern at $140 million and in this light has proposed the following new capital structure for the reorganized firm:

Unsecured debt	$ 20,000,000
Income debentures	20,000,000
Preferred stock	20,000,000
Common stock	80,000,000
	$140,000,000

If the court accepts this plan, what will be the distribution of the new securities to the old security holders?

4 Grandeur, Inc. has voluntarily filed a petition of bankruptcy under Chapter 7. Grandeur's balance sheet prior to liquidation is given on page 736 (all figures shown are in 000s):

Cash	$ 2,000	Accounts payable	$ 4,000
Marketable securities	1,000	Accrued wages	1,000
Inventories	3,000	Accrued taxes	2,000
Receivables	4,000		$ 7,000
Net fixed assets	30,000	Mortgage payable	
Total assets	$40,000	(secured by fixed assets)	18,000
		Bonds	3,000
		Subordinated debentures	
		(subordinated to bonds)	1,000
		Preferred stock	2,000
		Common stock	9,000
		Liabilities *plus* equity	$40,000

Total proceeds from the liquidation were $24 million, of which $16 million was received from the sale of the fixed assets. The administrative costs incurred in supervising the bankruptcy and orderly liquidation were $1,000,000. All the fixed assets represented security on the mortgage.

a What are the amounts allocated to each claimant?

b What amount would Grandeur's bondholders receive if the debentures were not subordinated?

The following is a list of readings that can be used to supplement and extend the material covered in this text.

SUGGESTED READINGS

CHAPTER 1

Anthony, Robert N., "The Trouble with Profit Maximization," *Harvard Business Review*, 38 (November–December 1960), pp. 126–134.

Daniells, Lorna M., "On Business, Society, and the Environment," *Harvard Business Review*, 54 (September–October 1976) pp. 170–172.

Donaldson, Gordon, "Financial Goals: Management vs. Stockholders," *Harvard Business Review*, 41 (May–June 1963), pp. 116–129.

Geneen, Harold S., "Why Directors Can't Protect the Shareholders," *Fortune*, 110 (September 17, 1984), pp. 28–32.

Hill, Lawrence W., "The Growth of the Corporate Finance Function," *Financial Executive*, 44 (July 1976), pp. 38–43.

Jensen, M. C., and W. H. Meckling, "Can the Corporation Survive?" *Financial Analysts Journal* (January–February 1978), pp. 31–37.

Wunthow, Robert, "The Moral Crisis in American Capitalism," *Harvard Business Review*, 60 (March–April 1982), pp. 76–84.

CHAPTER 2

Friedman, Milton, "Factors Affecting the Level of Interest Rates," *Proceedings of the Conference on Savings and Residential Financing* (U.S. Savings and Loan League, 1968), pp. 11–27.

Instruments of the Money Market, Federal Reserve Bank of Richmond, 5th Edition, 1981.

Santoni, G. J., and Courtenay C. Stone, "What Really Happened to Interest Rates?: A Longer-Run Analysis," *Review*, Federal Reserve Bank of St. Louis (November 1981), pp. 3–14.

Seligman, Daniel, "Why Americans Don't Save Enough," *Fortune*, 109 (April 2, 1984), pp. 26–36.

"Signals from the Future: The Emerging Financial Services Industry," *Economic Review*, Federal Reserve Bank of Atlanta, 68 (September 1983), pp. 20–32.

Sivesind, Charles M., "Mortgage-Backed Securities: The Revolution in Real Estate Finance," *Quarterly Review*, Federal Reserve Bank of New York, 4 (Autumn 1979), pp. 1–10.

Van Horne, James C., *Financial Market Rates and Flows*, 2d ed. (Englewood Cliffs, N.J.: Prentice-Hall, 1984), pp. 79–102.

CHAPTER 3

Farrell, Kevin, "The Small Pay More," *Venture* (August 1984), pp. 58–62.

Gehan, Raymond F., "How the Accelerated Cost Recovery System Affects Property," *Financial Executive*, 50 (March 1982), pp. 12–15.

Hoeber, Ralph C., et al., *Contemporary Business Law*, 2d ed. (New York: McGraw-Hill, 1982), chaps. 39–42.

CHAPTER 4

Grant, Eugene L., et al., *Principles of Engineering Economy*, 6th ed. (New York: Ronald Press, 1976), pp. 25–61.

CHAPTER 5

Bauman, W. Scott, "Investment Returns and Present Values," *Financial Management*, 27 (September–October 1971), pp. 107–118.

Fisher, Anne N., "How Good Are Wall Street's Security Analysts?" *Fortune*, 110 (October 1, 1984), pp. 130–136.

Piper, Thomas R., and William E. Fruhan, "Is Your Stock Worth Its Price?" *Harvard Business Review*, 59 (May–June 1981), pp. 124–132.

Van Horne, James C., *Financial Market Rates and Flows*, 2d ed. (Englewood Cliffs, N.J.: Prentice-Hall, 1984), pp. 103–133.

CHAPTER 6

Malkiel, Burton G., *A Random Walk Down Wall Street*, 4th ed. (New York: W. W. Norton, 1985).

Modigliani, Franco, and Gerald A. Pogue, "An Introduction to Risk and Return: Concepts and Evidence, Part I," *Financial Analysts Journal*, 30 (March–April 1974), pp. 68–80.

Mullins, David W., Jr., "Does the Capital Asset Pricing Model Work?" *Harvard Business Review*, 60 (January–February 1982), pp. 105–114.

Weston, J. Fred, "Developments in Finance Theory," *Financial Management*, 10 (Tenth Anniversary Issue 1981), pp. 5–22.

CHAPTER 7

Brennan, Michael J., "A New Look at the Weighted Average Cost of Capital," *Journal of Business Finance*, 5 (Spring 1973), pp. 24–30.

Gitman, Lawrence J, and Vincent A. Mercurio, "Cost of Capital Techniques Used by Major U.S. Firms: Survey and Analysis of Fortune's 1000," *Financial Management*, 11 (Winter 1982), pp. 21–29.

McDonald, John G., "Market Measures of Capital Cost," *Journal of Business Finance*, 2 (Autumn 1970), pp. 27–36.

Solomon, Ezra, "Measuring a Company's Cost of Capital," *Journal of Business*, 28 (October 1955), pp. 240–252.

CHAPTER 8

Brigham, Eugene F., and Richard H. Pettway, "Capital Budgeting by Utilities," *Financial Management*, 2 (Autumn 1973), pp. 11–22.

Corr, Arthur V., "Capital Investment Planning," *Financial Executive*, 50 (April 1982), pp. 12–15.

Fogler, H. Russell, "Ranking Technique and Capital Rationing," *Accounting Review*, 47 (January 1972), pp. 134–143.

Hendricks, James A., "Capital Budgeting Practices Including Inflation Adjustments: A Survey," *Managerial Planning* (January/February 1983), pp. 22–28.

Lewellen, Wilbur G., H. P. Lanser, and J. J. McConnell, "Payback Substitutes for Discounted Cash Flow," *Financial Management*, 2 (Summer 1973), pp. 17–25.

Mao, James C. T., "Survey of Capital Budgeting: Theory and Practice," *Journal of Finance*, 25 (May 1970), pp. 349–360.

Rappaport, Alfred, and Robert A. Taggart, Jr., "Evaluation of Capital Expenditure Proposals Under Inflation," *Financial Management*, 11 (Spring 1982), pp. 5–13.

CHAPTER 9

Hertz, David B., "Risk Analysis in Capital Investment," *Harvard Business Review*, 42 (January–February 1964), pp. 95–106.

————, "Investment Policies that Pay Off," *Harvard Business Review*, 46 (January–February 1968), pp. 96–108.

Kabus, Irwin, "You Can Bank on Uncertainty," *Harvard Business Review*, 54 (May–June 1976), pp. 95–105.

Lewellen, Wilbur G., and Michael S. Long, "Simulation versus Single-Value Estimates in Capital Expenditure Analysis," *Decision Sciences*, 3 (1972).

Magee, John F., "How to Use Decision Trees in Capital Investment," *Harvard Business Review*, 42 (September–October 1964), pp. 79–96.

Van Horne, James C., "An Application of the Capital Asset Pricing Model to Divisional Required Returns," *Financial Management*, 9 (Spring 1980), pp. 14–19.

Weston, J. Fred, "Investment Decisions Using the Capital Asset Pricing Model," *Financial Management*, 2 (Spring 1973), pp. 25–33.

CHAPTER 10

Brigham, Eugene F., and Myron J. Gordon, "Leverage, Dividend Policy, and the Cost of Capital," *Journal of Finance*, 23 (March 1968), pp. 85–104.

Clemente, Holly A., "Innovative Financing," *Financial Executive*, 50 (April 1982), pp. 14–19.

Donaldson, Gordon, "In Defense of Preferred Stock," *Harvard Business Review*, 40 (July–August 1962), pp. 123–136.

Marsh, Paul, "The Choice Between Equity and Debt: An Empirical Study," *Journal of Finance*, 37 (March 1982), pp. 121–144.

Myers, Stewart C., "The Capital Structure Puzzle," *Journal of Finance*, 39 (July 1984), pp. 575–592.

Scott, David F., Jr., and D. J. Johnson, "Financing Policies and Practices in Large Corporations," *Financial Management* (Summer 1982), pp. 51–59.

———, and John D. Martin, "Industry Influence on Financial Structure," *Financial Management*, 4 (Spring 1975), pp. 67–73.

Sihler, William W., "Framework for Financial Decisions," *Harvard Business Review*, 49 (March–April 1971), pp. 123–125.

Solomon, Ezra, "Leverage and the Cost of Capital," *Journal of Finance*, 18 (May 1963), pp. 273–279.

CHAPTER 11

Black, Fisher, "The Dividend Puzzle," *Journal of Portfolio Management*, 2 (Winter 1976).

Eiseman, Peter C., and Edward A. Moses, "Stock Dividends: Management's View," *Financial Analysts Journal*, 34 (July–August 1978), pp. 77–80.

Higgins, Robert C., "The Corporate Dividend-Savings Decision," *Journal of Financial and Quantitative Analysis*, 7 (March 1972), pp. 1527–1541.

Millar, James A., and Bruce D. Fielitz, "Stock-Split and Stock-Dividend Decisions," *Financial Management*, 2 (Winter 1973), pp. 35–45.

Soter, Dennis S., "The Dividend Controversy—What It Means for Corporate Policy," *Financial Executive*, 47 (May 1979), pp. 38–43.

West, Richard R., and Alan B. Brouilette, "Reverse Stock Splits," *Financial Executive*, 38 (January 1970), pp. 12–17.

CHAPTER 12

Altman, Edward I., "Financial Ratios, Discriminant Analysis, and the Prediction of Corporate Bankruptcy," *Journal of Finance*, 23 (September 1968), pp. 589–609.

Beaver, William, "Financial Ratios as Predictors of Failure," *Empirical Research in Accounting: Selected Studies, 1966* (Institute of Professional Accounting, January 1967), pp. 71–111.

Dambolena, Ismael G., and Sarkis J. Khoury, "Ratio Stability and Corporate Failure," *Journal of Finance*, 35 (September 1980), pp. 1017–1026.

Helfert, Erich A., *Techniques of Financial Analysis*, 5th ed. (Homewood, Ill.: R. D. Irwin, 1982), chaps. 1 and 2.

Largay, James A., III, and Clyde P. Stickney, "Cash Flows, Ratio Analysis, and the W. T. Grant Company Bankruptcy," *Financial Analysts Journal*, 36 (July–August 1980), pp. 51–54.

Murray, Roger, "Lessons for Financial Analysis," *Journal of Finance*, 26 (May 1971), pp. 327–332.

Scott, David F., and John D. Martin, "Industry Influence on Financial Structure," *Financial Management*, 4 (Spring 1975), pp. 67–73.

CHAPTER 13

Heath, Loyd C., "Let's Scrap the Funds Statement," *The Journal of Accountancy* (October 1978), pp. 94–103.

Kelvie, William E., and John M. Sinclair, "New Techniques for Break-Even Charts," *Financial Executive*, 36 (June 1968), pp. 31–43.

Packer Stephen B., "Flow of Funds Analysis—Its Uses and Limitations," *Financial Analysts Journal*, 20 (July–August 1964), pp. 117–123.

Raun, D. L., "The Limitations of Profit Graphs, Break-Even Analysis, and Budgets," *Accounting Review*, 39 (October 1964), pp. 927–945.

Reinhardt, U. E., "Break-Even Analysis for Lockheed's Tri Star," *Journal of Finance*, 28 (September 1973), pp. 821–838.

CHAPTER 14

Chambers, John C., et al., "How to Choose the Right Forecasting Technique," *Harvard Business Review*, 49 (July–August 1971), pp. 45–74.

Parker, George C., and Edilberto L. Segura, "How to Get a Better Forecast," *Harvard Business Review*, 49 (March–April 1971), pp. 99–109.

Preston, Gerald R., "Considerations in Long-Range Planning," *Financial Executive*, 36 (May 1968), pp. 44–49.

Wheelwright, Steven C., and Daniel G. Clarke, "Corporate Forecasting: Promise and Reality," *Harvard Business Review*, 54 (November–December 1976), pp. 40–68.

Readings for Chapter 15, 16, and 17 preceded by * are included in Smith, Keith V., *Management of Working Capital* (St. Paul: West, 1974).

CHAPTER 15

Cohen, Allen M., "Treasury Terminal Systems and Cash Management Information Support," *Journal of Cash Management*, 3 (August–September 1983), pp. 9–18.

Gitman, Lawrence J., Edward A. Moses, and I. Thomas White, "An Assessment of Corporate Cash Management Practices," *Financial Management*, 8 (Spring 1979), pp. 32–41.

* Marrah, George L., "Managing Receivables," *Financial Executive*, 38 (July 1970), pp. 40–44.

* Reed, Ward L., Jr., "Profits from Better Cash Management," *Financial Executive*, 40 (May 1972), pp. 40–56.

* Schiff, Michael, "Credit and Inventory Management—Separate or Together," *Financial Executive*, 40 (November 1972), pp. 28–33.

* Snyder, Arthur, "Principles of Inventory Management," *Financial Executive*, 32 (April 1964), pp. 13–21.

CHAPTER 16

* Conover, C. Todd, "The Case of the Costly Credit Agreement," *Financial Executive*, 39 (September 1971), pp. 40–48.

* Diener, Royce, "Analyzing the Financing Potential of a Small Business," in I. Pfeffer (ed.), *The Financing of Small Business* (New York: Macmillan, 1967), pp. 211–228.

* Nadler, Paul S., "Compensating Balances and the Prime at Twilight," *Harvard Business Review*, 50 (January–February 1972), pp. 112–120.

CHAPTER 17

Donaldson, Gordon, "Strategy for Financial Emergencies," *Harvard Business Review*, 47 (November–December 1969), pp. 67–79.

Johnson, James M., David R. Campbell, and James L. Wittenbach, "Problems in Corporate Liquidity," *Financial Executive*, 48 (March 1980), pp. 44–53.

Osteryoung, Jerome S., Gordon S. Roberts, and Daniel E. McCarty, "Ride the Yield Curve When Investing Idle Funds in Treasury Bills?" *Financial Executive*, 47 (April 1979), pp. 10–15.

* Van Horne, James C., "A Risk-Return Analysis of a Firm's Working Capital Position," *Engineering Economist*, 14 (Winter 1969), pp. 71–88.

CHAPTER 18

Arnold, Jasper H., III, "How to Negotiate a Term Loan," *Harvard Business Review*, 60 (March–April 1982), pp. 131–138.

Block, Stanley, and Marjorie Stanley, "The Financial Characteristics and Price Movement Patterns of Companies Approaching the Unseasoned Securities Market in the Late 1970's," *Financial Management*, 9 (Winter 1980), pp. 30–36.

Militello, Frederick C., Jr., "Swap Financing," *Financial Executive* (October 1984), pp. 34–39.

Sears, Gerald A., "Public Offerings for Smaller Companies," *Harvard Business Review*, 46 (September–October 1968), pp. 112–120.

Smith, Adam, *Supermoney* (New York: Random House, 1972).

CHAPTER 19

Anderson, Paul F., and John D. Martin, "Lease vs. Purchase Decisions: A Survey of Current Practice," *Financial Management*, 6 (Spring 1977), pp. 41–47.

Bower, R. S., "Issues in Lease Financing," *Financial Management*, 2 (Winter 1973), pp. 25–33.

Ingberman, Monroe, Joshua Ronen, and George H. Sorter, "How Lease Capitalization Under FASB Statement No. 13 Will Affect Financial Ratios," *Financial Analysts Journal*, 35 (January–February 1979), pp. 28–31.

McGugan, V. J., and R. E. Caves, "Integration and Competition in the Equipment Leasing Industry," *Journal of Business* (July 1974), pp. 382–396.

Peller, Philip R., John E. Stewart, and Benjamin S. Neuhausen, "The 1981 Tax Act: Accounting for Leases," *Financial Executive*, 50 (January 1982), pp. 16–26 (and update in March 1982 issue, p. 24).

Smith, Pierce R., "A Straightforward Approach to Leveraged Leasing," *The Journal of Commercial Bank Lending* (July 1973), pp. 19–39.

Sorensen, Ivar W., and Ramon E. Johnson, "Equipment Financial Leasing Practices and Costs: An Empirical Study," *Financial Management*, 6 (Spring 1977), pp. 33–40.

CHAPTER 20

Bacon, P. W., "The Subscription Price in Rights Offerings," *Financial Management*, 1 (Summer 1972), pp. 59–64.

Finnerty, Joseph E., "Corporate Stock Issue and Repurchase," *Financial Management*, 4 (Autumn 1975), pp. 62–66.

Furst, Richard W., "Does Listing Increase the Market Price of Common Stocks?" *Journal of Business*, 43 (April 1970), pp. 174–180.

Rosenberg, M., and A. Young, "Firm Repurchasing Stock: Financial, Security Market, and Operating Characteristics," *University of Michigan Business Review* (May 1978), pp. 17–22.

Stewart, S. S., "Should a Corporation Repurchase Its Own Shares?" *Journal of Finance*, 31 (June 1976), pp. 911–926.

Young, Alan, and W. Marshall, "Controlling Shareholder Servicing Costs," *Harvard Business Review*, 49 (January–February 1971), pp. 71–78.

CHAPTER 21

Brown, Bowman, "Why Corporations Should Consider Income Bonds," *Financial Executive*, 35 (October 1967), pp. 74–78.

Donaldson, Gordon, "In Defense of Preferred Stock," *Harvard Business Review*, 40 (July–August 1962), pp. 123–136.

Elsaid, Hussein H., "The Function of Preferred Stock in the Corporate Financial Plan," *Financial Analysts Journal*, 25 (July–August 1969), pp. 112–117.

McConnell, John J., and Gary G. Schlarbaum, "Returns, Risks, and Pricing of Income Bonds, 1956–76 (Does Money Have an Odor?)," *Journal of Business*, 54 (January 1981), pp. 33–63.

Marks, Kenneth R., and Warren A. Law, "Hedging Against Inflation with Floating-Rate Notes," *Harvard Business Review*, 58 (March–April 1980), pp. 106–112.

Ofer, Aharon R., and Robert A. Taggart, Jr., "Bond Refunding: A Clarifying Analysis," *Journal of Finance*, 32 (March 1977), pp. 21–30.

Pogue, Thomas F., and Robert M. Soldofsky, "What's in a Bond Rating?" *Journal of Financial and Quantitative Analysis*, 4 (July 1969), pp. 201–228.

Wyant, Larry, "Essential Elements of Project Financing," *Harvard Business Review*, 58 (May–June 1980), pp. 165–173.

CHAPTER 22

Bond, F. M., "Yields on Convertible Securities: 1969–1974," *The Journal of Business Finance and Accounting*, 3 (Summer 1976), pp. 93–114.

Brennan, M. J., and E. S. Schwartz, "Convertible Bonds: Valuation and Optimal Strategies for Call and Conversion," *Journal of Finance*, 32 (December 1977), pp. 1699–1715.

Hayes, Samuel L., III, and Henry B. Reiling, "Sophisticated Financing Tool: The Warrant," *Harvard Business Review*, 47 (January–February 1969), pp. 137–150.

Melicher, Ronald W., and J. Ronald Hoffmeister, "Issuing Convertible Bonds," *Financial Executive*, 48 (June 1980), pp. 20–23.

Pinches, George E., "Financing with Convertible Preferred Stocks, 1960–1967," *Journal of Finance*, 25 (March 1970), pp. 53–64.

Rush, David, and Ronald Melicher, "An Empirical Examination of Factors Which Influence Warrant Prices," *Journal of Finance*, 29 (December 1974), pp. 1449–1466.

Soldofsky, Robert M., "Yield-Rate Performance of Convertible Securities," *Financial Analysts Journal*, 27 (March–April 1971), pp. 61–65.

CHAPTER 23

Balog, James,"Market Reaction to Merger Announcements," *Financial Analysts Journal*, 31 (January–February 1975), pp. 24–27.

Biggadike, Ralph, "The Risky Business of Diversification," *Harvard Business Review*, 57 (May–June 1979), pp. 103–111.

Bradley, Michael, "Interfirm Tender Offers and the Market for Corporate Control," *Journal of Business*, 53 (October 1980), pp. 345–376.

Briloff, Abraham L., "The Funny-Money Game," *Financial Analysts Journal*, 25 (May–June 1969), pp. 73–79.

Emmett, Robert, "How to Value a Potential Acquisition," *Financial Executive*, 50 (February 1982), pp. 16–19.

Hector, Gary, "Is any Company Safe from Takeover?" *Fortune* (April 2, 1984), pp. 18–20.

Hogarty, Thomas F., "The Profitability of Corporate Mergers," *Journal of Business*, 44 (July 1970), pp. 317–327.

CHAPTER 24

Anderson, Gerald L., "International Project Financing," *Financial Executive*, 45 (May 1977), pp. 40–45.

Dufey, Gunter, "Corporate Finance and Exchange Rate Variations," *Financial Management*, 1 (Summer 1972), pp. 51–57.

———, and S. L. Srinivasulu, "The Case for Corporate Management of Foreign Exchange Risk," *Financial Management*, 12 (Winter 1983), pp. 54–62.

Franko, Lawrence G., "Multinationals: The End of U.S. Dominance," *Harvard Business Review*, 56 (November–December 1978), pp. 93–101.

Oblak, David J., and Roy J. Helm, Jr., "Survey and Analysis of Capital Budgeting Methods Used by Multinationals," *Financial Management*, 9 (Winter 1980), pp. 37–41.

Parkinson, Kenneth C., "Dealing with the Problem of International Cash Management," *Journal of Cash Management*, 3 (February–March 1983), pp. 16–25.

Robbins, Sidney M., and Robert B. Stobaugh, "Financing Foreign Affiliates," *Financial Management*, 1 (Winter 1972), pp. 56–65.

Robichek, Alexander A., and Mark R. Eaker, "Debt Denomination and Exchange Risk in International Capital Markets," *Financial Management*, 5 (Autumn 1976), pp. 11–18.

Rummel, R. J., and David A. Heenan, "How Multinationals Analyze Political Risk," *Harvard Business Review*, 56 (January–February 1978), pp. 67–76.

Shapiro, Alan C., "Capital Budgeting for the Multinational Corporation," *Financial Management*, 7 (Spring 1978), pp. 7–16.

CHAPTER 25

Aharony, Joseph, Charles P. Jones, and Itzhak Swary, "An Analysis of Risk and Return Characteristics of Corporate Bankruptcy Using Market Data," *Journal of Finance*, 35 (September 1980), pp. 1001–1016.

Altman, Edward I., "Corporate Bankruptcy Potential, Stockholder Returns, and Share Valuation," *Journal of Finance*, 24 (December 1969), pp. 887–900.

Gordon, Myron, "Toward a Theory of Financial Distress," *Journal of Finance*, 26 (May 1971), pp. 347–356.

APPENDIX A   Interest rate of ⅓ percent

Interest rate of ⅓ percent

N	Capital recovery — Annuity repaying a present amount A/P	Annuity present value — Present value of an annuity P/A	Sinking fund — Annuity providing a future amount A/F	Annuity compound amount — Future value of an annuity F/A	Present value — Present value of a future amount P/F	Compound amount — Future value of a present amount F/P	N
48	.0226	44.2888	.0192	51.9596	.8524	1.1732	48
60	.0184	54.2991	.0151	66.2990	.8190	1.2210	60
72	.0156	63.9174	.0123	81.2226	.7869	1.2707	72
84	.0137	73.1593	.0103	96.7541	.7561	1.3225	84
96	.0122	82.0393	.0089	112.9185	.7265	1.3764	96
108	.0110	90.5718	.0077	129.7414	.6981	1.4325	108
120	.0101	98.7702	.0068	147.2498	.6708	1.4908	120
132	.0094	106.6477	.0060	165.4714	.6445	1.5516	132
144	.0088	114.2168	.0054	184.4354	.6193	1.6148	144
156	.0082	121.4896	.0049	204.1721	.5950	1.6806	156
168	.0078	128.4777	.0045	224.7128	.5717	1.7490	168
180	.0074	135.1922	.0041	246.0904	.5494	1.8203	180
192	.0071	141.6439	.0037	268.3390	.5279	1.8945	192
204	.0068	147.8430	.0034	291.4940	.5072	1.9716	204
216	.0065	153.7994	.0032	315.5923	.4873	2.0520	216
228	.0063	159.5227	.0029	340.6725	.4683	2.1356	228
240	.0061	165.0219	.0027	366.7745	.4499	2.2226	240
252	.0059	170.3059	.0025	393.9399	.4323	2.3131	252
264	.0057	175.3830	.0024	422.2120	.4154	2.4074	264
276	.0055	180.2613	.0022	451.6360	.3991	2.5055	276
288	.0054	184.9487	.0021	482.2588	.3835	2.6075	288
300	.0053	189.4526	.0019	514.1293	.3685	2.7138	300
312	.0052	193.7801	.0018	547.2981	.3541	2.8243	312
324	.0051	197.9383	.0017	581.8183	.3402	2.9394	324
336	.0050	201.9337	.0016	617.7449	.3269	3.0591	336
348	.0049	205.7726	.0015	655.1353	.3141	3.1838	348
360	.0048	209.4613	.0014	694.0489	.3018	3.1135	360
∞	.0033	300.0000					∞

N	Compound amount — Future value of a present amount F/P	Present value — Present value of a future amount P/F	Annuity compound amount — Future value of an annuity F/A	Sinking fund — Annuity providing a future amount A/F	Annuity present value — Present value of an annuity P/A	Capital recovery — Annuity repaying a present amount A/P	N
1	1.0033	.9967	1.0000	1.0000	.9967	1.0033	1
2	1.0067	.9934	2.0033	.4992	1.9900	.5025	2
3	1.0100	.9901	3.0100	.3322	2.9801	.3356	3
4	1.0134	.9868	4.0200	.2488	3.9669	.2521	4
5	1.0168	.9835	5.0334	.1987	4.9504	.2020	5
6	1.0202	.9802	6.0502	.1653	5.9306	.1686	6
7	1.0236	.9770	7.0704	.1414	6.9076	.1448	7
8	1.0270	.9737	8.0940	.1235	7.8813	.1269	8
9	1.0304	.9705	9.1209	.1096	8.8518	.1130	9
10	1.0338	.9673	10.1513	.0985	9.8191	.1018	10
11	1.0373	.9641	11.1852	.0894	10.7831	.0927	11
12	1.0407	.9609	12.2225	.0818	11.7440	.0851	12
13	1.0442	.9577	13.2632	.0754	12.7017	.0787	13
14	1.0477	.9545	14.3074	.0699	13.6561	.0732	14
15	1.0512	.9513	15.3551	.0651	14.6074	.0685	15
16	1.0547	.9481	16.4063	.0610	15.5556	.0643	16
17	1.0582	.9450	17.4610	.0573	16.5006	.0606	17
18	1.0617	.9419	18.5192	.0540	17.4424	.0573	18
19	1.0653	.9387	19.5809	.0511	18.3812	.0544	19
20	1.0688	.9356	20.6462	.0484	19.3168	.0518	20
21	1.0724	.9325	21.7150	.0461	20.2493	.0494	21
22	1.0760	.9294	22.7874	.0439	21.1787	.0472	22
23	1.0795	.9263	23.8633	.0419	22.1050	.0452	23
24	1.0831	.9232	24.9429	.0401	23.0283	.0434	24
25	1.0868	.9202	26.0260	.0384	23.9484	.0418	25
26	1.0904	.9171	27.1128	.0369	24.8655	.0402	26
27	1.0940	.9141	28.2032	.0355	25.7796	.0388	27
28	1.0977	.9110	29.2972	.0341	26.6906	.0375	28
29	1.1013	.9080	30.3948	.0329	27.5986	.0362	29
30	1.1050	.9050	31.4961	.0317	28.5036	.0351	30
31	1.1087	.9020	32.6011	.0307	29.4056	.0340	31
32	1.1124	.8990	33.7098	.0297	30.3046	.0330	32
33	1.1161	.8960	34.8222	.0287	31.2006	.0321	33
34	1.1198	.8930	35.9382	.0278	32.0936	.0312	34
35	1.1235	.8901	37.0580	.0270	32.9837	.0303	35
36	1.1273	.8871	38.1816	.0262	33.8708	.0295	36

Interest rate of ⅔ percent

Interest rate of ½ percent (N = 48 to 360, ∞)

N	Capital recovery / Annuity repaying a present amount / A/P	Annuity present value / Present value of an annuity / P/A	Sinking fund / Annuity providing a future amount / A/F	Annuity compound amount / Future value of an annuity / F/A	Present value / Present value of a future amount / P/F	Compound amount / Future value of a present amount / F/P	N
48	.0235	42.5803	.0185	54.0978	.7871	1.2705	48
60	.0193	51.7256	.0143	69.7700	.7414	1.3489	60
72	.0166	60.3395	.0116	86.4089	.6983	1.4320	72
84	.0146	68.4530	.0096	104.0739	.6577	1.5204	84
96	.0131	76.0952	.0081	122.8285	.6195	1.6141	96
108	.0120	83.2934	.0070	142.7399	.5835	1.7137	108
120	.0111	90.0735	.0061	163.8793	.5496	1.8194	120
132	.0104	96.4596	.0054	186.3226	.5177	1.9316	132
144	.0098	102.4747	.0048	210.1502	.4876	2.0508	144
156	.0092	108.1404	.0042	235.4473	.4593	2.1772	156
168	.0088	113.4770	.0038	262.3048	.4326	2.3115	168
180	.0084	118.5035	.0034	290.8187	.4075	2.4541	180
192	.0081	123.2380	.0031	321.0913	.3838	2.6055	192
204	.0078	127.6975	.0028	353.2311	.3615	2.7662	204
216	.0076	131.8979	.0026	387.3532	.3405	2.9368	216
228	.0074	135.8542	.0024	423.5799	.3207	3.1179	228
240	.0072	139.5808	.0022	462.0409	.3021	3.3102	240
252	.0070	143.0908	.0020	502.8741	.2845	3.5144	252
264	.0068	146.3969	.0018	546.2259	.2680	3.7311	264
276	.0067	149.5110	.0017	592.2514	.2524	3.9613	276
288	.0066	152.4441	.0016	641.1158	.2378	4.2056	288
300	.0064	155.2069	.0014	692.9940	.2240	4.4650	300
312	.0063	157.8091	.0013	748.0719	.2110	4.7404	312
324	.0062	160.2602	.0012	806.5469	.1987	5.0327	324
336	.0062	162.5688	.0012	868.6285	.1872	5.3431	336
348	.0061	164.7434	.0011	934.5392	.1763	5.6727	348
360	.0060	166.7916	.0010	1004.5150	.1660	6.0226	360
∞	.0050	200.0000					∞

Interest rate of ½ percent (N = 1 to 36)

N	Compound amount / Future value of a present amount / F/P	Present value / Present value of a future amount / P/F	Annuity compound amount / Future value of an annuity / F/A	Sinking fund / Annuity providing a future amount / A/F	Annuity present value / Present value of an annuity / P/A	Capital recovery / Annuity repaying a present amount / A/P	N
1	1.0050	.9950	1.0000	1.0000	.9950	1.0050	1
2	1.0100	.9901	2.0050	.4988	1.9851	.5038	2
3	1.0151	.9851	3.0150	.3317	2.9702	.3367	3
4	1.0202	.9802	4.0301	.2481	3.9505	.2531	4
5	1.0253	.9754	5.0503	.1980	4.9259	.2030	5
6	1.0304	.9705	6.0755	.1646	5.8964	.1696	6
7	1.0355	.9657	7.1059	.1407	6.8621	.1457	7
8	1.0407	.9609	8.1414	.1228	7.8230	.1278	8
9	1.0459	.9561	9.1821	.1089	8.7791	.1139	9
10	1.0511	.9513	10.2280	.0978	9.7304	.1028	10
11	1.0564	.9466	11.2792	.0887	10.6770	.0937	11
12	1.0617	.9419	12.3356	.0811	11.6189	.0861	12
13	1.0670	.9372	13.3972	.0746	12.5562	.0796	13
14	1.0723	.9326	14.4642	.0691	13.4887	.0741	14
15	1.0777	.9279	15.5365	.0644	14.4166	.0694	15
16	1.0831	.9233	16.6142	.0602	15.3399	.0652	16
17	1.0885	.9187	17.6973	.0565	16.2586	.0615	17
18	1.0939	.9141	18.7858	.0532	17.1728	.0582	18
19	1.0994	.9096	19.8797	.0503	18.0824	.0553	19
20	1.1049	.9051	20.9791	.0477	18.9874	.0527	20
21	1.1104	.9006	22.0840	.0453	19.8880	.0503	21
22	1.1160	.8961	23.1944	.0431	20.7841	.0481	22
23	1.1216	.8916	24.3104	.0411	21.6757	.0461	23
24	1.1272	.8872	25.4320	.0393	22.5629	.0443	24
25	1.1328	.8828	26.5591	.0377	23.4456	.0427	25
26	1.1385	.8784	27.6919	.0361	24.3240	.0411	26
27	1.1442	.8740	28.8304	.0347	25.1980	.0397	27
28	1.1499	.8697	29.9745	.0334	26.0677	.0384	28
29	1.1556	.8653	31.1244	.0321	26.9330	.0371	29
30	1.1614	.8610	32.2800	.0310	27.7941	.0360	30
31	1.1672	.8567	33.4414	.0299	28.6508	.0349	31
32	1.1730	.8525	34.6086	.0289	29.5033	.0339	32
33	1.1789	.8482	35.7817	.0279	30.3515	.0329	33
34	1.1848	.8440	36.9606	.0271	31.1955	.0321	34
35	1.1907	.8398	38.1454	.0262	32.0354	.0312	35
36	1.1967	.8356	39.3361	.0254	32.8710	.0304	36

Interest rate of ⅔ percent

N	Compound amount — Future value of a present amount F/P	Present value — Present value of a future amount P/F	Annuity compound amount — Future value of an annuity F/A	Sinking fund — Annuity providing a future amount A/F	Annuity present value — Present value of an annuity P/A	Capital recovery — Annuity repaying a present amount A/P	N
1	1.0067	.9934	1.0000	1.0000	.9934	1.0067	1
2	1.0134	.9868	2.0067	.4983	1.9802	.5050	2
3	1.0201	.9803	3.0200	.3311	2.9604	.3378	3
4	1.0269	.9738	4.0402	.2475	3.9342	.2542	4
5	1.0338	.9673	5.0671	.1974	4.9015	.2040	5
6	1.0407	.9609	6.1009	.1639	5.8625	.1706	6
7	1.0476	.9546	7.1416	.1400	6.8170	.1467	7
8	1.0546	.9482	8.1892	.1221	7.7652	.1288	8
9	1.0616	.9420	9.2438	.1082	8.7072	.1148	9
10	1.0687	.9357	10.3054	.0970	9.6429	.1037	10
11	1.0758	.9295	11.3741	.0879	10.5724	.0946	11
12	1.0830	.9234	12.4499	.0803	11.4958	.0870	12
13	1.0902	.9172	13.5329	.0739	12.4130	.0806	13
14	1.0975	.9112	14.6231	.0684	13.3242	.0751	14
15	1.1048	.9051	15.7206	.0636	14.2293	.0703	15
16	1.1122	.8991	16.8254	.0594	15.1285	.0661	16
17	1.1196	.8932	17.9376	.0557	16.0217	.0624	17
18	1.1270	.8873	19.0572	.0525	16.9089	.0591	18
19	1.1346	.8814	20.1842	.0495	17.7903	.0562	19
20	1.1421	.8756	21.3188	.0469	18.6659	.0536	20
21	1.1497	.8698	22.4609	.0445	19.5357	.0512	21
22	1.1574	.8640	23.6107	.0424	20.3997	.0490	22
23	1.1651	.8583	24.7681	.0404	21.2579	.0470	23
24	1.1729	.8526	25.9332	.0386	22.1105	.0452	24
25	1.1807	.8470	27.1061	.0369	22.9575	.0436	25
26	1.1886	.8413	28.2868	.0354	23.7988	.0420	26
27	1.1965	.8358	29.4754	.0339	24.6346	.0406	27
28	1.2045	.8302	30.6719	.0326	25.4648	.0393	28
29	1.2125	.8247	31.8763	.0314	26.2896	.0380	29
30	1.2206	.8193	33.0889	.0302	27.1088	.0369	30
31	1.2287	.8138	34.3094	.0291	27.9227	.0358	31
32	1.2369	.8085	35.5382	.0281	28.7312	.0348	32
33	1.2452	.8031	36.7751	.0272	29.5343	.0339	33
34	1.2535	.7978	38.0203	.0263	30.3320	.0330	34
35	1.2618	.7925	39.2737	.0255	31.1246	.0321	35
36	1.2702	.7873	40.5356	.0247	31.9118	.0313	36

N	Compound amount — Future value of a present amount F/P	Present value — Present value of a future amount P/F	Annuity compound amount — Future value of an annuity F/A	Sinking fund — Annuity providing a future amount A/F	Annuity present value — Present value of an annuity P/A	Capital recovery — Annuity repaying a present amount A/P	N
48	1.3757	.7269	56.3499	.0177	40.9619	.0244	48
60	1.4898	.6712	73.4769	.0136	49.3184	.0203	60
72	1.6135	.6198	92.0253	.0109	57.0345	.0175	72
84	1.7474	.5723	112.1133	.0089	64.1593	.0156	84
96	1.8925	.5284	133.8686	.0075	70.7380	.0141	96
108	2.0495	.4879	157.4295	.0064	76.8125	.0130	108
120	2.2196	.4505	182.9460	.0055	82.4215	.0121	120
132	2.4039	.4160	210.5804	.0047	87.6006	.0114	132
144	2.6034	.3841	240.5084	.0042	92.3828	.0108	144
156	2.8195	.3547	272.9204	.0037	96.7985	.0103	156
168	3.0535	.3275	308.0226	.0032	100.8758	.0099	168
180	3.3069	.3024	346.0382	.0029	104.6406	.0096	180
192	3.5814	.2792	387.2092	.0026	108.1169	.0092	192
204	3.8786	.2578	431.7973	.0023	111.3267	.0090	204
216	4.2006	.2381	480.0861	.0021	114.2906	.0087	216
228	4.5492	.2198	532.3830	.0019	117.0273	.0085	228
240	4.9268	.2030	589.0204	.0017	119.5543	.0084	240
252	5.3357	.1874	650.3588	.0015	121.8876	.0082	252
264	5.7786	.1731	716.7882	.0014	124.0421	.0081	264
276	6.2582	.1598	788.7312	.0013	126.0315	.0079	276
288	6.7776	.1475	866.6454	.0012	127.8684	.0078	288
300	7.3402	.1362	951.0265	.0011	129.5645	.0077	300
312	7.9494	.1258	1042.4111	.0010	131.1307	.0076	312
324	8.6092	.1162	1141.3807	.0009	132.5768	.0075	324
336	9.3238	.1073	1248.5646	.0008	133.9121	.0075	336
348	10.0976	.0990	1364.6448	.0007	135.1450	.0074	348
360	10.9357	.0914	1490.3596	.0007	136.2835	.0073	360
∞					150.0000	.0067	∞

Interest rate of ¾ percent

N	Compound amount — Future value of a present amount F/P	Present value — Present value of a future amount P/F	Annuity compound amount — Future value of an annuity F/A	Sinking fund — Annuity providing a future amount A/F	Annuity present value — Present value of an annuity P/A	Capital recovery — Annuity repaying a present amount A/P	N
1	1.0075	.9926	1.0000	1.0000	.9926	1.0075	1
2	1.0151	.9852	2.0075	.4981	1.9777	.5056	2
3	1.0227	.9778	3.0226	.3308	2.9556	.3383	3
4	1.0303	.9706	4.0452	.2472	3.9261	.2547	4
5	1.0381	.9633	5.0756	.1970	4.8894	.2045	5
6	1.0459	.9562	6.1136	.1636	5.8456	.1711	6
7	1.0537	.9490	7.1595	.1397	6.7946	.1472	7
8	1.0616	.9420	8.2132	.1218	7.7366	.1293	8
9	1.0696	.9350	9.2748	.1078	8.6716	.1153	9
10	1.0776	.9280	10.3443	.0967	9.5996	.1042	10
11	1.0857	.9211	11.4219	.0876	10.5207	.0951	11
12	1.0938	.9142	12.5076	.0800	11.4349	.0875	12
13	1.1020	.9074	13.6014	.0735	12.3423	.0810	13
14	1.1103	.9007	14.7034	.0680	13.2430	.0755	14
15	1.1186	.8940	15.8137	.0632	14.1370	.0707	15
16	1.1270	.8873	16.9323	.0591	15.0243	.0666	16
17	1.1354	.8807	18.0593	.0554	15.9050	.0629	17
18	1.1440	.8742	19.1947	.0521	16.7792	.0596	18
19	1.1525	.8676	20.3387	.0492	17.6468	.0567	19
20	1.1612	.8612	21.4912	.0465	18.5080	.0540	20
21	1.1699	.8548	22.6524	.0441	19.3628	.0516	21
22	1.1787	.8484	23.8223	.0420	20.2112	.0495	22
23	1.1875	.8421	25.0010	.0400	21.0533	.0475	23
24	1.1964	.8358	26.1885	.0382	21.8891	.0457	24
25	1.2054	.8296	27.3849	.0365	22.7188	.0440	25
26	1.2144	.8234	28.5903	.0350	23.5422	.0425	26
27	1.2235	.8173	29.8047	.0336	24.3595	.0411	27
28	1.2327	.8112	31.0282	.0322	25.1707	.0397	28
29	1.2420	.8052	32.2609	.0310	25.9759	.0385	29
30	1.2513	.7992	33.5029	.0298	26.7751	.0373	30
31	1.2607	.7932	34.7542	.0288	27.5683	.0363	31
32	1.2701	.7873	36.0148	.0278	28.3557	.0353	32
33	1.2796	.7815	37.2849	.0268	29.1371	.0343	33
34	1.2892	.7757	38.5646	.0259	29.9128	.0334	34
35	1.2989	.7699	39.8538	.0251	30.6827	.0326	35
36	1.3086	.7641	41.1527	.0243	31.4468	.0318	36

N	Compound amount — Future value of a present amount F/P	Present value — Present value of a future amount P/F	Annuity compound amount — Future value of an annuity F/A	Sinking fund — Annuity providing a future amount A/F	Annuity present value — Present value of an annuity P/A	Capital recovery — Annuity repaying a present amount A/P	N
48	1.4314	.6986	57.5207	.0174	40.1848	.0249	48
60	1.5657	.6387	75.4241	.0133	48.1734	.0208	60
72	1.7126	.5839	95.0070	.0105	55.4768	.0180	72
84	1.8732	.5338	116.4269	.0086	62.1540	.0161	84
96	2.0489	.4881	139.8562	.0072	68.2584	.0147	96
108	2.2411	.4462	165.4832	.0060	73.8394	.0135	108
120	2.4514	.4079	193.5143	.0052	78.9417	.0127	120
132	2.6813	.3730	224.1748	.0045	83.6064	.0120	132
144	2.9328	.3410	257.7116	.0039	87.8711	.0114	144
156	3.2080	.3117	294.3943	.0034	91.7700	.0109	156
168	3.5089	.2850	334.5181	.0030	95.3346	.0105	168
180	3.8380	.2605	378.4058	.0026	98.5934	.0101	180
192	4.1981	.2382	426.4104	.0023	101.5728	.0098	192
204	4.5919	.2178	478.9183	.0021	104.2966	.0096	204
216	5.0226	.1991	536.3517	.0019	106.7869	.0094	216
228	5.4938	.1820	599.1727	.0017	109.0635	.0092	228
240	6.0092	.1664	667.8869	.0015	111.1450	.0090	240
252	6.5729	.1521	743.0469	.0013	113.0479	.0088	252
264	7.1894	.1391	825.2574	.0012	114.7876	.0087	264
276	7.8638	.1272	915.1798	.0011	116.3781	.0086	276
288	8.6015	.1163	1013.5375	.0010	117.8322	.0085	288
300	9.4084	.1063	1121.1219	.0009	119.1616	.0084	300
312	10.2910	.0972	1238.7985	.0008	120.3770	.0083	312
324	11.2564	.0888	1367.5139	.0007	121.4882	.0082	324
336	12.3123	.0812	1508.3037	.0007	122.5040	.0082	336
348	13.4673	.0743	1662.3006	.0006	123.4328	.0081	348
360	14.7306	.0679	1830.7435	.0005	124.2819	.0080	360
∞					133.3333	.0075	∞

Interest rate of 1.00 percent

N	Compound amount — Future value of a present amount — F/P	Present value — Present value of a future amount — P/F	Annuity compound amount — Future value of an annuity — F/A	Sinking fund — Annuity providing a future amount — A/F	Annuity present value — Present value of an annuity — P/A	Capital recovery — Annuity repaying a present amount — A/P	N
48	1.6122	.6203	61.2226	.0163	37.9740	.0263	48
60	1.8167	.5504	81.6697	.0122	44.9550	.0222	60
72	2.0471	.4885	104.7099	.0096	51.1504	.0196	72
84	2.3067	.4335	130.6723	.0077	56.6485	.0177	84
96	2.5993	.3847	159.9273	.0063	61.5277	.0163	96
108	2.9289	.3414	192.8926	.0052	65.8578	.0152	108
120	3.3004	.3030	230.0387	.0043	69.7005	.0143	120
132	3.7190	.2689	271.8959	.0037	73.1108	.0137	132
144	4.1906	.2386	319.0616	.0031	76.1372	.0131	144
156	4.7221	.2118	372.2091	.0027	78.8229	.0127	156
168	5.3210	.1879	432.0970	.0023	81.2064	.0123	168
180	5.9958	.1668	499.5802	.0020	83.3217	.0120	180
192	6.7562	.1480	575.6220	.0017	85.1988	.0117	192
204	7.6131	.1314	661.3078	.0015	86.8647	.0115	204
216	8.5786	.1166	757.8606	.0013	88.3431	.0113	216
228	9.6666	.1034	866.6588	.0012	89.6551	.0112	228
240	10.8926	.0918	989.2554	.0010	90.8194	.0110	240
252	12.2740	.0815	1127.4002	.0009	91.8527	.0109	252
264	13.8307	.0723	1283.0653	.0008	92.7697	.0108	264
276	15.5847	.0642	1458.4726	.0007	93.5835	.0107	276
288	17.5613	.0569	1656.1259	.0006	94.3056	.0106	288
300	19.7885	.0505	1878.8466	.0005	94.9466	.0106	300
312	22.2981	.0448	2129.8139	.0005	95.5153	.0105	312
324	25.1261	.0398	2412.6101	.0004	96.0201	.0104	324
336	28.3127	.0353	2731.2720	.0004	96.4680	.0104	336
348	31.9035	.0313	3090.3481	.0003	96.8655	.0103	348
360	35.9496	.0278	3494.9641	.0003	97.2183	.0103	360
∞					100.0000	.0100	∞

N	Compound amount — Future value of a present amount — F/P	Present value — Present value of a future amount — P/F	Annuity compound amount — Future value of an annuity — F/A	Sinking fund — Annuity providing a future amount — A/F	Annuity present value — Present value of an annuity — P/A	Capital recovery — Annuity repaying a present amount — A/P	N
1	1.0100	.9901	1.0000	1.0000	.9901	1.0100	1
2	1.0201	.9803	2.0100	.4975	1.9704	.5075	2
3	1.0303	.9706	3.0301	.3300	2.9410	.3400	3
4	1.0406	.9610	4.0604	.2463	3.9020	.2563	4
5	1.0510	.9515	5.1010	.1960	4.8534	.2060	5
6	1.0615	.9420	6.1520	.1625	5.7955	.1725	6
7	1.0721	.9327	7.2135	.1386	6.7282	.1486	7
8	1.0829	.9235	8.2857	.1207	7.6517	.1307	8
9	1.0937	.9143	9.3685	.1067	8.5660	.1167	9
10	1.1046	.9053	10.4622	.0956	9.4713	.1056	10
11	1.1157	.8963	11.5668	.0865	10.3676	.0965	11
12	1.1268	.8874	12.6825	.0788	11.2551	.0888	12
13	1.1381	.8787	13.8093	.0724	12.1337	.0824	13
14	1.1495	.8700	14.9474	.0669	13.0037	.0769	14
15	1.1610	.8613	16.0969	.0621	13.8651	.0721	15
16	1.1726	.8528	17.2579	.0579	14.7179	.0679	16
17	1.1843	.8444	18.4304	.0543	15.5623	.0643	17
18	1.1961	.8360	19.6147	.0510	16.3983	.0610	18
19	1.2081	.8277	20.8109	.0481	17.2260	.0581	19
20	1.2202	.8195	22.0190	.0454	18.0456	.0554	20
21	1.2324	.8114	23.2392	.0430	18.8570	.0530	21
22	1.2447	.8034	24.4716	.0409	19.6604	.0509	22
23	1.2572	.7954	25.7163	.0389	20.4558	.0489	23
24	1.2697	.7876	26.9735	.0371	21.2434	.0471	24
25	1.2824	.7798	28.2432	.0354	22.0232	.0454	25
26	1.2953	.7720	29.5256	.0339	22.7952	.0439	26
27	1.3082	.7644	30.8209	.0324	23.5596	.0424	27
28	1.3213	.7568	32.1291	.0311	24.3164	.0411	28
29	1.3345	.7493	33.4504	.0299	25.0658	.0399	29
30	1.3478	.7419	34.7849	.0287	25.8077	.0387	30
31	1.3613	.7346	36.1327	.0277	26.5423	.0377	31
32	1.3749	.7273	37.4941	.0267	27.2696	.0367	32
33	1.3887	.7201	38.8690	.0257	27.9897	.0357	33
34	1.4026	.7130	40.2577	.0248	28.7027	.0348	34
35	1.4166	.7059	41.6603	.0240	29.4086	.0340	35
36	1.4308	.6989	43.0769	.0232	30.1075	.0332	36

Interest rate of 1.25 percent

N	Compound amount Future value of a present amount F/P	Present value Present value of a future amount P/F	Annuity compound amount Future value of an annuity F/A	Sinking fund Annuity providing a future amount A/F	Annuity present value Present value of an annuity P/A	Capital recovery Annuity repaying a present amount A/P
1	1.0125	.9877	1.0000	1.0000	.9877	1.0125
2	1.0252	.9755	2.0125	.4969	1.9631	.5094
3	1.0380	.9634	3.0377	.3292	2.9265	.3417
4	1.0509	.9515	4.0756	.2454	3.8781	.2579
5	1.0641	.9398	5.1266	.1951	4.8178	.2076
6	1.0774	.9282	6.1907	.1615	5.7460	.1740
7	1.0909	.9167	7.2680	.1376	6.6627	.1501
8	1.1045	.9054	8.3589	.1196	7.5681	.1321
9	1.1183	.8942	9.4634	.1057	8.4623	.1182
10	1.1323	.8832	10.5817	.0945	9.3455	.1070
11	1.1464	.8723	11.7139	.0854	10.2178	.0979
12	1.1608	.8615	12.8604	.0778	11.0793	.0903
13	1.1753	.8509	14.0211	.0713	11.9302	.0838
14	1.1900	.8404	15.1964	.0658	12.7706	.0783
15	1.2048	.8300	16.3863	.0610	13.6005	.0735
16	1.2199	.8197	17.5912	.0568	14.4203	.0693
17	1.2351	.8096	18.8111	.0532	15.2299	.0657
18	1.2506	.7996	20.0462	.0499	16.0295	.0624
19	1.2662	.7898	21.2968	.0470	16.8193	.0595
20	1.2820	.7800	22.5630	.0443	17.5993	.0568
21	1.2981	.7704	23.8450	.0419	18.3697	.0544
22	1.3143	.7609	25.1431	.0398	19.1306	.0523
23	1.3307	.7515	26.4574	.0378	19.8820	.0503
24	1.3474	.7422	27.7881	.0360	20.6242	.0485
25	1.3642	.7330	29.1354	.0343	21.3573	.0468
26	1.3812	.7240	30.4996	.0328	22.0813	.0453
27	1.3985	.7150	31.8809	.0314	22.7963	.0439
28	1.4160	.7062	33.2794	.0300	23.5025	.0425
29	1.4337	.6975	34.6954	.0288	24.2000	.0413
30	1.4516	.6889	36.1291	.0277	24.8889	.0402
31	1.4698	.6804	37.5807	.0266	25.5693	.0391
32	1.4881	.6720	39.0504	.0256	26.2413	.0381
33	1.5067	.6637	40.5386	.0247	26.9050	.0372
34	1.5256	.6555	42.0453	.0238	27.5605	.0363
35	1.5446	.6474	43.5709	.0230	28.2079	.0355
36	1.5639	.6394	45.1155	.0222	28.8473	.0347
48	1.8154	.5509	65.2284	.0153	35.9315	.0278
60	2.1072	.4746	88.5745	.0113	42.0346	.0238
72	2.4459	.4088	115.6736	.0086	47.2925	.0211
84	2.8391	.3522	147.1290	.0068	51.8222	.0193
96	3.2955	.3034	183.6411	.0054	55.7246	.0179
108	3.8253	.2614	226.0226	.0044	59.0865	.0169
120	4.4402	.2252	275.2171	.0036	61.9828	.0161
132	5.1540	.1940	332.3198	.0030	64.4781	.0155
144	5.9825	.1672	398.6021	.0025	66.6277	.0150
156	6.9442	.1440	475.5395	.0021	68.4797	.0146
168	8.0606	.1241	564.8450	.0018	70.0751	.0143
180	9.3563	.1069	668.5068	.0015	71.4496	.0140
192	10.8604	.0921	788.8326	.0013	72.6338	.0138
204	12.6063	.0793	928.5014	.0011	73.6540	.0136
216	14.6328	.0683	1090.6225	.0009	74.5328	.0134
228	16.9851	.0589	1278.8054	.0008	75.2900	.0133
240	19.7155	.0507	1497.2395	.0007	75.9423	.0132
252	22.8848	.0437	1750.7879	.0006	76.5042	.0131
264	26.5637	.0376	2045.0953	.0005	76.9984	.0130
276	30.8339	.0324	2386.7139	.0004	77.4055	.0129
288	35.7906	.0279	2783.2493	.0004	77.7648	.0129
300	41.5441	.0241	3243.5296	.0003	78.0743	.0128
312	48.2225	.0207	3777.8020	.0003	78.3410	.0128
324	55.9745	.0179	4397.9611	.0002	78.5708	.0127
336	64.9727	.0154	5117.8136	.0002	78.7687	.0127
348	75.4173	.0133	5953.3856	.0002	78.9392	.0127
360	87.5410	.0114	6923.2796	.0001	79.0861	.0126
∞					80.0000	.0125

Interest rate of 1.50 percent

N	Compound amount — Future value of a present amount — F/P	Present value — Present value of a future amount — P/F	Annuity compound amount — Future value of an annuity — F/A	Sinking fund — Annuity providing a future amount — A/F	Annuity present value — Present value of an annuity — P/A	Capital recovery — Annuity repaying a present amount — A/P	N
1	1.0150	.9852	1.0000	1.0000	.9852	1.0150	1
2	1.0302	.9707	2.0150	.4963	1.9559	.5113	2
3	1.0457	.9563	3.0452	.3284	2.9122	.3434	3
4	1.0614	.9422	4.0909	.2444	3.8544	.2594	4
5	1.0773	.9283	5.1523	.1941	4.7826	.2091	5
6	1.0934	.9145	6.2296	.1605	5.6972	.1755	6
7	1.1098	.9010	7.3230	.1366	6.5982	.1516	7
8	1.1265	.8877	8.4328	.1186	7.4859	.1336	8
9	1.1434	.8746	9.5593	.1046	8.3605	.1196	9
10	1.1605	.8617	10.7027	.0934	9.2222	.1084	10
11	1.1779	.8489	11.8633	.0843	10.0711	.0993	11
12	1.1956	.8364	13.0412	.0767	10.9075	.0917	12
13	1.2136	.8240	14.2368	.0702	11.7315	.0852	13
14	1.2318	.8118	15.4504	.0647	12.5434	.0797	14
15	1.2502	.7999	16.6821	.0599	13.3432	.0749	15
16	1.2690	.7880	17.9324	.0558	14.1313	.0708	16
17	1.2880	.7764	19.2014	.0521	14.9076	.0671	17
18	1.3073	.7649	20.4894	.0488	15.6726	.0638	18
19	1.3270	.7536	21.7967	.0459	16.4262	.0609	19
20	1.3469	.7425	23.1237	.0432	17.1686	.0582	20
21	1.3671	.7315	24.4705	.0409	17.9001	.0559	21
22	1.3876	.7207	25.8376	.0387	18.6208	.0537	22
23	1.4084	.7100	27.2251	.0367	19.3309	.0517	23
24	1.4295	.6995	28.6335	.0349	20.0304	.0499	24
25	1.4509	.6892	30.0630	.0333	20.7196	.0483	25
26	1.4727	.6790	31.5140	.0317	21.3986	.0467	26
27	1.4948	.6690	32.9867	.0303	22.0676	.0453	27
28	1.5172	.6591	34.4815	.0290	22.7267	.0440	28
29	1.5400	.6494	35.9987	.0278	23.3761	.0428	29
30	1.5631	.6398	37.5387	.0266	24.0158	.0416	30
31	1.5865	.6303	39.1018	.0256	24.6461	.0406	31
32	1.6103	.6210	40.6883	.0246	25.2671	.0396	32
33	1.6345	.6118	42.2986	.0236	25.8790	.0386	33
34	1.6590	.6028	43.9331	.0228	26.4817	.0378	34
35	1.6839	.5939	45.5921	.0219	27.0756	.0369	35
36	1.7091	.5851	47.2760	.0212	27.6607	.0362	36

N	Compound amount — Future value of a present amount — F/P	Present value — Present value of a future amount — P/F	Annuity compound amount — Future value of an annuity — F/A	Sinking fund — Annuity providing a future amount — A/F	Annuity present value — Present value of an annuity — P/A	Capital recovery — Annuity repaying a present amount — A/P	N
40	1.8140	.5513	54.2679	.0184	29.9158	.0334	40
44	1.9253	.5194	61.6889	.0162	32.0406	.0312	44
48	2.0435	.4894	69.5652	.0144	34.0426	.0294	48
52	2.1689	.4611	77.9249	.0128	35.9287	.0278	52
56	2.3020	.4344	86.7975	.0115	37.7059	.0265	56
60	2.4432	.4039	96.2147	.0104	39.3803	.0254	60
64	2.5931	.3856	106.2096	.0094	40.9579	.0244	64
68	2.7523	.3633	116.8179	.0086	42.4442	.0236	68
72	2.9212	.3423	128.0772	.0078	43.8447	.0228	72
76	3.1004	.3225	140.0274	.0071	45.1641	.0221	76
80	3.2907	.3039	152.7109	.0065	46.4073	.0215	80
84	3.4926	.2863	166.1726	.0060	47.5786	.0210	84
88	3.7069	.2698	180.4605	.0055	48.6822	.0205	88
92	3.9344	.2542	195.6251	.0051	49.7220	.0201	92
96	4.1758	.2395	211.7202	.0047	50.7017	.0197	96
100	4.4320	.2256	228.8030	.0044	51.6247	.0194	100
104	4.7040	.2126	246.9341	.0040	52.4944	.0190	104
108	4.9927	.2003	266.1778	.0038	53.3137	.0188	108
112	5.2990	.1887	286.6023	.0035	54.0858	.0185	112
116	5.6242	.1778	308.2801	.0032	54.8131	.0182	116
120	5.9693	.1675	331.2882	.0030	55.4985	.0180	120
∞					66.6667	.0150	∞

Interest rate of 2.00 percent

N	Compound amount — Future value of a present amount F/P	Present value — Present value of a future amount P/F	Annuity compound amount — Future value of an annuity F/A	Sinking fund — Annuity providing a future amount A/F	Annuity present value — Present value of an annuity P/A	Capital recovery — Annuity repaying a present amount A/P	N
1	1.0200	.9804	1.0000	1.0000	.9804	1.0200	1
2	1.0404	.9612	2.0200	.4950	1.9416	.5150	2
3	1.0612	.9423	3.0604	.3268	2.8839	.3468	3
4	1.0824	.9238	4.1216	.2426	3.8077	.2626	4
5	1.1041	.9057	5.2040	.1922	4.7135	.2122	5
6	1.1262	.8880	6.3081	.1585	5.6014	.1785	6
7	1.1487	.8706	7.4343	.1345	6.4720	.1545	7
8	1.1717	.8535	8.5830	.1165	7.3255	.1365	8
9	1.1951	.8368	9.7546	.1025	8.1622	.1225	9
10	1.2190	.8203	10.9497	.0913	8.9826	.1113	10
11	1.2434	.8043	12.1687	.0822	9.7868	.1022	11
12	1.2682	.7885	13.4121	.0746	10.5753	.0946	12
13	1.2936	.7730	14.6803	.0681	11.3484	.0881	13
14	1.3195	.7579	15.9739	.0626	12.1062	.0826	14
15	1.3459	.7430	17.2934	.0578	12.8493	.0778	15
16	1.3728	.7284	18.6393	.0537	13.5777	.0737	16
17	1.4002	.7142	20.0121	.0500	14.2919	.0700	17
18	1.4282	.7002	21.4123	.0467	14.9920	.0667	18
19	1.4568	.6864	22.8406	.0438	15.6785	.0638	19
20	1.4859	.6730	24.2974	.0412	16.3514	.0612	20
21	1.5157	.6598	25.7833	.0388	17.0112	.0588	21
22	1.5460	.6468	27.2990	.0366	17.6580	.0566	22
23	1.5769	.6342	28.8450	.0347	18.2922	.0547	23
24	1.6084	.6217	30.4219	.0329	18.9139	.0529	24
25	1.6406	.6095	32.0303	.0312	19.5235	.0512	25
26	1.6734	.5976	33.6709	.0297	20.1210	.0497	26
27	1.7069	.5859	35.3443	.0283	20.7069	.0483	27
28	1.7410	.5744	37.0512	.0270	21.2813	.0470	28
29	1.7758	.5631	38.7922	.0258	21.8444	.0458	29
30	1.8114	.5521	40.5681	.0246	22.3965	.0446	30
31	1.8476	.5412	42.3794	.0236	22.9377	.0436	31
32	1.8845	.5306	44.2270	.0226	23.4683	.0426	32
33	1.9222	.5202	46.1116	.0217	23.9886	.0417	33
34	1.9607	.5100	48.0338	.0208	24.4986	.0408	34
35	1.9999	.5000	49.9945	.0200	24.9986	.0400	35
36	2.0399	.4902	51.9944	.0192	25.4888	.0392	36

N	Compound amount — Future value of a present amount F/P	Present value — Present value of a future amount P/F	Annuity compound amount — Future value of an annuity F/A	Sinking fund — Annuity providing a future amount A/F	Annuity present value — Present value of an annuity P/A	Capital recovery — Annuity repaying a present amount A/P	N
40	2.2080	.4529	60.4020	.0166	27.3555	.0366	40
44	2.3901	.4184	69.5027	.0144	29.0800	.0344	44
48	2.5871	.3865	79.3535	.0126	30.6731	.0326	48
52	2.8003	.3571	90.0164	.0111	32.1449	.0311	52
56	3.0312	.3299	101.5583	.0098	33.5047	.0298	56
60	3.2810	.3048	114.0515	.0088	34.7609	.0288	60
64	3.5515	.2816	127.5747	.0078	35.9214	.0278	64
68	3.8443	.2601	142.2125	.0070	36.9936	.0270	68
72	4.1611	.2403	158.0570	.0063	37.9841	.0263	72
76	4.5042	.2220	175.2076	.0057	38.8991	.0257	76
80	4.8754	.2051	193.7720	.0052	39.7445	.0252	80
84	5.2773	.1895	213.8666	.0047	40.5255	.0247	84
88	5.7124	.1751	235.6177	.0042	41.2470	.0242	88
92	6.1832	.1617	259.1618	.0039	41.9136	.0239	92
96	6.6929	.1494	284.6467	.0035	42.5294	.0235	96
100	7.2446	.1380	312.2323	.0032	43.0984	.0232	100
104	7.8418	.1275	342.0919	.0029	43.6239	.0229	104
108	8.4883	.1178	374.4129	.0027	44.1095	.0227	108
112	9.1880	.1088	409.3981	.0024	44.5581	.0224	112
116	9.9453	.1005	447.2673	.0022	44.9725	.0222	116
120	10.7652	.0929	488.2582	.0020	45.3554	.0220	120
∞					50.0000	.0200	∞

Interest rate of 3.00 percent

N	Compound amount — Future value of a present amount F/P	Present value — Present value of a future amount P/F	Annuity compound amount — Future value of an annuity F/A	Sinking fund — Annuity providing a future amount A/F	Annuity present value — Present value of an annuity P/A	Capital recovery — Annuity repaying a present amount A/P	N
1	1.0300	.9709	1.0000	1.0000	.9709	1.0300	1
2	1.0609	.9426	2.0300	.4926	1.9135	.5226	2
3	1.0927	.9151	3.0909	.3235	2.8286	.3535	3
4	1.1255	.8885	4.1836	.2390	3.7171	.2690	4
5	1.1593	.8626	5.3091	.1884	4.5797	.2184	5
6	1.1941	.8375	6.4684	.1546	5.4172	.1846	6
7	1.2299	.8131	7.6625	.1305	6.2303	.1605	7
8	1.2668	.7894	8.8923	.1125	7.0197	.1425	8
9	1.3048	.7664	10.1591	.0984	7.7861	.1284	9
10	1.3439	.7441	11.4639	.0872	8.5302	.1172	10
11	1.3842	.7224	12.8078	.0781	9.2526	.1081	11
12	1.4258	.7014	14.1920	.0705	9.9540	.1005	12
13	1.4685	.6810	15.6178	.0640	10.6350	.0940	13
14	1.5126	.6611	17.0863	.0585	11.2961	.0885	14
15	1.5580	.6419	18.5989	.0538	11.9379	.0838	15
16	1.6047	.6232	20.1569	.0496	12.5611	.0796	16
17	1.6528	.6050	21.7616	.0460	13.1661	.0760	17
18	1.7024	.5874	23.4144	.0427	13.7535	.0727	18
19	1.7535	.5703	25.1169	.0398	14.3238	.0698	19
20	1.8061	.5537	26.8704	.0372	14.8775	.0672	20
21	1.8603	.5375	28.6765	.0349	15.4150	.0649	21
22	1.9161	.5219	30.5368	.0327	15.9369	.0627	22
23	1.9736	.5067	32.4529	.0308	16.4436	.0608	23
24	2.0328	.4919	34.4265	.0290	16.9355	.0590	24
25	2.0938	.4776	36.4593	.0274	17.4131	.0574	25
26	2.1566	.4637	38.5530	.0259	17.8768	.0559	26
27	2.2213	.4502	40.7096	.0246	18.3270	.0546	27
28	2.2879	.4371	42.9309	.0233	18.7641	.0533	28
29	2.3566	.4243	45.2189	.0221	19.1885	.0521	29
30	2.4273	.4120	47.5754	.0210	19.6004	.0510	30
31	2.5001	.4000	50.0027	.0200	20.0004	.0500	31
32	2.5751	.3883	52.5028	.0190	20.3888	.0490	32
33	2.6523	.3770	55.0778	.0182	20.7658	.0482	33
34	2.7319	.3660	57.7302	.0173	21.1318	.0473	34
35	2.8139	.3554	60.4621	.0165	21.4872	.0465	35
36	2.8983	.3450	63.2759	.0158	21.8323	.0458	36

N	Compound amount — Future value of a present amount F/P	Present value — Present value of a future amount P/F	Annuity compound amount — Future value of an annuity F/A	Sinking fund — Annuity providing a future amount A/F	Annuity present value — Present value of an annuity P/A	Capital recovery — Annuity repaying a present amount A/P	N
40	3.2620	.3066	75.4013	.0133	23.1148	.0433	40
44	3.6715	.2724	89.0484	.0112	24.2543	.0412	44
48	4.1323	.2420	104.4084	.0096	25.2667	.0396	48
52	4.6509	.2150	121.6962	.0082	26.1662	.0382	52
56	5.2346	.1910	141.1538	.0071	26.9655	.0371	56
60	5.8916	.1697	163.0534	.0061	27.6756	.0361	60
64	6.6311	.1508	187.7017	.0053	28.3065	.0353	64
68	7.4633	.1340	215.4436	.0046	28.8670	.0346	68
72	8.4000	.1190	246.6672	.0041	29.3651	.0341	72
76	9.4543	.1058	281.8098	.0035	29.8076	.0335	76
80	10.6409	.0940	321.3630	.0031	30.0208	.0331	80
84	11.9764	.0835	365.8805	.0027	30.5501	.0327	84
88	13.4796	.0742	415.9854	.0024	30.8605	.0324	88
92	15.1714	.0659	472.3789	.0021	31.1362	.0321	92
96	17.0755	.0586	535.8502	.0019	31.3812	.0319	96
100	19.2186	.0520	607.2877	.0016	31.5989	.0316	100
104	21.6307	.0462	687.6913	.0015	31.7923	.0315	104
108	24.3456	.0411	778.1863	.0013	31.9642	.0313	108
112	27.4012	.0365	880.0391	.0011	32.1168	.0311	112
116	30.8403	.0324	994.6754	.0010	32.2525	.0310	116
120	34.7110	.0288	1123.6996	.0009	32.3730	.0309	120
∞					33.3333	.0300	∞

Interest rate of 4.00 percent

N	Compound amount — Future value of a present amount F/P	Present value — Present value of a future amount P/F	Annuity compound amount — Future value of an annuity F/A	Sinking fund — Annuity providing a future amount A/F	Annuity present value — Present value of an annuity P/A	Capital recovery — Annuity repaying a present amount A/P	N
1	1.0400	.9615	1.0000	1.0000	.9615	1.0400	1
2	1.0816	.9246	2.0400	.4902	1.8861	.5302	2
3	1.1249	.8890	3.1216	.3203	2.7751	.3603	3
4	1.1699	.8548	4.2465	.2355	3.6299	.2755	4
5	1.2167	.8219	5.4163	.1846	4.4518	.2246	5
6	1.2653	.7903	6.6330	.1508	5.2421	.1908	6
7	1.3159	.7599	7.8983	.1266	6.0021	.1666	7
8	1.3686	.7307	9.2142	.1085	6.7327	.1485	8
9	1.4233	.7026	10.5828	.0945	7.4353	.1345	9
10	1.4802	.6756	12.0061	.0833	8.1109	.1233	10
11	1.5395	.6496	13.4864	.0741	8.7605	.1141	11
12	1.6010	.6246	15.0258	.0666	9.3851	.1066	12
13	1.6651	.6006	16.6268	.0601	9.9856	.1001	13
14	1.7317	.5775	18.2919	.0547	10.5631	.0947	14
15	1.8009	.5553	20.0236	.0499	11.1184	.0899	15
16	1.8730	.5339	21.8245	.0458	11.6523	.0858	16
17	1.9479	.5134	23.6975	.0422	12.1657	.0822	17
18	2.0258	.4936	25.6454	.0390	12.6593	.0790	18
19	2.1068	.4746	27.6712	.0361	13.1339	.0761	19
20	2.1911	.4564	29.7781	.0336	13.5903	.0736	20
21	2.2788	.4388	31.9692	.0313	14.0292	.0713	21
22	2.3699	.4220	34.2480	.0292	14.4511	.0692	22
23	2.4647	.4057	36.6179	.0273	14.8568	.0673	23
24	2.5633	.3901	39.0826	.0256	15.2470	.0656	24
25	2.6658	.3751	41.6459	.0240	15.6221	.0640	25
26	2.7725	.3607	44.3117	.0226	15.9828	.0626	26
27	2.8834	.3468	47.0842	.0212	16.3296	.0612	27
28	2.9987	.3335	49.9676	.0200	16.6631	.0600	28
29	3.1187	.3207	52.9663	.0189	16.9837	.0589	29
30	3.2434	.3083	56.0849	.0178	17.2920	.0578	30
31	3.3731	.2965	59.3283	.0169	17.5885	.0569	31
32	3.5081	.2851	62.7015	.0159	17.8736	.0559	32
33	3.6484	.2741	66.2095	.0151	18.1476	.0551	33
34	3.7943	.2636	69.8579	.0143	18.4112	.0543	34
35	3.9461	.2534	73.6522	.0136	18.6646	.0536	35
36	4.1039	.2437	77.5983	.0129	18.9083	.0529	36

N	Compound amount — Future value of a present amount F/P	Present value — Present value of a future amount P/F	Annuity compound amount — Future value of an annuity F/A	Sinking fund — Annuity providing a future amount A/F	Annuity present value — Present value of an annuity P/A	Capital recovery — Annuity repaying a present amount A/P	N
40	4.8010	.2083	95.0255	.0105	19.7928	.0505	40
44	5.6165	.1780	115.4129	.0087	20.5488	.0487	44
48	6.6705	.1522	139.2632	.0072	21.1951	.0472	48
52	7.6866	.1301	167.1647	.0060	21.7476	.0460	52
56	8.9922	.1112	199.8055	.0050	22.2198	.0450	56
60	10.5196	.0951	237.9907	.0042	22.6235	.0442	60
64	12.3065	.0813	282.6619	.0035	22.9685	.0435	64
68	14.3968	.0695	334.9209	.0030	23.2635	.0430	68
72	16.8423	.0594	396.0566	.0025	23.5156	.0425	72
76	19.7031	.0508	467.5766	.0021	23.7312	.0421	76
80	23.0498	.0434	551.2450	.0018	23.9154	.0418	80
84	26.9650	.0371	649.1251	.0015	24.0729	.0415	84
88	31.5452	.0317	763.6310	.0013	24.2075	.0413	88
92	36.9035	.0271	897.5868	.0011	24.3226	.0411	92
96	43.1718	.0232	1054.2960	.0009	24.4209	.0409	96
100	50.5049	.0198	1237.6237	.0008	24.5050	.0408	100
104	59.0836	.0169	1452.0911	.0007	24.5769	.0407	104
108	69.1195	.0145	1702.9877	.0006	24.6383	.0406	108
112	80.8600	.0124	1996.5012	.0005	24.6908	.0405	112
116	94.5948	.0106	2339.8705	.0004	24.7357	.0404	116
120	110.6626	.0090	2741.5640	.0004	24.7741	.0404	120
∞					25.0000	.0400	∞

Interest rate of 5.00 percent

N	Compound amount — Future value of a present amount F/P	Present value — Present value of a future amount P/F	Annuity compound amount — Future value of an annuity F/A	Sinking fund — Annuity providing a future amount A/F	Annuity present value — Present value of an annuity P/A	Capital recovery — Annuity repaying a present amount A/P	N
1	1.0500	.9524	1.0000	1.0000	.9524	1.0500	1
2	1.1025	.9070	2.0500	.4878	1.8594	.5378	2
3	1.1576	.8638	3.1525	.3172	2.7232	.3672	3
4	1.2155	.8227	4.3101	.2320	3.5460	.2820	4
5	1.2763	.7835	5.5256	.1810	4.3295	.2310	5
6	1.3401	.7462	6.8019	.1470	5.0757	.1970	6
7	1.4071	.7107	8.1420	.1228	5.7864	.1728	7
8	1.4775	.6768	9.5491	.1047	6.4632	.1547	8
9	1.5513	.6446	11.0266	.0907	7.1078	.1407	9
10	1.6289	.6139	12.5779	.0795	7.7217	.1295	10
11	1.7103	.5847	14.2068	.0704	8.3064	.1204	11
12	1.7959	.5568	15.9171	.0628	8.8633	.1128	12
13	1.8856	.5303	17.7130	.0565	9.3936	.1065	13
14	1.9799	.5051	19.5986	.0510	9.8886	.1010	14
15	2.0789	.4810	21.5786	.0463	10.3797	.0963	15
16	2.1829	.4581	23.6575	.0423	10.8378	.0923	16
17	2.2920	.4363	25.8404	.0387	11.2741	.0887	17
18	2.4066	.4155	28.1324	.0355	11.6896	.0855	18
19	2.5270	.3957	30.5390	.0327	12.0853	.0827	19
20	2.6533	.3769	33.0660	.0302	12.4622	.0802	20
21	2.7860	.3589	35.7193	.0280	12.8212	.0780	21
22	2.9253	.3418	38.5052	.0260	13.1630	.0760	22
23	3.0715	.3256	41.4305	.0241	13.4886	.0741	23
24	3.2251	.3101	44.5020	.0225	13.7986	.0725	24
25	3.3864	.2953	47.7271	.0210	14.0939	.0710	25
26	3.5557	.2812	51.1135	.0196	14.3752	.0696	26
27	3.7335	.2678	54.6691	.0183	14.6430	.0683	27
28	3.9201	.2551	58.4026	.0171	14.8981	.0671	28
29	4.1161	.2429	62.3227	.0160	15.1411	.0660	29
30	4.3219	.2314	66.4388	.0151	15.3725	.0651	30
31	4.5380	.2204	70.7608	.0141	15.5928	.0641	31
32	4.7649	.2099	75.2988	.0133	15.8027	.0633	32
33	5.0032	.1999	80.0638	.0125	16.0025	.0625	33
34	5.2533	.1904	85.0670	.0118	16.1929	.0618	34
35	5.5160	.1813	90.3203	.0111	16.3742	.0611	35
36	5.7918	.1727	95.8363	.0104	16.5469	.0604	36

N	Compound amount — Future value of a present amount F/P	Present value — Present value of a future amount P/F	Annuity compound amount — Future value of an annuity F/A	Sinking fund — Annuity providing a future amount A/F	Annuity present value — Present value of an annuity P/A	Capital recovery — Annuity repaying a present amount A/P	N
40	7.0400	.1420	120.7998	.0083	17.1591	.0583	40
44	8.5572	.1169	151.1430	.0066	17.6628	.0566	44
48	10.4013	.0961	188.0254	.0053	18.0772	.0553	48
52	12.6428	.0791	232.8562	.0043	18.4181	.0543	52
56	15.3674	.0651	287.3482	.0035	18.6985	.0535	56
60	18.6792	.0535	353.5837	.0028	18.9293	.0528	60
64	22.7047	.0440	434.0933	.0023	19.1191	.0523	64
68	27.5977	.0362	531.9533	.0019	19.2753	.0519	68
72	33.5451	.0298	650.9027	.0015	19.4038	.0515	72
76	40.7743	.0245	795.4864	.0013	19.5095	.0513	76
80	49.5614	.0202	971.2288	.0010	19.5965	.0510	80
84	60.2422	.0166	1184.8448	.0008	19.6680	.0508	84
88	73.2248	.0137	1444.4964	.0007	19.7269	.0507	88
92	89.0052	.0112	1760.1045	.0006	19.7753	.0506	92
96	108.1864	.0092	2143.7282	.0005	19.8151	.0505	96
100	131.5013	.0076	2610.0252	.0004	19.8479	.0504	100
104	159.8406	.0063	3176.8120	.0003	19.8749	.0503	104
108	194.2872	.0051	3865.7450	.0003	19.8971	.0503	108
112	236.1574	.0042	4703.1473	.0002	19.9153	.0502	112
116	287.0508	.0035	5721.0151	.0002	19.9303	.0502	116
120	348.9120	.0029	6958.2397	.0001	19.9427	.0501	120
∞					20.0000	.0500	∞

Interest rate of 6.00 percent

N	Compound amount — Future value of a present amount — F/P	Present value — Present value of a future amount — P/F	Annuity compound amount — Future value of an annuity — F/A	Sinking fund — Annuity providing a future amount — A/F	Annuity present value — Present value of an annuity — P/A	Capital recovery — Annuity repaying a present amount — A/P
1	1.0600	.9434	1.0000	1.0000	.9434	1.0600
2	1.1236	.8900	2.0600	.4854	1.8334	.5454
3	1.1910	.8396	3.1836	.3141	2.6730	.3741
4	1.2625	.7921	4.3746	.2286	3.4651	.2886
5	1.3382	.7473	5.6371	.1774	4.2124	.2374
6	1.4185	.7050	6.9753	.1434	4.9173	.2034
7	1.5036	.6651	8.3938	.1191	5.5824	.1791
8	1.5938	.6274	9.8975	.1010	6.2098	.1610
9	1.6895	.5919	11.4913	.0870	6.8017	.1470
10	1.7908	.5584	13.1808	.0759	7.3601	.1359
11	1.8983	.5268	14.9716	.0668	7.8869	.1268
12	2.0122	.4970	16.8699	.0593	8.3838	.1193
13	2.1329	.4688	18.8821	.0530	8.8527	.1130
14	2.2609	.4423	21.0151	.0476	9.2950	.1076
15	2.3966	.4173	23.2760	.0430	9.7122	.1030
16	2.5404	.3936	25.6725	.0390	10.1059	.0990
17	2.6928	.3714	28.2129	.0354	10.4773	.0954
18	2.8543	.3503	30.9057	.0324	10.8276	.0924
19	3.0256	.3305	33.7600	.0296	11.1581	.0896
20	3.2071	.3118	36.7856	.0272	11.4699	.0872
21	3.3996	.2942	39.9927	.0250	11.7641	.0850
22	3.6035	.2775	43.3923	.0230	12.0416	.0830
23	3.8197	.2618	46.9958	.0213	12.3034	.0813
24	4.0489	.2470	50.8156	.0197	12.5504	.0797
25	4.2919	.2330	54.8645	.0182	12.7834	.0782
26	4.5494	.2198	59.1564	.0169	13.0032	.0769
27	4.8223	.2074	63.7058	.0157	13.2105	.0757
28	5.1117	.1956	68.5281	.0146	13.4062	.0746
29	5.4184	.1846	73.6398	.0136	13.5907	.0736
30	5.7435	.1741	79.0582	.0126	13.7648	.0726
31	6.0881	.1643	84.8017	.0118	13.9291	.0718
32	6.4534	.1550	90.8898	.0110	14.0840	.0710
33	6.8406	.1462	97.3432	.0103	14.2302	.0703
34	7.2510	.1379	104.1838	.0096	14.3681	.0696
35	7.6861	.1301	111.4348	.0090	14.4982	.0690
36	8.1473	.1227	119.1209	.0084	14.6210	.0684

N	Compound amount — Future value of a present amount — F/P	Present value — Present value of a future amount — P/F	Annuity compound amount — Future value of an annuity — F/A	Sinking fund — Annuity providing a future amount — A/F	Annuity present value — Present value of an annuity — P/A	Capital recovery — Annuity repaying a present amount — A/P
40	10.2857	.0972	154.7620	.0065	15.0463	.0665
44	12.9855	.0770	199.7580	.0050	15.3832	.0650
48	16.3939	.0610	256.5645	.0039	15.6500	.0639
52	20.6969	.0483	328.2814	.0030	15.8614	.0630
56	26.1293	.0383	418.8223	.0024	16.0288	.0624
60	32.9877	.0303	533.1282	.0019	16.1614	.0619
64	41.6462	.0240	677.4367	.0015	16.2665	.0615
68	52.5774	.0190	859.6228	.0012	16.3497	.0612
72	66.3777	.0151	1089.6286	.0009	16.4156	.0609
76	83.8003	.0119	1380.0056	.0007	16.4678	.0607
80	105.7960	.0095	1746.5999	.0006	16.5091	.0606
84	133.5650	.0075	2209.4167	.0005	16.5419	.0605
88	168.6227	.0059	2793.7123	.0004	16.5678	.0604
92	212.8823	.0047	3531.3721	.0003	16.5884	.0603
96	268.7590	.0037	4462.6505	.0002	16.6047	.0602
100	339.3021	.0029	5638.3681	.0002	16.6175	.0602
104	428.3611	.0023	7122.6844	.0001	16.6278	.0601
108	540.7960	.0018	8996.5995	.0001	16.6358	.0601
112	682.7425	.0015	11362.3743	.0001	16.6423	.0601
116	861.9466	.0012	14349.1103	.0001	16.6473	.0601
120	1088.1877	.0009	18119.7958	.0001	16.6514	.0601
∞					16.6667	.0600

APPENDIX A Interest rates of 7.00 and 8.00 percent

Interest rate of 8.00 percent

N	Compound amount — Future value of a present amount (F/P)	Present value — Present value of a future amount (P/F)	Annuity compound amount — Future value of an annuity (F/A)	Sinking fund — Annuity providing a future amount (A/F)	Annuity present value — Present value of an annuity (P/A)	Capital recovery — Annuity repaying a present amount (A/P)	N
1	1.0800	.9259	1.0000	1.0000	.9259	1.0800	1
2	1.1664	.8573	2.0800	.4808	1.7833	.5608	2
3	1.2597	.7938	3.2464	.3080	2.5771	.3880	3
4	1.3605	.7350	4.5061	.2219	3.3121	.3019	4
5	1.4693	.6806	5.8666	.1705	3.9927	.2505	5
6	1.5869	.6302	7.3359	.1363	4.6229	.2163	6
7	1.7138	.5835	8.9228	.1121	5.2064	.1921	7
8	1.8509	.5403	10.6366	.0940	5.7466	.1740	8
9	1.9990	.5002	12.4876	.0801	6.2469	.1601	9
10	2.1589	.4632	14.4866	.0690	6.7101	.1490	10
11	2.3316	.4289	16.6455	.0601	7.1390	.1401	11
12	2.5182	.3971	18.9771	.0527	7.5361	.1327	12
13	2.7196	.3677	21.4953	.0465	7.9038	.1265	13
14	2.9372	.3405	24.2149	.0413	8.2442	.1213	14
15	3.1722	.3152	27.1521	.0368	8.5595	.1168	15
16	3.4259	.2919	30.3243	.0330	8.8514	.1130	16
17	3.7000	.2703	33.7502	.0296	9.1216	.1096	17
18	3.9960	.2502	37.4502	.0267	9.3719	.1067	18
19	4.3157	.2317	41.4463	.0241	9.6036	.1041	19
20	4.6610	.2145	45.7620	.0219	9.8181	.1019	20
21	5.0338	.1987	50.4229	.0198	10.0168	.0998	21
22	5.4365	.1839	55.4568	.0180	10.2007	.0980	22
23	5.8715	.1703	60.8933	.0164	10.3711	.0964	23
24	6.3412	.1577	66.7648	.0150	10.5288	.0950	24
25	6.8485	.1460	73.1059	.0137	10.6748	.0937	25
26	7.3964	.1352	79.9544	.0125	10.8100	.0925	26
27	7.9881	.1252	87.3508	.0114	10.9352	.0914	27
28	8.6271	.1159	95.3388	.0105	11.0511	.0905	28
29	9.3173	.1073	103.9659	.0096	11.1584	.0896	29
30	10.0627	.0994	113.2832	.0088	11.2578	.0888	30
35	14.7853	.0676	172.3168	.0058	11.6546	.0858	35
40	21.7245	.0460	259.0565	.0039	11.9246	.0839	40
45	31.9204	.0313	386.5056	.0026	12.1084	.0826	45
50	46.9016	.0213	573.7702	.0017	12.2335	.0817	50
55	68.9139	.0145	848.9232	.0012	12.3186	.0812	55
60	101.2571	.0099	1253.2133	.0008	12.3766	.0808	60
∞					12.5000	.0800	∞

Interest rate of 7.00 percent

N	Compound amount — Future value of a present amount (F/P)	Present value — Present value of a future amount (P/F)	Annuity compound amount — Future value of an annuity (F/A)	Sinking fund — Annuity providing a future amount (A/F)	Annuity present value — Present value of an annuity (P/A)	Capital recovery — Annuity repaying a present amount (A/P)	N
1	1.0700	.9346	1.0000	1.0000	.9346	1.0700	1
2	1.1449	.8734	2.0700	.4831	1.8080	.5531	2
3	1.2250	.8163	3.2149	.3111	2.6243	.3811	3
4	1.3108	.7629	4.4399	.2252	3.3872	.2952	4
5	1.4026	.7130	5.7507	.1739	4.1002	.2439	5
6	1.5007	.6663	7.1533	.1398	4.7665	.2098	6
7	1.6058	.6227	8.6540	.1156	5.3893	.1856	7
8	1.7182	.5820	10.2598	.0975	5.9713	.1675	8
9	1.8385	.5439	11.9780	.0835	6.5152	.1535	9
10	1.9672	.5083	13.8164	.0724	7.0236	.1424	10
11	2.1049	.4751	15.7836	.0634	7.4987	.1334	11
12	2.2522	.4440	17.8885	.0559	7.9427	.1259	12
13	2.4098	.4150	20.1406	.0497	8.3577	.1197	13
14	2.5785	.3878	22.5505	.0443	8.7455	.1143	14
15	2.7590	.3624	25.1290	.0398	9.1079	.1098	15
16	2.9522	.3387	27.8881	.0359	9.4466	.1059	16
17	3.1588	.3166	30.8402	.0324	9.7632	.1024	17
18	3.3799	.2959	33.9990	.0294	10.0591	.0994	18
19	3.6165	.2765	37.3790	.0268	10.3356	.0968	19
20	3.8697	.2584	40.9955	.0244	10.5940	.0944	20
21	4.1406	.2415	44.8652	.0223	10.8355	.0923	21
22	4.4304	.2257	49.0057	.0204	11.0612	.0904	22
23	4.7405	.2109	53.4361	.0187	11.2722	.0887	23
24	5.0724	.1971	58.1767	.0172	11.4693	.0872	24
25	5.4274	.1842	63.2490	.0158	11.6536	.0858	25
26	5.8074	.1722	68.6765	.0146	11.8258	.0846	26
27	6.2139	.1609	74.4838	.0134	11.9867	.0834	27
28	6.6488	.1504	80.6977	.0124	12.1371	.0824	28
29	7.1143	.1406	87.3465	.0114	12.2777	.0814	29
30	7.6123	.1314	94.4608	.0106	12.4090	.0806	30
35	10.6766	.0937	138.2369	.0072	12.9477	.0772	35
40	14.9745	.0668	199.6351	.0050	13.3317	.0750	40
45	21.0025	.0476	285.7493	.0035	13.6055	.0735	45
50	29.4570	.0339	406.5289	.0025	13.8007	.0725	50
55	41.3150	.0242	575.9286	.0017	13.9399	.0717	55
60	57.9464	.0173	813.5204	.0012	14.0392	.0712	60
∞					14.2857	.0700	∞

Interest rate of 10.00 percent

N	Compound amount — Future value of a present amount — F/P	Present value — Present value of a future amount — P/F	Annuity compound amount — Future value of an annuity — F/A	Sinking fund — Annuity providing a future amount — A/F	Annuity present value — Present value of an annuity — P/A	Capital recovery — Annuity repaying a present amount — A/P	N
1	1.1000	.9091	1.0000	1.0000	.9091	1.1000	1
2	1.2100	.8264	2.1000	.4762	1.7355	.5762	2
3	1.3310	.7513	3.3100	.3021	2.4869	.4021	3
4	1.4641	.6830	4.6410	.2155	3.1699	.3155	4
5	1.6105	.6209	6.1051	.1638	3.7908	.2638	5
6	1.7716	.5645	7.7156	.1296	4.3553	.2296	6
7	1.9487	.5132	9.4872	.1054	4.8684	.2054	7
8	2.1436	.4665	11.4359	.0874	5.3349	.1874	8
9	2.3579	.4241	13.5795	.0736	5.7590	.1736	9
10	2.5937	.3855	15.9374	.0627	6.1446	.1627	10
11	2.8531	.3505	18.5312	.0540	6.4951	.1540	11
12	3.1384	.3186	21.3843	.0468	6.8137	.1468	12
13	3.4523	.2897	24.5227	.0408	7.1034	.1408	13
14	3.7975	.2633	27.9750	.0357	7.3667	.1357	14
15	4.1772	.2394	31.7725	.0315	7.6061	.1315	15
16	4.5950	.2176	35.9497	.0278	7.8237	.1278	16
17	5.0545	.1978	40.5447	.0247	8.0216	.1247	17
18	5.5599	.1799	45.5992	.0219	8.2014	.1219	18
19	6.1159	.1635	51.1591	.0195	8.3649	.1195	19
20	6.7275	.1486	57.2750	.0175	8.5136	.1175	20
21	7.4002	.1351	64.0025	.0156	8.6487	.1156	21
22	8.1403	.1228	71.4027	.0140	8.7715	.1140	22
23	8.9543	.1117	79.5430	.0126	8.8832	.1126	23
24	9.8497	.1015	88.4973	.0113	8.9847	.1113	24
25	10.8347	.0923	98.3471	.0102	9.0770	.1102	25
26	11.9182	.0839	109.1818	.0092	9.1609	.1092	26
27	13.1100	.0763	121.0999	.0083	9.2372	.1083	27
28	14.4210	.0693	134.2099	.0075	9.3066	.1075	28
29	15.8631	.0630	148.6309	.0067	9.3696	.1067	29
30	17.4494	.0573	164.4940	.0061	9.4269	.1061	30
35	28.1024	.0356	271.0244	.0037	9.6442	.1037	35
40	45.2593	.0221	442.5926	.0023	9.7791	.1023	40
45	72.8905	.0137	718.9048	.0014	9.8628	.1014	45
50	117.3909	.0085	1163.9085	.0009	9.9148	.1009	50
55	189.0591	.0053	1880.5914	.0005	9.9471	.1005	55
60	304.4816	.0033	3034.8164	.0003	9.9672	.1003	60
∞					10.0000	.1000	∞

Interest rate of 9.00 percent

N	Compound amount — Future value of a present amount — F/P	Present value — Present value of a future amount — P/F	Annuity compound amount — Future value of an annuity — F/A	Sinking fund — Annuity providing a future amount — A/F	Annuity present value — Present value of an annuity — P/A	Capital recovery — Annuity repaying a present amount — A/P	N
1	1.0900	.9174	1.0000	1.0000	.9174	1.0900	1
2	1.1881	.8417	2.0900	.4785	1.7591	.5685	2
3	1.2950	.7722	3.2781	.3051	2.5313	.3951	3
4	1.4116	.7084	4.5731	.2187	3.2397	.3087	4
5	1.5386	.6499	5.9847	.1671	3.8897	.2571	5
6	1.6771	.5963	7.5233	.1329	4.4859	.2229	6
7	1.8280	.5470	9.2004	.1087	5.0330	.1987	7
8	1.9926	.5019	11.0285	.0907	5.5348	.1807	8
9	2.1719	.4604	13.0210	.0768	5.9952	.1668	9
10	2.3674	.4224	15.1929	.0658	6.4177	.1558	10
11	2.5804	.3875	17.5603	.0569	6.8052	.1469	11
12	2.8127	.3555	20.1407	.0497	7.1607	.1397	12
13	3.0658	.3262	22.9534	.0436	7.4869	.1336	13
14	3.3417	.2992	26.0192	.0384	7.7862	.1284	14
15	3.6425	.2745	29.3609	.0341	8.0607	.1241	15
16	3.9703	.2519	33.0034	.0303	8.3126	.1203	16
17	4.3276	.2311	36.9737	.0270	8.5436	.1170	17
18	4.7171	.2120	41.3013	.0242	8.7556	.1142	18
19	5.1417	.1945	46.0185	.0217	8.9501	.1117	19
20	5.6044	.1784	51.1601	.0195	9.1285	.1095	20
21	6.1088	.1637	56.7645	.0176	9.2922	.1076	21
22	6.6586	.1502	62.8733	.0159	9.4424	.1059	22
23	7.2579	.1378	69.5319	.0144	9.5802	.1044	23
24	7.9111	.1264	76.7898	.0130	9.7066	.1030	24
25	8.6231	.1160	84.7009	.0118	9.8226	.1018	25
26	9.3992	.1064	93.3240	.0107	9.9290	.1007	26
27	10.2451	.0976	102.7231	.0097	10.0266	.0997	27
28	11.1671	.0895	112.9682	.0089	10.1161	.0989	28
29	12.1722	.0822	124.1354	.0081	10.1983	.0981	29
30	13.2677	.0754	136.3075	.0073	10.2737	.0973	30
35	20.4140	.0490	215.7108	.0046	10.5668	.0946	35
40	31.4094	.0318	337.8824	.0030	10.7574	.0930	40
45	48.3273	.0207	525.8587	.0019	10.8812	.0919	45
50	74.3575	.0134	815.0836	.0012	10.9617	.0912	50
55	114.4083	.0087	1260.0918	.0008	11.0140	.0908	55
60	176.0313	.0057	1944.7921	.0005	11.0480	.0905	60
∞					11.1111	.0900	∞

Interest rate of 11.00 percent

N	Compound amount — Future value of a present amount — F/P	Present value — Present value of a future amount — P/F	Annuity compound amount — Future value of an annuity — F/A	Sinking fund — Annuity providing a future amount — A/F	Annuity present value — Present value of an annuity — P/A	Capital recovery — Annuity repaying a present amount — A/P	N
1	1.1100	.9009	1.0000	1.0000	.9009	1.1100	1
2	1.2321	.8116	2.1100	.4739	1.7125	.5839	2
3	1.3676	.7312	3.3421	.2992	2.4437	.4092	3
4	1.5181	.6587	4.7097	.2123	3.1024	.3223	4
5	1.6851	.5935	6.2278	.1606	3.6959	.2706	5
6	1.8704	.5346	7.9129	.1264	4.2305	.2364	6
7	2.0762	.4817	9.7833	.1022	4.7122	.2122	7
8	2.3045	.4339	11.8594	.0843	5.1461	.1943	8
9	2.5580	.3909	14.1640	.0706	5.5370	.1806	9
10	2.8394	.3522	16.7220	.0598	5.8892	.1698	10
11	3.1518	.3173	19.5614	.0511	6.2065	.1611	11
12	3.4985	.2858	22.7132	.0440	6.4924	.1540	12
13	3.8833	.2575	26.2116	.0382	6.7499	.1482	13
14	4.3104	.2320	30.0949	.0332	6.9819	.1432	14
15	4.7846	.2090	34.4054	.0291	7.1909	.1391	15
16	5.3109	.1883	39.1899	.0255	7.3792	.1355	16
17	5.8951	.1696	44.5008	.0225	7.5488	.1325	17
18	6.5436	.1528	50.3959	.0198	7.7016	.1298	18
19	7.2633	.1377	56.9395	.0176	7.8393	.1276	19
20	8.0623	.1240	64.2028	.0156	7.9633	.1256	20
21	8.9492	.1117	72.2651	.0138	8.0751	.1238	21
22	9.9336	.1007	81.2143	.0123	8.1757	.1223	22
23	11.0263	.0907	91.1479	.0110	8.2664	.1210	23
24	12.2392	.0817	102.1742	.0098	8.3481	.1198	24
25	13.5855	.0736	114.4133	.0087	8.4217	.1187	25
26	15.0799	.0663	127.9988	.0078	8.4881	.1178	26
27	16.7386	.0597	143.0786	.0070	8.5478	.1170	27
28	18.5799	.0538	159.8173	.0063	8.6016	.1163	28
29	20.6237	.0485	178.3972	.0056	8.6501	.1156	29
30	22.8923	.0437	199.0209	.0050	8.6938	.1150	30
35	38.5749	.0259	341.5896	.0029	8.8552	.1129	35
40	65.0009	.0154	581.8261	.0017	8.9511	.1117	40
45	109.5302	.0091	986.6386	.0010	9.0079	.1110	45
50	184.5648	.0054	1668.7712	.0006	9.0417	.1106	50
55	311.0025	.0032	2818.2042	.0004	9.0617	.1104	55
60	524.0572	.0019	4755.0658	.0002	9.0736	.1102	60
∞					9.0909	.1100	∞

Interest rate of 12.00 percent

N	Compound amount — Future value of a present amount — F/P	Present value — Present value of a future amount — P/F	Annuity compound amount — Future value of an annuity — F/A	Sinking fund — Annuity providing a future amount — A/F	Annuity present value — Present value of an annuity — P/A	Capital recovery — Annuity repaying a present amount — A/P	N
1	1.1200	.8929	1.0000	1.0000	.8929	1.1200	1
2	1.2544	.7972	2.1200	.4717	1.6901	.5917	2
3	1.4049	.7118	3.3744	.2963	2.4018	.4163	3
4	1.5735	.6355	4.7793	.2092	3.0373	.3292	4
5	1.7623	.5674	6.3528	.1574	3.6048	.2774	5
6	1.9738	.5066	8.1152	.1232	4.1114	.2432	6
7	2.2107	.4523	10.0890	.0991	4.5638	.2191	7
8	2.4760	.4039	12.2997	.0813	4.9676	.2013	8
9	2.7731	.3606	14.7757	.0677	5.3282	.1877	9
10	3.1058	.3220	17.5487	.0570	5.6502	.1770	10
11	3.4785	.2875	20.6546	.0484	5.9377	.1684	11
12	3.8960	.2567	24.1331	.0414	6.1944	.1614	12
13	4.3635	.2292	28.0291	.0357	6.4235	.1557	13
14	4.8871	.2046	32.3926	.0309	6.6282	.1509	14
15	5.4736	.1827	37.2797	.0268	6.8109	.1468	15
16	6.1304	.1631	42.7533	.0234	6.9740	.1434	16
17	6.8660	.1456	48.8837	.0205	7.1196	.1405	17
18	7.6900	.1300	55.7497	.0179	7.2497	.1379	18
19	8.6128	.1161	63.4397	.0158	7.3658	.1358	19
20	9.6463	.1037	72.0524	.0139	7.4694	.1339	20
21	10.8038	.0926	81.6987	.0122	7.5620	.1322	21
22	12.1003	.0826	92.5026	.0108	7.6446	.1308	22
23	13.5523	.0738	104.6029	.0096	7.7184	.1296	23
24	15.1786	.0659	118.1552	.0085	7.7843	.1285	24
25	17.0001	.0588	133.3339	.0075	7.8431	.1275	25
26	19.0401	.0525	150.3339	.0067	7.8957	.1267	26
27	21.3249	.0469	169.6989	.0059	7.9426	.1259	27
28	23.8839	.0419	190.6989	.0052	7.9844	.1252	28
29	26.7499	.0374	214.5828	.0047	8.0218	.1247	29
30	29.9599	.0334	241.3327	.0041	8.0552	.1241	30
35	52.7996	.0189	431.6635	.0023	8.1755	.1223	35
40	93.0510	.0107	767.0914	.0013	8.2438	.1213	40
45	163.9876	.0061	1358.2300	.0007	8.2825	.1207	45
50	289.0022	.0035	2400.0182	.0004	8.3045	.1204	50
55	509.3206	.0020	4236.0050	.0002	8.3170	.1202	55
60	897.5969	.0011	7471.6411	.0001	8.3240	.1201	60
∞					8.3333	.1200	∞

Interest rate of 14.00 percent

N	Compound amount — Future value of a present amount (F/P)	Present value — Present value of a future amount (P/F)	Annuity compound amount — Future value of an annuity (F/A)	Sinking fund — Annuity providing a future amount (A/F)	Annuity present value — Present value of an annuity (P/A)	Capital recovery — Annuity repaying a present amount (A/P)	N
1	1.1400	.8772	1.0000	1.0000	.8772	1.1400	1
2	1.2996	.7695	2.1400	.4673	1.6467	.6073	2
3	1.4815	.6750	3.4396	.2907	2.3216	.4307	3
4	1.6890	.5921	4.9211	.2032	2.9137	.3432	4
5	1.9254	.5194	6.6101	.1513	3.4331	.2913	5
6	2.1950	.4556	8.5355	.1172	3.8887	.2572	6
7	2.5023	.3996	10.7305	.0932	4.2883	.2332	7
8	2.8526	.3506	13.2328	.0756	4.6389	.2156	8
9	3.2519	.3075	16.0853	.0622	4.9464	.2022	9
10	3.7072	.2697	19.3373	.0517	5.2161	.1917	10
11	4.2262	.2366	23.0445	.0434	5.4527	.1834	11
12	4.8179	.2076	27.2707	.0367	5.6603	.1767	12
13	5.4924	.1821	32.0887	.0312	5.8424	.1712	13
14	6.2613	.1597	37.5811	.0266	6.0021	.1666	14
15	7.1379	.1401	43.8424	.0228	6.1422	.1628	15
16	8.1372	.1229	50.9804	.0196	6.2651	.1596	16
17	9.2765	.1078	59.1176	.0169	6.3729	.1569	17
18	10.5752	.0946	68.3941	.0146	6.4674	.1546	18
19	12.0557	.0829	78.9692	.0127	6.5504	.1527	19
20	13.7435	.0728	91.0249	.0110	6.6231	.1510	20
21	15.6676	.0638	104.7684	.0095	6.6870	.1495	21
22	17.8610	.0560	120.4360	.0083	6.7429	.1483	22
23	20.3616	.0491	138.2970	.0072	6.7921	.1472	23
24	23.2122	.0431	158.6586	.0063	6.8351	.1463	24
25	26.4619	.0378	181.8708	.0055	6.8729	.1455	25
26	30.1666	.0331	208.3327	.0048	6.9061	.1448	26
27	34.3899	.0291	238.4993	.0042	6.9352	.1442	27
28	39.2045	.0255	272.8892	.0037	6.9607	.1437	28
29	44.6931	.0224	312.0937	.0032	6.9830	.1432	29
30	50.9502	.0196	356.7868	.0028	7.0027	.1428	30
35	98.1002	.0102	693.5727	.0014	7.0700	.1414	35
40	188.8835	.0053	1342.0251	.0007	7.1050	.1407	40
45	363.6791	.0027	2590.5648	.0004	7.1232	.1404	45
50	700.2330	.0014	4994.5213	.0002	7.1327	.1402	50
55	1348.2388	.0007	9623.1343	.0001	7.1376	.1401	55
60	2595.9187	.0004	18535.1333	.0001	7.1401	.1401	60
∞					7.1429	.1400	∞

Interest rate of 13.00 percent

N	Compound amount — Future value of a present amount (F/P)	Present value — Present value of a future amount (P/F)	Annuity compound amount — Future value of an annuity (F/A)	Sinking fund — Annuity providing a future amount (A/F)	Annuity present value — Present value of an annuity (P/A)	Capital recovery — Annuity repaying a present amount (A/P)	N
1	1.1300	.8850	1.0000	1.0000	.8850	1.1300	1
2	1.2769	.7831	2.1300	.4695	1.6681	.5995	2
3	1.4429	.6931	3.4069	.2935	2.3612	.4235	3
4	1.6305	.6133	4.8498	.2062	2.9745	.3362	4
5	1.8424	.5428	6.4803	.1543	3.5172	.2843	5
6	2.0820	.4803	8.3227	.1202	3.9975	.2502	6
7	2.3526	.4251	10.4047	.0961	4.4226	.2261	7
8	2.6584	.3762	12.7573	.0784	4.7988	.2084	8
9	3.0040	.3329	15.4157	.0649	5.1317	.1949	9
10	3.3946	.2946	18.4197	.0543	5.4262	.1843	10
11	3.8359	.2607	21.8143	.0458	5.6869	.1758	11
12	4.3345	.2307	25.6502	.0390	5.9176	.1690	12
13	4.8980	.2042	29.9847	.0334	6.1218	.1634	13
14	5.5348	.1807	34.8827	.0287	6.3025	.1587	14
15	6.2543	.1599	40.4175	.0247	6.4624	.1547	15
16	7.0673	.1415	46.6717	.0214	6.6039	.1514	16
17	7.9861	.1252	53.7391	.0186	6.7291	.1486	17
18	9.0243	.1108	61.7251	.0162	6.8399	.1462	18
19	10.1974	.0981	70.7494	.0141	6.9380	.1441	19
20	11.5231	.0868	80.9468	.0124	7.0248	.1424	20
21	13.0211	.0768	92.4699	.0108	7.1016	.1408	21
22	14.7138	.0680	105.4910	.0095	7.1695	.1395	22
23	16.6266	.0601	120.2048	.0083	7.2297	.1383	23
24	18.7881	.0532	136.8315	.0073	7.2829	.1373	24
25	21.2305	.0471	155.6196	.0064	7.3300	.1364	25
26	23.9905	.0417	176.8501	.0057	7.3717	.1357	26
27	27.1093	.0369	200.8406	.0050	7.4086	.1350	27
28	30.6335	.0326	227.9499	.0044	7.4412	.1344	28
29	34.6158	.0289	258.5834	.0039	7.4701	.1339	29
30	39.1159	.0256	293.1992	.0034	7.4957	.1334	30
35	72.0685	.0139	546.6808	.0018	7.5856	.1318	35
40	132.7816	.0075	1013.7042	.0010	7.6344	.1310	40
45	244.6414	.0041	1874.1646	.0005	7.6609	.1305	45
50	450.7359	.0022	3459.5071	.0003	7.6752	.1303	50
55	830.4517	.0012	6380.3979	.0002	7.6830	.1302	55
60	1530.0535	.0007	11761.9498	.0001	7.6873	.1301	60
∞					7.6923	.1300	∞

APPENDIX A   Interest rates of 15.00 and 16.00 percent

Interest rate of 16.00 percent

N	Compound amount — Future value of a present amount — F/P	Present value — Present value of a future amount — P/F	Annuity compound amount — Future value of an annuity — F/A	Sinking fund — Annuity providing a future amount — A/F	Annuity present value — Present value of an annuity — P/A	Capital recovery — Annuity repaying a present amount — A/P
1	1.1600	.8621	1.0000	1.0000	.8621	1.1600
2	1.3456	.7432	2.1600	.4630	1.6052	.6230
3	1.5609	.6407	3.5056	.2853	2.2459	.4453
4	1.8106	.5523	5.0665	.1974	2.7982	.3574
5	2.1003	.4761	6.8771	.1454	3.2743	.3054
6	2.4364	.4104	8.9775	.1114	3.6847	.2714
7	2.8262	.3538	11.4139	.0876	4.0386	.2476
8	3.2784	.3050	14.2401	.0702	4.3436	.2302
9	3.8030	.2630	17.5185	.0571	4.6065	.2171
10	4.4114	.2267	21.3215	.0469	4.8332	.2069
11	5.1173	.1954	25.7329	.0389	5.0286	.1989
12	5.9360	.1685	30.8502	.0324	5.1971	.1924
13	6.8858	.1452	36.7862	.0272	5.3423	.1872
14	7.9875	.1252	43.6720	.0229	5.4675	.1829
15	9.2655	.1079	51.6595	.0194	5.5755	.1794
16	10.7480	.0930	60.9250	.0164	5.6685	.1764
17	12.4677	.0802	71.6730	.0140	5.7487	.1740
18	14.4625	.0691	84.1407	.0119	5.8178	.1719
19	16.7765	.0596	98.6032	.0101	5.8775	.1701
20	19.4608	.0514	115.3797	.0087	5.9288	.1687
21	22.5745	.0443	134.8405	.0074	5.9731	.1674
22	26.1864	.0382	157.4150	.0064	6.0113	.1664
23	30.3762	.0329	183.6014	.0054	6.0442	.1654
24	35.2364	.0284	213.9776	.0047	6.0726	.1647
25	40.8742	.0245	249.2140	.0040	6.0971	.1640
26	47.4141	.0211	290.0883	.0034	6.1182	.1634
27	55.0004	.0182	337.5024	.0030	6.1364	.1630
28	63.8004	.0157	392.5028	.0025	6.1520	.1625
29	74.0085	.0135	456.3032	.0022	6.1656	.1622
30	85.8499	.0116	530.3117	.0019	6.1772	.1619
35	180.3141	.0055	1120.7130	.0009	6.2153	.1609
40	378.7212	.0026	2360.7572	.0004	6.2335	.1604
45	795.4438	.0013	4965.2739	.0002	6.2421	.1602
50	1670.7038	.0006	10435.6488	.0001	6.2463	.1601
55	3509.0488	.0003	21925.3050	.0000	6.2482	.1600
60	7370.2014	.0001	46057.5085	.0000	6.2492	.1600
8					6.2500	.1600

Interest rate of 15.00 percent

N	Compound amount — Future value of a present amount — F/P	Present value — Present value of a future amount — P/F	Annuity compound amount — Future value of an annuity — F/A	Sinking fund — Annuity providing a future amount — A/F	Annuity present value — Present value of an annuity — P/A	Capital recovery — Annuity repaying a present amount — A/P
1	1.1500	.8696	1.0000	1.0000	.8696	1.1500
2	1.3225	.7561	2.1500	.4651	1.6257	.6151
3	1.5209	.6575	3.4725	.2880	2.2832	.4380
4	1.7490	.5718	4.9934	.2003	2.8550	.3503
5	2.0114	.4972	6.7424	.1483	3.3522	.2983
6	2.3131	.4323	8.7537	.1142	3.7845	.2642
7	2.6600	.3759	11.0668	.0904	4.1604	.2404
8	3.0590	.3269	13.7268	.0729	4.4873	.2229
9	3.5179	.2843	16.7858	.0596	4.7716	.2096
10	4.0456	.2472	20.3037	.0493	5.0188	.1993
11	4.6524	.2149	24.3493	.0411	5.2337	.1911
12	5.3503	.1869	29.0017	.0345	5.4206	.1845
13	6.1528	.1625	34.3519	.0291	5.5831	.1791
14	7.0757	.1413	40.5047	.0247	5.7245	.1747
15	8.1371	.1229	47.5804	.0210	5.8474	.1710
16	9.3576	.1069	55.7175	.0179	5.9542	.1679
17	10.7613	.0929	65.0751	.0154	6.0472	.1654
18	12.3755	.0808	75.8364	.0132	6.1280	.1632
19	14.2318	.0703	88.2118	.0113	6.1982	.1613
20	16.3665	.0611	102.4436	.0098	6.2593	.1598
21	18.8215	.0531	118.8101	.0084	6.3125	.1584
22	21.6447	.0462	137.6316	.0073	6.3587	.1573
23	24.8915	.0402	159.2764	.0063	6.3988	.1563
24	28.6252	.0349	184.1678	.0054	6.4338	.1554
25	32.9190	.0304	212.7930	.0047	6.4641	.1547
26	37.8568	.0264	245.7120	.0041	6.4906	.1541
27	43.5353	.0230	283.5688	.0035	6.5135	.1535
28	50.0656	.0200	327.1041	.0031	6.5335	.1531
29	57.5755	.0174	377.1697	.0027	6.5509	.1527
30	66.2118	.0151	434.7451	.0023	6.5660	.1523
35	133.1755	.0075	881.1702	.0011	6.6166	.1511
40	267.8635	.0037	1779.0903	.0006	6.6418	.1506
45	538.7693	.0019	3585.1285	.0003	6.6543	.1503
50	1083.6574	.0009	7217.7163	.0001	6.6605	.1501
55	2179.6222	.0005	14524.1479	.0001	6.6636	.1501
60	4383.9987	.0002	29219.9916	.0000	6.6651	.1500
8					6.6667	.1500

Interest rate of 18.00 percent

N	Compound amount: Future value of a present amount F/P	Present value: Present value of a future amount P/F	Annuity compound amount: Future value of an annuity F/A	Sinking fund: Annuity providing a future amount A/F	Annuity present value: Present value of an annuity P/A	Capital recovery: Annuity repaying a present amount A/P	N
1	1.1800	.8475	1.0000	1.0000	.8475	1.1800	1
2	1.3924	.7182	2.1800	.4587	1.5656	.6387	2
3	1.6430	.6086	3.5724	.2799	2.1743	.4599	3
4	1.9388	.5158	5.2154	.1917	2.6901	.3717	4
5	2.2878	.4371	7.1542	.1398	3.1272	.3198	5
6	2.6996	.3704	9.4420	.1059	3.4976	.2859	6
7	3.1855	.3139	12.1415	.0824	3.8115	.2624	7
8	3.7589	.2660	15.3270	.0652	4.0776	.2452	8
9	4.4355	.2255	19.0859	.0524	4.3030	.2324	9
10	5.2338	.1911	23.5213	.0425	4.4941	.2225	10
11	6.1759	.1619	28.7551	.0348	4.6560	.2148	11
12	7.2876	.1372	34.9311	.0286	4.7932	.2086	12
13	8.5994	.1163	42.2187	.0237	4.9095	.2037	13
14	10.1472	.0985	50.8180	.0197	5.0081	.1997	14
15	11.9737	.0835	60.9653	.0164	5.0916	.1964	15
16	14.1290	.0708	72.9390	.0137	5.1624	.1937	16
17	16.6722	.0600	87.0680	.0115	5.2223	.1915	17
18	19.6733	.0508	103.7403	.0096	5.2732	.1896	18
19	23.2144	.0431	123.4135	.0081	5.3162	.1881	19
20	27.3930	.0365	146.6280	.0068	5.3527	.1868	20
21	32.3238	.0309	174.0210	.0057	5.3837	.1857	21
22	38.1421	.0262	206.3448	.0048	5.4099	.1848	22
23	45.0076	.0222	244.4868	.0041	5.4321	.1841	23
24	53.1090	.0188	289.4945	.0035	5.4509	.1835	24
25	62.6686	.0160	342.6035	.0029	5.4669	.1829	25
26	73.9490	.0135	405.2721	.0025	5.4804	.1825	26
27	87.2598	.0115	479.2211	.0021	5.4919	.1821	27
28	102.9666	.0097	566.4809	.0018	5.5016	.1818	28
29	121.5005	.0082	669.4475	.0015	5.5098	.1815	29
30	143.3706	.0070	790.9480	.0013	5.5168	.1813	30
∞					5.5556	.1800	∞

Interest rate of 20.00 percent

N	Compound amount: Future value of a present amount F/P	Present value: Present value of a future amount P/F	Annuity compound amount: Future value of an annuity F/A	Sinking fund: Annuity providing a future amount A/F	Annuity present value: Present value of an annuity P/A	Capital recovery: Annuity repaying a present amount A/P	N
1	1.2000	.8333	1.0000	1.0000	.8333	1.2000	1
2	1.4400	.6944	2.2000	.4545	1.5278	.6545	2
3	1.7280	.5787	3.6400	.2747	2.1065	.4747	3
4	2.0736	.4823	5.3680	.1863	2.5887	.3863	4
5	2.4883	.4019	7.4416	.1344	2.9906	.3344	5
6	2.9860	.3349	9.9299	.1007	3.3255	.3007	6
7	3.5832	.2791	12.9159	.0774	3.6046	.2774	7
8	4.2998	.2326	16.4991	.0606	3.8372	.2606	8
9	5.1598	.1938	20.7989	.0481	4.0310	.2481	9
10	6.1917	.1615	25.9587	.0385	4.1925	.2385	10
11	7.4301	.1346	32.1504	.0311	4.3271	.2311	11
12	8.9161	.1122	39.5805	.0253	4.4392	.2253	12
13	10.6993	.0935	48.4966	.0206	4.5327	.2206	13
14	12.8392	.0779	59.1959	.0169	4.6106	.2169	14
15	15.4070	.0649	72.0351	.0139	4.6755	.2139	15
16	18.4884	.0541	87.4421	.0114	4.7296	.2114	16
17	22.1861	.0451	105.9306	.0094	4.7746	.2094	17
18	26.6233	.0376	128.1167	.0078	4.8122	.2078	18
19	31.9480	.0313	154.7400	.0065	4.8435	.2065	19
20	38.3376	.0261	186.6880	.0054	4.8696	.2054	20
21	46.0051	.0217	225.0256	.0044	4.8913	.2044	21
22	55.2061	.0181	271.0307	.0037	4.9094	.2037	22
23	66.2474	.0151	326.2369	.0031	4.9245	.2031	23
24	79.4968	.0126	392.4842	.0025	4.9371	.2025	24
25	95.3962	.0105	471.9811	.0021	4.9476	.2021	25
26	114.4755	.0087	567.3773	.0018	4.9563	.2018	26
27	137.3706	.0073	681.8528	.0015	4.9636	.2015	27
28	164.8447	.0061	819.2233	.0012	4.9697	.2012	28
29	197.8136	.0051	984.0680	.0010	4.9747	.2010	29
30	237.3763	.0042	1181.8816	.0008	4.9789	.2008	30
∞					5.0000	.2000	∞

Interest rate of 30.00 percent

N	Compound amount Future value of a present amount F/P	Present value Present value of a future amount P/F	Annuity compound amount Future value of an annuity F/A	Sinking fund Annuity providing a future amount A/F	Annuity present value Present value of an annuity P/A	Capital recovery Annuity repaying a present amount A/P	N
1	1.3000	.7692	1.0000	1.0000	.7692	1.3000	1
2	1.6900	.5917	2.3000	.4348	1.3609	.7348	2
3	2.1970	.4552	3.9900	.2506	1.8161	.5506	3
4	2.8561	.3501	6.1870	.1616	2.1662	.4616	4
5	3.7129	.2693	9.0431	.1106	2.4356	.4106	5
6	4.8268	.2072	12.7560	.0784	2.6427	.3784	6
7	6.2749	.1594	17.5828	.0569	2.8021	.3569	7
8	8.1573	.1226	23.8577	.0419	2.9247	.3419	8
9	10.6045	.0943	32.0150	.0312	3.0190	.3312	9
10	13.7858	.0725	42.6195	.0235	3.0915	.3235	10
11	17.9216	.0558	56.4053	.0177	3.1473	.3177	11
12	23.2981	.0429	74.3270	.0135	3.1903	.3135	12
13	30.2875	.0330	97.6250	.0102	3.2233	.3102	13
14	39.3738	.0254	127.9125	.0078	3.2487	.3078	14
15	51.1859	.0195	167.2863	.0060	3.2682	.3060	15
16	66.5417	.0150	218.4722	.0046	3.2832	.3046	16
17	86.5042	.0116	285.0139	.0035	3.2948	.3035	17
18	112.4554	.0089	371.5180	.0027	3.3037	.3027	18
19	146.1920	.0068	483.9734	.0021	3.3105	.3021	19
20	190.0496	.0053	630.1655	.0016	3.3158	.3016	20
21	247.0645	.0040	820.2151	.0012	3.3198	.3012	21
22	321.1839	.0031	1067.2796	.0009	3.3230	.3009	22
23	417.5391	.0024	1388.4635	.0007	3.3254	.3007	23
24	542.8008	.0018	1806.0026	.0006	3.3272	.3006	24
25	705.6410	.0014	2348.8033	.0004	3.3286	.3004	25
26	917.3333	.0011	3054.4443	.0003	3.3297	.3003	26
27	1192.5333	.0008	3971.7776	.0003	3.3305	.3003	27
28	1550.2933	.0006	5164.3109	.0002	3.3312	.3002	28
29	2015.3813	.0005	6714.6042	.0001	3.3317	.3001	29
30	2619.9956	.0004	8729.9855	.0001	3.3321	.3001	30
∞					3.3333	.3000	∞

Interest rate of 25.00 percent

N	Compound amount Future value of a present amount F/P	Present value Present value of a future amount P/F	Annuity compound amount Future value of an annuity F/A	Sinking fund Annuity providing a future amount A/F	Annuity present value Present value of an annuity P/A	Capital recovery Annuity repaying a present amount A/P	N
1	1.2500	.8000	1.0000	1.0000	.8000	1.2500	1
2	1.5625	.6400	2.2500	.4444	1.4400	.6944	2
3	1.9531	.5120	3.8125	.2623	1.9520	.5123	3
4	2.4414	.4096	5.7656	.1734	2.3616	.4234	4
5	3.0518	.3277	8.2070	.1218	2.6893	.3718	5
6	3.8147	.2621	11.2588	.0888	2.9514	.3388	6
7	4.7684	.2097	15.0735	.0663	3.1611	.3163	7
8	5.9605	.1678	19.8419	.0504	3.3289	.3004	8
9	7.4506	.1342	25.8023	.0388	3.4631	.2888	9
10	9.3132	.1074	33.2529	.0301	3.5705	.2801	10
11	11.6415	.0859	42.5661	.0235	3.6564	.2735	11
12	14.5519	.0687	54.2077	.0184	3.7251	.2684	12
13	18.1899	.0550	68.7596	.0145	3.7801	.2645	13
14	22.7374	.0440	86.9495	.0115	3.8241	.2615	14
15	28.4217	.0352	109.6868	.0091	3.8593	.2591	15
16	35.5271	.0281	138.1085	.0072	3.8874	.2572	16
17	44.4089	.0225	173.6357	.0058	3.9099	.2558	17
18	55.5112	.0180	218.0446	.0046	3.9279	.2546	18
19	69.3889	.0144	273.5558	.0037	3.9424	.2537	19
20	86.7362	.0115	342.9447	.0029	3.9539	.2529	20
21	108.4202	.0092	429.6809	.0023	3.9631	.2523	21
22	135.5253	.0074	538.1011	.0019	3.9705	.2519	22
23	169.4066	.0059	673.6264	.0015	3.9764	.2515	23
24	211.7582	.0047	843.0329	.0012	3.9811	.2512	24
25	264.6978	.0038	1054.7912	.0009	3.9849	.2509	25
26	330.8722	.0030	1319.4890	.0008	3.9879	.2508	26
27	413.5903	.0024	1650.3612	.0006	3.9903	.2506	27
28	516.9879	.0019	2063.9515	.0005	3.9923	.2505	28
29	646.2349	.0015	2580.9394	.0004	3.9938	.2504	29
30	807.7936	.0012	3227.1743	.0003	3.9950	.2503	30
∞					4.0000	.2500	∞

Interest rate of 40.00 percent

N	Compound amount — Future value of a present amount — F/P	Present value — Present value of a future amount — P/F	Annuity compound amount — Future value of an annuity — F/A	Sinking fund — Annuity providing a future amount — A/F	Annuity present value — Present value of an annuity — P/A	Capital recovery — Annuity repaying a present amount — A/P	N
1	1.4000	.7143	1.0000	1.0000	.7143	1.4000	1
2	1.9600	.5102	2.4000	.4167	1.2245	.8167	2
3	2.7440	.3644	4.3600	.2294	1.5889	.6294	3
4	3.8416	.2603	7.1040	.1408	1.8492	.5408	4
5	5.3782	.1859	10.9456	.0914	2.0352	.4914	5
6	7.5295	.1328	16.3238	.0613	2.1680	.4613	6
7	10.5414	.0949	23.8534	.0419	2.2628	.4419	7
8	14.7579	.0678	34.3947	.0291	2.3306	.4291	8
9	20.6610	.0484	49.1526	.0203	2.3790	.4203	9
10	28.9255	.0346	69.8137	.0143	2.4136	.4143	10
11	40.4957	.0247	98.7391	.0101	2.4383	.4101	11
12	56.6939	.0176	139.2348	.0072	2.4559	.4072	12
13	79.3715	.0126	195.9287	.0051	2.4685	.4051	13
14	111.1201	.0090	275.3002	.0036	2.4775	.4036	14
15	155.5681	.0064	386.4202	.0026	2.4839	.4026	15
16	217.7953	.0046	541.9883	.0018	2.4885	.4018	16
17	304.9135	.0033	759.7837	.0013	2.4918	.4013	17
18	426.8789	.0023	1064.6971	.0009	2.4941	.4009	18
19	597.6304	.0017	1491.5760	.0007	2.4958	.4007	19
20	836.6826	.0012	2089.2064	.0005	2.4970	.4005	20
21	1171.3556	.0009	2925.8889	.0003	2.4979	.4003	21
22	1639.8978	.0006	4097.2445	.0002	2.4985	.4002	22
23	2295.8569	.0004	5737.1423	.0002	2.4989	.4002	23
24	3214.1997	.0003	8032.9993	.0001	2.4992	.4001	24
25	4499.8796	.0002	11247.1990	.0001	2.4994	.4001	25
∞					2.5000	.4000	∞

Interest rate of 50.00 percent

N	Compound amount — Future value of a present amount — F/P	Present value — Present value of a future amount — P/F	Annuity compound amount — Future value of an annuity — F/A	Sinking fund — Annuity providing a future amount — A/F	Annuity present value — Present value of an annuity — P/A	Capital recovery — Annuity repaying a present amount — A/P	N
1	1.5000	.6667	1.0000	1.0000	.6667	1.5000	1
2	2.2500	.4444	2.5000	.4000	1.1111	.9000	2
3	3.3750	.2963	4.7500	.2105	1.4074	.7105	3
4	5.0625	.1975	8.1250	.1231	1.6049	.6231	4
5	7.5938	.1317	13.1875	.0758	1.7366	.5758	5
6	11.3906	.0878	20.7813	.0481	1.8244	.5481	6
7	17.0859	.0585	32.1719	.0311	1.8829	.5311	7
8	25.6289	.0390	49.2578	.0203	1.9220	.5203	8
9	38.4434	.0260	74.8867	.0134	1.9480	.5134	9
10	57.6650	.0173	113.3301	.0088	1.9653	.5088	10
11	86.4976	.0116	170.9951	.0058	1.9769	.5058	11
12	129.7463	.0077	257.4927	.0039	1.9846	.5039	12
13	194.6195	.0051	387.2390	.0026	1.9897	.5026	13
14	291.9293	.0034	581.8585	.0017	1.9931	.5017	14
15	437.8939	.0023	873.7878	.0011	1.9954	.5011	15
16	656.8408	.0015	1311.6817	.0008	1.9970	.5008	16
17	985.2613	.0010	1968.5225	.0005	1.9980	.5005	17
18	1477.8919	.0007	2953.7838	.0003	1.9986	.5003	18
19	2216.8378	.0005	4431.6756	.0002	1.9991	.5002	19
20	3325.2567	.0003	6648.5135	.0002	1.9994	.5002	20
21	4987.8851	.0002	9973.7702	.0001	1.9996	.5001	21
22	7481.8276	.0001	14961.6553	.0001	1.9997	.5001	22
23	11222.7415	.0001	22443.4829	.0000	1.9998	.5000	23
24	16834.1122	.0001	33666.2244	.0000	1.9999	.5000	24
25	25251.1683	.0000	50500.3366	.0000	1.9999	.5000	25
∞					2.0000	.5000	∞

accelerated depreciation Any method of depreciating an asset that produces higher depreciation in earlier years than in later years.

accounting rate of return The rate of return on an investment computed as accounting profit divided by some measure of investment; e.g., average profit per year divided by initial investment.

acid test ratio See **quick ratio.**

activity ratio A financial ratio that indicates how efficiently a firm uses its assets; inventory turnover, average collection period, fixed-asset turnover, and total-asset turnover are activity ratios.

adjustable rate preferred stock Preferred stock with a dividend that varies with some stipulated market interest rate (e.g., the U.S. Treasury bill rate).

after-acquired property clause A provision in a bond indenture that provides that all property acquired by the firm in the future will also serve as collateral for the bonds.

agency issue See **best efforts issue.**

annuity A series of equal periodic payments or receipts.

arrangement An adjustment between a debtor and a creditor for the settlement of the debtor's obligations; usually covers small- and medium-sized debtor firms.

authorized shares Shares authorized under the company's charter for issuance. For example, a firm with 1 million authorized shares may issue up to but no more than 1 million shares unless the corporate charter is amended to increase this number.

balance sheet method Forecasts of future financing requirements and available cash based only on forecast income statements and balance sheets.

bankruptcy The condition in which a firm (or individual) is unable to pay its debts, and its assets are consequently surrendered to a court for administration.

bearer security Security for which ownership is primarily evidenced by possession of the certificate (compare with **registered securities**).

benefit-cost ratio For an investment, the ratio of the present value of its future cash flows to its initial cost. The benefit-cost ratio method uses the ratio to evaluate investment opportunities.

best efforts issue Issuing securities without underwriting. Securities are sold on a commission basis by the investment bankers with no guarantee of the total amount that will be sold.

beta A measure of the response of the rate of return on an asset or a portfolio of assets to changes in the rate of return of the entire capital market, and a measure of the risk of an asset or portfolio in the Capital Asset Pricing Model.

blanket mortgage A mortgage that covers many assets; e.g., a blanket mortgage covering several buildings in a real estate complex.

bond A long-term promise to pay a specified dollar amount; a long-term debt security.

book value The original cost of an asset minus total depreciation deductions made to date; this is the value indicated by the firm's financial statements.

break-even point The level of output at which the firm is just breaking even, i.e., earning a zero profit.

broker One who arranges the purchase and sale of assets; e.g., a securities (stock) broker, a mortgage broker, and a real estate broker. A broker does not buy or sell the asset but simply brings buyers and sellers together (contrast with **dealer**).

business risk Risk arising from the uncertainty of the future revenues and expenses (not including debt interest) of a firm (i.e., riskiness of the firm's EBIT).

call option See **option.**

call premium The difference between the call price and the face value of a bond.

call price The price that the firm must pay per bond to bondholders if the bonds are called (repurchased by the firm directly from bondholders).

call provision A stipulation in a bond or preferred stock agreement that the firm has the right to repurchase (call) the outstanding bonds or preferred stock at a given price from the securityholder.

capital asset A physical asset (plant and equipment) used by a firm in producing goods or services.

Capital Asset Pricing Model (CAPM) A model of equilibrium rates of return (prices) in the financial markets. The CAPM provides an explicit equation for the expected rate of return on an asset and for the equilibrium value of an asset.

capital budget A statement of the firm's planned investments, generally based upon estimates of future sales, costs, production needs, and availability of capital.

capital gains (losses) The difference between the original cost of an asset and its selling price. Capital gains (losses) are *realized* when the asset is sold.

capital income Income produced from investing money, such as dividends and interest. See also **earned income**.

capital market line A line showing the relationship between the expected rate of return and the risk borne by investors in the capital markets.

capital rationing The use of funds by the firm in a situation in which the funds are limited, i.e., no additional capital can be obtained regardless of the profitability of the investment opportunity.

capital structure The composition of a firm's financing; often refers to the proportions of long-term debt, preferred stock, and common equity on the firm's balance sheet.

cash budget Planned cash receipts and payments for one or more future periods.

cash flow forecasts Forecasts of cash receipts and payments for one or more periods.

cash flow from an investment The dollars coming to the firm (**cash inflow**) or paid out by the firm (**cash outflow**) as a result of adopting the investment.

CBOE Chicago Board Options Exchange.

certainty equivalent An amount, to be received for certain at a particular point in time, which is equal in desirability to a risky cash flow occurring at the same point in time.

chattel mortgage A pledge of personal proeprty as collateral on a debt.

clientele effect The attraction of investors who purchase the company's stock because they prefer the company's policies, such as the company's long-run dividend policy.

closed-end mortgage A mortgage that forbids the borrower from using the security (collateral) provided by the mortgage to cover any additional debt unless the additional debt is of lower priority than the existing debt backed by the mortgage.

coefficient of variation The standard deviation of a variable divided by the variable's expected level, for example, standard deviation of cash flow divided by the expected cash flow.

collateral Property pleged by a borrower as security on a loan.

collateral trust bonds Bonds that are secured by marketable securities, inventories, or intangible assets (e.g., patents).

collection period The time period from the date of sale of the firm's product to the date of collection of cash from the customer.

combined leverage The combination of operating and financial leverage.

commercial paper Short-term debt issued by corporations to the public.

common stock A document that represents the ownership of a corporation.

compensating balance Money that must be on deposit at a bank to compensate the bank for services; may be a requirement of a loan.

competitive bid A bid for securities that are ultimately sold to the investment banker that bids the highest price for the issue.

composition An agreement between the firm and its creditors under which creditors receive less than the amount due to them in satisfaction of the debt (e.g., $0.50 on the dollar).

compound interest Interest that is paid or received on interest accumulated from prior periods.

conglomerate A group of firms in different lines of business that are controlled by a single corporation.

consolidation The combination of two or more firms into a completely new firm (e.g., firm A consolidating with firm B to form firm C).

contractual (financial) failure Inability to fulfill debt commitments.

conversion premium The difference between a convertible's market value and the higher of its investment and conversion values.

conversion price The price, in terms of dollars of par of the convertible security, paid per share of common stock acquired through conversion.

conversion ratio The number of common shares received for converting a convertible security.

conversion value The market value of the common stock into which the convertible security can be converted.

convertible bond A bond that can be converted at the option of the owner into common stock of the corporation.

convertible security A security (usually a bond or preferred stock) that can be converted at the option of the holder into some other type of security (usually common stock) issued by the same corporation.

corporation A business that has been chartered by a state and whose owners are not personally responsible for the business's debts.

correlation coefficient A measure of how closely the two variables move together; this covariation is also indicated by the **covariance** of the two variables.

cost of capital The minimum acceptable rate of return on an investment undertaken by a company; often measured as an average of the rates on the individual securities issued by the company.

cost recovery The term used for depreciation for tax purposes under the Economic Recovery Tax Act of 1981.

coupon The interest payment to the bondholder made periodically (usually semiannually).

coupon rate The percentage of a bond's par value that is paid each year as interest to the bondholder (a $1000 face value bond with a 6 percent coupon rate pays $60 per year in interest).

covariance A measure of the statistical relationship between two variables.

covenant A promise by the firm, included in the debt contract, to perform a certain act (e.g., to pay interest on the debt); a **restrictive covenant** is one that imposes constraints upon the firm in order to protect the debtholders' interests (e.g., a restriction on dividends or a requirement that the firm maintain a particular current ratio).

cover To eliminate risk of a position by taking an offsetting position. For example, to buy or sell a futures contract in the forward exchange market to protect against a loss that may occur as a result of exchange rate changes.

cum dividend With the dividend (compare with **ex-dividend**).

cum rights With rights; shares which entitle the owner to rights to buy shares of the company's stock are cum rights (compare with **ex rights** and also see **rights**).

cumulative dividends Unpaid preferred dividends from prior years that must be paid before any dividends are paid to common stockholders.

cumulative preferred stock Preferred stock for which any past unpaid preferred dividends must be paid in full before any dividends are issued on the firm's common stock.

cumulative voting A system of electing directors under which a significant minority of the shares is ensured of being able to elect at least one director.

current ratio Current assets divided by current liabilities; a measure of a firm's liquidity.

current yield (on a bond) The annual interest paid on a bond divided by the current price of the bond.

dealer One who is in the occupation of buying or selling some type of asset; e.g., a securities dealer (contrast with **broker**).

debenture A long-term debt instrument issued by a corporation that is not secured by specific property but instead by the general credit of the corporation.

debt capacity The maximum amount of debt that can feasibly be outstanding for a firm at a given point in time.

debt ratio Total firm debt divided by total assets; a measure of a firm's debt burden.

decision tree analysis A way of formulating a problem—often represented by a figure that looks like a tree—which involves choosing a best alternative or strategy. Dynamic programming is a solution technique for efficiently solving such a problem.

degree of combined leverage (DCL) The percentage change in aftertax earnings per share from a 1 percent change in sales.

degree of financial leverage (DFL) The percentage change in aftertax earnings per share from a 1 percent change in EBIT.

degree of operating leverage (DOL) The percentage change in earnings before interest and taxes (EBIT) from a 1 percent change in sales.

depletion A tax deduction reflecting the using up of a natural resource.

depreciation A deduction of part of the cost of an asset from income in each year of the asset's life. **Economic depreciation** is the decline in the value of an asset over time.

dilution A reduction in earnings per share due to an increase in the number of shares outstanding.

direct issue Securities sold directly to investors by the issuing firm.

discount (bond) The difference between the face value and market value of a bond if the face value is greater; e.g., the discount is $100 on a $1000 (face value) bond selling in the market for $900.

disintermediation The withdrawal of money from financial intermediaries in order to reinvest it in the securities issued by business firms and governmental units.

diversification Investing in more than one risky asset at a time.

divestiture The sale of a division or subsidiary of a company.

dividend payout ratio The proportion of earnings paid out in dividends.

earned income Income produced by an individual's personal services. See also **capital income**.

EBIT Earnings before debt interest and income taxes are deducted.

economic failure The inability of the firm to earn an adequate return on investment regardless of the company's financial structure.

economic order quantity The amount of purchased goods per order that minimizes the cost of inventory.

efficient frontier A curve that indicates the expected returns and standard deviations of all efficient portfolios.

efficient market A market in which asset prices reflect available information instantaneously.

efficient portfolio A portfolio which provides the lowest risk (standard deviation) for its expected return and the highest expected return for its level of risk.

EPS Earnings per share.

equipment trust certificate Bonds that are secured by equipment.

equity investment That portion of firm investment financed from retained earnings or from the sale of equity securities such as common stock or warrants.

exchange rate The ratio of the value of one currency relative to another; the rate at which one currency may be exchanged for another.

ex-dividend Without the dividend; the term describes a purchase of shares under which the purchaser is not entitled to the latest dividend (compare with **cum dividend**).

exercise price The dollar amount that must be paid for a share of common stock when it is bought by exercising a warrant or a call option. The exercise price is sometimes referred to as the **option price**.

expected cash flow An average of the possible cash flows in a period; this average equals the sum of all possible cash flows each multiplied by its probability of occurrence.

ex-rights Without rights; shares which do not entitle the owner (buyer) to rights to buy shares of the company's stock are ex-rights (compare with **cum rights** and also see **rights**).

extension An agreement between the firm and its creditors to postpone payments on the firm's debt.

external financing Raising money by issuing new securities or by borrowing.

external investment Expansion by acquiring another firm (contrast with **internal investment**).

extra dividend A dividend payment, in addition to the firm's regular dividend, which is paid only if the firm has been particularly profitable during the period.

face value See **maturity value**.

factoring Selling accounts receivable. The purchasing firm is called a **factor**.

field warehouse An area set aside on a borrower's premises in which goods used as collateral are placed.

financial asset A claim to a present or future payment of dollars; e.g., a corporate bond that is a claim to future interest and principal payments by a corporation.

financial failure See **contractual failure**.

financial intermediaries Financial institutions that borrow money from some people in order to lend it to others.

financial lease A lease that is noncancellable (except by mutual consent of both lessor and lessee) and that generally has a duration equal to most of the economic life of the asset.

financial leverage The effect of debt financing on stockholder income. Often also used to refer to the use of debt financing by a firm. May also include the impact of preferred stock financing on stockholder income.

financial ratio A ratio of dollar magnitudes obtained from a firm's financial statements that reflects some aspect of the firm's performance.

financial risk The uncertainty as to the future returns to a firm's owners resulting from the use of debt or preferred stock.

fixed charge A payment by the firm required under a contractual agreement; e.g., interest on debt, sinking fund contributions, and lease payments.

fixed cost A cost that does not change as output changes.

floating rate bond Bond with an interest rate which varies with short-term interest rates.

floor plan Loan agreement used to finance "large-ticket" items such as automobiles and appliances. Each item is separately identified as being collateral for the loan.

flotation costs The accounting, legal, underwriting, and other costs of issuing securities (new stock, bonds, etc.).

forward contract A futures contract in a currency.

forward rate The rate of exchange as set currently for a transaction to occur at a specified future time.

full service lease Lease under which the lessor (owner) maintains and insures the asset and pays property taxes on the asset.

fundamental analysis The analysis of a company's stock based upon the company's business performance and financial position (contrast with **technical analysis**).

fundamentalist Someone who believes that analysis of information about a company can be helpful in determining whether the securities of the company would be a good investment.

funded debt A term used to refer to any long-term debt of the firm; sometimes used to refer to any debt for which there is a written agreement covering the indebtedness.

funding See refunding.

funds A term that normally refers either to cash or to working capital (current assets minus current liabilities).

funds flow The flow of funds through the firm; this flow is described by a sources and uses statement.

future value The value at a future date of money that has been paid or received in prior periods.

futures contract A contract for future delivery of a specified amount of an asset (commodity, currency, or security) at a fixed price on a particular date in the future.

general lien Claim against all assets of a given type; used to secure a loan.

general partnerships A business in which each partner is personally responsible for any debts of the business.

going public The selling of stock by the issuing corporation to the general public for the first time.

holding company A firm that owns a controlling interest in one or more other firms (which are referred to as subsidiaries).

horizontal combination The union of firms which are in similar lines of business, e.g., two electronics manufacturers.

illiquidity The condition in which a firm (or individual) has inadequate cash to meet its obligations.

income bond A bond that pays interest only to the extent that the firm issuing the bond has earnings (EBIT) to cover the interest.

incremental internal rate of return method A method for comparing two or more mutually exclusive investments using the IRR approach. This method examines the IRR on the additional (or "incremental") cash flow produced by one investment relative to any mutually exclusive alternative in order to determine which is more profitable.

indenture The contract between the corporation and the bondholders specifying the provisions of the debt agreement.

insolvency The condition in which a firm (or individual's) liabilities exceed its assets.

interim financing Short-term loans to be repaid from long-term debt or other financing in the future.

internal financing Financing with money earned and retained in the business.

internal investment A firm's investment that involves the direct acquisition of productive assets rather than the acquisition of another firm or the productive assets of another firm (**external investment**).

internal rate of return The discount rate that discounts an investment's expected net cash flows to a net present value of zero.

interrelated investment opportunities Investments that affect each other's cash flows.

investment banker Financial institution specializing in underwriting and selling new securities issues.

investment company A company whose primary business is the purchase and ownership of government securities and the stocks and bonds of other firms. Mutual funds, closed-end investment companies, and venture capital firms are investment companies.

investment tax credit An income tax credit that is given to firms for investing in plant and equipment.

investment value The value that a convertible security would have if it were not convertible but had all its other features.

legal list A list of securities that fiduciary institutions (e.g., insurance companies and banks) may, under various state laws, acquire as investments.

lessee The user of a leased asset who pays the lessor for the usage right.

lessor The owner of a leased asset.

letter of credit A written statement by a bank that money will be paid provided conditions specified in the letter are met.

letter stock Privately placed common stock for which, under SEC regulation, the purchaser is required to provide a letter indicating that the stock is not intended for resale.

leverage The degree of firm borrowing.

leverage ratio A financial ratio that measures a firm's debt burden; the debt, times interest earned, and fixed-charges coverage ratios are leverage ratios.

leveraged buyout The sale of a subsidiary or division of a company to parties (often the purchased company's management) who borrow to make the purchase.

leveraged lease (or "third-party lease") An arrangement under which the lessor borrows funds to cover part or all of the purchase price of the asset.

limited liability A legal term that means that the owner of a business is not personally responsible for its debts; only his investment in the business is available to its creditors.

limited partnerships A business in which some partners (the general partners) are personally responsible for any debts, but the other partners (the limited partners) are not.

line of credit An agreement by a bank to loan money to a customer as needed up to a stated maximum amount.

liquidation The sale of a firm's assets when the company is dissolved.

liquidity premium The additional return earned on securities of greater term to maturity.

liquidity ratio A financial ratio that measures a firm's ability to fulfill short-run financial commitments; the current and quick ratios are liquidity ratios.

listed stock Stock that is traded on an organized securities exchange.

lock box A post office box to which local payments to a company will be sent. A local bank will collect the payments and deposit them in the company's account.

loss carryback (-forward) Using a business loss in the current year as a deduction from taxable income in prior years (carryback) or future years (carryforward).

maintenance lease A lease under which the lessor pays for all maintenance and upkeep of the asset.

majority rule voting A system of electing directors under which a majority of the shares has the power to elect the entire board of directors.

margin The amount paid by an investor in acquiring a security, usually expressed as a percentage of the security's purchase price. The Federal Reserve sets minimum margin requirements for securities traded on the organized securities exchanges.

market rate of discount The rate of discount used by investors to discount returns of a particular level of risk.

market value (or market price) The value that an asset (e.g., a security such as a share of stock or a physical asset such as a machine) is bought and sold for in the market.

matching principle A principle that holds that the firm should finance short-term needs with short-term sources and long-term needs with long-term sources.

maturity date The date on which the firm is to retire a bond by repaying the principal (maturity value); that is, when the bond matures.

maturity value The amount the firm promises to pay the bondholder, in addition to interest, when the bond matures. The maturity value is also referred to as the bond's **par value, face value,** or **principal value.**

merger The combination of two or more firms with one of them surviving (e.g., firm A merging with firm B with firm A surviving).

minimum acceptable rate of return The lowest rate of return that an investment can be expected to earn and still be acceptable; same as the investment's **cost of capital.**

mortgage A pledge of specific property given by a borrower as security on a loan.

mortgage bond A bond secured by a mortgage.

multinational company A company that has direct investments in more than one country.

mutual fund A company that invests in securities using money raised from selling shares to individual investors at their net asset value (market value of assets divided by number of shares). Shares will be redeemed by the fund at their net asset value at the request of the investor. Also called "open-end investment companies."

mutually exclusive alternatives Alternatives or options of which only one can be adopted (adopting one eliminates the chance of adopting any of the others).

negative pledge clause A provision in a bond agreement that the firm will issue no new debt which will take priority over the bonds covered by the agreement.

negotiated underwriting A process of issuing securities whereby a firm selects an investment banker and negotiates the terms of the issue.

net lease A lease under which the lessee pays all maintenance and upkeep of the asset.

net present value The present value of the future cash flows of an investment less the investment's current cost.

net profit Aftertax net income to stockholders; sometimes also used to refer to the annual annuity that is equivalent to a given net present value.

net working capital See **working capital.**

note (loan) Written and signed evidence of a debt.

note (United States) A type of United States government security with an original maturity of one to ten years. Similar to a bond but with a shorter maturity.

open account A credit arrangement under which sales are made to the buyer without a formal debt agreement (such as a note).

open-end mortgage A mortgage that allows the security (collateral) provided by the mortgage to be used as collateral on additional debt. A **limited open-end mortgage** allows the issuance of further debt up to some specified limit.

operating lease A lease that is cancellable by the lessee at any time upon due notice to the lessor. Also refers to a short-term lease that is cancellable by the lessor or lessee upon due notice to the other party.

operating leverage The existence of fixed operating costs in the firm's cost structure.

operating margin Operating income divided by sales; a measure of a firm's profitability.

option A right to buy (call) or sell (put) a specified amount of a particular asset (e.g., Ford common stock) at a given price within a specified period of time.

over-the-counter market A market for securities made up of securities dealers who may or may not be members of an organized exchange.

owner of record The individual recorded on the corporation's books as the owner of the company's outstanding securities.

par value The stated value of a security. The par value of a bond is its maturity value, the amount paid per bond at maturity. The par value of a share of preferred stock is the amount on which preferred dividends are based (a $100 par value 6 percent preferred stock pays $6 annually in dividends). The preferred's par value is also the amount owed to the preferred shareholder upon liquidation or bankruptcy of the corporation. The par value of common stock is the value of a share of stock set by the board of directors and is generally less than market value; the primary significance of this value is that, in most states, the firm may not pay dividends if such dividends reduce common shareholders' equity in the firm below the total par on all common stock outstanding.

participating preferred stock Preferred stock with a provision for increased dividends if the firm's earnings exceed some minimum amount.

partnership A business owned by two or more people who agree on how the profits will be divided and who are personally liable for firm debts. See also **limited partnership.**

payback period The amount of time required for an asset to generate enough cash flow to just cover the initial outlay for that asset.

payback period method A capital budgeting technique that specifies that an investment is acceptable only if it has a payback period less than or equal to some specified time period, e.g., three years.

personal property All property other than **real property.**

pooling of interests A method of accounting for a business combination under which the assets of the acquired firm are subsequently carried on the merged firm's books at the same value that they were carried by the selling firm.

portfolio A combination of assets owned for investment.

preemptive right The stockholder's right to purchase additional stock of the company before it is offered for sale to outsiders.

preferred stock Stock that has a claim against income and assets before common stock but after debt.

premiuum (bond) The difference between the market value and the face value of a bond if the market value is greater; e.g., the premium is $200 on a $1000 (face value) bond selling in the market for $1200.

premium (warrant) The difference between the market value and the theoretical value of the warrant.

present value The value of money at a given date that will be paid or received in future periods.

price-earnings ratio The price per share of stock divided by the annual earnings per share.

primary markets The market in which financial assets are originally issued.

prime rate Interest rate charged by banks on short-term loans to large, low-risk businesses.

principal The amount on which interest is paid by a borrower or the amount on which interest is received by a lender.

principal value The **maturity value** of a bond.

private issue Security issue sold to only a few investors that need not be registered with the Securities and Exchange Commission. Also called **private placement.**

profitability index A measure of the profitability of an investment computed by dividing the net present value (or simply present value of future cash flows) by the initial cost of the investment.

profitability ratio A financial ratio that indicates the net returns on sales or assets; net operating margin, profit margin on sales, return on total assets, and return on net worth are profitability ratios.

proprietorship A business owned by an individual who is personally responsible for all its debts.

prospectus Information supplied to potential investors in a new securities issue that describes the current condition and history of the firm.

protective covenant See **covenant.**

proxy The authorization given by a shareholder to another party to exercise the shareholder's voting rights at a stockholders' meeting.

public issue Security issue sold to many investors. Large issues of most types of securities must be registered with the Securities and Exchange Commission.

public warehouse A place where goods belonging to other people are stored; sometimes used to maintain control over collateral.

purchase method A method of accounting for a business combination in which the assets of the acquired firm are carried on the merged firm's books at the price paid for them in the merger acquisition.

pure residual dividend policy See **residual dividend policy.**

put option See **option.**

quick ratio (or acid test ratio) A measure of the firm's liquidity equal to [(current assets − inventory) ÷ current liabilities].

rate of return The interest rate earned on an investment; may be the actual rate or an expected rate.

real property Land and buildings.

realized capital gain See **capital gain.**

red herring Preliminary prospectus in a securities offering.

refunding The issuance of new securities to pay off outstanding old debt; **funding,** on the other hand, specifically refers to issuing long-term debt to pay off short-term debt.

registered security Security whose ownership is recorded by the issuing company's registrar (compare with **bearer security**).

reorganization An adjustment under Chapter 11 of the Bankruptcy Reform Act for settlement of the firm's debts; covers most public corporations except railroads.

residual dividend policy A policy under which all equity investment is financed first with retained earnings and then, if such earnings are inadequate, by selling additional equity securities such as common stock and warrants. Earnings that are left over after equity investment is made are paid out as a dividend. A **pure residual dividend policy** requires that the above residual policy be followed every year; a **smoothed residual dividend policy** requires following a residual policy over the long run with dividends kept stable from year to year.

restrictive provisions Restrictions on various activities of a borrower included as part of a loan agreement to protect the lender. See **covenant**.

retained earnings The earnings in a given period that have been retained by the firm rather than paid out as dividends; also refers to the balance sheet account that is the sum of all earnings retained to date.

reverse split The reduction in the number of the firm's shares produced by exchanging all outstanding shares for a smaller number of new shares; each shareholder's percentage ownership of the firm is unaffected.

revolving credit Legal commitment by a bank to loan money to a customer as needed up to a stated maximum amount. The time period covered by the agreement may extend for several years.

rights A privilege offered to stockholders of buying a specified number of additional shares of the company's stock before the stock is offered to outsiders for sale. A stockholder is issued one right per share of stock already owned.

rights-off See **ex-rights**.

rights-on See **cum rights**.

sale and leaseback An arrangement under which the user of the asset sells the asset and then leases it back from the purchaser.

salvage value (residual value) The money that the firm can receive for an asset after it has held it for a period of time.

secondary market The market in which previously issued financial assets are traded.

security market line A line indicating the relationship between the risks and expected rates of return of available assets (securities) in the market.

semistrong-form efficient market A market in which asset prices instantaneously reflect all publicly available information.

sensitivity analysis Analysis of the effect on a project's cash flows or profitability of possible changes in factors which affect the project (e.g., sales, various costs, etc.).

serial bonds Bonds issued at the same time but which mature at different times in the future. For example, a $50 million serial bond issue may provide for $5 million of bonds maturing in five years, another $5 million of bonds maturing in six years, etc., until all bonds have matured in fourteen years.

simulation The use of a set of mathematical relationships to duplicate the operations of a system (e.g., a firm), in order to analyze the system. Simulation could be used to analyze the effect of a new project on firm profits.

sinking fund contribution A periodic payment made by the firm into a fund ("sinking fund") that will be paid to bondholders in retiring the bonds.

sinking fund provision A stipulation in the bond agreement (indenture) that the firm establish a sinking fund. The fund is used to retire part or all of the bonds by buying them on the open market, calling them, or retiring them at maturity.

skewness A measure of the nonsymmetry of a probability distribution.

Small Business Administration (SBA) A federal agency established to aid small businesses.

Small Business Investment Company (SBIC) A financial institution established under certain federal laws to provide financing to small businesses.

smoothed residual dividend policy See **residual dividend policy.**

spinoff The sale of a division or subsidiary of a company.

spot rate The current rate of exchange between two currencies; the rate of exchange at which currencies are presently being traded.

standard deviation A measure of the degree of dispersion of a probability distribution; a higher standard deviation of a cash flow implies a greater uncertainty regarding its level. Standard deviation is the square root of the **variance.** To adjust for scale in making risk comparisons between projects, a useful parameter is the project cash flow's **coefficient of variation,** which equals the cash flow's standard deviation divided by the expected cash flow.

stated value A value set by the board of directors for no-par stock. Stated value has essentially the same meaning as **par value,** in that dividends may not be paid which reduce shareholders' equity below the stated value of all the outstanding shares.

stock dividend New shares distributed to existing shareholders as a dividend.

stock exchange A financial institution that provides a central location for the purchase and sale of stocks.

stock split An increase in the number of firm shares effected by giving stockholders additional shares in proportion to the number of shares already owned.

strong-form efficient market A market in which asset prices instantaneously reflect all available information (compare with **weak-form efficient market** and **semistrong-form efficient market**).

subordination Relegation to a lower-priority position in receiving interest and principal; if an issue of debentures is subordinated to other debt, the latter debt is paid the amount due before the **subordinated debentures** receive anything.

syndicate A group of investment bankers formed to handle a large security issue, or a group of lenders formed to handle a large loan.

synergy Benefits from joining two or more economic units; e.g., the benefits from merging two firms if the merger lowers the cost per unit of output.

taxable income The income of an individual or business on which income taxes are levied as defined by the tax laws. Various deductions are made from total income to arrive at taxable income.

technical analysis The analysis of a firm's stock based on historical trends in the stock's market price (contrast with **fundamental analysis**).

technician Someone who believes that analysis of the history of past prices of an asset can be useful in forecasting the future price of the asset.

term to maturity The amount of time until a debt instrument matures; a twenty-year bond that was issued five years ago has a term to maturity of fifteen years.

term structure (of interest rates) The relationship between the market interest rate and the term to maturity of fixed-income securities that differ only in their term to maturity.

theoretical value For a warrant, the market price minus the option price of the common stock acquired with the warrant multiplied by the number of shares purchased per warrant; this is equal to the value of the common stock acquired with the warrant less the exercise price paid for that stock.

third-party lease See leveraged lease.

trade credit Credit on goods purchased by a company from its supplier on open account.

treasury bill A security issued at a discount by the United States government with a maturity of one year or less, paying its face value at maturity with no interest payments.

treasury stock Shares repurchased from a stockholder by the issuing company.

trustee In bankruptcy, a court-appointed official who draws up a reorganization plan and supervises the firm's assets until the plan goes into effect. In a public bond issue, an individual or firm who represents the bondholders in dealing with the issuing company.

underwriting The purchase of securities from the issuing company by an investment banker for resale to the public.

variable cost A cost that changes as output changes.

variable rate loan A loan with an interest rate that varies according to the general level of interest rates. The interest rate is not fixed over the period of the loan.

variance See standard deviation.

venture capital Money invested in a small or new business as an investment by persons not direclty managing the business.

vertical combination The union of firms engaged in different stages of production for the same type of product; e.g., a food retailer and food wholesaler.

warrant An option to buy a security (e.g., a share of stock) issued by the firm that issued the warrant.

weak-form efficient market Market in which asset prices instantaneously reflect information contained in the past history of asset prices (compare with **semistrong-form efficient market** and **strong-form efficient market**).

with dividend See cum dividend.

with rights See cum rights.

working capital Current assets *minus* current liabilities (sometimes referred to as net working capital).

yield curve A plot of **yield to maturity** and **term to maturity** for fixed-income securities that differ only in their term to maturity. Often used as a synonym for the **term structure of interest rates**.

yield to maturity The rate of return earned on a bond if it is purchased at a given price and held to maturity.

INDEX

FUTURE VALUE OF $1 IN N PERIODS (F/P, i, N)

N	0.33%	0.50%	0.67%	0.75%	0.83%	1%	2%	3%	4%	5%	6%	7%
1	1.0033	1.0050	1.0067	1.0075	1.0083	1.0100	1.0200	1.0300	1.0400	1.0500	1.0600	1.0700
2	1.0067	1.0100	1.0134	1.0151	1.0167	1.0201	1.0404	1.0609	1.0816	1.1025	1.1236	1.1449
3	1.0100	1.0151	1.0201	1.0227	1.0252	1.0303	1.0612	1.0927	1.1249	1.1576	1.1910	1.2250
4	1.0134	1.0202	1.0269	1.0303	1.0338	1.0406	1.0824	1.1255	1.1699	1.2155	1.2625	1.3108
5	1.0168	1.0253	1.0338	1.0381	1.0424	1.0510	1.1041	1.1593	1.2167	1.2763	1.3382	1.4026
6	1.0202	1.0304	1.0407	1.0459	1.0511	1.0615	1.1262	1.1941	1.2653	1.3401	1.4185	1.5007
7	1.0236	1.0355	1.0476	1.0537	1.0598	1.0721	1.1487	1.2299	1.3159	1.4071	1.5036	1.6058
8	1.0270	1.0407	1.0546	1.0616	1.0686	1.0829	1.1717	1.2668	1.3686	1.4775	1.5938	1.7182
9	1.0304	1.0459	1.0616	1.0696	1.0775	1.0937	1.1951	1.3048	1.4233	1.5513	1.6895	1.8385
10	1.0338	1.0511	1.0687	1.0776	1.0865	1.1046	1.2190	1.3439	1.4802	1.6289	1.7908	1.9672
11	1.0373	1.0564	1.0758	1.0857	1.0956	1.1157	1.2434	1.3842	1.5395	1.7103	1.8983	2.1049
12	1.0407	1.0617	1.0830	1.0938	1.1047	1.1268	1.2682	1.4258	1.6010	1.7959	2.0122	2.2522
13	1.0442	1.0670	1.0902	1.1020	1.1139	1.1381	1.2936	1.4685	1.6651	1.8856	2.1329	2.4098
14	1.0477	1.0723	1.0975	1.1103	1.1232	1.1495	1.3195	1.5126	1.7317	1.9799	2.2609	2.5785
15	1.0512	1.0777	1.1048	1.1186	1.1326	1.1610	1.3459	1.5580	1.8009	2.0789	2.3966	2.7590
16	1.0547	1.0831	1.1122	1.1270	1.1420	1.1726	1.3728	1.6047	1.8730	2.1829	2.5404	2.9522
17	1.0582	1.0885	1.1196	1.1354	1.1515	1.1843	1.4002	1.6528	1.9479	2.2920	2.6928	3.1588
18	1.0617	1.0939	1.1270	1.1440	1.1611	1.1961	1.4282	1.7024	2.0258	2.4066	2.8543	3.3799
19	1.0653	1.0994	1.1346	1.1525	1.1708	1.2081	1.4568	1.7535	2.1068	2.5270	3.0256	3.6165
20	1.0688	1.1049	1.1421	1.1612	1.1805	1.2202	1.4859	1.8061	2.1911	2.6533	3.2071	3.8697
21	1.0724	1.1104	1.1497	1.1699	1.1904	1.2324	1.5157	1.8603	2.2788	2.7860	3.3996	4.1406
22	1.0760	1.1160	1.1574	1.1787	1.2003	1.2447	1.5460	1.9161	2.3699	2.9253	3.6035	4.4304
23	1.0795	1.1216	1.1651	1.1875	1.2103	1.2572	1.5769	1.9736	2.4647	3.0715	3.8197	4.7405
24	1.0831	1.1272	1.1729	1.1964	1.2204	1.2697	1.6084	2.0328	2.5633	3.2251	4.0489	5.0724
25	1.0867	1.1328	1.1807	1.2054	1.2306	1.2824	1.6406	2.0938	2.6658	3.3864	4.2919	5.4274
30	1.1050	1.1614	1.2206	1.2513	1.2827	1.3478	1.8114	2.4273	3.2434	4.3219	5.7435	7.6123
40	1.1424	1.2208	1.3045	1.3483	1.3937	1.4889	2.2080	3.2620	4.8010	7.0400	10.2857	14.9745
50	1.1810	1.2832	1.3941	1.4530	1.5143	1.6446	2.6916	4.3839	7.1067	11.4674	18.4202	29.4570
60	1.2210	1.3489	1.4898	1.5657	1.6453	1.8167	3.2810	5.8916	10.5196	18.6792	32.9877	57.9464
80	1.3050	1.4903	1.7016	1.8180	1.9424	2.2167	4.8754	10.6409	23.0498	49.5614	105.79	224.23
120	147.25	163.88	182.95	193.51	204.84	230.04	488.26	1,124	2,742	6,958	18,120	47,954

N	8%	9%	10%	11%	12%	13%	14%	15%	16%	18%	20%	25%
1	1.0800	1.0900	1.1000	1.1100	1.1200	1.1300	1.1400	1.1500	1.1600	1.1800	1.2000	1.2500
2	1.1664	1.1881	1.2100	1.2321	1.2544	1.2769	1.2996	1.3225	1.3456	1.3924	1.4400	1.5625
3	1.2597	1.2950	1.3310	1.3676	1.4049	1.4429	1.4815	1.5209	1.5609	1.6430	1.7280	1.9531
4	1.3605	1.4116	1.4641	1.5181	1.5735	1.6305	1.6890	1.7490	1.8106	1.9388	2.0736	2.4414
5	1.4693	1.5386	1.6105	1.6851	1.7623	1.8424	1.9254	2.0114	2.1003	2.2878	2.4883	3.0518
6	1.5869	1.6771	1.7716	1.8704	1.9738	2.0820	2.1950	2.3131	2.4364	2.6996	2.9860	3.8147
7	1.7138	1.8280	1.9487	2.0762	2.2107	2.3526	2.5023	2.6600	2.8262	3.1855	3.5832	4.7684
8	1.8509	1.9926	2.1436	2.3045	2.4760	2.6584	2.8526	3.0590	3.2784	3.7589	4.2998	5.9605
9	1.9990	2.1719	2.3579	2.5580	2.7731	3.0040	3.2519	3.5179	3.8030	4.4355	5.1598	7.4506
10	2.1589	2.3674	2.5937	2.8394	3.1058	3.3946	3.7072	4.0456	4.4114	5.2338	6.1917	9.3132
11	2.3316	2.5804	2.8531	3.1518	3.4785	3.8359	4.2262	4.6524	5.1173	6.1759	7.4301	11.6415
12	2.5182	2.8127	3.1384	3.4985	3.8960	4.3345	4.8179	5.3503	5.9360	7.2876	8.9161	14.5519
13	2.7196	3.0658	3.4523	3.8833	4.3635	4.8980	5.4924	6.1528	6.8858	8.5994	10.6993	18.1899
14	2.9372	3.3417	3.7975	4.3104	4.8871	5.5348	6.2613	7.0757	7.9875	10.1472	12.8392	22.7374
15	3.1722	3.6425	4.1772	4.7846	5.4736	6.2543	7.1379	8.1371	9.2655	11.9737	15.4070	28.4217
16	3.4259	3.9703	4.5950	5.3109	6.1304	7.0673	8.1372	9.3576	10.7480	14.1290	18.4884	35.5271
17	3.7000	4.3276	5.0545	5.8951	6.8660	7.9861	9.2765	10.7613	12.4677	16.6722	22.1861	44.4089
18	3.9960	4.7171	5.5599	6.5436	7.6900	9.0243	10.5752	12.3755	14.4625	19.6733	26.6233	55.5112
19	4.3157	5.1417	6.1159	7.2633	8.6128	10.1974	12.0557	14.2318	16.7765	23.2144	31.9480	69.3889
20	4.6610	5.6044	6.7275	8.0623	9.6463	11.5231	13.7435	16.3665	19.4608	27.3930	38.3376	86.7362
25	6.8485	8.6231	10.8347	13.5855	17.0001	21.2305	26.4619	32.9190	40.8742	62.6686	95.3962	264.6978
30	10.06	13.27	17.45	22.89	29.96	39.12	50.95	66.21	85.85	143.37	237.38	807.79
40	21.72	31.41	45.26	65.00	93.05	132.78	188.88	267.86	378.72	750.38	1,470	7,523
50	46.90	74.36	117.39	184.56	289.00	450.74	700.23	1,084	1,671	3,927	9,100	70,065